Handbook of U.S. Labor Statistics

Employment, Earnings, Prices, Productivity, and Other Labor Data

10th Edition
2007

HANDBOOK OF U.S. LABOR STATISTICS

Employment, Earnings, Prices, Productivity, and Other Labor Data

10th Edition
2007

Edited by Eva E. Jacobs

Associate Editor
Mary Meghan Ryan

BERNAN PRESS
Lanham, MD

ISBN-13: 978-1-59888-074-8

ISSN: 1526-2553

Printed by Automated Graphic Systems, Inc., White Plains, MD, on acid-free paper that meets the American National Standards Institute Z39-48 standard.

2008 2007   4 3 2 1

BERNAN PRESS
4611-F Assembly Drive
Lanham, MD 20706
800-274-4447
email: info@bernan.com
www.bernanpress.com

CONTENTS

LIST OF TABLES

CHAPTER 9: OCCUPATIONAL SAFETY AND HEALTH 399

CHAPTER 10: LABOR MANAGEMENT RELATIONS .... .413

CHAPTER 11: FOREIGN LABOR AND PRICE STATISTICS .... .425

LIST OF FIGURES

ABOUT THE EDITORS

Eva E. Jacobs has been the editor of the *Handbook of U.S. Labor Statistics* since its first edition. She served as chief of the Division of Consumer Expenditure Surveys at the Bureau of Labor Statistics (BLS) for over 20 years. As the manager of this division, Ms. Jacobs was responsible for the ongoing Consumer Expenditure Survey, which tracks the expenditure patterns of U.S. households over time. Ms. Jacobs also held positions in BLS's Productivity Division and the Economic Growth Division. More recently, she acted as an adviser on cost-of-living projects for both government and private consultants. She currently serves as chair of a panel advising the Safe Harbor Working Group on issues related to cost-of-living adjustments for federal employees in Alaska, Hawaii, Guam, Puerto Rico, and the Virgin Islands. Ms. Jacobs was the 1998 recipient of the Julius Shiskin Award, given by the National Association of Business Economists and the Washington Statistical Society for distinguished contributions to the field of economic statistics.

Mary Meghan Ryan is a data analyst with Bernan Press. She received her bachelor's degree in economics from the University of Maryland and is a former economist with the American Economics Group. She has also worked as a research assistant for FRANDATA. Ms. Ryan is also an associate editor of *Business Statistics of the United States: Patterns of Economic Change* and of *Vital Statistics of the United States: Birth, Life Expectancy, Deaths, and Selected Health Data*, both published by Bernan Press.

ACKNOWLEDGMENTS

The preparation of this publication was very much a team activity. Mary Meghan Ryan capably researched the data and compiled the tables. Deirdre Gaquin prepared the special tabulations of data from the Current Population Survey. Jo A. Wilson, assisted by Lateef Padgett, prepared the graphics and layout. Shana Hertz copyedited this edition. Publisher Kenneth E. Lawrence and managing editor Katherine A. DeBrandt supervised the overall editorial and production aspects of this publication. I extend my sincere gratitude to these individuals for their skills, professionalism, and cooperative effort—all of which made this publication possible.

Particular thanks also go to BLS staff members, too numerous to mention by name, who patiently answered questions and provided essential information.

Bernan Press is pleased to present a compilation of Bureau of Labor Statistics (BLS) data in this 10th edition of its award-winning *Handbook of U.S Labor Statistics*. BLS provides a treasure trove of historical information about all aspects of labor and employment in the United States. The current edition maintains the content of previous editions and updates the text with additional data and new features. The editors have also added some tables on income derived from data from the Census Bureau; these tables are described later in the preface. The data in this publication are excellent sources of information for analysts in government and business.

This edition represents a significant milestone for the *Handbook of U.S. Labor Statistics*, and such a milestone invites a moment of introspection and reflective questioning. What problems in the nation and the economy are of interest now compared to 10 years ago? How do the numbers in this book draw attention to problems and provide quantitative assistance to the analysts who search for possible solutions? The short answer is that while the numbers change, the questions still remain with us—even as new questions are being added.

In earlier editions, this publication analyzed some of the issues that were then being addressed: the decline in employment in the manufacturing sector, the high unemployment rates for young minorities, the aging labor force, the cost of health care services and prescription drugs, the changing pension plans, the specter of inflation as a result of the rise in fuel prices, the impact of changing technology on the educational and occupational requirements of industry, and the impact of immigration on the structure of the labor force. Policy decisions on these questions are still relevant today. New issues include the stagnation of real wages despite an increase in productivity, which has led to concern that this trend indicates a lack of progress in improving the standard of living of workers.

It is important to examine the historical movement of various series; as a result, some tables in this publication show data back to 1985. This *Handbook* includes tables on employment and unemployment and employer costs for employee health care. Tables of projections of industry output and employment show the expected trends in the technology sector and the educational requirements of jobs in this sector. Other tables show how workers have fared in terms of wages (which have been adjusted for changing prices).

FEATURES OF THIS PUBLICATION

- Approximately 200 tables present authoritative data for labor market statistics, including employment and employment costs and hours, prices, productivity, comparisons with other countries, and other labor market statistics.

- Each section is preceded by one or more figures that call attention to noteworthy trends in the data. The

first edition had 8 figures, while the current edition has more than 20 figures. A summary of the most important trends (in figure form) can be found on page xxxi of this *Handbook*.

- In addition to the figures, the introductory material for each chapter also contains highlights of other salient data. For example, the highlights in Chapter 1 showcase the trend of labor force participation rate by age and the disparity in labor force participation rates for various demographic groups. A highlight in Chapter 4 calls attention to the difference between the rate of growth in projected employment and the level of growth in projected employment.

- The tables in each section are also preceded by notes and definitions, which contain concise descriptions of the data sources, concepts, definitions, and methodology from which the data are derived.

- The introductory notes also include references to more comprehensive reports. These reports provide additional data and more extensive descriptions of estimation methods, sampling, and reliability measures.

ARTICLES OVERVIEW

The introduction to the text provides articles that describe current information on developments, such as the planning or introduction of new surveys, the introduction of new classification definitions, and current research on economic topics that make use of the data contained in this *Handbook*.

The first article in the introduction, "Price Measurement in the United States: A Decade After the Boskin Report" describes the steps BLS has taken to address the problems raised in the Report by the U.S. Advisory Commission to Study the Consumer Price Index (more commonly known as the Boskin Report), which was issued on December 4, 1996. The Boskin Report focused attention on three key problems inherent in the calculation of Consumer Price Indexes: consumer substitution, quality change, and new goods. BLS subsequently reaffirmed its cost-of-living conceptual framework and built on prior research in order to introduce methodological changes; these changes corrected the issues with substitution, quality, and new goods.

The second article, "Employment Outlook, 2004–2014: A Summary of BLS Projections to 2014," summarizes a series of four articles that appeared in the November 2005 edition of the *Monthly Labor Review*. This summary presents a detailed picture of U.S. employment trends as they are likely to evolve over the 2004–2014 decade, under the assumptions used to develop those projections. The summary also updates the 2002–2012 projections published in February 2004. It presents a synopsis of the content of each article, a short statement of methods, an overview of what is new in this round of projections, and some thoughts about which factors might pose the greatest risks to the accuracy of the projections.

The third article, "Hurricane Katrina and the Bureau of Labor Statistics: A Summary of Articles from the August 2006 Edition of the Monthly Labor Review" concerns the impact of Hurricane Katrina. The entire August 2006 edition of the *Monthly Labor Review* was devoted to the impact of the hurricane on the collection and substance of BLS statistical series, particularly the employment and wages series. The article provided in this *Handbook* contains excerpts from articles published in the August 2006 edition.

NEW TABLES IN THIS EDITION

Income data. Chapter 13, a new addition to the publication, presents income data for the United States compiled by the Census Bureau. The *Handbook of U.S. Labor Statistics* has traditionally included tables with a great deal of information on wages. However, much of the recent public discussion about income inequality has focused on both wages and non-wage income (such as interest and dividends, Social Security, and other pension income). The Census Bureau collects this information in the March supplement to the Current Population Survey.

Consumer Price Index Research Series Using Current Methods (CPI-U-RS). BLS has made many improvements in the way the Consumer Price Index (CPI) is calculated, but these changes are not carried back historically in the official CPI. Some users would like to see the effect of these improvements over time. To this end, the CPI-U-RS attempts to answer the following question: "What would have been the measured rate of inflation from 1978 forward had the methods currently used in calculating the CPI-U been in use since 1978?"

North American Industry Classification System (NAICS). More series have been converted to NAICS industry classification. However, this conversion has caused some delays in data availability. See the notes and definitions in each chapter for more information on conversion of the applicable series. While conversion sometimes creates a comparability problem, the new classification system is more descriptive of the current structure of the economy. NAICS was described in a summary article in the sixth edition of this *Handbook*. More information about NAICS can be found on the BLS Web site at <http://www.bls.gov/bls/naics.htm>.

SOURCES OF ADDITIONAL INFORMATION

BLS data are primarily derived from surveys conducted by the federal government or through federal-state cooperative arrangements. The comparability of data over time can be affected by changes in the surveys, which are essential for keeping pace with the current structure of economic institutions and for taking advantage of improved survey techniques. Revisions of current data are also periodically made as a result of the availability of new information. In addition, some tables in this *Handbook* were dropped due to the data being from a one-time survey that is now outdated—such as the data on training (1995)—or due to the survey being entirely restructured. Introductory notes to each chapter summarize specific factors that may affect the data. In the tables, an ellipsis ("...") indicates that data are not available.

More extensive methodological information, including further discussion of the sampling and estimation procedures used for each BLS program, is contained in the *BLS Handbook of Methods*. This publication is in the process of being updated, and completed chapters are available on the BLS Web site at <http://www.bls.gov>. Other sources of current data and analytical include the *Monthly Labor Review* and a daily Internet publication, *The Editor's Desk* (TED). All of these publications can be found on the BLS Web site. Other relevant publications are noted in the notes and definitions for each applicable chapter.

OTHER PUBLICATIONS BY BERNAN PRESS

The *Handbook of U.S. Labor Statistics* is one of a number of publications in Bernan Press's award-winning U.S. DataBook Series. Other titles include *Business Statistics of the United States: Patterns of Economic Change*; *The Almanac of American Education*; *United States Foreign Trade Highlights: Trends in the Global Market*; *Datapedia of the United States, American History in Numbers*; and *Vital Statistics of the United States: Births, Life Expectancy, Deaths, and Selected Health Data*. Each of these titles provides the public with statistical information from official government sources.

If you have any questions or suggestions as to how we could make future editions even more useful, please contact us by email at bpress@bernan.com or by letter at Bernan Press, 4611-F Assembly Drive, Lanham, MD 20706. Please visit our Web site at <http://www.bernan press.com>.

ARTICLE 1
PRICE MEASUREMENT IN THE UNITED STATES: A DECADE AFTER THE BOSKIN REPORT

This is a brief summary of an article written by David S. Johnson, Stephen B. Reed, and Kenneth J. Stewart.[1] The full article appeared in the May 2006 edition of the Monthly Labor Review *and can be found online at <http://www.bls.gov/opub/mlr/2006/05/art2full.pdf>.*

The December 1996 Boskin Report (also called the Report by the U.S. Advisory Commission to Study the Consumer Price Index), estimated that the Consumer Price Index (CPI) was biased upwards by around 1.1 percent per year. The Boskin Commission divided the types of potential biases into three groups: consumer substitution bias, quality change bias, and new goods bias.

Since the publication of the Boskin Report, and by building on prior research, the Bureau of Labor Statistics (BLS) has introduced methodological changes that have addressed each of these issues. These include: 1) the introduction of the geometric means formula in 1999; 2) the introduction of the Chained Consumer Price Index for All Urban Consumers (C-CPU-U) in 2002; 3) the expansion of the use of hedonic models to improve the measurement of quality change; and 4) the institution of procedures to introduce new goods into the index more quickly. This article summarizes those methodological changes.

CONSUMER SUBSTITUTION BIAS IN THE CPI

Substitution bias arises in a fixed-weight CPI if consumers change their purchasing behavior in response to relative price changes. Until 1999, the CPI used Laspeyres formulas to calculate the CPI; Laspeyres formulas effectively assume zero consumer substitution. In other words, these formulas assume an elasticity of substitution of zero. To the extent that consumers can and do change their purchasing behavior in response to relative price changes, a Laspeyres formula will result in an upward bias in the index and overstate the cost of living. The Boskin Report estimated a total consumer substitution bias of 0.4 percent.

In 1999, the CPI converted to a geometric means formula for averaging prices within most CPI item categories. The geometric means formula effectively assumes constant relative expenditure on a given item, rather than constant quantity. As the relative price increases, the assumed quantity proportionally decreases. Thus, this formula implicitly assumes a unitary elasticity of substitution. The geometric mean formula was adopted to account for what is sometimes called "lower-level" consumer substitution; in other words, the substitution that takes place *within* item categories, such as apples, as relative prices change.

In 2002, the CPI began producing an additional index, the Chained Consumer Price Index for All Urban Consumers (C-CPI-U). This index uses a "superlative" formula—one in which expenditure data from both the base and current period are used to calculate the indexes. Thus, the final version of the C-CPI-U is based on actual consumer behavior, rather than on assumptions about substitution behavior. However, since expenditure data are only available with a time lag, the indexes are subject to revision until the final expenditure data are available. The C-CPI-U was created to account for what is sometimes called "upper-level" consumer substitution; that is, the substitution that takes place *across* item categories, such as apples and oranges, as relative prices change. Since the C-CPI-U uses both geometric means to account for lower-level substitution and a superlative formula to account for upper-level substitution, it is designed to be a closer approximation to a cost-of-living index than the more familiar CPI-U.

NEW GOODS AND QUALITY CHANGE BIAS IN THE CPI

Perhaps the most fundamental problem in creating a price index is that the market basket available to consumers constantly changes, while the goal is to produce a constant-quality CPI. The Boskin Report estimated an upward "quality change" bias in the CPI (the alleged inability of BLS to fully account for the increased variety and quality of goods and services over time) of 0.6 percent per year, larger than that estimated for the consumer substitution bias.

Operationally, the CPI deals with quality change in several different ways. If an item included in the CPI sample is no longer sold in the outlet, a new item is priced in its place. If the new item is substantially different than the discontinued item, then some sort of quality adjustment procedures must be used in order to estimate constant-quality price change.

One way to estimate constant-quality price change is to make an estimate of the quantitative value of the quality change. This is based on either manufacturer cost data or on estimates of the value to consumers of particular features of the good in question. These values are often estimated with hedonic models, a technique referred to as "hedonics." This technique is widely considered the most promising for quality adjustment, and the CPI has employed this technique for an increasing number of goods since the Boskin Report was issued. While hedonics is important for particular categories, it is still used for only a small part of the total index; its net impact on indexes has thus been relatively small.

Along with quality adjustment of goods in the sample, there is also the issue of goods entering the economy that were not included in the sample. It is important that the CPI gets new goods into the sample quickly, in order to have a market basket that accurately reflects consumer purchases. The CPI program has taken several steps in recent years to keep the market basket up to date. Since 2002, updated Consumer Expenditure Survey weights have been introduced every 2 years (as opposed to roughly every 10 years in the past). Moreover, the lag time from survey to implementation is shorter, and the survey is completed over a shorter period of time. The result is that weights used in the CPI reflect much more recent consumer behavior than those used in years past.

Additionally, the CPI has changed its sample and outlet rotation procedures. In 1998, the CPI went from rotating 20 percent of the outlet sample each year to 25 percent, making the entire sample rotate every 4 years instead of every 5 years. Some items in selected categories (particularly those that tend to change rapidly) are rotated every 2 years. The market basket of the CPI is thus considerably more up to date than it used to be, particularly in terms of high-tech goods.

CONCLUSION

Improving the CPI is an ongoing process. Since the Boskin Report was issued in 1996, there have been important changes to improve the index. The implementation of the geometric means formula to calculate basic indexes addresses lower-level substitution bias, and the creation of the C-CPI-U provides a measure that accounts for upper-level substitution. The expanded use of hedonic models to directly adjust for changes in quality has given BLS commodity analysts another sophisticated option with which to address this issue. More frequent weight updates and sample rotation make the market basket used in calculating the CPI more up to date and reflective of current consumer behavior than ever before.

ENDNOTES

[1]David S. Johnson is chief of the Division of Housing and Household Economic Statistics, U.S. Census Bureau. Stephen B. Reed and Kenneth J. Stewart are economists in the Division of Consumer Prices and Price Indexes, Bureau of Labor Statistics.

ARTICLE 2
EMPLOYMENT OUTLOOK: 2004–2014—
A SUMMARY OF BLS PROJECTIONS TO 2014

This article, written by Norman C. Saunders, is condensed from the summary article in the November 2005 edition of the Monthly Labor Review.[1] *The issue contains four other articles and tables concerning the projections and can be found on the Bureau of Labor Statistics (BLS) Web site at <http://www.bls.gov/opub/mlr/2005/11/contents.htm>. A short description of the methodology and the detailed tables can be found in Chapter 4 of this* Handbook.

The U.S. economy is expected to expand at a moderately strong pace over the coming decade, with restrained inflation, continued strong productivity growth, and labor force growth at a steady rate with a favorable outlook for a wide array of job opportunities.

The 2014 projections are the 19th in a series of biennial examinations of the aggregate economy; labor force by age, sex, race, and ethnicity; and industry and occupational employment.[2] The following four articles present a detailed picture of U.S. employment trends as they are likely to evolve over the 2004–2014 decade under the assumptions used to develop those projections. The articles update the 2002–2012 projections that were published in February 2004. This article presents a synopsis of the conclusions of the projections, a summary of what is new in this round of projections, and some thoughts about the factors that might pose the greatest risks to the accuracy of the projections.

SUMMARY OF ARTICLES

Aggregate economy. The first article of the series examines the overall economic outlook for the coming decade. Gross domestic product (GDP), which measures the sales of domestically produced goods and services to final users, is projected to grow by an average annual rate of 3.1 percent between 2004 and 2014. Consumer spending continues to account for more than 70 percent of GDP and is projected to grow at an annual rate of 2.8 percent in real terms. Gross private domestic investment is expected to grow 4.7 percent annually between 2004 and 2014. As the dollar continues its expected depreciation against the currencies in major trading partner countries, exports are projected to grow more strongly than they did during the 10 years preceding the projections. Conversely, imports are expected to grow less rapidly than during the past decade. On the government side, a slow but deliberate increase in federal defense spending is expected throughout the projection period, offset by like declines in nondefense spending. State and local government is projected to grow at 2.0 percent per year, slowing a bit from the 1994–2004 period, when it grew by 2.7 percent each year in chained 2000 dollars.

The aggregate projections are based on assumptions of an unemployment rate at 5.0 percent in 2014, nonfarm business labor productivity growth of 2.7 percent each year, continuing steady devaluation of the dollar vis-à-vis the currencies of our major trading partners, a per capita real disposable income increasing from $27,200 in 2004 to $33,200 in 2014, and a personal savings rate climbing slowly from 1.8 percent in 2004 to 3.4 percent a decade later. Improvements in the federal deficit and the current

account deficit are expected as well, though neither item is projected to reach a balance or a surplus position by 2014.

Labor force. The second article reviews the factors affecting the growth of the labor force by age, sex, race, and ethnicity. The civilian labor force is projected to increase annually by 1.0 percent, the same growth rate as that of the population, representing considerable slowing in growth from previous decades.

The labor force is defined as the portion of the population age 16 years and over that is either at work or actively seeking work. The labor force participation rate is the labor force as a proportion of the population age 16 years and over. Growth of the labor force is the result of simultaneous changes in the civilian noninstitutional population and in labor force participation rates. Participation rates are projected to remain flat or to decrease slightly over the next 10 years; therefore, the growth of the labor force will be entirely due to population growth. Population growth itself is a product of changes in fertility, mortality, and migration. Because changes in mortality and fertility rates tend to be very gradual, the main component of population change has been and will continue to be immigration.

A closer look at the 2004–2014 labor force shows that certain demographic groups are projected to grow more rapidly than others. The labor force will continue to age, with a projected 4.1 percent annual growth rate for the 55 years old and over age group, more than four times the rate of growth of the overall labor force. Baby boomers entered the labor market beginning in the late 1960s as a huge wave of workers who swelled the level and growth of the labor force. During the 1990s, baby boomers were in the prime-age working group of 25- to 54-year-olds and were still contributing to a relatively high annual growth of the workforce. They will be concentrated in the 50- to 68-year-old age group in 2014. Because older workers tend to have significantly lower participation rates, the baby boomer exit from the workforce, as with their entrance, will have significant impacts on the growth of the labor force.

Another interesting fact is that the labor force participation rate of workers over 55 years old has been increasing since the mid-1980s. The increase is projected to continue at least to 2014. The willingness of the 55 years old and over age group to participate in the future labor force or to retire is a multidimensional decision. This decision may be the result of various factors, such as the individual's health status and the status of pensions, savings, and anticipated Social Security payments. A growing proportion of the retirement-age population appears to be staging their transition from full-time work to full retirement as well. One of the most important factors in the increase of the labor force participation rate of older workers has been governmental policies and legislation aimed at eliminating mandatory retirement and outlawing age discrimination.

In summary, the labor force is projected to grow steadily into the future, albeit at a slower pace than in the past. BLS assumes that because labor markets clear, slower growth in labor supply will be reflected in slower growth in labor demand. Care should be taken not to compare household-based measures of employment with establishment-based versions discussed at the industry level of detail. Such comparisons could lead to a belief that BLS is predicting shortages when, by assumption, none exist in the projections.

Industry employment. The third article examines the outlook for output and employment growth for detailed industries. Nonfarm wage and salary employment is projected to increase by 18.7 million employees between 2004 and 2014, an annual average rate of growth of 1.3 percent. Goods-producing industries are expected to have no growth in employment, as the 1.1 percent annual increase predicted for the construction sector is expected to be offset by declines in manufacturing and mining employment. Employment in the service-providing industries, on the other hand, is expected to continue to grow strongly at a projected annual rate of 1.6 percent.

The decline in manufacturing employment does not mean that the manufacturing sector is disappearing from the U.S. economy. Output of manufacturing industries (sales of produced goods to final users and also to other industries) is expected to grow at a healthy 3.5 percent annual rate over the projection period, with declines in employment explained by the offsetting high growth in manufacturing labor productivity.

Among the service-providing sectors, the most rapidly-growing industries are in the health care and social assistance sector and the educational services sector. These two sectors are predicted to account for a little more than 22 million jobs in 2014 and to grow at an annual average rate of 2.8 percent from 2004 to 2014. The largest nongovernment sector is the professional and business services sector, comprising almost 21 million jobs in 2014 and projected to grow at an annual rate of 2.5 percent.

Occupational employment. The fourth article reviews the demand for occupations. Among the 10 major occupational groups, employment in the 2 largest in 2004—professional and related occupations and service occupations—will increase the most rapidly and add the most jobs from 2004 to 2014. These major groups, which are on opposite ends of the educational attainment and earnings spectrum, are expected to provide almost 60 percent of the total job growth from 2004 to 2014. Employment is projected to grow a bit faster than overall employment in management, business, and financial occupations. Employment in con-

struction and extraction occupations; installation, maintenance, and repair occupations; transportation and material moving occupations; and sales and related occupations will grow somewhat more slowly. Office and administrative support occupations are projected to grow at only half the rate projected for the total, while farming, fishing, and forestry occupations and production occupations are projected to decline slightly.

As a result of the different growth rates among the major occupational groups, the occupational distribution of total employment will change somewhat by the year 2014, but the relative ranking of the groups by employment size is not expected to change much. Professional and related occupations will continue to rank first, while farming, fishing, and forestry occupations will continue to rank last. Professional and related occupations and service occupations will significantly increase their relative share of employment—by 1.4 and 1.0 percentage points, respectively. However, office and administrative support occupations and production occupations should decrease significantly—by 1.0 and 0.9 points, respectively.

DEVELOPING ENHANCEMENTS

Two innovative projects were part of the 2004–2014 round of projections: 1) a scoring algorithm that allowed occupational analysts to more precisely identify occupations at significant risk of job movement offshore; and 2) a measurement of the actual educational attainment of individuals in occupations as a way of identifying alternative paths to success in specific occupations.

Offshoring. In this context, the term "offshoring" refers specifically to white-collar service-providing jobs that were formerly carried out in the United States but are now contracted to service-providing firms in other countries. In the 2012 projections, BLS occupational analysts knew that certain occupations, most notably those in the information technology sector, were at significant risk of offshoring, and the growth in occupational coefficients for these jobs was curtailed. However, the desire still remained to develop a more formalized approach that could be used by the entire occupational staff in the process of determining whether or not specific occupations were at risk of offshoring.

The purpose of the offshore scoring exercise was to identify the characteristics of occupations that made them more likely to be at risk for offshoring, and then to have the occupation analysts rate the incidence of those characteristics for all of the service-providing occupations in order to assign a potential risk level, although there was no quantitative use of the score as part of the projections presented in this issue. Where a risk of offshoring was identified, appropriate external information documented such activity, and no other mitigating circumstances were identified, additions were made to the "Job Outlook" section of the affected detailed occupational statements in the forthcoming *Occupational Outlook Handbook.* This addition alerts users interested in those occupations of the potential for offshoring as a factor affecting job growth in the future.

Full details regarding the approach and the resulting lists of occupations believed to be at risk are not presented in the article on occupational projections due to space constraints. However, a detailed explanation of the methodology and the results will be presented in the forthcoming 2006–2007 edition of *Occupational Projections and Training Data*. This is the first time this formalized approach to identifying occupations potentially at risk of offshore outsourcing has been attempted, and the process will continue to undergo evaluation and refinement for future rounds of projections.

Educational attainment of occupations. In prior rounds of projections, each occupation was assigned to 1 of 11 training or education categories, based on the occupation's most significant source of education and training. The assigned category was judged to represent the best avenue for entrance into and for ultimate success in the occupation. While this approach was useful for guidance purposes, further examination found some disparity between the actual educational attainment of individuals in specific occupations and BLS judgment as to the best avenue for success in the occupation. In short, the analysis pointed out that there were many different ways to attain success in an occupation. For example, higher educational attainments often were seen as an alternative to extensive on-the-job training. In other cases, it became apparent that a high school education allowed certain chances of success in occupations formerly believed to be bachelor's degree or higher jobs.

For this round of projections, the educational attainment of occupations will be compared, contrasted, and discussed in the *Occupational Outlook Handbook* and in *Occupational Projections and Training Data*.

RISKS TO THE PROJECTIONS

Projections are normally accompanied with a standard disclaimer that assumes no major wars, no natural catas-trophes, nor any other unanticipated factors which could upset the behavior of the various models used in the projections process. These standard disclaimers may not be completely appropriate at this point.

In addition to the financing of the two military engagements underway in Afganistan and Iraq, the potential exists for even higher military spending than assumed in these projections. Thus, military spending may well have greater impacts than anticipated in these projections. Hurricanes Katrina and Rita hit Mississippi and Louisiana with catastrophic effects, especially on the city of New Orleans, and Hurricane Wilma devastated South Florida. It remains to be seen what the longer-term impact on GDP growth will be in response to lost production as well as potential rebuilding efforts.

All of these factors and more may serve to modify to some extent the path of the projections from 2004. Overall, however, the U.S. economy is healthy and resilient. It has demonstrated a number of times in the past decade its ability to shrug off serious dislocations and continue to grow apace. Even though the factors mentioned above are worrying, it is believed that the 2014 projections of growth are reasonable and attainable and that the occupational demand estimates provide excellent guidance to students and others making critical career and educational decisions.

ENDNOTES

[1]The full article is by Norman C. Saunders, who coordinates the Research Program in the BLS Office of Occupational Statistics and Employment Projections and supervises the aggregate economic and labor force projections.

[2]The 19 projection groups span projections from 1970 (published in 1966) to the current projections to 2014 and represent the unified aggregate labor force, industry, and occupational demand estimates presented as a linked set of outlook estimates. The occupational demand projections predate these unified sets of projections by 17 years, as the first *Occupational Outlook Handbook* was published in 1949. See the series of articles in the May 1999 edition of the *Monthly Labor Review*, which can be found on the Internet at <http://www.bls.gov/opub/mlr/1999/05/contents.htm>. These articles provide a comprehensive look at the history of BLS's occupational projections program.

ARTICLE 3
HURRICANE KATRINA AND THE BUREAU OF LABOR STATISTICS:
A SUMMARY OF ARTICLES FROM THE AUGUST 2006 EDITION OF THE
MONTHLY LABOR REVIEW

The August 2006 issue of the Monthly Labor Review *was devoted to articles describing the impact of Hurricane Katrina on the Bureau of Labor Statistics's (BLS), collection activities and results. The following are excerpts from these articles, which were written by both BLS and non-BLS staff. The* Monthly Labor Review *can be found on the BLS Web site at <http://www.bls.gov>.*

THE LABOR MARKET IMPACT OF HURRICANE KATRINA: AN OVERVIEW

Prepared by staff members from several BLS data programs and assembled by Karen Kosanovich

This overview provides a look at Hurricane Katrina's impact on the labor markets of Louisiana and Mississippi and, to some extent, Alabama and Florida. An estimated 17 percent of Louisiana's employment and 5 percent of Mississippi's employment were located within the Federal Emergency Management Agency (FEMA)–designated damage zones. The two states experienced a sharp rise in mass layoff events and unemployment rates after Hurricane Katrina. In June 2006, Mississippi's employment level had returned to its pre-Katrina level, while Louisiana's had not. Evacuees once again living in their pre-Katrina homes in June 2006 had a lower unemployment rate than those who were not living in their pre-Katrina homes.

HURRICANE KATRINA'S EFFECTS ON INDUSTRY EMPLOYMENT AND WAGES

Written by Molly Garber, Linda Unger, James White, and Linda Wohlford[1]

BLS has two programs that measure employment and wages by industry: the Current Employment Statistics (CES) program and the Quarterly Census of Employment and Wages (QCEW) program. Both operate as federal-state cooperative programs in which BLS partners with workforce agencies in each state.

The CES program surveys approximately 400,000 business establishments nationwide and publishes estimates of employment, hours, and earnings for the nation, states, and metropolitan areas. Estimates are released 1 month after the reference month; for example, March estimates are published in April.

The QCEW provides a virtual census (97 percent) of monthly employment and quarterly total wages, derived from Unemployment Insurance tax records that almost all employers are required to file quarterly. QCEW series for the nation, states, metropolitan areas, and counties are published 7 months after the end of the reference quarter. For example, first quarter (January through March) employment and wage counts are published in October.

Thus, the CES estimates are timelier, but the QCEW series are more comprehensive and publish far more industry and geographic detail. The CES employment estimates are benchmarked annually to the QCEW employment counts.

The benchmarking process is intended to correct for sampling error and nonsampling error in the CES estimates.

Both the CES and the QCEW programs faced major operational and analytical challenges while collecting data following Hurricane Katrina. At the same time, there was great demand for these data as policymakers tried to assess the immediate and long-term effects of the storm.

THE CURRENT POPULATION SURVEY RESPONSE TO HURRICANE KATRINA

Written by Lawrence S. Cahoon, Diane E. Herz, Richard C. Ning, Anne E. Polivka, Maria E. Reed, Edwin L. Robison, and Gregory D. Weyland[2]

On August 29, 2005, Hurricane Katrina struck the coast of the Gulf of Mexico, devastating the city of New Orleans and the surrounding Louisiana parishes, as well as Gulf Coast towns in Mississippi. The immediate emergency and the storm's widespread reach and long-lasting devastation presented unprecedented challenges to statistical agencies charged with measuring the economic situation in the affected areas and in the United States as a whole. At the time of the storm, BLS and the Census Bureau were discussing a proposed disaster estimation strategy for the Current Population Survey (CPS) program, the U.S. national labor force survey. However, no formal plan was in place for dealing with such a situation when the hurricane struck the coast.

At news of the storm's approach, representatives from the two agencies, which co-sponsor the monthly survey of approximately 60,000 occupied housing units, began meeting to discuss how different scenarios might affect operations and estimation. After landfall, when the severity of the damage became more clear, the two bureaus met several times a day and worked between meetings to locate and support staff in the affected areas, assess problems with operations, and determine how to proceed with estimation and data dissemination.

THE EFFECT OF HURRICANE KATRINA ON EMPLOYMENT AND UNEMPLOYMENT

Written by Sharon P. Brown, Sandra L. Mason, and Richard B. Tiller[3]

The Local Area Unemployment Statistics (LAUS) estimates for the month of September 2005 were among the first subnational data to reflect the impact of Hurricane Katrina, which struck the Gulf Coast on August 29, 2005, with catastrophic effects in parts of Louisiana, Mississippi, and Alabama. Beginning in September and continuing into the present, BLS and its state partners made a number of critical modifications to standard estimating procedures to better reflect the employment and unemployment situation in the affected areas. BLS analyzed the subnational Current Population Survey (CPS) estimates and verified that they did not reflect the economic upheaval created by the hurricane and its aftermath. BLS also evaluated unemployment insurance statistics and state and area nonfarm employment estimates. To address estimating issues at the state level, models were modified to allow the state-supplied inputs of nonfarm employment and unemployment insurance claimants to have far greater weight in the calculations of estimates. In addition, breaking with long-standing practice, BLS introduced special intervention variables into the models in real time in order to immediately reflect the effect of Katrina. Area estimation procedures also were modified. The identification and implementation of revised estimation approaches at the state and area levels and of model interventions necessary each month in Louisiana and Mississippi required innovation and risk taking, as standard methods were adapted in an attempt to fully reflect the impact of Katrina.

HURRICANE DAMAGE TO THE OCEAN ECONOMY IN THE U.S. GULF REGION IN 2005

Written by Charles S. Colgan and Jefferey Adkins[4]

In 2005, insured losses from hurricanes and other catastrophes were greater than in any other year in U.S. history. The National Oceanic and Atmospheric Administration's (NOAA) National Hurricane Center estimates that $85 billion of total damages resulted from Hurricanes Katrina and Rita alone. One year later, the region affected by these two hurricanes still struggles to recover, both as a place to live and as a viable economy.

Using data from the BLS Quarterly Census of Employment and Wages, the National Ocean Economics Program has developed a data series that allows the economic damage to coastal regions to be seen in a new light: what happens to the economic value derived from the ocean when the ocean turns from resource and respite to a massive engine of destruction?[5]

According to federal disaster declarations, Hurricane Katrina affected all counties and parishes within Mississippi and Louisiana, plus 22 counties in Alabama and 9 counties in Florida. Hurricane Rita affected all parishes in Louisiana and 26 counties in Texas. The greatest effects were in areas closest to the coast, where the storm's effects were at their maximum intensity. Coastal counties and parishes include those designated as such by each state under the Federal Coastal Zone Management Program, as well as those designated as coastal watershed counties or parishes by the U.S. Geological Survey.

Virtually all of the coastal zone and watershed counties[6] and parishes of Alabama, Mississippi, and Louisiana, plus the coastal counties in Texas from Houston eastward, were affected by the two hurricanes. The coastal zone counties and parishes of the four states account for nearly a quarter of employment and wages in those states. In Louisiana, the coastal parishes are more than half of the state's economy. The combined coastal zone and watershed counties and parishes on the Gulf of Mexico constituted 14 percent of employment in Alabama, 4 percent in Mississippi, 6 percent in Florida, a considerably greater 33 percent in Texas, and 80 percent in Louisiana.

ENDNOTES

[1]Molly Garber and James White are economists in the Division of Current Employment Statistics, and Linda Unger is a statistician and Linda Wohlford is an economist for the Quarterly Census of Employment and Wages program in the Division of Administrative Statistics and Labor Turnover. All four work in the Office of Employment and Unemployment Statistics at the Bureau of Labor Statistics.

[2]Lawrence S. Cahoon is the assistant division chief for Census Design, Decennial Statistical Studies Division; Richard C. Ning is the chief of the Labor and Crime Surveys Branch, Field Division; Maria E. Reed is the chief of the Current Population Surveys Branch, Demographic Surveys Division; and Gregory D. Weyland is a survey statistician in the Current Population Survey (CPS) Branch, Demographic Surveys Division. All of these divisions are located in the Census Bureau. Diane E. Herz is the chief of the Division of Labor Force Statistics, Anne E. Polivka is a supervisory economist in the Division of Employment Research, and Edwin Robison is a supervisory mathematical statistician in the Division of the CPS and Local Area Unemployment Statistics (LAUS). All of these divisions are located within the Office of Employment and Unemployment Statistics, Bureau of Labor Statistics.

[3]Sharon P. Brown is the chief of the Division of LAUS, Office of Employment and Unemployment Statistics, Bureau of Labor Statistics. Sandra L. Mason is a supervisory economist in the Division of Research and Methods, Office of Employment and Unemployment Statistics, Bureau of Labor Statistics. Richard B. Tiller is a mathematical statistician in the Division of CPS and LAUS, Office of Employment and Unemployment Statistics, Bureau of Labor Statistics.

[4]Charles S. Colgan is a professor in the National Ocean Economics Program, Muskie School of Public Service, University of Southern Maine (Portland, Maine) and the chief economist for market data for the National Ocean Economics Program. Jefferey Adkins is an economist and program manager with the National Oceanic and Atmospheric Administration's Coastal Services (Charleston, South Carolina).

[5]For information on the definitions of the ocean economy, visit the National Ocean Economics Program Web site at <http://www.oceaneconomics.org>.

[6]Coastal zone counties are those within a state's defined coastal zone management program. Watershed counties are defined by the U.S. Geological Survey.

SUMMARY OF SELECTED ECONOMIC INDICATORS

These figures, which also appear in the relevant chapters of this publication, show the significant economic changes that took place during the recovery from the recession of 2000. They are also important indicators of the factors that will affect the economy in the future. While employment has recovered, manufacturing employment is still declining (although at a much slower rate than in during previous years). The costs of providing employee benefits continue to have important implications for total compensation costs, especially as real wages stagnate and the labor force ages. Finally, problems have been created by the rapid increase in fuel prices.

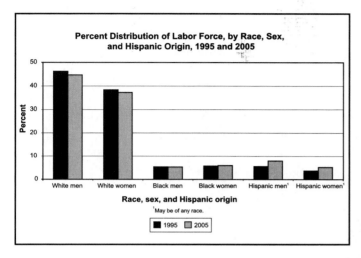

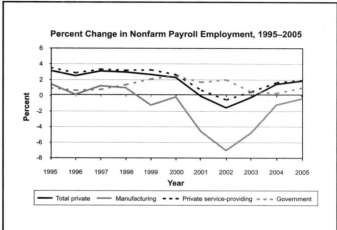

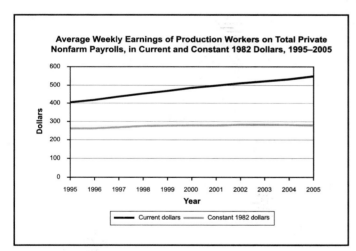

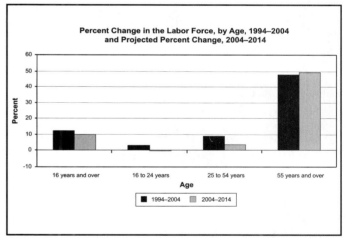

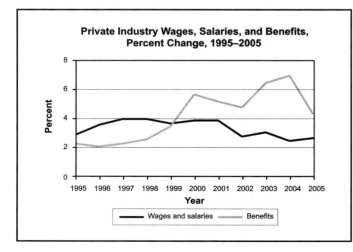

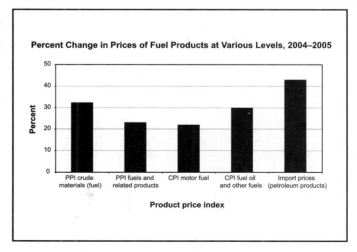

CHAPTER ONE

POPULATION, LABOR FORCE, AND EMPLOYMENT STATUS

POPULATION, LABOR FORCE, AND EMPLOYMENT STATUS

HIGHLIGHTS

This chapter presents the detailed historical information collected in the Current Population Survey (CPS), a monthly survey of households that gathers data on the employment status of the population. Basic data on labor force, employment, and unemployment are shown for various characteristics of the population, including age, sex, race, and marital status.

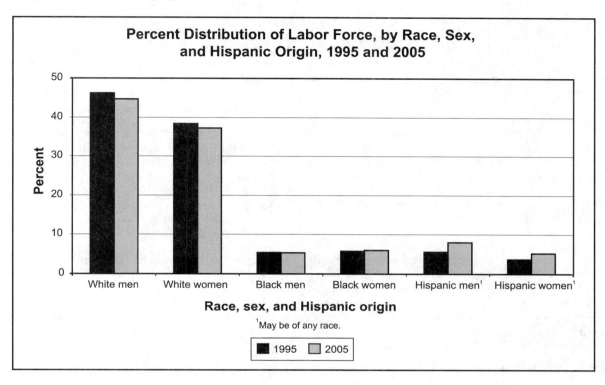

The proportion of the labor force made up of Whites declined over the 1995–2005 decade, dropping from 84.6 percent to 81.9 percent; the proportion made up of Blacks increased slightly from 11.2 percent in 1995 to 11.4 percent in 2005, mainly due to the increasing number of Black women in the labor force. Hispanic representation rose significantly, increasing from 9.3 percent in 1995 to 13.3 percent in 2005. Hispanics may be of any race. (See Table 1-3.)

OTHER HIGHLIGHTS

- The labor force increased more quickly in 2005 than in 2004 (1.3 percent compared to 0.6 percent). However, the total labor force participation rate was 66 percent in both years. (See Tables 1-1 and 1-8.)

- The labor force participation rate of persons age 65 years and over grew in 2005, a continuation of the steady increase in this group's participation rate over the past 10 years. From 1995 to 2005, the participation rate for this age group grew from 12.1 percent to 15.1 percent. (See Table 1-8.)

- In 2005, the number of Black women in the labor force exceeded the number of Black men in the labor force by nearly 1.02 million. This gap was smaller than in 2004 due to a 2.9 percent increase in the labor force of Black men. (See Table 1-7.)

- The labor force participation rate for married women rose from 53.8 percent in 1985 to 60.7 percent in 2005. (See Table 1-4.)

- The Midwest continued to have the highest labor force participation rate at 68.2 percent, 2.2 percentage points above the national average. The south had the lowest labor force participation rate at 64.9 percent. (See Table 1-5.)

NOTES AND DEFINITIONS

CURRENT POPULATION SURVEY OF HOUSEHOLDS

Collection and Coverage

The Bureau of Labor Statistics (BLS) uses data from the Current Population Survey (CPS) to compile statistics on the employment status of the population and related data. The Census Bureau—using a scientifically selected sample of the civilian noninstitutional population—conducts the CPS, a monthly survey of households, for BLS.

The CPS sample has been increased from 50,000 to 60,000 households. The new sample was introduced in September 2000. However, in order to evaluate the impact of the change, the estimates of the national labor force from the additional sample were not introduced at that time. Since the estimates from the two samples were virtually the same, BLS began incorporating the additional sample into official national estimates in July 2001.

Respondents are interviewed to obtain information about the employment status of each household member age 16 years and over. The inquiry relates to the household member's employment status during the calendar week, Sunday through Saturday, that contains the 12th day of the month. This is known as the "reference week." Actual field interviewing is conducted during the following week (the week that contains the 19th day of the month).

Concepts and Definitions

The concepts and definitions underlying the labor force data have been modified—but not substantially altered—since the inception of the survey in 1940. Current definitions of some of the major concepts used in the CPS are described below.

The *civilian noninstitutional population* includes persons 16 years of age and over who reside in the 50 states and the District of Columbia, who are not inmates of institutions (such as penal and mental facilities and homes for the aged), and who are not on active duty in the armed forces.

An *employed person* is any person who, during the reference week: (1) did any work at all (at least one hour) as a paid employee in his or her own business, profession, or on their own farm, or who worked 15 hours or more as an unpaid worker in an enterprise operated by a member of the family; and (2) any person who was not working but who had a job or business from which he or she was temporarily absent due to vacation, illness, bad weather, child-care problems, maternity or paternity leave, labor-management disputes, job training, or other family or personal reasons, despite whether the employee was being paid for the time off or was seeking other jobs.

Each employed person is counted only once, even if he or she holds more than one job. For purposes of occupation and industry classification, multiple jobholders are counted as being in the job at which they worked the greatest number of hours during the reference week.

Included in the total are employed citizens of foreign countries who were temporarily in the United States but not living on the premises of an embassy. Excluded are persons whose only activity during the reference week consisted of work around their own house (painting, repairing, or own home housework) or volunteer work for religious, charitable, and similar organizations.

Unemployed persons are all persons who had no employment during the reference week, but who were available for work (except for temporary illness) and had made specific efforts to find employment some time during the four-week period ending with the reference week. Persons who were waiting to be recalled to a job from which they had been laid off need not have been looking for work to be classified as unemployed.

Duration of *unemployment* represents the length of time (through the current reference week) that persons classified as unemployed had been looking for work. For persons on layoff, duration of unemployment represents the number of full weeks they had been on layoff. Mean duration of unemployment is the arithmetic average computed from single weeks of unemployment; median duration of unemployment is the midpoint of the distribution of weeks of unemployment.

Reasons for unemployment are divided into four major groups: (1) job losers, defined as (a) persons on temporary layoff, who have been given a date to return to work or who expect to return to work within six months; (b) permanent job losers, whose employment ended involuntarily and who began looking for work; and (c) persons who completed a temporary job and began looking for work after the job ended; (2) job leavers, defined as persons who quit or otherwise terminated their employment voluntarily and immediately began looking for work; (3) reentrants, defined as persons who previously worked but were out of the labor force prior to beginning their job search; and (4) new entrants, defined as persons who had never worked but were currently searching for work.

The *civilian labor force* comprises all civilians classified as employed or unemployed.

The *unemployment rate* is the number of unemployed persons as a percentage of the civilian labor force.

The *participation rate* represents the proportion of the civilian noninstitutional population currently in the labor force.

The *employment-population ratio* represents the proportion of the population that is currently employed.

Persons not in the labor force are all persons in the civilian noninstitutional population who are neither employed nor unemployed. Information is collected about their desire for and availability to take a job at the time of the CPS interview, job search activity during the prior year, and reason for not looking for work during the four-week period ending with the reference week. Persons not in the labor force who want and are available for a job and who have looked for work within the past 12 months (or since the end of their last job, if they had held one within the past 12 months), but who are not currently looking, are designated as *marginally attached to the labor force*. The marginally attached are divided into those not currently looking because they believe their search would be futile—so-called *discouraged workers*—and those not currently looking for other reasons, such as family responsibilities, ill health, or lack of transportation.

Discouraged workers are defined as persons not in the labor force who want and are available for a job and who have looked for work within in the past 12 months (or since the end of their last job, if they held one within the past 12 months), but who are not currently looking because they believe that there are no jobs available or there are none for which they would qualify. The reasons for not currently looking for work include a person's belief that no work is available in his or her line of work or area; he or she could not find any work; he or she lacks necessary schooling, training, skills, or experience; employers would think he or she is too young or too old; or he or she would encounter hiring discrimination.

Usual full- or part-time status refers to hours usually worked per week. Full-time workers are those who usually work 35 hours or more (at all jobs). This group includes some individuals who worked less than 35 hours during the reference week for economic or noneconomic reasons. Part-time workers are those who usually work less than 35 hours per week (at all jobs), regardless of the number of hours worked during the reference week. These concepts are used to differentiate a person's normal schedule from his or her specific activity during the reference week. Unemployed persons who are looking for full-time work or who are on layoff from full-time jobs are counted as part of the full-time labor force; unemployed persons who are seeking part-time work or who are on layoff from part-time jobs are counted as part of the part-time labor force.

Occupation, industry, and class of worker for members of the employed population are determined by the job held during the reference week. Persons with two or more jobs are classified as being in the job at which they worked the greatest number of hours. The unemployed are classified according to their last job. Beginning with data published in 2003, the systems used to classify occupational and industry data changed. They are currently based on the Standard Occupational Classification (SOC) system and the North American Industry Classification System (NAICS). (See the following section on historical comparability for a discussion of previous classification systems used in the CPS.) The class-of-worker breakdown assigns

workers to one of the following categories: private and government wage and salary workers, self-employed workers, and unpaid family workers. Wage and salary workers receive wages, salaries, commissions, tips, or pay in kind from a private employer or from a government unit. Self-employed workers are those who work for profit or fees in their own businesses, professions, trades, or on their own farms. Only the unincorporated self-employed are included in the self-employed category in the class-of-worker typology. Self-employed workers who respond that their businesses are incorporated are included among wage and salary workers, because they are technically paid employees of a corporation. An unpaid family worker is a person who works without pay for 15 hours or more per week on a farm or in a business operated by a member of the household to whom the worker is related by birth or marriage.

A *multiple jobholder* is an employed person who, during the reference week, had two or more jobs as a wage and salary worker, was self-employed and also held a wage and salary job, or worked as an unpaid family worker and also held a wage and salary job. A person only employed in private households (as a cleaner, gardener, babysitter, etc.) who worked for two or more employers during the reference week is not counted as a multiple jobholder, since working for several employers is considered an inherent characteristic of private household work. Also excluded are self-employed persons with multiple businesses and persons with multiple jobs as unpaid family workers.

At work part-time for economic reasons, sometimes called involuntary part-time, refers to individuals who gave an economic reason for working 1 to 34 hours during the reference week. Economic reasons include slack work or unfavorable business conditions, inability to find full-time work, and seasonal declines in demand. Those who usually work part-time must also indicate that they want and are available to work full-time to be classified as working part-time for economic reasons.

At work part-time for noneconomic reasons refers to persons who usually work part-time and were at work 1 to 34 hours during the reference week for a noneconomic reason. Noneconomic reasons include illness or other medical limitations, childcare problems or other family or personal obligations, school or training, retirement or Social Security limits on earnings, and being in a job where full-time work is less than 35 hours. This also includes workers who gave an economic reason for usually working 1 to 34 hours but said they did not want to work full-time or were unavailable for full-time work.

White, Black, and Asian are terms used to describe the race of persons. Persons in these categories are those who selected that race only. Persons in the remaining race categories—American Indian or Alaskan Native, Native Hawaiian or Other Pacific Islander, and persons who selected more than one race category—are included in the estimates of total employment and unemployment but are not shown separately because the number of survey respondents is too small to develop estimates of sufficient quality for monthly publication.

Hispanic origin refers to persons who identified themselves in the enumeration process as being Spanish, Hispanic, or Latino. Persons of Hispanic or Latino origin may be of any race.

Single, never married; married, spouse present; and *other marital status* are the terms used to define the marital status of individuals at the time of the CPS interview. Married, spouse present, applies to a husband and wife if both were living in the same household, even though one may be temporarily absent on business, vacation, in a hospital, etc. Other marital status applies to persons who are married, spouse absent; widowed; or divorced. Married, spouse absent relates to persons who are separated due to marital problems, as well as husbands and wives living apart because one was employed elsewhere, on duty with the armed forces, or for any other reason.

A *household* consists of all persons—related family members and all unrelated persons—who occupy a housing unit and have no other usual address. A house, an apartment, a group of rooms, or a single room is regarded as a housing unit when occupied or intended for occupancy as separate living quarters. A householder is the person (or one of the persons) in whose name the housing unit is owned or rented. The term is not applied to either husbands or wives in married-couple families; it refers only to persons in families maintained by either men or women without a spouse.

A *family* is defined as a group of two or more persons residing together who are related by birth, marriage, or adoption. All such persons are considered members of one family. Families are classified as either married-couple families or families maintained by women or men without spouses.

Children refer to "own" children of the husband, wife, or person maintaining the family, including sons and daughters, stepchildren, and adopted children. Excluded are other related children, such as grandchildren, nieces, nephews, cousins, and unrelated children.

The annual CPS data on the employment characteristics of families and family members began with data for 1995. These data are not strictly comparable with family data derived from the March supplement to the CPS. The annual data are derived by averaging the data for each month of the year, whereas the March data refer to that specific month. The annual average data provide a larger sample size, while the March data provide a longer historical series.

Additional Concepts and Definitions: CPS Supplements

In addition to the above concepts and definitions, the definitions below apply to the special labor force data collected annually in the March supplement to the CPS and

to the data on tenure usually collected in the February supplement to the CPS.

Persons with work experience are civilians who worked at any time during the preceding calendar year at full- or part-time jobs for pay or profit (including paid vacations and sick leave) or who worked without pay on farms or in family-operated businesses. From 1989 onward, these supplementary tables also include members of the armed forces.

Tenure refers to length of time a worker has been continuously employed by his or her current employer. These data are collected through a supplement to the CPS. All employed persons were asked how long they had been working continuously for their present employer and, if the length of time was one or two years, a follow-up question was asked about the exact number of months. The follow-up question was included for the first time in the February 1996 supplement to the CPS. CPS supplements that obtained information on tenure in the Januaries of 1983, 1987, and 1991 did not include the follow-up question. Prior to 1983, the question was asked differently. Data prior to 1983 are thus not strictly comparable to data for subsequent years.

Year-round, full-time workers are workers who primarily worked at full-time jobs for 50 weeks or more during the preceding calendar year. Part-year workers worked either full- or part-time for 1 to 49 weeks.

A *spell of unemployment* is a continuous period of unemployment of at least one week's duration and is terminated by either employment or withdrawal from the labor force.

Extent of unemployment refers to the number of workers and proportion of the labor force that were unemployed at some time during the year. The number of weeks unemployed is the total number of weeks accumulated during the entire calendar year.

Earnings are all money income of $1 or more from wages and salaries and all net money income of $1 or more from farm and nonfarm self-employment.

Educational attainment refers to years of school completed in regular schools, which include graded public, private, and parochial elementary, and high schools, whether day or night school. Colleges, universities, and professional schools are also included.

Minimum wage refers to the prevailing federal minimum wage, which was $5.15 per hour in 2005. Data are for wage and salary workers who were paid hourly rates and refer to a person's earnings at the sole or principal job.

Absences are defined as instances in which persons who usually work 35 or more hours a week worked less than that during the reference period for reasons of illness or family obligations. Excluded are situations in which work was missed for vacation, holidays, or other reasons. The estimates are based on one-fourth of the sample only.

Historical Comparability

While current survey concepts and methods are very similar to those used for the inaugural CPS in 1940, a number of changes have been made over the years to improve the accuracy and usefulness of the data. Only the latest changes are described here.

Major changes to the CPS, such as the complete redesign of the questionnaire and the use of computer-assisted interviewing for the entire survey, were introduced in 1994. In addition, there were revisions to some of the labor force concepts and definitions, including the implementation of changes recommended in 1979 by the National Commission on Employment and Unemployment Statistics (NCEUS, also known as the Levitan Commission). Some of the major changes to the survey at this time included the following:

1) A redesigned and automated questionnaire was implemented. The CPS questionnaire was totally redesigned in order to obtain more accurate, comprehensive, and relevant information, and to take advantage of state-of-the-art computer interviewing techniques.

2) The addition of two criteria made the definition of discouraged workers more objective. Beginning in 1994, persons classified as discouraged workers must have looked for a job within the past year (or since their last job, if they worked during the year), and must have been available for work during the reference week. (A direct question on availability was added in 1994.) These changes were made because the NCEUS and others felt that the previous definition of discouraged workers was too subjective, relying mainly on an individual's stated desire for a job and not on prior testing of the labor market.

3) Similarly, the identification of persons employed part-time for economic reasons (working less than 35 hours during the reference week because of poor business conditions or an inability to find full-time work) was tightened by adding two new criteria for persons who usually work part-time: these persons must now want and be available for full-time work. (Persons who usually work full-time but worked part-time for economic reasons during the reference week are assumed to meet these criteria.)

4) Specific questions were added about the expectation of recall for persons who indicate that they are on layoff. To be classified as "on temporary layoff," persons must expect to be recalled to their jobs.

Comparability of Labor Force Levels

In addition to the refinements in concepts, definitions, and methods made over the years, other changes—made to improve the accuracy of the estimates—have also affected the comparability of the labor force data. The most important of these changes is the adjustment of the population

totals as a result of new information from the decennial censuses. It is also crucial to correct for estimating errors during the intercensal years.

Beginning in January 1997, updated information on the demographic characteristics of immigrants and emigrants was introduced. This increased the overall population by about 470,000, the labor force by about 320,000, and employment by about 290,000, with similar upward adjustments for Hispanics. Unemployment and other percentage rates were not affected.

Beginning in January 1998, new estimating procedures were introduced, which reduced labor force by about 229,000 and employment by about 256,000. However, these new procedures raised unemployment by about 27,000. New information about immigration and emigration was also incorporated, which increased the Hispanic population by about 57,000. Unemployment rates were not significantly affected.

Beginning in January 1999, new information on immigration raised the population by about 310,000, with differing impacts on different demographic groups. The population of men was lowered by about 185,000, but the population of women was raised by about 490,000. The Hispanic population was lowered by about 165,000 while the rest of the population was raised by about 470,000. Hispanic labor force and employment estimates were each reduced by over 200,000. The impact on unemployment rates and other percentages was small.

Beginning in January 2003, several other changes were introduced into the CPS. These changes included the following:

1) Population controls that reflected the results of the 2000 census were introduced into the monthly CPS estimation process. These new population size controls substantially increased the size of the civilian noninstitutional population and the civilian labor force. Data from January 2000 through December 2002 were revised to reflect the higher population estimates from the 2000 census and the higher rates of population growth since the census. The entire amount of this adjustment was added to the labor force data in January 2003, resulting in the increases of about 941,000 to the civilian noninstitutional population and about 614,000 to the civilian labor force. The unemployment rate and other ratios were not substantially affected by either of these population control adjustments.

2) Questions on race and Hispanic origin were modified to comply with the new standards for maintaining, collecting, and presenting federal data on race and ethnicity for federal statistical agencies. The questions were reworded to indicate that individuals could select more than once race category and to convey more clearly that individuals should report their own perception of what race is. These changes had no impact on the overall civilian noninstitutional population and civilian labor force. However, they

did reduce the population and labor force levels of Whites, Blacks, and Asians beginning in January 2003.

3) Improvements were introduced to both the second stage and composite weighting procedures. These changes adapted the weighting procedures to the new race/ethnicity classification system and enhanced the stability over time for demographic groups. The second-stage weighting procedure substantially reduced the variability of estimates and corrected, to some extent, for CPS underreporting.

Changes in the Occupational and Industrial Classification System

Beginning in January 1983, the occupational and industrial classification systems used in the 1980 census were introduced into the CPS. The 1980 census occupational classification system was so radically different in concepts and nomenclature from the 1970 system that comparisons of historical data are not possible without major adjustments.

The industrial classification system used in the 1980 census was based on the 1972 Standard Industrial Classification (SIC) system, as modified in 1977. The adoption of the new industrial system had much less of an adverse effect on historical comparability than did the new occupational system.

Beginning in January 1992, the occupational and industrial classification systems used in the 1990 census were introduced into the CPS. There were a few breaks in comparability between the 1980 and 1990 census–based systems, particularly within the technical, sales, and administrative support categories. The most notable changes in industry classification were the shift of several industries from business services to professional services and the splitting of some industries into smaller, more detailed categories.

In January 2003, the CPS adopted the 2002 census industry and occupational classification systems, which were derived, respectively, from the 2002 North American Industry Classification System (NAICS) and the 2000 Standard Occupational Classification (SOC) system. The introduction of the new industry and occupational classification systems created a complete break in comparability at all levels of industry and occupation aggregation. For more information about the January 2003 change in the CPS classification systems, see the BLS Web site at <http://www.bls.gov/cps/cpsoccind.htm>.

Sources of Additional Information

A complete description of sampling and estimation procedures and further information on the impact of historical changes in the surveys can be found in the February issues of *Employment and Earnings*, a BLS publication, and in the updated version of Chapter 1 of the *BLS Handbook of*

Table 1-1. Employment Status of the Civilian Noninstitutional Population, 1947–2005

(Thousands of people, percent.)

Year	Civilian noninstitutional population	Civilian labor force								Not in labor force
		Total	Participation rate	Employed				Unemployed		
				Total	Percent of population	Agriculture	Nonagricultural industries	Number	Unemployment rate	
1947	101 827	59 350	58.3	57 038	56.0	7 890	49 148	2 311	3.9	42 477
1948	103 068	60 621	58.8	58 343	56.6	7 629	50 714	2 276	3.8	42 447
1949	103 994	61 286	58.9	57 651	55.4	7 658	49 993	3 637	5.9	42 708
1950	104 995	62 208	59.2	58 918	56.1	7 160	51 758	3 288	5.3	42 787
1951	104 621	62 017	59.2	59 961	57.3	6 726	53 235	2 055	3.3	42 604
1952	105 231	62 138	59.0	60 250	57.3	6 500	53 749	1 883	3.0	43 093
1953[1]	107 056	63 015	58.9	61 179	57.1	6 260	54 919	1 834	2.9	44 041
1954	108 321	63 643	58.8	60 109	55.5	6 205	53 904	3 532	5.5	44 678
1955	109 683	65 023	59.3	62 170	56.7	6 450	55 722	2 852	4.4	44 660
1956	110 954	66 552	60.0	63 799	57.5	6 283	57 514	2 750	4.1	44 402
1957	112 265	66 929	59.6	64 071	57.1	5 947	58 123	2 859	4.3	45 336
1958	113 727	67 639	59.5	63 036	55.4	5 586	57 450	4 602	6.8	46 088
1959	115 329	68 369	59.3	64 630	56.0	5 565	59 065	3 740	5.5	46 960
1960[1]	117 245	69 628	59.4	65 778	56.1	5 458	60 318	3 852	5.5	47 617
1961	118 771	70 459	59.3	65 746	55.4	5 200	60 546	4 714	6.7	48 312
1962[1]	120 153	70 614	58.8	66 702	55.5	4 944	61 759	3 911	5.5	49 539
1963	122 416	71 833	58.7	67 762	55.4	4 687	63 076	4 070	5.7	50 583
1964	124 485	73 091	58.7	69 305	55.7	4 523	64 782	3 786	5.2	51 394
1965	126 513	74 455	58.9	71 088	56.2	4 361	66 726	3 366	4.5	52 058
1966	128 058	75 770	59.2	72 895	56.9	3 979	68 915	2 875	3.8	52 288
1967	129 874	77 347	59.6	74 372	57.3	3 844	70 527	2 975	3.8	52 527
1968	132 028	78 737	59.6	75 920	57.5	3 817	72 103	2 817	3.6	53 291
1969	134 335	80 734	60.1	77 902	58.0	3 606	74 296	2 832	3.5	53 602
1970	137 085	82 771	60.4	78 678	57.4	3 463	75 215	4 093	4.9	54 315
1971	140 216	84 382	60.2	79 367	56.6	3 394	75 972	5 016	5.9	55 834
1972[1]	144 126	87 034	60.4	82 153	57.0	3 484	78 669	4 882	5.6	57 091
1973[1]	147 096	89 429	60.8	85 064	57.8	3 470	81 594	4 365	4.9	57 667
1974	150 120	91 949	61.3	86 794	57.8	3 515	83 279	5 156	5.6	58 171
1975	153 153	93 774	61.2	85 846	56.1	3 408	82 438	7 929	8.5	59 377
1976	156 150	96 158	61.6	88 752	56.8	3 331	85 421	7 406	7.7	59 991
1977	159 033	99 008	62.3	92 017	57.9	3 283	88 734	6 991	7.1	60 025
1978[1]	161 910	102 250	63.2	96 048	59.3	3 387	92 661	6 202	6.1	59 659
1979	164 863	104 962	63.7	98 824	59.9	3 347	95 477	6 137	5.8	59 900
1980	167 745	106 940	63.8	99 302	59.2	3 364	95 938	7 637	7.1	60 806
1981	170 130	108 670	63.9	100 397	59.0	3 368	97 030	8 273	7.6	61 460
1982	172 271	110 204	64.0	99 526	57.8	3 401	96 125	10 678	9.7	62 067
1983	174 215	111 550	64.0	100 834	57.9	3 383	97 450	10 717	9.6	62 665
1984	176 383	113 544	64.4	105 005	59.5	3 321	101 685	8 539	7.5	62 839
1985	178 206	115 461	64.8	107 150	60.1	3 179	103 971	8 312	7.2	62 744
1986[1]	180 587	117 834	65.3	109 597	60.7	3 163	106 434	8 237	7.0	62 752
1987	182 753	119 865	65.6	112 440	61.5	3 208	109 232	7 425	6.2	62 888
1988	184 613	121 669	65.9	114 968	62.3	3 169	111 800	6 701	5.5	62 944
1989	186 393	123 869	66.5	117 342	63.0	3 199	114 142	6 528	5.3	62 523
1990[1]	189 164	125 840	66.5	118 793	62.8	3 223	115 570	7 047	5.6	63 324
1991	190 925	126 346	66.2	117 718	61.7	3 269	114 449	8 628	6.8	64 578
1992	192 805	128 105	66.4	118 492	61.5	3 247	115 245	9 613	7.5	64 700
1993	194 838	129 200	66.3	120 259	61.7	3 115	117 144	8 940	6.9	65 638
1994[1]	196 814	131 056	66.6	123 060	62.5	3 409	119 651	7 996	6.1	65 758
1995	198 584	132 304	66.6	124 900	62.9	3 440	121 460	7 404	5.6	66 280
1996	200 591	133 943	66.8	126 708	63.2	3 443	123 264	7 236	5.4	66 647
1997[1]	203 133	136 297	67.1	129 558	63.8	3 399	126 159	6 739	4.9	66 836
1998[1]	205 220	137 673	67.1	131 463	64.1	3 378	128 085	6 210	4.5	67 547
1999[1]	207 753	139 368	67.1	133 488	64.3	3 281	130 207	5 880	4.2	68 385
2000[1]	212 577	142 583	67.1	136 891	64.4	2 464	134 427	5 692	4.0	69 994
2001	215 092	143 734	66.8	136 933	63.7	2 299	134 635	6 801	4.7	71 359
2002	217 570	144 863	66.6	136 485	62.7	2 311	134 174	8 378	5.8	72 707
2003[1]	221 168	146 510	66.2	137 736	62.3	2 275	135 461	8 774	6.0	74 658
2004[1]	223 357	147 401	66.0	139 252	62.3	2 232	137 020	8 149	5.5	75 956
2005[1]	226 082	149 320	66.0	141 730	62.7	2 197	139 532	7 591	5.1	76 762

[1]Not strictly comparable with data for prior years. See notes and definitions for information on historical comparability.

Table 1-2. Employment Status of the Civilian Noninstitutional Population, by Sex, 1970–2005

(Thousands of people, percent.)

Sex and year	Civilian noninstitutional population	Civilian labor force		Employed				Unemployed		Not in labor force
		Total	Participation rate	Total	Percent of population	Agriculture	Non-agricultural industries	Number	Unemployment rate	
Men										
1970	64 304	51 228	79.7	48 990	76.2	2 862	46 128	2 238	4.4	13 076
1971	65 942	52 180	79.1	49 390	74.9	2 795	46 595	2 789	5.3	13 762
1972[1]	67 835	53 555	78.9	50 896	75.0	2 849	48 047	2 659	5.0	14 280
1973[1]	69 292	54 624	78.8	52 349	75.5	2 847	49 502	2 275	4.2	14 667
1974	70 808	55 739	78.7	53 024	74.9	2 919	50 105	2 714	4.9	15 069
1975	72 291	56 299	77.9	51 857	71.7	2 824	49 032	4 442	7.9	15 993
1976	73 759	57 174	77.5	53 138	72.0	2 744	50 394	4 036	7.1	16 585
1977	75 193	58 396	77.7	54 728	72.8	2 671	52 057	3 667	6.3	16 797
1978[1]	76 576	59 620	77.9	56 479	73.8	2 718	53 761	3 142	5.3	16 956
1979	78 020	60 726	77.8	57 607	73.8	2 686	54 921	3 120	5.1	17 293
1980	79 398	61 453	77.4	57 186	72.0	2 709	54 477	4 267	6.9	17 945
1981	80 511	61 974	77.0	57 397	71.3	2 700	54 697	4 577	7.4	18 537
1982	81 523	62 450	76.6	56 271	69.0	2 736	53 534	6 179	9.9	19 073
1983	82 531	63 047	76.4	56 787	68.8	2 704	54 083	6 260	9.9	19 484
1984	83 605	63 835	76.4	59 091	70.7	2 668	56 423	4 744	7.4	19 771
1985	84 469	64 411	76.3	59 891	70.9	2 535	57 356	4 521	7.0	20 058
1986[1]	85 798	65 422	76.3	60 892	71.0	2 511	58 381	4 530	6.9	20 376
1987	86 899	66 207	76.2	62 107	71.5	2 543	59 564	4 101	6.2	20 692
1988	87 857	66 927	76.2	63 273	72.0	2 493	60 780	3 655	5.5	20 930
1989	88 762	67 840	76.4	64 315	72.5	2 513	61 802	3 525	5.2	20 923
1990[1]	90 377	69 011	76.4	65 104	72.0	2 546	62 559	3 906	5.7	21 367
1991	91 278	69 168	75.8	64 223	70.4	2 589	61 634	4 946	7.2	22 110
1992	92 270	69 964	75.8	64 440	69.8	2 575	61 866	5 523	7.9	22 306
1993	93 332	70 404	75.4	65 349	70.0	2 478	62 871	5 055	7.2	22 927
1994[1]	94 354	70 817	75.1	66 450	70.4	2 554	63 896	4 367	6.2	23 538
1995	95 178	71 360	75.0	67 377	70.8	2 559	64 818	3 983	5.6	23 818
1996	96 206	72 086	74.9	68 207	70.9	2 573	65 634	3 880	5.4	24 119
1997[1]	97 715	73 261	75.0	69 685	71.3	2 552	67 133	3 577	4.9	24 454
1998[1]	98 758	73 959	74.9	70 693	71.6	2 553	68 140	3 266	4.4	24 799
1999[1]	99 722	74 512	74.7	71 446	71.6	2 432	69 014	3 066	4.1	25 210
2000[1]	101 964	76 280	74.8	73 305	71.9	1 861	71 444	2 975	3.9	25 684
2001	103 282	76 886	74.4	73 196	70.9	1 708	71 488	3 690	4.8	26 396
2002	104 585	77 500	74.1	72 903	69.7	1 724	71 179	4 597	5.9	27 085
2003[1]	106 435	78 238	73.5	73 332	68.9	1 695	71 636	4 906	6.3	28 197
2004[1]	107 710	78 980	73.3	74 524	69.2	1 687	72 838	4 456	5.6	28 730
2005[1]	109 151	80 033	73.3	75 973	69.6	1 654	74 319	4 059	5.1	29 119
Women										
1970	72 782	31 543	43.3	29 688	40.8	601	29 087	1 855	5.9	41 239
1971	74 274	32 202	43.4	29 976	40.4	599	29 377	2 227	6.9	42 072
1972[1]	76 290	33 479	43.9	31 257	41.0	635	30 622	2 222	6.6	42 811
1973[1]	77 804	34 804	44.7	32 715	42.0	622	32 093	2 089	6.0	43 000
1974	79 312	36 211	45.7	33 769	42.6	596	33 173	2 441	6.7	43 101
1975	80 860	37 475	46.3	33 989	42.0	584	33 404	3 486	9.3	43 386
1976	82 390	38 983	47.3	35 615	43.2	588	35 027	3 369	8.6	43 406
1977	83 840	40 613	48.4	37 289	44.5	612	36 677	3 324	8.2	43 227
1978[1]	85 334	42 631	50.0	39 569	46.4	669	38 900	3 061	7.2	42 703
1979	86 843	44 235	50.9	41 217	47.5	661	40 556	3 018	6.8	42 608
1980	88 348	45 487	51.5	42 117	47.7	656	41 461	3 370	7.4	42 861
1981	89 618	46 696	52.1	43 000	48.0	667	42 333	3 696	7.9	42 922
1982	90 748	47 755	52.6	43 256	47.7	665	42 591	4 499	9.4	42 993
1983	91 684	48 503	52.9	44 047	48.0	680	43 367	4 457	9.2	43 181
1984	92 778	49 709	53.6	45 915	49.5	653	45 262	3 794	7.6	43 068
1985	93 736	51 050	54.5	47 259	50.4	644	46 615	3 791	7.4	42 686
1986[1]	94 789	52 413	55.3	48 706	51.4	652	48 054	3 707	7.1	42 376
1987	95 853	53 658	56.0	50 334	52.5	666	49 668	3 324	6.2	42 195
1988	96 756	54 742	56.6	51 696	53.4	676	51 020	3 046	5.6	42 014
1989	97 630	56 030	57.4	53 027	54.3	687	52 341	3 003	5.4	41 601
1990[1]	98 787	56 829	57.5	53 689	54.3	678	53 011	3 140	5.5	41 957
1991	99 646	57 178	57.4	53 496	53.7	680	52 815	3 683	6.4	42 468
1992	100 535	58 141	57.8	54 052	53.8	672	53 380	4 090	7.0	42 394
1993	101 506	58 795	57.9	54 910	54.1	637	54 273	3 885	6.6	42 711
1994[1]	102 460	60 239	58.8	56 610	55.3	855	55 755	3 629	6.0	42 221
1995	103 406	60 944	58.9	57 523	55.6	881	56 642	3 421	5.6	42 462
1996	104 385	61 857	59.3	58 501	56.0	871	57 630	3 356	5.4	42 528
1997[1]	105 418	63 036	59.8	59 873	56.8	847	59 026	3 162	5.0	42 382
1998[1]	106 462	63 714	59.8	60 771	57.1	825	59 945	2 944	4.6	42 748
1999[1]	108 031	64 855	60.0	62 042	57.4	849	61 193	2 814	4.3	43 175
2000[1]	110 613	66 303	59.9	63 586	57.5	602	62 983	2 717	4.1	44 310
2001	111 811	66 848	59.8	63 737	57.0	591	63 147	3 111	4.7	44 962
2002	112 985	67 363	59.6	63 582	56.3	587	62 995	3 781	5.6	45 621
2003[1]	114 733	68 272	59.5	64 404	56.1	580	63 824	3 868	5.7	46 461
2004[1]	115 647	68 421	59.2	64 728	56.0	546	64 182	3 694	5.4	47 225
2005[1]	116 931	69 288	59.3	65 757	56.2	544	65 213	3 531	5.1	47 643

[1]Not strictly comparable with data for prior years. See notes and definitions for information on historical comparability.

Table 1-3. Employment Status of the Civilian Noninstitutional Population, by Sex, Age, Race, and Hispanic Origin, 1985–2005

(Thousands of people.)

Characteristic	1985	1986	1987	1988	1989	1990	1991	1992	1993	1994	1995
ALL RACES											
Both Sexes											
Civilian noninstitutional population	178 206	180 587	182 753	184 613	186 393	189 164	190 925	192 805	194 838	196 814	198 584
Civilian labor force	115 461	117 834	119 865	121 669	123 869	125 840	126 346	128 105	129 200	131 056	132 304
Employed	107 150	109 597	112 440	114 968	117 342	118 793	117 718	118 492	120 259	123 060	124 900
Agriculture	3 179	3 163	3 208	3 169	3 199	3 223	3 269	3 247	3 115	3 409	3 440
Nonagricultural industries	103 971	106 434	109 232	111 800	114 142	115 570	114 449	115 245	117 144	119 651	121 460
Unemployed	8 312	8 237	7 425	6 701	6 528	7 047	8 628	9 613	8 940	7 996	7 404
Not in labor force	62 744	62 752	62 888	62 944	62 523	63 324	64 578	64 700	65 638	65 758	66 280
Men, 16 Years and Over											
Civilian noninstitutional population	84 469	85 798	86 899	87 857	88 762	90 377	91 278	92 270	93 332	94 355	95 178
Civilian labor force	64 411	65 422	66 207	66 927	67 840	69 011	69 168	69 964	70 404	70 817	71 360
Employed	59 891	60 892	62 107	63 273	64 315	65 104	64 223	64 440	65 349	66 450	67 377
Agriculture	2 535	2 511	2 543	2 493	2 513	2 546	2 589	2 575	2 478	2 554	2 559
Nonagricultural industries	57 356	58 381	59 564	60 780	61 802	62 559	61 634	61 866	62 871	63 896	64 818
Unemployed	4 521	4 530	4 101	3 655	3 525	3 906	4 946	5 523	5 055	4 367	3 983
Not in labor force	20 058	20 376	20 692	20 930	20 923	21 367	22 110	22 306	22 927	23 538	23 818
Men, 20 Years and Over											
Civilian noninstitutional population	77 195	78 523	79 565	80 553	81 619	83 030	84 144	85 247	86 256	87 151	87 811
Civilian labor force	60 277	61 320	62 095	62 768	63 704	64 916	65 374	66 213	66 642	66 921	67 324
Employed	56 562	57 569	58 726	59 781	60 837	61 678	61 178	61 496	62 355	63 294	64 085
Agriculture	2 278	2 292	2 329	2 271	2 307	2 329	2 383	2 385	2 293	2 351	2 335
Nonagricultural industries	54 284	55 277	56 397	57 510	58 530	59 349	58 795	59 111	60 063	60 943	61 750
Unemployed	3 715	3 751	3 369	2 987	2 867	3 239	4 195	4 717	4 287	3 627	3 239
Not in labor force	16 918	17 203	17 470	17 785	17 915	18 114	18 770	19 034	19 613	20 230	20 487
Women, 16 Years and Over											
Civilian noninstitutional population	93 736	94 789	95 853	96 756	97 630	98 787	99 646	100 535	101 506	102 460	103 406
Civilian labor force	51 050	52 413	53 658	54 742	56 030	56 829	57 178	58 141	58 795	60 239	60 944
Employed	47 259	48 706	50 334	51 696	53 027	53 689	53 496	54 052	54 910	56 610	57 523
Agriculture	644	652	666	676	687	678	680	672	637	855	881
Nonagricultural industries	46 615	48 054	49 668	51 020	52 341	53 011	52 815	53 380	54 273	55 755	56 642
Unemployed	3 791	3 707	3 324	3 046	3 003	3 140	3 683	4 090	3 885	3 629	3 421
Not in labor force	42 686	42 376	42 195	42 014	41 601	41 957	42 468	42 394	42 711	42 221	42 462
Women, 20 Years and Over											
Civilian noninstitutional population	86 506	87 567	88 583	89 532	90 550	91 614	92 708	93 718	94 647	95 467	96 262
Civilian labor force	47 283	48 589	49 783	50 870	52 212	53 131	53 708	54 796	55 388	56 655	57 215
Employed	44 154	45 556	47 074	48 383	49 745	50 535	50 634	51 328	52 099	53 606	54 396
Agriculture	596	614	622	625	642	631	639	625	598	809	830
Nonagricultural industries	43 558	44 943	46 453	47 757	49 103	49 904	49 995	50 702	51 501	52 796	53 566
Unemployed	3 129	3 032	2 709	2 487	2 467	2 596	3 074	3 469	3 288	3 049	2 819
Not in labor force	39 222	38 979	38 800	38 662	38 339	38 483	39 000	38 922	39 260	38 813	39 047
Both Sexes, 16 to 19 Years											
Civilian noninstitutional population	14 506	14 496	14 606	14 527	14 223	14 520	14 073	13 840	13 935	14 196	14 511
Civilian labor force	7 901	7 926	7 988	8 031	7 954	7 792	7 265	7 096	7 170	7 481	7 765
Employed	6 434	6 472	6 640	6 805	6 759	6 581	5 906	5 669	5 805	6 161	6 419
Agriculture	305	258	258	273	250	264	247	237	224	249	275
Nonagricultural industries	6 129	6 215	6 382	6 532	6 510	6 317	5 659	5 432	5 580	5 912	6 144
Unemployed	1 468	1 454	1 347	1 226	1 194	1 212	1 359	1 427	1 365	1 320	1 346
Not in labor force	6 604	6 570	6 618	6 497	6 270	6 727	6 808	6 745	6 765	6 715	6 746
WHITE[1]											
Both Sexes											
Civilian noninstitutional population	153 679	155 432	156 958	158 194	159 338	160 625	161 759	162 972	164 289	165 555	166 914
Civilian labor force	99 926	101 801	103 290	104 756	106 355	107 447	107 743	108 837	109 700	111 082	111 950
Employed	93 736	95 660	97 789	99 812	101 584	102 261	101 182	101 669	103 045	105 190	106 490
Agriculture	2 936	2 958	2 986	2 965	2 996	2 998	3 026	3 018	2 895	3 162	3 194
Nonagricultural industries	90 799	92 703	94 803	96 846	98 588	99 263	98 157	98 650	100 150	102 027	103 296
Unemployed	6 191	6 140	5 501	4 944	4 770	5 186	6 560	7 169	6 655	5 892	5 459
Not in labor force	53 753	53 631	53 669	53 349	52 983	53 178	54 061	54 135	54 589	54 473	54 965
Men, 16 Years and Over											
Civilian noninstitutional population	73 373	74 390	75 189	75 855	76 468	77 369	77 977	78 651	79 371	80 059	80 733
Civilian labor force	56 472	57 217	57 779	58 317	58 988	59 638	59 656	60 168	60 484	60 727	61 146
Employed	53 046	53 785	54 647	55 550	56 352	56 703	55 797	55 959	56 656	57 452	58 146
Agriculture	2 325	2 340	2 354	2 318	2 345	2 353	2 384	2 378	2 286	2 347	2 347
Nonagricultural industries	50 720	51 444	52 293	53 232	54 007	54 350	53 413	53 580	54 370	55 104	55 800
Unemployed	3 426	3 433	3 132	2 766	2 636	2 935	3 859	4 209	3 828	3 275	2 999
Not in labor force	16 901	17 173	17 410	17 538	17 480	17 731	18 321	18 484	18 887	19 332	19 587
Men, 20 Years and Over											
Civilian noninstitutional population	67 386	68 413	69 175	69 887	70 654	71 457	72 274	73 040	73 721	74 311	74 879
Civilian labor force	52 895	53 675	54 232	54 734	55 441	56 116	56 387	56 976	57 284	57 411	57 719
Employed	50 061	50 818	51 649	52 466	53 292	53 685	53 103	53 357	54 021	54 676	55 254
Agriculture	2 085	2 131	2 150	2 104	2 149	2 148	2 192	2 197	2 114	2 151	2 132
Nonagricultural industries	47 976	48 687	49 499	50 362	51 143	51 537	50 912	51 160	51 907	52 525	53 122
Unemployed	2 834	2 857	2 584	2 268	2 149	2 431	3 284	3 620	3 263	2 735	2 465
Not in labor force	14 490	14 738	14 942	15 153	15 213	15 340	15 887	16 064	16 436	16 900	17 161

[1]Beginning in 2003, persons who selected this race group only; persons who selected more than one race group are not included. Prior to 2003, persons who reported more than one race group were included in the group they identified as the main race.

Table 1-3. Employment Status of the Civilian Noninstitutional Population, by Sex, Age, Race, and Hispanic Origin, 1985–2005—*Continued*

(Thousands of people.)

Characteristic	1996	1997	1998	1999	2000	2001	2002	2003	2004	2005
ALL RACES										
Both Sexes										
Civilian noninstitutional population	200 591	203 133	205 220	207 753	212 577	215 092	217 570	221 168	223 357	226 082
Civilian labor force	133 943	136 297	137 673	139 368	142 583	143 734	144 863	146 510	147 401	149 320
Employed	126 708	129 558	131 463	133 488	136 891	136 933	136 485	137 736	139 252	141 730
Agriculture	3 443	3 399	3 378	3 281	2 464	2 299	2 311	2 275	2 232	2 197
Nonagricultural industries	123 264	126 159	128 085	130 207	134 427	134 635	134 174	135 461	137 020	139 532
Unemployed	7 236	6 739	6 210	5 880	5 692	6 801	8 378	8 774	8 149	7 591
Not in labor force	66 647	66 837	67 547	68 385	69 994	71 359	72 707	74 658	75 956	76 762
Men, 16 Years and Over										
Civilian noninstitutional population	96 206	97 715	98 758	99 722	101 964	103 282	104 585	106 435	107 710	109 151
Civilian labor force	72 087	73 261	73 959	74 512	76 280	76 886	77 500	78 238	78 980	80 033
Employed	68 207	69 685	70 693	71 446	73 305	73 196	72 903	73 332	74 524	75 973
Agriculture	2 573	2 552	2 553	2 432	1 861	1 708	1 724	1 695	1 688	1 654
Nonagricultural industries	65 634	67 133	68 140	69 014	71 444	71 488	71 179	71 636	72 836	74 319
Unemployed	3 880	3 577	3 266	3 066	2 975	3 690	4 597	4 906	4 456	4 059
Not in labor force	24 119	24 454	24 799	25 210	25 684	26 396	27 085	28 197	28 730	29 119
Men, 20 Years and Over										
Civilian noninstitutional population	88 606	89 879	90 790	91 555	93 875	95 181	96 439	98 272	99 476	100 835
Civilian labor force	68 044	69 166	69 715	70 194	72 010	72 816	73 630	74 623	75 364	76 443
Employed	64 897	66 284	67 135	67 761	69 634	69 776	69 734	70 415	71 572	73 050
Agriculture	2 356	2 356	2 350	2 244	1 756	1 613	1 629	1 614	1 596	1 577
Nonagricultural industries	62 541	63 927	64 785	65 517	67 878	68 163	68 104	68 801	69 976	71 473
Unemployed	3 146	2 882	2 580	2 433	2 376	3 040	3 896	4 209	3 791	3 392
Not in labor force	20 563	20 713	21 075	21 362	21 864	22 365	22 809	23 649	24 113	24 392
Women, 16 Years and Over										
Civilian noninstitutional population	104 385	105 418	106 462	108 031	110 613	111 811	112 985	114 733	115 647	116 931
Civilian labor force	61 857	63 036	63 714	64 855	66 303	66 848	67 363	68 272	68 421	69 288
Employed	58 501	59 873	60 771	62 042	63 586	63 737	63 582	64 404	64 728	65 757
Agriculture	871	847	825	849	602	591	587	580	547	544
Nonagricultural industries	57 630	59 026	59 945	61 193	62 983	63 147	62 995	63 824	64 181	65 213
Unemployed	3 356	3 162	2 944	2 814	2 717	3 111	3 781	3 868	3 694	3 531
Not in labor force	42 528	42 382	42 748	43 175	44 310	44 962	45 621	46 461	47 225	47 643
Women, 20 Years and Over										
Civilian noninstitutional population	97 050	97 889	98 786	100 158	102 790	103 983	105 136	106 800	107 658	108 850
Civilian labor force	58 094	59 198	59 702	60 840	62 301	63 016	63 648	64 716	64 923	65 714
Employed	55 311	56 613	57 278	58 555	60 067	60 417	60 420	61 402	61 773	62 702
Agriculture	827	798	768	803	567	558	557	550	515	519
Nonagricultural industries	54 484	55 815	56 510	57 752	59 500	59 860	59 863	60 852	61 258	62 182
Unemployed	2 783	2 585	2 424	2 285	2 235	2 599	3 228	3 314	3 150	3 013
Not in labor force	38 956	38 691	39 084	39 318	40 488	40 967	41 488	42 083	42 735	43 136
Both Sexes, 16 to 19 Years										
Civilian noninstitutional population	14 934	15 365	15 644	16 040	15 912	15 929	15 994	16 096	16 222	16 398
Civilian labor force	7 806	7 932	8 256	8 333	8 271	7 902	7 585	7 170	7 114	7 164
Employed	6 500	6 661	7 051	7 172	7 189	6 740	6 332	5 919	5 907	5 978
Agriculture	261	244	261	234	141	128	124	111	121	100
Nonagricultural industries	6 239	6 417	6 790	6 938	7 049	6 611	6 207	5 808	5 786	5 877
Unemployed	1 306	1 271	1 205	1 162	1 081	1 162	1 253	1 251	1 208	1 186
Not in labor force	7 128	7 433	7 388	7 706	7 642	8 027	8 409	8 926	9 108	9 234
WHITE[1]										
Both Sexes										
Civilian noninstitutional population	168 317	169 993	171 478	173 085	176 220	178 111	179 783	181 292	182 643	184 446
Civilian labor force	113 108	114 693	115 415	116 509	118 545	119 399	120 150	120 546	121 086	122 299
Employed	107 808	109 856	110 931	112 235	114 424	114 430	114 013	114 235	115 239	116 949
Agriculture	3 276	3 208	3 160	3 083	2 320	2 174	2 171	2 148	2 103	2 077
Nonagricultural industries	104 532	106 648	107 770	109 152	112 104	112 256	111 841	112 087	113 136	114 872
Unemployed	5 300	4 836	4 484	4 273	4 121	4 969	6 137	6 311	5 847	5 350
Not in labor force	55 209	55 301	56 064	56 577	57 675	58 713	59 633	60 746	61 558	62 148
Men, 16 Years and Over										
Civilian noninstitutional population	81 489	82 577	83 352	83 930	85 370	86 452	87 361	88 249	89 044	90 027
Civilian labor force	61 783	62 639	63 034	63 413	64 466	64 966	65 308	65 509	65 994	66 694
Employed	58 888	59 998	60 604	61 139	62 289	62 212	61 849	61 866	62 712	63 763
Agriculture	2 436	2 389	2 376	2 273	1 743	1 606	1 611	1 597	1 583	1 562
Nonagricultural industries	56 452	57 608	58 228	58 866	60 546	60 606	60 238	60 269	61 129	62 201
Unemployed	2 896	2 641	2 431	2 274	2 177	2 754	3 459	3 643	3 282	2 931
Not in labor force	19 706	19 938	20 317	20 517	20 905	21 486	22 053	22 740	23 050	23 334
Men, 20 Years and Over										
Civilian noninstitutional population	75 454	76 320	76 966	77 432	78 966	80 029	80 922	81 860	82 615	83 556
Civilian labor force	58 340	59 126	59 421	59 747	60 850	61 519	62 067	62 473	62 944	63 705
Employed	55 977	56 986	57 500	57 934	59 119	59 245	59 124	59 348	60 159	61 255
Agriculture	2 224	2 201	2 182	2 094	1 640	1 512	1 519	1 517	1 495	1 488
Nonagricultural industries	53 753	54 785	55 319	55 839	57 479	57 733	57 605	57 831	58 664	59 767
Unemployed	2 363	2 140	1 920	1 813	1 731	2 275	2 943	3 125	2 785	2 450
Not in labor force	17 114	17 194	17 545	17 685	18 116	18 510	18 855	19 386	19 671	19 851

[1]Beginning in 2003, persons who selected this race group only; persons who selected more than one race group are not included. Prior to 2003, persons who reported more than one race group were included in the group they identified as the main race.

Table 1-3. Employment Status of the Civilian Noninstitutional Population, by Sex, Age, Race, and Hispanic Origin, 1985–2005—*Continued*

(Thousands of people.)

Characteristic	1985	1986	1987	1988	1989	1990	1991	1992	1993	1994	1995
WHITE[1]											
Women, 16 Years and Over											
Civilian noninstitutional population	80 306	81 042	81 769	82 340	82 871	83 256	83 781	84 321	84 918	85 496	86 181
Civilian labor force	43 455	44 584	45 510	46 439	47 367	47 809	48 087	48 669	49 216	50 356	50 804
Employed	40 690	41 876	43 142	44 262	45 232	45 558	45 385	45 710	46 390	47 738	48 344
Agriculture	611	617	632	648	651	645	641	640	609	815	847
Nonagricultural industries	40 079	41 259	42 509	43 614	44 581	44 913	44 744	45 070	45 780	46 923	47 497
Unemployed	2 765	2 708	2 369	2 177	2 135	2 251	2 701	2 959	2 827	2 617	2 460
Not in labor force	36 852	36 458	36 258	35 901	35 504	35 447	35 695	35 651	35 702	35 141	35 377
Women, 20 Years and Over											
Civilian noninstitutional population	74 394	75 140	75 845	76 470	77 154	77 539	78 285	78 928	79 490	79 980	80 567
Civilian labor force	40 190	41 264	42 164	43 081	44 105	44 648	45 111	45 839	46 311	47 314	47 686
Employed	37 907	39 050	40 242	41 316	42 346	42 796	42 862	43 327	43 910	45 116	45 643
Agriculture	566	580	590	599	608	598	601	594	572	772	799
Nonagricultural industries	37 341	38 471	39 652	40 717	41 738	42 198	42 261	42 733	43 339	44 344	44 844
Unemployed	2 283	2 213	1 922	1 766	1 758	1 852	2 248	2 512	2 400	2 197	2 042
Not in labor force	34 204	33 876	33 681	33 389	33 050	32 891	33 174	33 089	33 179	32 666	32 881
Both Sexes, 16 to 19 Years											
Civilian noninstitutional population	11 900	11 879	11 939	11 838	11 530	11 630	11 200	11 004	11 078	11 264	11 468
Civilian labor force	6 841	6 862	6 893	6 940	6 809	6 683	6 245	6 022	6 105	6 357	6 545
Employed	5 768	5 792	5 898	6 030	5 946	5 779	5 216	4 985	5 113	5 398	5 593
Agriculture	285	247	246	263	239	252	233	228	209	239	262
Nonagricultural industries	5 483	5 545	5 652	5 767	5 707	5 528	4 984	4 757	4 904	5 158	5 331
Unemployed	1 074	1 070	995	910	863	903	1 029	1 037	992	960	952
Not in labor force	5 058	5 017	5 045	4 897	4 721	4 947	4 955	4 982	4 973	4 907	4 923
BLACK[1]											
Both Sexes											
Civilian noninstitutional population	19 664	19 989	20 352	20 692	21 021	21 477	21 799	22 147	22 521	22 879	23 246
Civilian labor force	12 364	12 654	12 993	13 205	13 497	13 740	13 797	14 162	14 225	14 502	14 817
Employed	10 501	10 814	11 309	11 658	11 953	12 175	12 074	12 151	12 382	12 835	13 279
Agriculture	189	155	164	153	150	142	160	153	143	136	101
Nonagricultural industries	10 312	10 659	11 145	11 505	11 803	12 034	11 914	11 997	12 239	12 699	13 178
Unemployed	1 864	1 840	1 684	1 547	1 544	1 565	1 723	2 011	1 844	1 666	1 538
Not in labor force	7 299	7 335	7 359	7 487	7 524	7 737	8 002	7 985	8 296	8 377	8 429
Men, 16 Years and Over											
Civilian noninstitutional population	8 790	8 956	9 128	9 289	9 439	9 573	9 725	9 896	10 083	10 258	10 411
Civilian labor force	6 220	6 373	6 486	6 596	6 701	6 802	6 851	6 997	7 019	7 089	7 183
Employed	5 270	5 428	5 661	5 824	5 928	5 995	5 961	5 930	6 047	6 241	6 422
Agriculture	167	133	142	133	127	124	139	*138	128	118	93
Nonagricultural industries	5 103	5 295	5 519	5 691	5 802	5 872	5 822	5 791	5 919	6 122	6 329
Unemployed	951	946	826	771	773	806	890	1 067	971	848	762
Not in labor force	2 570	2 583	2 642	2 694	2 738	2 772	2 874	2 899	3 064	3 169	3 228
Men, 20 Years and Over											
Civilian noninstitutional population	7 731	7 907	8 063	8 063	8 215	8 364	8 479	8 652	8 840	9 171	9 280
Civilian labor force	5 749	5 915	6 023	6 023	6 127	6 221	6 357	6 451	6 568	6 646	6 730
Employed	4 992	5 150	5 357	5 357	5 509	5 602	5 692	5 706	5 681	5 964	6 137
Agriculture	154	125	135	135	129	119	117	131	131	115	89
Nonagricultural industries	4 837	5 025	5 222	5 222	5 381	5 483	5 576	5 575	5 550	5 849	6 048
Unemployed	757	765	666	666	617	619	664	745	886	682	593
Not in labor force	1 982	1 991	2 040	2 040	2 089	2 143	2 122	2 202	801	2 525	2 550
Women, 16 Years and Over											
Civilian noninstitutional population	10 873	11 033	11 224	11 402	11 582	11 904	12 074	12 251	12 438	12 621	12 835
Civilian labor force	6 144	6 281	6 507	6 609	6 796	6 938	6 946	7 166	7 206	7 413	7 634
Employed	5 231	5 386	5 648	5 834	6 025	6 180	6 113	6 221	6 334	6 595	6 857
Agriculture	22	22	22	20	24	18	21	15	15	18	8
Nonagricultural industries	5 209	5 364	5 626	5 814	6 001	6 162	6 092	6 206	6 320	6 577	6 849
Unemployed	913	894	858	776	772	758	833	944	872	818	777
Not in labor force	4 729	4 752	4 717	4 793	4 786	4 965	5 129	5 086	5 231	5 208	5 201
Women, 20 Years and Over											
Civilian noninstitutional population	9 773	9 945	10 126	10 298	10 482	10 760	10 959	11 152	11 332	11 496	11 682
Civilian labor force	5 727	5 855	6 071	6 190	6 352	6 517	6 572	6 778	6 824	7 004	7 175
Employed	4 977	5 128	5 365	5 548	5 727	5 884	5 874	5 978	6 095	6 320	6 556
Agriculture	19	22	20	18	23	18	20	15	14	17	7
Nonagricultural industries	4 959	5 106	5 345	5 530	5 703	5 867	5 853	5 963	6 081	6 303	6 548
Unemployed	750	728	706	642	625	633	698	800	729	685	620
Not in labor force	4 046	4 090	4 054	4 108	4 130	4 243	4 388	4 374	4 508	4 492	4 507
Both Sexes, 16 to 19 Years											
Civilian noninstitutional population	2 160	2 137	2 163	2 179	2 176	2 238	2 187	2 155	2 181	2 211	2 284
Civilian labor force	889	883	899	889	925	866	774	816	807	852	911
Employed	532	536	587	601	625	598	494	492	494	552	586
Agriculture	16	8	9	7	8	7	8	7	9	1	5
Nonagricultural industries	516	529	578	594	617	591	486	485	485	547	581
Unemployed	357	347	312	288	300	268	280	324	313	300	325
Not in labor force	1 271	1 254	1 264	1 291	1 251	1 372	1 413	1 339	1 374	1 360	1 372

[1]Beginning in 2003, persons who selected this race group only; persons who selected more than one race group are not included. Prior to 2003, persons who reported more than one race group were included in the group they identified as the main race.

Table 1-3. Employment Status of the Civilian Noninstitutional Population, by Sex, Age, Race, and Hispanic Origin, 1985–2005—*Continued*

(Thousands of people.)

Characteristic	1996	1997	1998	1999	2000	2001	2002	2003	2004	2005
WHITE[1]										
Women, 16 Years and Over										
Civilian noninstitutional population	86 828	87 417	88 126	89 156	90 850	91 660	92 422	93 043	93 599	94 419
Civilian labor force	51 325	52 054	52 380	53 096	54 079	54 433	54 842	55 037	55 092	55 605
Employed	48 920	49 859	50 327	51 096	52 136	52 218	52 164	52 369	52 527	53 186
Agriculture	840	819	784	810	578	568	560	551	520	515
Nonagricultural industries	48 080	49 040	49 543	50 286	51 558	51 650	51 604	51 818	52 007	52 672
Unemployed	2 404	2 195	2 053	1 999	1 944	2 215	2 678	2 668	2 565	2 419
Not in labor force	35 503	35 363	35 746	36 060	36 770	37 227	37 581	38 006	38 508	38 814
Women, 20 Years and Over										
Civilian noninstitutional population	81 041	81 492	82 073	82 953	84 718	85 526	86 266	86 905	87 430	88 200
Civilian labor force	48 162	48 847	49 029	49 714	50 740	51 218	51 717	52 099	52 212	52 643
Employed	46 164	47 063	47 342	48 098	49 145	49 369	49 448	49 823	50 040	50 589
Agriculture	798	771	729	765	546	537	532	522	488	492
Nonagricultural industries	45 366	46 292	46 612	47 333	48 599	48 831	48 916	49 301	49 552	50 097
Unemployed	1 998	1 784	1 688	1 616	1 595	1 849	2 269	2 276	2 172	2 054
Not in labor force	32 879	32 645	33 044	33 239	33 978	34 308	34 548	34 806	35 218	35 557
Both Sexes, 16 to 19 Years										
Civilian noninstitutional population	11 822	12 181	12 439	12 700	12 535	12 556	12 596	12 527	12 599	12 690
Civilian labor force	6 607	6 720	6 965	7 048	6 955	6 661	6 366	5 973	5 929	5 950
Employed	5 667	5 807	6 089	6 204	6 160	5 817	5 441	5 064	5 039	5 105
Agriculture	254	236	250	224	135	125	121	109	116	97
Nonagricultural industries	5 413	5 571	5 839	5 980	6 025	5 692	5 320	4 955	4 923	5 008
Unemployed	939	912	876	844	795	845	925	909	890	845
Not in labor force	5 215	5 462	5 475	5 652	5 581	5 894	6 230	6 554	6 669	6 739
BLACK[1]										
Both Sexes										
Civilian noninstitutional population	23 604	24 003	24 373	24 855	24 902	25 138	25 578	25 686	26 065	26 517
Civilian labor force	15 134	15 529	15 982	16 365	16 397	16 421	16 565	16 526	16 638	17 013
Employed	13 542	13 969	14 556	15 056	15 156	15 006	14 872	14 739	14 909	15 313
Agriculture	98	117	138	117	77	62	69	63	50	51
Nonagricultural industries	13 444	13 852	14 417	14 939	15 079	14 944	14 804	14 676	14 859	15 261
Unemployed	1 592	1 560	1 426	1 309	1 241	1 416	1 693	1 787	1 729	1 700
Not in labor force	8 470	8 474	8 391	8 490	8 505	8 717	9 013	9 161	9 428	9 504
Men, 16 Years and Over										
Civilian noninstitutional population	10 575	10 763	10 927	11 143	11 129	11 172	11 391	11 454	11 656	11 882
Civilian labor force	7 264	7 354	7 542	7 652	7 702	7 647	7 794	7 711	7 773	7 998
Employed	6 456	6 607	6 871	7 027	7 082	6 938	6 959	6 820	6 912	7 155
Agriculture	86	103	118	99	67	56	63	52	43	43
Nonagricultural industries	6 371	6 504	6 752	6 952	7 015	6 882	6 896	6 768	6 869	7 111
Unemployed	808	747	671	671	620	709	835	891	860	844
Not in labor force	3 311	3 409	3 386	3 386	3 427	3 525	3 597	3 743	3 884	3 884
Men, 20 Years and Over										
Civilian noninstitutional population	9 414	9 575	9 727	9 926	9 952	9 993	10 196	10 278	11 656	10 659
Civilian labor force	6 806	6 910	7 053	7 182	7 240	7 200	7 347	7 346	7 773	7 600
Employed	6 167	6 325	6 530	6 702	6 741	6 627	6 652	6 586	6 912	6 901
Agriculture	83	101	112	96	67	55	62	51	274	43
Nonagricultural industries	6 084	6 224	6 418	6 606	6 675	55	6 591	6 535	6 638	6 858
Unemployed	639	585	524	480	499	573	695	760	860	699
Not in labor force	2 608	2 665	2 673	2 743	2 711	2 792	2 848	2 932	3 884	3 060
Women, 16 Years and Over										
Civilian noninstitutional population	13 029	13 241	13 446	13 711	13 772	13 966	14 187	14 232	14 409	14 635
Civilian labor force	7 869	8 175	8 441	8 713	8 695	8 774	8 772	8 815	8 865	9 014
Employed	7 086	7 362	7 685	8 029	8 073	8 068	7 914	7 919	7 997	8 158
Agriculture	13	14	20	18	10	6	6	11	7	8
Nonagricultural industries	7 073	7 348	7 665	8 011	8 064	8 062	7 907	7 908	7 990	8 150
Unemployed	784	813	756	684	621	706	858	895	868	856
Not in labor force	5 159	5 066	5 005	4 999	5 078	5 192	5 415	5 418	5 544	5 621
Women, 20 Years and Over										
Civilian noninstitutional population	11 833	12 016	12 023	12 451	12 561	12 758	12 966	13 026	14 409	13 377
Civilian labor force	7 405	7 686	7 912	8 224	8 215	8 323	8 348	8 409	8 865	8 610
Employed	6 762	7 013	7 290	7 663	7 703	7 741	7 610	7 636	7 997	7 876
Agriculture	12	13	19	17	9	6	5	10	7	7
Nonagricultural industries	6 749	7 000	7 272	7 646	7 694	7 735	7 604	7 626	7 701	7 868
Unemployed	643	673	622	561	512	582	738	772	868	734
Not in labor force	4 428	4 330	4 291	4 226	4 346	4 434	4 618	4 618	5 544	4 768
Both Sexes, 16 to 19 Years										
Civilian noninstitutional population	2 356	2 412	2 443	2 479	2 389	2 388	2 416	2 382	2 423	2 481
Civilian labor force	923	933	1 017	959	941	898	870	771	762	803
Employed	613	631	736	691	711	637	611	516	520	536
Agriculture	3	3	8	4	1	1	2	1	0	1
Nonagricultural industries	611	611	728	687	710	637	609	515	520	535
Unemployed	310	310	281	268	230	260	260	255	241	267
Not in labor force	1 434	1 434	1 427	1 520	1 448	1 490	1 546	1 611	1 661	1 677

[1]Beginning in 2003, persons who selected this race group only; persons who selected more than one race group are not included. Prior to 2003, persons who reported more than one race group were included in the group they identified as the main race.

Table 1-3. Employment Status of the Civilian Noninstitutional Population, by Sex, Age, Race, and Hispanic Origin, 1985–2005—*Continued*

(Thousands of people.)

Characteristic	1985	1986	1987	1988	1989	1990	1991	1992	1993	1994	1995
HISPANIC[2]											
Both Sexes											
Civilian noninstitutional population	11 915	12 344	12 867	13 325	13 791	15 904	16 425	16 961	17 532	18 117	18 629
Civilian labor force	7 698	8 076	8 541	8 982	9 323	10 720	10 920	11 338	11 610	11 975	12 267
Employed	6 888	7 219	7 790	8 250	8 573	9 845	9 828	10 027	10 361	10 788	11 127
Agriculture	302	329	398	407	440	517	512	524	523	560	604
Nonagricultural industries	6 586	6 890	7 391	7 843	8 133	9 328	9 315	9 503	9 838	10 227	10 524
Unemployed	811	857	751	732	750	876	1 092	1 311	1 248	1 187	1 140
Not in labor force	4 217	4 268	4 327	4 342	4 468	5 184	5 506	5 623	5 922	6 142	6 362
Men, 16 Years and Over											
Civilian noninstitutional population	5 885	6 106	6 371	6 604	6 825	8 041	8 296	8 553	8 824	9 104	9 329
Civilian labor force	4 729	4 948	5 163	5 409	5 595	6 546	6 664	6 900	7 076	7 210	7 376
Employed	4 245	4 428	4 713	4 972	5 172	6 021	5 979	6 093	6 328	6 530	6 725
Agriculture	264	287	351	356	393	449	453	468	469	494	527
Nonagricultural industries	3 981	4 140	4 361	4 616	4 779	5 572	5 526	5 625	5 860	6 036	6 198
Unemployed	483	520	451	437	423	524	685	807	747	680	651
Not in labor force	1 157	1 158	1 208	1 195	1 230	1 495	1 632	1 654	1 749	1 894	1 952
Men, 20 Years and Over											
Civilian noninstitutional population	5 232	5 451	5 700	5 921	6 114	7 126	7 392	7 655	7 930	8 178	8 375
Civilian labor force	4 395	4 612	4 818	5 031	5 195	6 034	6 198	6 432	6 621	6 747	6 898
Employed	3 994	4 174	4 444	4 680	4 853	5 609	5 623	5 757	5 992	6 189	6 367
Agriculture	239	263	327	327	366	415	419	437	441	466	501
Nonagricultural industries	3 754	3 911	4 118	4 353	4 487	5 195	5 204	5 320	5 551	5 722	5 866
Unemployed	401	438	374	351	342	425	575	675	629	558	530
Not in labor force	837	839	882	890	919	1 092	1 194	1 223	1 309	1 431	1 477
Women, 16 Years and Over											
Civilian noninstitutional population	6 029	6 238	6 496	6 721	6 965	7 863	8 130	8 408	8 708	9 014	9 300
Civilian labor force	2 970	3 128	3 377	3 573	3 728	4 174	4 256	4 439	4 534	4 765	4 891
Employed	2 642	2 791	3 077	3 278	3 401	3 823	3 848	3 934	4 033	4 258	4 403
Agriculture	38	42	47	51	48	68	59	57	55	66	76
Nonagricultural industries	2 604	2 749	3 030	3 227	3 353	3 755	3 789	3 877	3 978	4 191	4 326
Unemployed	327	337	300	296	327	351	407	504	501	508	488
Not in labor force	3 059	3 110	3 119	3 147	3 237	3 689	3 874	3 969	4 174	4 248	4 409
Women, 20 Years and Over											
Civilian noninstitutional population	5 385	5 591	5 835	6 050	6 278	7 041	7 301	7 569	7 846	8 122	8 382
Civilian labor force	2 893	3 112	3 281	3 448	3 857	3 941	4 110	4 218	4 421	4 520	4 779
Employed	2 456	2 615	2 872	3 047	3 172	3 567	3 603	3 693	3 800	3 989	4 116
Agriculture	31	39	45	49	44	62	53	51	49	61	72
Nonagricultural industries	2 424	2 576	2 827	2 998	3 128	3 505	3 549	3 642	3 751	3 928	4 044
Unemployed	269	278	241	234	276	289	339	418	418	431	404
Not in labor force	2 660	2 698	2 723	2 769	2 830	3 184	3 360	3 459	3 628	3 701	3 863
Both Sexes, 16 to 19 Years											
Civilian noninstitutional population	1 298	1 302	1 332	1 354	1 399	1 737	1 732	1 737	1 756	1 818	1 872
Civilian labor force	579	571	610	671	680	829	781	796	771	807	850
Employed	438	430	474	523	548	668	602	577	570	609	645
Agriculture	31	27	27	32	31	40	41	36	33	32	31
Nonagricultural industries	407	403	447	492	517	628	562	541	537	577	614
Unemployed	141	141	136	148	132	161	179	219	201	198	205
Not in labor force	719	730	722	683	719	907	951	941	985	1 010	1 022

[2]May be of any race.

Table 1-3. Employment Status of the Civilian Noninstitutional Population, by Sex, Age, Race, and Hispanic Origin, 1985–2005—*Continued*

(Thousands of people.)

Characteristic	1996	1997	1998	1999	2000	2001	2002	2003	2004	2005
HISPANIC[2]										
Both Sexes										
Civilian noninstitutional population	19 213	20 321	21 070	21 650	23 938	24 942	25 963	27 551	28 109	29 133
Civilian labor force	12 774	13 796	14 317	14 665	16 689	17 328	17 943	18 813	19 272	19 824
Employed	11 642	12 726	13 291	13 720	15 735	16 190	16 590	17 372	17 930	18 632
Agriculture	609	660	742	734	536	423	448	446	441	423
Nonagricultural industries	11 033	12 067	12 549	12 986	15 199	15 767	16 141	16 927	17 489	18 209
Unemployed	1 132	1 069	1 026	945	954	1 138	1 353	1 441	1 342	1 191
Not in labor force	6 439	6 526	6 753	6 985	7 249	7 614	8 020	8 738	8 837	9 310
Men, 16 Years and Over										
Civilian noninstitutional population	9 604	10 368	10 734	10 713	12 174	12 695	13 221	14 098	14 417	14 962
Civilian labor force	7 646	8 309	8 571	8 546	9 923	10 279	10 609	11 288	11 587	11 985
Employed	7 039	7 728	8 018	8 067	9 428	9 668	9 845	10 479	10 832	11 337
Agriculture	537	571	651	642	449	345	361	350	356	350
Nonagricultural industries	6 502	7 157	7 367	7 425	8 979	9 323	9 484	10 129	10 476	10 987
Unemployed	607	582	552	480	494	611	764	809	755	647
Not in labor force	1 957	2 059	2 164	2 167	2 252	2 416	2 613	2 810	2 831	2 977
Men, 20 Years and Over										
Civilian noninstitutional population	8 611	9 250	9 573	9 523	10 841	11 386	11 928	12 797	13 082	13 586
Civilian labor force	7 150	7 779	8 005	7 950	9 247	9 595	9 977	10 756	11 020	11 408
Employed	6 655	7 307	7 570	7 576	8 859	9 100	9 341	10 063	10 385	10 872
Agriculture	510	544	621	602	423	328	345	336	335	341
Nonagricultural industries	6 145	6 763	6 949	6 974	8 435	8 773	8 996	9 727	10 050	10 532
Unemployed	495	471	436	374	388	495	636	693	635	536
Not in labor force	1 461	1 471	1 568	1 573	1 595	1 791	1 951	2 041	2 061	2 177
Women, 16 Years and Over										
Civilian noninstitutional population	9 610	9 953	10 335	10 937	11 764	12 247	12 742	13 452	13 692	14 172
Civilian labor force	5 128	5 486	5 746	6 119	6 767	7 049	7 334	7 525	7 685	7 839
Employed	4 602	4 999	5 273	5 653	6 307	6 522	6 744	6 894	7 098	7 295
Agriculture	72	89	91	92	87	77	87	96	85	73
Nonagricultural industries	4 531	4 910	5 182	5 561	6 220	6 445	6 657	6 798	7 013	7 222
Unemployed	525	488	473	466	460	527	590	631	587	544
Not in labor force	4 482	4 466	4 589	4 819	4 997	5 198	5 408	5 928	6 007	6 333
Women, 20 Years and Over										
Civilian noninstitutional population	8 654	8 950	9 292	9 821	10 574	11 049	11 528	12 211	12 420	12 858
Civilian labor force	5 106	5 304	5 666	6 275	6 557	6 863	7 096	7 096	7 257	7 377
Employed	4 341	4 705	4 928	5 290	5 903	6 121	6 367	6 541	6 752	6 913
Agriculture	69	83	85	88	81	73	84	91	78	70
Nonagricultural industries	4 272	4 622	4 843	5 202	5 822	6 048	6 283	6 450	6 674	6 843
Unemployed	438	401	376	376	371	436	496	555	504	464
Not in labor force	3 875	3 845	3 988	4 155	4 299	4 492	4 666	5 114	5 163	5 481
Both Sexes, 16 to 19 Years										
Civilian noninstitutional population	1 948	2 121	2 204	2 307	2 523	2 508	2 507	2 543	2 608	2 689
Civilian labor force	845	911	1 007	1 049	1 168	1 176	1 103	960	995	1 038
Employed	646	714	793	854	973	969	882	768	792	847
Agriculture	29	33	36	45	31	22	19	19	25	13
Nonagricultural industries	617	682	757	809	942	947	863	749	767	834
Unemployed	199	197	214	196	194	208	221	192	203	191
Not in labor force	1 103	1 210	1 197	1 257	1 355	1 331	1 404	1 583	1 612	1 651

[2]May be of any race.

Table 1-4. Employment Status of the Civilian Noninstitutional Population, by Sex, Race, and Marital Status, 1985–2005

(Thousands of people.)

	Men				Women			
Race, marital status, and year	Civilian noninstitutional population	Civilian labor force			Civilian noninstitutional population	Civilian labor force		
		Total	Employed	Unemployed		Total	Employed	Unemployed
ALL RACES								
Single								
1985	23 328	17 208	15 022	2 186	19 768	13 163	11 758	1 404
1986	23 662	17 553	15 407	2 146	20 113	13 512	12 071	1 442
1987	23 947	17 772	15 794	1 978	20 596	13 885	12 561	1 323
1988	24 572	18 345	16 521	1 824	20 961	14 194	12 979	1 215
1989	24 831	18 738	16 936	1 801	21 141	14 377	13 175	1 202
1990	25 870	19 357	17 405	1 952	21 901	14 612	13 336	1 276
1991	26 197	19 411	17 011	2 400	22 173	14 681	13 198	1 482
1992	26 436	19 709	17 098	2 611	22 475	14 872	13 263	1 609
1993	26 570	19 706	17 261	2 445	22 713	15 031	13 484	1 547
1994	26 786	19 786	17 604	2 181	23 000	15 333	13 847	1 486
1995	26 918	19 841	17 833	2 007	23 151	15 467	14 053	1 413
1996	27 387	20 071	18 055	2 016	23 623	15 842	14 403	1 439
1997	28 311	20 689	18 783	1 906	24 285	16 492	15 037	1 455
1998	28 693	21 037	19 240	1 798	24 941	17 087	15 755	1 332
1999	29 104	21 351	19 686	1 665	25 576	17 575	16 267	1 308
2000	29 887	22 002	20 339	1 663	25 920	17 849	16 628	1 221
2001	30 646	22 285	20 298	1 988	26 462	18 021	16 635	1 386
2002	31 072	22 289	19 983	2 306	26 999	18 203	16 583	1 621
2003	31 691	22 297	19 841	2 457	27 802	18 397	16 723	1 674
2004	32 422	22 776	20 395	2 381	28 228	18 616	16 995	1 621
2005	33 125	23 214	21 006	2 209	29 046	19 183	17 588	1 595
Married, Spouse Present								
1985	52 128	41 014	39 248	1 767	51 832	27 894	26 336	1 558
1986	52 769	41 477	39 658	1 819	52 158	28 623	27 144	1 479
1987	53 223	41 889	40 265	1 625	52 532	29 381	28 107	1 273
1988	53 246	41 832	40 472	1 360	52 775	29 921	28 756	1 166
1989	53 530	42 036	40 760	1 276	52 885	30 548	29 404	1 145
1990	53 793	42 275	40 829	1 446	52 917	30 901	29 714	1 188
1991	54 158	42 303	40 429	1 875	53 169	31 112	29 698	1 415
1992	54 509	42 491	40 341	2 150	53 501	31 700	30 100	1 600
1993	55 178	42 834	40 935	1 899	53 838	31 980	30 499	1 482
1994	55 560	43 005	41 414	1 592	54 155	32 888	31 536	1 352
1995	56 100	43 472	42 048	1 424	54 716	33 359	32 063	1 296
1996	56 363	43 739	42 417	1 322	54 970	33 618	32 406	1 211
1997	56 396	43 808	42 642	1 167	54 915	33 802	32 755	1 047
1998	56 670	43 957	42 923	1 034	55 331	33 857	32 872	985
1999	57 089	44 244	43 254	990	56 178	34 372	33 450	921
2000	58 167	44 987	44 078	908	57 557	35 146	34 209	937
2001	58 448	45 233	44 007	1 226	57 610	35 236	34 153	1 083
2002	59 102	45 766	44 116	1 650	58 165	35 477	34 153	1 323
2003	60 063	46 404	44 653	1 751	59 069	36 046	34 695	1 352
2004	60 412	46 550	45 084	1 466	59 278	35 845	34 600	1 244
2005	60 545	46 771	45 483	1 287	59 205	35 941	34 773	1 168
Divorced, Widowed, or Separated								
1985	9 013	6 190	5 621	568	22 136	9 993	9 165	828
1986	9 367	6 392	5 827	565	22 518	10 277	9 491	787
1987	9 729	6 546	6 048	498	22 726	10 393	9 665	727
1988	10 039	6 751	6 280	471	23 020	10 627	9 962	665
1989	10 401	7 066	6 618	448	23 604	11 104	10 448	656
1990	10 714	7 378	6 871	508	23 968	11 315	10 639	676
1991	10 924	7 454	6 783	671	24 304	11 385	10 600	786
1992	11 325	7 763	7 001	762	24 559	11 570	10 689	881
1993	11 584	7 864	7 153	711	24 955	11 784	10 927	856
1994	12 008	2 076	7 432	594	25 304	12 018	11 227	791
1995	12 160	2 018	7 496	551	25 539	12 118	11 407	712
1996	12 456	2 103	7 735	541	25 791	12 397	11 691	706
1997	13 009	2 316	8 260	504	26 218	12 742	12 082	660
1998	13 394	2 332	8 530	435	26 190	12 771	12 143	628
1999	13 528	2 290	8 507	411	26 276	12 909	12 324	585
2000	13 910	9 291	8 888	403	27 135	13 308	12 748	559
2001	14 188	9 367	8 892	476	27 738	13 592	12 949	642
2002	14 411	9 445	8 804	641	27 821	13 683	12 846	837
2003	14 680	9 537	8 838	699	27 862	13 828	12 986	842
2004	14 875	9 654	9 045	608	28 141	13 961	13 133	828
2005	15 481	10 048	9 484	563	28 680	14 163	13 396	768

Note: See notes and definitions for information on historical comparability.

Table 1-4. Employment Status of the Civilian Noninstitutional Population, by Sex, Race, and Marital Status, 1985–2005—Continued

(Thousands of people.)

Race, marital status, and year	Men				Women			
	Civilian noninstitutional population	Civilian labor force			Civilian noninstitutional population	Civilian labor force		
		Total	Employed	Unemployed		Total	Employed	Unemployed
WHITE[1]								
Single								
1985	19 100	14 426	12 875	1 550	15 472	10 705	9 828	877
1986	19 316	14 672	13 162	1 510	15 686	10 965	10 060	906
1987	19 526	14 850	13 449	1 401	15 990	11 196	10 382	815
1988	19 966	15 279	13 982	1 297	16 218	11 428	10 674	754
1989	20 076	15 511	14 249	1 263	16 289	11 474	10 741	734
1990	20 746	15 993	14 617	1 376	16 555	11 522	10 729	794
1991	20 899	15 989	14 233	1 756	16 569	11 497	10 557	939
1992	21 025	16 129	14 285	1 844	16 684	11 502	10 526	976
1993	20 974	16 033	14 303	1 730	16 768	11 613	10 633	980
1994	21 071	16 074	14 539	1 535	16 936	11 805	10 885	920
1995	21 132	16 080	14 674	1 406	17 046	11 830	10 967	864
1996	21 454	16 285	14 891	1 394	17 282	11 977	11 099	878
1997	22 236	16 810	15 507	1 303	17 728	12 322	11 443	879
1998	22 513	17 007	15 746	1 261	18 247	12 742	11 945	797
1999	22 788	17 272	16 116	1 157	18 635	13 029	12 206	823
2000	23 266	17 659	16 504	1 154	18 808	13 215	12 449	766
2001	23 979	17 970	16 561	1 409	19 253	13 368	12 491	877
2002	24 289	17 924	16 289	1 635	19 625	13 556	12 550	1 006
2003	24 419	17 755	16 031	1 723	19 924	13 462	12 461	1 001
2004	24 929	18 090	16 435	1 655	20 210	13 597	12 628	969
2005	25 436	18 338	16 833	1 505	20 702	13 906	12 957	949
Married, Spouse Present								
1985	46 925	36 934	35 472	1 462	46 728	24 777	23 468	1 308
1986	47 399	37 230	35 727	1 503	46 892	25 368	24 141	1 226
1987	47 690	37 486	36 127	1 359	47 180	26 014	24 969	1 045
1988	47 685	37 429	36 304	1 125	47 364	26 499	25 540	959
1989	47 883	37 589	36 545	1 044	47 382	27 030	26 083	947
1990	47 841	37 515	36 338	1 177	47 240	27 271	26 285	986
1991	48 137	37 507	35 923	1 585	47 456	27 479	26 290	1 189
1992	48 416	37 671	35 886	1 785	47 705	27 951	26 623	1 329
1993	48 937	37 953	36 396	1 557	47 944	28 221	26 993	1 228
1994	49 169	38 008	36 719	1 288	48 120	29 017	27 888	1 129
1995	49 597	38 376	37 211	1 165	48 497	29 360	28 290	1 070
1996	49 800	38 616	37 522	1 094	48 684	29 517	28 496	1 020
1997	49 719	38 593	37 636	957	48 542	29 664	28 809	855
1998	49 901	38 629	37 793	836	48 722	29 534	28 727	808
1999	50 091	38 765	37 968	797	49 296	29 806	29 056	749
2000	50 775	39 169	38 451	717	50 194	30 344	29 582	762
2001	50 850	39 246	38 265	981	50 077	30 336	29 472	864
2002	51 284	39 580	38 261	1 319	50 489	30 511	29 463	1 048
2003	51 859	39 908	38 529	1 379	50 957	30 805	29 740	1 065
2004	51 992	39 935	38 774	1 161	50 939	30 544	29 549	996
2005	52 034	40 141	39 130	1 011	50 865	30 599	29 676	922
Divorced, Widowed, or Separated								
1985	7 348	5 112	4 698	414	18 106	7 973	7 393	580
1986	7 675	5 315	4 896	420	18 463	8 251	7 675	576
1987	7 974	5 443	5 070	373	18 599	8 300	7 791	509
1988	8 204	5 608	5 265	344	18 758	8 512	8 047	464
1989	8 509	5 887	5 558	329	19 200	8 863	8 409	454
1990	8 782	6 131	5 748	382	19 461	9 016	8 544	471
1991	8 941	6 159	5 641	518	19 757	9 111	8 538	573
1992	9 210	6 368	5 788	580	19 931	9 216	8 561	654
1993	9 459	6 498	5 957	541	20 206	9 382	8 764	618
1994	9 819	6 644	6 193	451	20 439	9 533	8 965	569
1995	10 005	6 689	6 261	428	20 638	9 613	9 087	526
1996	10 234	6 883	6 474	408	20 862	9 831	9 325	506
1997	10 622	7 236	6 855	382	21 147	10 068	9 607	461
1998	10 937	7 398	7 064	334	21 157	10 104	9 656	449
1999	11 050	7 375	7 056	320	21 225	10 261	9 834	427
2000	11 329	7 638	7 333	305	21 847	10 521	10 105	416
2001	11 623	7 750	7 386	364	22 330	10 729	10 255	474
2002	11 789	7 804	7 299	505	22 308	10 775	10 151	624
2003	11 971	7 846	7 305	541	22 162	10 769	10 168	602
2004	12 124	7 969	7 503	466	22 450	10 950	10 350	600
2005	12 558	8 215	7 800	415	22 853	11 101	10 552	548

Note: See notes and definitions for information on historical comparability.

[1]Beginning in 2003, persons who selected this race group only; persons who selected more than one race group are not included. Prior to 2003, persons who reported more than one race group were included in the group they identified as their main race.

Table 1-4. Employment Status of the Civilian Noninstitutional Population, by Sex, Race, and Marital Status, 1985–2005—*Continued*

(Thousands of people.)

Race, marital status, and year	Men				Women			
	Civilian noninstitutional population	Civilian labor force			Civilian noninstitutional population	Civilian labor force		
		Total	Employed	Unemployed		Total	Employed	Unemployed
BLACK AND OTHER RACES[1]								
Single								
1985	4 228	2 782	2 147	635	4 297	2 458	1 930	528
1986	4 345	2 881	2 245	636	4 427	2 547	2 011	536
1987	4 421	2 922	2 345	577	4 606	2 688	2 179	509
1988	4 606	3 066	2 539	527	4 743	2 766	2 304	461
1989	4 755	3 227	2 687	538	4 852	2 903	2 434	468
1990	5 124	3 364	2 788	576	5 346	3 090	2 607	482
1991	5 298	3 422	2 778	644	5 604	3 184	2 641	543
1992	5 411	3 580	2 813	767	5 791	3 370	2 737	633
1993	5 596	3 673	2 958	715	5 945	3 418	2 851	567
1994	5 715	3 712	3 065	646	6 064	3 528	2 962	566
1995	5 786	3 761	3 159	601	6 105	3 637	3 086	549
1996	5 933	3 786	3 164	622	6 341	3 865	3 304	561
1997	6 075	3 879	3 276	603	6 557	4 170	3 594	576
1998	6 180	4 030	3 494	537	6 694	4 345	3 810	535
1999	6 316	4 079	3 570	508	6 941	4 546	4 061	485
2000	6 621	4 343	3 835	509	7 112	4 634	4 179	455
2001	6 667	4 315	3 737	579	7 209	4 653	4 144	509
2002	6 783	4 365	3 694	671	7 374	4 647	4 033	615
2003	7 272	4 542	3 810	734	7 878	4 935	4 262	673
2004	7 493	4 686	3 960	726	8 018	5 019	4 367	652
2005	7 689	4 876	4 173	704	8 344	5 277	4 631	646
Married, Spouse Present								
1985	5 203	4 080	3 775	305	5 104	3 118	2 868	250
1986	5 370	4 247	3 931	316	5 266	3 255	3 003	253
1987	5 534	4 403	4 137	266	5 352	3 367	3 138	228
1988	5 560	4 403	4 168	234	5 411	3 422	3 215	207
1989	5 647	4 447	4 215	232	5 503	3 518	3 321	198
1990	5 952	4 760	4 491	269	5 677	3 630	3 429	202
1991	6 021	4 796	4 506	290	5 713	3 633	3 408	226
1992	6 093	4 820	4 455	365	5 796	3 749	3 477	271
1993	6 241	4 881	4 539	342	5 894	3 759	3 506	254
1994	6 391	4 997	4 695	304	6 035	3 871	3 648	223
1995	6 503	5 096	4 837	259	6 219	3 999	3 773	226
1996	6 563	5 123	4 895	228	6 286	4 101	3 910	191
1997	6 677	5 215	5 006	210	6 373	4 138	3 946	192
1998	6 769	5 328	5 130	198	6 609	4 323	4 145	177
1999	6 998	5 479	5 286	193	6 882	4 566	4 394	172
2000	7 392	5 818	5 627	191	7 363	4 802	4 627	175
2001	7 598	5 987	5 742	245	7 533	4 900	4 681	219
2002	7 818	6 186	5 855	331	7 676	4 966	4 690	275
2003	8 204	6 496	6 124	372	8 112	5 241	4 955	287
2004	8 420	6 615	6 310	305	8 339	5 301	5 051	248
2005	8 511	6 630	6 353	276	8 340	5 342	5 097	246
Divorced, Widowed, or Separated								
1985	1 665	1 078	923	155	4 030	2 020	1 772	248
1986	1 692	1 076	931	146	4 055	2 026	1 816	210
1987	1 755	1 103	977	125	4 127	2 093	1 875	218
1988	1 836	1 142	1 015	127	4 262	2 115	1 914	201
1989	1 892	1 179	1 060	119	4 404	2 241	2 039	202
1990	1 932	1 247	1 123	126	4 507	2 299	2 095	205
1991	1 983	1 295	1 142	153	4 547	2 274	2 062	213
1992	2 115	1 395	1 213	182	4 628	2 354	2 128	227
1993	2 125	1 366	1 196	170	4 749	2 402	2 163	238
1994	2 189	1 382	1 239	143	4 865	2 485	2 262	222
1995	2 155	1 358	1 235	123	4 901	2 505	2 320	186
1996	2 222	1 394	1 261	133	4 929	2 566	2 366	200
1997	2 387	1 528	1 405	122	5 071	2 674	2 475	199
1998	2 457	1 567	1 466	101	5 033	2 667	2 487	179
1999	2 478	1 543	1 451	91	5 051	2 648	2 490	158
2000	2 581	1 653	1 555	98	5 288	2 787	2 643	143
2001	2 565	1 617	1 506	112	5 408	2 863	2 694	168
2002	2 622	1 641	1 505	136	5 513	2 908	2 695	213
2003	2 709	1 691	1 533	158	5 700	3 059	2 818	240
2004	2 751	1 685	1 542	142	5 691	3 011	2 783	228
2005	2 923	1 833	1 684	148	5 827	3 062	2 844	220

Note: See notes and definitions for information on historical comparability.

[1]Beginning in 2003, persons who selected this race group only; persons who selected more than one race group are not included. Prior to 2003, persons who reported more than one race group were included in the group they identified as their main race.

Table 1-5. Employment Status of the Civilian Noninstitutional Population, by Region, Division, and State, 2004–2005

(Thousands of people, percent.)

Region, division, and state	2004						2005					
	Civilian noninstitutional population	Civilian labor force					Civilian noninstitutional population	Civilian labor force				
		Total	Participation rate	Employed	Unemployed	Unemploy-ment rate		Total	Participation rate	Employed	Unemployed	Unemploy-ment rate
UNITED STATES[1]	223 357	147 401	66.0	139 252	8 149	5.5	226 082	149 320	66.0	141 730	7 591	5.1
Northeast	42 447	27 508	64.8	26 042	1 466	5.3	42 584	27 689	65.0	26 358	1 331	4.8
New England	11 135	7 517	67.5	7 149	368	4.9	11 180	7 551	67.5	7 198	353	4.7
Connecticut	2 697	1 803	66.9	1 714	89	4.9	2 714	1 817	66.9	1 728	89	4.9
Maine	1 052	700	66.5	667	32	4.6	1 063	712	67.0	677	34	4.8
Massachusetts	5 025	3 375	67.2	3 199	176	5.2	5 027	3 364	66.9	3 203	162	4.8
New Hampshire	1 017	724	71.2	696	28	3.9	1 030	732	71.1	706	26	3.6
Rhode Island	845	562	66.5	533	29	5.2	843	569	67.5	541	29	5.0
Vermont	499	353	70.7	340	13	3.7	503	356	70.8	344	12	3.5
Middle Atlantic	31 312	19 991	63.8	18 893	1 098	5.5	31 405	20 139	64.1	19 160	979	4.9
New Jersey	6 655	4 380	65.8	4 164	215	4.9	6 687	4 430	66.2	4 236	194	4.4
New York	14 964	9 362	62.6	8 820	542	5.8	14 971	9 416	62.9	8 944	472	5.0
Pennsylvania	9 693	6 249	64.5	5 909	341	5.4	9 747	6 292	64.6	5 980	312	5.0
Midwest	50 340	34 397	68.3	32 426	1 971	5.7	50 726	34 602	68.2	32 725	1 878	5.4
East North Central	35 186	23 567	67.0	22 129	1 438	6.1	35 406	23 718	67.0	22 338	1 380	5.8
Illinois	9 639	6 405	66.4	6 008	398	6.2	9 700	6 469	66.7	6 101	369	5.7
Indiana	4 715	3 172	67.3	3 004	168	5.3	4 760	3 209	67.4	3 035	174	5.4
Michigan	7 738	5 073	65.6	4 717	356	7.0	7 771	5 097	65.6	4 754	344	6.7
Ohio	8 820	5 875	66.6	5 512	363	6.2	8 859	5 900	66.6	5 550	350	5.9
Wisconsin	4 273	3 041	71.2	2 888	153	5.0	4 317	3 041	70.4	2 897	144	4.7
West North Central	15 155	10 830	71.5	10 296	534	4.9	15 321	10 885	71.0	10 387	498	4.6
Iowa	2 307	1 636	70.9	1 559	77	4.7	2 329	1 660	71.3	1 584	76	4.6
Kansas	2 068	1 469	71.0	1 387	82	5.6	2 089	1 476	70.7	1 401	75	5.1
Minnesota	3 939	2 942	74.7	2 807	134	4.6	3 985	2 947	74.0	2 829	119	4.0
Missouri	4 428	3 014	68.1	2 841	174	5.8	4 479	3 024	67.5	2 862	162	5.4
Nebraska	1 331	986	74.1	947	38	3.9	1 344	986	73.4	949	37	3.8
North Dakota	497	355	71.4	343	12	3.5	501	359	71.7	347	12	3.4
South Dakota	585	428	73.2	412	16	3.8	593	432	72.8	415	17	3.9
South	80 049	51 895	64.8	49 168	2 727	5.3	81 442	52 867	64.9	50 234	2 633	5.0
South Atlantic	42 141	27 398	65.0	26 075	1 324	4.8	42 966	28 058	65.3	26 788	1 270	4.5
Delaware	641	429	66.9	412	17	4.0	655	438	66.9	420	18	4.2
District of Columbia	442	296	67.0	274	22	7.5	437	296	67.7	277	19	6.5
Florida	13 512	8 407	62.2	8 016	391	4.7	13 868	8 654	62.4	8 329	325	3.8
Georgia	6 624	4 443	67.1	4 231	212	4.8	6 769	4 588	67.8	4 346	242	5.3
Maryland	4 222	2 888	68.4	2 764	124	4.3	4 261	2 935	68.9	2 814	121	4.1
North Carolina	6 441	4 251	66.0	4 017	234	5.5	6 567	4 333	66.0	4 106	227	5.2
South Carolina	3 192	2 039	63.9	1 900	139	6.8	3 251	2 081	64.0	1 939	142	6.8
Virginia	5 616	3 855	68.6	3 713	142	3.7	5 704	3 934	69.0	3 798	136	3.5
West Virginia	1 450	791	54.6	749	42	5.3	1 456	800	54.9	761	40	5.0
East South Central	13 395	8 353	62.4	7 889	464	5.6	13 559	8 407	62.0	7 932	475	5.6
Alabama	3 481	2 145	61.6	2 034	111	5.2	3 521	2 155	61.2	2 069	86	4.0
Kentucky	3 189	1 976	62.0	1 867	110	5.5	3 222	2 000	62.1	1 878	121	6.1
Mississippi	2 165	1 334	61.6	1 250	85	6.3	2 185	1 343	61.5	1 237	106	7.9
Tennessee	4 560	2 897	63.5	2 739	158	5.5	4 631	2 910	62.8	2 748	162	5.6
West South Central	24 513	16 144	65.9	15 205	939	5.8	24 916	16 401	65.8	15 514	887	5.4
Arkansas	2 100	1 309	62.3	1 236	73	5.6	2 132	1 362	63.9	1 295	67	4.9
Louisiana	3 375	2 062	61.1	1 944	118	5.7	3 344	2 071	61.9	1 923	148	7.1
Oklahoma	2 671	1 715	64.2	1 630	84	4.9	2 704	1 742	64.4	1 665	76	4.4
Texas	16 367	11 058	67.6	10 394	664	6.0	16 736	11 226	67.1	10 630	596	5.3
West	50 522	33 605	66.5	31 622	1 983	5.9	51 313	34 150	66.6	32 391	1 759	5.2
Mountain	14 821	10 077	68.0	9 568	510	5.1	15 236	10 328	67.8	9 855	473	4.6
Arizona	4 268	2 763	64.7	2 626	137	5.0	4 433	2 844	64.2	2 710	134	4.7
Colorado	3 472	2 510	72.3	2 371	140	5.6	3 526	2 548	72.3	2 419	129	5.0
Idaho	1 041	711	68.3	678	33	4.7	1 073	739	68.9	711	28	3.8
Montana	729	484	66.4	463	21	4.3	741	493	66.5	474	20	4.0
Nevada	1 757	1 179	67.1	1 125	54	4.6	1 826	1 216	66.6	1 167	49	4.1
New Mexico	1 433	915	63.9	862	52	5.7	1 463	936	64.0	887	49	5.3
Utah	1 728	1 236	71.5	1 173	62	5.0	1 774	1 268	71.5	1 214	54	4.3
Wyoming	394	279	70.8	269	11	3.9	400	285	71.3	274	10	3.6
Pacific	35 700	23 528	65.9	22 054	1 474	6.3	36 077	23 822	66.0	22 536	1 286	5.4
Alaska	466	336	72.1	311	25	7.4	473	339	71.7	316	23	6.8
California	26 715	17 500	65.5	16 408	1 092	6.2	26 935	17 696	65.7	16 747	949	5.4
Hawaii	945	619	65.5	599	20	3.3	958	635	66.3	617	18	2.8
Oregon	2 799	1 850	66.1	1 714	135	7.3	2 848	1 860	65.3	1 746	114	6.1
Washington	4 776	3 224	67.5	3 022	202	6.3	4 862	3 292	67.7	3 110	182	5.5
Puerto Rico[2]	2 938	1 371	46.7	1 226	145	10.6	2 957	1 410	47.7	1 250	160	11.3

Note: Data refer to place of residence. Region and division data are derived from summing the component states. Sub-national data (except for Puerto Rico) reflect revised population controls and model reestimation.

[1]Due to separate processing and weighing procedures, totals for the United States differ from the results obtained by aggregating data for regions, divisions, or states.
[2]Data from Puerto Rico are derived from a monthly household survey similar to the Current Population Survey (CPS).

Table 1-6. Civilian Noninstitutional Population, by Age, Race, Sex, and Hispanic Origin, 1948–2005

(Thousands of people.)

Race, Hispanic origin, sex, and year	16 years and over	16 to 19 years			20 years and over						
		Total	16 to 17 years	18 to 19 years	Total	20 to 24 years	25 to 34 years	35 to 44 years	45 to 54 years	55 to 64 years	65 years and over
ALL RACES											
Both Sexes											
1948	103 068	8 449	4 265	4 185	94 618	11 530	22 610	20 097	16 771	12 885	10 720
1949	103 994	8 215	4 139	4 079	95 778	11 312	22 822	20 401	17 002	13 201	11 035
1950	104 995	8 143	4 076	4 068	96 851	11 080	23 013	20 681	17 240	13 469	11 363
1951	104 621	7 865	4 096	3 771	96 755	10 167	22 843	20 863	17 464	13 692	11 724
1952	105 231	7 922	4 234	3 689	97 305	9 389	23 044	21 137	17 716	13 889	12 126
1953	107 056	8 014	4 241	3 773	99 041	8 960	23 266	21 922	17 991	13 830	13 075
1954	108 321	8 224	4 336	3 889	100 095	8 885	23 304	22 135	18 305	14 085	13 375
1955	109 683	8 364	4 440	3 925	101 318	9 036	23 249	22 348	18 643	14 309	13 728
1956	110 954	8 434	4 482	3 953	102 518	9 271	23 072	22 567	19 012	14 516	14 075
1957	112 265	8 612	4 587	4 026	103 653	9 486	22 849	22 786	19 424	14 727	14 376
1958	113 727	8 986	4 872	4 114	104 737	9 733	22 563	23 025	19 832	14 923	14 657
1959	115 329	9 618	5 337	4 282	105 711	9 975	22 201	23 207	20 203	15 134	14 985
1960	117 245	10 187	5 573	4 615	107 056	10 273	21 998	23 437	20 601	15 409	15 336
1961	118 771	10 513	5 462	5 052	108 255	10 583	21 829	23 585	20 893	15 675	15 685
1962	120 153	10 652	5 503	5 150	109 500	10 852	21 503	23 797	20 916	15 874	16 554
1963	122 416	11 370	6 301	5 070	111 045	11 464	21 400	23 948	21 144	16 138	16 945
1964	124 485	12 111	6 974	5 139	112 372	12 017	21 367	23 940	21 452	16 442	17 150
1965	126 513	12 930	6 936	5 995	113 582	12 442	21 417	23 832	21 728	16 727	17 432
1966	128 058	13 592	6 914	6 679	114 463	12 638	21 543	23 579	21 977	17 007	17 715
1967	129 874	13 480	7 003	6 480	116 391	13 421	22 057	23 313	22 256	17 310	18 029
1968	132 028	13 698	7 200	6 499	118 328	13 891	22 912	23 036	22 534	17 614	18 338
1969	134 335	14 095	7 422	6 673	120 238	14 488	23 645	22 709	22 806	17 930	18 657
1970	137 085	14 519	7 643	6 876	122 566	15 323	24 435	22 489	23 059	18 250	19 007
1971	140 216	15 022	7 849	7 173	125 193	16 345	25 337	22 274	23 244	18 581	19 406
1972	144 126	15 510	8 076	7 435	128 614	17 143	26 740	22 358	23 338	19 007	20 023
1973	147 096	15 840	8 227	7 613	131 253	17 692	28 172	22 287	23 431	19 281	20 389
1974	150 120	16 180	8 373	7 809	133 938	17 994	29 439	22 461	23 578	19 517	20 945
1975	153 153	16 418	8 419	7 999	136 733	18 595	30 710	22 526	23 535	19 844	21 525
1976	156 150	16 614	8 442	8 171	139 536	19 109	31 953	22 796	23 409	20 185	22 083
1977	159 033	16 688	8 482	8 206	142 345	19 582	33 117	23 296	23 197	20 557	22 597
1978	161 910	16 695	8 484	8 211	145 216	20 007	34 091	24 099	22 977	20 875	23 166
1979	164 863	16 657	8 389	8 268	148 205	20 353	35 261	24 861	22 752	21 210	23 767
1980	167 745	16 543	8 279	8 264	151 202	20 635	36 558	25 578	22 563	21 520	24 350
1981	170 130	16 214	8 068	8 145	153 916	20 820	37 777	26 291	22 422	21 756	24 850
1982	172 271	15 763	7 714	8 049	156 508	20 845	38 492	27 611	22 264	21 909	25 387
1983	174 215	15 274	7 385	7 889	158 941	20 799	39 147	28 932	22 167	22 003	25 892
1984	176 383	14 735	7 196	7 538	161 648	20 688	39 999	30 251	22 226	22 052	26 433
1985	178 206	14 506	7 232	7 274	163 700	20 097	40 670	31 379	22 418	22 140	26 997
1986	180 587	14 496	7 386	7 110	166 091	19 569	41 731	32 550	22 732	22 011	27 497
1987	182 753	14 606	7 501	7 104	168 147	18 970	42 297	33 755	23 183	21 835	28 108
1988	184 613	14 527	7 284	7 243	170 085	18 434	42 611	34 784	24 004	21 641	28 612
1989	186 393	14 223	6 886	7 338	172 169	18 025	42 845	35 977	24 744	21 406	29 173
1990	189 164	14 520	6 893	7 626	174 644	18 902	42 976	37 719	25 081	20 719	29 247
1991	190 925	14 073	6 901	7 173	176 852	18 963	42 688	39 116	25 709	20 675	29 700
1992	192 805	13 840	6 907	6 933	178 965	18 846	42 278	39 852	27 206	20 604	30 179
1993	194 838	13 935	7 010	6 925	180 903	18 642	41 771	40 733	28 549	20 574	30 634
1994	196 814	14 196	7 245	6 951	182 619	18 353	41 306	41 534	29 778	20 635	31 012
1995	198 584	14 511	7 407	7 104	184 073	17 864	40 798	42 254	30 974	20 735	31 448
1996	200 591	14 934	7 678	7 256	185 656	17 409	40 252	43 086	32 167	20 990	31 751
1997	203 133	15 365	7 861	7 504	187 769	17 442	39 559	43 883	33 391	21 505	31 989
1998	205 220	15 644	7 895	7 749	189 576	17 593	38 778	44 299	34 373	22 296	32 237
1999	207 753	16 040	8 060	7 979	191 713	17 968	37 976	44 635	35 587	23 064	32 484
2000	212 577	15 912	7 978	7 934	196 664	18 311	38 703	44 312	37 642	24 230	33 466
2001	215 092	15 929	8 020	7 909	199 164	18 877	38 505	44 195	38 904	25 011	33 672
2002	217 570	15 994	8 099	7 895	201 576	19 348	38 472	43 894	39 711	26 343	33 808
2003	221 168	16 096	8 561	7 535	205 072	19 801	39 021	43 746	40 522	27 728	34 253
2004	223 357	16 222	8 574	7 648	207 134	20 197	38 939	43 226	41 245	28 919	34 609
2005	226 082	16 398	8 778	7 619	209 685	20 276	39 064	43 005	42 107	30 165	35 068

Table 1-6. Civilian Noninstitutional Population, by Age, Race, Sex, and Hispanic Origin, 1948–2005
—Continued

(Thousands of people.)

Race, Hispanic origin, sex, and year	16 years and over	16 to 19 years			20 years and over						
		Total	16 to 17 years	18 to 19 years	Total	20 to 24 years	25 to 34 years	35 to 44 years	45 to 54 years	55 to 64 years	65 years and over
ALL RACES											
Men											
1948	49 996	4 078	2 128	1 951	45 918	5 527	10 767	9 798	8 290	6 441	5 093
1949	50 321	3 946	2 062	1 884	46 378	5 405	10 871	9 926	8 379	6 568	5 226
1950	50 725	3 962	2 043	1 920	46 763	5 270	10 963	10 034	8 472	6 664	5 357
1951	49 727	3 725	2 039	1 687	46 001	4 451	10 709	10 049	8 551	6 737	5 503
1952	49 700	3 767	2 121	1 647	45 932	3 788	10 855	10 164	8 655	6 798	5 670
1953	50 750	3 823	2 122	1 701	46 927	3 482	11 020	10 632	8 878	6 798	6 119
1954	51 395	3 953	2 174	1 780	47 441	3 509	11 067	10 718	9 018	6 885	6 241
1955	52 109	4 022	2 225	1 798	48 086	3 708	11 068	10 804	9 164	6 960	6 380
1956	52 723	4 020	2 238	1 783	48 704	3 970	10 983	10 889	9 322	7 032	6 505
1957	53 315	4 083	2 284	1 800	49 231	4 166	10 889	10 965	9 499	7 109	6 602
1958	54 033	4 293	2 435	1 858	49 740	4 339	10 787	11 076	9 675	7 179	6 683
1959	54 793	4 652	2 681	1 971	50 140	4 488	10 625	11 149	9 832	7 259	6 785
1960	55 662	4 963	2 805	2 159	50 698	4 679	10 514	11 230	10 000	7 373	6 901
1961	56 286	5 112	2 742	2 371	51 173	4 844	10 440	11 286	10 112	7 483	7 006
1962	56 831	5 150	2 764	2 386	51 681	4 925	10 207	11 389	10 162	7 610	7 386
1963	57 921	5 496	3 162	2 334	52 425	5 240	10 165	11 476	10 274	7 740	7 526
1964	58 847	5 866	3 503	2 364	52 981	5 520	10 144	11 466	10 402	7 873	7 574
1965	59 782	6 318	3 488	2 831	53 463	5 701	10 182	11 427	10 512	7 990	7 649
1966	60 262	6 658	3 478	3 180	53 603	5 663	10 224	11 294	10 598	8 099	7 723
1967	60 905	6 537	3 528	3 010	54 367	5 977	10 495	11 161	10 705	8 218	7 809
1968	61 847	6 683	3 634	3 049	55 165	6 127	10 944	11 040	10 819	8 336	7 897
1969	62 898	6 928	3 741	3 187	55 969	6 379	11 309	10 890	10 935	8 464	7 990
1970	64 304	7 145	3 848	3 299	57 157	6 861	11 750	10 810	11 052	8 590	8 093
1971	65 942	7 430	3 954	3 477	58 511	7 511	12 227	10 721	11 129	8 711	8 208
1972	67 835	7 705	4 081	3 624	60 130	8 061	12 911	10 762	11 167	8 895	8 330
1973	69 292	7 855	4 152	3 703	61 436	8 429	13 641	10 746	11 202	8 990	8 426
1974	70 808	8 012	4 231	3 781	62 796	8 600	14 262	10 834	11 315	9 140	8 641
1975	72 291	8 134	4 252	3 882	64 158	8 950	14 899	10 874	11 298	9 286	8 852
1976	73 759	8 244	4 266	3 978	65 515	9 237	15 528	11 010	11 243	9 444	9 053
1977	75 193	8 288	4 290	4 000	66 904	9 477	16 108	11 260	11 144	9 616	9 297
1978	76 576	8 309	4 295	4 014	68 268	9 693	16 598	11 665	11 045	9 758	9 509
1979	78 020	8 310	4 251	4 060	69 709	9 873	17 193	12 046	10 944	9 907	9 746
1980	79 398	8 260	4 195	4 064	71 138	10 023	17 833	12 400	10 861	10 042	9 979
1981	80 511	8 092	4 087	4 005	72 419	10 116	18 427	12 758	10 797	10 151	10 170
1982	81 523	7 879	3 911	3 968	73 644	10 136	18 787	13 410	10 726	10 215	10 371
1983	82 531	7 659	3 750	3 908	74 872	10 140	19 143	14 067	10 689	10 261	10 573
1984	83 605	7 386	3 655	3 731	76 219	10 108	19 596	14 719	10 724	10 285	10 788
1985	84 469	7 275	3 689	3 586	77 195	9 746	19 864	15 265	10 844	10 392	11 084
1986	85 798	7 275	3 768	3 507	78 523	9 498	20 498	15 858	10 986	10 336	11 347
1987	86 899	7 335	3 824	3 510	79 565	9 195	20 781	16 475	11 215	10 267	11 632
1988	87 857	7 304	3 715	3 588	80 553	8 931	20 937	17 008	11 625	10 193	11 859
1989	88 762	7 143	3 524	3 619	81 619	8 743	21 080	17 590	11 981	10 092	12 134
1990	90 377	7 347	3 534	3 813	83 030	9 320	21 117	18 529	12 238	9 778	12 049
1991	91 278	7 134	3 548	3 586	84 144	9 367	20 977	19 213	12 554	9 780	12 254
1992	92 270	7 023	3 542	3 481	85 247	9 326	20 792	19 585	13 271	9 776	12 496
1993	93 332	7 076	3 595	3 481	86 256	9 216	20 569	20 037	13 944	9 773	12 717
1994	94 355	7 203	3 718	3 486	87 151	9 074	20 361	20 443	14 545	9 810	12 918
1995	95 178	7 367	3 794	3 573	87 811	8 835	20 079	20 800	15 111	9 856	13 130
1996	96 206	7 600	3 955	3 645	88 606	8 611	19 775	21 222	15 674	9 997	13 327
1997	97 715	7 836	4 053	3 783	89 879	8 706	19 478	21 669	16 276	10 282	13 469
1998	98 758	7 968	4 059	3 909	90 790	8 804	19 094	21 857	16 773	10 649	13 613
1999	99 722	8 167	4 143	4 024	91 555	8 899	18 565	21 969	17 335	11 008	13 779
2000	101 964	8 089	4 096	3 993	93 875	9 101	19 106	21 683	18 365	11 583	14 037
2001	103 282	8 101	4 102	3 999	95 181	9 368	19 056	21 643	18 987	11 972	14 155
2002	104 585	8 146	4 140	4 006	96 439	9 627	19 037	21 523	19 379	12 641	14 233
2003	106 435	8 163	4 365	3 797	98 272	9 878	19 347	21 463	19 784	13 305	14 496
2004	107 710	8 234	4 318	3 916	99 476	10 125	19 358	21 255	20 160	13 894	14 684
2005	109 151	8 317	4 481	3 836	100 835	10 181	19 446	21 177	20 585	14 502	14 944

Table 1-6. Civilian Noninstitutional Population, by Age, Race, Sex, and Hispanic Origin, 1948–2005
—Continued

(Thousands of people.)

Race, Hispanic origin, sex, and year	16 years and over	16 to 19 years			20 years and over						
		Total	16 to 17 years	18 to 19 years	Total	20 to 24 years	25 to 34 years	35 to 44 years	45 to 54 years	55 to 64 years	65 years and over
ALL RACES											
Women											
1948	53 071	4 371	2 137	2 234	48 700	6 003	11 843	10 299	8 481	6 444	5 627
1949	53 670	4 269	2 077	2 195	49 400	5 907	11 951	10 475	8 623	6 633	5 809
1950	54 270	4 181	2 033	2 148	50 088	5 810	12 050	10 647	8 768	6 805	6 006
1951	54 895	4 140	2 057	2 084	50 754	5 716	12 134	10 814	8 913	6 955	6 221
1952	55 529	4 155	2 113	2 042	51 373	5 601	12 189	10 973	9 061	7 091	6 456
1953	56 305	4 191	2 119	2 072	52 114	5 478	12 246	11 290	9 113	7 032	6 956
1954	56 925	4 271	2 162	2 109	52 654	5 376	12 237	11 417	9 287	7 200	7 134
1955	57 574	4 342	2 215	2 127	53 232	5 328	12 181	11 544	9 479	7 349	7 348
1956	58 228	4 414	2 244	2 170	53 814	5 301	12 089	11 678	9 690	7 484	7 570
1957	58 951	4 529	2 303	2 226	54 421	5 320	11 960	11 821	9 925	7 618	7 774
1958	59 690	4 693	2 437	2 256	54 997	5 394	11 776	11 949	10 157	7 744	7 974
1959	60 534	4 966	2 656	2 311	55 570	5 487	11 576	12 058	10 371	7 875	8 200
1960	61 582	5 224	2 768	2 456	56 358	5 594	11 484	12 207	10 601	8 036	8 435
1961	62 484	5 401	2 720	2 681	57 082	5 739	11 389	12 299	10 781	8 192	8 679
1962	63 321	5 502	2 739	2 764	57 819	5 927	11 296	12 408	10 754	8 264	9 168
1963	64 494	5 874	3 139	2 736	58 620	6 224	11 235	12 472	10 870	8 398	9 419
1964	65 637	6 245	3 471	2 775	59 391	6 497	11 223	12 474	11 050	8 569	9 576
1965	66 731	6 612	3 448	3 164	60 119	6 741	11 235	12 405	11 216	8 737	9 783
1966	67 795	6 934	3 436	3 499	60 860	6 975	11 319	12 285	11 379	8 908	9 992
1967	68 968	6 943	3 475	3 470	62 026	7 445	11 562	12 152	11 551	9 092	10 220
1968	70 179	7 015	3 566	3 450	63 164	7 764	11 968	11 996	11 715	9 278	10 441
1969	71 436	7 167	3 681	3 486	64 269	8 109	12 336	11 819	11 871	9 466	10 667
1970	72 782	7 373	3 796	3 578	65 408	8 462	12 684	11 679	12 008	9 659	10 914
1971	74 274	7 591	3 895	3 697	66 682	8 834	13 110	11 553	12 115	9 870	11 198
1972	76 290	7 805	3 994	3 811	68 484	9 082	13 829	11 597	12 171	10 113	11 693
1973	77 804	7 985	4 076	3 909	69 819	9 263	14 531	11 541	12 229	10 290	11 963
1974	79 312	8 168	4 142	4 028	71 144	9 393	15 177	11 627	12 263	10 377	12 304
1975	80 860	8 285	4 168	4 117	72 576	9 645	15 811	11 652	12 237	10 558	12 673
1976	82 390	8 370	4 176	4 194	74 020	9 872	16 425	11 786	12 166	10 742	13 030
1977	83 840	8 400	4 193	4 206	75 441	10 103	17 008	12 036	12 053	10 940	13 300
1978	85 334	8 386	4 189	4 197	76 948	10 315	17 493	12 435	11 932	11 118	13 658
1979	86 843	8 347	4 139	4 208	78 496	10 480	18 070	12 815	11 808	11 303	14 021
1980	88 348	8 283	4 083	4 200	80 065	10 612	18 725	13 177	11 701	11 478	14 372
1981	89 618	8 121	3 981	4 140	81 497	10 705	19 350	13 533	11 625	11 605	14 680
1982	90 748	7 884	3 804	4 081	82 864	10 709	19 705	14 201	11 538	11 694	15 017
1983	91 684	7 616	3 635	3 981	84 069	10 660	20 004	14 865	11 478	11 742	15 319
1984	92 778	7 349	3 542	3 807	85 429	10 580	20 403	15 532	11 501	11 768	15 645
1985	93 736	7 231	3 543	3 688	86 506	10 351	20 805	16 114	11 574	11 748	15 913
1986	94 789	7 221	3 618	3 603	87 567	10 072	21 233	16 692	11 746	11 675	16 150
1987	95 853	7 271	3 677	3 594	88 583	9 776	21 516	17 279	11 968	11 567	16 476
1988	96 756	7 224	3 569	3 655	89 532	9 503	21 674	17 776	12 378	11 448	16 753
1989	97 630	7 080	3 361	3 719	90 550	9 282	21 765	18 387	12 763	11 314	17 039
1990	98 787	7 173	3 359	3 813	91 614	9 582	21 859	19 190	12 843	10 941	17 198
1991	99 646	6 939	3 353	3 586	92 708	9 597	21 711	19 903	13 155	10 895	17 446
1992	100 535	6 818	3 366	3 452	93 718	9 520	21 486	20 267	13 935	10 828	17 682
1993	101 506	6 859	3 415	3 444	94 647	9 426	21 202	20 696	14 605	10 801	17 917
1994	102 460	6 993	3 528	3 465	95 467	9 279	20 945	21 091	15 233	10 825	18 094
1995	103 406	7 144	3 613	3 531	96 262	9 029	20 719	21 454	15 862	10 879	18 318
1996	104 385	7 335	3 723	3 612	97 050	8 798	20 477	21 865	16 493	10 993	18 424
1997	105 418	7 528	3 808	3 721	97 889	8 736	20 081	22 214	17 115	11 224	18 520
1998	106 462	7 676	3 835	3 840	98 786	8 790	19 683	22 442	17 600	11 646	18 625
1999	108 031	7 873	3 917	3 955	100 158	9 069	19 411	22 666	18 251	12 056	18 705
2000	110 613	7 823	3 882	3 941	102 790	9 211	19 597	22 628	19 276	12 647	19 430
2001	111 811	7 828	3 917	3 910	103 983	9 509	19 449	22 552	19 917	13 039	19 517
2002	112 985	7 848	3 959	3 889	105 136	9 721	19 435	22 371	20 332	13 703	19 575
2003	114 733	7 934	4 195	3 738	106 800	9 924	19 674	22 283	20 738	14 423	19 758
2004	115 647	7 989	4 257	3 732	107 658	10 072	19 581	21 970	21 085	15 025	19 925
2005	116 931	8 081	4 297	3 784	108 850	10 095	19 618	21 828	21 521	15 663	20 125

Table 1-6. Civilian Noninstitutional Population, by Age, Race, Sex, and Hispanic Origin, 1948–2005
—Continued

(Thousands of people.)

Race, Hispanic origin, sex, and year	16 years and over	16 to 19 years			20 years and over						
		Total	16 to 17 years	18 to 19 years	Total	20 to 24 years	25 to 34 years	35 to 44 years	45 to 54 years	55 to 64 years	65 years and over
WHITE[1]											
Both Sexes											
1954	97 705	7 180	3 786	3 394	90 524	7 794	20 818	19 915	16 569	12 993	12 438
1955	98 880	7 292	3 874	3 419	91 586	7 912	20 742	20 110	16 869	13 169	12 785
1956	99 976	7 346	3 908	3 438	92 629	8 106	20 564	20 314	17 198	13 341	13 105
1957	101 119	7 505	4 007	3 498	93 612	8 293	20 342	20 514	17 562	13 518	13 383
1958	102 392	7 843	4 271	3 573	94 547	8 498	20 063	20 734	17 924	13 681	13 645
1959	103 803	8 430	4 707	3 725	95 370	8 697	19 715	20 893	18 257	13 858	13 951
1960	105 282	8 924	4 909	4 016	96 355	8 927	19 470	21 049	18 578	14 070	14 260
1961	106 604	9 211	4 785	4 427	97 390	9 203	19 289	21 169	18 845	14 304	14 581
1962	107 715	9 343	4 818	4 526	98 371	9 484	18 974	21 293	18 872	14 450	15 297
1963	109 705	9 978	5 549	4 430	99 725	10 069	18 867	21 398	19 082	14 681	15 629
1964	111 534	10 616	6 137	4 481	100 916	10 568	18 838	21 375	19 360	14 957	15 816
1965	113 284	11 319	6 049	5 271	101 963	10 935	18 882	21 258	19 604	15 215	16 070
1966	114 566	11 862	5 993	5 870	102 702	11 094	18 989	21 005	19 822	15 469	16 322
1967	116 100	11 682	6 051	5 632	104 417	11 797	19 464	20 745	20 067	15 745	16 602
1968	117 948	11 840	6 225	5 616	106 107	12 184	20 245	20 474	20 310	16 018	16 875
1969	119 913	12 179	6 418	5 761	107 733	12 677	20 892	20 156	20 546	16 305	17 156
1970	122 174	12 521	6 591	5 931	109 652	13 359	21 546	19 929	20 760	16 591	17 469
1971	124 758	12 937	6 750	6 189	111 821	14 208	22 295	19 694	20 907	16 884	17 833
1972	127 906	13 301	6 910	6 392	114 603	14 897	23 555	19 673	20 950	17 250	18 278
1973	130 097	13 533	7 021	6 512	116 563	15 264	24 685	19 532	20 991	17 484	18 607
1974	132 417	13 784	7 114	6 671	118 632	15 502	25 711	19 628	21 061	17 645	19 085
1975	134 790	13 941	7 132	6 808	120 849	15 980	26 746	19 641	20 981	17 918	19 587
1976	137 106	14 055	7 125	6 930	123 050	16 368	27 757	19 827	20 816	18 220	20 064
1977	139 380	14 095	7 150	6 944	125 285	16 728	28 703	20 231	20 575	18 540	20 508
1978	141 612	14 060	7 132	6 928	127 552	17 038	29 453	20 932	20 322	18 799	21 007
1979	143 894	13 994	7 029	6 964	129 900	17 284	30 371	21 579	20 058	19 071	21 538
1980	146 122	13 854	6 912	6 943	132 268	17 484	31 407	22 174	19 837	19 316	22 050
1981	147 908	13 516	6 704	6 813	134 392	17 609	32 367	22 778	19 666	19 485	22 487
1982	149 441	13 076	6 383	6 693	136 366	17 579	32 863	23 910	19 478	19 591	22 945
1983	150 805	12 623	6 089	6 534	138 183	17 492	33 286	25 027	19 349	19 625	23 403
1984	152 347	12 147	5 918	6 228	140 200	17 304	33 889	26 124	19 348	19 629	23 906
1985	153 679	11 900	5 922	5 978	141 780	16 853	34 450	27 100	19 405	19 620	24 352
1986	155 432	11 879	6 036	5 843	143 553	16 353	35 293	28 062	19 587	19 477	24 780
1987	156 958	11 939	6 110	5 829	145 020	15 808	35 667	29 036	19 965	19 242	25 301
1988	158 194	11 838	5 893	5 945	146 357	15 276	35 876	29 818	20 652	18 996	25 739
1989	159 338	11 530	5 506	6 023	147 809	14 879	35 951	30 774	21 287	18 743	26 175
1990	160 625	11 630	5 464	6 166	148 996	15 538	35 661	31 739	21 535	18 204	26 319
1991	161 759	11 200	5 451	5 749	150 558	15 516	35 342	32 854	22 052	18 074	26 721
1992	162 972	11 004	5 478	5 526	151 968	15 354	34 885	33 305	23 364	17 951	27 108
1993	164 289	11 078	5 562	5 516	153 210	15 087	34 365	33 919	24 456	17 892	27 493
1994	165 555	11 264	5 710	5 554	154 291	14 708	33 865	34 582	25 435	17 924	27 776
1995	166 914	11 468	5 822	5 646	155 446	14 313	33 355	35 222	26 418	17 986	28 153
1996	168 317	11 822	6 026	5 796	156 495	13 907	32 852	35 810	27 403	18 136	28 387
1997	169 993	12 181	6 213	5 968	157 812	13 983	32 091	36 325	28 388	18 511	28 514
1998	171 478	12 439	6 264	6 176	159 039	14 138	31 286	36 610	29 132	19 231	28 642
1999	173 085	12 700	6 342	6 358	160 385	14 394	30 516	36 755	30 048	19 855	28 818
2000	176 220	12 535	6 264	6 271	163 685	14 552	30 948	36 261	31 550	20 757	29 617
2001	178 111	12 556	6 291	6 265	165 556	15 001	30 770	36 113	32 475	21 434	29 762
2002	179 783	12 596	6 346	6 250	167 187	15 360	30 676	35 750	33 012	22 540	29 849
2003	181 292	12 527	6 629	5 898	168 765	15 536	30 789	35 352	33 466	23 589	30 033
2004	182 643	12 599	6 561	6 038	170 045	15 817	30 585	34 845	34 005	24 549	30 245
2005	184 446	12 690	6 768	5 921	171 757	15 871	30 592	34 554	34 649	25 534	30 556

[1]Beginning in 2003, persons who selected this race group only; persons who selected more than one race group are not included. Prior to 2003, persons who reported more than one race group were included in the group identified as their main race.

Table 1-6. Civilian Noninstitutional Population, by Age, Race, Sex, and Hispanic Origin, 1948–2005
—Continued

(Thousands of people.)

Race, Hispanic origin, sex, and year	16 years and over	16 to 19 years			20 years and over						
		Total	16 to 17 years	18 to 19 years	Total	20 to 24 years	25 to 34 years	35 to 44 years	45 to 54 years	55 to 64 years	65 years and over
WHITE[1]											
Men											
1954	46 462	3 455	1 902	1 553	43 007	3 074	9 948	9 688	8 172	6 341	5 787
1955	47 076	3 507	1 945	1 563	43 569	3 241	9 936	9 768	8 303	6 398	5 923
1956	47 602	3 500	1 955	1 546	44 102	3 464	9 851	9 848	8 446	6 455	6 038
1957	48 119	3 556	2 000	1 557	44 563	3 638	9 758	9 917	8 605	6 518	6 127
1958	48 745	3 747	2 140	1 607	44 998	3 783	9 656	10 018	8 765	6 574	6 203
1959	49 408	4 079	2 370	1 710	45 329	3 903	9 499	10 081	8 909	6 639	6 298
1960	50 065	4 349	2 476	1 874	45 716	4 054	9 373	10 131	9 042	6 721	6 395
1961	50 608	4 479	2 407	2 073	46 129	4 204	9 290	10 178	9 148	6 819	6 490
1962	51 054	4 520	2 426	2 094	46 534	4 306	9 080	10 239	9 191	6 917	6 801
1963	52 031	4 827	2 792	2 036	47 204	4 610	9 039	10 309	9 297	7 031	6 919
1964	52 869	5 148	3 090	2 059	47 721	4 862	9 024	10 301	9 417	7 153	6 963
1965	53 681	5 541	3 050	2 492	48 140	5 017	9 056	10 262	9 516	7 261	7 028
1966	54 061	5 820	3 023	2 798	48 241	4 974	9 085	10 136	9 592	7 362	7 092
1967	54 608	5 671	3 058	2 613	48 937	5 257	9 339	10 013	9 688	7 474	7 167
1968	55 434	5 787	3 153	2 635	49 647	5 376	9 752	9 902	9 790	7 585	7 242
1969	56 348	6 005	3 246	2 759	50 343	5 589	10 074	9 760	9 895	7 705	7 320
1970	57 516	6 179	3 329	2 851	51 336	5 988	10 441	9 678	9 999	7 822	7 409
1971	58 900	6 420	3 412	3 008	52 481	6 546	10 841	9 578	10 066	7 933	7 517
1972	60 473	6 627	3 503	3 125	53 845	7 042	11 495	9 568	10 078	8 089	7 573
1973	61 577	6 737	3 555	3 182	54 842	7 312	12 075	9 514	10 099	8 178	7 664
1974	62 791	6 851	3 604	3 247	55 942	7 476	12 599	9 564	10 165	8 288	7 849
1975	63 981	6 929	3 609	3 320	57 052	7 766	13 131	9 578	10 134	8 413	8 031
1976	65 132	6 993	3 609	3 384	58 138	7 987	13 655	9 674	10 063	8 556	8 203
1977	66 301	7 024	3 625	3 399	59 278	8 175	14 139	9 880	9 957	8 708	8 420
1978	67 401	7 022	3 619	3 404	60 378	8 335	14 528	10 236	9 845	8 826	8 608
1979	68 547	7 007	3 568	3 439	61 540	8 470	15 008	10 563	9 730	8 949	8 820
1980	69 634	6 941	3 508	3 433	62 694	8 581	15 529	10 863	9 636	9 059	9 027
1981	70 480	6 764	3 401	3 363	63 715	8 644	16 005	11 171	9 560	9 139	9 195
1982	71 211	6 556	3 249	3 307	64 655	8 621	16 260	11 756	9 463	9 188	9 367
1983	71 922	6 340	3 098	3 242	65 581	8 597	16 499	12 314	9 408	9 208	9 556
1984	72 723	6 113	3 019	3 094	66 610	8 522	16 816	12 853	9 434	9 217	9 768
1985	73 373	5 987	3 026	2 961	67 386	8 246	17 042	13 337	9 488	9 262	10 010
1986	74 390	5 977	3 084	2 894	68 413	8 002	17 564	13 840	9 578	9 201	10 229
1987	75 189	6 015	3 125	2 890	69 175	7 729	17 754	14 338	9 771	9 101	10 481
1988	75 855	5 968	3 015	2 953	69 887	7 473	17 867	14 743	10 114	9 001	10 688
1989	76 468	5 813	2 817	2 996	70 654	7 279	17 908	15 237	10 434	8 900	10 897
1990	77 369	5 913	2 809	3 103	71 457	7 764	17 766	15 770	10 598	8 680	10 879
1991	77 977	5 704	2 805	2 899	72 274	7 748	17 615	16 340	10 856	8 640	11 074
1992	78 651	5 611	2 819	2 792	73 040	7 676	17 403	16 579	11 513	8 602	11 268
1993	79 371	5 650	2 862	2 788	73 721	7 545	17 158	16 900	12 058	8 590	11 470
1994	80 059	5 748	2 938	2 810	74 311	7 357	16 915	17 247	12 545	8 618	11 629
1995	80 733	5 854	2 995	2 859	74 879	7 163	16 653	17 567	13 028	8 653	11 815
1996	81 489	6 035	3 099	2 936	75 454	6 971	16 395	17 868	13 518	8 734	11 968
1997	82 577	6 257	3 209	3 048	76 320	7 087	16 043	18 163	14 030	8 929	12 067
1998	83 352	6 386	3 233	3 153	76 966	7 170	15 644	18 310	14 400	9 286	12 155
1999	83 930	6 498	3 266	3 232	77 432	7 244	15 150	18 340	14 834	9 581	12 283
2000	85 370	6 404	3 224	3 181	78 966	7 329	15 528	18 003	15 578	10 028	12 501
2001	86 452	6 422	3 229	3 194	80 029	7 564	15 486	17 960	16 047	10 369	12 604
2002	87 361	6 439	3 251	3 189	80 922	7 750	15 470	17 792	16 317	10 918	12 676
2003	88 249	6 390	3 378	3 012	81 860	7 856	15 569	17 620	16 555	11 442	12 818
2004	89 044	6 429	3 301	3 129	82 615	8 024	15 486	17 404	16 834	11 922	12 946
2005	90 027	6 471	3 464	3 006	83 556	8 057	15 507	17 286	17 169	12 415	13 123

[1]Beginning in 2003, persons who selected this race group only; persons who selected more than one race group are not included. Prior to 2003, persons who reported more than one race group were included in the group identified as their main race.

Table 1-6. Civilian Noninstitutional Population, by Age, Race, Sex, and Hispanic Origin, 1948–2005
—Continued

(Thousands of people.)

Race, Hispanic origin, sex, and year	16 years and over	16 to 19 years			20 years and over						
		Total	16 to 17 years	18 to 19 years	Total	20 to 24 years	25 to 34 years	35 to 44 years	45 to 54 years	55 to 64 years	65 years and over
WHITE[1]											
Women											
1954	51 242	3 725	1 884	1 841	47 517	4 720	10 870	10 227	8 397	6 652	6 651
1955	51 802	3 785	1 929	1 856	48 017	4 671	10 806	10 342	8 566	6 771	6 862
1956	52 373	3 846	1 953	1 892	48 527	4 642	10 713	10 466	8 752	6 886	7 067
1957	52 998	3 949	2 007	1 941	49 049	4 655	10 584	10 597	8 957	7 000	7 256
1958	53 645	4 096	2 131	1 966	49 549	4 715	10 407	10 716	9 159	7 107	7 442
1959	54 392	4 351	2 337	2 015	50 041	4 794	10 216	10 812	9 348	7 219	7 653
1960	55 214	4 575	2 433	2 142	50 639	4 873	10 097	10 918	9 536	7 349	7 865
1961	55 993	4 732	2 378	2 354	51 261	4 999	9 999	10 991	9 697	7 485	8 091
1962	56 660	4 823	2 392	2 432	51 837	5 178	9 894	11 054	9 681	7 533	8 496
1963	57 672	5 151	2 757	2 394	52 521	5 459	9 828	11 089	9 785	7 650	8 710
1964	58 663	5 468	3 047	2 422	53 195	5 706	9 814	11 074	9 943	7 804	8 853
1965	59 601	5 778	2 999	2 779	53 823	5 918	9 826	10 996	10 088	7 954	9 042
1966	60 503	6 042	2 970	3 072	54 461	6 120	9 904	10 869	10 230	8 107	9 230
1967	61 491	6 011	2 993	3 019	55 480	6 540	10 125	10 732	10 379	8 271	9 435
1968	62 512	6 053	3 072	2 981	56 460	6 809	10 493	10 572	10 520	8 433	9 633
1969	63 563	6 174	3 172	3 002	57 390	7 089	10 818	10 396	10 651	8 600	9 836
1970	64 656	6 342	3 262	3 080	58 315	7 370	11 105	10 251	10 761	8 769	10 060
1971	65 857	6 518	3 338	3 180	59 340	7 662	11 454	10 117	10 841	8 951	10 315
1972	67 431	6 673	3 407	3 267	60 758	7 855	12 060	10 105	10 872	9 161	10 705
1973	68 517	6 796	3 466	3 331	61 721	7 951	12 610	10 018	10 891	9 306	10 943
1974	69 623	6 933	3 510	3 424	62 690	8 026	13 112	10 064	10 896	9 356	11 236
1975	70 810	7 011	3 523	3 488	63 798	8 214	13 615	10 063	10 847	9 505	11 556
1976	71 974	7 062	3 516	3 546	64 912	8 381	14 102	10 153	10 752	9 664	11 860
1977	73 077	7 071	3 525	3 545	66 007	8 553	14 564	10 351	10 618	9 832	12 088
1978	74 213	7 038	3 513	3 524	67 174	8 704	14 926	10 696	10 476	9 974	12 399
1979	75 347	6 987	3 460	3 527	68 360	8 815	15 363	11 017	10 327	10 122	12 717
1980	76 489	6 914	3 403	3 511	69 575	8 904	15 878	11 313	10 201	10 256	13 022
1981	77 428	6 752	3 303	3 449	70 677	8 965	16 362	11 606	10 106	10 346	13 292
1982	78 230	6 519	3 134	3 385	71 711	8 959	16 603	12 154	10 015	10 402	13 579
1983	78 884	6 282	2 991	3 292	72 601	8 895	16 788	12 714	9 941	10 418	13 847
1984	79 624	6 034	2 899	3 135	73 590	8 782	17 073	13 271	9 914	10 412	14 138
1985	80 306	5 912	2 895	3 017	74 394	8 607	17 409	13 762	9 917	10 358	14 342
1986	81 042	5 902	2 953	2 949	75 140	8 351	17 728	14 223	10 009	10 277	14 551
1987	81 769	5 924	2 985	2 939	75 845	8 079	17 913	14 698	10 194	10 141	14 820
1988	82 340	5 869	2 878	2 991	76 470	7 804	18 009	15 074	10 537	9 994	15 052
1989	82 871	5 716	2 690	3 027	77 154	7 600	18 043	15 537	10 853	9 843	15 278
1990	83 256	5 717	2 654	3 063	77 539	7 774	17 895	15 969	10 937	9 524	15 440
1991	83 781	5 497	2 646	2 850	78 285	7 768	17 726	16 514	11 196	9 435	15 647
1992	84 321	5 393	2 659	2 734	78 928	7 678	17 482	16 727	11 851	9 350	15 841
1993	84 918	5 428	2 700	2 728	79 490	7 542	17 206	17 019	12 398	9 302	16 023
1994	85 496	5 516	2 772	2 744	79 980	7 351	16 950	17 335	12 890	9 306	16 148
1995	86 181	5 614	2 827	2 787	80 567	7 150	16 702	17 654	13 390	9 333	16 337
1996	86 828	5 787	2 927	2 860	81 041	6 936	16 457	17 943	13 884	9 402	16 419
1997	87 417	5 924	3 004	2 920	81 492	6 896	16 047	18 162	14 357	9 582	16 447
1998	88 126	6 053	3 031	3 023	82 073	6 969	15 642	18 300	14 732	9 944	16 486
1999	89 156	6 202	3 076	3 127	82 953	7 150	15 366	18 415	15 214	10 274	16 536
2000	90 850	6 131	3 041	3 090	84 718	7 223	15 420	18 258	15 972	10 729	17 116
2001	91 660	6 134	3 062	3 071	85 526	7 438	15 284	18 153	16 428	11 065	17 158
2002	92 422	6 157	3 096	3 061	86 266	7 611	15 207	17 958	16 695	11 622	17 173
2003	93 043	6 137	3 251	2 886	86 905	7 680	15 220	17 731	16 911	12 147	17 216
2004	93 599	6 169	3 260	2 909	87 430	7 794	15 099	17 441	17 170	12 627	17 299
2005	94 419	6 219	3 304	2 915	88 200	7 814	15 086	17 268	17 480	13 119	17 433

[1]Beginning in 2003, persons who selected this race group only; persons who selected more than one race group are not included. Prior to 2003, persons who reported more than one race group were included in the group identified as their main race.

Table 1-6. Civilian Noninstitutional Population, by Age, Race, Sex, and Hispanic Origin, 1948–2005
—Continued

(Thousands of people.)

Race, Hispanic origin, sex, and year	16 years and over	16 to 19 years			20 years and over						
		Total	16 to 17 years	18 to 19 years	Total	20 to 24 years	25 to 34 years	35 to 44 years	45 to 54 years	55 to 64 years	65 years and over
BLACK[1]											
Both Sexes											
1972	14 526	2 018	1 061	956	12 508	2 027	2 809	2 329	2 139	1 601	1 605
1973	14 917	2 095	1 095	1 000	12 823	2 132	2 957	2 333	2 156	1 616	1 628
1974	15 329	2 137	1 122	1 014	13 192	2 137	3 103	2 382	2 202	1 679	1 689
1975	15 751	2 191	1 146	1 046	13 560	2 228	3 258	2 395	2 211	1 717	1 755
1976	16 196	2 264	1 165	1 098	13 932	2 303	3 412	2 435	2 220	1 736	1 826
1977	16 605	2 273	1 175	1 097	14 332	2 400	3 566	2 493	2 225	1 765	1 883
1978	16 970	2 270	1 169	1 101	14 701	2 483	3 717	2 547	2 226	1 794	1 932
1979	17 397	2 276	1 167	1 109	15 121	2 556	3 899	2 615	2 240	1 831	1 980
1980	17 824	2 289	1 171	1 119	15 535	2 606	4 095	2 687	2 249	1 870	2 030
1981	18 219	2 288	1 161	1 127	15 931	2 642	4 290	2 758	2 260	1 913	2 069
1982	18 584	2 252	1 119	1 134	16 332	2 697	4 438	2 887	2 263	1 935	2 113
1983	18 925	2 225	1 092	1 133	16 700	2 734	4 607	2 999	2 260	1 964	2 135
1984	19 348	2 161	1 056	1 105	17 187	2 783	4 789	3 167	2 288	1 977	2 183
1985	19 664	2 160	1 083	1 077	17 504	2 649	4 873	3 290	2 372	2 060	2 259
1986	19 989	2 137	1 090	1 048	17 852	2 625	5 026	3 410	2 413	2 079	2 298
1987	20 352	2 163	1 123	1 040	18 189	2 578	5 139	3 563	2 460	2 097	2 352
1988	20 692	2 179	1 130	1 049	18 513	2 527	5 234	3 716	2 524	2 110	2 402
1989	21 021	2 176	1 116	1 060	18 846	2 479	5 308	3 900	2 587	2 118	2 454
1990	21 477	2 238	1 101	1 138	19 239	2 554	5 407	4 328	2 618	1 970	2 362
1991	21 799	2 187	1 085	1 102	19 612	2 585	5 419	4 538	2 682	1 985	2 403
1992	22 147	2 155	1 086	1 069	19 992	2 615	5 404	4 722	2 809	1 996	2 446
1993	22 521	2 181	1 113	1 069	20 339	2 600	5 409	4 886	2 941	2 016	2 487
1994	22 879	2 211	1 168	1 044	20 668	2 616	5 362	5 038	3 084	2 045	2 524
1995	23 246	2 284	1 198	1 086	20 962	2 554	5 337	5 178	3 244	2 079	2 571
1996	23 604	2 356	1 238	1 118	21 248	2 519	5 311	5 290	3 408	2 110	2 609
1997	24 003	2 412	1 255	1 158	21 591	2 515	5 279	5 410	3 571	2 164	2 653
1998	24 373	2 443	1 241	1 202	21 930	2 546	5 221	5 510	3 735	2 224	2 695
1999	24 855	2 479	1 250	1 229	22 376	2 615	5 197	5 609	3 919	2 295	2 741
2000	24 902	2 389	1 205	1 183	22 513	2 611	5 089	5 488	4 168	2 407	2 750
2001	25 138	2 388	1 212	1 176	22 750	2 686	5 003	5 467	4 343	2 478	2 775
2002	25 578	2 416	1 235	1 181	23 162	2 779	5 015	5 460	4 513	2 571	2 823
2003	25 686	2 382	1 309	1 074	23 304	2 773	4 978	5 387	4 628	2 692	2 846
2004	26 065	2 423	1 350	1 072	23 643	2 821	5 020	5 335	4 739	2 827	2 899
2005	26 517	2 481	1 341	1 140	24 036	2 835	5 075	5 311	4 869	2 980	2 967
Men											
1972	6 538	978	525	453	5 559	921	1 251	1 026	963	720	679
1973	6 704	1 007	539	468	5 697	979	1 327	1 027	962	718	684
1974	6 875	1 027	554	471	5 848	956	1 381	1 055	997	753	707
1975	7 060	1 051	565	486	6 009	1 002	1 452	1 060	997	769	730
1976	7 265	1 099	579	518	6 167	1 036	1 521	1 077	999	774	756
1977	7 431	1 102	586	516	6 329	1 080	1 589	1 102	998	786	774
1978	7 577	1 093	579	514	6 484	1 120	1 657	1 128	995	794	789
1979	7 761	1 100	581	519	6 661	1 151	1 738	1 159	998	809	804
1980	7 944	1 110	583	526	6 834	1 171	1 828	1 191	999	825	822
1981	8 117	1 110	577	534	7 007	1 189	1 914	1 224	1 003	844	835
1982	8 283	1 097	556	542	7 186	1 225	1 983	1 282	1 003	848	846
1983	8 447	1 087	542	545	7 360	1 254	2 068	1 333	1 000	857	847
1984	8 654	1 055	524	531	7 599	1 292	2 164	1 411	1 012	858	861
1985	8 790	1 059	543	517	7 731	1 202	2 180	1 462	1 060	924	902
1986	8 956	1 049	548	503	7 907	1 195	2 264	1 517	1 072	934	924
1987	9 128	1 065	566	499	8 063	1 173	2 320	1 587	1 092	944	947
1988	9 289	1 074	569	505	8 215	1 151	2 367	1 656	1 121	951	970
1989	9 439	1 075	575	501	8 364	1 128	2 403	1 741	1 145	956	989
1990	9 573	1 094	555	540	8 479	1 144	2 412	1 968	1 183	855	917
1991	9 725	1 072	546	526	8 652	1 168	2 417	2 060	1 211	864	933
1992	9 896	1 056	544	512	8 840	1 194	2 409	2 150	1 268	868	951
1993	10 083	1 075	559	516	9 008	1 181	2 425	2 228	1 330	874	969
1994	10 258	1 087	586	501	9 171	1 207	2 399	2 300	1 392	889	985
1995	10 411	1 131	601	530	9 280	1 161	2 388	2 362	1 462	901	1 006
1996	10 575	1 161	623	538	9 414	1 154	2 373	2 413	1 534	914	1 025
1997	10 763	1 188	634	553	9 575	1 153	2 363	2 471	1 607	936	1 045
1998	10 927	1 201	623	578	9 727	1 166	2 335	2 520	1 682	956	1 068
1999	11 143	1 218	628	589	9 926	1 197	2 321	2 566	1 765	986	1 091
2000	11 129	1 178	605	572	9 952	1 195	2 277	2 471	1 889	1 067	1 053
2001	11 172	1 179	606	573	9 993	1 224	2 212	2 440	1 960	1 096	1 060
2002	11 391	1 195	615	580	10 196	1 281	2 223	2 437	2 042	1 137	1 075
2003	11 454	1 176	661	515	10 278	1 291	2 210	2 401	2 094	1 189	1 093
2004	11 656	1 195	680	516	10 461	1 326	2 242	2 382	2 150	1 250	1 111
2005	11 882	1 223	682	541	10 659	1 341	2 277	2 372	2 202	1 319	1 148

[1]Beginning in 2003, persons who selected this race group only; persons who selected more than one race group are not included. Prior to 2003, persons who reported more than one race group were included in the group identified as their main race.

Table 1-6. Civilian Noninstitutional Population, by Age, Race, Sex, and Hispanic Origin, 1948–2005
—Continued

(Thousands of people.)

Race, Hispanic origin, sex, and year	16 years and over	16 to 19 years			20 years and over						
		Total	16 to 17 years	18 to 19 years	Total	20 to 24 years	25 to 34 years	35 to 44 years	45 to 54 years	55 to 64 years	65 years and over
BLACK[1]											
Women											
1972	7 988	1 040	536	503	6 948	1 106	1 558	1 302	1 176	881	925
1973	8 214	1 088	556	532	7 126	1 153	1 631	1 306	1 194	898	944
1974	8 454	1 110	567	542	7 344	1 181	1 723	1 327	1 206	926	981
1975	8 691	1 141	581	560	7 550	1 226	1 806	1 334	1 213	948	1 025
1976	8 931	1 165	585	580	7 765	1 266	1 890	1 357	1 220	962	1 070
1977	9 174	1 171	590	581	8 003	1 320	1 978	1 390	1 228	979	1 108
1978	9 394	1 177	589	588	8 217	1 363	2 061	1 419	1 231	999	1 143
1979	9 636	1 176	586	589	8 460	1 405	2 160	1 455	1 242	1 022	1 176
1980	9 880	1 180	587	593	8 700	1 435	2 267	1 496	1 250	1 045	1 208
1981	10 102	1 178	584	593	8 924	1 453	2 376	1 534	1 257	1 069	1 234
1982	10 300	1 155	563	592	9 146	1 472	2 455	1 605	1 260	1 087	1 267
1983	10 477	1 138	550	588	9 340	1 480	2 539	1 666	1 260	1 107	1 288
1984	10 694	1 106	532	574	9 588	1 491	2 625	1 756	1 276	1 119	1 322
1985	10 873	1 101	540	560	9 773	1 447	2 693	1 828	1 312	1 136	1 357
1986	11 033	1 088	542	545	9 945	1 430	2 762	1 893	1 341	1 145	1 374
1987	11 224	1 098	557	541	10 126	1 405	2 819	1 976	1 368	1 153	1 405
1988	11 402	1 105	561	544	10 298	1 376	2 867	2 060	1 403	1 159	1 432
1989	11 582	1 100	541	559	10 482	1 351	2 905	2 159	1 441	1 162	1 464
1990	11 904	1 144	546	598	10 760	1 410	2 995	2 360	1 435	1 114	1 446
1991	12 074	1 115	539	576	10 959	1 417	3 003	2 478	1 471	1 121	1 470
1992	12 251	1 099	542	557	11 152	1 421	2 995	2 573	1 542	1 127	1 495
1993	12 438	1 106	554	552	11 332	1 419	2 983	2 659	1 611	1 142	1 518
1994	12 621	1 125	582	543	11 496	1 410	2 963	2 738	1 692	1 156	1 538
1995	12 835	1 153	597	556	11 682	1 392	2 948	2 816	1 782	1 178	1 565
1996	13 029	1 195	615	580	11 833	1 364	2 938	2 877	1 874	1 196	1 584
1997	13 241	1 225	620	604	12 016	1 362	2 916	2 939	1 964	1 228	1 608
1998	13 446	1 243	618	624	12 203	1 380	2 886	2 991	2 053	1 268	1 626
1999	13 711	1 261	621	640	12 451	1 418	2 876	3 043	2 153	1 310	1 650
2000	13 772	1 211	600	611	12 561	1 416	2 812	3 017	2 279	1 340	1 697
2001	13 966	1 209	606	603	12 758	1 462	2 790	3 026	2 383	1 382	1 714
2002	14 187	1 221	620	601	12 966	1 498	2 792	3 023	2 471	1 434	1 747
2003	14 232	1 206	648	558	13 026	1 482	2 768	2 986	2 534	1 504	1 753
2004	14 409	1 227	670	557	13 182	1 495	2 778	2 954	2 590	1 577	1 789
2005	14 635	1 258	659	598	13 377	1 494	2 797	2 939	2 666	1 661	1 819
HISPANIC[2]											
Both Sexes											
1973	6 104	867	. . .	. . .	5 238	. . .	. . .	. . .	. . .	. . .	. . .
1974	6 564	926	. . .	. . .	5 645	. . .	. . .	. . .	. . .	. . .	. . .
1975	6 862	962	. . .	. . .	5 900	. . .	. . .	. . .	. . .	. . .	. . .
1976	6 910	953	494	480	6 075	1 053	1 775	1 261	936	570	479
1977	7 362	1 024	513	508	6 376	1 163	1 869	1 283	989	587	485
1978	7 912	1 076	561	515	6 836	1 265	2 004	1 378	1 033	627	529
1979	8 207	1 095	544	551	7 113	1 296	2 117	1 458	1 015	659	566
1980	9 598	1 281	638	643	8 317	1 564	2 508	1 575	1 190	782	698
1981	10 120	1 301	641	660	8 819	1 650	2 698	1 680	1 231	832	728
1982	10 580	1 307	639	668	9 273	1 724	2 871	1 779	1 264	880	755
1983	11 029	1 304	635	670	9 725	1 790	3 045	1 883	1 298	928	781
1984	11 478	1 300	633	667	10 178	1 839	3 224	1 996	1 336	973	810
1985	11 915	1 298	638	661	10 617	1 864	3 401	2 117	1 377	1 015	843
1986	12 344	1 302	658	644	11 042	1 899	3 510	2 239	1 496	1 023	875
1987	12 867	1 332	651	681	11 536	1 910	3 714	2 464	1 492	1 061	895
1988	13 325	1 354	662	692	11 970	1 948	3 807	2 565	1 571	1 159	920
1989	13 791	1 399	672	727	12 392	1 950	3 953	2 658	1 649	1 182	1 001
1990	15 904	1 737	821	915	14 167	2 428	4 589	3 001	1 817	1 247	1 084
1991	16 425	1 732	819	913	14 693	2 481	4 674	3 243	1 879	1 283	1 134
1992	16 961	1 737	836	901	15 224	2 444	4 806	3 458	1 980	1 321	1 216
1993	17 532	1 756	855	901	15 776	2 487	4 887	3 632	2 094	1 324	1 353
1994	18 117	1 818	902	916	16 300	2 518	5 000	3 756	2 223	1 401	1 401
1995	18 629	1 872	903	969	16 757	2 528	5 050	3 965	2 294	1 483	1 437
1996	19 213	1 948	962	986	17 265	2 524	5 181	4 227	2 275	1 546	1 512
1997	20 321	2 121	1 088	1 033	18 200	2 623	5 405	4 453	2 581	1 580	1 558
1998	21 070	2 204	1 070	1 135	18 865	2 731	5 447	4 636	2 775	1 615	1 662
1999	21 650	2 307	1 113	1 194	19 344	2 700	5 512	4 833	2 868	1 713	1 718
2000	23 938	2 523	1 214	1 309	21 415	3 255	6 466	5 189	3 061	1 736	1 708
2001	24 942	2 508	1 173	1 334	22 435	3 417	6 726	5 346	3 339	1 816	1 792
2002	25 963	2 507	1 216	1 291	23 456	3 508	7 010	5 606	3 494	1 953	1 885
2003	27 551	2 543	1 346	1 197	25 008	3 533	7 506	6 003	3 845	2 093	2 027
2004	28 109	2 608	1 337	1 270	25 502	3 666	7 470	6 055	3 987	2 208	2 115
2005	29 133	2 689	1 415	1 274	26 444	3 647	7 684	6 293	4 217	2 361	2 242

[1]Beginning in 2003, persons who selected this race group only; persons who selected more than one race group are not included. Prior to 2003, persons who reported more than one race group were included in the group identified as their main race.
[2]May be of any race.
. . . = Not available.

Table 1-6. Civilian Noninstitutional Population, by Age, Race, Sex, and Hispanic Origin, 1948–2005
—*Continued*

(Thousands of people.)

Race, Hispanic origin, sex, and year	16 years and over	16 to 19 years			20 years and over						
		Total	16 to 17 years	18 to 19 years	Total	20 to 24 years	25 to 34 years	35 to 44 years	45 to 54 years	55 to 64 years	65 years and over
HISPANIC[2]											
Men											
1973	2 891	...	...	...	2 472	...	...	...	...	...	...
1974	3 130	...	...	...	2 680	...	...	...	...	...	...
1975	3 219	...	...	...	2 741	...	...	...	...	...	...
1976	3 241	...	...	...	2 764	...	...	...	...	...	...
1977	3 483	...	...	...	2 982	...	...	...	...	...	...
1978	3 750	...	...	...	3 228	...	...	...	...	...	...
1979	3 917	...	...	...	3 362	...	...	...	...	...	...
1980	4 689	...	...	...	4 036	...	...	...	...	...	...
1981	4 968	...	...	...	4 306	...	...	...	...	...	...
1982	5 203	...	...	...	4 539	...	...	...	...	...	...
1983	5 432	...	...	...	4 771	...	...	...	...	...	...
1984	5 661	...	...	...	5 005	...	...	...	...	...	...
1985	5 885	...	...	...	5 232	...	...	...	...	...	...
1986	6 106	...	...	...	5 451	...	...	...	...	...	...
1987	6 371	...	...	...	5 700	...	...	...	...	...	...
1988	6 604	...	...	...	5 921	...	...	...	...	...	...
1989	6 825	...	...	...	6 114	...	...	...	...	...	...
1990	8 041	...	...	...	7 126	...	...	...	...	...	...
1991	8 296	...	...	...	7 392	...	...	...	...	...	...
1992	8 553	...	...	...	7 655	...	...	...	...	...	...
1993	8 824	...	...	...	7 930	...	...	...	...	...	...
1994	9 104	926	472	454	8 178	1 346	2 627	1 871	1 076	644	614
1995	9 329	954	481	473	8 375	1 337	2 657	1 966	1 127	668	619
1996	9 604	992	485	507	8 611	1 321	2 692	2 144	1 111	712	630
1997	10 368	1 119	585	534	9 250	1 439	2 872	2 275	1 266	747	651
1998	10 734	1 161	586	575	9 573	1 462	2 907	2 377	1 342	771	714
1999	10 713	1 190	571	619	9 523	1 398	2 805	2 407	1 397	767	749
2000	12 174	1 333	640	693	10 841	1 784	3 380	2 626	1 527	799	725
2001	12 695	1 310	619	690	11 386	1 846	3 529	2 765	1 650	848	749
2002	13 221	1 293	615	678	11 928	1 890	3 727	2 875	1 716	902	817
2003	14 098	1 301	674	627	12 797	1 905	4 033	3 098	1 910	989	862
2004	14 417	1 336	664	672	13 082	1 981	4 024	3 147	1 990	1 046	894
2005	14 962	1 376	730	646	13 586	1 956	4 155	3 284	2 114	1 123	953
Women											
1973	3 213	...	...	...	2 766	...	...	...	...	...	...
1974	3 434	...	...	...	2 959	...	...	...	...	...	...
1975	3 644	...	...	...	3 161	...	...	...	...	...	...
1976	3 669	...	...	...	3 263	...	...	...	...	...	...
1977	3 879	...	...	...	3 377	...	...	...	...	...	...
1978	4 159	...	...	...	3 608	...	...	...	...	...	...
1979	4 291	...	...	...	3 751	...	...	...	...	...	...
1980	4 909	...	...	...	4 281	...	...	...	...	...	...
1981	5 151	...	...	...	4 513	...	...	...	...	...	...
1982	5 377	...	...	...	4 734	...	...	...	...	...	...
1983	5 597	...	...	...	4 954	...	...	...	...	...	...
1984	5 816	...	...	...	5 173	...	...	...	...	...	...
1985	6 029	...	...	...	5 385	...	...	...	...	...	...
1986	6 238	...	...	...	5 591	...	...	...	...	...	...
1987	6 496	...	...	...	5 835	...	...	...	...	...	...
1988	6 721	...	...	...	6 050	...	...	...	...	...	...
1989	6 965	...	...	...	6 278	...	...	...	...	...	...
1990	7 863	...	...	...	7 041	...	...	...	...	...	...
1991	8 130	...	...	...	7 301	...	...	...	...	...	...
1992	8 408	...	...	...	7 569	...	...	...	...	...	...
1993	8 708	...	...	...	7 846	...	...	...	...	...	...
1994	9 014	892	430	462	8 122	1 173	2 373	1 885	1 147	757	787
1995	9 300	918	422	496	8 382	1 191	2 393	1 999	1 167	815	818
1996	9 610	956	477	479	8 654	1 203	2 489	2 082	1 164	834	882
1997	9 953	1 003	503	500	8 950	1 184	2 533	2 178	1 315	833	907
1998	10 335	1 044	483	560	9 292	1 269	2 539	2 259	1 433	844	948
1999	10 937	1 116	542	575	9 821	1 302	2 707	2 425	1 470	947	969
2000	11 764	1 190	574	616	10 574	1 471	3 086	2 564	1 534	937	982
2001	12 247	1 198	554	644	11 049	1 571	3 198	2 581	1 689	968	1 043
2002	12 742	1 214	601	613	11 528	1 617	3 283	2 732	1 777	1 051	1 068
2003	13 452	1 242	672	570	12 211	1 628	3 473	2 905	1 935	1 105	1 166
2004	13 692	1 272	674	598	12 420	1 685	3 447	2 908	1 997	1 162	1 221
2005	14 172	1 313	685	628	12 858	1 692	3 529	3 009	2 103	1 237	1 289

[2]May be of any race.
. . . = Not available.

Table 1-7. Civilian Labor Force, by Age, Sex, Race, and Hispanic Origin, 1948–2005

(Thousands of people.)

Race, Hispanic origin, sex, and year	16 years and over	16 to 19 years			20 years and over						
		Total	16 to 17 years	18 to 19 years	Total	20 to 24 years	25 to 34 years	35 to 44 years	45 to 54 years	55 to 64 years	65 years and over
ALL RACES											
Both Sexes											
1948	60 621	4 435	1 780	2 654	56 187	7 392	14 258	13 397	10 914	7 329	2 897
1949	61 286	4 288	1 704	2 583	57 000	7 340	14 415	13 711	11 107	7 426	3 010
1950	62 208	4 216	1 659	2 557	57 994	7 307	14 619	13 954	11 444	7 633	3 036
1951	62 017	4 103	1 743	2 360	57 914	6 594	14 668	14 100	11 739	7 796	3 020
1952	62 138	4 064	1 806	2 257	58 075	5 840	14 904	14 383	11 961	7 980	3 005
1953	63 015	4 027	1 727	2 299	58 989	5 481	14 898	15 099	12 249	8 024	3 236
1954	63 643	3 976	1 643	2 300	59 666	5 475	14 983	15 221	12 524	8 269	3 192
1955	65 023	4 092	1 711	2 382	60 931	5 666	15 058	15 400	12 992	8 513	3 305
1956	66 552	4 296	1 878	2 418	62 257	5 940	14 961	15 694	13 407	8 830	3 423
1957	66 929	4 275	1 843	2 433	62 653	6 071	14 826	15 847	13 768	8 853	3 290
1958	67 639	4 260	1 818	2 442	63 377	6 272	14 668	16 028	14 179	9 031	3 199
1959	68 369	4 492	1 971	2 522	63 876	6 413	14 435	16 127	14 518	9 227	3 158
1960	69 628	4 841	2 095	2 747	64 788	6 702	14 382	16 269	14 852	9 385	3 195
1961	70 459	4 936	1 984	2 951	65 524	6 950	14 319	16 402	15 071	9 636	3 146
1962	70 614	4 916	1 919	2 997	65 699	7 082	14 023	16 589	15 096	9 757	3 154
1963	71 833	5 139	2 171	2 966	66 695	7 473	14 050	16 788	15 338	10 006	3 041
1964	73 091	5 388	2 449	2 940	67 702	7 963	14 056	16 771	15 637	10 182	3 090
1965	74 455	5 910	2 486	3 425	68 543	8 259	14 233	16 840	15 756	10 350	3 108
1966	75 770	6 558	2 664	3 893	69 219	8 410	14 458	16 738	15 984	10 575	3 053
1967	77 347	6 521	2 734	3 786	70 825	9 010	15 055	16 703	16 172	10 792	3 097
1968	78 737	6 619	2 817	3 803	72 118	9 305	15 708	16 591	16 397	10 964	3 153
1969	80 734	6 970	3 009	3 959	73 763	9 879	16 336	16 458	16 730	11 135	3 227
1970	82 771	7 249	3 135	4 115	75 521	10 597	17 036	16 437	16 949	11 283	3 222
1971	84 382	7 470	3 192	4 278	76 913	11 331	17 714	16 305	17 024	11 390	3 149
1972	87 034	8 054	3 420	4 636	78 980	12 130	18 960	16 398	16 967	11 412	3 114
1973	89 429	8 507	3 665	4 839	80 924	12 846	20 376	16 492	16 983	11 256	2 974
1974	91 949	8 871	3 810	5 059	83 080	13 314	21 654	16 763	17 131	11 284	2 934
1975	93 775	8 870	3 740	5 131	84 904	13 750	22 864	16 903	17 084	11 346	2 956
1976	96 158	9 056	3 767	5 288	87 103	14 284	24 203	17 317	16 982	11 422	2 895
1977	99 009	9 351	3 919	5 431	89 658	14 825	25 500	17 943	16 878	11 577	2 934
1978	102 251	9 652	4 127	5 526	92 598	15 370	26 703	18 821	16 891	11 744	3 070
1979	104 962	9 638	4 079	5 559	95 325	15 769	27 938	19 685	16 897	11 931	3 104
1980	106 940	9 378	3 883	5 496	97 561	15 922	29 227	20 463	16 910	11 985	3 054
1981	108 670	8 988	3 647	5 340	99 682	16 099	30 392	21 211	16 970	11 969	3 042
1982	110 204	8 526	3 336	5 189	101 679	16 082	31 186	22 431	16 889	12 062	3 030
1983	111 550	8 171	3 073	5 098	103 379	16 052	31 834	23 611	16 851	11 992	3 040
1984	113 544	7 943	3 050	4 894	105 601	16 046	32 723	24 933	17 006	11 961	2 933
1985	115 461	7 901	3 154	4 747	107 560	15 718	33 550	26 073	17 322	11 991	2 907
1986	117 834	7 926	3 287	4 639	109 908	15 441	34 591	27 232	17 739	11 894	3 010
1987	119 865	7 988	3 384	4 604	111 878	14 977	35 233	28 460	18 210	11 877	3 119
1988	121 669	8 031	3 286	4 745	113 638	14 505	35 503	29 435	19 104	11 808	3 284
1989	123 869	7 954	3 125	4 828	115 916	14 180	35 896	30 601	19 916	11 877	3 446
1990	125 840	7 792	2 937	4 856	118 047	14 700	35 929	32 145	20 248	11 575	3 451
1991	126 346	7 265	2 789	4 476	119 082	14 548	35 507	33 312	20 828	11 473	3 413
1992	128 105	7 096	2 769	4 327	121 009	14 521	35 369	33 899	22 160	11 587	3 473
1993	129 200	7 170	2 831	4 338	122 030	14 354	34 780	34 562	23 296	11 599	3 439
1994	131 056	7 481	3 134	4 347	123 576	14 131	34 353	35 226	24 318	11 713	3 834
1995	132 304	7 765	3 225	4 540	124 539	13 688	34 198	35 751	25 223	11 860	3 819
1996	133 943	7 806	3 263	4 543	126 137	13 377	33 833	36 556	26 397	12 146	3 828
1997	136 297	7 932	3 237	4 695	128 365	13 532	33 380	37 326	27 574	12 665	3 887
1998	137 673	8 256	3 335	4 921	129 417	13 638	32 813	37 536	28 368	13 215	3 847
1999	139 368	8 333	3 337	4 996	131 034	13 933	32 143	37 882	29 388	13 682	4 005
2000	142 583	8 271	3 261	5 010	134 312	14 250	32 755	37 567	31 071	14 356	4 312
2001	143 734	7 902	3 088	4 814	135 832	14 557	32 361	37 404	32 025	15 104	4 382
2002	144 863	7 585	2 870	4 715	137 278	14 781	32 196	36 926	32 597	16 309	4 469
2003	146 510	7 170	2 857	4 313	139 340	14 928	32 343	36 695	33 270	17 312	4 792
2004	147 401	7 114	2 747	4 367	140 287	15 154	32 207	36 158	33 758	18 013	4 998
2005	149 320	7 164	2 825	4 339	142 157	15 127	32 341	36 030	34 402	18 979	5 278

Table 1-7. Civilian Labor Force, by Age, Sex, Race, and Hispanic Origin, 1948–2005—*Continued*

(Thousands of people.)

Race, Hispanic origin, sex, and year	16 years and over	16 to 19 years			20 years and over						
		Total	16 to 17 years	18 to 19 years	Total	20 to 24 years	25 to 34 years	35 to 44 years	45 to 54 years	55 to 64 years	65 years and over
ALL RACES											
Men											
1948	43 286	2 600	1 109	1 490	40 687	4 673	10 327	9 596	7 943	5 764	2 384
1949	43 498	2 477	1 056	1 420	41 022	4 682	10 418	9 722	8 008	5 748	2 454
1950	43 819	2 504	1 048	1 456	41 316	4 632	10 527	9 793	8 117	5 794	2 453
1951	43 001	2 347	1 081	1 266	40 655	3 935	10 375	9 799	8 205	5 873	2 469
1952	42 869	2 312	1 101	1 210	40 558	3 338	10 585	9 945	8 326	5 949	2 416
1953	43 633	2 320	1 070	1 249	41 315	3 053	10 736	10 437	8 570	5 975	2 543
1954	43 965	2 295	1 023	1 272	41 669	3 051	10 771	10 513	8 702	6 105	2 526
1955	44 475	2 369	1 070	1 299	42 106	3 221	10 806	10 595	8 838	6 122	2 526
1956	45 091	2 433	1 142	1 291	42 658	3 485	10 685	10 663	9 002	6 220	2 602
1957	45 197	2 415	1 127	1 289	42 780	3 629	10 571	10 731	9 153	6 222	2 477
1958	45 521	2 428	1 133	1 295	43 092	3 771	10 475	10 843	9 320	6 304	2 378
1959	45 886	2 596	1 206	1 390	43 289	3 940	10 346	10 899	9 438	6 345	2 322
1960	46 388	2 787	1 290	1 496	43 603	4 123	10 251	10 967	9 574	6 399	2 287
1961	46 653	2 794	1 210	1 583	43 860	4 253	10 176	11 012	9 668	6 530	2 220
1962	46 600	2 770	1 178	1 592	43 831	4 279	9 920	11 115	9 715	6 560	2 241
1963	47 129	2 907	1 321	1 586	44 222	4 514	9 876	11 187	9 836	6 675	2 135
1964	47 679	3 074	1 499	1 575	44 604	4 754	9 876	11 156	9 956	6 741	2 124
1965	48 255	3 397	1 532	1 866	44 857	4 894	9 903	11 120	10 045	6 763	2 132
1966	48 471	3 685	1 609	2 075	44 788	4 820	9 948	10 983	10 100	6 847	2 089
1967	48 987	3 634	1 658	1 976	45 354	5 043	10 207	10 859	10 189	6 937	2 118
1968	49 533	3 681	1 687	1 995	45 852	5 070	10 610	10 725	10 267	7 025	2 154
1969	50 221	3 870	1 770	2 100	46 351	5 282	10 941	10 556	10 344	7 058	2 170
1970	51 228	4 008	1 810	2 199	47 220	5 717	11 327	10 469	10 417	7 126	2 165
1971	52 180	4 172	1 856	2 315	48 009	6 233	11 731	10 347	10 451	7 155	2 090
1972	53 555	4 476	1 955	2 522	49 079	6 766	12 350	10 372	10 412	7 155	2 026
1973	54 624	4 693	2 073	2 618	49 932	7 183	13 056	10 338	10 416	7 028	1 913
1974	55 739	4 861	2 138	2 721	50 879	7 387	13 665	10 401	10 431	7 063	1 932
1975	56 299	4 805	2 065	2 740	51 494	7 565	14 192	10 398	10 401	7 023	1 914
1976	57 174	4 886	2 069	2 817	52 288	7 866	14 784	10 500	10 293	7 020	1 826
1977	58 396	5 048	2 155	2 893	53 348	8 109	15 353	10 771	10 158	7 100	1 857
1978	59 620	5 149	2 227	2 923	54 471	8 327	15 814	11 159	10 083	7 151	1 936
1979	60 726	5 111	2 192	2 919	55 615	8 535	16 387	11 531	10 008	7 212	1 943
1980	61 453	4 999	2 102	2 897	56 455	8 607	16 971	11 836	9 905	7 242	1 893
1981	61 974	4 777	1 957	2 820	57 197	8 648	17 479	12 166	9 868	7 170	1 866
1982	62 450	4 470	1 776	2 694	57 980	8 604	17 793	12 781	9 784	7 174	1 845
1983	63 047	4 303	1 621	2 682	58 744	8 601	18 038	13 398	9 746	7 119	1 842
1984	63 835	4 134	1 591	2 542	59 701	8 594	18 488	14 037	9 776	7 050	1 755
1985	64 411	4 134	1 663	2 471	60 277	8 283	18 808	14 506	9 870	7 060	1 750
1986	65 422	4 102	1 707	2 395	61 320	8 148	19 383	15 029	9 994	6 954	1 811
1987	66 207	4 112	1 745	2 367	62 095	7 837	19 656	15 587	10 176	6 940	1 899
1988	66 927	4 159	1 714	2 445	62 768	7 594	19 742	16 074	10 566	6 831	1 960
1989	67 840	4 136	1 630	2 505	63 704	7 458	19 905	16 622	10 919	6 783	2 017
1990	69 011	4 094	1 537	2 557	64 916	7 866	19 872	17 481	11 103	6 627	1 967
1991	69 168	3 795	1 452	2 343	65 374	7 820	19 641	18 077	11 362	6 550	1 924
1992	69 964	3 751	1 453	2 297	66 213	7 770	19 495	18 347	12 040	6 551	2 010
1993	70 404	3 762	1 497	2 265	66 642	7 671	19 214	18 713	12 562	6 502	1 980
1994	70 817	3 896	1 630	2 266	66 921	7 540	18 854	18 966	12 962	6 423	2 176
1995	71 360	4 036	1 668	2 368	67 324	7 338	18 670	19 189	13 421	6 504	2 201
1996	72 087	4 043	1 665	2 378	68 044	7 104	18 430	19 602	13 967	6 693	2 247
1997	73 261	4 095	1 676	2 419	69 166	7 184	18 110	20 058	14 564	6 952	2 298
1998	73 959	4 244	1 728	2 516	69 715	7 221	17 796	20 242	14 963	7 253	2 240
1999	74 512	4 318	1 732	2 587	70 194	7 291	17 318	20 382	15 394	7 477	2 333
2000	76 280	4 269	1 676	2 594	72 010	7 521	17 844	20 093	16 269	7 795	2 488
2001	76 886	4 070	1 568	2 501	72 816	7 640	17 671	20 018	16 804	8 171	2 511
2002	77 500	3 870	1 431	2 439	73 630	7 769	17 596	19 828	17 143	8 751	2 542
2003	78 238	3 614	1 405	2 209	74 623	7 906	17 767	19 762	17 352	9 144	2 692
2004	78 980	3 616	1 329	2 288	75 364	8 057	17 798	19 539	17 635	9 547	2 787
2005	80 033	3 590	1 368	2 222	76 443	8 054	17 837	19 495	18 053	10 045	2 959

Table 1-7. Civilian Labor Force, by Age, Sex, Race, and Hispanic Origin, 1948–2005—*Continued*

(Thousands of people.)

Race, Hispanic origin, sex, and year	16 years and over	16 to 19 years			20 years and over						
		Total	16 to 17 years	18 to 19 years	Total	20 to 24 years	25 to 34 years	35 to 44 years	45 to 54 years	55 to 64 years	65 years and over
ALL RACES											
Women											
1948	17 335	1 835	671	1 164	15 500	2 719	3 931	3 801	2 971	1 565	513
1949	17 788	1 811	648	1 163	15 978	2 658	3 997	3 989	3 099	1 678	556
1950	18 389	1 712	611	1 101	16 678	2 675	4 092	4 161	3 327	1 839	583
1951	19 016	1 756	662	1 094	17 259	2 659	4 293	4 301	3 534	1 923	551
1952	19 269	1 752	705	1 047	17 517	2 502	4 319	4 438	3 635	2 031	589
1953	19 382	1 707	657	1 050	17 674	2 428	4 162	4 662	3 679	2 049	693
1954	19 678	1 681	620	1 028	17 997	2 424	4 212	4 708	3 822	2 164	666
1955	20 548	1 723	641	1 083	18 825	2 445	4 252	4 805	4 154	2 391	779
1956	21 461	1 863	736	1 127	19 599	2 455	4 276	5 031	4 405	2 610	821
1957	21 732	1 860	716	1 144	19 873	2 442	4 255	5 116	4 615	2 631	813
1958	22 118	1 832	685	1 147	20 285	2 501	4 193	5 185	4 859	2 727	821
1959	22 483	1 896	765	1 132	20 587	2 473	4 089	5 228	5 080	2 882	836
1960	23 240	2 054	805	1 251	21 185	2 579	4 131	5 302	5 278	2 986	908
1961	23 806	2 142	774	1 368	21 664	2 697	4 143	5 390	5 403	3 106	926
1962	24 014	2 146	741	1 405	21 868	2 803	4 103	5 474	5 381	3 197	913
1963	24 704	2 232	850	1 380	22 473	2 959	4 174	5 601	5 502	3 331	906
1964	25 412	2 314	950	1 365	23 098	3 209	4 180	5 615	5 681	3 441	966
1965	26 200	2 513	954	1 559	23 686	3 365	4 330	5 720	5 711	3 587	976
1966	27 299	2 873	1 055	1 818	24 431	3 590	4 510	5 755	5 884	3 728	964
1967	28 360	2 887	1 076	1 810	25 475	3 966	4 848	5 844	5 983	3 855	979
1968	29 204	2 938	1 130	1 808	26 266	4 235	5 098	5 866	6 130	3 939	999
1969	30 513	3 100	1 239	1 859	27 413	4 597	5 395	5 902	6 386	4 077	1 057
1970	31 543	3 241	1 325	1 916	28 301	4 880	5 708	5 968	6 532	4 157	1 056
1971	32 202	3 298	1 336	1 963	28 904	5 098	5 983	5 957	6 573	4 234	1 059
1972	33 479	3 578	1 464	2 114	29 901	5 364	6 610	6 027	6 555	4 257	1 089
1973	34 804	3 814	1 592	2 221	30 991	5 663	7 320	6 154	6 567	4 228	1 061
1974	36 211	4 010	1 672	2 338	32 201	5 926	7 989	6 362	6 699	4 221	1 002
1975	37 475	4 065	1 674	2 391	33 410	6 185	8 673	6 505	6 683	4 323	1 042
1976	38 983	4 170	1 698	2 470	34 814	6 418	9 419	6 817	6 689	4 402	1 069
1977	40 613	4 303	1 765	2 538	36 310	6 717	10 149	7 171	6 720	4 477	1 078
1978	42 631	4 503	1 900	2 603	38 128	7 043	10 888	7 662	6 807	4 593	1 134
1979	44 235	4 527	1 887	2 639	39 708	7 234	11 551	8 154	6 889	4 719	1 161
1980	45 487	4 381	1 781	2 599	41 106	7 315	12 257	8 627	7 004	4 742	1 161
1981	46 696	4 211	1 691	2 520	42 485	7 451	12 912	9 045	7 101	4 799	1 176
1982	47 755	4 056	1 561	2 495	43 699	7 477	13 393	9 651	7 105	4 888	1 185
1983	48 503	3 868	1 452	2 416	44 636	7 451	13 796	10 213	7 105	4 873	1 198
1984	49 709	3 810	1 458	2 351	45 900	7 451	14 234	10 896	7 230	4 911	1 177
1985	51 050	3 767	1 491	2 276	47 283	7 434	14 742	11 567	7 452	4 932	1 156
1986	52 413	3 824	1 580	2 244	48 589	7 293	15 208	12 204	7 746	4 940	1 199
1987	53 658	3 875	1 638	2 237	49 783	7 140	15 577	12 873	8 034	4 937	1 221
1988	54 742	3 872	1 572	2 300	50 870	6 910	15 761	13 361	8 537	4 977	1 324
1989	56 030	3 818	1 495	2 323	52 212	6 721	15 990	13 980	8 997	5 095	1 429
1990	56 829	3 698	1 400	2 298	53 131	6 834	16 058	14 663	9 145	4 948	1 483
1991	57 178	3 470	1 337	2 133	53 708	6 728	15 867	15 235	9 465	4 924	1 489
1992	58 141	3 345	1 316	2 030	54 796	6 750	15 875	15 552	10 120	5 035	1 464
1993	58 795	3 408	1 335	2 073	55 388	6 683	15 566	15 849	10 733	5 097	1 459
1994	60 239	3 585	1 504	2 081	56 655	6 592	15 499	16 259	11 357	5 289	1 658
1995	60 944	3 729	1 557	2 172	57 215	6 349	15 528	16 562	11 801	5 356	1 618
1996	61 857	3 763	1 599	2 164	58 094	6 273	15 403	16 954	12 430	5 452	1 581
1997	63 036	3 837	1 561	2 277	59 198	6 348	15 271	17 268	13 010	5 713	1 590
1998	63 714	4 012	1 607	2 405	59 702	6 418	15 017	17 294	13 405	5 962	1 607
1999	64 855	4 015	1 606	2 410	60 840	6 643	14 826	17 501	13 994	6 204	1 673
2000	66 303	4 002	1 585	2 416	62 301	6 730	14 912	17 473	14 802	6 561	1 823
2001	66 848	3 832	1 520	2 313	63 016	6 917	14 690	17 386	15 221	6 932	1 870
2002	67 363	3 715	1 439	2 277	63 648	7 012	14 600	17 098	15 454	7 559	1 926
2003	68 272	3 556	1 452	2 104	64 716	7 021	14 576	16 933	15 919	8 168	2 099
2004	68 421	3 498	1 418	2 080	64 923	7 097	14 409	16 619	16 123	8 466	2 211
2005	69 288	3 574	1 457	2 117	65 714	7 073	14 503	16 535	16 349	8 934	2 319

Table 1-7. Civilian Labor Force, by Age, Sex, Race, and Hispanic Origin, 1948–2005—*Continued*

(Thousands of people.)

Race, Hispanic origin, sex, and year	16 years and over	16 to 19 years			20 years and over						
		Total	16 to 17 years	18 to 19 years	Total	20 to 24 years	25 to 34 years	35 to 44 years	45 to 54 years	55 to 64 years	65 years and over
WHITE[1]											
Both Sexes											
1954	56 816	3 501	1 448	2 054	53 315	4 752	13 226	13 540	11 258	7 591	2 946
1955	58 085	3 598	1 511	2 087	54 487	4 941	13 267	13 729	11 680	7 810	3 062
1956	59 428	3 771	1 656	2 113	55 657	5 194	13 154	14 000	12 061	8 080	3 166
1957	59 754	3 775	1 637	2 135	55 979	5 283	13 044	14 117	12 382	8 091	3 049
1958	60 293	3 757	1 615	2 144	56 536	5 449	12 884	14 257	12 727	8 254	2 964
1959	60 952	4 000	1 775	2 225	56 952	5 544	12 670	14 355	13 048	8 411	2 925
1960	61 915	4 275	1 871	2 405	57 640	5 787	12 594	14 450	13 322	8 522	2 964
1961	62 656	4 362	1 767	2 594	58 294	6 026	12 503	14 557	13 517	8 773	2 917
1962	62 750	4 354	1 709	2 645	58 396	6 164	12 218	14 695	13 551	8 856	2 912
1963	63 830	4 559	1 950	2 608	59 271	6 537	12 229	14 859	13 789	9 067	2 790
1964	64 921	4 784	2 211	2 572	60 137	6 952	12 235	14 852	14 043	9 239	2 817
1965	66 137	5 267	2 221	3 044	60 870	7 189	12 391	14 900	14 162	9 392	2 839
1966	67 276	5 827	2 367	3 460	61 449	7 324	12 591	14 785	14 370	9 583	2 793
1967	68 699	5 749	2 432	3 318	62 950	7 886	13 123	14 765	14 545	9 817	2 821
1968	69 976	5 839	2 519	3 320	64 137	8 109	13 740	14 683	14 756	9 968	2 884
1969	71 778	6 168	2 698	3 470	65 611	8 614	14 289	14 564	15 057	10 132	2 954
1970	73 556	6 442	2 824	3 617	67 113	9 238	14 896	14 525	15 269	10 255	2 930
1971	74 963	6 681	2 894	3 787	68 282	9 889	15 445	14 374	15 343	10 351	2 880
1972	77 275	7 193	3 096	4 098	70 082	10 605	16 584	14 399	15 283	10 402	2 809
1973	79 151	7 579	3 320	4 260	71 572	11 182	17 764	14 440	15 256	10 240	2 687
1974	81 281	7 899	3 441	4 459	73 381	11 600	18 862	14 644	15 375	10 241	2 656
1975	82 831	7 899	3 375	4 525	74 932	12 019	19 897	14 753	15 308	10 287	2 668
1976	84 767	8 088	3 410	4 679	76 678	12 444	20 990	15 088	15 187	10 371	2 599
1977	87 141	8 352	3 562	4 790	78 789	12 892	22 099	15 604	15 053	10 495	2 647
1978	89 634	8 555	3 715	4 839	81 079	13 309	23 067	16 353	15 004	10 602	2 745
1979	91 923	8 548	3 668	4 881	83 375	13 632	24 101	17 123	14 965	10 767	2 787
1980	93 600	8 312	3 485	4 827	85 286	13 769	25 181	17 811	14 956	10 812	2 759
1981	95 052	7 962	3 274	4 688	87 089	13 926	26 208	18 445	14 993	10 764	2 753
1982	96 143	7 518	3 001	4 518	88 625	13 866	26 814	19 491	14 879	10 832	2 742
1983	97 021	7 186	2 765	4 421	89 835	13 816	27 237	20 488	14 798	10 732	2 766
1984	98 492	6 952	2 720	4 232	91 540	13 733	27 958	21 588	14 899	10 701	2 660
1985	99 926	6 841	2 777	4 065	93 085	13 469	28 640	22 591	15 101	10 679	2 605
1986	101 801	6 862	2 895	3 967	94 939	13 176	29 497	23 571	15 379	10 583	2 732
1987	103 290	6 893	2 963	3 931	96 396	12 764	29 956	24 581	15 792	10 497	2 806
1988	104 756	6 940	2 861	4 079	97 815	12 311	30 167	25 358	16 573	10 462	2 943
1989	106 355	6 809	2 685	4 124	99 546	11 940	30 388	26 312	17 278	10 533	3 094
1990	107 447	6 683	2 543	4 140	100 764	12 397	30 174	27 265	17 515	10 290	3 123
1991	107 743	6 245	2 432	3 813	101 498	12 248	29 794	28 213	18 028	10 129	3 086
1992	108 837	6 022	2 388	3 633	102 815	12 187	29 518	28 580	19 200	10 196	3 135
1993	109 700	6 105	2 458	3 647	103 595	11 987	29 027	29 056	20 181	10 215	3 129
1994	111 082	6 357	2 681	3 677	104 725	11 688	28 580	29 626	21 026	10 319	3 486
1995	111 950	6 545	2 749	3 796	105 404	11 266	28 325	30 112	21 804	10 432	3 466
1996	113 108	6 607	2 780	3 826	106 502	11 003	27 901	30 683	22 781	10 648	3 485
1997	114 693	6 720	2 779	3 941	107 973	11 127	27 362	31 171	23 709	11 086	3 517
1998	115 415	6 965	2 860	4 105	108 450	11 244	26 707	31 221	24 282	11 548	3 448
1999	116 509	7 048	2 849	4 199	109 461	11 436	25 978	31 391	25 102	11 960	3 595
2000	118 545	6 955	2 768	4 186	111 590	11 626	26 336	30 968	26 353	12 463	3 846
2001	119 399	6 661	2 626	4 035	112 737	11 883	26 010	30 778	27 062	13 121	3 883
2002	120 150	6 366	2 445	3 921	113 784	12 073	25 908	30 286	27 405	14 148	3 965
2003	120 546	5 973	2 414	3 560	114 572	12 064	25 752	29 788	27 786	14 944	4 238
2004	121 086	5 929	2 309	3 620	115 156	12 192	25 548	29 305	28 181	15 522	4 408
2005	122 299	5 950	2 390	3 560	116 349	12 109	25 548	29 107	28 685	16 275	4 624

[1]Beginning in 2003, persons who selected this race group only; persons who selected more than one race group are not included. Prior to 2003, persons who reported more than one race group were included in the group they identified as their main race.

Table 1-7. Civilian Labor Force, by Age, Sex, Race, and Hispanic Origin, 1948–2005—*Continued*

(Thousands of people.)

Race, Hispanic origin, sex, and year	16 years and over	16 to 19 years			20 years and over						
		Total	16 to 17 years	18 to 19 years	Total	20 to 24 years	25 to 34 years	35 to 44 years	45 to 54 years	55 to 64 years	65 years and over
WHITE[1]											
Men											
1954	39 759	1 989	896	1 095	37 770	2 654	9 695	9 516	7 913	5 653	2 339
1955	40 197	2 056	935	1 121	38 141	2 803	9 721	9 597	8 025	5 654	2 343
1956	40 734	2 114	1 002	1 110	38 620	3 036	9 595	9 661	8 175	5 736	2 417
1957	40 826	2 108	992	1 114	38 718	3 152	9 483	9 719	8 317	5 735	2 307
1958	41 080	2 116	1 001	1 116	38 964	3 278	9 386	9 822	8 465	5 800	2 213
1959	41 397	2 279	1 077	1 202	39 118	3 409	9 261	9 876	8 581	5 833	2 158
1960	41 743	2 433	1 140	1 293	39 310	3 559	9 153	9 919	8 689	5 861	2 129
1961	41 986	2 439	1 067	1 372	39 547	3 681	9 072	9 961	8 776	5 988	2 068
1962	41 931	2 432	1 041	1 391	39 499	3 726	8 846	10 029	8 820	5 995	2 082
1963	42 404	2 563	1 183	1 380	39 841	3 955	8 805	10 079	8 944	6 090	1 967
1964	42 894	2 716	1 345	1 371	40 178	4 166	8 800	10 055	9 053	6 161	1 942
1965	43 400	2 999	1 359	1 639	40 401	4 279	8 824	10 023	9 130	6 188	1 959
1966	43 572	3 253	1 423	1 830	40 319	4 200	8 859	9 892	9 189	6 250	1 928
1967	44 041	3 191	1 464	1 727	40 851	4 416	9 102	9 785	9 260	6 348	1 944
1968	44 553	3 236	1 504	1 732	41 318	4 432	9 477	9 662	9 340	6 427	1 981
1969	45 185	3 413	1 583	1 830	41 772	4 615	9 773	9 509	9 413	6 467	1 996
1970	46 035	3 551	1 629	1 922	42 483	4 988	10 099	9 414	9 487	6 517	1 978
1971	46 904	3 719	1 681	2 039	43 185	5 448	10 444	9 294	9 528	6 550	1 922
1972	48 118	3 980	1 758	2 223	44 138	5 937	11 039	9 278	9 473	6 562	1 846
1973	48 920	4 174	1 875	2 300	44 747	6 274	11 621	9 212	9 445	6 452	1 740
1974	49 843	4 312	1 922	2 391	45 532	6 470	12 135	9 246	9 455	6 464	1 759
1975	50 324	4 290	1 871	2 418	46 034	6 642	12 579	9 231	9 415	6 425	1 742
1976	51 033	4 357	1 869	2 489	46 675	6 890	13 092	9 289	9 310	6 437	1 657
1977	52 033	4 496	1 949	2 548	47 537	7 097	13 575	9 509	9 175	6 492	1 688
1978	52 955	4 565	2 002	2 563	48 390	7 274	13 939	9 858	9 068	6 508	1 744
1979	53 856	4 537	1 974	2 563	49 320	7 421	14 415	10 183	8 968	6 571	1 761
1980	54 473	4 424	1 881	2 543	50 049	7 479	14 893	10 455	8 877	6 618	1 727
1981	54 895	4 224	1 751	2 473	50 671	7 521	15 340	10 740	8 836	6 530	1 704
1982	55 133	3 933	1 602	2 331	51 200	7 438	15 549	11 289	8 727	6 520	1 677
1983	55 480	3 764	1 452	2 312	51 716	7 406	15 707	11 817	8 649	6 446	1 691
1984	56 062	3 609	1 420	2 189	52 453	7 370	16 037	12 348	8 683	6 410	1 606
1985	56 472	3 576	1 467	2 109	52 895	7 122	16 306	12 767	8 730	6 376	1 595
1986	57 217	3 542	1 502	2 040	53 675	6 986	16 769	13 207	8 791	6 260	1 663
1987	57 779	3 547	1 524	2 023	54 232	6 717	16 963	13 674	8 945	6 200	1 733
1988	58 317	3 583	1 487	2 095	54 734	6 468	17 018	14 068	9 285	6 108	1 787
1989	58 988	3 546	1 401	2 146	55 441	6 316	17 077	14 516	9 615	6 082	1 835
1990	59 638	3 522	1 333	2 189	56 116	6 688	16 920	15 026	9 713	5 957	1 811
1991	59 656	3 269	1 266	2 003	56 387	6 619	16 709	15 523	9 926	5 847	1 763
1992	60 168	3 192	1 260	1 932	56 976	6 542	16 512	15 701	10 570	5 821	1 830
1993	60 484	3 200	1 292	1 908	57 284	6 449	16 244	15 971	11 010	5 784	1 825
1994	60 727	3 315	1 403	1 912	57 411	6 294	15 879	16 188	11 327	5 726	1 998
1995	61 146	3 427	1 429	1 998	57 719	6 096	15 669	16 414	11 730	5 809	2 000
1996	61 783	3 444	1 421	2 023	58 340	5 922	15 475	16 728	12 217	5 943	2 054
1997	62 639	3 513	1 440	2 073	59 126	6 029	15 120	17 019	12 710	6 154	2 094
1998	63 034	3 614	1 487	2 127	59 421	6 063	14 770	17 157	13 003	6 415	2 013
1999	63 413	3 666	1 478	2 188	59 747	6 151	14 292	17 201	13 368	6 618	2 117
2000	64 466	3 615	1 422	2 193	60 850	6 244	14 666	16 880	13 977	6 840	2 243
2001	64 966	3 446	1 334	2 112	61 519	6 363	14 536	16 809	14 400	7 169	2 241
2002	65 308	3 241	1 215	2 026	62 067	6 444	14 499	16 583	14 615	7 665	2 261
2003	65 509	3 036	1 193	1 843	62 473	6 479	14 529	16 398	14 708	7 973	2 386
2004	65 994	3 050	1 127	1 923	62 944	6 586	14 429	16 192	14 934	8 326	2 478
2005	66 694	2 988	1 162	1 826	63 705	6 562	14 426	16 080	15 273	8 734	2 631

[1]Beginning in 2003, persons who selected this race group only; persons who selected more than one race group are not included. Prior to 2003, persons who reported more than one race group were included in the group they identified as their main race.

Table 1-7. Civilian Labor Force, by Age, Sex, Race, and Hispanic Origin, 1948–2005—*Continued*

(Thousands of people.)

Race, Hispanic origin, sex, and year	16 years and over	16 to 19 years			20 years and over						
		Total	16 to 17 years	18 to 19 years	Total	20 to 24 years	25 to 34 years	35 to 44 years	45 to 54 years	55 to 64 years	65 years and over
WHITE[1]											
Women											
1954	17 057	1 512	552	959	15 545	2 098	3 531	4 024	3 345	1 938	607
1955	17 888	1 542	576	966	16 346	2 138	3 546	4 132	3 655	2 156	719
1956	18 694	1 657	654	1 003	17 037	2 158	3 559	4 339	3 886	2 344	749
1957	18 928	1 667	645	1 021	17 261	2 131	3 561	4 398	4 065	2 356	742
1958	19 213	1 641	614	1 028	17 572	2 171	3 498	4 435	4 262	2 454	751
1959	19 555	1 721	698	1 023	17 834	2 135	3 409	4 479	4 467	2 578	767
1960	20 172	1 842	731	1 112	18 330	2 228	3 441	4 531	4 633	2 661	835
1961	20 670	1 923	700	1 222	18 747	2 345	3 431	4 596	4 741	2 785	849
1962	20 819	1 922	668	1 254	18 897	2 438	3 372	4 666	4 731	2 861	830
1963	21 426	1 996	767	1 228	19 430	2 582	3 424	4 780	4 845	2 977	823
1964	22 027	2 068	866	1 201	19 959	2 786	3 435	4 797	4 990	3 078	875
1965	22 737	2 268	862	1 405	20 469	2 910	3 567	4 877	5 032	3 204	880
1966	23 704	2 574	944	1 630	21 130	3 124	3 732	4 893	5 181	3 333	865
1967	24 658	2 558	968	1 591	22 100	3 471	4 021	4 980	5 285	3 469	877
1968	25 423	2 603	1 015	1 588	22 821	3 677	4 263	5 021	5 416	3 541	903
1969	26 593	2 755	1 115	1 640	23 839	3 999	4 516	5 055	5 644	3 665	958
1970	27 521	2 891	1 195	1 695	24 630	4 250	4 797	5 111	5 781	3 738	952
1971	28 060	2 962	1 213	1 748	25 097	4 441	5 001	5 080	5 816	3 801	958
1972	29 157	3 213	1 338	1 875	25 945	4 668	5 544	5 121	5 810	3 839	963
1973	30 231	3 405	1 445	1 960	26 825	4 908	6 143	5 228	5 811	3 788	947
1974	31 437	3 588	1 520	2 068	27 850	5 131	6 727	5 399	5 920	3 777	897
1975	32 508	3 610	1 504	2 107	28 898	5 378	7 318	5 522	5 892	3 862	926
1976	33 735	3 731	1 541	2 189	30 004	5 554	7 898	5 799	5 877	3 935	940
1977	35 108	3 856	1 614	2 243	31 253	5 795	8 523	6 095	5 877	4 003	959
1978	36 679	3 990	1 713	2 276	32 689	6 035	9 128	6 495	5 936	4 094	1 001
1979	38 067	4 011	1 694	2 318	34 056	6 211	9 687	6 940	5 997	4 196	1 024
1980	39 127	3 888	1 605	2 284	35 239	6 290	10 289	7 356	6 079	4 194	1 032
1981	40 157	3 739	1 523	2 216	36 418	6 406	10 868	7 704	6 157	4 235	1 049
1982	41 010	3 585	1 399	2 186	37 425	6 428	11 264	8 202	6 152	4 313	1 065
1983	41 541	3 422	1 314	2 109	38 119	6 410	11 530	8 670	6 149	4 285	1 074
1984	42 431	3 343	1 300	2 043	39 087	6 363	11 922	9 240	6 217	4 292	1 054
1985	43 455	3 265	1 310	1 955	40 190	6 348	12 334	9 824	6 371	4 303	1 010
1986	44 584	3 320	1 393	1 927	41 264	6 191	12 729	10 364	6 588	4 323	1 069
1987	45 510	3 347	1 439	1 908	42 164	6 047	12 993	10 907	6 847	4 297	1 073
1988	46 439	3 358	1 374	1 984	43 081	5 844	13 149	11 291	7 288	4 354	1 156
1989	47 367	3 262	1 284	1 978	44 105	5 625	13 311	11 796	7 663	4 451	1 259
1990	47 809	3 161	1 210	1 951	44 648	5 709	13 254	12 239	7 802	4 333	1 312
1991	48 087	2 976	1 166	1 810	45 111	5 629	13 085	12 689	8 101	4 282	1 324
1992	48 669	2 830	1 128	1 702	45 839	5 645	13 006	12 879	8 630	4 375	1 305
1993	49 216	2 905	1 167	1 739	46 311	5 539	12 783	13 085	9 171	4 430	1 304
1994	50 356	3 042	1 278	1 764	47 314	5 394	12 702	13 439	9 699	4 593	1 487
1995	50 804	3 118	1 320	1 798	47 686	5 170	12 656	13 697	10 074	4 622	1 466
1996	51 325	3 163	1 360	1 803	48 162	5 081	12 426	13 955	10 563	4 706	1 431
1997	52 054	3 207	1 339	1 867	48 847	5 099	12 242	14 153	10 999	4 932	1 422
1998	52 380	3 351	1 373	1 977	49 029	5 180	11 937	14 064	11 279	5 133	1 435
1999	53 096	3 382	1 371	2 010	49 714	5 285	11 685	14 190	11 734	5 342	1 478
2000	54 079	3 339	1 346	1 993	50 740	5 381	11 669	14 088	12 376	5 623	1 602
2001	54 433	3 215	1 292	1 923	51 218	5 519	11 474	13 969	12 662	5 952	1 642
2002	54 842	3 125	1 229	1 895	51 717	5 628	11 409	13 703	12 790	6 482	1 704
2003	55 037	2 937	1 221	1 716	52 099	5 584	11 223	13 390	13 078	6 970	1 852
2004	55 092	2 879	1 182	1 697	52 212	5 606	11 119	13 114	13 247	7 197	1 930
2005	55 605	2 962	1 228	1 733	52 643	5 546	11 123	13 027	13 413	7 542	1 993

[1]Beginning in 2003, persons who selected this race group only; persons who selected more than one race group are not included. Prior to 2003, persons who reported more than one race group were included in the group they identified as their main race.

Table 1-7. Civilian Labor Force, by Age, Sex, Race, and Hispanic Origin, 1948–2005—*Continued*

(Thousands of people.)

Race, Hispanic origin, sex, and year	16 years and over	16 to 19 years			20 years and over						
		Total	16 to 17 years	18 to 19 years	Total	20 to 24 years	25 to 34 years	35 to 44 years	45 to 54 years	55 to 64 years	65 years and over
BLACK[1]											
Both Sexes											
1972	8 707	788	293	496	7 919	1 393	2 107	1 735	1 496	909	281
1973	8 976	833	307	525	8 143	1 489	2 242	1 741	1 513	901	258
1974	9 167	851	317	534	8 317	1 492	2 358	1 777	1 517	917	253
1975	9 263	838	312	524	8 426	1 477	2 466	1 775	1 519	929	258
1976	9 561	837	304	532	8 724	1 544	2 646	1 824	1 518	925	268
1977	9 932	861	304	557	9 072	1 641	2 798	1 894	1 530	943	267
1978	10 432	930	341	589	9 501	1 739	2 961	1 975	1 560	978	289
1979	10 678	912	340	572	9 766	1 793	3 094	2 039	1 584	974	281
1980	10 865	891	326	565	9 975	1 802	3 259	2 081	1 596	978	257
1981	11 086	862	308	554	10 224	1 828	3 365	2 164	1 608	1 009	249
1982	11 331	824	268	556	10 507	1 849	3 492	2 303	1 610	1 012	243
1983	11 647	809	248	561	10 838	1 871	3 675	2 406	1 630	1 032	224
1984	12 033	827	268	558	11 206	1 926	3 800	2 565	1 671	1 020	224
1985	12 364	889	311	578	11 476	1 854	3 888	2 681	1 742	1 059	252
1986	12 654	883	322	562	11 770	1 881	4 028	2 793	1 793	1 051	224
1987	12 993	899	336	563	12 094	1 818	4 147	2 942	1 838	1 098	251
1988	13 205	889	344	545	12 316	1 782	4 226	3 069	1 894	1 069	276
1989	13 497	925	353	572	12 573	1 789	4 295	3 227	1 954	1 023	285
1990	13 740	866	306	560	12 874	1 758	4 307	3 566	2 003	977	262
1991	13 797	774	266	508	13 023	1 750	4 254	3 719	2 042	1 001	256
1992	14 162	816	285	532	13 346	1 763	4 309	3 843	2 142	1 029	259
1993	14 225	807	283	524	13 418	1 764	4 232	3 960	2 212	1 013	237
1994	14 502	852	351	501	13 650	1 800	4 199	4 068	2 308	1 007	267
1995	14 817	911	366	545	13 906	1 754	4 267	4 165	2 404	1 046	271
1996	15 134	923	366	556	14 211	1 738	4 305	4 287	2 553	1 073	255
1997	15 529	933	352	580	14 596	1 783	4 329	4 401	2 724	1 093	265
1998	15 982	1 017	370	646	14 966	1 797	4 332	4 531	2 863	1 163	278
1999	16 365	959	352	607	15 406	1 866	4 430	4 653	2 992	1 180	285
2000	16 397	941	356	585	15 456	1 873	4 281	4 515	3 203	1 264	320
2001	16 421	898	332	565	15 524	1 878	4 180	4 483	3 298	1 335	350
2002	16 565	870	297	574	15 695	1 908	4 134	4 458	3 435	1 407	353
2003	16 526	771	289	482	15 755	1 892	4 060	4 465	3 506	1 466	366
2004	16 638	762	272	489	15 876	1 926	4 076	4 380	3 578	1 538	380
2005	17 013	803	279	525	16 209	1 957	4 145	4 370	3 686	1 647	403
Men											
1972	4 816	453	180	272	4 364	761	1 158	935	824	522	165
1973	4 924	460	175	286	4 464	819	1 217	935	842	499	153
1974	5 020	480	189	291	4 540	798	1 279	953	838	519	152
1975	5 016	447	168	279	4 569	790	1 328	948	833	520	150
1976	5 101	454	168	285	4 648	820	1 383	969	824	504	149
1977	5 263	476	178	299	4 787	856	1 441	1 003	818	515	154
1978	5 435	491	186	306	4 943	883	1 504	1 022	829	540	166
1979	5 559	480	179	301	5 079	928	1 577	1 049	844	524	156
1980	5 612	479	181	298	5 134	935	1 659	1 061	830	509	138
1981	5 685	462	169	293	5 223	940	1 702	1 093	829	524	134
1982	5 804	436	137	300	5 368	964	1 769	1 152	824	525	135
1983	5 966	433	134	300	5 533	997	1 840	1 196	845	536	119
1984	6 126	440	141	299	5 686	1 022	1 924	1 270	847	505	118
1985	6 220	471	162	310	5 749	950	1 937	1 313	879	544	125
1986	6 373	458	164	294	5 915	957	2 029	1 359	901	552	116
1987	6 486	463	179	284	6 023	914	2 074	1 406	915	586	130
1988	6 596	469	186	283	6 127	913	2 114	1 459	936	565	139
1989	6 701	480	190	291	6 221	904	2 157	1 544	945	530	141
1990	6 802	445	161	284	6 357	879	2 142	1 733	988	496	119
1991	6 851	400	140	260	6 451	896	2 111	1 806	1 010	507	122
1992	6 997	429	149	280	6 568	900	2 121	1 859	1 037	521	130
1993	7 019	425	154	270	6 594	875	2 118	1 918	1 065	506	112
1994	7 089	443	176	266	6 646	891	2 068	1 975	1 102	484	125
1995	7 183	453	184	269	6 730	866	2 089	1 987	1 148	490	150
1996	7 264	458	182	276	6 806	848	2 077	2 036	1 204	509	132
1997	7 354	444	178	266	6 910	832	2 052	2 096	1 287	508	134
1998	7 542	488	181	307	7 053	837	2 034	2 142	1 343	548	150
1999	7 652	470	180	291	7 182	835	2 069	2 206	1 387	547	138
2000	7 702	462	181	281	7 240	875	1 999	2 105	1 497	612	151
2001	7 647	447	166	281	7 200	853	1 915	2 073	1 537	645	177
2002	7 794	446	149	297	7 347	906	1 909	2 064	1 623	664	181
2003	7 711	365	138	228	7 346	918	1 872	2 058	1 627	685	186
2004	7 773	359	128	231	7 414	927	1 931	2 000	1 654	714	188
2005	7 998	399	139	260	7 600	940	1 948	2 028	1 732	756	196

[1]Beginning in 2003, persons who selected this race group only; persons who selected more than one race group are not included. Prior to 2003, persons who reported more than one race group were included in the group they identified as their main race.

Table 1-7. Civilian Labor Force, by Age, Sex, Race, and Hispanic Origin, 1948–2005—*Continued*

(Thousands of people.)

Race, Hispanic origin, sex, and year	16 years and over	16 to 19 years			20 years and over						
		Total	16 to 17 years	18 to 19 years	Total	20 to 24 years	25 to 34 years	35 to 44 years	45 to 54 years	55 to 64 years	65 years and over
BLACK[1]											
Women											
1972	3 890	335	113	224	3 555	632	949	800	672	387	116
1973	4 052	373	133	240	3 678	670	1 026	806	670	402	105
1974	4 148	371	128	243	3 777	694	1 079	824	679	398	100
1975	4 247	391	144	245	3 857	687	1 138	827	686	409	108
1976	4 460	384	136	247	4 076	723	1 264	855	694	421	119
1977	4 670	385	127	258	4 286	785	1 357	891	712	429	113
1978	4 997	439	155	283	4 558	856	1 456	953	731	439	124
1979	5 119	432	161	271	4 687	865	1 517	990	740	451	124
1980	5 253	412	144	267	4 841	867	1 600	1 020	767	469	119
1981	5 401	400	139	261	5 001	888	1 663	1 071	779	485	115
1982	5 527	387	131	256	5 140	885	1 723	1 151	786	487	108
1983	5 681	375	114	261	5 306	874	1 835	1 210	785	496	105
1984	5 907	387	127	260	5 520	904	1 876	1 294	823	515	106
1985	6 144	417	149	268	5 727	904	1 951	1 368	862	515	127
1986	6 281	425	157	268	5 855	924	1 999	1 434	892	499	107
1987	6 507	435	157	278	6 071	904	2 073	1 537	924	512	121
1988	6 609	419	158	262	6 190	869	2 112	1 610	958	504	137
1989	6 796	445	163	281	6 352	885	2 138	1 683	1 009	493	144
1990	6 938	421	145	276	6 517	879	2 165	1 833	1 015	481	143
1991	6 946	374	126	248	6 572	854	2 143	1 913	1 032	494	135
1992	7 166	387	135	252	6 778	863	2 188	1 985	1 105	508	129
1993	7 206	383	129	254	6 824	889	2 115	2 042	1 147	506	125
1994	7 413	409	174	235	7 004	909	2 131	2 093	1 206	523	142
1995	7 634	458	182	276	7 175	887	2 177	2 178	1 256	556	121
1996	7 869	464	184	280	7 405	890	2 228	2 251	1 349	565	122
1997	8 175	489	175	314	7 686	951	2 277	2 305	1 437	585	131
1998	8 441	528	189	339	7 912	960	2 298	2 390	1 520	615	128
1999	8 713	489	172	316	8 224	1 031	2 360	2 447	1 606	633	147
2000	8 695	479	175	305	8 215	998	2 282	2 409	1 706	652	168
2001	8 774	451	166	284	8 323	1 025	2 265	2 410	1 762	690	173
2002	8 772	424	148	276	8 348	1 002	2 225	2 394	1 812	743	171
2003	8 815	406	151	255	8 409	973	2 188	2 407	1 879	781	180
2004	8 865	403	144	259	8 462	999	2 144	2 380	1 924	824	192
2005	9 014	405	140	265	8 610	1 017	2 197	2 342	1 954	891	207
HISPANIC[2]											
Both Sexes											
1973	3 673	407	. . .	. . .	. . .	. . .	. . .	. . .	. . .	. . .	. . .
1974	4 012	442	. . .	. . .	. . .	. . .	. . .	. . .	. . .	. . .	. . .
1975	4 171	444	. . .	. . .	. . .	. . .	. . .	. . .	. . .	. . .	. . .
1976	4 205	447	176	285	3 820	729	1 248	875	625	294	48
1977	4 536	493	184	305	4 059	813	1 325	916	656	293	55
1978	4 979	533	221	312	4 446	901	1 446	1 008	701	323	67
1979	5 219	551	207	343	4 668	960	1 532	1 062	704	339	72
1980	6 146	645	241	404	5 502	1 136	1 843	1 163	860	414	85
1981	6 492	603	215	388	5 888	1 231	2 015	1 239	886	430	87
1982	6 734	585	192	393	6 148	1 251	2 163	1 313	891	444	85
1983	7 033	590	189	401	6 442	1 282	2 267	1 380	931	495	86
1984	7 451	618	209	409	6 833	1 325	2 436	1 509	954	524	84
1985	7 698	579	199	379	7 119	1 358	2 571	1 595	985	527	82
1986	8 076	571	203	368	7 505	1 414	2 685	1 713	1 097	511	84
1987	8 541	610	206	404	7 931	1 425	2 890	1 904	1 086	545	81
1988	8 982	671	234	437	8 311	1 486	2 957	1 996	1 147	621	103
1989	9 323	680	224	456	8 643	1 483	3 118	2 092	1 205	625	120
1990	10 720	829	276	554	9 891	1 839	3 590	2 386	1 320	647	110
1991	10 920	781	249	532	10 139	1 835	3 596	2 539	1 376	681	111
1992	11 338	796	263	533	10 542	1 815	3 740	2 735	1 442	687	122
1993	11 610	771	246	525	10 839	1 811	3 800	2 865	1 534	684	145
1994	11 975	807	285	522	11 168	1 863	3 865	2 965	1 626	698	151
1995	12 267	850	291	559	11 417	1 818	3 943	3 113	1 671	720	152
1996	12 774	845	284	561	11 929	1 845	4 054	3 361	1 697	806	166
1997	13 796	911	315	596	12 884	2 004	4 298	3 601	1 945	850	186
1998	14 317	1 007	320	688	13 310	2 077	4 372	3 707	2 090	894	169
1999	14 665	1 049	333	717	13 616	2 052	4 330	3 929	2 178	927	199
2000	16 689	1 168	368	800	15 521	2 546	5 197	4 241	2 387	940	209
2001	17 328	1 176	352	824	16 152	2 616	5 380	4 377	2 583	1 000	195
2002	17 943	1 103	335	769	16 840	2 678	5 645	4 545	2 657	1 091	224
2003	18 813	960	322	638	17 853	2 672	5 960	4 867	2 894	1 201	259
2004	19 272	995	297	698	18 277	2 732	5 931	4 931	3 093	1 284	306
2005	19 824	1 038	331	708	18 785	2 651	6 080	5 110	3 256	1 378	311

[1]Beginning in 2003, persons who selected this race group only; persons who selected more than one race group are not included. Prior to 2003, persons who reported more than one race group were included in the group they identified as their main race.
[2]May be any race.
. . . = Not available.

Table 1-7. Civilian Labor Force, by Age, Sex, Race, and Hispanic Origin, 1948–2005—*Continued*

(Thousands of people.)

Race, Hispanic origin, sex, and year	16 years and over	16 to 19 years			20 years and over						
		Total	16 to 17 years	18 to 19 years	Total	20 to 24 years	25 to 34 years	35 to 44 years	45 to 54 years	55 to 64 years	65 years and over
HISPANIC[2]											
Men											
1973	2 356	...	...	...	2 124	...	...	...	...	...	...
1974	2 556	...	...	...	2 306	...	...	...	...	...	...
1975	2 597	...	...	...	2 343	...	...	...	...	...	...
1976	2 580	260	104	155	2 326	433	771	541	398	189	34
1977	2 817	285	105	179	2 530	485	828	567	416	197	42
1978	3 041	299	129	171	2 742	546	882	620	425	217	52
1979	3 184	315	121	194	2 869	562	941	648	445	216	56
1980	3 818	392	147	245	3 426	697	1 161	713	522	270	62
1981	4 005	359	130	229	3 647	747	1 269	756	535	278	61
1982	4 148	333	111	221	3 815	759	1 361	808	539	290	58
1983	4 362	348	109	239	4 014	789	1 447	852	557	311	58
1984	4 563	345	113	232	4 218	822	1 540	910	570	325	51
1985	4 729	334	116	218	4 395	835	1 629	957	591	331	53
1986	4 948	336	114	222	4 612	888	1 669	1 015	661	323	56
1987	5 163	345	112	233	4 818	865	1 801	1 121	652	325	55
1988	5 409	378	123	255	5 031	897	1 834	1 189	686	355	69
1989	5 595	400	129	271	5 195	909	1 899	1 221	719	375	71
1990	6 546	512	165	346	6 034	1 182	2 230	1 403	775	380	65
1991	6 664	466	141	325	6 198	1 202	2 260	1 487	780	401	67
1992	6 900	468	154	314	6 432	1 141	2 366	1 593	844	414	74
1993	7 076	455	145	310	6 621	1 147	2 417	1 675	900	394	88
1994	7 210	463	163	300	6 747	1 184	2 430	1 713	922	410	89
1995	7 376	479	168	311	6 898	1 153	2 469	1 795	965	417	98
1996	7 646	496	156	340	7 150	1 132	2 510	1 966	967	469	105
1997	8 309	531	177	354	7 779	1 267	2 684	2 091	1 112	511	113
1998	8 571	565	188	377	8 005	1 288	2 733	2 173	1 164	541	106
1999	8 546	596	181	415	7 950	1 231	2 633	2 219	1 205	526	136
2000	9 923	676	204	471	9 247	1 590	3 181	2 451	1 337	555	134
2001	10 279	684	200	484	9 595	1 602	3 294	2 562	1 430	582	125
2002	10 609	632	183	449	9 977	1 627	3 484	2 647	1 478	607	134
2003	11 288	532	164	368	10 756	1 642	3 776	2 877	1 630	680	150
2004	11 587	567	156	410	11 020	1 671	3 765	2 934	1 736	728	186
2005	11 985	577	179	398	11 408	1 645	3 879	3 058	1 855	779	192
Women											
1973	1 317	...	...	...	1 142	...	...	...	...	...	...
1974	1 456	...	...	...	1 264	...	...	...	...	...	...
1975	1 574	...	...	...	1 384	...	...	...	...	...	...
1976	1 625	201	71	130	1 454	295	479	334	227	105	13
1977	1 720	204	80	125	1 523	327	497	349	240	96	13
1978	1 938	233	93	142	1 704	354	564	388	275	106	16
1979	2 035	235	86	149	1 800	397	590	413	258	124	15
1980	2 328	252	93	159	2 076	439	682	450	337	144	22
1981	2 486	244	85	159	2 242	484	745	483	351	152	27
1982	2 586	252	81	172	2 333	492	802	504	352	155	28
1983	2 671	242	80	162	2 429	493	820	529	374	184	29
1984	2 888	273	96	177	2 615	503	896	599	384	199	34
1985	2 970	245	84	161	2 725	524	943	639	394	196	29
1986	3 128	236	89	147	2 893	526	1 016	698	436	189	28
1987	3 377	265	94	171	3 112	559	1 090	783	434	220	27
1988	3 573	293	111	182	3 281	589	1 123	806	461	267	34
1989	3 728	280	95	185	3 448	574	1 219	871	486	251	49
1990	4 174	318	110	207	3 857	657	1 360	983	545	268	45
1991	4 256	315	107	207	3 941	633	1 336	1 052	596	279	44
1992	4 439	328	110	219	4 110	674	1 374	1 142	599	273	48
1993	4 534	316	101	215	4 218	664	1 383	1 190	633	290	57
1994	4 765	345	122	222	4 421	679	1 435	1 252	704	288	62
1995	4 891	371	123	249	4 520	666	1 473	1 318	706	303	54
1996	5 128	349	128	221	4 779	713	1 544	1 395	729	338	61
1997	5 486	381	138	242	5 106	737	1 614	1 510	833	338	73
1998	5 746	442	132	310	5 304	789	1 639	1 533	927	353	62
1999	6 119	453	151	302	5 666	821	1 698	1 710	973	401	63
2000	6 767	492	164	328	6 275	956	2 016	1 791	1 051	386	75
2001	7 049	492	152	340	6 557	1 014	2 086	1 815	1 153	418	70
2002	7 334	471	152	320	6 863	1 051	2 161	1 897	1 179	484	90
2003	7 525	428	158	271	7 096	1 030	2 183	1 990	1 264	520	109
2004	7 685	429	141	288	7 257	1 060	2 166	1 998	1 357	556	119
2005	7 839	462	152	310	7 377	1 005	2 201	2 052	1 401	599	119

[2]May be any race.
... = Not available.

Table 1-8. Civilian Labor Force Participation Rates, by Age, Sex, Race, and Hispanic Origin, 1948–2005

(Percent.)

Race, Hispanic origin, sex, and year	16 years and over	16 to 19 years	20 years and over						
			Total	20 to 24 years	25 to 34 years	35 to 44 years	45 to 54 years	55 to 64 years	65 years and over
ALL RACES									
Both Sexes									
1948	58.8	52.5	59.4	64.1	63.1	66.7	65.1	56.9	27.0
1949	58.9	52.2	59.5	64.9	63.2	67.2	65.3	56.2	27.3
1950	59.2	51.8	59.9	65.9	63.5	67.5	66.4	56.7	26.7
1951	59.2	52.2	59.8	64.8	64.2	67.6	67.2	56.9	25.8
1952	59.0	51.3	59.7	62.2	64.7	68.0	67.5	57.5	24.8
1953	58.9	50.2	59.6	61.2	64.0	68.9	68.1	58.0	24.8
1954	58.8	48.3	59.6	61.6	64.3	68.8	68.4	58.7	23.9
1955	59.3	48.9	60.1	62.7	64.8	68.9	69.7	59.5	24.1
1956	60.0	50.9	60.7	64.1	64.8	69.5	70.5	60.8	24.3
1957	59.6	49.6	60.4	64.0	64.9	69.5	70.9	60.1	22.9
1958	59.5	47.4	60.5	64.4	65.0	69.6	71.5	60.5	21.8
1959	59.3	46.7	60.4	64.3	65.0	69.5	71.9	61.0	21.1
1960	59.4	47.5	60.5	65.2	65.4	69.4	72.2	60.9	20.8
1961	59.3	46.9	60.5	65.7	65.6	69.5	72.1	61.5	20.1
1962	58.8	46.1	60.0	65.3	65.2	69.7	72.2	61.5	19.1
1963	58.7	45.2	60.1	65.1	65.6	70.1	72.5	62.0	17.9
1964	58.7	44.5	60.2	66.3	65.8	70.0	72.9	61.9	18.0
1965	58.9	45.7	60.3	66.4	66.4	70.7	72.5	61.9	17.8
1966	59.2	48.2	60.5	66.5	67.1	71.0	72.7	62.2	17.2
1967	59.6	48.4	60.9	67.1	68.2	71.6	72.7	62.3	17.2
1968	59.6	48.3	60.9	67.0	68.6	72.0	72.8	62.2	17.2
1969	60.1	49.4	61.3	68.2	69.1	72.5	73.4	62.1	17.3
1970	60.4	49.9	61.6	69.2	69.7	73.1	73.5	61.8	17.0
1971	60.2	49.7	61.4	69.3	69.9	73.2	73.2	61.3	16.2
1972	60.4	51.9	61.4	70.8	70.9	73.3	72.7	60.0	15.6
1973	60.8	53.7	61.7	72.6	72.3	74.0	72.5	58.4	14.6
1974	61.3	54.8	62.0	74.0	73.6	74.6	72.7	57.8	14.0
1975	61.2	54.0	62.1	73.9	74.4	75.0	72.6	57.2	13.7
1976	61.6	54.5	62.4	74.7	75.7	76.0	72.5	56.6	13.1
1977	62.3	56.0	63.0	75.7	77.0	77.0	72.8	56.3	13.0
1978	63.2	57.8	63.8	76.8	78.3	78.1	73.5	56.3	13.3
1979	63.7	57.9	64.3	77.5	79.2	79.2	74.3	56.2	13.1
1980	63.8	56.7	64.5	77.2	79.9	80.0	74.9	55.7	12.5
1981	63.9	55.4	64.8	77.3	80.5	80.7	75.7	55.0	12.2
1982	64.0	54.1	65.0	77.1	81.0	81.2	75.9	55.1	11.9
1983	64.0	53.5	65.0	77.2	81.3	81.6	76.0	54.5	11.7
1984	64.4	53.9	65.3	77.6	81.8	82.4	76.5	54.2	11.1
1985	64.8	54.5	65.7	78.2	82.5	83.1	77.3	54.2	10.8
1986	65.3	54.7	66.2	78.9	82.9	83.7	78.0	54.0	10.9
1987	65.6	54.7	66.5	78.9	83.3	84.3	78.6	54.4	11.1
1988	65.9	55.3	66.8	78.7	83.3	84.6	79.6	54.6	11.5
1989	66.5	55.9	67.3	78.7	83.8	85.1	80.5	55.5	11.8
1990	66.5	53.7	67.6	77.8	83.6	85.2	80.7	55.9	11.8
1991	66.2	51.6	67.3	76.7	83.2	85.2	81.0	55.5	11.5
1992	66.4	51.3	67.6	77.0	83.7	85.1	81.5	56.2	11.5
1993	66.3	51.5	67.5	77.0	83.3	84.9	81.6	56.4	11.2
1994	66.6	52.7	67.7	77.0	83.2	84.8	81.7	56.8	12.4
1995	66.6	53.5	67.7	76.6	83.8	84.6	81.4	57.2	12.1
1996	66.8	52.3	67.9	76.8	84.1	84.8	82.1	57.9	12.1
1997	67.1	51.6	68.4	77.6	84.4	85.1	82.6	58.9	12.2
1998	67.1	52.8	68.3	77.5	84.6	84.7	82.5	59.3	11.9
1999	67.1	52.0	68.3	77.5	84.6	84.9	82.6	59.3	12.3
2000	67.1	52.0	68.3	77.8	84.6	84.8	82.5	59.2	12.9
2001	66.8	49.6	68.2	77.1	84.0	84.6	82.3	60.4	13.0
2002	66.6	47.4	68.1	76.4	83.7	84.1	82.1	61.9	13.2
2003	66.2	44.5	67.9	75.4	82.9	83.9	82.1	62.4	14.0
2004	66.0	43.9	67.7	75.0	82.7	83.6	81.8	62.3	14.4
2005	66.0	43.7	67.8	74.6	82.8	83.8	81.7	62.9	15.1

Table 1-8. Civilian Labor Force Participation Rates, by Age, Sex, Race, and Hispanic Origin, 1948–2005 —Continued

(Percent.)

Race, Hispanic origin, sex, and year	16 years and over	16 to 19 years	20 years and over						
			Total	20 to 24 years	25 to 34 years	35 to 44 years	45 to 54 years	55 to 64 years	65 years and over
ALL RACES									
Men									
1948	86.6	63.7	88.6	84.6	95.9	97.9	95.8	89.5	46.8
1949	86.4	62.8	88.5	86.6	95.8	97.9	95.6	87.5	47.0
1950	86.4	63.2	88.4	87.9	96.0	97.6	95.8	86.9	45.8
1951	86.3	63.0	88.2	88.4	96.9	97.5	95.9	87.2	44.9
1952	86.3	61.3	88.3	88.1	97.5	97.8	96.2	87.5	42.6
1953	86.0	60.7	88.0	87.7	97.4	98.2	96.5	87.9	41.6
1954	85.5	58.0	87.8	86.9	97.3	98.1	96.5	88.7	40.5
1955	85.4	58.9	87.6	86.9	97.6	98.1	96.4	87.9	39.6
1956	85.5	60.5	87.6	87.8	97.3	97.9	96.6	88.5	40.0
1957	84.8	59.1	86.9	87.1	97.1	97.9	96.3	87.5	37.5
1958	84.2	56.6	86.6	86.9	97.1	97.9	96.3	87.8	35.6
1959	83.7	55.8	86.3	87.8	97.4	97.8	96.0	87.4	34.2
1960	83.3	56.1	86.0	88.1	97.5	97.7	95.7	86.8	33.1
1961	82.9	54.6	85.7	87.8	97.5	97.6	95.6	87.3	31.7
1962	82.0	53.8	84.8	86.9	97.2	97.6	95.6	86.2	30.3
1963	81.4	52.9	84.4	86.1	97.1	97.5	95.7	86.2	28.4
1964	81.0	52.4	84.2	86.1	97.3	97.3	95.7	85.6	28.0
1965	80.7	53.8	83.9	85.8	97.2	97.3	95.6	84.6	27.9
1966	80.4	55.3	83.6	85.1	97.3	97.2	95.3	84.5	27.1
1967	80.4	55.6	83.4	84.4	97.2	97.3	95.2	84.4	27.1
1968	80.1	55.1	83.1	82.8	96.9	97.1	94.9	84.3	27.3
1969	79.8	55.9	82.8	82.8	96.7	96.9	94.6	83.4	27.2
1970	79.7	56.1	82.6	83.3	96.4	96.9	94.3	83.0	26.8
1971	79.1	56.1	82.1	83.0	95.9	96.5	93.9	82.1	25.5
1972	78.9	58.1	81.6	83.9	95.7	96.4	93.2	80.4	24.3
1973	78.8	59.7	81.3	85.2	95.7	96.2	93.0	78.2	22.7
1974	78.7	60.7	81.0	85.9	95.8	96.0	92.2	77.3	22.4
1975	77.9	59.1	80.3	84.5	95.2	95.6	92.1	75.6	21.6
1976	77.5	59.3	79.8	85.2	95.2	95.4	91.6	74.3	20.2
1977	77.7	60.9	79.7	85.6	95.3	95.7	91.1	73.8	20.0
1978	77.9	62.0	79.8	85.9	95.3	95.7	91.3	73.3	20.4
1979	77.8	61.5	79.8	86.4	95.3	95.7	91.4	72.8	19.9
1980	77.4	60.5	79.4	85.9	95.2	95.5	91.2	72.1	19.0
1981	77.0	59.0	79.0	85.5	94.9	95.4	91.4	70.6	18.4
1982	76.6	56.7	78.7	84.9	94.7	95.3	91.2	70.2	17.8
1983	76.4	56.2	78.5	84.8	94.2	95.2	91.2	69.4	17.4
1984	76.4	56.0	78.3	85.0	94.4	95.4	91.2	68.5	16.3
1985	76.3	56.8	78.1	85.0	94.7	95.0	91.0	67.9	15.8
1986	76.3	56.4	78.1	85.8	94.6	94.8	91.0	67.3	16.0
1987	76.2	56.1	78.0	85.2	94.6	94.6	90.7	67.6	16.3
1988	76.2	56.9	77.9	85.0	94.3	94.5	90.9	67.0	16.5
1989	76.4	57.9	78.1	85.3	94.4	94.5	91.1	67.2	16.6
1990	76.4	55.7	78.2	84.4	94.1	94.3	90.7	67.8	16.3
1991	75.8	53.2	77.7	83.5	93.6	94.1	90.5	67.0	15.7
1992	75.8	53.4	77.7	83.3	93.8	93.7	90.7	67.0	16.1
1993	75.4	53.2	77.3	83.2	93.4	93.4	90.1	66.5	15.6
1994	75.1	54.1	76.8	83.1	92.6	92.8	89.1	65.5	16.8
1995	75.0	54.8	76.7	83.1	93.0	92.3	88.8	66.0	16.8
1996	74.9	53.2	76.8	82.5	93.2	92.4	89.1	67.0	16.9
1997	75.0	52.3	77.0	82.5	93.0	92.6	89.5	67.6	17.1
1998	74.9	53.3	76.8	82.0	93.2	92.6	89.2	68.1	16.5
1999	74.7	52.9	76.7	81.9	93.3	92.8	88.8	67.9	16.9
2000	74.8	52.8	76.7	82.6	93.4	92.7	88.6	67.3	17.7
2001	74.4	50.2	76.5	81.6	92.7	92.5	88.5	68.3	17.7
2002	74.1	47.5	76.3	80.7	92.4	92.1	88.5	69.2	17.9
2003	73.5	44.3	75.9	80.0	91.8	92.1	87.7	68.7	18.6
2004	73.3	43.9	75.8	79.6	91.9	91.9	87.5	68.7	19.0
2005	73.3	43.2	75.8	79.1	91.7	92.1	87.7	69.3	19.8

Table 1-8. Civilian Labor Force Participation Rates, by Age, Sex, Race, and Hispanic Origin, 1948–2005
—Continued

(Percent.)

Race, Hispanic origin, sex, and year	16 years and over	16 to 19 years	20 years and over						
			Total	20 to 24 years	25 to 34 years	35 to 44 years	45 to 54 years	55 to 64 years	65 years and over
ALL RACES									
Women									
1948	32.7	42.0	31.8	45.3	33.2	36.9	35.0	24.3	9.1
1949	33.1	42.4	32.3	45.0	33.4	38.1	35.9	25.3	9.6
1950	33.9	41.0	33.3	46.0	34.0	39.1	37.9	27.0	9.7
1951	34.6	42.4	34.0	46.5	35.4	39.8	39.7	27.6	8.9
1952	34.7	42.2	34.1	44.7	35.4	40.4	40.1	28.7	9.1
1953	34.4	40.7	33.9	44.3	34.0	41.3	40.4	29.1	10.0
1954	34.6	39.4	34.2	45.1	34.4	41.2	41.2	30.0	9.3
1955	35.7	39.7	35.4	45.9	34.9	41.6	43.8	32.5	10.6
1956	36.9	42.2	36.4	46.3	35.4	43.1	45.5	34.9	10.8
1957	36.9	41.1	36.5	45.9	35.6	43.3	46.5	34.5	10.5
1958	37.1	39.0	36.9	46.3	35.6	43.4	47.8	35.2	10.3
1959	37.1	38.2	37.1	45.1	35.3	43.4	49.0	36.6	10.2
1960	37.7	39.3	37.6	46.1	36.0	43.4	49.9	37.2	10.8
1961	38.1	39.7	38.0	47.0	36.4	43.8	50.1	37.9	10.7
1962	37.9	39.0	37.8	47.3	36.3	44.1	50.0	38.7	10.0
1963	38.3	38.0	38.3	47.5	37.2	44.9	50.6	39.7	9.6
1964	38.7	37.0	38.9	49.4	37.2	45.0	51.4	40.2	10.1
1965	39.3	38.0	39.4	49.9	38.5	46.1	50.9	41.1	10.0
1966	40.3	41.4	40.1	51.5	39.8	46.8	51.7	41.8	9.6
1967	41.1	41.6	41.1	53.3	41.9	48.1	51.8	42.4	9.6
1968	41.6	41.9	41.6	54.5	42.6	48.9	52.3	42.4	9.6
1969	42.7	43.2	42.7	56.7	43.7	49.9	53.8	43.1	9.9
1970	43.3	44.0	43.3	57.7	45.0	51.1	54.4	43.0	9.7
1971	43.4	43.4	43.3	57.7	45.6	51.6	54.3	42.9	9.5
1972	43.9	45.8	43.7	59.1	47.8	52.0	53.9	42.1	9.3
1973	44.7	47.8	44.4	61.1	50.4	53.3	53.7	41.1	8.9
1974	45.7	49.1	45.3	63.1	52.6	54.7	54.6	40.7	8.1
1975	46.3	49.1	46.0	64.1	54.9	55.8	54.6	40.9	8.2
1976	47.3	49.8	47.0	65.0	57.3	57.8	55.0	41.0	8.2
1977	48.4	51.2	48.1	66.5	59.7	59.6	55.8	40.9	8.1
1978	50.0	53.7	49.6	68.3	62.2	61.6	57.1	41.3	8.3
1979	50.9	54.2	50.6	69.0	63.9	63.6	58.3	41.7	8.3
1980	51.5	52.9	51.3	68.9	65.5	65.5	59.9	41.3	8.1
1981	52.1	51.8	52.1	69.6	66.7	66.8	61.1	41.4	8.0
1982	52.6	51.4	52.7	69.8	68.0	68.0	61.6	41.8	7.9
1983	52.9	50.8	53.1	69.9	69.0	68.7	61.9	41.5	7.8
1984	53.6	51.8	53.7	70.4	69.8	70.1	62.9	41.7	7.5
1985	54.5	52.1	54.7	71.8	70.9	71.8	64.4	42.0	7.3
1986	55.3	53.0	55.5	72.4	71.6	73.1	65.9	42.3	7.4
1987	56.0	53.3	56.2	73.0	72.4	74.5	67.1	42.7	7.4
1988	56.6	53.6	56.8	72.7	72.7	75.2	69.0	43.5	7.9
1989	57.4	53.9	57.7	72.4	73.5	76.0	70.5	45.0	8.4
1990	57.5	51.6	58.0	71.3	73.5	76.4	71.2	45.2	8.6
1991	57.4	50.0	57.9	70.1	73.1	76.5	72.0	45.2	8.5
1992	57.8	49.1	58.5	70.9	73.9	76.7	72.6	46.5	8.3
1993	57.9	49.7	58.5	70.9	73.4	76.6	73.5	47.2	8.1
1994	58.8	51.3	59.3	71.0	74.0	77.1	74.6	48.9	9.2
1995	58.9	52.2	59.4	70.3	74.9	77.2	74.4	49.2	8.8
1996	59.3	51.3	59.9	71.3	75.2	77.5	75.4	49.6	8.6
1997	59.8	51.0	60.5	72.7	76.0	77.7	76.0	50.9	8.6
1998	59.8	52.3	60.4	73.0	76.3	77.1	76.2	51.2	8.6
1999	60.0	51.0	60.7	73.2	76.4	77.2	76.7	51.5	8.9
2000	59.9	51.2	60.6	73.1	76.1	77.2	76.8	51.9	9.4
2001	59.8	49.0	60.6	72.7	75.5	77.1	76.4	53.2	9.6
2002	59.6	47.3	60.5	72.1	75.1	76.4	76.0	55.2	9.8
2003	59.5	44.8	60.6	70.8	74.1	76.0	76.8	56.6	10.6
2004	59.2	43.8	60.3	70.5	73.6	75.6	76.5	56.3	11.1
2005	59.3	44.2	60.4	70.1	73.9	75.8	76.0	57.0	11.5

Table 1-8. Civilian Labor Force Participation Rates, by Age, Sex, Race, and Hispanic Origin, 1948–2005
—*Continued*

(Percent.)

Race, Hispanic origin, sex, and year	16 years and over	16 to 19 years	20 years and over						
			Total	20 to 24 years	25 to 34 years	35 to 44 years	45 to 54 years	55 to 64 years	65 years and over
WHITE[1]									
Both Sexes									
1954	58.2	48.8	58.9	61.0	63.5	68.0	67.9	58.4	23.7
1955	58.7	49.3	59.5	62.4	64.0	68.3	69.2	59.3	23.9
1956	59.4	51.3	60.1	64.1	64.0	68.9	70.1	60.6	24.2
1957	59.1	50.3	59.8	63.7	64.1	68.8	70.5	59.9	22.8
1958	58.9	47.9	59.8	64.1	64.2	68.8	71.0	60.3	21.7
1959	58.7	47.4	59.7	63.7	64.3	68.7	71.5	60.7	21.0
1960	58.8	47.9	59.8	64.8	64.7	68.6	71.7	60.6	20.8
1961	58.8	47.4	59.9	65.5	64.8	68.8	71.7	61.3	20.0
1962	58.3	46.6	59.4	65.0	64.4	69.0	71.8	61.3	19.0
1963	58.2	45.7	59.4	64.9	64.8	69.4	72.3	61.8	17.9
1964	58.2	45.1	59.6	65.8	64.9	69.5	72.5	61.8	17.8
1965	58.4	46.5	59.7	65.7	65.6	70.1	72.2	61.7	17.7
1966	58.7	49.1	59.8	66.0	66.3	70.4	72.5	61.9	17.1
1967	59.2	49.2	60.3	66.8	67.4	71.2	72.5	62.3	17.0
1968	59.3	49.3	60.4	66.6	67.9	71.7	72.7	62.2	17.1
1969	59.9	50.6	60.9	67.9	68.4	72.3	73.3	62.1	17.2
1970	60.2	51.4	61.2	69.2	69.1	72.9	73.5	61.8	16.8
1971	60.1	51.6	61.1	69.6	69.3	73.0	73.4	61.3	16.1
1972	60.4	54.1	61.2	71.2	70.4	73.2	72.9	60.3	15.4
1973	60.8	56.0	61.4	73.3	72.0	73.9	72.7	58.6	14.4
1974	61.4	57.3	61.9	74.8	73.4	74.6	73.0	58.0	13.9
1975	61.5	56.7	62.0	75.2	74.4	75.1	73.0	57.4	13.6
1976	61.8	57.5	62.3	76.0	75.6	76.1	73.0	56.9	13.0
1977	62.5	59.3	62.9	77.1	77.0	77.1	73.2	56.6	12.9
1978	63.3	60.8	63.6	78.1	78.3	78.1	73.8	56.4	13.1
1979	63.9	61.1	64.2	78.9	79.4	79.3	74.6	56.5	12.9
1980	64.1	60.0	64.5	78.7	80.2	80.3	75.4	56.0	12.5
1981	64.3	58.9	64.8	79.1	81.0	81.0	76.2	55.2	12.2
1982	64.3	57.5	65.0	78.9	81.6	81.5	76.4	55.3	12.0
1983	64.3	56.9	65.0	79.0	81.8	81.9	76.5	54.7	11.8
1984	64.6	57.2	65.3	79.4	82.5	82.6	77.0	54.5	11.1
1985	65.0	57.5	65.7	79.9	83.1	83.4	77.8	54.4	10.7
1986	65.5	57.8	66.1	80.6	83.6	84.0	78.5	54.3	11.0
1987	65.8	57.7	66.5	80.7	84.0	84.7	79.1	54.6	11.1
1988	66.2	58.6	66.8	80.6	84.1	85.0	80.3	55.1	11.4
1989	66.7	59.1	67.3	80.2	84.5	85.5	81.2	56.2	11.8
1990	66.9	57.5	67.6	79.8	84.6	85.9	81.3	56.5	11.9
1991	66.6	55.8	67.4	78.9	84.3	85.9	81.8	56.0	11.6
1992	66.8	54.7	67.7	79.4	84.6	85.8	82.2	56.8	11.6
1993	66.8	55.1	67.6	79.5	84.5	85.7	82.5	57.1	11.4
1994	67.1	56.4	67.9	79.5	84.4	85.7	82.7	57.6	12.5
1995	67.1	57.1	67.8	78.7	84.9	85.5	82.5	58.0	12.3
1996	67.2	55.9	68.1	79.1	84.9	85.7	83.1	58.7	12.3
1997	67.5	55.2	68.4	79.6	85.3	85.8	83.5	59.9	12.3
1998	67.3	56.0	68.2	79.5	85.4	85.3	83.4	60.1	12.0
1999	67.3	55.5	68.2	79.5	85.1	85.4	83.5	60.2	12.5
2000	67.3	55.5	68.2	79.9	85.1	85.4	83.5	60.0	13.0
2001	67.0	53.1	68.1	79.2	84.5	85.2	83.3	61.2	13.0
2002	66.8	50.5	68.1	78.6	84.5	84.7	83.0	62.8	13.3
2003	66.5	47.7	67.9	77.7	83.6	84.3	83.0	63.3	14.1
2004	66.3	47.1	67.7	77.1	83.5	84.1	82.9	63.2	14.6
2005	66.3	46.9	67.7	76.3	83.5	84.2	82.8	63.7	15.1

[1]Beginning in 2003, persons who selected this race group only; persons who selected more than one race group are not included. Prior to 2003, persons who reported more than one race group were included in the group they identified as their main race.

Table 1-8. Civilian Labor Force Participation Rates, by Age, Sex, Race, and Hispanic Origin, 1948–2005
—Continued

(Percent.)

Race, Hispanic origin, sex, and year	16 years and over	16 to 19 years	20 years and over						
			Total	20 to 24 years	25 to 34 years	35 to 44 years	45 to 54 years	55 to 64 years	65 years and over
WHITE[1]									
Men									
1954	85.6	57.6	87.8	86.3	97.5	98.2	96.8	89.1	40.4
1955	85.4	58.6	87.5	86.5	97.8	98.2	96.7	88.4	39.6
1956	85.6	60.4	87.6	87.6	97.4	98.1	96.8	88.9	40.0
1957	84.8	59.2	86.9	86.6	97.2	98.0	96.7	88.0	37.7
1958	84.3	56.5	86.6	86.7	97.2	98.0	96.6	88.2	35.7
1959	83.8	55.9	86.3	87.3	97.5	98.0	96.3	87.9	34.3
1960	83.4	55.9	86.0	87.8	97.7	97.9	96.1	87.2	33.3
1961	83.0	54.5	85.7	87.6	97.7	97.9	95.9	87.8	31.9
1962	82.1	53.8	84.9	86.5	97.4	97.9	96.0	86.7	30.6
1963	81.5	53.1	84.4	85.8	97.4	97.8	96.2	86.6	28.4
1964	81.1	52.7	84.2	85.7	97.5	97.6	96.1	86.1	27.9
1965	80.8	54.1	83.9	85.3	97.4	97.7	95.9	85.2	27.9
1966	80.6	55.9	83.6	84.4	97.5	97.6	95.8	84.9	27.2
1967	80.6	56.3	83.5	84.0	97.5	97.7	95.6	84.9	27.1
1968	80.4	55.9	83.2	82.4	97.2	97.6	95.4	84.7	27.4
1969	80.2	56.8	83.0	82.6	97.0	97.4	95.1	83.9	27.3
1970	80.0	57.5	82.8	83.3	96.7	97.3	94.9	83.3	26.7
1971	79.6	57.9	82.3	83.2	96.3	97.0	94.7	82.6	25.6
1972	79.6	60.1	82.0	84.3	96.0	97.0	94.0	81.1	24.4
1973	79.4	62.0	81.6	85.8	96.2	96.8	93.5	78.9	22.7
1974	79.4	62.9	81.4	86.6	96.3	96.7	93.0	78.0	22.4
1975	78.7	61.9	80.7	85.5	95.8	96.4	92.9	76.4	21.7
1976	78.4	62.3	80.3	86.3	95.9	96.0	92.5	75.2	20.2
1977	78.5	64.0	80.2	86.8	96.0	96.2	92.1	74.6	20.0
1978	78.6	65.0	80.1	87.3	95.9	96.3	92.1	73.7	20.3
1979	78.6	64.8	80.1	87.6	96.0	96.4	92.2	73.4	20.0
1980	78.2	63.7	79.8	87.2	95.9	96.2	92.1	73.1	19.1
1981	77.9	62.4	79.5	87.0	95.8	96.1	92.4	71.5	18.5
1982	77.4	60.0	79.2	86.3	95.6	96.0	92.2	71.0	17.9
1983	77.1	59.4	78.9	86.1	95.2	96.0	91.9	70.0	17.7
1984	77.1	59.0	78.7	86.5	95.4	96.1	92.0	69.5	16.4
1985	77.0	59.7	78.5	86.4	95.7	95.7	92.0	68.8	15.9
1986	76.9	59.3	78.5	87.3	95.5	95.4	91.8	68.0	16.3
1987	76.8	59.0	78.4	86.9	95.5	95.4	91.6	68.1	16.5
1988	76.9	60.0	78.3	86.6	95.2	95.4	91.8	67.9	16.7
1989	77.1	61.0	78.5	86.8	95.4	95.3	92.2	68.3	16.8
1990	77.1	59.6	78.5	86.2	95.2	95.3	91.7	68.6	16.6
1991	76.5	57.3	78.0	85.4	94.9	95.0	91.4	67.7	15.9
1992	76.5	56.9	78.0	85.2	94.9	94.7	91.8	67.7	16.2
1993	76.2	56.6	77.7	85.5	94.7	94.5	91.3	67.3	15.9
1994	75.9	57.7	77.3	85.5	93.9	93.9	90.3	66.4	17.2
1995	75.7	58.5	77.1	85.1	94.1	93.4	90.0	67.1	16.9
1996	75.8	57.1	77.3	85.0	94.4	93.6	90.4	68.0	17.2
1997	75.9	56.1	77.5	85.1	94.2	93.7	90.6	68.9	17.4
1998	75.6	56.6	77.2	84.6	94.4	93.7	90.3	69.1	16.6
1999	75.6	56.4	77.2	84.9	94.3	93.8	90.1	69.1	17.2
2000	75.5	56.5	77.1	85.2	94.5	93.8	89.7	68.2	17.9
2001	75.1	53.7	76.9	84.1	93.9	93.6	89.7	69.1	17.8
2002	74.8	50.3	76.7	83.2	93.7	93.2	89.6	70.2	17.8
2003	74.2	47.5	76.3	82.5	93.3	93.1	88.8	69.7	18.6
2004	74.1	47.4	76.2	82.1	93.2	93.0	88.7	69.8	19.1
2005	74.1	46.2	76.2	81.4	93.0	93.0	89.0	70.4	20.0

[1]Beginning in 2003, persons who selected this race group only; persons who selected more than one race group are not included. Prior to 2003, persons who reported more than one race group were included in the group they identified as their main race.

Table 1-8. Civilian Labor Force Participation Rates, by Age, Sex, Race, and Hispanic Origin, 1948–2005 —Continued

(Percent.)

Race, Hispanic origin, sex, and year	16 years and over	16 to 19 years	20 years and over						
			Total	20 to 24 years	25 to 34 years	35 to 44 years	45 to 54 years	55 to 64 years	65 years and over
WHITE[1]									
Women									
1954	33.3	40.6	32.7	44.4	32.5	39.3	39.8	29.1	9.1
1955	34.5	40.7	34.0	45.8	32.8	40.0	42.7	31.8	10.5
1956	35.7	43.1	35.1	46.5	33.2	41.5	44.4	34.0	10.6
1957	35.7	42.2	35.2	45.8	33.6	41.5	45.4	33.7	10.2
1958	35.8	40.1	35.5	46.0	33.6	41.4	46.5	34.5	10.1
1959	36.0	39.6	35.6	44.5	33.4	41.4	47.8	35.7	10.0
1960	36.5	40.3	36.2	45.7	34.1	41.5	48.6	36.2	10.6
1961	36.9	40.6	36.6	46.9	34.3	41.8	48.9	37.2	10.5
1962	36.7	39.8	36.5	47.1	34.1	42.2	48.9	38.0	9.8
1963	37.2	38.7	37.0	47.3	34.8	43.1	49.5	38.9	9.4
1964	37.5	37.8	37.5	48.8	35.0	43.3	50.2	39.4	9.9
1965	38.1	39.2	38.0	49.2	36.3	44.4	49.9	40.3	9.7
1966	39.2	42.6	38.8	51.0	37.7	45.0	50.6	41.1	9.4
1967	40.1	42.5	39.8	53.1	39.7	46.4	50.9	41.9	9.3
1968	40.7	43.0	40.4	54.0	40.6	47.5	51.5	42.0	9.4
1969	41.8	44.6	41.5	56.4	41.7	48.6	53.0	42.6	9.7
1970	42.6	45.6	42.2	57.7	43.2	49.9	53.7	42.6	9.5
1971	42.6	45.4	42.3	58.0	43.7	50.2	53.6	42.5	9.3
1972	43.2	48.1	42.7	59.4	46.0	50.7	53.4	41.9	9.0
1973	44.1	50.1	43.5	61.7	48.7	52.2	53.4	40.7	8.7
1974	45.2	51.7	44.4	63.9	51.3	53.6	54.3	40.4	8.0
1975	45.9	51.5	45.3	65.5	53.8	54.9	54.3	40.6	8.0
1976	46.9	52.8	46.2	66.3	56.0	57.1	54.7	40.7	7.9
1977	48.0	54.5	47.3	67.8	58.5	58.9	55.3	40.7	7.9
1978	49.4	56.7	48.7	69.3	61.2	60.7	56.7	41.1	8.1
1979	50.5	57.4	49.8	70.5	63.1	63.0	58.1	41.5	8.1
1980	51.2	56.2	50.6	70.6	64.8	65.0	59.6	40.9	7.9
1981	51.9	55.4	51.5	71.5	66.4	66.4	60.9	40.9	7.9
1982	52.4	55.0	52.2	71.8	67.8	67.5	61.4	41.5	7.8
1983	52.7	54.5	52.5	72.1	68.7	68.2	61.9	41.1	7.8
1984	53.3	55.4	53.1	72.5	69.8	69.6	62.7	41.2	7.5
1985	54.1	55.2	54.0	73.8	70.9	71.4	64.2	41.5	7.0
1986	55.0	56.3	54.9	74.1	71.8	72.9	65.8	42.1	7.3
1987	55.7	56.5	55.6	74.8	72.5	74.2	67.2	42.4	7.2
1988	56.4	57.2	56.3	74.9	73.0	74.9	69.2	43.6	7.7
1989	57.2	57.1	57.2	74.0	73.8	75.9	70.6	45.2	8.2
1990	57.4	55.3	57.6	73.4	74.1	76.6	71.3	45.5	8.5
1991	57.4	54.1	57.6	72.5	73.8	76.8	72.4	45.4	8.5
1992	57.7	52.5	58.1	73.5	74.4	77.0	72.8	46.8	8.2
1993	58.0	53.5	58.3	73.4	74.3	76.9	74.0	47.6	8.1
1994	58.9	55.1	59.2	73.4	74.9	77.5	75.2	49.4	9.2
1995	59.0	55.5	59.2	72.3	75.8	77.6	75.2	49.5	9.0
1996	59.1	54.7	59.4	73.3	75.5	77.8	76.1	50.1	8.7
1997	59.5	54.1	59.9	73.9	76.3	77.9	76.6	51.5	8.6
1998	59.4	55.4	59.7	74.3	76.3	76.9	76.6	51.6	8.7
1999	59.6	54.5	59.9	73.9	76.0	77.1	77.1	52.0	8.9
2000	59.5	54.5	59.9	74.5	75.7	77.2	77.5	52.4	9.4
2001	59.4	52.4	59.9	74.2	75.1	77.0	77.1	53.8	9.6
2002	59.3	50.8	60.0	74.0	75.0	76.3	76.6	55.8	9.9
2003	59.2	47.9	59.9	72.7	73.7	75.5	77.3	57.4	10.8
2004	58.9	46.7	59.7	71.9	73.6	75.2	77.1	57.0	11.2
2005	58.9	47.6	59.7	71.0	73.7	75.4	76.7	57.5	11.4

[1] Beginning in 2003, persons who selected this race group only; persons who selected more than one race group are not included. Prior to 2003, persons who reported more than one race group were included in the group they identified as their main race.

Table 1-8. Civilian Labor Force Participation Rates, by Age, Sex, Race, and Hispanic Origin, 1948–2005
—Continued

(Percent.)

Race, Hispanic origin, sex, and year	16 years and over	16 to 19 years	20 years and over						
			Total	20 to 24 years	25 to 34 years	35 to 44 years	45 to 54 years	55 to 64 years	65 years and over
BLACK[1]									
Both Sexes									
1972	59.9	39.1	63.3	68.6	74.9	74.4	70.0	56.9	17.5
1973	60.2	39.8	63.4	69.7	75.7	74.5	70.3	55.9	16.0
1974	59.8	39.8	63.0	69.8	75.8	74.6	69.1	54.7	15.1
1975	58.8	38.2	62.0	66.1	75.6	74.1	69.0	54.3	14.9
1976	59.0	37.0	62.5	66.8	77.4	74.9	68.6	53.4	14.9
1977	59.8	37.9	63.2	68.2	78.3	75.9	69.0	53.7	14.5
1978	61.5	41.0	64.5	69.9	79.6	77.4	70.4	54.8	15.3
1979	61.4	40.1	64.5	70.0	79.2	77.9	71.1	53.5	14.5
1980	61.0	38.9	64.1	69.0	79.5	77.4	71.4	52.6	13.0
1981	60.8	37.7	64.2	69.2	78.5	78.4	71.2	52.8	12.0
1982	61.0	36.6	64.3	68.6	78.7	79.8	71.1	52.3	11.5
1983	61.5	36.4	64.9	68.4	79.8	80.2	72.1	52.5	10.5
1984	62.2	38.3	65.2	69.2	79.3	81.0	73.0	51.6	10.3
1985	62.9	41.2	65.6	70.0	79.8	81.5	73.4	51.4	11.2
1986	63.3	41.3	65.9	71.7	80.1	81.9	74.3	50.6	9.7
1987	63.8	41.6	66.5	70.5	80.7	82.6	74.7	52.4	10.7
1988	63.8	40.8	66.5	70.5	80.8	82.6	75.0	50.6	11.5
1989	64.2	42.5	66.7	72.2	80.9	82.7	75.5	48.3	11.6
1990	64.0	38.7	66.9	68.8	79.7	82.4	76.5	49.6	11.1
1991	63.3	35.4	66.4	67.7	78.5	82.0	76.2	50.4	10.7
1992	63.9	37.9	66.8	67.4	79.7	81.4	76.2	51.6	10.6
1993	63.2	37.0	66.0	67.8	78.3	81.0	75.2	50.2	9.5
1994	63.4	38.5	66.0	68.8	78.3	80.8	74.8	49.3	10.6
1995	63.7	39.9	66.3	68.7	80.0	80.4	74.1	50.3	10.5
1996	64.1	39.2	66.9	69.0	81.1	81.0	74.9	50.9	9.8
1997	64.7	38.7	67.6	70.9	82.0	81.4	76.3	50.5	10.0
1998	65.6	41.6	68.2	70.6	83.0	82.2	76.7	52.3	10.3
1999	65.8	38.7	68.9	71.4	85.2	83.0	76.4	51.4	10.4
2000	65.8	39.4	68.7	71.8	84.1	82.3	76.9	52.5	11.6
2001	65.3	37.6	68.2	69.9	83.6	82.0	75.9	53.9	12.6
2002	64.8	36.0	67.8	68.6	82.4	81.6	76.1	54.7	12.5
2003	64.3	32.4	67.6	68.2	81.6	82.9	75.8	54.4	12.9
2004	63.8	31.4	67.2	68.3	81.2	82.1	75.5	54.4	13.1
2005	64.2	32.4	67.4	69.0	81.7	82.3	75.7	55.3	13.6
Men									
1972	73.6	46.3	78.5	82.7	92.7	91.1	85.4	72.5	24.2
1973	73.4	45.7	78.4	83.7	91.8	91.0	87.4	69.5	22.3
1974	72.9	46.7	77.6	83.6	92.8	90.4	84.0	68.9	21.6
1975	70.9	42.6	76.0	78.7	91.6	89.4	83.5	67.7	20.7
1976	70.0	41.3	75.4	79.0	90.9	89.9	82.4	65.1	19.8
1977	70.6	43.2	75.6	79.2	90.7	91.0	82.0	65.5	20.0
1978	71.5	44.9	76.2	78.8	90.9	90.5	83.2	67.9	21.1
1979	71.3	43.6	76.3	80.7	90.8	90.4	84.5	64.8	19.5
1980	70.3	43.2	75.1	79.9	90.9	89.1	83.0	61.9	16.9
1981	70.0	41.6	74.5	79.2	88.9	89.3	82.7	62.1	16.0
1982	70.1	39.8	74.7	78.7	89.2	89.8	82.2	61.9	15.9
1983	70.6	39.9	75.2	79.4	89.0	89.7	84.5	62.6	14.0
1984	70.8	41.7	74.8	79.1	88.9	90.0	83.7	58.9	13.7
1985	70.8	44.6	74.4	79.0	88.8	89.8	83.0	58.9	13.9
1986	71.2	43.7	74.8	80.1	89.6	89.6	84.1	59.1	12.6
1987	71.1	43.6	74.7	77.8	89.4	88.6	83.7	62.1	13.7
1988	71.0	43.8	74.6	79.3	89.3	88.2	83.5	59.4	14.3
1989	71.0	44.6	74.4	80.2	89.7	88.7	82.5	55.5	14.3
1990	71.0	40.7	75.0	76.8	88.8	88.1	83.5	58.0	13.0
1991	70.4	37.3	74.6	76.7	87.3	87.7	83.4	58.7	13.0
1992	70.7	40.6	74.3	75.4	88.0	86.5	81.8	60.0	13.7
1993	69.6	39.5	73.2	74.1	87.3	86.1	80.0	57.9	11.6
1994	69.1	40.8	72.5	73.9	86.2	85.9	79.1	54.5	12.7
1995	69.0	40.1	72.5	74.6	87.5	84.1	78.5	54.4	14.9
1996	68.7	39.5	72.3	73.4	87.5	84.4	78.5	55.6	12.9
1997	68.3	37.4	72.2	72.1	86.8	84.8	80.1	54.3	12.9
1998	69.0	40.7	72.5	71.8	87.1	85.0	79.9	57.3	14.0
1999	68.7	38.6	72.4	69.8	89.2	86.0	78.5	55.5	12.7
2000	69.2	39.2	72.8	73.3	87.8	85.2	79.2	57.4	14.4
2001	68.4	37.9	72.1	69.7	86.6	84.9	78.4	58.9	16.7
2002	68.4	37.3	72.1	70.7	85.9	84.7	79.5	58.4	16.9
2003	67.3	31.1	71.5	71.1	84.7	85.7	77.7	57.6	17.0
2004	66.7	30.0	70.9	69.9	86.1	84.0	76.9	57.1	17.0
2005	67.3	32.6	71.3	70.1	85.5	85.5	78.6	57.3	17.1

[1]Beginning in 2003, persons who selected this race group only; persons who selected more than one race group are not included. Prior to 2003, persons who reported more than one race group were included in the group they identified as their main race.

Table 1-8. Civilian Labor Force Participation Rates, by Age, Sex, Race, and Hispanic Origin, 1948–2005 *—Continued*

(Percent.)

Race, Hispanic origin, sex, and year	16 years and over	16 to 19 years	20 years and over						
			Total	20 to 24 years	25 to 34 years	35 to 44 years	45 to 54 years	55 to 64 years	65 years and over
BLACK[1]									
Women									
1972	48.7	32.2	51.2	57.0	60.8	61.4	57.2	44.0	12.6
1973	49.3	34.2	51.6	58.0	62.7	61.7	56.1	44.7	11.4
1974	49.0	33.4	51.4	58.8	62.4	62.2	56.4	42.8	10.4
1975	48.8	34.2	51.1	55.9	62.8	62.0	56.6	43.1	10.7
1976	49.8	32.9	52.5	56.9	66.7	63.0	56.8	43.7	11.3
1977	50.8	32.9	53.6	59.3	68.5	64.1	57.9	43.7	10.5
1978	53.1	37.3	55.5	62.7	70.6	67.2	59.4	43.8	11.1
1979	53.1	36.8	55.4	61.5	70.1	68.0	59.6	44.0	10.9
1980	53.1	34.9	55.6	60.2	70.5	68.1	61.4	44.8	10.2
1981	53.5	34.0	56.0	61.1	70.0	69.8	62.0	45.4	9.3
1982	53.7	33.5	56.2	60.1	70.2	71.7	62.4	44.8	8.5
1983	54.2	33.0	56.8	59.1	72.3	72.6	62.3	44.8	8.2
1984	55.2	35.0	57.6	60.7	71.5	73.7	64.5	46.1	8.0
1985	56.5	37.9	58.6	62.5	72.4	74.8	65.7	45.3	9.4
1986	56.9	39.1	58.9	64.6	72.4	75.8	66.5	43.6	7.8
1987	58.0	39.6	60.0	64.4	73.5	77.8	67.5	44.4	8.6
1988	58.0	37.9	60.1	63.2	73.7	78.1	68.3	43.4	9.6
1989	58.7	40.4	60.6	65.5	73.6	78.0	70.0	42.4	9.8
1990	58.3	36.8	60.6	62.4	72.3	77.7	70.7	43.2	9.9
1991	57.5	33.5	60.0	60.3	71.4	77.2	70.2	44.1	9.2
1992	58.5	35.2	60.8	60.8	73.1	77.1	71.7	45.1	8.6
1993	57.9	34.6	60.2	62.6	70.9	76.8	71.2	44.4	8.3
1994	58.7	36.3	60.9	64.5	71.9	76.4	71.3	45.3	9.2
1995	59.5	39.8	61.4	63.7	73.9	77.3	70.5	47.2	7.7
1996	60.4	38.9	62.6	65.2	75.9	78.2	72.0	47.2	7.7
1997	61.7	39.9	64.0	69.9	78.1	78.4	73.2	47.6	8.2
1998	62.8	42.5	64.8	69.6	79.6	79.9	74.0	48.5	7.9
1999	63.5	38.8	66.1	72.7	82.1	80.4	74.6	48.4	8.9
2000	63.1	39.6	65.4	70.5	81.1	79.9	74.9	48.6	9.9
2001	62.8	37.3	65.2	70.1	81.2	79.6	73.9	49.9	10.1
2002	61.8	34.7	64.4	66.9	79.7	79.2	73.3	51.8	9.8
2003	61.9	33.7	64.6	65.7	79.1	80.6	74.2	51.9	10.3
2004	61.5	32.8	64.2	66.8	77.2	80.6	74.3	52.3	10.7
2005	61.6	32.2	64.4	68.1	78.5	79.7	73.3	53.7	11.4
HISPANIC[2]									
Both Sexes									
1973	60.2	46.9	...	...	...	...	...	...	...
1974	61.1	47.7	...	...	...	...	...	...	...
1975	60.8	46.2	...	...	...	...	...	...	...
1976	60.8	46.9	...	...	...	...	...	...	...
1977	61.6	48.2	...	...	...	...	...	...	...
1978	62.9	49.6	...	...	...	...	...	...	...
1979	63.6	50.3	...	...	...	...	...	...	...
1980	64.0	50.3	...	...	...	...	...	...	...
1981	64.1	46.4	...	...	...	...	...	...	...
1982	63.6	44.8	...	...	...	...	...	...	...
1983	63.8	45.3	...	...	...	...	...	...	...
1984	64.9	47.5	...	...	...	...	...	...	...
1985	64.6	44.6	...	...	...	...	...	...	...
1986	65.4	43.9	...	...	...	...	...	...	...
1987	66.4	45.8	...	...	...	...	...	...	...
1988	67.4	49.6	...	...	...	...	...	...	...
1989	67.6	48.6	...	...	...	...	...	...	...
1990	67.4	47.8	...	...	...	...	...	...	...
1991	66.5	45.1	...	...	...	...	...	...	...
1992	66.8	45.8	...	...	...	...	...	...	...
1993	66.2	43.9	...	...	...	...	...	...	...
1994	66.1	44.4	68.5	74.0	77.3	78.9	73.1	49.8	10.7
1995	65.8	45.4	68.1	71.9	78.1	78.5	72.8	48.6	10.5
1996	66.5	43.4	69.1	73.1	78.2	79.5	74.6	52.2	11.0
1997	67.9	43.0	70.8	76.4	79.5	80.9	75.4	53.8	11.9
1998	67.9	45.7	70.6	76.1	80.3	80.0	75.3	55.4	10.1
1999	67.7	45.5	70.4	76.0	78.6	81.3	75.9	54.1	11.6
2000	69.7	46.3	72.5	78.2	80.4	81.7	78.0	54.2	12.3
2001	69.5	46.9	72.0	76.6	80.0	81.9	77.4	55.1	10.9
2002	69.1	44.0	71.8	76.3	80.5	81.1	76.1	55.8	11.9
2003	68.3	37.7	71.4	75.6	79.4	81.1	75.3	57.4	12.8
2004	68.6	38.2	71.7	74.5	79.4	81.4	77.6	58.1	14.5
2005	68.0	38.6	71.0	72.7	79.1	81.2	77.2	58.4	13.9

[1]Beginning in 2003, persons who selected this race group only; persons who selected more than one race group are not included. Prior to 2003, persons who reported more than one race group were included in the group they identified as their main race.
[2]May be of any race.
... = Not available.

Table 1-8. Civilian Labor Force Participation Rates, by Age, Sex, Race, and Hispanic Origin, 1948–2005 —*Continued*

(Percent.)

Race, Hispanic origin, sex, and year	16 years and over	16 to 19 years	20 years and over						
			Total	20 to 24 years	25 to 34 years	35 to 44 years	45 to 54 years	55 to 64 years	65 years and over
HISPANIC[2]									
Men									
1973	81.5	. . .	85.9	. . .	. . .	. . .	. . .	. . .	. . .
1974	81.7	. . .	86.0	. . .	. . .	. . .	. . .	. . .	. . .
1975	80.7	. . .	85.5	. . .	. . .	. . .	. . .	. . .	. . .
1976	79.6	. . .	84.2	. . .	. . .	. . .	. . .	. . .	. . .
1977	80.9	. . .	84.8	. . .	. . .	. . .	. . .	. . .	. . .
1978	81.1	. . .	84.9	. . .	. . .	. . .	. . .	. . .	. . .
1979	81.3	. . .	85.3	. . .	. . .	. . .	. . .	. . .	. . .
1980	81.4	. . .	84.9	. . .	. . .	. . .	. . .	. . .	. . .
1981	80.6	. . .	84.7	. . .	. . .	. . .	. . .	. . .	. . .
1982	79.7	. . .	84.0	. . .	. . .	. . .	. . .	. . .	. . .
1983	80.3	. . .	84.1	. . .	. . .	. . .	. . .	. . .	. . .
1984	80.6	. . .	84.3	. . .	. . .	. . .	. . .	. . .	. . .
1985	80.3	. . .	84.0	. . .	. . .	. . .	. . .	. . .	. . .
1986	81.0	. . .	84.6	. . .	. . .	. . .	. . .	. . .	. . .
1987	81.0	. . .	84.5	. . .	. . .	. . .	. . .	. . .	. . .
1988	81.9	. . .	85.0	. . .	. . .	. . .	. . .	. . .	. . .
1989	82.0	. . .	85.0	. . .	. . .	. . .	. . .	. . .	. . .
1990	81.4	. . .	84.7	. . .	. . .	. . .	. . .	. . .	. . .
1991	80.3	. . .	83.8	. . .	. . .	. . .	. . .	. . .	. . .
1992	80.7	. . .	84.0	. . .	. . .	. . .	. . .	. . .	. . .
1993	80.2	. . .	83.5	. . .	. . .	. . .	. . .	. . .	. . .
1994	79.2	50.0	82.5	88.0	92.5	91.5	85.7	63.6	14.4
1995	79.1	50.2	82.4	86.2	92.9	91.3	85.6	62.4	15.8
1996	79.6	50.0	83.0	85.7	93.2	91.7	87.0	65.9	16.7
1997	80.1	47.4	84.1	88.1	93.5	91.9	87.8	68.4	17.3
1998	79.8	48.7	83.6	88.1	94.0	91.4	86.7	70.2	14.9
1999	79.8	50.1	83.5	88.1	93.9	92.2	86.2	68.6	18.2
2000	81.5	50.7	85.3	89.1	94.1	93.3	87.6	69.4	18.5
2001	81.0	52.2	84.3	86.8	93.4	92.7	86.7	68.6	16.8
2002	80.2	48.8	83.6	86.1	93.5	92.1	86.1	67.3	16.3
2003	80.1	40.9	84.1	86.2	93.6	92.9	85.4	68.8	17.4
2004	80.4	42.4	84.2	84.4	93.6	93.2	87.2	69.6	20.8
2005	80.1	41.9	84.0	84.1	93.3	93.1	87.7	69.3	20.1
Women									
1973	41.0	. . .	41.3	. . .	. . .	. . .	. . .	. . .	. . .
1974	42.4	. . .	42.7	. . .	. . .	. . .	. . .	. . .	. . .
1975	43.2	. . .	43.8	. . .	. . .	. . .	. . .	. . .	. . .
1976	44.3	. . .	44.6	. . .	. . .	. . .	. . .	. . .	. . .
1977	44.3	. . .	45.1	. . .	. . .	. . .	. . .	. . .	. . .
1978	46.6	. . .	47.2	. . .	. . .	. . .	. . .	. . .	. . .
1979	47.4	. . .	48.0	. . .	. . .	. . .	. . .	. . .	. . .
1980	47.4	. . .	48.5	. . .	. . .	. . .	. . .	. . .	. . .
1981	48.3	. . .	49.7	. . .	. . .	. . .	. . .	. . .	. . .
1982	48.1	. . .	49.3	. . .	. . .	. . .	. . .	. . .	. . .
1983	47.7	. . .	49.0	. . .	. . .	. . .	. . .	. . .	. . .
1984	49.6	. . .	50.5	. . .	. . .	. . .	. . .	. . .	. . .
1985	49.3	. . .	50.6	. . .	. . .	. . .	. . .	. . .	. . .
1986	50.1	. . .	51.7	. . .	. . .	. . .	. . .	. . .	. . .
1987	52.0	. . .	53.3	. . .	. . .	. . .	. . .	. . .	. . .
1988	53.2	. . .	54.2	. . .	. . .	. . .	. . .	. . .	. . .
1989	53.5	. . .	54.9	. . .	. . .	. . .	. . .	. . .	. . .
1990	53.1	. . .	54.8	. . .	. . .	. . .	. . .	. . .	. . .
1991	52.4	. . .	54.0	. . .	. . .	. . .	. . .	. . .	. . .
1992	52.8	. . .	54.3	. . .	. . .	. . .	. . .	. . .	. . .
1993	52.1	. . .	53.8	. . .	. . .	. . .	. . .	. . .	. . .
1994	52.9	38.7	54.4	57.9	60.5	66.4	61.4	38.1	7.9
1995	52.6	40.4	53.9	55.9	61.6	65.9	60.5	37.2	6.6
1996	53.4	36.5	55.2	59.2	62.0	67.0	62.7	40.5	6.9
1997	55.1	38.0	57.0	62.3	63.7	69.3	63.3	40.6	8.1
1998	55.6	42.4	57.1	62.2	64.5	67.9	64.7	41.9	6.6
1999	55.9	40.6	57.7	63.0	62.7	70.5	66.2	42.4	6.5
2000	57.5	41.4	59.3	65.0	65.3	69.9	68.5	41.2	7.7
2001	57.6	41.1	59.3	64.6	65.2	70.3	68.3	43.2	6.7
2002	57.6	38.8	59.5	65.0	65.8	69.5	66.3	46.1	8.5
2003	55.9	34.5	58.1	63.3	62.9	68.5	65.3	47.1	9.4
2004	56.1	33.7	58.4	62.9	62.9	68.7	67.9	47.8	9.8
2005	55.3	35.2	57.4	59.4	62.4	68.2	66.6	48.4	9.3

[2]May be of any race.
. . . = Not available.

Table 1-9. Employed and Unemployed Full- and Part-Time Workers, by Age, Sex, and Race, 1995–2005

(Thousands of people.)

Race, sex, age, and year	Employed[1]								Unemployed	
	Full-time workers				Part-time workers					
		At work				At work[2]				
	Total	35 hours or more	1 to 34 hours for economic or noneconomic reasons	Not at work	Total	For economic reasons	For noneconomic reasons	Not at work	Looking for full-time work	Looking for part-time work

ALL RACES

Both Sexes, 16 Years and Over

1995	101 679	87 736	9 924	4 020	23 220	3 215	18 443	1 562	5 909	1 495
1996	103 537	89 020	10 381	4 137	23 170	3 080	18 459	1 631	5 803	1 433
1997	106 334	92 399	9 922	4 013	23 224	2 826	18 856	1 542	5 395	1 344
1998	108 202	91 880	12 260	4 062	23 261	2 497	19 239	1 524	4 916	1 293
1999	110 302	96 276	10 079	3 947	23 186	2 216	19 509	1 461	4 669	1 211
2000	113 846	100 533	9 125	4 188	23 044	2 003	19 548	1 493	4 538	1 154
2001	113 573	99 047	10 464	4 061	23 361	2 297	19 494	1 570	5 546	1 254
2002	112 700	99 042	9 746	3 912	23 785	2 755	19 549	1 481	7 063	1 314
2003	113 324	99 539	9 841	3 944	24 412	3 184	19 702	1 525	7 361	1 413
2004	114 518	100 496	10 053	3 969	24 734	3 113	20 109	1 513	6 762	1 388
2005	117 016	103 044	9 983	3 990	24 714	2 963	20 229	1 522	6 175	1 415

Both Sexes, 20 Years and Over

1995	99 651	86 043	9 643	3 965	18 830	2 853	14 613	1 365	5 253	806
1996	101 496	87 344	10 070	4 083	18 712	2 733	14 556	1 423	5 157	773
1997	104 168	90 613	9 601	3 954	18 729	2 500	14 872	1 357	4 748	719
1998	105 882	89 966	11 915	4 001	18 530	2 197	15 007	1 326	4 332	672
1999	107 917	94 270	9 754	3 893	18 399	1 939	15 187	1 273	4 094	624
2000	111 353	98 439	8 787	4 127	18 348	1 747	15 297	1 304	3 978	632
2001	111 323	97 161	10 156	4 006	18 870	2 013	15 486	1 371	4 956	682
2002	110 679	97 342	9 474	3 862	19 475	2 448	15 704	1 322	6 395	730
2003	111 578	98 087	9 587	3 904	20 239	2 875	16 001	1 363	6 705	818
2004	112 747	99 034	9 789	3 924	20 598	2 817	16 436	1 345	6 178	764
2005	115 206	101 534	9 729	3 942	20 546	2 698	16 489	1 359	5 619	786

Men, 16 Years and Over

1995	59 936	52 833	5 120	1 984	7 441	1 401	5 626	414	3 374	609
1996	60 762	53 425	5 290	2 047	7 445	1 322	5 692	431	3 276	604
1997	62 258	55 216	5 040	2 001	7 427	1 187	5 821	418	3 012	564
1998	63 189	55 080	6 136	1 973	7 504	1 063	6 026	416	2 707	559
1999	63 930	57 034	4 971	1 924	7 516	946	6 178	392	2 548	518
2000	65 930	59 345	4 555	2 030	7 375	856	6 105	414	2 486	488
2001	65 623	58 386	5 241	1 996	7 573	1 021	6 129	424	3 144	546
2002	65 205	58 318	4 971	1 916	7 697	1 246	6 050	401	4 029	568
2003	65 379	58 428	5 023	1 927	7 953	1 473	6 056	423	4 291	615
2004	66 444	59 363	5 148	1 933	8 080	1 405	6 258	417	3 843	613
2005	67 858	60 825	5 096	1 937	8 115	1 316	6 370	429	3 444	616

Men, 20 Years and Over

1995	58 707	51 793	4 960	1 955	5 377	1 228	3 828	322	2 988	251
1996	59 543	52 411	5 117	2 015	5 354	1 155	3 859	341	2 899	248
1997	60 974	54 148	4 857	1 969	5 310	1 023	3 944	343	2 644	239
1998	61 837	53 947	5 950	1 940	5 297	925	4 050	322	2 366	214
1999	62 514	55 827	4 790	1 897	5 247	809	4 127	311	2 222	211
2000	64 464	58 095	4 370	2 000	5 170	733	4 109	328	2 162	214
2001	64 311	57 273	5 072	1 966	5 465	881	4 253	331	2 801	239
2002	64 006	57 302	4 815	1 889	5 728	1 093	4 299	336	3 642	254
2003	64 364	57 580	4 879	1 905	6 051	1 314	4 388	348	3 906	302
2004	65 377	58 471	5 000	1 906	6 196	1 251	4 600	345	3 511	281
2005	66 803	59 934	4 955	1 914	6 247	1 182	4 705	360	3 118	274

Women, 16 Years and Over

1995	41 743	34 903	4 805	2 036	15 779	1 814	12 817	1 148	2 535	886
1996	42 776	35 594	5 091	2 090	15 725	1 758	12 767	1 200	2 527	829
1997	44 076	37 183	4 882	2 011	15 797	1 638	13 035	1 124	2 383	779
1998	45 014	36 800	6 124	2 090	15 757	1 435	13 214	1 108	2 210	734
1999	46 372	39 242	5 108	2 022	15 670	1 270	13 330	1 069	2 121	693
2000	47 916	41 188	4 570	2 158	15 670	1 147	13 443	1 080	2 052	666
2001	47 950	40 661	5 223	2 065	15 788	1 276	13 365	1 146	2 402	709
2002	47 494	40 723	4 775	1 996	16 088	1 509	13 498	1 080	3 034	747
2003	47 946	41 111	4 818	2 017	16 459	1 711	13 646	1 102	3 070	798
2004	48 073	41 133	4 905	2 036	16 654	1 708	13 851	1 096	2 919	775
2005	49 158	42 219	4 887	2 052	16 598	1 647	13 859	1 092	2 732	799

Note: Beginning in January 2004, data reflect revised population controls used in the household survey. See notes and definitions for information on historical comparability.

[1]Employed persons are classified as full- or part-time workers based on their usual weekly hours at all jobs, regardless of the number of hours they were at work during the reference week. Persons absent from work are also classified according to their usual status.
[2]Includes some persons at work 35 hours or more classified by their reason for working part time.

Table 1-9. Employed and Unemployed Full- and Part-Time Workers, by Age, Sex, and Race, 1995–2005
—Continued

(Thousands of people.)

Race, sex, age, and year	Employed[1]								Unemployed	
	Full-time workers				Part-time workers				Looking for full-time work	Looking for part-time work
		At work		Not at work		At work[2]		Not at work		
	Total	35 hours or more	1 to 34 hours for economic or noneconomic reasons		Total	For economic reasons	For noneconomic reasons			
ALL RACES										
Women, 20 Years and Over										
1995	40 943	34 250	4 683	2 010	13 453	1 623	10 785	1 043	2 265	554
1996	41 953	34 933	4 953	2 068	13 357	1 579	10 697	1 082	2 258	525
1997	43 194	36 465	4 744	1 985	13 419	1 477	10 927	1 015	2 105	480
1998	44 045	36 019	5 965	2 061	13 233	1 272	10 957	1 004	1 966	458
1999	45 403	38 443	4 964	1 996	13 152	1 131	11 059	962	1 872	413
2000	46 889	40 344	4 417	2 128	13 178	1 013	11 188	976	1 816	419
2001	47 012	39 889	5 083	2 040	13 405	1 132	11 233	1 040	2 155	444
2002	46 673	40 040	4 660	1 973	13 747	1 355	11 406	986	2 752	476
2003	47 215	40 507	4 708	2 000	14 188	1 560	11 613	1 015	2 799	515
2004	47 371	40 563	4 790	2 017	14 402	1 567	11 836	1 000	2 667	483
2005	48 403	41 600	4 774	2 028	14 299	1 516	11 784	999	2 501	512
WHITE[3]										
Men, 16 Years and Over										
1995	51 768	45 634	4 406	1 728	6 378	1 100	4 921	357	2 525	475
1996	52 527	46 208	4 547	1 772	6 361	1 046	4 941	374	2 426	470
1997	53 640	47 563	4 358	1 719	6 358	909	5 084	365	2 202	440
1998	54 206	47 239	5 257	1 709	6 398	829	5 209	360	1 999	432
1999	54 756	48 834	4 274	1 647	6 383	730	5 314	339	1 883	391
2000	56 068	50 434	3 896	1 738	6 221	656	5 213	351	1 798	379
2001	55 830	49 625	4 504	1 701	6 381	793	5 225	364	2 323	431
2002	55 369	49 459	4 267	1 644	6 480	980	5 150	350	3 017	443
2003	55 216	49 323	4 266	1 628	6 650	1 146	5 148	357	3 164	479
2004	55 926	49 891	4 396	1 638	6 786	1 092	5 331	363	2 805	477
2005	56 955	50 965	4 334	1 656	6 808	1 014	5 424	370	2 459	471
Men, 20 Years and Over										
1995	50 691	44 726	4 263	1 702	4 563	958	3 330	275	2 260	204
1996	51 442	45 300	4 397	1 745	4 534	907	3 330	297	2 167	197
1997	52 498	46 609	4 199	1 691	4 488	771	3 419	298	1 946	194
1998	53 017	46 240	5 095	1 682	4 483	716	3 487	280	1 756	164
1999	53 513	47 764	4 124	1 626	4 420	618	3 534	268	1 651	162
2000	54 778	49 335	3 733	1 710	4 341	558	3 505	278	1 566	165
2001	54 666	48 636	4 354	1 676	4 579	677	3 616	285	2 080	195
2002	54 333	48 581	4 133	1 619	4 790	857	3 640	293	2 743	200
2003	54 339	48 585	4 145	1 609	5 010	1 016	3 703	291	2 893	231
2004	55 005	49 124	4 267	1 614	5 154	961	3 895	299	2 567	217
2005	56 050	50 203	4 213	1 634	5 205	905	3 990	310	2 242	209
Women, 16 Years and Over										
1995	34 422	28 685	4 039	1 697	13 922	1 431	11 448	1 043	1 755	705
1996	35 057	29 124	4 196	1 737	13 863	1 388	11 398	1 077	1 749	656
1997	35 965	30 286	4 036	1 643	13 894	1 260	11 623	1 011	1 587	608
1998	36 553	29 792	5 039	1 722	13 774	1 089	11 695	990	1 481	572
1999	37 417	31 577	4 157	1 684	13 679	947	11 768	964	1 469	530
2000	38 438	32 942	3 729	1 767	13 698	867	11 870	961	1 422	521
2001	38 445	32 491	4 252	1 702	13 773	971	11 787	1 015	1 664	551
2002	38 152	32 623	3 896	1 633	14 011	1 152	11 903	956	2 084	595
2002	38 249	32 659	3 939	1 652	14 120	1 304	11 860	956	2 038	629
2004	38 240	32 555	4 018	1 667	14 287	1 280	12 038	969	1 968	597
2005	38 973	33 325	3 976	1 672	14 213	1 207	12 043	963	1 807	612
Women, 20 Years and Over										
1995	33 728	28 116	3 938	1 674	11 916	1 277	9 690	949	1 579	463
1996	34 350	28 553	4 078	1 719	11 814	1 243	9 598	973	1 570	427
1997	35 216	29 677	3 919	1 620	11 847	1 136	9 788	923	1 396	388
1998	35 738	29 130	4 910	1 698	11 604	953	9 749	902	1 318	370
1999	36 602	30 905	4 036	1 662	11 496	839	9 789	867	1 297	319
2000	37 585	32 242	3 600	1 743	11 560	754	9 935	872	1 256	339
2001	37 658	31 839	4 139	1 680	11 711	853	9 933	924	1 492	357
2002	37 467	32 049	3 803	1 615	11 981	1 029	10 079	873	1 888	381
2003	37 640	32 158	3 845	1 637	12 183	1 180	10 124	879	1 866	411
2004	37 663	32 085	3 927	1 652	12 377	1 166	10 326	885	1 795	377
2005	38 354	32 820	3 882	1 652	12 235	1 108	10 248	879	1 653	401

Note: Beginning in January 2004, data reflect revised population controls used in the household survey. See notes and definitions for information on historical comparability.

[1]Employed persons are classified as full- or part-time workers based on their usual weekly hours at all jobs, regardless of the number of hours they were at work during the reference week. Persons absent from work are also classified according to their usual status.
[2]Includes some persons at work 35 hours or more classified by their reason for working part time.
[3]Beginning in 2003, persons who selected this race group only; persons who selected more than one race group are not included. Prior to 2003, persons who reported more than one race group were included in the group they identified as their main race.

Table 1-9. Employed and Unemployed Full- and Part-Time Workers, by Age, Sex, and Race, 1995–2005 —Continued

(Thousands of people.)

Race, sex, age, and year	Employed[1]								Unemployed	
	Full-time workers				Part-time workers				Looking for full-time work	Looking for part-time work
		At work				At work[2]				
	Total	35 hours or more	1 to 34 hours for economic or noneconomic reasons	Not at work	Total	For economic reasons	For noneconomic reasons	Not at work		

BLACK[3]

Men, 16 Years and Over

Race, sex, age, and year	Total	35 hours or more	1 to 34 hours	Not at work	Total	For economic reasons	For noneconomic reasons	Not at work	Looking for full-time work	Looking for part-time work
1995	5 685	4 995	513	177	737	216	479	43	660	101
1996	5 723	4 971	547	206	733	199	494	40	705	103
1997	5 894	5 193	490	211	713	203	474	36	648	98
1998	6 148	5 322	637	189	723	168	520	34	572	99
1999	6 263	5 574	494	196	764	163	568	33	528	97
2000	6 350	5 704	445	202	732	144	548	41	542	78
2001	6 178	5 509	468	200	761	165	557	39	626	83
2002	6 194	5 541	480	173	765	188	546	30	749	86
2003	6 055	5 414	453	188	765	221	505	39	804	87
2004	6 177	5 538	460	179	736	205	499	32	763	98
2005	6 381	5 745	463	174	773	207	533	33	742	102

Men, 20 Years and Over

	Total	35 hours or more	1 to 34 hours	Not at work	Total	For economic reasons	For noneconomic reasons	Not at work	Looking for full-time work	Looking for part-time work
1995	5 582	4 906	502	175	554	193	326	36	558	35
1996	5 622	4 892	528	201	545	177	338	30	602	37
1997	5 790	5 111	471	208	535	179	326	30	549	35
1998	6 023	5 218	620	185	507	147	334	25	487	37
1999	6 140	5 477	471	192	561	142	392	27	446	35
2000	6 222	5 594	429	199	520	125	363	32	468	31
2001	6 069	5 417	455	197	558	145	382	31	542	31
2002	6 073	5 437	465	171	579	166	387	26	660	35
2003	5 980	5 355	439	185	607	201	372	34	717	43
2004	6 089	5 463	449	177	592	189	376	27	689	44
2005	6 287	5 662	452	174	614	189	397	28	655	44

Women, 16 Years and Over

	Total	35 hours or more	1 to 34 hours	Not at work	Total	For economic reasons	For noneconomic reasons	Not at work	Looking for full-time work	Looking for part-time work
1995	5 542	4 679	594	268	1 315	290	952	74	637	140
1996	5 776	4 785	710	280	1 310	289	933	88	652	132
1997	6 026	5 085	652	289	1 336	305	952	79	677	136
1998	6 281	5 166	828	288	1 404	278	1 045	81	624	131
1999	6 641	5 651	734	256	1 388	257	1 059	72	554	130
2000	6 780	5 862	632	287	1 293	211	1 005	77	515	106
2001	6 761	5 777	715	270	1 307	223	998	85	584	122
2002	6 588	5 685	640	263	1 326	259	991	76	744	114
2003	6 552	5 709	595	247	1 367	274	1 017	76	774	121
2004	6 597	5 740	611	246	1 399	306	1 022	71	744	124
2005	6 750	5 871	619	260	1 407	320	1 018	70	723	133

Women, 20 Years and Over

	Total	35 hours or more	1 to 34 hours	Not at work	Total	For economic reasons	For noneconomic reasons	Not at work	Looking for full-time work	Looking for part-time work
1995	5 469	4 623	580	266	1 087	263	757	66	553	66
1996	5 684	4 714	693	277	1 078	263	737	79	570	73
1997	5 921	5 001	634	286	1 092	273	755	64	603	70
1998	6 159	5 073	803	283	1 131	256	807	68	555	66
1999	6 519	5 549	717	252	1 145	230	850	65	486	75
2000	6 651	5 753	615	283	1 052	197	788	67	456	56
2001	6 647	5 684	695	268	1 094	203	816	75	521	61
2002	6 492	5 605	626	261	1 117	234	816	68	671	67
2003	6 468	5 639	583	246	1 168	257	842	69	698	75
2004	6 512	5 674	595	243	1 195	287	844	64	679	76
2005	6 653	5 789	606	258	1 222	298	861	63	660	74

Note: Beginning in January 2004, data reflect revised population controls used in the household survey. See notes and definitions for information on historical comparability.

[1]Employed persons are classified as full- or part-time workers based on their usual weekly hours at all jobs, regardless of the number of hours they were at work during the reference week. Persons absent from work are also classified according to their usual status.
[2]Includes some persons at work 35 hours or more classified by their reason for working part time.
[3]Beginning in 2003, persons who selected this race group only; persons who selected more than one race group are not included. Prior to 2003, persons who reported more than one race group were included in the group they identified as their main race.

Table 1-10. Persons Not in the Labor Force, by Age, Sex, and Desire and Availability for Work, 2000–2005

(Thousands of people.)

Category	Total 2000	Total 2001	16 to 24 years 2000	16 to 24 years 2001	25 to 54 years 2000	25 to 54 years 2001	55 years and over 2000	55 years and over 2001	Men 2000	Men 2001	Women 2000	Women 2001
TOTAL, NOT IN THE LABOR FORCE	69 994	71 359	11 702	12 347	19 263	19 814	39 029	39 198	25 684	26 396	44 310	44 962
Do Not Want a Job Now[1]	65 581	66 769	10 083	10 616	17 286	17 797	38 212	38 355	23 818	24 403	41 762	42 366
Want a Job[1]	4 413	4 590	1 619	1 730	1 977	2 017	817	842	1 866	1 993	2 547	2 597
Did not search for work in the previous year	2 705	2 731	899	939	1 164	1 150	642	642	1 076	1 134	1 628	1 597
Searched for work in the previous year[2]	1 708	1 859	720	791	813	867	175	201	789	859	919	1 000
Not available to work now	552	593	276	300	242	256	34	37	216	228	335	365
Available to work now	1 157	1 266	444	492	571	611	142	163	573	631	584	634
Reason not currently looking:												
Discouragement over job prospects[3]	266	321	79	104	148	170	40	47	164	192	102	129
Reasons other than discouragement	891	945	365	388	423	441	102	116	409	440	482	505
Family responsibilities	120	133	26	32	84	89	10	13	23	29	96	105
In school or training	184	203	157	172	27	30	1	1	97	111	88	92
Ill health or disability	96	96	15	16	58	56	22	25	49	45	47	51
Other[4]	491	513	167	168	254	266	69	77	240	255	251	257

Category	Total 2002	Total 2003	16 to 24 years 2002	16 to 24 years 2003	25 to 54 years 2002	25 to 54 years 2003	55 years and over 2002	55 years and over 2003	Men 2002	Men 2003	Women 2002	Women 2003
TOTAL, NOT IN THE LABOR FORCE	72 707	74 658	12 976	13 800	20 358	20 980	39 373	39 878	27 085	28 730	45 621	47 225
Do Not Want a Job Now[1]	68 029	69 932	11 254	12 079	18 286	18 857	38 489	38 996	24 994	26 565	43 035	44 538
Want a Job[1]	4 677	4 726	1 722	1 721	2 071	2 124	884	882	2 091	2 165	2 586	2 687
Did not search for work in the previous year	2 673	2 631	910	882	1 112	1 129	651	620	1 135	1 126	1 538	1 590
Searched for work in the previous year[2]	2 004	2 096	812	838	960	995	233	262	956	1 040	1 048	1 097
Not available to work now	565	564	272	274	252	248	41	43	227	230	338	333
Available to work now	1 439	1 531	540	565	708	747	191	220	729	809	710	765
Reason not currently looking:												
Discouragement over job prospects[3]	369	457	110	134	209	248	51	75	226	288	143	178
Reasons other than discouragement	1 070	1 075	430	431	499	499	141	145	503	521	567	587
Family responsibilities	150	153	31	37	99	94	20	22	34	38	116	119
In school or training	238	239	195	194	41	42	2	3	126	131	112	112
Ill health or disability	107	113	16	15	61	72	30	26	50	56	56	67
Other[4]	575	570	188	184	299	292	88	94	292	296	283	2

Category	Total 2004	Total 2005	16 to 24 years 2004	16 to 24 years 2005	25 to 54 years 2004	25 to 54 years 2005	55 years and over 2004	55 years and over 2005	Men 2004	Men 2005	Women 2004	Women 2005
TOTAL, NOT IN THE LABOR FORCE	75 956	76 762	14 151	14 383	21 288	21 403	40 517	40 976	28 730	29 119	47 225	47 643
Do Not Want a Job Now[1]	71 103	71 777	12 422	12 585	19 136	19 238	39 545	39 954	26 565	26 926	44 538	44 851
Want a Job[1]	4 852	4 985	1 729	1 798	2 152	2 165	971	1 022	2 165	2 193	2 687	2 792
Did not search for work in the previous year	2 715	2 841	886	963	1 145	1 163	684	715	1 126	1 173	1 590	1 668
Searched for work in the previous year[2]	2 137	2 144	843	836	1 006	1 002	288	307	1 040	1 020	1 097	1 124
Not available to work now	563	599	279	285	242	260	42	54	230	231	333	368
Available to work now	1 574	1 545	565	551	764	742	245	252	809	789	765	756
Reason not currently looking:												
Discouragement over job prospects[3]	466	436	142	141	240	217	84	78	288	260	178	176
Reasons other than discouragement	1 108	1 109	423	410	524	525	161	175	521	529	587	580
Family responsibilities	157	159	28	32	104	105	24	22	38	36	119	123
In school or training	244	217	199	179	43	35	2	2	131	118	112	99
Ill health or disability	123	119	18	16	71	69	35	34	56	64	67	55
Other[4]	584	614	178	182	306	316	100	116	296	311	288	302

Note: Beginning in January 2004, data reflect revised population controls used in the household survey. See notes and definitions for information on historical comparability.

[1]Includes some persons who were not asked if they wanted a job.
[2]Persons who had a job during the prior 12 months must have searched since the end of that job.
[3]Includes believes no work available, could not find work, lacks necessary schooling or training, employer thinks too young or old, and other types of discrimination.
[4]Includes those who did not actively look for work in the prior four weeks for reasons such as childcare and transportation problems, as well as a small number for whom reason for nonparticipation was not ascertained.

EMPLOYMENT

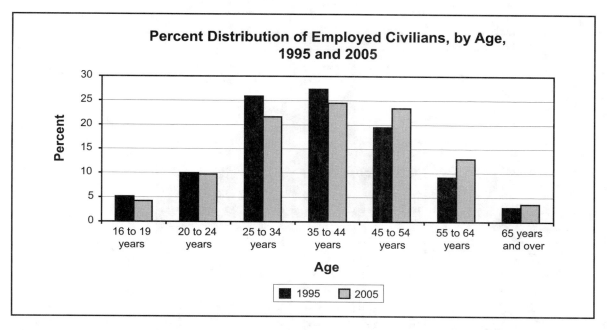

The aging of the working population is evidenced by in the figure above. From 1995 to 2005, the proportion of employed persons age 16 to 44 years declined, while the percentage of employed persons age 45 years and over increased. Workers age 45 years and over made up 40 percent of employed civilians, up from 32 percent in 1995. (See Table 1-11.)

OTHER HIGHLIGHTS

- Total employment increased 1.8 percent from 2004 to 2005. The largest percentage increase was in the 55- to 64-year-old age group (5.9 percent), followed closely by the 65 years and over age group (5.7 percent). (See Table 1-11.)

- There were declines in the number of employed civilians in two age groups from 1995 to 2005. The number of employed civilians age 16 to 19 years dropped by over 400,000 and the number of employed civilians age 25 to 34 years decreased by nearly 1.7 million. (See Table 1-11.)

- The Hispanic work force is younger than average: 70 percent of the total number of employed Hispanics belonged in the 20- to 44-year-old age group in 2005. In contrast, only 56 percent of all workers were between 20 and 44 years of age. (See Table 1-11.)

- In 2005, 58 percent of management, business, and financial occupations employees were men and 42 percent were women. The reverse was true for professional and related occupations, which included teachers; 56 percent were women and 44 percent were men. Service occupations accounted for 20 percent of female employment and 13 percent of male employment. (See Table 1-13.)

- Employment in the construction industry rose 4 percent in 2005 and provided 17 percent of the total employment increase. Retail trade and health care services also contributed to the increase in employment, while employment in manufacturing declined slightly. (See Table 1-14.)

- The number of employed persons age 25 years and over increased 15 percent from 1995 to 2005, while the employment of those with a bachelor's degree or higher increased 32 percent during this period. (See Table 1-16.)

Table 1-11. Employed Civilians, by Age, Sex, Race, and Hispanic Origin, 1948–2005

(Thousands of people.)

Race, Hispanic origin, sex, and year	16 years and over	16 to 19 years			20 years and over						
		Total	16 to 17 years	18 to 19 years	Total	20 to 24 years	25 to 34 years	35 to 44 years	45 to 54 years	55 to 64 years	65 years and over
ALL RACES											
Both Sexes											
1948	58 343	4 026	1 600	2 426	54 318	6 937	13 801	13 050	10 624	7 103	2 804
1949	57 651	3 712	1 466	2 246	53 940	6 660	13 639	13 108	10 636	7 042	2 864
1950	58 918	3 703	1 433	2 270	55 218	6 746	13 917	13 424	10 966	7 265	2 899
1951	59 961	3 767	1 575	2 192	56 196	6 321	14 233	13 746	11 421	7 558	2 917
1952	60 250	3 719	1 626	2 092	56 536	5 572	14 515	14 058	11 687	7 785	2 919
1953	61 179	3 720	1 577	2 142	57 460	5 225	14 519	14 774	11 969	7 806	3 166
1954	60 109	3 475	1 422	2 053	56 634	4 971	14 190	14 541	11 976	7 895	3 060
1955	62 170	3 642	1 500	2 143	58 528	5 270	14 481	14 879	12 556	8 158	3 185
1956	63 799	3 818	1 647	2 171	59 983	5 545	14 407	15 218	12 978	8 519	3 314
1957	64 071	3 778	1 613	2 167	60 291	5 641	14 253	15 348	13 320	8 553	3 179
1958	63 036	3 582	1 519	2 063	59 454	5 571	13 675	15 157	13 448	8 559	3 045
1959	64 630	3 838	1 670	2 168	60 791	5 870	13 709	15 454	13 915	8 822	3 023
1960	65 778	4 129	1 770	2 360	61 648	6 119	13 630	15 598	14 238	8 989	3 073
1961	65 746	4 108	1 621	2 486	61 638	6 227	13 429	15 552	14 320	9 120	2 987
1962	66 702	4 195	1 607	2 588	62 508	6 446	13 311	15 901	14 491	9 346	3 013
1963	67 762	4 255	1 751	2 504	63 508	6 815	13 318	16 114	14 749	9 596	2 915
1964	69 305	4 516	2 013	2 503	64 789	7 303	13 449	16 166	15 094	9 804	2 973
1965	71 088	5 036	2 075	2 962	66 052	7 702	13 704	16 294	15 320	10 028	3 005
1966	72 895	5 721	2 269	3 452	67 178	7 964	14 017	16 312	15 615	10 310	2 961
1967	74 372	5 682	2 334	3 348	68 690	8 499	14 575	16 281	15 789	10 536	3 011
1968	75 920	5 781	2 403	3 377	70 141	8 762	15 265	16 220	16 083	10 745	3 065
1969	77 902	6 117	2 573	3 543	71 785	9 319	15 883	16 100	16 410	10 919	3 155
1970	78 678	6 144	2 598	3 546	72 534	9 731	16 318	15 922	16 473	10 974	3 118
1971	79 367	6 208	2 596	3 613	73 158	10 201	16 781	15 675	16 451	11 009	3 040
1972	82 153	6 746	2 787	3 959	75 407	10 999	18 082	15 822	16 457	11 044	3 003
1973	85 064	7 271	3 032	4 239	77 793	11 839	19 509	16 041	16 553	10 966	2 886
1974	86 794	7 448	3 111	4 338	79 347	12 101	20 610	16 203	16 633	10 964	2 835
1975	85 846	7 104	2 941	4 162	78 744	11 885	21 087	15 953	16 190	10 827	2 801
1976	88 752	7 336	2 972	4 363	81 416	12 570	22 493	16 468	16 224	10 912	2 747
1977	92 017	7 688	3 138	4 550	84 329	13 196	23 850	17 157	16 212	11 126	2 787
1978	96 048	8 070	3 330	4 739	87 979	13 887	25 281	18 128	16 338	11 400	2 946
1979	98 824	8 083	3 340	4 743	90 741	14 327	26 492	18 981	16 357	11 585	2 999
1980	99 303	7 710	3 106	4 605	91 593	14 087	27 204	19 523	16 234	11 586	2 960
1981	100 397	7 225	2 866	4 359	93 172	14 122	28 180	20 145	16 255	11 525	2 945
1982	99 526	6 549	2 505	4 044	92 978	13 690	28 149	20 879	15 923	11 414	2 923
1983	100 834	6 342	2 320	4 022	94 491	13 722	28 756	21 960	15 812	11 315	2 927
1984	105 005	6 444	2 404	4 040	98 562	14 207	30 348	23 598	16 178	11 395	2 835
1985	107 150	6 434	2 492	3 941	100 716	13 980	31 208	24 732	16 509	11 474	2 813
1986	109 597	6 472	2 622	3 850	103 125	13 790	32 201	25 861	16 949	11 405	2 919
1987	112 440	6 640	2 736	3 905	105 800	13 524	33 105	27 179	17 487	11 465	3 041
1988	114 968	6 805	2 713	4 092	108 164	13 244	33 574	28 269	18 447	11 433	3 197
1989	117 342	6 759	2 588	4 172	110 582	12 962	34 045	29 443	19 279	11 499	3 355
1990	118 793	6 581	2 410	4 171	112 213	13 401	33 935	30 817	19 525	11 189	3 346
1991	117 718	5 906	2 202	3 704	111 812	12 975	33 061	31 593	19 882	11 001	3 300
1992	118 492	5 669	2 128	3 540	112 824	12 872	32 667	31 923	21 022	10 998	3 341
1993	120 259	5 805	2 226	3 579	114 455	12 840	32 385	32 666	22 175	11 058	3 331
1994	123 060	6 161	2 510	3 651	116 899	12 758	32 286	33 599	23 348	11 228	3 681
1995	124 900	6 419	2 573	3 846	118 481	12 443	32 356	34 202	24 378	11 435	3 666
1996	126 708	6 500	2 646	3 853	120 208	12 138	32 077	35 051	25 514	11 739	3 690
1997	129 558	6 661	2 648	4 012	122 897	12 380	31 809	35 908	26 744	12 296	3 761
1998	131 463	7 051	2 762	4 289	124 413	12 557	31 394	36 278	27 587	12 872	3 725
1999	133 488	7 172	2 793	4 379	126 316	12 891	30 865	36 728	28 635	13 315	3 882
2000	136 891	7 189	2 759	4 431	129 701	13 229	31 549	36 433	30 310	14 002	4 179
2001	136 933	6 740	2 558	4 182	130 194	13 348	30 863	36 049	31 036	14 645	4 253
2002	136 485	6 332	2 330	4 002	130 154	13 351	30 306	35 235	31 281	15 674	4 306
2003	137 736	5 919	2 312	3 607	131 817	13 433	30 383	34 881	31 914	16 598	4 608
2004	139 252	5 907	2 193	3 714	133 345	13 723	30 423	34 580	32 469	17 331	4 819
2005	141 730	5 978	2 284	3 694	135 752	13 792	30 680	34 630	33 207	18 349	5 094

Table 1-11. Employed Civilians, by Age, Sex, Race, and Hispanic Origin, 1948–2005—*Continued*

(Thousands of people.)

Race, Hispanic origin, sex, and year	16 years and over	16 to 19 years			20 years and over						
		Total	16 to 17 years	18 to 19 years	Total	20 to 24 years	25 to 34 years	35 to 44 years	45 to 54 years	55 to 64 years	65 years and over
ALL RACES											
Men											
1948	41 725	2 344	996	1 348	39 382	4 349	10 038	9 363	7 742	5 587	2 303
1949	40 925	2 124	911	1 213	38 803	4 197	9 879	9 308	7 661	5 438	2 329
1950	41 578	2 186	909	1 277	39 394	4 255	10 060	9 445	7 790	5 508	2 336
1951	41 780	2 156	979	1 177	39 626	3 780	10 134	9 607	8 012	5 711	2 382
1952	41 682	2 107	985	1 121	39 578	3 183	10 352	9 753	8 144	5 804	2 343
1953	42 430	2 136	976	1 159	40 296	2 901	10 500	10 229	8 374	5 808	2 483
1954	41 619	1 985	881	1 104	39 634	2 724	10 254	10 082	8 330	5 830	2 414
1955	42 621	2 095	936	1 159	40 526	2 973	10 453	10 267	8 553	5 857	2 424
1956	43 379	2 164	1 008	1 156	41 216	3 245	10 337	10 385	8 732	6 004	2 512
1957	43 357	2 115	987	1 130	41 239	3 346	10 222	10 427	8 851	6 002	2 394
1958	42 423	2 012	948	1 064	40 411	3 293	9 790	10 291	8 828	5 955	2 254
1959	43 466	2 198	1 015	1 183	41 267	3 597	9 862	10 492	9 048	6 058	2 210
1960	43 904	2 361	1 090	1 271	41 543	3 754	9 759	10 552	9 182	6 105	2 191
1961	43 656	2 315	989	1 325	41 342	3 795	9 591	10 505	9 195	6 155	2 098
1962	44 177	2 362	990	1 372	41 815	3 898	9 475	10 711	9 333	6 260	2 138
1963	44 657	2 406	1 073	1 334	42 251	4 118	9 431	10 801	9 478	6 385	2 038
1964	45 474	2 587	1 242	1 345	42 886	4 370	9 531	10 832	9 637	6 478	2 039
1965	46 340	2 918	1 285	1 634	43 422	4 583	9 611	10 837	9 792	6 542	2 057
1966	46 919	3 253	1 389	1 863	43 668	4 599	9 709	10 764	9 904	6 668	2 024
1967	47 479	3 186	1 417	1 769	44 294	4 809	9 988	10 674	9 990	6 774	2 058
1968	48 114	3 255	1 453	1 802	44 859	4 812	10 405	10 554	10 102	6 893	2 093
1969	48 818	3 430	1 526	1 904	45 388	5 012	10 736	10 401	10 187	6 931	2 122
1970	48 990	3 409	1 504	1 905	45 581	5 237	10 936	10 216	10 170	6 928	2 094
1971	49 390	3 478	1 510	1 968	45 912	5 593	11 218	10 028	10 139	6 916	2 019
1972	50 896	3 765	1 598	2 167	47 130	6 138	11 884	10 088	10 139	6 929	1 953
1973	52 349	4 039	1 721	2 318	48 310	6 655	12 617	10 126	10 197	6 857	1 856
1974	53 024	4 103	1 744	2 359	48 922	6 739	13 119	10 135	10 181	6 880	1 869
1975	51 857	3 839	1 621	2 219	48 018	6 484	13 205	9 891	9 902	6 722	1 811
1976	53 138	3 947	1 626	2 321	49 190	6 915	13 869	10 069	9 881	6 724	1 732
1977	54 728	4 174	1 733	2 441	50 555	7 232	14 483	10 399	9 832	6 848	1 761
1978	56 479	4 336	1 800	2 535	52 143	7 559	15 124	10 845	9 806	6 954	1 855
1979	57 607	4 300	1 799	2 501	53 308	7 791	15 688	11 202	9 735	7 015	1 876
1980	57 186	4 085	1 672	2 412	53 101	7 532	15 832	11 355	9 548	6 999	1 835
1981	57 397	3 815	1 526	2 289	53 582	7 504	16 266	11 613	9 478	6 909	1 812
1982	56 271	3 379	1 307	2 072	52 891	7 197	16 002	11 902	9 234	6 781	1 776
1983	56 787	3 300	1 213	2 087	53 487	7 232	16 216	12 450	9 133	6 686	1 770
1984	59 091	3 322	1 244	2 078	55 769	7 571	17 166	13 309	9 326	6 694	1 703
1985	59 891	3 328	1 300	2 029	56 562	7 339	17 564	13 800	9 411	6 753	1 695
1986	60 892	3 323	1 352	1 971	57 569	7 250	18 092	14 266	9 554	6 654	1 753
1987	62 107	3 381	1 393	1 988	58 726	7 058	18 487	14 898	9 750	6 682	1 850
1988	63 273	3 492	1 403	2 089	59 781	6 918	18 702	15 457	10 201	6 591	1 911
1989	64 315	3 477	1 327	2 150	60 837	6 799	18 952	16 002	10 569	6 548	1 968
1990	65 104	3 427	1 254	2 173	61 678	7 151	18 779	16 771	10 690	6 378	1 909
1991	64 223	3 044	1 135	1 909	61 178	6 909	18 265	17 086	10 813	6 245	1 860
1992	64 440	2 944	1 096	1 848	61 496	6 819	17 966	17 230	11 365	6 173	1 943
1993	65 349	2 994	1 155	1 839	62 355	6 805	17 877	17 665	11 927	6 166	1 916
1994	66 450	3 156	1 288	1 868	63 294	6 771	17 741	18 111	12 439	6 142	2 089
1995	67 377	3 292	1 316	1 977	64 085	6 665	17 709	18 374	12 958	6 272	2 108
1996	68 207	3 310	1 318	1 992	64 897	6 429	17 527	18 816	13 483	6 470	2 172
1997	69 685	3 401	1 355	2 045	66 284	6 548	17 338	19 327	14 107	6 735	2 229
1998	70 693	3 558	1 398	2 161	67 135	6 638	17 097	19 634	14 544	7 052	2 171
1999	71 446	3 685	1 437	2 249	67 761	6 729	16 694	19 811	14 991	7 274	2 263
2000	73 305	3 671	1 394	2 276	69 634	6 974	17 241	19 537	15 871	7 606	2 406
2001	73 196	3 420	1 268	2 151	69 776	6 952	16 915	19 305	16 268	7 900	2 437
2002	72 903	3 169	1 130	2 040	69 734	6 978	16 573	18 932	16 419	8 378	2 455
2003	73 332	2 917	1 115	1 802	70 415	7 065	16 670	18 774	16 588	8 733	2 585
2004	74 524	2 952	1 037	1 915	71 572	7 246	16 818	18 700	16 951	9 174	2 683
2005	75 973	2 923	1 067	1 855	73 050	7 279	16 993	18 780	17 429	9 714	2 857

Table 1-11. Employed Civilians, by Age, Sex, Race, and Hispanic Origin, 1948–2005—*Continued*

(Thousands of people.)

Race, Hispanic origin, sex, and year	16 years and over	16 to 19 years			20 years and over						
		Total	16 to 17 years	18 to 19 years	Total	20 to 24 years	25 to 34 years	35 to 44 years	45 to 54 years	55 to 64 years	65 years and over
ALL RACES											
Women											
1948	16 617	1 682	604	1 078	14 936	2 588	3 763	3 687	2 882	1 516	501
1949	16 723	1 588	555	1 033	15 137	2 463	3 760	3 800	2 975	1 604	535
1950	17 340	1 517	524	993	15 824	2 491	3 857	3 979	3 176	1 757	563
1951	18 181	1 611	596	1 015	16 570	2 541	4 099	4 139	3 409	1 847	535
1952	18 568	1 612	641	971	16 958	2 389	4 163	4 305	3 543	1 981	576
1953	18 749	1 584	601	983	17 164	2 324	4 019	4 545	3 595	1 998	683
1954	18 490	1 490	541	949	17 000	2 247	3 936	4 459	3 646	2 065	646
1955	19 551	1 547	564	984	18 002	2 297	4 028	4 612	4 003	2 301	761
1956	20 419	1 654	639	1 015	18 767	2 300	4 070	4 833	4 246	2 515	802
1957	20 714	1 663	626	1 037	19 052	2 295	4 031	4 921	4 469	2 551	785
1958	20 613	1 570	571	999	19 043	2 278	3 885	4 866	4 620	2 604	791
1959	21 164	1 640	655	985	19 524	2 273	3 847	4 962	4 867	2 764	813
1960	21 874	1 768	680	1 089	20 105	2 365	3 871	5 046	5 056	2 884	882
1961	22 090	1 793	632	1 161	20 296	2 432	3 838	5 047	5 125	2 965	889
1962	22 525	1 833	617	1 216	20 693	2 548	3 836	5 190	5 158	3 086	875
1963	23 105	1 849	678	1 170	21 257	2 697	3 887	5 313	5 271	3 211	877
1964	23 831	1 929	771	1 158	21 903	2 933	3 918	5 334	5 457	3 326	934
1965	24 748	2 118	790	1 328	22 630	3 119	4 093	5 457	5 528	3 486	948
1966	25 976	2 468	880	1 589	23 510	3 365	4 308	5 548	5 711	3 642	937
1967	26 893	2 496	917	1 579	24 397	3 690	4 587	5 607	5 799	3 762	953
1968	27 807	2 526	950	1 575	25 281	3 950	4 860	5 666	5 981	3 852	972
1969	29 084	2 687	1 047	1 639	26 397	4 307	5 147	5 699	6 223	3 988	1 033
1970	29 688	2 735	1 094	1 641	26 952	4 494	5 382	5 706	6 303	4 046	1 023
1971	29 976	2 730	1 086	1 645	27 246	4 609	5 563	5 647	6 313	4 093	1 021
1972	31 257	2 980	1 188	1 792	28 276	4 861	6 197	5 734	6 318	4 115	1 051
1973	32 715	3 231	1 310	1 920	29 484	5 184	6 893	5 915	6 356	4 109	1 029
1974	33 769	3 345	1 367	1 978	30 424	5 363	7 492	6 068	6 451	4 084	966
1975	33 989	3 263	1 320	1 943	30 726	5 401	7 882	6 061	6 288	4 105	989
1976	35 615	3 389	1 346	2 043	32 226	5 655	8 624	6 400	6 343	4 188	1 017
1977	37 289	3 514	1 403	2 110	33 775	5 965	9 367	6 758	6 380	4 279	1 027
1978	39 569	3 734	1 530	2 204	35 836	6 328	10 157	7 282	6 532	4 446	1 091
1979	41 217	3 783	1 541	2 242	37 434	6 538	10 802	7 779	6 622	4 569	1 124
1980	42 117	3 625	1 433	2 192	38 492	6 555	11 370	8 168	6 686	4 587	1 125
1981	43 000	3 411	1 340	2 070	39 590	6 618	11 914	8 532	6 777	4 616	1 133
1982	43 256	3 170	1 198	1 972	40 086	6 492	12 147	8 977	6 689	4 634	1 147
1983	44 047	3 043	1 107	1 935	41 004	6 490	12 540	9 510	6 678	4 629	1 157
1984	45 915	3 122	1 161	1 962	42 793	6 636	13 182	10 289	6 852	4 700	1 133
1985	47 259	3 105	1 193	1 913	44 154	6 640	13 644	10 933	7 097	4 721	1 118
1986	48 706	3 149	1 270	1 879	45 556	6 540	14 109	11 595	7 395	4 751	1 165
1987	50 334	3 260	1 343	1 917	47 074	6 466	14 617	12 281	7 737	4 783	1 191
1988	51 696	3 313	1 310	2 003	48 383	6 326	14 872	12 811	8 246	4 841	1 286
1989	53 027	3 282	1 261	2 021	49 745	6 163	15 093	13 440	8 711	4 950	1 388
1990	53 689	3 154	1 156	1 998	50 535	6 250	15 155	14 046	8 835	4 811	1 437
1991	53 496	2 862	1 067	1 794	50 634	6 066	14 796	14 507	9 069	4 756	1 440
1992	54 052	2 724	1 032	1 692	51 328	6 053	14 701	14 693	9 657	4 825	1 398
1993	54 910	2 811	1 071	1 740	52 099	6 035	14 508	15 002	10 248	4 892	1 414
1994	56 610	3 005	1 222	1 783	53 606	5 987	14 545	15 488	10 908	5 085	1 592
1995	57 523	3 127	1 258	1 869	54 396	5 779	14 647	15 828	11 421	5 163	1 558
1996	58 501	3 190	1 328	1 862	55 311	5 709	14 549	16 235	12 031	5 269	1 518
1997	59 873	3 260	1 293	1 967	56 613	5 831	14 471	16 581	12 637	5 561	1 532
1998	60 771	3 493	1 364	2 128	57 278	5 919	14 298	16 644	13 043	5 820	1 554
1999	62 042	3 487	1 357	2 130	58 555	6 163	14 171	16 917	13 644	6 041	1 619
2000	63 586	3 519	1 364	2 154	60 067	6 255	14 308	16 897	14 438	6 396	1 773
2001	63 737	3 320	1 289	2 031	60 417	6 396	13 948	16 744	14 768	6 745	1 815
2002	63 582	3 162	1 200	1 962	60 420	6 374	13 733	16 303	14 863	7 296	1 851
2003	64 404	3 002	1 197	1 805	61 402	6 367	13 714	16 106	15 326	7 866	2 023
2004	64 728	2 955	1 156	1 799	61 773	6 477	13 605	15 880	15 518	8 157	2 135
2005	65 757	3 055	1 217	1 838	62 702	6 513	13 687	15 850	15 779	8 635	2 238

Table 1-11. Employed Civilians, by Age, Sex, Race, and Hispanic Origin, 1948–2005—*Continued*

(Thousands of people.)

Race, Hispanic origin, sex, and year	16 years and over	16 to 19 years			20 years and over						
		Total	16 to 17 years	18 to 19 years	Total	20 to 24 years	25 to 34 years	35 to 44 years	45 to 54 years	55 to 64 years	65 years and over
WHITE[1]											
Both Sexes											
1954	53 957	3 078	1 257	1 822	50 879	4 358	12 616	13 000	10 811	7 262	2 831
1955	55 833	3 225	1 330	1 896	52 608	4 637	12 855	13 327	11 322	7 510	2 957
1956	57 269	3 389	1 465	1 922	53 880	4 897	12 748	13 637	11 706	7 822	3 068
1957	57 465	3 374	1 442	1 931	54 091	4 952	12 619	13 716	12 009	7 829	2 951
1958	56 613	3 216	1 370	1 847	53 397	4 908	12 128	13 571	12 113	7 849	2 828
1959	58 006	3 475	1 520	1 955	54 531	5 138	12 144	13 830	12 552	8 063	2 805
1960	58 850	3 700	1 598	2 103	55 150	5 331	12 021	13 930	12 820	8 192	2 855
1961	58 913	3 693	1 472	2 220	55 220	5 460	11 835	13 905	12 906	8 335	2 778
1962	59 698	3 774	1 447	2 327	55 924	5 676	11 703	14 173	13 066	8 511	2 795
1963	60 622	3 851	1 600	2 250	56 771	6 036	11 689	14 341	13 304	8 718	2 683
1964	61 922	4 076	1 846	2 230	57 846	6 444	11 794	14 380	13 596	8 916	2 717
1965	63 446	4 562	1 892	2 670	58 884	6 752	11 992	14 473	13 804	9 116	2 748
1966	65 021	5 176	2 052	3 124	59 845	6 986	12 268	14 449	14 072	9 356	2 713
1967	66 361	5 114	2 121	2 993	61 247	7 493	12 763	14 429	14 224	9 596	2 746
1968	67 750	5 195	2 193	3 002	62 555	7 687	13 410	14 386	14 487	9 781	2 804
1969	69 518	5 508	2 347	3 161	64 010	8 182	13 935	14 270	14 788	9 947	2 888
1970	70 217	5 571	2 386	3 185	64 645	8 559	14 326	14 092	14 854	9 979	2 835
1971	70 878	5 670	2 404	3 266	65 208	9 000	14 713	13 858	14 843	10 014	2 780
1972	73 370	6 173	2 581	3 592	67 197	9 718	15 904	13 940	14 845	10 077	2 714
1973	75 708	6 623	2 806	3 816	69 086	10 424	17 099	14 083	14 886	9 983	2 610
1974	77 184	6 796	2 881	3 916	70 388	10 676	18 040	14 196	14 948	9 958	2 568
1975	76 411	6 487	2 721	3 770	69 924	10 546	18 485	13 979	14 555	9 827	2 533
1976	78 853	6 724	2 762	3 962	72 129	11 119	19 662	14 407	14 549	9 923	2 470
1977	81 700	7 068	2 926	4 142	74 632	11 696	20 844	14 984	14 483	10 107	2 518
1978	84 936	7 367	3 085	4 282	77 569	12 251	22 008	15 809	14 550	10 311	2 642
1979	87 259	7 356	3 079	4 278	79 904	12 594	23 033	16 578	14 522	10 477	2 699
1980	87 715	7 021	2 861	4 161	80 694	12 405	23 653	17 071	14 405	10 475	2 684
1981	88 709	6 588	2 645	3 943	82 121	12 477	24 551	17 617	14 414	10 386	2 676
1982	87 903	5 984	2 317	3 667	81 918	12 097	24 531	18 268	14 083	10 283	2 656
1983	88 893	5 799	2 156	3 643	83 094	12 138	24 955	19 194	13 961	10 169	2 678
1984	92 120	5 836	2 209	3 627	86 284	12 451	26 235	20 552	14 239	10 227	2 580
1985	93 736	5 768	2 270	3 498	87 968	12 235	26 945	21 552	14 459	10 247	2 530
1986	95 660	5 792	2 386	3 406	89 869	12 027	27 746	22 515	14 750	10 176	2 654
1987	97 789	5 898	2 468	3 431	91 890	11 748	28 429	23 596	15 216	10 164	2 738
1988	99 812	6 030	2 424	3 606	93 782	11 438	28 796	24 468	16 054	10 153	2 874
1989	101 584	5 946	2 278	3 668	95 638	11 084	29 091	25 442	16 775	10 223	3 024
1990	102 261	5 779	2 141	3 638	96 481	11 498	28 773	26 282	16 933	9 960	3 035
1991	101 182	5 216	1 971	3 246	95 966	11 116	27 989	26 883	17 269	9 719	2 990
1992	101 669	4 985	1 904	3 081	96 684	11 031	27 552	27 097	18 285	9 701	3 019
1993	103 045	5 113	1 990	3 123	97 932	10 931	27 274	27 645	19 273	9 772	3 037
1994	105 190	5 398	2 210	3 188	99 792	10 736	27 101	28 442	20 247	9 912	3 354
1995	106 490	5 593	2 273	3 320	100 897	10 400	27 014	28 951	21 127	10 070	3 335
1996	107 808	5 667	2 325	3 343	102 141	10 149	26 678	29 566	22 071	10 313	3 364
1997	109 856	5 807	2 341	3 466	104 049	10 362	26 294	30 137	23 061	10 785	3 411
1998	110 931	6 089	2 436	3 653	104 842	10 512	25 729	30 320	23 662	11 272	3 347
1999	112 235	6 204	2 435	3 769	106 032	10 716	25 113	30 548	24 507	11 657	3 491
2000	114 424	6 160	2 383	3 777	108 264	10 944	25 500	30 151	25 762	12 169	3 738
2001	114 430	5 817	2 224	3 593	108 613	11 054	24 948	29 793	26 301	12 743	3 774
2002	114 013	5 441	2 037	3 404	108 572	11 096	24 568	29 049	26 401	13 630	3 828
2003	114 235	5 064	1 999	3 065	109 171	11 052	24 399	28 501	26 762	14 375	4 083
2004	115 239	5 039	1 895	3 145	110 199	11 233	24 337	28 176	27 228	14 965	4 260
2005	116 949	5 105	1 999	3 106	111 844	11 231	24 443	28 102	27 801	15 788	4 480

[1]Beginning in 2003, persons who selected this race group only; persons who selected more than one race group are not included. Prior to 2003, persons who reported more than one race group were included in the group they identified as the main race.

Table 1-11. Employed Civilians, by Age, Sex, Race, and Hispanic Origin, 1948–2005—*Continued*

(Thousands of people.)

Race, Hispanic origin, sex, and year	16 years and over	16 to 19 years			20 years and over						
		Total	16 to 17 years	18 to 19 years	Total	20 to 24 years	25 to 34 years	35 to 44 years	45 to 54 years	55 to 64 years	65 years and over
WHITE[1]											
Men											
1954	37 846	1 723	771	953	36 123	2 394	9 287	9 175	7 614	5 412	2 241
1955	38 719	1 824	821	1 004	36 895	2 607	9 461	9 351	7 792	5 431	2 254
1956	39 368	1 893	890	1 002	37 475	2 850	9 330	9 449	7 950	5 559	2 336
1957	39 349	1 865	874	990	37 484	2 930	9 226	9 480	8 067	5 542	2 234
1958	38 591	1 783	852	932	36 808	2 896	8 861	9 386	8 061	5 501	2 103
1959	39 494	1 961	915	1 046	37 533	3 153	8 911	9 560	8 261	5 588	2 060
1960	39 755	2 092	973	1 119	37 663	3 264	8 777	9 589	8 372	5 618	2 043
1961	39 588	2 055	891	1 164	37 533	3 311	8 630	9 566	8 394	5 670	1 961
1962	40 016	2 098	883	1 215	37 918	3 426	8 514	9 718	8 512	5 749	1 998
1963	40 428	2 156	972	1 184	38 272	3 646	8 463	9 782	8 650	5 844	1 887
1964	41 115	2 316	1 128	1 188	38 799	3 856	8 538	9 800	8 787	5 945	1 872
1965	41 844	2 612	1 159	1 453	39 232	4 025	8 598	9 795	8 924	5 998	1 892
1966	42 331	2 913	1 245	1 668	39 418	4 028	8 674	9 719	9 029	6 096	1 871
1967	42 833	2 849	1 278	1 571	39 985	4 231	8 931	9 632	9 093	6 208	1 892
1968	43 411	2 908	1 319	1 589	40 503	4 226	9 315	9 522	9 198	6 316	1 926
1969	44 048	3 070	1 385	1 685	40 978	4 401	9 608	9 379	9 279	6 359	1 953
1970	44 178	3 066	1 374	1 692	41 112	4 601	9 784	9 202	9 271	6 340	1 914
1971	44 595	3 157	1 393	1 764	41 438	4 935	10 026	9 026	9 256	6 339	1 856
1972	45 944	3 416	1 470	1 947	42 528	5 431	10 664	9 047	9 236	6 363	1 786
1973	47 085	3 660	1 590	2 071	43 424	5 863	11 268	9 046	9 257	6 299	1 689
1974	47 674	3 728	1 611	2 117	43 946	5 965	11 701	9 027	9 242	6 304	1 706
1975	46 697	3 505	1 502	2 002	43 192	5 770	11 783	8 818	9 005	6 160	1 656
1976	47 775	3 604	1 501	2 103	44 171	6 140	12 362	8 944	8 968	6 176	1 579
1977	49 150	3 824	1 607	2 217	45 326	6 437	12 893	9 212	8 898	6 279	1 605
1978	50 544	3 950	1 664	2 286	46 594	6 717	13 413	9 608	8 840	6 339	1 677
1979	51 452	3 904	1 654	2 250	47 546	6 868	13 888	9 930	8 748	6 406	1 707
1980	51 127	3 708	1 534	2 174	47 419	6 652	14 009	10 077	8 586	6 412	1 684
1981	51 315	3 469	1 402	2 066	47 846	6 652	14 398	10 307	8 518	6 309	1 662
1982	50 287	3 079	1 214	1 865	47 209	6 372	14 164	10 593	8 267	6 188	1 624
1983	50 621	3 003	1 124	1 879	47 618	6 386	14 297	11 062	8 152	6 084	1 637
1984	52 462	3 001	1 140	1 861	49 461	6 647	15 045	11 776	8 320	6 108	1 564
1985	53 046	2 985	1 185	1 800	50 061	6 428	15 374	12 214	8 374	6 118	1 552
1986	53 785	2 966	1 225	1 741	50 818	6 340	15 790	12 620	8 442	6 012	1 612
1987	54 647	2 999	1 252	1 747	51 649	6 150	16 084	13 138	8 596	5 991	1 690
1988	55 550	3 084	1 248	1 836	52 466	5 987	16 241	13 590	8 992	5 909	1 748
1989	56 352	3 060	1 171	1 889	53 292	5 839	16 383	14 046	9 335	5 891	1 797
1990	56 703	3 018	1 119	1 899	53 685	6 179	16 124	14 496	9 383	5 744	1 760
1991	55 797	2 694	1 017	1 677	53 103	5 942	15 644	14 743	9 488	5 578	1 707
1992	55 959	2 602	990	1 612	53 357	5 855	15 357	14 842	10 027	5 503	1 772
1993	56 656	2 634	1 031	1 603	54 021	5 830	15 230	15 178	10 497	5 514	1 772
1994	57 452	2 776	1 144	1 632	54 676	5 738	15 052	15 562	10 910	5 490	1 925
1995	58 146	2 892	1 169	1 723	55 254	5 613	14 958	15 793	11 359	5 609	1 921
1996	58 888	2 911	1 161	1 750	55 977	5 444	14 820	16 136	11 834	5 755	1 987
1997	59 998	3 011	1 206	1 806	56 986	5 590	14 567	16 470	12 352	5 972	2 037
1998	60 604	3 103	1 233	1 870	57 500	5 659	14 259	16 715	12 661	6 251	1 955
1999	61 139	3 205	1 254	1 951	57 934	5 753	13 851	16 781	13 046	6 447	2 056
2000	62 289	3 169	1 205	1 965	59 119	5 876	14 238	16 477	13 675	6 678	2 175
2001	62 212	2 967	1 102	1 865	59 245	5 870	13 989	16 280	13 987	6 941	2 178
2002	61 849	2 725	987	1 738	59 124	5 882	13 727	15 910	14 060	7 360	2 184
2003	61 866	2 518	972	1 546	59 348	5 890	13 731	15 675	14 117	7 640	2 295
2004	62 712	2 553	903	1 650	60 159	6 026	13 735	15 572	14 418	8 018	2 390
2005	63 763	2 508	942	1 566	61 255	6 041	13 840	15 544	14 810	8 471	2 550

[1]Beginning in 2003, persons who selected this race group only; persons who selected more than one race group are not included. Prior to 2003, persons who reported more than one race group were included in the group they identified as the main race.

Table 1-11. Employed Civilians, by Age, Sex, Race, and Hispanic Origin, 1948–2005—Continued

(Thousands of people.)

Race, Hispanic origin, sex, and year	16 years and over	16 to 19 years			20 years and over						
		Total	16 to 17 years	18 to 19 years	Total	20 to 24 years	25 to 34 years	35 to 44 years	45 to 54 years	55 to 64 years	65 years and over
WHITE[1]											
Women											
1954	16 111	1 355	486	869	14 756	1 964	3 329	3 825	3 197	1 850	590
1955	17 114	1 401	509	892	15 713	2 030	3 394	3 976	3 530	2 079	703
1956	17 901	1 496	575	920	16 405	2 047	3 418	4 188	3 756	2 263	732
1957	18 116	1 509	568	941	16 607	2 022	3 393	4 236	3 942	2 287	717
1958	18 022	1 433	518	915	16 589	2 012	3 267	4 185	4 052	2 348	725
1959	18 512	1 514	605	909	16 998	1 985	3 233	4 270	4 291	2 475	745
1960	19 095	1 608	625	984	17 487	2 067	3 244	4 341	4 448	2 574	812
1961	19 325	1 638	581	1 056	17 687	2 149	3 205	4 339	4 512	2 665	817
1962	19 682	1 676	564	1 112	18 006	2 250	3 189	4 455	4 554	2 762	797
1963	20 194	1 695	628	1 066	18 499	2 390	3 226	4 559	4 654	2 874	796
1964	20 807	1 760	718	1 042	19 047	2 588	3 256	4 580	4 809	2 971	845
1965	21 602	1 950	733	1 217	19 652	2 727	3 394	4 678	4 880	3 118	856
1966	22 690	2 263	807	1 456	20 427	2 958	3 594	4 730	5 043	3 260	842
1967	23 528	2 265	843	1 422	21 263	3 262	3 832	4 797	5 131	3 388	854
1968	24 339	2 287	874	1 413	22 052	3 461	4 095	4 864	5 289	3 465	878
1969	25 470	2 438	962	1 476	23 032	3 781	4 327	4 891	5 509	3 588	935
1970	26 039	2 505	1 012	1 493	23 534	3 959	4 542	4 890	5 582	3 640	921
1971	26 283	2 513	1 011	1 502	23 770	4 065	4 687	4 831	5 588	3 675	924
1972	27 426	2 755	1 111	1 645	24 669	4 286	5 240	4 893	5 608	3 714	928
1973	28 623	2 962	1 217	1 746	25 661	4 562	5 831	5 036	5 628	3 684	920
1974	29 511	3 069	1 269	1 799	26 442	4 711	6 340	5 169	5 706	3 654	862
1975	29 714	2 983	1 215	1 767	26 731	4 775	6 701	5 161	5 550	3 667	877
1976	31 078	3 120	1 260	1 860	27 958	4 978	7 300	5 462	5 580	3 746	891
1977	32 550	3 244	1 319	1 923	29 306	5 259	7 950	5 772	5 585	3 829	912
1978	34 392	3 416	1 420	1 996	30 975	5 535	8 595	6 201	5 710	3 972	964
1979	35 807	3 451	1 423	2 027	32 357	5 726	9 145	6 648	5 773	4 071	993
1980	36 587	3 314	1 327	1 986	33 275	5 753	9 644	6 994	5 818	4 064	1 001
1981	37 394	3 119	1 242	1 877	34 275	5 826	10 153	7 311	5 896	4 077	1 013
1982	37 615	2 905	1 103	1 802	34 710	5 724	10 367	7 675	5 816	4 095	1 032
1983	38 272	2 796	1 032	1 764	35 476	5 751	10 659	8 132	5 809	4 084	1 041
1984	39 659	2 835	1 069	1 766	36 823	5 804	11 190	8 776	5 920	4 118	1 015
1985	40 690	2 783	1 085	1 698	37 907	5 807	11 571	9 338	6 084	4 128	978
1986	41 876	2 825	1 160	1 665	39 050	5 687	11 956	9 895	6 307	4 164	1 042
1987	43 142	2 900	1 216	1 684	40 242	5 598	12 345	10 459	6 620	4 172	1 047
1988	44 262	2 946	1 176	1 770	41 316	5 450	12 555	10 878	7 062	4 244	1 126
1989	45 232	2 886	1 107	1 779	42 346	5 245	12 708	11 395	7 440	4 332	1 227
1990	45 558	2 762	1 023	1 739	42 796	5 319	12 649	11 785	7 551	4 217	1 275
1991	45 385	2 523	954	1 569	42 862	5 174	12 344	12 139	7 781	4 141	1 283
1992	45 710	2 383	915	1 468	43 327	5 176	12 195	12 254	8 258	4 198	1 246
1993	46 390	2 479	959	1 520	43 910	5 101	12 044	12 467	8 776	4 258	1 265
1994	47 738	2 622	1 066	1 556	45 116	4 997	12 049	12 880	9 338	4 423	1 429
1995	48 344	2 701	1 104	1 597	45 643	4 787	12 056	13 157	9 768	4 461	1 415
1996	48 920	2 756	1 164	1 592	46 164	4 705	11 858	13 430	10 237	4 558	1 376
1997	49 859	2 796	1 136	1 660	47 063	4 773	11 727	13 667	10 709	4 813	1 374
1998	50 327	2 986	1 203	1 783	47 342	4 853	11 470	13 604	11 001	5 021	1 392
1999	51 096	2 999	1 181	1 817	48 098	4 963	11 262	13 767	11 461	5 211	1 435
2000	52 136	2 991	1 178	1 813	49 145	5 068	11 262	13 674	12 087	5 490	1 564
2001	52 218	2 850	1 122	1 727	49 369	5 184	10 959	13 513	12 314	5 802	1 597
2002	52 164	2 716	1 050	1 665	49 448	5 214	10 842	13 138	12 341	6 269	1 644
2003	52 369	2 546	1 027	1 519	49 823	5 161	10 668	12 826	12 645	6 735	1 788
2004	52 527	2 486	991	1 495	50 040	5 207	10 602	12 604	12 810	6 947	1 870
2005	53 186	2 597	1 057	1 540	50 589	5 190	10 603	12 558	12 991	7 317	1 930

[1]Beginning in 2003, persons who selected this race group only; persons who selected more than one race group are not included. Prior to 2003, persons who reported more than one race group were included in the group they identified as the main race.

Table 1-11. Employed Civilians, by Age, Sex, Race, and Hispanic Origin, 1948–2005—*Continued*

(Thousands of people.)

Race, Hispanic origin, sex, and year	16 years and over	16 to 19 years			20 years and over						
		Total	16 to 17 years	18 to 19 years	Total	20 to 24 years	25 to 34 years	35 to 44 years	45 to 54 years	55 to 64 years	65 years and over
BLACK[1]											
Both Sexes											
1972	7 802	509	180	329	7 292	1 166	1 924	1 629	1 434	872	269
1973	8 128	570	194	378	7 559	1 258	2 062	1 659	1 460	872	249
1974	8 203	554	190	364	7 649	1 231	2 157	1 682	1 452	884	243
1975	7 894	507	183	325	7 386	1 115	2 145	1 617	1 393	874	241
1976	8 227	508	170	338	7 719	1 193	2 309	1 679	1 416	870	252
1977	8 540	508	169	339	8 031	1 244	2 443	1 754	1 448	892	251
1978	9 102	571	191	380	8 531	1 359	2 641	1 848	1 479	932	273
1979	9 359	579	204	376	8 780	1 424	2 759	1 902	1 502	927	266
1980	9 313	547	192	356	8 765	1 376	2 827	1 910	1 487	925	239
1981	9 355	505	170	335	8 849	1 346	2 872	1 957	1 489	954	231
1982	9 189	428	138	290	8 761	1 283	2 830	2 025	1 469	928	225
1983	9 375	416	123	294	8 959	1 280	2 976	2 107	1 456	937	204
1984	10 119	474	146	328	9 645	1 423	3 223	2 311	1 533	945	209
1985	10 501	532	175	356	9 969	1 399	3 325	2 427	1 598	985	235
1986	10 814	536	183	353	10 278	1 429	3 464	2 524	1 666	982	214
1987	11 309	587	203	385	10 722	1 421	3 614	2 695	1 714	1 036	241
1988	11 658	601	223	378	11 057	1 433	3 725	2 839	1 783	1 018	261
1989	11 953	625	237	388	11 328	1 467	3 801	2 981	1 844	970	265
1990	12 175	598	194	404	11 577	1 409	3 803	3 287	1 897	933	248
1991	12 074	494	161	334	11 580	1 373	3 714	3 401	1 892	957	243
1992	12 151	492	157	335	11 659	1 343	3 699	3 441	1 964	965	246
1993	12 382	494	171	323	11 888	1 377	3 700	3 584	2 059	941	226
1994	12 835	552	224	328	12 284	1 449	3 732	3 722	2 178	953	251
1995	13 279	586	223	363	12 693	1 443	3 844	3 861	2 288	1 004	253
1996	13 542	613	233	380	12 929	1 411	3 851	3 974	2 426	1 025	241
1997	13 969	631	229	401	13 339	1 456	3 903	4 094	2 588	1 048	249
1998	14 556	736	246	490	13 820	1 496	3 967	4 238	2 739	1 118	262
1999	15 056	691	243	448	14 365	1 594	4 091	4 404	2 872	1 134	271
2000	15 156	711	260	451	14 444	1 593	3 993	4 261	3 073	1 226	300
2001	15 006	637	230	408	14 368	1 571	3 840	4 200	3 139	1 283	335
2002	14 872	611	193	417	14 262	1 543	3 726	4 109	3 220	1 332	332
2003	14 739	516	196	320	14 222	1 516	3 618	4 080	3 289	1 373	346
2004	14 909	520	169	351	14 389	1 572	3 635	4 039	3 332	1 452	359
2005	15 313	536	164	372	14 776	1 599	3 722	4 060	3 464	1 555	375
Men											
1972	4 368	309	114	195	4 058	648	1 074	890	793	499	156
1973	4 527	330	112	220	4 197	711	1 142	898	816	483	148
1974	4 527	322	114	209	4 204	668	1 176	912	803	500	145
1975	4 275	276	98	179	3 998	595	1 159	865	755	487	137
1976	4 404	283	100	184	4 120	635	1 217	897	763	472	137
1977	4 565	291	105	186	4 273	659	1 271	940	777	484	143
1978	4 796	312	106	206	4 483	697	1 357	969	788	516	155
1979	4 923	316	111	205	4 606	754	1 425	983	801	498	147
1980	4 798	299	109	191	4 498	713	1 438	975	770	478	126
1981	4 794	273	95	178	4 520	693	1 457	991	764	492	123
1982	4 637	223	65	158	4 414	660	1 414	997	750	471	122
1983	4 753	222	64	158	4 531	684	1 483	1 034	749	477	105
1984	5 124	252	79	173	4 871	750	1 635	1 138	780	460	108
1985	5 270	278	92	186	4 992	726	1 669	1 187	795	501	114
1986	5 428	278	96	182	5 150	732	1 756	1 211	831	507	112
1987	5 661	304	109	195	5 357	728	1 821	1 283	853	547	124
1988	5 824	316	122	193	5 509	736	1 881	1 348	878	536	131
1989	5 928	327	124	202	5 602	742	1 931	1 415	886	498	131
1990	5 995	303	99	204	5 692	702	1 895	1 586	926	469	114
1991	5 961	255	85	170	5 706	695	1 859	1 634	923	481	114
1992	5 930	249	78	170	5 681	679	1 819	1 650	930	478	124
1993	6 047	254	88	166	5 793	674	1 858	1 717	978	461	106
1994	6 241	276	107	169	5 964	718	1 850	1 795	1 030	455	115
1995	6 422	285	111	174	6 137	714	1 895	1 836	1 085	468	138
1996	6 456	289	109	180	6 167	685	1 867	1 878	1 129	482	126
1997	6 607	282	108	174	6 325	668	1 874	1 955	1 215	487	127
1998	6 871	341	120	221	6 530	686	1 886	2 008	1 284	524	142
1999	7 027	325	120	205	6 702	700	1 926	2 092	1 327	525	131
2000	7 082	341	129	211	6 741	730	1 865	1 984	1 425	596	142
2001	6 938	311	115	196	6 627	703	1 757	1 931	1 452	614	170
2002	6 959	306	95	212	6 652	725	1 729	1 899	1 503	624	172
2003	6 820	234	89	145	6 586	726	1 660	1 868	1 518	638	176
2004	6 912	231	76	155	6 681	739	1 720	1 840	1 534	668	180
2005	7 155	254	76	178	6 901	748	1 759	1 886	1 616	711	182

[1]Beginning in 2003, persons who selected this race group only; persons who selected more than one race group are not included. Prior to 2003, persons who reported more than one race group were included in the group they identified as the main race.

Table 1-11. Employed Civilians, by Age, Sex, Race, and Hispanic Origin, 1948–2005—*Continued*

(Thousands of people.)

Race, Hispanic origin, sex, and year	16 years and over	16 to 19 years			20 years and over						
		Total	16 to 17 years	18 to 19 years	Total	20 to 24 years	25 to 34 years	35 to 44 years	45 to 54 years	55 to 64 years	65 years and over
BLACK[1]											
Women											
1972	3 433	200	65	134	3 233	519	850	739	641	373	113
1973	3 601	239	81	158	3 362	546	920	761	644	389	101
1974	3 677	232	77	155	3 445	562	981	770	649	383	98
1975	3 618	231	85	146	3 388	520	985	752	638	387	104
1976	3 823	224	70	154	3 599	558	1 092	782	653	398	115
1977	3 975	217	64	153	3 758	585	1 172	814	671	408	109
1978	4 307	260	85	175	4 047	662	1 283	879	691	416	118
1979	4 436	263	92	171	4 174	670	1 333	919	702	428	119
1980	4 515	248	82	165	4 267	663	1 389	936	717	448	113
1981	4 561	232	75	157	4 329	653	1 415	966	725	462	108
1982	4 552	205	73	132	4 347	623	1 416	1 028	719	457	103
1983	4 622	194	59	136	4 428	596	1 493	1 073	707	460	99
1984	4 995	222	67	155	4 773	673	1 588	1 173	753	485	101
1985	5 231	254	83	171	4 977	673	1 656	1 240	804	484	121
1986	5 386	259	87	171	5 128	696	1 708	1 313	835	475	102
1987	5 648	283	93	190	5 365	693	1 793	1 412	860	489	117
1988	5 834	285	101	184	5 548	697	1 844	1 491	905	482	129
1989	6 025	298	113	185	5 727	725	1 870	1 566	959	472	134
1990	6 180	296	96	200	5 884	707	1 907	1 701	971	464	135
1991	6 113	239	76	164	5 874	677	1 855	1 768	969	476	129
1992	6 221	243	79	164	5 978	664	1 880	1 791	1 034	487	123
1993	6 334	239	82	157	6 095	703	1 842	1 867	1 081	480	121
1994	6 595	275	117	158	6 320	731	1 882	1 926	1 147	497	136
1995	6 857	301	112	189	6 556	729	1 949	2 025	1 202	536	114
1996	7 086	324	124	200	6 762	726	1 984	2 096	1 297	543	115
1997	7 362	349	122	227	7 013	789	2 029	2 139	1 373	561	122
1998	7 685	395	126	268	7 290	810	2 081	2 230	1 455	594	120
1999	8 029	366	123	243	7 663	893	2 165	2 312	1 545	609	139
2000	8 073	370	131	240	7 703	862	2 128	2 277	1 647	630	158
2001	8 068	327	115	212	7 741	868	2 084	2 269	1 686	668	165
2002	7 914	304	99	205	7 610	819	1 997	2 209	1 717	708	160
2003	7 919	283	107	175	7 636	790	1 959	2 211	1 770	735	171
2004	7 997	289	93	196	7 707	833	1 914	2 199	1 798	784	179
2005	8 158	282	88	194	7 876	852	1 964	2 175	1 848	844	193
HISPANIC[2]											
Both Sexes											
1973	3 396	325	...	...	...	...	...	...	...	...	...
1974	3 687	355	...	...	...	...	...	...	...	...	...
1975	3 663	322	...	...	...	...	...	...	...	...	...
1976	3 720	341	124	230	3 436	614	1 135	803	573	269	42
1977	4 079	381	135	245	3 715	715	1 212	860	608	269	50
1978	4 527	423	159	264	4 104	803	1 330	942	661	307	62
1979	4 785	445	152	292	4 340	860	1 430	996	666	319	69
1980	5 527	500	174	325	5 028	998	1 675	1 074	811	389	80
1981	5 813	459	155	304	5 354	1 060	1 837	1 147	829	399	82
1982	5 805	410	119	291	5 394	1 030	1 896	1 173	816	399	80
1983	6 072	423	125	297	5 649	1 068	1 997	1 224	837	441	81
1984	6 651	468	148	320	6 182	1 160	2 201	1 385	883	474	79
1985	6 888	438	144	294	6 449	1 187	2 316	1 473	913	486	75
1986	7 219	430	146	284	6 789	1 231	2 427	1 570	1 011	474	76
1987	7 790	474	149	325	7 316	1 273	2 668	1 775	1 010	512	76
1988	8 250	523	171	353	7 727	1 341	2 749	1 876	1 078	585	97
1989	8 573	548	165	383	8 025	1 325	2 900	1 968	1 129	589	114
1990	9 845	668	208	460	9 177	1 672	3 327	2 229	1 235	611	103
1991	9 828	602	169	433	9 225	1 622	3 264	2 333	1 266	637	103
1992	10 027	577	169	408	9 450	1 575	3 350	2 468	1 316	628	112
1993	10 361	570	160	410	9 792	1 574	3 446	2 605	1 402	630	135
1994	10 788	609	195	415	10 178	1 643	3 517	2 737	1 495	647	139
1995	11 127	645	194	450	10 483	1 609	3 618	2 889	1 565	666	135
1996	11 642	646	199	447	10 996	1 628	3 758	3 115	1 595	748	152
1997	12 726	714	228	487	12 012	1 798	4 029	3 371	1 846	794	173
1998	13 291	793	230	563	12 498	1 883	4 113	3 504	1 994	846	158
1999	13 720	854	254	600	12 866	1 881	4 097	3 738	2 074	886	190
2000	15 735	973	285	688	14 762	2 356	4 950	4 052	2 308	898	197
2001	16 190	969	268	701	15 221	2 404	5 065	4 149	2 472	944	187
2002	16 590	882	254	628	15 708	2 413	5 272	4 273	2 511	1 029	209
2003	17 372	768	242	525	16 604	2 399	5 541	4 573	2 711	1 132	249
2004	17 930	792	211	581	17 138	2 477	5 560	4 671	2 932	1 210	288
2005	18 632	847	253	595	17 785	2 423	5 756	4 879	3 114	1 317	296

[1]Beginning in 2003, persons who selected this race group only; persons who selected more than one race group are not included. Prior to 2003, persons who reported more than one race group were included in the group they identified as the main race.
[2]May be of any race.
. . . = Not available.

Table 1-11. Employed Civilians, by Age, Sex, Race, and Hispanic Origin, 1948–2005—*Continued*

(Thousands of people.)

Race, Hispanic origin, sex, and year	16 years and over	16 to 19 years			20 years and over						
		Total	16 to 17 years	18 to 19 years	Total	20 to 24 years	25 to 34 years	35 to 44 years	45 to 54 years	55 to 64 years	65 years and over
HISPANIC[2]											
Men											
1973	2 198	...	...	...	2 010	...	...	...	...	...	...
1974	2 369	...	...	...	2 165	...	...	...	...	...	...
1975	2 301	...	...	...	2 117	...	...	...	...	...	...
1976	2 303	199	74	125	2 109	364	708	504	369	173	...
1977	2 564	225	78	147	2 335	427	763	540	394	184	...
1978	2 808	241	93	147	2 568	494	824	590	405	207	...
1979	2 962	260	93	168	2 701	511	891	615	427	205	...
1980	3 448	306	109	198	3 142	611	1 065	662	491	254	...
1981	3 597	272	90	182	3 325	642	1 157	707	504	259	...
1982	3 583	229	66	162	3 354	621	1 192	729	498	261	...
1983	3 771	248	71	177	3 523	655	1 280	760	499	275	...
1984	4 083	258	78	180	3 825	718	1 398	841	530	292	...
1985	4 245	251	82	169	3 994	727	1 473	888	550	308	...
1986	4 428	254	82	172	4 174	773	1 510	929	614	297	...
1987	4 713	268	81	188	4 444	777	1 664	1 044	606	303	...
1988	4 972	292	87	205	4 680	815	1 706	1 120	645	331	...
1989	5 172	319	94	225	4 853	821	1 787	1 152	676	350	...
1990	6 021	412	126	286	5 609	1 083	2 076	1 312	722	355	...
1991	5 979	356	94	263	5 623	1 063	2 050	1 360	719	369	...
1992	6 093	336	97	238	5 757	985	2 127	1 437	768	372	...
1993	6 328	337	95	242	5 992	1 003	2 200	1 527	822	360	...
1994	6 530	341	109	233	6 189	1 056	2 227	1 600	847	379	79
1995	6 725	358	110	248	6 367	1 030	2 284	1 675	908	384	85
1996	7 039	384	107	277	6 655	1 015	2 345	1 842	918	438	96
1997	7 728	420	130	290	7 307	1 142	2 547	1 978	1 059	477	105
1998	8 018	449	133	315	7 570	1 173	2 592	2 077	1 115	512	101
1999	8 067	491	139	352	7 576	1 135	2 524	2 135	1 151	502	130
2000	9 428	570	159	411	8 859	1 486	3 063	2 358	1 295	532	126
2001	9 668	568	149	419	9 100	1 473	3 142	2 446	1 375	545	119
2002	9 845	504	141	363	9 341	1 476	3 271	2 503	1 396	569	125
2003	10 479	415	121	294	10 063	1 485	3 537	2 724	1 533	639	144
2004	10 832	446	108	338	10 385	1 514	3 557	2 801	1 654	687	174
2005	11 337	465	137	328	10 872	1 511	3 711	2 939	1 781	748	183
Women											
1973	1 198	...	...	...	1 060	...	...	...	...	...	...
1974	1 319	...	...	...	1 166	...	...	...	...	...	...
1975	1 362	...	...	...	1 224	...	...	...	...	...	...
1976	1 417	155	50	106	1 288	249	427	300	204	96	...
1977	1 516	155	57	98	1 370	288	449	320	214	86	...
1978	1 719	182	65	117	1 537	308	506	352	256	99	...
1979	1 824	185	60	125	1 638	349	539	381	241	115	...
1980	2 079	193	65	128	1 886	387	610	412	320	136	...
1981	2 216	187	65	122	2 029	418	680	440	326	139	...
1982	2 222	181	52	129	2 040	409	704	444	318	139	...
1983	2 301	175	54	120	2 127	413	717	464	338	166	...
1984	2 568	211	71	140	2 357	442	804	544	354	181	...
1985	2 642	187	62	125	2 456	460	843	585	362	178	...
1986	2 791	176	64	112	2 615	458	917	641	397	177	...
1987	3 077	206	69	137	2 872	496	1 004	732	405	209	...
1988	3 278	231	84	147	3 047	526	1 042	756	434	254	...
1989	3 401	229	71	158	3 172	504	1 114	816	453	239	...
1990	3 823	256	82	174	3 567	588	1 251	917	513	256	...
1991	3 848	246	76	170	3 603	559	1 214	972	548	268	...
1992	3 934	242	72	170	3 693	591	1 223	1 031	548	256	...
1993	4 033	233	65	168	3 800	571	1 246	1 077	581	269	...
1994	4 258	268	86	182	3 989	587	1 290	1 137	648	268	59
1995	4 403	287	85	202	4 116	579	1 334	1 213	657	282	50
1996	4 602	261	92	169	4 341	612	1 412	1 273	677	310	56
1997	4 999	294	98	196	4 705	656	1 482	1 393	787	318	69
1998	5 273	345	97	247	4 928	710	1 521	1 428	879	334	57
1999	5 653	363	115	248	5 290	746	1 574	1 603	923	384	60
2000	6 307	404	127	277	5 903	870	1 887	1 695	1 013	366	72
2001	6 522	401	119	282	6 121	931	1 923	1 703	1 097	398	67
2002	6 744	378	113	265	6 367	937	2 001	1 770	1 114	460	84
2003	6 894	353	121	231	6 541	914	2 004	1 849	1 178	493	105
2004	7 098	346	103	243	6 752	964	2 003	1 870	1 279	523	114
2005	7 295	382	116	266	6 913	912	2 045	1 940	1 333	569	113

[2]May be of any race.
. . . = Not available.

Table 1-12. Civilian Employment-Population Ratios, by Sex, Age, Race, and Hispanic Origin, 1948–2005

(Percent.)

Race, Hispanic origin, and year	Both sexes			Men			Women		
	16 years and over	16 to 19 years	20 years and over	16 years and over	16 to 19 years	20 years and over	16 years and over	16 to 19 years	20 years and over
All Races									
1948	56.6	47.7	57.4	83.5	57.5	85.8	31.3	38.5	30.7
1949	55.4	45.2	56.3	81.3	53.8	83.7	31.2	37.2	30.6
1950	56.1	45.5	57.0	82.0	55.2	84.2	32.0	36.3	31.6
1951	57.3	47.9	58.1	84.0	57.9	86.1	33.1	38.9	32.6
1952	57.3	46.9	58.1	83.9	55.9	86.2	33.4	38.8	33.0
1953	57.1	46.4	58.0	83.6	55.9	85.9	33.3	37.8	32.9
1954	55.5	42.3	56.6	81.0	50.2	83.5	32.5	34.9	32.3
1955	56.7	43.5	57.8	81.8	52.1	84.3	34.0	35.6	33.8
1956	57.5	45.3	58.5	82.3	53.8	84.6	35.1	37.5	34.9
1957	57.1	43.9	58.2	81.3	51.8	83.8	35.1	36.7	35.0
1958	55.4	39.9	56.8	78.5	46.9	81.2	34.5	33.5	34.6
1959	56.0	39.9	57.5	79.3	47.2	82.3	35.0	33.0	35.1
1960	56.1	40.5	57.6	78.9	47.6	81.9	35.5	33.8	35.7
1961	55.4	39.1	56.9	77.6	45.3	80.8	35.4	33.2	35.6
1962	55.5	39.4	57.1	77.7	45.9	80.9	35.6	33.3	35.8
1963	55.4	37.4	57.2	77.1	43.8	80.6	35.8	31.5	36.3
1964	55.7	37.3	57.7	77.3	44.1	80.9	36.3	30.9	36.9
1965	56.2	38.9	58.2	77.5	46.2	81.2	37.1	32.0	37.6
1966	56.9	42.1	58.7	77.9	48.9	81.5	38.3	35.6	38.6
1967	57.3	42.2	59.0	78.0	48.7	81.5	39.0	35.9	39.3
1968	57.5	42.2	59.3	77.8	48.7	81.3	39.6	36.0	40.0
1969	58.0	43.4	59.7	77.6	49.5	81.1	40.7	37.5	41.1
1970	57.4	42.3	59.2	76.2	47.7	79.7	40.8	37.1	41.2
1971	56.6	41.3	58.4	74.9	46.8	78.5	40.4	36.0	40.9
1972	57.0	43.5	58.6	75.0	48.9	78.4	41.0	38.2	41.3
1973	57.8	45.9	59.3	75.5	51.4	78.6	42.0	40.5	42.2
1974	57.8	46.0	59.2	74.9	51.2	77.9	42.6	41.0	42.8
1975	56.1	43.3	57.6	71.7	47.2	74.8	42.0	39.4	42.3
1976	56.8	44.2	58.3	72.0	47.9	75.1	43.2	40.5	43.5
1977	57.9	46.1	59.2	72.8	50.4	75.6	44.5	41.8	44.8
1978	59.3	48.3	60.6	73.8	52.2	76.4	46.4	44.5	46.6
1979	59.9	48.5	61.2	73.8	51.7	76.5	47.5	45.3	47.7
1980	59.2	46.6	60.6	72.0	49.5	74.6	47.7	43.8	48.1
1981	59.0	44.6	60.5	71.3	47.1	74.0	48.0	42.0	48.6
1982	57.8	41.5	59.4	69.0	42.9	71.8	47.7	40.2	48.4
1983	57.9	41.5	59.5	68.8	43.1	71.4	48.0	40.0	48.8
1984	59.5	43.7	61.0	70.7	45.0	73.2	49.5	42.5	50.1
1985	60.1	44.4	61.5	70.9	45.7	73.3	50.4	42.9	51.0
1986	60.7	44.6	62.1	71.0	45.7	73.3	51.4	43.6	52.0
1987	61.5	45.5	62.9	71.5	46.1	73.8	52.5	44.8	53.1
1988	62.3	46.8	63.6	72.0	47.8	74.2	53.4	45.9	54.0
1989	63.0	47.5	64.2	72.5	48.7	74.5	54.3	46.4	54.9
1990	62.8	45.3	64.3	72.0	46.6	74.3	54.3	44.0	55.2
1991	61.7	42.0	63.2	70.4	42.7	72.7	53.7	41.2	54.6
1992	61.5	41.0	63.0	69.8	41.9	72.1	53.8	40.0	54.8
1993	61.7	41.7	63.3	70.0	42.3	72.3	54.1	41.0	55.0
1994	62.5	43.4	64.0	70.4	43.8	72.6	55.3	43.0	56.2
1995	62.9	44.2	64.4	70.8	44.7	73.0	55.6	43.8	56.5
1996	63.2	43.5	64.7	70.9	43.6	73.2	56.0	43.5	57.0
1997	63.8	43.4	65.5	71.3	43.4	73.7	56.8	43.3	57.8
1998	64.1	45.1	65.6	71.6	44.7	73.9	57.1	45.5	58.0
1999	64.3	44.7	65.9	71.6	45.1	74.0	57.4	44.3	58.5
2000	64.4	45.2	66.0	71.9	45.4	74.2	57.5	45.0	58.4
2001	63.7	42.3	65.4	70.9	42.2	73.3	57.0	42.4	58.1
2002	62.7	39.6	64.6	69.7	38.9	72.3	56.3	40.3	57.5
2003	62.3	36.8	64.3	68.9	35.7	71.7	56.1	37.8	57.5
2004	62.3	36.4	64.4	69.2	35.9	71.9	56.0	37.0	57.4
2005	62.7	36.5	64.7	69.6	35.1	72.4	56.2	37.8	57.6

Table 1-12. Civilian Employment-Population Ratios, by Sex, Age, Race, and Hispanic Origin, 1948–2005
—*Continued*

(Percent.)

Race, Hispanic origin, and year	Both sexes			Men			Women		
	16 years and over	16 to 19 years	20 years and over	16 years and over	16 to 19 years	20 years and over	16 years and over	16 to 19 years	20 years and over
White[1]									
1954	55.2	42.9	56.2	81.5	49.9	84.0	31.4	36.4	31.1
1955	56.5	44.2	57.4	82.2	52.0	84.7	33.0	37.0	32.7
1956	57.3	46.1	58.2	82.7	54.1	85.0	34.2	38.9	33.8
1957	56.8	45.0	57.8	81.8	52.4	84.1	34.2	38.2	33.9
1958	55.3	41.0	56.5	79.2	47.6	81.8	33.6	35.0	33.5
1959	55.9	41.2	57.2	79.9	48.1	82.8	34.0	34.8	34.0
1960	55.9	41.5	57.2	79.4	48.1	82.4	34.6	35.1	34.5
1961	55.3	40.1	56.7	78.2	45.9	81.4	34.5	34.6	34.5
1962	55.4	40.4	56.9	78.4	46.4	81.5	34.7	34.8	34.7
1963	55.3	38.6	56.9	77.7	44.7	81.1	35.0	32.9	35.2
1964	55.5	38.4	57.3	77.8	45.0	81.3	35.5	32.2	35.8
1965	56.0	40.3	57.8	77.9	47.1	81.5	36.2	33.7	36.5
1966	56.8	43.6	58.3	78.3	50.1	81.7	37.5	37.5	37.5
1967	57.2	43.8	58.7	78.4	50.2	81.7	38.3	37.7	38.3
1968	57.4	43.9	59.0	78.3	50.3	81.6	38.9	37.8	39.1
1969	58.0	45.2	59.4	78.2	51.1	81.4	40.1	39.5	40.1
1970	57.5	44.5	59.0	76.8	49.6	80.1	40.3	39.5	40.4
1971	56.8	43.8	58.3	75.7	49.2	79.0	39.9	38.6	40.1
1972	57.4	46.4	58.6	76.0	51.5	79.0	40.7	41.3	40.6
1973	58.2	48.9	59.3	76.5	54.3	79.2	41.8	43.6	41.6
1974	58.3	49.3	59.3	75.9	54.4	78.6	42.4	44.3	42.2
1975	56.7	46.5	57.9	73.0	50.6	75.7	42.0	42.5	41.9
1976	57.5	47.8	58.6	73.4	51.5	76.0	43.2	44.2	43.1
1977	58.6	50.1	59.6	74.1	54.4	76.5	44.5	45.9	44.4
1978	60.0	52.4	60.8	75.0	56.3	77.2	46.3	48.5	46.1
1979	60.6	52.6	61.5	75.1	55.7	77.3	47.5	49.4	47.3
1980	60.0	50.7	61.0	73.4	53.4	75.6	47.8	47.9	47.8
1981	60.0	48.7	61.1	72.8	51.3	75.1	48.3	46.2	48.5
1982	58.8	45.8	60.1	70.6	47.0	73.0	48.1	44.6	48.4
1983	58.9	45.9	60.1	70.4	47.4	72.6	48.5	44.5	48.9
1984	60.5	48.0	61.5	72.1	49.1	74.3	49.8	47.0	50.0
1985	61.0	48.5	62.0	72.3	49.9	74.3	50.7	47.1	51.0
1986	61.5	48.8	62.6	72.3	49.6	74.3	51.7	47.9	52.0
1987	62.3	49.4	63.4	72.7	49.9	74.7	52.8	49.0	53.1
1988	63.1	50.9	64.1	73.2	51.7	75.1	53.8	50.2	54.0
1989	63.8	51.6	64.7	73.7	52.6	75.4	54.6	50.5	54.9
1990	63.7	49.7	64.8	73.3	51.0	75.1	54.7	48.3	55.2
1991	62.6	46.6	63.7	71.6	47.2	73.5	54.2	45.9	54.8
1992	62.4	45.3	63.6	71.1	46.4	73.1	54.2	44.2	54.9
1993	62.7	46.2	63.9	71.4	46.6	73.3	54.6	45.7	55.2
1994	63.5	47.9	64.7	71.8	48.3	73.6	55.8	47.5	56.4
1995	63.8	48.8	64.9	72.0	49.4	73.8	56.1	48.1	56.7
1996	64.1	47.9	65.3	72.3	48.2	74.2	56.3	47.6	57.0
1997	64.6	47.7	65.9	72.7	48.1	74.7	57.0	47.2	57.8
1998	64.7	48.9	65.9	72.7	48.6	74.7	57.1	49.3	57.7
1999	64.8	48.8	66.1	72.8	49.3	74.8	57.3	48.3	58.0
2000	64.9	49.1	66.1	73.0	49.5	74.9	57.4	48.8	58.0
2001	64.2	46.3	65.6	72.0	46.2	74.0	57.0	46.5	57.7
2002	63.4	43.2	64.9	70.8	42.3	73.1	56.4	44.1	57.3
2003	63.0	40.4	64.7	70.1	39.4	72.5	56.3	41.5	57.3
2004	63.1	40.0	64.8	70.4	39.7	72.8	56.1	40.3	57.2
2005	63.4	40.2	65.1	70.8	38.8	73.3	56.3	41.8	57.4

[1]Beginning in 2003, persons who selected this race group only; persons who selected more than one race group are not included. Prior to 2003, persons who reported more than one race group were included in the group they identified as their main race.

Table 1-12. Civilian Employment-Population Ratios, by Sex, Age, Race, and Hispanic Origin, 1948–2005
—*Continued*

(Percent.)

Race, Hispanic origin, and year	Both sexes			Men			Women		
	16 years and over	16 to 19 years	20 years and over	16 years and over	16 to 19 years	20 years and over	16 years and over	16 to 19 years	20 years and over
Black[1]									
1972	53.7	25.2	58.3	66.8	31.6	73.0	43.0	19.2	46.5
1973	54.5	27.2	58.9	67.5	32.8	73.7	43.8	22.0	47.2
1974	53.5	25.9	58.0	65.8	31.4	71.9	43.5	20.9	46.9
1975	50.1	23.1	54.5	60.6	26.3	66.5	41.6	20.2	44.9
1976	50.8	22.4	55.4	60.6	25.8	66.8	42.8	19.2	46.4
1977	51.4	22.3	56.0	61.4	26.4	67.5	43.3	18.5	47.0
1978	53.6	25.2	58.0	63.3	28.5	69.1	45.8	22.1	49.3
1979	53.8	25.4	58.1	63.4	28.7	69.1	46.0	22.4	49.3
1980	52.3	23.9	56.4	60.4	27.0	65.8	45.7	21.0	49.1
1981	51.3	22.1	55.5	59.1	24.6	64.5	45.1	19.7	48.5
1982	49.4	19.0	53.6	56.0	20.3	61.4	44.2	17.7	47.5
1983	49.5	18.7	53.6	56.3	20.4	61.6	44.1	17.0	47.4
1984	52.3	21.9	56.1	59.2	23.9	64.1	46.7	20.1	49.8
1985	53.4	24.6	57.0	60.0	26.3	64.6	48.1	23.1	50.9
1986	54.1	25.1	57.6	60.6	26.5	65.1	48.8	23.8	51.6
1987	55.6	27.1	58.9	62.0	28.5	66.4	50.3	25.8	53.0
1988	56.3	27.6	59.7	62.7	29.4	67.1	51.2	25.8	53.9
1989	56.9	28.7	60.1	62.8	30.4	67.0	52.0	27.1	54.6
1990	56.7	26.7	60.2	62.6	27.7	67.1	51.9	25.8	54.7
1991	55.4	22.6	59.0	61.3	23.8	65.9	50.6	21.5	53.6
1992	54.9	22.8	58.3	59.9	23.6	64.3	50.8	22.1	53.6
1993	55.0	22.6	58.4	60.0	23.6	64.3	50.9	21.6	53.8
1994	56.1	24.9	59.4	60.8	25.4	65.0	52.3	24.5	55.0
1995	57.1	25.7	60.5	61.7	25.2	66.1	53.4	26.1	56.1
1996	57.4	26.0	60.8	61.1	24.9	65.5	54.4	27.1	57.1
1997	58.2	26.1	61.8	61.4	23.7	66.1	55.6	28.5	58.4
1998	59.7	30.1	63.0	62.9	28.4	67.1	57.2	31.8	59.7
1999	60.6	27.9	64.2	63.1	26.7	67.5	58.6	29.0	61.5
2000	60.9	29.8	64.2	63.6	28.9	67.7	58.6	30.6	61.3
2001	59.7	26.7	63.2	62.1	26.4	66.3	57.8	27.0	60.7
2002	58.1	25.3	61.6	61.1	25.6	65.2	55.8	24.9	58.7
2003	57.4	21.7	61.0	59.5	19.9	64.1	55.6	23.4	58.6
2004	57.2	21.5	60.9	59.3	19.3	63.9	55.5	23.6	58.5
2005	57.7	21.6	61.5	60.2	20.8	64.7	55.7	22.4	58.9
Hispanic[2]									
1973	55.6	. . .	55.6	. . .	. . .	. . .	. . .	. . .	. . .
1974	56.2	. . .	56.2	. . .	. . .	. . .	. . .	. . .	. . .
1975	53.4	. . .	53.4	. . .	. . .	. . .	. . .	. . .	. . .
1976	53.8	. . .	53.8	. . .	. . .	. . .	. . .	. . .	. . .
1977	55.4	. . .	55.4	. . .	. . .	. . .	. . .	. . .	. . .
1978	57.2	. . .	57.2	. . .	. . .	. . .	. . .	. . .	. . .
1979	58.3	. . .	58.3	. . .	. . .	. . .	. . .	. . .	. . .
1980	57.6	. . .	57.6	. . .	. . .	. . .	. . .	. . .	. . .
1981	57.4	. . .	57.4	. . .	. . .	. . .	. . .	. . .	. . .
1982	54.9	. . .	54.9	. . .	. . .	. . .	. . .	. . .	. . .
1983	55.1	. . .	55.1	. . .	. . .	. . .	. . .	. . .	. . .
1984	57.9	. . .	57.9	. . .	. . .	. . .	. . .	. . .	. . .
1985	57.8	. . .	57.8	. . .	. . .	. . .	. . .	. . .	. . .
1986	58.5	. . .	58.5	. . .	. . .	. . .	. . .	. . .	. . .
1987	60.5	. . .	60.5	. . .	. . .	. . .	. . .	. . .	. . .
1988	61.9	. . .	61.9	. . .	. . .	. . .	. . .	. . .	. . .
1989	62.2	. . .	62.2	. . .	. . .	. . .	. . .	. . .	. . .
1990	61.9	. . .	61.9	. . .	. . .	. . .	. . .	. . .	. . .
1991	59.8	. . .	59.8	. . .	. . .	. . .	. . .	. . .	. . .
1992	59.1	. . .	59.1	. . .	. . .	. . .	. . .	. . .	. . .
1993	59.1	. . .	59.1	. . .	. . .	. . .	. . .	. . .	. . .
1994	59.5	33.5	59.5	71.7	36.8	. . .	47.2	30.1	. . .
1995	59.7	34.4	59.7	72.1	37.5	. . .	47.3	31.3	. . .
1996	60.6	33.1	60.6	73.3	38.8	. . .	47.9	27.3	. . .
1997	62.6	33.7	62.6	74.5	37.6	. . .	50.2	29.3	. . .
1998	63.1	36.0	63.1	74.7	38.6	. . .	51.0	33.0	. . .
1999	63.4	37.0	63.4	75.3	41.2	. . .	51.7	32.5	. . .
2000	65.7	38.6	65.7	77.4	42.8	81.7	53.6	33.9	55.8
2001	64.9	38.6	64.9	76.2	43.3	79.9	53.3	33.5	55.4
2002	63.9	35.2	63.9	74.5	39.0	78.3	52.9	31.1	55.2
2003	63.1	30.2	63.1	74.3	31.9	78.6	51.2	28.4	53.6
2004	63.8	30.4	63.8	75.1	33.4	79.4	51.8	27.2	54.4
2005	64.0	31.5	64.0	75.8	33.8	80.0	51.5	29.1	53.8

[1]Beginning in 2003, persons who selected this race group only; persons who selected more than one race group are not included. Prior to 2003, persons who reported more than one race group were included in the group they identified as their main race.
[2]May be of any race.
. . . = Not available.

Table 1-13. Employed Civilians, by Sex, Race, Hispanic Origin, and Occupation, 2003–2005

(Thousands of people.)

Year and occupation	Total	Men	Women	White[1]	Black[1]	Hispanic[2]
2003						
All Occupations	137 736	73 332	64 404	114 235	14 739	17 372
Management, professional, and related	47 929	23 735	24 194	40 558	3 923	2 925
Management, business, and financial operations	19 934	11 534	8 400	17 377	1 368	1 176
Professional and related	27 995	12 201	15 794	23 181	2 555	1 749
Life, physical, and social science	1 375	783	592	1 113	86	81
Community and social services	2 184	862	1 323	1 663	408	184
Services	22 086	9 460	12 626	17 132	3 408	4 175
Health care support	2 926	311	2 616	1 996	738	365
Protective services	2 727	2 164	563	2 098	511	276
Food preparation and serving related	7 254	3 151	4 104	5 797	842	1 441
Building and grounds cleaning and maintenance	4 947	2 920	2 027	3 920	740	1 542
Personal care and services	4 232	915	3 316	3 321	578	550
Sales and office	35 496	12 851	22 645	29 555	3 881	3 820
Office and administrative support	19 536	4 714	14 823	15 968	2 465	2 167
Natural resources, construction, and maintenance	14 205	13 541	665	12 600	1 022	3 023
Farming, fishing, and forestry	1 050	819	231	954	49	423
Construction and extraction	8 114	7 891	223	7 242	578	1 926
Installation, maintenance, and repair	5 041	4 830	211	4 404	395	674
Production, transportation, and material moving	18 020	13 745	4 274	14 391	2 504	3 430
Transportation and material moving	8 320	7 049	1 270	6 625	1 301	8 320
2004						
All Occupations	139 252	74 524	64 728	115 239	14 909	17 930
Management, professional, and related	48 532	24 136	24 396	41 027	3 949	3 101
Management, business, and financial operations	20 235	11 718	8 517	17 590	1 408	1 290
Professional and related	28 297	12 418	15 879	23 438	2 541	1 811
Life, physical, and social science	1 365	777	588	1 143	76	69
Community and social services	2 170	845	1 325	1 650	415	203
Services	22 720	9 826	12 894	17 544	3 543	4 336
Health care support	2 921	311	2 609	1 991	758	384
Protective services	2 847	2 230	616	2 197	510	315
Food preparation and serving related	7 279	3 196	4 084	5 854	835	1 405
Building and grounds cleaning and maintenance	5 185	3 085	2 100	4 094	773	1 661
Personal care and services	4 488	1 004	3 484	3 407	667	571
Sales and office	35 464	12 805	22 660	29 399	3 918	3 818
Office and administrative support	19 481	4 700	14 781	15 842	2 487	2 164
Natural resources, construction, and maintenance	14 582	13 930	652	12 928	1 012	3 229
Farming, fishing, and forestry	991	786	204	885	53	387
Construction and extraction	8 522	8 306	216	7 642	572	2 127
Installation, maintenance, and repair	5 069	4 838	231	4 401	387	715
Production, transportation, and material moving	17 954	13 827	4 126	14 340	2 488	3 446
Transportation and material moving	8 491	7 240	1 251	6 746	1 364	1 552
2005						
All Occupations	141 730	75 973	65 757	116 949	15 313	18 632
Management, professional, and related	49 245	24 349	24 896	41 475	3 985	3 174
Management, business, and financial operations	20 450	11 761	8 689	17 668	1 451	1 330
Professional and related	28 795	12 588	16 207	23 807	2 533	1 844
Life, physical, and social science	1 406	808	598	1 171	71	63
Community and social services	2 138	827	1 311	1 654	365	209
Services	23 133	9 882	13 251	17 817	3 656	4 434
Health care support	3 092	339	2 753	2 121	766	426
Protective services	2 894	2 246	648	2 195	560	300
Food preparation and serving related	7 374	3 202	4 173	5 888	857	1 519
Building and grounds cleaning and maintenance	5 241	3 111	2 130	4 130	828	1 605
Personal care and services	4 531	984	3 548	3 484	645	584
Sales and office	35 962	13 190	22 772	29 658	4 033	4 000
Office and administrative support	19 529	4 829	14 700	15 777	2 526	2 258
Natural resources, construction, and maintenance	15 348	14 635	713	13 582	1 086	3 552
Farming, fishing, and forestry	976	756	220	882	50	394
Construction and extraction	9 145	8 871	274	8 158	643	2 450
Installation, maintenance, and repair	5 226	5 008	219	4 542	394	709
Production, transportation, and material moving	18 041	13 917	4 124	14 418	2 552	3 473
Transportation and material moving	8 664	7 377	1 286	6 892	1 393	1 597

[1]Beginning in 2003, persons who selected this race group only; persons who selected more than one race group are not included. Prior to 2003, persons who reported more than one race group were included in the group they identified as the main race.
[2]May be of any race.

Table 1-14. Employed Civilians, by Selected Occupation and Industry, 2003–2005

(Thousands of people.)

Year and industry	Total employed	Management, professional, and related occupations	Life, physical, and social science occupations	Service occupations	Sales and office occupations	Natural resources, construction, and maintenance occupations	Production, transportation, and material moving occupations
2003							
All Industries	137 736	47 929	1 375	22 086	35 496	14 205	18 020
Agriculture, forestry, fishing, and hunting	2 275	1 088	29	80	112	901	94
Mining	525	133	18	6	57	203	127
Construction	10 138	1 590	6	60	693	7 277	519
Manufacturing	16 902	4 733	287	252	2 340	1 150	8 428
Durable goods	10 520	3 207	58	128	1 370	756	5 060
Nondurable goods	6 382	1 526	229	123	970	394	3 368
Wholesale trade	4 486	782	20	47	2 477	239	941
Retail trade	16 220	1 679	15	569	11 273	888	1 811
Transportation and warehousing	5 758	630	6	268	1 614	401	2 845
Utilities	1 193	376	28	21	252	293	251
Information	3 687	1 852	12	91	1 188	380	176
Finance and insurance	6 834	3 142	26	67	3 561	36	29
Real estate and rental and leasing	2 914	881	6	304	1 421	194	114
Professional and technical services	8 243	6 237	320	122	1 627	130	128
Management, administrative, and waste services	5 636	1 131	25	2 321	1 286	262	637
Educational services	11 826	8 808	170	1 274	1 236	187	322
Health care and social assistance	16 434	8 665	201	4 785	2 565	127	291
Arts, entertainment, and recreation	2 587	891	9	1 193	361	92	50
Accommodation and food services	9 021	1 267	2	6 393	988	57	315
Other services	6 815	1 482	14	2 321	1 064	1 144	804
Public administration	6 243	2 563	182	1 912	1 384	245	138
2004							
All Industries	139 252	48 532	1 365	22 720	35 464	14 582	17 954
Agriculture, forestry, fishing, and hunting	2 232	1 092	28	95	106	837	103
Mining	539	118	13	5	51	232	133
Construction	10 768	1 696	5	70	732	7 743	527
Manufacturing	16 484	4 719	265	225	2 185	1 151	8 203
Durable goods	10 329	3 202	53	113	1 247	771	4 996
Nondurable goods	6 155	1 517	212	113	938	380	3 207
Wholesale trade	4 600	754	12	60	2 553	292	940
Retail trade	16 269	1 759	16	571	11 295	815	1 830
Transportation and warehousing	5 844	593	3	277	1 636	383	2 955
Utilities	1 168	373	35	22	266	276	231
Information	3 463	1 766	19	93	1 102	341	161
Finance and insurance	6 940	3 311	17	69	3 495	34	30
Real estate and rental and leasing	3 029	931	2	280	1 502	201	115
Professional and technical services	8 386	6 333	326	108	1 651	139	156
Management, administrative, and waste services	5 722	1 050	26	2 503	1 249	278	642
Educational services	12 058	9 036	170	1 298	1 201	184	338
Health care and social assistance	16 661	8 756	211	4 860	2 634	127	285
Arts, entertainment, and recreation	2 690	898	15	1 266	372	86	67
Accommodation and food services	9 131	1 286	4	6 487	1 000	70	289
Other services	6 903	1 467	16	2 408	1 082	1 134	812
Public administration	6 365	2 594	181	2 021	1 354	259	138
2005							
All Industries	141 730	49 245	1 406	23 133	35 962	15 348	18 041
Agriculture, forestry, fishing, and hunting	2 197	1 086	29	82	96	836	97
Mining	624	141	23	6	64	264	150
Construction	11 197	1 688	5	76	736	8 208	489
Manufacturing	16 253	4 612	247	242	2 127	1 179	8 092
Durable goods	10 333	3 170	60	112	1 216	787	5 048
Nondurable goods	5 919	1 443	187	130	911	392	3 044
Wholesale trade	4 579	751	21	55	2 479	295	1 000
Retail trade	16 825	1 817	14	559	11 790	830	1 830
Transportation and warehousing	6 184	650	4	270	1 678	414	3 172
Utilities	1 176	353	31	23	234	307	261
Information	3 402	1 717	13	90	1 096	336	164
Finance and insurance	7 035	3 408	14	72	3 497	33	25
Real estate and rental and leasing	3 168	980	1	284	1 588	206	110
Professional and technical services	8 584	6 545	329	113	1 610	172	144
Management, administrative, and waste services	5 709	1 005	25	2 542	1 260	268	635
Educational services	12 264	9 197	179	1 318	1 222	202	323
Health care and social assistance	16 910	8 805	230	5 047	2 653	146	259
Arts, entertainment, and recreation	2 765	979	17	1 256	358	102	71
Accommodation and food services	9 306	1 367	2	6 535	1 045	61	297
Other services	7 020	1 498	15	2 448	1 078	1 219	778
Public administration	6 530	2 646	207	2 115	1 353	272	144

Table 1-15. Employed Civilians in Agriculture and Nonagricultural Industries, by Class of Worker and Sex, 1980–2005

(Thousands of people.)

Sex and year	Total employed	Agriculture				Nonagricultural industries						
		Total	Wage and salary workers	Self-employed workers	Unpaid family workers	Total	Wage and salary workers				Self-employed workers	Unpaid family workers
							Total	Govern-ment	Private household	Other private		
Both Sexes												
1980	99 302	3 364	1 425	1 642	297	95 938	88 525	15 912	1 192	71 421	7 000	413
1981	100 398	3 368	1 464	1 638	266	97 030	89 543	15 689	1 208	72 646	7 097	390
1982	99 526	3 401	1 505	1 636	261	96 125	88 462	15 516	1 207	71 739	7 262	401
1983	100 833	3 383	1 579	1 565	240	97 450	89 500	15 537	1 244	72 719	7 575	376
1984	105 006	3 321	1 555	1 553	213	101 685	93 565	15 770	1 238	76 557	7 785	335
1985	107 150	3 179	1 535	1 458	185	103 971	95 871	16 031	1 249	78 591	7 811	289
1986	109 597	3 163	1 547	1 447	169	106 434	98 299	16 342	1 235	80 722	7 881	255
1987	112 440	3 208	1 632	1 423	153	109 232	100 771	16 800	1 208	82 763	8 201	260
1988	114 969	3 169	1 621	1 398	150	111 800	103 021	17 114	1 153	84 754	8 519	260
1989	117 341	3 199	1 665	1 403	131	114 142	105 259	17 469	1 101	86 689	8 605	279
1990	118 793	3 223	1 740	1 378	105	115 570	106 598	17 769	1 027	87 802	8 719	253
1991	117 718	3 269	1 729	1 423	118	114 449	105 373	17 934	1 010	86 429	8 851	226
1992	118 492	3 247	1 750	1 385	112	115 245	106 437	18 136	1 135	87 166	8 575	233
1993	120 259	3 115	1 689	1 320	106	117 144	107 966	18 579	1 126	88 261	8 959	218
1994	123 060	3 409	1 715	1 645	49	119 651	110 517	18 293	966	91 258	9 003	131
1995	124 900	3 440	1 814	1 580	45	121 460	112 448	18 362	963	93 123	8 902	110
1996	126 707	3 443	1 869	1 518	56	123 264	114 171	18 217	928	95 026	8 971	122
1997	129 558	3 399	1 890	1 457	51	126 159	116 983	18 131	915	97 937	9 056	120
1998	131 463	3 378	2 000	1 341	38	128 085	119 019	18 383	962	99 674	8 962	103
1999	133 488	3 281	1 944	1 297	40	130 207	121 323	18 903	933	101 487	8 790	95
2000	136 891	2 464	1 421	1 010	33	134 427	125 114	19 248	718	105 148	9 205	108
2001	136 933	2 299	1 283	988	28	134 635	125 407	19 335	694	105 378	9 121	107
2002	136 485	2 311	1 282	1 003	26	134 174	125 156	19 636	757	104 764	8 923	95
2003	137 736	2 275	1 299	951	25	135 461	126 015	19 634	764	105 616	9 344	101
2004	139 252	2 232	1 242	964	27	137 020	127 463	19 983	779	106 701	9 467	90
2005	141 730	2 197	1 212	955	30	139 532	129 931	20 357	812	108 761	9 509	93
Men												
1980	57 186	2 709	1 149	1 458	101	54 477	49 517	7 822	149	41 546	4 904	56
1981	57 397	2 700	1 168	1 442	91	54 697	49 745	7 676	192	41 877	4 905	47
1982	56 270	2 736	1 208	1 433	95	53 534	48 529	7 598	188	40 743	4 954	52
1983	56 787	2 704	1 265	1 355	84	54 083	48 896	7 623	208	41 065	5 136	51
1984	59 091	2 668	1 254	1 350	65	56 423	51 151	7 720	178	43 253	5 219	52
1985	59 891	2 535	1 230	1 244	60	57 356	52 111	7 757	170	44 184	5 207	38
1986	60 892	2 511	1 230	1 227	54	58 381	53 075	7 805	180	45 090	5 271	35
1987	62 107	2 543	1 290	1 194	58	59 564	54 102	8 013	180	45 909	5 423	39
1988	63 273	2 493	1 268	1 174	50	60 780	55 177	8 074	157	46 946	5 564	39
1989	64 315	2 513	1 302	1 167	44	61 802	56 202	8 116	156	47 930	5 562	38
1990	65 105	2 546	1 355	1 151	39	62 559	56 913	8 245	149	48 519	5 597	48
1991	64 223	2 589	1 359	1 185	45	61 634	55 899	8 300	143	47 456	5 700	35
1992	64 441	2 575	1 371	1 164	40	61 866	56 212	8 348	156	47 708	5 613	41
1993	65 349	2 478	1 323	1 117	39	62 871	56 926	8 435	146	48 345	5 894	50
1994	66 450	2 554	1 330	1 197	27	63 896	58 300	8 327	99	49 874	5 560	37
1995	67 377	2 559	1 395	1 138	26	64 818	59 332	8 267	96	50 969	5 461	25
1996	68 207	2 573	1 418	1 124	31	65 634	60 133	8 110	99	51 924	5 465	36
1997	69 685	2 552	1 439	1 084	29	67 133	61 595	8 015	81	53 499	5 506	31
1998	70 693	2 553	1 526	1 005	23	68 140	62 630	8 178	86	54 366	5 480	29
1999	71 446	2 432	1 450	962	20	69 014	63 624	8 278	74	55 272	5 366	25
2000	73 305	1 861	1 116	725	20	71 444	65 838	8 309	71	57 458	5 573	33
2001	73 196	1 708	990	703	15	71 488	65 930	8 342	63	57 524	5 527	31
2002	72 903	1 724	979	731	14	71 179	65 726	8 437	76	57 212	5 425	29
2003	73 332	1 695	991	694	11	71 636	65 871	8 368	59	57 444	5 736	30
2004	74 525	1 687	970	702	15	72 838	66 951	8 616	60	58 275	5 860	27
2005	75 973	1 654	949	688	17	74 319	68 345	8 760	67	59 518	5 944	30
Women												
1980	42 117	656	275	184	197	41 461	39 007	8 090	1 044	29 873	2 097	357
1981	43 000	667	296	196	176	42 333	39 798	8 013	1 016	30 769	2 192	343
1982	43 256	665	296	203	166	42 591	39 934	7 918	1 019	30 997	2 309	348
1983	44 047	680	314	210	156	43 367	40 603	7 913	1 036	31 654	2 439	325
1984	45 915	653	301	203	148	45 262	42 413	8 050	1 061	33 302	2 566	283
1985	47 259	644	305	214	125	46 615	43 761	8 274	1 078	34 409	2 603	251
1986	48 706	652	317	220	115	48 054	45 225	8 537	1 055	35 633	2 610	219
1987	50 334	666	342	229	95	49 668	46 669	8 788	1 029	36 852	2 778	221
1988	51 696	676	353	224	99	51 020	47 844	9 039	996	37 809	2 955	220
1989	53 028	687	363	236	87	52 341	49 057	9 353	945	38 759	3 043	240
1990	53 689	678	385	227	66	53 011	49 685	9 524	879	39 282	3 122	205
1991	53 495	680	369	237	73	52 815	49 474	9 635	867	38 972	3 150	191
1992	54 052	672	379	221	73	53 380	50 225	9 788	979	39 458	2 963	192
1993	54 910	637	367	204	67	54 273	51 040	10 144	980	39 916	3 065	168
1994	56 610	855	384	448	23	55 755	52 217	9 965	867	41 385	3 443	95
1995	57 523	881	419	442	20	56 642	53 115	10 095	867	42 153	3 440	86
1996	58 501	871	452	394	25	57 630	54 037	10 107	830	43 100	3 506	87
1997	59 873	847	451	373	23	59 026	55 388	10 116	834	44 438	3 550	89
1998	60 770	825	474	336	15	59 945	56 389	10 205	876	45 308	3 482	74
1999	62 042	849	494	335	20	61 193	57 699	10 625	859	46 215	3 424	70
2000	63 586	602	305	285	12	62 983	59 277	10 939	647	47 690	3 631	76
2001	63 737	591	293	284	13	63 147	59 477	10 993	630	47 853	3 594	75
2002	63 582	587	303	272	12	62 995	59 431	11 199	680	47 552	3 499	66
2003	64 404	580	309	257	14	63 824	60 144	11 267	705	48 172	3 609	72
2004	64 728	546	271	262	12	64 182	60 512	11 367	719	48 426	3 607	63
2005	65 757	544	263	267	13	65 213	61 586	11 598	745	49 243	3 565	63

Note: See notes and definitions for information on historical comparabilty.

Table 1-16. Number of Employed Persons Age 25 Years and Over, by Educational Attainment, Sex, Race, and Hispanic Origin, 1995–2005

(Thousands of people.)

Race, Hispanic origin, sex, and year	Total	Less than a high school diploma	High school graduate, no college	Some college, no degree	Associate degree	College graduate or higher	
						Total	Bachelor's degree only
All Races							
1995	106 037	10 945	34 999	20 436	9 245	30 412	19 924
1996	108 070	11 317	36 300	20 590	9 404	31 459	20 742
1997	110 518	11 546	36 163	20 678	9 643	32 488	21 524
1998	111 855	11 673	35 976	20 626	9 850	33 730	22 260
1999	113 425	11 294	36 017	21 129	10 079	34 905	22 973
2000	116 473	11 692	36 452	21 601	10 707	36 020	23 706
2001	116 846	11 669	36 078	21 459	11 127	36 514	23 907
2002	116 802	11 535	35 779	20 928	11 166	37 395	24 570
2003	118 385	11 537	35 857	21 107	11 313	38 570	25 188
2004	119 622	11 408	35 944	21 284	11 693	39 293	25 484
2005	121 960	11 712	36 398	21 380	12 245	40 225	26 027
Men							
1995	57 420	6 691	18 426	10 653	4 394	17 255	10 983
1996	58 468	7 058	18 639	10 759	4 416	17 596	11 266
1997	59 736	7 210	19 124	10 876	4 517	18 010	11 587
1998	60 497	7 238	19 188	10 684	4 731	18 656	12 028
1999	61 032	6 921	19 125	10 941	4 838	19 208	12 343
2000	62 661	7 199	19 388	11 260	5 013	19 800	12 742
2001	62 824	7 188	19 274	11 076	5 226	20 060	12 872
2002	62 756	7 220	19 154	10 811	5 221	20 350	13 076
2003	63 349	7 290	19 200	10 858	5 231	20 770	13 354
2004	64 326	7 276	19 535	10 896	5 426	21 192	13 575
2005	65 772	7 487	20 127	10 993	5 739	21 427	13 687
Women							
1995	48 617	4 254	16 573	9 783	4 851	13 157	8 941
1996	49 602	4 259	16 661	9 831	4 988	13 863	9 475
1997	50 782	4 336	17 039	9 802	5 126	14 478	9 937
1998	51 359	4 435	16 788	9 943	5 119	15 074	10 231
1999	52 392	4 372	16 893	10 189	5 242	15 697	10 630
2000	53 812	4 493	17 064	10 341	5 694	16 220	10 964
2001	54 021	4 480	16 804	10 383	5 901	16 453	11 035
2002	54 046	4 315	16 624	10 117	5 945	17 045	11 493
2003	55 035	4 248	16 657	10 249	6 081	17 800	11 834
2004	55 296	4 132	16 409	10 387	6 267	18 101	11 908
2005	56 188	4 226	16 271	10 388	6 506	18 798	12 340
White[1]							
1995	90 498	8 690	29 776	17 265	7 970	26 796	17 434
1996	91 992	9 258	30 042	17 249	8 072	27 371	17 978
1997	93 687	9 414	30 552	17 302	8 271	28 148	18 801
1998	94 330	9 510	30 249	17 101	8 426	29 044	19 107
1999	95 316	9 235	30 211	17 388	8 556	29 925	19 668
2000	97 320	9 544	30 438	17 770	9 075	30 493	20 078
2001	97 560	9 550	30 126	17 671	9 393	30 821	20 136
2002	97 476	9 394	29 836	17 209	9 440	31 597	20 670
2003	98 120	9 437	29 645	17 227	9 476	32 335	21 103
2004	98 967	9 335	29 571	17 445	9 817	32 799	21 299
2005	100 613	9 579	29 911	17 515	10 256	33 352	21 550
Black[1]							
1995	11 249	1 482	4 142	2 517	960	2 149	1 538
1996	11 518	1 534	4 192	2 640	969	2 183	1 539
1997	11 882	1 578	4 409	2 681	984	2 230	1 591
1998	12 324	1 579	4 504	2 776	1 020	2 446	1 741
1999	12 771	1 488	4 631	2 924	1 108	2 621	1 814
2000	12 852	1 499	4 571	2 910	1 160	2 713	1 866
2001	12 797	1 492	4 492	2 871	1 216	2 727	1 921
2002	12 719	1 498	4 453	2 843	1 210	2 715	1 955
2003	12 706	1 376	4 465	2 780	1 199	2 887	2 056
2004	12 817	1 326	4 606	2 717	1 195	2 973	2 097
2005	13 177	1 369	4 742	2 720	1 288	3 057	2 106
Hispanic[2]							
1995	8 873	3 204	2 624	1 427	534	1 084	759
1996	9 368	3 450	2 746	1 453	568	1 151	813
1997	10 214	3 738	2 945	1 603	611	1 316	926
1998	10 615	3 889	3 018	1 622	660	1 427	1 007
1999	10 985	3 926	3 213	1 696	660	1 491	1 034
2000	12 406	4 468	3 658	1 828	756	1 696	1 198
2001	12 817	4 601	3 796	1 916	781	1 723	1 223
2002	13 294	4 744	3 921	1 900	823	1 906	1 370
2003	14 205	5 073	4 169	2 037	889	2 039	1 468
2004	14 661	5 135	4 330	2 137	931	2 127	1 538
2005	15 362	5 367	4 535	2 230	997	2 232	1 595

[1]Beginning in 2003, persons who selected this race group only; persons who selected more than one race group are not included. Prior to 2003, persons who reported more than one race group were included in the group they identified as their main race.
[2]May be of any race.

Table 1-16. Number of Employed Persons Age 25 Years and Over, by Educational Attainment, Sex, Race, and Hispanic Origin, 1995–2005—*Continued*

(Thousands of people.)

Race, Hispanic origin, sex, and year	Total	Less than a high school diploma	High school graduate, no college	Some college, no degree	Associate degree	College graduate or higher	
						Total	Bachelor's degree only
White Men[1]							
1995	49 641	5 444	15 760	9 155	3 856	15 426	9 780
1996	50 533	5 920	15 995	9 197	3 861	15 559	9 965
1997	51 397	6 049	16 330	9 245	3 941	15 832	10 191
1998	51 842	6 123	16 308	9 009	4 118	16 284	10 490
1999	52 180	5 883	16 193	9 182	4 160	16 763	10 806
2000	53 243	6 085	16 373	9 435	4 320	17 030	11 029
2001	53 375	6 080	16 292	9 344	4 501	17 158	11 060
2002	53 242	6 072	16 148	9 102	4 497	17 423	11 217
2003	53 458	6 192	16 068	9 042	4 431	17 725	11 461
2004	54 133	6 188	16 297	9 125	4 613	17 910	11 555
2005	55 214	6 368	16 750	9 225	4 851	18 021	11 551
White Women[1]							
1995	40 857	3 246	14 016	8 110	4 115	11 370	7 655
1996	41 459	3 337	14 046	8 052	4 211	11 812	8 012
1997	42 290	3 365	14 222	8 058	4 330	12 316	8 410
1998	42 488	3 387	13 941	8 092	4 308	12 760	8 618
1999	43 135	3 352	14 018	8 207	4 396	13 162	8 862
2000	44 077	3 459	14 065	8 335	4 755	13 463	9 049
2001	44 184	3 469	13 834	8 327	4 891	13 663	9 075
2002	44 234	3 322	13 688	8 107	4 944	14 173	9 453
2003	44 662	3 245	13 576	8 185	5 045	14 610	9 643
2004	44 834	3 146	13 275	8 320	5 203	14 888	9 744
2005	45 399	3 211	13 162	8 290	5 405	15 331	9 999
Black Men[1]							
1995	5 423	778	2 101	1 142	393	1 010	717
1996	5 483	861	2 104	1 177	382	960	666
1997	5 658	868	2 181	1 241	385	983	710
1998	5 844	811	2 248	1 267	413	1 104	802
1999	6 001	741	2 339	1 313	469	1 140	789
2000	6 011	755	2 253	1 326	466	1 210	828
2001	5 924	762	2 232	1 258	486	1 186	834
2002	5 928	785	2 212	1 264	482	1 185	855
2003	5 860	693	2 190	1 256	492	1 230	890
2004	5 942	676	2 287	1 172	503	1 305	931
2005	6 153	697	2 417	1 171	558	1 310	938
Black Women[1]							
1995	5 826	704	2 042	1 375	566	1 139	822
1996	6 035	673	2 088	1 463	587	1 224	873
1997	6 225	710	2 229	1 439	600	1 247	882
1998	6 480	768	2 256	1 509	607	1 341	939
1999	6 770	746	2 292	1 612	639	1 481	1 025
2000	6 841	743	2 318	1 583	694	1 503	1 038
2001	6 873	730	2 260	1 612	729	1 541	1 087
2002	6 791	713	2 241	1 579	729	1 530	1 101
2003	6 846	683	2 275	1 524	707	1 657	1 166
2004	6 874	650	2 319	1 545	691	1 668	1 166
2005	7 024	672	2 325	1 549	730	1 748	1 169
Hispanic Men[2]							
1995	5 337	2 125	1 501	818	279	615	408
1996	5 640	2 320	1 588	790	271	671	456
1997	6 165	2 502	1 714	899	302	747	502
1998	6 397	2 594	1 764	913	336	790	547
1999	6 441	2 554	1 839	917	334	797	540
2000	7 373	2 937	2 128	995	397	916	634
2001	7 628	3 041	2 174	1 082	386	945	669
2002	7 865	3 141	2 244	1 029	415	1 035	732
2003	8 578	3 424	2 461	1 105	451	1 137	806
2004	8 872	3 508	2 583	1 158	468	1 155	837
2005	9 361	3 639	2 775	1 251	503	1 193	847
Hispanic Women[2]							
1995	3 536	1 079	1 123	609	255	470	351
1996	3 729	1 131	1 159	663	297	480	357
1997	4 049	1 236	1 231	704	309	569	425
1998	4 219	1 295	1 254	708	325	637	459
1999	4 544	1 372	1 373	778	327	694	494
2000	5 033	1 531	1 529	833	359	780	564
2001	5 190	1 560	1 622	834	395	778	553
2002	5 429	1 604	1 676	871	408	871	638
2003	5 627	1 649	1 708	932	438	901	661
2004	5 789	1 628	1 746	980	463	972	701
2005	6 000	1 728	1 759	979	495	1 039	748

[1]Beginning in 2003, persons who selected this race group only; persons who selected more than one race group are not included. Prior to 2003, persons who reported more than one race group were included in the group they identified as their main race.
[2]May be of any race.

Table 1-17. Multiple Jobholders and Multiple Jobholding Rates, by Selected Characteristics, May of Selected Years, 1970–2006

(Thousands of people, percent, not seasonally adjusted.)

Year	Total employed	Multiple jobholders				Multiple jobholding rate[1]				
		Total	Men	Women		Total	Men	Women	White	Black[2]
				Number	Percent of all multiple jobholders					
1970	78 358	4 048	3 412	636	15.7	5.2	7.0	2.2	5.3	4.4
1971	78 708	4 035	3 270	765	19.0	5.1	6.7	2.6	5.3	3.8
1972	81 224	3 770	3 035	735	19.5	4.6	6.0	2.4	4.8	3.7
1973	83 758	4 262	3 393	869	20.4	5.1	6.6	2.7	5.1	4.7
1974	85 786	3 889	3 022	867	22.3	4.5	5.8	2.6	4.6	3.8
1975	84 146	3 918	2 962	956	24.4	4.7	5.8	2.9	4.8	3.7
1976	87 278	3 948	3 037	911	23.1	4.5	5.8	2.6	4.7	2.8
1977	90 482	4 558	3 317	1 241	27.2	5.0	6.2	3.4	5.3	2.6
1978	93 904	4 493	3 212	1 281	28.5	4.8	5.8	3.3	5.0	3.1
1979	96 327	4 724	3 317	1 407	29.8	4.9	5.9	3.5	5.1	3.0
1980	96 809	4 759	3 210	1 549	32.5	4.9	5.8	3.8	5.1	3.2
1985	106 878	5 730	3 537	2 192	38.3	5.4	5.9	4.7	5.7	3.2
1989	117 084	7 225	4 115	3 109	43.0	6.2	6.4	5.9	6.5	4.3
1991	116 626	7 183	4 054	3 129	43.6	6.2	6.4	5.9	6.4	4.9
1994	122 946	7 316	3 973	3 343	45.7	6.0	6.0	5.9	6.1	4.9
1995	124 554	7 952	4 225	3 727	46.9	6.4	6.3	6.5	6.6	5.2
1996	126 391	7 846	4 352	3 494	44.5	6.2	6.4	6.0	6.4	5.1
1997	129 565	8 197	4 398	3 800	46.4	6.3	6.3	6.4	6.5	5.7
1998	131 476	8 126	4 438	3 688	45.4	6.2	6.3	6.1	6.3	5.5
1999	133 411	7 895	4 117	3 778	47.9	5.9	5.8	6.1	6.0	5.5
2000	136 685	7 751	4 084	3 667	47.3	5.7	5.6	5.8	5.9	4.9
2001	137 121	7 540	3 914	3 626	48.1	5.5	5.3	5.7	5.6	5.3
2002	136 559	7 247	3 736	3 511	48.4	5.3	5.1	5.5	5.5	4.7
2003	137 567	7 338	3 841	3 498	47.7	5.3	5.3	5.4	5.5	4.3
2004	138 867	7 258	3 653	3 605	49.7	5.2	4.9	5.6	5.3	5.1
2005	141 591	7 348	3 741	3 607	49.1	5.2	4.9	5.5	5.4	4.4
2006	144 041	7 641	3 863	3 778	49.4	5.3	5.0	5.7	5.3	5.4

Note: Data prior to 1985 reflect 1970 census–based population controls; for 1985 to 1991, data reflect 1980 census–based controls; and for 1994 to 1997, data reflect 1990 census–based controls adjusted for the estimated undercount. Beginning in 1994, data reflect the introduction of a major redesign of the Current Population Survey (CPS). Beginning in 1997, data reflect revised population controls. Beginning in 1998, data reflect new composite estimation procedures and revised population controls. Beginning in 1999, 2000, and 2004, data reflect revised population controls. These changes affect comparability with data for prior periods. Comprehensive surveys of multiple jobholders were not conducted in 1981–1984, 1986–1988, 1990, or 1992–1993.

[1]Multiple jobholders as a percent of all employed persons in specified group.
[2]Data for years prior to 1977 refer to the Black-and-Other population group.

Table 1-18. Multiple Jobholders, by Sex, Age, Marital Status, Race, Hispanic Origin, and Job Status, 2002–2005

(Thousands of people, percent.)

Characteristic	Both sexes				Men				Women			
	Number		Rate[1]		Number		Rate[1]		Number		Rate[1]	
	2002	2003	2002	2003	2002	2003	2002	2003	2002	2003	2002	2003
Age												
Total, 16 years and over[2]	7 291	7 315	5.3	5.3	3 734	3 716	5.0	5.1	3 557	3 599	5.6	5.6
16 to 19 years	286	280	4.5	4.7	114	107	3.6	3.7	171	173	5.4	5.7
20 to 24 years	740	778	5.5	5.8	335	350	4.8	5.0	405	428	6.4	6.7
25 to 34 years	1 551	...	5.1	...	833	...	5.0	...	718	696	5.2	5.1
35 to 44 years	2 016	...	5.7	...	1 055	...	5.6	...	961	920	5.9	5.7
45 to 54 years	1 808	...	5.8	...	927	...	5.6	...	881	908	5.9	5.9
55 to 64 years	752	837	4.8	5.0	394	430	4.7	4.9	358	407	4.9	5.2
65 years and over	139	154	3.2	3.3	76	87	3.1	3.4	63	67	3.4	3.3
Marital Status												
Single	1 980	1 978	5.4	5.4	920	907	4.6	4.6	1 060	1 070	6.4	6.4
Married, spouse present	3 998	4 067	5.1	5.1	2 362	2 398	5.4	5.4	1 636	1 669	4.8	4.8
Widowed, divorced, or separated	1 313	1 270	6.1	5.8	452	410	5.1	4.6	861	860	6.7	6.6
Race and Hispanic Origin												
White[3]	6 270	6 273	5.5	5.5	3 233	3 190	5.2	5.2	3 037	3 083	5.8	5.9
Black[3]	709	645	4.8	4.4	343	328	4.9	4.8	366	317	4.6	4.0
Hispanic[4]	579	554	3.5	3.2	347	325	3.5	3.1	232	229	3.4	3.3
Full- or Part-time Status												
Primary job full time, secondary job part time	3 937	3 825	...	...	2 235	2 164	...	...	1 701	1 661	...	...
Primary and secondary jobs, both part time	1 590	1 651	...	...	493	510	...	...	1 097	1 141	...	...
Primary and secondary jobs, both full time	276	273	...	...	186	187	...	...	90	86	...	...
Hours vary on primary or secondary job	1 449	1 523	...	...	801	831	...	...	647	692	...	...

Characteristic	Both sexes				Men				Women			
	Number		Rate[1]		Number		Rate[1]		Number		Rate[1]	
	2004	2005	2004	2005	2004	2005	2004	2005	2004	2005	2004	2005
Age												
Total, 16 years and over[2]	7 473	7 546	5.4	5.3	3 835	3 855	5.1	5.1	3 638	3 691	5.6	5.6
16 to 19 years	274	298	4.6	5.0	107	118	3.6	4.0	167	180	5.7	5.9
20 to 24 years	795	798	5.8	5.8	377	373	5.2	5.1	419	425	6.5	6.5
25 to 34 years	1 608	1 582	5.3	5.2	853	827	5.1	4.9	755	755	5.6	5.5
35 to 44 years	1 898	1 900	5.5	5.5	1 012	1 016	5.4	5.4	886	884	5.6	5.6
45 to 54 years	1 855	1 879	5.7	5.7	935	939	5.5	5.4	920	940	5.9	6.0
55 to 64 years	869	900	5.0	4.9	451	473	4.9	4.9	417	426	5.1	4.9
65 years and over	173	189	3.6	3.7	100	109	3.7	3.8	74	80	3.4	3.6
Marital Status												
Single	2 044	2 113	5.5	5.5	964	987	4.7	4.7	1 080	1 125	6.4	6.4
Married, spouse present	4 125	4 109	5.2	5.1	2 408	2 416	5.3	5.3	1 718	1 693	5.0	4.9
Widowed, divorced, or separated	1 303	1 324	5.9	5.8	463	452	5.1	4.8	840	872	6.4	6.5
Race and Hispanic Origin												
White[3]	6 357	6 342	5.5	5.4	3 266	3 268	5.2	5.1	3 091	3 074	5.9	5.8
Black[3]	705	763	4.7	5.0	360	363	5.2	5.1	345	400	4.3	4.9
Hispanic[4]	612	582	3.4	3.1	363	333	3.4	2.9	248	248	3.5	3.4
Full- or Part-time Status												
Primary job full time, secondary job part time	3 908	3 942	...	...	2 210	2 219	...	...	1 697	1 724	...	...
Primary and secondary jobs, both part time	1 678	1 708	...	...	540	570	...	...	1 138	1 138	...	...
Primary and secondary jobs, both full time	286	294	...	...	187	188	...	...	100	105	...	...
Hours vary on primary or secondary job	1 564	1 558	...	...	879	859	...	...	685	698	...	...

Note: Estimates for the above race groups (White or Black) do not sum to totals because data are not presented for all races. Beginning in January 2003, data reflect the revised population controls used in the household survey.

[1]Multiple jobholders as a percent of all employed persons in specified group.
[2]Includes a small number of persons who work part time at their primary job and full time at their secondary job(s), not shown separately.
[3]Beginning in 2003, persons who selected this race group only; persons who selected more than one race group are not included. Prior to 2003, persons who reported more than one race group were included in the group they identified as their main race.
[4]May be of any race.
. . . = Not available.

Table 1-19. Multiple Jobholders, by Sex and Industry of Principal Secondary Job, Annual Averages, 2003–2005

(Thousands of people.)

Year and industry of secondary job	Both sexes	Men	Women
2003			
All Nonagricultural Industries, Wage and Salary Workers	5 134	2 402	2 732
Mining	3	2	1
Construction	141	90	51
Manufacturing	147	94	53
Durable goods	80	55	25
Nondurable goods	67	39	28
Wholesale and retail trade	875	382	493
Wholesale trade	76	57	19
Retail trade	799	325	474
Transportation and utilities	173	122	51
Transportation and warehousing	160	112	48
Utilities	13	10	4
Information	144	92	52
Financial activities	251	142	109
Professional and business services	483	270	213
Education and health services	1 296	437	859
Leisure and hospitality	966	444	521
Other services	439	181	258
Other services, except private households	364	175	189
Other servces, private households	75	6	68
Public administration	217	146	71
2004			
All Nonagricultural Industries, Wage and Salary Workers	5 149	2 444	2 705
Mining	9	6	4
Construction	246	196	49
Manufacturing	169	102	67
Durable goods	92	60	32
Nondurable goods	77	42	35
Wholesale and retail trade	1 137	488	648
Wholesale trade	89	48	40
Retail trade	1 048	440	608
Transportation and utilities	185	137	49
Transportation and warehousing	172	127	45
Utilities	13	10	3
Information	197	123	74
Financial activities	371	224	147
Professional and business services	850	483	366
Education and health services	1 455	511	945
Leisure and hospitality	1 114	560	554
Other services	533	235	298
Other services, except private households	455	228	226
Other servces, private households	79	7	71
Public administration	196	133	63
2005			
All Nonagricultural Industries, Wage and Salary Workers	5 209	2 458	2 751
Mining	7	3	4
Construction	239	199	40
Manufacturing	195	122	73
Durable goods	124	86	38
Nondurable goods	72	36	36
Wholesale and retail trade	1 126	464	661
Wholesale trade	112	78	34
Retail trade	1 014	387	627
Transportation and utilities	186	138	48
Transportation and warehousing	172	131	41
Utilities	14	7	7
Information	175	113	62
Financial activities	369	225	144
Professional and business services	836	499	337
Education and health services	1 527	535	992
Leisure and hospitality	1 120	547	573
Other services	536	245	291
Other services, except private households	453	235	218
Other servces, private households	84	10	73
Public administration	215	130	85

Table 1-20. Employment and Unemployment in Families, by Race and Hispanic Origin, Annual Averages, 1995–2005

(Thousands of people, percent.)

Characteristic	1995	1996	1997	1998	1999	2000	2001	2002	2003	2004	2005
ALL RACES											
Total Families	68 552	69 203	69 714	70 218	71 250	71 680	73 306	74 169	75 301	75 872	76 443
With employed member(s)	55 633	56 342	57 289	57 986	59 185	59 626	60 707	61 121	61 761	62 424	62 933
As percent of total families	81.2	81.4	82.2	82.6	83.1	83.2	82.8	82.4	82.0	82.3	82.3
Some usually work full time[1]	51 473	52 249	53 226	53 945	55 123	55 683	56 519	56 742	57 229	57 813	58 276
With no employed member	12 919	12 860	12 425	12 232	12 065	12 054	12 600	13 048	13 540	13 447	13 509
As percent of total families	18.8	18.6	17.8	17.4	16.9	16.8	17.2	17.6	18.0	17.7	17.7
With unemployed member(s)	5 404	5 270	4 913	4 503	4 260	4 110	4 847	5 809	6 079	5 593	5 318
As percent of total families	7.9	7.6	7.0	6.4	6.0	5.7	6.6	7.8	8.1	7.4	7.0
Some member(s) employed	3 795	3 678	3 445	3 177	3 091	2 973	3 494	4 126	4 285	3 915	3 717
As percent of families with unemployed member(s)	70.2	69.8	70.1	70.6	72.6	72.3	72.1	71.0	70.5	70.0	69.9
Some usually work full time[1]	3 334	3 265	3 070	2 830	2 771	2 675	3 122	3 668	3 790	3 494	3 310
As percent of families with unemployed member(s)	61.7	62.0	62.5	62.8	65.0	65.1	64.4	63.1	62.3	62.5	62.2
WHITE[2]											
Total Families	57 650	58 315	58 514	58 930	59 661	59 918	60 921	61 494	61 995	62 250	62 567
With employed member(s)	47 216	47 882	48 378	48 850	49 632	49 877	50 505	50 785	51 002	51 350	51 645
As percent of total families	81.9	82.1	82.7	82.9	83.2	83.2	83.0	82.6	82.3	82.5	82.5
Some usually work full time[1]	43 804	44 522	45 069	45 567	46 333	46 639	47 060	47 193	47 356	47 620	47 883
With no employed member	10 433	10 434	10 135	10 080	10 029	10 042	10 416	10 709	10 993	10 900	10 922
As percent of total families	18.1	17.9	17.3	17.1	16.8	16.8	17.0	17.4	17.7	17.5	17.5
With unemployed member(s)	4 002	3 896	3 566	3 299	3 134	3 010	3 553	4 275	4 411	4 078	3 801
As percent of total families	6.9	6.7	6.1	5.6	5.3	5.0	5.8	7.0	7.1	6.6	6.1
Some member(s) employed	2 934	2 875	2 632	2 463	2 374	2 276	2 661	3 164	3 245	3 000	2 782
As percent of families with unemployed member(s)	73.3	73.8	73.8	74.7	75.8	75.6	74.9	74.0	73.6	73.6	73.2
Some usually work full time[1]	2 579	2 557	2 353	2 204	2 132	2 052	2 379	2 808	2 873	2 677	2 477
As percent of families with unemployed member(s)	64.4	65.6	66.0	66.8	68.0	68.2	67.0	65.7	65.1	65.7	65.2
BLACK[2]											
Total Families	8 015	8 149	8 308	8 317	8 498	8 600	8 674	8 845	8 869	8 860	8 952
With employed member(s)	5 991	6 137	6 409	6 554	6 847	6 964	6 933	6 987	6 906	6 920	6 986
As percent of total families	74.7	75.3	77.1	78.8	80.6	81.0	80.0	79.0	77.9	78.1	78.0
Some usually work full time[1]	5 419	5 563	5 810	5 953	6 249	6 401	6 373	6 390	6 270	6 292	6 353
With no employed member	2 024	2 012	1 899	1 763	1 652	1 636	1 742	1 858	1 963	1 940	1 966
As percent of total families	25.3	24.7	22.9	21.2	19.4	19.0	20.1	21.0	22.1	21.9	22.0
With unemployed member(s)	1 080	1 121	1 104	984	905	881	990	1 162	1 213	1 127	1 140
As percent of total families	13.5	13.8	13.3	11.8	10.6	10.2	11.4	13.1	13.7	12.7	12.7
Some member(s) employed	631	627	631	555	551	535	596	689	695	625	657
As percent of families with unemployed member(s)	58.4	55.9	57.2	56.4	60.9	60.8	60.2	59.3	57.3	55.5	57.7
Some usually work full time[1]	556	553	553	485	486	476	533	611	612	556	583
As percent of families with unemployed member(s)	51.5	49.3	50.1	49.3	53.7	54.1	53.8	52.6	50.5	49.3	51.1
HISPANIC[3]											
Total Families	6 233	6 465	6 779	7 025	7 403	7 581	8 140	8 650	9 185	9 305	9 603
With employed member(s)	5 086	5 312	5 701	5 947	6 405	6 633	7 100	7 485	7 907	8 071	8 312
As percent of total families	81.6	82.2	84.1	84.7	86.5	87.5	87.2	86.5	86.1	86.7	86.6
Some usually work full time[1]	4 673	4 917	5 285	5 545	6 017	6 255	6 692	6 989	7 383	7 566	7 786
With no employed member	1 147	1 153	1 078	1 078	998	947	1 040	1 165	1 277	1 235	1 291
As percent of total families	18.4	17.8	15.9	15.3	13.5	12.5	12.8	13.5	13.9	13.3	13.4
With unemployed member(s)	841	841	789	744	715	679	809	965	1 020	950	860
As percent of total families	13.5	13.0	11.6	10.6	9.7	9.0	9.9	11.2	11.1	10.2	9.0
Some member(s) employed	568	563	532	522	518	493	592	686	715	664	606
As percent of families with unemployed member(s)	67.5	66.9	67.4	70.2	72.4	72.7	73.2	71.1	70.1	69.9	70.5
Some usually work full time[1]	490	497	473	467	467	446	537	615	640	594	544
As percent of families with unemployed member(s)	58.3	59.1	59.9	62.8	65.3	65.8	66.4	63.7	62.7	62.5	63.2

Note: The race or ethnicity of the family is determined by the race of the householder. Estimates for the above race groups (White or Black) do not sum to totals because data are not presented for all races. Detail may not sum to total due to rounding. Data for 2003 reflect the revised population controls used in the Current Population Survey (CPS).

[1]Usually work 35 hours or more a week at all jobs.
[2]Beginning in 2003, families where the householder selected this race group only; families where the householder selected more than one race group are excluded. Prior to 2003, families where the householder selected more than one race group were included in the group that the householder identified as the main race.
[3]May be of any race.

Table 1-21. Families, by Presence and Relationship of Employed Members and Family Type, Annual Averages, 2000–2005

(Thousands of people, percent.)

Characteristic	Number						Percent distribution					
	2000	2001	2002	2003	2004	2005	2000	2001	2002	2003	2004	2005
MARRIED-COUPLE FAMILIES												
Total	54 704	55 749	56 280	57 074	57 188	57 167	100.0	100.0	100.0	100.0	100.0	100.0
Member(s) employed, total	45 967	46 680	46 976	47 535	47 767	47 895	84.0	83.7	83.5	83.3	83.5	83.8
Husband only	10 500	10 833	11 174	11 403	11 712	11 562	19.2	19.4	19.9	20.0	20.5	20.2
Wife only	2 946	3 257	3 613	3 863	3 843	3 715	5.4	5.8	6.4	6.8	6.7	6.5
Husband and wife	29 128	29 241	28 873	29 077	28 991	29 330	53.2	52.5	51.3	50.9	50.7	51.3
Other employment combinations	3 394	3 350	3 317	3 193	3 222	3 288	6.2	6.0	5.9	5.6	5.6	5.8
No member(s) employed	8 737	9 068	9 303	9 539	9 420	9 272	16.0	16.3	16.5	16.7	16.5	16.2
FAMILIES MAINTAINED BY WOMEN[1]												
Total	12 775	13 037	13 215	13 450	13 614	14 035	100.0	100.0	100.0	100.0	100.0	100.0
Member(s) employed, total	10 026	10 131	10 169	10 187	10 358	10 609	78.5	77.7	77.0	75.7	76.1	75.6
Householder only	5 581	5 667	5 944	5 987	6 021	6 052	43.7	43.5	45.0	44.5	44.2	43.1
Householder and other member(s)	2 806	2 778	2 559	2 539	2 701	2 830	22.0	21.3	19.4	18.9	19.8	20.2
Other member(s), not householder	1 639	1 686	1 666	1 660	1 636	1 727	12.8	12.9	12.6	12.3	12.0	12.3
No member(s) employed	2 749	2 906	3 047	3 263	3 255	3 426	21.5	22.3	23.1	24.3	23.9	24.4
FAMILIES MAINTAINED BY MEN[1]												
Total	4 200	4 521	4 674	4 777	5 071	5 242	100.0	100.0	100.0	100.0	100.0	100.0
Member(s) employed, total	3 632	3 895	3 976	4 039	4 299	4 430	86.5	86.2	85.1	84.6	84.8	84.5
Householder only	1 761	1 875	1 939	1 954	2 060	2 093	41.9	41.5	41.5	40.9	40.6	39.9
Householder and other member(s)	1 358	1 450	1 440	1 427	1 557	1 639	32.3	32.1	30.8	29.9	30.7	31.3
Other member(s), not householder	514	570	598	658	682	698	12.2	12.6	12.8	13.8	13.5	13.3
No member(s) employed	567	625	698	739	772	812	13.5	13.8	14.9	15.5	15.2	15.5

Note: Detail may not sum to total due to rounding.

[1]No spouse present.

Table 1-22. Unemployment in Families, by Presence and Relationship of Employed Members and Family Type, Annual Averages, 2000–2005

(Thousands of people, percent.)

Characteristic	Number						Percent distribution					
	2000	2001	2002	2003	2004	2005	2000	2001	2002	2003	2004	2005
MARRIED-COUPLE FAMILIES												
With Unemployed Member(s), Total	2 584	3 081	3 772	3 857	3 521	3 243	100.0	100.0	100.0	100.0	100.0	100.0
No member employed	411	531	676	713	615	580	15.9	17.2	17.9	18.5	17.5	17.9
Some member(s) employed	2 174	2 550	3 096	3 144	2 906	2 664	84.1	82.8	82.1	81.5	82.5	82.1
Husband unemployed	836	1 160	1 523	1 600	1 333	1 190	32.3	37.7	40.4	41.5	37.9	36.7
Wife employed	531	736	993	1 023	850	753	20.5	23.9	26.3	26.5	24.2	23.2
Wife unemployed	789	918	1 117	1 129	1 041	1 004	30.5	29.8	29.6	29.3	29.6	31.0
Husband employed	694	809	969	991	913	873	26.8	26.3	25.7	25.7	25.9	26.9
Other family member unemployed	959	1 003	1 133	1 129	1 147	1 049	37.1	32.6	30.0	29.3	32.6	32.4
FAMILIES MAINTAINED BY WOMEN[1]												
With Unemployed Member(s), Total	1 194	1 324	1 504	1 612	1 521	1 539	100.0	100.0	100.0	100.0	100.0	100.0
No member employed	587	643	787	842	829	797	49.1	48.6	52.3	52.2	54.5	51.8
Some member(s) employed	607	681	717	770	692	743	50.9	51.4	47.7	47.8	45.5	48.2
Householder unemployed	522	593	737	791	758	746	43.7	44.8	49.0	49.1	49.8	48.5
Other member(s) employed	102	129	147	162	146	161	85.0	9.7	9.8	10.0	9.6	10.5
Other member(s) unemployed	672	731	767	821	764	793	56.3	55.2	51.0	50.9	50.2	51.5
FAMILIES MAINTAINED BY MEN[1]												
With Unemployed Member(s), Total	331	442	533	610	551	536	100.0	100.0	100.0	100.0	100.0	100.0
No member employed	139	178	220	239	234	225	42.0	40.3	41.3	39.2	42.5	42.1
Some member(s) employed	192	264	313	371	316	310	58.0	59.7	58.7	60.8	57.5	57.9
Householder unemployed	173	234	303	340	296	301	52.2	52.9	56.8	55.7	53.7	56.1
Other member(s) employed	67	96	129	158	117	122	20.4	21.7	24.2	25.9	21.3	22.8
Other member(s) unemployed	158	208	230	270	255	235	47.8	47.1	43.2	44.3	46.3	43.9

Note: Detail may not sum to total due to rounding.

[1]No spouse present.

Table 1-23. Employment Status of the Population, by Sex, Marital Status, and Presence and Age of Own Children Under 18 Years, Annual Averages, 2000–2005

(Thousands of people, percent.)

Characteristic	2000			2001			2002		
	Both sexes	Men	Women	Both sexes	Men	Women	Both sexes	Men	Women
With Own Children Under 18 Years, Total									
Civilian noninstitutional population	63 267	27 673	35 595	64 100	28 076	36 024	64 399	28 137	36 263
Civilian labor force	51 944	26 202	25 742	52 489	26 551	25 938	52 566	26 529	26 036
Participation rate	82.1	94.7	72.3	81.9	94.6	72.0	81.6	94.3	71.8
Employed	50 259	25 622	24 637	50 455	25 750	24 704	50 022	25 474	24 549
Employment-population ratio	79.4	92.6	69.2	78.7	91.7	68.6	77.7	90.5	67.7
Full-time workers[1]	43 365	24 922	18 443	43 424	24 964	18 460	42 884	24 644	18 240
Part-time workers[2]	6 894	699	6 195	7 031	787	6 244	7 138	829	6 308
Unemployed	1 685	581	1 104	2 034	801	1 233	2 543	1 056	1 488
Unemployment rate	3.2	2.2	4.3	3.9	3.0	4.8	4.8	4.0	5.7
Married, Spouse Present									
Civilian noninstitutional population	51 415	25 540	25 874	51 981	25 796	26 185	51 947	25 781	26 166
Civilian labor force	42 361	24 290	18 072	42 712	24 512	18 201	42 492	24 425	18 067
Participation rate	82.4	95.1	69.8	82.2	95.0	69.5	81.8	94.7	69.0
Employed	41 357	23 816	17 541	41 431	23 849	17 581	40 867	23 533	17 334
Employment-population ratio	80.4	93.2	67.8	79.7	92.5	67.1	78.7	91.3	66.2
Full-time workers[1]	35 793	23 212	12 581	35 772	23 169	12 603	35 180	22 825	12 356
Part-time workers[2]	5 564	604	4 960	5 659	680	4 979	5 687	708	4 979
Unemployed	1 004	474	531	1 282	662	619	1 625	893	733
Unemployment rate	2.4	2.0	2.9	3.0	2.7	3.4	3.8	3.7	4.1
Other Marital Status[3]									
Civilian noninstitutional population	11 853	2 132	9 720	12 119	2 280	9 839	12 452	2 355	10 096
Civilian labor force	9 583	1 913	7 670	9 777	2 039	7 737	10 073	2 103	7 970
Participation rate	80.8	89.7	78.9	80.7	89.4	78.6	80.9	89.3	78.9
Employed	8 902	1 806	7 096	9 024	1 902	7 123	9 155	1 941	7 215
Employment-population ratio	75.1	84.7	73.0	74.5	83.4	72.4	73.5	82.4	71.5
Full-time workers[1]	7 572	1 710	5 862	7 652	1 795	5 857	7 704	1 820	5 885
Part-time workers[2]	1 330	96	1 234	1 372	107	1 265	1 451	122	1 329
Unemployed	681	107	574	752	138	614	918	163	755
Unemployment rate	7.1	5.6	7.5	7.7	6.8	7.9	9.1	7.8	9.5
With Own Children 6 to 17 Years, None Younger									
Civilian noninstitutional population	34 737	15 165	19 572	35 523	15 486	20 038	35 829	15 580	20 250
Civilian labor force	29 576	14 178	15 398	30 182	14 489	15 693	30 371	14 541	15 830
Participation rate	85.1	93.5	78.7	85.0	93.6	78.3	84.8	93.3	78.2
Employed	28 744	13 877	14 868	29 174	14 096	15 078	29 122	14 023	15 099
Employment-population ratio	82.7	91.5	76.0	82.1	91.0	75.2	81.3	90.0	74.6
Full-time workers[1]	25 042	13 513	11 529	25 382	13 689	11 693	25 225	13 586	11 638
Part-time workers[2]	3 703	364	3 339	3 792	407	3 385	3 898	437	3 461
Unemployed	832	302	530	1 008	393	615	1 249	518	731
Unemployment rate	2.8	2.1	3.4	3.3	2.7	3.9	4.1	3.6	4.6
With Own Children Under 6 Years									
Civilian noninstitutional population	28 530	12 508	16 022	28 577	12 590	15 986	28 570	12 557	16 013
Civilian labor force	22 368	12 024	10 344	22 307	12 062	10 245	22 194	11 988	10 206
Participation rate	78.4	96.1	64.6	78.1	95.8	64.1	77.7	95.5	63.7
Employed	21 515	11 745	9 770	21 280	11 654	9 626	20 900	11 450	9 450
Employment-population ratio	75.4	93.9	61.0	74.5	92.6	60.2	73.2	91.2	59.0
Full-time workers[1]	18 323	11 410	6 914	18 041	11 274	6 767	17 660	11 058	6 602
Part-time workers[2]	3 191	335	2 856	3 239	380	2 859	3 240	392	2 848
Unemployed	853	279	574	1 026	408	619	1 294	538	757
Unemployment rate	3.8	2.3	5.6	4.6	3.4	6.0	5.8	4.5	7.4
With No Own Children Under 18 Years									
Civilian noninstitutional population	145 199	71 825	73 374	149 643	73 857	75 786	151 715	74 993	76 722
Civilian labor force	88 014	48 140	39 874	90 171	49 249	40 922	90 971	49 644	41 327
Participation rate	60.6	67.0	54.3	60.3	66.7	54.0	60.0	66.2	53.9
Employed	84 058	45 781	38 278	85 421	46 371	39 050	85 187	46 154	39 034
Employment-population ratio	57.9	63.7	52.2	57.1	62.8	51.5	56.1	61.5	50.9
Full-time workers[1]	68 046	39 136	28 910	69 074	39 596	29 478	68 574	39 319	29 254
Part-time workers[2]	16 012	6 645	9 367	16 347	6 776	9 572	16 614	6 834	9 779
Unemployed	3 956	2 359	1 596	4 750	2 878	1 872	5 784	3 491	2 293
Unemployment rate	4.5	4.9	4.0	5.3	5.8	4.6	6.4	7.0	5.5

Note: Own children include sons, daughters, stepchildren, and adopted children. Not included are nieces, nephews, grandchildren, and other related and unrelated children. Detail may not sum to total due to rounding.

[1]Usually work 35 hours or more a week at all jobs.
[2]Usually work less than 35 hours a week at all jobs.
[3]Includes never-married, divorced, separated, and widowed persons.

Table 1-23. Employment Status of the Population, by Sex, Marital Status, and Presence and Age of Own Children Under 18 Years, Annual Averages, 2000–2005—*Continued*

(Thousands of people, percent.)

Characteristic	2003			2004			2005		
	Both sexes	Men	Women	Both sexes	Men	Women	Both sexes	Men	Women
With Own Children Under 18 Years, Total									
Civilian noninstitutional population	64 932	28 402	36 530	64 758	28 272	36 486	64 482	28 065	36 417
Civilian labor force	52 727	26 739	25 988	52 288	26 607	25 681	52 056	26 399	25 657
Participation rate	81.2	94.1	71.1	80.7	94.1	70.4	80.7	94.1	70.5
Employed	50 103	25 638	24 466	49 957	25 696	24 261	49 882	25 587	24 294
Employment-population ratio	77.2	90.3	67.0	77.1	90.9	66.5	77.4	91.2	66.7
Full-time workers[1]	42 880	24 762	18 118	42 758	24 794	17 964	42 852	24 713	18 139
Part-time workers[2]	7 223	876	6 347	7 200	902	6 298	7 029	875	6 155
Unemployed	2 624	1 101	1 523	2 331	911	1 420	2 174	811	1 363
Unemployment rate	5.0	4.1	5.9	4.5	3.4	5.5	4.2	3.1	5.3
Married, Spouse Present									
Civilian noninstitutional population	52 476	26 049	26 427	52 109	25 852	26 258	51 519	25 578	25 942
Civilian labor force	42 776	24 638	18 138	42 247	24 449	17 798	41 905	24 215	17 690
Participation rate	81.5	94.6	68.6	81.1	94.6	67.8	81.3	94.7	68.2
Employed	41 128	23 712	17 416	40 847	23 703	17 144	40 614	23 556	17 058
Employment-population ratio	78.4	91.0	65.9	78.4	91.7	65.3	78.8	92.1	65.8
Full-time workers[1]	35 315	22 954	12 360	35 141	22 935	12 206	35 086	22 808	12 278
Part-time workers[2]	5 813	757	5 056	5 706	768	4 938	5 528	748	4 780
Unemployed	1 648	926	722	1 400	747	653	1 291	659	632
Unemployment rate	3.9	3.8	4.0	3.3	3.1	3.7	3.1	2.7	3.6
Other Marital Status[3]									
Civilian noninstitutional population	12 455	2 354	10 102	12 649	2 420	10 229	12 963	2 487	10 475
Civilian labor force	9 950	2 100	7 850	10 042	2 158	7 883	10 151	2 184	7 967
Participation rate	79.9	89.2	77.7	79.4	89.2	77.1	78.3	87.8	76.1
Employed	8 975	1 926	7 050	9 110	1 993	7 117	9 268	2 032	7 236
Employment-population ratio	72.1	81.8	69.8	72.0	82.4	69.6	71.5	81.7	69.1
Full-time workers[1]	7 566	1 807	5 759	7 617	1 859	5 757	7 766	1 905	5 861
Part-time workers[2]	1 411	118	1 291	1 494	134	1 360	1 502	127	1 375
Unemployed	976	175	800	931	165	766	883	152	731
Unemployment rate	9.8	8.3	10.2	9.3	7.6	9.7	8.7	7.0	9.2
With Own Children 6 to 17 Years, None Younger									
Civilian noninstitutional population	35 943	15 653	20 290	35 874	15 597	20 277	35 937	15 590	20 348
Civilian labor force	30 362	14 572	15 790	30 182	14 516	15 666	30 068	14 496	15 572
Participation rate	84.5	93.1	77.8	84.1	93.1	77.3	83.7	93.0	76.5
Employed	29 040	14 008	15 032	29 013	14 056	14 957	28 953	14 066	14 887
Employment-population ratio	80.8	89.5	74.1	80.9	90.1	73.8	80.6	90.2	73.2
Full-time workers[1]	25 116	13 558	11 557	25 069	13 597	11 473	25 074	13 606	11 468
Part-time workers[2]	3 925	450	3 475	3 944	459	3 485	3 880	460	3 419
Unemployed	1 322	564	758	1 170	460	709	1 115	430	684
Unemployment rate	4.4	3.9	4.8	3.9	3.2	4.5	3.7	3.0	4.4
With Own Children Under 6 Years									
Civilian noninstitutional population	28 988	12 749	16 240	28 884	12 675	16 210	28 545	12 475	16 070
Civilian labor force	22 365	12 167	10 198	22 106	12 091	10 014	21 988	11 903	10 085
Participation rate	77.2	95.4	62.8	76.5	95.4	61.8	77.0	95.4	62.8
Employed	21 063	11 630	9 433	20 944	11 640	9 304	20 928	11 521	9 407
Employment-population ratio	72.7	91.2	58.1	72.5	91.8	57.4	73.3	92.4	58.5
Full-time workers[1]	17 764	11 203	6 561	17 689	11 197	6 491	17 778	11 107	6 671
Part-time workers[2]	3 299	426	2 872	3 256	443	2 813	3 150	414	2 736
Unemployed	1 302	538	765	1 162	451	710	1 060	381	678
Unemployment rate	5.8	4.4	7.5	5.3	3.7	7.1	4.8	3.2	6.7
With No Own Children Under 18 Years									
Civilian noninstitutional population	154 714	76 510	78 204	156 900	77 739	79 160	159 751	79 237	80 514
Civilian labor force	92 319	50 036	42 284	93 511	50 771	42 740	95 545	51 914	43 631
Participation rate	59.7	65.4	54.1	59.6	65.3	54.0	59.8	65.5	54.2
Employed	86 233	46 294	39 939	87 748	47 282	40 467	90 171	48 709	41 462
Employment-population ratio	55.7	60.5	51.1	55.9	60.8	51.1	56.4	61.5	51.5
Full-time workers[1]	69 073	39 245	29 827	70 244	40 134	30 110	72 515	41 496	31 019
Part-time workers[2]	17 160	7 049	10 111	17 505	7 148	10 357	17 657	7 213	10 444
Unemployed	6 087	3 741	2 345	5 763	3 489	2 274	5 374	3 205	2 169
Unemployment rate	6.6	7.5	5.5	6.2	6.9	5.3	5.6	6.2	5.0

Note: Own children include sons, daughters, stepchildren, and adopted children. Not included are nieces, nephews, grandchildren, and other related and unrelated children. Detail may not sum to total due to rounding.

[1] Usually work 35 hours or more a week at all jobs.
[2] Usually work less than 35 hours a week at all jobs.
[3] Includes never-married, divorced, separated, and widowed persons.

Table 1-24. Employment Status of Mothers with Own Children Under 3 Years of Age, by Age of Youngest Child and Marital Status, Annual Averages, 2001–2005

(Thousands of people, percent.)

Year and characteristic	Civilian noninsti-tutional population	Civilian labor force		Employed				Unemployed	
		Total	Percent of population	Total	Percent of population	Full-time workers[1]	Part-time workers[2]	Number	Percent of labor force
2001									
Total Mothers with Own Children Under 3 Years	9 352	5 613	60.0	5 227	55.9	3 591	1 636	387	6.9
2 years	2 844	1 868	65.7	1 751	61.6	1 218	533	117	6.3
1 year	3 405	2 050	60.2	1 911	56.1	1 308	603	140	6.8
Under 1 year	3 103	1 695	54.6	1 565	50.4	1 065	500	130	7.7
Married, Spouse Present with Own Children Under 3 Years	7 079	4 058	57.3	3 884	54.9	2 601	1 282	175	4.3
2 years	2 120	1 310	61.8	1 258	59.3	839	419	53	4.0
1 year	2 589	1 479	57.1	1 416	54.7	940	475	63	4.3
Under 1 year	2 370	1 269	53.5	1 210	51.1	822	388	59	4.6
Other Marital Status with Own Children Under 3 Years[3]	2 269	1 555	68.5	1 343	59.2	989	352	212	13.6
2 years	723	558	77.2	493	68.2	379	114	65	11.6
1 year	814	571	70.1	495	60.8	367	127	76	13.3
Under 1 year	732	426	58.2	355	48.5	243	111	71	16.7
2002									
Total Mothers with Own Children Under 3 Years	9 350	5 632	60.2	5 181	55.4	3 513	1 667	451	8.0
2 years	2 949	1 895	64.3	1 758	59.6	1 234	524	137	7.2
1 year	3 310	2 003	60.5	1 852	56.0	1 241	610	151	7.5
Under 1 year	3 091	1 734	56.1	1 571	50.8	1 038	533	163	9.4
Married, Spouse Present with Own Children Under 3 Years	7 073	4 071	57.6	3 869	54.7	2 572	1 297	203	5.0
2 years	2 201	1 333	60.6	1 274	57.9	870	404	59	4.4
1 year	2 509	1 446	57.6	1 379	55.0	902	477	67	4.6
Under 1 year	2 363	1 292	54.7	1 216	51.5	800	416	77	6.0
Other Marital Status with Own Children Under 3 Years[3]	2 278	1 562	68.6	1 313	57.6	941	372	248	15.9
2 years	748	562	75.1	484	64.7	364	120	77	13.7
1 year	802	557	69.5	473	59.0	340	134	84	15.1
Under 1 year	728	443	60.9	356	48.9	237	118	87	19.6
2003									
Total Mothers with Own Children Under 3 Years	9 450	5 563	58.9	5 115	54.1	3 430	1 685	446	8.0
2 years	2 987	1 896	63.5	1 752	58.7	1 205	547	143	7.5
1 year	3 353	1 997	59.6	1 842	54.9	1 223	619	154	7.7
Under 1 year	3 110	1 670	53.7	1 521	48.9	1 002	519	149	8.9
Married, Spouse Present with Own Children Under 3 Years	7 165	4 068	56.8	3 872	54.0	2 529	1 342	197	4.8
2 years	2 243	1 350	60.2	1 281	57.1	853	428	69	5.1
1 year	2 541	1 458	57.4	1 395	54.9	906	488	64	4.4
Under 1 year	2 381	1 260	52.9	1 196	50.2	770	426	64	5.1
Other Marital Status with Own Children Under 3 Years[3]	2 287	1 495	65.4	1 244	54.4	902	341	250	16.7
2 years	744	546	73.4	471	63.3	352	118	75	13.7
1 year	813	539	66.3	448	55.1	317	131	91	16.9
Under 1 year	730	410	56.2	325	44.5	233	92	84	20.5
2004									
Total Mothers with Own Children Under 3 Years	9 345	5 377	57.5	4 964	53.1	3 360	1 604	414	7.7
2 years	2 813	1 746	62.1	1 630	57.9	1 152	477	116	6.6
1 year	3 273	1 906	58.2	1 759	53.7	1 172	587	147	7.7
Under 1 year	3 259	1 725	52.9	1 575	48.3	1 035	540	151	8.7
Married, Spouse Present with Own Children Under 3 Years	7 071	3 910	55.3	3 740	52.9	2 513	1 227	170	4.4
2 years	2 111	1 246	59.0	1 200	56.8	839	361	46	3.7
1 year	2 519	1 401	55.6	1 337	53.1	877	459	65	4.6
Under 1 year	2 441	1 262	51.7	1 203	49.3	797	406	59	4.7
Other Marital Status with Own Children Under 3 Years[3]	2 274	1 467	64.5	1 224	53.8	847	377	243	16.6
2 years	702	499	71.1	430	61.2	314	116	70	13.9
1 year	754	505	66.9	422	56.0	295	127	82	16.3
Under 1 year	818	463	56.6	372	45.4	238	134	91	19.7
2005									
Total Mothers with Own Children Under 3 Years	9 365	5 470	58.4	5 077	54.2	3 501	1 576	393	7.2
2 years	2 845	1 773	62.3	1 654	58.1	1 162	492	119	6.7
1 year	3 287	1 958	59.6	1 823	55.5	1 247	576	135	6.9
Under 1 year	3 233	1 740	53.8	1 600	49.5	1 092	508	140	8.0
Married, Spouse Present with Own Children Under 3 Years	6 951	3 939	56.7	3 776	54.3	2 588	1 188	164	4.2
2 years	2 118	1 268	59.9	1 214	57.3	840	374	55	4.3
1 year	2 435	1 389	57.0	1 337	54.9	901	436	52	3.7
Under 1 year	2 398	1 282	53.5	1 225	51.1	847	378	58	4.5
Other Marital Status with Own Children Under 3 Years[3]	2 414	1 531	63.4	1 301	53.9	913	388	230	15.0
2 years	726	504	69.5	440	60.6	322	118	64	12.7
1 year	852	569	66.8	486	57.0	346	139	83	14.6
Under 1 year	836	457	54.7	375	44.9	245	130	82	18.0

Note: Own children include sons, daughters, stepchildren, and adopted children. Not included are nieces, nephews, grandchildren, and other related and unrelated children. Detail may not sum to total due to rounding. Data for 2003 reflect the revised population controls used in the Current Population Survey (CPS).

[1]Usually work 35 hours or more a week at all jobs.
[2]Usually work less than 35 hours a week at all jobs.
[3]Includes never-married, divorced, separated, and widowed persons.

UNEMPLOYMENT

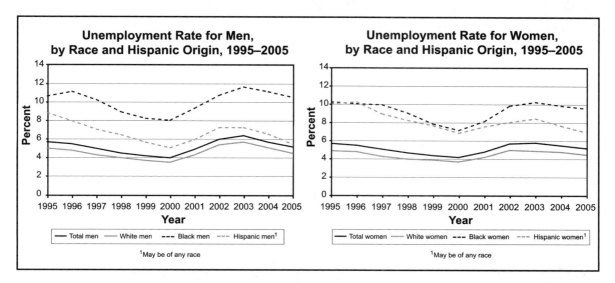

The unemployment rate fell for all groups in 2005. The overall unemployment rate dropped to 5.1 percent; however, it was still much higher than the recent low of 4.0 percent, which occured in 2000. The rates for Black men and women continued to be more than double the rates for White men and women. (See Table 1-27.)

OTHER HIGHLIGHTS

• The number of unemployed persons dropped by over 500,000 from 2004 to 2005, but the total was still 1.9 million higher than the total in 2000. (See Table 1-26.)

• The disparity in unemployment rates among age and race groups continued to be substantial in 2005. For example, the unemployment rate for White men age 20 to 24 years was 7.9 percent; for Black men of the same age, the unemployment rate was 20.5 percent. Black women age 20 to 24 years had an unemployment rate of 16.3 percent, while White women in that age group had an unemployment rate of 6.4 percent. (See Table 1-27.)

• From 2004 to 2005, the median duration of unemployment dropped from 9.8 to 8.9 weeks. (See Table 1-30.)

• In 2005, the states with the highest unemployment rates and the largest increases in unemployment from the previous year were Louisiana and Mississippi, the two states hardest hit by Hurricane Katrina. In Louisiana, the unemployment rate increased from 5.7 percent to 7.1 percent. In Mississippi, the unemployment rate increased from 6.3 percent to 7.9 percent. (See Table 1-5.)

Table 1-25. Unemployment Rate, by Selected Characteristics, 1948–2005

(Unemployment as a percent of civilian labor force.)

Year	All civilian workers	Both sexes, 16 to 19 years	Men, 20 years and over	Women, 20 years and over	White[1]	Black[1]	Asian[1]	Hispanic[2]	Married men, spouse present	Married women, spouse present	Women who maintain families
1948	3.8	9.2	3.2	3.6	...	...	...	...	...	...	...
1949	5.9	13.4	5.4	5.3	...	...	...	...	...	...	...
1950	5.3	12.2	4.7	5.1	...	...	...	...	...	...	...
1951	3.3	8.2	2.5	4.0	...	...	...	...	...	...	...
1952	3.0	8.5	2.4	3.2	...	...	...	...	...	...	...
1953	2.9	7.6	2.5	2.9	...	...	...	...	...	...	...
1954	5.5	12.6	4.9	5.5	5.0	...	...	...	...	...	...
1955	4.4	11.0	3.8	4.4	3.9	...	...	...	2.6	3.7	...
1956	4.1	11.1	3.4	4.2	3.6	...	...	...	2.3	3.6	...
1957	4.3	11.6	3.6	4.1	3.8	...	...	...	2.8	4.3	...
1958	6.8	15.9	6.2	6.1	6.1	...	...	...	5.1	6.5	...
1959	5.5	14.6	4.7	5.2	4.8	...	...	...	3.6	5.2	...
1960	5.5	14.7	4.7	5.1	5.0	...	...	...	3.7	5.2	...
1961	6.7	16.8	5.7	6.3	6.0	...	...	...	4.6	6.4	...
1962	5.5	14.7	4.6	5.4	4.9	...	...	...	3.6	5.4	...
1963	5.7	17.2	4.5	5.4	5.0	...	...	...	3.4	5.4	...
1964	5.2	16.2	3.9	5.2	4.6	...	...	...	2.8	5.1	...
1965	4.5	14.8	3.2	4.5	4.1	...	...	...	2.4	4.5	...
1966	3.8	12.8	2.5	3.8	3.4	...	...	...	1.9	3.7	...
1967	3.8	12.9	2.3	4.2	3.4	...	...	...	1.8	4.5	4.9
1968	3.6	12.7	2.2	3.8	3.2	...	...	...	1.6	3.9	4.4
1969	3.5	12.2	2.1	3.7	3.1	...	...	...	1.5	3.9	4.4
1970	4.9	15.3	3.5	4.8	4.5	...	...	...	2.6	4.9	5.4
1971	5.9	16.9	4.4	5.7	5.4	...	...	...	3.2	5.7	7.3
1972	5.6	16.2	4.0	5.4	5.1	10.4	...	...	2.8	5.4	7.2
1973	4.9	14.5	3.3	4.9	4.3	9.4	...	7.5	2.3	4.7	7.1
1974	5.6	16.0	3.8	5.5	5.0	10.5	...	8.1	2.7	5.3	7.0
1975	8.5	19.9	6.8	8.0	7.8	14.8	...	12.2	5.1	7.9	10.0
1976	7.7	19.0	5.9	7.4	7.0	14.0	...	11.5	4.2	7.1	10.1
1977	7.1	17.8	5.2	7.0	6.2	14.0	...	10.1	3.6	6.5	9.4
1978	6.1	16.4	4.3	6.0	5.2	12.8	...	9.1	2.8	5.5	8.5
1979	5.8	16.1	4.2	5.7	5.1	12.3	...	8.3	2.8	5.1	8.3
1980	7.1	17.8	5.9	6.4	6.3	14.3	...	10.1	4.2	5.8	9.2
1981	7.6	19.6	6.3	6.8	6.7	15.6	...	10.4	4.3	6.0	10.4
1982	9.7	23.2	8.8	8.3	8.6	18.9	...	13.8	6.5	7.4	11.7
1983	9.6	22.4	8.9	8.1	8.4	19.5	...	13.7	6.5	7.0	12.2
1984	7.5	18.9	6.6	6.8	6.5	15.9	...	10.7	4.6	5.7	10.3
1985	7.2	18.6	6.2	6.6	6.2	15.1	...	10.5	4.3	5.6	10.4
1986	7.0	18.3	6.1	6.2	6.0	14.5	...	10.6	4.4	5.2	9.8
1987	6.2	16.9	5.4	5.4	5.3	13.0	...	8.8	3.9	4.3	9.2
1988	5.5	15.3	4.8	4.9	4.7	11.7	...	8.2	3.3	3.9	8.1
1989	5.3	15.0	4.5	4.7	4.5	11.4	...	8.0	3.0	3.7	8.1
1990	5.6	15.5	5.0	4.9	4.8	11.4	...	8.2	3.4	3.8	8.3
1991	6.8	18.7	6.4	5.7	6.1	12.5	...	10.0	4.4	4.5	9.3
1992	7.5	20.1	7.1	6.3	6.6	14.2	...	11.6	5.1	5.0	10.0
1993	6.9	19.0	6.4	5.9	6.1	13.0	...	10.8	4.4	4.6	9.7
1994	6.1	17.6	5.4	5.4	5.3	11.5	...	9.9	3.7	4.1	8.9
1995	5.6	17.3	4.8	4.9	4.9	10.4	...	9.3	3.3	3.9	8.0
1996	5.4	16.7	4.6	4.8	4.7	10.5	...	8.9	3.0	3.6	8.2
1997	4.9	16.0	4.2	4.4	4.2	10.0	...	7.7	2.7	3.1	8.1
1998	4.5	14.6	3.7	4.1	3.9	8.9	...	7.2	2.4	2.9	7.2
1999	4.2	13.9	3.5	3.8	3.7	8.0	...	6.4	2.2	2.7	6.4
2000	4.0	13.1	3.3	3.6	3.5	7.6	3.6	5.7	2.0	2.7	5.9
2001	4.7	14.7	4.2	4.1	4.2	8.6	4.5	6.6	2.7	3.1	6.6
2002	5.8	16.5	5.3	5.1	5.1	10.2	5.9	7.5	3.6	3.7	8.0
2003	6.0	17.5	5.6	5.1	5.2	10.8	6.0	7.7	3.8	3.7	8.5
2004	5.5	17.0	5.0	4.9	4.8	10.4	4.4	7.0	3.1	3.5	8.0
2005	5.1	16.6	4.4	4.6	4.4	10.0	4.0	6.0	2.8	3.3	7.8

Note: See notes and definitions for information on historical comparability.

[1]Beginning in 2003, persons who selected this race group only; persons who selected more than one race group are not included. Prior to 2003, persons who reported more than one race group were included in the group they identified as their main race.
[2]May be of any race.
... = Not available.

Table 1-26. Unemployed Persons, by Age, Sex, Race, and Hispanic Origin, 1948–2005

(Thousands of people.)

Race, Hispanic origin, sex, and year	16 years and over	16 to 19 years			20 years and over						
		Total	16 to 17 years	18 to 19 years	Total	20 to 24 years	25 to 34 years	35 to 44 years	45 to 54 years	55 to 64 years	65 years and over
ALL RACES											
Both Sexes											
1948	2 276	409	180	228	1 869	455	457	347	290	226	93
1949	3 637	576	238	337	3 060	680	776	603	471	384	146
1950	3 288	513	226	287	2 776	561	702	530	478	368	137
1951	2 055	336	168	168	1 718	273	435	354	318	238	103
1952	1 883	345	180	165	1 539	268	389	325	274	195	86
1953	1 834	307	150	157	1 529	256	379	325	280	218	70
1954	3 532	501	221	247	3 032	504	793	680	548	374	132
1955	2 852	450	211	239	2 403	396	577	521	436	355	120
1956	2 750	478	231	247	2 274	395	554	476	429	311	109
1957	2 859	497	230	266	2 362	430	573	499	448	300	111
1958	4 602	678	299	379	3 923	701	993	871	731	472	154
1959	3 740	654	301	354	3 085	543	726	673	603	405	135
1960	3 852	712	325	387	3 140	583	752	671	614	396	122
1961	4 714	828	363	465	3 886	723	890	850	751	516	159
1962	3 911	721	312	409	3 191	636	712	688	605	411	141
1963	4 070	884	420	462	3 187	658	732	674	589	410	126
1964	3 786	872	436	437	2 913	660	607	605	543	378	117
1965	3 366	874	411	463	2 491	557	529	546	436	322	103
1966	2 875	837	395	441	2 041	446	441	426	369	265	92
1967	2 975	839	400	438	2 140	511	480	422	383	256	86
1968	2 817	838	414	426	1 978	543	443	371	314	219	88
1969	2 832	853	436	416	1 978	560	453	358	320	216	72
1970	4 093	1 106	537	569	2 987	866	718	515	476	309	104
1971	5 016	1 262	596	665	3 755	1 130	933	630	573	381	109
1972	4 882	1 308	633	676	3 573	1 132	878	576	510	368	111
1973	4 365	1 235	634	600	3 130	1 008	866	451	430	290	88
1974	5 156	1 422	699	722	3 733	1 212	1 044	559	498	321	99
1975	7 929	1 767	799	968	6 161	1 865	1 776	951	893	520	155
1976	7 406	1 719	796	924	5 687	1 714	1 710	849	758	510	147
1977	6 991	1 663	781	881	5 330	1 629	1 650	785	666	450	147
1978	6 202	1 583	796	787	4 620	1 483	1 422	694	552	345	123
1979	6 137	1 555	739	816	4 583	1 442	1 446	705	540	346	104
1980	7 637	1 669	778	890	5 969	1 835	2 024	940	676	399	94
1981	8 273	1 763	781	981	6 510	1 976	2 211	1 065	715	444	98
1982	10 678	1 977	831	1 145	8 701	2 392	3 037	1 552	966	647	107
1983	10 717	1 829	753	1 076	8 888	2 330	3 078	1 650	1 039	677	114
1984	8 539	1 499	646	854	7 039	1 838	2 374	1 335	828	566	97
1985	8 312	1 468	662	806	6 844	1 738	2 341	1 340	813	518	93
1986	8 237	1 454	665	789	6 783	1 651	2 390	1 371	790	489	91
1987	7 425	1 347	648	700	6 077	1 453	2 129	1 281	723	412	78
1988	6 701	1 226	573	653	5 475	1 261	1 929	1 166	657	375	87
1989	6 528	1 194	537	657	5 333	1 218	1 851	1 159	637	379	91
1990	7 047	1 212	527	685	5 835	1 299	1 995	1 328	723	386	105
1991	8 628	1 359	587	772	7 269	1 573	2 447	1 719	946	473	113
1992	9 613	1 427	641	787	8 186	1 649	2 702	1 976	1 138	589	132
1993	8 940	1 365	606	759	7 575	1 514	2 395	1 896	1 121	541	108
1994	7 996	1 320	624	696	6 676	1 373	2 067	1 627	971	485	153
1995	7 404	1 346	652	695	6 058	1 244	1 841	1 549	844	425	153
1996	7 236	1 306	617	689	5 929	1 239	1 757	1 505	883	406	139
1997	6 739	1 271	589	683	5 467	1 152	1 571	1 418	830	369	127
1998	6 210	1 205	573	632	5 005	1 081	1 419	1 258	782	343	122
1999	5 880	1 162	544	618	4 718	1 042	1 278	1 154	753	367	124
2000	5 692	1 081	502	579	4 611	1 022	1 207	1 133	762	355	132
2001	6 801	1 162	531	632	5 638	1 209	1 498	1 355	989	458	129
2002	8 378	1 253	540	714	7 124	1 430	1 890	1 691	1 315	635	163
2003	8 774	1 251	545	706	7 523	1 495	1 960	1 815	1 356	713	183
2004	8 149	1 208	554	653	6 942	1 431	1 784	1 578	1 288	682	179
2005	7 591	1 186	541	645	6 405	1 335	1 661	1 400	1 195	630	184

Table 1-26. Unemployed Persons, by Age, Sex, Race, and Hispanic Origin, 1948–2005—*Continued*

(Thousands of people.)

Race, Hispanic origin, sex, and year	16 years and over	16 to 19 years			20 years and over						
		Total	16 to 17 years	18 to 19 years	Total	20 to 24 years	25 to 34 years	35 to 44 years	45 to 54 years	55 to 64 years	65 years and over
ALL RACES											
Men											
1948	1 559	256	113	142	1 305	324	289	233	201	177	81
1949	2 572	353	145	207	2 219	485	539	414	347	310	125
1950	2 239	318	139	179	1 922	377	467	348	327	286	117
1951	1 221	191	102	89	1 029	155	241	192	193	162	87
1952	1 185	205	116	89	980	155	233	192	182	145	73
1953	1 202	184	94	90	1 019	152	236	208	196	167	60
1954	2 344	310	142	168	2 035	327	517	431	372	275	112
1955	1 854	274	134	140	1 580	248	353	328	285	265	102
1956	1 711	269	134	135	1 442	240	348	278	270	216	90
1957	1 841	300	140	159	1 541	283	349	304	302	220	83
1958	3 098	416	185	231	2 681	478	685	552	492	349	124
1959	2 420	398	191	207	2 022	343	484	407	390	287	112
1960	2 486	426	200	225	2 060	369	492	415	392	294	96
1961	2 997	479	221	258	2 518	458	585	507	473	375	122
1962	2 423	408	188	220	2 016	381	445	404	382	300	103
1963	2 472	501	248	252	1 971	396	445	386	358	290	97
1964	2 205	487	257	230	1 718	384	345	324	319	263	85
1965	1 914	479	247	232	1 435	311	292	283	253	221	75
1966	1 551	432	220	212	1 120	221	239	219	196	179	65
1967	1 508	448	241	207	1 060	235	219	185	199	163	60
1968	1 419	426	234	193	993	258	205	171	165	132	61
1969	1 403	440	244	196	963	270	205	155	157	127	48
1970	2 238	599	306	294	1 638	479	391	253	247	198	71
1971	2 789	693	346	347	2 097	640	513	320	313	239	71
1972	2 659	711	357	355	1 948	628	466	284	272	227	73
1973	2 275	653	352	300	1 624	528	439	211	219	171	57
1974	2 714	757	394	362	1 957	649	546	266	250	183	63
1975	4 442	966	445	521	3 476	1 081	986	507	499	302	103
1976	4 036	939	443	496	3 098	951	914	431	411	296	94
1977	3 667	874	421	453	2 794	877	869	373	326	252	97
1978	3 142	813	426	388	2 328	768	691	314	277	198	81
1979	3 120	811	393	418	2 308	744	699	329	272	196	67
1980	4 267	913	429	485	3 353	1 076	1 137	482	357	243	58
1981	4 577	962	431	531	3 615	1 144	1 213	552	390	261	55
1982	6 179	1 090	469	621	5 089	1 407	1 791	879	550	393	69
1983	6 260	1 003	408	595	5 257	1 369	1 822	947	613	433	73
1984	4 744	812	348	464	3 932	1 023	1 322	728	450	356	53
1985	4 521	806	363	443	3 715	944	1 244	706	459	307	55
1986	4 530	779	355	424	3 751	899	1 291	763	440	301	58
1987	4 101	732	353	379	3 369	779	1 169	689	426	258	49
1988	3 655	667	311	356	2 987	676	1 040	617	366	240	49
1989	3 525	658	303	355	2 867	660	953	619	351	234	49
1990	3 906	667	283	384	3 239	715	1 092	711	413	249	59
1991	4 946	751	317	433	4 195	911	1 375	990	550	305	64
1992	5 523	806	357	449	4 717	951	1 529	1 118	675	378	67
1993	5 055	768	342	426	4 287	865	1 338	1 049	636	336	64
1994	4 367	740	342	398	3 627	768	1 113	855	522	281	88
1995	3 983	744	352	391	3 239	673	961	815	464	233	94
1996	3 880	733	347	387	3 146	675	903	786	484	223	76
1997	3 577	694	321	373	2 882	636	772	732	457	217	69
1998	3 266	686	330	355	2 580	583	699	609	420	201	69
1999	3 066	633	295	338	2 433	562	624	571	403	203	70
2000	2 975	599	281	317	2 376	547	602	557	398	189	83
2001	3 690	650	300	350	3 040	688	756	714	536	272	74
2002	4 597	700	301	399	3 896	792	1 023	897	725	373	87
2003	4 906	697	291	407	4 209	841	1 097	988	764	412	107
2004	4 456	664	292	372	3 791	811	980	839	684	373	104
2005	4 059	667	300	367	3 392	775	844	715	624	331	102

Table 1-26. Unemployed Persons, by Age, Sex, Race, and Hispanic Origin, 1948–2005—*Continued*

(Thousands of people.)

Race, Hispanic origin, sex, and year	16 years and over	16 to 19 years			20 years and over						
		Total	16 to 17 years	18 to 19 years	Total	20 to 24 years	25 to 34 years	35 to 44 years	45 to 54 years	55 to 64 years	65 years and over
ALL RACES											
Women											
1948	717	153	67	86	564	131	168	114	89	49	12
1949	1 065	223	93	130	841	195	237	189	124	74	21
1950	1 049	195	87	108	854	184	235	182	151	82	20
1951	834	145	66	79	689	118	194	162	125	76	16
1952	698	140	64	76	559	113	156	133	92	50	13
1953	632	123	56	67	510	104	143	117	84	51	10
1954	1 188	191	79	79	997	177	276	249	176	99	20
1955	998	176	77	99	823	148	224	193	151	90	18
1956	1 039	209	97	112	832	155	206	198	159	95	19
1957	1 018	197	90	107	821	147	224	195	146	80	28
1958	1 504	262	114	148	1 242	223	308	319	239	123	30
1959	1 320	256	110	147	1 063	200	242	266	213	118	23
1960	1 366	286	125	162	1 080	214	260	256	222	102	26
1961	1 717	349	142	207	1 368	265	305	343	278	141	37
1962	1 488	313	124	189	1 175	255	267	284	223	111	38
1963	1 598	383	172	210	1 216	262	287	288	231	120	29
1964	1 581	385	179	207	1 195	276	262	281	224	115	32
1965	1 452	395	164	231	1 056	246	237	263	183	101	28
1966	1 324	405	175	229	921	225	202	207	173	86	27
1967	1 468	391	159	231	1 078	277	261	237	184	93	26
1968	1 397	412	180	233	985	285	238	200	149	87	27
1969	1 429	413	192	220	1 015	290	248	203	163	89	24
1970	1 855	506	231	275	1 349	387	327	262	229	111	33
1971	2 227	568	250	318	1 658	489	420	310	260	142	38
1972	2 222	598	276	322	1 625	503	413	293	237	141	38
1973	2 089	583	282	301	1 507	480	427	240	212	119	31
1974	2 441	665	305	360	1 777	564	497	294	248	137	36
1975	3 486	802	355	447	2 684	783	791	444	395	219	52
1976	3 369	780	352	429	2 588	763	795	417	346	214	53
1977	3 324	789	361	428	2 535	752	782	412	340	198	50
1978	3 061	769	370	399	2 292	714	731	381	275	148	43
1979	3 018	743	346	396	2 276	697	748	375	268	150	38
1980	3 370	755	349	407	2 615	760	886	459	318	155	36
1981	3 696	800	350	450	2 895	833	998	513	325	184	43
1982	4 499	886	362	524	3 613	985	1 246	673	416	254	38
1983	4 457	825	344	481	3 632	961	1 255	703	427	244	41
1984	3 794	687	298	390	3 107	815	1 052	607	378	211	45
1985	3 791	661	298	363	3 129	794	1 098	634	355	211	39
1986	3 707	675	310	365	3 032	752	1 099	609	350	189	33
1987	3 324	616	295	321	2 709	674	960	592	298	155	30
1988	3 046	558	262	297	2 487	585	889	550	291	136	38
1989	3 003	536	234	302	2 467	558	897	540	286	144	41
1990	3 140	544	243	301	2 596	584	902	617	310	137	46
1991	3 683	608	270	338	3 074	662	1 071	728	396	168	49
1992	4 090	621	283	338	3 469	698	1 173	858	463	210	66
1993	3 885	597	264	333	3 288	648	1 058	847	485	205	45
1994	3 629	580	282	298	3 049	605	954	772	449	204	66
1995	3 421	602	299	303	2 819	571	880	735	381	193	60
1996	3 356	573	270	303	2 783	564	854	720	399	183	63
1997	3 162	577	268	310	2 585	516	800	686	373	152	58
1998	2 944	519	242	277	2 424	498	720	650	362	141	53
1999	2 814	529	249	280	2 285	480	654	584	350	163	54
2000	2 717	483	221	262	2 235	475	604	577	364	165	50
2001	3 111	512	230	282	2 599	521	742	641	453	187	55
2002	3 781	553	238	315	3 228	638	866	795	591	263	76
2003	3 868	554	255	299	3 314	654	863	827	592	302	76
2004	3 694	543	262	281	3 150	619	804	739	605	309	75
2005	3 531	519	240	278	3 013	560	817	685	571	299	82

Table 1-26. Unemployed Persons, by Age, Sex, Race, and Hispanic Origin, 1948–2005—*Continued*

(Thousands of people.)

Race, Hispanic origin, sex, and year	16 years and over	16 to 19 years			20 years and over						
		Total	16 to 17 years	18 to 19 years	Total	20 to 24 years	25 to 34 years	35 to 44 years	45 to 54 years	55 to 64 years	65 years and over
WHITE[1]											
Both Sexes											
1954	2 859	423	191	232	2 436	394	610	540	447	329	115
1955	2 252	373	181	191	1 879	304	412	402	358	300	105
1956	2 159	382	191	191	1 777	297	406	363	355	258	98
1957	2 289	401	195	204	1 888	331	425	401	373	262	98
1958	3 680	541	245	297	3 139	541	756	686	614	405	136
1959	2 946	525	255	270	2 421	406	526	525	496	348	120
1960	3 065	575	273	302	2 490	456	573	520	502	330	109
1961	3 743	669	295	374	3 074	566	668	652	611	438	139
1962	3 052	580	262	318	2 472	488	515	522	485	345	117
1963	3 208	708	350	358	2 500	501	540	518	485	349	107
1964	2 999	708	365	342	2 291	508	441	472	447	323	100
1965	2 691	705	329	374	1 986	437	399	427	358	276	91
1966	2 255	651	315	336	1 604	338	323	336	298	227	80
1967	2 338	635	311	325	1 703	393	360	336	321	221	75
1968	2 226	644	326	318	1 582	422	330	297	269	187	80
1969	2 260	660	351	309	1 601	432	354	294	269	185	66
1970	3 339	871	438	432	2 468	679	570	433	415	275	95
1971	4 085	1 011	491	521	3 074	887	732	517	500	338	100
1972	3 906	1 021	515	506	2 885	887	679	459	439	324	95
1973	3 442	955	513	443	2 486	758	664	358	371	257	77
1974	4 097	1 104	561	544	2 993	925	821	448	427	283	88
1975	6 421	1 413	657	755	5 007	1 474	1 413	774	753	460	136
1976	5 914	1 364	649	715	4 550	1 326	1 329	682	637	448	128
1977	5 441	1 284	636	648	4 157	1 195	1 255	621	569	388	129
1978	4 698	1 189	631	558	3 509	1 059	1 059	543	453	290	104
1979	4 664	1 193	589	603	3 472	1 038	1 068	545	443	290	87
1980	5 884	1 291	625	666	4 593	1 364	1 528	740	550	335	74
1981	6 343	1 374	629	745	4 968	1 449	1 658	827	578	379	77
1982	8 241	1 534	683	851	6 707	1 770	2 283	1 223	796	549	86
1983	8 128	1 387	609	778	6 741	1 678	2 282	1 294	837	563	88
1984	6 372	1 116	510	605	5 256	1 282	1 723	1 036	660	475	81
1985	6 191	1 074	507	567	5 117	1 235	1 695	1 039	642	432	75
1986	6 140	1 070	509	561	5 070	1 149	1 751	1 056	629	407	78
1987	5 501	995	495	500	4 506	1 017	1 527	984	576	333	68
1988	4 944	910	437	473	4 033	874	1 371	890	520	309	69
1989	4 770	863	407	456	3 908	856	1 297	871	503	311	70
1990	5 186	903	401	502	4 283	899	1 401	983	582	330	88
1991	6 560	1 029	461	568	5 532	1 132	1 805	1 330	759	410	96
1992	7 169	1 037	484	553	6 132	1 156	1 967	1 483	915	495	116
1993	6 655	992	468	523	5 663	1 057	1 754	1 411	907	442	92
1994	5 892	960	471	489	4 933	952	1 479	1 184	779	407	132
1995	5 459	952	476	476	4 507	866	1 311	1 161	676	362	131
1996	5 300	939	456	484	4 361	854	1 223	1 117	709	336	122
1997	4 836	912	438	475	3 924	765	1 068	1 035	648	302	106
1998	4 484	876	424	451	3 608	731	978	901	620	276	101
1999	4 273	844	414	430	3 429	720	865	843	595	303	104
2000	4 121	795	386	409	3 326	682	835	817	591	294	107
2001	4 969	845	402	443	4 124	829	1 062	985	761	378	109
2002	6 137	925	407	518	5 212	977	1 340	1 237	1 004	518	137
2003	6 311	909	414	495	5 401	1 012	1 354	1 287	1 025	569	155
2004	5 847	890	414	476	4 957	959	1 211	1 130	953	557	148
2005	5 350	845	391	454	4 505	878	1 106	1 006	884	488	144

[1]Beginning in 2003, persons who selected this race group only; persons who selected more than one race group are not included. Prior to 2003, persons who reported more than one race group were included in the group they identified as their main race.

Table 1-26. Unemployed Persons, by Age, Sex, Race, and Hispanic Origin, 1948–2005—*Continued*

(Thousands of people.)

Race, Hispanic origin, sex, and year	16 years and over	16 to 19 years			20 years and over						
		Total	16 to 17 years	18 to 19 years	Total	20 to 24 years	25 to 34 years	35 to 44 years	45 to 54 years	55 to 64 years	65 years and over
WHITE[1]											
Men											
1954	1 913	266	125	142	1 647	260	408	341	299	241	98
1955	1 478	232	114	117	1 246	196	260	246	233	223	89
1956	1 366	221	112	108	1 145	186	265	212	225	177	81
1957	1 477	243	118	124	1 234	222	257	239	250	193	73
1958	2 489	333	149	184	2 156	382	525	436	404	299	110
1959	1 903	318	162	156	1 585	256	350	316	320	245	98
1960	1 988	341	167	174	1 647	295	376	330	317	243	86
1961	2 398	384	176	208	2 014	370	442	395	382	318	107
1962	1 915	334	158	176	1 581	300	332	311	308	246	84
1963	1 976	407	211	196	1 569	309	342	297	294	246	80
1964	1 779	400	217	183	1 379	310	262	255	266	216	70
1965	1 556	387	200	186	1 169	254	226	228	206	190	67
1966	1 241	340	178	162	901	172	185	173	160	154	57
1967	1 208	342	186	156	866	185	171	153	167	140	52
1968	1 142	328	185	143	814	206	162	140	142	111	55
1969	1 137	343	198	145	794	214	165	130	134	108	43
1970	1 857	485	255	230	1 372	388	316	212	216	177	64
1971	2 309	562	288	275	1 747	513	418	268	272	211	66
1972	2 173	564	288	276	1 610	506	375	231	237	199	60
1973	1 836	513	284	229	1 323	411	353	166	188	153	51
1974	2 169	584	311	274	1 585	505	434	218	213	161	53
1975	3 627	785	369	416	2 841	871	796	412	411	265	86
1976	3 258	754	368	385	2 504	750	730	346	341	259	78
1977	2 883	672	342	330	2 211	660	682	297	276	213	82
1978	2 411	615	338	277	1 797	558	525	250	227	169	68
1979	2 405	633	319	313	1 773	553	526	253	220	165	56
1980	3 345	716	347	369	2 629	827	884	378	291	206	44
1981	3 580	755	349	406	2 825	869	943	433	317	221	42
1982	4 846	854	387	467	3 991	1 066	1 385	696	460	331	53
1983	4 859	761	328	433	4 098	1 019	1 410	755	497	362	54
1984	3 600	608	280	328	2 992	722	991	572	363	302	42
1985	3 426	592	282	310	2 834	694	931	553	356	257	43
1986	3 433	576	276	299	2 857	645	978	586	349	248	51
1987	3 132	548	272	276	2 584	568	879	536	350	209	43
1988	2 766	499	239	260	2 268	480	777	477	293	200	40
1989	2 636	487	230	257	2 149	476	694	470	280	191	38
1990	2 935	504	214	290	2 431	510	796	530	330	214	51
1991	3 859	575	249	327	3 284	677	1 064	780	438	269	55
1992	4 209	590	270	319	3 620	686	1 155	858	543	318	58
1993	3 828	565	261	305	3 263	619	1 015	793	512	270	53
1994	3 275	540	259	280	2 735	555	827	626	417	236	74
1995	2 999	535	260	275	2 465	483	711	621	371	200	79
1996	2 896	532	260	273	2 363	478	655	592	383	188	67
1997	2 641	502	234	268	2 140	439	553	549	358	182	58
1998	2 431	510	254	257	1 920	405	512	441	342	164	58
1999	2 274	461	223	237	1 813	398	441	419	322	172	61
2000	2 177	446	217	229	1 731	368	428	403	302	162	68
2001	2 754	479	232	247	2 275	494	547	529	413	229	64
2002	3 459	516	228	288	2 943	562	772	672	554	305	77
2003	3 643	518	221	298	3 125	589	798	723	591	333	91
2004	3 282	497	224	274	2 785	560	694	620	516	307	88
2005	2 931	480	220	260	2 450	522	586	536	463	263	81

[1]Beginning in 2003, persons who selected this race group only; persons who selected more than one race group are not included. Prior to 2003, persons who reported more than one race group were included in the group they identified as their main race.

Table 1-26. Unemployed Persons, by Age, Sex, Race, and Hispanic Origin, 1948–2005—*Continued*

(Thousands of people.)

Race, Hispanic origin, sex, and year	16 years and over	16 to 19 years			20 years and over						
		Total	16 to 17 years	18 to 19 years	Total	20 to 24 years	25 to 34 years	35 to 44 years	45 to 54 years	55 to 64 years	65 years and over
WHITE[1]											
Women											
1954	946	157	66	90	789	134	202	199	148	88	17
1955	774	141	67	74	633	108	152	156	125	77	16
1956	793	161	79	83	632	111	141	151	130	81	17
1957	812	158	77	80	654	109	168	162	123	69	25
1958	1 191	208	96	113	983	159	231	250	210	106	26
1959	1 043	207	93	114	836	150	176	209	176	103	22
1960	1 077	234	106	128	843	161	197	190	185	87	23
1961	1 345	285	119	166	1 060	196	226	257	229	120	32
1962	1 137	246	104	142	891	188	183	211	177	99	33
1963	1 232	301	139	162	931	192	198	221	191	103	27
1964	1 220	308	148	159	912	198	179	217	181	107	30
1965	1 135	318	129	188	817	183	173	199	152	86	24
1966	1 014	311	137	174	703	166	138	163	138	73	23
1967	1 130	293	125	169	837	209	189	183	154	81	23
1968	1 084	316	141	175	768	216	168	157	127	76	25
1969	1 123	317	153	164	806	218	189	164	135	77	23
1970	1 482	386	183	202	1 096	291	254	221	199	98	31
1971	1 777	449	203	246	1 328	376	314	249	228	126	34
1972	1 733	457	227	230	1 275	381	304	227	202	125	35
1973	1 606	442	228	214	1 164	347	311	192	183	104	26
1974	1 927	519	250	270	1 408	420	387	230	214	122	35
1975	2 794	628	288	340	2 166	602	617	362	342	195	49
1976	2 656	611	280	330	2 045	577	598	336	296	188	49
1977	2 558	612	294	318	1 946	536	573	323	293	175	47
1978	2 287	574	292	281	1 713	500	533	294	226	122	37
1979	2 260	560	270	290	1 699	485	542	293	223	125	32
1980	2 540	576	278	298	1 964	537	645	362	259	129	31
1981	2 762	620	281	339	2 143	580	715	394	261	158	36
1982	3 395	680	296	384	2 715	704	898	527	337	217	33
1983	3 270	626	282	345	2 643	659	872	539	340	201	33
1984	2 772	508	231	277	2 264	559	731	464	297	173	39
1985	2 765	482	225	257	2 283	541	763	486	286	175	32
1986	2 708	495	233	262	2 213	504	773	470	281	159	27
1987	2 369	447	223	224	1 922	449	648	448	227	124	25
1988	2 177	412	198	214	1 766	393	594	413	227	110	30
1989	2 135	376	177	199	1 758	380	603	401	223	120	32
1990	2 251	399	187	212	1 852	389	605	453	251	116	37
1991	2 701	453	212	241	2 248	455	741	550	320	141	41
1992	2 959	447	214	233	2 512	469	811	625	372	177	58
1993	2 827	426	208	219	2 400	438	739	618	395	172	39
1994	2 617	420	211	208	2 197	397	652	558	361	170	58
1995	2 460	418	216	201	2 042	384	600	540	306	162	52
1996	2 404	407	196	211	1 998	376	568	525	326	148	55
1997	2 195	411	204	207	1 784	326	515	486	290	119	49
1998	2 053	365	171	195	1 688	327	467	460	279	112	43
1999	1 999	383	190	193	1 616	322	423	423	273	131	43
2000	1 944	349	168	180	1 595	314	407	414	289	133	39
2001	2 215	366	170	196	1 849	335	515	456	348	150	45
2002	2 678	409	179	230	2 269	415	567	565	449	213	60
2003	2 668	391	194	197	2 276	423	555	564	434	235	64
2004	2 565	393	191	202	2 172	399	516	510	437	250	60
2005	2 419	365	172	193	2 054	356	520	469	421	225	63

[1]Beginning in 2003, persons who selected this race group only; persons who selected more than one race group are not included. Prior to 2003, persons who reported more than one race group were included in the group they identified as their main race.

Table 1-26. Unemployed Persons, by Age, Sex, Race, and Hispanic Origin, 1948–2005—*Continued*

(Thousands of people.)

Race, Hispanic origin, sex, and year	16 years and over	16 to 19 years			20 years and over						
		Total	16 to 17 years	18 to 19 years	Total	20 to 24 years	25 to 34 years	35 to 44 years	45 to 54 years	55 to 64 years	65 years and over
BLACK¹											
Both Sexes											
1972	906	279	113	167	627	226	183	106	62	37	12
1973	846	262	114	148	584	231	181	82	53	29	9
1974	965	297	127	170	666	261	201	95	65	33	10
1975	1 369	330	130	200	1 040	362	321	157	126	54	17
1976	1 334	330	134	195	1 005	350	338	145	101	54	16
1977	1 393	354	135	218	1 040	397	355	140	81	51	16
1978	1 330	360	150	210	972	379	320	127	82	47	17
1979	1 319	333	137	197	986	369	335	137	82	48	15
1980	1 553	343	134	210	1 209	426	433	171	109	53	18
1981	1 731	357	138	219	1 374	483	493	207	119	55	17
1982	2 142	396	130	266	1 747	565	662	278	141	84	17
1983	2 272	392	125	267	1 879	591	700	299	174	95	21
1984	1 914	353	122	230	1 561	504	577	253	138	75	15
1985	1 864	357	135	221	1 507	455	562	254	143	74	18
1986	1 840	347	138	209	1 493	453	564	269	127	69	10
1987	1 684	312	134	178	1 373	397	533	247	124	62	10
1988	1 547	288	121	167	1 259	349	502	230	111	51	15
1989	1 544	300	116	184	1 245	322	494	246	109	53	20
1990	1 565	268	112	156	1 297	349	505	278	106	44	14
1991	1 723	280	105	175	1 443	378	539	318	151	44	13
1992	2 011	324	127	197	1 687	421	610	402	178	64	13
1993	1 844	313	112	201	1 530	387	532	376	153	72	11
1994	1 666	300	127	173	1 366	351	468	346	130	55	16
1995	1 538	325	143	182	1 213	311	423	303	116	42	18
1996	1 592	310	133	177	1 282	327	454	313	127	48	13
1997	1 560	302	123	179	1 258	327	426	307	136	45	16
1998	1 426	281	124	156	1 146	301	366	294	125	45	16
1999	1 309	268	109	159	1 041	273	339	249	121	46	14
2000	1 241	230	96	134	1 011	281	289	254	131	38	20
2001	1 416	260	102	158	1 155	307	340	283	159	52	15
2002	1 693	260	103	156	1 433	365	407	349	215	76	21
2003	1 787	255	93	162	1 532	375	442	385	217	93	20
2004	1 729	241	103	138	1 487	353	441	341	245	86	21
2005	1 700	267	115	152	1 433	358	423	310	222	92	28
Men											
1972	448	143	66	77	305	113	84	45	31	23	9
1973	395	128	62	66	267	108	75	37	27	16	5
1974	494	159	75	82	336	129	103	41	35	19	8
1975	741	170	71	100	571	195	169	83	78	33	13
1976	698	170	69	103	528	185	166	73	60	32	13
1977	698	187	73	114	512	197	170	63	40	31	12
1978	641	180	80	101	462	185	148	53	40	24	11
1979	636	164	68	97	473	174	152	66	44	27	10
1980	815	179	72	108	636	222	222	88	60	32	12
1981	891	188	73	115	703	248	245	102	65	32	10
1982	1 167	213	72	141	954	304	355	154	74	54	12
1983	1 213	211	70	142	1 002	313	358	162	96	59	14
1984	1 003	188	62	126	815	272	289	132	67	45	9
1985	951	193	69	124	757	224	268	127	85	43	11
1986	946	180	68	112	765	225	273	148	70	44	5
1987	826	160	70	90	666	186	253	122	61	39	6
1988	771	154	64	90	617	177	233	111	58	30	8
1989	773	153	65	88	619	162	226	129	59	33	10
1990	806	142	62	80	664	177	247	146	62	27	6
1991	890	145	54	91	745	201	252	172	87	25	7
1992	1 067	180	71	109	886	221	301	208	107	42	6
1993	971	170	66	104	801	201	260	201	87	46	7
1994	848	167	69	97	682	173	218	180	72	29	10
1995	762	168	73	95	593	153	195	150	63	21	11
1996	808	169	73	96	639	163	210	158	75	26	7
1997	747	162	70	92	585	165	178	141	72	22	7
1998	671	147	61	86	524	151	148	133	60	24	8
1999	626	145	60	85	480	135	143	114	60	22	7
2000	620	121	52	70	499	145	134	121	72	17	9
2001	709	136	51	85	573	150	159	142	84	31	7
2002	835	140	54	85	695	181	180	165	120	40	9
2003	891	132	49	83	760	192	212	189	109	47	10
2004	860	128	52	75	733	188	211	160	120	46	8
2005	844	145	63	82	699	192	189	143	116	45	14

¹Beginning in 2003, persons who selected this race group only; persons who selected more than one race group are not included. Prior to 2003, persons who reported more than one race group were included in the group they identified as their main race.

Table 1-26. Unemployed Persons, by Age, Sex, Race, and Hispanic Origin, 1948–2005—*Continued*

(Thousands of people.)

Race, Hispanic origin, sex, and year	16 years and over	16 to 19 years			20 years and over						
		Total	16 to 17 years	18 to 19 years	Total	20 to 24 years	25 to 34 years	35 to 44 years	45 to 54 years	55 to 64 years	65 years and over
BLACK[1]											
Women											
1972	458	136	47	90	322	113	99	61	31	14	3
1973	451	134	51	82	317	123	105	45	26	13	4
1974	470	139	51	87	331	132	98	55	30	14	2
1975	629	160	60	100	469	167	153	75	48	22	4
1976	637	160	66	93	477	165	172	73	41	23	3
1977	695	167	63	104	528	200	185	77	41	21	4
1978	690	179	70	110	510	194	173	74	41	23	6
1979	683	169	69	100	513	195	183	71	38	21	5
1980	738	164	62	102	574	204	211	83	49	21	6
1981	840	169	65	104	671	235	248	105	54	23	7
1982	975	182	58	124	793	261	307	123	67	29	5
1983	1 059	181	56	125	878	278	342	137	77	36	7
1984	911	165	60	104	747	231	288	121	71	30	5
1985	913	164	66	98	750	231	295	127	58	31	7
1986	894	167	70	97	728	228	291	121	57	25	5
1987	858	152	64	88	706	211	280	125	63	23	4
1988	776	134	57	78	642	172	269	118	53	22	7
1989	772	147	51	96	625	160	267	118	50	21	9
1990	758	126	49	76	633	172	258	132	44	17	8
1991	833	135	51	84	698	177	288	145	64	19	6
1992	944	144	56	88	800	200	308	194	71	22	6
1993	872	143	46	97	729	186	272	175	66	26	5
1994	818	133	57	76	685	178	249	166	59	26	6
1995	777	157	87	620	158	228	153	53	20	. . .	. . .
1996	784	141	60	80	643	164	244	155	52	21	7
1997	813	140	53	87	673	163	248	166	64	24	9
1998	756	134	63	71	622	150	218	160	65	21	8
1999	684	123	49	74	561	138	196	135	61	25	7
2000	621	109	44	65	512	136	154	132	59	22	10
2001	706	124	52	72	582	157	181	141	75	21	8
2002	858	120	49	71	738	183	228	185	95	35	12
2003	895	123	44	79	772	183	230	195	109	46	10
2004	868	114	51	63	755	166	230	180	126	40	13
2005	856	123	52	70	734	166	233	168	106	47	14
HISPANIC[2]											
Both Sexes											
1973	277	80	. . .	. . .	. . .	. . .	. . .	. . .	. . .	. . .	. . .
1974	325	88	. . .	. . .	. . .	. . .	. . .	. . .	. . .	. . .	. . .
1975	508	123	. . .	. . .	. . .	. . .	. . .	. . .	. . .	. . .	. . .
1976	485	106	51	55	385	116	113	72	53	26	6
1977	456	113	50	60	344	98	114	56	48	24	5
1978	452	110	63	47	342	98	116	65	41	16	5
1979	434	106	54	51	329	100	102	65	37	20	4
1980	620	145	66	79	474	138	168	90	49	24	5
1981	678	144	60	84	533	171	178	92	57	31	5
1982	929	175	73	102	754	221	267	140	75	45	6
1983	961	167	64	104	793	214	270	156	93	54	5
1984	800	149	60	88	651	164	235	124	71	51	5
1985	811	141	55	85	670	171	256	123	73	41	7
1986	857	141	57	84	716	183	258	143	85	38	9
1987	751	136	57	79	615	152	222	128	75	33	5
1988	732	148	63	84	585	145	209	120	69	36	6
1989	750	132	59	73	618	158	218	124	76	36	6
1990	876	161	68	94	714	167	263	156	85	36	7
1991	1 092	179	79	99	913	214	332	206	110	44	8
1992	1 311	219	94	124	1 093	240	390	267	126	59	10
1993	1 248	201	86	115	1 047	237	354	261	132	54	10
1994	1 187	198	90	108	989	220	348	227	132	51	12
1995	1 140	205	96	109	934	209	325	224	106	54	16
1996	1 132	199	85	114	933	217	296	246	101	59	14
1997	1 069	197	87	110	872	206	269	229	99	56	13
1998	1 026	214	89	125	812	194	260	203	96	48	11
1999	945	196	79	117	750	171	233	190	104	42	10
2000	954	194	83	112	759	190	247	189	79	42	12
2001	1 138	208	84	123	931	212	315	228	111	56	9
2002	1 353	221	81	140	1 132	265	373	271	146	62	15
2003	1 441	192	79	113	1 249	273	419	294	183	69	10
2004	1 342	203	86	117	1 139	255	371	261	161	74	18
2005	1 191	191	78	113	1 000	227	324	231	142	61	15

[1]Beginning in 2003, persons who selected this race group only; persons who selected more than one race group are not included. Prior to 2003, persons who reported more than one race group were included in the group they identified as their main race.
[2]May be of any race.
. . . = Not available.

Table 1-26. Unemployed Persons, by Age, Sex, Race, and Hispanic Origin, 1948–2005—*Continued*

(Thousands of people.)

Race, Hispanic origin, sex, and year	16 years and over	16 to 19 years			20 years and over						
		Total	16 to 17 years	18 to 19 years	Total	20 to 24 years	25 to 34 years	35 to 44 years	45 to 54 years	55 to 64 years	65 years and over
HISPANIC[2]											
Men											
1973	158	114	...	...	...	...	...	...	...	...	...
1974	187	139	...	...	...	...	...	...	...	...	...
1975	296	225	...	...	...	...	...	...	...	...	...
1976	278	60	30	31	217	69	63	38	29	16	...
1977	253	60	27	33	195	57	65	28	22	15	...
1978	234	59	35	24	175	51	59	30	20	10	...
1979	223	55	29	27	168	52	50	33	19	11	...
1980	370	86	39	47	284	85	96	51	31	16	...
1981	408	87	40	47	321	105	113	49	31	19	...
1982	565	104	45	59	461	138	169	80	40	29	...
1983	591	100	38	62	491	134	168	92	57	36	...
1984	480	87	36	51	393	103	142	69	41	33	...
1985	483	82	34	49	401	108	156	69	40	23	...
1986	520	82	33	50	438	115	159	86	46	26	...
1987	451	77	32	45	374	88	137	77	46	22	...
1988	437	86	36	50	351	83	128	70	42	24	...
1989	423	81	36	45	342	88	113	69	43	25	...
1990	524	100	40	60	425	99	154	91	53	25	...
1991	685	110	47	62	575	139	210	126	62	33	...
1992	807	132	56	75	675	156	239	156	75	42	...
1993	747	118	50	68	629	144	217	148	79	33	...
1994	680	121	54	67	558	128	203	113	75	30	9
1995	651	121	59	63	530	123	185	120	57	33	13
1996	607	112	49	63	495	117	165	124	49	31	9
1997	582	110	47	63	471	125	137	113	54	35	8
1998	552	117	54	62	436	115	142	97	49	29	5
1999	480	106	42	63	374	96	109	83	54	24	7
2000	494	106	46	60	388	105	118	93	42	23	8
2001	611	117	52	65	495	129	152	116	55	36	6
2002	764	127	42	86	636	151	213	144	82	38	8
2003	809	116	42	74	693	157	239	153	98	41	5
2004	755	120	48	72	635	158	207	133	82	41	13
2005	647	112	42	70	536	134	168	119	74	31	9
Women											
1973	119	83	...	...	...	...	...	...	...	...	...
1974	137	98	...	...	...	...	...	...	...	...	...
1975	212	160	...	...	...	...	...	...	...	...	...
1976	207	45	22	24	166	47	52	33	22	10	...
1977	204	50	23	27	153	40	49	28	25	11	...
1978	219	51	28	23	168	46	58	36	20	8	...
1979	211	50	26	24	160	48	52	32	18	10	...
1980	249	59	28	31	190	53	72	39	18	8	...
1981	269	57	20	37	212	65	65	43	25	13	...
1982	364	71	28	43	293	83	98	60	35	16	...
1983	369	68	26	42	302	80	102	65	36	18	...
1984	320	62	25	37	258	61	93	55	30	17	...
1985	327	58	22	37	269	63	100	54	32	18	...
1986	337	59	25	35	278	68	99	57	39	12	...
1987	300	59	25	34	241	64	85	51	29	11	...
1988	296	62	27	34	234	63	81	50	27	12	...
1989	327	51	23	28	276	70	105	55	33	11	...
1990	351	62	28	34	289	68	109	65	32	11	...
1991	407	69	32	37	339	74	122	80	48	12	...
1992	504	87	38	49	418	84	151	111	51	17	...
1993	501	83	36	47	418	93	136	113	53	21	...
1994	508	77	36	40	431	92	145	115	57	21	2
1995	488	84	38	46	404	86	140	104	50	21	3
1996	525	88	36	52	438	100	131	122	52	27	5
1997	488	87	40	46	401	81	132	117	46	21	4
1998	473	98	35	63	376	80	118	106	48	19	5
1999	466	90	36	54	376	75	124	107	50	17	3
2000	460	88	37	51	371	86	129	96	38	19	4
2001	527	91	33	58	436	83	163	112	56	20	3
2002	590	94	39	54	496	113	160	127	65	24	7
2003	631	76	37	39	555	116	180	141	86	28	5
2004	587	83	38	45	504	97	164	128	78	32	5
2005	544	80	36	43	464	93	156	112	68	30	6

[2]May be of any race.
. . . = Not available.

Table 1-27. Unemployment Rates of Civilian Workers, by Age, Sex, Race, and Hispanic Origin, 1948–2005

(Percent of labor force.)

Race, Hispanic origin, sex, and year	16 years and over	16 to 19 years			20 years and over						
		Total	16 to 17 years	18 to 19 years	Total	20 to 24 years	25 to 34 years	35 to 44 years	45 to 54 years	55 to 64 years	65 years and over
ALL RACES											
Both Sexes											
1948	3.8	9.2	10.1	8.6	3.3	6.2	3.2	2.6	2.7	3.1	3.2
1949	5.9	13.4	14.0	13.0	5.4	9.3	5.4	4.4	4.2	5.2	4.9
1950	5.3	12.2	13.6	11.2	4.8	7.7	4.8	3.8	4.2	4.8	4.5
1951	3.3	8.2	9.6	7.1	3.0	4.1	3.0	2.5	2.7	3.1	3.4
1952	3.0	8.5	10.0	7.3	2.7	4.6	2.6	2.3	2.3	2.4	2.9
1953	2.9	7.6	8.7	6.8	2.6	4.7	2.5	2.2	2.3	2.7	2.2
1954	5.5	12.6	13.5	10.7	5.1	9.2	5.3	4.5	4.4	4.5	4.1
1955	4.4	11.0	12.3	10.0	3.9	7.0	3.8	3.4	3.4	4.2	3.6
1956	4.1	11.1	12.3	10.2	3.7	6.6	3.7	3.0	3.2	3.5	3.2
1957	4.3	11.6	12.5	10.9	3.8	7.1	3.9	3.1	3.3	3.4	3.4
1958	6.8	15.9	16.4	15.5	6.2	11.2	6.8	5.4	5.2	5.2	4.8
1959	5.5	14.6	15.3	14.0	4.8	8.5	5.0	4.2	4.2	4.4	4.3
1960	5.5	14.7	15.5	14.1	4.8	8.7	5.2	4.1	4.1	4.2	3.8
1961	6.7	16.8	18.3	15.8	5.9	10.4	6.2	5.2	5.0	5.4	5.1
1962	5.5	14.7	16.3	13.6	4.9	9.0	5.1	4.1	4.0	4.2	4.5
1963	5.7	17.2	19.3	15.6	4.8	8.8	5.2	4.0	3.8	4.1	4.1
1964	5.2	16.2	17.8	14.9	4.3	8.3	4.3	3.6	3.5	3.7	3.8
1965	4.5	14.8	16.5	13.5	3.6	6.7	3.7	3.2	2.8	3.1	3.3
1966	3.8	12.8	14.8	11.3	2.9	5.3	3.1	2.5	2.3	2.5	3.0
1967	3.8	12.9	14.6	11.6	3.0	5.7	3.2	2.5	2.4	2.4	2.8
1968	3.6	12.7	14.7	11.2	2.7	5.8	2.8	2.2	1.9	2.0	2.8
1969	3.5	12.2	14.5	10.5	2.7	5.7	2.8	2.2	1.9	1.9	2.2
1970	4.9	15.3	17.1	13.8	4.0	8.2	4.2	3.1	2.8	2.7	3.2
1971	5.9	16.9	18.7	15.5	4.9	10.0	5.3	3.9	3.4	3.3	3.5
1972	5.6	16.2	18.5	14.6	4.5	9.3	4.6	3.5	3.0	3.2	3.6
1973	4.9	14.5	17.3	12.4	3.9	7.8	4.2	2.7	2.5	2.6	3.0
1974	5.6	16.0	18.3	14.3	4.5	9.1	4.8	3.3	2.9	2.8	3.4
1975	8.5	19.9	21.4	18.9	7.3	13.6	7.8	5.6	5.2	4.6	5.2
1976	7.7	19.0	21.1	17.5	6.5	12.0	7.1	4.9	4.5	4.5	5.1
1977	7.1	17.8	19.9	16.2	5.9	11.0	6.5	4.4	3.9	3.9	5.0
1978	6.1	16.4	19.3	14.2	5.0	9.6	5.3	3.7	3.3	2.9	4.0
1979	5.8	16.1	18.1	14.7	4.8	9.1	5.2	3.6	3.2	2.9	3.4
1980	7.1	17.8	20.0	16.2	6.1	11.5	6.9	4.6	4.0	3.3	3.1
1981	7.6	19.6	21.4	18.4	6.5	12.3	7.3	5.0	4.2	3.7	3.2
1982	9.7	23.2	24.9	22.1	8.6	14.9	9.7	6.9	5.7	5.4	3.5
1983	9.6	22.4	24.5	21.1	8.6	14.5	9.7	7.0	6.2	5.6	3.7
1984	7.5	18.9	21.2	17.4	6.7	11.5	7.3	5.4	4.9	4.7	3.3
1985	7.2	18.6	21.0	17.0	6.4	11.1	7.0	5.1	4.7	4.3	3.2
1986	7.0	18.3	20.2	17.0	6.2	10.7	6.9	5.0	4.5	4.1	3.0
1987	6.2	16.9	19.1	15.2	5.4	9.7	6.0	4.5	4.0	3.5	2.5
1988	5.5	15.3	17.4	13.8	4.8	8.7	5.4	4.0	3.4	3.2	2.7
1989	5.3	15.0	17.2	13.6	4.6	8.6	5.2	3.8	3.2	3.2	2.6
1990	5.6	15.5	17.9	14.1	4.9	8.8	5.6	4.1	3.6	3.3	3.0
1991	6.8	18.7	21.0	17.2	6.1	10.8	6.9	5.2	4.5	4.1	3.3
1992	7.5	20.1	23.1	18.2	6.8	11.4	7.6	5.8	5.1	5.1	3.8
1993	6.9	19.0	21.4	17.5	6.2	10.5	6.9	5.5	4.8	4.7	3.2
1994	6.1	17.6	19.9	16.0	5.4	9.7	6.0	4.6	4.0	4.1	4.0
1995	5.6	17.3	20.2	15.3	4.9	9.1	5.4	4.3	3.3	3.6	4.0
1996	5.4	16.7	18.9	15.2	4.7	9.3	5.2	4.1	3.3	3.3	3.6
1997	4.9	16.0	18.2	14.5	4.3	8.5	4.7	3.8	3.0	2.9	3.3
1998	4.5	14.6	17.2	12.8	3.9	7.9	4.3	3.4	2.8	2.6	3.2
1999	4.2	13.9	16.3	12.4	3.6	7.5	4.0	3.0	2.6	2.7	3.1
2000	4.0	13.1	15.4	11.6	3.4	7.2	3.7	3.0	2.5	2.5	3.1
2001	4.7	14.7	17.2	13.1	4.2	8.3	4.6	3.6	3.1	3.0	2.9
2002	5.8	16.5	18.8	15.1	5.2	9.7	5.9	4.6	4.0	3.9	3.6
2003	6.0	17.5	19.1	16.4	5.4	10.0	6.1	4.9	4.1	4.1	3.8
2004	5.5	17.0	20.2	15.0	4.9	9.4	5.5	4.4	3.8	3.8	3.6
2005	5.1	16.6	19.1	14.9	4.5	8.8	5.1	3.9	3.5	3.3	3.5

Table 1-27. Unemployment Rates of Civilian Workers, by Age, Sex, Race, and Hispanic Origin, 1948–2005 —*Continued*

(Percent of labor force.)

Race, Hispanic origin, sex, and year	16 years and over	16 to 19 years			20 years and over						
		Total	16 to 17 years	18 to 19 years	Total	20 to 24 years	25 to 34 years	35 to 44 years	45 to 54 years	55 to 64 years	65 years and over
ALL RACES											
Men											
1948	3.6	9.8	10.2	9.5	3.2	6.9	2.8	2.4	2.5	3.1	3.4
1949	5.9	14.3	13.7	14.6	5.4	10.4	5.2	4.3	4.3	5.4	5.1
1950	5.1	12.7	13.3	12.3	4.7	8.1	4.4	3.6	4.0	4.9	4.8
1951	2.8	8.1	9.4	7.0	2.5	3.9	2.3	2.0	2.4	2.8	3.5
1952	2.8	8.9	10.5	7.4	2.4	4.6	2.2	1.9	2.2	2.4	3.0
1953	2.8	7.9	8.8	7.2	2.5	5.0	2.2	2.0	2.3	2.8	2.4
1954	5.3	13.5	13.9	13.2	4.9	10.7	4.8	4.1	4.3	4.5	4.4
1955	4.2	11.6	12.5	10.8	3.8	7.7	3.3	3.1	3.2	4.3	4.0
1956	3.8	11.1	11.7	10.5	3.4	6.9	3.3	2.6	3.0	3.5	3.5
1957	4.1	12.4	12.4	12.3	3.6	7.8	3.3	2.8	3.3	3.5	3.4
1958	6.8	17.1	16.3	17.8	6.2	12.7	6.5	5.1	5.3	5.5	5.2
1959	5.2	15.3	15.8	14.9	4.7	8.7	4.7	3.7	4.1	4.5	4.8
1960	5.4	15.3	15.5	15.0	4.7	8.9	4.8	3.8	4.1	4.6	4.2
1961	6.4	17.1	18.3	16.3	5.7	10.8	5.7	4.6	4.9	5.7	5.5
1962	5.2	14.7	16.0	13.8	4.6	8.9	4.5	3.6	3.9	4.6	4.6
1963	5.2	17.2	18.8	15.9	4.5	8.8	4.5	3.5	3.6	4.3	4.5
1964	4.6	15.8	17.1	14.6	3.9	8.1	3.5	2.9	3.2	3.9	4.0
1965	4.0	14.1	16.1	12.4	3.2	6.4	2.9	2.5	2.5	3.3	3.5
1966	3.2	11.7	13.7	10.2	2.5	4.6	2.4	2.0	1.9	2.6	3.1
1967	3.1	12.3	14.5	10.5	2.3	4.7	2.1	1.7	2.0	2.3	2.8
1968	2.9	11.6	13.9	9.7	2.2	5.1	1.9	1.6	1.6	1.9	2.8
1969	2.8	11.4	13.8	9.3	2.1	5.1	1.9	1.5	1.5	1.8	2.2
1970	4.4	15.0	16.9	13.4	3.5	8.4	3.5	2.4	2.4	2.8	3.3
1971	5.3	16.6	18.7	15.0	4.4	10.3	4.4	3.1	3.0	3.3	3.4
1972	5.0	15.9	18.3	14.1	4.0	9.3	3.8	2.7	2.6	3.2	3.6
1973	4.2	13.9	17.0	11.4	3.3	7.3	3.4	2.0	2.1	2.4	3.0
1974	4.9	15.6	18.4	13.3	3.8	8.8	4.0	2.6	2.4	2.6	3.3
1975	7.9	20.1	21.6	19.0	6.8	14.3	6.9	4.9	4.8	4.3	5.4
1976	7.1	19.2	21.4	17.6	5.9	12.1	6.2	4.1	4.0	4.2	5.1
1977	6.3	17.3	19.5	15.6	5.2	10.8	5.7	3.5	3.2	3.6	5.2
1978	5.3	15.8	19.1	13.3	4.3	9.2	4.4	2.8	2.7	2.8	4.2
1979	5.1	15.9	17.9	14.3	4.2	8.7	4.3	2.9	2.7	2.7	3.4
1980	6.9	18.3	20.4	16.7	5.9	12.5	6.7	4.1	3.6	3.4	3.1
1981	7.4	20.1	22.0	18.8	6.3	13.2	6.9	4.5	4.0	3.6	2.9
1982	9.9	24.4	26.4	23.1	8.8	16.4	10.1	6.9	5.6	5.5	3.7
1983	9.9	23.3	25.2	22.2	8.9	15.9	10.1	7.1	6.3	6.1	3.9
1984	7.4	19.6	21.9	18.3	6.6	11.9	7.2	5.2	4.6	5.0	3.0
1985	7.0	19.5	21.9	17.9	6.2	11.4	6.6	4.9	4.6	4.3	3.1
1986	6.9	19.0	20.8	17.7	6.1	11.0	6.7	5.1	4.4	4.3	3.2
1987	6.2	17.8	20.2	16.0	5.4	9.9	5.9	4.4	4.2	3.7	2.6
1988	5.5	16.0	18.2	14.6	4.8	8.9	5.3	3.8	3.5	3.5	2.5
1989	5.2	15.9	18.6	14.2	4.5	8.8	4.8	3.7	3.2	3.5	2.4
1990	5.7	16.3	18.4	15.0	5.0	9.1	5.5	4.1	3.7	3.8	3.0
1991	7.2	19.8	21.8	18.5	6.4	11.6	7.0	5.5	4.8	4.6	3.3
1992	7.9	21.5	24.6	19.5	7.1	12.2	7.8	6.1	5.6	5.8	3.3
1993	7.2	20.4	22.9	18.8	6.4	11.3	7.0	5.6	5.1	5.2	3.2
1994	6.2	19.0	21.0	17.6	5.4	10.2	5.9	4.5	4.0	4.4	4.0
1995	5.6	18.4	21.1	16.5	4.8	9.2	5.1	4.2	3.5	3.6	4.3
1996	5.4	18.1	20.8	16.3	4.6	9.5	4.9	4.0	3.5	3.3	3.4
1997	4.9	16.9	19.1	15.4	4.2	8.9	4.3	3.6	3.1	3.1	3.0
1998	4.4	16.2	19.1	14.1	3.7	8.1	3.9	3.0	2.8	2.8	3.1
1999	4.1	14.7	17.0	13.1	3.5	7.7	3.6	2.8	2.6	2.7	3.0
2000	3.9	14.0	16.8	12.2	3.3	7.3	3.4	2.8	2.4	2.4	3.3
2001	4.8	16.0	19.1	14.0	4.2	9.0	4.3	3.6	3.2	3.3	3.0
2002	5.9	18.1	21.1	16.4	5.3	10.2	5.8	4.5	4.2	4.3	3.4
2003	6.3	19.3	20.7	18.4	5.6	10.6	6.2	5.0	4.4	4.5	4.0
2004	5.6	18.4	22.0	16.3	5.0	10.1	5.5	4.3	3.9	3.9	3.7
2005	5.1	18.6	22.0	16.5	4.4	9.6	4.7	3.7	3.5	3.3	3.4

Table 1-27. Unemployment Rates of Civilian Workers, by Age, Sex, Race, and Hispanic Origin, 1948–2005
—Continued

(Percent of labor force.)

Race, Hispanic origin, sex, and year	16 years and over	16 to 19 years			20 years and over						
		Total	16 to 17 years	18 to 19 years	Total	20 to 24 years	25 to 34 years	35 to 44 years	45 to 54 years	55 to 64 years	65 years and over
ALL RACES											
Women											
1948	4.1	8.3	10.0	7.4	3.6	4.8	4.3	3.0	3.0	3.1	2.3
1949	6.0	12.3	14.4	11.2	5.3	7.3	5.9	4.7	4.0	4.4	3.8
1950	5.7	11.4	14.2	9.8	5.1	6.9	5.7	4.4	4.5	4.5	3.4
1951	4.4	8.3	10.0	7.2	4.0	4.4	4.5	3.8	3.5	4.0	2.9
1952	3.6	8.0	9.1	7.3	3.2	4.5	3.6	3.0	2.5	2.5	2.2
1953	3.3	7.2	8.5	6.4	2.9	4.3	3.4	2.5	2.3	2.5	1.4
1954	6.0	11.4	12.7	7.7	5.5	7.3	6.6	5.3	4.6	4.6	3.0
1955	4.9	10.2	12.0	9.1	4.4	6.1	5.3	4.0	3.6	3.8	2.3
1956	4.8	11.2	13.2	9.9	4.2	6.3	4.8	3.9	3.6	3.6	2.3
1957	4.7	10.6	12.6	9.4	4.1	6.0	5.3	3.8	3.2	3.0	3.4
1958	6.8	14.3	16.6	12.9	6.1	8.9	7.3	6.2	4.9	4.5	3.7
1959	5.9	13.5	14.4	13.0	5.2	8.1	5.9	5.1	4.2	4.1	2.8
1960	5.9	13.9	15.5	12.9	5.1	8.3	6.3	4.8	4.2	3.4	2.9
1961	7.2	16.3	18.3	15.1	6.3	9.8	7.4	6.4	5.1	4.5	4.0
1962	6.2	14.6	16.7	13.5	5.4	9.1	6.5	5.2	4.1	3.5	4.2
1963	6.5	17.2	20.2	15.2	5.4	8.9	6.9	5.1	4.2	3.6	3.2
1964	6.2	16.6	18.8	15.2	5.2	8.6	6.3	5.0	3.9	3.3	3.3
1965	5.5	15.7	17.2	14.8	4.5	7.3	5.5	4.6	3.2	2.8	2.9
1966	4.8	14.1	16.6	12.6	3.8	6.3	4.5	3.6	2.9	2.3	2.8
1967	5.2	13.5	14.8	12.8	4.2	7.0	5.4	4.1	3.1	2.4	2.7
1968	4.8	14.0	15.9	12.9	3.8	6.7	4.7	3.4	2.4	2.2	2.7
1969	4.7	13.3	15.5	11.8	3.7	6.3	4.6	3.4	2.6	2.2	2.3
1970	5.9	15.6	17.4	14.4	4.8	7.9	5.7	4.4	3.5	2.7	3.1
1971	6.9	17.2	18.7	16.2	5.7	9.6	7.0	5.2	4.0	3.3	3.6
1972	6.6	16.7	18.8	15.2	5.4	9.4	6.2	4.9	3.6	3.3	3.5
1973	6.0	15.3	17.7	13.5	4.9	8.5	5.8	3.9	3.2	2.8	2.9
1974	6.7	16.6	18.2	15.4	5.5	9.5	6.2	4.6	3.7	3.2	3.6
1975	9.3	19.7	21.2	18.7	8.0	12.7	9.1	6.8	5.9	5.1	5.0
1976	8.6	18.7	20.8	17.4	7.4	11.9	8.4	6.1	5.2	4.9	5.0
1977	8.2	18.3	20.5	16.9	7.0	11.2	7.7	5.7	5.1	4.4	4.7
1978	7.2	17.1	19.5	15.3	6.0	10.1	6.7	5.0	4.0	3.2	3.8
1979	6.8	16.4	18.3	15.0	5.7	9.6	6.5	4.6	3.9	3.2	3.3
1980	7.4	17.2	19.6	15.6	6.4	10.4	7.2	5.3	4.5	3.3	3.1
1981	7.9	19.0	20.7	17.9	6.8	11.2	7.7	5.7	4.6	3.8	3.6
1982	9.4	21.9	23.2	21.0	8.3	13.2	9.3	7.0	5.9	5.2	3.2
1983	9.2	21.3	23.7	19.9	8.1	12.9	9.1	6.9	6.0	5.0	3.4
1984	7.6	18.0	20.4	16.6	6.8	10.9	7.4	5.6	5.2	4.3	3.8
1985	7.4	17.6	20.0	16.0	6.6	10.7	7.4	5.5	4.8	4.3	3.3
1986	7.1	17.6	19.6	16.3	6.2	10.3	7.2	5.0	4.5	3.8	2.8
1987	6.2	15.9	18.0	14.3	5.4	9.4	6.2	4.6	3.7	3.1	2.4
1988	5.6	14.4	16.6	12.9	4.9	8.5	5.6	4.1	3.4	2.7	2.9
1989	5.4	14.0	15.7	13.0	4.7	8.3	5.6	3.9	3.2	2.8	2.9
1990	5.5	14.7	17.4	13.1	4.9	8.5	5.6	4.2	3.4	2.8	3.1
1991	6.4	17.5	20.2	15.9	5.7	9.8	6.8	4.8	4.2	3.4	3.3
1992	7.0	18.6	21.5	16.6	6.3	10.3	7.4	5.5	4.6	4.2	4.5
1993	6.6	17.5	19.8	16.1	5.9	9.7	6.8	5.3	4.5	4.0	3.1
1994	6.0	16.2	18.7	14.3	5.4	9.2	6.2	4.7	4.0	3.9	4.0
1995	5.6	16.1	19.2	14.0	4.9	9.0	5.7	4.4	3.2	3.6	3.7
1996	5.4	15.2	16.9	14.0	4.8	9.0	5.5	4.2	3.2	3.4	4.0
1997	5.0	15.0	17.2	13.6	4.4	8.1	5.2	4.0	2.9	2.7	3.6
1998	4.6	12.9	15.1	11.5	4.1	7.8	4.8	3.8	2.7	2.4	3.3
1999	4.3	13.2	15.5	11.6	3.8	7.2	4.4	3.3	2.5	2.6	3.2
2000	4.1	12.1	13.9	10.8	3.6	7.1	4.1	3.3	2.5	2.5	2.7
2001	4.7	13.4	15.2	12.2	4.1	7.5	5.1	3.7	3.0	2.7	2.9
2002	5.6	14.9	16.6	13.8	5.1	9.1	5.9	4.6	3.8	3.5	3.9
2003	5.7	15.6	17.5	14.2	5.1	9.3	5.9	4.9	3.7	3.7	3.6
2004	5.4	15.5	18.5	13.5	4.9	8.7	5.6	4.4	3.7	3.6	3.4
2005	5.1	14.5	16.5	13.1	4.6	7.9	5.6	4.1	3.5	3.3	3.5

Table 1-27. Unemployment Rates of Civilian Workers, by Age, Sex, Race, and Hispanic Origin, 1948–2005
—*Continued*

(Percent of labor force.)

Race, Hispanic origin, sex, and year	16 years and over	16 to 19 years			20 years and over						
		Total	16 to 17 years	18 to 19 years	Total	20 to 24 years	25 to 34 years	35 to 44 years	45 to 54 years	55 to 64 years	65 years and over
WHITE[1]											
Both Sexes											
1954	5.0	12.1	13.2	11.3	4.6	8.3	4.6	4.0	4.0	4.3	3.9
1955	3.9	10.4	12.0	9.2	3.4	6.2	3.1	2.9	3.1	3.8	3.4
1956	3.6	10.1	11.5	9.0	3.2	5.7	3.1	2.6	2.9	3.2	3.1
1957	3.8	10.6	11.9	9.6	3.4	6.3	3.3	2.8	3.0	3.2	3.2
1958	6.1	14.4	15.2	13.9	5.6	9.9	5.9	4.8	4.8	4.9	4.6
1959	4.8	13.1	14.4	12.1	4.3	7.3	4.2	3.7	3.8	4.1	4.1
1960	5.0	13.5	14.6	12.6	4.3	7.9	4.5	3.6	3.8	3.9	3.7
1961	6.0	15.3	16.7	14.4	5.3	9.4	5.3	4.5	4.5	5.0	4.8
1962	4.9	13.3	15.3	12.0	4.2	7.9	4.2	3.6	3.6	3.9	4.0
1963	5.0	15.5	17.9	13.7	4.2	7.7	4.4	3.5	3.5	3.8	3.8
1964	4.6	14.8	16.5	13.3	3.8	7.3	3.6	3.2	3.2	3.5	3.5
1965	4.1	13.4	14.8	12.3	3.3	6.1	3.2	2.9	2.5	2.9	3.2
1966	3.4	11.2	13.3	9.7	2.6	4.6	2.6	2.3	2.1	2.4	2.9
1967	3.4	11.0	12.8	9.8	2.7	5.0	2.7	2.3	2.2	2.3	2.7
1968	3.2	11.0	12.9	9.6	2.5	5.2	2.4	2.0	1.8	1.9	2.8
1969	3.1	10.7	13.0	8.9	2.4	5.0	2.5	2.0	1.8	1.8	2.2
1970	4.5	13.5	15.5	11.9	3.7	7.3	3.8	3.0	2.7	2.7	3.2
1971	5.4	15.1	17.0	13.8	4.5	9.0	4.7	3.6	3.3	3.3	3.5
1972	5.1	14.2	16.6	12.3	4.1	8.4	4.1	3.2	2.9	3.1	3.4
1973	4.3	12.6	15.4	10.4	3.5	6.8	3.7	2.5	2.4	2.5	2.9
1974	5.0	14.0	16.3	12.2	4.1	8.0	4.4	3.1	2.8	2.8	3.3
1975	7.8	17.9	19.5	16.7	6.7	12.3	7.1	5.2	4.9	4.5	5.1
1976	7.0	16.9	19.0	15.3	5.9	10.7	6.3	4.5	4.2	4.3	4.9
1977	6.2	15.4	17.9	13.5	5.3	9.3	5.7	4.0	3.8	3.7	4.9
1978	5.2	13.9	17.0	11.5	4.3	8.0	4.6	3.3	3.0	2.7	3.8
1979	5.1	14.0	16.1	12.4	4.2	7.6	4.4	3.2	3.0	2.7	3.1
1980	6.3	15.5	17.9	13.8	5.4	9.9	6.1	4.2	3.7	3.1	2.7
1981	6.7	17.3	19.2	15.9	5.7	10.4	6.3	4.5	3.9	3.5	2.8
1982	8.6	20.4	22.8	18.8	7.6	12.8	8.5	6.3	5.4	5.1	3.1
1983	8.4	19.3	22.0	17.6	7.5	12.1	8.4	6.3	5.7	5.2	3.2
1984	6.5	16.0	18.8	14.3	5.7	9.3	6.2	4.8	4.4	4.4	3.0
1985	6.2	15.7	18.3	13.9	5.5	9.2	5.9	4.6	4.3	4.0	2.9
1986	6.0	15.6	17.6	14.1	5.3	8.7	5.9	4.5	4.1	3.8	2.9
1987	5.3	14.4	16.7	12.7	4.7	8.0	5.1	4.0	3.7	3.2	2.4
1988	4.7	13.1	15.3	11.6	4.1	7.1	4.5	3.5	3.1	3.0	2.4
1989	4.5	12.7	15.2	11.1	3.9	7.2	4.3	3.3	2.9	3.0	2.3
1990	4.8	13.5	15.8	12.1	4.3	7.3	4.6	3.6	3.3	3.2	2.8
1991	6.1	16.5	19.0	14.9	5.5	9.2	6.1	4.7	4.2	4.0	3.1
1992	6.6	17.2	20.3	15.2	6.0	9.5	6.7	5.2	4.8	4.9	3.7
1993	6.1	16.2	19.0	14.4	5.5	8.8	6.0	4.9	4.5	4.3	3.0
1994	5.3	15.1	17.6	13.3	4.7	8.1	5.2	4.0	3.7	3.9	3.8
1995	4.9	14.5	17.3	12.5	4.3	7.7	4.6	3.9	3.1	3.5	3.8
1996	4.7	14.2	16.4	12.6	4.1	7.8	4.4	3.6	3.1	3.2	3.5
1997	4.2	13.6	15.8	12.0	3.6	6.9	3.9	3.3	2.7	2.7	3.0
1998	3.9	12.6	14.8	11.0	3.3	6.5	3.7	2.9	2.6	2.4	2.9
1999	3.7	12.0	14.5	10.2	3.1	6.3	3.3	2.7	2.4	2.5	2.9
2000	3.5	11.4	13.9	9.8	3.0	5.9	3.2	2.6	2.2	2.4	2.8
2001	4.2	12.7	15.3	11.0	3.7	7.0	4.1	3.2	2.8	2.9	2.8
2002	5.1	14.5	16.7	13.2	4.6	8.1	5.2	4.1	3.7	3.7	3.5
2003	5.2	15.2	17.2	13.9	4.7	8.4	5.3	4.3	3.7	3.8	3.7
2004	4.8	15.0	17.9	13.1	4.3	7.9	4.7	3.9	3.4	3.6	3.3
2005	4.4	14.2	16.4	12.7	3.9	7.2	4.3	3.5	3.1	3.0	3.1

[1]Beginning in 2003, persons who selected this race group only; persons who selected more than one race group are not included. Prior to 2003, persons who reported more than one race group were included in the group they identified as their main race.

Table 1-27. Unemployment Rates of Civilian Workers, by Age, Sex, Race, and Hispanic Origin, 1948–2005
—*Continued*

(Percent of labor force.)

Race, Hispanic origin, sex, and year	16 years and over	16 to 19 years			20 years and over						
		Total	16 to 17 years	18 to 19 years	Total	20 to 24 years	25 to 34 years	35 to 44 years	45 to 54 years	55 to 64 years	65 years and over
WHITE[1]											
Men											
1954	4.8	13.4	14.0	13.0	4.4	9.8	4.2	3.6	3.8	4.3	4.2
1955	3.7	11.3	12.2	10.4	3.3	7.0	2.7	2.6	2.9	3.9	3.8
1956	3.4	10.5	11.2	9.7	3.0	6.1	2.8	2.2	2.8	3.1	3.4
1957	3.6	11.5	11.9	11.1	3.2	7.0	2.7	2.5	3.0	3.4	3.2
1958	6.1	15.7	14.9	16.5	5.5	11.7	5.6	4.4	4.8	5.2	5.0
1959	4.6	14.0	15.0	13.0	4.1	7.5	3.8	3.2	3.7	4.2	4.5
1960	4.8	14.0	14.6	13.5	4.2	8.3	4.1	3.3	3.6	4.1	4.0
1961	5.7	15.7	16.5	15.2	5.1	10.1	4.9	4.0	4.4	5.3	5.2
1962	4.6	13.7	15.2	12.7	4.0	8.1	3.8	3.1	3.5	4.1	4.0
1963	4.7	15.9	17.8	14.2	3.9	7.8	3.9	2.9	3.3	4.0	4.1
1964	4.1	14.7	16.1	13.3	3.4	7.4	3.0	2.5	2.9	3.5	3.6
1965	3.6	12.9	14.7	11.3	2.9	5.9	2.6	2.3	2.3	3.1	3.4
1966	2.8	10.5	12.5	8.9	2.2	4.1	2.1	1.7	1.7	2.5	3.0
1967	2.7	10.7	12.7	9.0	2.1	4.2	1.9	1.6	1.8	2.2	2.7
1968	2.6	10.1	12.3	8.3	2.0	4.6	1.7	1.4	1.5	1.7	2.8
1969	2.5	10.0	12.5	7.9	1.9	4.6	1.7	1.4	1.4	1.7	2.2
1970	4.0	13.7	15.7	12.0	3.2	7.8	3.1	2.3	2.3	2.7	3.2
1971	4.9	15.1	17.1	13.5	4.0	9.4	4.0	2.9	2.9	3.2	3.4
1972	4.5	14.2	16.4	12.4	3.6	8.5	3.4	2.5	2.5	3.0	3.3
1973	3.8	12.3	15.2	10.0	3.0	6.6	3.0	1.8	2.0	2.4	2.9
1974	4.4	13.5	16.2	11.5	3.5	7.8	3.6	2.4	2.2	2.5	3.0
1975	7.2	18.3	19.7	17.2	6.2	13.1	6.3	4.5	4.4	4.1	5.0
1976	6.4	17.3	19.7	15.5	5.4	10.9	5.6	3.7	3.7	4.0	4.7
1977	5.5	15.0	17.6	13.0	4.7	9.3	5.0	3.1	3.0	3.3	4.9
1978	4.6	13.5	16.9	10.8	3.7	7.7	3.8	2.5	2.5	2.6	3.9
1979	4.5	13.9	16.1	12.2	3.6	7.5	3.7	2.5	2.5	2.5	3.2
1980	6.1	16.2	18.5	14.5	5.3	11.1	5.9	3.6	3.3	3.1	2.5
1981	6.5	17.9	19.9	16.4	5.6	11.6	6.1	4.0	3.6	3.4	2.4
1982	8.8	21.7	24.2	20.0	7.8	14.3	8.9	6.2	5.3	5.1	3.2
1983	8.8	20.2	22.6	18.7	7.9	13.8	9.0	6.4	5.7	5.6	3.2
1984	6.4	16.8	19.7	15.0	5.7	9.8	6.2	4.6	4.2	4.7	2.6
1985	6.1	16.5	19.2	14.7	5.4	9.7	5.7	4.3	4.1	4.0	2.7
1986	6.0	16.3	18.4	14.7	5.3	9.2	5.8	4.4	4.0	4.0	3.0
1987	5.4	15.5	17.9	13.7	4.8	8.4	5.2	3.9	3.9	3.4	2.5
1988	4.7	13.9	16.1	12.4	4.1	7.4	4.6	3.4	3.2	3.3	2.2
1989	4.5	13.7	16.4	12.0	3.9	7.5	4.1	3.2	2.9	3.1	2.1
1990	4.9	14.3	16.1	13.2	4.3	7.6	4.7	3.5	3.4	3.6	2.8
1991	6.5	17.6	19.7	16.3	5.8	10.2	6.4	5.0	4.4	4.6	3.1
1992	7.0	18.5	21.5	16.5	6.4	10.5	7.0	5.5	5.1	5.5	3.2
1993	6.3	17.7	20.2	16.0	5.7	9.6	6.2	5.0	4.7	4.7	2.9
1994	5.4	16.3	18.5	14.7	4.8	8.8	5.2	3.9	3.7	4.1	3.7
1995	4.9	15.6	18.2	13.8	4.3	7.9	4.5	3.8	3.2	3.4	4.0
1996	4.7	15.5	18.3	13.5	4.1	8.1	4.2	3.5	3.1	3.2	3.2
1997	4.2	14.3	16.3	12.9	3.6	7.3	3.7	3.2	2.8	3.0	2.7
1998	3.9	14.1	17.1	12.1	3.2	6.7	3.5	2.6	2.6	2.6	2.9
1999	3.6	12.6	15.1	10.8	3.0	6.5	3.1	2.4	2.4	2.6	2.9
2000	3.4	12.3	15.3	10.4	2.8	5.9	2.9	2.4	2.2	2.4	3.0
2001	4.2	13.9	17.4	11.7	3.7	7.8	3.8	3.1	2.9	3.2	2.8
2002	5.3	15.9	18.8	14.2	4.7	8.7	5.3	4.1	3.8	4.0	3.4
2003	5.6	17.1	18.5	16.1	5.0	9.1	5.5	4.4	4.0	4.2	3.8
2004	5.0	16.3	19.8	14.2	4.4	8.5	4.8	3.8	3.5	3.7	3.5
2005	4.4	16.1	18.9	14.3	3.8	7.9	4.1	3.3	3.0	3.0	3.1

[1]Beginning in 2003, persons who selected this race group only; persons who selected more than one race group are not included. Prior to 2003, persons who reported more than one race group were included in the group they identified as their main race.

Table 1-27. Unemployment Rates of Civilian Workers, by Age, Sex, Race, and Hispanic Origin, 1948–2005
—Continued

(Percent of labor force.)

Race, Hispanic origin, sex, and year	16 years and over	16 to 19 years			20 years and over						
		Total	16 to 17 years	18 to 19 years	Total	20 to 24 years	25 to 34 years	35 to 44 years	45 to 54 years	55 to 64 years	65 years and over
WHITE[1]											
Women											
1954	5.5	10.4	12.0	9.4	5.1	6.4	5.7	4.9	4.4	4.5	2.8
1955	4.3	9.1	11.6	7.7	3.9	5.1	4.3	3.8	3.4	3.6	2.2
1956	4.2	9.7	12.1	8.3	3.7	5.1	4.0	3.5	3.3	3.5	2.3
1957	4.3	9.5	11.9	7.8	3.8	5.1	4.7	3.7	3.0	2.9	3.4
1958	6.2	12.7	15.6	11.0	5.6	7.3	6.6	5.6	4.9	4.3	3.5
1959	5.3	12.0	13.3	11.1	4.7	7.0	5.2	4.7	3.9	4.0	2.9
1960	5.3	12.7	14.5	11.5	4.6	7.2	5.7	4.2	4.0	3.3	2.8
1961	6.5	14.8	17.0	13.6	5.7	8.4	6.6	5.6	4.8	4.3	3.8
1962	5.5	12.8	15.6	11.3	4.7	7.7	5.4	4.5	3.7	3.5	4.0
1963	5.8	15.1	18.1	13.2	4.8	7.4	5.8	4.6	3.9	3.5	3.3
1964	5.5	14.9	17.1	13.2	4.6	7.1	5.2	4.5	3.6	3.5	3.4
1965	5.0	14.0	15.0	13.4	4.0	6.3	4.9	4.1	3.0	2.7	2.7
1966	4.3	12.1	14.5	10.7	3.3	5.3	3.7	3.3	2.7	2.2	2.7
1967	4.6	11.5	12.9	10.6	3.8	6.0	4.7	3.7	2.9	2.3	2.6
1968	4.3	12.1	13.9	11.0	3.4	5.9	3.9	3.1	2.3	2.1	2.8
1969	4.2	11.5	13.7	10.0	3.4	5.5	4.2	3.2	2.4	2.1	2.4
1970	5.4	13.4	15.3	11.9	4.4	6.9	5.3	4.3	3.4	2.6	3.3
1971	6.3	15.1	16.7	14.1	5.3	8.5	6.3	4.9	3.9	3.3	3.6
1972	5.9	14.2	17.0	12.3	4.9	8.2	5.5	4.4	3.5	3.3	3.7
1973	5.3	13.0	15.8	10.9	4.3	7.1	5.1	3.7	3.2	2.7	2.8
1974	6.1	14.5	16.4	13.0	5.1	8.2	5.8	4.3	3.6	3.2	3.9
1975	8.6	17.4	19.2	16.1	7.5	11.2	8.4	6.5	5.8	5.0	5.3
1976	7.9	16.4	18.2	15.1	6.8	10.4	7.6	5.8	5.0	4.8	5.3
1977	7.3	15.9	18.2	14.2	6.2	9.3	6.7	5.3	5.0	4.4	4.9
1978	6.2	14.4	17.1	12.4	5.2	8.3	5.8	4.5	3.8	3.0	3.7
1979	5.9	14.0	15.9	12.5	5.0	7.8	5.6	4.2	3.7	3.0	3.1
1980	6.5	14.8	17.3	13.1	5.6	8.5	6.3	4.9	4.3	3.1	3.0
1981	6.9	16.6	18.4	15.3	5.9	9.1	6.6	5.1	4.2	3.7	3.4
1982	8.3	19.0	21.2	17.6	7.3	10.9	8.0	6.4	5.5	5.0	3.1
1983	7.9	18.3	21.4	16.4	6.9	10.3	7.6	6.2	5.5	4.7	3.1
1984	6.5	15.2	17.8	13.6	5.8	8.8	6.1	5.0	4.8	4.0	3.7
1985	6.4	14.8	17.2	13.1	5.7	8.5	6.2	4.9	4.5	4.1	3.1
1986	6.1	14.9	16.7	13.6	5.4	8.1	6.1	4.5	4.3	3.7	2.6
1987	5.2	13.4	15.5	11.7	4.6	7.4	5.0	4.1	3.3	2.9	2.4
1988	4.7	12.3	14.4	10.8	4.1	6.7	4.5	3.7	3.1	2.5	2.6
1989	4.5	11.5	13.8	10.1	4.0	6.8	4.5	3.4	2.9	2.7	2.5
1990	4.7	12.6	15.5	10.9	4.1	6.8	4.6	3.7	3.2	2.7	2.8
1991	5.6	15.2	18.2	13.3	5.0	8.1	5.7	4.3	4.0	3.3	3.1
1992	6.1	15.8	18.9	13.7	5.5	8.3	6.2	4.9	4.3	4.0	4.5
1993	5.7	14.7	17.8	12.6	5.2	7.9	5.8	4.7	4.3	3.9	3.0
1994	5.2	13.8	16.6	11.8	4.6	7.4	5.1	4.2	3.7	3.7	3.9
1995	4.8	13.4	16.4	11.2	4.3	7.4	4.7	3.9	3.0	3.5	3.5
1996	4.7	12.9	14.4	11.7	4.1	7.4	4.6	3.8	3.1	3.1	3.8
1997	4.2	12.8	15.2	11.1	3.7	6.4	4.2	3.4	2.6	2.4	3.4
1998	3.9	10.9	12.4	9.8	3.4	6.3	3.9	3.3	2.5	2.2	3.0
1999	3.8	11.3	13.9	9.6	3.3	6.1	3.6	3.0	2.3	2.5	2.9
2000	3.6	10.4	12.5	9.0	3.1	5.8	3.5	2.9	2.3	2.4	2.4
2001	4.1	11.4	13.1	10.2	3.6	6.1	4.5	3.3	2.7	2.5	2.7
2002	4.9	13.1	14.6	12.1	4.4	7.4	5.0	4.1	3.5	3.3	3.5
2003	4.8	13.3	15.9	11.5	4.4	7.6	4.9	4.2	3.3	3.4	3.5
2004	4.7	13.6	16.1	11.9	4.2	7.1	4.6	3.9	3.3	3.5	3.1
2005	4.4	12.3	14.0	11.1	3.9	6.4	4.7	3.6	3.1	3.0	3.2

[1]Beginning in 2003, persons who selected this race group only; persons who selected more than one race group are not included. Prior to 2003, persons who reported more than one race group were included in the group they identified as their main race.

Table 1-27. Unemployment Rates of Civilian Workers, by Age, Sex, Race, and Hispanic Origin, 1948–2005
—Continued

(Percent of labor force.)

Race, Hispanic origin, sex, and year	16 years and over	16 to 19 years			20 years and over						
		Total	16 to 17 years	18 to 19 years	Total	20 to 24 years	25 to 34 years	35 to 44 years	45 to 54 years	55 to 64 years	65 years and over
BLACK[1]											
Both Sexes											
1972	10.4	35.4	38.7	33.6	7.9	16.3	8.7	6.1	4.2	4.1	4.3
1973	9.4	31.5	37.0	28.1	7.2	15.5	8.1	4.7	3.5	3.2	3.5
1974	10.5	35.0	40.0	31.8	8.0	17.5	8.5	5.4	4.3	3.6	3.9
1975	14.8	39.5	41.6	38.1	12.3	24.5	13.0	8.9	8.3	5.9	6.6
1976	14.0	39.3	44.2	36.7	11.5	22.7	12.8	8.0	6.7	5.9	5.9
1977	14.0	41.1	44.5	39.2	11.5	24.2	12.7	7.4	5.3	5.5	5.9
1978	12.8	38.7	43.9	35.7	10.2	21.8	10.8	6.4	5.2	4.8	5.8
1979	12.3	36.5	40.2	34.4	10.1	20.6	10.8	6.7	5.2	4.9	5.3
1980	14.3	38.5	41.1	37.1	12.1	23.6	13.3	8.2	6.8	5.4	6.9
1981	15.6	41.4	44.8	39.5	13.4	26.4	14.7	9.5	7.4	5.5	7.0
1982	18.9	48.0	48.6	47.8	16.6	30.6	19.0	12.1	8.7	8.3	7.1
1983	19.5	48.5	50.5	47.6	17.3	31.6	19.0	12.4	10.7	9.2	9.2
1984	15.9	42.7	45.7	41.2	13.9	26.1	15.2	9.9	8.2	7.4	6.5
1985	15.1	40.2	43.6	38.3	13.1	24.5	14.5	9.5	8.2	7.0	7.0
1986	14.5	39.3	43.0	37.2	12.7	24.1	14.0	9.6	7.1	6.6	4.5
1987	13.0	34.7	39.7	31.6	11.3	21.8	12.8	8.4	6.8	5.6	3.9
1988	11.7	32.4	35.1	30.7	10.2	19.6	11.9	7.5	5.9	4.8	5.5
1989	11.4	32.4	32.9	32.2	9.9	18.0	11.5	7.6	5.6	5.2	6.9
1990	11.4	30.9	36.5	27.8	10.1	19.9	11.7	7.8	5.3	4.6	5.3
1991	12.5	36.1	39.5	34.4	11.1	21.6	12.7	8.5	7.4	4.4	5.2
1992	14.2	39.7	44.7	37.1	12.6	23.8	14.2	10.5	8.3	6.2	4.9
1993	13.0	38.8	39.7	38.4	11.4	21.9	12.6	9.5	6.9	7.1	4.7
1994	11.5	35.2	36.1	34.6	10.0	19.5	11.1	8.5	5.6	5.4	6.2
1995	10.4	35.7	39.1	33.4	8.7	17.7	9.9	7.3	4.8	4.0	6.7
1996	10.5	33.6	36.3	31.7	9.0	18.8	10.5	7.3	5.0	4.4	5.3
1997	10.0	32.4	35.0	30.8	8.6	18.3	9.9	7.0	5.0	4.2	6.1
1998	8.9	27.6	33.6	24.2	7.7	16.8	8.4	6.5	4.4	3.9	5.6
1999	8.0	27.9	31.0	26.2	6.8	14.6	7.6	5.3	4.0	3.9	5.0
2000	7.6	24.5	26.9	22.9	6.5	15.0	6.7	5.6	4.1	3.0	6.1
2001	8.6	29.0	30.8	27.9	7.4	16.3	8.1	6.3	4.8	3.9	4.3
2002	10.2	29.8	34.9	27.2	9.1	19.1	9.9	7.8	6.3	5.4	5.9
2003	10.8	33.0	32.2	33.5	9.7	19.8	10.9	8.6	6.2	6.3	5.4
2004	10.4	31.7	37.8	28.3	9.4	18.4	10.8	7.8	6.9	5.6	5.5
2005	10.0	33.3	41.2	29.0	8.8	18.3	10.2	7.1	6.0	5.6	6.9
Men											
1972	9.3	31.7	36.7	28.4	7.0	14.9	7.2	4.8	3.8	4.4	5.4
1973	8.0	27.8	35.7	23.0	6.0	13.2	6.2	3.9	3.2	3.2	3.3
1974	9.8	33.1	39.9	28.3	7.4	16.2	8.1	4.3	4.2	3.6	5.3
1975	14.8	38.1	41.9	35.9	12.5	24.7	12.7	8.7	9.3	6.3	8.7
1976	13.7	37.5	40.8	36.0	11.4	22.6	12.0	7.5	7.3	6.3	8.7
1977	13.3	39.2	41.0	38.2	10.7	23.0	11.8	6.2	4.9	6.0	7.8
1978	11.8	36.7	43.0	32.9	9.3	21.0	9.8	5.1	4.9	4.4	6.6
1979	11.4	34.2	37.9	32.2	9.3	18.7	9.6	6.3	5.2	5.1	6.4
1980	14.5	37.5	39.7	36.2	12.4	23.7	13.4	8.2	7.2	6.2	8.7
1981	15.7	40.7	43.2	39.2	13.5	26.4	14.4	9.3	7.8	6.1	7.5
1982	20.1	48.9	52.7	47.1	17.8	31.5	20.1	13.4	9.0	10.3	9.3
1983	20.3	48.8	52.2	47.3	18.1	31.4	19.4	13.5	11.4	11.0	11.8
1984	16.4	42.7	44.0	42.2	14.3	26.6	15.0	10.4	7.9	8.9	7.9
1985	15.3	41.0	42.9	40.0	13.2	23.5	13.8	9.6	9.7	7.9	8.9
1986	14.8	39.3	41.4	38.2	12.9	23.5	13.5	10.9	7.8	8.0	4.3
1987	12.7	34.4	39.0	31.6	11.1	20.3	12.2	8.7	6.7	6.6	4.3
1988	11.7	32.7	34.4	31.7	10.1	19.4	11.0	7.6	6.2	5.2	5.6
1989	11.5	31.9	34.4	30.3	10.0	17.9	10.5	8.4	6.2	6.2	7.4
1990	11.9	31.9	38.8	28.0	10.4	20.1	11.5	8.4	6.3	5.4	4.6
1991	13.0	36.3	39.0	34.8	11.5	22.4	11.9	9.5	8.6	5.0	6.1
1992	15.2	42.0	47.5	39.1	13.5	24.6	14.2	11.2	10.3	8.1	4.9
1993	13.8	40.1	42.7	38.6	12.1	23.0	12.3	10.5	8.1	9.0	5.8
1994	12.0	37.6	39.3	36.5	10.3	19.4	10.6	9.1	6.5	6.0	8.2
1995	10.6	37.1	39.7	35.4	8.8	17.6	9.3	7.6	5.5	4.4	7.6
1996	11.1	36.9	39.9	34.9	9.4	19.2	10.1	7.8	6.3	5.2	5.0
1997	10.2	36.5	39.5	34.4	8.5	19.8	8.7	6.7	5.6	4.2	5.5
1998	8.9	30.1	33.9	27.9	7.4	18.0	7.3	6.2	4.4	4.5	5.2
1999	8.2	30.9	33.3	29.4	6.7	16.2	6.9	5.2	4.3	3.9	5.0
2000	8.0	26.2	28.5	24.7	6.9	16.6	6.7	5.8	4.8	2.7	6.3
2001	9.3	30.4	30.5	30.4	8.0	17.6	8.3	6.9	5.5	4.8	4.0
2002	10.7	31.3	36.6	28.7	9.5	20.0	9.4	8.0	7.4	6.1	5.0
2003	11.6	36.0	35.6	36.3	10.3	20.9	11.3	9.2	6.7	6.8	5.6
2004	11.1	35.6	40.8	32.7	9.9	20.3	10.9	8.0	7.2	6.4	4.2
2005	10.5	36.3	45.1	31.5	9.2	20.5	9.7	7.0	6.7	5.9	7.1

[1]Beginning in 2003, persons who selected this race group only; persons who selected more than one race group are not included. Prior to 2003, persons who reported more than one race group were included in the group they identified as their main race.

Table 1-27. Unemployment Rates of Civilian Workers, by Age, Sex, Race, and Hispanic Origin, 1948–2005 —Continued

(Percent of labor force.)

Race, Hispanic origin, sex, and year	16 years and over	16 to 19 years			20 years and over						
		Total	16 to 17 years	18 to 19 years	Total	20 to 24 years	25 to 34 years	35 to 44 years	45 to 54 years	55 to 64 years	65 years and over
BLACK[1]											
Women											
1972	11.8	40.5	42.0	40.1	9.0	17.9	10.5	7.6	4.6	3.7	2.6
1973	11.1	36.1	38.6	34.2	8.6	18.4	10.3	5.6	3.9	3.3	3.7
1974	11.3	37.4	40.2	36.0	8.8	19.0	9.0	6.6	4.4	3.6	1.9
1975	14.8	41.0	41.2	40.6	12.2	24.3	13.4	9.0	7.0	5.3	3.6
1976	14.3	41.6	48.4	37.6	11.7	22.8	13.6	8.5	5.9	5.4	2.4
1977	14.9	43.4	49.5	40.4	12.3	25.5	13.6	8.7	5.8	4.8	3.4
1978	13.8	40.8	45.0	38.7	11.2	22.7	11.9	7.8	5.6	5.2	4.7
1979	13.3	39.1	42.7	36.9	10.9	22.6	12.1	7.2	5.2	4.7	3.9
1980	14.0	39.8	42.9	38.2	11.9	23.5	13.2	8.2	6.4	4.5	4.9
1981	15.6	42.2	46.5	39.8	13.4	26.4	14.9	9.8	6.9	4.7	6.0
1982	17.6	47.1	44.2	48.6	15.4	29.6	17.8	10.7	8.5	6.1	4.5
1983	18.6	48.2	48.6	48.0	16.5	31.8	18.6	11.4	9.9	7.3	6.3
1984	15.4	42.6	47.5	40.2	13.5	25.6	15.4	9.4	8.6	5.9	4.9
1985	14.9	39.2	44.3	36.4	13.1	25.6	15.1	9.3	6.8	6.0	5.2
1986	14.2	39.2	44.6	36.1	12.4	24.7	14.6	8.5	6.4	5.0	4.9
1987	13.2	34.9	40.5	31.7	11.6	23.3	13.5	8.1	6.9	4.5	3.4
1988	11.7	32.0	35.9	29.6	10.4	19.8	12.7	7.4	5.6	4.3	5.4
1989	11.4	33.0	31.1	34.0	9.8	18.1	12.5	7.0	5.0	4.2	6.4
1990	10.9	29.9	34.1	27.6	9.7	19.6	11.9	7.2	4.3	3.6	5.9
1991	12.0	36.0	40.1	33.9	10.6	20.7	13.4	7.6	6.2	3.8	4.4
1992	13.2	37.2	41.7	34.8	11.8	23.1	14.1	9.8	6.4	4.2	5.0
1993	12.1	37.4	36.1	38.1	10.7	20.9	12.9	8.6	5.8	5.1	3.6
1994	11.0	32.6	32.9	32.5	9.8	19.6	11.7	8.0	4.9	4.9	4.4
1995	10.2	34.3	38.5	31.5	8.6	17.8	10.5	7.0	4.2	3.6	. . .
1996	10.0	30.3	32.8	28.6	8.7	18.4	11.0	6.9	3.8	3.8	5.6
1997	9.9	28.7	30.3	27.8	8.8	17.1	10.9	7.2	4.4	4.1	6.6
1998	9.0	25.3	33.2	20.9	7.9	15.7	9.5	6.7	4.3	3.4	6.1
1999	7.8	25.1	28.5	23.3	6.8	13.4	8.3	5.5	3.8	3.9	5.0
2000	7.1	22.8	25.3	21.3	6.2	13.6	6.8	5.5	3.4	3.3	6.0
2001	8.1	27.5	31.2	25.4	7.0	15.3	8.0	5.8	4.3	3.1	4.6
2002	9.8	28.3	33.2	25.6	8.8	18.3	10.2	7.7	5.3	4.7	6.9
2003	10.2	30.3	29.1	31.1	9.2	18.8	10.5	8.1	5.8	5.9	5.3
2004	9.8	28.2	35.2	24.3	8.9	16.6	10.7	7.6	6.5	4.8	6.8
2005	9.5	30.3	37.3	26.6	8.5	16.3	10.6	7.2	5.4	5.3	6.6
HISPANIC[2]											
Both Sexes											
1973	7.5	19.7	23.4	17.3	6.0	8.5	5.7	5.6	4.7	5.5	3.9
1974	8.1	19.8	23.5	17.2	6.6	9.8	6.3	5.9	4.6	6.1	6.3
1975	12.2	27.7	30.0	26.5	10.3	16.7	9.9	8.6	8.1	7.7	9.9
1976	11.5	23.8	29.2	19.2	10.1	15.9	9.1	8.2	8.4	8.8	12.6
1977	10.1	22.9	27.0	19.6	8.5	12.0	8.6	6.1	7.3	8.2	9.2
1978	9.1	20.7	28.3	15.1	7.7	10.9	8.0	6.5	5.8	5.0	7.5
1979	8.3	19.2	26.0	14.9	7.0	10.4	6.7	6.2	5.2	6.0	5.7
1980	10.1	22.5	27.6	19.5	8.6	12.1	9.1	7.7	5.7	5.9	6.0
1981	10.4	23.9	28.0	21.7	9.1	13.9	8.8	7.4	6.4	7.3	5.4
1982	13.8	29.9	38.1	25.9	12.3	17.7	12.3	10.7	8.4	10.1	6.5
1983	13.7	28.4	33.8	25.8	12.3	16.7	11.9	11.3	10.0	10.9	5.8
1984	10.7	24.1	28.9	21.6	9.5	12.4	9.7	8.2	7.5	9.7	6.1
1985	10.5	24.3	27.8	22.5	9.4	12.6	9.9	7.7	7.4	7.8	8.1
1986	10.6	24.7	28.1	22.9	9.5	12.9	9.6	8.4	7.8	7.3	10.1
1987	8.8	22.3	27.7	19.5	7.8	10.6	7.7	6.7	6.9	6.0	6.5
1988	8.2	22.0	27.1	19.3	7.0	9.8	7.1	6.0	6.0	5.8	5.6
1989	8.0	19.4	26.4	16.0	7.2	10.7	7.0	5.9	6.3	5.8	5.3
1990	8.2	19.5	24.5	16.9	7.2	9.1	7.3	6.6	6.4	5.6	6.0
1991	10.0	22.9	31.9	18.7	9.0	11.6	9.2	8.1	8.0	6.5	7.0
1992	11.6	27.5	35.7	23.4	10.4	13.2	10.4	9.8	8.8	8.6	8.1
1993	10.8	26.1	35.1	21.8	9.7	13.1	9.3	9.1	8.6	8.0	6.6
1994	9.9	24.5	31.7	20.6	8.9	11.8	9.0	7.7	8.1	7.3	7.9
1995	9.3	24.1	33.1	19.5	8.2	11.5	8.2	7.2	6.4	7.5	10.6
1996	8.9	23.6	30.0	20.3	7.8	11.8	7.3	7.3	6.0	7.3	8.2
1997	7.7	21.6	27.7	18.4	6.8	10.3	6.3	6.4	5.1	6.5	6.8
1998	7.2	21.3	28.0	18.1	6.1	9.4	5.9	5.5	4.6	5.3	6.4
1999	6.4	18.6	23.7	16.3	5.5	8.3	5.4	4.8	4.8	4.5	5.0
2000	5.7	16.6	22.5	13.9	4.9	7.5	4.8	4.5	3.3	4.5	5.7
2001	6.6	17.7	24.0	15.0	5.8	8.1	5.9	5.2	4.3	5.6	4.5
2002	7.5	20.1	24.2	18.2	6.7	9.9	6.6	6.0	5.5	5.7	6.8
2003	7.7	20.0	24.6	17.7	7.0	10.2	7.0	6.0	6.3	5.7	3.9
2004	7.0	20.4	29.0	16.8	6.2	9.3	6.3	5.3	5.2	5.8	6.0
2005	6.0	18.4	23.6	16.0	5.3	8.6	5.3	4.5	4.4	4.4	4.9

[1]Beginning in 2003, persons who selected this race group only; persons who selected more than one race group are not included. Prior to 2003, persons who reported more than one race group were included in the group they identified as their main race.
[2]May be of any race.
. . . = Not available.

Table 1-27. Unemployment Rates of Civilian Workers, by Age, Sex, Race, and Hispanic Origin, 1948–2005 —Continued

(Percent of labor force.)

Race, Hispanic origin, sex, and year	16 years and over	16 to 19 years			20 years and over						
		Total	16 to 17 years	18 to 19 years	Total	20 to 24 years	25 to 34 years	35 to 44 years	45 to 54 years	55 to 64 years	65 years and over
HISPANIC[2]											
Men											
1973	6.7	19.0	20.9	17.7	5.4	8.2	5.0	4.2	4.5	5.4	. . .
1974	7.3	19.0	22.0	17.1	6.0	9.9	5.5	5.0	4.3	5.4	. . .
1975	11.4	27.6	29.3	26.5	9.6	16.3	9.6	7.9	7.0	6.8	. . .
1976	10.8	23.3	28.7	19.7	9.4	16.0	8.1	7.0	7.4	8.7	. . .
1977	9.0	20.9	25.9	18.2	7.7	11.7	7.9	4.9	5.4	7.4	. . .
1978	7.7	19.7	27.5	13.9	6.4	9.4	6.6	4.8	4.8	4.4	. . .
1979	7.0	17.5	23.5	13.8	5.8	9.2	5.3	5.1	4.4	5.0	. . .
1980	9.7	21.9	26.2	19.3	8.3	12.2	8.3	7.1	6.0	5.9	. . .
1981	10.2	24.3	30.9	20.3	8.8	14.1	8.9	6.5	5.9	6.7	. . .
1982	13.6	31.3	40.2	26.8	12.1	18.2	12.4	9.9	7.5	10.0	. . .
1983	13.6	28.7	34.7	25.9	12.2	17.0	11.6	10.8	10.3	11.7	. . .
1984	10.5	25.2	31.5	22.2	9.3	12.5	9.2	7.6	7.2	10.2	. . .
1985	10.2	24.7	29.1	22.4	9.1	12.9	9.6	7.2	6.8	7.0	. . .
1986	10.5	24.5	28.5	22.4	9.5	13.0	9.5	8.5	7.0	8.0	. . .
1987	8.7	22.2	28.2	19.3	7.8	10.2	7.6	6.9	7.1	6.7	. . .
1988	8.1	22.7	29.5	19.5	7.0	9.2	7.0	5.9	6.1	6.7	. . .
1989	7.6	20.2	27.6	16.8	6.6	9.7	5.9	5.7	6.0	6.6	. . .
1990	8.0	19.5	24.0	17.4	7.0	8.4	6.9	6.5	6.8	6.5	. . .
1991	10.3	23.5	33.6	19.2	9.3	11.6	9.3	8.5	7.9	8.1	. . .
1992	11.7	28.2	36.6	24.0	10.5	13.7	10.1	9.8	8.9	10.2	. . .
1993	10.6	25.9	34.5	21.9	9.5	12.6	9.0	8.8	8.8	8.5	. . .
1994	9.4	26.3	33.3	22.5	8.3	10.8	8.4	6.6	8.1	7.4	10.5
1995	8.8	25.3	34.8	20.2	7.7	10.6	7.5	6.7	5.9	7.9	12.9
1996	7.9	22.5	31.5	18.4	6.9	10.3	6.6	6.3	5.1	6.7	8.3
1997	7.0	20.8	26.5	17.9	6.1	9.8	5.1	5.4	4.8	6.8	7.2
1998	6.4	20.6	29.0	16.4	5.4	8.9	5.2	4.5	4.2	5.3	5.0
1999	5.6	17.8	23.4	15.3	4.7	7.8	4.1	3.8	4.5	4.6	5.0
2000	5.0	15.7	22.3	12.8	4.2	6.6	3.7	3.8	3.1	4.1	6.2
2001	5.9	17.1	25.8	13.4	5.2	8.1	4.6	4.5	3.8	6.3	4.8
2002	7.2	20.2	22.9	19.1	6.4	9.3	6.1	5.4	5.5	6.2	6.3
2003	7.2	21.9	25.9	20.1	6.4	9.6	6.3	5.3	6.0	6.0	3.6
2004	6.5	21.2	30.7	17.6	5.8	9.4	5.5	4.5	4.7	5.7	6.9
2005	5.4	19.3	23.4	17.5	4.7	8.2	4.3	3.9	4.0	4.0	4.8
Women											
1973	9.0	20.7	26.8	16.7	7.3	9.0	6.9	8.3	5.1	5.6	. . .
1974	9.4	20.8	25.3	17.4	7.7	9.7	7.7	7.5	5.3	7.5	. . .
1975	13.5	27.9	31.0	26.4	11.5	17.2	10.5	9.9	10.0	9.3	. . .
1976	12.7	22.2	30.3	18.7	11.4	15.8	10.8	10.0	9.8	9.0	. . .
1977	11.9	24.4	28.5	21.9	10.1	12.1	9.8	8.2	10.6	11.0	. . .
1978	11.3	21.8	29.9	16.6	9.8	13.0	10.3	9.2	7.4	7.2	. . .
1979	10.3	21.2	30.0	15.8	8.9	12.1	8.9	7.7	7.1	7.9	. . .
1980	10.7	23.4	29.7	19.8	9.2	12.0	10.6	8.6	5.3	5.8	. . .
1981	10.8	23.4	23.5	23.4	9.5	13.5	8.7	8.9	7.2	8.4	. . .
1982	14.1	28.2	35.1	25.0	12.5	16.8	12.2	11.9	9.9	10.4	. . .
1983	13.8	28.0	32.5	25.7	12.4	16.2	12.5	12.2	9.7	9.6	. . .
1984	11.1	22.8	26.1	21.0	9.9	12.2	10.3	9.1	7.9	8.8	. . .
1985	11.0	23.8	26.2	22.6	9.9	12.1	10.6	8.5	8.1	9.2	. . .
1986	10.8	25.1	27.6	23.6	9.6	12.9	9.8	8.2	8.9	6.2	. . .
1987	8.9	22.4	27.1	19.9	7.7	11.4	7.8	6.5	6.7	5.0	. . .
1988	8.3	21.0	24.5	18.9	7.1	10.7	7.2	6.2	5.9	4.6	. . .
1989	8.8	18.2	24.7	14.9	8.0	12.2	8.6	6.3	6.7	4.5	. . .
1990	8.4	19.4	25.4	16.2	7.5	10.4	8.0	6.7	6.0	4.3	. . .
1991	9.6	21.9	29.6	17.9	8.6	11.7	9.1	7.6	8.1	4.1	. . .
1992	11.4	26.4	34.5	22.4	10.2	12.4	11.0	9.7	8.5	6.2	. . .
1993	11.0	26.3	36.0	21.7	9.9	14.0	9.9	9.5	8.3	7.2	. . .
1994	10.7	22.2	29.7	18.1	9.8	13.5	10.1	9.2	8.0	7.1	3.6
1995	10.0	22.6	30.7	18.7	8.9	13.0	9.5	7.9	7.0	6.8	6.4
1996	10.2	25.1	28.2	23.3	9.2	14.1	8.5	8.7	7.2	8.1	8.0
1997	8.9	22.7	29.2	19.1	7.9	11.0	8.2	7.7	5.5	6.1	6.0
1998	8.2	22.1	26.4	20.2	7.1	10.1	7.2	6.9	5.1	5.4	8.8
1999	7.6	19.8	24.0	17.7	6.6	9.1	7.3	6.3	5.1	4.3	4.8
2000	6.8	18.0	22.7	15.6	5.9	9.0	6.4	5.4	3.6	5.0	4.8
2001	7.5	18.5	21.6	17.1	6.6	8.2	7.8	6.2	4.8	4.8	4.0
2002	8.0	19.9	25.8	17.0	7.2	10.8	7.4	6.7	5.5	5.0	7.5
2003	8.4	17.7	23.2	14.4	7.8	11.3	8.2	7.1	6.8	5.3	4.4
2004	7.6	19.3	27.0	15.5	7.0	9.1	7.6	6.4	5.8	5.8	4.6
2005	6.9	17.2	23.8	14.0	6.3	9.2	7.1	5.5	4.8	5.0	5.1

[2]May be of any race.
. . . = Not available.

Table 1-28. Unemployed Persons and Unemployment Rates, by Selected Occupation, 2000–2005

(Thousands of people, percent of civilian labor force.)

Occupation	2000	2001	2002	2003	2004	2005
Total Unemployed Persons, 16 Years and Over[1]	5 692	6 801	8 378	8 774	8 149	7 591
Management, professional, and related	827	1 102	1 482	1 556	1 346	1 172
Management, business, and financial operations	320	455	622	627	544	464
Professional and related	507	647	859	929	801	708
Services	1 132	1 311	1 544	1 681	1 617	1 587
Sales and office	1 446	1 652	2 110	2 070	1 937	1 820
Sales and related	673	779	998	995	912	874
Office and administrative support	773	873	1 112	1 076	1 025	946
Natural resources, construction, and maintenance	758	943	1 155	1 244	1 140	1 069
Farming, fishing, and forestry	133	163	142	136	132	103
Construction and extraction	507	626	788	814	786	751
Installation, maitenance, and repair	119	154	225	295	222	214
Production, transportation, and material moving	1 081	1 318	1 530	1 555	1 393	1 245
Production	575	759	848	807	714	677
Transportation and material moving	505	559	682	748	679	568
Total Unemployment Rate, 16 Years and Over[1]	4.0	4.7	5.8	6.0	5.5	5.1
Management, professional, and related	1.8	2.3	3.0	3.1	2.7	2.3
Management, business, and financial operations	1.6	2.2	3.0	3.1	2.6	2.2
Professional and related	1.9	2.3	3.0	3.2	2.8	2.4
Services	5.2	5.8	6.6	7.1	6.6	6.4
Sales and office	3.8	4.4	5.6	5.5	5.2	4.8
Sales and related	4.1	4.7	5.9	5.9	5.4	5.0
Office and administrative support	3.6	4.2	5.4	5.2	5.0	4.6
Natural resources, construction, and maintenance	5.3	6.4	7.8	8.1	7.3	6.5
Farming, fishing, and forestry	10.2	13.4	12.0	11.4	11.8	9.6
Construction and extraction	6.2	7.3	9.1	9.1	8.4	7.6
Installation, maintenance, and repair	2.4	3.2	4.6	5.5	4.2	3.9
Production, transportation, and material moving	5.1	6.4	7.6	7.9	7.2	6.5
Production	4.8	6.6	7.8	7.7	7.0	6.7
Transportation and material moving	5.6	6.2	7.4	8.2	7.4	6.2

[1]Includes persons with no work experience and those whose last job was in the armed forces.

Table 1-29. Unemployed Persons and Unemployment Rates, by Class of Worker and Industry, 2000–2005

(Thousands of people, percent.)

Class of worker and industry	2000	2001	2002	2003	2004	2005
Total Unemployed Persons, 16 Years and Over	5 692	6 801	8 378	8 774	8 149	7 591
Nonagricultural private wage and salary workers	4 483	5 540	6 926	7 131	6 484	5 989
Mining	21	23	33	37	21	20
Construction	513	609	800	810	769	712
Manufacturing	691	992	1 205	1 166	966	812
Durable goods	400	630	789	762	590	485
Nondurable goods	290	362	416	404	375	326
Wholesale trade and retail trade	837	945	1 202	1 237	1 197	1 137
Transportation and utilities	193	236	274	283	236	232
Information	124	190	253	246	189	163
Financial activities	208	252	320	319	332	272
Professional and business services	573	768	1 009	1 042	861	792
Education and health services	383	463	570	640	617	627
Leisure and hospitality	720	833	961	1 006	972	921
Other services	219	229	301	347	324	301
Agriculture and related private wage and salary workers	134	153	139	140	129	104
Government workers	422	430	512	568	548	534
Self-employed and unpaid family workers	219	218	265	294	303	298
Total Unemployment Rate, 16 Years and Over[1]	4.0	4.7	5.8	6.0	5.5	5.1
Nonagricultural private wage and salary workers	4.1	5.0	6.2	6.3	5.7	5.2
Mining	4.4	4.2	6.3	6.7	3.9	3.1
Construction	6.2	7.1	9.2	9.3	8.4	7.4
Manufacturing	3.5	5.2	6.7	6.6	5.7	4.9
Durable goods	3.2	5.2	6.9	6.9	5.5	4.6
Nondurable goods	4.0	5.2	6.2	6.1	5.9	5.3
Wholesale trade and retail trade	4.3	4.9	6.1	6.0	5.8	5.4
Transportation and utilities	3.4	4.3	4.9	5.3	4.4	4.1
Information	3.2	4.9	6.9	6.8	5.7	5.0
Financial activities	2.4	2.9	3.5	3.5	3.6	2.9
Professional and business services	4.8	6.1	7.9	8.2	6.8	6.2
Education and health services	2.5	2.8	3.4	3.6	3.4	3.4
Leisure and hospitality	6.6	7.5	8.4	8.7	8.3	7.8
Other services	3.9	4.0	5.1	5.7	5.3	4.8
Agriculture and related private wage and salary workers	9.0	11.2	10.1	10.2	9.9	8.3
Government workers	2.1	2.2	2.5	2.8	2.7	2.6
Self-employed and unpaid family workers	2.1	2.1	2.6	2.7	2.8	2.7

Note: See notes and definitions for information on historical comparability.

[1]Includes persons with no work experience and persons whose last job was in the armed forces.

Table 1-30. Unemployed Persons, by Duration of Unemployment, 1948–2005

(Thousands of people, number of weeks.)

Year	Total unemployed	Duration of unemployment					Average duration, in weeks	Median duration, in weeks
		Less than 5 weeks	5 to 14 weeks	15 weeks and over				
				Total	15 to 26 weeks	27 weeks and over		
1948	2 276	1 300	669	309	193	116	8.6	. . .
1949	3 637	1 756	1 194	684	428	256	10.0	. . .
1950	3 288	1 450	1 055	782	425	357	12.1	. . .
1951	2 055	1 177	574	303	166	137	9.7	. . .
1952	1 883	1 135	516	232	148	84	8.4	. . .
1953	1 834	1 142	482	210	132	78	8.0	. . .
1954	3 532	1 605	1 116	812	495	317	11.8	. . .
1955	2 852	1 335	815	702	366	336	13.0	. . .
1956	2 750	1 412	805	533	301	232	11.3	. . .
1957	2 859	1 408	891	560	321	239	10.5	. . .
1958	4 602	1 753	1 396	1 452	785	667	13.9	. . .
1959	3 740	1 585	1 114	1 040	469	571	14.4	. . .
1960	3 852	1 719	1 176	957	503	454	12.8	. . .
1961	4 714	1 806	1 376	1 532	728	804	15.6	. . .
1962	3 911	1 663	1 134	1 119	534	585	14.7	. . .
1963	4 070	1 751	1 231	1 088	535	553	14.0	. . .
1964	3 786	1 697	1 117	973	491	482	13.3	. . .
1965	3 366	1 628	983	755	404	351	11.8	. . .
1966	2 875	1 573	779	526	287	239	10.4	. . .
1967	2 975	1 634	893	448	271	177	8.7	2.3
1968	2 817	1 594	810	412	256	156	8.4	4.5
1969	2 832	1 629	827	375	242	133	7.8	4.4
1970	4 093	2 139	1 290	663	428	235	8.6	4.9
1971	5 016	2 245	1 585	1 187	668	519	11.3	6.3
1972	4 882	2 242	1 472	1 167	601	566	12.0	6.2
1973	4 365	2 224	1 314	826	483	343	10.0	5.2
1974	5 156	2 604	1 597	955	574	381	9.8	5.2
1975	7 929	2 940	2 484	2 505	1 303	1 203	14.2	8.4
1976	7 406	2 844	2 196	2 366	1 018	1 348	15.8	8.2
1977	6 991	2 919	2 132	1 942	913	1 028	14.3	7.0
1978	6 202	2 865	1 923	1 414	766	648	11.9	5.9
1979	6 137	2 950	1 946	1 241	706	535	10.8	5.4
1980	7 637	3 295	2 470	1 871	1 052	820	11.9	6.5
1981	8 273	3 449	2 539	2 285	1 122	1 162	13.7	6.9
1982	10 678	3 883	3 311	3 485	1 708	1 776	15.6	8.7
1983	10 717	3 570	2 937	4 210	1 652	2 559	20.0	10.1
1984	8 539	3 350	2 451	2 737	1 104	1 634	18.2	7.9
1985	8 312	3 498	2 509	2 305	1 025	1 280	15.6	6.8
1986	8 237	3 448	2 557	2 232	1 045	1 187	15.0	6.9
1987	7 425	3 246	2 196	1 983	943	1 040	14.5	6.5
1988	6 701	3 084	2 007	1 610	801	809	13.5	5.9
1989	6 528	3 174	1 978	1 375	730	646	11.9	4.8
1990	7 047	3 265	2 257	1 525	822	703	12.0	5.3
1991	8 628	3 480	2 791	2 357	1 246	1 111	13.7	6.8
1992	9 613	3 376	2 830	3 408	1 453	1 954	17.7	8.7
1993	8 940	3 262	2 584	3 094	1 297	1 798	18.0	8.3
1994	7 996	2 728	2 408	2 860	1 237	1 623	18.8	9.2
1995	7 404	2 700	2 342	2 363	1 085	1 278	16.6	8.3
1996	7 236	2 633	2 287	2 316	1 053	1 262	16.7	8.3
1997	6 739	2 538	2 138	2 062	995	1 067	15.8	8.0
1998	6 210	2 622	1 950	1 637	763	875	14.5	6.7
1999	5 880	2 568	1 832	1 480	755	725	13.4	6.4
2000	5 692	2 558	1 815	1 318	669	649	12.6	5.9
2001	6 801	2 853	2 196	1 752	951	801	13.1	6.8
2002	8 378	2 893	2 580	2 904	1 369	1 535	16.6	9.1
2003	8 774	2 785	2 612	3 378	1 442	1 936	19.2	10.1
2004	8 149	2 696	2 382	3 072	1 293	1 779	19.6	9.8
2005	7 591	2 667	2 304	2 619	1 130	1 490	18.4	8.9

. . . = Not available.

Table 1-31. Long-Term Unemployment, by Industry and Selected Occupation, 2000–2005

(Thousands of people.)

Length of unemployment, industry, and occupation	2000	2001	2002	2003	2004	2005
UNEMPLOYED 15 WEEKS AND OVER						
Total	1 318	1 752	2 904	3 378	3 072	2 619
Wage and Salary Workers, by Industry						
Agriculture and related	32	44	39	44	38	29
Mining	7	7	11	17	8	8
Construction	107	130	236	262	248	216
Manufacturing	184	303	528	575	467	326
Durable goods	99	183	348	389	293	199
Nondurable goods	86	120	180	186	174	127
Wholesale and retail trade	186	241	423	472	455	415
Transportation and utilities	57	71	124	132	114	91
Information	33	52	119	128	87	76
Financial activities	58	75	131	144	139	91
Professional and business services	143	217	377	440	345	299
Education and health services	124	149	232	300	304	271
Leisure and hospitality	146	196	279	328	321	277
Other services	54	58	95	132	126	117
Public administration	41	36	51	59	72	62
Experienced Workers, by Occupation						
Management, professional, and related	213	313	603	692	571	436
Services	246	323	447	564	565	511
Sales and office	331	419	759	810	750	641
Natural resources, construction, and maintenance ..	161	212	346	424	386	341
Production, transportation, and material moving	273	360	575	654	561	461
UNEMPLOYED 27 WEEKS AND OVER						
Total	649	801	1 535	1 936	1 779	1 490
Wage and Salary Workers, by Industry						
Agriculture and related	13	16	18	21	18	16
Mining	4	3	5	10	6	4
Construction	44	60	111	132	133	108
Manufacturing	100	132	291	366	302	195
Durable goods	50	75	191	255	196	124
Nondurable goods	50	57	100	111	106	71
Wholesale and retail trade	80	114	226	261	261	230
Transportation and utilities	27	33	67	74	63	50
Information	18	21	62	80	58	41
Financial activities	32	34	131	88	79	56
Professional and business services	67	90	377	262	193	172
Education and health services	63	71	232	167	168	156
Leisure and hospitality	69	90	279	166	169	148
Other services	26	31	95	71	76	74
Public administration	23	18	51	33	44	38
Experienced Workers, by Occupation						
Management, professional, and related	101	135	340	429	356	269
Services	128	156	225	295	307	284
Sales and office	151	185	397	459	419	354
Natural resources, construction, and maintenance ..	74	96	164	229	221	186
Production, transportation, and material moving	140	162	313	388	336	261

Note: Beginning in January 2004, data reflect revised population controls used in the household survey. See notes and definitions for information on historical comparability.

Table 1-32. Unemployed Persons and Unemployment Rates, by Reason for Unemployment, Sex, and Age, 1970–2005

(Thousands of people, percent.)

Sex, age, and year	Number of unemployed					Unemployed as a percent of the total civilian labor force			
	Total	Job losers	Job leavers	Entrants		Job losers	Job leavers	Entrants	
				Reentrants	New entrants			Reentrants	New entrants
Both Sexes, 16 Years and Over									
1970	4 093	1 811	550	1 228	504	2.2	0.7	1.5	0.6
1971	5 016	2 323	590	1 472	630	2.8	0.7	1.7	0.7
1972	4 882	2 108	641	1 456	677	2.4	0.7	1.7	0.8
1973	4 365	1 694	683	1 340	649	1.9	0.8	1.5	0.7
1974	5 156	2 242	768	1 463	681	2.4	0.8	1.6	0.7
1975	7 929	4 386	827	1 892	823	4.7	0.9	2.0	0.9
1976	7 406	3 679	903	1 928	895	3.8	0.9	2.0	0.9
1977	6 991	3 166	909	1 963	953	3.2	0.9	2.0	1.0
1978	6 202	2 585	874	1 857	885	2.5	0.9	1.8	0.9
1979	6 137	2 635	880	1 806	817	2.5	0.8	1.7	0.8
1980	7 637	3 947	891	1 927	872	3.7	0.8	1.8	0.8
1981	8 273	4 267	923	2 102	981	3.9	0.8	1.9	0.9
1982	10 678	6 268	840	2 384	1 185	5.7	0.8	2.2	1.1
1983	10 717	6 258	830	2 412	1 216	5.6	0.7	2.2	1.1
1984	8 539	4 421	823	2 184	1 110	3.9	0.7	1.9	1.0
1985	8 312	4 139	877	2 256	1 039	3.6	0.8	2.0	0.9
1986	8 237	4 033	1 015	2 160	1 029	3.4	0.9	1.8	0.9
1987	7 425	3 566	965	1 974	920	3.0	0.8	1.6	0.8
1988	6 701	3 092	983	1 809	816	2.5	0.8	1.5	0.7
1989	6 528	2 983	1 024	1 843	677	2.4	0.8	1.5	0.5
1990	7 047	3 387	1 041	1 930	688	2.7	0.8	1.5	0.5
1991	8 628	4 694	1 004	2 139	792	3.7	0.8	1.7	0.6
1992	9 613	5 389	1 002	2 285	937	4.2	0.8	1.8	0.7
1993	8 940	4 848	976	2 198	919	3.8	0.8	1.7	0.7
1994	7 996	3 815	791	2 786	604	2.9	0.6	2.1	0.5
1995	7 404	3 476	824	2 525	579	2.6	0.6	1.9	0.4
1996	7 236	3 370	774	2 512	580	2.5	0.6	1.9	0.4
1997	6 739	3 037	795	2 338	569	2.2	0.6	1.7	0.4
1998	6 210	2 822	734	2 132	520	2.1	0.5	1.5	0.4
1999	5 880	2 622	783	2 005	469	1.9	0.6	1.4	0.3
2000	5 692	2 517	780	1 961	434	1.8	0.5	1.4	0.3
2001	6 801	3 476	835	2 031	459	2.4	0.6	1.4	0.3
2002	8 378	4 607	866	2 368	536	3.2	0.6	1.6	0.4
2003	8 774	4 838	818	2 477	641	3.3	0.6	1.7	0.4
2004	8 149	4 197	858	2 408	686	2.8	0.6	1.6	0.5
2005	7 591	3 667	872	2 386	666	2.5	0.6	1.6	0.4
Both Sexes, 16 to 19 Years									
1970	1 106	200	126	378	401	2.8	1.7	5.2	5.5
1971	1 262	233	117	410	501	3.1	1.6	5.5	6.7
1972	1 308	248	129	395	536	3.1	1.6	4.9	6.6
1973	1 235	212	146	364	513	2.4	1.7	4.3	6.0
1974	1 422	280	173	436	533	3.1	2.0	4.9	6.0
1975	1 767	450	155	529	634	5.1	1.7	6.0	7.1
1976	1 719	387	153	496	683	4.3	1.7	5.5	7.5
1977	1 663	318	156	477	711	3.4	1.7	5.1	7.6
1978	1 583	300	167	455	660	3.1	1.7	4.7	6.8
1979	1 555	319	184	452	599	3.3	1.9	4.7	6.2
1980	1 669	388	156	481	643	4.1	1.7	5.1	6.9
1981	1 763	385	162	487	728	4.3	1.8	5.4	8.1
1982	1 977	460	134	509	874	5.4	1.6	6.0	10.2
1983	1 829	370	110	482	867	4.6	1.3	5.9	10.6
1984	1 499	271	114	370	745	3.4	1.4	4.7	9.4
1985	1 468	275	113	390	689	3.5	1.4	4.9	8.7
1986	1 454	240	145	374	695	3.0	1.8	4.7	8.8
1987	1 347	210	146	375	617	2.7	1.8	4.7	7.7
1988	1 226	207	159	310	550	2.6	2.0	3.9	6.8
1989	1 194	198	200	345	452	2.5	2.5	4.3	5.7
1990	1 212	233	181	338	460	3.0	2.3	4.3	5.9
1991	1 359	289	180	365	524	4.0	2.5	5.0	7.2
1992	1 427	259	149	377	643	3.6	2.1	5.3	9.1
1993	1 365	233	151	353	628	3.3	2.1	4.9	8.8
1994	1 320	185	84	634	416	2.5	1.1	8.5	5.6
1995	1 346	214	102	615	415	2.8	1.3	7.9	5.3
1996	1 306	182	91	625	409	2.3	1.2	8.0	5.2
1997	1 271	174	104	606	388	2.2	1.3	7.6	4.9
1998	1 205	181	86	577	361	2.2	1.0	7.0	4.4
1999	1 162	173	114	547	328	2.1	1.4	6.6	3.9
2000	1 081	157	109	516	299	1.9	1.3	6.2	3.6
2001	1 162	185	98	568	311	2.3	1.2	7.2	3.9
2002	1 253	197	91	597	368	2.6	1.2	7.9	4.9
2003	1 251	188	85	554	424	2.6	1.2	7.7	5.9
2004	1 208	165	76	510	456	2.3	1.1	7.2	6.4
2005	1 186	155	76	489	466	2.2	1.1	6.8	6.5

Note: See notes and definitions for information on historical comparability.

Table 1-32. Unemployed Persons and Unemployment Rates, by Reason for Unemployment, Sex, and Age, 1970–2005—Continued

(Thousands of people, percent.)

Sex, age, and year	Number of unemployed					Unemployed as a percent of the total civilian labor force			
	Total	Job losers	Job leavers	Entrants		Job losers	Job leavers	Entrants	
				Reentrants	New entrants			Reentrants	New entrants
Men, 20 Years and Over									
1970	1 638	1 066	209	318	44	2.2	0.4	0.7	0.1
1971	2 097	1 391	239	411	57	2.9	0.5	0.9	0.1
1972	1 948	1 219	248	420	60	2.5	0.5	0.9	0.1
1973	1 624	959	258	350	56	1.9	0.5	0.7	0.1
1974	1 957	1 276	276	356	48	2.5	0.5	0.7	0.1
1975	3 476	2 598	298	506	76	5.0	0.6	1.0	0.1
1976	3 098	2 167	323	521	86	4.1	0.6	1.0	0.2
1977	2 794	1 816	335	540	103	3.4	0.6	1.0	0.2
1978	2 328	1 433	337	471	86	2.6	0.6	0.9	0.2
1979	2 308	1 464	325	446	73	2.6	0.6	0.8	0.1
1980	3 353	2 389	359	516	90	4.2	0.6	0.9	0.2
1981	3 615	2 565	356	592	102	4.5	0.6	1.0	0.2
1982	5 089	3 965	327	678	119	6.8	0.6	1.2	0.2
1983	5 257	4 088	336	695	138	6.9	0.6	1.2	0.2
1984	3 932	2 800	324	663	146	4.7	0.5	1.1	0.2
1985	3 715	2 568	352	671	124	4.3	0.6	1.1	0.2
1986	3 751	2 568	444	611	128	4.1	0.7	1.0	0.2
1987	3 369	2 289	413	558	108	3.7	0.7	0.9	0.2
1988	2 987	1 939	416	534	98	3.1	0.7	0.9	0.2
1989	2 867	1 843	394	541	88	2.9	0.6	0.8	0.1
1990	3 239	2 100	431	626	82	3.2	0.7	1.0	0.1
1991	4 195	2 982	411	698	105	4.6	0.6	1.1	0.2
1992	4 717	3 420	421	765	111	5.2	0.6	1.2	0.2
1993	4 287	2 996	429	747	114	4.5	0.6	1.1	0.2
1994	3 627	2 296	367	898	65	3.4	0.5	1.3	0.1
1995	3 239	2 051	356	775	57	3.0	0.5	1.2	0.1
1996	3 146	2 043	322	731	51	3.0	0.5	1.1	0.1
1997	2 882	1 795	358	675	55	2.6	0.5	1.0	0.1
1998	2 580	1 588	318	611	63	2.3	0.5	0.9	0.1
1999	2 433	1 459	336	592	46	2.1	0.5	0.8	0.1
2000	2 376	1 416	328	577	55	2.0	0.5	0.8	0.1
2001	3 040	1 999	372	612	56	2.7	0.5	0.8	0.1
2002	3 896	2 702	386	743	65	3.7	0.5	1.0	0.1
2003	4 209	2 899	376	846	88	3.9	0.5	1.1	0.1
2004	3 791	2 503	398	791	99	3.3	0.5	1.0	0.1
2005	4 059	2 188	445	1 067	359	2.7	0.5	1.0	0.1
Women, 20 Years and Over									
1970	1 349	546	214	531	58	1.9	0.8	1.9	0.2
1971	1 658	700	235	651	72	2.5	0.8	2.3	0.2
1972	1 625	641	264	641	80	2.2	0.9	2.1	0.3
1973	1 507	522	280	625	80	1.6	0.9	2.0	0.3
1974	1 777	685	319	673	100	2.1	1.0	2.1	0.3
1975	2 684	1 339	375	858	114	4.0	1.1	2.6	0.3
1976	2 588	1 124	427	912	126	3.2	1.2	2.6	0.4
1977	2 535	1 031	419	945	140	2.8	1.2	2.6	0.4
1978	2 292	852	371	930	138	2.2	1.0	2.4	0.4
1979	2 276	851	370	908	145	2.1	0.9	2.3	0.4
1980	2 615	1 170	376	930	139	2.8	0.9	2.3	0.3
1981	2 895	1 317	404	1 023	151	3.1	1.0	2.4	0.4
1982	3 613	1 844	379	1 197	192	4.2	0.9	2.7	0.4
1983	3 632	1 801	384	1 235	212	4.0	0.9	2.8	0.5
1984	3 107	1 350	386	1 151	220	2.9	0.8	2.5	0.5
1985	3 129	1 296	412	1 195	227	2.7	0.9	2.5	0.5
1986	3 032	1 225	426	1 175	206	2.5	0.9	2.4	0.4
1987	2 709	1 067	406	1 041	194	2.2	0.8	2.1	0.4
1988	2 487	946	408	965	168	1.9	0.8	1.9	0.3
1989	2 467	942	430	958	137	1.8	0.8	1.8	0.3
1990	2 596	1 054	429	966	146	2.0	0.8	1.8	0.3
1991	3 074	1 423	413	1 075	163	2.6	0.8	2.0	0.3
1992	3 469	1 710	433	1 142	183	3.1	0.8	2.1	0.3
1993	3 288	1 619	395	1 098	176	2.9	0.7	2.0	0.3
1994	3 049	1 334	339	1 253	122	2.4	0.6	2.2	0.2
1995	2 819	1 211	366	1 135	107	2.1	0.6	2.0	0.2
1996	2 783	1 145	361	1 156	120	2.0	0.6	2.0	0.2
1997	2 585	1 069	333	1 057	126	1.8	0.6	1.8	0.2
1998	2 424	1 053	330	944	97	1.8	0.6	1.6	0.2
1999	2 285	990	333	866	96	1.6	0.5	1.4	0.2
2000	2 235	943	343	868	80	1.5	0.6	1.4	0.1
2001	2 599	1 291	365	850	92	2.0	0.6	1.3	0.1
2002	3 228	1 708	389	1 028	102	2.7	0.6	1.6	0.2
2003	3 314	1 751	357	1 076	130	2.7	0.6	1.7	0.2
2004	3 150	1 529	384	1 107	131	2.4	0.6	1.7	0.2
2005	3 013	1 417	391	1 103	101	2.2	0.6	1.7	0.2

Note: See notes and definitions for information on historical comparability.

Table 1-33. Percent of the Population with Work Experience During the Year, by Age and Sex, 1987–2005

(Percent.)

Sex and year	Total	16 to 17 years	18 to 19 years	20 to 24 years	25 to 34 years	35 to 44 years	45 to 54 years	55 to 59 years	60 to 64 years	65 to 69 years	70 years and over
Both Sexes											
1987	69.7	51.8	76.6	85.5	85.7	86.1	81.6	69.4	51.3	26.2	10.2
1988	70.2	50.6	75.5	85.7	86.0	86.8	82.2	70.5	52.2	27.9	10.3
1989	70.5	51.9	75.4	84.9	86.6	86.9	82.8	70.4	52.5	28.4	10.0
1990	70.2	48.6	74.2	84.1	86.2	87.0	82.8	70.9	53.4	28.3	10.2
1991	69.5	43.4	70.8	83.4	85.9	86.6	83.0	70.3	52.9	27.2	9.8
1992	69.1	43.8	69.9	82.7	85.2	85.9	82.8	70.8	53.5	25.5	9.8
1993	69.2	42.1	70.4	82.0	85.0	85.3	82.8	71.6	51.6	27.5	10.7
1994	69.6	44.1	71.5	82.5	85.5	85.6	83.8	72.2	52.8	27.5	10.0
1995	69.6	44.4	71.2	82.0	85.6	85.9	83.4	72.2	53.3	28.0	10.2
1996	69.9	43.3	70.5	83.1	86.1	85.7	84.3	73.3	54.3	27.8	10.4
1997	70.1	43.6	70.5	83.0	87.1	85.9	84.4	73.8	53.8	28.5	10.0
1998	70.1	42.1	69.9	82.9	86.7	86.3	84.2	73.7	54.5	29.2	10.6
1999	70.7	43.7	71.2	82.7	87.3	86.9	85.0	72.3	55.8	30.5	11.6
2000	70.5	42.2	69.6	82.6	87.1	87.0	84.6	72.9	55.1	30.8	11.4
2001	69.4	37.7	66.7	80.8	86.1	85.8	83.7	73.5	56.7	30.6	10.5
2002	68.5	34.5	62.8	78.5	84.4	85.0	83.7	74.7	56.8	33.1	10.4
2003	67.8	32.0	61.7	77.5	83.7	84.0	82.9	73.9	56.5	33.2	11.4
2004	67.7	32.6	59.8	76.9	83.3	84.2	82.6	73.9	57.0	32.7	12.2
2005	67.8	31.1	60.1	77.3	83.7	84.1	82.8	74.4	58.2	32.0	12.1
Men											
1987	78.9	52.4	77.4	90.4	94.3	94.1	91.9	83.3	63.2	34.2	15.4
1988	79.1	51.8	78.9	90.7	94.3	94.6	91.6	82.1	63.1	35.6	15.6
1989	79.4	53.2	77.7	89.9	94.7	94.7	91.9	82.0	64.2	35.4	15.1
1990	78.9	50.3	76.7	88.7	94.4	94.7	91.3	82.0	65.8	35.8	14.0
1991	77.9	45.4	72.2	87.9	93.5	93.6	91.3	81.5	63.6	35.0	14.4
1992	77.4	46.6	73.7	87.1	93.3	92.8	89.9	80.9	63.2	32.4	14.3
1993	76.8	43.9	71.4	86.6	92.5	92.0	89.3	79.8	59.1	34.3	15.3
1994	77.2	44.4	74.7	87.2	92.9	92.0	90.0	81.3	61.4	33.9	14.8
1995	77.0	43.7	73.6	86.4	92.6	92.2	89.7	81.5	62.1	34.5	14.9
1996	77.2	44.1	71.8	86.7	93.4	92.1	90.4	81.8	62.5	33.6	15.2
1997	77.1	43.4	70.3	86.6	94.1	92.3	90.7	81.4	62.9	33.8	13.9
1998	76.9	40.4	71.6	86.4	93.5	92.7	90.1	81.7	63.5	35.5	14.7
1999	77.3	44.7	72.3	85.5	93.9	93.2	89.9	79.2	65.1	37.4	16.5
2000	77.1	42.1	70.2	85.1	93.4	93.6	89.8	80.6	64.4	38.4	16.0
2001	76.3	37.4	67.7	84.8	93.2	92.2	89.1	80.4	64.3	37.8	14.5
2002	75.2	34.7	62.8	82.1	91.6	91.8	88.9	80.7	64.3	39.3	14.6
2003	74.3	32.8	61.7	80.2	90.8	90.9	87.7	80.9	63.1	37.3	15.8
2004	74.2	32.1	58.9	80.2	91.0	91.1	87.9	80.1	64.5	37.1	16.7
2005	74.6	31.1	60.7	80.8	91.3	91.6	88.2	80.1	64.3	37.6	17.0
Women											
1987	61.3	51.1	75.8	81.0	77.3	78.5	71.9	56.7	41.0	19.6	6.8
1988	62.1	49.3	72.2	81.0	78.1	79.4	73.5	60.0	42.5	21.4	6.8
1989	62.3	50.6	73.1	80.2	78.6	79.3	74.2	59.9	42.4	22.5	6.7
1990	62.2	46.8	71.7	79.6	78.0	79.6	74.9	60.4	42.5	22.1	7.7
1991	61.8	41.4	69.4	79.0	78.3	79.9	75.3	59.9	43.6	20.6	6.7
1992	61.5	40.9	66.1	78.4	77.2	79.1	76.1	61.5	44.4	20.0	6.7
1993	62.1	40.3	69.4	77.5	77.6	78.7	76.5	63.9	44.7	22.1	7.7
1994	62.5	43.7	68.4	77.8	78.1	79.4	78.0	63.9	45.0	22.2	6.8
1995	62.8	45.2	68.7	77.7	78.8	79.8	77.6	63.2	45.6	22.4	7.1
1996	63.2	42.5	69.2	79.5	78.9	79.5	78.4	65.4	46.9	23.0	7.1
1997	63.6	43.9	70.7	79.5	80.1	79.6	78.4	66.7	45.6	24.0	7.3
1998	63.7	44.1	68.2	79.4	80.1	80.0	78.6	66.3	46.2	23.8	7.8
1999	64.5	42.6	70.1	79.9	80.9	80.7	80.3	66.2	47.3	24.4	8.2
2000	64.3	42.3	69.0	80.2	80.9	80.5	79.5	65.7	47.0	23.9	8.2
2001	63.1	38.1	65.7	76.9	79.2	79.5	78.6	67.1	49.8	24.2	7.9
2002	62.3	34.3	62.8	74.9	77.2	78.4	78.7	69.1	50.0	27.8	7.4
2003	61.7	31.2	61.6	74.6	76.6	77.2	78.4	67.3	50.7	29.6	8.3
2004	61.5	33.1	60.7	73.7	75.6	77.4	77.5	68.2	50.3	28.7	9.0
2005	61.4	31.2	59.6	73.7	76.1	76.8	77.6	68.9	52.7	27.1	8.7

Note: See notes and definitions for information on historical comparability.

Table 1-34. Persons with Work Experience During the Year, by Industry and Class of Worker of Job Held the Longest, 2002–2005

(Thousands of people.)

Industry and class of worker	2002	2003	2004	2005
TOTAL	151 546	151 553	153 024	155 127
Agriculture	2 490	2 521	2 492	2 344
Wage and salary workers	1 583	1 605	1 549	1 501
Self-employed workers	875	894	918	829
Unpaid family workers	33	22	25	14
Nonagricultural Industries	149 055	149 032	150 532	152 783
Wage and salary workers	139 909	139 747	140 885	143 002
Mining	594	576	630	696
Construction	9 488	9 423	10 076	10 423
Manufacturing	17 660	17 349	17 196	17 243
Durable goods	11 013	10 622	10 814	10 930
Nondurable goods	6 647	6 727	6 382	6 313
Wholesale and retail trade	21 615	21 650	22 091	22 479
Wholesale trade	4 402	4 691	4 470	4 517
Retail trade	17 213	16 959	17 621	17 962
Transportation and utilities	7 039	6 934	7 040	7 248
Transportation and warehousing	5 745	5 736	5 827	6 095
Utilities	1 294	1 198	1 213	1 153
Information	3 989	3 755	3 359	3 495
Financial activities	9 591	9 822	9 956	9 748
Finance and insurance	6 986	7 135	7 192	7 011
Real estate and rental and leasing	2 605	2 687	2 764	2 737
Professional and business services	13 883	13 485	13 277	13 537
Professional, scientific, and technical services	7 989	7 855	7 793	7 768
Management, administration, and waste management services	5 894	5 629	5 484	5 769
Education and health services	29 343	29 571	29 814	30 552
Education services	12 765	13 026	13 169	13 282
Health care and social assistance services	16 578	16 544	16 645	17 270
Leisure and hospitality	13 260	13 110	13 345	13 405
Arts, entertainment, and recreation	2 852	2 789	2 888	2 877
Accommodation and food services	10 408	10 321	10 457	10 528
Other services and private household	6 416	6 529	6 473	6 490
Private households	873	897	907	866
Public administration	6 290	6 734	6 897	6 917
Self-employed workers	9 023	9 169	9 520	9 658
Unpaid family workers	124	116	128	123

Note: See notes and definitions for information on historical comparability.

Table 1-35. Number of Persons with Work Experience During the Year, by Extent of Employment and Sex, 1987–2005

(Thousands of people.)

Sex and year	Total	Full-time workers				Part-time workers			
		Total	50 to 52 weeks	27 to 49 weeks	1 to 26 weeks	Total	50 to 52 weeks	27 to 49 weeks	1 to 26 weeks
Both Sexes									
1987	128 315	100 288	77 015	13 361	9 912	28 027	10 973	6 594	10 460
1988	130 451	102 131	79 627	12 875	9 629	28 320	11 384	6 624	10 312
1989	132 817	104 876	81 117	14 271	9 488	27 941	11 275	6 987	9 679
1990	133 535	105 323	80 932	14 758	9 633	28 212	11 507	7 012	9 693
1991	133 410	104 472	80 385	14 491	9 596	28 938	11 946	7 003	9 989
1992	133 912	104 813	81 523	13 587	9 703	29 099	12 326	6 841	9 932
1993	136 354	106 299	83 384	13 054	9 861	30 055	12 818	6 777	10 460
1994	138 468	108 141	85 764	13 051	9 326	30 327	12 936	6 956	10 435
1995	139 724	110 063	88 173	12 970	8 920	29 661	12 725	6 831	10 105
1996	142 201	112 313	90 252	12 997	9 064	29 888	13 382	6 643	9 863
1997	143 968	113 879	92 631	12 508	8 740	30 089	13 810	6 565	9 714
1998	145 566	116 412	95 772	12 156	8 484	29 155	13 538	6 480	9 137
1999	148 295	119 096	97 941	12 294	8 861	29 199	13 680	6 317	9 202
2000	149 361	120 591	100 349	12 071	8 171	28 770	13 865	6 161	8 744
2001	151 042	121 921	100 357	13 172	8 392	29 121	14 038	6 139	8 944
2002	151 546	121 726	100 659	12 544	8 523	29 819	14 635	6 184	9 000
2003	151 553	121 158	100 700	11 972	8 486	30 395	15 333	6 027	9 035
2004	153 024	122 404	102 427	11 862	8 115	30 621	15 552	6 077	8 992
2005	155 127	124 683	104 876	11 816	7 991	30 444	15 374	6 161	8 909
Men									
1987	69 144	59 736	47 040	7 503	5 193	9 408	3 260	2 191	3 957
1988	70 021	60 504	48 299	7 329	4 876	9 517	3 468	2 199	3 850
1989	71 640	62 108	49 693	7 642	4 773	9 532	3 619	2 254	3 659
1990	71 953	62 319	49 175	8 188	4 956	9 634	3 650	2 322	3 662
1991	71 700	61 636	47 895	8 324	5 417	10 064	3 820	2 342	3 902
1992	72 007	61 722	48 300	7 965	5 457	10 285	3 864	2 354	4 067
1993	72 872	62 513	49 832	7 317	5 364	10 359	4 005	2 144	4 210
1994	73 958	63 634	51 582	7 094	4 958	10 324	3 948	2 358	4 018
1995	74 381	64 145	52 671	6 973	4 501	10 236	4 034	2 257	3 945
1996	75 760	65 356	53 795	6 891	4 670	10 404	4 321	2 136	3 947
1997	76 408	66 089	54 918	6 638	4 533	10 319	4 246	2 274	3 799
1998	76 918	67 250	56 953	6 208	4 089	9 669	4 197	2 090	3 382
1999	78 145	68 347	57 520	6 401	4 426	9 797	4 297	2 062	3 438
2000	78 804	68 925	58 756	6 094	4 075	9 879	4 485	1 957	3 437
2001	79 971	70 074	58 715	7 087	4 272	9 897	4 306	1 989	3 602
2002	80 282	70 132	58 765	6 804	4 563	10 151	4 519	2 042	3 590
2003	80 317	69 766	58 778	6 479	4 509	10 551	5 042	1 872	3 637
2004	81 261	70 780	60 096	6 428	4 256	10 482	4 987	1 992	3 503
2005	82 735	72 056	61 510	6 299	4 247	10 679	5 153	2 074	3 452
Women									
1987	59 171	40 552	29 975	5 858	4 719	18 619	7 713	4 403	6 503
1988	60 430	41 627	31 328	5 546	4 753	18 803	7 916	4 425	6 462
1989	61 178	42 768	31 424	6 629	4 715	18 410	7 656	4 733	6 021
1990	61 582	43 004	31 757	6 570	4 677	18 578	7 857	4 690	6 031
1991	61 712	42 837	32 491	6 167	4 179	18 875	8 126	4 662	6 087
1992	61 904	43 090	33 223	5 621	4 246	18 814	8 462	4 487	5 865
1993	63 481	43 785	33 552	5 736	4 497	19 696	8 813	4 633	6 250
1994	64 511	44 508	34 182	5 957	4 369	20 003	8 988	4 598	6 417
1995	65 342	45 917	35 502	5 997	4 418	19 425	8 691	4 574	6 160
1996	66 439	46 955	36 457	6 105	4 393	19 484	9 061	4 507	5 916
1997	67 559	47 790	37 713	5 870	4 207	19 769	9 564	4 291	5 914
1998	68 648	49 162	38 819	5 948	4 395	19 486	9 341	4 390	5 755
1999	70 150	50 748	40 421	5 892	4 435	19 402	9 383	4 255	5 764
2000	70 556	51 665	41 593	5 977	4 095	18 891	9 380	4 204	5 307
2001	71 071	51 848	41 642	6 085	4 120	19 223	9 731	4 150	5 342
2002	71 263	51 593	41 893	5 741	3 959	19 671	10 117	4 143	5 411
2003	71 236	51 391	41 921	5 493	3 977	19 844	10 291	4 155	5 398
2004	71 763	51 624	42 331	5 434	3 859	20 139	10 565	4 085	5 489
2005	72 392	52 627	43 366	5 517	3 744	19 765	10 222	4 087	5 456

Note: See notes and definitions for information on historical comparability.

Table 1-36. Percent Distribution of the Population with Work Experience During the Year, by Extent of Employment and Sex, 1987–2005

(Percent of total people with work experience.)

Sex and year	Total	Full-time workers				Part-time workers			
		Total	50 to 52 weeks	27 to 49 weeks	1 to 26 weeks	Total	50 to 52 weeks	27 to 49 weeks	1 to 26 weeks
Both Sexes									
1987	100.0	78.1	60.0	10.4	7.7	21.9	8.6	5.1	8.2
1988	100.0	78.3	61.0	9.9	7.4	21.7	8.7	5.1	7.9
1989	100.0	78.9	61.1	10.7	7.1	21.1	8.5	5.3	7.3
1990	100.0	78.9	60.6	11.1	7.2	21.2	8.6	5.3	7.3
1991	100.0	78.4	60.3	10.9	7.2	21.7	9.0	5.2	7.5
1992	100.0	78.2	60.9	10.1	7.2	21.7	9.2	5.1	7.4
1993	100.0	78.0	61.2	9.6	7.2	22.1	9.4	5.0	7.7
1994	100.0	78.0	61.9	9.4	6.7	21.8	9.3	5.0	7.5
1995	100.0	78.8	63.1	9.3	6.4	21.2	9.1	4.9	7.2
1996	100.0	79.0	63.5	9.1	6.4	21.0	9.4	4.7	6.9
1997	100.0	79.1	64.3	8.7	6.1	20.9	9.6	4.6	6.7
1998	100.0	80.0	65.8	8.4	5.8	20.1	9.3	4.5	6.3
1999	100.0	80.3	66.0	8.3	6.0	19.7	9.2	4.3	6.2
2000	100.0	80.8	67.2	8.1	5.5	19.3	9.3	4.1	5.9
2001	100.0	80.7	66.4	8.7	5.6	19.3	9.3	4.1	5.9
2002	100.0	80.3	66.4	8.3	5.6	19.7	9.7	4.1	5.9
2003	100.0	79.9	66.4	7.9	5.6	20.1	10.1	4.0	6.0
2004	100.0	80.0	66.9	7.8	5.3	20.1	10.2	4.0	5.9
2005	100.0	80.4	67.6	7.6	5.2	19.6	9.9	4.0	5.7
Men									
1987	100.0	86.4	68.0	10.9	7.5	13.6	4.7	3.2	5.7
1988	100.0	86.5	69.0	10.5	7.0	13.6	5.0	3.1	5.5
1989	100.0	86.8	69.4	10.7	6.7	13.3	5.1	3.1	5.1
1990	100.0	86.6	68.3	11.4	6.9	13.4	5.1	3.2	5.1
1991	100.0	86.0	66.8	11.6	7.6	14.0	5.3	3.3	5.4
1992	100.0	85.8	67.1	11.1	7.6	14.3	5.4	3.3	5.6
1993	100.0	85.8	68.4	10.0	7.4	14.2	5.5	2.9	5.8
1994	100.0	86.0	69.7	9.6	6.7	13.9	5.3	3.2	5.4
1995	100.0	86.3	70.8	9.4	6.1	13.7	5.4	3.0	5.3
1996	100.0	86.3	71.0	9.1	6.2	13.7	5.7	2.8	5.2
1997	100.0	86.5	71.9	8.7	5.9	13.6	5.6	3.0	5.0
1998	100.0	87.4	74.0	8.1	5.3	12.6	5.5	2.7	4.4
1999	100.0	87.5	73.6	8.2	5.7	12.5	5.5	2.6	4.4
2000	100.0	87.5	74.6	7.7	5.2	12.6	5.7	2.5	4.4
2001	100.0	87.6	73.4	8.9	5.3	12.4	5.4	2.5	4.5
2002	100.0	87.4	73.2	8.5	5.7	12.6	5.6	2.5	4.5
2003	100.0	86.9	73.2	8.1	5.6	13.1	6.3	2.3	4.5
2004	100.0	87.1	74.0	7.9	5.2	12.9	6.1	2.5	4.3
2005	100.0	87.0	74.3	7.6	5.1	12.9	6.2	2.5	4.2
Women									
1987	100.0	68.6	50.7	9.9	8.0	31.4	13.0	7.4	11.0
1988	100.0	68.9	51.8	9.2	7.9	31.1	13.1	7.3	10.7
1989	100.0	69.9	51.4	10.8	7.7	30.0	12.5	7.7	9.8
1990	100.0	69.9	51.6	10.7	7.6	30.2	12.8	7.6	9.8
1991	100.0	69.4	52.6	10.0	6.8	30.7	13.2	7.6	9.9
1992	100.0	69.7	53.7	9.1	6.9	30.4	13.7	7.2	9.5
1993	100.0	69.0	52.9	9.0	7.1	31.0	13.9	7.3	9.8
1994	100.0	69.0	53.0	9.2	6.8	30.9	13.9	7.1	9.9
1995	100.0	70.3	54.3	9.2	6.8	29.7	13.3	7.0	9.4
1996	100.0	70.7	54.9	9.2	6.6	29.3	13.6	6.8	8.9
1997	100.0	70.7	55.8	8.7	6.2	29.4	14.2	6.4	8.8
1998	100.0	71.6	56.5	8.7	6.4	28.4	13.6	6.4	8.4
1999	100.0	72.3	57.6	8.4	6.3	27.7	13.4	6.1	8.2
2000	100.0	73.2	58.9	8.5	5.8	26.8	13.3	6.0	7.5
2001	100.0	73.0	58.6	8.6	5.8	27.0	13.7	5.8	7.5
2002	100.0	72.5	58.8	8.1	5.6	27.6	14.2	5.8	7.6
2003	100.0	72.1	58.8	7.7	5.6	27.8	14.4	5.8	7.6
2004	100.0	72.0	59.0	7.6	5.4	28.0	14.7	5.7	7.6
2005	100.0	72.7	59.9	7.6	5.2	27.2	14.1	5.6	7.5

Note: See notes and definitions for information on historical comparability.

Table 1-37. Extent of Unemployment During the Year, by Sex, 1995–2005

(Thousands of people, percent.)

Sex and extent of unemployment	1995	1996	1997	1998	1999	2000	2001	2002	2003	2004	2005
BOTH SEXES											
Total Who Worked or Looked for Work	142 413	144 528	146 096	147 295	149 798	150 786	153 056	154 205	154 315	155 576	157 549
Percent with unemployment	12.7	11.6	10.7	9.5	8.7	8.1	10.4	10.9	10.7	9.7	9.2
Total with Unemployment	18 067	16 789	15 637	14 044	13 068	12 269	15 843	16 824	16 462	15 074	14 558
Did not work but looked for work	2 690	2 329	2 129	1 729	1 503	1 425	2 014	2 660	2 762	2 551	2 422
Worked during the year	15 377	14 460	13 508	12 316	11 566	10 845	13 829	14 164	13 699	12 522	12 136
Year-round workers with 1 or 2 weeks of unemployment	715	589	611	630	562	573	602	584	534	465	431
Part-year workers with unemployment	14 662	13 871	12 897	11 686	11 004	10 272	13 227	13 580	13 165	12 057	11 705
1 to 4 weeks	2 812	2 550	2 582	2 323	2 361	2 233	2 368	2 002	1 839	1 985	1 941
5 to 10 weeks	2 725	2 671	2 601	2 495	2 218	2 014	2 557	2 373	2 264	2 100	2 170
11 to 14 weeks	2 147	2 020	1 822	1 701	1 594	1 505	2 038	1 970	1 749	1 773	1 698
15 to 26 weeks	4 013	3 662	3 378	3 019	2 803	2 641	3 683	3 848	3 778	3 448	3 349
27 weeks or more	2 965	2 968	2 514	2 148	2 028	1 879	2 582	3 387	3 535	2 751	2 547
With 2 or more spells of unemployment	4 468	4 237	4 044	3 628	3 225	3 079	3 421	3 226	3 093	2 896	3 095
2 spells	1 963	1 982	1 853	1 650	1 449	1 397	1 643	1 556	1 585	1 344	1 477
3 or more spells	2 505	2 255	2 191	1 978	1 776	1 682	1 779	1 670	1 508	1 552	1 618
MEN											
Total Who Worked or Looked for Work	75 698	76 786	77 385	77 704	78 905	79 546	80 975	81 651	81 804	82 478	83 951
Percent with unemployment	13.2	11.9	11.1	9.4	9.0	8.6	11.0	11.8	11.4	10.0	9.7
Total with Unemployment	9 996	9 157	8 604	7 284	7 091	6 806	8 928	9 621	9 339	8 256	8 116
Did not work but looked for work	1 317	1 026	978	787	760	742	1 004	1 369	1 487	1 217	1 216
Worked during the year	8 679	8 130	7 626	6 497	6 332	6 064	7 924	8 252	7 854	7 039	6 899
Year-round workers with 1 or 2 weeks of unemployment	462	395	382	386	373	379	421	365	359	289	296
Part-year workers with unemployment	8 217	7 735	7 244	6 111	5 959	5 685	7 502	7 887	7 495	6 750	6 603
1 to 4 weeks	1 398	1 272	1 275	1 085	1 166	1 070	1 247	1 075	958	1 028	1 052
5 to 10 weeks	1 434	1 478	1 474	1 363	1 168	1 135	1 446	1 342	1 314	1 170	1 209
11 to 14 weeks	1 253	1 258	1 068	980	937	880	1 207	1 186	1 039	1 021	1 024
15 to 26 weeks	2 439	2 076	1 949	1 585	1 655	1 595	2 191	2 282	2 178	2 065	1 923
27 weeks or more	1 693	1 651	1 478	1 098	1 033	1 005	1 412	2 002	2 006	1 466	1 395
With 2 or more spells of unemployment	2 793	2 554	2 437	2 014	1 845	1 809	2 100	1 920	1 882	1 828	1 975
2 spells	1 110	1 109	1 078	880	787	804	1 002	914	946	808	940
3 or more spells	1 683	1 445	1 359	1 134	1 058	1 005	1 099	1 006	936	1 020	1 035
WOMEN											
Total Who Worked or Looked for Work	66 716	67 742	68 710	69 591	70 893	71 240	72 081	72 554	72 511	73 097	73 598
Percent with unemployment	12.1	11.3	10.2	9.7	8.4	7.7	9.6	9.9	9.8	9.3	8.8
Total with Unemployment	8 070	7 632	7 033	6 760	5 976	5 463	6 915	7 203	7 123	6 818	6 442
Did not work but looked for work	1 373	1 303	1 151	942	743	683	1 010	1 291	1 275	1 334	1 206
Worked during the year	6 696	6 330	5 882	5 816	5 234	4 779	5 905	5 913	5 848	5 484	5 236
Year-round workers with 1 or 2 weeks of unemployment	253	194	229	243	189	193	180	220	176	177	136
Part-year workers with unemployment	6 443	6 136	5 653	5 573	5 045	4 586	5 725	5 693	5 672	5 307	5 100
1 to 4 weeks	1 413	1 279	1 307	1 237	1 194	1 164	1 121	927	882	957	888
5 to 10 weeks	1 291	1 192	1 127	1 131	1 050	878	1 111	1 031	950	929	961
11 to 14 weeks	893	762	754	721	657	625	831	784	710	752	674
15 to 26 weeks	1 574	1 586	1 429	1 434	1 148	1 045	1 492	1 566	1 600	1 384	1 426
27 weeks or more	1 272	1 317	1 036	1 050	996	874	1 170	1 385	1 530	1 285	1 151
With 2 or more spells of unemployment	1 675	1 682	1 607	1 614	1 379	1 270	1 321	1 306	1 211	1 069	1 120
2 spells	853	872	775	770	662	593	641	642	639	537	537
3 or more spells	822	810	832	844	717	677	680	664	572	532	583

Note: See notes and definitions for information on historical comparability.

Table 1-38. Percent Distribution of Persons with Unemployment During the Year, by Sex and Extent of Unemployment, 1995–2005

(Percent.)

Sex and extent of unemployment	1995	1996	1997	1998	1999	2000	2001	2002	2003	2004	2005
BOTH SEXES											
Total with Unemployment Who Worked During the Year	100.0	100.0	100.0	100.0	100.0	100.0	100.0	100.0	100.0	100.0	100.0
Year-round workers with 1 or 2 weeks of unemployment	4.6	4.1	4.5	5.1	4.9	5.3	4.4	4.1	3.9	3.7	3.6
Part-year workers with unemployment	95.4	96.0	95.5	95.0	95.1	94.8	95.6	95.9	96.1	96.3	96.4
1 to 4 weeks	18.3	17.6	19.1	18.9	20.4	20.6	17.1	14.1	13.4	15.9	16.0
5 to 10 weeks	17.7	18.5	19.3	20.3	19.2	18.6	18.5	16.8	16.5	16.8	17.9
11 to 14 weeks	14.0	14.0	13.5	13.8	13.8	13.9	14.7	13.9	12.8	14.2	14.0
15 to 26 weeks	26.1	25.3	25.0	24.5	24.2	24.4	26.6	27.2	27.6	27.5	27.6
27 weeks or more	19.3	20.6	18.6	17.5	17.5	17.3	18.7	23.9	25.8	22.0	20.9
With 2 or more spells of unemployment	29.1	29.3	29.9	29.5	27.9	28.4	24.8	22.8	22.6	23.1	25.5
2 spells	12.8	13.7	13.7	13.4	12.5	12.9	11.9	11.0	11.6	10.7	12.2
3 or more spells	16.3	15.6	16.2	16.1	15.4	15.5	12.9	11.8	11.0	12.4	13.3
MEN											
Total with Unemployment Who Worked During the Year	100.0	100.0	100.0	100.0	100.0	100.0	100.0	100.0	100.0	100.0	100.0
Year-round workers with 1 or 2 weeks of unemployment	5.3	4.9	5.0	5.9	5.9	6.3	5.3	4.4	4.6	4.1	4.3
Part-year workers with unemployment	94.7	95.1	95.1	94.1	94.0	93.6	94.7	95.6	95.4	95.9	95.7
1 to 4 weeks	16.1	15.6	16.7	16.7	18.4	17.6	15.7	13.0	12.2	14.6	15.3
5 to 10 weeks	16.5	18.2	19.3	21.0	18.4	18.7	18.2	16.3	16.7	16.6	17.5
11 to 14 weeks	14.4	15.5	14.0	15.1	14.8	14.5	15.2	14.4	13.2	14.5	14.8
15 to 26 weeks	28.1	25.5	25.6	24.4	26.1	26.3	27.6	27.7	27.7	29.3	27.9
27 weeks or more	19.5	20.3	19.4	16.9	16.3	16.5	17.8	24.3	25.5	20.8	20.2
With 2 or more spells of unemployment	32.2	31.4	31.9	31.0	29.1	29.9	26.5	23.3	24.0	26.0	28.6
2 spells	12.8	13.6	14.1	13.5	12.4	13.3	12.6	11.1	12.1	11.5	13.6
3 or more spells	19.4	17.8	17.8	17.5	16.7	16.6	13.9	12.2	11.9	14.5	15.0
WOMEN											
Total With Unemployment Who Worked During the Year	100.0	100.0	100.0	100.0	100.0	100.0	100.0	100.0	100.0	100.0	100.0
Year-round workers with 1 or 2 weeks of unemployment	3.8	3.1	3.9	4.2	3.6	4.0	3.1	3.7	3.0	3.2	2.6
Part-year workers with unemployment	96.2	96.9	96.1	95.8	96.4	96.0	96.9	96.3	97.0	96.8	97.4
1 to 4 weeks	21.1	20.2	22.2	21.3	22.8	24.3	19.0	15.7	15.1	17.4	17.0
5 to 10 weeks	19.3	18.8	19.2	19.4	20.1	18.4	18.8	17.4	16.2	16.9	18.4
11 to 14 weeks	13.3	12.0	12.8	12.4	12.6	13.1	14.1	13.3	12.1	13.7	12.9
15 to 26 weeks	23.5	25.1	24.3	24.7	21.9	21.9	25.3	26.5	27.4	25.2	27.2
27 weeks or more	19.0	20.8	17.6	18.0	19.0	18.3	19.8	23.4	26.2	23.5	22.0
With 2 or more spells of unemployment	25.0	26.6	27.3	27.7	26.3	26.6	22.4	22.1	20.7	19.5	21.4
2 spells	12.7	13.8	13.2	13.2	12.6	12.4	10.9	10.9	10.9	9.8	10.3
3 or more spells	12.3	12.8	14.1	14.5	13.7	14.2	11.5	11.2	9.8	9.7	11.1

Note: See notes and definitions for information on historical comparability.

Table 1-39. Number of and Median Annual Earnings of Year-Round Full-Time Wage and Salary Workers, by Age, Sex, and Race, 1990–2005

(Thousands of people, dollars.)

Sex, age, and race	1990	1991	1992	1993	1994	1995	1996	1997	1998	1999	2000	2001	2002	2003	2004	2005
NUMBER																
Both Sexes, 16 Years and Over	74 728	74 449	75 517	77 427	79 875	83 407	85 611	86 905	89 748	91 722	94 359	94 531	94 526	94 731	96 098	98 632
16 to 24 years	6 978	6 571	6 224	6 685	6 684	6 892	6 809	7 063	7 618	7 631	8 384	7 989	7 903	7 631	7 702	7 956
25 to 44 years	45 086	44 811	45 022	45 951	47 150	48 695	49 225	49 513	50 264	50 532	51 159	49 939	49 120	48 343	48 421	49 149
25 to 34 years	23 201	22 541	22 469	22 637	23 193	23 310	23 071	23 186	23 048	22 952	23 044	22 744	22 657	22 512	22 405	22 808
35 to 44 years	21 885	22 270	22 553	23 314	23 957	25 385	26 154	26 327	27 216	27 580	28 115	27 195	26 463	25 831	26 016	26 341
45 to 54 years	14 070	14 718	15 652	16 424	17 366	18 436	19 714	20 109	21 274	22 375	23 307	23 855	23 999	24 507	25 074	25 661
55 to 64 years	7 458	7 219	7 590	7 208	7 500	8 122	8 455	8 901	9 273	9 594	9 870	10 948	11 584	12 207	12 812	13 605
65 years and over	1 137	1 130	1 029	1 159	1 174	1 263	1 408	1 318	1 318	1 590	1 639	1 800	1 921	2 042	2 090	2 262
Men, 16 Years and Over	44 574	43 523	43 894	45 494	47 255	49 334	50 407	50 772	52 509	53 132	54 477	54 630	54 420	54 575	55 610	57 020
16 to 24 years	3 982	3 596	3 457	3 853	3 918	4 094	3 942	4 021	4 479	4 347	4 602	4 605	4 570	4 421	4 493	4 663
25 to 44 years	27 069	26 353	26 335	27 161	28 000	28 940	29 282	29 453	29 763	29 738	30 080	29 271	28 855	28 499	28 763	29 151
25 to 34 years	13 941	13 303	13 146	13 400	13 749	13 844	13 817	13 735	13 612	13 471	13 497	13 386	13 400	13 288	13 430	13 629
35 to 44 years	13 128	13 050	13 189	13 761	14 251	15 096	15 465	15 718	16 151	16 267	16 583	15 885	15 455	15 211	15 333	15 522
45 to 54 years	8 168	8 479	8 908	9 522	10 120	10 589	11 372	11 388	12 030	12 546	13 045	13 363	13 330	13 616	13 975	14 382
55 to 64 years	4 650	4 403	4 588	4 238	4 460	4 884	4 908	5 133	5 438	5 498	5 693	6 253	6 502	6 872	7 165	7 489
65 years and over	705	694	606	719	757	827	903	775	801	1 003	1 057	1 138	1 163	1 165	1 213	1 334
Women, 16 Years and Over	30 155	30 925	31 622	31 933	32 619	34 073	35 203	36 133	37 239	38 591	39 887	39 901	40 106	40 156	40 488	41 613
16 to 24 years	2 995	2 976	2 767	2 832	2 767	2 798	2 867	3 041	3 140	3 285	3 782	3 384	3 333	3 210	3 209	3 293
25 to 44 years	18 017	18 458	18 688	18 790	19 150	19 755	19 942	20 060	20 503	20 794	21 081	20 668	20 264	19 844	19 656	19 997
25 to 34 years	9 260	9 238	9 323	9 237	9 444	9 467	9 254	9 451	9 437	9 481	9 548	9 358	9 257	9 224	8 974	9 179
35 to 44 years	8 757	9 220	9 365	9 553	9 706	10 288	10 688	10 609	11 066	11 313	11 533	11 310	11 007	10 620	10 682	10 818
45 to 54 years	5 902	6 239	6 744	6 902	7 246	7 847	8 343	8 721	9 244	9 829	10 263	10 493	10 669	10 891	11 099	11 279
55 to 64 years	2 808	2 816	3 002	2 970	3 040	3 238	3 547	3 767	3 836	4 096	4 178	4 695	5 082	5 335	5 647	6 116
65 years and over	433	436	423	439	417	436	505	543	517	586	583	662	758	877	877	927
White, 16 Years and Over	64 128	63 926	64 706	65 656	67 370	70 430	72 068	72 650	75 046	76 203	77 790	78 306	77 632	77 545	78 236	80 546
Men	38 915	38 018	38 267	39 347	40 589	42 608	43 554	43 429	44 901	45 211	46 105	46 373	45 823	45 816	46 317	47 790
Women	25 213	25 908	26 439	26 309	26 782	27 822	28 514	29 221	30 145	30 992	31 685	31 933	31 809	31 729	31 919	32 756
Black, 16 Years and Over	8 027	7 941	7 995	8 478	9 074	9 446	9 706	10 248	10 532	11 145	11 899	11 001	10 966	10 979	11 301	11 417
Men	4 162	4 001	4 011	4 259	4 598	4 686	4 682	5 026	5 202	5 411	5 636	5 281	5 150	5 196	5 470	5 402
Women	3 865	3 940	3 984	4 219	4 476	4 759	5 024	5 222	5 329	5 734	6 264	5 720	5 816	5 783	5 832	6 015
MEDIAN ANNUAL EARNINGS																
Both Sexes, 16 Years and Over	24 000	25 000	25 871	26 000	26 620	27 000	28 000	30 000	30 000	31 000	32 000	34 000	35 000	35 000	35 672	36 400
16 to 24 years	14 400	14 100	15 000	15 000	15 000	15 500	15 600	16 000	18 000	18 000	19 000	20 000	20 000	20 000	20 000	20 000
25 to 34 years	22 000	23 000	24 000	24 000	24 480	25 000	25 300	27 000	28 500	30 000	30 000	31 000	31 800	32 000	33 000	33 000
35 to 44 years	27 970	28 000	29 483	30 000	30 000	30 000	31 000	32 000	33 000	34 992	35 000	36 000	37 000	39 000	40 000	40 000
45 to 54 years	28 000	29 000	30 000	30 500	32 343	32 000	33 000	35 000	35 000	36 000	38 000	39 500	40 000	40 000	40 000	42 000
55 to 64 years	26 000	27 000	27 430	28 000	30 000	30 000	30 000	32 000	34 000	35 000	35 000	36 400	39 145	40 000	40 000	41 000
65 years and over	23 841	22 000	24 000	24 000	24 377	29 600	26 496	28 200	26 000	30 000	32 000	32 000	33 000	32 000	35 000	35 000
Men, 16 Years and Over	28 000	29 120	30 000	30 000	30 000	31 000	32 000	34 000	35 000	36 000	37 600	38 500	40 000	40 000	40 000	40 051
16 to 24 years	15 000	15 000	15 000	15 000	15 000	16 000	17 000	17 000	18 720	19 000	20 000	20 000	20 000	20 800	20 800	20 800
25 to 34 years	25 000	25 000	26 000	25 000	26 000	27 000	28 000	29 852	30 000	32 000	33 500	34 000	34 740	35 000	35 000	35 000
35 to 44 years	32 000	33 000	34 000	35 000	35 000	35 000	36 000	37 000	38 000	40 000	40 000	42 000	43 000	43 900	45 000	45 000
45 to 54 years	35 000	36 000	37 000	38 000	40 000	40 000	40 000	41 000	42 000	44 616	45 000	45 000	47 000	48 000	48 000	50 000
55 to 64 years	31 875	33 000	33 000	34 000	36 000	36 000	36 000	39 000	40 000	40 853	44 000	45 000	47 000	50 000	50 000	50 000
65 years and over	29 000	28 000	30 000	28 000	30 000	36 000	33 000	36 400	35 000	36 000	35 999	35 000	37 861	42 000	40 000	41 000
Women, 16 Years and Over	20 000	20 000	21 500	22 000	22 150	23 000	24 000	25 000	25 000	26 000	27 500	29 000	30 000	30 000	30 001	32 000
16 to 24 years	13 392	13 800	14 000	14 872	14 560	15 000	15 000	15 000	17 000	17 000	18 000	19 000	19 000	20 000	20 000	20 000
25 to 34 years	19 500	20 000	21 000	21 000	22 000	22 000	23 000	24 000	25 000	26 000	27 000	28 080	29 500	30 000	30 000	30 000
35 to 44 years	22 000	22 510	23 397	24 000	25 000	25 000	25 000	26 000	27 200	28 000	29 000	30 000	30 400	32 000	32 800	35 000
45 to 54 years	21 000	24 000	24 000	24 000	25 000	25 000	26 000	27 040	28 132	30 000	30 000	32 000	32 000	33 466	34 771	35 000
55 to 64 years	19 000	20 000	22 000	21 500	22 000	22 500	24 000	24 800	25 775	27 000	28 000	30 000	31 410	32 000	33 000	33 000
65 years and over	18 586	17 000	18 500	20 000	19 000	23 290	20 800	24 000	22 000	20 800	24 000	25 000	28 000	26 000	27 000	28 768
White, 16 Years and Over	25 000	25 000	26 200	27 000	28 000	28 000	29 000	30 000	31 000	32 000	34 000	35 000	35 000	36 000	37 000	38 000
Men	29 000	30 000	31 000	30 700	32 000	32 000	33 000	35 000	36 000	37 200	39 000	40 000	40 000	40 000	42 000	42 000
Women	20 000	20 500	22 000	22 000	23 000	23 000	24 000	25 000	26 000	27 000	28 000	30 000	30 000	31 000	31 800	32 000
Black, 16 Years and Over	19 350	20 000	21 000	20 800	21 000	22 000	23 784	24 000	25 000	25 760	26 000	28 500	29 000	30 000	30 000	30 000
Men	20 800	22 000	22 312	23 000	23 500	24 500	26 000	26 000	27 000	30 000	30 000	30 000	30 000	32 000	30 000	33 000
Women	18 000	18 500	20 000	19 843	20 000	20 000	21 000	22 000	23 000	24 000	25 000	26 000	26 000	27 000	28 000	29 141

Note: Detail for the above race groups will not sum to totals because data for other race groups are not presented. See notes and definitions for information on historical comparability.

Table 1-40. Number of and Median Annual Earnings of Year-Round Full-Time Wage and Salary Workers, by Sex and Occupation of Job Held the Longest, 2002–2005

(Thousands of people, dollars.)

Sex and occupation	2002	2003	2004	2005
Both Sexes, Number of Workers				
Management, business, and financial operations	15 707	15 552	15 575	16 299
Management	11 350	11 102	11 125	11 685
Business and financial operations	4 357	4 450	4 451	4 613
Professional and related	19 149	19 607	19 592	20 093
Computer and mathematical	2 644	2 598	2 680	2 779
Architecture and engineering	2 257	2 273	2 349	2 361
Life, physical, and social science	1 094	1 010	999	1 096
Community and social services	1 694	1 698	1 632	1 728
Legal	1 006	1 149	1 087	1 093
Education, training, and library	4 606	4 918	4 742	4 894
Arts, design, entertainment, sports, and media	1 453	1 374	1 416	1 362
Health care practitioner and technical	4 395	4 586	4 688	4 780
Services	12 011	11 990	12 457	13 117
Health care support	1 767	1 703	1 781	2 027
Protective services	2 042	2 385	2 406	2 429
Food preparation and serving related	3 592	3 223	3 383	3 586
Building and grounds cleaning and maintenance	2 843	2 942	3 116	3 285
Personal care and services	1 767	1 735	1 771	1 790
Sales and office	23 791	23 766	23 619	24 010
Sales and related	9 929	9 804	9 951	10 251
Office and administrative support	13 862	13 962	13 668	13 758
Natural resources, construction, and maintenance	9 823	9 709	10 574	10 864
Farming, fishing, and forestry	573	562	629	556
Construction and extraction	5 256	5 070	5 711	6 145
Installation, maintenance, and repair	3 994	4 077	4 234	4 163
Production, transportation, and material moving	13 386	13 391	13 648	13 586
Production	7 736	7 670	7 787	7 623
Transportation and material moving	5 650	5 721	5 861	5 963
Armed forces	658	717	632	664
Both Sexes, Median Annual Earnings				
Management, business, and financial operations	50 000	52 000	55 000	57 000
Management	55 000	58 000	60 000	60 000
Business and financial operations	44 000	45 000	45 000	49 000
Professional and related	46 000	46 000	48 000	50 000
Computer and mathematical	60 000	60 000	62 000	62 400
Architecture and engineering	59 400	62 000	60 000	65 000
Life, physical, and social science	50 000	50 000	50 000	53 500
Community and social services	34 000	34 349	36 000	36 000
Legal	61 860	75 000	70 000	72 000
Education, training, and library	38 000	39 000	40 000	40 000
Arts, design, entertainment, sports, and media	43 500	40 000	40 000	42 000
Health care practitioner and technical	46 000	48 000	50 000	50 000
Services	22 000	22 000	22 000	23 000
Health care support	22 100	22 000	22 000	22 000
Protective services	38 000	42 000	42 000	42 000
Food preparation and serving related	18 000	18 000	18 000	19 656
Building and grounds cleaning and maintenance	20 000	20 000	20 000	21 000
Personal care and services	21 840	20 678	22 537	23 000
Sales and office	30 000	30 000	30 000	31 200
Sales and related	35 000	35 000	35 000	35 000
Office and administrative support	28 000	29 000	30 000	30 000
Natural resources, construction, and maintenance	33 000	34 000	35 000	35 000
Farming, fishing, and forestry	20 000	20 000	20 000	21 000
Construction and extraction	31 200	32 000	33 000	32 000
Installation, maintenance, and repair	36 000	38 000	38 300	40 000
Production, transportation, and material moving	28 704	30 000	30 000	30 200
Production	28 000	30 000	30 000	30 000
Transportation and material moving	29 000	30 000	30 000	30 800
Armed forces	36 000	36 000	40 000	39 000

Note: See notes and definitions for information on historical comparability.

Table 1-40. Number of and Median Annual Earnings of Year-Round Full-Time Wage and Salary Workers, by Sex and Occupation of Job Held the Longest, 2002–2005—*Continued*

(Thousands of people, dollars.)

Sex and occupation	2002	2003	2004	2005
Men, Number of Workers				
Management, business, and financial operations	9 178	8 961	8 849	9 496
Management	7 145	6 991	6 911	7 477
Business and financial operations	2 033	1 970	1 938	2 019
Professional and related	9 299	9 535	9 497	9 561
Computer and mathematical	1 953	1 913	1 972	2 060
Architecture and engineering	1 984	2 004	2 049	2 041
Life, physical, and social science	667	668	626	668
Community and social services	726	730	705	713
Legal	490	610	537	490
Education, training, and library	1 407	1 476	1 386	1 421
Arts, design, entertainment, sports, and media	847	811	848	789
Health care practitioner and technical	1 225	1 323	1 374	1 378
Services	5 988	6 204	6 314	6 658
Health care support	181	178	208	240
Protective services	1 689	1 967	1 906	1 919
Food preparation and serving related	1 836	1 638	1 716	1 873
Building and grounds cleaning and maintenance	1 788	1 914	2 002	2 153
Personal care and services	494	508	482	473
Sales and office	9 453	9 398	9 380	9 464
Sales and related	5 933	5 891	5 892	5 896
Office and administrative support	3 520	3 507	3 488	3 568
Natural resources, construction, and maintenance	9 434	9 348	10 178	10 503
Farming, fishing, and forestry	463	470	536	469
Construction and extraction	5 156	4 972	5 576	6 026
Installation, maintenance, and repair	3 815	3 905	4 065	4 008
Production, transportation, and material moving	10 472	10 492	10 812	10 747
Production	5 517	5 513	5 637	5 503
Transportation and material moving	4 955	4 979	5 176	5 244
Armed forces	600	636	580	591
Men, Median Annual Earnings				
Management, business, and financial operations	60 000	60 200	65 000	69 000
Management	65 000	65 000	70 000	70 000
Business and financial operations	52 000	51 000	55 000	60 000
Professional and related	55 000	58 000	58 000	60 000
Computer and mathematical	60 000	65 000	65 000	65 000
Architecture and engineering	60 000	64 558	61 785	66 921
Life, physical, and social science	52 000	50 801	55 000	62 000
Community and social services	35 000	35 000	38 000	40 000
Legal	100 000	100 000	101 000	108 000
Education, training, and library	45 600	48 000	47 000	50 000
Arts, design, entertainment, sports, and media	46 000	45 000	45 000	50 000
Health care practitioner and technical	72 000	65 500	70 000	70 000
Services	25 000	26 000	25 000	26 000
Health care support	24 000	22 537	20 400	22 880
Protective services	40 000	44 000	44 000	45 000
Food preparation and serving related	20 000	18 720	18 720	20 000
Building and grounds cleaning and maintenance	24 500	22 156	24 000	24 000
Personal care and services	30 000	28 559	26 000	30 000
Sales and office	38 000	39 000	40 000	40 000
Sales and related	41 600	41 000	44 000	42 000
Office and administrative support	32 000	32 000	34 000	34 000
Natural resources, construction, and maintenance	33 592	34 283	35 000	35 000
Farming, fishing, and forestry	22 000	22 000	22 000	22 500
Construction and extraction	31 304	32 000	33 000	32 000
Installation, maintenance, and repair	36 000	38 000	38 870	40 000
Production, transportation, and material moving	30 000	32 000	33 000	34 000
Production	30 360	32 000	34 000	35 000
Transportation and material moving	30 000	30 000	32 000	32 760
Armed forces	36 000	36 000	40 000	40 000

Note: See notes and definitions for information on historical comparability.

Table 1-40. Number of and Median Annual Earnings of Year-Round Full-Time Wage and Salary Workers, by Sex and Occupation of Job Held the Longest, 2002–2005—*Continued*

(Thousands of people, dollars.)

Sex and occupation	2002	2003	2004	2005
Women, Number of Workers				
Management, business, and financial operations	6 529	6 591	6 726	6 803
Management	4 205	4 111	4 214	4 209
Business and financial operations	2 324	2 479	2 512	2 594
Professional and related	9 851	10 071	10 095	10 532
Computer and mathematical	691	685	708	718
Architecture and engineering	273	269	300	320
Life, physical, and social science	428	342	373	428
Community and social services	968	968	927	1 015
Legal	516	539	550	603
Education, training, and library	3 199	3 441	3 356	3 473
Arts, design, entertainment, sports, and media	606	563	568	573
Health care practitioner and technical	3 170	3 263	3 314	3 403
Services	6 026	5 786	6 144	6 459
Health care support	1 586	1 525	1 573	1 787
Protective services	354	419	500	510
Food preparation and serving related	1 757	1 585	1 668	1 713
Building and grounds cleaning and maintenance	1 055	1 029	1 115	1 132
Personal care and services	1 274	1 228	1 289	1 317
Sales and office	14 338	14 368	14 239	14 546
Sales and related	3 996	3 913	4 060	4 355
Office and administrative support	10 342	10 455	10 180	10 191
Natural resources, construction, and maintenance	391	361	396	360
Farming, fishing, and forestry	111	92	93	87
Construction and extraction	100	97	135	119
Installation, maintenance, and repair	180	172	169	155
Production, transportation, and material moving	2 914	2 899	2 835	2 839
Production	2 219	2 157	2 150	2 120
Transportation and material moving	695	742	685	719
Armed forces	58	81	52	73
Women, Median Annual Earnings				
Management, business, and financial operations	41 000	43 000	43 000	46 000
Management	44 000	47 000	46 000	50 000
Business and financial operations	38 500	40 000	40 000	41 000
Professional and related	40 000	40 000	40 000	42 000
Computer and mathematical	51 627	52 000	57 000	57 000
Architecture and engineering	50 000	48 000	47 500	55 000
Life, physical, and social science	44 000	45 000	45 995	50 000
Community and social services	33 000	33 000	35 000	35 000
Legal	45 000	45 000	46 000	47 500
Education, training, and library	35 000	35 000	37 000	38 000
Arts, design, entertainment, sports, and media	40 000	35 000	36 000	35 000
Health care practitioner and technical	41 000	43 000	45 000	46 000
Services	20 000	20 000	20 000	20 000
Health care support	22 000	22 000	22 000	21 000
Protective services	30 900	32 000	32 000	34 344
Food preparation and serving related	16 160	17 000	16 000	18 000
Building and grounds cleaning and maintenance	16 491	16 000	16 866	18 000
Personal care and services	20 000	20 000	21 000	20 800
Sales and office	26 989	28 000	28 000	29 000
Sales and related	25 000	26 000	26 000	26 000
Office and administrative support	27 000	28 000	28 000	29 800
Natural resources, construction, and maintenance	26 000	28 000	30 000	30 200
Farming, fishing, and forestry	17 000	16 000	15 700	18 000
Construction and extraction	26 000	29 500	40 000	31 200
Installation, maintenance, and repair	34 000	37 000	33 000	36 000
Production, transportation, and material moving	22 000	22 100	23 000	23 000
Production	21 632	22 000	23 000	23 400
Transportation and material moving	22 000	22 710	23 000	21 000
Armed forces	40 000	32 000	35 100	32 652

Note: See notes and definitions for information on historical comparability.

Table 1-41. Wage and Salary Workers Paid Hourly Rates with Earnings at or Below the Prevailing Federal Minimum Wage, by Selected Characteristics, 2004–2005

(Thousands of people, percent.)

Characteristic	Workers paid hourly rates				
	Total	Below prevailing federal minimum wage	At prevailing federal minimum wage	Total at or below prevailing federal minimum wage	
				Number	Percent of hourly-paid workers
2004					
Age and Sex					
Both sexes, 16 years and over	73 939	1 483	520	2 003	2.7
16 to 24 years	16 174	750	272	1 021	6.3
25 years and over	57 765	733	249	982	1.7
Men, 16 years and over	36 806	470	210	680	1.8
16 to 24 years	8 305	239	127	366	4.4
25 years and over	28 500	231	83	314	1.1
Women, 16 years and over	37 133	1 013	310	1 323	3.6
16 to 24 years	7 869	510	145	655	8.3
25 years and over	29 265	502	166	668	2.3
Race, Sex, and Hispanic Origin					
White, 16 years and over	59 877	1 286	395	1 681	2.8
Men	30 255	393	161	555	1.8
Women	29 621	892	234	1 126	3.8
Black, 16 years and over	9 417	128	99	228	2.4
Men	4 243	49	40	89	2.1
Women	5 174	79	59	138	2.7
Hispanic, 16 years and over[1]	12 073	168	82	250	2.1
Men	7 183	66	32	99	1.4
Women	4 890	102	49	151	3.1
Full- and Part-Time Status and Sex[2]					
Full-time workers	55 739	583	177	760	1.4
Men	30 951	223	77	300	1.0
Women	24 788	360	100	460	1.9
Part-time workers	18 046	897	343	1 240	6.9
Men	5 770	246	132	378	6.6
Women	12 276	651	210	861	7.0
2005					
Age and Sex					
Both sexes, 16 years and over	75 609	1 403	479	1 882	2.5
16 to 24 years	16 374	720	283	1 002	6.1
25 years and over	59 235	683	196	880	1.5
Men, 16 years and over	37 652	459	189	648	1.7
16 to 24 years	8 288	223	130	353	4.3
25 years and over	29 364	236	60	296	1.0
Women, 16 years and over	37 957	944	290	1 234	3.3
16 to 24 years	8 086	496	153	650	8.0
25 years and over	29 871	447	137	584	2.0
Race, Sex, and Hispanic Origin					
White, 16 years and over	60 978	1 188	349	1 537	2.5
Men	30 901	352	133	485	1.6
Women	30 078	836	216	1 053	3.5
Black, 16 years and over	9 793	119	96	215	2.2
Men	4 421	63	42	105	2.4
Women	5 372	57	54	111	2.1
Hispanic, 16 years and over[1]	12 527	210	71	282	2.2
Men	7 467	85	29	114	1.5
Women	5 060	125	42	167	3.3
Full- and Part-Time Status and Sex[2]					
Full-time workers	57 385	608	143	752	1.3
Men	31 911	252	69	321	1.0
Women	25 474	356	74	430	1.7
Part-time workers	18 084	790	336	1 126	6.2
Men	5 669	207	120	327	5.8
Women	12 415	583	216	799	6.4

Note: The prevailing federal minimum wage was $5.15 per hour in 2005. Data are for wage and salary workers, excluding the incorporated self-employed. They refer to a person's earnings for their sole or principal job and pertain only to workers who are paid hourly rates. Salaried workers and other non-hourly workers are not included. The presence of workers with hourly earnings below the minimum wage does not necessarily indicate violations of the Fair Labor Standards Act, as there are exceptions to the minimum wage provisions of the law. In addition, some survey respondents might have rounded hourly earnings to the nearest dollar, and, as a result, reported hourly earnings below the minimum wage even though they earned the minimum wage or higher. Beginning in January 2005, data reflect the revised population controls used in the household survey.

[1]May be of any race.
[2]The distinction between full- and part-time workers is based on the hours usually worked. These data will not sum to totals because full- or part-time status on the principal job is not identifiable for a small number of multiple jobholders.

Table 1-42. Absences from Work of Employed Full-Time Wage and Salary Workers, by Age and Sex, 2003–2005

(Thousands of people, percent.)

Year, sex, and age	Total employed	Absence rate[1]			Lost worktime rate[2]		
		Total	Illness or injury	Other reasons	Total	Illness or injury	Other reasons
2003							
Both Sexes, 16 Years and Over	100 198	3.3	2.4	1.0	1.8	1.3	0.5
16 to 19 years	1 633	2.8	2.0	0.8	1.4	0.9	0.5
20 to 24 years	9 183	3.1	2.0	1.1	1.5	0.9	0.6
25 years and over	89 382	3.4	2.4	0.9	1.8	1.3	0.5
25 to 54 years	76 216	3.3	2.3	1.0	1.8	1.2	0.5
55 years and over	13 166	3.6	2.9	0.6	2.1	1.8	0.3
Men, 16 Years and Over	56 159	2.5	1.9	0.6	1.3	1.1	0.3
16 to 19 years	956	2.2	1.6	0.6	1.1	0.8	0.3
20 to 24 years	5 201	2.1	1.5	0.5	1.0	0.7	0.3
25 years and over	50 001	2.5	1.9	0.6	1.4	1.1	0.3
25 to 54 years	42 863	2.4	1.8	0.6	1.3	1.0	0.3
55 years and over	7 138	2.9	2.4	0.5	1.7	1.5	0.2
Women, 16 Years and Over	44 039	4.4	3.0	1.4	2.4	1.6	0.8
16 to 19 years	677	3.7	2.6	1.1	1.7	1.0	0.7
20 to 24 years	3 981	4.5	2.7	1.8	2.2	1.1	1.1
25 years and over	39 381	4.4	3.0	1.4	2.4	1.6	0.8
25 to 54 years	33 353	4.4	2.9	1.5	2.4	1.5	0.9
55 years and over	6 028	4.3	3.5	0.8	2.5	2.1	0.4
2004							
Both Sexes, 16 Years and Over	101 011	3.2	2.3	0.9	1.7	1.2	0.5
16 to 19 years	1 663	3.2	2.4	0.8	1.7	1.2	0.5
20 to 24 years	9 191	3.1	2.0	1.1	1.6	0.9	0.6
25 years and over	90 157	3.2	2.3	0.9	1.8	1.3	0.5
25 to 54 years	76 458	3.1	2.2	1.0	1.7	1.2	0.5
55 years and over	13 699	3.5	2.9	0.7	2.1	1.8	0.3
Men, 16 Years and Over	56 922	2.3	1.8	0.5	1.2	1.0	0.2
16 to 19 years	1 015	2.9	2.4	0.5	1.7	1.4	0.3
20 to 24 years	5 242	2.2	1.6	0.5	1.1	0.8	0.2
25 years and over	50 665	2.3	1.8	0.5	1.3	1.0	0.2
25 to 54 years	43 177	2.2	1.7	0.5	1.2	0.9	0.2
55 years and over	7 489	3.0	2.4	0.5	1.9	1.6	0.2
Women, 16 Years and Over	44 088	4.4	2.9	1.4	2.4	1.5	0.9
16 to 19 years	648	3.7	2.3	1.3	1.8	0.9	0.9
20 to 24 years	3 949	4.4	2.6	1.8	2.3	1.1	1.2
25 years and over	39 492	4.4	3.0	1.4	2.4	1.6	0.8
25 to 54 years	33 282	4.4	2.9	1.5	2.4	1.5	0.9
55 years and over	6 210	4.2	3.4	0.9	2.4	2.0	0.4
2005							
Both Sexes, 16 Years and Over	103 410	3.3	2.4	0.9	1.8	1.3	0.5
16 to 19 years	1 691	2.8	1.9	0.9	1.5	0.9	0.5
20 to 24 years	9 376	3.2	2.2	1.0	1.6	1.0	0.6
25 years and over	92 344	3.4	2.4	0.9	1.8	1.3	0.5
25 to 54 years	77 674	3.3	2.3	1.0	1.8	1.2	0.5
55 years and over	14 670	3.8	3.1	0.7	2.1	1.8	0.3
Men, 16 Years and Over	58 287	2.5	1.9	0.6	1.3	1.1	0.3
16 to 19 years	997	1.8	1.4	0.4	0.8	0.7	0.1
20 to 24 years	5 343	2.3	1.8	0.5	1.1	0.9	0.2
25 years and over	51 947	2.5	1.9	0.6	1.4	1.1	0.3
25 to 54 years	43 953	2.4	1.8	0.6	1.3	1.0	0.3
55 years and over	7 994	3.1	2.6	0.6	1.8	1.6	0.3
Women, 16 Years and Over	45 123	4.4	3.0	1.4	2.4	1.5	0.8
16 to 19 years	694	4.2	2.6	1.6	2.4	1.3	1.1
20 to 24 years	4 033	4.4	2.7	1.8	2.3	1.1	1.2
25 years and over	40 397	4.5	3.1	1.4	2.4	1.6	0.8
25 to 54 years	33 720	4.4	2.9	1.5	2.4	1.5	0.9
55 years and over	6 676	4.5	3.6	0.9	2.4	2.1	0.4

Note: Beginning in January 2003, data reflect the revised population controls used in the household survey.

[1]Absences are defined as instances when persons who usually work 35 or more hours a week worked less than 35 hours during the reference week for reasons including own illness, injury, or medical problems; childcare problems; other family or personal obligations; civic or military duty; and maternity or paternity leave. Excluded are situations in which work was missed due to vacation or personal days, holidays, labor disputes, and other reasons. For multiple jobholders, absence data refer only to work missed at their main jobs. The absence rate is the ratio of workers with absences to total full-time wage and salary employment. The estimates of full-time wage and salary employment shown in this table do not match those in other tables because the estimates in this table are based on the full Current Population Survey (CPS) sample. Those in the other tables are based on a quarter of the sample only.

[2]Hours absent as a percentage of hours usually worked.

Table 1-43. Median Years of Tenure with Current Employer for Employed Wage and Salary Workers, by Age and Sex, Selected Years, February 1996–January 2006

(Number of years.)

Sex and age	February 1996	February 1998	February 2000	January 2002	January 2004	January 2006
Both Sexes						
16 years and over	3.8	3.6	3.5	3.7	4.0	4.0
16 to 17 years	0.7	0.6	0.6	0.7	0.7	0.6
18 to 19 years	0.7	0.7	0.7	0.8	0.8	0.7
20 to 24 years	1.2	1.1	1.1	1.2	1.3	1.3
25 years and over	5.0	4.7	4.7	4.7	4.9	4.9
25 to 34 years	2.8	2.7	2.6	2.7	2.9	2.9
35 to 44 years	5.3	5.0	4.8	4.6	4.9	4.9
45 to 54 years	8.3	8.1	8.2	7.6	7.7	7.3
55 to 64 years	10.2	10.1	10.0	9.9	9.6	9.3
65 years and over	8.4	7.8	9.4	8.6	9.0	8.8
Men						
16 years and over	4.0	3.8	3.8	3.9	4.1	4.1
16 to 17 years	0.6	0.6	0.6	0.8	0.7	0.7
18 to 19 years	0.7	0.7	0.7	0.8	0.8	0.7
20 to 24 years	1.2	1.2	1.2	1.4	1.3	1.4
25 years and over	5.3	4.9	4.9	4.9	5.1	5.0
25 to 34 years	3.0	2.8	2.7	2.8	3.0	2.9
35 to 44 years	6.1	5.5	5.3	5.0	5.2	5.1
45 to 54 years	10.1	9.4	9.5	9.1	9.6	8.1
55 to 64 years	10.5	11.2	10.2	10.2	9.8	9.5
65 years and over	8.3	7.1	9.0	8.1	8.2	8.3
Women						
16 years and over	3.5	3.4	3.3	3.4	3.8	3.9
16 to 17 years	0.7	0.6	0.6	0.7	0.6	0.6
18 to 19 years	0.7	0.7	0.7	0.8	0.8	0.7
20 to 24 years	1.2	1.1	1.0	1.1	1.3	1.2
25 years and over	4.7	4.4	4.4	4.4	4.7	4.8
25 to 34 years	2.7	2.5	2.5	2.5	2.8	2.8
35 to 44 years	4.8	4.5	4.3	4.2	4.5	4.6
45 to 54 years	7.0	7.2	7.3	6.5	6.4	6.7
55 to 64 years	10.0	9.6	9.9	9.6	9.2	9.2
65 years and over	8.4	8.7	9.7	9.4	9.6	9.5

Note: Data for 1996 and 1998 are based on population controls from the 1990 census. Data beginning in 2000 reflect the introduction of Census 2000 population controls and are not strictly comparable with data for prior years. In addition, data for 2004 reflect the introduction of revised population controls in January 2003 and January 2004 and data for January 2006 reflect the introduction of revisions to the population controls in January 2005 and 2006.

Table 1-44. Median Years of Tenure with Current Employer for Employed Wage and Salary Workers, by Industry, Selected Years, February 2000–January 2006

(Number of years.)

Industry	February 2000	January 2002	January 2004	January 2006
TOTAL, 16 YEARS AND OVER	3.5	3.7	4.0	4.0
Private Sector	3.2	3.3	3.5	3.6
Agriculture and related industries	3.7	4.2	3.7	3.8
Nonagricultural industries	3.2	3.3	3.5	3.6
Mining	4.8	4.5	5.2	3.8
Construction	2.7	3.0	3.0	3.0
Manufacturing	4.9	5.4	5.8	5.5
Durable goods manufacturing	4.8	5.5	6.0	5.6
Nonmetallic mineral product	5.5	5.3	4.8	5.0
Primary metals and fabricated metal product	5.0	6.3	6.4	6.2
Machinery manufacturing	5.3	6.8	6.4	6.6
Computers and electronic product	3.9	4.7	5.2	5.9
Electrical equipment and appliances	5.0	5.5	9.8	6.2
Transportation equipment	6.4	7.0	7.7	7.2
Wood product	3.7	4.3	5.0	4.7
Furniture and fixtures	4.4	4.7	4.7	4.2
Miscellaneous manufacturing	3.7	4.5	4.6	3.9
Nondurable goods manufacturing	5.0	5.3	5.5	5.4
Food manufacturing	4.6	5.0	4.9	5.2
Beverage and tobacco product	5.5	4.6	8.0	5.4
Textiles, apparel, and leather	4.7	5.0	5.0	4.4
Paper and printing	5.1	6.2	6.9	6.3
Petroleum and coal product	9.5	9.8	11.4	5.0
Chemicals	6.0	5.7	5.3	6.1
Plastics and rubber product	4.6	5.3	5.7	5.0
Wholesale and retail trade	2.7	2.8	3.1	3.1
Wholesale trade	3.9	3.9	4.3	4.6
Retail trade	2.5	2.6	2.8	2.8
Transportation and utilities	4.7	4.9	5.3	4.9
Transportation and warehousing	4.0	4.3	4.7	4.3
Utilities	11.5	13.4	13.3	10.4
Information[1]	3.4	3.3	4.3	4.8
Publishing, except Internet	4.2	4.8	4.7	5.3
Motion picture and sound recording industries	1.6	2.3	2.2	1.9
Broadcasting, except Internet	3.6	3.1	4.0	4.6
Telecommunications	4.3	3.4	4.6	5.3
Financial activities	3.5	3.6	3.9	4.0
Finance and insurance	3.6	3.9	4.1	4.1
Finance	3.3	3.6	4.0	3.9
Insurance	4.4	4.5	4.4	4.7
Real estate and rental and leasing	3.1	3.0	3.3	3.4
Real estate	3.1	3.2	3.5	3.5
Rental and leasing services	3.0	2.2	2.9	3.1
Professional and business services	2.4	2.7	3.2	3.2
Professional and technical services	2.6	3.1	3.6	3.8
Management, administrative, and waste services[1]	2.0	2.1	2.6	2.5
Administrative and support services	1.8	1.9	2.4	2.4
Waste management and remediation services	3.6	4.3	3.4	4.1
Education and health services	3.4	3.5	3.6	4.0
Education services	3.2	3.6	3.8	4.0
Health care and social assistance	3.5	3.5	3.6	4.1
Hospitals	5.1	4.9	4.7	5.2
Health services, except hospitals	3.2	3.1	3.3	3.6
Social assistance	2.4	2.5	2.8	3.1
Leisure and hospitality	1.7	1.8	2.0	1.9
Arts, entertainment, and recreation	2.6	2.3	2.8	3.1
Accommodation and food services	1.5	1.6	1.9	1.6
Accommodation	2.8	2.7	3.1	2.5
Food services and drinking places	1.4	1.4	1.6	1.4
Other services	3.1	3.3	3.3	3.2
Other services, except private households	3.2	3.3	3.5	3.3
Repair and maintenance	3.0	3.0	3.2	2.9
Personal and laundry services	2.7	2.8	3.4	2.8
Membership associations and organizations	4.0	4.1	3.9	4.2
Other services, private households	3.0	2.7	2.3	2.8
Public Sector	7.1	6.7	6.9	6.9
Federal government	11.5	11.3	10.4	9.9
State government	5.5	5.4	6.4	6.3
Local government	6.7	6.2	6.4	6.6

Note: Data for January 2004 reflect the introduction of revisions to the population controls in January 2003 and 2004. Data for January 2006 reflect the introduction of revisions to the population controls in January 2005 and 2006.

[1]Includes other industries not shown separately.

Table 1-45. Employment Status of the Population, by Sex and Marital Status, March 1990–March 2006

(Thousands of people, percent.)

Marital status and year	Men						Women					
	Population	Labor force					Population	Labor force				
		Total		Employed	Unemployed			Total		Employed	Unemployed	
		Number	Percent of population		Number	Percent of labor force		Number	Percent of population		Number	Percent of labor force
Single												
1990	25 757	18 829	73.1	16 893	1 936	10.3	21 088	14 003	66.4	12 856	1 147	8.2
1991	26 220	19 014	72.5	16 418	2 596	13.7	21 688	14 125	65.1	12 887	1 238	8.8
1992	26 529	19 229	72.5	16 401	2 828	14.7	21 738	14 072	64.7	12 793	1 279	9.1
1993	26 951	19 625	72.8	16 858	2 767	14.1	21 848	14 091	64.5	12 711	1 380	9.8
1994	28 350	20 365	71.8	17 826	2 539	12.5	22 885	14 903	65.1	13 419	1 484	10.0
1995	28 318	20 449	72.2	18 286	2 163	10.6	22 853	14 974	65.5	13 673	1 301	8.7
1996	28 695	20 561	71.7	18 097	2 464	12.0	23 632	15 417	65.2	14 084	1 333	8.6
1997	29 294	20 942	71.5	18 683	2 259	10.8	24 215	16 178	66.8	14 747	1 431	8.8
1998	29 558	21 255	71.9	19 124	2 131	10.0	24 808	16 885	68.1	15 626	1 259	7.5
1999	29 883	21 329	71.4	19 465	1 864	8.7	25 674	17 486	68.1	16 185	1 301	7.4
2000	30 232	21 641	71.6	19 823	1 818	8.4	25 863	17 749	68.6	16 446	1 303	7.3
2001	30 968	22 232	71.8	20 239	1 993	9.0	26 180	17 900	68.4	16 631	1 269	7.1
2002	32 220	22 761	70.6	20 066	2 695	11.8	26 942	18 079	67.1	16 499	1 580	8.7
2003	32 852	22 821	69.5	20 194	2 627	11.5	27 527	17 901	65.0	16 219	1 682	9.4
2004	33 786	23 212	68.7	20 434	2 778	12.0	28 033	18 089	64.5	16 506	1 583	8.8
2005	34 069	23 335	68.5	20 831	2 504	10.7	28 508	18 554	65.1	16 902	1 652	8.9
2006	34 906	24 369	69.8	21 961	2 408	9.9	29 357	18 989	64.7	17 444	1 545	8.1
Married, Spouse Present												
1990	52 464	41 020	78.2	39 562	1 458	3.6	53 207	30 967	58.2	29 870	1 097	3.5
1991	52 460	40 883	77.9	38 843	2 040	5.0	53 176	31 103	58.5	29 668	1 435	4.6
1992	52 780	40 930	77.5	38 650	2 280	5.6	53 464	31 686	59.3	30 130	1 556	4.9
1993	53 488	41 255	77.1	39 069	2 186	5.3	54 146	32 158	59.4	30 757	1 401	4.4
1994	53 436	40 993	76.7	39 085	1 908	4.7	54 198	32 863	60.6	31 397	1 466	4.5
1995	54 166	41 806	77.2	40 262	1 544	3.7	54 902	33 563	61.1	32 267	1 296	3.9
1996	53 996	41 837	77.5	40 356	1 481	3.5	54 640	33 382	61.1	32 258	1 124	3.4
1997	53 981	41 967	77.7	40 628	1 339	3.2	54 611	33 907	62.1	32 836	1 071	3.2
1998	54 685	42 288	77.3	41 039	1 249	3.0	55 241	34 136	61.8	33 028	1 108	3.2
1999	55 256	42 557	77.0	41 476	1 081	2.5	55 801	34 349	61.6	33 403	946	2.8
2000	55 897	43 254	77.4	42 261	993	2.3	56 432	34 959	61.9	33 998	961	2.7
2001	56 152	43 463	77.4	42 245	1 218	2.8	56 740	35 234	62.1	34 273	961	2.7
2002	57 325	44 271	77.2	42 508	1 763	4.0	57 883	35 624	61.5	34 295	1 329	3.7
2003	57 940	44 700	77.1	42 797	1 903	4.3	58 545	36 185	61.8	34 806	1 379	3.8
2004	58 395	44 860	76.8	43 247	1 613	3.6	59 008	35 918	60.9	34 582	1 336	3.7
2005	58 854	45 263	76.9	43 763	1 500	3.3	59 449	35 809	60.2	34 738	1 071	3.0
2006	58 850	45 082	76.6	43 877	1 205	2.7	59 476	36 192	60.9	35 185	1 007	2.8
Widowed, Divorced, or Separated												
1990	11 152	7 513	67.4	6 959	554	7.4	23 857	11 168	46.8	10 530	638	5.7
1991	11 588	7 804	67.3	6 985	819	10.5	24 105	11 145	46.2	10 386	759	6.8
1992	11 927	8 049	67.5	7 140	909	11.3	24 582	11 486	46.7	10 610	876	7.6
1993	11 861	7 956	67.1	7 055	901	11.3	24 661	11 308	45.9	10 528	780	6.9
1994	12 239	8 156	66.6	7 382	774	9.5	25 098	11 879	47.3	10 995	884	7.4
1995	12 410	8 315	67.0	7 632	683	8.2	25 373	12 001	47.3	11 308	693	5.8
1996	13 176	8 697	66.0	7 976	721	8.3	25 786	12 430	48.2	11 742	688	5.5
1997	14 113	9 420	66.7	8 715	705	7.5	26 301	12 814	48.7	12 071	743	5.8
1998	14 166	9 482	66.9	8 954	528	5.6	26 092	12 880	49.4	12 235	645	5.0
1999	14 225	9 449	66.4	8 971	478	5.1	26 199	12 951	49.4	12 307	644	5.0
2000	14 289	9 623	67.3	9 152	471	4.9	26 354	13 228	50.2	12 657	571	4.3
2001	14 392	9 421	65.5	8 927	494	5.2	26 747	13 454	50.3	12 887	567	4.2
2002	14 617	9 650	66.0	8 931	719	7.5	27 802	13 716	49.3	12 855	861	6.3
2003	15 180	9 855	64.9	9 020	835	8.5	28 240	14 154	50.1	13 240	914	6.5
2004	15 059	9 789	65.0	9 059	730	7.5	28 228	14 194	50.3	13 324	870	6.1
2005	15 779	10 256	65.0	9 569	687	6.7	28 576	14 233	49.8	13 472	761	5.3
2006	16 405	10 815	65.9	10 141	674	6.2	28 981	14 220	49.1	13 539	681	4.8

Note: See notes and definitions for information on historical comparability.

Table 1-45. Employment Status of the Population, by Sex and Marital Status, March 1990–March 2006
—*Continued*

(Thousands of people, percent.)

Marital status and year	Men						Women					
	Population	Labor force					Population	Labor force				
		Total		Employed	Unemployed			Total		Employed	Unemployed	
		Number	Percent of population		Number	Percent of labor force		Number	Percent of population		Number	Percent of labor force
Widowed												
1990	2 331	519	22.3	490	29	5.6	11 477	2 243	19.5	2 149	94	4.2
1991	2 385	486	20.4	448	38	7.8	11 288	2 150	19.0	2 044	106	4.9
1992	2 529	566	22.4	501	65	11.5	11 325	2 131	18.8	2 029	102	4.8
1993	2 468	596	24.1	535	61	10.2	11 214	1 961	17.5	1 856	105	5.4
1994	2 220	474	21.4	440	34	7.2	11 073	1 945	17.6	1 825	120	6.2
1995	2 282	496	21.7	469	27	5.4	11 080	1 941	17.5	1 844	97	5.0
1996	2 476	487	19.7	466	21	4.3	11 070	1 916	17.3	1 820	96	5.0
1997	2 686	559	20.8	529	30	5.4	11 058	2 018	18.2	1 926	92	4.6
1998	2 567	563	21.9	551	12	2.1	11 027	2 157	19.6	2 071	86	4.0
1999	2 540	562	22.1	532	30	5.3	10 943	2 039	18.6	1 942	97	4.8
2000	2 601	583	22.4	547	36	6.2	11 061	2 011	18.2	1 911	100	5.0
2001	2 638	568	21.5	546	22	3.9	11 182	2 137	19.1	2 045	92	4.3
2002	2 635	629	23.9	581	48	7.6	11 411	2 001	17.5	1 887	114	5.7
2003	2 694	628	23.3	588	40	6.4	11 295	2 087	18.5	1 991	96	4.6
2004	2 651	581	21.9	558	23	4.0	11 159	2 157	19.3	2 048	109	5.1
2005	2 729	618	22.6	590	28	4.5	11 125	2 111	19.0	2 005	106	5.0
2006	2 626	610	23.2	563	47	7.7	11 305	2 164	19.1	2 094	70	3.2
Divorced												
1990	6 256	5 004	80.0	4 639	365	7.3	8 845	6 678	75.5	6 333	345	5.2
1991	6 586	5 262	79.9	4 722	540	10.3	9 152	6 779	74.1	6 365	414	6.1
1992	6 743	5 418	80.3	4 823	595	11.0	9 569	7 076	73.9	6 578	498	7.0
1993	6 770	5 330	78.7	4 736	594	11.1	9 879	7 183	72.7	6 736	447	6.2
1994	7 222	5 548	76.8	5 028	520	9.4	10 113	7 473	73.9	6 962	511	6.8
1995	7 343	5 739	78.2	5 266	473	8.2	10 262	7 559	73.7	7 206	353	4.7
1996	7 734	5 954	77.0	5 468	486	8.2	10 508	7 829	74.5	7 468	361	4.6
1997	8 191	6 298	76.9	5 851	447	7.1	11 102	8 092	72.9	7 666	426	5.3
1998	8 307	6 378	76.8	6 045	333	5.2	11 065	8 038	72.6	7 687	351	4.4
1999	8 529	6 481	76.0	6 151	330	5.1	11 130	8 171	73.4	7 841	330	4.0
2000	8 532	6 583	77.2	6 279	304	4.6	11 061	8 505	76.9	8 217	288	3.4
2001	8 580	6 403	74.6	6 074	329	5.1	11 719	8 662	73.9	8 335	327	3.8
2002	8 643	6 519	75.4	6 053	466	7.1	12 227	8 902	72.8	8 416	486	5.5
2003	8 938	6 621	74.1	6 052	569	8.6	12 653	9 191	72.6	8 673	518	5.6
2004	8 942	6 622	74.1	6 104	518	7.8	12 817	9 246	72.1	8 706	540	5.8
2005	9 196	6 754	73.4	6 281	473	7.0	12 950	9 253	71.5	8 836	417	4.5
2006	9 646	7 065	73.2	6 631	434	6.1	13 107	9 188	70.1	8 799	389	4.2
Separated												
1990	2 565	1 990	77.6	1 830	160	8.0	3 535	2 247	63.6	2 048	199	8.9
1991	2 616	2 057	78.6	1 816	241	11.7	3 665	2 216	60.5	1 977	239	10.8
1992	2 655	2 065	77.8	1 816	249	12.1	3 688	2 279	61.8	2 003	276	12.1
1993	2 623	2 030	77.4	1 784	246	12.1	3 568	2 165	60.7	1 937	228	10.5
1994	2 797	2 134	76.3	1 914	220	10.3	3 911	2 461	62.9	2 208	253	10.3
1995	2 784	2 081	74.7	1 898	183	8.8	4 031	2 501	62.0	2 258	243	9.7
1996	2 966	2 255	76.0	2 041	214	9.5	4 209	2 684	63.8	2 453	231	8.6
1997	3 236	2 563	79.2	2 335	228	8.9	4 141	2 705	65.3	2 480	225	8.3
1998	3 293	2 542	77.2	2 358	184	7.2	4 000	2 683	67.1	2 476	207	7.7
1999	3 156	2 405	76.2	2 287	118	4.9	4 126	2 740	66.4	2 523	217	7.9
2000	3 157	2 456	77.8	2 326	130	5.3	4 012	2 711	67.6	2 528	183	6.8
2001	3 174	2 450	77.2	2 307	143	5.8	3 846	2 654	69.0	2 507	147	5.5
2002	3 339	2 502	74.9	2 297	205	8.2	4 164	2 812	67.5	2 551	261	9.3
2003	3 548	2 606	73.4	2 380	226	8.7	4 293	2 877	67.0	2 576	301	10.5
2004	3 466	2 586	74.6	2 397	189	7.3	4 251	2 791	65.7	2 569	222	8.0
2005	3 855	2 884	74.8	2 698	186	6.4	4 501	2 870	63.8	2 632	238	8.3
2006	4 132	3 141	76.0	2 947	194	6.2	4 569	2 869	62.8	2 647	222	7.7

Note: See notes and definitions for information on historical comparability.

Table 1-46. Employment Status of All Women and Single Women, by Presence and Age of Children, March 1990–March 2006

(Thousands of people, percent.)

Presence and age of children and year	All women						Single women					
	Civilian labor force	Civilian labor force as percent of population	Employed		Unemployed		Civilian labor force	Civilian labor force as percent of population	Employed		Unemployed	
			Number	Percent full time	Percent part time	Number	Percent of labor force			Number	Percent full time	Percent part time	Number	Percent of labor force

(Note: header spans — data columns below are: Civilian labor force | Civ. as % of pop | Number | % full time | % part time | Number | % of labor force | Civilian labor force | Civ. as % of pop | Number | % full time | % part time | Number | % of labor force)

Presence and age of children and year	Civ. LF	% pop	Number	% FT	% PT	Unemp Number	% LF	Civ. LF	% pop	Number	% FT	% PT	Unemp Number	% LF
Women with No Children Under 18 Years														
1990	33 942	52.3	32 391	74.4	25.6	1 551	4.6	12 478	68.1	11 611	65.9	34.1	866	6.9
1991	34 047	52.0	32 167	74.0	26.0	1 880	5.5	12 472	67.0	11 529	66.2	33.8	943	7.6
1992	34 487	52.3	32 481	74.3	25.7	2 006	5.8	12 355	66.9	11 374	66.6	33.4	982	7.9
1993	34 495	52.1	32 476	74.6	25.4	2 020	5.9	12 223	66.4	11 201	66.1	33.9	1 022	8.4
1994	35 454	53.1	33 343	72.7	27.3	2 110	6.0	12 737	66.8	11 674	64.5	35.5	1 063	8.3
1995	35 843	52.9	34 054	72.9	27.1	1 789	5.0	12 870	67.1	11 919	64.5	35.5	951	7.4
1996	36 509	53.0	34 698	73.3	26.7	1 811	5.0	13 172	66.1	12 255	64.6	35.4	918	7.0
1997	37 295	53.6	35 572	73.7	26.3	1 723	4.6	13 405	66.5	12 442	64.0	36.0	964	7.2
1998	38 253	54.1	36 680	74.1	25.9	1 573	4.1	13 888	67.2	13 082	64.8	35.2	806	5.8
1999	39 316	54.3	37 589	74.6	25.4	1 727	4.4	14 435	67.1	13 491	65.6	34.4	944	6.5
2000	40 142	54.8	38 408	75.4	24.6	1 733	4.3	14 677	67.6	13 713	66.6	33.4	964	6.6
2001	40 836	54.9	39 219	75.7	24.3	1 617	4.0	14 877	67.4	13 993	67.3	32.7	884	5.9
2002	41 278	54.0	39 038	75.1	24.9	2 241	5.4	14 855	65.6	13 682	65.9	34.1	1 173	7.9
2003	42 039	54.1	39 667	74.8	25.2	2 372	5.6	14 678	63.5	13 430	65.1	34.9	1 249	8.5
2004	42 289	53.8	40 000	74.6	25.4	2 289	5.4	14 828	63.0	13 670	65.5	34.5	1 157	7.8
2005	42 039	54.1	39 667	74.8	25.2	2 372	5.6	14 678	63.5	13 430	65.1	34.9	1 249	8.5
2006	43 392	53.6	41 440	75.3	24.7	1 952	4.5	15 673	63.4	14 547	66.5	33.5	1 125	7.2
Women with Children Under 18 Years														
1990	22 196	66.7	20 865	73.0	27.0	1 331	6.0	1 525	55.2	1 244	79.1	20.9	280	18.4
1991	22 327	66.6	20 774	73.0	27.0	1 552	7.0	1 654	53.6	1 358	76.4	23.6	296	17.9
1992	22 756	67.2	21 052	73.8	26.2	1 704	7.5	1 716	52.5	1 420	75.9	24.1	297	17.3
1993	23 063	66.9	21 521	73.9	26.1	1 541	6.7	1 869	54.4	1 510	74.8	25.2	359	19.2
1994	24 191	68.4	22 467	70.8	29.2	1 724	7.1	2 166	56.9	1 745	73.9	26.1	421	19.4
1995	24 695	69.7	23 195	71.7	28.3	1 500	6.1	2 104	57.5	1 754	73.6	26.4	350	16.6
1996	24 720	70.2	23 386	72.6	27.4	1 334	5.4	2 245	60.5	1 829	73.5	26.5	416	18.5
1997	25 604	72.1	24 082	74.1	25.9	1 522	5.9	2 772	68.1	2 305	76.6	23.4	467	16.8
1998	25 647	72.3	24 209	74.0	26.0	1 438	5.6	2 997	72.5	2 544	75.6	24.4	453	15.1
1999	25 469	72.1	24 305	74.1	25.9	1 165	4.6	3 051	73.4	2 694	75.8	24.2	357	11.7
2000	25 795	72.9	24 693	74.6	25.4	1 102	4.3	3 073	73.9	2 734	79.7	20.3	339	11.0
2001	25 751	73.1	24 572	75.6	24.4	1 179	4.6	3 022	73.8	2 638	81.8	18.2	385	12.7
2002	26 140	72.2	24 612	74.8	25.2	1 529	5.8	3 224	75.3	2 818	79.1	20.9	406	12.6
2003	26 202	71.7	24 598	74.3	25.7	1 603	6.1	3 222	73.1	2 789	79.5	20.5	433	13.4
2004	25 913	70.7	24 413	74.2	25.8	1 501	5.8	3 262	72.6	2 836	76.8	23.2	426	13.1
2005	26 202	71.7	24 598	74.3	25.7	1 603	6.1	3 222	73.1	2 789	79.5	20.5	433	13.4
2006	26 009	70.6	24 728	75.6	24.4	1 281	4.9	3 317	71.5	2 896	77.8	22.2	420	12.7
Women with Children Under 6 Years														
1990	9 397	58.2	8 732	69.6	30.4	664	7.1	929	48.7	736	75.0	25.0	194	20.9
1991	9 636	58.4	8 758	69.5	30.5	878	9.1	1 050	48.8	819	72.2	27.8	231	22.0
1992	9 573	58.0	8 662	70.2	29.8	911	9.5	1 029	45.8	829	73.2	26.8	200	19.4
1993	9 621	57.9	8 764	70.1	29.9	857	8.9	1 125	47.4	869	70.0	30.0	257	22.8
1994	10 328	60.3	9 394	67.1	32.9	935	9.1	1 379	52.2	1 062	70.0	30.0	317	23.0
1995	10 395	62.3	9 587	67.5	32.5	809	7.8	1 328	53.0	1 069	68.6	31.4	259	19.5
1996	10 293	62.3	9 592	68.4	31.6	701	6.8	1 378	55.1	1 099	67.3	32.7	279	20.2
1997	10 610	65.0	9 800	70.5	29.5	810	7.6	1 755	65.1	1 424	71.6	28.4	330	18.8
1998	10 619	65.2	9 839	69.8	30.2	780	7.3	1 755	67.3	1 448	71.7	28.3	307	17.5
1999	10 322	64.4	9 674	69.0	31.0	648	6.3	1 811	68.1	1 565	71.0	29.0	246	13.6
2000	10 316	65.3	9 763	70.5	29.5	553	5.4	1 835	70.5	1 603	75.3	24.7	232	12.6
2001	10 200	64.9	9 618	71.2	28.8	582	5.7	1 783	69.7	1 542	79.1	20.9	242	13.6
2002	10 193	64.1	9 441	70.4	29.6	752	7.4	1 819	71.0	1 568	74.5	25.5	251	13.8
2003	10 209	62.9	9 433	70.0	30.0	776	7.6	1 893	70.2	1 614	75.2	24.8	279	14.7
2004	10 131	62.2	9 407	69.4	30.6	724	7.1	1 885	68.4	1 605	70.1	29.9	279	14.8
2005	10 209	62.9	9 433	70.0	30.0	776	7.6	1 893	70.2	1 614	75.2	24.8	279	14.7
2006	10 430	63.0	9 779	72.0	28.0	651	6.2	1 934	68.6	1 659	72.8	27.2	276	14.3

Note: See notes and definitions for information on historical comparability.

Table 1-47. Employment Status of Ever-Married Women and Married Women, Spouse Present, by Presence and Age of Children, March 1990–March 2006

(Thousands of people, percent.)

Presence and age of children and year	Ever-married women[1]							Married women, spouse present						
	Civilian labor force	Civilian labor force as percent of population	Employed			Unemployed		Civilian labor force	Civilian labor force as percent of population	Employed			Unemployed	
			Number	Percent full time	Percent part time	Number	Percent of labor force			Number	Percent full time	Percent part time	Number	Percent of labor force
Women with No Children Under 18 Years														
1990	21 464	46.1	20 779	79.1	20.9	685	3.2	14 467	51.1	14 068	77.3	22.7	399	2.8
1991	21 575	46.1	20 637	78.4	21.6	937	4.3	14 529	51.2	13 976	77.6	22.4	552	3.8
1992	22 132	46.6	21 108	78.5	21.5	1 024	4.6	14 851	51.9	14 247	77.8	22.2	604	4.1
1993	22 273	46.6	21 275	79.0	21.0	998	4.5	15 211	52.4	14 630	77.6	22.4	581	3.8
1994	22 716	47.6	21 669	77.1	22.9	1 047	4.6	15 234	53.2	14 641	75.6	24.4	593	3.9
1995	22 973	47.3	22 134	77.4	22.6	839	3.7	15 594	53.2	15 072	76.3	23.7	522	3.3
1996	23 337	47.7	22 444	78.1	21.9	893	3.8	15 628	53.4	15 123	76.8	23.2	506	3.2
1997	23 890	48.3	23 130	78.9	21.1	760	3.2	15 750	54.2	15 315	77.7	22.3	435	2.8
1998	24 366	48.7	23 598	79.3	20.7	767	3.1	16 007	54.1	15 581	78.3	21.7	426	2.7
1999	24 881	48.9	24 098	79.7	20.3	783	3.1	16 484	54.4	16 061	78.2	21.8	423	2.6
2000	25 465	49.4	24 695	80.3	19.7	769	3.0	16 786	54.7	16 357	79.1	20.9	429	2.6
2001	25 959	49.6	25 226	80.4	19.6	733	2.8	16 909	54.8	16 528	78.7	21.3	381	2.3
2002	26 423	49.1	25 356	80.0	20.0	1 068	4.0	17 353	54.8	16 780	78.4	21.6	573	3.3
2003	27 361	50.1	26 238	79.7	20.3	1 123	4.1	17 901	55.7	17 273	78.6	21.4	628	3.5
2004	27 461	49.8	26 329	79.3	20.7	1 131	4.1	17 965	55.0	17 367	78.6	21.4	598	3.3
2005	27 361	50.1	26 238	79.7	20.3	1 123	4.1	17 901	55.7	17 273	78.6	21.4	628	3.5
2006	27 719	49.3	26 893	80.1	19.9	827	3.0	18 124	54.8	17 691	79.3	20.7	434	2.4
Women with Children Under 18 Years														
1990	20 671	67.8	19 621	72.6	27.4	1 051	5.1	16 500	66.3	15 803	69.8	30.2	698	4.2
1991	20 673	67.9	19 416	72.8	27.2	1 257	6.1	16 575	66.8	15 692	70.1	29.9	883	5.3
1992	21 040	68.8	19 633	73.6	26.4	1 407	6.7	16 835	67.8	15 884	71.3	28.7	952	5.7
1993	21 194	68.3	20 011	73.9	26.1	1 183	5.6	16 947	67.5	16 127	71.4	28.6	820	4.8
1994	22 025	69.8	20 722	70.5	29.5	1 303	5.9	17 628	69.0	16 755	68.0	32.0	873	5.0
1995	22 591	71.1	21 441	71.5	28.5	1 150	5.1	17 969	70.2	17 195	68.8	31.2	774	4.3
1996	22 475	71.4	21 556	72.5	27.5	919	4.1	17 754	70.0	17 136	69.6	30.4	618	3.5
1997	22 831	72.6	21 777	73.9	26.1	1 054	4.6	18 157	71.1	17 521	71.6	28.4	636	3.5
1998	22 650	72.3	21 665	73.8	26.2	985	4.3	18 129	70.6	17 447	71.5	28.5	682	3.8
1999	22 419	71.9	21 611	73.9	26.1	808	3.6	17 865	70.1	17 342	71.5	28.5	523	2.9
2000	22 722	72.7	21 960	74.0	26.0	763	3.4	18 174	70.6	17 641	71.7	28.3	533	2.9
2001	22 729	73.0	21 934	74.9	25.1	795	3.5	18 325	70.8	17 745	72.6	27.4	580	3.2
2002	22 917	71.8	21 794	74.3	25.7	1 122	4.9	18 271	69.6	17 515	71.7	28.3	756	4.1
2003	22 979	71.5	21 809	73.7	26.3	1 170	5.1	18 284	69.2	17 533	71.0	29.0	751	4.1
2004	22 651	70.5	21 576	73.8	26.2	1 075	4.7	17 953	68.2	17 215	71.3	28.7	738	4.1
2005	22 979	71.5	21 809	73.7	26.3	1 170	5.1	18 284	69.2	17 533	71.0	29.0	751	4.1
2006	22 692	70.5	21 831	75.3	24.7	861	3.8	18 067	68.4	17 494	73.0	27.0	574	3.2
Women with Children Under 6 Years														
1990	8 467	59.5	7 996	69.1	30.9	471	5.6	7 247	58.9	6 901	67.4	32.6	346	4.8
1991	8 585	59.9	7 938	69.2	30.8	647	7.5	7 434	59.9	6 933	67.5	32.5	501	6.7
1992	8 544	60.0	7 832	69.9	30.1	711	8.3	7 333	59.9	6 819	68.5	31.5	514	7.0
1993	8 496	59.6	7 895	70.2	29.8	600	7.1	7 289	59.6	6 840	68.8	31.2	450	6.2
1994	8 949	61.8	8 332	66.7	33.3	617	6.9	7 723	61.7	7 291	65.4	34.6	432	5.6
1995	9 067	63.9	8 517	67.4	32.6	550	6.1	7 759	63.5	7 349	66.1	33.9	409	5.3
1996	8 915	63.6	8 493	68.6	31.4	422	4.7	7 590	62.7	7 297	66.5	33.5	293	3.9
1997	8 856	64.9	8 376	70.3	29.7	480	5.4	7 582	63.6	7 252	69.1	30.9	330	4.4
1998	8 864	64.8	8 391	69.5	30.5	473	5.3	7 655	63.7	7 309	68.1	31.9	346	4.5
1999	8 511	63.7	8 109	68.6	31.4	402	4.7	7 246	61.8	6 979	67.1	32.9	267	3.7
2000	8 481	64.3	8 159	69.5	30.5	321	3.8	7 341	62.8	7 087	68.1	31.9	254	3.5
2001	8 417	64.0	8 077	69.7	30.3	340	4.0	7 319	62.5	7 062	68.5	31.5	257	3.5
2002	8 373	62.8	7 873	69.6	30.4	501	6.0	7 166	60.8	6 804	67.7	32.3	363	5.1
2003	8 315	61.4	7 818	68.9	31.1	497	6.0	7 175	59.8	6 826	67.1	32.9	349	4.9
2004	8 246	61.0	7 801	69.3	30.7	445	5.4	7 107	59.3	6 774	68.1	31.9	332	4.7
2005	8 315	61.4	7 818	68.9	31.1	497	6.0	7 175	59.8	6 826	67.1	32.9	349	4.9
2006	8 496	61.9	8 121	71.8	28.2	375	4.4	7 366	60.3	7 092	70.6	29.4	274	3.7

[1] Ever-married women are women who are, or have ever been, married.

Table 1-48. Employment Status of Women Who Maintain Families, by Marital Status and Presence and Age of Children, March 1990–March 2006

(Thousands of people, percent.)

Marital status, age of children, and year	Civilian noninstitutional population	Civilian labor force					Not in the labor force
		Number	Percent of the population	Employed	Unemployed		
					Number	Percent of the labor force	
Total, Women Who Maintain Families							
1990	11 309	7 088	62.7	6 471	617	8.7	4 221
1991	11 765	7 329	62.3	6 657	672	9.2	4 436
1992	12 214	7 517	61.5	6 798	719	9.6	4 697
1993	12 489	7 777	62.3	7 093	684	8.8	4 712
1994	12 963	8 214	63.4	7 413	801	9.8	4 750
1995	12 762	8 192	64.2	7 527	665	8.1	4 570
1996	12 993	8 460	65.1	7 832	628	7.4	4 532
1997	13 258	8 998	67.9	8 192	806	9.0	4 260
1998	13 102	8 976	68.5	8 309	667	7.4	4 127
1999	13 191	9 213	69.8	8 596	617	6.7	3 978
2000	13 145	9 226	70.2	8 592	634	6.9	3 918
2001	12 930	9 034	69.9	8 453	581	6.4	3 897
2002	13 489	9 523	70.6	8 755	768	8.1	3 966
2003	14 000	9 759	69.7	8 898	861	8.8	4 241
2004	14 165	9 869	69.7	9 054	815	8.3	4 297
2005	14 391	9 941	69.1	9 140	801	8.1	4 450
2006	14 485	9 966	68.8	9 227	739	7.4	4 520
Women with No Children Under 18 Years							
1990	4 290	2 227	51.9	2 132	95	4.3	2 062
1991	4 447	2 364	53.2	2 231	133	5.6	2 083
1992	4 651	2 427	52.2	2 307	120	4.9	2 223
1993	4 708	2 466	52.4	2 339	127	5.2	2 242
1994	4 758	2 609	54.8	2 489	120	4.6	2 149
1995	4 610	2 471	53.6	2 394	77	3.1	2 139
1996	4 847	2 552	52.7	2 462	90	3.5	2 295
1997	4 909	2 663	54.2	2 571	92	3.5	2 246
1998	4 952	2 649	53.5	2 578	71	2.7	2 303
1999	4 942	2 667	54.0	2 556	111	4.2	2 275
2000	5 097	2 707	53.1	2 546	161	5.9	2 390
2001	5 185	2 772	53.5	2 668	104	3.8	2 413
2002	5 119	2 764	54.0	2 628	136	4.9	2 355
2003	5 457	2 934	53.8	2 728	206	7.0	2 522
2004	5 551	3 052	55.0	2 855	197	6.5	2 499
2005	5 692	3 095	54.4	2 961	134	4.3	2 597
2006	5 693	3 088	54.2	2 945	143	4.6	2 604
Women with Children Under 18 Years							
1990	7 018	4 860	69.3	4 338	522	10.7	2 159
1991	7 318	4 965	67.8	4 426	539	10.9	2 353
1992	7 564	5 090	67.3	4 491	599	11.8	2 473
1993	7 781	5 311	68.3	4 755	556	10.5	2 470
1994	8 205	5 604	68.3	4 924	680	12.1	2 601
1995	8 152	5 720	70.2	5 132	588	10.3	2 431
1996	8 146	5 908	72.5	5 370	538	9.1	2 237
1997	8 348	6 335	75.9	5 621	714	11.3	2 014
1998	8 151	6 327	77.6	5 731	596	9.4	1 823
1999	8 248	6 546	79.4	6 040	506	7.7	1 702
2000	8 048	6 520	81.0	6 046	474	7.3	1 528
2001	7 746	6 261	80.8	5 785	476	7.6	1 484
2002	8 370	6 759	80.8	6 127	632	9.4	1 611
2003	8 543	6 825	79.9	6 170	655	9.6	1 718
2004	8 614	6 817	79.1	6 199	618	9.1	1 798
2005	8 699	6 846	78.7	6 179	667	9.7	1 853
2006	8 793	6 878	78.2	6 282	596	8.7	1 915
Single Women with No Children Under 18 Years							
1990	642	450	70.1	425	25	5.6	192
1991	682	469	68.8	441	28	6.0	214
1992	745	505	67.8	475	30	5.9	241
1993	752	531	70.6	494	37	7.0	221
1994	704	490	69.6	451	39	8.0	213
1995	779	534	68.5	508	26	4.9	245
1996	895	588	65.7	572	16	2.7	308
1997	860	585	68.0	563	22	3.8	275
1998	893	637	71.3	613	24	3.8	256
1999	969	674	69.6	638	36	5.3	295
2000	1 004	720	71.7	642	78	10.8	284
2001	1 096	787	71.8	756	31	3.9	309
2002	1 154	796	69.0	747	49	6.2	358
2003	1 254	814	64.9	713	101	12.4	440
2004	1 381	977	70.7	887	90	9.2	404
2005	1 388	926	66.7	855	71	7.7	463
2006	1 370	933	68.1	861	72	7.7	437

Note: See notes and definitions for information on historical comparability.

Table 1-48. Employment Status of Women Who Maintain Families, by Marital Status and Presence and Age of Children, March 1990–March 2006—Continued

(Thousands of people, percent.)

Marital status, age of children, and year	Civilian noninstitutional population	Civilian labor force					Not in the labor force
		Number	Percent of the population	Employed	Unemployed		
					Number	Percent of the labor force	
Single Women with Children Under 18 Years							
1990	1 953	1 095	56.1	874	221	20.2	858
1991	2 208	1 187	53.8	985	202	17.0	1 021
1992	2 376	1 256	52.9	1 067	189	15.0	1 120
1993	2 445	1 414	57.8	1 161	253	17.9	1 031
1994	2 790	1 625	58.2	1 328	297	18.3	1 165
1995	2 613	1 510	57.8	1 261	249	16.5	1 102
1996	2 639	1 633	61.9	1 346	287	17.6	1 006
1997	3 012	2 087	69.3	1 749	338	16.2	925
1998	3 083	2 280	74.0	1 960	320	14.0	803
1999	3 163	2 415	76.4	2 146	269	11.1	748
2000	3 167	2 413	76.2	2 151	262	10.9	754
2001	3 097	2 351	75.9	2 055	296	12.6	745
2002	3 315	2 566	77.4	2 241	325	12.7	749
2003	3 421	2 584	75.5	2 272	312	12.1	837
2004	3 414	2 568	75.2	2 233	335	13.0	846
2005	3 591	2 708	75.4	2 325	383	14.1	882
2006	3 671	2 710	73.8	2 370	340	12.5	961
Widowed, Divorced, or Separated Women with No Children Under 18 Years							
1990	3 648	1 778	48.7	1 708	70	3.9	1 870
1991	3 765	1 896	50.4	1 791	105	5.5	1 869
1992	3 905	1 923	49.2	1 832	91	4.7	1 982
1993	3 956	1 935	48.9	1 845	90	4.7	2 021
1994	4 054	2 118	52.2	2 037	81	3.8	1 936
1995	3 831	1 938	50.6	1 887	51	2.6	1 894
1996	3 952	1 964	49.7	1 890	74	3.8	1 988
1997	4 049	2 077	51.3	2 008	69	3.3	1 971
1998	4 058	2 011	49.6	1 965	46	2.3	2 047
1999	3 974	1 993	50.2	1 918	75	3.8	1 980
2000	4 093	1 987	48.5	1 904	83	4.2	2 106
2001	4 088	1 985	48.6	1 912	73	3.7	2 104
2002	3 964	1 968	49.6	1 882	86	4.4	1 997
2003	4 203	2 121	50.5	2 016	105	5.0	2 082
2004	4 170	2 075	49.8	1 968	107	5.2	2 095
2005	4 304	2 170	50.4	2 106	64	2.9	2 135
2006	4 323	2 156	49.9	2 084	72	3.3	2 168
Widowed, Divorced, or Separated Women with Children Under 18 Years							
1990	5 065	3 765	74.3	3 464	301	8.0	1 301
1991	5 109	3 778	73.9	3 441	337	8.9	1 331
1992	5 187	3 834	73.9	3 424	410	10.7	1 353
1993	5 336	3 897	73.0	3 594	303	7.8	1 439
1994	5 415	3 979	73.5	3 596	383	9.6	1 436
1995	5 539	4 210	76.0	3 871	339	8.1	1 329
1996	5 507	4 275	77.6	4 024	251	5.9	1 231
1997	5 337	4 248	79.6	3 872	376	8.9	1 089
1998	5 068	4 047	79.9	3 771	276	6.8	1 020
1999	5 086	4 131	81.2	3 894	237	5.7	955
2000	4 881	4 107	84.1	3 895	212	5.2	774
2001	4 649	3 910	84.1	3 730	180	4.6	739
2002	5 056	4 193	82.9	3 886	307	7.3	862
2003	5 122	4 241	82.8	3 898	343	8.1	881
2004	5 201	4 249	81.7	3 966	283	6.7	952
2005	5 108	4 137	81.0	3 854	283	6.8	971
2006	5 121	4 167	81.4	3 912	255	6.1	955

Note: See notes and definitions for information on historical comparability.

Table 1-49. Number and Age of Children in Families, by Type of Family and Labor Force Status of Mother, March 1990–March 2006

(Thousands of children.)

Age of children and year	Total children	Mother in labor force	Mother not in labor force	Married-couple families			Families maintained by women			Families maintained by men
				Total	Mother in labor force	Mother not in labor force	Total	Mother in labor force	Mother not in labor force	
Children Under 18 Years										
1990	59 596	36 712	21 110	45 898	29 077	16 820	11 925	7 635	4 290	1 774
1991	60 330	36 968	21 526	45 912	29 056	16 856	12 582	7 912	4 670	1 836
1992	61 262	38 081	21 176	45 966	29 882	16 084	13 291	8 199	5 093	2 005
1993	62 020	38 542	21 444	46 499	30 054	16 445	13 487	8 488	4 999	2 034
1994	63 407	40 186	21 188	47 247	31 279	15 968	14 127	8 907	5 220	2 033
1995	63 989	41 365	20 421	47 675	32 190	15 486	14 111	9 176	4 935	2 202
1996	64 506	41 573	20 449	47 484	31 764	15 720	14 538	9 809	4 729	2 484
1997	64 710	42 747	19 223	47 529	32 263	15 265	14 441	10 483	3 958	2 740
1998	65 043	43 156	19 069	47 909	32 533	15 376	14 317	10 623	3 694	2 818
1999	65 191	43 419	19 074	47 945	32 193	15 752	14 547	11 226	3 322	2 699
2000	65 601	44 188	18 674	48 902	33 149	15 753	13 960	11 039	2 921	2 739
2001	65 777	44 051	18 864	49 352	33 436	15 916	13 563	10 615	2 948	2 862
2002	65 978	43 821	19 243	48 836	32 673	16 163	14 228	11 149	3 079	2 914
2003	66 521	43 769	19 782	49 004	32 411	16 593	14 547	11 359	3 189	2 970
2004	66 386	43 144	20 229	48 656	31 892	16 764	14 717	11 252	3 465	3 014
2005	66 526	43 239	20 179	48 688	31 886	16 802	14 729	11 352	3 377	3 108
2006	66 883	43 278	20 440	48 853	31 946	16 908	14 865	11 332	3 532	3 165
Children from 6 to 17 Years										
1990	39 095	25 805	12 079	29 726	20 067	9 659	8 157	5 737	2 420	1 211
1991	39 470	25 806	12 392	29 598	19 907	9 691	8 599	5 899	2 701	1 272
1992	40 064	26 666	12 067	29 673	20 586	9 087	9 060	6 079	2 980	1 331
1993	40 622	27 046	12 291	30 233	20 796	9 437	9 104	6 249	2 854	1 285
1994	41 795	28 179	12 287	30 895	21 663	9 233	9 570	6 516	3 054	1 329
1995	42 423	28 931	12 000	31 298	22 239	9 059	9 633	6 692	2 941	1 492
1996	42 964	29 381	11 897	31 231	22 092	9 139	10 047	7 289	2 758	1 685
1997	43 488	30 308	11 400	31 509	22 602	8 906	10 199	7 705	2 493	1 781
1998	43 771	30 579	11 367	31 707	22 706	9 001	10 238	7 873	2 365	1 826
1999	44 110	30 885	11 370	31 975	22 706	9 269	10 281	8 179	2 101	1 855
2000	44 562	31 531	11 198	32 732	23 393	9 339	9 997	8 138	1 859	1 833
2001	44 458	31 411	11 153	32 957	23 599	9 358	9 608	7 813	1 795	1 894
2002	44 865	31 437	11 510	32 799	23 296	9 504	10 148	8 142	2 006	1 918
2003	45 273	31 559	11 635	32 782	23 160	9 622	10 412	8 399	2 013	2 080
2004	45 066	31 040	11 968	32 506	22 736	9 769	10 502	8 304	2 199	2 058
2005	45 027	30 930	11 995	32 412	22 565	9 847	10 514	8 366	2 148	2 102
2006	45 039	30 591	12 250	32 311	22 315	9 996	10 530	8 276	2 254	2 198
Children Under 6 Years										
1990	20 502	10 907	9 031	16 171	9 010	7 161	3 767	1 897	1 870	563
1991	20 860	11 162	9 134	16 313	9 148	7 165	3 983	2 013	1 969	563
1992	21 198	11 415	9 109	16 293	9 296	6 997	4 232	2 119	2 112	674
1993	21 398	11 496	9 153	16 266	9 258	7 008	4 383	2 239	2 145	749
1994	21 612	12 007	8 901	16 352	9 617	6 735	4 556	2 391	2 166	704
1995	21 566	12 435	8 421	16 377	9 951	6 427	4 478	2 484	1 995	710
1996	21 542	12 192	8 552	16 253	9 672	6 581	4 491	2 520	1 971	799
1997	21 222	12 439	7 823	16 020	9 661	6 359	4 243	2 778	1 464	959
1998	21 272	12 577	7 703	16 201	9 827	6 375	4 079	2 751	1 328	992
1999	21 081	12 533	7 704	15 971	9 487	6 484	4 267	3 046	1 220	844
2000	21 039	12 657	7 476	16 170	9 757	6 413	3 963	2 901	1 062	906
2001	21 318	12 640	7 711	16 395	9 837	6 558	3 956	2 802	1 153	968
2002	21 113	12 384	7 733	16 037	9 377	6 660	4 080	3 007	1 073	996
2003	21 248	12 210	8 147	16 222	9 251	6 971	4 136	2 960	1 176	890
2004	21 321	12 104	8 261	16 151	9 156	6 995	4 214	2 948	1 266	956
2005	21 498	12 308	8 184	16 276	9 321	6 955	4 216	2 987	1 229	1 006
2006	21 844	12 687	8 190	16 542	9 631	6 911	4 335	3 057	1 278	968

Note: See notes and definitions for information on historical comparability.

Table 1-50. Number of Families and Median Family Income, by Type of Family and Earner Status of Members, 1995–2005

(Thousands of families, dollars.)

Number and type of families and median family income	1995	1996	1997	1998	1999	2000	2001	2002	2003	2004	2005
NUMBER OF FAMILIES											
Married-Couple Families, Total	53 621	53 654	54 362	54 829	55 352	55 650	56 798	57 362	57 767	58 180	58 225
No earners	7 276	7 145	7 286	7 257	7 160	7 297	7 662	7 803	8 043	7 998	8 017
One earner	11 708	11 493	11 700	12 246	12 290	12 450	12 852	13 503	14 061	14 385	14 301
Husband	8 792	8 611	8 770	9 173	9 062	9 319	9 573	10 121	10 478	10 853	10 611
Wife	2 251	2 207	2 298	2 411	2 585	2 545	2 689	2 821	3 027	2 993	3 097
Other family member	666	674	632	662	643	586	590	560	557	539	593
Two earners	27 180	27 260	27 712	27 593	28 010	28 329	28 779	28 891	28 693	28 806	28 802
Husband and wife	25 274	25 274	25 731	25 696	26 134	26 447	26 829	26 966	26 860	26 758	26 833
Husband and other family member	1 393	1 483	1 406	1 306	1 325	1 277	1 424	1 391	1 322	1 462	1 376
Husband not an earner	513	502	575	590	552	605	526	534	511	586	594
Three earners or more	7 456	7 756	7 664	7 733	7 892	7 575	7 504	7 165	6 970	6 991	7 104
Husband and wife	6 770	7 126	7 023	7 102	7 220	6 917	6 859	6 565	6 349	6 459	6 535
Husband, not wife	531	479	478	456	528	537	530	455	467	381	445
Husband not an earner	155	150	163	176	144	120	115	145	154	152	124
Families Maintained by Women, Total	13 007	13 277	13 115	13 206	13 164	12 950	13 517	14 033	14 196	14 404	14 505
No earners	2 664	2 574	2 332	2 143	1 883	1 786	2 076	2 228	2 451	2 610	2 616
One earner	6 815	7 027	7 091	7 351	7 441	7 462	7 693	8 153	8 012	8 074	8 052
Householder	5 590	5 817	5 841	6 167	6 127	6 132	6 436	6 832	6 725	6 788	6 724
Other family member	1 225	1 211	1 251	1 183	1 314	1 331	1 257	1 321	1 286	1 285	1 329
Two earners or more	3 527	3 675	3 692	3 712	3 840	3 702	3 748	3 652	3 733	3 720	3 836
Householder and other family member(s)	3 225	3 431	3 398	3 399	3 508	3 376	3 442	3 290	3 364	3 399	3 468
Householder not an earner	302	245	294	313	332	325	306	362	369	321	368
Families Maintained by Men, Total	3 557	3 924	3 982	4 041	4 086	4 316	4 499	4 747	4 778	4 953	5 193
No earners	357	359	344	381	376	380	461	466	530	492	537
One earner	1 800	1 972	2 104	2 027	2 044	2 223	2 319	2 434	2 466	2 573	2 661
Householder	1 548	1 667	1 791	1 725	1 721	1 879	1 911	2 026	2 053	2 152	2 196
Other family member	253	305	313	302	323	344	408	408	413	421	464
Two earners or more	1 400	1 593	1 534	1 634	1 666	1 713	1 719	1 847	1 782	1 888	1 995
Householder and other family member(s)	1 302	1 469	1 427	1 532	1 522	1 585	1 629	1 709	1 625	1 736	1 848
Householder not an earner	98	124	107	102	143	128	90	138	157	152	147
MEDIAN FAMILY INCOME											
Married-Couple Families, Total	47 000	49 614	51 475	54 043	56 792	59 200	60 100	61 000	62 388	63 627	65 586
No earners	21 888	22 622	23 782	24 525	25 262	25 356	25 900	25 954	26 312	26 798	28 376
One earner	35 100	36 468	39 140	40 519	41 261	44 424	44 400	45 000	46 546	47 749	50 000
Husband	36 052	38 150	40 300	42 000	44 200	47 010	47 500	48 004	48 948	50 000	52 000
Wife	32 098	30 301	34 050	35 625	35 546	36 458	36 140	39 072	41 180	41 000	43 505
Other family member	37 784	39 644	40 317	42 414	41 120	45 492	44 270	40 927	45 936	46 324	50 263
Two earners	53 500	56 000	58 020	61 300	64 007	67 500	69 543	71 282	73 309	75 100	76 960
Husband and wife	53 626	56 392	58 564	61 900	64 950	68 132	70 000	72 150	74 500	76 000	77 539
Husband and other family member	52 530	49 610	53 854	57 680	53 541	56 503	65 240	62 848	60 100	66 120	67 350
Husband not an earner	47 121	46 990	47 979	50 955	52 466	53 430	58 725	54 840	58 000	63 050	65 622
Three earners or more	68 996	70 400	75 593	78 973	81 940	83 990	86 090	88 632	93 000	94 212	98 000
Husband and wife	69 371	71 148	76 105	79 907	83 000	84 634	87 000	89 962	94 353	95 524	99 800
Husband, not wife	60 360	61 824	68 890	71 001	69 561	79 050	76 230	82 180	77 316	87 000	79 417
Husband not an earner	61 196	55 495	62 684	63 205	69 275	68 050	80 661	68 400	91 771	73 137	84 638
Families Maintained by Women, Total	19 306	19 416	20 470	21 875	23 100	25 000	25 064	26 000	26 000	26 400	27 000
No earners	7 440	7 092	7 476	7 737	8 010	8 988	8 160	8 808	8 344	8 400	8 228
One earner	18 824	18 500	19 000	20 000	20 092	22 306	23 008	24 597	24 752	25 040	25 308
Householder	17 890	18 000	18 000	18 800	19 000	21 400	22 001	23 760	23 832	24 801	24 505
Other family member	23 166	21 000	22 870	25 981	26 800	27 524	28 476	29 524	28 857	29 700	31 700
Two earners or more	35 000	36 400	39 275	40 000	41 144	43 035	45 244	46 580	47 576	48 549	50 000
Householder and other family member(s)	34 674	36 400	39 000	39 713	40 855	43 000	44 842	46 000	46 701	47 974	48 989
Householder not an earner	39 444	38 249	47 471	43 725	48 004	45 600	51 000	51 248	57 267	56 799	64 805
Families Maintained by Men, Total	30 000	31 500	32 984	35 000	37 000	37 040	36 000	37 440	37 914	40 000	40 293
No earners	12 240	12 030	14 252	15 468	13 752	14 946	12 840	15 200	15 408	14 167	13 950
One earner	25 337	26 100	26 897	29 125	31 038	30 160	30 800	30 139	32 097	35 000	35 001
Householder	25 069	25 874	27 000	29 125	30 483	30 816	30 500	30 014	31 355	35 000	35 075
Other family member	27 291	28 584	25 486	28 241	34 756	29 118	31 052	32 000	35 525	35 438	35 000
Two earners or more	43 100	44 275	49 900	51 288	51 040	55 010	55 024	55 000	57 840	57 600	60 024
Householder and other family member(s)	43 000	43 065	50 000	50 954	50 960	55 400	54 850	55 220	57 400	57 058	60 000
Householder not an earner	55 133	47 001	44 786	68 257	57 407	51 945	61 824	49 852	64 658	65 400	70 879

Note: See notes and definitions for information on historical comparability.

Table 1-51. Employment Status of the Foreign-Born and Native-Born Populations, by Selected Characteristics, 2004–2005

(Thousands of people, percent.)

Year and characteristic	Civilian noninstitutional population	Civilian labor force				
		Total	Participation rate	Employed	Unemployed	
					Number	Rate
2004						
TOTAL						
Both sexes, 16 years and over	223 357	147 401	66.0	139 252	8 149	5.5
Men	107 710	78 980	73.3	74 524	4 456	5.6
Women	115 647	68 421	59.2	64 728	3 694	5.4
FOREIGN BORN						
Both sexes, 16 years and over	31 763	21 433	67.5	20 255	1 178	5.5
Men	15 913	12 905	81.1	12 263	642	5.0
Women	15 849	8 528	53.8	7 992	536	6.3
Age						
16 to 24 years	4 191	2 497	59.6	2 278	219	8.8
25 to 34 years	7 821	5 988	76.6	5 670	318	5.3
35 to 44 years	7 481	6 085	81.3	5 787	298	4.9
45 to 54 years	5 342	4 305	80.6	4 096	210	4.9
55 to 64 years	3 294	2 050	62.2	1 945	105	5.1
65 years and over	3 634	507	14.0	479	28	5.5
Race and Hispanic Origin						
White, non-Hispanic	7 141	4 282	60.0	4 088	194	4.5
Black, non-Hispanic	2 360	1 731	73.4	1 595	136	7.9
Asian, non-Hispanic	7 062	4 738	67.1	4 530	208	4.4
Hispanic[1]	14 878	10 439	70.2	9 808	631	6.0
Educational Attainment						
Total, 25 years and over	27 572	18 936	68.7	17 977	959	5.1
Less than a high school diploma	8 796	5 351	60.8	4 974	377	7.0
High school graduate, no college[2]	6 929	4 707	67.9	4 493	214	4.5
Some college or associate degree	4 259	3 104	72.9	2 944	161	5.2
Bachelor's degree or higher[3]	7 587	5 773	76.1	5 566	207	3.6
NATIVE BORN						
Both sexes, 16 years and over	191 594	125 968	65.7	118 997	6 971	5.5
Men	91 797	66 075	72.0	62 261	3 813	5.8
Women	99 797	59 893	60.0	56 736	3 158	5.3
Age						
16 to 24 years	32 228	19 771	61.3	17 352	2 419	12.2
25 to 34 years	31 118	26 219	84.3	24 753	1 466	5.6
35 to 44 years	35 745	30 072	84.1	28 793	1 280	4.3
45 to 54 years	35 904	29 452	82.0	28 374	1 079	3.7
55 to 64 years	25 625	15 963	62.3	15 386	577	3.6
65 years and over	30 975	4 490	14.5	4 339	151	3.4
Race and Hispanic Origin						
White, non-Hispanic	149 414	98 920	66.2	94 480	4 440	4.5
Black, non-Hispanic	22 876	14 355	62.8	12 817	1 537	10.7
Asian, non-Hispanic	2 358	1 455	61.7	1 391	64	4.4
Hispanic[1]	13 231	8 833	66.8	8 122	711	8.0
Educational Attainment						
Total, 25 years and over	159 366	106 197	66.6	101 645	4 552	4.3
Less than a high school diploma	18 873	7 118	37.7	6 434	684	9.6
High school graduates, no college[2]	52 930	33 128	62.6	31 451	1 676	5.1
Some college or associate degree	43 297	31 334	72.4	30 033	1 301	4.2
Bachelor's degree or higher[3]	44 266	34 617	78.2	33 727	891	2.6

Note: Due to the introduction of revised population controls in January 2005, estimated levels for 2005 are not strictly comparable with those for 2004. Data for race/ethnicity groups do not sum to total because data are not presented for all races.

[1]May be of any race.
[2]Includes persons with a high school diploma or equivalent.
[3]Includes persons with bachelor's, master's, professional, and/or doctoral degrees.

Table 1-51. Employment Status of the Foreign-Born and Native-Born Populations, by Selected Characteristics, 2004–2005—*Continued*

(Thousands of people, percent.)

Year and characteristic	Civilian noninstitutional population	Civilian labor force				
		Total	Participation rate	Employed	Unemployed	
					Number	Rate
2005						
TOTAL						
Both sexes, 16 years and over	226 082	149 320	66.0	141 730	7 591	5.1
Men	109 151	80 033	73.3	75 973	4 059	5.1
Women	116 931	69 288	59.3	65 757	3 531	5.1
FOREIGN BORN						
Both sexes, 16 years and over	32 558	22 042	67.7	21 022	1 020	4.6
Men	16 321	13 263	81.3	12 720	544	4.1
Women	16 236	8 779	54.1	8 302	477	5.4
Age						
16 to 24 years	4 168	2 469	59.2	2 277	192	7.8
25 to 34 years	7 902	6 094	77.1	5 824	270	4.4
35 to 44 years	7 620	6 162	80.9	5 930	232	3.8
45 to 54 years	5 578	4 473	80.2	4 285	188	4.2
55 to 64 years	3 499	2 278	65.1	2 163	115	5.1
65 years and over	3 791	566	14.9	542	24	4.2
Race and Hispanic Origin						
White, non-Hispanic	7 239	4 351	60.1	4 187	165	3.8
Black, non-Hispanic	2 360	1 746	74.0	1 631	115	6.6
Asian, non-Hispanic	7 289	4 922	67.5	4 728	194	3.9
Hispanic[1]	15 360	10 794	70.3	10 252	541	5.0
Educational Attainment						
Total, 25 years and over	28 389	19 573	68.9	18 745	828	4.2
Less than a high school diploma	9 053	5 545	61.2	5 227	318	5.7
High school graduates, no college[2]	7 106	4 804	67.6	4 599	205	4.3
Some college or associate degree	4 354	3 181	73.1	3 064	118	3.7
Bachelor's degree and higher[3]	7 876	6 043	76.7	5 856	188	3.1
NATIVE BORN						
Both sexes, 16 years and over	193 525	127 278	65.8	120 708	6 570	5.2
Men	92 830	66 769	71.9	63 254	3 516	5.3
Women	100 695	60 509	60.1	57 454	3 055	5.0
Age						
16 to 24 years	32 505	19 821	61.0	17 493	2 328	11.7
25 to 34 years	31 162	26 247	84.2	24 856	1 391	5.3
35 to 44 years	35 385	29 868	84.4	28 699	1 168	3.9
45 to 54 years	36 529	29 930	81.9	28 922	1 008	3.4
55 to 64 years	26 666	16 701	62.6	16 186	515	3.1
65 years and over	31 278	4 712	15.1	4 552	160	3.4
Race and Hispanic Origin						
White, non-Hispanic	150 155	99 539	66.3	95 430	4 109	4.1
Black, non-Hispanic	23 283	14 694	63.1	13 155	1 538	10.5
Asian, non-Hispanic	2 444	1 496	61.2	1 434	62	4.2
Hispanic[1]	13 773	9 030	65.6	8 380	650	7.2
Educational Attainment						
Total, 25 years and over	161 019	107 457	66.7	103 215	4 242	3.9
Less than a high school diploma	18 818	7 135	37.9	6 485	649	9.1
High school graduates, no college[2]	53 302	33 392	62.6	31 799	1 593	4.8
Some college or associate degree	43 915	31 793	72.4	30 561	1 232	3.9
Bachelor's degree or higher[3]	44 984	35 137	78.1	34 369	768	2.2

Note: Due to the introduction of revised population controls in January 2005, estimated levels for 2005 are not strictly comparable with those for 2004. Data for race/ethnicity groups do not sum to total because data are not presented for all races.

[1]May be of any race.
[2]Includes persons with a high school diploma or equivalent.
[3]Includes persons with bachelor's, master's, professional, and/or doctoral degrees.

Table 1-52. Employment Status of the Foreign-Born and Native-Born Populations Age 16 Years and Over, by Sex and Presence and Age of Youngest Child, Annual Averages, 2004–2005

(Thousands of people, percent.)

Characteristic	2004			2005		
	Both sexes	Men	Women	Both sexes	Men	Women
FOREIGN BORN						
With Own Children Under 18 Years						
Civilian noninstitutional population	12 740	6 060	6 680	12 781	6 084	6 697
Civilian labor force	9 614	5 710	3 904	9 653	5 737	3 916
Participation rate	75.5	94.2	58.4	75.5	94.3	58.5
Employed	9 125	5 474	3 652	9 247	5 547	3 700
Employment-population ratio	71.6	90.3	54.7	72.3	91.2	55.2
Unemployed	489	236	253	406	190	216
Unemployment rate	5.1	4.1	6.5	4.2	3.3	5.5
With Own Children 6 to 17 Years, None Younger						
Civilian noninstitutional population	6 268	2 907	3 361	6 353	2 950	3 403
Civilian labor force	5 024	2 715	2 309	5 053	2 750	2 303
Participation rate	80.1	93.4	68.7	79.5	93.2	67.7
Employed	4 785	2 605	2 180	4 852	2 658	2 194
Employment-population ratio	76.3	89.6	64.9	76.4	90.1	64.5
Unemployed	238	110	129	201	93	108
Unemployment rate	4.7	4.0	5.6	4.0	3.4	4.7
With Own Children Under 6 Years						
Civilian noninstitutional population	6 472	3 153	3 319	6 428	3 134	3 294
Civilian labor force	4 590	2 995	1 595	4 600	2 987	1 613
Participation rate	70.9	95.0	48.1	71.6	95.3	49.0
Employed	4 340	2 869	1 471	4 395	2 889	1 505
Employment-population ratio	67.1	91.0	44.3	68.4	92.2	45.7
Unemployed	250	126	124	206	98	108
Unemployment rate	5.5	4.2	7.8	4.5	3.3	6.7
With Own Children Under 3 Years						
Civilian noninstitutional population	3 789	1 865	1 924	3 732	1 841	1 891
Civilian labor force	2 596	1 778	819	2 595	1 760	835
Participation rate	68.5	95.3	42.6	69.5	95.6	44.2
Employed	2 457	1 705	751	2 489	1 711	778
Employment-population ratio	64.8	91.4	39.1	66.7	93.0	41.1
Unemployed	139	72	67	106	49	57
Unemployment rate	5.4	4.1	8.2	4.1	2.8	6.8
With No Own Children Under 18 Years						
Civilian noninstitutional population	19 023	9 853	9 170	19 777	10 237	9 539
Civilian labor force	11 819	7 195	4 624	12 389	7 526	4 863
Participation rate	62.1	73.0	50.4	62.6	73.5	51.0
Employed	11 130	6 789	4 340	11 775	7 173	4 603
Employment-population ratio	58.5	68.9	47.3	59.5	70.1	48.2
Unemployed	690	406	283	614	354	260
Unemployment rate	5.8	5.6	6.1	5.0	4.7	5.4

Note: Due to the introduction of revised population controls in January 2005, estimated levels for 2005 are not strictly comparable with those for 2004.

Table 1-52. Employment Status of the Foreign-Born and Native-Born Populations Age 16 Years and Over, by Sex and Presence and Age of Youngest Child, Annual Averages, 2004–2005—*Continued*

(Thousands of people, percent.)

Characteristic	2004			2005		
	Both sexes	Men	Women	Both sexes	Men	Women
NATIVE BORN						
With Own Children Under 18 Years						
Civilian noninstitutional population	53 136	23 424	29 712	52 845	23 226	29 619
Civilian labor force	43 757	22 053	21 703	43 521	21 852	21 669
Participation rate	82.3	94.1	73.0	82.4	94.1	73.2
Employed	41 882	21 342	20 540	41 727	21 202	20 524
Employment-population ratio	78.8	91.1	69.1	79.0	91.3	69.3
Unemployed	1 875	711	1 163	1 794	650	1 145
Unemployment rate	4.3	3.2	5.4	4.1	3.0	5.3
With Own Children 6 to 17 Years, None Younger						
Civilian noninstitutional population	30 101	13 279	16 821	30 095	13 252	16 843
Civilian labor force	25 642	12 358	13 284	25 526	12 329	13 197
Participation rate	85.2	93.1	79.0	84.8	93.0	78.4
Employed	24 700	11 993	12 707	24 600	11 977	12 623
Employment-population ratio	82.1	90.3	75.5	81.7	90.4	74.9
Unemployed	942	365	577	926	351	574
Unemployment rate	3.7	3.0	4.3	3.6	2.9	4.4
With Own Children Under 6 Years						
Civilian noninstitutional population	23 036	10 145	12 891	22 749	9 974	12 776
Civilian labor force	18 115	9 696	8 419	17 995	9 524	8 472
Participation rate	78.6	95.6	65.3	79.1	95.5	66.3
Employed	17 182	9 349	7 833	17 127	9 225	7 901
Employment-population ratio	74.6	92.2	60.8	75.3	92.5	61.8
Unemployed	933	347	586	869	298	570
Unemployment rate	5.1	3.6	7.0	4.8	3.1	6.7
With Own Children Under 3 Years						
Civilian noninstitutional population	13 363	5 941	7 422	13 384	5 910	7 474
Civilian labor force	10 252	5 693	4 559	10 285	5 650	4 635
Participation rate	76.7	95.8	61.4	76.8	95.6	62.0
Employed	9 696	5 483	4 212	9 769	5 470	4 299
Employment-population ratio	72.6	92.3	56.8	73.0	92.6	57.5
Unemployed	556	210	346	516	180	336
Unemployment rate	5.4	3.7	7.6	5.0	3.2	7.3
With No Own Children Under 18 Years						
Civilian noninstitutional population	138 458	68 373	70 085	140 680	69 605	71 076
Civilian labor force	82 212	44 021	38 190	83 757	44 917	38 840
Participation rate	59.4	64.4	54.5	59.5	64.5	54.6
Employed	77 115	40 919	36 196	78 981	42 051	36 930
Employment-population ratio	55.7	59.8	51.6	56.1	60.4	52.0
Unemployed	5 096	3 102	1 994	4 776	2 866	1 910
Unemployment rate	6.2	7.0	5.2	5.7	6.4	4.9

Note: Due to the introduction of revised population controls in January 2005, estimated levels for 2005 are not strictly comparable with those for 2004.

Table 1-53. Employment Status of the Foreign-Born and Native-Born Populations Age 25 Years and Over, by Educational Attainment, Race, and Hispanic Origin, Annual Averages, 2004–2005

(Thousands of people, percent.)

Characteristic	2004				2005			
	Less than a high school diploma	High school graduate, no college[1]	Some college or associate degree	Bachelor's degree or higher[2]	Less than a high school diploma	High school graduate, no college[1]	Some college or associate degree	Bachelor's degree or higher[2]
FOREIGN BORN								
White, Non-Hispanic								
Civilian noninstitutional population	899	1 833	1 281	2 474	928	1 869	1 258	2 525
Civilian labor force	298	981	811	1 814	345	988	797	1 862
Participation rate	33.2	53.5	63.3	73.3	37.1	52.8	63.4	73.8
Employed	279	948	768	1 747	325	955	766	1 805
Employment-population ratio	31.1	51.7	60.0	70.6	35.0	51.1	60.9	71.5
Unemployed	19	33	43	67	19	33	31	57
Unemployment rate	6.4	3.4	5.3	3.7	5.6	3.4	3.9	3.1
Black, Non-Hispanic								
Civilian noninstitutional population	371	650	451	569	361	641	499	558
Civilian labor force	220	495	364	487	219	490	407	468
Participation rate	59.4	76.1	80.7	85.6	60.7	76.5	81.5	83.9
Employed	198	463	332	463	203	458	382	452
Employment-population ratio	53.4	71.1	73.7	81.3	56.1	71.5	76.6	80.9
Unemployed	22	32	31	25	17	32	25	17
Unemployment rate	10.1	6.5	8.6	5.0	7.5	6.5	6.1	3.6
Asian, Non-Hispanic								
Civilian noninstitutional population	874	1 291	986	3 163	857	1 332	998	3 385
Civilian labor force	390	862	727	2 394	402	845	725	2 606
Participation rate	44.6	66.8	73.8	75.7	46.9	63.5	72.7	77.0
Employed	366	819	688	2 321	378	804	702	2 524
Employment-population ratio	41.9	63.4	69.8	73.4	44.1	60.4	70.3	74.6
Unemployed	24	43	40	72	24	41	23	82
Unemployment rate	6.1	5.0	5.4	3.0	5.9	4.9	3.2	3.2
Hispanic[3]								
Civilian noninstitutional population	6 618	3 088	1 474	1 280	6 870	3 207	1 534	1 309
Civilian labor force	4 422	2 315	1 147	997	4 558	2 437	1 202	1 026
Participation rate	66.8	75.0	77.9	77.9	66.4	76.0	78.3	78.4
Employed	4 111	2 209	1 102	957	4 301	2 340	1 164	997
Employment-population ratio	62.1	71.5	74.8	74.8	62.6	72.9	75.9	76.2
Unemployed	311	105	46	40	257	98	38	29
Unemployment rate	7.0	4.6	4.0	4.0	5.6	4.0	3.1	2.9
NATIVE BORN								
White, Non-Hispanic								
Civilian noninstitutional population	12 622	42 042	34 302	38 440	12 313	42 100	34 792	38 847
Civilian labor force	4 546	25 719	24 536	29 797	4 479	25 768	24 879	30 102
Participation rate	36.0	61.0	72.0	78.0	36.0	61.0	71.5	77.5
Employed	4 193	24 615	23 681	29 079	4 157	24 740	24 058	29 490
Employment-population ratio	33.0	59.0	69.0	76.0	34.0	59.0	69.1	75.9
Unemployed	353	1 103	854	718	322	1 027	821	612
Unemployment rate	7.8	4.3	3.5	2.4	7.2	4.0	3.3	2.0
Black, Non-Hispanic								
Civilian noninstitutional population	3 391	6 600	5 068	3 097	3 464	6 778	5 039	3 211
Civilian labor force	1 228	4 400	3 768	2 554	1 277	4 538	3 780	2 617
Participation rate	36.2	66.7	74.4	82.5	36.9	66.9	75.0	81.5
Employed	1 025	4 004	3 483	2 451	1 077	4 135	3 518	2 528
Employment-population ratio	30.0	61.0	69.0	79.0	31.0	61.0	69.8	78.7
Unemployed	203	396	285	104	200	403	263	89
Unemployment rate	16.5	9.0	7.6	4.1	15.7	8.9	6.9	3.4
Asian, Non-Hispanic								
Civilian noninstitutional population	142	320	381	807	158	303	380	859
Civilian labor force	55	174	259	640	57	162	257	680
Participation rate	38.4	54.6	68.0	79.2	36.3	53.5	67.8	79.2
Employed	52	170	252	624	56	158	249	664
Employment-population ratio	37.0	53.0	66.0	77.0	35.0	52.0	65.5	77.3
Unemployed	2	4	8	16	2	5	9	17
Unemployment rate	4.2	2.4	3.0	2.5	2.8	2.8	3.4	2.4
Hispanic[3]								
Civilian noninstitutional population	2 297	3 084	2 590	1 406	2 455	3 182	2 735	1 504
Civilian labor force	1 131	2 251	2 075	1 207	1 163	2 313	2 164	1 272
Participation rate	49.2	73.0	80.1	85.9	47.4	72.7	79.1	84.5
Employed	1 024	2 120	1 966	1 170	1 066	2 195	2 064	1 235
Employment-population ratio	45.0	69.0	76.0	83.0	43.0	69.0	75.5	82.1
Unemployed	106	131	109	37	97	118	100	36
Unemployment rate	9.4	5.8	5.2	3.1	8.4	5.1	4.6	2.9

Note: Due to the introduction of revised population controls in January 2005, estimated levels for 2005 are not strictly comparable with those for 2004. Data for race/ethnicity groups do not sum to total because data are not presented for all races.

[1]Includes persons with a high school diploma or equivalent.
[2]Includes persons with bachelor's, master's, professional, and/or doctoral degrees.
[3]May be of any race.

Table 1-54. Employed Foreign-Born and Native-Born Persons Age 16 Years and Over, by Occupation and Sex, 2005 Averages

(Thousands of people, percent.)

Occupation	Foreign born			Native born		
	Both sexes	Male	Female	Both sexes	Male	Female
TOTAL EMPLOYED	21 022	12 720	8 302	120 708	63 254	57 454
Percent Employed	100.0	100.0	100.0	100.0	100.0	100.0
Management, professional, and related	26.2	23.9	29.6	36.2	33.7	39.1
Management, business, and financial operations	9.5	9.2	10.0	15.3	16.7	13.7
Management	6.6	7.2	5.7	11.0	13.1	8.7
Business and financial operations	2.9	2.0	4.3	4.3	3.6	5.0
Professional and related	16.7	14.7	19.6	21.0	16.9	25.4
Computer and mathematical	3.2	3.9	2.1	2.1	3.0	1.2
Architecture and engineering	2.2	3.0	0.9	1.9	3.2	0.5
Life, physical, and social science	1.1	1.1	1.2	1.0	1.1	0.9
Community and social services	0.9	0.8	1.2	1.6	1.2	2.1
Legal	0.5	0.3	0.6	1.3	1.2	1.3
Education, training, and library	3.2	1.9	5.2	6.2	3.0	9.7
Arts, design, entertainment, sports, and media	1.2	1.1	1.4	2.0	2.0	2.1
Health care practitioner and technical	4.3	2.6	7.1	4.8	2.3	7.6
Services	22.8	17.8	30.4	15.2	12.0	18.7
Health care support	2.6	0.6	5.6	2.1	0.4	4.0
Protective services	0.9	1.1	0.5	2.2	3.3	1.1
Food preparation and serving related	7.8	7.6	8.1	4.8	3.5	6.1
Building and grounds cleaning and maintenance	8.1	7.0	9.7	2.9	3.5	2.3
Personal care and services	3.5	1.4	6.7	3.1	1.3	5.2
Sales and office	18.0	12.9	25.9	26.7	18.3	35.9
Sales and related	9.1	8.0	11.0	12.0	11.6	12.5
Office and administrative support	8.9	5.0	14.9	14.6	6.6	23.4
Natural resources, construction, and maintenance	16.0	25.2	1.9	9.9	18.1	1.0
Farming, fishing, and forestry	1.8	2.3	1.0	0.5	0.7	0.2
Construction and extraction	11.1	17.9	0.6	5.6	10.4	0.4
Installation, maintenance, and repair	3.2	5.1	0.3	3.8	6.9	0.3
Production, transportation, and material moving	17.0	20.1	12.3	12.0	18.0	5.4
Production	10.0	10.4	9.3	6.0	8.2	3.6
Transportation and material moving	7.0	9.6	3.0	6.0	9.7	1.8

Note: Due to the introduction of revised population controls in January 2005, estimated levels for 2005 are not strictly comparable with those for 2004.

Table 1-55. Median Usual Weekly Earnings of Full-Time Wage and Salary Workers for the Foreign-Born and Native-Born Populations, by Selected Characteristics, Annual Averages, 2004–2005

(Thousands of people, dollars, percent.)

Year and characteristic	Foreign born		Native born		Earnings of foreign born as a percent of earnings of native born[1]
	Number	Median weekly earnings	Number	Median weekly earnings	
2004					
Both Sexes, 16 Years and Over	15 580	502	85 644	664	75.6
Men	9 902	518	47 099	749	69.1
Women	5 678	473	38 545	585	81.0
Age					
16 to 24 years	1 551	341	9 325	397	85.8
25 to 34 years	4 631	491	20 126	624	78.7
35 to 44 years	4 538	540	22 323	741	72.9
45 to 54 years	3 187	565	21 799	764	73.9
55 to 64 years	1 409	607	10 523	740	82.0
65 years and over	264	552	1 548	562	98.2
Race and Hispanic Origin					
White, non-Hispanic	2 852	731	66 563	702	104.1
Black, non-Hispanic	1 268	533	10 374	529	100.8
Asian, non-Hispanic	3 383	699	1 009	738	94.8
Hispanic[2]	7 899	402	6 163	539	74.5
Educational Attainment					
Total, 25 years and over	14 029	524	76 319	710	73.7
Less than a high school diploma	4 094	373	4 439	433	86.2
High school graduate, no college[3]	3 486	478	23 655	586	81.5
Some college	2 216	595	22 630	668	89.0
Bachelor's degree or higher[4]	4 234	943	25 595	994	94.9
2005					
Both Sexes, 16 Years and Over	16 340	511	87 220	677	75.6
Men	10 396	523	48 011	760	68.9
Women	5 945	487	39 210	596	81.7
Age					
16 to 24 years	1 578	353	9 529	404	87.3
25 to 34 years	4 831	495	20 181	633	78.3
35 to 44 years	4 700	587	22 403	755	77.8
45 to 54 years	3 352	563	22 299	772	73.0
55 to 64 years	1 582	607	11 192	757	80.2
65 years and over	297	494	1 616	578	85.4
Race and Hispanic Origin					
White, non-Hispanic	2 978	733	67 458	720	101.8
Black, non-Hispanic	1 326	521	10 671	521	100.0
Asian, non-Hispanic	3 541	747	1 041	777	96.1
Hispanic[2]	8 331	412	6 343	555	74.2
Educational Attainment					
Total, 25 years and over	14 762	543	77 691	724	74.9
Less than a high school diploma	4 305	385	4 557	442	87.0
High school graduates, no college[3]	3 589	496	23 926	594	83.4
Some college	2 316	592	23 155	679	87.2
Bachelor's degree and higher[4]	4 553	960	26 053	1 023	93.8

Note: Due to the introduction of revised population controls in January 2005, estimated levels for 2005 are not strictly comparable with those for 2004. Data for race/ethnicity groups do not sum to total because data are not presented for all races.

[1]These figures are computed using unrounded medians and may differ slightly from percentages computed using the rounded medians displayed in this table.
[2]May be of any race.
[3]Includes persons with a high school diploma or equivalent.
[4]Includes persons with bachelor's, master's, professional, and/or doctoral degrees.

Table 1-56. Percent Distribution of the Civilian Labor Force Age 25 to 64 Years, by Educational Attainment, Sex, and Race, March 1990–March 2006

(Thousands of people, percent.)

Sex, race, and year	Civilian labor force	Percent distribution				
		Total	Less than a high school diploma	4 years of high school only	1 to 3 years of college	4 or more years of college
Both Sexes						
1990	99 175	100.0	13.4	39.5	20.7	26.4
1991	100 480	100.0	13.0	39.4	21.1	26.5
1992	102 387	100.0	12.2	36.2	25.2	26.4
1993	103 504	100.0	11.5	35.2	26.3	27.0
1994	104 868	100.0	11.0	34.0	27.7	27.3
1995	106 519	100.0	10.8	33.1	27.8	28.3
1996	108 037	100.0	10.9	32.9	27.7	28.5
1997	110 514	100.0	10.9	33.0	27.4	28.6
1998	111 857	100.0	10.7	32.8	27.4	29.1
1999	112 542	100.0	10.3	32.3	27.4	30.0
2000	114 052	100.0	9.8	31.8	27.9	30.4
2001	115 073	100.0	9.8	31.4	28.1	30.7
2002	117 738	100.0	10.1	30.6	27.7	31.6
2003	119 261	100.0	10.1	30.1	27.8	31.9
2004	119 392	100.0	9.7	30.1	27.8	32.4
2005	120 461	100.0	9.8	30.1	27.8	32.3
2006	122 541	100.0	9.8	29.6	28.0	32.6
Men						
1990	54 476	100.0	15.1	37.2	19.7	28.0
1991	55 165	100.0	14.7	37.5	20.2	27.6
1992	55 917	100.0	13.9	34.7	23.8	27.5
1993	56 544	100.0	13.2	33.9	24.7	28.1
1994	56 633	100.0	12.7	32.9	25.8	28.6
1995	57 454	100.0	12.2	32.3	25.7	29.7
1996	58 121	100.0	12.7	32.2	26.0	29.1
1997	59 268	100.0	12.8	32.2	25.8	29.2
1998	59 905	100.0	12.3	32.3	25.8	29.6
1999	60 030	100.0	11.7	32.0	25.8	30.5
2000	60 510	100.0	11.1	31.8	26.1	30.9
2001	61 091	100.0	11.0	31.6	26.3	31.1
2002	62 794	100.0	11.8	30.6	25.9	31.7
2003	63 466	100.0	12.0	30.1	25.8	32.1
2004	63 699	100.0	11.5	30.5	25.8	32.2
2005	64 562	100.0	11.6	31.4	25.4	31.6
2006	65 708	100.0	11.8	30.7	25.7	31.8
Women						
1990	44 699	100.0	11.3	42.4	21.9	24.5
1991	45 315	100.0	10.9	41.6	22.2	25.2
1992	46 469	100.0	10.2	37.9	26.9	25.0
1993	46 961	100.0	9.3	36.7	28.2	25.8
1994	48 235	100.0	9.1	35.3	29.8	25.8
1995	49 065	100.0	9.1	34.1	30.2	26.6
1996	49 916	100.0	8.8	33.7	29.7	27.8
1997	51 246	100.0	8.7	34.0	29.3	28.0
1998	51 953	100.0	8.8	33.3	29.3	28.6
1999	52 512	100.0	8.7	32.7	29.2	29.5
2000	53 541	100.0	8.4	31.8	30.0	29.8
2001	53 982	100.0	8.5	31.1	30.1	30.2
2002	54 944	100.0	8.2	30.6	29.7	31.5
2003	55 795	100.0	8.0	30.1	30.1	31.8
2004	55 693	100.0	7.7	29.6	30.2	32.5
2005	55 899	100.0	7.8	28.6	30.5	33.1
2006	56 833	100.0	7.6	28.2	30.6	33.6

Table 1-56. Percent Distribution of the Civilian Labor Force Age 25 to 64 Years, by Educational Attainment, Sex, and Race, March 1990–March 2006—*Continued*

(Thousands of people, percent.)

Sex, race, and year	Civilian labor force	Percent distribution				
		Total	Less than a high school diploma	4 years of high school only	1 to 3 years of college	4 or more years of college
White[1]						
1990	85 238	100.0	12.6	39.6	20.6	27.1
1991	86 344	100.0	12.2	39.3	21.1	27.4
1992	87 656	100.0	11.3	36.1	25.5	27.1
1993	88 457	100.0	10.7	35.0	26.4	27.9
1994	89 009	100.0	10.5	33.7	27.7	28.1
1995	90 192	100.0	10.0	32.8	27.8	29.3
1996	91 506	100.0	10.4	32.8	27.5	29.3
1997	93 179	100.0	10.4	32.8	27.3	29.5
1998	93 527	100.0	10.2	32.7	27.4	29.8
1999	94 216	100.0	9.8	32.2	27.2	30.8
2000	95 073	100.0	9.5	31.8	27.7	31.0
2001	95 562	100.0	9.5	31.0	28.0	31.4
2002	97 699	100.0	9.8	30.6	27.6	32.0
2003	98 241	100.0	9.9	30.0	27.7	32.4
2004	98 030	100.0	9.5	29.8	27.8	32.9
2005	98 581	100.0	9.7	29.8	27.8	32.7
2006	100 205	100.0	9.7	29.3	28.1	32.9
Black[1]						
1990	10 537	100.0	19.9	42.5	22.1	15.5
1991	10 650	100.0	19.5	42.9	22.1	15.4
1992	10 936	100.0	19.2	40.3	24.9	15.6
1993	11 051	100.0	16.8	39.5	27.6	16.1
1994	11 368	100.0	14.5	39.3	29.2	17.0
1995	11 695	100.0	14.1	38.6	29.6	17.7
1996	11 891	100.0	14.2	37.2	31.2	17.4
1997	12 253	100.0	14.3	37.8	31.3	16.6
1998	12 893	100.0	14.3	37.3	30.1	18.2
1999	12 945	100.0	13.0	37.2	30.4	19.5
2000	13 383	100.0	11.8	36.1	31.5	20.7
2001	13 617	100.0	12.0	37.1	31.1	19.8
2002	13 319	100.0	12.4	34.5	32.0	21.0
2003	13 315	100.0	11.3	35.6	31.5	21.6
2004	13 372	100.0	11.0	36.6	30.5	21.9
2005	13 635	100.0	11.2	37.3	29.9	21.6
2006	13 855	100.0	10.9	35.6	30.4	23.0

[1]Beginning in 2003, persons who selected this race group only; persons who selected more than one race group are not included. Prior to 2003, persons who reported more than one race group were included in the group they identified as their main race.

Table 1-57. Labor Force Participation Rates of Persons Age 25 to 64 Years, by Educational Attainment, Sex, and Race, March 1990–March 2006

(Civilian labor force as a percent of the civilian noninstitutional population.)

Sex, race, and year	Participation rates				
	Total	Less than a high school diploma	4 years of high school only	1 to 3 years of college	4 or more years of college
Both Sexes					
1990	78.6	60.7	78.2	83.3	88.4
1991	78.6	60.7	78.1	83.2	88.4
1992	79.0	60.3	78.3	83.5	88.4
1993	78.9	59.6	77.7	82.9	88.3
1994	78.9	58.3	77.8	83.2	88.2
1995	79.3	59.8	77.3	83.2	88.7
1996	79.4	60.2	77.9	83.7	87.8
1997	80.1	61.7	78.5	83.7	88.5
1998	80.2	63.0	78.4	83.5	88.0
1999	80.0	62.7	78.1	83.0	87.6
2000	80.3	62.7	78.4	83.2	87.8
2001	80.2	63.5	78.4	83.0	87.0
2002	79.7	63.5	77.7	82.1	86.7
2003	79.4	64.1	76.9	81.9	86.2
2004	78.8	63.2	76.1	81.2	85.9
2005	78.5	62.9	75.7	81.1	85.7
2006	78.7	63.2	75.9	81.0	85.9
Men					
1990	88.8	75.1	89.9	91.5	94.5
1991	88.6	75.1	89.3	92.0	94.2
1992	88.6	75.1	89.0	91.8	93.7
1993	88.1	74.9	88.1	90.6	93.7
1994	87.0	71.5	86.8	90.3	93.2
1995	87.4	72.0	86.9	90.1	93.8
1996	87.5	74.3	86.9	90.0	92.9
1997	87.7	75.2	86.4	90.6	93.5
1998	87.8	75.3	86.7	90.0	93.4
1999	87.5	74.4	86.6	89.4	93.0
2000	87.5	74.9	86.2	88.9	93.3
2001	87.4	75.4	85.8	89.1	92.9
2002	87.0	75.5	85.3	88.8	92.4
2003	86.4	76.1	84.3	87.5	92.2
2004	85.9	75.2	83.8	87.0	91.9
2005	86.0	75.7	83.7	87.5	91.7
2006	86.0	76.3	83.4	87.8	91.7
Women					
1990	68.9	46.2	68.7	75.9	81.1
1991	69.1	46.2	68.6	75.2	81.8
1992	70.0	45.6	69.1	76.2	82.2
1993	70.0	44.2	68.8	76.1	82.2
1994	71.1	44.7	70.0	77.0	82.5
1995	71.5	47.2	68.9	77.3	82.8
1996	71.8	45.7	69.8	78.1	82.3
1997	72.8	47.1	71.4	77.6	83.2
1998	73.0	49.8	70.9	77.8	82.3
1999	72.8	50.5	70.4	77.4	81.9
2000	73.5	50.4	71.2	78.3	82.0
2001	73.4	51.7	71.3	77.7	80.9
2002	72.7	50.4	70.4	76.4	81.0
2003	72.6	50.5	69.8	77.1	80.1
2004	72.0	49.7	68.6	76.2	80.0
2005	71.4	48.7	67.4	75.8	79.8
2006	71.7	48.3	68.2	75.3	80.4

Table 1-57. Labor Force Participation Rates of Persons Age 25 to 64 Years, by Educational Attainment, Sex, and Race, March 1990–March 2006—*Continued*

(Civilian labor force as a percent of the civilian noninstitutional population.)

Sex, race, and year	Participation rates				
	Total	Less than a high school diploma	4 years of high school only	1 to 3 years of college	4 or more years of college
White[1]					
1990	79.2	62.5	78.4	83.3	88.3
1991	79.4	62.5	78.3	83.1	88.6
1992	79.8	61.5	78.7	83.8	88.7
1993	79.7	61.1	78.2	83.1	88.8
1994	79.8	60.3	78.3	83.5	88.5
1995	80.1	61.6	77.9	83.4	88.8
1996	80.4	62.5	78.6	83.9	88.2
1997	81.0	63.8	79.2	83.9	89.0
1998	80.6	63.8	78.6	83.5	88.3
1999	80.6	64.2	78.5	83.3	87.9
2000	80.8	64.2	78.7	83.1	87.9
2001	80.7	64.5	78.7	83.1	87.2
2002	80.3	65.0	78.2	82.4	87.0
2003	80.1	65.7	77.5	82.3	86.5
2004	79.5	64.6	76.7	81.6	86.2
2005	79.2	63.8	76.4	81.5	86.1
2006	79.5	65.1	76.5	81.4	86.2
Black[1]					
1990	74.6	54.5	78.2	84.2	92.0
1991	73.9	53.9	77.1	84.1	90.2
1992	74.4	55.4	76.9	83.4	89.1
1993	73.8	53.4	74.7	83.0	89.6
1994	73.5	49.4	75.2	82.4	89.5
1995	74.2	51.0	74.5	82.8	90.9
1996	73.7	50.1	74.3	83.0	87.9
1997	74.9	52.9	75.0	83.8	89.0
1998	77.7	59.3	77.0	85.0	88.8
1999	76.5	55.1	76.5	82.9	88.6
2000	77.9	55.5	77.0	84.2	90.3
2001	78.1	58.7	76.8	83.0	90.5
2002	76.4	56.6	75.0	81.7	88.9
2003	75.8	55.4	73.9	81.2	88.2
2004	75.0	55.2	73.4	79.0	87.9
2005	75.2	58.2	72.6	79.5	87.2
2006	75.0	54.0	73.3	79.6	87.7

[1]Beginning in 2003, persons who selected this race group only; persons who selected more than one race group are not included. Prior to 2003, persons who reported more than one race group were included in the group they identified as their main race.

Table 1-58. Unemployment Rates of Persons Age 25 to 64 Years, by Educational Attainment and Sex, March 1990–March 2006

(Unemployment as a percent of the civilian labor force.)

Sex, race, and year	Unemployment rates				
	Total	Less than a high school diploma	4 years of high school only	1 to 3 years of college	4 or more years of college
Both Sexes					
1990	4.5	9.6	4.9	3.7	1.9
1991	6.1	12.3	6.7	5.0	2.9
1992	6.7	13.5	7.7	5.9	2.9
1993	6.4	13.0	7.3	5.5	3.2
1994	5.8	12.6	6.7	5.0	2.9
1995	4.8	10.0	5.2	4.5	2.5
1996	4.8	10.9	5.5	4.1	2.2
1997	4.4	10.4	5.1	3.8	2.0
1998	4.0	8.5	4.8	3.6	1.8
1999	3.5	7.7	4.0	3.1	1.9
2000	3.3	7.9	3.8	3.0	1.5
2001	3.5	8.1	4.2	2.9	2.0
2002	5.0	10.2	6.1	4.5	2.8
2003	5.3	9.9	6.4	5.2	3.0
2004	5.1	10.5	5.9	4.9	2.9
2005	4.4	9.0	5.5	4.1	2.3
2006	4.1	8.3	4.7	3.9	2.3
Men					
1990	4.8	9.6	5.3	3.9	2.1
1991	6.8	13.4	7.7	5.2	3.2
1992	7.5	14.8	8.8	6.4	3.2
1993	7.3	14.1	8.7	6.3	3.4
1994	6.2	12.8	7.2	5.3	2.9
1995	5.1	10.9	5.7	4.4	2.6
1996	5.3	11.0	6.4	4.5	2.3
1997	4.7	9.9	5.6	4.0	2.1
1998	4.1	8.0	5.1	3.7	1.7
1999	3.5	7.0	4.1	3.2	1.9
2000	3.3	7.1	3.9	3.1	1.6
2001	3.7	7.5	4.6	3.2	1.9
2002	5.5	9.9	6.7	4.9	3.0
2003	5.8	9.5	6.9	6.0	3.2
2004	5.4	9.4	6.6	5.4	3.0
2005	4.7	7.9	6.0	4.3	2.5
2006	4.3	7.6	5.0	4.2	2.4
Women					
1990	4.2	9.5	4.6	3.5	1.7
1991	5.2	10.7	5.5	4.8	2.5
1992	5.7	11.4	6.5	5.3	2.5
1993	5.2	11.2	5.8	4.6	2.9
1994	5.4	12.4	6.2	4.7	2.9
1995	4.4	8.6	4.6	4.5	2.4
1996	4.1	10.7	4.4	3.8	2.1
1997	4.1	11.3	4.5	3.6	2.0
1998	3.9	9.3	4.4	3.5	1.9
1999	3.5	8.8	3.9	3.0	1.9
2000	3.2	9.1	3.6	2.9	1.4
2001	3.3	8.9	3.8	2.6	2.0
2002	4.6	10.6	5.4	4.1	2.6
2003	4.8	10.6	5.9	4.4	2.8
2004	4.7	12.2	5.2	4.3	2.9
2005	4.2	10.9	4.8	4.0	2.2
2006	3.8	9.4	4.4	3.7	2.1

Table 1-58. Unemployment Rates of Persons Age 25 to 64 Years, by Educational Attainment and Sex, March 1990–March 2006—*Continued*

(Unemployment as a percent of the civilian labor force.)

Sex, race, and year	Unemployment rates				
	Total	Less than a high school diploma	4 years of high school only	1 to 3 years of college	4 or more years of college
White[1]					
1990	4.0	8.3	4.4	3.3	1.8
1991	5.6	11.6	6.2	4.6	2.7
1992	6.0	12.9	6.8	5.3	2.7
1993	5.8	12.4	6.5	5.0	3.1
1994	5.2	11.7	5.8	4.5	2.6
1995	4.3	9.2	4.6	4.2	2.3
1996	4.2	10.2	4.6	3.7	2.1
1997	3.9	9.4	4.6	3.4	1.8
1998	3.5	7.5	4.2	3.2	1.7
1999	3.1	7.0	3.4	2.8	1.7
2000	3.0	7.5	3.3	2.7	1.4
2001	3.1	7.2	3.6	2.7	1.8
2002	4.6	9.1	5.5	4.1	2.6
2003	4.7	9.0	5.7	4.5	2.7
2004	4.6	9.6	5.4	4.4	2.8
2005	3.9	7.7	4.9	3.6	2.2
2006	3.5	7.1	4.0	3.5	2.1
Black[1]					
1990	8.6	15.9	8.6	6.5	1.9
1991	10.1	15.9	10.3	8.0	5.2
1992	12.4	17.2	14.1	10.7	4.8
1993	10.9	17.3	12.4	8.7	4.1
1994	10.6	17.4	12.2	8.3	4.9
1995	7.7	13.7	8.4	6.3	4.1
1996	8.9	15.3	10.8	6.9	3.3
1997	8.1	16.6	8.2	6.1	4.4
1998	7.3	13.4	8.4	6.4	2.1
1999	6.3	12.0	6.7	5.2	3.3
2000	5.4	10.4	6.3	4.3	2.5
2001	6.5	14.0	7.7	4.3	3.3
2002	8.1	15.4	9.7	6.0	4.1
2003	9.0	14.7	9.9	8.9	4.7
2004	8.4	15.8	9.3	7.9	3.7
2005	8.3	17.9	8.6	7.5	3.6
2006	7.8	16.4	9.0	6.5	3.6

[1]Beginning in 2003, persons who selected this race group only; persons who selected more than one race group are not included. Prior to 2003, persons who reported more than one race group were included in the group they identified as their main race.

Table 1-59. Workers Age 25 to 64 Years, by Educational Attainment, Occupation of Longest Job Held, and Sex, 2004–2005

(Thousands of people with work experience during the year.)

Year, sex, and occupation	Total	Less than a high school diploma	4 years of high school only	1 to 3 years of college	4 or more years of college
2004					
Both Sexes	123 578	12 018	37 168	34 480	39 913
Management, business, and financial operations	18 667	396	3 308	4 890	10 073
Management	13 311	347	2 586	3 444	6 934
Business and financial operations	5 356	50	722	1 446	3 139
Professional and related	26 599	203	2 290	6 031	18 075
Computer and mathematical	3 137	13	230	840	2 053
Architecture and engineering	2 470	6	263	604	1 597
Life, physical, and social science	1 249	2	99	118	1 031
Community and social services	1 918	23	188	358	1 348
Legal	1 427	5	87	251	1 083
Education, training, and library	7 740	61	652	993	6 034
Arts, design, entertainment, sports, and media	2 392	45	321	633	1 393
Health care practitioner and technical	6 267	47	450	2 234	3 537
Services	18 016	3 437	7 238	5 163	2 179
Health care support	2 526	314	997	997	219
Protective services	2 564	92	717	1 098	658
Food preparation and serving related	4 672	1 096	2 078	1 071	426
Building and grounds cleaning and maintenance	4 708	1 541	2 068	804	295
Personal care and services	3 547	395	1 379	1 193	581
Sales and office	29 571	1 490	10 335	10 658	7 087
Sales and related	12 839	825	3 991	3 983	4 040
Office and administrative support	16 732	665	6 344	6 675	3 047
Natural resources, construction, and maintenance	13 718	3 139	5 938	3 623	1 018
Farming, fishing, and forestry	947	474	297	108	68
Construction and extraction	8 076	2 095	3 585	1 883	514
Installation, maintenance, and repair	4 694	571	2 056	1 632	436
Production, transportation, and material moving	16 436	3 345	7 930	3 890	1 271
Production	9 062	1 890	4 298	2 167	706
Transportation and material moving	7 374	1 455	3 632	1 723	565
Armed forces	571	8	129	225	210
Men	65 840	7 582	20 572	16 845	20 841
Management, business, and financial operations	10 428	273	1 798	2 446	5 910
Management	8 208	249	1 596	2 011	4 352
Business and financial operations	2 219	24	203	435	1 558
Professional and related	11 365	75	867	2 116	8 306
Computer and mathematical	2 272	10	161	603	1 498
Architecture and engineering	2 135	5	230	521	1 380
Life, physical, and social science	724	. . .	67	70	586
Community and social services	773	10	68	126	569
Legal	701	. . .	10	23	668
Education, training, and library	1 916	4	85	159	1 669
Arts, design, entertainment, sports, and media	1 249	34	161	346	707
Health care practitioner and technical	1 594	11	86	268	1 228
Services	7 540	1 402	2 873	2 144	1 121
Health care support	274	28	93	119	35
Protective services	1 983	56	550	851	526
Food preparation and serving related	1 890	490	749	430	221
Building and grounds cleaning and maintenance	2 703	784	1 212	524	183
Personal care and services	688	45	269	219	157
Sales and office	10 605	520	3 210	3 437	3 439
Sales and related	6 826	304	1 873	2 068	2 582
Office and administrative support	3 779	216	1 337	1 369	857
Natural resources, construction, and maintenance	13 015	2 960	5 700	3 432	923
Farming, fishing, and forestry	704	346	228	77	53
Construction and extraction	7 826	2 056	3 493	1 798	479
Installation, maintenance, and repair	4 484	558	1 979	1 557	391
Production, transportation, and material moving	12 363	2 344	6 006	3 059	954
Production	6 231	1 157	3 011	1 588	474
Transportation and material moving	6 132	1 187	2 995	1 470	480
Armed forces	524	8	118	211	188
Women	57 740	4 436	16 594	17 636	19 070
Management, business, and financial operations	8 240	123	1 509	2 445	4 162
Management	5 103	97	990	1 433	2 582
Business and financial operations	3 137	26	519	1 011	1 581
Professional and related	15 234	127	1 423	3 915	9 769
Computer and mathematical	864	3	70	237	555
Architecture and engineering	335	2	33	84	217
Life, physical, and social science	525	2	32	47	445
Community and social services	1 144	12	120	233	779
Legal	726	5	78	228	415
Education, training, and library	5 824	57	567	834	4 365
Arts, design, entertainment, sports, and media	1 143	11	159	287	686
Health care practitioner and technical	4 673	36	364	1 966	2 308
Services	10 477	2 034	4 365	3 019	1 058
Health care support	2 251	286	904	877	184
Protective services	580	36	166	247	132
Food preparation and serving related	2 782	606	1 329	641	206
Building and grounds cleaning and maintenance	2 004	757	856	280	112
Personal care and services	2 859	350	1 110	975	424
Sales and office	18 965	971	7 125	7 221	3 648
Sales and related	6 012	521	2 117	1 915	1 459
Office and administrative support	12 953	449	5 008	5 306	2 190
Natural resources, construction, and maintenance	703	180	238	191	94
Farming, fishing, and forestry	243	128	69	31	14
Construction and extraction	250	38	92	85	35
Installation, maintenance, and repair	210	14	77	75	45
Production, transportation, and material moving	4 073	1 001	1 923	831	317
Production	2 831	733	1 287	579	232
Transportation and material moving	1 242	268	636	252	85
Armed forces	48	. . .	11	14	22

. . . = Not available.

Table 1-59. Workers Age 25 to 64 Years, by Educational Attainment, Occupation of Longest Job Held, and Sex, 2004–2005—*Continued*

(Thousands of people with work experience during the year.)

Year, sex, and occupation	Total	Less than a high school diploma	4 years of high school only	1 to 3 years of college	4 or more years of college
2005					
Both Sexes	125 664	12 170	37 080	35 438	40 976
Management, business, and financial operations	19 624	442	3 348	5 132	10 702
Management	14 083	394	2 633	3 674	7 382
Business and financial operations	5 541	48	715	1 458	3 320
Professional and related	26 851	173	2 245	6 184	18 249
Computer and mathematical	3 116	19	258	799	2 040
Architecture and engineering	2 509	3	253	662	1 592
Life, physical, and social science	1 317	. . .	87	172	1 057
Community and social services	1 992	18	163	361	1 449
Legal	1 389	6	96	237	1 050
Education, training, and library	7 659	33	574	1 030	6 022
Arts, design, entertainment, sports, and media	2 400	62	304	682	1 352
Health care practitioner and technical	6 469	30	510	2 240	3 688
Services	18 586	3 336	7 499	5 425	2 325
Health care support	2 772	301	1 092	1 044	335
Protective services	2 576	84	691	1 179	621
Food preparation and serving related	4 771	1 034	2 132	1 124	481
Building and grounds cleaning and maintenance	4 787	1 492	2 143	847	304
Personal care and services	3 680	425	1 441	1 231	584
Sales and office	29 770	1 653	9 939	10 963	7 214
Sales and related	12 984	917	3 998	4 052	4 016
Office and administrative support	16 786	736	5 941	6 912	3 198
Natural resources, construction, and maintenance	13 977	3 287	5 964	3 684	1 042
Farming, fishing, and forestry	818	431	262	74	51
Construction and extraction	8 430	2 263	3 679	1 917	571
Installation, maintenance, and repair	4 729	594	2 023	1 693	420
Production, transportation, and material moving	16 255	3 273	7 955	3 806	1 221
Production	8 835	1 887	4 220	2 098	631
Transportation and material moving	7 420	1 386	3 736	1 708	590
Armed forces	602	7	129	244	222
Men	67 099	7 739	20 592	17 354	21 416
Management, business, and financial operations	11 244	309	1 846	2 618	6 472
Management	8 840	287	1 646	2 127	4 780
Business and financial operations	2 403	21	199	491	1 692
Professional and related	11 428	75	790	2 281	8 282
Computer and mathematical	2 271	16	179	562	1 514
Architecture and engineering	2 165	3	217	590	1 355
Life, physical, and social science	728	. . .	57	103	568
Community and social services	751	5	47	116	583
Legal	636	3	4	12	618
Education, training, and library	1 958	3	51	162	1 742
Arts, design, entertainment, sports, and media	1 266	33	156	418	658
Health care practitioner and technical	1 652	12	78	318	1 244
Services	7 824	1 386	2 990	2 286	1 162
Health care support	296	12	98	108	78
Protective services	1 959	61	523	895	479
Food preparation and serving related	2 007	482	804	490	231
Building and grounds cleaning and maintenance	2 781	761	1 288	541	191
Personal care and services	781	70	276	252	183
Sales and office	10 528	583	3 076	3 500	3 369
Sales and related	6 688	329	1 826	2 131	2 403
Office and administrative support	3 840	254	1 250	1 369	967
Natural resources, construction, and maintenance	13 326	3 115	5 761	3 479	971
Farming, fishing, and forestry	612	321	209	47	35
Construction and extraction	8 185	2 215	3 597	1 830	543
Installation, maintenance, and repair	4 529	579	1 955	1 603	392
Production, transportation, and material moving	12 222	2 266	6 011	2 986	960
Production	5 988	1 106	2 861	1 570	451
Transportation and material moving	6 234	1 160	3 150	1 416	509
Armed forces	527	5	118	204	200
Women	58 567	4 432	16 488	18 085	19 561
Management, business, and financial operations	8 380	133	1 502	2 514	4 231
Management	5 243	107	986	1 547	2 602
Business and financial operations	3 138	26	516	967	1 628
Professional and related	15 424	98	1 455	3 903	9 967
Computer and mathematical	846	3	79	237	527
Architecture and engineering	344	. . .	36	72	237
Life, physical, and social science	589	. . .	30	69	489
Community and social services	1 241	13	116	245	866
Legal	753	4	92	225	432
Education, training, and library	5 701	31	523	869	4 279
Arts, design, entertainment, sports, and media	1 134	29	148	264	693
Health care practitioner and technical	4 817	18	432	1 922	2 444
Services	10 762	1 949	4 510	3 139	1 163
Health care support	2 476	289	994	936	257
Protective services	617	23	168	284	142
Food preparation and serving related	2 765	552	1 328	634	250
Building and grounds cleaning and maintenance	2 005	731	855	306	113
Personal care and services	2 899	355	1 165	979	400
Sales and office	19 242	1 070	6 863	7 464	3 845
Sales and related	6 296	589	2 173	1 921	1 614
Office and administrative support	12 946	481	4 690	5 543	2 232
Natural resources, construction, and maintenance	651	172	203	205	71
Farming, fishing, and forestry	206	110	53	28	16
Construction and extraction	245	48	82	87	28
Installation, maintenance, and repair	200	15	68	90	28
Production, transportation, and material moving	4 033	1 008	1 944	820	261
Production	2 847	781	1 359	528	179
Transportation and material moving	1 186	226	585	293	82
Armed forces	75	2	11	40	23

. . . = Not available.

Table 1-60. Percent Distribution of Workers Age 25 to 64 Years, by Educational Attainment, Occupation of Longest Job Held, and Sex, 2004–2005

(Percent of total workers in occupation.)

Year, sex, and occupation	Total	Less than a high school diploma	4 years of high school only	1 to 3 years of college	4 or more years of college
2004					
Both Sexes	100.0	9.7	30.1	27.9	32.3
Management, business, and financial operations	100.0	2.1	17.7	26.2	54.0
Management	100.0	2.6	19.4	25.9	52.1
Business and financial operations	100.0	0.9	13.5	27.0	58.6
Professional and related	100.0	0.8	8.6	22.7	68.0
Computer and mathematical	100.0	0.4	7.3	26.8	65.5
Architecture and engineering	100.0	0.3	10.6	24.5	64.6
Life, physical, and social science	100.0	0.1	7.9	9.4	82.5
Community and social services	100.0	1.2	9.8	18.7	70.3
Legal	100.0	0.4	6.1	17.6	75.9
Education, training, and library	100.0	0.8	8.4	12.8	78.0
Arts, design, entertainment, sports, and media	100.0	1.9	13.4	26.5	58.2
Health care practitioner and technical	100.0	0.7	7.2	35.6	56.4
Services	100.0	19.1	40.2	28.7	12.1
Health care support	100.0	12.4	39.5	39.5	8.7
Protective services	100.0	3.6	27.9	42.8	25.7
Food preparation and serving related	100.0	23.5	44.5	22.9	9.1
Building and grounds cleaning and maintenance	100.0	32.7	43.9	17.1	6.3
Personal care and services	100.0	11.1	38.9	33.6	16.4
Sales and office	100.0	5.0	35.0	36.0	24.0
Sales and related	100.0	6.4	31.1	31.0	31.5
Office and administrative support	100.0	4.0	37.9	39.9	18.2
Natural resources, construction, and maintenance	100.0	22.9	43.3	26.4	7.4
Farming, fishing, and forestry	100.0	50.0	31.4	11.4	7.1
Construction and extraction	100.0	25.9	44.4	23.3	6.4
Installation, maintenance, and repair	100.0	12.2	43.8	34.8	9.3
Production, transportation, and material moving	100.0	20.4	48.2	23.7	7.7
Production	100.0	20.9	47.4	23.9	7.8
Transportation and material moving	100.0	19.7	49.3	23.4	7.7
Armed forces	100.0	1.4	22.6	39.3	36.7
Men	100.0	11.5	30.7	25.9	31.9
Management, business, and financial operations	100.0	2.6	17.2	23.5	56.7
Management	100.0	3.0	19.4	24.5	53.0
Business and financial operations	100.0	1.1	9.1	19.6	70.2
Professional and related	100.0	0.7	7.6	18.6	73.1
Computer and mathematical	100.0	0.5	7.1	26.5	65.9
Architecture and engineering	100.0	0.2	10.8	24.4	64.6
Life, physical, and social science	100.0	. . .	9.3	9.7	81.0
Community and social services	100.0	1.4	8.8	16.3	73.6
Legal	100.0	. . .	1.4	3.3	95.3
Education, training, and library	100.0	0.2	4.4	8.3	87.1
Arts, design, entertainment, sports, and media	100.0	2.8	12.9	27.7	56.6
Health care practitioner and technical	100.0	0.7	5.4	16.8	77.1
Services	100.0	18.6	38.1	28.4	14.9
Health care support	100.0	10.2	33.8	43.4	12.6
Protective services	100.0	2.8	27.7	42.9	26.5
Food preparation and serving related	100.0	25.9	39.6	22.8	11.7
Building and grounds cleaning and maintenance	100.0	29.0	44.8	19.4	6.8
Personal care and services	100.0	6.5	39.0	31.8	22.7
Sales and office	100.0	4.9	30.3	32.4	32.4
Sales and related	100.0	4.4	27.4	30.3	37.8
Office and administrative support	100.0	5.7	35.4	36.2	22.7
Natural resources, construction, and maintenance	100.0	22.7	43.8	26.4	7.1
Farming, fishing, and forestry	100.0	49.1	32.4	10.9	7.6
Construction and extraction	100.0	26.3	44.6	23.0	6.1
Installation, maintenance, and repair	100.0	12.4	44.1	34.7	8.7
Production, transportation, and material moving	100.0	19.0	48.6	24.7	7.7
Production	100.0	18.6	48.3	25.5	7.6
Transportation and material moving	100.0	19.3	48.8	24.0	7.8
Armed forces	100.0	1.5	22.5	40.2	35.8
Women	100.0	7.6	28.2	30.9	33.4
Management, business, and financial operations	100.0	1.5	18.3	29.7	50.5
Management	100.0	1.9	19.4	28.1	50.6
Business and financial operations	100.0	0.8	16.5	32.2	50.4
Professional and related	100.0	0.8	9.3	25.7	64.1
Computer and mathematical	100.0	0.4	8.1	27.4	64.2
Architecture and engineering	100.0	0.4	9.8	25.0	64.7
Life, physical, and social science	100.0	0.3	6.1	9.0	84.6
Community and social services	100.0	1.1	10.5	20.3	68.1
Legal	100.0	0.7	10.7	31.5	57.1
Education, training, and library	100.0	1.0	9.7	14.3	75.0
Arts, design, entertainment, sports, and media	100.0	1.0	13.9	25.1	60.0
Health care practitioner and technical	100.0	0.8	7.8	42.1	49.4
Services	100.0	19.4	41.7	28.8	10.1
Health care support	100.0	12.7	40.2	39.0	8.2
Protective services	100.0	6.2	28.7	42.5	22.7
Food preparation and serving related	100.0	21.8	47.8	23.0	7.4
Building and grounds cleaning and maintenance	100.0	37.8	42.7	14.0	5.6
Personal care and services	100.0	12.2	38.8	34.1	14.8
Sales and office	100.0	5.1	37.6	38.1	19.2
Sales and related	100.0	8.7	35.2	31.9	24.3
Office and administrative support	100.0	3.5	38.7	41.0	16.9
Natural resources, construction, and maintenance	100.0	25.6	33.9	27.2	13.4
Farming, fishing, and forestry	100.0	52.7	28.5	12.9	5.9
Construction and extraction	100.0	15.4	36.7	33.9	14.0
Installation, maintenance, and repair	100.0	6.4	36.6	35.6	21.3
Production, transportation, and material moving	100.0	24.6	47.2	20.4	7.8
Production	100.0	25.9	45.5	20.4	8.2
Transportation and material moving	100.0	21.6	51.3	20.3	6.8
Armed forces	100.0	. . .	23.9	29.6	46.5

. . . = Not available.

Table 1-60. Percent Distribution of Workers Age 25 to 64 Years, by Educational Attainment, Occupation of Longest Job Held, and Sex, 2004–2005—*Continued*

(Percent of total workers in occupation.)

Year, sex, and occupation	Total	Less than a high school diploma	4 years of high school only	1 to 3 years of college	4 or more years of college
2005					
Both Sexes	100.0	9.7	29.5	28.2	32.6
Management, business, and financial operations	100.0	2.3	17.1	26.2	54.5
Management	100.0	2.8	18.7	26.1	52.4
Business and financial operations	100.0	0.9	12.9	26.3	59.9
Professional and related	100.0	0.6	8.4	23.0	68.0
Computer and mathematical	100.0	0.6	8.3	25.6	65.5
Architecture and engineering	100.0	0.1	10.1	26.4	63.4
Life, physical, and social science	100.0	. . .	6.6	13.1	80.3
Community and social services	100.0	0.9	8.2	18.1	72.7
Legal	100.0	0.5	6.9	17.1	75.6
Education, training, and library	100.0	0.4	7.5	13.5	78.6
Arts, design, entertainment, sports, and media	100.0	2.6	12.7	28.4	56.3
Health care practitioner and technical	100.0	0.5	7.9	34.6	57.0
Services	100.0	17.9	40.4	29.2	12.5
Health care support	100.0	10.8	39.4	37.7	12.1
Protective services	100.0	3.3	26.8	45.8	24.1
Food preparation and serving related	100.0	21.7	44.7	23.6	10.1
Building and grounds cleaning and maintenance	100.0	31.2	44.8	17.7	6.4
Personal care and services	100.0	11.6	39.2	33.4	15.9
Sales and office	100.0	5.6	33.4	36.8	24.2
Sales and related	100.0	7.1	30.8	31.2	30.9
Office and administrative support	100.0	4.4	35.4	41.2	19.1
Natural resources, construction, and maintenance	100.0	23.5	42.7	26.4	7.5
Farming, fishing, and forestry	100.0	52.7	32.0	9.1	6.2
Construction and extraction	100.0	26.8	43.6	22.7	6.8
Installation, maintenance, and repair	100.0	12.6	42.8	35.8	8.9
Production, transportation, and material moving	100.0	20.1	48.9	23.4	7.5
Production	100.0	21.4	47.8	23.7	7.1
Transportation and material moving	100.0	18.7	50.3	23.0	8.0
Armed forces	100.0	1.1	21.4	40.5	37.0
Men	100.0	. . .	. . .	. . .	. . .
Management, business, and financial operations	100.0	2.7	16.4	23.3	57.6
Management	100.0	3.3	18.6	24.1	54.1
Business and financial operations	100.0	0.9	8.3	20.4	70.4
Professional and related	100.0	0.7	6.9	20.0	72.5
Computer and mathematical	100.0	0.7	7.9	24.7	66.7
Architecture and engineering	100.0	0.1	10.0	27.2	62.6
Life, physical, and social science	100.0	. . .	7.8	14.1	78.0
Community and social services	100.0	0.7	6.3	15.4	77.6
Legal	100.0	0.4	0.6	1.9	97.0
Education, training, and library	100.0	0.1	2.6	8.3	89.0
Arts, design, entertainment, sports, and media	100.0	2.6	12.4	33.0	52.0
Health care practitioner and technical	100.0	0.7	4.7	19.3	75.3
Services	100.0	17.7	38.2	29.2	14.8
Health care support	100.0	4.1	33.0	36.5	26.4
Protective services	100.0	3.1	26.7	45.7	24.5
Food preparation and serving related	100.0	24.0	40.1	24.4	11.5
Building and grounds cleaning and maintenance	100.0	27.4	46.3	19.4	6.9
Personal care and services	100.0	9.0	35.4	32.2	23.4
Sales and office	100.0	5.5	29.2	33.2	32.0
Sales and related	100.0	4.9	27.3	31.9	35.9
Office and administrative support	100.0	6.6	32.6	35.6	25.2
Natural resources, construction, and maintenance	100.0	23.4	43.2	26.1	7.3
Farming, fishing, and forestry	100.0	52.4	34.2	7.6	5.8
Construction and extraction	100.0	27.1	43.9	22.4	6.6
Installation, maintenance, and repair	100.0	12.8	43.2	35.4	8.7
Production, transportation, and material moving	100.0	18.5	49.2	24.4	7.9
Production	100.0	18.5	47.8	26.2	7.5
Transportation and material moving	100.0	18.6	50.5	22.7	8.2
Armed forces	100.0	0.9	22.5	38.7	37.9
Women	100.0	. . .	. . .	. . .	. . .
Management, business, and financial operations	100.0	1.6	17.9	30.0	50.5
Management	100.0	2.0	18.8	29.5	49.6
Business and financial operations	100.0	0.8	16.4	30.8	51.9
Professional and related	100.0	0.6	9.4	25.3	64.6
Computer and mathematical	100.0	0.4	9.3	28.0	62.3
Architecture and engineering	100.0	. . .	10.4	20.9	68.7
Life, physical, and social science	100.0	. . .	5.1	11.8	83.1
Community and social services	100.0	1.1	9.3	19.8	69.8
Legal	100.0	0.5	12.2	29.9	57.4
Education, training, and library	100.0	0.5	9.2	15.2	75.1
Arts, design, entertainment, sports, and media	100.0	2.6	13.0	23.3	61.1
Health care practitioner and technical	100.0	0.4	9.0	39.9	50.7
Services	100.0	18.1	41.9	29.2	10.8
Health care support	100.0	11.7	40.1	37.8	10.4
Protective services	100.0	3.8	27.2	46.0	23.0
Food preparation and serving related	100.0	20.0	48.0	22.9	9.1
Building and grounds cleaning and maintenance	100.0	36.5	42.6	15.3	5.6
Personal care and services	100.0	12.2	40.2	33.8	13.8
Sales and office	100.0	5.6	35.7	38.8	20.0
Sales and related	100.0	9.4	34.5	30.5	25.6
Office and administrative support	100.0	3.7	36.2	42.8	17.2
Natural resources, construction, and maintenance	100.0	26.5	31.1	31.5	10.9
Farming, fishing, and forestry	100.0	53.4	25.6	13.5	7.6
Construction and extraction	100.0	19.5	33.6	35.6	11.4
Installation, maintenance, and repair	100.0	7.4	33.9	45.0	13.8
Production, transportation, and material moving	100.0	25.0	48.2	20.3	6.5
Production	100.0	27.4	47.7	18.5	6.3
Transportation and material moving	100.0	19.1	49.4	24.7	6.9
Armed forces	100.0	2.2	14.2	53.4	30.3

. . . = Not available.

Table 1-61. Median Annual Earnings of Year-Round Full-Time Wage and Salary Workers Age 25 to 64 Years, by Educational Attainment and Sex, 2000–2005

(Thousands of workers, dollars.)

Year and sex	Total	Less than a high school diploma	4 years of high school only	1 to 3 years of college	4 or more years of college
2000					
Both Sexes					
Number of workers	84 337	7 354	26 144	24 064	26 775
Median annual earnings	35 000	20 000	28 600	34 000	50 000
Men					
Number of workers	48 816	4 738	15 057	13 242	15 780
Median annual earnings	40 000	22 500	33 000	40 000	60 000
Women					
Number of workers	35 521	2 616	11 087	10 822	10 995
Median annual earnings	29 000	16 000	24 000	28 000	40 000
2001					
Both Sexes					
Number of workers	84 743	7 623	25 522	23 719	27 879
Median annual earnings	35 000	20 800	29 000	35 000	50 000
Men					
Number of workers	48 887	5 049	14 655	12 968	16 215
Median annual earnings	40 000	24 000	33 800	40 000	60 000
Women					
Number of workers	35 856	2 574	10 867	10 751	11 664
Median annual earnings	30 000	17 000	24 000	30 000	42 000
2002					
Both Sexes					
Number of workers	84 702	7 578	25 078	23 604	28 443
Median annual earnings	36 000	21 000	30 000	35 100	52 000
Men					
Number of workers	48 687	5 102	14 306	12 677	16 602
Median annual earnings	41 000	23 400	34 000	41 500	61 000
Women					
Number of workers	36 015	2 476	10 772	10 927	11 841
Median annual earnings	30 000	18 000	25 000	30 000	43 500
2003					
Both Sexes					
Number of workers	85 058	7 245	25 352	23 702	28 759
Median annual earnings	37 752	21 000	30 000	36 000	53 000
Men					
Number of workers	48 988	4 879	14 657	12 766	16 686
Median annual earnings	42 000	24 000	35 000	42 000	62 000
Women					
Number of workers	36 070	2 366	10 695	10 936	12 073
Median annual earnings	32 000	18 000	25 111	31 000	45 000
2004					
Both Sexes					
Number of workers	86 306	7 648	25 786	23 897	28 976
Median annual earnings	38 000	21 840	30 000	37 000	55 000
Men					
Number of workers	49 904	5 178	15 263	12 822	16 642
Median annual earnings	42 900	24 000	35 000	43 000	65 000
Women					
Number of workers	36 402	2 470	10 523	11 074	12 334
Median annual earnings	32 000	18 000	25 280	31 200	45 000
2005					
Both Sexes					
Number of workers	88 415	7 758	26 023	24 623	30 012
Median annual earnings	39 768	22 880	31 000	38 000	55 000
Men					
Number of workers	51 022	5 376	15 451	13 199	16 996
Median annual earnings	44 000	25 000	35 360	45 000	65 000
Women					
Number of workers	37 393	2 381	10 571	11 424	13 016
Median annual earnings	33 644	18 200	26 000	32 000	46 700

NOTES AND DEFINITIONS

CONTINGENT AND ALTERNATIVE EMPLOYMENT

Data on contingent workers is collected through a supplement to the Current Population Survey (CPS), a monthly survey of about 60,000 households that provides data on employment and unemployment for the nation. The Census Bureau conducts the CPS for the Bureau of Labor Statistics (BLS). The purpose of this supplement is to obtain information from workers on whether they held contingent jobs (jobs expected to last for only a limited period of time). Information is also collected on several alternative employment arrangements, namely working on call and as an independent contractor, as well as working through temporary help agencies or contract firms.

Several major changes introduced into the CPS in 2003 affect the data that presented in this *Handbook*. These include the introduction of Census 2000 population controls, the use of new questions about race and Hispanic or Latino ethnicity, the presentation of data for Asians, and the introduction of new industry and occupational classification systems. For a detailed discussion of these changes and their impact on CPS data, see "Revisions to the Current Population Survey Effective in January 2003" in the February 2003 issue of *Employment and Earnings*, available on the BLS Web site at <http://www.bls.gov/c ps/rvcps03.pdf>. All employed persons, except unpaid family workers, were included in the February 2005 supplement. For persons holding more than one job, the questions referred to the characteristics of their main job—the job at which they worked the most hours. Similar surveys were conducted in the Februaries of 1995, 1997, 1999, and 2001, and 2005.

Defining and Estimating the Contingent Workforce

Contingent workers are defined as those who do not have an explicit or implicit contract for long-term employment. Several pieces of data are collected in the supplement; these allow the existence of a contingent employment arrangement to be discerned. Included information consists of the following: whether the job is temporary or not expected to continue, how long the worker expects to be able to hold the job, and how long the worker has held the job. For workers who have a job with an intermediary (namely a temporary help agency or a contract company), information is collected about their employment at the place they are assigned to work by the intermediary as well as about their employment with the intermediary itself.

The key factor used to determine whether a worker's job fits the conceptual definition of contingent is whether the job is temporary or not expected to continue. The first questions in the supplement ask: (1) "Some people are in temporary jobs that last only for a limited time or until the completion of a project. Is your job temporary?" (2) "Provided the economy does not change and your job performance is adequate, can you continue to work for your current employer as long as you wish?" Respondents who answer "yes" to the first question or "no" to the second are then asked a series of questions designed to distinguish persons in temporary jobs from those who, for personal reasons, are temporarily holding jobs that offer the opportunity of ongoing employment.

To assess the impact of altering some of the defining factors on the estimated size of the contingent workforce, three measures of contingent employment were developed:

1) Estimate one, which is the narrowest of the three estimates, measures contingent workers as wage and salary workers who expect to work in their current job for one year or less and who have worked for their current employer for one year or less. Self-employed workers, both incorporated and unincorporated, and independent contractors are excluded from the count of contingent workers under estimate one; individuals who work for temporary help agencies or contract companies are considered contingent under estimate one only if they expect their employment arrangement with the temporary help or contract company to last for one year or less and they have worked for the company for one year or less.

2) Estimate two expands the measure of the contingent work force by including the self-employed—both the incorporated and the unincorporated—and independent contractors who expect to be, and have been, in such employment arrangements for one year or less. (The questions asked of the self-employed are different from those asked of wage and salary workers.) In addition, temporary help and contract company workers are classified as contingent under estimate two if they have worked and expect to work with customers to whom they have been assigned for one year or less.

3) Estimate three expands the count of contingency by removing the one-year requirement on both expected duration of the job and current tenure for wage and salary workers. The estimate effectively includes all the wage and salary workers who do not expect their employment to last, except for those who, for personal reasons, expect to leave jobs that they would otherwise be able to keep. Thus, a worker who has held a job for five years could be considered contingent if he or she now views the job as temporary.

Sources of Additional Information

A complete description of the survey and additional tables are available from BLS news release USDL 05-1433, "Contingent and Alternative Employment Arrangements," available at <http://www.bls.gov>.

Table 1-62. Employed Contingent and Noncontingent Workers, by Selected Characteristics, February 2005

(Thousands of people.)

Characteristic	Total employed	Contingent workers			Noncontingent workers
		Estimate 1	Estimate 2	Estimate 3	
Age and Sex					
Both sexes, 16 years and over	138 952	2 504	3 177	5 705	133 247
16 to 19 years	5 510	308	338	476	5 035
20 to 24 years	13 114	606	688	1 077	12 036
25 to 34 years	30 103	693	874	1 447	28 656
35 to 44 years	34 481	415	580	1 044	33 437
45 to 54 years	32 947	263	387	875	32 072
55 to 64 years	17 980	143	198	536	17 445
65 years and over	4 817	76	111	250	4 567
Men, 16 years and over	73 946	1 325	1 648	2 914	71 032
16 to 19 years	2 579	145	157	229	2 351
20 to 24 years	6 928	358	394	597	6 331
25 to 34 years	16 624	395	512	829	15 794
35 to 44 years	18 523	245	303	540	17 983
45 to 54 years	17 193	95	140	368	16 825
55 to 64 years	9 485	70	107	261	9 224
65 years and over	2 615	17	35	92	2 523
Women, 16 years and over	65 006	1 180	1 529	2 790	62 216
16 to 19 years	2 931	163	182	247	2 684
20 to 24 years	6 186	249	294	481	5 705
25 to 34 years	13 480	298	362	618	12 862
35 to 44 years	15 958	171	277	504	15 454
45 to 54 years	15 754	168	247	508	15 247
55 to 64 years	8 495	73	91	275	8 220
65 years and over	2 202	58	76	158	2 044
Race and Hispanic Origin					
White	115 043	2 007	2 534	4 521	110 522
Black	14 688	296	387	660	14 028
Asian	6 083	121	161	350	5 733
Hispanic[1]	18 062	603	704	1 185	16 876
Full- or Part-Time Status					
Full-time workers	113 798	1 367	1 812	3 410	110 387
Part-time workers	25 154	1 137	1 364	2 294	22 860

Note: Noncontingent workers are those who do not fall into any estimate of contingent workers. Estimates for the above race groups (White, Black, and Asian) do not sum to total because data are not presented for all races. Detail for other characteristics may not sum to total due to rounding.

[1]May be of any race.

Table 1-63. Employed Contingent and Noncontingent Workers, by Occupation and Industry, February 2005

(Thousands of people, percent.)

Characteristic	Contingent workers			Noncontingent workers
	Estimate 1	Estimate 2	Estimate 3	
OCCUPATION				
Total, 16 years and over	2 504	3 177	5 705	133 247
Percent Distribution	100.0	100.0	100.0	100.0
Management, professional, and related	28.4	30.7	35.9	35.2
Management, business, and financial operations	5.5	8.0	8.7	14.6
Professional and related	22.8	22.6	27.2	20.6
Services	17.3	17.6	15.7	15.6
Sales and office	24.3	22.5	20.6	26.0
Sales and related	4.9	6.0	5.7	12.1
Office and administrative support	19.4	16.5	14.8	13.9
Natural resources, construction, and maintenance	16.5	16.7	16.1	10.2
Farming, fishing, and forestry	2.4	2.0	2.1	0.5
Construction and extraction	11.4	12.3	11.1	5.8
Installation, maintenance, and repair	2.7	2.4	2.9	3.8
Production, transportation, and material moving	13.6	12.5	11.7	13.1
Production	4.5	4.0	5.2	6.8
Transportation and material moving	9.1	8.5	6.5	6.2
INDUSTRY				
Total, 16 years and over	2 504	3 177	5 705	133 247
Percent Distribution	100.0	100.0	100.0	100.0
Agriculture and related industries	2.5	2.3	1.7	1.3
Mining	0.7	0.6	0.4	0.4
Construction	13.0	14.0	12.3	7.2
Manufacturing	6.7	6.0	6.4	11.9
Wholesale trade	3.2	2.9	2.2	3.2
Retail trade	6.4	6.7	6.4	12.4
Transportation and utilities	5.0	4.7	3.7	5.3
Information	1.6	1.3	2.1	2.3
Financial activities	1.4	2.6	3.1	7.7
Professional and business services	18.2	20.7	18.2	9.7
Education and health services	23.5	21.8	27.1	20.8
Leisure and hospitality	10.1	8.9	7.4	8.1
Other services	5.0	5.3	4.9	4.7
Public administration	2.8	2.3	4.0	4.9

Note: Noncontingent workers are those who do not fall into any estimate of contingent workers. Detail may not sum to total due to rounding.

Table 1-64. Employed Workers with Alternative and Traditional Work Arrangements, by Selected Characteristics, February 2005

(Thousands of people.)

Characteristic	Total employed	Workers with alternative arrangements				Workers with traditional arrangements
		Independent contractors	On-call workers	Temporary help agency workers	Workers provided by contract firms	
Age and Sex						
Both sexes, 16 years and over	138 952	10 342	2 454	1 217	813	123 843
16 to 19 years	5 510	89	133	33	7	5 194
20 to 24 years	13 114	356	355	202	87	12 055
25 to 34 years	30 103	1 520	535	362	205	27 427
35 to 44 years	34 481	2 754	571	253	196	30 646
45 to 54 years	32 947	2 799	417	200	186	29 324
55 to 64 years	17 980	1 943	267	135	114	15 496
65 years and over	4 817	881	175	33	18	3 701
Men, 16 years and over	73 946	6 696	1 241	574	561	64 673
16 to 19 years	2 579	32	82	24	7	2 389
20 to 24 years	6 928	194	200	107	61	6 331
25 to 34 years	16 624	1 006	299	185	138	14 950
35 to 44 years	18 523	1 824	252	120	140	16 130
45 to 54 years	17 193	1 764	209	71	143	15 003
55 to 64 years	9 485	1 287	108	52	70	7 954
65 years and over	2 615	589	91	16	3	1 917
Women, 16 years and over	65 006	3 647	1 212	643	252	59 170
16 to 19 years	2 931	57	52	9	0	2 805
20 to 24 years	6 186	162	155	95	27	5 724
25 to 34 years	13 480	514	236	177	67	12 477
35 to 44 years	15 958	930	319	133	57	14 516
45 to 54 years	15 754	1 035	208	129	43	14 322
55 to 64 years	8 495	656	158	83	44	7 542
65 years and over	2 202	292	84	17	15	1 785
Race and Hispanic Origin						
White	115 043	9 169	2 097	840	637	102 052
Black	14 688	583	212	276	121	13 471
Asian	6 083	370	64	63	43	5 538
Hispanic[1]	18 062	951	385	255	133	16 202
Full- or Part-time Status						
Full-time workers	113 798	7 732	1 370	979	695	102 889
Part-time workers	25 154	2 611	1 084	238	119	20 954

Note: Workers with traditional arrangements are those who do not fall into any of the "alternative arrangements" categories. Detail may not add to totals because the total employed includes day laborers (an alternative arrangement not shown separately) and a small number of workers who were both "on call" and "provided by contract firms." Estimates for the above race groups (White, Black, and Asian) do not sum to totals because data are not presented for all races. Detail for other characteristics may not sum to total due to rounding.

[1]May be of any race.

Table 1-65. Employed Contingent and Noncontingent Workers and Those with Alternative and Traditional Work Arrangements, by Health Insurance Coverage and Eligibility for Employer-Provided Pension Plans, February 2005

(Thousands of people, percent.)

Characteristic	Total employed	Percent with health insurance coverage		Percent eligible for employer-provided pension plan[1]	
		Total	Provided by employer[2]	Total	Included in employer-provided pension plan
Contingent Workers					
Estimate 1	2 504	51.8	9.4	9.2	4.6
Estimate 2	3 177	52.5	7.9	8.3	4.1
Estimate 3	5 705	59.1	18.1	18.6	12.4
Noncontingent Workers	133 247	79.4	52.1	49.6	44.7
With Alternative Arrangements					
Independent contractors	10 342	69.3	X	2.6	1.9
On-call workers	2 454	66.9	25.7	33.2	27.8
Temporary help agency workers	1 217	39.7	8.3	8.9	3.8
Workers provided by contract firms	813	80.2	48.9	42.6	33.5
With Traditional Arrangements	123 843	80.0	56.0	52.9	47.7

Note: Noncontingent workers are those who do not fall into any estimate of contingent workers. Workers with traditional arrangements are those who do not fall into any of the "alternative arrangements" categories.

[1]Excludes the self-employed (incorporated and unincorporated); includes independent contractors who were self-employed.
[2]Excludes the self-employed (incorporated and unincorporated) and independent contractors.
X = Not applicable.

Table 1-66. Median Usual Weekly Earnings of Full- and Part-Time Contingent Wage and Salary Workers and Those with Alternative Work Arrangements, by Sex, Race, and Hispanic Origin, February 2005

(Dollars.)

Characteristic	Contingent workers			Workers with alternative arrangements			
	Estimate 1	Estimate 2	Estimate 3	Independent contractors	On-call workers	Temporary help agency workers	Workers provided by contract firms
Full-Time Workers							
Total, 16 years and over	405	411	488	716	519	414	756
Men	427	440	505	794	586	405	860
Women	376	383	423	462	394	424	595
White	413	421	498	731	561	418	772
Black	344	375	387	474	303	375	(1)
Asian	(1)	(1)	619	889	(1)	(1)	(1)
Hispanic[2]	335	331	370	603	417	311	513
Part-Time Workers							
Total, 16 years and over	152	152	161	253	173	224	204
Men	165	169	183	330	206	253	(1)
Women	142	138	149	216	159	202	(1)
White	154	154	163	252	177	247	(1)
Black	133	133	145	196	(1)	(1)	(1)
Asian	(1)	(1)	190	(1)	(1)	(1)	0
Hispanic[2]	152	153	175	207	249	(1)	(1)

Note: Earnings data for contingent workers exclude the incorporated self-employed and independent contractors. Data for independent contractors include the incorporated and unincorporated self-employed. However, these groups are excluded from the data for workers with other arrangements. Full- or part-time status is determined by hours usually worked at the sole or primary job.

[1] Data not shown where base is less than 100,000.
[2] May be of any race.

NOTES AND DEFINITIONS

FLEXIBLE WORKERS

These data and other information on work schedules were obtained from a supplement to the May 2004 Current Population Survey (CPS). This was the first time since 2001 that this supplemental survey was conducted. Respondents to the May 2004 supplement answered questions about flexible and shift schedules, their reasons for working particular shifts, the beginning and ending hours of their workdays, the availability of formal flextime programs and home-based work, and other related topics. The data cover the incidence and nature of flexible and shift schedules and pertain to wage and salary workers who usually work 35 hours or more per week at their principal job. The data exclude all self-employed persons, regardless of whether or not their businesses were incorporated.

Sources of Additional Information

For further information see BLS news release USDL 05-1198, "Workers on Flexible and Shift Schedules in May 2004," at <http://www.bls.gov>.

Table 1-67. Flexible Schedules: Full-Time Wage and Salary Workers, by Selected Characteristics, May 2004

(Thousands of people, percent.)

Characteristic	Both sexes			Men			Women		
	Total[1]	With flexible schedules		Total[1]	With flexible schedules		Total[1]	With flexible schedules	
		Number	Percent of total		Number	Percent of total		Number	Percent of total
Age									
Total, 16 years and over	99 778	27 411	27.5	56 412	15 853	28.1	43 366	11 558	26.7
16 to 19 years	1 427	336	23.6	903	185	20.5	524	151	28.9
20 years and over	98 351	27 075	27.5	55 509	15 668	28.2	42 842	11 406	26.6
20 to 24 years	9 004	2 058	22.9	5 147	1 065	20.7	3 856	993	25.8
25 to 34 years	24 640	6 902	28.0	14 358	4 051	28.2	10 283	2 851	27.7
35 to 44 years	26 766	7 807	29.2	15 424	4 605	29.9	11 342	3 202	28.2
45 to 54 years	24 855	6 651	26.8	13 440	3 769	28.0	11 415	2 882	25.2
55 to 64 years	11 745	3 181	27.1	6 383	1 865	29.2	5 361	1 316	24.5
65 years and over	1 341	475	35.4	757	314	41.4	585	161	27.6
Race and Hispanic Origin									
White	80 498	23 121	28.7	46 222	13 582	29.4	34 276	9 539	27.8
Black	12 578	2 476	19.7	6 447	1 193	18.5	6 131	1 283	20.9
Asian	4 136	1 132	27.4	2 300	720	31.3	1 836	412	22.4
Hispanic[2]	14 110	2 596	18.4	8 621	1 430	16.6	5 489	1 166	21.2
Marital Status									
Married, spouse present	57 630	16 270	28.2	34 926	10 382	29.7	22 704	5 888	25.9
Not married	42 148	11 141	26.4	21 486	5 471	25.5	20 662	5 670	27.4
Never married	25 144	6 693	26.6	14 469	3 605	24.9	10 676	3 088	28.9
Other marital status	17 004	4 448	26.2	7 018	1 866	26.6	9 986	2 582	25.9
Presence and Age of Children									
Without own children under 18 years	61 761	16 759	27.1	34 680	9 410	27.1	27 081	7 349	27.1
With own children under 18 years	38 018	10 652	28.0	21 733	6 443	29.6	16 285	4 209	25.8
With youngest child 6 to 17 years	21 739	5 960	27.4	11 477	3 341	29.1	10 262	2 619	25.5
With youngest child under 6 years	16 279	4 692	28.8	10 256	3 102	30.2	6 023	1 590	26.4

Note: Data relate to the sole or principal job of full-time wage and salary workers and exclude all self-employed persons, regardless of whether or not their businesses were incorporated. Detail for the above race and Hispanic origin groups will not sum to total because data for the "other races" group are not presented. Own children include sons, daughters, stepchildren, and adopted children. Not included are nieces, nephews, grandchildren, and other related and unrelated children.

[1]Includes persons who did not provide information on flexible schedules.
[2]May be of any race.

Table 1-68. Flexible Schedules: Full-Time Wage and Salary Workers, by Sex, Occupation, and Industry, May 2004

(Thousands of people, percent.)

Occupation and industry	Both sexes			Men			Women		
	Total[1]	With flexible schedules		Total[1]	With flexible schedules		Total[1]	With flexible schedules	
		Number	Percent of total		Number	Percent of total		Number	Percent of total
Occupation									
Total, 16 years and over	99 778	27 411	27.5	56 412	15 853	28.1	43 366	11 558	26.7
Management, professional, and related	36 200	13 325	36.8	17 911	7 832	43.7	18 289	5 492	30.0
Management, business, and financial operations	14 496	6 483	44.7	7 969	3 741	46.9	6 527	2 742	42.0
Management	10 036	4 598	45.8	6 000	2 862	47.7	4 035	1 736	43.0
Business and financial operations	4 461	1 885	42.3	1 969	879	44.7	2 492	1 006	40.4
Professional and related	21 704	6 842	31.5	9 942	4 091	41.1	11 762	2 751	23.4
Computer and mathematical	2 683	1 405	52.4	2 023	1 085	53.6	660	320	48.5
Architecture and engineering	2 478	1 080	43.6	2 147	917	42.7	330	163	49.3
Life, physical, and social science	1 016	483	47.5	640	285	44.6	376	198	52.6
Community and social services	1 866	860	46.1	786	430	54.7	1 080	430	39.8
Legal	1 118	497	44.5	536	312	58.2	582	185	31.8
Education, training, and library	6 414	843	13.1	1 779	374	21.0	4 635	469	10.1
Arts, design, entertainment, sports, and media	1 502	613	40.8	915	396	43.3	587	217	37.0
Health care practitioner and technical	4 626	1 060	22.9	1 115	291	26.1	3 511	769	21.9
Services	13 423	2 849	21.2	6 858	1 339	19.5	6 566	1 510	23.0
Health care support	1 908	315	16.5	199	37	18.7	1 708	278	16.3
Protective services	2 224	419	18.8	1 807	312	17.2	417	107	25.7
Food preparation and serving related	3 881	972	25.0	2 086	524	25.1	1 795	448	25.0
Building and grounds cleaning and maintenance	3 481	531	15.2	2 260	318	14.1	1 221	213	17.4
Personal care and services	1 929	612	31.7	505	148	29.2	1 424	465	32.6
Sales and office	24 359	7 196	29.5	9 561	3 069	32.1	14 798	4 127	27.9
Sales and related	9 634	3 669	38.1	5 683	2 305	40.6	3 952	1 364	34.5
Office and administrative support	14 724	3 527	24.0	3 878	764	19.7	10 847	2 763	25.5
Natural resources, construction, and maintenance	10 848	1 908	17.6	10 403	1 820	17.5	445	88	19.8
Farming, fishing, and forestry	744	172	23.1	591	132	22.4	152	39	25.7
Construction and extraction	5 825	942	16.2	5 750	925	16.1	74	17	(2)
Installation, maintenance, and repair	4 280	795	18.6	4 061	762	18.8	218	32	14.7
Production, transportation, and material moving	14 948	2 133	14.3	11 679	1 793	15.3	3 268	340	10.4
Production	8 281	1 030	12.4	5 928	806	13.6	2 353	224	9.5
Transportation and material moving	6 666	1 102	16.5	5 751	986	17.1	915	116	12.7
Industry									
Private sector	82 870	23 978	28.9	48 724	14 119	29.0	34 145	9 859	28.9
Agriculture and related industries	888	233	26.3	702	180	25.6	186	53	28.7
Nonagricultural industries	81 982	23 745	29.0	48 023	13 939	29.0	33 959	9 806	28.9
Mining	446	102	22.9	416	84	20.2	30	18	(2)
Construction	6 617	1 341	20.3	6 059	1 153	19.0	558	188	33.7
Manufacturing	15 125	3 631	24.0	10 659	2 638	24.7	4 466	993	22.2
Durable goods	9 249	2 351	25.4	6 881	1 794	26.1	2 368	558	23.6
Nondurable goods	5 875	1 280	21.8	3 777	844	22.3	2 098	436	20.8
Wholesale and retail trade	14 008	4 100	29.3	8 717	2 544	29.2	5 291	1 557	29.4
Wholesale trade	3 771	1 209	32.1	2 698	910	33.7	1 072	300	27.9
Retail trade	10 237	2 891	28.2	6 019	1 634	27.1	4 219	1 257	29.8
Transportation and utilities	4 226	1 086	25.7	3 454	906	26.2	771	179	23.2
Transportation and warehousing	3 482	912	26.2	2 858	767	26.8	624	145	23.3
Utilities	744	173	23.3	596	139	23.4	147	34	23.0
Information[3]	2 716	948	34.9	1 674	600	35.8	1 041	348	33.4
Publishing, except Internet	648	274	42.3	364	165	45.4	284	109	38.4
Motion picture and sound recording industries	211	74	35.3	162	62	38.5	49	12	(2)
Broadcasting, except Internet	512	116	22.7	319	79	24.7	193	37	19.4
Telecommunications	1 180	419	35.5	732	254	34.7	448	164	36.7
Financial activities	7 341	2 767	37.7	3 117	1 323	42.4	4 224	1 444	34.2
Finance and insurance	5 537	2 056	37.1	2 100	943	44.9	3 437	1 113	32.4
Finance	3 633	1 218	33.5	1 443	584	40.5	2 190	633	28.9
Insurance	1 904	838	44.0	657	359	54.6	1 247	480	38.5
Real estate and rental and leasing	1 805	711	39.4	1 017	380	37.3	787	332	42.1
Professional and business services	8 997	3 381	37.6	5 342	2 072	38.8	3 655	1 309	35.8
Professional and technical services	5 476	2 570	46.9	3 113	1 596	51.3	2 364	974	41.2
Management, administrative, and waste services	3 521	811	23.0	2 229	477	21.4	1 292	335	25.9
Education and health services	12 485	3 202	25.6	2 969	862	29.0	9 517	2 339	24.6
Educational services	2 260	541	23.9	812	246	30.3	1 448	295	20.4
Health care and social assistance	10 226	2 661	26.0	2 157	616	28.6	8 069	2 045	25.3
Leisure and hospitality	6 111	1 686	27.6	3 458	956	27.6	2 653	730	27.5
Arts, entertainment, and recreation	1 134	312	27.5	630	165	26.2	504	147	29.2
Accommodation and food services	4 977	1 374	27.6	2 828	791	28.0	2 149	583	27.1
Accommodation	1 123	252	22.4	546	147	26.9	577	105	18.2
Food services and drinking places	3 854	1 122	29.1	2 282	644	28.2	1 572	478	30.4
Other services	3 911	1 502	38.4	2 158	801	37.1	1 753	701	40.0
Other services, except private households	3 584	1 370	38.2	2 140	792	37.0	1 444	577	40.0
Other services, private households	327	132	40.4	18	9	(2)	309	123	39.9
Public sector	16 909	3 433	20.3	7 688	1 734	22.6	9 221	1 699	18.4
Federal government	2 786	803	28.8	1 617	453	28.0	1 169	351	30.0
State government	4 724	1 340	28.4	2 089	640	30.7	2 635	700	26.6
Local government	9 399	1 289	13.7	3 982	641	16.1	5 417	648	12.0

Note: Data relate to the sole or principal job of full-time wage and salary workers and exclude all self-employed persons, regardless of whether or not their businesses were incorporated.

[1]Includes persons who did not provide information on flexible schedules.
[2]Percent not shown where base is less than 75,000.
[3]Includes other industries not shown separately.

Table 1-69. Flexible Schedules: Full-Time Wage and Salary Workers, by Formal Flextime Program Status, Occupation, and Industry, May 2004

(Thousands of people, percent.)

Occupation and industry	Total[1]	With flexible schedules	With a formal flextime program		
			Number	Percent of total employed	Percent of workers with flexible schedules
Occupation					
Total, 16 years and over	99 778	27 411	10 642	10.7	38.8
Management, professional, and related	36 200	13 325	5 137	14.2	38.6
Management, business, and financial operations	14 496	6 483	2 293	15.8	35.4
Management	10 036	4 598	1 436	14.3	31.2
Business and financial operations	4 461	1 885	857	19.2	45.5
Professional and related	21 704	6 842	2 844	13.1	41.6
Computer and mathematical	2 683	1 405	729	27.1	51.8
Architecture and engineering	2 478	1 080	509	20.5	47.1
Life, physical, and social science	1 016	483	203	19.9	42.0
Community and social services	1 866	860	325	17.4	37.8
Legal	1 118	497	140	12.6	28.2
Education, training, and library	6 414	843	278	4.3	33.0
Arts, design, entertainment, sports, and media	1 502	613	272	18.1	44.4
Health care practitioner and technical	4 626	1 060	389	8.4	36.6
Services	13 423	2 849	1 188	8.9	41.7
Health care support	1 908	315	139	7.3	44.3
Protective services	2 224	419	192	8.6	45.8
Food preparation and serving related	3 881	972	423	10.9	43.5
Building and grounds cleaning and maintenance ...	3 481	531	178	5.1	33.5
Personal care and services	1 929	612	256	13.3	41.8
Sales and office	24 359	7 196	2 734	11.2	38.0
Sales and related	9 634	3 669	1 175	12.2	32.0
Office and administrative support	14 724	3 527	1 559	10.6	44.2
Natural resources, construction, and maintenance ...	10 848	1 908	697	6.4	36.5
Farming, fishing, and forestry	744	172	47	6.3	27.1
Construction and extraction	5 825	942	416	7.1	44.2
Installation, maintenance, and repair	4 280	795	234	5.5	29.5
Production, transportation, and material moving	14 948	2 133	885	5.9	41.5
Production	8 281	1 030	490	5.9	47.6
Transportation and material moving	6 666	1 102	395	5.9	35.8
Industry					
Private sector	82 870	23 978	8 816	10.6	36.8
Agriculture and related industries	888	233	53	6.0	22.9
Nonagricultural industries	81 982	23 745	8 762	10.7	36.9
Mining	446	102	47	10.5	46.1
Construction	6 617	1 341	493	7.5	36.8
Manufacturing	15 125	3 631	1 618	10.7	44.6
Durable goods	9 249	2 351	1 061	11.5	45.1
Nondurable goods	5 875	1 280	557	9.5	43.5
Wholesale and retail trade	14 008	4 100	1 302	9.3	31.8
Wholesale trade	3 771	1 209	300	8.0	24.8
Retail trade	10 237	2 891	1 002	9.8	34.6
Transportation and utilities	4 226	1 086	432	10.2	39.8
Transportation and warehousing	3 482	912	335	9.6	36.7
Utilities	744	173	97	13.0	55.9
Information[2]	2 716	948	371	13.7	39.2
Publishing, except Internet	648	274	102	15.8	37.3
Motion picture and sound recording industries ...	211	74	33	15.9	(3)
Broadcasting, except Internet	512	116	43	8.4	37.2
Telecommunications	1 180	419	170	14.4	40.5
Financial activities	7 341	2 767	1 066	14.5	38.5
Finance and insurance	5 537	2 056	868	15.7	42.2
Finance	3 633	1 218	425	11.7	34.9
Insurance	1 904	838	443	23.3	52.9
Real estate and rental and leasing	1 805	711	198	11.0	27.9
Professional and business services	8 997	3 381	1 294	14.4	38.3
Professional and technical services	5 476	2 570	991	18.1	38.6
Management, administrative, and waste services ...	3 521	811	303	8.6	37.3
Education and health services	12 485	3 202	1 118	9.0	34.9
Educational services	2 260	541	156	6.9	28.8
Health care and social assistance	10 226	2 661	962	9.4	36.2
Leisure and hospitality	6 111	1 686	598	9.8	35.4
Arts, entertainment, and recreation	1 134	312	84	7.4	27.1
Accommodation and food services	4 977	1 374	513	10.3	37.4
Accommodation	1 123	252	105	9.3	41.5
Food services and drinking places	3 854	1 122	408	10.6	36.4
Other services	3 911	1 502	422	10.8	28.1
Other services, except private households	3 584	1 370	404	11.3	29.5
Other services, private households	327	132	18	5.5	13.6
Public sector	16 909	3 433	1 826	10.8	53.2
Federal government	2 786	803	561	20.1	69.9
State government	4 724	1 340	665	14.1	49.6
Local government	9 399	1 289	600	6.4	46.5

Note: Data relate to the sole or principal job of full-time wage and salary workers and exclude all self-employed persons, regardless of whether or not their businesses were incorporated.

[1]Includes persons who did not provide information on flexible schedules.
[2]Includes other industries not shown separately.
[3]Percent not shown where base is less than 75,000.

Table 1-70. Shift Usually Worked: Full-Time Wage and Salary Workers, by Selected Characteristics, May 2004

(Thousands of people, percent.)

Characteristic	Total[1]	Regular daytime schedule	Shift workers						
			Total	Evening shift	Night shift	Rotating shift	Split shift	Employer-arranged irregular schedule	Other shift
Age and Sex									
Both sexes, 16 years and over	99 778	84.6	14.8	4.7	3.2	2.5	0.5	3.1	0.7
16 to 19 years	1 427	64.9	34.6	14.5	4.4	6.1	1.0	8.3	0.2
20 years and over	98 351	84.9	14.6	4.6	3.2	2.5	0.5	3.0	0.7
20 to 24 years	9 004	76.8	22.3	8.8	3.7	3.3	0.9	4.6	0.9
25 to 34 years	24 640	84.1	15.2	5.0	3.4	2.7	0.5	2.8	0.8
35 to 44 years	26 766	85.4	14.1	4.1	3.2	2.5	0.4	3.1	0.7
45 to 54 years	24 855	86.8	12.8	3.6	3.2	2.3	0.5	2.5	0.7
55 to 64 years	11 745	87.1	12.5	3.8	2.6	2.0	0.4	3.0	0.7
65 years and over	1 341	88.8	10.3	3.5	1.8	1.4	0.5	2.9	0.2
Men	56 412	82.7	16.7	5.2	3.6	2.8	0.5	3.6	0.9
Women	43 366	87.0	12.4	4.1	2.8	2.2	0.5	2.4	0.4
Race and Hispanic Origin									
White	80 498	85.8	13.7	4.1	3.0	2.3	0.5	3.1	0.7
Black	12 578	78.0	20.8	7.9	4.5	4.1	0.4	3.0	0.7
Asian	4 136	83.6	15.7	5.4	4.1	1.6	1.2	2.6	0.8
Hispanic[2]	14 110	83.1	16.0	5.8	3.9	2.1	0.6	2.6	0.9
Marital Status and Presence and Age of Children									
Men									
Married, spouse present	34 926	84.8	14.9	3.9	3.3	2.9	0.5	3.4	0.9
Not married	21 486	79.5	19.7	7.4	3.9	2.6	0.7	4.0	1.0
Never married	14 469	78.6	20.6	8.1	3.8	2.6	0.8	4.2	1.0
Other marital status	7 018	81.4	17.8	5.9	4.2	2.8	0.4	3.6	1.0
Without own children under 18 years	34 680	81.8	17.6	6.0	3.6	2.7	0.6	3.8	0.9
With own children under 18 years	21 733	84.3	15.3	4.0	3.6	3.0	0.5	3.2	1.0
With youngest child 6 to 17 years	11 477	85.1	14.6	3.9	3.2	3.1	0.2	3.4	0.8
With youngest child under 6 years	10 256	83.5	16.1	4.2	3.9	2.9	0.8	3.0	1.2
Women									
Married, spouse present	22 704	90.4	9.2	2.8	2.4	1.4	0.3	1.9	0.3
Not married	20 662	83.2	16.0	5.6	3.2	3.0	0.6	2.9	0.6
Never married	10 676	81.2	17.9	6.3	3.0	3.6	0.8	3.6	0.6
Other marital status	9 986	85.5	13.9	4.8	3.5	2.3	0.4	2.1	0.6
Without own children under 18 years	27 081	86.4	13.0	4.1	2.7	2.5	0.6	2.7	0.4
With own children under 18 years	16 285	87.9	11.5	4.3	2.9	1.7	0.3	1.9	0.4
With youngest child 6 to 17 years	10 262	89.1	10.5	3.4	3.0	1.6	0.2	1.8	0.5
With youngest child under 6 years	6 023	86.0	13.2	5.8	2.7	1.8	0.4	2.1	0.4

Note: Data relate to the sole or principal job of full-time wage and salary workers and exclude all self-employed persons, regardless of whether or not their businesses were incorporated. Detail for the above race and Hispanic origin groups will not sum to total because data for the "other races" group are not presented. Own children include sons, daughters, stepchildren, and adopted children. Not included are nieces, nephews, grandchildren, and other related and unrelated children.

[1] Includes persons who did not provide information on shift usually worked.
[2] May be of any race.

Table 1-71. Shift Usually Worked: Full-Time Wage and Salary Workers, by Occupation and Industry, May 2004

(Thousands of people, civilian labor force as a percent of the civilian noninstitutional population.)

Occupation and industry	Total[1]	Regular daytime schedule	Shift workers						
			Total	Evening shift	Night shift	Rotating shift	Split shift	Employer-arranged irregular schedule	Other shift
Occupation									
Total, 16 years and over	99 778	84.6	14.8	4.7	3.2	2.5	0.5	3.1	0.7
Management, professional, and related	36 200	91.9	7.6	1.7	1.6	1.3	0.3	2.2	0.5
Management, business, and financial operations	14 496	94.6	5.0	1.1	0.5	0.9	0.2	2.0	0.3
Management	10 036	93.6	6.1	1.4	0.5	1.1	0.3	2.4	0.4
Business and financial operations	4 461	96.8	2.7	0.5	0.6	0.4	0.1	0.9	0.2
Professional and related	21 704	90.1	9.4	2.1	2.4	1.6	0.3	2.3	0.7
Computer and mathematical	2 683	95.2	4.1	1.1	1.3	0.8	0.3	0.4	0.4
Architecture and engineering	2 478	95.7	3.9	0.9	1.2	0.7	0.1	0.7	0.4
Life, physical, and social science	1 016	93.9	5.8	1.1	1.4	2.0	0.0	1.2	0.1
Community and social services	1 866	87.0	12.7	1.9	1.3	2.2	0.3	4.9	2.0
Legal	1 118	97.4	1.8	0.0	0.0	0.0	0.2	1.4	0.2
Education, training, and library	6 414	97.3	2.3	0.6	0.1	0.2	0.4	0.9	0.2
Arts, design, entertainment, sports, and media	1 502	84.7	14.7	3.1	1.6	2.2	0.4	6.0	1.2
Health care practitioner and technical	4 626	74.5	24.6	5.8	8.3	4.4	0.5	4.4	1.1
Services	13 423	66.5	32.6	12.5	6.2	5.2	1.4	5.5	1.7
Health care support	1 908	70.4	28.0	12.5	7.1	3.8	0.7	3.1	0.7
Protective services	2 224	48.3	50.6	14.4	12.9	11.9	0.6	6.2	4.3
Food preparation and serving related	3 881	58.7	40.4	17.6	3.4	5.8	3.3	8.9	1.1
Building and grounds cleaning and maintenance	3 481	82.1	17.5	8.3	5.4	1.5	0.5	1.1	0.7
Personal care and services	1 929	70.9	28.1	7.3	4.6	4.5	1.0	8.1	2.7
Sales and office	24 359	87.3	12.0	3.5	2.6	2.3	0.3	2.8	0.3
Sales and related	9 634	83.8	15.2	3.5	1.9	3.8	0.6	5.0	0.4
Office and administrative support	14 724	89.6	9.9	3.6	3.0	1.4	0.2	1.4	0.3
Natural resources, construction, and maintenance	10 848	92.0	7.5	2.1	1.9	1.3	0.1	1.5	0.5
Farming, fishing, and forestry	744	89.8	9.8	0.6	2.4	1.4	1.0	2.4	2.0
Construction and extraction	5 825	95.1	4.4	0.8	0.8	1.2	0.1	1.3	0.3
Installation, maintenance, and repair	4 280	88.2	11.4	4.3	3.4	1.5	0.0	1.7	0.5
Production, transportation, and material moving	14 948	73.3	26.2	9.1	6.5	4.2	0.8	4.6	1.1
Production	8 281	75.0	24.4	10.1	7.1	4.7	0.3	1.4	0.8
Transportation and material moving	6 666	71.2	28.5	7.8	5.7	3.7	1.4	8.4	1.5
Industry									
Private sector	82 870	84.0	15.4	5.0	3.3	2.6	0.5	3.3	0.7
Agriculture and related industries	888	90.1	9.9	1.4	2.3	1.1	1.0	3.2	1.0
Nonagricultural industries	81 982	83.9	15.5	5.1	3.3	2.6	0.5	3.3	0.7
Mining	446	68.0	31.9	3.6	4.9	15.1	0.2	6.1	2.1
Construction	6 617	96.6	2.9	0.5	0.5	0.3	0.0	1.3	0.2
Manufacturing	15 125	81.5	18.1	7.2	5.2	3.3	0.3	1.2	0.8
Durable goods	9 249	85.3	14.4	6.7	4.2	1.9	0.2	0.7	0.7
Nondurable goods	5 875	75.6	23.8	8.1	6.8	5.4	0.5	1.9	1.1
Wholesale and retail trade	14 008	82.9	16.3	4.4	3.2	3.6	0.4	4.1	0.5
Wholesale trade	3 771	91.5	8.0	2.7	1.8	0.7	0.1	2.3	0.2
Retail trade	10 237	79.8	19.4	5.0	3.7	4.6	0.5	4.8	0.6
Transportation and utilities	4 226	71.4	27.9	5.0	4.8	4.0	1.7	11.0	1.3
Transportation and warehousing	3 482	67.5	31.8	5.6	5.6	3.9	1.9	13.1	1.4
Utilities	744	89.5	9.5	1.9	0.8	4.4	0.9	1.1	0.5
Information[2]	2 716	87.3	11.7	4.2	2.4	1.7	0.1	2.6	0.6
Publishing, except Internet	648	87.6	10.3	2.3	3.6	0.8	0.3	2.0	1.3
Motion picture and sound recording industries	211	85.0	15.0	5.5	2.2	1.8	0.0	5.5	0.0
Broadcasting, except Internet	512	84.4	15.0	6.4	0.1	2.9	0.3	3.3	1.3
Telecommunications	1 180	88.8	10.5	3.6	2.7	1.9	0.0	2.3	0.0
Financial activities	7 341	94.0	5.4	2.0	0.6	0.6	0.1	1.8	0.3
Finance and insurance	5 537	96.7	2.8	1.2	0.4	0.5	0.1	0.5	0.1
Finance	3 633	96.8	2.6	1.2	0.5	0.5	0.0	0.3	0.1
Insurance	1 904	96.5	3.1	1.2	0.3	0.4	0.2	0.8	0.2
Real estate and rental and leasing	1 805	85.6	13.4	4.3	1.4	1.0	0.2	5.9	0.7
Professional and business services	8 997	92.0	7.8	2.7	2.4	0.7	0.1	1.4	0.5
Professional and technical services	5 476	96.5	3.2	0.6	0.5	0.4	0.1	1.3	0.4
Management, administrative, and waste services ...	3 521	84.9	15.0	6.1	5.3	1.1	0.2	1.5	0.8
Education and health services	12 485	83.2	16.0	5.5	4.5	2.4	0.5	2.3	0.7
Educational services	2 260	93.9	5.6	3.0	0.4	0.3	0.5	1.3	0.2
Health care and social assistance	10 226	80.9	18.3	6.0	5.4	2.9	0.5	2.6	0.8
Leisure and hospitality	6 111	60.8	38.3	15.2	4.8	5.2	2.4	9.4	1.2
Arts, entertainment, and recreation	1 134	67.7	31.9	10.2	7.9	1.6	0.7	9.2	2.1
Accommodation and food services	4 977	59.3	39.8	16.4	4.1	6.0	2.9	9.5	1.0
Accommodation	1 123	70.2	29.4	11.1	6.6	4.2	0.7	5.9	0.9
Food services and drinking places	3 854	56.1	42.8	17.9	3.3	6.6	3.5	10.5	1.0
Other services	3 911	88.9	10.6	1.5	1.0	1.9	0.3	4.8	1.0
Other services, except private households	3 584	89.3	10.3	1.4	1.0	1.9	0.3	4.9	0.8
Other services, private households	327	85.0	14.1	3.3	0.6	2.7	0.6	4.0	3.0
Public sector	16 909	87.6	11.9	3.4	2.9	2.4	0.4	1.9	0.9
Federal government	2 786	84.8	14.7	4.4	4.9	1.2	0.2	3.1	0.7
State government	4 724	87.9	11.5	3.8	3.3	1.9	0.4	1.4	0.7
Local government	9 399	88.3	11.3	2.9	2.0	3.0	0.4	1.8	1.1

Note: Data relate to the sole or principal job of full-time wage and salary workers and exclude all self-employed persons, regardless of whether or not their businesses were incorporated.

[1]Includes persons who did not provide information on shift usually worked.
[2]Includes other industries not shown seperately.

CHAPTER TWO

EMPLOYMENT, HOURS, AND EARNINGS

EMPLOYMENT AND HOURS

HIGHLIGHTS

The employment, hours, and earnings data in this section are derived from the Current Employment Statistics (CES) survey, which covers 400,000 establishments, and are presented by industry and state. The employment numbers differ from those presented in Chapter 1 from the household survey because of the dissimilarities in methodology, concepts, definitions, and coverage. As the CES survey data are obtained from payroll records, they are consistent with industry classifications. The data on hours and earnings are also likely to be more accurate.

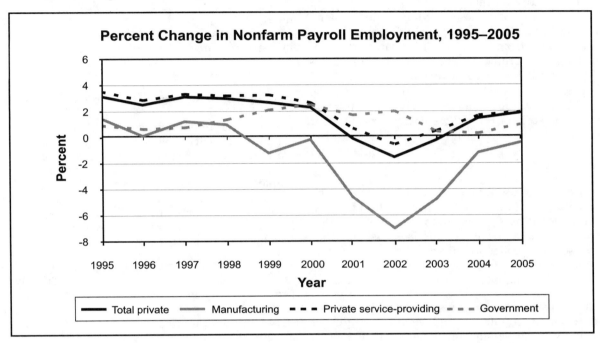

Total employment increased 1.5 percent from 2004 to 2005, as private sector employment rose 1.7 percent and government employment went up 0.8 percent. Manufacturing employment continued to decline; it dropped very slowly, decreasing at a rate of less than 1 percent. (See Table 2-1.)

OTHER HIGHLIGHTS

- In 2005, total employment increased by more than 2 million jobs, with the private service-providing sector contributing 1.8 million jobs (more than 90 percent of the total). (See Table 2-1.)

- The construction industry was again a leader in employment gains in 2005, adding 300,000 jobs and increasing by 4.3 percent from 2004. The information sector declined slightly, with a drop in employment of 52,000 jobs. (See Table 2-1.)

- Total government employment increased by 180,000 jobs in 2005; this was largely the result of an increase in local government employment. (See Table 2-1.)

- Average weekly hours of production or nonsupervisory workers in private industry increased by 0.1 hours; however, the index of aggregate hours increased by 2.4 hours as employment increased. (See Tables 2-6 and 2-9.)

NOTES AND DEFINITIONS

EMPLOYMENT, HOURS, AND EARNINGS

Collection and Coverage

The Bureau of Labor Statistics (BLS) works with State Employment Security Agencies (SESAs) to conduct the Current Employment Statistics (CES), or establishment, survey. This survey collects monthly data on employment, hours, and earnings from a sample of nonfarm establishments (including government). The CES sample includes about 160,000 businesses and government agencies and covers approximately 400,000 individual worksites. The active CES sample includes approximately one-third of all nonfarm payroll workers. From these data, a large number of employment, hours, and earnings series with considerable industrial and geographic detail are prepared and published.

The most frequently used data collection method is the touchtone data entry (TDE) system. Under the TDE system, the respondent uses a touchtone telephone to call a toll-free number and activate an interview session. Other frequently used data collection methods include computer-assisted telephone interviewing (CATI), electronic files transmission (EDI), and interviews over the Internet.

Establishment survey data are adjusted annually to accord with comprehensive counts of employment in March of the preceding year; these adjustments are called "benchmarks." All estimates back to the most recent benchmark month are subject to revision each year when new benchmarks become available. National benchmarks are published 11 months after the benchmark month (March). For example, the revised estimates based on the March 2003 benchmarks were released in February 2004. The benchmarks are derived mainly from employment reports from all employers subject to unemployment insurance. The related series on production and nonsupervisory workers, hours, and earnings are recalculated to be consistent with the employment benchmarks.

Concepts and Definitions

Industry classification

The CES survey completed a conversion from its original quota sample design to a probability-based sample survey design and switched from the Standard Industrial Classification (SIC) system to the North American Industry Classification System (NAICS) in 2003. The industry-coding update included reconstruction of historical estimates in order to preserve time series for data users. The foundation of industrial classification with NAICS has changed how establishments are classified into industries and how businesses, as they exist today, are recognized.

Establishments reporting on BLS Form 790 are classified into industries on the basis of their primary activity. Those that use comparable capital equipment, labor, and raw material inputs are classified together. This information is collected on a supplement to the quarterly unemployment insurance tax reports filed by employers. For an establishment engaging in more than one activity, the entire employment of the establishment is included under the industry indicated by the principal activity.

Industry employment

Employment data refer to persons on establishment payrolls who received pay for any part of the pay period containing the 12th day of the month. The data exclude proprietors, the self-employed, unpaid volunteer or family workers, farm workers, and domestic workers. Salaried officers of corporations are included. Government employment covers only civilian employees; military personnel are excluded. Employees of the Central Intelligence Agency, the National Security Agency, the National Imagery and Mapping Agency, and the Defense Intelligence Agency are also excluded.

Persons on establishment payrolls who are on paid sick leave (for cases in which pay is received directly from the firm), paid holiday, or vacation leave, or who work during part of the pay period despite being unemployed or on strike during the rest of the period are counted as employed. Not counted as employed are persons who are on layoff, on leave without pay, on strike for the entire period, or who had been hired but had not yet reported during to their new jobs.

Beginning with the June 2003 publication of May 2003 data, the CES national federal government employment series has been estimated from a sample of federal establishments and benchmarked annually to counts from unemployment insurance tax records. It reflects employee counts as of the pay period containing the 12th day of the month, which is consistent with other CES industry series. Previously, the national series was an end-of-month count produced by the Office of Personnel Management.

The exclusion of farm employment, self-employment, and domestic service employment accounts from the payroll survey accounts for the differences in employment figures between the household and payroll surveys. The payroll survey also excludes workers on leave without pay. (These workers are counted as employed in the household survey.) Persons who worked in more than one establishment during the reporting period are counted each time their names appear on payrolls; these persons are only counted once in the household survey.

Production and related workers. This category includes working supervisors and all nonsupervisory workers (including group leaders and trainees) engaged in fabricating, processing, assembling, inspecting, receiving, storing, handling, packing, warehousing, shipping, trucking, hauling, maintenance, repair, janitorial, guard services, product development, auxiliary production for plant's own use (such as a power plant), record keeping, and other services closely associated with production operations.

Construction workers. This group includes the following employees in the construction division: working supervisors, qualified craft workers, mechanics, apprentices, helpers, and laborers engaged in new work, alterations, demolition, repair, maintenance, and the like, whether working at the site of construction or at jobs in shops or yards at jobs (such as precutting and pre-assembling) ordinarily performed by members of the construction trades.

Nonsupervisory workers. This category consists of employees such as office and clerical workers, repairers, salespersons, operators, drivers, physicians, lawyers, accountants, nurses, social workers, research aides, teachers, drafters, photographers, beauticians, musicians, restaurant workers, custodial workers, attendants, line installers and repairers, laborers, janitors, guards, and other employees at similar occupational levels whose services are closely associated with those of the employees listed. It excludes persons in executive, managerial, and supervisory positions.

Payroll. This refers to payments made to full- and part-time production, construction, or nonsupervisory workers who received pay for any part of the pay period containing the 12th day of the month. The payroll is reported before deductions of any kind, such as those for old age and unemployment insurance, group insurance, withholding tax, bonds, or union dues. Also included is pay for overtime, holidays, and vacation, as well as for sick leave paid directly by the firm. Bonuses (unless earned and paid regularly each pay period), other pay not earned in the pay period reported (such as retroactive pay), tips, and the value of free rent, fuel, meals, or other payment-in-kind are excluded. Employee benefits (such as health and other types of insurance and contributions to retirement, as paid by the employer) are also excluded.

Total hours. During the pay period, total hours include all hours worked (including overtime hours), hours paid for standby or reporting time, and equivalent hours for which employees received pay directly from the employer for sick leave, holidays, vacations, and other leave. Overtime and other premium pay hours are not converted to straight-time equivalent hours. The concept of total hours differs from those of scheduled hours and hours worked. The average weekly hours derived from paid total hours reflect the effects of such factors as unpaid absenteeism, labor turnover, part-time work, and work stoppages, as well as fluctuations in work schedules.

Overtime hours. These are hours worked by production or related workers for which overtime premiums were paid because the hours were in excess of the number of hours of either the straight-time workday or the total workweek. Weekend and holiday hours are included only if overtime premiums were paid. Hours for which only shift differential, hazard, incentive, or other similar types of premiums were paid are excluded.

Average weekly hours. The workweek information relates to the average hours for which pay was received and is different from standard or scheduled hours. Such factors as unpaid absenteeism, labor turnover, part-time work, and work stoppages cause average weekly hours to be lower than scheduled hours of work for an establishment. Group averages further reflect changes in the workweeks of component industries.

Industry hours and earnings. Average hours and earnings data are derived from reports of payrolls and hours for production and related workers in manufacturing and natural resources and mining, construction workers in construction, and nonsupervisory employees in private service-providing industries. All dollar amounts refer to current dollars unless otherwise specified.

Indexes of aggregate weekly hours and payrolls. The indexes of aggregate weekly hours are calculated by dividing the current month's aggregate by the average of the 12 monthly figures for 1982. For basic industries, the hours aggregates are the product of average weekly hours and production worker or nonsupervisory worker employment. At all higher levels of industry aggregation, hours aggregates are the sum of the component aggregates.

The indexes of aggregate weekly payrolls are calculated by dividing the current month's aggregate by the average of the 12 monthly figures for 1982. For basic industries, the payroll aggregates are the product of average hourly earnings and aggregate weekly hours. At all higher levels of industry aggregation, payroll aggregates are the sum of the component aggregates.

Average overtime hours. Overtime hours represent the portion of average weekly hours that exceeded regular hours and for which overtime premiums were paid. If an employee worked during a paid holiday at regular rates, receiving as total compensation his or her holiday pay plus straight-time pay for hours worked that day, no overtime hours would be reported.

Since overtime hours are premium hours by definition, weekly hours and overtime hours do not necessarily move in the same direction from month to month. Factors such as work stoppages, absenteeism, and labor turnover may not have the same influence on overtime hours as on average hours. Diverse trends at the industry group level may also be caused by a marked change in hours for a component industry in which little or no overtime was worked in both the previous and current months.

Average hourly earnings. Average hourly earnings are on a "gross" basis. They reflect not only changes in basic hourly and incentive wage rates, but also such variable factors as premium pay for overtime and late-shift work and changes in output of workers paid on an incentive plan. They also reflect shifts in the number of employees between relatively high-paid and low-paid work and changes in workers' earnings in individual establishments. Averages for groups and divisions further reflect changes in average hourly earnings for individual industries.

Averages of hourly earnings differ from wage rates. Earnings are the actual return to the worker for a stated period; rates are the amount stipulated for a given unit of work or time. The earnings series do not measure the level of total labor costs on the part of the employer because the following items are excluded: irregular bonuses, retroactive items, payroll taxes paid by employers, and earnings for those employees not covered under the definitions of production workers, construction workers, or nonsupervisory employees.

Average hourly earnings, excluding overtime-premium pay, are computed by dividing the total production worker payroll for the industry group by the sum of total production worker hours and one-half of total overtime hours. No adjustments are made for other premium payment provisions, such as holiday pay, late-shift premiums, and overtime rates other than time and one-half.

Average weekly earnings. These estimates are derived by multiplying average weekly hours estimates by average hourly earnings estimates. Therefore, weekly earnings are affected not only by changes in average hourly earnings but also by changes in the length of the workweek. Monthly variations in factors, such as the proportion of part-time workers, work stoppages, labor turnover during the survey period, and absenteeism for which employees are not paid may cause the average workweek to fluctuate.

Long-term trends of average weekly earnings can be affected by structural changes in the makeup of the work-force. For example, persistent long-term increases in the proportion of part-time workers in retail trade and many of the services industries have reduced average workweeks in these industries and have affected the average weekly earnings series.

The earnings in constant 1982 dollars are calculated from the earnings averages for the current month using a deflator derived from the Consumer Price Index for Urban Wage Earnings and Clerical Workers (CPI-W). The reference year for this series is 1982.

Future Plans

BLS is planning several changes to the CES survey to improve its relevance to the needs of data users, and enhance its value as an input to other key economic statistics. The planned improvements to the CES survey are new data on the hours and regular earnings of all employees, and new data on total earnings—both regular and irregular pay—for all employees. Publication of the CES series on women workers, which was discontinued to accommodate these improvements, resumed in September 2006 with estimates for the missing period.

BLS plans to discontinue the production and nonsupervisory worker hours and earnings series after the new all-employee hours and earning series are well established.

Sources of Additional Information

For further information on sampling and estimation methods see the updated version of Chapter 2 in the *BLS Handbook of Methods*, BLS news releases, and the publication *Employment and Earnings*. All of these resources are available on the BLS Web site at <http://www.bls.gov>

Table 2-1. Employees on Nonfarm Payrolls, by Super Sector and Selected Component Groups, NAICS Basis, 1995–2005

(Thousands of people.)

Industry	1995	1996	1997	1998	1999	2000	2001	2002	2003	2004	2005
TOTAL	117 298	119 708	122 776	125 930	128 993	131 785	131 826	130 341	129 999	131 435	133 463
Total Private	97 866	100 169	103 113	106 021	108 686	110 996	110 707	108 828	108 416	109 814	111 660
Goods-Producing	23 156	23 410	23 886	24 354	24 465	24 649	23 873	22 557	21 816	21 882	22 133
Natural Resources and Mining	641	637	654	645	598	599	606	583	572	591	625
Mining	558	556	571	565	517	520	532	512	503	523	561
Logging	82	81	82	80	81	79	74	70	69	68	64
Construction	5 274	5 536	5 813	6 149	6 545	6 787	6 826	6 716	6 735	6 976	7 277
Construction of buildings	1 325	1 380	1 435	1 509	1 586	1 632	1 589	1 575	1 576	1 630	1 695
Heavy and civil engineering	775	800	825	865	909	937	953	931	903	907	953
Specialty trade contractors	3 174	3 355	3 553	3 775	4 050	4 217	4 284	4 210	4 256	4 439	4 629
Manufacturing	17 241	17 237	17 419	17 560	17 322	17 263	16 441	15 259	14 510	14 315	14 232
Durable goods	10 372	10 485	10 704	10 910	10 830	10 876	10 335	9 483	8 963	8 924	8 953
Wood product	574	583	595	609	620	613	574	555	538	550	555
Nonmetallic mineral product	513	517	526	535	541	554	544	516	494	506	503
Primary metals	642	639	639	642	625	622	571	509	477	467	469
Fabricated metal product	1 623	1 648	1 696	1 740	1 728	1 753	1 676	1 548	1 479	1 497	1 519
Machinery	1 440	1 467	1 494	1 512	1 466	1 455	1 368	1 230	1 149	1 143	1 162
Computer and electronic product	1 688	1 747	1 803	1 831	1 780	1 820	1 749	1 507	1 355	1 323	1 320
Electrical equipment and appliances	593	591	586	592	588	591	557	496	460	445	436
Transportation equipment	1 977	1 974	2 026	2 077	2 087	2 056	1 938	1 829	1 774	1 766	1 772
Furniture and related product	607	604	615	641	665	680	642	604	573	573	563
Miscellaneous manufacturing	714	716	723	732	729	733	714	688	663	656	654
Nondurable goods	6 869	6 752	6 716	6 650	6 492	6 388	6 107	5 775	5 547	5 391	5 278
Food manufacturing	1 560	1 562	1 558	1 555	1 550	1 553	1 551	1 526	1 518	1 494	1 472
Beverage and tobacco product	203	204	206	209	208	207	209	207	200	195	192
Textile mills	468	443	436	425	397	378	333	291	261	237	218
Textile product mills	219	216	217	217	217	216	206	195	179	176	172
Apparel	814	743	700	639	556	497	426	360	312	286	260
Paper and paper product	640	631	631	625	616	605	578	547	516	496	484
Printing and related support activities	817	816	821	828	815	807	768	707	680	663	648
Petroleum and coal product	140	137	136	134	128	123	121	118	114	112	113
Chemicals	988	984	987	993	982	980	959	928	906	887	879
Plastics and rubber product	915	920	934	943	948	952	897	848	815	806	800
Private Service-Providing	74 710	76 759	79 227	81 667	84 221	86 346	86 834	86 271	86 599	87 932	89 527
Trade, Transportation, and Utilities	23 834	24 239	24 700	25 186	25 771	26 225	25 983	25 497	25 287	25 533	25 909
Wholesale Trade	5 433	5 522	5 664	5 795	5 892	5 933	5 773	5 652	5 608	5 663	5 750
Durable goods	2 909	2 978	3 072	3 162	3 220	3 251	3 130	3 008	2 941	2 951	2 992
Nondurable goods	1 969	1 978	2 008	2 033	2 061	2 065	2 031	2 015	2 005	2 010	2 022
Electronic markets, agents, and brokers	555	567	584	600	612	618	611	629	662	702	735
Retail Trade	13 897	14 142	14 389	14 609	14 970	15 280	15 239	15 025	14 917	15 058	15 255
Motor vehicle and parts dealers	1 627	1 686	1 723	1 741	1 797	1 847	1 855	1 879	1 883	1 902	1 919
Furniture and home furnishing stores	461	474	485	499	524	544	541	539	547	563	578
Electronic and appliance stores	449	470	494	510	542	564	554	525	512	516	533
Building material and garden supply stores	982	1 007	1 043	1 062	1 101	1 142	1 152	1 176	1 185	1 227	1 272
Food and beverage stores	2 880	2 928	2 957	2 966	2 984	2 993	2 950	2 882	2 838	2 822	2 814
Health and personal care stores	812	826	853	876	898	928	952	939	938	941	955
Gasoline stations	922	946	961	961	944	936	925	896	882	876	871
Clothing and clothing accessories stores	1 246	1 221	1 236	1 269	1 307	1 322	1 321	1 312	1 304	1 364	1 414
Sporting goods, hobby, and music stores	606	614	626	635	664	686	679	661	647	641	642
General merchandise stores	2 635	2 657	2 658	2 686	2 752	2 820	2 842	2 812	2 822	2 863	2 919
Miscellaneous store retailers	841	874	913	950	986	1 007	993	960	931	914	903
Nonstore retailers	435	438	444	453	472	492	474	444	427	429	435
Transportation and Warehousing	3 838	3 935	4 026	4 168	4 300	4 410	4 372	4 224	4 185	4 249	4 347
Air transportation	511	526	542	563	586	614	615	564	528	514	501
Rail transportation	232	225	221	225	229	232	227	218	218	226	228
Water transportation	51	51	51	50	52	56	54	53	54	56	61
Truck transportation	1 249	1 282	1 308	1 354	1 392	1 406	1 387	1 339	1 326	1 352	1 393
Transit and ground passenger transportation	328	339	350	363	371	372	375	381	382	385	388
Pipeline transportation	54	51	50	48	47	46	45	42	40	38	38
Scenic and sightseeing transportation	22	23	24	25	26	28	29	26	27	27	30
Support activities for transportation	430	446	473	497	518	537	539	525	520	535	551
Couriers and messengers	517	540	546	568	586	605	587	561	562	557	572
Warehousing and storage	444	452	462	474	494	514	514	517	528	558	585

Table 2-1. Employees on Nonfarm Payrolls, by Super Sector and Selected Component Groups, NAICS Basis, 1995–2005—*Continued*

(Thousands of people.)

Industry	1995	1996	1997	1998	1999	2000	2001	2002	2003	2004	2005
Utilities	666	640	621	613	608	601	599	596	577	564	558
Information	2 843	2 940	3 084	3 218	3 419	3 631	3 629	3 395	3 188	3 118	3 066
Publishing industries, except Internet	911	927	956	982	1 005	1 035	1 021	964	925	909	904
Motion picture and sound recording industry	311	335	353	370	384	383	377	388	376	385	379
Broadcasting, except Internet	298	309	313	321	329	344	345	334	324	325	327
Internet publishing and broadcasting	19	21	24	27	37	50	46	34	29	30	30
Telecommunications	976	997	1 060	1 108	1 180	1 263	1 302	1 186	1 082	1 035	999
ISPs, search portals, and data processing	291	312	339	369	439	510	494	441	402	384	377
Other information services	38	39	40	41	44	46	46	46	47	49	51	50
Financial Activities	6 827	6 969	7 178	7 462	7 648	7 687	7 807	7 847	7 977	8 031	8 141
Finance and insurance	5 072	5 154	5 305	5 532	5 668	5 680	5 773	5 817	5 923	5 949	6 012
Monetary authorities, central bank	23	23	22	22	23	23	23	23	23	22	21
Credit intermediation	2 314	2 368	2 434	2 532	2 591	2 548	2 598	2 686	2 792	2 817	2 866
Securities, commodity contracts, and investments	562	590	636	692	737	804	830	789	758	766	783
Insurance carriers and related activities	2 108	2 108	2 144	2 209	2 236	2 221	2 234	2 233	2 266	2 259	2 255
Funds, trust, and other financial vehicles	64	66	70	77	82	85	88	85	84	85	87
Real estate and rental and leasing	1 755	1 814	1 873	1 930	1 979	2 007	2 034	2 030	2 054	2 082	2 129
Real estate	1 179	1 206	1 241	1 274	1 299	1 312	1 340	1 353	1 384	1 415	1 456
Rental and leasing services	557	588	610	631	653	667	666	649	643	641	646
Lessors of nonfinancial intangible assets	19	21	23	25	27	28	29	28	27	26	27
Professional and Business Services	12 844	13 462	14 335	15 147	15 957	16 666	16 476	15 976	15 987	16 395	16 882
Professional and technical services	5 101	5 337	5 656	6 021	6 375	6 734	6 902	6 676	6 630	6 774	7 013
Management of companies and enterprises	1 686	1 703	1 730	1 756	1 774	1 796	1 779	1 705	1 687	1 724	1 752
Administrative and waste services	6 057	6 422	6 950	7 369	7 807	8 136	7 795	7 595	7 670	7 896	8 117
Administrative and support services	5 783	6 140	6 659	7 070	7 497	7 823	7 478	7 277	7 348	7 567	7 783
Waste management and remediation services	273	282	290	299	310	313	317	318	322	329	334
Education and Health Services	13 289	13 683	14 087	14 446	14 798	15 109	15 645	16 199	16 588	16 953	17 342
Educational services	2 010	2 078	2 155	2 233	2 320	2 390	2 511	2 643	2 695	2 762	2 819
Health care and social assistance	11 278	11 605	11 932	12 214	12 477	12 718	13 134	13 556	13 893	14 190	14 523
Ambulatory health care services	3 768	3 940	4 093	4 161	4 227	4 320	4 462	4 633	4 786	4 952	5 110
Hospitals	3 734	3 773	3 822	3 892	3 936	3 954	4 051	4 160	4 245	4 285	4 347
Nursing and residential health facilities	2 308	2 380	2 443	2 487	2 529	2 583	2 676	2 743	2 786	2 818	2 856
Social assistance	1 470	1 512	1 574	1 673	1 786	1 860	1 946	2 020	2 075	2 135	2 210
Leisure and Hospitality	10 501	10 777	11 018	11 232	11 543	11 862	12 036	11 986	12 173	12 493	12 802
Arts, entertainment, and recreation	1 459	1 522	1 600	1 645	1 709	1 788	1 824	1 783	1 813	1 850	1 891
Performing arts and spectator sports	308	329	350	350	361	382	382	364	372	368	369
Museums, historical sites	84	89	94	97	103	110	115	114	115	118	121
Amusements, gambling, and recreation	1 068	1 104	1 156	1 198	1 245	1 296	1 327	1 305	1 326	1 364	1 401
Accommodation and food services	9 042	9 254	9 418	9 586	9 834	10 074	10 211	10 203	10 360	10 643	10 911
Accommodation	1 652	1 699	1 730	1 774	1 832	1 884	1 852	1 779	1 775	1 790	1 812
Food services and drinking places	7 389	7 555	7 688	7 813	8 002	8 189	8 359	8 425	8 584	8 854	9 099
Other Services	4 572	4 690	4 825	4 976	5 087	5 168	5 258	5 372	5 401	5 409	5 386
Repair and maintenance	1 079	1 136	1 169	1 189	1 222	1 242	1 256	1 247	1 234	1 229	1 236
Personal and laundry services	1 144	1 166	1 180	1 206	1 220	1 243	1 255	1 257	1 264	1 273	1 273
Membership associations and organizations	2 349	2 389	2 475	2 581	2 644	2 683	2 746	2 868	2 904	2 908	2 877
Government	19 432	19 539	19 664	19 909	20 307	20 790	21 118	21 513	21 583	21 621	21 803
Federal	2 949	2 877	2 806	2 772	2 769	2 865	2 764	2 766	2 761	2 730	2 724
Federal, excluding U.S. Postal Service	2 099	2 010	1 940	1 891	1 880	1 985	1 891	1 924	1 952	1 948	1 951
State	4 635	4 606	4 582	4 612	4 709	4 786	4 905	5 029	5 002	4 982	5 021
State, excluding education	2 716	2 695	2 678	2 690	2 726	2 756	2 792	2 786	2 748	2 744	2 771
Local	11 849	12 056	12 276	12 525	12 829	13 139	13 449	13 718	13 820	13 909	14 058
Local, excluding education	5 396	5 464	5 517	5 604	5 709	5 845	5 970	6 063	6 110	6 144	6 194

Table 2-2. Women Employees on Nonfarm Payrolls, by Super Sector and Selected Component Groups, NAICS Basis, 1990–2005

(Thousands of people.)

Industry	1990	1991	1992	1993	1994	1995	1996	1997	1998	1999	2000	2001	2002	2003	2004	2005
TOTAL NONFARM	51 586	51 681	52 132	53 175	54 759	56 213	57 406	58 914	60 309	61 810	63 222	63 683	63 360	63 237	63 739	64 633
Total Private	41 731	41 696	41 970	42 849	44 228	45 514	46 573	47 923	49 144	50 358	51 452	51 669	51 033	50 901	51 404	52 239
Goods-Producing	6 470	6 243	6 119	6 090	6 168	6 225	6 214	6 294	6 353	6 299	6 297	5 961	5 486	5 192	5 117	5 102
Natural resources and mining	112	114	109	105	102	98	96	99	100	96	92	90	85	80	80	79
Construction	656	628	599	609	636	666	700	730	769	818	846	832	827	822	841	882
Manufacturing	5 702	5 501	5 410	5 377	5 430	5 462	5 417	5 466	5 484	5 386	5 359	5 039	4 574	4 290	4 197	4 141
Private Service-Providing	35 262	35 453	35 851	36 759	38 061	39 289	40 360	41 629	42 791	44 059	45 155	45 708	45 547	45 709	46 287	47 137
Trade, transportation, and utilities	9 363	9 243	9 176	9 259	9 564	9 870	10 043	10 230	10 413	10 658	10 859	10 768	10 466	10 321	10 364	10 517
Wholesale trade	1 611	1 587	1 565	1 554	1 607	1 668	1 701	1 746	1 778	1 809	1 826	1 770	1 718	1 700	1 714	1 734
Retail trade	6 696	6 588	6 534	6 599	6 813	7 020	7 142	7 272	7 380	7 542	7 680	7 635	7 449	7 339	7 387	7 512
Transportation and warehousing	879	891	901	932	974	1 018	1 042	1 060	1 103	1 154	1 202	1 212	1 149	1 134	1 117	1 127
Utilities	177	177	176	174	169	163	157	153	152	152	151	151	150	147	146	144
Information	1 324	1 319	1 295	1 304	1 334	1 380	1 433	1 481	1 514	1 600	1 697	1 684	1 554	1 428	1 366	1 335
Financial activities	4 055	4 036	4 022	4 114	4 196	4 164	4 241	4 359	4 515	4 605	4 638	4 726	4 755	4 830	4 831	4 891
Professional and business services	5 105	5 026	5 160	5 399	5 682	5 979	6 273	6 705	7 030	7 370	7 680	7 591	7 314	7 248	7 360	7 542
Educational and health services	8 422	8 840	9 141	9 454	9 822	10 181	10 474	10 779	11 042	11 323	11 586	12 037	12 474	12 786	13 073	13 386
Leisure and hospitality	4 829	4 806	4 876	4 994	5 192	5 382	5 520	5 640	5 760	5 933	6 082	6 224	6 215	6 319	6 516	6 699
Other services	2 164	2 184	2 181	2 236	2 269	2 333	2 376	2 435	2 517	2 570	2 614	2 677	2 769	2 779	2 776	2 767
Government	9 855	9 985	10 162	10 326	10 531	10 698	10 832	10 991	11 164	11 452	11 771	12 015	12 327	12 337	12 335	12 394
Federal	1 378	1 329	1 335	1 321	1 306	1 285	1 261	1 240	1 184	1 174	1 231	1 148	1 155	1 173	1 168	1 174
State	2 137	2 173	2 197	2 238	2 281	2 326	2 316	2 324	2 354	2 412	2 464	2 534	2 621	2 599	2 562	2 569
Local	6 340	6 483	6 630	6 767	6 943	7 088	7 255	7 426	7 627	7 866	8 076	8 333	8 551	8 565	8 606	8 652

Table 2-3. Production Workers on Private Nonfarm Payrolls, by Super Sector, NAICS Basis, 1990–2005

(Thousands of people.)

Industry	1990	1991	1992	1993	1994	1995	1996	1997	1998	1999	2000	2001	2002	2003	2004	2005
TOTAL PRIVATE	73 684	72 520	72 786	74 591	77 382	79 845	81 773	84 158	86 316	88 430	90 336	89 983	88 393	87 658	88 937	90 944
Goods-Producing	17 322	16 352	16 043	16 236	16 795	17 137	17 318	17 698	18 008	18 067	18 169	17 466	16 400	15 732	15 821	16 099
Natural resources and mining	538	515	478	462	461	458	461	479	473	438	446	457	436	420	440	471
Construction	4 115	3 674	3 546	3 704	3 973	4 113	4 325	4 546	4 807	5 105	5 295	5 332	5 196	5 123	5 309	5 566
Manufacturing	12 669	12 164	12 020	12 070	12 361	12 566	12 532	12 673	12 729	12 524	12 428	11 677	10 768	10 190	10 072	10 062
Private Service-Providing	56 362	56 168	56 743	58 355	60 587	62 708	64 455	66 460	68 308	70 363	72 167	72 517	71 993	71 926	73 116	74 844
Trade, transportation, and utilities	19 032	18 640	18 506	18 752	19 392	19 984	20 325	20 698	21 059	21 576	21 965	21 709	21 337	21 078	21 319	21 788
Wholesale trade	4 198	4 122	4 071	4 072	4 196	4 361	4 423	4 523	4 605	4 673	4 686	4 555	4 474	4 396	4 444	4 572
Retail trade	11 308	11 008	10 931	11 104	11 502	11 841	12 057	12 274	12 440	12 772	13 040	12 952	12 774	12 655	12 788	13 007
Transportation and warehousing	2 941	2 928	2 934	3 019	3 153	3 260	3 339	3 407	3 522	3 642	3 753	3 718	3 611	3 563	3 637	3 762
Utilities	585	582	570	557	541	522	506	494	492	489	485	483	478	464	450	446
Information	1 866	1 871	1 871	1 896	1 928	2 007	2 096	2 181	2 217	2 351	2 502	2 530	2 398	2 347	2 371	2 390
Financial activities	4 973	4 911	4 908	5 057	5 183	5 165	5 279	5 415	5 605	5 728	5 737	5 810	5 872	5 967	5 989	6 084
Professional and business services	8 889	8 748	8 971	9 451	10 078	10 645	11 161	11 896	12 566	13 184	13 790	13 588	13 049	12 910	13 287	13 797
Educational and health services	9 748	10 212	10 555	10 908	11 338	11 765	12 123	12 478	12 791	13 089	13 362	13 846	14 311	14 532	14 771	15 103
Leisure and hospitality	8 299	8 247	8 406	8 667	8 979	9 330	9 565	9 780	9 947	10 216	10 516	10 662	10 576	10 666	10 955	11 252
Other services	3 555	3 539	3 526	3 623	3 689	3 812	3 907	4 013	4 124	4 219	4 296	4 373	4 449	4 426	4 425	4 432

Table 2-4. Production Workers on Durable Goods Manufacturing Payrolls, by Industry, NAICS Basis, 1990–2005

(Thousands of people.)

Industry	1990	1991	1992	1993	1994	1995	1996	1997	1998	1999	2000	2001	2002	2003	2004	2005
Total Durable Goods	7 396	7 000	6 852	6 879	7 132	7 351	7 425	7 597	7 720	7 650	7 658	7 163	6 529	6 152	6 139	6 217
Wood product	450	413	417	437	469	478	485	497	508	514	506	468	449	433	444	450
Nonmetallic mineral product	413	384	378	381	392	400	405	412	421	426	440	427	399	375	388	386
Primary metals	525	497	479	473	487	500	500	502	505	492	490	447	396	370	364	365
Fabricated metal product	1 190	1 132	1 101	1 117	1 172	1 223	1 242	1 285	1 320	1 305	1 326	1 254	1 147	1 092	1 109	1 127
Machinery	938	884	856	874	921	968	983	1 006	1 015	977	960	889	785	731	728	747
Computer and electronic product	980	926	876	856	864	890	915	951	965	933	949	876	744	673	656	702
Electrical equipment and appliances	465	436	425	422	435	438	434	428	432	433	433	402	352	320	307	302
Transportation equipment	1 472	1 406	1 388	1 366	1 415	1 471	1 480	1 521	1 529	1 525	1 497	1 398	1 309	1 268	1 264	1 277
Furniture and related product	475	440	443	454	476	480	478	490	512	532	544	509	475	444	444	434
Miscellaneous manufacturing	487	484	489	498	502	502	503	507	514	512	513	493	472	445	435	429

Table 2-5. Production Workers on Nondurable Goods Manufacturing Payrolls, by Industry, NAICS Basis, 1990–2005

(Thousands of people.)

Industry	1990	1991	1992	1993	1994	1995	1996	1997	1998	1999	2000	2001	2002	2003	2004	2005
Total Nondurable Goods	5 273	5 164	5 168	5 192	5 229	5 215	5 107	5 076	5 009	4 873	4 770	4 514	4 239	4 038	3 933	3 846
Food manufacturing	1 165	1 174	1 182	1 195	1 200	1 221	1 228	1 228	1 228	1 229	1 228	1 221	1 202	1 192	1 178	1 166
Beverage and tobacco product	117	117	116	118	118	117	120	121	122	120	117	116	120	106	106	112
Textile mills	418	407	406	404	403	393	372	367	357	334	315	276	242	217	194	174
Textile product mills	170	161	163	167	176	176	173	175	174	173	172	164	154	141	141	140
Apparel	830	805	810	788	763	719	650	612	550	472	415	351	294	249	225	200
Leather and allied product	117	108	104	101	97	88	78	74	67	60	55	47	40	35	33	31
Paper and paper product	493	488	490	491	493	494	488	489	484	474	468	446	421	393	374	365
Printing and related support	598	582	574	580	591	599	594	597	598	585	576	544	493	471	460	448
Petroleum and coal product	98	97	97	93	91	89	87	88	87	85	83	81	78	74	77	76
Chemicals	620	600	586	590	596	598	595	593	601	595	588	562	532	525	520	515
Plastics and rubber product	648	625	640	665	700	720	721	733	740	747	754	705	663	634	626	619

Table 2-6. Average Weekly Hours of Production Workers on Private Nonfarm Payrolls, by Super Sector, NAICS Basis, 1990–2005

(Hours.)

Industry	1990	1991	1992	1993	1994	1995	1996	1997	1998	1999	2000	2001	2002	2003	2004	2005
TOTAL PRIVATE	34.3	34.1	34.2	34.3	34.5	34.3	34.3	34.5	34.5	34.3	34.3	34.0	33.9	33.7	33.7	33.8
Goods-Producing	40.1	40.1	40.2	40.6	41.1	40.8	40.8	41.1	40.8	40.8	40.7	39.9	39.9	39.8	40.0	40.1
Natural resources and mining	45.0	45.3	44.6	44.9	45.3	45.3	46.0	46.2	44.9	44.2	44.4	44.6	43.2	43.6	44.5	45.6
Construction	38.3	38.1	38.0	38.4	38.8	38.8	38.9	38.9	38.8	39.0	39.2	38.7	38.4	38.4	38.3	38.6
Manufacturing	40.5	40.4	40.7	41.1	41.7	41.3	41.3	41.7	41.4	41.4	41.3	40.3	40.5	40.4	40.8	40.7
Private Service-Providing	32.5	32.4	32.5	32.5	32.7	32.6	32.6	32.8	32.8	32.7	32.7	32.5	32.5	32.4	32.3	32.4
Trade, transportation, and utilities	33.7	33.7	33.8	34.1	34.3	34.1	34.1	34.3	34.2	33.9	33.8	33.5	33.6	33.6	33.5	33.4
Wholesale trade	38.4	38.4	38.6	38.5	38.8	38.6	38.6	38.8	38.6	38.6	38.8	38.4	38.0	37.9	37.8	37.7
Retail trade	30.6	30.4	30.7	30.7	30.9	30.8	30.7	30.9	30.9	30.8	30.7	30.7	30.9	30.9	30.7	30.6
Transportation and warehousing	37.7	37.4	37.4	38.9	39.5	38.9	39.1	39.4	38.7	37.6	37.4	36.7	36.8	36.8	37.2	37.0
Utilities	41.5	41.5	41.7	42.1	42.3	42.3	42.0	42.0	42.0	42.0	42.0	41.4	40.9	41.1	40.9	41.1
Information	35.8	35.6	35.8	36.0	36.0	36.0	36.4	36.3	36.6	36.7	36.8	36.9	36.5	36.2	36.3	36.5
Financial activities	35.5	35.5	35.6	35.5	35.5	35.5	35.5	35.7	36.0	35.8	35.9	35.8	35.6	35.5	35.5	35.9
Professional and business services	34.2	34.0	34.0	34.0	34.1	34.0	34.1	34.3	34.3	34.4	34.5	34.2	34.2	34.1	34.2	34.2
Educational and health services	31.9	31.9	32.0	32.0	32.0	32.0	31.9	32.2	32.2	32.1	32.2	32.3	32.4	32.3	32.4	32.6
Leisure and hospitality	26.0	25.6	25.7	25.9	26.0	25.9	25.9	26.0	26.2	26.1	26.1	25.8	25.8	25.6	25.7	25.7
Other services	32.8	32.7	32.6	32.6	32.7	32.6	32.5	32.7	32.6	32.5	32.5	32.3	32.0	31.4	31.0	30.9

Table 2-7. Average Weekly Hours of Production Workers on Manufacturing Payrolls, by Industry, NAICS Basis, 1990–2005

(Hours.)

Industry	1990	1991	1992	1993	1994	1995	1996	1997	1998	1999	2000	2001	2002	2003	2004	2005
DURABLE GOODS																
Total	41.1	40.9	41.3	41.9	42.6	42.1	42.1	42.6	42.1	41.9	41.8	40.6	40.8	40.8	41.3	41.1
Wood product	40.4	40.2	40.9	41.2	41.7	41.0	41.2	41.4	41.4	41.3	41.0	40.2	39.9	40.4	40.7	40.0
Nonmetallic mineral product	40.9	40.5	41.0	41.5	42.2	41.8	42.0	41.9	42.2	42.1	41.6	41.6	42.0	42.2	42.3	42.2
Primary metals	42.0	41.5	42.4	43.1	44.1	43.4	43.6	44.3	43.5	43.8	44.2	42.4	42.4	42.3	43.1	43.1
Fabricated metal product	41.0	40.8	41.2	41.6	42.3	41.9	41.9	42.3	41.9	41.7	41.9	40.6	40.6	40.7	41.1	41.0
Machinery	42.1	41.9	42.4	43.2	43.9	43.5	43.3	44.0	43.1	42.3	42.3	40.9	40.5	40.8	41.9	42.1
Computer and electronic product	41.3	40.9	41.4	41.8	42.2	42.2	41.9	42.5	41.8	41.5	41.4	39.8	39.7	40.4	40.4	40.0
Electrical equipment and appliances	41.2	41.5	41.8	42.4	43.0	41.9	42.1	42.1	41.8	41.8	41.6	39.8	40.1	40.6	40.7	40.6
Transportation equipment	42.0	41.9	41.9	43.0	44.3	43.7	43.8	44.2	43.2	43.6	43.3	41.9	42.5	41.9	42.5	42.5
Furniture and related product	38.0	37.8	38.7	39.0	39.3	38.5	38.3	39.1	39.4	39.3	39.2	38.3	39.2	38.9	39.5	39.2
Miscellaneous manufacturing	39.0	39.1	39.3	39.2	39.4	39.2	39.1	39.7	39.2	39.3	39.0	38.8	38.6	38.4	38.5	38.7
NONDURABLE GOODS																
Total	39.6	39.7	40.0	40.1	40.5	40.1	40.1	40.5	40.5	40.4	40.3	39.9	40.1	39.8	40.0	39.9
Food manufacturing	39.3	39.2	39.2	39.3	39.8	39.6	39.5	39.8	40.1	40.2	40.1	39.6	39.6	39.3	39.3	39.0
Beverage and tobacco product	38.9	38.8	38.7	38.3	39.3	39.3	39.7	40.0	40.3	41.0	42.0	40.9	39.4	39.1	39.2	40.0
Textile mills	40.2	40.7	41.3	41.6	41.9	40.9	40.8	41.6	41.0	41.0	41.4	40.0	40.6	39.1	40.1	40.3
Textile product mills	39.0	39.1	39.2	39.8	39.9	39.1	39.2	39.2	39.6	39.5	39.4	39.0	38.6	39.2	39.6	39.0
Apparel	34.8	35.4	35.6	35.5	35.7	35.3	35.2	35.5	35.5	35.4	35.7	36.0	36.7	35.6	36.0	35.7
Leather and allied product	37.4	37.6	37.9	38.4	38.2	37.7	37.8	38.2	37.4	37.2	37.5	36.4	37.5	39.3	38.4	38.4
Paper and paper product	43.6	43.6	43.8	43.8	44.2	43.4	43.5	43.9	43.6	43.6	42.8	42.1	41.9	41.5	42.1	42.5
Printing and related support	38.7	38.6	39.0	39.2	39.6	39.1	39.1	39.5	39.3	39.1	39.2	38.7	38.4	38.2	38.4	38.4
Petroleum and coal product	44.4	43.9	43.6	44.0	44.3	43.7	43.7	43.1	43.6	42.6	42.7	43.8	43.0	44.5	44.9	45.6
Chemicals	42.8	43.1	43.3	43.2	43.4	43.3	43.3	43.4	43.2	42.7	42.2	41.9	42.3	42.4	42.8	42.3
Plastics and rubber product	40.6	40.5	41.2	41.4	41.8	41.1	41.0	41.4	41.3	41.3	40.8	40.0	40.6	40.4	40.4	40.0

Table 2-8. Average Weekly Overtime Hours of Production Workers on Manufacturing Payrolls, by Industry, NAICS Basis, 1990–2005

(Hours.)

Industry	1990	1991	1992	1993	1994	1995	1996	1997	1998	1999	2000	2001	2002	2003	2004	2005
TOTAL MANUFACTURING	3.8	3.8	4.0	4.4	5.0	4.7	4.8	5.1	4.8	4.8	4.7	4.0	4.2	4.2	4.6	4.6
Total Durable Goods	3.9	3.7	3.9	4.5	5.3	5.0	5.0	5.4	5.0	5.0	4.8	3.9	4.2	4.3	4.7	4.6
Wood product	3.3	3.1	3.6	3.9	4.3	3.9	4.0	4.0	4.0	4.2	4.1	3.7	3.9	4.1	4.4	4.1
Nonmetallic mineral product	5.0	4.7	5.0	5.4	5.9	5.7	6.1	6.0	6.4	6.1	6.1	5.5	5.9	5.8	6.1	6.3
Primary metals	4.6	4.2	4.7	5.2	6.2	5.7	5.8	6.3	5.9	6.3	6.5	5.5	5.6	5.5	6.5	6.3
Fabricated metal product	3.9	3.7	3.9	4.4	5.1	4.8	4.8	5.3	4.9	4.8	4.9	4.1	4.1	4.1	4.5	4.6
Machinery	4.0	3.8	4.1	4.8	5.6	5.3	5.2	5.8	5.1	5.0	5.1	3.9	4.0	4.2	4.8	5.0
Computer and electronic product	3.8	3.8	3.9	4.3	4.8	4.9	4.7	5.2	4.8	4.6	4.6	3.2	3.4	3.8	3.7	3.6
Electrical equipment and appliances	3.0	3.0	3.2	3.7	4.2	3.5	3.7	3.9	3.6	3.6	3.7	3.0	3.1	3.4	4.0	3.8
Transportation equipment	4.5	4.3	4.3	5.5	7.0	6.5	6.7	7.2	6.4	6.1	5.5	4.5	5.1	5.0	5.5	5.3
Furniture and related product	2.3	2.2	2.7	2.9	3.3	2.8	2.9	3.3	3.6	3.9	3.5	2.7	3.4	3.5	3.6	3.2
Miscellaneous manufacturing	3.0	3.1	3.1	3.2	3.5	3.4	3.4	3.7	3.4	3.7	3.1	2.8	2.9	2.7	3.2	3.3
Total Nondurable Goods	3.8	3.9	4.1	4.2	4.5	4.3	4.4	4.6	4.5	4.6	4.4	4.1	4.2	4.1	4.4	4.4
Food manufacturing	4.1	4.1	4.2	4.2	4.5	4.4	4.4	4.6	4.8	5.0	4.8	4.6	4.6	4.4	4.7	4.7
Beverage and tobacco product	3.8	3.9	3.8	4.0	4.9	4.8	5.0	4.8	5.0	5.3	5.8	4.9	4.8	4.0	4.3	5.7
Textile mills	4.2	4.7	5.1	5.3	5.5	5.0	5.0	5.5	5.2	5.0	4.8	3.8	4.2	4.0	4.4	3.9
Textile product mills	3.0	3.1	3.2	3.8	3.9	3.4	3.8	4.1	4.1	4.1	3.5	2.7	3.3	3.2	3.0	4.4
Apparel	2.0	2.3	2.4	2.2	2.4	2.2	2.3	2.4	2.2	2.4	2.1	1.8	2.3	2.0	2.2	2.1
Leather and allied product	4.0	4.6	4.9	5.3	4.9	4.0	4.0	4.7	4.7	4.1	4.6	2.2	2.9	2.7	2.2	2.2
Paper and paper product	4.9	5.1	5.5	5.6	5.9	5.5	5.7	6.0	5.8	5.9	5.7	4.9	5.1	5.1	5.4	5.6
Printing and related support	3.6	3.4	3.7	3.9	4.3	3.8	3.8	4.2	3.9	3.6	3.7	3.4	3.4	3.2	3.4	3.3
Petroleum and coal product	6.2	6.3	6.3	6.2	6.6	6.3	6.4	6.4	6.8	6.6	6.5	7.9	7.0	8.3	8.2	8.5
Chemicals	4.9	5.1	5.3	5.3	5.6	5.6	5.7	5.8	5.6	5.2	5.0	4.6	4.7	4.5	4.9	4.6
Plastics and rubber product	3.4	3.4	3.9	4.2	4.5	3.9	4.0	4.3	4.2	4.2	3.9	3.6	3.9	3.9	4.2	4.0

Table 2-9. Indexes of Aggregate Weekly Hours of Production Workers on Private Nonfarm Payrolls, by Super Sector, NAICS Basis, 1990–2005

(2002 = 100.)

Industry	1990	1991	1992	1993	1994	1995	1996	1997	1998	1999	2000	2001	2002	2003	2004	2005
TOTAL PRIVATE	84.4	82.6	83.1	85.5	89.2	91.6	93.8	97.1	99.4	101.5	103.6	102.1	100.0	98.7	100.2	102.6
Goods-Producing	106.1	100.1	98.7	100.8	105.6	106.8	108.1	111.2	112.3	112.6	113.1	106.6	100.0	95.8	96.8	98.6
Natural resources and mining	128.6	123.8	113.3	110.3	111.0	110.2	112.7	117.6	112.8	102.9	105.1	108.3	100.0	97.4	104.0	114.2
Construction	78.8	70.1	67.5	71.3	77.3	79.9	84.3	88.6	93.4	99.7	104.0	103.2	100.0	98.4	101.7	107.5
Manufacturing	117.7	112.8	112.4	113.9	118.3	119.0	118.8	121.4	121.0	118.9	117.7	108.1	100.0	94.5	94.3	93.9
Private Service-Providing	78.3	77.8	78.8	81.2	84.6	87.3	89.7	93.1	95.8	98.4	101.0	100.8	100.0	99.5	101.1	103.6
Trade, transportation, and utilities	89.5	87.4	87.3	89.0	92.7	95.1	96.6	98.8	100.3	101.9	103.5	101.5	100.0	98.6	99.6	101.5
Wholesale trade	94.9	93.3	92.4	92.4	95.8	99.2	100.7	103.4	104.8	106.2	107.1	102.9	100.0	98.0	98.9	101.6
Retail trade	87.5	84.8	85.1	86.3	89.8	92.3	93.7	95.9	97.2	99.5	101.3	100.5	100.0	98.9	99.4	100.6
Transportation and warehousing	83.5	82.4	82.7	88.4	93.8	95.6	98.3	101.0	102.7	103.2	105.6	102.8	100.0	98.8	101.9	104.9
Utilities	124.3	123.5	121.6	119.9	117.1	112.9	108.6	106.1	105.8	105.0	104.2	102.4	100.0	97.4	94.2	93.7
Information	76.2	76.1	76.5	78.0	79.2	82.5	86.9	90.4	92.6	98.5	104.9	106.6	100.0	97.0	98.2	99.6
Financial activities	84.5	83.3	83.5	85.9	88.0	87.8	89.8	92.6	96.5	98.0	98.5	99.5	100.0	101.5	101.9	104.6
Professional and business services	68.1	66.7	68.4	71.9	77.0	81.2	85.2	91.5	96.7	101.7	106.6	104.0	100.0	98.7	101.8	105.8
Educational and health services	67.2	70.2	72.9	75.4	78.3	81.2	83.4	86.7	88.9	90.6	92.8	96.6	100.0	101.4	103.3	106.2
Leisure and hospitality	78.9	77.3	79.3	82.2	85.6	88.5	90.8	93.4	95.5	97.9	100.6	100.7	100.0	100.1	103.0	106.2
Other services	81.8	81.2	80.6	82.8	84.5	87.1	89.1	91.9	94.3	96.3	97.8	99.1	100.0	97.5	96.1	96.1

Table 2-10. Indexes of Aggregate Weekly Hours of Production Workers on Manufacturing Payrolls, by Industry, NAICS Basis, 1990–2005

(2002 = 100.)

Industry	1990	1991	1992	1993	1994	1995	1996	1997	1998	1999	2000	2001	2002	2003	2004	2005
DURABLE GOODS																
Total	114.2	107.6	106.4	108.2	114.2	116.3	117.5	121.6	122.0	120.6	120.4	109.3	100.0	94.3	95.2	96.1
Wood product	101.5	92.6	95.2	100.5	109.1	109.3	111.6	114.8	117.5	118.6	115.8	105.0	100.0	97.8	100.9	100.5
Nonmetallic mineral product	100.8	92.8	92.6	94.2	98.8	99.7	101.5	103.2	105.8	106.9	109.1	106.1	100.0	94.3	98.0	97.0
Primary metals	131.5	122.9	120.8	121.4	128.0	129.3	129.9	132.3	131.1	128.4	128.9	113.0	100.0	93.4	93.3	93.6
Fabricated metal product	104.7	99.1	97.3	99.7	106.3	109.9	111.6	116.6	118.6	116.7	119.1	109.3	100.0	95.3	97.7	99.0
Machinery	123.9	116.3	113.9	118.6	127.0	132.3	133.8	139.0	137.4	129.9	127.6	114.1	100.0	93.6	95.9	98.7
Computer and electronic product	137.2	128.1	122.9	121.1	123.5	127.1	129.9	136.8	136.7	131.1	133.0	117.9	100.0	92.1	89.7	95.0
Electrical equipment and appliances	136.0	128.0	125.9	126.8	132.5	130.3	129.4	127.7	127.8	128.3	127.8	113.4	100.0	92.0	88.7	86.8
Transportation equipment	111.1	105.8	104.4	105.5	112.6	115.4	116.4	120.7	118.7	119.5	116.4	105.3	100.0	95.4	96.5	97.3
Furniture and related product	97.2	89.5	92.1	95.3	100.5	99.3	98.3	102.9	108.5	112.6	114.8	104.8	100.0	93.0	94.3	91.5
Miscellaneous manufacturing	104.0	103.8	105.2	106.9	108.2	107.7	107.7	110.0	110.3	110.3	109.5	104.8	100.0	93.6	91.8	90.9
NONDURABLE GOODS																
Total	123.0	120.8	121.7	122.6	124.7	123.1	120.5	120.9	119.4	116.1	113.3	106.0	100.0	94.7	92.7	90.3
Food manufacturing	96.2	96.6	97.3	98.7	100.5	101.6	101.8	102.6	103.4	103.8	103.5	101.5	100.0	98.4	97.1	95.4
Beverage and tobacco product	96.9	96.4	95.4	95.6	98.7	97.9	101.4	103.1	104.9	104.7	104.2	100.3	100.0	88.4	88.8	94.8
Textile mills	170.4	168.4	170.3	170.8	171.6	163.5	154.1	155.2	148.9	139.1	132.4	112.2	100.0	86.3	79.0	71.4
Textile product mills	110.3	104.5	106.0	110.6	116.6	114.4	112.8	114.8	114.1	113.5	111.1	105.0	100.0	92.9	91.0	90.6
Apparel	267.4	264.2	267.5	259.4	252.6	235.4	211.9	201.4	181.2	154.7	137.4	117.1	100.0	81.9	75.1	66.4
Leather and allied product	290.0	268.9	263.5	259.1	246.9	221.8	197.5	187.1	166.6	148.3	138.4	113.3	100.0	91.3	83.6	78.8
Paper and paper product	121.8	120.6	121.7	121.9	123.5	121.4	120.1	121.5	119.5	117.1	113.4	106.6	100.0	92.4	89.2	87.9
Printing and related support	122.3	118.7	118.4	120.3	123.8	123.9	122.8	124.6	124.3	120.9	119.4	111.5	100.0	95.3	93.4	91.1
Petroleum and coal product	128.9	127.5	126.0	122.0	120.0	115.5	113.5	112.7	113.4	107.6	105.8	105.6	100.0	98.7	102.6	102.9
Chemicals	118.2	115.0	112.9	113.4	115.1	115.4	114.7	114.6	115.4	113.1	110.4	104.7	100.0	98.9	99.0	96.8
Plastics and rubber product	97.7	94.2	98.1	102.4	108.8	109.9	110.1	112.7	113.8	114.6	114.3	105.0	100.0	95.2	94.2	92.0

Table 2-11. Employees on Total Nonfarm Payrolls, by State and Selected Territory, 1965–2005

(Thousands of people.)

State	1965	1966	1967	1968	1969	1970	1971	1972	1973	1974	1975	1976	1977	1978	1979
UNITED STATES	60 874	64 020	65 931	68 023	70 512	71 006	71 335	73 798	76 912	78 389	77 069	79 502	82 593	86 826	89 932
Alabama	886	936	952	970	1 000	1 010	1 022	1 072	1 136	1 170	1 155	1 207	1 269	1 336	1 362
Alaska	70	73	77	80	87	93	98	104	110	128	162	172	163	164	167
Arizona	404	435	446	473	517	547	581	646	714	746	729	759	809	895	980
Arkansas	459	490	501	515	534	536	551	582	614	641	624	660	696	733	750
California	5 800	6 145	6 368	6 642	6 932	6 946	6 917	7 210	7 622	7 834	7 847	8 154	8 600	9 200	9 665
Colorado	599	631	656	687	721	750	787	869	936	960	964	1 003	1 058	1 150	1 218
Connecticut	1 033	1 095	1 130	1 158	1 194	1 198	1 164	1 190	1 239	1 264	1 223	1 240	1 282	1 346	1 398
Delaware	184	193	197	203	212	217	225	232	239	233	230	237	239	248	257
District of Columbia	572	587	595	583	575	567	567	572	574	580	576	576	579	596	612
Florida	1 619	1 727	1 816	1 932	2 070	2 152	2 276	2 513	2 779	2 864	2 746	2 784	2 933	3 181	3 381
Georgia	1 257	1 338	1 395	1 456	1 532	1 558	1 603	1 695	1 802	1 828	1 756	1 839	1 926	2 050	2 128
Hawaii	219	232	242	255	276	294	302	313	328	336	343	349	359	377	394
Idaho	178	185	188	193	201	208	217	236	252	267	273	291	307	331	338
Illinois	3 880	4 095	4 210	4 285	4 376	4 346	4 296	4 315	4 467	4 546	4 419	4 565	4 656	4 789	4 880
Indiana	1 631	1 737	1 777	1 817	1 880	1 849	1 841	1 922	2 028	2 031	1 942	2 024	2 114	2 206	2 236
Iowa	752	804	833	852	873	877	883	912	961	999	999	1 037	1 079	1 119	1 132
Kansas	600	634	653	672	686	679	678	718	763	790	801	835	871	912	947
Kentucky	759	804	836	869	896	910	932	988	1 039	1 066	1 058	1 103	1 148	1 210	1 245
Louisiana	898	958	997	1 020	1 033	1 034	1 056	1 129	1 176	1 221	1 250	1 314	1 365	1 464	1 517
Maine	295	309	317	323	330	332	332	344	355	362	357	375	388	406	416
Maryland	1 058	1 132	1 178	1 224	1 272	1 349	1 372	1 415	1 472	1 494	1 479	1 498	1 546	1 626	1 691
Massachusetts	2 016	2 097	2 148	2 188	2 249	2 244	2 211	2 252	2 333	2 354	2 273	2 324	2 416	2 526	2 604
Michigan	2 685	2 861	2 900	2 960	3 081	2 999	2 995	3 119	3 284	3 278	3 137	3 283	3 442	3 609	3 637
Minnesota	1 081	1 148	1 200	1 243	1 300	1 315	1 310	1 357	1 436	1 481	1 474	1 521	1 597	1 689	1 767
Mississippi	487	522	535	552	573	584	602	649	693	711	692	728	766	814	838
Missouri	1 478	1 554	1 596	1 631	1 672	1 668	1 661	1 700	1 771	1 789	1 741	1 798	1 862	1 953	2 011
Montana	179	185	188	193	196	199	205	215	224	234	238	251	265	280	284
Nebraska	419	434	449	459	474	484	491	517	541	562	558	572	594	610	631
Nevada	157	162	166	177	194	203	210	224	245	256	263	280	308	350	384
New Hampshire	221	235	244	252	259	258	260	278	298	300	293	313	337	360	378
New Jersey	2 256	2 359	2 422	2 485	2 570	2 606	2 608	2 672	2 760	2 783	2 700	2 754	2 837	2 962	3 027
New Mexico	262	272	273	277	288	293	306	328	346	360	370	390	415	444	461
New York	6 519	6 710	6 858	7 002	7 182	7 156	7 011	7 038	7 132	7 077	6 830	6 790	6 858	7 044	7 179
North Carolina	1 431	1 534	1 601	1 679	1 747	1 783	1 814	1 912	2 018	2 048	1 980	2 083	2 171	2 278	2 373
North Dakota	146	148	152	156	158	164	167	176	184	194	204	215	221	234	244
Ohio	3 364	3 537	3 620	3 751	3 887	3 881	3 840	3 938	4 113	4 169	4 016	4 095	4 230	4 395	4 485
Oklahoma	642	676	700	720	748	762	774	812	852	887	900	931	972	1 036	1 088
Oregon	608	640	652	679	709	711	729	775	816	838	837	878	937	1 009	1 056
Pennsylvania	3 918	4 077	4 171	4 264	4 375	4 352	4 291	4 400	4 506	4 515	4 436	4 513	4 565	4 716	4 806
Rhode Island	316	330	338	343	346	344	343	358	366	367	349	367	382	396	400
South Carolina	686	735	754	783	820	842	863	920	984	1 016	983	1 038	1 082	1 138	1 176
South Dakota	156	160	164	168	173	175	179	190	199	207	209	219	227	237	241
Tennessee	1 108	1 184	1 219	1 264	1 310	1 328	1 357	1 450	1 531	1 558	1 506	1 575	1 648	1 737	1 777
Texas	2 932	3 109	3 259	3 424	3 597	3 625	3 684	3 884	4 142	4 360	4 463	4 684	4 907	5 272	5 602
Utah	300	317	327	335	348	357	369	393	415	434	440	463	489	525	548
Vermont	121	131	136	140	146	148	148	154	161	163	162	168	178	191	198
Virginia	1 219	1 285	1 330	1 385	1 436	1 519	1 567	1 656	1 753	1 805	1 779	1 848	1 930	2 034	2 115
Washington	896	988	1 045	1 099	1 120	1 079	1 064	1 100	1 152	1 199	1 226	1 283	1 367	1 485	1 581
West Virginia	477	495	504	508	512	516	520	540	562	572	575	596	612	633	659
Wisconsin	1 332	1 394	1 430	1 472	1 525	1 530	1 525	1 581	1 660	1 703	1 677	1 726	1 799	1 887	1 960
Wyoming	. . .	. . .	99	103	107	108	111	117	126	136	146	157	171	187	201
Puerto Rico	. . .	. . .	. . .	. . .	. . .	. . .	. . .	. . .	. . .	. . .	. . .	. . .	. . .	. . .	. . .
Virgin Islands	. . .	. . .	. . .	. . .	. . .	. . .	. . .	. . .	. . .	. . .	33	31	32	34	36

. . . = Not available.

Table 2-11. Employees on Total Nonfarm Payrolls, by State and Selected Territory, 1965–2005—*Continued*

(Thousands of people.)

State	1980	1981	1982	1983	1984	1985	1986	1987	1988	1989	1990	1991	1992
UNITED STATES	90 528	91 289	89 677	90 280	94 530	97 511	99 474	102 088	105 345	108 014	109 487	108 374	108 726
Alabama	1 356	1 348	1 312	1 329	1 388	1 427	1 463	1 508	1 559	1 601	1 636	1 642	1 674
Alaska	169	186	200	214	226	231	221	210	214	227	238	243	247
Arizona	1 014	1 041	1 030	1 078	1 182	1 279	1 338	1 386	1 419	1 454	1 483	1 491	1 517
Arkansas	742	740	720	741	780	797	814	837	865	893	923	936	963
California	9 849	9 985	9 810	9 918	10 390	10 770	11 086	11 473	11 912	12 238	12 500	12 359	12 154
Colorado	1 251	1 295	1 317	1 327	1 402	1 419	1 408	1 413	1 436	1 482	1 521	1 545	1 597
Connecticut	1 427	1 438	1 428	1 444	1 517	1 558	1 598	1 638	1 667	1 666	1 624	1 555	1 526
Delaware	259	259	259	266	280	293	303	321	334	344	347	342	341
District of Columbia	616	611	598	597	614	629	640	656	674	681	686	677	674
Florida	3 576	3 736	3 762	3 905	4 204	4 410	4 599	4 848	5 067	5 261	5 387	5 294	5 358
Georgia	2 159	2 199	2 202	2 280	2 449	2 570	2 672	2 782	2 876	2 941	2 992	2 938	2 987
Hawaii	404	405	399	406	413	426	439	460	478	506	528	539	543
Idaho	330	328	312	318	330	336	328	333	349	366	385	398	416
Illinois	4 850	4 732	4 593	4 531	4 672	4 755	4 791	4 928	5 098	5 214	5 288	5 232	5 235
Indiana	2 130	2 114	2 028	2 030	2 122	2 169	2 222	2 305	2 396	2 479	2 522	2 507	2 554
Iowa	1 110	1 089	1 042	1 040	1 075	1 074	1 074	1 109	1 156	1 200	1 226	1 238	1 252
Kansas	945	950	921	922	961	968	985	1 005	1 035	1 064	1 088	1 095	1 115
Kentucky	1 210	1 196	1 161	1 152	1 214	1 250	1 274	1 328	1 382	1 433	1 470	1 475	1 508
Louisiana	1 579	1 630	1 607	1 565	1 602	1 591	1 518	1 484	1 512	1 538	1 588	1 611	1 625
Maine	418	419	416	425	446	458	477	501	527	542	535	513	512
Maryland	1 712	1 716	1 676	1 724	1 814	1 888	1 952	2 028	2 102	2 155	2 173	2 102	2 084
Massachusetts	2 654	2 672	2 642	2 696	2 856	2 930	2 989	3 066	3 131	3 109	2 985	2 821	2 795
Michigan	3 443	3 364	3 193	3 223	3 381	3 562	3 657	3 736	3 819	3 922	3 970	3 891	3 928
Minnesota	1 770	1 761	1 707	1 718	1 820	1 866	1 892	1 962	2 028	2 087	2 136	2 146	2 194
Mississippi	829	819	791	793	821	839	848	864	896	919	936	938	960
Missouri	1 970	1 956	1 922	1 937	2 033	2 095	2 143	2 198	2 259	2 315	2 345	2 309	2 334
Montana	280	282	274	276	281	279	275	274	283	291	297	304	316
Nebraska	628	623	610	611	635	650	652	667	688	708	730	739	750
Nevada	400	411	401	403	426	446	468	500	538	581	621	629	639
New Hampshire	385	395	394	410	442	466	490	513	529	529	508	482	487
New Jersey	3 060	3 099	3 093	3 165	3 329	3 414	3 488	3 576	3 651	3 690	3 635	3 499	3 458
New Mexico	465	476	474	480	503	520	526	529	548	562	580	585	602
New York	7 207	7 287	7 255	7 313	7 570	7 751	7 908	8 059	8 187	8 247	8 212	7 887	7 730
North Carolina	2 380	2 392	2 347	2 419	2 565	2 651	2 744	2 863	2 987	3 074	3 118	3 072	3 125
North Dakota	245	249	250	251	252	252	250	252	257	260	266	271	277
Ohio	4 367	4 318	4 124	4 092	4 260	4 373	4 472	4 583	4 701	4 818	4 882	4 819	4 848
Oklahoma	1 138	1 201	1 217	1 171	1 180	1 165	1 124	1 108	1 132	1 164	1 196	1 211	1 222
Oregon	1 044	1 019	961	967	1 007	1 030	1 058	1 100	1 153	1 206	1 247	1 245	1 267
Pennsylvania	4 753	4 729	4 580	4 524	4 655	4 730	4 791	4 915	5 042	5 138	5 170	5 084	5 076
Rhode Island	398	401	390	396	416	429	443	452	459	462	451	422	425
South Carolina	1 189	1 196	1 162	1 189	1 262	1 296	1 338	1 392	1 449	1 500	1 545	1 514	1 528
South Dakota	238	236	230	235	247	249	252	257	266	276	289	296	308
Tennessee	1 747	1 755	1 703	1 719	1 812	1 868	1 930	2 012	2 092	2 167	2 193	2 184	2 245
Texas	5 851	6 180	6 263	6 194	6 492	6 663	6 564	6 517	6 678	6 840	7 097	7 176	7 271
Utah	551	558	561	567	601	624	634	640	660	691	724	745	769
Vermont	200	204	203	206	215	225	234	246	256	262	258	249	251
Virginia	2 157	2 161	2 146	2 207	2 333	2 455	2 558	2 680	2 772	2 862	2 896	2 829	2 848
Washington	1 608	1 612	1 569	1 586	1 660	1 710	1 770	1 852	1 941	2 047	2 143	2 177	2 222
West Virginia	646	628	608	582	597	597	598	599	610	615	630	629	640
Wisconsin	1 938	1 923	1 867	1 867	1 949	1 983	2 024	2 090	2 168	2 236	2 292	2 302	2 358
Wyoming	210	224	218	202	204	207	196	183	189	193	198	203	206
Puerto Rico	. . .	. . .	. . .	. . .	. . .	. . .	. . .	. . .	. . .	846	838	858	
Virgin Islands	37	38	36	36	37	37	38	40	42	42	43	44	45

. . . = Not available.

Table 2-11. Employees on Total Nonfarm Payrolls, by State and Selected Territory, 1965–2005—*Continued*

(Thousands of people.)

State	1993	1994	1995	1996	1997	1998	1999	2000	2001	2002	2003	2004	2005
UNITED STATES	110 844	114 291	117 298	119 708	122 776	125 930	128 993	131 785	131 826	130 341	129 999	131 435	133 463
Alabama	1 717	1 758	1 804	1 829	1 866	1 898	1 920	1 931	1 909	1 883	1 876	1 902	1 943
Alaska	253	259	262	264	269	275	278	284	289	295	299	304	310
Arizona	1 584	1 692	1 795	1 892	1 984	2 075	2 163	2 243	2 265	2 265	2 296	2 381	2 507
Arkansas	994	1 034	1 069	1 086	1 104	1 122	1 142	1 158	1 154	1 146	1 145	1 158	1 178
California	12 045	12 160	12 422	12 743	13 130	13 596	13 992	14 488	14 602	14 458	14 392	14 530	14 785
Colorado	1 671	1 756	1 835	1 901	1 980	2 058	2 133	2 214	2 227	2 184	2 153	2 180	2 226
Connecticut	1 531	1 544	1 562	1 584	1 612	1 643	1 669	1 693	1 681	1 665	1 644	1 650	1 663
Delaware	349	356	366	376	388	400	413	420	419	414	414	424	430
District of Columbia	670	659	643	623	618	614	627	650	654	664	666	674	682
Florida	5 571	5 799	5 996	6 183	6 414	6 636	6 827	7 080	7 171	7 180	7 261	7 510	7 810
Georgia	3 109	3 266	3 402	3 527	3 614	3 741	3 855	3 949	3 943	3 870	3 845	3 900	4 000
Hawaii	539	536	533	531	532	531	535	551	555	557	568	583	602
Idaho	436	461	477	491	508	521	539	560	568	568	572	588	613
Illinois	5 330	5 463	5 593	5 685	5 772	5 899	5 958	6 045	5 995	5 884	5 811	5 816	5 865
Indiana	2 627	2 713	2 786	2 814	2 858	2 917	2 970	3 000	2 933	2 901	2 895	2 929	2 956
Iowa	1 278	1 320	1 358	1 383	1 407	1 443	1 469	1 478	1 466	1 447	1 440	1 457	1 481
Kansas	1 133	1 166	1 198	1 227	1 268	1 312	1 327	1 345	1 348	1 335	1 312	1 325	1 335
Kentucky	1 548	1 597	1 643	1 672	1 711	1 753	1 795	1 825	1 804	1 789	1 783	1 799	1 825
Louisiana	1 656	1 720	1 770	1 808	1 848	1 887	1 894	1 918	1 915	1 896	1 906	1 918	1 870
Maine	519	532	538	542	554	569	586	603	608	606	607	612	612
Maryland	2 104	2 148	2 184	2 213	2 269	2 326	2 392	2 455	2 472	2 480	2 487	2 518	2 555
Massachusetts	2 840	2 904	2 977	3 035	3 109	3 179	3 237	3 323	3 327	3 247	3 185	3 181	3 196
Michigan	4 006	4 147	4 274	4 361	4 448	4 510	4 582	4 674	4 556	4 478	4 410	4 395	4 384
Minnesota	2 252	2 320	2 388	2 442	2 500	2 564	2 622	2 685	2 690	2 664	2 660	2 681	2 709
Mississippi	1 002	1 056	1 074	1 089	1 107	1 134	1 153	1 154	1 130	1 124	1 115	1 124	1 130
Missouri	2 395	2 470	2 521	2 567	2 639	2 684	2 727	2 749	2 730	2 699	2 680	2 693	2 728
Montana	326	340	351	360	365	373	380	388	392	396	401	411	421
Nebraska	767	796	817	837	857	880	897	914	920	912	914	922	936
Nevada	672	738	786	843	891	926	983	1 027	1 051	1 052	1 088	1 153	1 224
New Hampshire	502	523	540	554	570	589	606	622	627	618	618	627	635
New Jersey	3 493	3 553	3 600	3 639	3 724	3 801	3 901	3 994	3 997	3 984	3 979	3 999	4 043
New Mexico	626	657	682	694	708	720	730	745	757	766	776	790	809
New York	7 760	7 831	7 892	7 939	8 067	8 237	8 456	8 635	8 592	8 459	8 407	8 462	8 528
North Carolina	3 245	3 359	3 460	3 546	3 663	3 774	3 870	3 934	3 899	3 837	3 790	3 837	3 912
North Dakota	285	295	302	309	314	319	324	328	330	330	333	338	345
Ohio	4 918	5 076	5 221	5 296	5 392	5 482	5 564	5 625	5 543	5 445	5 398	5 408	5 429
Oklahoma	1 247	1 279	1 316	1 353	1 392	1 441	1 462	1 489	1 507	1 486	1 458	1 474	1 511
Oregon	1 308	1 363	1 418	1 474	1 526	1 552	1 575	1 607	1 607	1 587	1 576	1 608	1 658
Pennsylvania	5 123	5 192	5 253	5 306	5 406	5 495	5 586	5 691	5 682	5 641	5 611	5 644	5 704
Rhode Island	430	434	440	442	450	458	466	477	478	479	484	488	492
South Carolina	1 570	1 607	1 646	1 675	1 720	1 783	1 830	1 859	1 823	1 804	1 807	1 833	1 860
South Dakota	319	332	344	349	355	363	373	378	378	377	378	383	390
Tennessee	2 328	2 423	2 499	2 533	2 584	2 638	2 685	2 729	2 688	2 664	2 663	2 706	2 744
Texas	7 483	7 753	8 024	8 258	8 608	8 938	9 155	9 427	9 514	9 416	9 371	9 497	9 735
Utah	810	860	908	954	994	1 023	1 048	1 075	1 081	1 073	1 074	1 104	1 150
Vermont	257	264	270	275	279	285	292	299	302	299	299	303	305
Virginia	2 919	3 004	3 070	3 136	3 232	3 320	3 412	3 516	3 516	3 494	3 497	3 584	3 668
Washington	2 253	2 304	2 347	2 416	2 514	2 595	2 649	2 711	2 697	2 654	2 658	2 701	2 779
West Virginia	652	674	688	699	708	719	726	736	735	733	728	737	747
Wisconsin	2 413	2 491	2 559	2 601	2 656	2 718	2 784	2 834	2 814	2 782	2 775	2 807	2 840
Wyoming	210	217	219	221	224	228	233	239	245	248	250	255	263
Puerto Rico	872	898	930	973	989	997	1 011	1 025	1 009	1 005	1 022	1 046	1 044
Virgin Islands	48	44	42	41	42	42	41	42	44	43	42	43	44

Table 2-12. Employees on Manufacturing Payrolls, by State and Selected Territory, NAICS Basis, 1990–2005

(Thousands of people.)

State	1990	1991	1992	1993	1994	1995	1996	1997	1998	1999	2000	2001	2002	2003	2004	2005
UNITED STATES	17 695	17 068	16 799	16 774	17 021	17 241	17 237	17 419	17 560	17 322	17 263	16 441	15 259	14 510	14 315	14 232
Alabama	364	354	357	359	362	370	362	364	365	358	351	326	307	294	292	298
Alaska	14	15	16	15	14	15	14	14	13	12	12	12	11	12	12	12
Arizona	176	171	167	170	182	191	199	205	207	210	210	202	184	175	177	181
Arkansas	219	219	224	231	240	246	241	241	242	241	240	227	214	206	203	200
California	1 967	1 892	1 794	1 701	1 689	1 721	1 778	1 830	1 861	1 834	1 862	1 790	1 643	1 553	1 533	1 513
Colorado	170	165	164	166	172	178	181	187	191	187	189	180	164	154	152	151
Connecticut	298	285	274	262	253	248	245	245	248	240	236	227	211	200	197	195
Delaware	46	46	44	44	43	43	41	43	44	44	42	39	37	36	35	33
District of Columbia	7	6	5	5	5	5	4	4	4	4	4	3	3	2	2	2
Florida	493	463	457	463	459	464	470	471	467	463	462	440	413	395	396	400
Georgia	506	483	491	511	526	540	544	547	545	543	530	498	467	452	448	449
Hawaii	20	19	19	18	17	16	16	16	16	16	16	16	15	15	15	15
Idaho	53	55	58	61	63	63	66	68	69	69	70	68	65	62	62	63
Illinois	915	876	855	860	878	894	899	902	906	882	870	815	754	714	697	689
Indiana	609	590	600	614	625	651	646	651	657	665	664	615	588	573	572	571
Iowa	219	216	216	221	230	236	235	239	251	253	251	240	227	220	223	230
Kansas	178	174	174	172	176	180	186	198	206	204	201	195	184	175	177	180
Kentucky	273	267	271	279	289	299	298	302	306	309	310	292	275	265	264	262
Louisiana	177	178	177	177	179	182	183	186	185	181	177	172	161	156	153	151
Maine	93	88	84	82	83	83	81	81	81	80	80	75	68	64	63	61
Maryland	198	187	180	176	177	177	174	175	175	174	174	168	156	147	143	141
Massachusetts	486	452	437	425	418	417	416	417	418	405	408	389	349	324	313	306
Michigan	838	793	796	806	848	873	866	873	890	898	897	820	760	716	697	679
Minnesota	341	339	342	351	361	375	381	391	397	395	396	378	356	343	343	346
Mississippi	229	230	236	239	244	241	231	228	234	233	222	201	188	179	180	178
Missouri	392	373	366	365	366	377	376	377	379	374	364	345	325	314	311	308
Montana	20	19	20	20	21	21	22	22	22	22	22	21	20	19	19	19
Nebraska	98	97	98	100	106	110	111	113	114	113	114	111	106	102	101	102
Nevada	24	25	26	29	33	36	38	40	40	41	43	44	43	44	46	48
New Hampshire	98	92	90	91	94	97	99	102	104	101	102	97	85	80	80	80
New Jersey	530	498	474	463	456	449	437	435	429	422	422	401	368	350	338	329
New Mexico	38	38	37	39	42	42	43	43	42	41	42	41	38	36	36	36
New York	983	910	870	836	816	810	797	797	792	773	751	708	652	613	597	580
North Carolina	824	785	796	813	817	821	808	800	796	776	758	704	644	599	577	567
North Dakota	16	16	17	18	20	20	20	22	22	23	24	24	24	24	25	26
Ohio	1 065	1 023	994	980	1 004	1 037	1 030	1 028	1 031	1 028	1 021	953	885	843	822	813
Oklahoma	157	157	153	156	159	162	163	169	176	177	178	170	152	143	142	145
Oregon	203	195	192	192	200	208	216	225	227	223	223	216	202	195	200	204
Pennsylvania	947	909	888	875	878	878	865	869	872	862	862	821	759	712	690	682
Rhode Island	95	87	85	84	82	80	77	76	75	72	71	68	62	59	57	55
South Carolina	348	334	338	342	345	347	339	338	341	336	336	314	290	276	268	262
South Dakota	34	34	36	38	41	44	44	44	44	44	44	41	38	38	39	40
Tennessee	493	480	493	503	514	518	502	498	499	495	488	454	428	413	412	409
Texas	948	936	929	942	966	995	1 017	1 045	1 077	1 063	1 068	1 027	949	900	891	899
Utah	104	102	102	106	112	117	122	126	127	126	126	122	114	112	114	118
Vermont	43	40	40	40	40	41	43	44	45	45	46	46	40	38	37	37
Virginia	387	376	373	370	371	373	371	374	376	367	364	341	320	305	299	296
Washington	336	329	325	313	312	311	325	350	360	343	332	316	285	267	264	272
West Virginia	82	79	78	79	77	78	78	77	78	77	76	72	69	64	63	62
Wisconsin	523	513	517	526	546	567	568	579	593	595	594	560	528	504	503	506
Wyoming	9	9	9	10	10	10	10	10	10	10	10	10	10	9	9	10
Puerto Rico	159	154	154	155	156	159	158	155	148	144	143	132	121	118	118	116
Virgin Islands	2	2	2	3	3	2	2	2	2	2	2	2	2	2	2	2

Table 2-13. Employees on Government Payrolls, by State and Selected Territory, NAICS Basis, 1990–2005

(Thousands of people.)

State	1990	1991	1992	1993	1994	1995	1996	1997	1998	1999	2000	2001	2002	2003	2004	2005
UNITED STATES	18 415	18 545	18 787	18 989	19 275	19 432	19 539	19 664	19 909	20 307	20 790	21 118	21 513	21 583	21 621	21 803
Alabama	327	333	338	341	346	343	343	346	347	351	352	352	355	358	359	362
Alaska	71	72	73	75	74	73	73	73	74	74	74	79	81	82	81	81
Arizona	259	271	277	287	294	310	318	328	341	354	367	378	390	394	399	403
Arkansas	159	163	167	170	173	177	180	183	185	187	191	194	195	198	200	205
California	2 075	2 091	2 096	2 081	2 093	2 107	2 113	2 141	2 166	2 239	2 318	2 382	2 447	2 426	2 396	2 414
Colorado	277	283	291	297	299	304	309	316	322	328	337	344	355	356	358	363
Connecticut	210	208	207	211	217	221	223	226	228	235	242	244	249	246	243	244
Delaware	48	48	49	50	50	51	52	53	54	55	57	57	57	57	58	59
District of Columbia	277	281	286	285	270	255	240	233	226	222	224	226	232	231	231	233
Florida	847	859	870	882	910	918	928	942	955	966	1 002	1 023	1 039	1 053	1 066	1 081
Georgia	532	537	537	548	564	570	570	577	586	590	597	610	625	632	637	650
Hawaii	106	109	111	112	112	111	110	112	112	113	115	114	118	119	120	120
Idaho	81	84	88	90	93	96	97	100	103	105	109	110	112	113	114	115
Illinois	766	770	774	774	786	799	809	808	816	826	840	850	861	853	845	846
Indiana	378	380	388	391	391	392	391	392	399	403	410	410	417	423	426	427
Iowa	219	221	221	222	227	230	233	235	236	239	243	245	244	245	245	246
Kansas	214	219	226	230	233	237	234	236	240	240	245	248	251	250	251	252
Kentucky	260	267	273	276	280	287	289	291	295	301	305	311	315	312	310	314
Louisiana	326	332	340	342	351	358	362	364	367	370	373	374	375	379	382	379
Maine	96	96	96	95	94	93	93	93	95	97	100	102	103	104	105	105
Maryland	422	419	417	419	422	423	423	423	433	444	450	457	465	462	463	464
Massachusetts	402	390	382	387	390	395	400	404	412	417	424	428	423	413	408	410
Michigan	634	636	639	639	639	641	644	647	656	668	682	686	687	685	680	674
Minnesota	347	351	355	361	369	387	389	389	390	397	408	409	414	412	412	416
Mississippi	203	204	208	210	214	215	217	219	223	227	234	238	240	241	242	242
Missouri	370	371	371	377	385	390	401	413	414	421	426	429	431	432	429	429
Montana	71	72	74	74	76	77	77	77	78	79	80	84	85	86	87	86
Nebraska	143	146	148	149	152	151	151	152	151	151	154	157	159	160	160	161
Nevada	76	81	86	88	92	96	101	106	112	117	122	127	131	135	139	144
New Hampshire	73	72	73	74	76	76	78	79	80	82	84	86	88	90	90	90
New Jersey	577	572	572	571	573	573	571	570	572	578	589	603	614	622	633	642
New Mexico	150	152	156	159	163	166	171	177	178	180	183	186	191	195	198	202
New York	1 473	1 445	1 428	1 433	1 436	1 416	1 401	1 407	1 424	1 445	1 468	1 468	1 493	1 488	1 484	1 488
North Carolina	492	502	502	527	539	550	561	576	594	604	622	636	642	641	652	664
North Dakota	65	66	67	67	67	71	71	71	71	72	73	73	74	75	75	75
Ohio	722	728	735	736	741	749	752	758	763	772	785	794	800	803	802	799
Oklahoma	262	265	270	270	270	270	271	276	278	283	288	296	301	296	302	312
Oregon	224	226	231	233	235	240	247	250	255	261	267	283	287	281	284	286
Pennsylvania	699	695	693	702	706	712	712	715	712	716	725	728	739	746	744	745
Rhode Island	62	61	61	61	62	61	61	63	63	63	64	65	66	66	66	65
South Carolina	282	286	292	296	295	294	295	299	309	315	323	323	326	326	325	328
South Dakota	63	63	65	67	67	71	70	70	71	72	70	73	74	74	75	75
Tennessee	351	353	357	362	371	373	382	380	386	390	399	403	410	411	415	414
Texas	1 263	1 288	1 334	1 376	1 414	1 446	1 458	1 483	1 504	1 535	1 562	1 586	1 626	1 646	1 656	1 683
Utah	150	154	157	159	161	164	167	172	177	180	185	190	195	197	199	203
Vermont	44	44	44	44	45	45	45	46	46	48	49	50	51	52	52	53
Virginia	578	580	589	598	603	598	596	597	602	611	625	629	635	638	651	663
Washington	398	412	424	430	437	444	450	458	466	474	483	505	516	521	524	527
West Virginia	127	128	132	133	136	136	139	139	141	141	143	141	143	142	143	144
Wisconsin	343	346	357	362	367	379	384	387	393	399	406	414	415	413	412	413
Wyoming	55	56	57	57	58	58	58	58	58	59	61	62	63	64	64	65
Puerto Rico	295	291	296	290	300	305	316	310	308	291	286	282	295	301	307	306
Virgin Islands	14	13	14	14	14	14	14	14	14	13	13	12	13	13	12	12

Table 2-14. Average Weekly Hours of Production Workers on Manufacturing Payrolls, by State and Selected Territory, NAICS Basis, 2001–2005

(Hours.)

State	2001	2002	2003	2004	2005
UNITED STATES	40.3	40.5	40.4	40.8	40.7
Alabama	41.0	41.4	41.0	40.8	40.8
Alaska	43.1	37.4	43.0	40.6	32.9
Arizona	40.3	40.0	40.4	40.5	40.7
Arkansas	39.9	39.7	39.6	39.9	39.9
California	39.6	39.6	39.7	40.0	39.9
Colorado	40.7	40.6	40.4	40.4	38.5
Connecticut	41.7	41.6	41.4	41.8	42.2
Delaware	39.7	40.0	40.3	40.1	39.7
District of Columbia	. . .	. . .	. . .	. . .	. . .
Florida	40.6	42.1	41.0	41.1	41.7
Georgia	40.4	40.9	39.8	39.2	39.0
Hawaii	36.0	35.6	37.2	37.9	38.4
Idaho	39.1	39.6	41.3	40.5	40.3
Illinois	41.0	41.4	40.6	41.0	40.8
Indiana	41.0	42.4	42.1	42.1	41.9
Iowa	40.9	41.3	41.7	42.2	41.6
Kansas	40.7	40.8	40.5	41.0	41.1
Kentucky	41.5	42.2	41.7	40.8	40.6
Louisiana	43.1	43.9	44.1	43.9	42.0
Maine	39.8	39.9	40.0	39.6	39.6
Maryland	39.0	40.0	39.5	40.1	40.1
Massachusetts	40.3	40.8	40.6	41.1	41.5
Michigan	41.9	42.7	42.1	42.4	41.7
Minnesota	39.6	39.7	40.2	40.9	40.9
Mississippi	39.7	40.6	39.9	40.1	40.1
Missouri	40.3	39.3	40.5	40.2	39.6
Montana	38.8	38.2	38.4	38.3	40.1
Nebraska	41.2	41.9	41.6	41.6	40.0
Nevada	38.7	38.8	39.0	40.1	39.8
New Hampshire	40.6	39.8	40.0	40.0	41.2
New Jersey	40.6	40.9	41.0	42.1	42.0
New Mexico	39.0	39.9	39.4	39.6	39.1
New York	39.8	40.3	40.0	39.7	39.6
North Carolina	39.4	40.2	39.8	40.3	40.0
North Dakota	40.9	40.2	40.0	39.3	39.2
Ohio	41.2	41.4	41.0	41.7	41.4
Oklahoma	39.4	39.2	39.3	40.5	39.2
Oregon	39.1	39.1	39.3	39.1	40.2
Pennsylvania	40.4	40.3	40.0	40.3	40.5
Rhode Island	39.4	38.7	39.3	39.2	38.4
South Carolina	41.2	42.1	41.3	39.5	39.7
South Dakota	41.7	42.3	42.5	42.0	42.3
Tennessee	38.9	40.1	39.8	40.0	39.2
Texas	41.6	41.1	41.4	39.8	40.0
Utah	38.4	37.8	39.7	38.1	39.2
Vermont	39.6	40.0	40.0	40.2	39.2
Virginia	40.1	40.8	40.8	41.5	41.4
Washington	40.0	40.1	39.5	40.0	39.7
West Virginia	41.1	41.4	41.3	41.4	41.4
Wisconsin	40.2	40.5	40.3	40.3	40.4
Wyoming	38.6	39.3	40.2	39.7	40.5
Puerto Rico	. . .	. . .	40.9	41.0	40.8
Virgin Islands	43.9	43.7	42.8	46.4	43.8

. . . = Not available.

EARNINGS

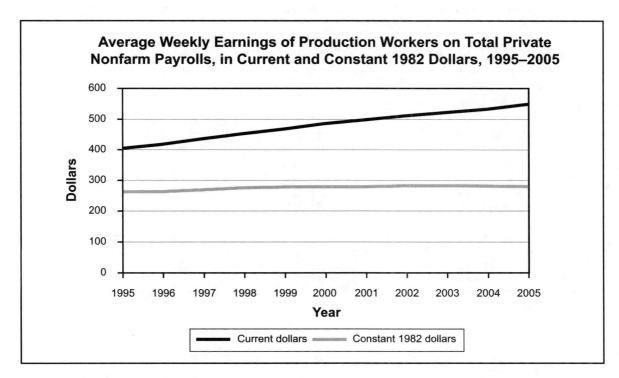

Average Weekly Earnings of Production Workers on Total Private Nonfarm Payrolls, in Current and Constant 1982 Dollars, 1995–2005

While weekly earnings of production workers rose 2.9 percent from 2004, real earnings declined 0.6 percent as consumer prices rose 3.4 percent. Real earnings in 2005 were the same as in 2000. (See Table 2-17.)

OTHER HIGHLIGHTS

• Natural resources was the only industry with a significant gain in real weekly earnings in 2005. However, it employed less than 1 percent of all workers. The education and health services industry, which employed 13 percent of all workers, increased 0.5 percent in 2005. (See Table 2-17.)

• Weekly earnings in current dollars ranged from $235.29 in leisure and hospitality to $1,097.16 in utilities in 2005. Wages in goods-producing industries were 38.7 percent higher than in private service-providing industries. (See Table 2-17.)

• Within manufacturing, the highest average weekly earnings were $1,117.94 in petroleum and coal products, followed by $938.37 in transportation equipment. (See Table 2-18.)

• In 2004, the District of Columbia had the highest average annual pay for all workers at $63,887. This was 62 percent above the national average, most likely due to the lack of production workers in the district. Industries with high pay included mining, utilities, and financial activities. (See Tables 2-21 and 2-22.)

Table 2-15. Average Hourly Earnings of Production Workers on Private Nonfarm Payrolls, by Super Sector, NAICS Basis, 1990–2005

(Dollars.)

Industry	1990	1991	1992	1993	1994	1995	1996	1997	1998	1999	2000	2001	2002	2003	2004	2005
TOTAL PRIVATE	10.19	10.50	10.76	11.03	11.32	11.64	12.03	12.49	13.00	13.47	14.00	14.53	14.95	15.35	15.67	16.11
Goods-Producing	11.46	11.76	11.99	12.28	12.63	12.96	13.38	13.82	14.23	14.71	15.27	15.78	16.33	16.80	17.19	17.60
Natural resources and mining	13.40	13.82	14.09	14.12	14.41	14.78	15.10	15.57	16.20	16.33	16.55	17.00	17.19	17.56	18.07	18.73
Construction	13.42	13.65	13.81	14.04	14.38	14.73	15.11	15.67	16.23	16.80	17.48	18.00	18.52	18.95	19.23	19.46
Manufacturing	10.78	11.13	11.40	11.70	12.04	12.34	12.75	13.14	13.45	13.85	14.32	14.76	15.29	15.74	16.15	16.56
Private Service-Providing	9.71	10.05	10.33	10.60	10.87	11.19	11.57	12.05	12.59	13.07	13.60	14.16	14.56	14.96	15.26	15.71
Trade, transportation, and utilities	9.83	10.08	10.30	10.55	10.80	11.10	11.46	11.90	12.39	12.82	13.31	13.70	14.02	14.34	14.58	14.93
Wholesale trade	11.58	11.95	12.21	12.57	12.93	13.34	13.80	14.41	15.07	15.62	16.28	16.77	16.98	17.36	17.65	18.16
Retail trade	7.71	7.89	8.12	8.36	8.61	8.85	9.21	9.59	10.05	10.45	10.86	11.29	11.67	11.90	12.08	12.36
Transportation and warehousing	12.50	12.61	12.77	12.71	12.84	13.18	13.45	13.78	14.12	14.55	15.05	15.33	15.76	16.25	16.52	16.71
Utilities	16.14	16.70	17.17	17.95	18.66	19.19	19.78	20.59	21.48	22.03	22.75	23.58	23.96	24.77	25.61	26.70
Information	13.40	13.90	14.29	14.86	15.32	15.68	16.30	17.14	17.67	18.40	19.07	19.80	20.20	21.01	21.40	22.07
Financial activities	9.99	10.42	10.86	11.36	11.82	12.28	12.71	13.22	13.93	14.47	14.98	15.59	16.17	17.14	17.52	17.94
Professional and business services ..	11.14	11.50	11.78	11.96	12.15	12.53	13.00	13.57	14.27	14.85	15.52	16.33	16.81	17.21	17.48	18.07
Educational and health services	10.00	10.49	10.87	11.21	11.50	11.80	12.17	12.56	13.00	13.44	13.95	14.64	15.21	15.64	16.15	16.72
Leisure and hospitality	5.88	6.06	6.20	6.32	6.46	6.62	6.82	7.13	7.48	7.76	8.11	8.35	8.58	8.76	8.91	9.14
Other services	9.08	9.39	9.66	9.90	10.18	10.51	10.85	11.29	11.79	12.26	12.73	13.27	13.72	13.84	13.98	14.33

Table 2-16. Average Hourly Earnings of Production Workers on Manufacturing Payrolls, by Industry, NAICS Basis, 1990–2005

(Dollars.)

Industry	1990	1991	1992	1993	1994	1995	1996	1997	1998	1999	2000	2001	2002	2003	2004	2005
DURABLE GOODS																
Total	11.40	11.81	12.09	12.41	12.78	13.05	13.45	13.83	14.07	14.46	14.93	15.38	16.02	16.45	16.82	17.34
Wood product	8.82	9.03	9.24	9.41	9.66	9.92	10.24	10.53	10.85	11.18	11.63	11.99	12.33	12.71	13.03	13.16
Nonmetallic mineral product	11.11	11.34	11.57	11.83	12.11	12.39	12.80	13.17	13.59	13.97	14.53	14.86	15.40	15.76	16.25	16.61
Primary metals	12.97	13.37	13.72	14.08	14.47	14.75	15.12	15.40	15.66	16.00	16.64	17.06	17.68	18.13	18.57	18.94
Fabricated metal product	10.64	10.97	11.16	11.40	11.64	11.91	12.26	12.64	12.97	13.34	13.77	14.19	14.68	15.01	15.31	15.80
Machinery	11.73	12.12	12.40	12.73	12.94	13.14	13.49	13.94	14.24	14.77	15.22	15.49	15.92	16.30	16.68	17.03
Computer and electronic product	10.89	11.35	11.64	11.95	12.19	12.29	12.75	13.24	13.85	14.37	14.73	15.42	16.20	16.69	17.27	18.40
Electrical equipment and appliances	10.00	10.30	10.50	10.65	10.94	11.25	11.80	12.24	12.51	12.90	13.23	13.78	13.98	14.36	14.90	15.25
Transportation equipment	14.44	15.12	15.59	16.22	16.94	17.21	17.67	18.00	17.92	18.24	18.89	19.48	20.64	21.23	21.49	22.10
Furniture and related product	8.52	8.74	9.00	9.24	9.51	9.75	10.08	10.50	10.88	11.27	11.72	12.14	12.61	12.98	13.16	13.44
Miscellaneous manufacturing	8.87	9.16	9.44	9.65	9.90	10.23	10.60	10.89	11.18	11.56	11.93	12.46	12.91	13.30	13.84	14.08
NONDURABLE GOODS																
Total	9.87	10.18	10.45	10.70	10.96	11.30	11.68	12.04	12.45	12.85	13.31	13.75	14.15	14.63	15.05	15.27
Food manufacturing	9.04	9.32	9.59	9.82	10.00	10.27	10.50	10.77	11.09	11.40	11.77	12.18	12.55	12.80	12.98	13.04
Beverage and tobacco product	13.24	13.65	14.07	14.30	14.97	15.40	15.73	16.00	16.03	16.54	17.40	17.67	17.73	17.96	19.14	18.79
Textile mills	8.17	8.49	8.82	9.12	9.35	9.63	9.88	10.22	10.58	10.90	11.23	11.40	11.73	11.99	12.13	12.38
Textile product mills	7.53	7.77	8.03	8.27	8.45	8.76	9.12	9.45	9.75	10.18	10.43	10.60	10.96	11.23	11.39	11.66
Apparel	6.22	6.43	6.60	6.74	6.95	7.22	7.45	7.76	8.05	8.35	8.60	8.82	9.10	9.56	9.75	10.24
Leather and allied product	7.18	7.43	7.68	7.88	8.23	8.50	8.94	9.31	9.68	9.93	10.35	10.69	11.00	11.66	11.63	11.50
Paper and paper product	12.06	12.45	12.78	13.13	13.49	13.94	14.38	14.76	15.20	15.58	15.91	16.38	16.85	17.33	17.91	17.98
Printing and related support	11.11	11.32	11.53	11.67	11.89	12.08	12.41	12.78	13.20	13.67	14.09	14.48	14.93	15.37	15.71	15.75
Petroleum and coal product	17.00	17.90	18.83	19.43	19.96	20.24	20.18	21.10	21.75	22.22	22.80	22.90	23.04	23.63	24.39	24.54
Chemicals	12.85	13.30	13.70	13.97	14.33	14.86	15.37	15.78	16.23	16.40	17.09	17.57	17.97	18.50	19.17	19.67
Plastics and rubber product	9.76	10.07	10.35	10.55	10.66	10.86	11.17	11.48	11.79	12.25	12.69	13.21	13.55	14.18	14.59	14.82

Table 2-17. Average Weekly Earnings of Production Workers on Nonfarm Payrolls, by Industry, in Current and Constant 1982 Dollars, NAICS Basis, 1990–2005

(Dollars.)

Industry	1990	1991	1992	1993	1994	1995	1996	1997	1998	1999	2000	2001	2002	2003	2004	2005
TOTAL PRIVATE																
Current dollars	349.29	358.06	367.83	378.40	390.73	399.53	412.74	431.25	448.04	462.49	480.41	493.20	506.07	517.30	528.36	543.65
Constant 1982 dollars	262.43	258.34	257.95	258.12	259.97	258.43	259.58	265.22	271.87	274.64	275.62	275.38	278.83	278.72	277.50	275.82
Goods-Producing																
Current dollars	459.55	471.32	482.58	498.82	519.58	528.62	546.48	568.43	580.99	599.99	621.86	630.04	651.61	669.13	688.17	705.28
Constant 1982 dollars	345.27	340.06	338.42	340.26	345.70	341.93	343.70	349.59	352.54	356.29	356.78	351.78	359.01	360.52	361.43	357.83
Natural resources and mining																
Current dollars	602.54	625.42	629.02	634.77	653.14	670.32	695.07	720.11	727.28	721.74	734.92	757.92	741.97	765.94	803.82	853.89
Constant 1982 dollars	452.70	451.24	441.11	432.99	434.56	433.58	437.15	442.87	441.31	428.59	421.64	423.18	408.80	412.68	422.17	433.23
Construction																
Current dollars	513.43	520.41	525.13	539.81	558.53	571.57	588.48	609.48	629.75	655.11	685.78	695.89	711.82	726.83	735.55	750.63
Constant 1982 dollars	385.75	375.48	368.25	368.22	371.61	369.71	370.11	374.83	382.13	389.02	393.45	388.55	392.19	391.61	386.32	380.84
Manufacturing																
Current dollars	436.16	449.73	464.43	480.80	502.12	509.26	526.55	548.22	557.12	573.17	590.65	595.19	618.75	635.99	658.59	673.61
Constant 1982 dollars	327.69	324.48	325.69	327.97	334.08	329.40	331.16	337.16	338.06	340.36	338.87	332.32	340.91	342.67	345.90	341.76
Private Service-Providing																
Current dollars	315.49	325.31	335.46	345.03	354.97	364.14	376.72	394.77	412.78	427.30	445.00	460.32	472.88	483.89	493.30	508.66
Constant 1982 dollars	237.03	234.71	235.25	235.35	236.17	235.54	236.93	242.79	250.47	253.74	255.31	257.02	260.54	260.72	259.09	258.07
Trade, transportation, and utilities																
Current dollars	331.55	339.19	348.68	359.33	370.38	378.79	390.64	407.57	423.30	434.31	449.88	459.53	471.27	481.14	488.42	498.59
Constant 1982 dollars	249.10	244.73	244.52	245.11	246.43	245.01	245.69	250.66	256.86	257.90	258.11	256.58	259.65	259.23	256.52	252.96
Wholesale trade																
Current dollars	444.48	459.27	470.51	484.46	501.17	515.14	533.29	559.39	582.21	602.77	631.40	643.45	644.38	657.29	667.09	684.91
Constant 1982 dollars	333.94	331.36	329.95	330.46	333.45	333.21	335.40	344.03	353.28	357.94	362.25	359.27	355.03	354.14	350.36	347.49
Retail trade																
Current dollars	235.62	240.15	249.63	256.89	265.77	272.56	282.76	295.97	310.34	321.63	333.38	346.16	360.81	367.15	371.13	377.68
Constant 1982 dollars	177.02	173.27	175.06	175.23	176.83	176.30	177.84	182.02	188.31	190.99	191.27	193.28	198.79	197.82	194.92	191.62
Transportation and warehousing																
Current dollars	471.72	471.12	478.02	494.36	507.27	513.37	525.60	542.55	546.86	547.97	562.31	562.70	579.75	598.41	614.82	618.64
Constant 1982 dollars	354.41	339.91	335.22	337.22	337.50	332.06	330.57	333.67	331.83	325.40	322.61	314.18	319.42	322.42	322.91	313.87
Utilities																
Current dollars	670.40	693.40	716.36	756.35	789.98	811.52	830.74	865.26	902.94	924.59	955.66	977.18	979.09	1 017.27	1 048.44	1 097.16
Constant 1982 dollars	503.68	500.29	502.36	515.93	525.60	524.92	522.48	532.14	547.90	549.04	548.28	545.61	539.44	548.10	550.65	556.65
Information																
Current dollars	479.50	495.20	512.01	535.25	551.28	564.98	592.68	622.40	646.52	675.32	700.89	731.11	738.17	760.81	777.05	805.89
Constant 1982 dollars	360.26	357.29	359.05	365.11	366.79	365.45	372.75	382.78	392.31	401.02	402.12	408.21	406.71	409.92	408.11	408.87
Financial activities																
Current dollars	354.65	369.57	386.01	403.02	419.20	436.12	451.49	472.37	500.95	517.57	537.37	558.02	575.51	609.08	622.87	644.71
Constant 1982 dollars	266.45	266.65	270.69	274.91	278.91	282.10	283.96	290.51	303.97	307.35	308.30	311.57	317.09	328.17	327.14	327.10
Professional and business services																
Current dollars	380.61	391.09	400.64	406.20	414.16	426.44	442.81	465.51	490.00	510.99	535.07	557.84	574.66	587.02	597.56	618.46
Constant 1982 dollars	285.96	282.17	280.95	277.08	275.56	275.83	278.50	286.29	297.33	303.44	306.98	311.47	316.62	316.28	313.84	313.78
Education and health services																
Current dollars	319.27	334.55	348.29	359.08	368.14	377.73	388.27	404.65	418.82	431.35	449.29	473.39	492.74	505.69	523.78	544.80
Constant 1982 dollars	239.87	241.38	244.24	244.94	244.94	244.33	244.19	248.86	254.14	256.15	257.77	264.32	271.48	272.46	275.09	276.41
Leisure and hospitality																
Current dollars	152.47	155.16	159.54	163.45	168.00	171.43	176.48	185.81	195.82	202.87	211.79	215.19	221.26	224.30	228.65	235.29
Constant 1982 dollars	114.55	111.95	111.88	111.49	111.78	110.89	110.99	114.27	118.82	120.47	121.51	120.15	121.91	120.85	120.09	119.38
Other services																
Current dollars	297.91	306.91	315.08	322.69	332.44	342.36	352.62	368.63	384.25	398.77	413.41	428.64	439.76	434.41	433.04	443.06
Constant 1982 dollars	223.82	221.44	220.95	220.12	221.18	221.45	221.77	226.71	233.16	236.80	237.18	239.33	242.29	234.06	227.44	224.79

Table 2-18. Average Weekly Earnings of Production Workers on Manufacturing Payrolls, by Industry, NAICS Basis, 1990–2005

(Dollars.)

Industry	1990	1991	1992	1993	1994	1995	1996	1997
TOTAL MANUFACTURING	436.16	449.73	464.43	480.80	502.12	509.26	526.55	548.22
Total Durable Goods	468.43	483.28	499.59	519.92	544.66	549.49	566.53	589.10
Wood product	356.38	362.69	377.76	387.38	402.86	406.51	422.32	435.78
Nonmetallic mineral product	453.98	459.20	474.55	490.54	510.92	517.68	537.81	552.02
Primary metals	545.22	555.37	581.34	606.37	637.69	639.70	658.68	681.47
Fabricated metal product	436.12	447.98	459.64	474.21	492.07	498.48	513.57	534.48
Machinery	493.39	507.96	525.53	549.98	568.12	571.25	584.69	613.49
Computer and electronic product	450.09	464.25	482.09	499.15	514.92	518.25	534.42	562.69
Electrical equipment and appliances	412.42	426.96	439.04	451.28	470.21	471.63	496.69	515.73
Transportation equipment	606.87	633.87	652.95	697.16	750.67	751.74	773.95	795.82
Furniture and related product	324.08	330.49	348.03	360.63	373.87	375.06	385.68	410.38
Miscellaneous manufacturing	346.02	358.56	370.75	378.28	389.79	400.85	414.13	431.89
Total Nondurable Goods	390.65	404.17	417.95	429.15	443.82	452.83	467.88	487.04
Food manufacturing	355.61	364.90	375.69	386.04	398.54	406.66	414.74	428.58
Beverage and tobacco product	515.73	530.09	544.25	547.60	588.39	605.00	624.82	639.69
Textile mills	328.11	345.48	364.45	379.74	391.64	394.17	403.08	425.53
Textile product mills	293.77	303.81	314.47	329.26	336.96	342.17	356.90	373.95
Apparel	216.10	227.76	235.20	239.45	248.33	254.85	261.90	275.61
Leather and allied product	268.32	279.41	291.11	302.85	314.18	319.98	337.86	355.63
Paper and paper product	525.71	542.26	560.27	575.49	596.19	604.74	625.38	647.55
Printing and related support	429.93	437.00	450.02	457.91	470.74	472.37	484.99	504.46
Petroleum and coal product	754.13	786.05	821.72	855.36	883.81	883.68	881.24	908.50
Chemicals	550.25	573.27	593.17	603.71	622.46	644.30	666.00	685.26
Plastics and rubber product	396.07	408.22	426.56	436.96	445.87	445.91	458.15	474.87

Industry	1998	1999	2000	2001	2002	2003	2004	2005
TOTAL MANUFACTURING	557.12	573.17	590.65	595.19	618.75	635.99	658.59	673.61
Total Durable Goods	591.68	606.67	624.38	624.54	652.97	671.21	694.13	713.05
Wood product	449.78	461.61	477.23	481.36	492.00	514.10	530.15	526.91
Nonmetallic mineral product	572.96	587.53	604.88	618.79	646.91	664.92	688.20	700.62
Primary metals	681.64	700.76	734.62	723.95	749.32	767.60	799.78	815.52
Fabricated metal product	543.20	555.86	576.68	576.60	596.38	610.37	628.80	647.32
Machinery	613.87	625.40	643.92	632.77	645.55	664.79	699.59	716.48
Computer and electronic product	579.70	596.25	609.70	613.07	642.87	674.72	697.83	735.82
Electrical equipment and appliances	522.51	538.98	550.56	548.00	560.24	583.23	606.97	619.19
Transportation equipment	774.82	796.25	817.98	817.08	877.87	889.48	912.98	938.37
Furniture and related product	428.50	443.38	459.69	464.57	494.01	505.30	519.62	527.11
Miscellaneous manufacturing	437.99	454.56	465.02	483.44	499.13	510.82	533.07	545.19
Total Nondurable Goods	503.99	519.91	536.82	548.41	566.84	582.61	602.53	609.13
Food manufacturing	444.81	458.63	472.09	481.67	496.91	502.92	509.55	508.03
Beverage and tobacco product	646.26	679.06	730.35	721.68	698.39	702.45	751.20	752.39
Textile mills	434.15	447.38	464.51	456.64	476.52	469.33	486.68	498.47
Textile product mills	385.13	401.01	406.24	408.56	429.01	444.70	443.12	455.19
Apparel	286.07	295.20	307.00	317.15	333.66	340.12	351.56	366.11
Leather and allied product	361.87	369.80	388.46	388.83	412.99	457.83	446.66	442.16
Paper and paper product	662.20	679.24	681.34	690.06	705.62	719.73	754.14	763.36
Printing and related support	518.32	534.15	552.15	560.89	573.05	587.58	603.97	604.80
Petroleum and coal product	949.28	947.60	973.53	1 003.34	990.88	1 052.32	1 095.00	1 117.94
Chemicals	700.53	700.45	721.90	735.54	759.53	783.95	819.73	831.40
Plastics and rubber product	487.00	505.31	517.74	528.69	549.85	572.26	589.84	592.50

Table 2-19. Average Hourly Earnings of Production Workers on Manufacturing Payrolls, by State and Selected Territory, NAICS Basis, 2001–2005

(Dollars.)

State	2001	2002	2003	2004	2005
UNITED STATES	14.76	15.29	15.74	16.15	16.56
Alabama	12.76	13.10	13.56	14.33	14.93
Alaska	11.70	13.24	12.18	12.01	14.22
Arizona	13.80	14.16	14.38	14.20	14.55
Arkansas	12.90	13.30	13.55	13.49	13.71
California	14.69	14.89	15.04	15.36	15.70
Colorado	14.72	15.44	16.89	16.46	15.91
Connecticut	16.42	17.24	17.74	18.35	18.96
Delaware	16.56	16.60	16.91	17.66	17.72
District of Columbia	. . .	. . .	. . .	. . .	. . .
Florida	12.68	13.30	14.09	13.84	13.89
Georgia	12.50	13.38	14.08	14.54	14.56
Hawaii	13.18	13.07	12.90	13.50	14.35
Idaho	13.85	13.80	13.72	14.15	14.96
Illinois	14.66	14.99	15.20	15.61	15.84
Indiana	16.42	17.15	17.84	17.92	18.14
Iowa	14.67	15.32	15.70	16.17	16.25
Kansas	15.48	15.98	15.83	16.57	17.14
Kentucky	15.44	15.73	16.01	16.50	16.64
Louisiana	16.18	17.03	16.86	16.40	17.30
Maine	14.71	15.55	16.28	16.97	17.28
Maryland	14.56	15.21	15.74	16.47	16.98
Massachusetts	15.75	16.25	16.53	16.89	17.67
Michigan	19.45	20.51	21.20	21.51	21.50
Minnesota	14.76	15.06	15.43	16.04	16.63
Mississippi	11.93	12.32	12.89	13.12	13.53
Missouri	16.11	16.80	18.22	17.92	17.43
Montana	14.03	14.43	14.02	14.87	15.61
Nebraska	13.64	14.05	14.86	15.19	15.44
Nevada	13.79	14.62	14.63	14.60	14.98
New Hampshire	13.98	14.21	14.85	15.48	15.87
New Jersey	14.74	15.19	15.45	15.89	16.33
New Mexico	13.27	13.41	13.19	13.13	13.66
New York	16.24	16.75	16.78	17.29	17.77
North Carolina	12.81	13.18	13.66	14.25	14.38
North Dakota	12.77	13.17	14.04	14.35	15.29
Ohio	16.79	17.49	17.99	18.47	19.07
Oklahoma	13.66	14.11	14.13	14.24	14.65
Oregon	14.74	15.06	15.20	15.34	15.49
Pennsylvania	14.37	14.75	14.99	15.16	15.26
Rhode Island	12.68	12.75	12.88	13.03	13.12
South Carolina	13.79	14.00	14.19	14.73	15.23
South Dakota	12.11	12.60	13.13	13.37	13.47
Tennessee	12.88	13.15	13.56	13.84	14.03
Texas	14.04	13.93	13.94	13.98	14.03
Utah	13.76	14.12	14.90	15.38	14.71
Vermont	14.18	14.33	14.54	14.60	15.06
Virginia	14.50	15.20	15.90	16.11	16.40
Washington	17.96	18.15	18.02	18.28	18.83
West Virginia	14.80	15.40	16.05	16.57	17.14
Wisconsin	15.44	15.86	16.12	16.19	16.29
Wyoming	17.26	17.72	16.75	16.58	17.07
Puerto Rico	. . .	. . .	10.46	10.84	11.09
Virgin Islands	22.57	22.98	23.37	23.35	23.50

. . . = Not available.

Table 2-20. Average Weekly Earnings of Production Workers on Manufacturing Payrolls, by State and Selected Territory, NAICS Basis, 2001–2005

(Dollars.)

State	2001	2002	2003	2004	2005
UNITED STATES	595.19	618.75	635.99	658.59	673.61
Alabama	523.16	542.34	555.96	584.66	609.14
Alaska	504.27	495.18	523.74	487.61	467.84
Arizona	556.14	566.40	580.95	575.10	592.19
Arkansas	514.71	528.01	536.58	538.25	547.03
California	581.72	589.64	597.09	614.40	626.43
Colorado	599.10	626.86	682.36	664.98	612.54
Connecticut	684.71	717.18	734.44	767.03	800.11
Delaware	657.43	664.00	681.47	708.17	703.48
District of Columbia	. . .	. . .	. . .	. . .	. . .
Florida	514.81	559.93	577.69	568.82	579.21
Georgia	505.00	547.24	560.38	569.97	567.84
Hawaii	474.48	465.29	479.88	511.65	551.04
Idaho	541.54	546.48	566.64	573.08	602.89
Illinois	601.06	620.59	617.12	640.01	646.27
Indiana	673.22	727.16	751.06	754.43	760.07
Iowa	600.00	632.72	654.69	682.37	676.00
Kansas	630.04	651.98	641.12	679.37	704.45
Kentucky	640.76	663.81	667.62	673.20	675.58
Louisiana	697.36	747.62	743.53	719.96	726.60
Maine	585.46	620.45	651.20	672.01	684.29
Maryland	567.84	608.40	621.73	660.45	680.90
Massachusetts	634.73	663.00	671.12	694.18	733.31
Michigan	814.96	875.78	892.52	912.02	896.55
Minnesota	584.50	597.88	620.29	656.04	680.17
Mississippi	473.62	500.19	514.31	526.11	542.55
Missouri	649.23	660.24	737.91	720.38	690.23
Montana	544.36	551.23	538.37	569.52	625.96
Nebraska	561.97	588.70	618.18	631.90	617.60
Nevada	533.67	567.26	570.57	585.46	596.20
New Hampshire	567.59	565.56	594.00	619.20	653.84
New Jersey	598.44	621.27	633.45	668.97	685.86
New Mexico	517.53	535.06	519.69	519.95	534.11
New York	646.35	675.03	671.20	686.41	703.69
North Carolina	504.71	529.84	543.67	574.28	575.20
North Dakota	522.29	529.43	561.60	563.96	599.37
Ohio	691.75	724.09	737.59	770.20	789.50
Oklahoma	538.20	553.11	555.31	576.72	574.28
Oregon	576.33	588.85	597.36	599.79	622.70
Pennsylvania	580.55	594.43	599.60	610.95	618.03
Rhode Island	499.59	493.43	506.18	510.78	503.81
South Carolina	568.15	589.40	586.05	581.84	604.63
South Dakota	504.99	532.98	558.03	561.54	569.78
Tennessee	501.03	527.32	539.69	553.60	549.98
Texas	584.06	572.52	577.12	556.40	561.20
Utah	528.38	533.74	591.53	585.98	576.63
Vermont	561.53	573.20	581.60	586.92	590.35
Virginia	581.30	621.30	647.70	668.57	678.96
Washington	718.40	727.82	711.79	731.20	747.55
West Virginia	608.28	637.56	662.87	686.00	709.60
Wisconsin	620.69	642.33	649.64	652.46	658.12
Wyoming	666.24	696.40	673.35	658.23	691.34
Puerto Rico	. . .	. . .	427.81	444.44	452.47
Virgin Islands	990.82	1 004.23	1 000.24	1 083.44	1 029.30

. . . = Not available.

NOTES AND DEFINITIONS

QUARTERLY CENSUS OF EMPLOYMENT AND WAGES

The Quarterly Census of Employment and Wages (QCEW) program, also referred to as the ES-202 program, is a cooperative endeavor of the Bureau of Labor Statistics (BLS) and the State Employment Security Agencies (SESAs). Using quarterly data submitted by the agencies, BLS summarizes the employment and wage data for workers covered by state unemployment insurance laws and civilian workers covered by the Unemployment Compensation for Federal Employees (UCFE) program.

The QCEW tables use the 2002 version of the North American Industry Classification System (NAICS) as the basis for the assignment and tabulation of economic data by industry. The structure of NAICS is significantly different than that of the 1987 Standard Industrial Classification (SIC) system, which was previously used for industry classification purposes. Due to these differences, results in NAICS-based data are not directly comparable with historical SIC-based data. The NAICS classification system was described in the sixth edition of this *Handbook* and more information about NAICS can be found on the BLS Web site at <http://www.bls.gov/bls/naics.htm>.

The QCEW data series is the most complete universe of employment and wage information by industry, county, and state. These data serve as the basic source of benchmark information for employment by industry in the Current Employment Statistics (CES) survey, which is described in the first section of notes in this chapter. Therefore, the entire employment series is not presented here. The wage series is presented because the CES only provides earnings only for production and nonsupervisory employees. The QCEW is more comprehensive. BLS aggregates the data by industry and ownership; these aggregations are available at the national, state, county, and metropolitan statistical area (MSA) levels.

Collection and Coverage

Employment data under the QCEW program represent the number of covered workers who worked during (or received pay for) the pay period containing the 12th of the month. Excluded are members of the armed forces, the self-employed, proprietors, domestic workers, unpaid family workers, and railroad workers covered by the railroad unemployment insurance system.

Annual pay data are compiled from reports submitted by employers subject to state and federal unemployment insurance (UI) laws, covering approximately 130 million full- and part-time workers. Average annual pay is computed by dividing total annual payrolls of employees covered by UI programs by the average monthly number of these employees. Pay differences among states reflect the varying composition of employment by occupation, industry, hours of work, and other factors, and pay differences among industries are similarly affected. For example, the relatively large share of part-time workers reduces average annual pay levels in retail trade industries. Correspondingly, pay levels in construction industries reflect the prevalence of part-year employment due to weather and seasonal factors. Over-the-year pay changes may reflect shifts in the composition of employment, as well as changes in the average level of pay.

Total wages, for purposes of the quarterly UI reports submitted by private industry employers in private industry in most states, include gross wages and salaries, bonuses, stock options, tips and other gratuities, and the value of meals and lodging (when supplied). In some of the states, employer contributions to certain deferred compensation plans, such as 401(k) plans, are included in total wages. Total wages, however, do not include employer contributions to Old Age, Survivors', and Disability Insurance (OASDI), health insurance, unemployment insurance, workers' compensation, and private pension and welfare funds.

In most states, firms report the total wages paid during the calendar quarter, regardless of the timing of the services performed. However, under the laws of a few states, the employers report total wages earned during the quarter (payable) rather than actual amounts paid. For federal workers, wages represent the gross amount of all payrolls for all pay periods paid within the quarter. This gross amount includes cash allowances and the cash equivalent of any type of remuneration. It includes all lump-sum payments for terminal leave, withholding taxes, and retirement deductions. Federal employee remuneration generally covers the same types of services as those for workers in private industry.

Sources of Additional Information

Additional information and the sub-national data are available in the annual BLS bulletin, *Employment and Wages, Annual Averages*, which can be found on the BLS Web site at <http://www.bls.gov >.

Table 2-21. Employment and Average Annual Pay for All Covered Workers,[1] by Industry, NAICS Basis, 2001–2004

(Number, dollars.)

Industry	2001		2002		2003		2004	
	Employment	Average annual pay	Employment	Average annual pay	Employment	Average annual pay	Employment	Average annual pay
Total Private	109 304 802	36 157	107 577 281	36 539	107 065 553	37 508	108 490 066	39 134
Agriculture, forestry, fishing, and hunting	1 170 570	20 188	1 155 890	20 890	1 156 242	21 366	1 155 106	22 337
Mining	535 189	59 686	505 979	60 392	500 103	62 313	519 931	66 632
Construction	6 773 512	38 412	6 683 553	39 027	6 672 360	39 509	6 916 398	40 521
Manufacturing	16 386 001	42 969	15 209 192	44 097	14 459 712	45 916	14 257 380	47 861
Wholesale trade	5 730 294	48 791	5 617 456	49 241	5 589 032	50 835	5 642 537	53 310
Retail trade	15 179 753	22 667	15 018 588	23 232	14 930 765	23 804	15 060 686	24 415
Transportation and warehousing	4 138 146	36 189	3 989 116	36 823	3 946 170	37 436	4 009 165	38 834
Utilities	599 899	65 561	592 152	67 374	575 877	68 651	563 931	72 403
Information	3 591 995	57 288	3 364 485	56 103	3 180 752	58 002	3 099 633	60 722
Financial activities	7 678 974	55 515	7 706 265	55 172	7 826 930	57 143	7 890 786	61 487
Professional and business services	16 324 890	43 566	15 939 596	43 899	15 858 457	45 052	16 294 776	47 401
Education and health services	14 849 666	32 718	15 346 718	33 931	15 738 013	35 071	16 084 963	36 548
Leisure and hospitality	11 884 966	15 426	11 995 950	15 777	12 162 238	16 138	12 467 597	16 624
Other services	4 206 345	23 220	4 246 011	23 784	4 261 165	24 348	4 287 999	25 152
Total Government	20 330 998	36 549	20 656 638	37 935	20 730 273	39 094	20 788 110	40 500
Federal	2 752 619	48 940	2 758 627	52 050	2 764 275	54 239	2 739 596	57 782
State	4 452 237	37 814	4 485 071	39 212	4 481 845	40 057	4 484 997	41 118
Local	13 126 143	33 521	13 412 941	34 605	13 484 153	35 669	13 563 517	36 805

[1]Includes workers covered by Unemployment Insurance (UI) and Unemployment Compensation for Federal Employees (UCFE) programs.

Table 2-22. Employment and Average Annual Pay for All Covered Workers,[1] by State and Selected Territory, 2001–2004

(Number, dollars.)

State	2001		2002		2003		2004	
	Employment	Average annual pay	Employment	Average annual pay	Employment	Average annual pay	Employment	Average annual pay
UNITED STATES	129 635 800	36 219	128 233 919	36 764	127 795 827	37 765	129 278 176	39 354
Alabama	1 854 462	30 102	1 830 620	31 163	1 823 573	32 236	1 851 769	33 414
Alaska	283 033	36 170	287 231	37 134	291 797	37 804	296 292	39 062
Arizona	2 243 652	33 411	2 240 234	34 036	2 272 393	35 056	2 354 660	36 646
Arkansas	1 127 151	27 260	1 119 428	28 074	1 115 891	28 893	1 129 018	30 245
California	14 981 757	41 327	14 837 334	41 419	14 807 656	42 592	14 953 022	44 641
Colorado	2 201 379	37 952	2 153 857	38 005	2 117 773	38 942	2 142 352	40 276
Connecticut	1 665 607	46 993	1 648 547	46 852	1 625 801	48 328	1 631 240	51 007
Delaware	406 736	38 427	401 971	39 684	402 166	40 954	411 298	42 487
District of Columbia	635 749	55 908	650 515	57 914	651 088	60 417	659 542	63 887
Florida	7 153 589	31 553	7 164 523	32 426	7 248 097	33 544	7 463 255	35 186
Georgia	3 871 763	35 136	3 807 915	35 734	3 783 232	36 626	3 840 663	37 866
Hawaii	557 146	31 253	558 651	32 671	569 532	33 742	585 131	35 198
Idaho	571 314	27 768	571 869	28 163	575 889	28 677	591 355	29 871
Illinois	5 886 248	39 083	5 771 132	39 688	5 698 184	40 540	5 700 643	42 277
Indiana	2 871 236	31 779	2 832 553	32 603	2 821 879	33 379	2 848 873	34 694
Iowa	1 429 543	28 837	1 412 203	29 668	1 404 377	30 708	1 422 454	32 097
Kansas	1 319 667	30 153	1 303 114	30 825	1 284 726	31 489	1 296 618	32 738
Kentucky	1 736 575	30 021	1 717 975	30 904	1 714 060	31 855	1 729 015	33 165
Louisiana	1 869 966	29 131	1 847 754	30 115	1 855 554	30 782	1 865 164	31 880
Maine	593 166	28 815	591 052	29 736	591 372	30 750	597 238	31 906
Maryland	2 421 899	38 253	2 427 257	39 382	2 434 245	40 686	2 459 362	42 579
Massachusetts	3 276 224	44 975	3 202 323	44 954	3 141 089	46 323	3 138 738	48 916
Michigan	4 476 659	37 391	4 390 209	38 135	4 321 094	39 433	4 301 743	40 373
Minnesota	2 609 669	36 587	2 585 650	37 458	2 576 452	38 610	2 600 360	40 398
Mississippi	1 111 255	25 923	1 104 225	26 665	1 096 802	27 591	1 105 915	28 535
Missouri	2 652 876	32 421	2 627 082	33 118	2 615 848	33 788	2 627 401	34 845
Montana	383 905	25 195	388 161	26 001	393 541	26 907	403 432	27 830
Nebraska	883 920	28 377	874 063	29 448	875 251	30 382	882 263	31 507
Nevada	1 043 748	33 121	1 045 012	33 993	1 080 624	35 329	1 145 762	37 106
New Hampshire	610 192	35 481	603 234	36 176	604 340	37 321	613 310	39 176
New Jersey	3 876 194	44 320	3 855 419	45 182	3 850 590	46 351	3 873 787	48 064
New Mexico	729 422	28 702	737 418	29 431	745 935	30 202	760 449	31 411
New York	8 423 312	46 727	8 272 274	46 328	8 224 387	47 247	8 271 927	49 941
North Carolina	3 805 498	32 024	3 751 648	32 689	3 719 444	33 532	3 777 872	34 791
North Dakota	311 632	25 707	311 800	26 550	314 283	27 628	321 108	28 987
Ohio	5 434 769	33 283	5 332 891	34 214	5 281 390	35 153	5 292 088	36 441
Oklahoma	1 463 622	28 016	1 439 701	28 654	1 411 640	29 699	1 427 618	30 743
Oregon	1 596 753	33 204	1 573 057	33 684	1 563 725	34 450	1 595 003	35 630
Pennsylvania	5 552 366	34 978	5 504 553	35 808	5 471 255	36 995	5 496 599	38 555
Rhode Island	468 952	33 603	468 557	34 810	472 586	36 415	475 628	37 651
South Carolina	1 786 899	29 255	1 765 717	30 003	1 766 861	30 750	1 789 447	31 839
South Dakota	364 715	25 601	363 292	26 360	364 263	27 210	369 632	28 281
Tennessee	2 625 746	31 520	2 601 518	32 531	2 598 748	33 581	2 644 749	34 925
Texas	9 350 770	36 045	9 261 089	36 248	9 208 473	36 968	9 323 537	38 511
Utah	1 050 674	30 077	1 041 707	30 585	1 041 938	31 106	1 071 855	32 171
Vermont	298 020	30 238	295 443	31 041	294 395	32 086	298 454	33 274
Virginia	3 436 172	36 733	3 404 760	37 222	3 410 834	38 585	3 495 767	40 534
Washington	2 689 507	37 459	2 643 754	38 242	2 653 237	39 021	2 694 933	39 361
West Virginia	685 754	27 981	683 183	28 612	677 901	29 284	686 936	30 382
Wisconsin	2 717 660	31 540	2 690 830	32 464	2 687 919	33 425	2 714 847	34 743
Wyoming	237 278	28 043	239 615	28 975	241 699	29 924	248 051	31 210
Puerto Rico	1 007 919	19 728	992 529	20 662	1 023 102	21 548	1 043 949	22 259
Virgin Islands	44 330	29 210	43 070	30 506	41 961	30 994	43 156	31 846

[1]Includes workers covered by the Unemployment Insurance (UI) and Unemployment Compensation for Federal Employees (UCFE) programs.

BUSINESS EMPLOYMENT DYNAMICS

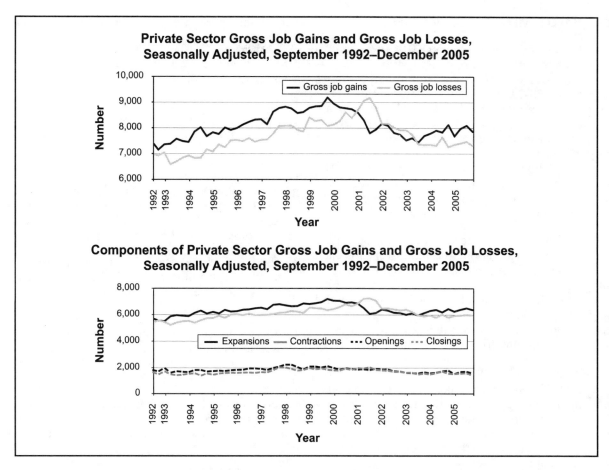

Private Sector Gross Job Gains and Gross Job Losses, Seasonally Adjusted, September 1992–December 2005

Components of Private Sector Gross Job Gains and Gross Job Losses, Seasonally Adjusted, September 1992–December 2005

Private sector business establishments gained about 7.82 million gross jobs in the fourth quarter of 2005, 237,000 fewer jobs than in the third quarter. However, job losses were also lower than the previous quarter, resulting in a net change (the difference between gross job gains and gross job losses) of 551,000. Although substantial, this net change contained more than 300,000 fewer jobs than the net change posted in the fourth quarter of 2004. Gross job gains and losses demonstrate that a sizable number of jobs appear and disappear within the short time from of one quarter. (See Table 2-23.)

OTHER HIGHLIGHTS

• During the fourth quarter of 2005, expanding establishments added 6.3 million jobs while opening establishments added another 1.5 million jobs. Gross job losses were 7.3 million, somewhat less than the third quarter for 2005 but about the same as the fourth quarter of 2004. Job losses due to closing establishments were 1.4 million, fewer than in the fourth quarter of 2004. (See Table 2-23.)

• In the fourth quarter of 2005, gross jobs gains represented 7.1 percent of private sector employment, a smaller proportion than in the third quarter of 2005. Gross jobs losses were at a low of 6.5 percent. (See Table 2-24.)

• The manufacturing sector had a small net job gain in the fourth quarter of 2005, after experiencing net losses for the previous four quarters. Service-providing industries contributed about 78 percent of the total net job gain. (See Table 2-25.)

NOTES AND DEFINITIONS

BUSINESS EMPLOYMENT DYNAMICS (BED)

The Business Employment Dynamics (BED) data are a product of a federal-state cooperative program known as the Quarterly Census of Employment and Wages (QCEW), or the ES-202 program. The Bureau of Labor Statistics (BLS) compiles the BED data from existing quarterly state unemployment insurance (UI) records. Most employers in the United States are required to file quarterly reports on the employment and wages of workers covered by UI laws and to pay quarterly UI taxes. The quarterly UI reports are sent by the State Workforce Agencies (SWAs) to BLS. These reports form the basis of the BLS establishment universe-sampling frame.

In the BED program, the quarterly UI records are linked across quarters to provide a longitudinal history for each establishment. The linkage process allows the tracking of net employment changes at the establishment level, which in turn allows estimations of jobs gained at opening and expanding establishments and of jobs lost at closing and contracting establishments. BLS publishes three different establishment-based employment measures for every given quarter. Each of these measures—the Current Employment Statistics (CES) survey, the QCEW program, and the BED data each make use of the quarterly UI employment reports. However, each measure has somewhat different types of universal coverage, estimation procedures, and publication products. (See the notes and corresponding tables for CES and QCEW in earlier sections of this chapter.)

Concepts and Definitions

The BED data measure the net change in employment at the establishment level. These changes can come about in four different ways. A net increase in employment can come from either opening establishments or expanding establishments. A net decrease in employment can come from either closing establishments or contracting establishments.

Gross job gains include the sum of all jobs added at either opening or expanding establishments.

Gross job losses include the sum of all jobs lost in either closing or contracting establishments. The net change in employment is the difference between gross job gains and gross job losses.

Openings consist of establishments with positive third-month employment for the first time in the current quarter, with no links to the prior quarter, or with positive third-month employment in the current quarter, following zero employment in the previous quarter.

Expansions include establishments with positive employment in the third month in both the previous and current quarters, with a net increase in employment over this period.

Closings consist of establishments with positive third-month employment in the previous quarter, with no employment or zero employment reported in the current quarter.

Contractions include establishments with positive employment in the third month in both the previous and current quarters, with a net decrease in employment over this period.

Sources of Additional Information

For additional information, see BLS news release 06-1562, "Business Employment Dynamics: Fourth Quarter 2005." An extensive article on the BED data appeared in the April 2004 edition of the *Monthly Labor Review*. These resources can be found on the BLS Web site at <http://www.bls.gov>.

Table 2-23. Private Sector Gross Job Gains and Job Losses, Seasonally Adjusted, September 1992– December 2005

(Thousands of jobs.)

Year and month	Net change[1]	Gross job gains			Gross job losses		
		Total	Expanding establishments	Opening establishments	Total	Contracting establishments	Closing establishments
1992							
September	455	7 377	5 632	1 745	6 922	5 351	1 571
December	216	7 101	5 465	1 636	6 885	5 487	1 398
1993							
March	313	7 309	5 410	1 899	6 996	5 354	1 642
June	786	7 330	5 794	1 536	6 544	5 136	1 408
September	874	7 523	5 881	1 642	6 649	5 316	1 333
December	641	7 436	5 840	1 596	6 795	5 420	1 375
1994							
March	517	7 400	5 807	1 593	6 883	5 435	1 448
June	1 021	7 807	6 060	1 747	6 786	5 295	1 491
September	1 175	7 972	6 227	1 745	6 797	5 493	1 304
December	507	7 630	5 998	1 632	7 123	5 647	1 476
1995							
March	746	7 782	6 129	1 653	7 036	5 660	1 376
June	402	7 714	6 017	1 697	7 312	5 839	1 473
September	771	7 970	6 291	1 679	7 199	5 680	1 519
December	407	7 877	6 153	1 724	7 470	5 934	1 536
1996							
March	460	7 943	6 190	1 753	7 483	5 957	1 526
June	642	8 080	6 302	1 778	7 438	5 894	1 544
September	632	8 189	6 326	1 863	7 557	5 998	1 559
December	861	8 278	6 409	1 869	7 417	5 889	1 528
1997							
March	799	8 292	6 448	1 844	7 493	5 900	1 593
June	594	8 098	6 342	1 756	7 504	5 925	1 579
September	854	8 593	6 680	1 913	7 739	5 981	1 758
December	702	8 731	6 727	2 004	8 029	6 068	1 961
1998							
March	747	8 788	6 633	2 155	8 041	6 107	1 934
June	666	8 722	6 569	2 153	8 056	6 218	1 838
September	659	8 539	6 574	1 965	7 880	6 161	1 719
December	759	8 576	6 778	1 798	7 817	6 060	1 757
1999							
March	380	8 744	6 733	2 011	8 364	6 466	1 898
June	569	8 800	6 788	2 012	8 231	6 419	1 812
September	548	8 817	6 871	1 946	8 269	6 397	1 872
December	1 105	9 144	7 112	2 032	8 039	6 264	1 775
2000							
March	818	8 906	6 988	1 918	8 088	6 361	1 727
June	541	8 764	6 975	1 789	8 223	6 509	1 714
September	146	8 724	6 834	1 890	8 578	6 719	1 859
December	336	8 690	6 862	1 828	8 354	6 582	1 772
2001							
March	-101	8 555	6 768	1 787	8 656	6 756	1 900
June	-771	8 254	6 439	1 815	9 025	7 149	1 876
September	-1 380	7 749	5 990	1 759	9 129	7 174	1 955
December	-871	7 893	6 055	1 838	8 764	6 995	1 769
2002							
March	-1	8 128	6 324	1 804	8 129	6 400	1 729
June	-80	8 050	6 246	1 804	8 130	6 411	1 719
September	-211	7 763	6 083	1 680	7 974	6 345	1 629
December	-175	7 702	6 059	1 643	7 877	6 267	1 610
2003							
March	-404	7 472	5 932	1 540	7 876	6 321	1 555
June	-142	7 560	6 033	1 527	7 702	6 138	1 564
September	72	7 396	5 897	1 499	7 324	5 893	1 431
December	344	7 646	6 063	1 583	7 302	5 816	1 486
2004							
March	435	7 745	6 231	1 514	7 310	5 871	1 439
June	594	7 857	6 292	1 565	7 263	5 726	1 537
September	191	7 789	6 123	1 666	7 598	5 953	1 645
December	869	8 081	6 365	1 716	7 212	5 727	1 485
2005							
March	325	7 635	6 171	1 464	7 310	5 852	1 458
June	574	7 932	6 311	1 621	7 358	5 873	1 485
September	628	8 055	6 423	1 632	7 427	5 915	1 512
December	551	7 818	6 293	1 525	7 267	5 888	1 379

[1]Net change is the difference between total gross job gains and total gross job losses.

Table 2-24. Private Sector Gross Job Gains and Job Losses, as a Percent of Employment,[1] Seasonally Adjusted, September 1992–December 2005

(Percent.)

Year and month	Net change[2]	Gross job gains			Gross job losses		
		Total	Expanding establishments	Opening establishments	Total	Expanding establishments	Closing establishments
1992							
September	0.5	8.3	6.3	2.0	7.8	6.0	1.8
December	0.2	7.9	6.1	1.8	7.7	6.1	1.6
1993							
March	0.3	8.1	6.0	2.1	7.8	6.0	1.8
June	0.8	8.1	6.4	1.7	7.3	5.7	1.6
September	0.9	8.2	6.4	1.8	7.3	5.8	1.5
December	0.6	8.0	6.3	1.7	7.4	5.9	1.5
1994							
March	0.5	8.0	6.3	1.7	7.5	5.9	1.6
June	1.1	8.4	6.5	1.9	7.3	5.7	1.6
September	1.2	8.4	6.6	1.8	7.2	5.8	1.4
December	0.6	8.0	6.3	1.7	7.4	5.9	1.5
1995							
March	0.8	8.1	6.4	1.7	7.3	5.9	1.4
June	0.5	8.0	6.2	1.8	7.5	6.0	1.5
September	0.8	8.2	6.5	1.7	7.4	5.8	1.6
December	0.4	8.1	6.3	1.8	7.7	6.1	1.6
1996							
March	0.4	8.1	6.3	1.8	7.7	6.1	1.6
June	0.6	8.2	6.4	1.8	7.6	6.0	1.6
September	0.7	8.3	6.4	1.9	7.6	6.0	1.6
December	0.9	8.3	6.4	1.9	7.4	5.9	1.5
1997							
March	0.7	8.2	6.4	1.8	7.5	5.9	1.6
June	0.5	7.9	6.2	1.7	7.4	5.8	1.6
September	0.8	8.4	6.5	1.9	7.6	5.9	1.7
December	0.6	8.4	6.5	1.9	7.8	5.9	1.9
1998							
March	0.7	8.5	6.4	2.1	7.8	5.9	1.9
June	0.6	8.4	6.3	2.1	7.8	6.0	1.8
September	0.7	8.2	6.3	1.9	7.5	5.9	1.6
December	0.7	8.1	6.4	1.7	7.4	5.7	1.7
1999							
March	0.3	8.2	6.3	1.9	7.9	6.1	1.8
June	0.6	8.3	6.4	1.9	7.7	6.0	1.7
September	0.5	8.2	6.4	1.8	7.7	6.0	1.7
December	1.1	8.5	6.6	1.9	7.4	5.8	1.6
2000							
March	0.8	8.2	6.4	1.8	7.4	5.8	1.6
June	0.4	7.9	6.3	1.6	7.5	5.9	1.6
September	0.1	7.9	6.2	1.7	7.8	6.1	1.7
December	0.3	7.9	6.2	1.7	7.6	6.0	1.6
2001							
March	-0.1	7.7	6.1	1.6	7.8	6.1	1.7
June	-0.8	7.4	5.8	1.6	8.2	6.5	1.7
September	-1.3	7.1	5.5	1.6	8.4	6.6	1.8
December	-0.8	7.3	5.6	1.7	8.1	6.5	1.6
2002							
March	0.1	7.6	5.9	1.7	7.5	5.9	1.6
June	-0.1	7.5	5.8	1.7	7.6	6.0	1.6
September	-0.1	7.3	5.7	1.6	7.4	5.9	1.5
December	-0.2	7.1	5.6	1.5	7.3	5.8	1.5
2003							
March	-0.5	6.9	5.5	1.4	7.4	5.9	1.5
June	-0.2	7.0	5.6	1.4	7.2	5.7	1.5
September	0.1	6.9	5.5	1.4	6.8	5.5	1.3
December	0.4	7.2	5.7	1.5	6.8	5.4	1.4
2004							
March	0.4	7.2	5.8	1.4	6.8	5.5	1.3
June	0.5	7.2	5.8	1.4	6.7	5.3	1.4
September	0.2	7.2	5.7	1.5	7.0	5.5	1.5
December	0.7	7.4	5.8	1.6	6.7	5.3	1.4
2005							
March	0.3	6.9	5.6	1.3	6.6	5.3	1.3
June	0.6	7.2	5.7	1.5	6.6	5.3	1.3
September	0.5	7.3	5.8	1.5	6.8	5.4	1.4
December	0.6	7.1	5.7	1.4	6.5	5.3	1.2

[1]The rates measure gross job gains and job losses as a percentage of the average of the previous and current employment.
[2]Net change is the difference between total gross job gains and total gross job losses.

Table 2-25. Three-Month Private Sector Job Gains and Losses, by Industry, Seasonally Adjusted, December 2004–December 2005

(Thousands of jobs.)

Industry	Gross job gains (3 months ended)					Gross job losses (3 months ended)				
	December 2004	March 2005	June 2005	September 2005	December 2005	December 2004	March 2005	June 2005	September 2005	December 2005
TOTAL PRIVATE[1]	8 081	7 635	7 932	8 055	7 818	7 212	7 310	7 358	7 427	7 267
Goods-Producing	1 734	1 720	1 713	1 698	1 722	1 637	1 686	1 679	1 663	1 606
Natural resources and mining	296	307	288	265	279	275	284	285	265	265
Construction	848	844	859	868	862	747	806	786	782	774
Manufacturing	590	569	566	565	581	615	596	608	616	567
Service-Providing[1]	6 347	5 915	6 219	6 357	6 096	5 575	5 624	5 679	5 764	5 661
Wholesale trade	329	319	337	338	320	294	310	300	311	302
Retail trade	1 090	1 020	1 047	1 074	1 058	992	980	989	1 063	1 015
Transportation and warehousing	255	243	248	254	268	217	231	262	236	231
Utilities	11	15	15	13	14	15	15	18	12	16
Information	188	143	155	170	152	169	164	153	154	156
Financial activities	497	452	475	480	472	451	443	439	413	434
Professional and business services	1 512	1 370	1 456	1 523	1 432	1 300	1 304	1 332	1 311	1 303
Education and health services	802	741	800	811	766	647	704	701	691	699
Leisure and hospitality	1 204	1 138	1 212	1 202	1 175	1 134	1 131	1 135	1 219	1 165
Other services	299	302	309	297	289	310	297	300	309	296

[1]Includes unclassified sector, not shown separately.

CHAPTER THREE

OCCUPATIONAL EMPLOYMENT AND WAGES

OCCUPATIONAL EMPLOYMENT AND WAGES

HIGHLIGHTS

This chapter presents employment and wage statistics for 801 occupations from the Bureau of Labor Statistics's Occupational Employment Statistics (OES) program.

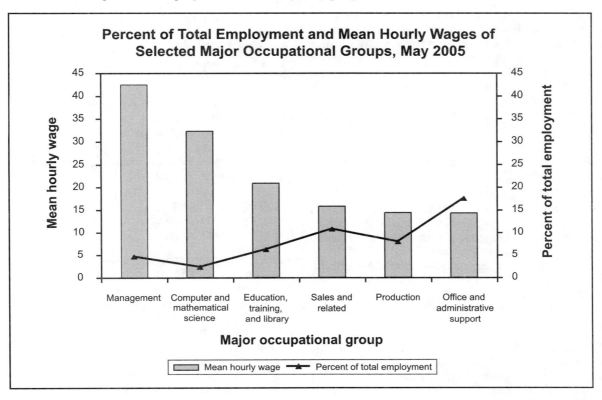

The distribution of employment and wages in occupations changed little between 2004 and 2005. Office and administrative support occupations continued to employ the largest percentage of workers in any major group (17.5 percent), while mean hourly wages for this occupational group remained relatively low at $14.28 per hour—more than 27 percent less than average. In contrast, management occupations employed only 4.6 percent of total workers, but workers in this occupational group earned a mean hourly wage of $42.52. (See Table 3-1.)

OTHER HIGHLIGHTS

* The gap between the earnings of management, the highest-paid major occupational group, and food preparation and serving, the lowest-paid major occupational group, continued to grow. Management earned 4.96 times as much as food preparation and serving in 2005 compared to 4.88 times as much (as food preparation and serving) in 2004. (See Table 3-1.)

* Other low-wage occupational groups were farming, fishing, and forestry; building and grounds cleaning and maintenance; and personal care and service. At least 38 percent of the workers in each of these groups earned less than $8.50 per hour in May 2005. (See Table 3-2.)

* Specialist physicians and dentists accounted for 12 of the 14 highest-paid detailed occupations in May 2005. Surgeons had the highest mean annual wages at $177,690. (See Table 3-3.)

* Among occupations with more than 2 million workers, registered nurses earned the most at $27.35 an hour in May 2005. (See Table 3-3.)

NOTES AND DEFINITIONS

Collection and Coverage

The Occupational Employment Statistics (OES) survey is a federal-state cooperative program conducted by the Bureau of Labor Statistics (BLS) and the State Workforce Agencies (SWAs). The OES survey provides estimates of employment and hourly and annual wages for wage and salary workers in 22 major occupational groups and 801 detailed occupations. BLS funds the survey and provides procedural and technical support, while the SWAs collect the necessary data.

Scope of the Survey

In 1999, the OES survey began using the Standard Occupational Classification (SOC) system. The SOC system is the first Office of Management and Budget (OMB)–required occupational classification system for federal agencies. The SOC system consists of 821 detailed occupations grouped into 449 broad occupations, 96 minor occupational groups, and 23 major occupational groups. The OES survey uses 22 of the 23 major occupational groups from the SOC to categorize workers into 801 detailed occupations. Military-specific occupations, which are not covered by the OES survey, are not included.

Prior to 2002, the OES survey was conducted annually by mail and measured occupational employment and occupational wage rates for wage and salary workers in nonfarm establishments by industry. The survey sampled and contacted approximately 400,000 establishments in the fourth quarter of each year.

Beginning in November 2002, the OES survey became a semi-annual survey that sampled approximately 200,000 establishments per panel. The OES also switched from the Standard Industrial Classification System (SIC) to the North American Industry Classification System (NAICS) in 2002. More information about NAICS can be found on the BLS Web site at <http://www.bls.gov/bls/naics.htm>.

The May 2005 OES estimates are benchmarked to the average of the May 2005 and November 2004 reference periods. May 2005 employment and wage estimates are based on all data collected from establishments in May 2005, November 2004, May 2004, November 2003, May 2003, and November 2002 semi-annual samples. Over the course of a 3-year cycle, approximately 1.2 million establishments are sampled.

Concepts and Definitions

Employment is the estimate of total wage and salary employment in an occupation across the industries in which it was reported. The OES survey defines employment as the number of workers who can be classified as full-time or part-time employees, including workers on paid vacations or other types of leave; workers on unpaid short-term absences; employees who are salaried officers, executives, or staff members of incorporated firms; employees temporarily assigned to other units; and employees for whom the reporting unit is their permanent duty station, regardless of whether that unit prepares their paycheck. Self-employed owners, partners in unincorporated firms, household workers, and unpaid family workers are excluded.

Occupations are classified based on work performed and on required skills. Employees are assigned to an occupation based on the work they perform and not on their education or training. For example, an employee trained as an engineer but working as a drafter is reported as a drafter. Employees who perform the duties of two or more occupations are reported as being in either the occupation that requires the highest level of skill or the occupation in which the most time is spent (if there is no measurable difference in skill requirements).

The OES survey form sent to an establishment contains between 50 and 225 SOC occupations selected on the basis of the industry classification and size class of the sampled establishment. To reduce paperwork and respondent burden, no survey form contains every SOC occupation. Data for specific occupations are thus primarily collected from establishments within the industries that are the predominant employers of labor for these occupations. However, each survey form is structured to allow a respondent to provide information for each detailed occupation at the establishment; unlisted occupations can be added to the survey form.

Wages are money that is paid or received for work or services performed in a specified period. Base rate, cost-of-living allowances, guaranteed pay, hazardous-duty pay, incentive pay (including commissions and production bonuses), tips, and on-call pay are included. Excluded are back pay, jury duty pay, overtime pay, severance pay, shift differentials, nonproduction bonuses, employer cost of supplementary benefits, and tuition reimbursements.

Mean wage refers to an average wage; an occupational mean wage estimate is calculated by summing the wages of all the employees in a given occupation and then dividing the total wages by the number of employees.

An *establishment* is defined as an economic unit that processes goods or provides services, such as a factory, store, or mine. The establishment is generally at a single physical location and is primarily engaged in one type of economic activity.

Additional Information

For additional data including area data, see BLS news release USDL 06-896, "Occupational Employment and Wages, May 2005," and special reports on the BLS Web site at <http://www.bls.gov>.

Table 3-1. Employment and Wages, by Major Occupational Group, May 2004 and May 2005

(Number, percent, dollars.)

Occupation	May 2004				May 2005			
	Employment		Mean hourly wage	Mean annual wage[1]	Employment		Mean hourly wage	Mean annual wage[1]
	Number	Percent			Number	Percent		
All Occupations	128 127 360	100.0	17.80	37 020	130 307 850	100.0	18.21	37 870
Management	6 200 940	4.8	41.12	85 530	5 960 560	4.6	42.52	88 450
Business and financial operations	5 131 840	4.0	27.10	56 380	5 410 410	4.2	27.85	57 930
Computer and mathematical science	2 915 300	2.3	31.50	65 510	2 952 740	2.3	32.26	67 100
Architecture and engineering	2 372 770	1.9	29.69	61 750	2 382 480	1.8	30.73	63 910
Life, physical, and social science	1 131 390	0.9	26.89	55 920	1 185 730	0.9	27.90	58 030
Community and social services	1 673 740	1.3	17.52	36 440	1 692 950	1.3	18.04	37 530
Legal	958 520	0.7	38.42	79 910	986 740	0.8	38.98	81 070
Education, training, and library	7 891 810	6.2	20.23	42 080	8 078 500	6.2	20.89	43 450
Arts, design, entertainment, sports, and media	1 595 710	1.2	21.01	43 710	1 683 310	1.3	21.30	44 310
Health care practitioner and technical	6 359 380	5.0	27.55	57 310	6 547 350	5.0	28.45	59 170
Health care support	3 271 350	2.6	11.17	23 220	3 363 800	2.6	11.47	23 850
Protective services	3 006 100	2.3	16.75	34 840	3 056 660	2.3	17.19	35 750
Food preparation and serving related	10 507 390	8.2	8.43	17 530	10 797 700	8.3	8.58	17 840
Building and grounds cleaning and maintenance	4 300 440	3.4	10.33	21 490	4 342 550	3.3	10.55	21 930
Personal care and services	3 099 550	2.4	10.48	21 800	3 188 850	2.4	10.67	22 180
Sales and related	13 507 840	10.5	15.49	32 210	13 930 320	10.7	15.77	32 800
Office and administrative support	22 649 080	17.7	13.95	29 020	22 784 330	17.5	14.28	29 710
Farming, fishing, and forestry	458 850	0.4	9.76	20 310	443 070	0.3	10.10	21 010
Construction and extraction	6 170 410	4.8	18.04	37 520	6 370 400	4.9	18.39	38 260
Installation, maintenance, and repair	5 215 390	4.1	17.89	37 220	5 305 260	4.1	18.30	38 050
Production	10 128 200	7.9	14.08	29 280	10 249 220	7.9	14.37	29 890
Transportation and material moving	9 581 320	7.5	13.41	27 880	9 594 920	7.4	13.85	28 820

[1]Annual wages have been calculated by multiplying the hourly mean wage by a "year-round, full-time" hours figure of 2,080 hours; for those occupations with no hourly mean wage published, the annual wage has been directly calculated from the reported survey data.

Table 3-2. Distribution of Employment, by Wage Range and Occupational Group, May 2004 and May 2005

(Percent distribution.)

Occupation	Total	Wage range (May 2004)								
		Under $8.50	$8.50 to $10.74	$10.75 to $13.49	$13.50 to $16.99	$17.00 to $21.49	$21.50 to $27.24	$27.25 to $34.49	$34.50 to $43.74	$43.75 and over
Management	100.0	1.3	1.0	2.4	5.0	8.6	13.2	15.9	17.4	35.2
Business and financial operations	100.0	1.6	2.0	5.2	11.8	18.9	21.6	17.8	11.6	9.5
Computer and mathematical science	100.0	0.6	1.2	3.1	6.6	12.0	17.8	21.8	20.5	16.4
Architecture and engineering	100.0	0.5	1.5	3.9	7.8	13.7	20.3	21.1	18.2	13.1
Life, physical, and social science	100.0	1.6	3.5	7.5	12.5	17.1	18.5	16.1	12.0	11.3
Community and social services	100.0	6.4	10.4	17.4	21.2	19.3	14.2	7.5	2.7	0.8
Legal	100.0	1.1	2.1	5.1	10.3	14.1	13.8	11.1	11.0	31.3
Education, training, and library	100.0	10.6	8.6	9.7	14.4	18.8	17.0	11.7	5.4	3.7
Arts, design, entertainment, sports, and media	100.0	12.1	9.8	11.8	14.8	15.8	13.8	9.6	6.1	6.2
Health care practitioner and technical	100.0	2.1	4.6	7.7	11.9	18.7	21.1	14.6	8.1	11.1
Health care support	100.0	23.2	31.1	24.2	14.0	5.5	1.5	0.4	0.1	-
Protective services	100.0	15.6	14.9	14.6	14.9	13.7	13.1	8.3	3.6	1.2
Food preparation and serving related	100.0	65.6	18.1	9.2	4.3	1.9	0.6	0.2	0.1	-
Building and grounds cleaning and maintenance	100.0	40.4	25.2	16.7	9.9	5.4	1.8	0.5	0.1	-
Personal care and services	100.0	47.5	22.8	12.2	7.5	4.8	2.7	1.3	0.7	0.6
Sales and related	100.0	34.5	17.1	11.6	9.6	8.3	6.6	4.6	3.2	4.5
Office and administrative support	100.0	13.7	18.9	22.7	20.1	14.6	7.0	2.1	0.7	0.3
Farming, fishing, and forestry	100.0	56.3	18.0	11.0	7.1	4.3	2.1	0.8	0.3	0.1
Construction and extraction	100.0	6.3	11.7	16.5	18.8	17.9	14.8	9.5	3.6	1.0
Installation, maintenance, and repair	100.0	6.5	10.0	14.6	19.4	21.3	17.2	8.1	2.3	0.7
Production	100.0	16.5	19.3	20.3	18.2	12.8	8.5	3.1	0.9	0.2
Transportation and material moving	100.0	25.2	19.3	18.1	15.4	11.6	6.3	2.2	0.8	1.0

Occupation	Total	Wage range (May 2005)								
		Under $8.50	$8.50 to $10.74	$10.75 to $13.49	$13.50 to $16.99	$17.00 to $21.49	$21.50 to $27.24	$27.25 to $34.49	$34.50 to $43.74	$43.75 and over
Management	100.0	1.0	0.8	2.0	4.3	7.8	12.6	15.8	18.0	37.8
Business and financial operations	100.0	1.4	1.8	4.6	10.9	18.4	21.6	18.3	12.4	10.5
Computer and mathematical science	100.0	0.4	1.2	2.9	6.3	11.4	17.4	21.3	20.7	18.2
Architecture and engineering	100.0	0.4	1.4	3.4	7.1	12.7	19.7	21.3	18.8	15.3
Life, physical, and social science	100.0	1.1	2.9	6.5	12.0	16.8	18.6	16.7	12.6	13.0
Community and social services	100.0	5.2	9.6	16.5	21.7	19.7	15.0	8.2	3.1	1.1
Legal	100.0	1.1	2.0	4.6	9.4	13.4	14.4	11.5	10.9	32.6
Education, training, and library	100.0	9.4	8.6	9.7	13.9	18.7	17.1	12.1	6.1	4.4
Arts, design, entertainment, sports, and media	100.0	11.2	9.5	11.4	15.2	16.0	13.8	9.8	6.6	6.5
Health care practitioner and technical	100.0	1.8	4.2	7.1	10.9	17.3	21.0	16.4	9.0	12.3
Health care support	100.0	20.6	30.8	24.9	15.1	6.2	1.7	0.4	0.1	-
Protective services	100.0	14.4	14.9	14.1	15.0	13.8	13.4	8.9	4.0	1.4
Food preparation and serving related	100.0	63.9	18.8	9.6	4.6	2.1	0.7	0.2	0.1	-
Building and grounds cleaning and maintenance	100.0	38.1	25.9	17.2	10.4	5.7	2.0	0.5	0.1	-
Personal care and services	100.0	45.0	23.9	12.9	8.0	4.9	2.6	1.4	0.6	0.6
Sales and related	100.0	33.7	17.1	11.6	9.7	8.4	6.8	4.7	3.4	4.6
Office and administrative support	100.0	12.8	18.3	22.2	20.6	14.6	8.2	2.3	0.7	0.3
Farming, fishing, and forestry	100.0	52.3	19.8	11.3	8.1	4.9	2.4	0.9	0.3	-
Construction and extraction	100.0	5.3	11.4	16.2	19.0	18.4	15.1	9.7	3.8	1.2
Installation, maintenance, and repair	100.0	5.7	9.7	14.2	19.1	21.3	17.7	8.8	2.7	0.7
Production	100.0	15.0	18.9	20.3	18.8	13.4	8.7	3.4	1.0	0.3
Transportation and material moving	100.0	22.9	19.1	18.4	16.0	12.2	6.9	2.5	0.9	1.1

- = Quantity represents or rounds to zero.

Table 3-3. Employment and Wages, by Occupation, May 2004 and May 2005

(Number of people, dollars.)

Occupation	May 2004				May 2005			
	Employ-ment	Median hourly wages	Mean hourly wages	Mean annual wages[1]	Employ-ment	Median hourly wages	Mean hourly wages	Mean annual wages[1]
ALL OCCUPATIONS	128 127 360	13.83	17.80	37 020	130 307 840	14.15	18.21	37 870
Management								
Chief executives	346 590	67.47	67.27	139 920	321 300	68.48	67.22	139 810
General and operations managers	1 752 910	37.22	44.24	92 010	1 663 810	39.17	45.90	95 470
Legislators	63 440	(2)	(2)	30 750	61 060	(2)	(2)	31 320
Advertising and promotions managers	57 100	30.58	36.76	76 460	41 710	33.10	39.06	81 250
Marketing managers	177 550	42.13	46.48	96 680	166 470	44.56	49.03	101 990
Sales managers	320 240	40.49	45.68	95 010	317 970	42.11	47.36	98 510
Public relations managers	50 670	33.65	38.26	79 580	43 770	36.75	41.26	85 820
Administrative services managers	254 610	28.99	31.98	66 530	239 410	30.78	33.44	69 540
Computer and information systems managers	267 390	44.51	47.24	98 260	259 330	46.41	49.21	102 360
Financial managers	493 360	39.37	44.04	91 610	471 950	41.48	46.45	96 620
Compensation and benefits managers	55 040	31.99	35.59	74 020	51 470	33.23	36.68	76 300
Training and development managers	35 510	32.43	35.45	73 730	28 720	35.66	38.55	80 180
Human resources managers, all other	58 770	39.33	42.11	87 580	57 830	40.47	43.24	89 950
Industrial production managers	155 980	35.09	38.06	79 170	153 950	36.34	39.41	81 960
Purchasing managers	73 480	34.83	37.51	78 020	69 300	36.67	39.16	81 440
Transportation, storage, and distribution managers	88 100	32.02	34.87	72 530	84 870	33.23	36.12	75 130
Farm, ranch, and other agricultural managers	4 810	24.38	26.51	55 140	4 070	24.60	26.81	55 760
Farmers and ranchers	540	19.44	20.78	43 230	350	16.41	19.09	39 720
Construction managers	185 580	33.59	37.83	78 690	192 610	34.74	39.31	81 760
Education administrators, preschool and childcare center/program	50 590	17.18	19.74	41 060	47 670	17.79	20.51	42 670
Education administrators, elementary and secondary school	209 630	(2)	(2)	75 640	213 250	(2)	(2)	76 890
Education administrators, postsecondary	101 530	32.86	36.44	75 800	105 360	33.82	37.78	78 590
Education administrators, all other	22 570	28.96	32.01	66 580	24 710	30.85	33.38	69 430
Engineering managers	186 380	46.94	49.33	102 600	187 410	48.44	50.71	105 470
Food service managers	206 340	19.04	21.13	43 940	191 420	19.87	21.60	44 930
Funeral directors	23 140	22.10	25.82	53 710	21 960	22.90	27.04	56 240
Gaming managers	3 520	28.17	31.77	66 090	3 310	28.82	31.69	65 920
Lodging managers	30 860	18.11	21.18	44 060	31 040	19.53	22.80	47 420
Medical and health services managers	224 070	32.42	36.12	75 140	230 130	33.51	37.09	77 140
Natural sciences managers	40 240	42.63	46.06	95 800	40 400	44.75	47.66	99 140
Postmasters and mail superintendents	26 430	24.32	24.43	50 820	26 120	25.34	25.83	53 740
Property, real estate, and community association managers	159 980	19.22	23.44	48 760	154 230	20.14	24.31	50 570
Social and community service managers	119 280	22.50	24.39	50 740	112 910	23.80	25.92	53 920
Managers, all other	354 730	37.19	39.28	81 700	340 720	38.06	40.16	83 530
Business and Financial Operations								
Agents and business managers of artists, performers, and athletes	10 860	26.48	33.42	69 520	10 640	25.87	33.68	70 060
Purchasing agents and buyers, farm products	14 300	21.02	24.03	49 980	12 970	22.44	25.47	52 970
Wholesale and retail buyers, except farm products	136 930	20.30	23.29	48 450	132 900	20.61	23.58	49 050
Purchasing agents, except wholesale, retail, and farm products	257 070	22.92	24.60	51 180	267 410	23.57	25.27	52 560
Claims adjusters, examiners, and investigators	234 950	21.26	22.74	47 310	234 030	22.21	23.66	49 210
Insurance appraisers, auto damage	12 520	21.79	22.01	45 780	12 900	23.12	23.43	48 740
Compliance officers, except agriculture, construction, health and safety, and transportation	167 650	22.78	24.64	51 260	161 810	23.73	25.63	53 320
Cost estimators	191 080	24.01	25.90	53 870	204 330	25.01	26.91	55 980
Emergency management specialists	10 070	21.82	23.73	49 350	11 240	22.10	23.90	49 720
Employment, recruitment, and placement specialists	169 750	19.80	22.76	47 330	181 260	20.08	23.31	48 470
Compensation, benefits, and job analysis specialists	92 940	22.83	24.10	50 130	97 740	23.49	24.88	51 750
Training and development specialists	200 440	21.43	22.97	47 780	206 860	22.05	23.58	49 060
Human resources, training, and labor relations specialists, all other	158 930	22.85	23.67	49 240	171 880	23.29	24.27	50 480
Logisticians	52 470	27.46	28.99	60 310	52 220	28.90	30.30	63 010
Management analysts	416 340	30.51	34.97	72 730	441 000	31.91	36.06	75 000
Meeting and convention planners	34 640	19.05	20.43	42 490	40 040	19.85	21.44	44 590
Business operations specialists, all other	847 170	25.70	27.72	57 660	916 290	26.22	28.38	59 030
Accountants and auditors	995 910	24.41	27.35	56 880	1 051 220	25.10	27.89	58 020
Appraisers and assessors of real estate	62 270	20.86	23.73	49 350	63 800	20.88	23.96	49 830
Budget analysts	53 300	26.94	28.41	59 100	53 510	28.32	29.89	62 180
Credit analysts	67 100	22.72	26.57	55 280	61 500	24.22	27.94	58 110
Financial analysts	177 780	29.76	33.89	70 500	180 910	30.70	35.16	73 130
Personal financial advisors	94 490	30.14	39.70	82 570	108 640	30.53	39.89	82 970
Insurance underwriters	96 110	23.34	26.08	54 240	98 970	24.65	27.15	56 480
Financial examiners	23 400	29.00	31.47	65 450	22 160	30.33	32.74	68 090

[1]Annual wages have been calculated by multiplying the hourly mean wage by a "year-round, full-time" hours figure of 2,080 hours; for those occupations with no hourly mean wage published, the annual wage has been directly calculated from the reported survey data.
[2]Hourly wage rates for occupations at which workers typically work fewer than 2,080 hours per year are not available.

Table 3-3. Employment and Wages, by Occupation, May 2004 and May 2005—*Continued*

(Number of people, dollars.)

Occupation	May 2004				May 2005			
	Employ-ment	Median hourly wages	Mean hourly wages	Mean annual wages[1]	Employ-ment	Median hourly wages	Mean hourly wages	Mean annual wages[1]
Business and Financial Operations—*Continued*								
Loan counselors	31 160	16.33	18.61	38 710	28 030	17.15	20.85	43 370
Loan officers	278 830	23.48	27.98	58 200	332 690	23.77	28.53	59 350
Tax examiners, collectors, and revenue agents	71 610	20.91	23.18	48 210	72 290	21.26	23.78	49 460
Tax preparers	51 950	13.33	16.50	34 330	58 850	12.36	14.90	31 000
Financial specialists, all other	119 840	23.82	26.64	55 420	122 320	24.64	27.47	57 130
Computer and Mathematical Science								
Computer and information scientists, research	24 720	40.96	42.32	88 020	25 890	43.86	45.21	94 030
Computer programmers	412 090	30.24	31.69	65 910	389 090	30.49	32.40	67 400
Computer software engineers, applications	425 890	36.05	37.18	77 330	455 980	37.06	38.24	79 540
Computer software engineers, systems software ...	318 020	38.34	39.50	82 160	320 720	39.48	40.54	84 310
Computer support specialists	488 540	19.44	20.97	43 620	499 860	19.52	20.86	43 380
Computer systems analysts	489 130	31.95	32.87	68 370	492 120	32.84	33.86	70 430
Database administrators	96 960	29.16	30.51	63 460	99 380	30.41	31.54	65 590
Network and computer systems administrators	259 320	27.98	29.55	61 470	270 330	28.81	30.39	63 210
Network systems and data communications analysts ...	169 200	29.14	30.49	63 410	185 190	29.69	31.23	64 970
Computer specialists, all other	130 420	28.60	30.31	63 030	116 760	28.57	30.38	63 190
Actuaries	16 350	36.70	42.05	87 460	15 770	39.25	43.63	90 760
Mathematicians	2 410	39.06	39.18	81 500	2 930	38.90	39.02	81 150
Operations research analysts	55 030	28.94	30.49	63 420	52 530	29.90	31.70	65 940
Statisticians	17 030	28.18	30.42	63 260	17 480	30.02	31.79	66 130
Mathematical technicians	1 720	18.49	20.99	43 650	1 430	17.54	22.23	46 230
Mathematical scientists, all other	8 500	29.98	29.67	61 710	7 320	29.74	29.60	61 560
Architecture and Engineering								
Architects, except landscape and naval	94 280	28.99	31.84	66 230	96 740	30.22	32.96	68 560
Landscape architects	17 960	25.54	27.73	57 680	20 220	26.07	28.62	59 540
Cartographers and photogrammetrists	9 870	22.15	23.48	48 830	11 260	23.20	24.68	51 340
Surveyors	52 680	20.66	22.15	46 080	54 220	22.05	23.53	48 950
Aerospace engineers	73 650	38.03	38.68	80 460	81 100	40.43	41.08	85 450
Agricultural engineers	3 220	27.17	29.04	60 400	3 170	31.20	31.91	66 370
Biomedical engineers	8 650	32.54	34.04	70 800	11 660	34.54	36.24	75 380
Chemical engineers	30 320	36.91	38.49	80 050	27 550	37.09	38.09	79 230
Civil engineers	218 220	30.88	32.18	66 930	229 700	31.82	33.41	69 480
Computer hardware engineers	74 760	39.02	40.39	84 010	78 580	40.59	41.91	87 170
Electrical engineers	148 310	34.43	35.68	74 220	144 920	35.34	36.57	76 060
Electronics engineers, except computer	135 560	36.43	37.24	77 450	130 050	37.52	38.46	79 990
Environmental engineers	47 690	31.96	32.86	68 350	50 140	32.74	34.00	70 720
Health and safety engineers, except mining safety engineers and inspectors	25 860	30.64	31.78	66 110	25 330	31.35	32.33	67 240
Industrial engineers	174 960	31.26	32.05	66 660	191 640	32.05	32.93	68 500
Marine engineers and naval architects	6 620	34.63	35.44	73 720	6 550	35.06	35.73	74 320
Materials engineers	21 130	32.26	33.36	69 390	20 950	33.49	34.32	71 390
Mechanical engineers	217 010	31.88	32.91	68 460	220 750	32.49	33.65	70 000
Mining and geological engineers, including mining safety engineers	5 050	31.10	32.77	68 160	5 680	33.69	36.09	75 070
Nuclear engineers	17 180	40.81	42.67	88 760	14 290	42.45	43.60	90 690
Petroleum engineers	14 690	42.55	44.15	91 820	14 860	44.71	46.80	97 350
Engineers, all other	159 720	35.78	36.32	75 540	152 940	37.09	37.29	77 570
Architectural and civil drafters	101 060	18.84	19.59	40 750	101 040	19.42	20.24	42 110
Electrical and electronics drafters	34 850	20.76	22.48	46 760	30 270	21.90	23.27	48 410
Mechanical drafters	76 610	20.67	21.70	45 140	74 650	20.84	21.87	45 490
Drafters, all other	22 620	20.13	21.91	45 560	20 870	20.34	21.84	45 420
Aerospace engineering and operations technicians ...	9 260	25.24	25.98	54 040	9 950	25.22	26.31	54 720
Civil engineering technicians	90 000	18.50	19.18	39 900	90 390	18.85	19.61	40 780
Electrical and electronic engineering technicians ...	178 560	22.26	22.66	47 130	165 850	23.10	23.42	48 710
Electromechanical technicians	18 770	19.92	20.74	43 130	15 130	21.10	21.96	45 670
Environmental engineering technicians	19 840	18.53	19.55	40 660	19 900	19.14	20.16	41 940
Industrial engineering technicians	68 210	20.96	22.64	47 080	73 310	21.77	23.67	49 220
Mechanical engineering technicians	46 990	20.87	21.66	45 050	46 580	21.55	22.37	46 520
Engineering technicians, except drafters, all other ...	88 100	23.77	23.86	49 630	78 300	25.25	25.19	52 400
Surveying and mapping technicians	60 530	14.60	15.76	32 780	63 910	15.04	16.05	33 390

[1]Annual wages have been calculated by multiplying the hourly mean wage by a "year-round, full-time" hours figure of 2,080 hours; for those occupations with no hourly mean wage published, the annual wage has been directly calculated from the reported survey data.

Table 3-3. Employment and Wages, by Occupation, May 2004 and May 2005—*Continued*

(Number of people, dollars.)

Occupation	May 2004				May 2005			
	Employ-ment	Median hourly wages	Mean hourly wages	Mean annual wages[1]	Employ-ment	Median hourly wages	Mean hourly wages	Mean annual wages[1]
Life, Physical, and Social Science								
Animal scientists	1 540	24.00	25.87	53 800	3 000	20.76	22.88	47 600
Food scientists and technologists	7 210	24.44	26.98	56 110	7 570	24.73	27.33	56 840
Soil and plant scientists	9 690	24.62	26.67	55 470	10 100	26.22	27.90	58 040
Biochemists and biophysicists	15 200	33.15	34.48	71 730	17 690	34.14	36.21	75 320
Microbiologists	13 880	26.37	29.45	61 250	15 250	27.34	30.46	63 360
Zoologists and wildlife biologists	15 050	24.20	25.54	53 120	16 440	25.02	26.58	55 280
Biological scientists, all other	26 180	27.05	29.03	60 370	26 200	28.94	30.61	63 670
Conservation scientists	14 290	25.23	25.72	53 500	15 540	25.65	26.27	54 640
Foresters	10 250	23.19	23.91	49 730	10 750	23.40	24.53	51 030
Epidemiologists	4 560	26.35	27.91	58 060	3 630	25.08	27.09	56 340
Medical scientists, except epidemiologists	66 450	29.48	33.04	68 730	73 670	29.68	33.24	69 140
Life scientists, all other	13 870	26.65	30.63	63 710	12 790	27.10	31.04	64 570
Astronomers	680	46.79	44.99	93 580	970	50.32	48.73	101 360
Physicists	14 150	42.04	42.83	89 090	15 160	43.18	43.98	91 480
Atmospheric and space scientists	7 070	33.70	33.46	69 590	7 050	35.55	35.11	73 020
Chemists	79 650	26.95	29.43	61 220	76 540	27.83	30.51	63 470
Materials scientists	7 330	34.80	35.77	74 390	7 880	34.35	35.74	74 350
Environmental scientists and specialists, including health	66 850	24.56	26.53	55 190	72 000	25.30	27.63	57 470
Geoscientists, except hydrologists and geographers	25 100	33.04	36.96	76 870	27 430	34.44	38.46	79 990
Hydrologists	7 290	29.57	30.82	64 100	8 360	30.68	32.33	67 260
Physical scientists, all other	25 260	38.53	39.21	81 560	23 800	40.05	40.57	84 380
Economists	12 030	34.99	38.35	79 770	12 470	35.43	38.90	80 900
Market research analysts	170 200	26.99	30.28	62 990	195 710	27.55	30.95	64 370
Survey researchers	19 480	12.74	15.39	32 010	21 650	14.97	18.13	37 710
Clinical, counseling, and school psychologists	96 540	26.42	29.24	60 810	98 820	27.49	30.75	63 960
Industrial-organizational psychologists	1 500	34.33	37.88	78 800	1 070	40.72	43.26	89 980
Psychologists, all other	6 480	34.57	33.53	69 740	6 750	35.70	35.70	74 250
Sociologists	3 640	27.82	30.46	63 350	3 500	25.37	29.66	61 700
Urban and regional planners	31 140	25.70	26.75	55 640	31 650	26.53	27.70	57 620
Anthropologists and archeologists	4 510	21.10	22.86	47 550	4 790	22.07	24.07	50 060
Geographers	750	28.35	28.65	59 600	810	30.56	31.07	64 620
Historians	2 350	21.39	23.48	48 850	2 850	21.35	23.86	49 620
Political scientists	4 370	41.71	41.24	85 770	5 010	40.43	40.78	84 820
Social scientists and related workers, all other	31 990	28.12	29.09	60 500	31 900	30.12	31.27	65 040
Agricultural and food science technicians	18 940	14.29	15.37	31 980	19 340	15.08	15.99	33 260
Biological technicians	59 710	15.97	17.04	35 450	67 080	16.47	17.54	36 480
Chemical technicians	61 700	18.35	19.04	39 600	59 790	18.51	19.29	40 120
Geological and petroleum technicians	10 420	19.35	20.85	43 360	11 130	21.03	23.82	49 550
Nuclear technicians	7 210	28.46	28.28	58 830	6 050	29.39	28.77	59 840
Social science research assistants	15 710	16.52	17.26	35 900	16 320	16.32	17.29	35 960
Environmental science and protection technicians, including health	29 460	16.99	17.90	37 230	32 460	17.43	18.52	38 520
Forensic science technicians	9 230	21.16	22.83	47 490	11 030	21.44	22.79	47 390
Forest and conservation technicians	29 910	13.14	14.79	30 770	29 940	13.72	15.13	31 480
Life, physical, and social science technicians, all other	72 580	18.19	20.52	42 680	63 810	19.25	21.72	45 180
Community and Social Services								
Substance abuse and behavioral disorder counselors	68 880	15.45	16.50	34 310	72 210	15.66	16.73	34 800
Educational, vocational, and school counselors	220 690	21.91	22.88	47 590	214 160	22.33	23.33	48 530
Marriage and family therapists	20 710	18.74	20.21	42 040	18 500	20.34	21.90	45 550
Mental health counselors	89 300	15.85	17.31	36 000	87 220	16.35	18.01	37 470
Rehabilitation counselors	115 150	13.40	14.76	30 710	117 230	13.62	15.07	31 350
Counselors, all other	21 970	16.82	18.21	37 880	21 390	17.91	19.01	39 540
Child, family, and school social workers	250 790	16.74	18.19	37 830	256 430	17.00	18.65	38 780
Medical and public health social workers	103 180	19.27	19.92	41 440	112 220	19.77	20.52	42 690
Mental health and substance abuse social workers	108 950	16.31	17.34	36 060	120 140	16.64	17.75	36 920
Social workers, all other	60 120	18.96	19.80	41 180	60 940	19.85	20.54	42 720
Health educators	46 490	18.50	20.25	42 120	51 970	19.10	20.89	43 440
Probation officers and correctional treatment specialists	89 170	19.04	20.53	42 690	90 600	19.33	20.92	43 510
Social and human service assistants	331 860	11.67	12.45	25 890	313 210	12.03	12.79	26 600
Community and social service specialists, all other	89 250	15.64	16.57	34 470	99 860	15.83	16.85	35 060
Clergy	35 790	17.64	19.23	40 000	36 590	18.53	20.05	41 700
Directors, religious activities and education	12 620	14.76	16.14	33 560	13 610	15.64	17.09	35 540
Religious workers, all other	8 810	9.01	11.41	23 730	6 670	11.43	13.48	28 050

[1]Annual wages have been calculated by multiplying the hourly mean wage by a "year-round, full-time" hours figure of 2,080 hours; for those occupations with no hourly mean wage published, the annual wage has been directly calculated from the reported survey data.

Table 3-3. Employment and Wages, by Occupation, May 2004 and May 2005—*Continued*

(Number of people, dollars.)

Occupation	May 2004				May 2005			
	Employ-ment	Median hourly wages	Mean hourly wages	Mean annual wages[1]	Employ-ment	Median hourly wages	Mean hourly wages	Mean annual wages[1]
Legal								
Lawyers	521 130	45.64	52.30	108 790	529 190	47.56	53.13	110 520
Administrative law judges, adjudicators, and hearing officers	14 830	33.14	35.44	73 710	15 350	33.98	36.89	76 730
Arbitrators, mediators, and conciliators	4 940	26.32	29.08	60 480	5 780	26.14	28.78	59 870
Judges, magistrate judges, and magistrates	25 500	44.75	42.96	89 360	25 330	46.91	43.99	91 500
Paralegals and legal assistants	210 020	18.81	19.95	41 490	217 700	19.79	20.92	43 510
Court reporters	15 520	20.63	22.63	47 070	17 130	20.02	21.84	45 420
Law clerks	43 300	16.34	16.92	35 180	40 620	17.12	17.78	36 980
Title examiners, abstractors, and searchers	53 700	16.77	18.93	39 360	64 580	16.88	19.26	40 070
Legal support workers, all other	69 590	20.26	21.79	45 330	71 060	21.06	22.54	46 890
Education, Training, and Library								
Business teachers, postsecondary	68 340	(2)	(2)	65 430	67 420	(2)	(2)	67 500
Computer science teachers, postsecondary	37 260	(2)	(2)	58 140	38 520	(2)	(2)	60 330
Mathematical science teachers, postsecondary	43 760	(2)	(2)	57 240	44 660	(2)	(2)	58 850
Architecture teachers, postsecondary	5 700	(2)	(2)	65 510	6 110	(2)	(2)	65 740
Engineering teachers, postsecondary	33 520	(2)	(2)	77 070	34 500	(2)	(2)	78 780
Agricultural sciences teachers, postsecondary	10 230	(2)	(2)	67 520	11 460	(2)	(2)	73 680
Biological science teachers, postsecondary	60 260	(2)	(2)	73 220	59 540	(2)	(2)	77 690
Forestry and conservation science teachers, postsecondary	2 970	(2)	(2)	67 660	2 990	(2)	(2)	67 550
Atmospheric, earth, marine, and space sciences teachers, postsecondary	8 660	(2)	(2)	70 300	8 810	(2)	(2)	70 960
Chemistry teachers, postsecondary	18 720	(2)	(2)	63 520	19 520	(2)	(2)	65 400
Environmental science teachers, postsecondary	3 860	(2)	(2)	66 790	4 340	(2)	(2)	66 020
Physics teachers, postsecondary	12 590	(2)	(2)	69 210	13 310	(2)	(2)	71 020
Anthropology and archeology teachers, postsecondary	4 990	(2)	(2)	66 060	5 320	(2)	(2)	66 700
Area, ethnic, and cultural studies teachers, postsecondary	7 670	(2)	(2)	62 940	7 970	(2)	(2)	62 480
Economics teachers, postsecondary	12 230	(2)	(2)	73 280	12 670	(2)	(2)	74 600
Geography teachers, postsecondary	4 180	(2)	(2)	61 020	4 250	(2)	(2)	61 790
Political science teachers, postsecondary	13 230	(2)	(2)	64 950	13 710	(2)	(2)	65 760
Psychology teachers, postsecondary	29 400	(2)	(2)	60 800	30 240	(2)	(2)	61 980
Sociology teachers, postsecondary	14 220	(2)	(2)	59 830	14 980	(2)	(2)	59 030
Social sciences teachers, postsecondary, all other	6 310	(2)	(2)	68 460	6 330	(2)	(2)	66 060
Health specialties teachers, postsecondary	105 610	(2)	.(2)	76 720	108 680	(2)	(2)	82 450
Nursing instructors and teachers, postsecondary	34 360	(2)	(2)	55 770	37 020	(2)	(2)	56 840
Education teachers, postsecondary	47 710	(2)	(2)	52 850	51 320	(2)	(2)	54 790
Library science teachers, postsecondary	3 740	(2)	(2)	54 590	3 960	(2)	(2)	56 630
Criminal justice and law enforcement teachers, postsecondary	9 550	(2)	(2)	51 500	9 880	(2)	(2)	52 930
Law teachers, postsecondary	12 580	(2)	(2)	95 300	13 560	(2)	(2)	95 570
Social work teachers, postsecondary	6 670	(2)	(2)	56 620	7 440	(2)	(2)	56 520
Art, drama, and music teachers, postsecondary	63 730	(2)	(2)	52 750	69 260	(2)	(2)	55 340
Communications teachers, postsecondary	20 760	(2)	(2)	53 130	22 320	(2)	(2)	54 010
English language and literature teachers, postsecondary	57 400	(2)	(2)	52 560	58 710	(2)	(2)	53 950
Foreign language and literature teachers, postsecondary	22 460	(2)	(2)	51 620	23 830	(2)	(2)	53 400
History teachers, postsecondary	19 190	(2)	(2)	58 490	20 520	(2)	(2)	59 450
Philosophy and religion teachers, postsecondary	17 170	(2)	(2)	56 630	18 340	(2)	(2)	57 960
Graduate teaching assistants	111 730	(2)	(2)	27 860	117 970	(2)	(2)	29 170
Home economics teachers, postsecondary	3 870	(2)	(2)	50 810	4 010	(2)	(2)	51 760
Recreation and fitness studies teachers, postsecondary	15 470	(2)	(2)	47 360	16 530	(2)	(2)	48 960
Vocational education teachers, postsecondary	112 990	19.59	21.19	44 060	105 980	20.07	21.69	45 110
Postsecondary teachers, all other	248 330	27.93	30.73	63 920	267 280	(2)	(2)	67 540
Preschool teachers, except special education	354 800	10.09	11.51	23 940	348 690	10.57	12.09	25 150
Kindergarten teachers, except special education	164 530	(2)	(2)	44 000	171 290	(2)	(2)	45 250
Elementary school teachers, except special education	1 422 840	(2)	(2)	45 670	1 486 650	(2)	(2)	46 990
Middle school teachers, except special and vocational education	623 400	(2)	(2)	46 510	637 340	(2)	(2)	47 890
Vocational education teachers, middle school	16 820	(2)	(2)	46 250	15 380	(2)	(2)	46 080
Secondary school teachers, except special and vocational education	1 021 180	(2)	(2)	48 420	1 015 740	(2)	(2)	49 400
Vocational education teachers, secondary school	102 210	(2)	(2)	48 000	96 600	(2)	(2)	49 240
Special education teachers, preschool, kindergarten, and elementary school	205 960	(2)	(2)	46 420	214 060	(2)	(2)	47 820
Special education teachers, middle school	98 840	(2)	(2)	48 910	103 480	(2)	(2)	50 340
Special education teachers, secondary school	138 470	(2)	(2)	49 620	136 290	(2)	(2)	50 880
Adult literacy, remedial education, and GED teachers and instructors	63 200	18.74	20.92	43 520	66 070	19.84	21.21	44 110
Self-enrichment education teachers	141 180	14.85	16.93	35 210	141 650	15.56	17.68	36 760
Teachers and instructors, all other	505 570	(2)	(2)	33 100	530 670	(2)	(2)	33 510
Archivists	5 190	17.54	19.05	39 630	5 410	17.99	19.64	40 850
Curators	8 590	20.97	23.04	47 920	8 790	21.75	23.64	49 180
Museum technicians and conservators	8 850	15.30	16.96	35 270	9 370	16.39	17.94	37 320
Librarians	149 680	22.07	22.88	47 590	146 740	22.79	23.61	49 110

[1]Annual wages have been calculated by multiplying the hourly mean wage by a "year-round, full-time" hours figure of 2,080 hours; for those occupations with no hourly mean wage published, the annual wage has been directly calculated from the reported survey data.
[2]Hourly wage rates for occupations at which workers typically work fewer than 2,080 hours per year are not available.

Table 3-3. Employment and Wages, by Occupation, May 2004 and May 2005—*Continued*

(Number of people, dollars.)

Occupation	May 2004				May 2005			
	Employ-ment	Median hourly wages	Mean hourly wages	Mean annual wages[1]	Employ-ment	Median hourly wages	Mean hourly wages	Mean annual wages[1]
Education, Training, and Library—*Continued*								
Library technicians	113 520	11.99	12.63	26 260	115 770	12.33	12.95	26 940
Audio-visual collections specialists	8 420	15.86	17.13	35 630	6 910	19.36	19.76	41 100
Farm and home management advisors	12 620	20.00	21.62	44 960	12 620	20.14	22.05	45 860
Instructional coordinators	106 590	23.46	24.74	51 450	112 880	24.24	25.66	53 360
Teacher assistants	1 242 760	(2)	(2)	20 400	1 260 400	(2)	(2)	21 100
Education, training, and library workers, all other	65 150	14.29	16.29	33 890	72 450	14.37	16.33	33 970
Arts, Design, Entertainment, Sports, and Media								
Art directors	26 870	30.69	35.21	73 240	29 350	30.75	35.48	73 790
Craft artists	3 890	11.31	13.33	27 720	4 300	10.78	13.15	27 360
Fine artists, including painters, sculptors, and illustrators	9 570	18.30	20.98	43 640	10 390	19.85	22.44	46 670
Multimedia artists and animators	30 210	24.21	27.65	57 520	23 790	24.18	27.53	57 270
Artists and related workers, all other	5 370	14.72	18.02	37 490	5 290	15.01	17.73	36 880
Commercial and industrial designers	33 050	25.15	26.77	55 670	31 650	25.10	27.30	56 780
Fashion designers	12 100	26.85	30.84	64 150	12 980	29.26	32.39	67 370
Floral designers	67 710	9.83	10.51	21 860	63 920	10.12	10.77	22 410
Graphic designers	159 720	18.28	20.25	42 120	178 530	18.46	20.45	42 530
Interior designers	46 360	19.56	21.59	44 900	50 020	19.88	22.60	47 010
Merchandise displayers and window trimmers	62 220	10.89	12.51	26 020	64 320	10.86	12.10	25 170
Set and exhibit designers	8 750	17.21	19.23	40 000	8 380	17.98	20.15	41 920
Designers, all other	12 650	20.31	22.27	46 320	12 410	20.96	22.99	47 810
Actors	59 000	11.28	22.48	(3)	59 590	13.60	23.73	(3)
Producers and directors	55 260	25.40	34.84	72 470	59 070	25.89	33.16	68 970
Athletes and sports competitors	12 250	(2)	(2)	86 690	12 230	(2)	(2)	71 900
Coaches and scouts	122 930	(2)	(2)	32 780	145 440	(2)	(2)	32 050
Umpires, referees, and other sports officials	11 440	(2)	(2)	27 850	12 800	(2)	(2)	27 150
Dancers	14 880	8.54	12.15	(3)	16 240	8.92	13.22	(3)
Choreographers	15 360	16.19	18.39	38 250	16 150	15.84	18.26	37 970
Music directors and composers	8 870	16.62	21.06	43 810	8 610	16.74	20.90	43 470
Musicians and singers	52 000	17.85	24.96	(3)	50 410	17.90	25.16	(3)
Entertainers and performers, sports and related workers, all other	54 800	16.73	18.82	(3)	68 540	15.73	17.92	(3)
Radio and television announcers	41 430	10.64	15.22	31 650	41 090	11.60	17.11	35 600
Public address system and other announcers	8 180	10.56	14.08	29 290	8 150	11.20	14.98	31 160
Broadcast news analysts	6 930	17.78	27.28	56 740	6 680	20.58	30.73	63 920
Reporters and correspondents	52 550	15.06	18.58	38 650	52 920	15.52	19.41	40 370
Public relations specialists	166 210	21.07	23.80	49 510	191 430	21.64	24.56	51 080
Editors	100 790	21.10	23.65	49 190	96 270	21.88	24.88	51 750
Technical writers	45 100	25.71	27.24	56 650	46 250	26.52	27.75	57 720
Writers and authors	42 780	21.32	25.52	53 080	43 020	22.32	25.89	53 850
Interpreters and translators	25 410	16.28	17.61	36 630	29 240	16.73	18.41	38 300
Media and communication workers, all other	27 380	19.64	21.66	45 060	25 660	20.14	22.13	46 030
Audio and video equipment technicians	40 050	15.66	17.62	36 650	40 390	15.84	17.48	36 350
Broadcast technicians	29 940	13.47	16.14	33 560	30 730	14.62	17.00	35 350
Radio operators	1 670	15.73	17.06	35 490	1 190	17.42	18.21	37 880
Sound engineering technicians	11 650	18.32	21.91	45 570	12 680	18.46	22.98	47 790
Photographers	54 400	12.54	15.00	31 200	58 260	12.55	15.10	31 410
Camera operators, television, video, and motion picture	21 600	18.08	20.04	41 690	22 530	20.01	22.13	46 040
Film and video editors	15 800	20.96	24.37	50 690	15 200	22.56	26.31	54 730
Media and communication equipment workers, all other	18 570	19.77	22.36	46 510	17 200	22.95	24.81	51 610
Health Care Practitioner and Technical								
Chiropractors	21 830	33.61	42.01	87 390	24 290	32.31	39.45	82 060
Dentists, general	84 240	59.16	63.87	132 850	86 270	60.24	64.27	133 680
Oral and maxillofacial surgeons	4 950	(4)	79.69	165 750	5 120	(4)	77.24	160 660
Orthodontists	6 190	(4)	72.45	150 700	4 820	(4)	78.56	163 410
Prosthodontists	730	(4)	70.04	145 670	560	(4)	70.23	146 080
Dentists, all other specialists	2 710	60.64	62.64	130 300	3 480	45.48	55.60	115 640
Dietitians and nutritionists	46 530	20.98	21.46	44 640	48 850	21.61	22.09	45 950
Optometrists	22 780	42.51	46.53	96 780	23 720	42.33	45.91	95 500
Pharmacists	222 960	40.82	40.56	84 370	229 740	43.18	42.62	88 650
Anesthesiologists	25 130	(4)	83.77	174 250	27 970	(4)	83.77	174 240
Family and general practitioners	106 750	65.91	66.58	138 490	112 150	67.50	67.49	140 370
Internists, general	51 180	(4)	76.06	158 200	48 210	(4)	75.27	156 550
Obstetricians and gynecologists	20 850	(4)	84.74	176 270	21 910	(4)	82.60	171 810
Pediatricians, general	26 520	65.26	68.04	141 520	26 400	65.67	66.94	139 230
Psychiatrists	22 440	(4)	72.17	150 110	23 450	(4)	70.26	146 150

[1]Annual wages have been calculated by multiplying the hourly mean wage by a "year-round, full-time" hours figure of 2,080 hours; for those occupations with no hourly mean wage published, the annual wage has been directly calculated from the reported survey data.
[2]Hourly wage rates for occupations at which workers typically work fewer than 2,080 hours per year are not available.
[3]There is a wide variation in the number of hours worked by those employed as actors, dancers, singers, and musicians. Many jobs are for the duration of 1 day or 1 week, and it is extremely rare for a performer to have guaranteed employment for a period that exceeds 3 to 6 months. Therefore, only hourly wages are available for these occupations.
[4]Median hourly wage is equal to or greater than $70.00 per hour.

Table 3-3. Employment and Wages, by Occupation, May 2004 and May 2005—*Continued*

(Number of people, dollars.)

Occupation	May 2004				May 2005			
	Employ-ment	Median hourly wages	Mean hourly wages	Mean annual wages[1]	Employ-ment	Median hourly wages	Mean hourly wages	Mean annual wages[1]
Health Care Practitioner and Technical—*Continued*								
Surgeons	55 800	(4)	87.31	181 610	52 930	(4)	85.43	177 690
Physicians and surgeons, all other	162 720	67.44	66.16	137 610	180 210	68.98	66.79	138 910
Physician assistants	59 470	33.37	33.07	68 780	63 350	34.63	34.17	71 070
Podiatrists	7 550	45.38	52.11	108 400	8 290	48.34	53.49	111 250
Registered nurses	2 311 970	25.16	26.06	54 210	2 368 070	26.28	27.35	56 880
Audiologists	9 810	24.74	26.47	55 050	10 330	25.72	27.72	57 660
Occupational therapists	83 560	26.28	27.19	56 550	87 430	27.34	28.41	59 100
Physical therapists	142 940	28.93	30.00	62 390	151 280	30.33	31.42	65 350
Radiation therapists	14 470	27.74	29.05	60 420	14 120	29.97	30.59	63 620
Recreational therapists	23 050	15.82	16.48	34 280	23 260	16.10	16.90	35 150
Respiratory therapists	91 350	20.74	21.24	44 180	95 320	21.70	22.24	46 270
Speech-language pathologists	89 260	25.20	26.71	55 550	94 660	26.38	27.89	58 000
Therapists, all other	8 090	19.32	21.45	44 620	9 730	20.22	21.96	45 680
Veterinarians	46 090	32.01	36.07	75 030	47 870	33.13	37.36	77 710
Health diagnosing and treating practitioners, all other	56 920	27.87	44.38	92 300	57 880	27.64	42.13	87 630
Medical and clinical laboratory technologists	151 240	21.99	22.41	46 600	155 250	22.94	23.37	48 600
Medical and clinical laboratory technicians	141 720	14.83	15.44	32 120	142 330	15.24	15.95	33 170
Dental hygienists	155 810	28.05	28.58	59 440	161 140	29.28	29.15	60 620
Cardiovascular technologists and technicians	43 540	18.60	19.09	39 710	43 560	19.43	19.99	41 580
Diagnostic medical sonographers	41 280	25.24	25.78	53 620	43 590	26.14	26.65	55 430
Nuclear medicine technologists	17 520	27.14	29.43	61 210	18 280	28.69	29.10	60 530
Radiologic technologists and technicians	177 220	20.84	21.41	44 530	184 580	22.09	22.60	47 010
Emergency medical technicians and paramedics	187 900	12.17	13.30	27 650	196 880	12.54	13.68	28 440
Dietetic technicians	24 630	11.05	11.89	24 730	23 780	11.28	12.20	25 380
Pharmacy technicians	255 290	11.37	11.87	24 700	266 790	11.73	12.19	25 350
Psychiatric technicians	59 010	12.28	13.43	27 940	62 040	12.87	14.04	29 210
Respiratory therapy technicians	24 190	17.67	18.00	37 440	22 060	18.37	18.57	38 620
Surgical technologists	82 280	16.35	16.72	34 770	83 680	16.75	17.27	35 920
Veterinary technologists and technicians	58 570	11.99	12.49	25 990	63 860	12.34	12.84	26 710
Licensed practical and licensed vocational nurses	702 740	16.33	16.75	34 840	710 020	16.94	17.41	36 210
Medical records and health information technicians	155 030	12.30	13.30	27 660	160 450	12.83	13.81	28 720
Opticians, dispensing	62 350	13.44	14.37	29 880	70 090	13.94	14.80	30 770
Orthotists and prosthetists	4 930	24.17	27.47	57 130	5 190	25.85	28.87	60 050
Health technologists and technicians, all other	72 390	16.46	18.10	37 650	71 140	16.49	18.04	37 520
Occupational health and safety specialists	36 360	24.79	25.54	53 110	35 460	25.82	26.83	55 800
Occupational health and safety technicians	11 190	20.25	21.31	44 320	9 510	20.75	22.17	46 120
Athletic trainers	13 100	(2)	(2)	36 350	15 110	(2)	(2)	36 520
Health care practitioners and technical workers, all other	52 240	16.04	18.20	37 860	50 880	16.12	19.03	39 590
Health Care Support								
Home health aides	596 330	8.81	9.13	18 980	663 280	9.04	9.34	19 420
Nursing aides, orderlies, and attendants	1 384 120	10.09	10.39	21 610	1 391 430	10.31	10.67	22 200
Psychiatric aides	54 520	11.19	11.70	24 340	56 150	11.02	11.47	23 860
Occupational therapist assistants	20 880	18.48	18.49	38 460	22 160	19.11	19.13	39 800
Occupational therapist aides	5 240	11.13	12.51	26 030	6 220	11.69	13.20	27 450
Physical therapist assistants	57 420	18.22	18.14	37 730	58 670	18.98	18.98	39 490
Physical therapist aides	41 910	10.28	11.14	23 160	41 930	10.34	11.01	22 900
Massage therapists	32 200	15.36	17.63	36 670	37 670	15.81	19.33	40 210
Dental assistants	264 820	13.62	13.97	29 060	270 720	14.19	14.41	29 970
Medical assistants	380 340	11.83	12.21	25 400	382 720	12.19	12.58	26 160
Medical equipment preparers	40 380	11.76	12.14	25 240	41 790	11.96	12.42	25 830
Medical transcriptionists	92 740	13.64	14.01	29 150	90 380	13.98	14.36	29 880
Pharmacy aides	47 720	8.86	9.52	19 810	46 610	9.09	9.76	20 310
Veterinary assistants and laboratory animal caretakers	70 200	8.97	9.44	19 640	69 890	9.43	9.90	20 590
Health care support workers, all other	182 550	12.01	12.62	26 250	184 200	12.51	13.05	27 150
Protective Services								
First-line supervisors/managers of correctional officers	35 880	21.50	22.83	47 490	37 530	23.35	24.37	50 700
First-line supervisors/managers of police and detectives	96 080	30.97	31.34	65 180	91 320	31.52	32.33	67 240
First-line supervisors/managers of fire fighting and prevention workers	54 170	28.33	29.26	60 860	53 490	29.25	30.06	62 510
First-line supervisors/managers of protective service workers, all other	47 280	17.91	20.05	41 690	49 330	19.78	21.95	45 650
Firefighters	273 630	18.43	19.06	39 640	282 180	18.80	19.43	40 420
Fire inspectors and investigators	12 500	22.28	23.03	47 890	12 820	22.64	23.44	48 760
Forest fire inspectors and prevention specialists	1 580	18.77	19.98	41 560	1 720	16.48	18.44	38 360
Bailiffs	17 270	16.28	16.80	34 950	17 160	16.25	16.90	35 160
Correctional officers and jailers	409 580	16.15	17.29	35 970	411 080	16.39	17.60	36 600
Detectives and criminal investigators	86 880	25.96	27.16	56 500	85 270	26.82	28.24	58 750

[1]Annual wages have been calculated by multiplying the hourly mean wage by a "year-round, full-time" hours figure of 2,080 hours; for those occupations with no hourly mean wage published, the annual wage has been directly calculated from the reported survey data.
[2]Hourly wage rates for occupations at which workers typically work fewer than 2,080 hours per year are not available.
[4]Median hourly wage is equal to or greater than $70.00 per hour.

Table 3-3. Employment and Wages, by Occupation, May 2004 and May 2005—*Continued*

(Number of people, dollars.)

Occupation	May 2004				May 2005			
	Employ-ment	Median hourly wages	Mean hourly wages	Mean annual wages[1]	Employ-ment	Median hourly wages	Mean hourly wages	Mean annual wages[1]
Protective Services—*Continued*								
Fish and game wardens	7 050	20.57	23.60	49 090	6 300	20.60	20.85	43 360
Parking enforcement workers	9 990	13.64	14.37	29 890	10 140	13.98	14.72	30 620
Police and sheriff's patrol officers	616 340	21.74	22.20	46 180	624 130	22.25	22.73	47 270
Transit and railroad police	4 610	21.84	22.77	47 370	5 090	23.49	24.20	50 330
Animal control workers	13 780	12.60	13.15	27 360	13 940	12.87	13.50	28 090
Private detectives and investigators	31 220	15.44	17.47	36 330	33 720	15.70	17.78	36 980
Gaming surveillance officers and gaming investigators	8 560	12.42	13.69	28 470	8 730	12.44	13.82	28 740
Security guards	978 570	9.77	10.61	22 070	994 220	9.98	10.91	22 690
Crossing guards	70 180	9.28	9.94	20 670	69 390	9.64	10.21	21 230
Lifeguards, ski patrol, and other recreational protective service workers	108 210	7.95	8.43	17 530	107 620	8.13	8.67	18 020
Protective service workers, all other	122 740	13.50	14.54	30 240	141 480	14.77	15.90	33 070
Food Preparation and Serving Related								
Chefs and head cooks	116 930	14.75	16.42	34 160	115 850	15.54	17.23	35 840
First-line supervisors/managers of food preparation and serving workers	733 680	12.22	13.21	27 480	748 550	12.53	13.44	27 960
Cooks, fast food	652 500	7.07	7.33	15 250	631 190	7.25	7.45	15 500
Cooks, institution and cafeteria	401 110	9.10	9.55	19 860	393 500	9.44	9.88	20 550
Cooks, private household	650	9.42	10.83	22 530	830	10.01	11.18	23 250
Cooks, restaurant	765 670	9.39	9.73	20 230	791 450	9.54	9.86	20 510
Cooks, short order	225 740	8.11	8.46	17 590	203 350	8.28	8.64	17 980
Cooks, all other	10 780	10.09	10.87	22 600	12 100	10.48	11.40	23 720
Food preparation workers	863 700	8.03	8.47	17 620	880 360	8.19	8.68	18 060
Bartenders	463 000	7.42	8.29	17 240	480 010	7.62	8.48	17 640
Combined food preparation and serving workers, including fast food	2 140 740	7.06	7.40	15 390	2 298 010	7.11	7.48	15 550
Counter attendants, cafeteria, food concession, and coffee shop	458 610	7.53	7.78	16 170	501 390	7.60	7.88	16 380
Waiters and waitresses	2 219 850	6.75	7.66	15 930	2 274 770	6.83	7.84	16 310
Food servers, nonrestaurant	186 770	7.95	8.58	17 840	188 750	8.28	8.98	18 680
Dining room and cafeteria attendants and bartender helpers	390 980	7.10	7.44	15 470	391 320	7.23	7.59	15 800
Dishwashers	497 650	7.35	7.50	15 600	498 620	7.45	7.58	15 760
Hosts and hostesses, restaurant, lounge, and coffee shop	316 400	7.52	7.82	16 260	328 930	7.62	7.90	16 430
Food preparation and serving related workers, all other	62 620	8.26	8.89	18 490	58 730	8.38	9.14	19 000
Building and Grounds Cleaning and Maintenance								
First-line supervisors/managers of housekeeping and janitorial workers	199 990	14.19	15.32	31 880	186 870	14.58	15.66	32 570
First-line supervisors/managers of landscaping, lawn service, and groundskeeping workers	102 380	16.99	18.38	38 230	106 280	17.46	18.82	39 150
Janitors and cleaners, except maids and housekeeping cleaners	2 103 490	9.04	9.91	20 620	2 107 360	9.32	10.15	21 120
Maids and housekeeping cleaners	880 150	8.13	8.62	17 930	893 820	8.21	8.74	18 180
Building cleaning workers, all other	13 580	10.17	10.74	22 350	15 610	11.25	12.99	27 020
Pest control workers	59 080	12.61	13.38	27 830	62 400	13.06	13.89	28 880
Landscaping and groundskeeping workers	860 200	9.82	10.62	22 080	896 690	9.94	10.74	22 350
Pesticide handlers, sprayers, and applicators, vegetation	24 200	12.30	12.74	26 500	25 770	12.56	13.22	27 500
Tree trimmers and pruners	39 600	12.57	13.37	27 800	29 790	13.42	14.35	29 850
Grounds maintenance workers, all other	17 760	9.57	11.18	23 250	17 960	10.04	11.78	24 510
Personal Care and Services								
First-line supervisors/managers of personal service workers	121 250	14.59	16.07	33 430	125 760	15.09	16.53	34 390
Gaming supervisors	25 040	19.64	19.98	41 570	24 180	19.38	19.87	41 320
Slot key persons	16 210	11.06	12.07	25 110	14 700	10.64	11.65	24 230
Animal trainers	8 060	10.60	12.48	25 950	8 320	11.92	14.19	29 510
Nonfarm animal caretakers	81 110	8.39	9.24	19 220	100 550	8.52	9.64	20 050
Gaming dealers	82 560	6.89	7.89	16 420	82 320	6.85	7.71	16 040
Gaming and sports book writers and runners	18 290	8.84	9.76	20 310	19 290	8.87	9.58	19 930
Gaming service workers, all other	14 860	10.01	10.85	22 570	16 070	10.37	11.53	23 980
Motion picture projectionists	10 290	8.32	9.55	19 870	10 230	8.07	9.30	19 340
Ushers, lobby attendants, and ticket takers	110 420	7.30	8.07	16 780	102 330	7.41	8.05	16 740
Amusement and recreation attendants	241 110	7.47	8.00	16 630	232 030	7.65	8.15	16 950
Costume attendants	3 460	12.04	13.81	28 720	3 900	12.19	13.94	28 990
Locker room, coatroom, and dressing room attendants	24 320	8.44	8.80	18 310	20 340	8.63	9.02	18 760
Entertainment attendants and related workers, all other	37 080	8.14	8.57	17 820	. . .	. . .	. . .	. . .
Embalmers	8 660	17.09	17.93	37 300	9 840	17.77	19.01	39 550
Funeral attendants	29 660	9.26	10.05	20 900	30 220	9.48	10.39	21 600
Barbers	15 830	10.19	12.04	25 040	13 630	10.46	11.88	24 700
Hairdressers, hairstylists, and cosmetologists	331 260	9.52	10.95	22 770	338 910	9.91	11.36	23 640
Makeup artists, theatrical and performance	1 060	11.74	15.28	31 780	1 070	11.29	15.70	32 660
Manicurists and pedicurists	38 030	8.89	9.65	20 080	42 960	8.79	9.81	20 400

[1]Annual wages have been calculated by multiplying the hourly mean wage by a "year-round, full-time" hours figure of 2,080 hours; for those occupations with no hourly mean wage published, the annual wage has been directly calculated from the reported survey data.

. . . = Not available.

Table 3-3. Employment and Wages, by Occupation, May 2004 and May 2005—Continued

(Number of people, dollars.)

Occupation	May 2004				May 2005			
	Employ-ment	Median hourly wages	Mean hourly wages	Mean annual wages[1]	Employ-ment	Median hourly wages	Mean hourly wages	Mean annual wages[1]
Personal Care and Services—Continued								
Shampooers	16 180	7.03	7.51	15 610	16 040	7.49	7.85	16 320
Skin care specialists	19 650	11.55	13.20	27 450	22 740	11.22	12.90	26 830
Baggage porters and bellhops	55 910	8.54	10.46	21 760	51 300	8.46	10.03	20 870
Concierges	17 310	11.23	11.93	24 820	16 810	11.30	12.08	25 130
Tour guides and escorts	28 660	9.32	9.92	20 640	28 320	9.61	10.42	21 670
Travel guides	4 140	13.20	14.30	29 750	3 120	14.06	15.03	31 270
Flight attendants	101 980	(2)	(2)	51 160	99 590	(2)	(2)	53 740
Transportation attendants, except flight attendants and baggage porters	27 730	9.17	9.99	20 780	24 810	9.28	9.88	20 550
Childcare workers	513 110	8.06	8.57	17 830	557 680	8.20	8.74	18 180
Personal and home care aides	532 490	8.12	8.38	17 430	566 860	8.34	8.52	17 710
Fitness trainers and aerobics instructors	182 280	12.25	14.98	31 170	189 220	12.43	14.93	31 060
Recreation workers	266 520	9.29	10.43	21 690	264 840	9.67	10.78	22 420
Residential advisors	49 960	10.30	11.17	23 240	50 490	10.51	11.39	23 690
Personal care and service workers, all other	65 070	8.63	9.81	20 410	60 260	8.91	10.20	21 210
Sales and Related								
First-line supervisors/managers of retail sales workers	1 087 830	15.73	18.01	37 470	1 083 890	15.79	18.08	37 600
First-line supervisors/managers of non-retail sales workers	307 610	28.51	34.33	71 420	294 010	29.79	35.42	73 670
Cashiers	3 438 070	7.81	8.29	17 250	3 481 420	7.82	8.32	17 300
Gaming change persons and booth cashiers	28 830	9.87	10.04	20 890	28 590	9.64	9.92	20 630
Counter and rental clerks	444 850	8.79	10.47	21 770	473 090	9.12	10.83	22 530
Parts salespersons	236 710	12.32	13.58	28 240	235 190	12.72	13.94	28 990
Retail salespersons	4 130 470	8.98	11.03	22 930	4 344 770	9.20	11.14	23 170
Advertising sales agents	144 690	19.37	23.76	49 420	153 890	20.08	24.23	50 400
Insurance sales agents	285 390	20.06	26.77	55 680	299 470	20.36	27.38	56 960
Securities, commodities, and financial services sales agents	240 500	33.27	43.77	91 040	251 710	32.28	42.30	87 990
Travel agents	90 500	13.29	14.25	29 650	88 590	13.78	14.78	30 750
Sales representatives, services, all other	352 050	22.60	25.93	53 940	439 450	22.50	26.07	54 230
Sales representatives, wholesale and manufacturing, technical and scientific products	378 080	28.17	32.37	67 330	379 890	29.21	33.14	68 940
Sales representatives, wholesale and manufacturing, except technical and scientific products	1 385 630	21.83	25.91	53 900	1 436 800	22.78	26.90	55 940
Demonstrators and product promoters	93 240	9.95	12.00	24 960	86 050	9.96	11.81	24 570
Models	1 410	10.50	13.21	27 480	1 430	10.92	13.26	27 570
Real estate brokers	40 050	28.23	37.43	77 850	41 760	27.49	36.98	76 930
Real estate sales agents	126 470	17.15	23.05	47 950	150 200	18.87	25.04	52 090
Sales engineers	71 690	33.95	36.42	75 740	69 790	35.68	38.16	79 370
Telemarketers	410 360	9.82	11.29	23 490	400 860	9.79	11.30	23 500
Door-to-door sales workers, news and street vendors, and related workers	15 200	10.85	13.36	27 790	10 970	9.83	12.19	25 350
Sales and related workers, all other	198 230	15.09	18.44	38 350	178 480	15.77	19.05	39 610
Office and Adminstrative Support								
First-line supervisors/managers of office and administrative support workers	1 406 240	19.72	21.15	43 990	1 352 130	20.38	21.89	45 540
Switchboard operators, including answering service	206 370	10.38	10.81	22 490	194 980	10.61	11.07	23 020
Telephone operators	38 500	13.65	14.53	30 220	29 290	15.09	14.92	31 030
Communications equipment operators, all other	4 040	15.23	15.98	33 240	3 870	15.64	16.36	34 030
Bill and account collectors	445 180	13.20	13.95	29 010	431 280	13.54	14.36	29 860
Billing and posting clerks and machine operators	496 780	13.00	13.50	28 070	513 020	13.36	13.87	28 860
Bookkeeping, accounting, and auditing clerks	1 770 860	13.74	14.34	29 830	1 815 340	14.18	14.76	30 700
Gaming cage workers	19 710	10.74	11.09	23 070	18 730	10.76	11.28	23 460
Payroll and timekeeping clerks	205 670	14.59	15.02	31 240	205 600	15.08	15.44	32 120
Procurement clerks	71 740	14.85	15.11	31 420	71 390	15.49	15.64	32 530
Tellers	552 860	10.15	10.30	21 420	599 220	10.24	10.59	22 020
Brokerage clerks	73 910	16.94	18.15	37 750	70 110	17.04	18.34	38 140
Correspondence clerks	21 590	13.51	14.19	29 510	17 990	13.66	14.51	30 180
Court, municipal, and license clerks	103 090	13.67	14.63	30 420	102 060	14.09	15.02	31 230
Credit authorizers, checkers, and clerks	66 010	13.97	15.15	31 520	65 410	14.10	14.90	30 990
Customer service representatives	2 021 350	12.99	14.01	29 130	2 067 700	13.22	14.27	29 680
Eligibility interviewers, government programs	93 250	15.92	16.25	33 800	85 550	16.22	16.53	34 390
File clerks	242 640	10.11	10.72	22 310	229 830	10.30	10.98	22 840
Hotel, motel, and resort desk clerks	190 300	8.51	8.93	18 570	207 190	8.56	9.05	18 820
Interviewers, except eligibility and loan	193 780	11.38	11.91	24 770	201 790	12.07	12.54	26 070
Library assistants, clerical	102 310	9.96	10.57	21 990	104 650	10.16	10.76	22 380
Loan interviewers and clerks	209 320	13.94	14.75	30 680	231 700	14.52	15.33	31 880
New accounts clerks	96 560	12.91	13.55	28 180	82 450	13.18	13.69	28 460
Order clerks	289 830	12.07	12.85	26 730	259 760	12.30	13.18	27 410

[1]Annual wages have been calculated by multiplying the hourly mean wage by a "year-round, full-time" hours figure of 2,080 hours; for those occupations with no hourly mean wage published, the annual wage has been directly calculated from the reported survey data.
[2]Hourly wage rates for occupations at which workers typically work fewer than 2,080 hours per year are not available.

Table 3-3. Employment and Wages, by Occupation, May 2004 and May 2005—*Continued*

(Number of people, dollars.)

Occupation	May 2004				May 2005			
	Employ-ment	Median hourly wages	Mean hourly wages	Mean annual wages[1]	Employ-ment	Median hourly wages	Mean hourly wages	Mean annual wages[1]
Office and Adminstrative Support—*Continued*								
Human resources assistants, except payroll and timekeeping	164 940	15.26	15.77	32 810	161 870	15.74	16.24	33 790
Receptionists and information clerks	1 071 230	10.50	10.91	22 690	1 088 400	10.65	11.12	23 120
Reservation and transportation ticket agents and travel clerks	159 910	13.34	14.48	30 120	160 120	13.52	14.45	30 050
All other information and record clerks	269 070	15.44	18.34	38 150	288 730	16.16	19.10	39 720
Cargo and freight agents	70 000	16.47	17.24	35 870	78 730	17.24	17.97	37 380
Couriers and messengers	111 700	9.71	10.26	21 330	106 520	10.03	10.80	22 460
Police, fire, and ambulance dispatchers	90 930	13.91	14.58	30 330	94 060	14.45	15.03	31 270
Dispatchers, except police, fire, and ambulance	165 910	14.87	16.01	33 310	172 550	15.09	16.15	33 590
Meter readers, utilities	48 830	14.15	15.03	31 260	46 920	14.09	14.92	31 030
Postal service clerks	76 870	19.69	19.82	41 230	78 710	23.23	22.51	46 820
Postal service mail carriers	344 050	21.37	20.85	43 370	347 180	22.27	21.38	44 460
Postal service mail sorters, processors, and processing machine operators	214 400	18.96	18.12	37 690	208 600	20.88	20.01	41 620
Production, planning, and expediting clerks	285 940	17.47	18.10	37 650	287 980	18.07	18.71	38 920
Shipping, receiving, and traffic clerks	747 270	11.73	12.43	25 850	759 910	12.10	12.80	26 620
Stock clerks and order fillers	1 561 530	9.66	10.52	21 890	1 625 430	9.66	10.60	22 060
Weighers, measurers, checkers, and samplers, recordkeeping	83 570	11.81	12.92	26 880	79 050	12.17	12.99	27 030
Executive secretaries and administrative assistants	1 422 610	16.81	17.69	36 790	1 442 040	17.29	18.18	37 810
Legal secretaries	264 070	17.65	18.40	38 280	265 000	18.15	18.78	39 070
Medical secretaries	360 850	12.76	13.42	27 900	381 020	13.13	13.65	28 390
Secretaries, except legal, medical, and executive	1 743 560	12.55	13.06	27 160	1 744 380	12.82	13.35	27 780
Computer operators	140 870	14.94	15.79	32 850	129 160	15.42	16.15	33 580
Data entry keyers	313 590	11.18	11.72	24 380	296 700	11.45	11.98	24 910
Word processors and typists	168 430	13.48	14.17	29 480	153 580	13.95	14.49	30 140
Desktop publishers	32 790	15.55	16.40	34 110	29 910	15.77	16.72	34 770
Insurance claims and policy processing clerks	239 250	14.06	14.70	30 580	239 120	14.49	15.24	31 700
Mail clerks and mail machine operators, except postal service	149 700	10.76	11.27	23 440	148 330	10.99	11.59	24 120
Office clerks, general	2 970 660	10.95	11.62	24 170	2 997 370	11.09	11.82	24 580
Office machine operators, except computer	97 140	11.16	11.83	24 610	87 900	11.53	12.24	25 460
Proofreaders and copy markers	20 530	12.18	12.99	27 010	18 070	12.30	13.30	27 660
Statistical assistants	18 560	14.55	15.19	31 600	18 700	13.92	15.04	31 270
Office and administrative support workers, all other	318 430	12.22	13.16	27 380	287 270	12.52	13.50	28 070
Farming, Fishing, and Forestry								
First-line supervisors/managers of farming, fishing, and forestry workers	19 890	17.06	18.50	38 480	19 750	17.32	18.65	38 790
Farm labor contractors	2 770	8.42	10.84	22 540	2 310	9.52	12.14	25 240
Agricultural inspectors	12 300	14.92	16.05	33 390	11 730	15.79	16.75	34 840
Animal breeders	1 530	13.55	15.74	32 730	1 860	12.90	15.23	31 690
Graders and sorters, agricultural products	50 110	7.90	8.52	17 710	45 010	8.06	8.74	18 170
Agricultural equipment operators	20 960	8.88	9.76	20 300	19 940	9.36	10.06	20 930
Farmworkers and laborers, crop, nursery, and greenhouse	240 000	7.70	8.07	16 780	227 750	7.91	8.35	17 370
Farmworkers, farm and ranch animals	43 250	8.31	9.07	18 870	49 740	8.76	9.56	19 890
Agricultural workers, all other	9 500	10.15	11.06	23 010	8 970	10.61	11.60	24 140
Fishers and related fishing workers	940	11.58	14.04	29 200	770	12.08	13.94	29 000
Forest and conservation workers	9 140	9.51	11.34	23 590	8 700	9.46	11.19	23 280
Fallers	10 180	13.23	15.15	31 510	9 780	13.64	15.26	31 740
Logging equipment operators	27 690	13.18	13.75	28 600	26 880	13.91	14.28	29 700
Log graders and scalers	4 870	12.29	13.21	27 480	4 520	13.31	14.21	29 550
Logging workers, all other	5 680	14.29	14.06	29 240	5 330	15.24	15.04	31 290
Construction and Extraction								
First-line supervisors/managers of construction trades and extraction workers	542 440	24.25	25.95	53 980	555 380	24.98	26.79	55 720
Boilermakers	18 520	21.68	22.29	46 360	17 760	23.10	23.62	49 130
Brickmasons and blockmasons	107 660	20.07	20.42	42 480	115 950	20.13	20.60	42 850
Stonemasons	16 320	16.82	17.75	36 920	17 030	16.66	17.53	36 450
Carpenters	882 490	16.78	18.26	37 970	935 920	17.11	18.62	38 720
Carpet installers	40 170	16.39	17.72	36 860	37 050	16.13	17.84	37 100
Floor layers, except carpet, wood, and hard tiles	15 800	15.68	17.13	35 640	14 520	15.87	17.92	37 270
Floor sanders and finishers	6 430	12.88	13.93	28 980	5 950	13.14	14.34	29 830
Tile and marble setters	42 930	17.02	18.28	38 020	47 410	17.56	18.81	39 130
Cement masons and concrete finishers	191 690	15.10	16.36	34 030	204 720	15.40	16.64	34 610
Terrazzo workers and finishers	6 700	13.45	15.47	32 170	5 440	15.40	16.69	34 720
Construction laborers	854 840	12.10	13.86	28 830	934 000	12.22	13.97	29 050
Paving, surfacing, and tamping equipment operators	61 860	14.42	16.07	33 430	63 220	14.58	15.93	33 140
Pile-driver operators	4 450	21.29	22.46	46 720	4 410	23.51	24.27	50 490

[1]Annual wages have been calculated by multiplying the hourly mean wage by a "year-round, full-time" hours figure of 2,080 hours; for those occupations with no hourly mean wage published, the annual wage has been directly calculated from the reported survey data.

Table 3-3. Employment and Wages, by Occupation, May 2004 and May 2005—*Continued*

(Number of people, dollars.)

Occupation	May 2004				May 2005			
	Employ- ment	Median hourly wages	Mean hourly wages	Mean annual wages[1]	Employ- ment	Median hourly wages	Mean hourly wages	Mean annual wages[1]
Construction and Extraction—*Continued*								
Operating engineers and other construction equipment operators	357 080	17.00	18.62	38 730	378 720	17.23	18.85	39 210
Drywall and ceiling tile installers	113 350	16.36	17.71	36 830	126 810	16.70	18.07	37 580
Tapers	36 370	18.78	19.25	40 040	38 570	19.17	19.91	41 410
Electricians	582 920	20.33	21.58	44 900	606 500	20.57	21.94	45 630
Glaziers	43 140	15.70	17.63	36 680	49 310	16.12	17.75	36 920
Insulation workers, floor, ceiling, and wall	37 000	14.57	16.12	33 530	34 250	15.08	16.59	34 510
Insulation workers, mechanical	17 110	16.03	17.48	36 350	22 100	17.07	19.16	39 840
Painters, construction and maintenance	249 560	14.55	15.87	33 010	249 850	14.81	16.08	33 450
Paperhangers	7 660	15.73	16.87	35 090	7 710	16.08	17.65	36 720
Pipelayers	54 470	13.68	15.40	32 040	56 280	13.83	15.53	32 290
Plumbers, pipefitters, and steamfitters	424 360	19.85	21.21	44 110	420 770	20.27	21.56	44 850
Plasterers and stucco masons	54 920	15.60	16.96	35 270	47 760	16.08	17.40	36 200
Reinforcing iron and rebar workers	32 660	16.90	19.32	40 190	30 270	16.78	19.32	40 190
Roofers	119 820	14.83	16.17	33 630	120 070	15.01	16.14	33 570
Sheet metal workers	184 740	17.09	18.63	38 760	174 550	17.50	19.03	39 570
Structural iron and steel workers	70 240	20.40	21.30	44 300	68 900	19.51	20.93	43 540
Helpers—brickmasons, blockmasons, stonemasons, and tile and marble setters	61 680	12.00	13.40	27 860	58 690	11.83	13.14	27 340
Helpers—carpenters	106 130	10.38	10.94	22 750	101 870	10.57	11.11	23 100
Helpers—electricians	92 820	11.26	11.97	24 890	90 370	11.17	11.86	24 670
Helpers—painters, paperhangers, plasterers, and stucco masons	26 090	9.87	10.87	22 610	21 820	9.88	10.61	22 070
Helpers—pipelayers, plumbers, pipefitters, and steamfitters	74 820	10.75	11.50	23 930	77 630	10.97	11.84	24 630
Helpers—roofers	21 530	9.93	10.58	22 000	20 510	9.97	10.41	21 660
Helpers—construction trades, all other	38 310	9.91	10.97	22 820	37 590	10.40	11.55	24 020
Construction and building inspectors	82 690	21.00	21.86	45 460	87 820	21.50	22.51	46 830
Elevator installers and repairers	21 110	28.23	27.98	58 190	21 000	28.46	28.12	58 500
Fence erectors	23 350	11.24	12.27	25 530	22 600	11.99	12.74	26 490
Hazardous materials removal workers	38 550	16.02	17.54	36 480	38 260	16.20	17.90	37 240
Highway maintenance workers	136 550	14.21	14.61	30 390	140 600	14.54	14.88	30 950
Rail-track laying and maintenance equipment operators	10 430	18.35	17.96	37 360	13 510	19.23	18.81	39 120
Septic tank servicers and sewer pipe cleaners	16 670	13.88	14.73	30 640	17 940	14.64	15.38	31 980
Segmental pavers	840	11.74	13.31	27 690	330	12.02	12.82	26 670
Construction and related workers, all other	81 260	11.40	12.71	26 440	63 340	14.36	15.50	32 230
Derrick operators, oil and gas	13 880	16.11	16.74	34 810	13 270	16.29	17.16	35 690
Rotary drill operators, oil and gas	13 860	17.11	18.68	38 860	15 500	18.03	19.18	39 880
Service unit operators, oil, gas, and mining	16 210	14.75	16.05	33 380	19 530	14.74	16.61	34 560
Earth drillers, except oil and gas	19 320	16.07	17.18	35 740	18 800	16.23	17.20	35 770
Explosives workers, ordnance handling experts, and blasters	5 290	17.16	17.85	37 130	4 800	18.65	19.33	40 210
Continuous mining machine operators	8 060	17.87	17.71	36 840	9 000	18.80	18.67	38 830
Mine cutting and channeling machine operators	3 900	17.96	17.95	37 330	6 080	18.64	18.12	37 680
Mining machine operators, all other	2 710	16.45	17.17	35 710	2 450	17.37	18.26	37 970
Rock splitters, quarry	3 180	12.54	13.43	27 940	3 600	13.10	13.56	28 200
Roof bolters, mining	4 290	18.70	18.54	38 570	4 140	18.91	18.84	39 180
Roustabouts, oil and gas	32 280	11.94	12.74	26 500	33 570	11.96	12.71	26 430
Helpers—extraction workers	26 430	12.66	13.23	27 520	25 550	13.19	13.76	28 620
Extraction workers, all other	10 450	15.66	16.37	34 050	9 060	16.35	17.32	36 010
Installation, Maintenance, and Repair								
First-line supervisors/managers of mechanics, installers, and repairers	459 440	24.20	25.34	52 700	455 690	24.99	26.15	54 390
Computer, automated teller, and office machine repairers	141 350	16.90	17.59	36 580	138 210	17.34	18.10	37 640
Radio mechanics	6 340	17.65	18.30	38 070	6 170	18.25	18.78	39 070
Telecommunications equipment installers and repairers, except line installers	202 160	23.96	23.10	48 050	198 350	24.33	23.72	49 330
Avionics technicians	22 310	21.30	21.38	44 460	22 490	22.42	22.57	46 940
Electric motor, power tool, and related repairers	21 910	15.54	16.11	33 520	20 070	16.09	16.77	34 880
Electrical and electronics installers and repairers, transportation equipment	17 390	19.25	19.46	40 470	20 560	19.95	20.20	42 010
Electrical and electronics repairers, commercial and industrial equipment	71 300	20.48	20.63	42 910	69 620	21.21	21.32	44 350
Electrical and electronics repairers, powerhouse, substation, and relay	20 660	25.86	25.51	53 060	21 250	26.43	26.26	54 620
Electronic equipment installers and repairers, motor vehicles	15 490	12.79	14.24	29 610	17 650	13.19	14.94	31 080
Electronic home entertainment equipment installers and repairers	32 210	13.44	14.25	29 640	35 360	13.91	14.83	30 840
Security and fire alarm systems installers	44 710	16.06	16.78	34 900	49 470	16.21	17.06	35 480
Aircraft mechanics and service technicians	112 830	21.77	22.69	47 190	115 120	22.74	23.68	49 260
Automotive body and related repairers	162 820	16.68	18.10	37 650	158 160	16.74	18.23	37 920
Automotive glass installers and repairers	18 150	13.45	13.98	29 080	17 760	14.18	14.67	30 510
Automotive service technicians and mechanics	668 540	15.60	16.61	34 550	654 800	15.89	16.90	35 140
Bus and truck mechanics and diesel engine specialists	251 430	17.20	17.66	36 730	248 280	17.61	17.96	37 360
Farm equipment mechanics	30 770	13.40	13.74	28 580	30 800	13.81	14.17	29 480
Mobile heavy equipment mechanics, except engines	112 000	18.34	18.68	38 860	117 500	18.95	19.32	40 190
Rail car repairers	18 140	19.48	19.01	39 550	24 270	20.45	20.32	42 270

[1] Annual wages have been calculated by multiplying the hourly mean wage by a "year-round, full-time" hours figure of 2,080 hours; for those occupations with no hourly mean wage published, the annual wage has been directly calculated from the reported survey data.

Table 3-3. Employment and Wages, by Occupation, May 2004 and May 2005—*Continued*

(Number of people, dollars.)

Occupation	May 2004				May 2005			
	Employ-ment	Median hourly wages	Mean hourly wages	Mean annual wages[1]	Employ-ment	Median hourly wages	Mean hourly wages	Mean annual wages[1]
Installation, Maintenance, and Repair—*Continued*								
Motorboat mechanics	17 680	14.74	15.16	31 530	18 190	15.76	16.31	33 920
Motorcycle mechanics	15 920	13.70	14.61	30 380	16 140	14.16	15.11	31 430
Outdoor power equipment and other small engine mechanics	25 170	11.98	12.66	26 340	24 680	12.41	12.95	26 930
Bicycle repairers	7 750	9.71	9.90	20 580	7 980	10.05	10.33	21 490
Recreational vehicle service technicians	12 340	13.93	14.73	30 630	13 540	14.65	15.43	32 100
Tire repairers and changers	87 110	10.01	10.75	22 350	100 860	10.08	10.72	22 300
Mechanical door repairers	10 470	15.38	16.92	35 190	14 400	14.57	15.81	32 890
Control and valve installers and repairers, except mechanical door	37 260	21.01	20.83	43 320	38 640	21.21	21.21	44 120
Heating, air conditioning, and refrigeration mechanics and installers	225 630	17.43	18.30	38 060	241 380	17.81	18.64	38 770
Home appliance repairers	40 300	15.47	16.00	33 280	43 110	15.86	16.38	34 060
Industrial machinery mechanics	212 770	18.78	19.28	40 090	234 650	19.11	19.74	41 060
Maintenance and repair workers, general	1 267 390	14.77	15.41	32 060	1 307 820	15.01	15.70	32 650
Maintenance workers, machinery	84 850	15.79	16.40	34 120	83 220	16.18	16.96	35 270
Millwrights	57 050	21.02	21.63	44 990	53 080	21.53	22.33	46 450
Refractory materials repairers, except brickmasons	3 570	18.09	18.76	39 020	3 250	19.35	19.74	41 070
Electrical power line installers and repairers	101 760	23.61	22.91	47 640	106 060	24.11	23.65	49 200
Telecommunications line installers and repairers	144 080	19.39	19.55	40 660	142 560	20.39	20.66	42 970
Camera and photographic equipment repairers	3 830	15.54	16.29	33 880	3 160	16.78	17.37	36 130
Medical equipment repairers	23 750	17.90	18.72	38 930	27 940	19.02	20.04	41 680
Musical instrument repairers and tuners	5 290	13.47	14.88	30 950	4 830	13.73	15.33	31 880
Watch repairers	3 450	13.87	15.23	31 670	3 080	15.21	16.00	33 280
Precision instrument and equipment repairers, all other	13 500	21.25	21.64	45 000	12 870	21.37	22.11	45 980
Coin, vending, and amusement machine servicers and repairers	37 230	13.47	13.95	29 020	39 570	13.56	14.11	29 340
Commercial divers	2 230	16.94	18.66	38 820	2 310	18.25	20.15	41 910
Fabric menders, except garment	2 150	15.62	15.60	32 440	2 140	16.77	16.37	34 040
Locksmiths and safe repairers	15 540	14.60	15.30	31 830	16 080	14.85	15.67	32 600
Manufactured building and mobile home installers	12 150	11.23	11.64	24 210	10 120	11.09	12.05	25 070
Riggers	12 480	16.98	17.55	36 500	11 840	17.79	18.17	37 790
Signal and track switch repairers	7 780	21.43	21.73	45 210	6 100	23.65	23.25	48 370
Helpers—installation, maintenance, and repair workers	157 310	10.25	11.18	23 250	158 520	10.21	11.17	23 230
Installation, maintenance, and repair workers, all other	137 650	16.23	17.23	35 830	135 560	16.39	17.43	36 260
Production								
First-line supervisors/managers of production and operating workers	696 750	21.51	22.96	47 760	679 930	22.18	23.66	49 210
Aircraft structure, surfaces, rigging, and systems assemblers	18 710	17.79	18.02	37 470	22 820	21.15	20.45	42 530
Coil winders, tapers, and finishers	27 360	12.24	12.69	26 400	23 190	12.32	12.65	26 320
Electrical and electronic equipment assemblers	217 360	11.68	12.63	26 270	207 270	12.08	13.05	27 150
Electromechanical equipment assemblers	51 370	12.71	13.29	27 650	57 200	12.97	13.71	28 520
Engine and other machine assemblers	45 730	16.73	17.29	35 960	49 430	16.72	17.38	36 150
Structural metal fabricators and fitters	86 240	14.34	14.94	31 070	93 490	14.56	15.09	31 390
Fiberglass laminators and fabricators	30 250	12.18	12.59	26 190	30 560	12.13	12.64	26 300
Team assemblers	1 208 270	11.42	12.36	25 720	1 242 370	11.60	12.50	26 000
Timing device assemblers, adjusters, and calibrators	3 150	13.76	14.57	30 310	2 460	13.54	14.23	29 600
Assemblers and fabricators, all other	259 830	11.90	14.14	29 410	258 240	12.62	14.49	30 140
Bakers	150 900	10.26	10.97	22 820	144 110	10.35	11.13	23 150
Butchers and meat cutters	131 490	12.45	13.12	27 300	128 660	12.78	13.37	27 810
Meat, poultry, and fish cutters and trimmers	137 370	9.09	9.60	19 970	136 690	9.53	9.99	20 780
Slaughterers and meat packers	134 140	10.03	10.20	21 220	132 000	10.20	10.33	21 490
Food and tobacco roasting, baking, and drying machine operators and tenders	18 110	11.46	12.12	25 210	18 160	11.17	12.15	25 280
Food batchmakers	85 010	10.62	11.34	23 590	89 400	10.82	11.61	24 140
Food cooking machine operators and tenders	41 810	10.02	10.72	22 290	43 100	10.29	11.03	22 950
Computer-controlled machine tool operators, metal and plastic	124 330	14.75	15.22	31 650	136 490	14.91	15.41	32 060
Numerical tool and process control programmers	17 310	19.31	20.27	42 160	17 860	20.11	21.15	43 990
Extruding and drawing machine setters, operators, and tenders, metal and plastic	88 980	13.18	13.54	28 170	87 290	13.46	13.84	28 790
Forging machine setters, operators, and tenders, metal and plastic	37 890	13.22	14.05	29 210	33 850	13.93	14.53	30 220
Rolling machine setters, operators, and tenders, metal and plastic	37 210	14.33	14.81	30 810	37 500	14.65	15.02	31 240
Cutting, punching, and press machine setters, operators, and tenders, metal and plastic	248 800	12.45	13.04	27 120	265 480	12.49	13.13	27 310
Drilling and boring machine tool setters, operators, and tenders, metal and plastic	41 940	13.69	14.72	30 620	43 180	13.85	14.72	30 610
Grinding, lapping, polishing, and buffing machine tool setters, operators, and tenders, metal and plastic	98 770	13.19	14.10	29 330	101 530	13.34	14.23	29 600
Lathe and turning machine tool setters, operators, and tenders, metal and plastic	70 230	15.04	15.47	32 190	71 410	15.26	15.74	32 750
Milling and planing machine setters, operators, and tenders, metal and plastic	30 280	14.91	15.16	31 530	29 140	15.13	15.44	32 120
Machinists	361 280	16.33	16.73	34 790	368 380	16.51	17.00	35 350
Metal refining furnace operators and tenders	17 150	15.74	16.13	33 560	17 960	15.83	16.26	33 820

[1]Annual wages have been calculated by multiplying the hourly mean wage by a "year-round, full-time" hours figure of 2,080 hours; for those occupations with no hourly mean wage published, the annual wage has been directly calculated from the reported survey data.

Table 3-3. Employment and Wages, by Occupation, May 2004 and May 2005—*Continued*

(Number of people, dollars.)

Occupation	May 2004				May 2005			
	Employ-ment	Median hourly wages	Mean hourly wages	Mean annual wages[1]	Employ-ment	Median hourly wages	Mean hourly wages	Mean annual wages[1]
Production—*Continued*								
Pourers and casters, metal	13 670	13.92	14.68	30 530	14 340	14.02	14.73	30 650
Model makers, metal and plastic	8 030	21.28	21.57	44 870	8 120	21.62	22.26	46 300
Patternmakers, metal and plastic	5 930	17.86	18.19	37 840	6 850	16.57	17.74	36 900
Foundry mold and coremakers	17 320	13.37	14.29	29 720	15 890	13.95	14.87	30 920
Molding, coremaking, and casting machine setters, operators, and tenders, metal and plastic	156 480	11.63	12.47	25 940	157 080	12.05	12.82	26 680
Multiple machine tool setters, operators, and tenders, metal and plastic	97 060	14.06	14.88	30 960	98 120	14.32	15.17	31 550
Tool and die makers	99 390	20.55	21.19	44 070	99 680	20.95	21.61	44 940
Welders, cutters, solderers, and brazers	344 970	14.72	15.41	32 050	358 050	14.90	15.52	32 280
Welding, soldering, and brazing machine setters, operators, and tenders	47 210	14.32	15.39	32 020	45 220	14.63	15.55	32 350
Heat treating equipment setters, operators, and tenders, metal and plastic	25 690	14.26	14.73	30 630	26 310	14.57	14.97	31 130
Lay out workers, metal and plastic	11 240	15.65	16.23	33 750	10 970	16.03	16.56	34 440
Plating and coating machine setters, operators, and tenders, metal and plastic	38 620	12.96	13.68	28 440	40 550	12.86	13.67	28 420
Tool grinders, filers, and sharpeners	19 750	14.52	15.10	31 410	18 180	15.05	15.64	32 530
Metal workers and plastic workers, all other	53 050	16.15	17.19	35 750	49 650	17.06	17.97	37 380
Bindery workers	73 240	11.31	12.33	25 650	64 330	12.04	12.92	26 880
Bookbinders	7 160	13.71	14.58	30 320	7 660	14.04	14.52	30 200
Job printers	56 770	15.41	16.23	33 750	50 580	15.35	16.02	33 320
Prepress technicians and workers	76 190	15.30	16.08	33 450	72 050	15.79	16.53	34 380
Printing machine operators	184 230	14.38	15.26	31 740	192 520	14.77	15.61	32 470
Laundry and dry-cleaning workers	218 610	8.28	8.74	18 170	218 360	8.38	8.87	18 450
Pressers, textile, garment, and related materials	80 520	8.33	8.62	17 920	78 620	8.45	8.76	18 220
Sewing machine operators	242 500	8.61	9.24	19 230	233 130	8.82	9.55	19 860
Shoe and leather workers and repairers	7 840	9.29	9.68	20 120	7 680	9.62	10.11	21 030
Shoe machine operators and tenders	4 530	9.44	9.85	20 500	3 850	9.90	10.31	21 440
Sewers, hand	12 430	9.13	10.20	21 210	11 090	9.51	10.61	22 060
Tailors, dressmakers, and custom sewers	27 180	10.79	11.76	24 450	30 150	10.95	11.79	24 530
Textile bleaching and dyeing machine operators and tenders	21 480	10.56	10.96	22 790	21 660	10.80	11.16	23 200
Textile cutting machine setters, operators, and tenders	25 320	9.80	10.44	21 700	21 420	10.30	10.83	22 530
Textile knitting and weaving machine setters, operators, and tenders	45 320	11.48	11.47	23 850	42 760	11.40	11.41	23 740
Textile winding, twisting, and drawing-out machine setters, operators, and tenders	53 490	10.87	11.41	23 740	47 670	11.04	11.30	23 510
Extruding and forming machine setters, operators, and tenders, synthetic and glass fibers	23 040	13.37	13.71	28 520	23 040	13.82	14.20	29 540
Fabric and apparel patternmakers	9 340	13.85	16.23	33 760	9 650	15.07	17.62	36 660
Upholsterers	38 550	12.35	13.05	27 140	41 040	12.84	13.46	27 990
Textile, apparel, and furnishings workers, all other	21 920	10.34	10.96	22 790	24 740	11.01	11.35	23 610
Cabinetmakers and bench carpenters	121 380	12.16	12.90	26 830	121 660	12.51	13.29	27 650
Furniture finishers	25 770	11.35	12.11	25 190	24 610	11.83	12.60	26 200
Model makers, wood	3 210	12.94	14.82	30 820	2 280	13.46	15.71	32 680
Patternmakers, wood	2 500	14.88	15.74	32 750	2 000	13.78	15.16	31 540
Sawing machine setters, operators, and tenders, wood	56 500	10.91	11.35	23 600	60 280	11.15	11.72	24 380
Woodworking machine setters, operators, and tenders, except sawing	88 870	10.93	11.43	23 780	94 690	11.25	11.83	24 610
Woodworkers, all other	12 190	10.16	10.94	22 760	10 550	10.20	11.13	23 150
Nuclear power reactor operators	4 300	30.81	30.71	63 880	3 730	31.84	32.17	66 900
Power distributors and dispatchers	8 290	27.56	28.03	58 300	7 520	28.44	28.61	59 510
Power plant operators	33 350	25.26	25.02	52 030	33 650	25.56	25.65	53 350
Stationary engineers and boiler operators	46 870	21.22	21.66	45 060	43 110	21.44	21.94	45 640
Water and liquid waste treatment plant and system operators	92 120	16.81	17.32	36 030	102 940	16.79	17.34	36 060
Chemical plant and system operators	59 980	21.55	21.61	44 940	58 640	22.45	22.55	46 900
Gas plant operators	10 670	24.36	24.36	50 660	10 530	24.96	25.15	52 310
Petroleum pump system operators, refinery operators, and gaugers	42 300	24.27	23.44	48 760	40 470	24.55	24.19	50 320
Plant and system operators, all other	14 930	20.10	20.14	41 900	13 920	21.57	21.50	44 730
Chemical equipment operators and tenders	48 450	18.69	18.94	39 390	50 610	18.77	19.05	39 620
Separating, filtering, clarifying, precipitating, and still machine setters, operators, and tenders	38 000	15.98	16.49	34 290	41 250	16.66	17.15	35 680
Crushing, grinding, and polishing machine setters, operators, and tenders	42 600	12.96	13.70	28 490	41 480	13.21	13.89	28 900
Grinding and polishing workers, hand	44 210	11.28	12.03	25 030	44 890	11.28	12.03	25 010
Mixing and blending machine setters, operators, and tenders	119 320	13.51	14.06	29 240	129 440	13.89	14.52	30 200
Cutters and trimmers, hand	28 780	10.59	11.60	24 120	28 360	10.50	11.57	24 070
Cutting and slicing machine setters, operators, and tenders	73 250	12.82	13.46	27 990	78 030	13.25	14.04	29 210
Extruding, forming, pressing, and compacting machine setters, operators, and tenders ...	73 970	13.20	13.88	28 880	80 420	13.36	14.15	29 420
Furnace, kiln, oven, dryer, and kettle operators and tenders	29 750	14.29	15.08	31 360	28 140	14.62	15.36	31 940
Inspectors, testers, sorters, samplers, and weighers	495 430	13.66	15.00	31 210	506 160	14.04	15.51	32 250

[1] Annual wages have been calculated by multiplying the hourly mean wage by a "year-round, full-time" hours figure of 2,080 hours; for those occupations with no hourly mean wage published, the annual wage has been directly calculated from the reported survey data.

Table 3-3. Employment and Wages, by Occupation, May 2004 and May 2005—*Continued*

(Number of people, dollars.)

Occupation	May 2004				May 2005			
	Employ-ment	Median hourly wages	Mean hourly wages	Mean annual wages¹	Employ-ment	Median hourly wages	Mean hourly wages	Mean annual wages¹
Production—*Continued*								
Jewelers and precious stone and metal workers	26 360	13.18	14.76	30 700	28 100	14.15	15.79	32 830
Dental laboratory technicians	44 540	14.93	16.21	33 720	45 600	15.50	16.47	34 260
Medical appliance technicians	10 080	13.38	15.19	31 600	10 810	13.98	15.61	32 460
Ophthalmic laboratory technicians	25 170	11.40	12.32	25 620	26 740	11.89	12.81	26 640
Packaging and filling machine operators and tenders	411 660	10.67	11.59	24 110	396 270	11.02	11.94	24 840
Coating, painting, and spraying machine setters, operators, and tenders	96 510	12.64	13.25	27 550	100 830	12.82	13.50	28 080
Painters, transportation equipment	49 810	16.89	18.17	37 800	52 650	16.75	18.14	37 720
Painting, coating, and decorating workers	26 990	10.95	12.01	24 970	27 830	10.89	12.15	25 280
Photographic process workers	31 610	9.63	11.07	23 010	28 000	10.51	12.05	25 070
Photographic processing machine operators	53 350	9.33	10.26	21 340	53 970	9.26	10.16	21 120
Semiconductor processors	44 440	13.85	14.46	30 070	44 720	14.92	15.80	32 870
Cementing and gluing machine operators and tenders	24 630	11.57	12.34	25 660	25 650	11.78	12.45	25 900
Cleaning, washing, and metal pickling equipment operators and tenders	16 860	11.18	12.15	25 270	15 250	10.95	12.19	25 350
Cooling and freezing equipment operators and tenders	8 790	10.96	12.18	25 340	9 640	11.13	12.16	25 290
Etchers and engravers	8 490	11.33	12.59	26 180	10 050	12.04	13.35	27 760
Molders, shapers, and casters, except metal and plastic	37 930	11.58	12.51	26 020	41 250	11.39	12.33	25 640
Paper goods machine setters, operators, and tenders	109 560	14.63	15.01	31 220	107 560	14.98	15.32	31 870
Tire builders	17 960	17.50	17.38	36 150	19 860	17.68	17.80	37 020
Helpers—production workers	480 430	9.70	10.35	21 530	528 610	9.80	10.45	21 730
Production workers, all other	299 950	11.38	13.47	28 010	296 340	11.36	13.49	28 070
Transportation and Material Moving								
Aircraft cargo handling supervisors	7 460	16.40	18.90	39 310	6 210	16.78	19.73	41 030
First-line supervisors/managers of helpers, laborers, and material movers, hand	169 860	18.40	19.45	40 460	176 030	18.75	19.81	41 210
First-line supervisors/managers of transportation and material moving machine and vehicle operators	222 590	21.54	23.23	48 320	221 520	22.85	24.63	51 230
Airline pilots, copilots, and flight engineers	78 490	(2)	(2)	129 620	76 240	(2)	(2)	135 040
Commercial pilots	21 370	(2)	(2)	62 290	24 860	(2)	(2)	65 560
Air traffic controllers	22 260	49.05	47.94	99 710	21 590	51.73	50.88	105 820
Airfield operations specialists	4 810	17.64	20.22	42 050	4 510	17.95	20.30	42 230
Ambulance drivers and attendants, except emergency medical technicians	17 410	9.49	10.17	21 140	18 320	9.03	9.72	20 220
Bus drivers, transit and intercity	183 710	14.30	15.09	31 390	183 450	14.91	15.37	31 960
Bus drivers, school	475 430	11.18	11.33	23 560	465 880	11.57	11.71	24 350
Driver/sales workers	406 910	9.66	11.36	23 620	400 530	9.67	11.44	23 800
Truck drivers, heavy and tractor-trailer	1 553 370	16.11	16.63	34 580	1 624 740	16.48	17.05	35 460
Truck drivers, light or delivery services	938 730	11.80	12.88	26 790	938 280	11.92	12.99	27 020
Taxi drivers and chauffeurs	132 650	9.41	10.34	21 510	144 280	9.60	10.36	21 550
Motor vehicle operators, all other	85 520	9.45	11.04	22 960	76 500	10.71	12.29	25 570
Locomotive engineers	31 180	24.30	26.29	54 680	37 390	26.69	28.96	60 230
Locomotive firers	620	21.56	22.23	46 230	540	18.65	20.54	42 710
Rail yard engineers, dinkey operators, and hostlers	6 170	17.70	18.41	38 280	6 970	18.28	18.99	39 500
Railroad brake, signal, and switch operators	16 410	21.46	23.03	47 900	20 700	23.89	25.07	52 150
Railroad conductors and yardmasters	35 720	22.28	25.28	52 580	38 330	25.98	27.50	57 200
Subway and streetcar operators	8 900	23.70	22.67	47 150	7 430	22.84	22.43	46 660
Rail transportation workers, all other	7 680	19.57	19.56	40 680	7 500	18.74	18.32	38 100
Sailors and marine oilers	27 570	14.00	14.98	31 160	31 090	14.11	15.19	31 590
Captains, mates, and pilots of water vessels	25 200	24.20	25.11	52 230	28 570	24.49	25.55	53 140
Motorboat operators	2 830	15.39	16.25	33 790	2 700	16.48	17.14	35 650
Ship engineers	10 330	26.42	27.80	57 830	13 240	25.38	27.54	57 290
Bridge and lock tenders	3 500	17.98	17.05	35 460	3 620	18.26	17.44	36 270
Parking lot attendants	120 080	8.08	8.48	17 650	124 250	8.14	8.64	17 970
Service station attendants	90 640	8.29	8.92	18 560	96 340	8.32	8.94	18 590
Traffic technicians	6 240	16.19	17.11	35 600	6 990	17.82	18.21	37 870
Transportation inspectors	24 140	24.22	24.89	51 780	25 570	23.79	25.59	53 230
Transportation workers, all other	51 850	15.47	16.11	33 510	54 010	15.68	15.98	33 240
Conveyor operators and tenders	54 380	12.23	12.85	26 720	49 220	12.81	13.24	27 530
Crane and tower operators	43 570	17.99	18.81	39 130	43 690	18.69	19.65	40 860
Dredge operators	1 730	13.47	14.43	30 010	1 720	14.92	16.08	33 450
Excavating and loading machine and dragline operators	67 080	15.37	16.40	34 120	66 030	15.57	16.64	34 610
Loading machine operators, underground mining	3 330	15.98	16.34	34 000	2 390	17.15	17.47	36 330
Hoist and winch operators	5 550	16.19	18.65	38 790	3 110	15.66	17.52	36 440
Industrial truck and tractor operators	631 530	12.78	13.57	28 230	627 060	13.02	13.86	28 830
Cleaners of vehicles and equipment	330 520	8.41	9.33	19 400	333 350	8.47	9.48	19 720
Laborers and freight, stock, and material movers, hand	2 390 910	9.67	10.53	21 910	2 363 960	9.91	10.80	22 460
Machine feeders and offbearers	149 500	10.68	11.31	23 530	145 740	10.74	11.41	23 730
Packers and packagers, hand	872 260	8.25	8.97	18 660	840 410	8.36	9.13	18 990
Gas compressor and gas pumping station operators	4 680	21.07	21.56	44 850	3 950	21.07	20.91	43 500
Pump operators, except wellhead pumpers	9 810	17.04	17.79	37 000	9 970	17.38	18.47	38 410
Wellhead pumpers	10 040	16.31	16.33	33 960	10 190	18.12	17.86	37 150
Refuse and recyclable material collectors	139 920	12.38	13.37	27 810	133 930	13.68	14.50	30 160
Shuttle car operators	3 000	18.08	17.58	36 570	3 100	18.42	18.28	38 030
Tank car, truck, and ship loaders	16 530	15.59	16.44	34 190	15 950	15.06	16.34	33 990
Material moving workers, all other	57 390	13.87	15.29	31 800	52 970	14.53	15.65	32 550

¹Annual wages have been calculated by multiplying the hourly mean wage by a "year-round, full-time" hours figure of 2,080 hours; for those occupations with no hourly mean wage published, the annual wage has been directly calculated from the reported survey data.

²Hourly wage rates for occupations at which workers typically work fewer than 2,080 hours per year are not available.

CHAPTER FOUR

LABOR FORCE AND EMPLOYMENT PROJECTIONS BY INDUSTRY AND OCCUPATION

LABOR FORCE AND EMPLOYMENT PROJECTIONS BY INDUSTRY AND OCCUPATION

HIGHLIGHTS

Every two years, the Bureau of Labor Statistics (BLS) develops decade-long projections for industry output, employment, and occupations. This chapter presents the employment outlook for the 2004–2014 period. The projections are based on a set of explicit assumptions and an application of a model of economic relationships.

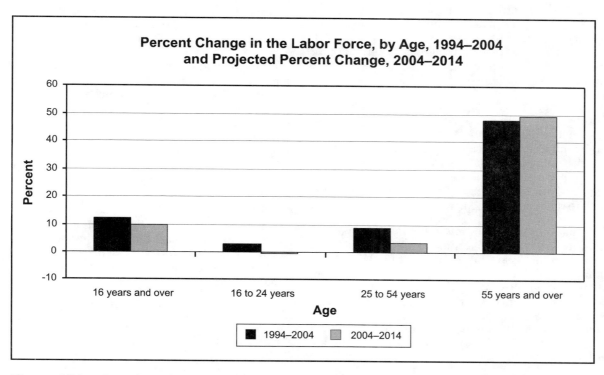

The total labor force is projected to grow by 10 percent (1 percentage point per year) between 2004 and 2014, a decrease of 2.5 percent (0.25 percentage points per year) from the 1994–2004 period. As the baby boomers age, the number of workers age 55 years and over in the civilian labor force will grow by a significant 49 percent. An increase is also predicted for the 25- to 54-year-old age group, but a decline is projected for the 35- to 44-year-old age group. The share of 16- to 24-year-old workers in the labor force is also expected to decline. (See Table 4-1.)

OTHER HIGHLIGHTS

- The proportion of men in the labor force is expected to continue to decline slightly, with a drop from 53.6 percent in 2004 to 53.2 percent in 2014. The female labor force is projected to increase a small amount, rising from 68,421 in 2004 to 75,906 in 2014. (See Table 4-1.)

- The Hispanic labor force is expected to rise rapidly during the 2004–2014 period, with a projected growth of 33.7 percent (3.37 percent per year)—a sizeable difference over the total labor force growth of 10.0 percent. However, this growth is not nearly as dramatic as the increase during the 1994–2004 period when it increased 60.9 percent. (See Table 4-1.)

- The Asian labor force, while relatively small in number, is also projected to experience a rapid increase, rising by 32.4 percent during the 2004–2014 period. (See Table 4-1.)

- The Black labor force is expected to grow at a faster-than-average rate of 16.8 percent, while the White labor force is expected to grow at a rate of only 7.3 percent during the 2004-2014 period. (See Table 4-1.)

NOTES AND DEFINITIONS

Concepts, Definitions, and Procedures

The Bureau of Labor Statistics (BLS) employment projections are carried out as a staged set of methodologies that move from the determination of labor supply and aggregate economic activity to the determination of jobs at a detailed industry level, and to the demand for specific occupations within each of the detailed industries. The following notes include a general discussion of the methods used; greater detail on the projection techniques is presented in the *BLS Handbook of Methods*.

The labor force projections are a function of two components—projections of the population and projections of labor force participation rates. Population projections are provided by the Census Bureau for detailed age, sex, race, and ethnicity groupings. BLS extrapolates participation rates for these same categories by applying well-specified smoothing and time series techniques to historical time series for the detailed participation rates.

The extrapolation results are multiplied by the projected population to arrive at initial estimates of the labor force categories. Both the participation rate and the labor force projections are carefully examined by BLS senior staff to ensure that relationships among the various categories do not change in unexplained ways over the forecast horizon. The total of all the categories in the labor force is used as one of the critical demographic assumptions in the next stage of the projections: the determination of aggregate economic activity.

The aggregate economic projections are carried out using the quarterly model of the U.S. economy produced by Macroeconomic Advisers, LLC (MA). MA is a team of economists based in St. Louis, MO, that provides monthly short-term forecasts of the U.S. economy, as well as quarterly long-term projections. The MA macroeconomic model comprises 609 variables that are descriptive of the aggregate U.S. economy. Of these variables, 160 are determined by stochastic behavioral relationships, 280 are identities, and 169 are exogenous variables determined outside the model. In order to use the MA model, quarterly estimates of the exogenous variables must be provided to the model over the forecast horizon. The model is then solved for the 440 behavioral and identity variables, and the results are evaluated for meaningfulness and acceptability.

The industry projections involve two primary tasks. The first is to translate the gross domestic product (GDP) categories from the aggregate economic model into a detailed commodity-by-category matrix. This redistribution of GDP, carried out using an eclectic grouping of models, techniques, and expert judgments, provides the demand component of an interindustry model of the U.S. economy. Approximately 200 commodities and 160 categories of demand are identified for this exercise. The second task is to derive input-output tables for the projection year, which when combined with the final demand matrix, yield estimates of both commodity and industry total output necessary to produce that level of GDP. Industry total output, also referred to as gross duplicated output, combines industry sales to final users with sales to intermediate users (other industries) in the economy and is the primary determinant of the factors of production (labor and capital) necessary to produce that total output.

The determination of detailed employment estimates begins with the specification of a production function for each of the 200 industries for which employment estimates are carried out. The production function is solved for the labor input component, and the resulting set of equations determines total hours paid as a function of industry output, sector wage rates, the unemployment rate, and a trend variable standing in as a proxy for technological change. A separate set of trend equations is estimated for industry-specific measures of average annual hours. Dividing hours paid by average hours yields a count of jobs by industry. The final stage of the industry employment projections process is to extrapolate the 200 industries to a full, 4-digit North American Industry Classification System (NAICS) level of detail (about 310 industries) for input to occupational demand.

The occupational projections also involve two basic tasks. The first is to extrapolate the latest historical industry-by-occupation staffing pattern matrix to the projection year. A staffing pattern matrix presents the proportional distribution of detailed occupations within each of the 310 4-digit NAICS industries. Analysts must determine whether each occupational ratio should remain unchanged, increase, or decrease relative to all the other ratios within a given industry. Straightforward balancing procedures are applied to ensure that the changed ratios still account for exactly 100 percent of industry employment. The projected industry employments from the previous step are then applied to the projected staffing pattern matrix and result in estimates of new job growth for about 700 detailed occupations. Estimates of job growth for the self-employed are carried out as a separate step.

In addition to the job growth estimates, analysts must also carry out estimates of replacement demand for individuals who have died, retired, or moved on to other occupations during the intervening decade. These estimates are based on relationships derived from the Current Population Survey, which is based on household employment behavior. In terms of occupational job opportunities, replacement demand often exceeds new job growth; thus, basing the analysis on measurements of new jobs alone could seriously underestimate job opportunities for many occupations.

A detailed review process is carried out during this entire process. Review feedback can affect occupational ratios, industry outputs, and/or employment totals; it could even impose changes at the aggregate level of detail. The purpose of the detailed review process is to derive a set of estimates which are consistent at all levels of detail, from the aggregate level to the most detailed occupational level. The ultimate review, of course, occurs when historical data finally overtakes the projected years. BLS has been carrying out and publishing these types of reviews since the 1970 projections. It has pointed the way toward improvements in the process and has allowed users to determine for themselves the places where weak points might impact their use of the projections.

Sources of Additional Information

A complete presentation of the projections, including analysis of results and additional tables and a comprehensive description of the methodology, can be found in the November 2005 edition of the *Monthly Labor Review*. A more detailed description of methods can be found in Chapter 13 of the *BLS Handbook of Methods* and in the 2006–2007 edition of *Occupational Projections and Training Data*. An article assessing labor force projections appeared in October 2003 edition of the Monthly Labor Review. All of these resources are available on the BLS Web site at <http://www.bls.gov>.

Table 4-1. Civilian Labor Force, by Age, Sex, Race, and Hispanic Origin, 1984, 1994, 2004, and Projected 2014

(Numbers in thousands, percent.)

Age, sex, race, and Hispanic origin	Labor force				Change			Percent change		
	1984	1994	2004	2014	1984–1994	1994–2004	2004–2014	1984–1994	1994–2004	2004–2014
Both Sexes, 16 Years and Over	113 544	131 056	147 401	162 100	17 512	16 345	14 699	15.4	12.5	10.0
16 to 24 years	23 989	21 612	22 268	22 158	-2 377	656	-110	-9.9	3.0	-0.5
16 to 19 years	7 943	7 481	7 114	6 243	-462	-367	-871	-5.8	-4.9	12.2
20 to 24 years	16 046	14 131	15 154	15 915	-1 915	1 023	761	-11.9	7.2	5.0
25 to 54 years	74 661	93 898	102 122	105 627	19 237	8 224	3 505	25.8	8.8	3.4
25 to 34 years	32 723	34 353	32 207	36 755	1 630	-2 146	4 548	5.0	-6.2	14.1
35 to 44 years	24 933	35 226	36 158	33 345	10 293	932	-2 813	41.3	2.6	-7.8
45 to 54 years	17 006	24 318	33 758	35 527	7 312	9 440	1 769	43.0	38.8	5.2
55 years and over	14 894	15 546	23 011	34 315	652	7 465	11 304	4.4	48.0	49.1
55 to 64 years	11 961	11 713	18 013	25 629	-248	6 300	7 616	-2.1	53.8	42.3
65 years and over	2 933	3 834	4 998	8 687	901	1 164	3 689	30.7	30.4	73.8
65 to 74 years	2 494	3 140	3 990	6 942	646	850	2 952	25.9	27.1	74.0
75 years and over	498	694	1 007	1 745	196	313	738	39.4	45.1	73.3
Men, 16 Years and Over	63 835	70 817	78 980	86 194	6 982	8 163	7 214	10.9	11.5	9.1
16 to 24 years	12 728	11 435	11 673	11 389	-1 293	238	-284	-10.2	2.1	-2.4
16 to 19 years	4 134	3 896	3 616	3 057	-238	-280	-559	-5.8	-7.2	-15.5
20 to 24 years	8 594	7 540	8 057	8 332	-1 054	517	275	-12.3	6.9	3.4
25 to 54 years	42 302	50 782	60 773	56 988	8 480	9 991	-3 785	20.0	19.7	-6.2
25 to 34 years	18 488	18 854	17 798	20 565	366	-1 056	2 767	2.0	-5.6	15.5
35 to 44 years	14 037	18 966	19 539	18 068	4 929	573	-1 471	35.1	3.0	-7.5
45 to 54 years	9 776	12 962	17 635	18 355	3 186	4 673	720	32.6	36.1	4.1
55 years and over	8 805	8 600	12 334	17 817	-205	3 734	5 483	-2.3	43.4	44.5
55 to 64 years	7 050	6 423	9 547	13 022	-627	3 124	3 475	-8.9	48.6	36.4
65 years and over	1 755	2 177	2 787	4 795	422	610	2 008	24.0	28.0	72.0
65 to 74 years	1 476	1 763	2 211	3 834	287	448	1 623	19.4	25.4	73.4
75 years and over	279	414	576	961	135	162	385	48.4	39.1	66.8
Women, 16 Years and Over	49 709	60 239	68 421	75 906	10 530	8 182	7 485	21.2	13.6	10.9
16 to 24 years	11 261	10 177	10 595	10 769	-1 084	418	174	-9.6	4.1	1.6
16 to 19 years	3 810	3 585	3 498	3 186	-225	-87	-312	-5.9	-2.4	-8.9
20 to 24 years	7 451	6 592	7 097	7 583	-859	505	486	-11.5	7.7	6.8
25 to 54 years	32 360	43 116	47 150	48 639	10 756	4 034	1 489	33.2	9.4	3.2
25 to 34 years	14 234	15 499	14 409	16 190	1 265	-1 090	1 781	8.9	-7.0	12.4
35 to 44 years	10 896	16 259	16 619	15 277	5 363	360	-1 342	49.2	2.2	-8.1
45 to 54 years	7 230	11 357	16 123	17 172	4 127	4 766	1 049	57.1	42.0	6.5
55 years and over	6 088	6 947	10 676	16 498	859	3 729	5 822	14.1	53.7	54.5
55 to 64 years	4 911	5 289	8 466	12 606	378	3 177	4 140	7.7	60.1	48.9
65 years and over	1 177	1 658	2 211	3 892	481	553	1 681	40.9	33.4	76.0
65 to 74 years	1 018	1 377	1 780	3 108	359	403	1 328	35.3	29.3	74.6
75 years and over	159	281	431	784	122	150	353	76.7	53.4	81.9
White, 16 Years and Over	98 492	111 082	121 086	129 936	12 590	10 004	8 850	12.8	9.0	7.3
Men	56 062	60 727	65 994	70 335	4 665	5 267	4 341	8.3	8.7	6.6
Women	42 431	50 356	55 092	59 601	7 925	4 736	4 509	18.7	9.4	8.2
Black, 16 Years and Over	12 033	14 502	16 638	19 434	2 469	2 136	2 796	20.5	14.7	16.8
Men	6 126	7 089	7 773	9 075	963	684	1 302	15.7	9.6	16.8
Women	5 907	7 413	8 865	10 359	1 506	1 452	1 494	25.5	19.6	16.9
Asian,[1] 16 Years and Over	3 019	5 472	6 271	8 304	2 456	799	2 033	81.4	14.6	32.4
Men	1 647	3 002	3 396	4 411	1 355	394	1 015	82.3	13.1	29.9
Women	1 369	2 472	2 876	3 893	1 103	404	1 017	80.6	16.3	35.4
All Other Groups,[2] 16 Years and Over	. . .	. . .	3 406	4 427	. . .	. . .	1 021	. . .	. . .	30.0
Men	. . .	. . .	1 817	2 373	. . .	. . .	556	. . .	. . .	30.6
Women	. . .	. . .	1 589	2 054	. . .	. . .	465	. . .	. . .	29.3
Hispanic,[3] 16 Years and Over	7 451	11 975	19 272	25 760	4 524	7 297	6 488	60.7	60.9	33.7
Men	4 563	7 210	11 587	14 921	2 647	4 377	3 334	58.0	60.7	28.8
Women	2 888	4 765	7 685	10 839	1 877	2 920	3 154	65.0	61.3	41.0
Non-Hispanic, 16 Years and Over	106 093	119 081	128 129	136 340	12 988	9 048	8 211	12.2	7.6	6.4
Men	59 272	63 607	67 393	71 273	4 335	3 786	3 880	7.3	6.0	5.8
Women	46 821	55 474	60 736	65 067	8 653	5 262	4 331	18.5	9.5	7.1
White Non-Hispanic, 16 Years and Over	91 296	100 462	103 202	106 373	9 166	2 740	3 171	10.0	2.7	3.1
Men	51 650	54 306	55 186	56 615	2 656	880	1 429	5.1	1.6	2.6
Women	39 646	46 157	48 017	49 758	6 511	1 860	1 741	16.4	4.0	3.6

[1]There was a disruption in the series for "Asian and other" and "Asian only" due to changes in the definition of the race categories for the 2000 census. Data for 1984–1994 represent the "Asian and other" race category with 1990 census weights. Data for 2004–2014 represent the "Asian only" race category with 2000 census weights.
[2]The "All other groups" category includes those reporting the racial categories of "American Indian and Alaska Native" or "Native Hawaiian and Other Pacific Islander," as well as those reporting two or more races. The category was not defined prior to 2003.
[3]May be of any race.
. . . = Not available.

Table 4-1. Civilian Labor Force, by Age, Sex, Race, and Hispanic Origin, 1984, 1994, 2004, and Projected 2014—*Continued*

(Numbers in thousands, percent.)

Age, sex, race, and Hispanic origin	Percent distribution				Annual growth rate (percent)		
	1984	1994	2004	2014	1984–1994	1994–2004	2004–2014
Both Sexes, 16 Years and Over	100.0	100.0	100.0	100.0	1.4	1.2	1.0
16 to 24 years	21.1	16.5	15.1	13.7	-1.0	0.3	0.0
16 to 19 years	7.0	5.7	4.8	3.9	-0.6	-0.5	-1.3
20 to 24 years	14.1	10.8	10.3	9.8	-1.3	0.7	0.5
25 to 54 years	65.8	71.6	69.3	65.2	2.3	0.8	0.3
25 to 34 years	28.8	26.2	21.8	22.7	0.5	-0.6	1.3
35 to 44 years	22.0	26.9	24.5	20.6	3.5	0.3	-0.8
45 to 54 years	15.0	18.6	22.9	21.9	3.6	3.3	0.5
55 years and over	13.1	11.9	15.6	21.2	0.4	4.0	4.1
55 to 64 years	10.5	8.9	12.2	15.8	-0.2	4.4	3.6
65 years and over	2.6	2.9	3.4	5.4	2.7	2.7	5.7
65 to 74 years	2.2	2.4	2.7	4.3	2.3	2.4	5.7
75 years and over	0.4	0.5	0.7	1.1	3.4	3.8	5.7
Men, 16 Years and Over	56.2	54.0	53.6	53.2	1.0	1.1	0.9
16 to 24 years	11.2	8.7	7.9	7.0	-1.1	0.2	-0.2
16 to 19 years	3.6	3.0	2.5	1.9	-0.6	-0.7	-1.7
20 to 24 years	7.6	5.8	5.5	5.1	-1.3	0.7	0.3
25 to 54 years	37.3	38.7	41.2	35.2	1.8	1.8	-0.6
25 to 34 years	16.3	14.4	12.1	12.7	0.2	-0.6	1.5
35 to 44 years	12.4	14.5	13.3	11.1	3.1	0.3	-0.8
45 to 54 years	8.6	9.9	12.0	11.3	2.9	3.1	0.4
55 years and over	7.8	6.6	8.4	11.0	-0.2	3.7	3.7
55 to 64 years	6.2	4.9	6.5	8.0	-0.9	4.0	3.2
65 years and over	1.5	1.7	1.9	3.0	2.2	2.5	5.6
65 to 74 years	1.3	1.3	1.5	2.4	1.8	2.3	5.7
75 years and over	0.2	0.3	0.4	0.6	4.0	3.4	5.3
Women, 16 Years and Over	43.8	46.0	46.4	46.8	1.9	1.3	1.0
16 to 24 years	9.9	7.8	7.2	6.6	-1.0	0.4	0.2
16 to 19 years	3.4	2.7	2.4	2.0	-0.6	-0.2	-0.9
20 to 24 years	6.6	5.0	4.8	4.7	-1.2	0.7	0.7
25 to 54 years	28.5	32.9	32.0	30.0	2.9	0.9	0.3
25 to 34 years	12.5	11.8	9.8	10.0	0.9	-0.7	1.2
35 to 44 years	9.6	12.4	11.3	9.4	4.1	0.2	-0.8
45 to 54 years	6.4	8.7	10.9	10.6	4.6	3.6	0.6
55 years and over	5.4	5.3	7.2	10.2	1.3	4.4	4.4
55 to 64 years	4.3	4.0	5.7	7.8	0.7	4.8	4.1
65 years and over	1.0	1.3	1.5	2.4	3.5	2.9	5.8
65 to 74 years	0.9	1.1	1.2	1.9	3.1	2.6	5.7
75 years and over	0.1	0.2	0.3	0.5	5.9	4.4	6.2
White, 16 Years and Over	86.7	84.8	82.1	80.2	1.2	0.9	0.7
Men	49.4	46.3	44.8	43.4	0.8	0.8	0.6
Women	37.4	38.4	37.4	36.8	1.7	0.9	0.8
Black, 16 Years and Over	10.6	11.1	11.3	12.0	1.9	1.4	1.6
Men	5.4	5.4	5.3	5.6	1.5	0.9	1.6
Women	5.2	5.7	6.0	6.4	2.3	1.8	1.6
Asian, [1] 16 Years and Over	2.7	4.2	4.3	5.1	6.1	1.4	2.8
Men	1.5	2.3	2.3	2.7	6.2	1.2	2.6
Women	1.2	1.9	2.0	2.4	6.1	1.5	3.1
All Other Groups, [2] 16 Years and Over	. . .	. . .	2.3	2.7	. . .	. . .	2.7
Men	. . .	. . .	1.2	1.5	. . .	. . .	2.7
Women	. . .	. . .	1.1	1.3	. . .	. . .	2.6
Hispanic, [3] 16 Years and Over	6.6	9.1	13.1	15.9	4.9	4.9	2.9
Men	4.0	5.5	7.9	9.2	4.7	4.9	2.6
Women	2.5	3.6	5.2	6.7	5.1	4.9	3.5
Non-Hispanic, 16 Years and Over	93.4	90.9	86.9	84.1	1.2	0.7	0.6
Men	52.2	48.5	45.7	44.0	0.7	0.6	0.6
Women	41.2	42.3	41.2	40.1	1.7	0.9	0.7
White Non-Hispanic, 16 Years and Over	80.4	76.7	70.0	65.6	1.0	0.3	0.3
Men	45.5	41.4	37.4	34.9	0.5	0.2	0.3
Women	34.9	35.2	32.6	30.7	1.5	0.4	0.4

[1]There was a disruption in the series for "Asian and other" and "Asian only" due to changes in the definition of the race categories for the 2000 census. Data for 1984–1994 represent the "Asian and other" race category with 1990 census weights. Data for 2004–2014 represent the "Asian only" race category with 2000 census weights.
[2]The "All other groups" category includes those reporting the racial categories of "American Indian and Alaska Native" or "Native Hawaiian and Other Pacific Islander," as well as those reporting two or more races. The category was not defined prior to 2003.
[3]May be of any race.
. . . = Not available.

PROJECTED EMPLOYMENT

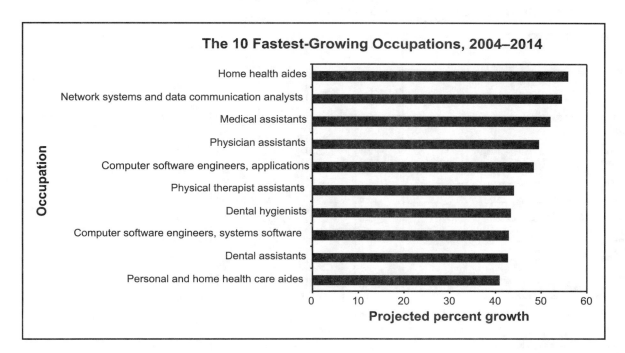

The 10 Fastest-Growing Occupations, 2004–2014

Seven of the ten fastest-growing occupations are in the health field, while only three are directly associated with computers. However, many of these fastest-growing occupations are relatively small, with total employment ranging from 59,000 to 700,000 workers. (See Table 4-2.)

OTHER HIGHLIGHTS

• The fastest-growing occupations do not necessarily provide the largest number of additional jobs. While employment in the fastest-growing occupations was relatively small in 2004, employment in the five largest-growing occupations ranged from 1.6 million to 4.3 million workers. Only one occupation was connected to health care and no occupations were directly related to computers. The occupations with the most employees in 2004 were retail sales and office administration. (See Table 4-3.)

• Of the ten occupations with the largest job growth in 2004, only two required a bachelor's degree or higher. Five were in the lowest quartile rank of median earnings. Meanwhile, of the ten fastest-growing occupations, four required a bachelor's degree or higher and only two were in the very low earnings group. (See Tables 4-2 and 4-3.)

• In 2014, 46 percent of the projected job openings will require a high school diploma and some college education. (See Table 4-5.)

• Total job openings result from growth and net replacements. Of the 54.7 million job openings expected in 2014, only about one-third will be from growth; the rest will be derived from replacements. (See Table 4-7.)

• While computer and peripheral equipment manufacturing is projected to have the largest output growth from 2004 to 2014, it is not expected to be a source of employment growth. Employment in computer manufacturing is predicted to decline. (See Tables 4-4 and 4-6.)

• The industries expected to have the largest employment growth from 2004 to 2014 are health care and social assistance, administrative and support services, and state and local government. (See Table 4-6.)

Table 4-2. Fastest-Growing Occupations, 2004–2014

(Numbers in thousands, percent.)

Occupation	Employment		Change		Quartile rank by 2004 median annual earnings[1]	Most significant source of postsecondary education or training[2]
	2004	2014	Number	Percent		
Home health aides	624	974	350	56.0	VL	Short term on-the-job training
Network systems and data communications analysts	231	357	126	54.6	VH	Bachelor's degree
Medical assistants	387	589	202	52.1	L	Moderate term on-the-job training
Physician assistants	62	93	31	49.6	VH	Bachelor's degree
Computer software engineers, applications	460	682	222	48.4	VH	Bachelor's degree
Physical therapist assistants	59	85	26	44.2	H	Associate's degree
Dental hygienists	158	226	68	43.3	VH	Associate's degree
Computer software engineers, systems software	340	486	146	43.0	VH	Bachelor's degree
Dental assistants	267	382	114	42.7	L	Moderate term on-the-job training
Personal and home care aides	701	988	287	41.0	VL	Short term on-the-job training
Network and computer systems administrators	278	385	107	38.4	VH	Bachelor's degree
Database administrators	104	144	40	38.2	VH	Bachelor's degree
Physical therapists	155	211	57	36.7	VH	Master's degree
Forensic science technicians	10	13	4	36.4	VH	Associate's degree
Veterinary technologists and technicians	60	81	21	35.3	L	Associate's degree
Diagnostic medical sonographers	42	57	15	34.8	VH	Associate's degree
Physical therapist aides	43	57	15	34.4	L	Short term on-the-job training
Occupational therapist assistants	21	29	7	34.1	H	Associate's degree
Medical scientists, except epidemiologists	72	97	25	34.1	VH	Doctoral degree
Occupational therapists	92	123	31	33.6	VH	Master's degree
Preschool teachers, except special education	431	573	143	33.1	L	Postsecondary vocational award
Cardiovascular technologists and technicians	45	60	15	32.6	H	Associate's degree
Postsecondary teachers	1 628	2 153	524	32.2	VH	Doctoral degree
Hydrologists	8	11	3	31.6	VH	Master's degree
Computer systems analysts	487	640	153	31.4	VH	Bachelor's degree
Hazardous materials removal workers	38	50	12	31.2	H	Moderate term on-the-job training
Biomedical engineers	10	13	3	30.7	VH	Bachelor's degree
Employment, recruitment, and placement specialists	182	237	55	30.5	H	Bachelor's degree
Environmental engineers	49	64	15	30.0	VH	Bachelor's degree
Paralegals and legal assistants	224	291	67	29.7	H	Associate's degree

[1]The quartile rankings of the BLS Occupational Employment Statistics Survey annual earnings data are presented in the following categories: VH = very high ($43,600 or more); H = high ($28,580 to $43,590); L = low ($20,190 to $28,570); and VL = very low (up to $20,180). The rankings were based on quartiles, with one-quarter of total employment defining each quartile. Earnings are for wage and salary workers.

[2]An occupation is placed into one of 11 categories that best describes the education or training needed by most workers to become fully qualified in that occupation.

Table 4-3. Occupations with the Largest Job Growth, 2004–2014

(Numbers in thousands, percent.)

Occupation	Employment		Change		Quartile rank by 2004 median annual earnings[1]	Most significant source of postsecondary education or training[2]
	2004	2014	Number	Percent		
Retail salespersons	4 256	4 992	736	17.3	VL	Short term on-the-job training
Registered nurses	2 394	3 096	703	29.4	VH	Associate's degree
Postsecondary teachers	1 628	2 153	524	32.2	VH	Doctoral degree
Customer service representatives	2 063	2 534	471	22.8	L	Moderate term on-the-job training
Janitors and cleaners, except maids and housekeeping cleaners	2 374	2 813	440	18.5	VL	Short term on-the-job training
Waiters and waitresses	2 252	2 627	376	16.7	VL	Short term on-the-job training
Combined food preparation and serving workers, including fast food	2 150	2 516	367	17.1	VL	Short term on-the-job training
Home health aides	624	974	350	56.0	VL	Short term on-the-job training
Nursing aides, orderlies, and attendants	1 455	1 781	325	22.3	L	Postsecondary vocational award
General and operations managers	1 807	2 115	308	17.0	VH	Bachelor's degree plus work experience
Personal and home care aides	701	988	287	41.0	VL	Short term on-the-job training
Elementary school teachers, except special education	1 457	1 722	265	18.2	H	Bachelor's degree
Accountants and auditors	1 176	1 440	264	22.4	VH	Bachelor's degree
Office clerks, general	3 138	3 401	263	8.4	L	Short term on-the-job training
Laborers and freight, stock, and material movers, hand	2 430	2 678	248	10.2	VL	Short term on-the-job training
Receptionists and information clerks	1 133	1 379	246	21.7	L	Short term on-the-job training
Landscaping and groundskeeping workers	1 177	1 407	230	19.5	L	Short term on-the-job training
Truck drivers, heavy and tractor trailer	1 738	1 962	223	12.9	H	Moderate term on-the-job training
Computer software engineers, applications	460	682	222	48.4	VH	Bachelor's degree
Maintenance and repair workers, general	1 332	1 533	202	15.2	H	Moderate term on-the-job training
Medical assistants	387	589	202	52.1	L	Moderate term on-the-job training
Executive secretaries and administrative assistants	1 547	1 739	192	12.4	H	Moderate term on-the-job training
Sales representatives, wholesale and manufacturing, except technical and scientific products	1 454	1 641	187	12.9	VH	Moderate term on-the-job training
Carpenters	1 349	1 535	186	13.8	H	Long term on-the-job training
Teacher assistants	1 296	1 478	183	14.1	VL	Short term on-the-job training
Childcare workers	1 280	1 456	176	13.8	VL	Short term on-the-job training
Food preparation workers	889	1 064	175	19.7	VL	Short term on-the-job training
Maids and housekeeping cleaners	1 422	1 587	165	11.6	VL	Short term on-the-job training
Truck drivers, light or delivery services	1 042	1 206	164	15.7	L	Short term on-the-job training
Computer systems analysts	487	640	153	31.4	VH	Bachelor's degree

[1]The quartile rankings of the BLS Occupational Employment Statistics Survey annual earnings data are presented in the following categories: VH = very high ($43,600 or more); H = high ($28,580 to $43,590); L = low ($20,190 to $28,570); and VL = very low (up to $20,180). The rankings were based on quartiles, with one-quarter of total employment defining each quartile. Earnings are for wage and salary workers.

[2]An occupation is placed into one of 11 categories that best describes the education or training needed by most workers to become fully qualified in that occupation.

Table 4-4. Industries with the Largest Output Growth and Declines, 2004–2014

(Dollars, number, percent.)

Industry	Billions of chained (1996) dollars		Change, 2004–2014	Average annual rate of change, 2004–2014
	2004	2014		
Largest Growth				
Computer and peripheral equipment manufacturing	171.8	1 367.6	1 195.8	23.1
Communications equipment manufacturing	92.2	318.8	226.7	13.2
Software publishers	101.1	281.2	180.0	10.8
Computer and peripheral equipment manufacturing	171.8	1 367.6	1 195.8	23.1
Wholesale trade	971.0	1 812.5	841.5	6.4
Retail trade	1 125.3	1 757.5	632.2	4.6
Monetary authorities, credit intermediation, and related activities	655.9	944.4	288.5	3.7
Management of companies and enterprises	397.4	681.4	284.0	5.5
Securities, commodity contracts, and other financial investments and related activity	296.2	565.4	269.2	6.7
Owner-occupied dwellings	858.3	1 123.9	265.6	2.7
Communications equipment manufacturing	92.2	318.8	226.7	13.2
Real estate	807.4	1 025.8	218.4	2.4
Telecommunications	463.6	667.0	203.4	3.7
Construction	841.0	1 043.8	202.7	2.2
Offices of health practitioners	400.0	600.0	200.0	4.1
Software publishers	101.1	281.2	180.0	10.8
Lessors of nonfinancial intangible assets (except copyrighted works)	122.7	291.8	169.1	9.0
Hospitals, private	384.8	544.0	159.2	3.5
Internet and other information services	119.9	271.8	152.0	8.5
Computer systems design and related services	154.6	305.4	150.8	7.0
Management, scientific, and technical consulting services	148.8	271.7	123.0	6.2
Scientific research and development services	120.6	239.9	119.3	7.1
Local government, excluding enterprises, educational services, and hospitals	360.5	469.1	108.6	2.7
Local government educational services	390.5	491.6	101.1	2.3
Semiconductor and other electronic component manufacturing	166.6	264.9	98.3	4.7
Largest Declines				
Tobacco manufacturing	42.5	25.7	-16.8	-4.9
Natural gas distribution	59.6	45.8	-13.8	-2.6
Cut and sew apparel manufacturing	43.9	32.8	-11.2	-2.9
Fabric mills	20.4	14.0	-6.5	-3.7
Commercial and service industry machinery manufacturing	25.9	22.3	-3.6	-1.5
Alumina and aluminum production and processing	35.2	31.7	-3.6	-1.1
Textile and fabric finishing and fabric coating mills	11.2	8.4	-2.8	-2.8
Foundries	29.3	26.5	-2.8	-1.0
Apparel knitting mills	8.0	5.6	-2.4	-3.5
Fiber, yarn, and thread mills	10.0	7.8	-2.2	-2.4
Rubber product manufacturing	30.2	28.4	-1.8	-0.6
Other support services	31.0	29.5	-1.6	-0.5
Pipeline transportation	26.3	24.9	-1.4	-0.5
Metal ore mining	6.6	5.5	-1.2	-1.9
Basic chemical manufacturing	111.2	110.3	-1.0	-0.1
Pesticide, fertilizer, and other agricultural chemical manufacturing	20.0	19.0	-1.0	-0.5
Footwear manufacturing	3.3	2.7	-0.6	-2.0
Leather and hide tanning and finishing	3.3	2.8	-0.5	-1.7
Apparel accessories and other apparel manufacturing	3.5	3.0	-0.5	-1.5
Spring and wire product manufacturing	8.2	7.9	-0.3	-0.4

Table 4-5. Employment and Total Job Openings, by Education Cluster, 2004–2014

(Numbers in thousands, percent.)

Education cluster	Employment				Change in employment, 2004–2014			Total job openings due to growth and net replacements[1]	
	Number		Percent distribution		Number	Percent	Percent distribution	Number	Percent distribution
	2004	2014	2004	2014					
Total	145 612	164 540	100.0	100.0	18 928	13.0	100.0	54 680	100.0
High school occupations	19 164	21 100	13.2	12.8	1 935	10.1	10.2	6 834	12.5
High school/some college occupations	67 944	74 671	46.7	45.4	6 727	9.9	35.5	25 220	46.1
Some college occupations	218	279	0.1	0.2	61	27.9	0.3	86	0.2
High school/some college/college occupations	24 894	28 019	17.1	17.0	3 126	12.6	16.5	9 078	16.6
Some college/college occupations	16 470	20 031	11.3	12.2	3 561	21.6	18.8	6 563	12.0
College occupations	16 922	20 440	11.6	12.4	3 517	20.8	18.6	6 898	12.6

Note: A high school occupation is defined as an occupation in which the percentage of employees age 25 to 44 years with high school as their highest level of educational attainment is greater than or equal to 60 percent, and the percentage of those with some college or a bachelor's degree or more are each less than 20 percent. Occupations requiring some college and college occupations are similarly defined. (That is, the definitions are identical to that of a high school occupation, except that the terms some college and high school, in the one case, and college and high school, in the other, are interchanged.) Three "mixture" occupations are also defined. An occupation requiring high school/some college is defined as an occupation in which the percentages of those with a high school diploma or some college as their highest level of educational attainment are each greater than or equal to 20 percent, while the percentage with a bachelor's degree or more is less than 20 percent. Occupations described as some college/college are similarly defined. (That is, the terms some college and college replace high school and some college, respectively.) High school/some college/college occupations are defined as occupations in which 20 or more percent of employees have an education level of high school, some college, or college. Data may not sum to totals or 100 percent, due to rounding.

[1]Total job openings are given by the sum of net employment increases and net replacements. If employment change is negative, job openings due to growth are zero and total job openings equal net replacements.

Table 4-6. Employment and Output, by Industry, 1994, 2004, and Projected 2014

(Number, percent, dollars.)

Industry	Employment							Output				
	Thousands of jobs			Change		Average annual rate of change (percent)		Billions of chained (1996) dollars			Average annual rate of change (percent)	
	1994	2004	2014	1994–2004	2004–2014	1994–2004	2004–2014	1994	2004	2014	1994–2004	2004–2014
TOTAL[1,2]	129 246	145 612	164 540	16 366	18 928	1.2	1.2	14 088	19 278	27 418	3.2	3.6
Nonagriculture Wage and Salary Workers[3]	114 984	132 192	150 877	17 208	18 685	1.4	1.3	13 850	19 003	27 089	3.2	3.6
Mining	576	523	477	-53	-46	-1.0	-0.9	211	224	230	0.6	0.2
Oil and gas extraction	162	123	107	-39	-16	-2.7	-1.4	145	137	144	-0.6	0.5
Mining (except oil and gas)	255	207	180	-48	-27	-2.1	-1.4	46	48	49	0.5	0.3
Coal mining	104	72	55	-32	-17	-3.6	-2.6	20	23	24	1.0	0.7
Metal ore mining	46	27	19	-19	-8	-5.1	-3.4	9	7	6	-2.9	-1.9
Nonmetallic mineral mining and quarrying	106	108	106	2	-2	0.2	-0.2	16	18	19	1.2	0.4
Mining support activities	159	193	190	34	-3	2.0	-0.2	24	39	38	4.7	-0.1
Utilities	689	570	563	-119	-7	-1.9	-0.1	305	323	351	0.6	0.8
Electric power generation, transmission, and distribution	504	412	400	-92	-12	-2.0	-0.3	225	256	298	1.3	1.5
Natural gas distribution	148	112	107	-36	-5	-2.8	-0.5	75	60	46	-2.3	-2.6
Water, sewage, and other systems	37	46	56	9	10	2.3	1.9	6	7	9	2.0	2.3
Construction	5 095	6 964	7 757	1 870	792	3.2	1.1	685	841	1 044	2.1	2.2
Manufacturing	17 020	14 330	13 553	2 691	-776	-1.7	-0.6	3 345	4 155	5 871	2.2	3.5
Food	1 539	1 498	1 555	-42	57	-0.3	0.4	384	420	499	0.9	1.7
Animal food	56	51	48	-6	-2	-1.0	-0.5	20	24	30	1.7	2.6
Grain and oilseed milling	70	61	57	-10	-4	-1.4	-0.7	40	39	51	0.0	2.6
Sugar and confectionery product	99	84	80	-16	-4	-1.7	-0.5	22	25	28	1.3	1.4
Fruit and vegetable preserving and specialty food	217	182	179	-35	-3	-1.7	-0.1	46	55	63	1.7	1.4
Dairy product	138	132	118	-6	-14	-0.4	-1.1	58	57	66	-0.2	1.6
Animal slaughtering and processing	456	505	570	50	65	1.0	1.2	98	107	125	0.8	1.6
Seafood product preparation and packaging	53	42	40	-11	-2	-2.4	-0.4	9	10	12	1.1	1.8
Bakery and tortilla	301	288	299	-13	11	-0.4	0.4	43	47	57	0.9	2.0
Other food	149	154	164	5	10	0.3	0.6	50	58	67	1.5	1.3
Beverage and tobacco product	205	194	181	-10	-14	-0.5	-0.7	126	110	102	-1.4	-0.7
Beverage	165	165	164	-0.2	-1	0.0	-0.1	67	68	81	0.2	1.7
Tobacco	40	29	17	-10	-13	-2.9	-5.6	61	42	26	-3.5	-4.9
Textile mills	478	239	120	-239	-119	-6.7	-6.6	54	42	30	-2.5	-3.2
Fiber, yarn, and thread mills	96	54	25	-42	-29	-5.5	-7.5	12	10	8	-1.4	-2.4
Fabric mills	252	116	60	-136	-56	-7.5	-6.4	29	20	14	-3.4	-3.7
Textile fabric finishing/fabric coating mills	130	68	35	-62	-34	-6.2	-6.5	14	11	8	-1.8	-2.8
Textile product mills	219	178	145	-41	-33	-2.1	-2.0	29	36	46	2.3	2.5
Textile furnishings mills	129	103	90	-26	-13	-2.3	-1.3	19	25	34	3.2	3.1
Other textile product mills	90	75	55	-14	-20	-1.7	-3.1	10	11	12	0.5	0.7
Apparel	856	285	115	-571	-170	-10.4	-8.7	68	55	41	-2.1	-2.9
Apparel knitting mills	108	42	20	-66	-22	-9.0	-7.2	11	8	6	-3.4	-3.5
Cut and sew apparel	704	220	80	-484	-140	-11.0	-9.6	52	44	33	-1.7	-2.9
Apparel accessories and other apparel	44	23	15	-21	-8	-6.3	-4.2	5	4	3	-3.0	-1.5
Leather and allied product	114	43	32	-71	-10	-9.3	-2.7	10	9	8	-1.0	-0.8
Leather and hide tanning and finishing[4]	15	7	6	-8	-1	-7.3	-1.7	3	3	3	0.5	-1.7
Footwear	65	19	12	-45	-7	-11.3	-4.3	5	3	3	-3.6	-2.0
Other leather and allied product[4]	34	16	14	-18	-2	-7.0	-1.6	2	3	3	1.1	1.3
Wood product	560	548	588	-12	40	-0.2	0.7	81	101	124	2.2	2.1
Sawmills and wood preservation	139	118	96	-21	-22	-1.7	-2.0	25	30	38	1.9	2.1
Veneer, plywood, and engineered wood product	102	117	125	15	8	1.4	0.7	18	21	27	1.5	2.5
Other wood product	319	314	367	-6	53	-0.2	1.6	38	49	59	2.8	1.8
Paper	639	499	487	-140	-12	-2.4	-0.2	162	171	184	0.6	0.8
Pulp, paper, and paperboard mills	224	147	124	-78	-23	-4.2	-1.7	74	83	87	1.2	0.5
Converted paper product	415	352	363	-63	11	-1.6	0.3	88	88	98	0.0	1.0
Printing and related support activities	802	665	600	-137	-65	-1.9	-1.0	97	92	103	-0.5	1.1
Petroleum and coal product	144	113	97	-31	-16	-2.4	-1.5	214	249	268	1.5	0.7
Chemical	1 005	887	877	-118	-10	-1.2	-0.1	403	452	539	1.2	1.8
Basic chemical	234	156	110	-78	-46	-4.0	-3.4	119	111	110	-0.6	-0.1
Resin, synthetic rubber, and artificial and synthetic fiber and filament	142	109	86	-33	-23	-2.6	-2.4	63	65	77	0.2	1.7
Pesticide, fertilizer, and other agricultural chemical	51	41	34	-10	-7	-2.1	-1.9	21	20	19	-0.6	-0.5
Pharmaceutical and medicine	230	291	367	60	76	2.4	2.3	90	125	173	3.3	3.3
Paint, coating, and adhesive	80	68	64	-12	-5	-1.6	-0.7	26	26	29	0.0	1.1
Soap, cleaning compound, and toilet preparation	126	114	120	-12	6	-1.0	0.5	48	63	77	2.7	2.0
Other chemical product and preparation	140	108	97	-33	-11	-2.6	-1.0	36	43	54	1.7	2.3
Plastics and rubber product	889	807	733	-83	-74	-1.0	-1.0	142	192	276	3.1	3.7
Plastics product	684	634	600	-51	-34	-0.8	-0.5	112	162	247	3.7	4.3
Rubber product	205	173	133	-32	-40	-1.7	-2.6	30	30	28	0.1	-0.6
Nonmetallic mineral product	505	505	525	-0.5	20	0.0	0.4	80	86	101	0.8	1.6
Clay product and refractory	83	66	69	-17	4	-2.3	0.6	9	8	10	-1.3	2.5
Glass and glass product	144	112	98	-32	-15	-2.5	-1.4	20	22	28	1.1	2.0
Cement and concrete product	189	235	260	46	25	2.2	1.0	32	37	42	1.4	1.2
Lime and gypsum product[3]	15	19	23	4	4	2.6	1.8	5	5	7	0.0	2.9
Other nonmetallic mineral product[3]	74	73	75	-2	2	-0.2	0.3	13	14	15	0.3	0.9
Primary metal	630	466	380	-164	-86	-3.0	-2.0	153	142	148	-0.7	0.4
Iron and steel mills ferroalloy	155	95	80	-59	-15	-4.7	-1.7	49	40	47	-1.9	1.6
Steel product from purchased steel	68	61	55	-7	-6	-1.1	-1.0	18	14	16	-2.8	1.6
Alumina and aluminum production and processing	98	73	57	-25	-16	-2.9	-2.5	35	35	32	0.1	-0.9
Nonferrous (except aluminum) production and processing	104	71	60	-32	-11	-3.7	-1.7	26	25	26	-0.6	0.7
Foundries	207	165	128	-41	-38	-2.2	-2.5	25	29	27	1.7	-1.0

[1]Employment data for wage and salary workers are from the BLS Current Employment Statistics (CES) Survey, which counts jobs, whereas data for self-employed, unpaid family workers and agriculture, forestry, fishing, and hunting workers are from the Current Population Survey (CPS or household survey), which counts workers.
[2]Output subcategories do not necessarily add to higher categories as a by-product of chain weighting.
[3]Includes wage and salary data from the CES Survey, except data for private households. Logging workers are excluded.
[4]Employment data are based on estimates from the CES Survey.

Table 4-6. Employment and Output, by Industry, 1994, 2004, and Projected 2014—*Continued*

(Number, percent, dollars.)

Industry	Employment							Output				
	Thousands of jobs			Change		Average annual rate of change (percent)		Billions of chained (1996) dollars			Average annual rate of change (percent)	
	1994	2004	2014	1994–2004	2004–2014	1994–2004	2004–2014	1994	2004	2014	1994–2004	2004–2014
Manufacturing—*Continued*												
Fabricated metal product	1 565	1 498	1 470	-68	-28	-0.4	-0.2	214	254	306	1.7	1.9
Forging and stamping	131	110	100	-22	-10	-1.8	-0.9	21	24	25	1.3	0.7
Cutlery and handtool	78	59	55	-19	-4	-2.7	-0.7	11	12	15	1.3	1.9
Architectural and structural metals	343	390	399	46	9	1.3	0.2	46	57	70	2.3	2.0
Boiler, tank, and shipping container	106	92	85	-14	-7	-1.4	-0.8	22	23	24	0.5	0.3
Hardware	55	38	35	-17	-4	-3.6	-1.0	11	11	13	-0.4	2.3
Spring and wire product	81	62	50	-19	-12	-2.6	-2.1	7	8	8	1.1	-0.3
Machine shops; turned product; and screw, nut, and bolt	313	326	340	13	14	0.4	0.4	35	45	64	2.7	3.4
Coating, engraving, heat treating, and allied activities	148	142	150	-5	8	-0.4	0.5	16	20	28	2.6	3.4
Other fabricated metal product	310	278	257	-32	-22	-1.1	-0.8	46	53	59	1.3	1.1
Machinery	1 379	1 142	995	-238	-146	-1.9	-1.4	225	273	298	2.0	0.9
Agriculture, construction, and mining machinery	211	195	190	-16	-5	-0.8	-0.3	43	50	54	1.5	0.8
Industrial machinery	149	119	104	-30	-15	-2.2	-1.3	30	34	37	1.5	0.8
Commercial and service industry machinery	142	115	85	-27	-30	-2.1	-3.0	24	26	22	0.8	-1.5
Ventilation, heating, air-conditioning, and commercial refrigeration	173	152	139	-21	-13	-1.3	-0.9	27	36	42	2.7	1.7
Metalworking machinery	258	202	169	-56	-33	-2.4	-1.8	26	28	29	0.8	0.2
Engine, turbine, and power transmission equipment	114	93	78	-21	-15	-2.1	-1.7	23	37	43	4.7	1.5
Other general purpose machinery	333	266	230	-67	-36	-2.2	-1.4	52	62	71	1.9	1.3
Computer and electronic product	1 651	1 326	1 232	-325	-94	-2.2	-0.7	203	543	1 795	10.4	12.7
Computer and peripheral equipment	298	212	175	-86	-37	-3.3	-1.9	26	172	1 368	21.0	23.1
Communications equipment	218	150	135	-68	-16	-3.6	-1.1	53	92	319	5.8	13.2
Audio and video equipment	58	32	25	-26	-7	-5.7	-2.4	9	6	6	-4.2	0.3
Semiconductor and other electronic component	535	453	400	-83	-53	-1.7	-1.2	50	167	265	12.8	4.7
Navigational, measuring, electromedical, and control instruments	493	432	450	-62	18	-1.3	0.4	80	108	154	3.1	3.6
Manufacturing and reproducing magnetic and optical media	49	47	47	-2	-0.1	-0.4	0.0	8	14	19	5.2	3.1
Electrical equipment, appliance, and component	588	447	363	-142	-84	-2.7	-2.1	100	103	128	0.3	2.2
Electric lighting equipment	78	65	55	-13	-10	-1.8	-1.7	11	12	14	0.8	1.4
Household appliance	113	90	66	-23	-24	-2.2	-3.1	21	22	29	0.4	2.9
Electrical equipment	218	153	117	-64	-36	-3.5	-2.7	32	30	32	-0.3	0.5
Other electrical equipment and component	180	138	125	-41	-14	-2.6	-1.0	36	39	53	0.7	3.2
Transportation equipment	1 936	1 764	1 859	-173	95	-0.9	0.5	514	634	898	2.1	3.5
Motor vehicle	282	256	262	-25	5	-0.9	0.2	194	252	325	2.7	2.6
Motor vehicle body and trailer	151	164	178	13	13	0.8	0.8	22	26	39	1.6	4.2
Motor vehicle parts	736	688	732	-47	43	-0.7	0.6	154	198	286	2.6	3.7
Aerospace product and parts	552	444	480	-108	36	-2.2	0.8	109	122	196	1.1	4.9
Railroad rolling stock	32	25	19	-8	-6	-2.7	-2.6	7	6	7	-1.4	1.4
Ship and boat building	145	148	145	3	-3	0.2	-0.2	16	18	26	1.2	3.3
Other transportation equipment	38	38	44	0.2	6	0.1	1.5	13	12	17	-0.4	3.6
Furniture and related product	600	573	563	-28	-10	-0.5	-0.2	56	71	91	2.3	2.5
Household and institutional furniture and kitchen cabinet	399	384	375	-14	-10	-0.4	-0.2	34	41	51	2.1	2.1
Office furniture (including fixtures)	154	136	138	-18	2	-1.3	0.1	17	23	32	3.0	3.3
Other furniture related product	47	52	50	5	-2	1.0	-0.4	6	7	8	1.7	1.8
Miscellaneous	714	656	637	-58	-19	-0.8	-0.3	92	138	198	4.1	3.7
Medical equipment and supplies	296	304	312	8	8	0.3	0.3	39	69	109	5.8	4.7
Other miscellaneous	418	352	325	-67	-26	-1.7	-0.8	54	69	89	2.6	2.6
Wholesale Trade	5 248	5 655	6 131	407	476	0.8	0.8	595	971	1 812	5.0	6.4
Retail Trade	13 491	15 034	16 683	1 543	1 649	1.1	1.0	741	1 125	1 758	4.3	4.6
Transportation and Warehousing	3 701	4 250	4 756	549	506	1.4	1.1	494	619	887	2.3	3.7
Air transportation	511	515	560	4	45	0.1	0.8	86	130	213	4.2	5.0
Rail transportation	235	224	215	-10	-9	-0.5	-0.4	40	43	60	0.7	3.3
Water transportation	52	57	58	5	1	0.9	0.2	28	22	27	-2.3	1.8
Truck transportation	1 206	1 351	1 480	145	129	1.1	0.9	175	224	318	2.5	3.5
Transit and ground passenger transportation	317	386	476	69	90	2.0	2.1	25	31	41	2.3	2.8
Pipeline transportation	57	39	37	-18	-2	-3.8	-0.5	28	26	25	-0.6	-0.5
Scenic and sightseeing transportation	21	27	35	6	8	2.3	2.8	2	2	4	1.8	4.8
Support activities for transportation	405	536	600	131	64	2.8	1.1	38	45	72	1.8	4.8
Couriers and messengers	466	560	600	94	40	1.9	0.7	45	60	76	3.0	2.3
Warehousing and storage	431	556	694	125	138	2.6	2.2	28	36	56	2.5	4.6
Information	2 739	3 138	3 502	400	364	1.4	1.1	546	947	1 571	5.7	5.2
Publishing industries, except Internet	891	910	1 115	19	205	0.2	2.1	158	230	435	3.8	6.6
Newspaper, periodical, book, and directory publishers	754	671	715	-83	44	-1.2	0.6	118	130	176	0.9	3.1
Software publishers	137	239	400	102	161	5.7	5.3	42	101	281	9.2	10.8
Motion picture, video, and sound recording industries	278	389	451	110	62	3.4	1.5	47	69	99	3.8	3.7
Broadcasting, except Internet	290	327	362	36	35	1.2	1.0	50	66	94	2.8	3.6
Telecommunications	961	1 043	975	82	-68	0.8	-0.7	257	464	667	6.1	3.7
Internet and other information services	318	470	600	152	130	4.0	2.5	32	120	272	14.1	8.5
Financial Activities	6 867	8 052	8 901	1 185	849	1.6	1.0	1 593	2 477	3 544	4.5	3.6
Monetary authorities, credit intermediation, and related activities	2 399	2 854	3 005	455	151	1.8	0.5	387	656	944	5.4	3.7
Securities, commodity contracts, and other financial investments and related activities	553	767	888	213	121	3.3	1.5	79	296	565	14.1	6.7
Insurance carriers	1 418	1 403	1 452	-15	49	-0.1	0.3	300	322	391	0.7	2.0
Agencies, brokerages, and other insurance-related activities	700	857	1 024	157	167	2.0	1.8	70	114	143	5.0	2.3
Funds, trusts, and other financial vehicles	64	85	93	21	8	2.8	0.9	57	71	88	2.2	2.2
Real estate	1 183	1 417	1 675	234	258	1.8	1.7	641	807	1 026	2.3	2.4
Automotive equipment rental and leasing	163	198	230	35	32	2.0	1.5	19	30	46	4.6	4.6
Consumer goods rental and general rental centers	287	341	378	54	37	1.7	1.0	18	24	32	2.9	2.6
Commercial and industrial machinery and equipment rental and leasing	80	105	129	25	24	2.8	2.1	30	36	50	1.9	3.5
Lessors of nonfinancial intangible assets (except copyrighted works)	18	25	28	7	2	3.3	0.9	55	123	292	8.3	9.0

Table 4-6. Employment and Output, by Industry, 1994, 2004, and Projected 2014—*Continued*

(Number, percent, dollars.)

Industry	Employment							Output				
	Thousands of jobs			Change		Average annual rate of change (percent)		Billions of chained (1996) dollars			Average annual rate of change (percent)	
	1994	2004	2014	1994–2004	2004–2014	1994–2004	2004–2014	1994	2004	2014	1994–2004	2004–2014
Professional, Scientific, and Technical Services	4 844	6 762	8 684	1 918	1 922	3.4	2.5	679	1 060	1 698	4.6	4.8
Legal services	966	1 162	1 340	196	178	1.9	1.4	169	189	236	1.1	2.2
Accounting, tax prepartion, bookkeeping, and payroll services	670	816	1 100	146	284	2.0	3.0	72	90	127	2.3	3.5
Architectural, engineering, and related services	952	1 261	1 460	309	199	2.8	1.5	124	180	248	3.8	3.3
Specialized design services	89	121	155	32	34	3.1	2.5	16	23	33	3.6	3.8
Computer systems design and related services	531	1 147	1 600	616	453	8.0	3.4	76	155	305	7.4	7.0
Management, scientific, and technical consulting services	417	779	1 250	362	471	6.5	4.8	71	149	272	7.6	6.2
Scientific research and development services	476	548	613	72	65	1.4	1.1	52	121	240	8.7	7.1
Advertising and related services	375	425	520	50	95	1.3	2.0	47	70	114	4.0	5.0
Other professional, scientific, and technical services	368	503	646	136	143	3.2	2.5	55	87	134	4.6	4.4
Management of companies and enterprises	1 666	1 718	1 900	52	182	0.3	1.0	218	397	681	6.2	5.5
Administrative and support and waste management and remediation services	5 664	7 934	10 396	2 270	2 462	3.4	2.7	298	496	762	5.2	4.4
Administrative and support services	5 404	7 608	9 983	2 205	2 374	3.5	2.8	255	439	686	5.6	4.6
Office administrative services	208	319	450	111	130	4.4	3.5	25	66	130	10.1	7.0
Facilities support services	72	116	170	43	54	4.8	3.9	7	11	15	4.5	3.4
Employment services	2 226	3 470	5 050	1 244	1 580	4.5	3.8	60	113	176	6.4	4.5
Business support services	574	754	830	180	76	2.8	1.0	36	60	107	5.3	5.9
Travel arrangement and reservation services	271	226	233	-46	7	-1.8	0.3	23	28	38	1.8	3.0
Investigation and security services	562	730	900	168	170	2.7	2.1	20	25	28	2.2	1.4
Services to buildings and dwellings	1 267	1 694	2 050	427	356	2.9	1.9	58	107	164	6.3	4.4
Other support services	221	299	300	77	1	3.0	0.0	26	31	30	1.8	-0.5
Waste management and remediation services	261	325	413	65	88	2.2	2.4	43	56	75	2.7	2.9
Waste collection	88	119	145	31	26	3.1	2.0	22	29	38	2.7	2.9
Waste treatment and disposal and waste mangement services	173	206	268	33	62	1.8	2.6	21	28	37	2.7	2.9
Education services	1 895	2 766	3 664	872	898	3.9	2.9	115	145	188	2.3	2.7
Elementary and secondary schools	544	829	1 050	285	220	4.3	2.4	25	27	37	0.8	3.4
Junior colleges, colleges, universities, and professional schools	1 074	1 462	1 965	388	503	3.1	3.0	68	85	108	2.3	2.5
Other education services	277	475	650	198	175	5.6	3.2	22	33	43	4.0	2.6
Health care and social assistance	10 912	14 187	18 482	3 275	4 295	2.7	2.7	829	1 147	1 639	3.3	3.6
Ambulatory health care services	3 579	4 946	7 031	1 367	2 085	3.3	3.6	376	550	822	3.9	4.1
Offices of health practitioners	2 430	3 337	4 561	907	1 224	3.2	3.2	273	400	600	3.9	4.1
Home health care services	553	773	1 310	220	537	3.4	5.4	30	42	67	3.3	4.8
Outpatient, laboratory, and other ambulatory services	595	836	1 160	241	324	3.5	3.3	73	108	156	4.1	3.7
Hospitals, private	3 724	4 294	4 982	570	688	1.4	1.5	284	385	544	3.1	3.5
Nursing and residential care facilities	2 227	2 815	3 597	588	782	2.4	2.5	90	115	144	2.5	2.3
Nursing care facilities	1 377	1 575	1 757	198	181	1.4	1.1	58	68	74	1.5	0.9
Residential care facilities	850	1 240	1 840	390	601	3.8	4.0	32	48	71	4.1	4.1
Social assistance	1 382	2 132	2 872	750	740	4.4	3.0	79	98	130	2.2	2.9
Individual, family, community, and vocational rehabilitation services	872	1 365	1 810	493	445	4.6	2.9	51	59	79	1.5	3.0
Child day care services	510	767	1 062	257	295	4.2	3.3	28	39	51	3.3	2.8
Arts, entertainment, and recreation	1 376	1 833	2 293	458	460	2.9	2.3	115	176	254	4.4	3.8
Performing arts, spectator sports, and related industries	296	365	443	69	78	2.1	2.0	52	63	86	2.0	3.2
Performing arts companies	107	115	135	8	20	0.8	1.6	10	9	10	-0.9	1.1
Spectator sports	96	120	150	24	30	2.3	2.3	16	22	31	3.2	3.5
Promoters of events, and agents, and managers	66	88	97	22	9	3.0	1.0	11	14	20	2.3	3.6
Independent artists, writers, and performers	28	42	61	14	19	4.2	3.8	15	19	26	2.0	3.4
Museums, historical sites, and similar institutions	82	117	140	35	23	3.7	1.8	5	7	10	4.9	3.1
Amusement, gambling, and recreation industries	998	1 351	1 710	354	358	3.1	2.4	59	106	158	6.0	4.1
Accommodation and food services	8 724	10 646	12 401	1 922	1 755	2.0	1.5	410	510	627	2.2	2.1
Accommodation	1 615	1 796	2 100	180	304	1.1	1.6	106	123	162	1.5	2.8
Food services and drinking places	7 109	8 850	10 301	1 741	1 451	2.2	1.5	304	387	465	2.4	1.9
Other services	5 202	6 210	6 944	1 008	734	1.8	1.1	344	430	565	2.2	2.8
Repair and maintenance	1 023	1 228	1 408	204	180	1.8	1.4	132	168	212	2.5	2.4
Automotive repair and maintenance	701	891	1 068	190	177	2.4	1.8	81	103	128	2.4	2.2
Electronic and precision equipment repair and maintenance	98	99	90	1	-9	0.1	-1.0	17	18	18	0.3	0.1
Commercial and industrial machinery and equipment (except automotive and electronic repair and maintenance)	144	158	170	14	12	0.9	0.8	16	28	44	5.8	4.6
Personal and household goods repair and maintenance	80	80	80	-0.2	0.5	0.0	0.1	18	20	23	1.1	1.7
Personal and laundry services	1 120	1 274	1 475	154	201	1.3	1.5	88	113	165	2.5	3.9
Personal care services	439	561	670	122	109	2.5	1.8	27	37	56	3.4	4.2
Death care services	120	138	157	18	19	1.4	1.3	12	13	14	0.7	0.5
Dry cleaning and laundry services	368	352	380	-16	28	-0.4	0.8	19	20	28	0.5	3.3
Other personal services	193	223	268	30	45	1.5	1.8	31	43	68	3.4	4.7
Religious, grantmaking, civic, professional, and similar organizations	2 285	2 929	3 310	644	381	2.5	1.2	112	134	172	1.8	2.5
Religious organizations	1 234	1 698	1 900	464	202	3.2	1.1	44	51	67	1.3	2.9
Grantmaking and giving services and social advocacy organizations	261	304	360	44	56	1.6	1.7	14	24	38	5.0	4.9
Civic, social, professional, and similar organizations	790	927	1 050	137	123	1.6	1.3	53	60	66	1.2	1.0
Private households	774	779	750	5	-29	0.1	-0.4	13	15	15	1.8	0.1
Federal Government	3 018	2 728	2 771	-290	43	-1.0	0.2	601	706	737	1.6	0.4
Postal service	821	784	778	-36	-6	-0.5	-0.1	56	59	65	0.6	0.9
Federal electric utilities	27	23	23	-4	-0.5	-1.6	-0.2	8	9	12	1.0	2.5
Federal enterprises, except postal service and electric utilities	124	70	53	-54	-18	-5.5	-2.8	9	8	10	-1.1	2.4
Federal government, except enterprises	2 046	1 850	1 917	-196	68	-1.0	0.4	448	544	560	2.0	0.3
Federal government capital services	. . .	. . .	. . .	. . .	. . .	. . .	. . .	81	85	90	0.4	0.6

. . . = Not available.

Table 4-6. Employment and Output, by Industry, 1994, 2004, and Projected 2014—*Continued*

(Number, percent, dollars.)

| Industry | Employment | | | | | | | Output | | | | |
| | Thousands of jobs | | | Change | | Average annual rate of change (percent) | | Billions of chained (1996) dollars | | | Average annual rate of change (percent) | |
	1994	2004	2014	1994–2004	2004–2014	1994–2004	2004–2014	1994	2004	2014	1994–2004	2004–2014
State and Local Government	16 257	18 891	21 019	2 634	2 128	1.5	1.1	1 113	1 402	1 798	2.3	2.5
Local government passenger transit	204	248	300	44	52	1.9	1.9	8	7	10	-0.5	3.3
Local government enterprises, except passenger transit	3 652	4 216	4 699	564	483	1.4	1.1	111	142	176	2.5	2.2
Local government hospitals	673	657	690	-16	33	-0.2	0.5	52	58	74	0.9	2.5
Local government educational services	6 329	7 762	8 546	1 433	783	2.1	1.0	303	390	494	2.6	2.4
Local government, excluding enterprises, education services, and hospitals	823	1 022	1 250	199	228	2.2	2.0	288	360	471	2.3	2.7
State government enterprises	1 783	1 853	1 947	70	94	0.4	0.5	16	20	25	2.3	2.1
State government hospitals	407	350	326	-57	-24	-1.5	-0.7	40	42	54	0.6	2.5
State government educational services	1 882	2 249	2 691	367	442	1.8	1.8	111	147	186	2.8	2.4
State government, excluding enterprises, education services, and hospitals	503	533	571	30	37	0.6	0.7	119	136	179	1.3	2.7
State and local government capital services	. . .	. . .	. . .	. . .	. . .	. . .	. . .	66	99	131	4.2	2.8
Owner-Occupied Dwellings	. . .	. . .	. . .	. . .	. . .	. . .	. . .	657	858	1 124	2.7	2.7
Agriculture, Forestry, Fishing, and Hunting[5]	2 890	2 140	1 910	-750	-230	-3.0	-1.1	232	275	322	1.7	1.6
Crop production	1 226	857	712	-369	-145	-3.5	-1.8	87	112	144	2.5	2.6
Animal production	1 331	953	877	-379	-75	-3.3	-0.8	94	114	126	2.0	1.0
Forestry	22	24	20	2	-5	0.9	-2.1	6	5	5	-0.6	0.0
Logging	119	100	91	-18	-9	-1.7	-1.0	28	26	28	-0.8	0.7
Fishing, hunting, and trapping	75	52	42	-23	-10	-3.6	-2.0	7	6	7	-1.4	0.6
Support activities for agriculture and forestry	117	154	168	36	14	2.7	0.9	11	11	12	0.2	1.1
Nonagriculture Self-Employed and Unpaid Family Workers[6]	9 360	9 556	10 012	196	456	0.2	. . .	. . .	. . .	. . .	. . .	. . .
Secondary Wage and Salary Jobs in Agriculture and Private Household Industries[7]	182	138	127	-44	-11	-2.8	-0.8	. . .	. . .	. . .	. . .	. . .
Secondary Jobs as a Self-Employed or Unpaid Family Workers[8]	1 830	1 587	1 614	-243	28	-1.4	0.2	. . .	. . .	. . .	. . .	. . .

[5]Includes agriculture, forestry, fishing, and hunting wage and salary, self-employed, and unpaid family worker data from the household survey (except logging, which is from the CES Survey). Government wage and salary workers are excluded.
[6]Comparable estimate of output growth is not available.
[7]Workers who hold a secondary wage and salary job in agricultural production, forestry, fishing, and private household industries.
[8]Output subcategories do not necessarily add to higher categories due to chain weighting.
. . . = Not available.

Table 4-7. Employment, by Occupation, 2004 and Projected 2014

(Numbers in thousands, percent.)

Occupation	Employment				Change, 2004–2014		Total job openings due to growth and net replacements, 2004–2014[1]
	Number		Percent distribution		Number	Percent	
	2004	2014	2004	2014			
ALL OCCUPATIONS	145 612	164 540	100.0	100.0	18 928	13.0	54 680
Management, Business, and Financial	14 987	17 142	10.3	10.4	2 155	14.4	4 920
Management	9 115	10 147	6.3	6.2	1 032	11.3	2 757
Top executives	2 317	2 692	1.6	1.6	375	16.2	808
Chief executives	444	510	0.3	0.3	66	14.9	150
General and operations managers	1 807	2 115	1.2	1.3	308	17.0	649
Legislators	66	67	0.0	0.0	1	2.0	10
Advertising, marketing, promotions, public relations, and sales managers	646	777	0.4	0.5	131	20.3	249
Advertising and promotions managers	64	77	0.0	0.0	13	20.3	25
Marketing and sales managers	525	630	0.4	0.4	105	20.1	202
Marketing managers	188	228	0.1	0.1	39	20.8	74
Sales managers	337	403	0.2	0.2	66	19.7	128
Public relations managers	58	70	0.0	0.0	12	21.7	22
Operations specialties managers	1 561	1 807	1.1	1.1	246	15.8	517
Administrative services managers	268	314	0.2	0.2	45	16.9	97
Computer and information systems managers	280	353	0.2	0.2	73	25.9	124
Financial managers	528	606	0.4	0.4	78	14.8	154
Human resources managers	157	189	0.1	0.1	32	20.3	58
Compensation and benefits managers	57	70	0.0	0.0	12	21.5	22
Training and development managers	37	47	0.0	0.0	10	25.9	16
Human resources managers, all other	62	72	0.0	0.0	10	15.9	20
Industrial production managers	160	162	0.1	0.1	1	0.8	32
Purchasing managers	75	80	0.1	0.0	5	7.0	21
Transportation, storage, and distribution managers	92	104	0.1	0.1	12	12.7	30
Other management occupations	4 591	4 870	3.2	3.0	280	6.1	1 183
Agricultural managers	1 285	1 139	0.9	0.7	-146	-11.3	109
Farm, ranch, and other agricultural managers	220	229	0.2	0.1	9	4.0	47
Farmers and ranchers	1 065	910	0.7	0.6	-155	-14.5	63
Construction managers	431	475	0.3	0.3	45	10.4	123
Education administrators	442	515	0.3	0.3	73	16.6	183
Education administrators, preschool and childcare center/program	58	75	0.0	0.0	16	27.9	31
Education administrators, elementary and secondary school	225	249	0.2	0.2	24	10.4	80
Education administrators, postsecondary	132	160	0.1	0.1	28	21.3	61
Education administrators, all other	26	31	0.0	0.0	5	20.3	12
Engineering managers	190	215	0.1	0.1	25	13.0	63
Food service managers	371	414	0.3	0.3	43	11.5	103
Funeral directors	30	32	0.0	0.0	2	6.7	10
Gaming managers	4	5	0.0	0.0	1	22.6	2
Lodging managers	58	68	0.0	0.0	10	16.6	19
Medical and health services managers	248	305	0.2	0.2	57	22.8	105
Natural sciences managers	42	48	0.0	0.0	6	13.6	14
Postmasters and mail superintendents	26	26	0.0	0.0	0	0.0	5
Property, real estate, and community association managers	361	416	0.2	0.3	55	15.3	123
Social and community service managers	134	169	0.1	0.1	34	25.5	60
Managers, all other	969	1 045	0.7	0.6	76	7.8	265
Business and Financial Operations	5 873	6 996	4.0	4.3	1 123	19.1	2 163
Business operations specialists	3 375	4 054	2.3	2.5	679	20.1	1 276
Agents and business managers of artists, performers, and athletes	21	23	0.0	0.0	2	11.8	7
Buyers and purchasing agents	445	482	0.3	0.3	36	8.1	151
Purchasing agents and buyers, farm products	16	17	0.0	0.0	1	7.0	6
Wholesale and retail buyers, except farm products	156	169	0.1	0.1	13	8.4	54
Purchasing agents, except wholesale, retail, and farm products	273	296	0.2	0.2	22	8.1	90
Claims adjusters, appraisers, examiners, and investigators	263	303	0.2	0.2	40	15.1	72
Claims adjusters, examiners, and investigators	250	288	0.2	0.2	38	15.1	69
Insurance appraisers, auto damage	13	15	0.0	0.0	2	16.6	4
Compliance officers, except agriculture, construction, health and safety, and transportation	177	197	0.1	0.1	21	11.6	62
Cost estimators	198	234	0.1	0.1	36	18.2	80
Emergency management specialists	10	13	0.0	0.0	2	22.8	5
Human resources, training, and labor relations specialists	663	823	0.5	0.5	161	24.2	265
Employment, recruitment, and placement specialists	182	237	0.1	0.1	55	30.5	83
Compensation, benefits, and job analysis specialists	99	119	0.1	0.1	20	20.4	35
Training and development specialists	216	261	0.1	0.2	45	20.8	78
Human resources, training, and labor relations specialists, all other	166	206	0.1	0.1	40	24.1	68
Logisticians	53	60	0.0	0.0	7	13.2	16
Management analysts	605	727	0.4	0.4	122	20.1	204
Meeting and convention planners	43	52	0.0	0.0	10	22.2	19
Business operation specialists, all other	897	1 139	0.6	0.7	242	27.0	395
Financial specialists	2 497	2 941	1.7	1.8	444	17.8	887
Accountants and auditors	1 176	1 440	0.8	0.9	264	22.4	486
Appraisers and assessors of real estate	102	125	0.1	0.1	23	22.8	45
Budget analysts	58	65	0.0	0.0	8	13.5	17
Credit analysts	68	70	0.0	0.0	2	3.6	13
Financial analysts and advisers	456	539	0.3	0.3	83	18.2	151
Financial analysts	197	231	0.1	0.1	34	17.3	63
Personal financial advisers	158	199	0.1	0.1	41	25.9	61
Insurance underwriters	101	109	0.1	0.1	8	8.0	26
Financial examiners	24	27	0.0	0.0	2	9.5	8
Loan counselors and officers	325	355	0.2	0.2	30	9.2	82
Loan counselors	34	40	0.0	0.0	6	17.7	11
Loan officers	291	315	0.2	0.2	24	8.3	71
Tax examiners, collectors, preparers, and revenue agents	162	175	0.1	0.1	13	8.0	45
Tax examiners, collectors, and revenue agents	76	80	0.1	0.0	4	5.1	21
Tax preparers	86	95	0.1	0.1	9	10.6	23
Financial specialists, all other	127	145	0.1	0.1	18	14.4	40

Note: Data may not sum to totals or 100 percent due to rounding.

[1]Total job openings represent the sum of employment increases and net replacements. If employment change is negative, job openings due to growth are zero and total job openings equal net replacements.

Table 4-7. Employment, by Occupation, 2004 and Projected 2014—*Continued*

(Numbers in thousands, percent.)

Occupation	Employment				Change, 2004–2014		Total job openings due to growth and net replacements, 2004–2014[1]
	Number		Percent distribution		Number	Percent	
	2004	2014	2004	2014			
Computer and Mathematical Science	3 153	4 120	2.2	2.5	967	30.7	1 389
Computer specialists	3 046	4 003	2.1	2.4	957	31.4	1 350
Computer and information scientists, research	22	28	0.0	0.0	6	25.6	8
Computer programmers	455	464	0.3	0.3	9	2.0	117
Computer software engineers	800	1 169	0.5	0.7	369	46.1	448
Computer software engineers, applications	460	682	0.3	0.4	222	48.4	268
Computer software engineers, systems software	340	486	0.2	0.3	146	43.0	180
Computer support specialists	518	638	0.4	0.4	119	23.0	183
Computer systems analysts	487	640	0.3	0.4	153	31.4	208
Database administrators	104	144	0.1	0.1	40	38.2	51
Network and computer systems administrators	278	385	0.2	0.2	107	38.4	138
Network systems and data communications analysts	231	357	0.2	0.2	126	54.6	153
Computer specialists, all other	149	177	0.1	0.1	28	19.0	45
Mathematical science occupations	107	117	0.1	0.1	10	9.7	39
Actuaries	18	22	0.0	0.0	4	23.2	12
Mathematicians	3	3	0.0	0.0	0	-1.3	1
Operations research analysts	58	62	0.0	0.0	5	8.4	17
Statisticians	19	20	0.0	0.0	1	4.6	6
Miscellaneous mathematical science occupations	10	11	0.0	0.0	1	5.7	3
Mathematical technicians	2	2	0.0	0.0	0	3.4	0
Mathematical scientists, all other	9	9	0.0	0.0	1	6.2	2
Architecture and engineering	2 520	2 835	1.7	1.7	315	12.5	876
Architects, surveyors, and cartographers	220	258	0.2	0.2	38	17.1	78
Architects, except naval	154	181	0.1	0.1	27	17.7	45
Architects, except landscape and naval	129	151	0.1	0.1	22	17.3	37
Landscape architects	25	30	0.0	0.0	5	19.4	8
Surveyors, cartographers, and photogrammetrists	67	77	0.0	0.0	11	15.8	33
Cartographers and photogrammetrists	11	12	0.0	0.0	2	15.3	5
Surveyors	56	65	0.0	0.0	9	15.9	28
Engineers	1 449	1 644	1.0	1.0	195	13.4	507
Aerospace engineers	76	82	0.1	0.0	6	8.3	25
Agricultural engineers	3	4	0.0	0.0	1	12.0	2
Biomedical engineers	10	13	0.0	0.0	3	30.7	5
Chemical engineers	31	34	0.0	0.0	3	10.6	12
Civil engineers	237	276	0.2	0.2	39	16.5	77
Computer hardware engineers	77	84	0.1	0.1	8	10.1	20
Electrical and electronics engineers	299	331	0.2	0.2	32	10.8	91
Electrical engineers	156	174	0.1	0.1	18	11.8	49
Electronics engineers, except computer	143	157	0.1	0.1	14	9.7	42
Environmental engineers	49	64	0.0	0.0	15	30.0	23
Industrial engineers, including health and safety	203	235	0.1	0.1	32	15.7	81
Health and safety engineers, except mining safety engineers and inspectors	27	30	0.0	0.0	4	13.4	10
Industrial engineers	177	205	0.1	0.1	28	16.0	71
Marine engineers and naval architects	7	7	0.0	0.0	1	8.5	4
Materials engineers	21	24	0.0	0.0	3	12.2	8
Mechanical engineers	226	251	0.2	0.2	25	11.1	87
Mining and geological engineers, including mining safety engineers	5	5	0.0	0.0	0	-1.5	2
Nuclear engineers	17	19	0.0	0.0	1	7.3	6
Petroleum engineers	16	16	0.0	0.0	0	-0.1	5
Engineers, all other	172	198	0.1	0.1	27	15.4	59
Drafters, engineering, and mapping technicians	851	933	0.6	0.6	83	9.7	291
Drafters	254	267	0.2	0.2	13	5.3	84
Architectural and civil drafters	110	115	0.1	0.1	5	4.6	36
Electrical and electronics drafters	38	38	0.0	0.0	0	1.2	11
Mechanical drafters	82	87	0.1	0.1	4	5.5	28
Drafters, all other	24	27	0.0	0.0	3	14.0	9
Engineering technicians, except drafters	532	595	0.4	0.4	63	11.8	177
Aerospace engineering and operations technicians	10	10	0.0	0.0	1	8.5	3
Civil engineering technicians	94	107	0.1	0.1	13	14.1	33
Electrical and electronic engineering technicians	182	199	0.1	0.1	18	9.8	56
Electromechanical technicians	19	21	0.0	0.0	2	9.7	6
Environmental engineering technicians	20	25	0.0	0.0	5	24.4	9
Industrial engineering technicians	69	76	0.0	0.0	7	10.5	22
Mechanical engineering technicians	48	54	0.0	0.0	6	12.3	16
Engineering technicians, except drafters, all other	91	102	0.1	0.1	11	12.3	33
Surveying and mapping technicians	65	71	0.0	0.0	6	9.6	30
Life, Physical, and Social Science	1 316	1 532	0.9	0.9	216	16.4	531
Life scientists	232	280	0.2	0.2	48	20.8	103
Agricultural and food scientists	30	34	0.0	0.0	4	12.8	9
Animal scientists	3	3	0.0	0.0	0	12.9	1
Food scientists and technologists	11	12	0.0	0.0	1	10.9	3
Soil and plant scientists	17	19	0.0	0.0	2	13.9	5
Biological scientists	77	90	0.1	0.1	13	17.0	37
Biochemists and biophysicists	16	20	0.0	0.0	3	21.0	8
Microbiologists	15	18	0.0	0.0	3	17.2	7
Zoologists and wildlife biologists	16	19	0.0	0.0	2	13.0	7
Biological scientists, all other	29	34	0.0	0.0	5	17.0	14
Conservation scientists and foresters	32	34	0.0	0.0	2	6.5	11
Conservation scientists	19	20	0.0	0.0	1	6.3	7
Foresters	13	14	0.0	0.0	1	6.7	5
Medical scientists	77	103	0.1	0.1	26	33.6	40
Epidemiologists	5	6	0.0	0.0	1	26.2	2
Medical scientists, except epidemiologists	72	97	0.0	0.1	25	34.1	37
Life scientists, all other	15	19	0.0	0.0	3	20.6	6

Note: Data may not sum to totals or 100 percent due to rounding.

[1]Total job openings represent the sum of employment increases and net replacements. If employment change is negative, job openings due to growth are zero and total job openings equal net replacements.

Table 4-7. Employment, by Occupation, 2004 and Projected 2014—*Continued*

(Numbers in thousands, percent.)

Occupation	Employment				Change, 2004–2014		Total job openings due to growth and net replacements, 2004–2014[1]
	Number		Percent distribution		Number	Percent	
	2004	2014	2004	2014			
Life, Physical, and Social Science—*Continued*							
Physical scientists	250	281	0.2	0.2	30	12.2	94
Astronomers and physicists	16	17	0.0	0.0	1	7.1	6
Astronomers	1	1	0.0	0.0	0	10.4	0
Physicists	15	16	0.0	0.0	1	7.0	6
Atmospheric and space scientists	7	9	0.0	0.0	1	16.5	4
Chemists and materials scientists	90	96	0.1	0.1	7	7.3	36
Chemists	82	88	0.1	0.1	6	7.3	33
Materials scientists	8	8	0.0	0.0	1	8.0	3
Environmental scientists and geoscientists	109	126	0.1	0.1	17	15.9	37
Environmental scientists and specialists, including health	73	86	0.1	0.1	13	17.1	26
Geoscientists, except hydrologists and geologists	28	30	0.0	0.0	2	8.3	7
Hydrologists	8	11	0.0	0.0	3	31.6	4
Physical scientists, all other	29	33	0.0	0.0	4	14.6	11
Social scientists and related	492	580	0.3	0.4	88	17.9	209
Economists	13	13	0.0	0.0	1	5.6	4
Market and survey researchers	212	255	0.1	0.2	43	20.2	98
Market research analysts	190	227	0.1	0.1	37	19.6	86
Survey researchers	22	28	0.0	0.0	6	25.9	12
Psychologists	179	212	0.1	0.1	33	18.7	72
Clinical, counseling, and school psychologists	167	199	0.1	0.1	32	19.1	68
Industrial-organizational psychologists	2	3	0.0	0.0	0	20.4	1
Psychologists, all other	10	11	0.0	0.0	1	9.9	3
Sociologists	5	5	0.0	0.0	0	4.7	2
Urban and regional planners	32	37	0.0	0.0	5	15.2	16
Miscellaneous social scientists and related workers	51	57	0.0	0.0	6	11.8	17
Anthropologists and archeologists	5	6	0.0	0.0	1	17.0	2
Geographers	1	1	0.0	0.0	0	6.8	0
Historians	3	3	0.0	0.0	0	4.3	1
Political scientists	5	5	0.0	0.0	0	7.3	1
Social scientists and related workers, all other	38	42	0.0	0.0	5	12.3	13
Life, physical, and social science technicians	342	391	0.2	0.2	49	14.4	126
Agricultural and food science technicians	23	26	0.0	0.0	3	13.4	7
Biological technicians	64	75	0.0	0.0	11	17.2	22
Chemical technicians	62	65	0.0	0.0	3	4.4	18
Geological and petroleum technicians	11	12	0.0	0.0	1	6.5	3
Nuclear technicians	7	8	0.0	0.0	1	13.7	3
Social science research assistants	18	21	0.0	0.0	3	17.4	7
Other life, physical, and social science technicians	157	184	0.1	0.1	27	17.5	64
Environmental science and protection technicians, including health	31	36	0.0	0.0	5	16.3	12
Forensic science technicians	10	13	0.0	0.0	4	36.4	6
Forest and conservation technicians	33	35	0.0	0.0	2	6.6	10
Life, physical, and social science technicians, all other	83	100	0.1	0.1	17	20.0	36
Community and Social Services	2 317	2 800	1.6	1.7	483	20.8	928
Counselors, social workers, and other community and social service specialists	1 755	2 165	1.2	1.3	410	23.4	749
Counselors	601	729	0.4	0.4	128	21.3	264
Substance abuse and behavioral disorder counselors	76	98	0.1	0.1	22	28.7	39
Educational, vocational, and school counselors	248	285	0.2	0.2	37	14.8	94
Marriage and family therapists	24	30	0.0	0.0	6	25.4	12
Mental health counselors	96	122	0.1	0.1	26	27.2	48
Rehabilitation counselors	131	162	0.1	0.1	31	23.9	61
Counselors, all other	25	31	0.0	0.0	6	23.1	10
Social workers	562	686	0.4	0.4	124	22.0	221
Child, family, and school social workers	272	324	0.2	0.2	52	19.0	98
Medical and public health social workers	110	139	0.1	0.1	29	25.9	48
Mental health and substance abuse social workers	116	147	0.1	0.1	31	26.7	51
Social workers, all other	64	76	0.0	0.0	12	19.6	24
Miscellaneous community and social service specialists	592	751	0.4	0.5	159	26.8	264
Health educators	49	60	0.0	0.0	11	22.5	20
Probation officers and correctional treatment specialists	93	105	0.1	0.1	12	12.8	28
Social and human service assistants	352	456	0.2	0.3	104	29.7	166
Community and social service specialists, all other	98	129	0.1	0.1	31	31.9	50
Religious workers	562	635	0.4	0.4	73	12.9	178
Clergy	422	474	0.3	0.3	52	12.4	139
Directors, religious activities and education	90	107	0.1	0.1	17	18.5	27
Religious workers, all other	50	54	0.0	0.0	4	7.4	13
Legal	1 220	1 414	0.8	0.9	194	15.9	336
Lawyers, judges, and related workers	783	897	0.5	0.5	114	14.6	215
Lawyers	735	845	0.5	0.5	110	15.0	205
Judges, magistrates, and other judicial workers	47	52	0.0	0.0	4	8.9	10
Administrative law judges, adjudicators, and hearing officers	16	17	0.0	0.0	2	10.1	4
Arbitrators, mediators, and conciliators	5	6	0.0	0.0	1	15.5	1
Judges, magistrate judges, and magistrates	27	28	0.0	0.0	2	6.9	5
Legal support workers	437	517	0.3	0.3	80	18.2	121
Paralegals and legal assistants	224	291	0.2	0.2	67	29.7	85
Miscellaneous legal support workers	213	227	0.1	0.1	13	6.1	36
Court reporters	18	21	0.0	0.0	3	14.8	5
Law clerks	51	55	0.0	0.0	4	7.7	9
Title examiners, abstractors, and searchers	61	62	0.0	0.0	1	0.9	7
Legal support workers, all other	83	89	0.1	0.1	6	7.1	15

Note: Data may not sum to totals or 100 percent due to rounding.

[1]Total job openings represent the sum of employment increases and net replacements. If employment change is negative, job openings due to growth are zero and total job openings equal net replacements.

Table 4-7. Employment, by Occupation, 2004 and Projected 2014—*Continued*

(Numbers in thousands, percent.)

Occupation	Employment				Change, 2004–2014		Total job openings due to growth and net replacements, 2004–2014[1]
	Number		Percent distribution		Number	Percent	
	2004	2014	2004	2014			
Education, Training, and Library	8 698	10 438	6.0	6.3	1 740	20.0	3 558
Postsecondary teachers	1 628	2 153	1.1	1.3	524	32.2	892
Primary, secondary, and special education teachers	4 270	5 051	2.9	3.1	781	18.3	1 739
Preschool and kindergarten teachers	601	782	0.4	0.5	181	30.1	252
Preschool teachers, except special education	431	573	0.3	0.3	143	33.1	194
Kindergarten teachers, except special education	171	209	0.1	0.1	38	22.4	59
Elementary and middle school teachers	2 102	2 453	1.4	1.5	351	16.7	815
Elementary school teachers, except special education	1 457	1 722	1.0	1.0	265	18.2	587
Middle school teachers, except special and vocational education	628	714	0.4	0.4	86	13.7	225
Vocational education teachers, middle school	17	16	0.0	0.0	-1	-0.9	4
Secondary school teachers	1 126	1 283	0.8	0.8	157	14.0	474
Secondary school teachers, except special and vocational education	1 024	1 172	0.7	0.7	148	14.4	436
Vocational education teachers, secondary school	101	110	0.1	0.1	9	9.1	38
Special education teachers	441	534	0.3	0.3	92	20.9	197
Special education teachers, preschool, kindergarten, and elementary school	205	253	0.1	0.2	48	23.3	97
Special education teachers, middle school	98	118	0.1	0.1	19	19.9	43
Special education teachers, secondary school	138	163	0.1	0.1	25	17.9	58
Other teachers and instructors	977	1 150	0.7	0.7	173	17.7	293
Adult literacy, remedial education, and GED teachers and instructors	98	113	0.1	0.1	15	15.6	27
Self-enrichment education teachers	253	317	0.2	0.2	64	25.3	95
Teachers and instructors, all other	626	720	0.4	0.4	93	14.9	170
Archivists, curators, and librarians	308	336	0.2	0.2	28	9.1	117
Archivists, curators, and museum technicians	27	31	0.0	0.0	4	14.5	10
Archivists	6	7	0.0	0.0	1	13.4	2
Curators	10	12	0.0	0.0	2	15.7	4
Museum technicians and conservators	10	12	0.0	0.0	1	14.1	4
Librarians	159	167	0.1	0.1	8	4.9	46
Library technicians	122	138	0.1	0.1	16	13.4	61
Other education, training, and library	1 515	1 748	1.0	1.1	233	15.4	517
Audio-visual collections specialists	9	11	0.0	0.0	2	18.6	3
Farm and home management advisers	16	17	0.0	0.0	1	7.7	4
Instructional coordinators	117	149	0.1	0.1	32	27.5	50
Teacher assistants	1 296	1 478	0.9	0.9	183	14.1	433
Education, training, and library workers, all other	77	92	0.1	0.1	16	20.5	27
Arts, Design, Entertainment, Sports, and Media	2 515	2 890	1.7	1.8	375	14.9	851
Art and design	780	880	0.5	0.5	100	12.8	221
Artists and related workers	208	234	0.1	0.1	26	12.4	71
Art directors	71	79	0.0	0.0	8	11.5	24
Craft artists	6	7	0.0	0.0	1	10.6	2
Fine artists, including painters, sculptors, and illustrators	29	32	0.0	0.0	3	10.2	9
Multimedia artists and animators	94	107	0.1	0.1	13	14.1	34
Artists and related workers, all other	9	9	0.0	0.0	1	10.0	2
Designers	572	645	0.4	0.4	74	12.9	151
Commercial and industrial designers	49	55	0.0	0.0	5	10.8	12
Fashion designers	17	18	0.0	0.0	1	8.4	4
Floral designers	98	108	0.1	0.1	10	10.3	23
Graphic designers	228	263	0.2	0.2	35	15.2	65
Interior designers	65	75	0.0	0.0	10	15.5	19
Merchandise displayers and window trimmers	86	95	0.1	0.1	9	10.3	20
Set and exhibit designers	13	14	0.0	0.0	1	9.3	3
Designers, all other	16	18	0.0	0.0	2	13.6	5
Entertainers and performers, sports and related	732	856	0.5	0.5	124	16.9	271
Actors, producers, and directors	157	182	0.1	0.1	26	16.4	47
Actors	74	85	0.1	0.1	12	16.1	21
Producers and directors	83	97	0.1	0.1	14	16.6	26
Athletes, coaches, umpires, and related workers	212	255	0.1	0.2	43	20.4	84
Athletes and sports competitors	17	21	0.0	0.0	4	21.1	7
Coaches and scouts	178	215	0.1	0.1	36	20.4	71
Umpires, referees, and other sports officials	16	19	0.0	0.0	3	19.0	6
Dancers and choreographers	38	45	0.0	0.0	6	16.8	30
Dancers	19	22	0.0	0.0	3	16.8	15
Choreographers	19	22	0.0	0.0	3	16.8	15
Musicians, singers, and related workers	249	282	0.2	0.2	33	13.2	85
Music directors and composers	60	66	0.0	0.0	6	10.4	19
Musicians and singers	189	216	0.1	0.1	26	14.0	66
Entertainers and performers, sports and related, all other	76	92	0.1	0.1	16	21.0	25
Media and communication	710	821	0.5	0.5	111	15.6	253
Announcers	69	66	0.0	0.0	-3	-4.8	18
Radio and television announcers	57	54	0.0	0.0	-4	-6.5	15
Public address system and other announcers	12	12	0.0	0.0	0	3.8	3
News analysts, reporters, and correspondents	64	67	0.0	0.0	3	4.8	19
Broadcast news analysts	8	8	0.0	0.0	0	4.3	2
Reporters and correspondents	56	59	0.0	0.0	3	4.9	16
Public relations specialists	188	231	0.1	0.1	43	22.9	70
Writers and editors	320	376	0.2	0.2	56	17.4	125
Editors	127	146	0.1	0.1	19	14.8	50
Technical writers	50	62	0.0	0.0	12	23.2	26
Writers and authors	142	167	0.1	0.1	25	17.7	50
Miscellaneous media and communication workers	70	82	0.0	0.1	12	17.5	21
Interpreters and translators	31	37	0.0	0.0	6	19.9	10
Media and communication workers, all other	39	46	0.0	0.0	6	15.7	11

Note: Data may not sum to totals or 100 percent due to rounding.

[1]Total job openings represent the sum of employment increases and net replacements. If employment change is negative, job openings due to growth are zero and total job openings equal net replacements.

Table 4-7. Employment, by Occupation, 2004 and Projected 2014—*Continued*

(Numbers in thousands, percent.)

Occupation	Employment				Change, 2004–2014		Total job openings due to growth and net replacements, 2004–2014[1]
	Number		Percent distribution		Number	Percent	
	2004	2014	2004	2014			
Arts, Design, Entertainment, Sports, and Media—*Continued*							
Media and communication equipment occupations	293	334	0.2	0.2	41	14.0	105
Broadcast and sound engineering technicians and radio operators	95	109	0.1	0.1	14	14.5	37
Audio and video equipment technicians	46	55	0.0	0.0	8	18.1	20
Broadcast technicians	34	37	0.0	0.0	3	9.8	12
Radio operators	2	2	0.0	0.0	0	-12.9	0
Sound engineering technicians	13	16	0.0	0.0	2	18.4	6
Photographers	129	145	0.1	0.1	16	12.3	42
Television, video, and motion picture camera operators and editors	49	56	0.0	0.0	8	16.0	18
Camera operators, television, video, and motion picture	28	32	0.0	0.0	4	14.2	10
Film and video editors	20	24	0.0	0.0	4	18.6	8
Media and communication equipment workers, all other	19	23	0.0	0.0	3	17.0	7
Health Care Practitioner and Technical	6 805	8 561	4.7	5.2	1 756	25.8	3 047
Health diagnosing and treating practitioners	4 190	5 330	2.9	3.2	1 140	27.2	1 960
Chiropractors	53	64	0.0	0.0	12	22.4	22
Dentists	150	171	0.1	0.1	20	13.5	46
Dentists, general	128	145	0.1	0.1	17	13.5	39
Oral and maxillofacial surgeons	6	7	0.0	0.0	1	16.2	2
Orthodontists	10	11	0.0	0.0	1	12.8	3
Prosthodontists	1	1	0.0	0.0	0	13.6	0
Dentists, all other specialists	5	6	0.0	0.0	1	12.2	1
Dietitians and nutritionists	50	59	0.0	0.0	9	18.3	22
Optometrists	34	40	0.0	0.0	7	19.7	16
Pharmacists	230	287	0.2	0.2	57	24.6	101
Physicians and surgeons	567	702	0.4	0.4	136	24.0	212
Physician assistants	62	93	0.0	0.1	31	49.6	40
Podiatrists	10	12	0.0	0.0	2	16.2	4
Registered nurses	2 394	3 096	1.6	1.9	703	29.4	1 203
Therapists	509	647	0.3	0.4	138	27.1	237
Audiologists	10	11	0.0	0.0	1	9.1	3
Occupational therapists	92	123	0.1	0.1	31	33.6	43
Physical therapists	155	211	0.1	0.1	57	36.7	72
Radiation therapists	15	19	0.0	0.0	4	26.3	7
Recreational therapists	24	25	0.0	0.0	1	5.7	7
Respiratory therapists	94	120	0.1	0.1	27	28.4	57
Speech-language pathologists	96	110	0.1	0.1	14	14.6	38
Therapists, all other	24	28	0.0	0.0	4	15.0	9
Veterinarians	61	71	0.0	0.0	11	17.4	25
Health diagnosing and treating practitioners, all other	72	88	0.0	0.1	16	22.5	32
Health technologists and technicians	2 494	3 086	1.7	1.9	592	23.7	1 038
Clinical laboratory technologists and technicians	302	371	0.2	0.2	69	22.7	150
Medical and clinical laboratory technologists	156	188	0.1	0.1	32	20.5	74
Medical and clinical laboratory technicians	147	183	0.1	0.1	37	25.0	76
Dental hygienists	158	226	0.1	0.1	68	43.3	82
Diagnostic related technologists and technicians	287	363	0.2	0.2	75	26.3	129
Cardiovascular technologists and technicians	45	60	0.0	0.0	15	32.6	23
Diagnostic medical sonographers	42	57	0.0	0.0	15	34.8	23
Nuclear medicine technologists	18	22	0.0	0.0	4	21.5	7
Radiologic technologists and technicians	182	224	0.1	0.1	42	23.2	76
Emergency medical technicians and paramedics	192	244	0.1	0.1	52	27.3	74
Health diagnosing and treating practitioner support technicians	514	641	0.4	0.4	127	24.8	194
Dietetic technicians	25	30	0.0	0.0	5	19.1	8
Pharmacy technicians	258	332	0.2	0.2	74	28.6	107
Psychiatric technicians	61	63	0.0	0.0	2	3.2	10
Respiratory therapy technicians	25	26	0.0	0.0	1	3.3	4
Surgical technologists	84	109	0.1	0.1	25	29.5	36
Veterinary technologists and technicians	60	81	0.0	0.0	21	35.3	29
Licensed practical and licensed vocational nurses	726	850	0.5	0.5	124	17.1	282
Medical records and health information technicians	159	205	0.1	0.1	46	28.9	69
Opticians, dispensing	66	75	0.0	0.0	9	13.6	21
Miscellaneous health technologists and technicians	91	112	0.1	0.1	21	22.5	37
Orthotists and prosthetists	6	7	0.0	0.0	1	18.0	2
Health care technologists and technicians, all other	85	104	0.1	0.1	19	22.9	35
Other health care practitioner and technical	121	145	0.1	0.1	24	20.1	49
Occupational health and safety specialists and technicians	51	58	0.0	0.0	7	13.5	18
Occupational health and safety specialists	40	45	0.0	0.0	5	12.4	14
Occupational health and safety technicians	12	14	0.0	0.0	2	17.1	5
Miscellaneous health practitioner and technical	70	87	0.0	0.1	17	25.0	31
Athletic trainers	15	19	0.0	0.0	4	29.3	8
Health care practitioner and technical workers, all other	55	68	0.0	0.0	13	23.8	23
Health Care Support	3 492	4 656	2.4	2.8	1 164	33.3	1 717
Nursing, psychiatric, and home health aides	2 139	2 815	1.5	1.7	676	31.6	956
Home health aides	624	974	0.4	0.6	350	56.0	431
Nursing aides, orderlies, and attendants	1 455	1 781	1.0	1.1	325	22.3	516
Psychiatric aides	59	61	0.0	0.0	1	2.3	9
Occupational and physical therapist assistants and aides	128	178	0.1	0.1	49	38.5	70
Occupational therapist assistants and aides	27	35	0.0	0.0	9	32.5	12
Occupational therapist assistants	21	29	0.0	0.0	7	34.1	10
Occupational therapist aides	5	7	0.0	0.0	1	26.3	2
Physical therapist assistants and aides	101	142	0.1	0.1	41	40.1	58
Physical therapist assistants	59	85	0.0	0.1	26	44.2	36
Physical therapist aides	43	57	0.0	0.0	15	34.4	22

Note: Data may not sum to totals or 100 percent due to rounding.

[1]Total job openings represent the sum of employment increases and net replacements. If employment change is negative, job openings due to growth are zero and total job openings equal net replacements.

Table 4-7. Employment, by Occupation, 2004 and Projected 2014—*Continued*

(Numbers in thousands, percent.)

Occupation	Employment				Change, 2004–2014		Total job openings due to growth and net replacements, 2004–2014[1]
	Number		Percent distribution		Number	Percent	
	2004	2014	2004	2014			
Health Care Support—*Continued*							
Other health care support	1 225	1 664	0.8	1.0	438	35.8	691
Massage therapists	97	120	0.1	0.1	23	23.6	42
Miscellaneous health care support	1 129	1 544	0.8	0.9	415	36.8	650
Dental assistants	267	382	0.2	0.2	114	42.7	189
Medical assistants	387	589	0.3	0.4	202	52.1	273
Medical equipment preparers	43	51	0.0	0.0	9	20.0	16
Medical transcriptionists	105	129	0.1	0.1	24	23.3	44
Pharmacy aides	50	59	0.0	0.0	9	17.4	18
Veterinary assistants and laboratory animal caretakers	74	90	0.1	0.1	16	21.0	29
Health care support workers, all other	202	244	0.1	0.1	42	20.9	80
Protective Services	3 138	3 578	2.2	2.2	440	14.0	1 329
First-line supervisors/managers of protective service workers	243	278	0.2	0.2	35	14.5	115
First-line supervisors/managers of law enforcement workers	138	157	0.1	0.1	19	13.8	63
First-line supervisors/managers of correctional officers	38	41	0.0	0.0	4	9.4	15
First-line supervisors/managers of police and detectives	100	115	0.1	0.1	16	15.5	48
First-line supervisors/managers of fire fighting and prevention workers	56	68	0.0	0.0	12	21.1	35
First-line supervisors/managers of protective service workers, all other	50	54	0.0	0.0	4	8.7	17
Fire fighting and prevention workers	297	365	0.2	0.2	68	22.9	155
Firefighters	282	351	0.2	0.2	69	24.3	150
Fire inspectors	15	14	0.0	0.0	-1	-5.2	4
Fire inspectors and investigators	13	12	0.0	0.0	-1	-5.5	4
Forest fire inspectors and prevention specialists	2	2	0.0	0.0	0	-3.1	0
Law enforcement workers	1 199	1 347	0.8	0.8	148	12.3	435
Bailiffs, correctional officers, and jailers	447	478	0.3	0.3	31	7.0	124
Bailiffs	18	20	0.0	0.0	2	13.2	6
Correctional officers and jailers	429	458	0.3	0.3	29	6.7	118
Detectives and criminal investigators	91	106	0.1	0.1	15	16.3	39
Fish and game wardens	7	8	0.0	0.0	1	10.5	3
Parking enforcement workers	11	12	0.0	0.0	2	15.1	4
Police officers	644	743	0.4	0.5	100	15.5	266
Police and sheriff's patrol officers	639	738	0.4	0.4	99	15.5	265
Transit and railroad police	5	5	0.0	0.0	0	9.2	1
Other protective services	1 399	1 588	1.0	1.0	189	13.5	624
Animal control workers	15	17	0.0	0.0	2	14.4	13
Private detectives and investigators	43	50	0.0	0.0	8	17.7	17
Security guards and gaming surveillance officers	1 025	1 155	0.7	0.7	130	12.7	353
Gaming surveillance officers and gaming investigators	9	11	0.0	0.0	2	24.5	4
Security guards	1 016	1 144	0.7	0.7	128	12.6	349
Miscellaneous protective services	316	366	0.2	0.2	50	15.8	242
Crossing guards	71	86	0.0	0.1	14	19.7	37
Lifeguards, ski patrol, and other recreational protective service workers	113	137	0.1	0.1	23	20.4	102
Protective service workers, all other	131	144	0.1	0.1	13	9.6	103
Food Preparation and Serving Related	10 739	12 453	7.4	7.6	1 714	16.0	5 981
Supervisors of food preparation and serving workers	898	1 047	0.6	0.6	149	16.6	370
Chefs and head cooks	125	146	0.1	0.1	21	16.7	58
First-line supervisors/managers of food preparation and serving workers	773	901	0.5	0.5	129	16.6	312
Cooks and food preparation workers	3 011	3 459	2.1	2.1	448	14.9	1 419
Cooks	2 122	2 395	1.5	1.5	272	12.8	930
Cooks, fast food	662	771	0.5	0.5	109	16.4	314
Cooks, institution and cafeteria	424	430	0.3	0.3	6	1.4	137
Cooks, private household	9	9	0.0	0.0	-1	-5.6	3
Cooks, restaurant	783	914	0.5	0.6	130	16.6	373
Cooks, short order	230	257	0.2	0.2	27	11.8	98
Cooks, all other	13	14	0.0	0.0	1	5.7	5
Food preparation workers	889	1 064	0.6	0.6	175	19.7	490
Food and beverage serving workers	5 530	6 440	3.8	3.9	911	16.5	3 555
Bartenders	474	545	0.3	0.3	70	14.8	258
Fast food and counter workers	2 614	3 062	1.8	1.9	448	17.1	1 683
Combined food preparation and serving workers, including fast food	2 150	2 516	1.5	1.5	367	17.1	1 298
Counter attendants, cafeteria, food concession, and coffee shop	465	546	0.3	0.3	81	17.5	385
Waiters and waitresses	2 252	2 627	1.5	1.6	376	16.7	1 534
Food servers, nonrestaurant	189	206	0.1	0.1	17	8.8	80
Other food preparation and serving related workers	1 301	1 507	0.9	0.9	206	15.9	636
Dining room and cafeteria attendants and bartender helpers	401	464	0.3	0.3	62	15.6	197
Dishwashers	507	587	0.3	0.4	80	15.8	251
Hosts and hostesses, restaurant, lounge, and coffee shop	328	381	0.2	0.2	53	16.3	157
Food preparation and serving related workers, all other	64	75	0.0	0.0	11	16.7	31
Building and Grounds Cleaning and Maintenance	5 582	6 530	3.8	4.0	948	17.0	2 062
Supervisors of building and grounds cleaning and maintenance workers	420	497	0.3	0.3	78	18.5	150
First-line supervisors/managers of housekeeping and janitorial workers	236	281	0.2	0.2	45	19.0	101
First-line supervisors/managers of landscaping, lawn service, and groundskeeping workers	184	217	0.1	0.1	33	17.8	50
Building cleaning and pest control workers	3 879	4 500	2.7	2.7	620	16.0	1 383
Building cleaning workers	3 811	4 418	2.6	2.7	608	16.0	1 360
Janitors and cleaners, except maids and housekeeping workers	2 374	2 813	1.6	1.7	440	18.5	890
Maids and housekeeping cleaners	1 422	1 587	1.0	1.0	165	11.6	464
Building cleaning workers, all other	15	18	0.0	0.0	3	19.8	6
Pest control workers	68	81	0.0	0.0	13	18.4	23
Grounds maintenance	1 283	1 533	0.9	0.9	250	19.4	529
Landscaping and groundskeeping	1 177	1 407	0.8	0.9	230	19.5	486
Pesticide handlers, sprayers, and applicators, vegetation	30	34	0.0	0.0	5	16.6	11
Tree trimmers and pruners	55	64	0.0	0.0	9	16.5	21
Grounds maintenance workers, all other	21	27	0.0	0.0	6	26.3	10

Note: Data may not sum to totals or 100 percent due to rounding.

[1] Total job openings represent the sum of employment increases and net replacements. If employment change is negative, job openings due to growth are zero and total job openings equal net replacements.

Table 4-7. Employment, by Occupation, 2004 and Projected 2014—*Continued*

(Numbers in thousands, percent.)

Occupation	Employment				Change, 2004–2014		Total job openings due to growth and net replacements, 2004–2014[1]
	Number		Percent distribution		Number	Percent	
	2004	2014	2004	2014			
Personal Care and Services	4 721	5 713	3.2	3.5	991	21.0	2 121
Supervisors of personal care and service workers	267	316	0.2	0.2	49	18.4	114
First-line supervisors/managers of gaming workers	61	72	0.0	0.0	11	18.8	24
Gaming supervisors	38	44	0.0	0.0	6	16.3	14
Slot key persons	23	28	0.0	0.0	5	23.0	10
First-line supervisors/managers of personal service workers	206	244	0.1	0.1	38	18.3	89
Animal care and service workers	172	214	0.1	0.1	42	24.3	83
Animal trainers	44	53	0.0	0.0	9	20.3	18
Nonfarm animal caretakers	128	161	0.1	0.1	33	25.6	65
Entertainment attendants and related workers	558	682	0.4	0.4	125	22.4	324
Gaming services workers	116	147	0.1	0.1	31	26.6	67
Gaming dealers	83	106	0.1	0.1	23	28.0	49
Gaming and sports book writers and runners	18	22	0.0	0.0	4	22.1	10
Gaming service workers, all other	15	19	0.0	0.0	4	24.2	8
Motion picture projectionists	12	11	0.0	0.0	-1	-9.9	6
Ushers, lobby attendants, and ticket takers	112	124	0.1	0.1	12	10.6	76
Miscellaneous entertainment attendants and related workers	318	401	0.2	0.2	83	26.2	175
Amusement and recreation attendants	252	322	0.2	0.2	70	28.0	143
Costume attendants	4	4	0.0	0.0	1	23.4	2
Locker room, coatroom, and dressing room attendants	25	29	0.0	0.0	4	17.3	11
Entertainment attendants and related workers, all other	38	45	0.0	0.0	8	20.0	19
Funeral service	38	46	0.0	0.0	8	19.7	16
Embalmers	9	10	0.0	0.0	1	15.6	3
Funeral attendants	30	36	0.0	0.0	6	20.8	12
Personal appearance	790	915	0.5	0.6	126	15.9	283
Barbers and cosmetologists	670	773	0.5	0.5	103	15.4	237
Barbers	60	65	0.0	0.0	5	8.2	22
Hairdressers, hairstylists, and cosmetologists	610	708	0.4	0.4	98	16.1	215
Miscellaneous personal appearance	120	142	0.1	0.1	23	18.9	46
Makeup artists, theatrical and performance	2	2	0.0	0.0	0	13.2	1
Manicurists and pedicurists	60	73	0.0	0.0	13	21.0	24
Shampooers	27	31	0.0	0.0	4	13.1	9
Skin care specialists	30	37	0.0	0.0	6	20.4	12
Transportation, tourism, and lodging attendants	248	287	0.2	0.2	39	15.6	87
Baggage porters, bellhops, and concierges	75	85	0.1	0.1	11	14.4	30
Baggage porters and bellhops	57	65	0.0	0.0	8	14.0	23
Concierges	18	21	0.0	0.0	3	16.0	8
Tour and travel guides	44	51	0.0	0.0	7	15.7	18
Tour guides and escorts	38	44	0.0	0.0	6	16.6	16
Travel guides	6	6	0.0	0.0	1	9.6	2
Transportation attendants	130	151	0.1	0.1	21	16.2	38
Flight attendants	102	119	0.1	0.1	17	16.3	30
Transportation attendants, except flight attendants and baggage porters	28	32	0.0	0.0	4	15.9	8
Other personal care and services	2 648	3 252	1.8	2.0	604	22.8	1 215
Childcare workers	1 280	1 456	0.9	0.9	176	13.8	525
Personal and home care aides	701	988	0.5	0.6	287	41.0	400
Recreation and fitness workers	514	623	0.4	0.4	109	21.2	227
Fitness trainers and aerobics instructors	205	260	0.1	0.2	55	27.1	102
Recreation workers	310	363	0.2	0.2	54	17.3	125
Residential advisors	56	72	0.0	0.0	16	28.9	28
Personal care and service workers, all other	96	112	0.1	0.1	15	15.9	36
Sales and Related	15 330	16 806	10.5	10.2	1 476	9.6	6 491
Supervisors of sales workers	2 183	2 256	1.5	1.4	74	3.4	471
First-line supervisors/managers of retail sales workers	1 667	1 731	1.1	1.1	64	3.8	363
First-line supervisors/managers of non-retail sales workers	516	526	0.4	0.3	10	1.9	107
Retail sales	8 445	9 382	5.8	5.7	937	11.1	4 444
Cashiers	3 499	3 612	2.4	2.2	113	3.2	1 815
Cashiers, except gaming	3 470	3 578	2.4	2.2	108	3.1	1 796
Gaming change persons and booth cashiers	29	35	0.0	0.0	5	18.5	20
Counter and rental clerks and parts salespersons	690	778	0.5	0.5	88	12.8	345
Counter and rental clerks	451	555	0.3	0.3	104	23.1	277
Parts salespersons	239	223	0.2	0.1	-16	-6.6	68
Retail salespersons	4 256	4 992	2.9	3.0	736	17.3	2 283
Sales representatives, services	1 318	1 467	0.9	0.9	149	11.3	408
Advertising sales agents	154	180	0.1	0.1	25	16.3	55
Insurance sales agents	400	426	0.3	0.3	26	6.6	122
Securities, commodities, and financial services sales agents	281	313	0.2	0.2	32	11.5	64
Travel agents	103	96	0.1	0.1	-6	-6.1	23
Sales representatives, services, all other	380	452	0.3	0.3	71	18.7	144
Sales representatives, wholesale and manufacturing	1 851	2 095	1.3	1.3	244	13.2	730
Sales representatives, wholesale and manufacturing, technical and scientific products	397	454	0.3	0.3	57	14.4	161
Sales representatives, wholesale and manufacturing, except technical and scientific products	1 454	1 641	1.0	1.0	187	12.9	569
Other sales and related workers	1 533	1 606	1.1	1.0	72	4.7	439
Models, demonstrators, and product promoters	120	140	0.1	0.1	20	16.5	47
Demonstrators and product promoters	118	138	0.1	0.1	19	16.5	46
Models	2	3	0.0	0.0	1	15.7	1
Real estate brokers and sales agents	460	520	0.3	0.3	60	13.0	151
Real estate brokers	111	120	0.1	0.1	9	7.8	31
Real estate sales agents	348	400	0.2	0.2	51	14.7	120
Sales engineers	74	84	0.1	0.1	10	14.0	32
Telemarketers	415	373	0.3	0.2	-42	-10.0	68

Note: Data may not sum to totals or 100 percent due to rounding.

[1]Total job openings represent the sum of employment increases and net replacements. If employment change is negative, job openings due to growth are zero and total job openings equal net replacements.

Table 4-7. Employment, by Occupation, 2004 and Projected 2014—*Continued*

(Numbers in thousands, percent.)

Occupation	Employment				Change, 2004–2014		Total job openings due to growth and net replacements, 2004–2014[1]
	Number		Percent distribution		Number	Percent	
	2004	2014	2004	2014			
Sales and Related—*Continued*							
Miscellaneous sales and related	465	489	0.3	0.3	24	5.1	141
Door-to-door sales workers, news and street vendors, and related workers	239	221	0.2	0.1	-18	-7.4	56
Sales and related workers, all other	226	267	0.2	0.2	42	18.4	85
Office and Administrative Support	23 907	25 287	16.4	15.4	1 380	5.8	7 455
Supervisors of office and administrative support workers	1 482	1 602	1.0	1.0	120	8.1	438
First-line supervisors/managers of office and administrative support workers	1 482	1 602	1.0	1.0	120	8.1	438
Communications equipment operators	256	223	0.2	0.1	-33	-12.9	66
Switchboard operators, including answering service	213	195	0.1	0.1	-19	-8.8	55
Telephone operators	39	25	0.0	0.0	-14	-35.7	10
Communications equipment operators, all other	4	4	0.0	0.0	0	10.8	1
Financial clerks	3 891	4 203	2.7	2.6	312	8.0	1 232
Bill and account collectors	456	554	0.3	0.3	98	21.4	184
Billing and posting clerks and machine operators	523	541	0.4	0.3	18	3.4	107
Bookkeeping, accounting, and auditing clerks	2 046	2 166	1.4	1.3	120	5.9	503
Gaming cage workers	20	23	0.0	0.0	3	17.0	13
Payroll and timekeeping clerks	214	251	0.1	0.2	37	17.3	94
Procurement clerks	74	72	0.1	0.0	-2	-2.7	19
Tellers	558	596	0.4	0.4	38	6.8	313
Information and record clerks	5 554	6 212	3.8	3.8	657	11.8	2 045
Brokerage clerks	75	81	0.1	0.0	6	7.5	16
Correspondence clerks	23	21	0.0	0.0	-2	-6.9	7
Court, municipal, and license clerks	110	131	0.1	0.1	21	18.6	45
Credit authorizers, checkers, and clerks	67	39	0.0	0.0	-27	-41.2	13
Customer service representatives	2 063	2 534	1.4	1.5	471	22.8	778
Eligibility interviewers, government programs	98	88	0.1	0.1	-9	-9.4	26
File clerks	255	163	0.2	0.1	-93	-36.3	76
Hotel, motel, and resort desk clerks	195	229	0.1	0.1	34	17.2	121
Interviewers, except eligibility and loan	199	251	0.1	0.2	52	26.0	103
Library assistants, clerical	109	122	0.1	0.1	14	12.5	58
Loan interviewers and clerks	218	217	0.1	0.1	-1	-0.6	30
New accounts clerks	98	99	0.1	0.1	2	1.7	26
Order clerks	293	230	0.2	0.1	-63	-21.4	66
Human resources assistants, except payroll and timekeeping	172	200	0.1	0.1	29	16.7	66
Receptionists and information clerks	1 133	1 379	0.8	0.8	246	21.7	524
Reservation and transportation ticket agents and travel clerks	163	167	0.1	0.1	4	2.4	46
Information and record clerks, all other	285	260	0.2	0.2	-24	-8.6	45
Material recording, scheduling, dispatching, and distributing occupations	3 849	3 761	2.6	2.3	-88	-2.3	1 204
Cargo and freight agents	70	67	0.0	0.0	-4	-5.6	16
Couriers and messengers	147	134	0.1	0.1	-13	-8.6	34
Dispatchers	266	291	0.2	0.2	25	9.4	82
Police, fire, and ambulance dispatchers	95	111	0.1	0.1	15	15.9	36
Dispatchers, except police, fire, and ambulance	171	181	0.1	0.1	10	5.7	46
Meter readers, utilities	50	27	0.0	0.0	-22	-44.9	16
Postal service workers	619	619	0.4	0.4	1	0.0	180
Postal service clerks	75	75	0.1	0.0	0	0.0	20
Postal service mail carriers	335	335	0.2	0.2	0	0.0	105
Postal service mail sorters, processors, and processing machine operators	209	209	0.1	0.1	0	0.0	55
Production, planning, and expediting clerks	292	315	0.2	0.2	23	7.7	93
Shipping, receiving, and traffic clerks	751	779	0.5	0.5	28	3.7	182
Stock clerks and order fillers	1 566	1 451	1.1	0.9	-115	-7.3	579
Weighers, measurers, checkers, and samplers, recordkeeping	88	78	0.1	0.0	-10	-11.3	22
Secretaries and administrative assistants	4 126	4 382	2.8	2.7	255	6.2	1 093
Executive secretaries and administrative assistants	1 547	1 739	1.1	1.1	192	12.4	488
Legal secretaries	272	319	0.2	0.2	47	17.4	99
Medical secretaries	373	436	0.3	0.3	63	17.0	135
Secretaries, except legal, medical, and executive	1 934	1 887	1.3	1.1	-48	-2.5	370
Other office and administrative support	4 748	4 905	3.3	3.0	157	3.3	1 378
Computer operators	149	101	0.1	0.1	-49	-32.6	32
Data entry and information processing	525	493	0.4	0.3	-32	-6.1	121
Data entry keyers	330	328	0.2	0.2	-2	-0.7	78
Word processors and typists	194	165	0.1	0.1	-30	-15.3	43
Desktop publishers	34	41	0.0	0.0	8	23.2	15
Insurance claims and policy processing clerks	251	262	0.2	0.2	11	4.5	52
Mail clerks and mail machine operators, except postal service	160	101	0.1	0.1	-59	-37.1	48
Office clerks, general	3 138	3 401	2.2	2.1	263	8.4	958
Office machine operators, except computer	100	78	0.1	0.0	-22	-21.9	25
Proofreaders and copy markers	23	24	0.0	0.0	1	1.7	5
Statistical assistants	19	20	0.0	0.0	1	5.7	4
Office and administrative support workers, all other	349	384	0.2	0.2	35	10.0	117
Farming, Fishing, and Forestry	1 026	1 013	0.7	0.6	-13	-1.3	286
Supervisors of farming, fishing, and forestry workers	61	63	0.0	0.0	2	3.6	14
Agricultural workers	834	824	0.6	0.5	-10	-1.2	240
Agricultural inspectors	14	15	0.0	0.0	1	6.8	4
Animal breeders	12	12	0.0	0.0	1	5.6	3
Graders and sorters, agricultural products	45	49	0.0	0.0	4	7.9	16
Miscellaneous agricultural	764	749	0.5	0.5	-15	-2.0	217
Agricultural equipment operators	60	60	0.0	0.0	0	-0.1	17
Farmworkers and laborers, crop, nursery, and greenhouse	611	595	0.4	0.4	-16	-2.7	173
Farmworkers, farm and ranch animals	79	80	0.1	0.0	1	0.9	23
Agricultural workers, all other	14	15	0.0	0.0	1	4.3	4
Fishing and hunting	39	33	0.0	0.0	-7	-16.6	12
Fishers and related fishing	38	32	0.0	0.0	-7	-17.2	11
Hunters and trappers	1	1	0.0	0.0	0	5.2	1

Note: Data may not sum to totals or 100 percent due to rounding.

[1]Total job openings represent the sum of employment increases and net replacements. If employment change is negative, job openings due to growth are zero and total job openings equal net replacements.

Table 4-7. Employment, by Occupation, 2004 and Projected 2014—*Continued*

(Numbers in thousands, percent.)

Occupation	Employment				Change, 2004–2014		Total job openings due to growth and net replacements, 2004–2014[1]
	Number		Percent distribution		Number	Percent	
	2004	2014	2004	2014			
Farming, Fishing, and Forestry—*Continued*							
Forest, conservation, and logging	92	93	0.1	0.1	1	1.6	21
Forest and conservation	17	18	0.0	0.0	1	6.0	5
Logging	75	75	0.1	0.0	0	0.6	16
Fallers	15	14	0.0	0.0	-1	-5.7	3
Logging equipment operators	43	45	0.0	0.0	1	3.4	9
Log graders and scalers	9	9	0.0	0.0	0	1.7	2
Logging workers, all other	7	7	0.0	0.0	0	-4.2	2
Construction and Extraction	7 738	8 669	5.3	5.3	931	12.0	2 459
Supervisors of construction and extraction workers	750	832	0.5	0.5	82	10.9	209
First-line supervisors/managers of construction and extraction workers	750	832	0.5	0.5	82	10.9	209
Construction trades and related	5 929	6 627	4.1	4.0	699	11.8	1 785
Boilermakers	19	20	0.0	0.0	2	8.7	8
Brickmasons, blockmasons, and stonemasons	177	198	0.1	0.1	21	12.1	48
Brickmasons and blockmasons	155	174	0.1	0.1	19	12.0	42
Stonemasons	22	25	0.0	0.0	3	13.0	6
Carpenters	1 349	1 535	0.9	0.9	186	13.8	405
Carpet, floor, and tile installers and finishers	184	209	0.1	0.1	25	13.4	53
Carpet installers	79	86	0.1	0.1	7	8.4	19
Floor layers, except carpet, wood, and hard tiles	31	34	0.0	0.0	3	10.2	8
Floor sanders and finishers	15	16	0.0	0.0	1	8.2	4
Tile and marble setters	59	73	0.0	0.0	14	22.9	23
Cement masons, concrete finishers, and terrazzo workers	208	241	0.1	0.1	33	15.9	75
Cement masons and concrete finishers	201	233	0.1	0.1	32	15.9	72
Terrazzo workers and finishers	7	8	0.0	0.0	1	15.2	2
Construction laborers	1 009	1 069	0.7	0.6	60	5.9	194
Construction equipment operators	449	504	0.3	0.3	55	12.2	162
Paving, surfacing, and tamping equipment operators	63	73	0.0	0.0	10	15.6	19
Pile-driver operators	4	5	0.0	0.0	1	11.9	1
Operating engineers and other construction equipment operators	382	426	0.3	0.3	44	11.6	142
Drywall installers, ceiling tile installers, and tapers	196	212	0.1	0.1	16	8.3	59
Drywall and ceiling tile installers	149	162	0.1	0.1	13	9.0	46
Tapers	47	50	0.0	0.0	3	5.9	13
Electricians	656	734	0.5	0.4	77	11.8	207
Glaziers	49	56	0.0	0.0	7	14.2	17
Insulation workers	61	63	0.0	0.0	1	2.4	20
Insulation workers, floor, ceiling, and wall	42	44	0.0	0.0	1	3.0	14
Insulation workers, mechanical	19	19	0.0	0.0	0	1.0	6
Painters and paperhangers	486	546	0.3	0.3	60	12.4	134
Painters, construction and maintenance	471	531	0.3	0.3	60	12.6	131
Paperhangers	14	15	0.0	0.0	0	3.2	2
Pipelayers, plumbers, pipefitters, and steamfitters	561	645	0.4	0.4	84	15.0	213
Pipelayers	62	69	0.0	0.0	6	9.9	21
Plumbers, pipefitters, and steamfitters	499	577	0.3	0.4	78	15.7	193
Plasterers and stucco masons	59	64	0.0	0.0	5	8.2	16
Reinforcing iron and rebar workers	34	38	0.0	0.0	5	14.1	11
Roofers	162	189	0.1	0.1	27	16.8	65
Sheet metal workers	198	222	0.1	0.1	24	12.2	72
Structural iron and steel workers	73	83	0.0	0.1	11	15.0	25
Helpers—construction trades	431	480	0.3	0.3	49	11.4	228
Helpers—brickmasons, blockmasons, stonemasons, and tile and marble setters	62	71	0.0	0.0	9	14.9	35
Helpers—carpenters	109	125	0.1	0.1	16	14.5	61
Helpers—electricians	95	99	0.1	0.1	4	4.0	43
Helpers—painters, paperhangers, plasterers, and stucco masons	27	30	0.0	0.0	3	11.5	14
Helpers—pipelayers, plumbers, pipefitters, and steamfitters	76	89	0.1	0.1	13	16.6	44
Helpers—roofers	22	26	0.0	0.0	4	16.5	13
Helpers—construction trades, all other	39	40	0.0	0.0	1	1.8	17
Other construction and related	460	562	0.3	0.3	102	22.2	189
Construction and building inspectors	94	115	0.1	0.1	21	22.3	42
Elevator installers and repairers	22	25	0.0	0.0	3	14.8	9
Fence erectors	38	42	0.0	0.0	4	9.9	9
Hazardous materials removal	38	50	0.0	0.0	12	31.2	22
Highway maintenance	143	177	0.1	0.1	33	23.3	54
Rail-track laying and maintenance equipment operators	11	10	0.0	0.0	-1	-10.9	2
Septic tank servicers and sewer pipe cleaners	20	24	0.0	0.0	4	21.8	10
Miscellaneous construction and related	94	119	0.1	0.1	26	27.3	40
Segmental pavers	1	1	0.0	0.0	0	12.5	0
Construction and related workers, all other	92	118	0.1	0.1	25	27.5	40
Extraction workers	169	169	0.1	0.1	-1	-0.4	48
Derrick, rotary drill, and service unit operators, oil, gas, and mining	47	47	0.0	0.0	0	-0.3	14
Derrick operators, oil and gas	15	15	0.0	0.0	0	-0.5	4
Rotary drill operators, oil and gas	15	15	0.0	0.0	0	0.1	4
Service unit operators, oil, gas, and mining	17	17	0.0	0.0	0	-0.6	5
Earth drillers, except oil and gas	22	23	0.0	0.0	2	7.9	6
Explosives workers, ordnance handling experts, and blasters	5	6	0.0	0.0	0	2.2	2
Mining machine operators	15	14	0.0	0.0	-1	-9.6	4
Continuous mining machine operators	8	7	0.0	0.0	-1	-12.4	2
Mine cutting and channeling machine operators	4	4	0.0	0.0	0	-11.1	1
Mining machine operators, all other	3	3	0.0	0.0	0	0.9	1
Rock splitters, quarry	3	4	0.0	0.0	0	4.1	1
Roof bolters, mining	4	3	0.0	0.0	-1	-29.5	1
Roustabouts, oil and gas	34	34	0.0	0.0	0	1.0	10
Helpers—extraction workers	27	27	0.0	0.0	0	-0.1	8
Extraction workers, all other	12	12	0.0	0.0	0	-0.7	3

Note: Data may not sum to totals or 100 percent due to rounding.

[1]Total job openings represent the sum of employment increases and net replacements. If employment change is negative, job openings due to growth are zero and total job openings equal net replacements.

Table 4-7. Employment, by Occupation, 2004 and Projected 2014—*Continued*

(Numbers in thousands, percent.)

Occupation	Employment				Change, 2004–2014		Total job openings due to growth and net replacements, 2004–2014[1]
	Number		Percent distribution		Number	Percent	
	2004	2014	2004	2014			
Installation, Maintenance, and Repair	5 747	6 404	3.9	3.9	657	11.4	1 984
Supervisors of installation, maintenance, and repair workers	469	527	0.3	0.3	58	12.4	175
First-line supervisors/managers of mechanics, installers, and repairers	469	527	0.3	0.3	58	12.4	175
Electrical and electronic equipment mechanics, installers, and repairers	664	686	0.5	0.4	22	3.3	159
Computer, automated teller, and office machine repairers	168	174	0.1	0.1	6	3.8	27
Radio and telecommunications equipment installers and reporters	222	211	0.2	0.1	-11	-4.7	46
Radio mechanics	7	7	0.0	0.0	0	-1.1	1
Telecommunications equipment installers and repairers, except line installers	215	204	0.1	0.1	-10	-4.9	44
Miscellaneous electrical and electronic equipment mechanics, installers, and repairers	275	301	0.2	0.2	26	9.6	86
Avionics technicians	23	25	0.0	0.0	2	9.1	8
Electric motor, power tool, and related repairers	28	29	0.0	0.0	1	4.1	8
Electrical and electronics installers and repairers, transportation equipment	18	19	0.0	0.0	1	6.6	5
Electrical and electronics repairers, commercial and industrial equipment	72	79	0.0	0.0	7	9.7	23
Electrical and electronics repairers, powerhouse, substation, and relay	21	21	0.0	0.0	0	-0.4	5
Electronic equipment installers and repairers, motor vehicles	19	21	0.0	0.0	3	13.6	7
Electronic home entertainment equipment installers and repairers	47	49	0.0	0.0	2	4.7	11
Security and fire alarm systems installers	47	57	0.0	0.0	10	21.7	19
Vehicle and mobile equipment mechanics, installers, and repairers	1 778	2 012	1.2	1.2	234	13.2	695
Aircraft mechanics and service technicians	119	135	0.1	0.1	16	13.4	44
Automotive technicians and repairers	1 026	1 175	0.7	0.7	150	14.6	408
Automotive body and related repairers	201	221	0.1	0.1	21	10.3	61
Automotive glass installers and repairers	22	26	0.0	0.0	3	15.1	8
Automotive service technicians and mechanics	803	929	0.6	0.6	126	15.7	339
Bus and truck mechanics and diesel engine specialists	270	309	0.2	0.2	39	14.4	108
Heavy vehicle and mobile equipment service technicians and mechanics	178	189	0.1	0.1	12	6.7	51
Farm equipment mechanics	33	34	0.0	0.0	1	3.3	8
Mobile heavy equipment mechanics, except engines	125	136	0.1	0.1	11	8.8	38
Rail car repairers	20	20	0.0	0.0	0	-1.2	4
Small engine mechanics	73	83	0.1	0.1	10	14.2	28
Motorboat mechanics	23	26	0.0	0.0	3	15.1	9
Motorcycle mechanics	19	22	0.0	0.0	3	13.7	7
Outdoor power equipment and other small engine mechanics	31	36	0.0	0.0	4	14.0	12
Miscellaneous vehicle and mobile equipment mechanics, installers, and repairers	112	120	0.1	0.1	8	6.9	55
Bicycle repairers	8	9	0.0	0.0	1	14.3	5
Recreational vehicle service technicians	13	15	0.0	0.0	3	19.5	8
Tire repairers and changers	91	96	0.1	0.1	4	4.5	43
Other installation, maintenance, and repair occupations	2 837	3 180	1.9	1.9	342	12.1	955
Control and valve installers and repairers	48	52	0.0	0.0	4	7.3	16
Mechanical door repairers	11	12	0.0	0.0	2	15.8	4
Control and valve installers and repairers, except mechanical door	38	40	0.0	0.0	2	4.9	11
Heating, air conditioning, and refrigeration mechanics and installers	270	321	0.2	0.2	51	19.0	87
Home appliance repairers	50	51	0.0	0.0	1	2.6	13
Industrial machinery installation, repair, and maintenance	1 700	1 907	1.2	1.2	207	12.2	542
Industrial machinery mechanics	220	220	0.2	0.1	0	-0.2	44
Maintenance and repair workers, general	1 332	1 533	0.9	0.9	202	15.2	457
Maintenance workers, machinery	86	89	0.1	0.1	2	2.8	22
Millwrights	59	62	0.0	0.0	3	5.9	18
Refractory materials repairers, except brickmasons	4	3	0.0	0.0	-1	-5.2	1
Line installers and repairers	251	269	0.2	0.2	18	7.4	91
Electrical power line installers and repairers	104	107	0.1	0.1	3	2.5	36
Telecommunications line installers and repairers	147	163	0.1	0.1	16	10.8	56
Precision instrument and equipment repairers	62	67	0.0	0.0	5	8.7	23
Camera and photographic equipment repairers	5	5	0.0	0.0	0	-9.1	1
Medical equipment repairers	29	34	0.0	0.0	4	14.8	13
Musical instrument repairers and tuners	6	6	0.0	0.0	0	2.8	2
Watch repairers	4	4	0.0	0.0	0	0.6	1
Precision instrument and equipment repairers, all other	17	18	0.0	0.0	1	7.7	6
Miscellaneous installation, maintenance, and repair	456	512	0.3	0.3	55	12.1	182
Coin, vending, and amusement machine servicers and repairers	46	47	0.0	0.0	1	2.4	12
Commercial divers	3	3	0.0	0.0	0	9.5	1
Fabric menders, except garment	3	3	0.0	0.0	0	-0.6	1
Locksmiths and safe repairers	28	33	0.0	0.0	5	16.1	14
Manufactured building and mobile home installers	15	16	0.0	0.0	1	7.9	5
Riggers	13	14	0.0	0.0	2	13.9	5
Signal and track switch repairers	8	8	0.0	0.0	0	2.3	3
Helpers—installation, maintenance, and repair	163	190	0.1	0.1	27	16.4	82
Installation, maintenance, and repair workers, all other	178	197	0.1	0.1	20	11.0	60
Production	10 562	10 483	7.3	6.4	-79	-0.7	2 909
Supervisors of production workers	731	750	0.5	0.5	20	2.7	173
First-line supervisors/managers of production and operating workers	731	750	0.5	0.5	20	2.7	173
Assemblers and fabricators	1 997	2 075	1.4	1.3	78	3.9	616
Aircraft structure, surfaces, rigging, and systems assemblers	19	21	0.0	0.0	1	7.8	7
Electrical, electronics, and electromechanical assemblers	301	272	0.2	0.2	-29	-9.8	71
Coil winders, tapers, and finishers	28	20	0.0	0.0	-8	-28.5	7
Electrical and electronic equipment assemblers	221	207	0.2	0.1	-14	-6.4	52
Electromechanical equipment assemblers	52	45	0.0	0.0	-7	-13.9	12
Engine and other machine assemblers	46	46	0.0	0.0	0	0.2	13
Structural metal fabricators and fitters	90	93	0.1	0.1	3	2.9	24
Miscellaneous assemblers and fabricators	1 541	1 644	1.1	1.0	103	6.7	502
Fiberglass laminators and fabricators	31	32	0.0	0.0	1	4.0	9
Team assemblers	1 239	1 329	0.9	0.8	90	7.3	410
Timing device assemblers, adjusters, and calibrators	3	3	0.0	0.0	0	-1.5	1
Assemblers and fabricators, all other	268	280	0.2	0.2	12	4.5	81

Note: Data may not sum to totals or 100 percent due to rounding.

[1]Total job openings represent the sum of employment increases and net replacements. If employment change is negative, job openings due to growth are zero and total job openings equal net replacements.

Table 4-7. Employment, by Occupation, 2004 and Projected 2014—*Continued*

(Numbers in thousands, percent.)

Occupation	Employment				Change, 2004–2014		Total job openings due to growth and net replacements, 2004–2014[1]
	Number		Percent distribution		Number	Percent	
	2004	2014	2004	2014			
Production—*Continued*							
Food processing	725	810	0.5	0.5	86	11.8	251
Bakers	166	191	0.1	0.1	25	15.2	64
Butchers and other meat, poultry, and fish processing	411	462	0.3	0.3	51	12.5	142
Butchers and meat cutters	134	145	0.1	0.1	11	7.9	40
Meat, poultry, and fish cutters and trimmers	140	163	0.1	0.1	22	15.8	53
Slaughterers and meat packers	136	155	0.1	0.1	19	13.8	49
Miscellaneous food processing	148	157	0.1	0.1	9	6.0	45
Food and tobacco roasting, baking, and drying machine operators and tenders	18	19	0.0	0.0	1	4.7	6
Food batchmakers	87	94	0.1	0.1	7	7.9	28
Food cooking machine operators and tenders	43	44	0.0	0.0	1	2.9	11
Metal workers and plastic	2 175	2 085	1.5	1.3	-90	-4.1	562
Computer control programmers and operators	143	141	0.1	0.1	-2	-1.2	24
Computer-controlled machine tool operators, metal and plastic	126	124	0.1	0.1	-1	-1.2	21
Numerical tool and process control programmers	18	17	0.0	0.0	-1	-1.1	3
Forming machine setters, operators, and tenders, metal and plastic	165	143	0.1	0.1	-22	-13.5	44
Extruding and drawing machine setters, operators, and tenders, metal and plastic	89	70	0.1	0.0	-19	-21.3	30
Forging machine setters, operators, and tenders, metal and plastic	38	37	0.0	0.0	-2	-4.6	6
Rolling machine setters, operators, and tenders, metal and plastic	37	36	0.0	0.0	-1	-3.9	8
Machine tool cutting setters, operators, and tenders, metal and plastic	495	431	0.3	0.3	-65	-13.1	109
Cutting, punching, and press machine setters, operators, and tenders, metal and plastic	251	208	0.2	0.1	-43	-17.2	58
Drilling and boring machine tool setters, operators, and tenders, metal and plastic	42	39	0.0	0.0	-4	-8.4	12
Grinding, lapping, polishing, and buffing machine, tool setters, operators, and tenders, metal and plastic	101	91	0.1	0.1	-10	-10.0	19
Lathe and turning machine tool setters, operators, and tenders, metal and plastic	71	64	0.0	0.0	-6	-9.0	14
Milling and planing machine setters, operators, and tenders, metal and plastic	31	29	0.0	0.0	-2	-5.3	5
Machinists	370	386	0.3	0.2	16	4.3	102
Metal furnace and kiln operators and tenders	31	26	0.0	0.0	-5	-14.7	7
Metal-refining furnace operators and tenders	17	15	0.0	0.0	-2	-13.5	4
Pourers and casters, metal	14	12	0.0	0.0	-2	-16.1	3
Model makers and patternmakers, metal and plastic	14	13	0.0	0.0	-1	-5.5	4
Model makers, metal and plastic	8	8	0.0	0.0	0	-4.0	3
Patternmakers, metal and plastic	6	6	0.0	0.0	0	-7.5	2
Molders and molding machine setters, operators, and tenders, metal and plastic	175	157	0.1	0.1	-17	-9.9	43
Foundry mold and coremakers	17	15	0.0	0.0	-2	-13.3	4
Molding, coremaking, and casting machine setters, operators and tenders, metal and plastic	157	142	0.1	0.1	-15	-9.5	39
Multiple machine tool setters, operators, and tenders, metal and plastic	97	98	0.1	0.1	1	0.3	27
Tool and die makers	103	100	0.1	0.1	-3	-2.6	23
Welding, soldering, and brazing	429	448	0.3	0.3	19	4.5	140
Welders, cutters, solderers, and brazers	377	396	0.3	0.2	19	5.0	125
Welding, soldering, and brazing machine setters, operators, and tenders	52	52	0.0	0.0	0	0.4	15
Miscellaneous metalworkers and plastic	153	142	0.1	0.1	-11	-7.4	38
Heat treating equipment setters, operators, and tenders, matal and plastic	26	26	0.0	0.0	0	-0.4	8
Lay out workers, metal and plastic	11	11	0.0	0.0	-1	-4.6	2
Plating and coating machine setters, operators, and tenders, metal and plastic	40	38	0.0	0.0	-2	-4.0	9
Tool grinders, filers, and sharpeners	21	19	0.0	0.0	-2	-7.7	7
Metal workers and plastic workers, all other	55	47	0.0	0.0	-7	-13.6	13
Printing occupations	413	405	0.3	0.2	-8	-1.9	106
Bookbinders and bindery workers	81	73	0.1	0.0	-8	-9.9	22
Bindery workers	74	66	0.1	0.0	-8	-10.4	20
Bookbinders	7	7	0.0	0.0	0	-4.5	2
Printers	332	332	0.2	0.2	0	0.1	84
Job printers	63	64	0.0	0.0	1	1.8	16
Prepress technicians and workers	78	71	0.1	0.0	-7	-8.4	18
Printing machine operators	191	197	0.1	0.1	6	2.9	50
Textile, apparel, and furnishings occupations	929	768	0.6	0.5	-161	-17.3	214
Laundry and dry cleaning	235	265	0.2	0.2	30	12.7	94
Pressers, textile, garment, and related materials	82	84	0.1	0.1	2	2.9	15
Sewing machine operators	256	163	0.2	0.1	-93	-36.5	32
Shoe and leather	15	12	0.0	0.0	-3	-19.4	4
Shoe and leather workers and repairers	10	9	0.0	0.0	-2	-16.0	3
Shoe machine operators and tenders	5	3	0.0	0.0	-1	-27.3	1
Tailors, dressmakers, and sewers	85	79	0.1	0.0	-6	-7.0	15
Sewers, hand	31	25	0.0	0.0	-6	-19.7	5
Tailors, dressmakers, and custom sewers	54	54	0.0	0.0	0	0.3	10
Textile machine setters, operators, and tenders	148	81	0.1	0.0	-66	-45.0	26
Textile bleaching and dyeing machine operators and tenders	21	12	0.0	0.0	-10	-45.3	5
Textile cutting machine operators, operators, and tenders	28	21	0.0	0.0	-7	-25.0	6
Textile knitting and weaving machine setters, operators, and tenders	46	20	0.0	0.0	-26	-56.2	5
Textile winding, twisting, and drawing out machine setters, operators, and tenders	53	29	0.0	0.0	-24	-45.5	10
Miscellaneous textile, apparel, and furnishings workers	109	84	0.1	0.1	-24	-22.4	28
Extruding and forming machine setters, operators, and tenders, synthetic or glass fibers	23	17	0.0	0.0	-6	-25.3	4
Fabric and apparel patternmakers	9	6	0.0	0.0	-3	-30.5	4
Upholsterers	53	44	0.0	0.0	-9	-16.5	14
Textile, apparel, and furnishings workers, all other	23	16	0.0	0.0	-7	-29.8	6
Woodworkers	364	345	0.2	0.2	-18	-5.0	100
Cabinetmakers and bench carpenters	148	154	0.1	0.1	6	4.1	43
Furniture finishers	34	30	0.0	0.0	-5	-13.3	7
Model makers and patternmakers, wood	6	6	0.0	0.0	0	6.5	2
Model makers, wood	3	4	0.0	0.0	1	9.0	1
Patternmakers, wood	3	3	0.0	0.0	0	3.3	1
Woodworking machine setters, operators, and tenders	150	133	0.1	0.1	-17	-11.1	40
Sawing machine setters, operators, and tenders, wood	58	51	0.0	0.0	-7	-11.3	16
Woodworking machine setters, operators, and tenders, except sawing	92	82	0.1	0.0	-10	-11.0	24

Note: Data may not sum to totals or 100 percent due to rounding.

[1]Total job openings represent the sum of employment increases and net replacements. If employment change is negative, job openings due to growth are zero and total job openings equal net replacements.

Table 4-7. Employment, by Occupation, 2004 and Projected 2014—*Continued*

(Numbers in thousands, percent.)

Occupation	Employment				Change, 2004–2014		Total job openings due to growth and net replacements, 2004–2014[1]
	Number		Percent distribution		Number	Percent	
	2004	2014	2004	2014			
Production—*Continued*							
Woodworkers, all other	26	23	0.0	0.0	-4	-13.9	8
Plant and system operators	320	324	0.2	0.2	4	1.4	113
Power plant operators, distributors, and dispatchers	47	46	0.0	0.0	-1	-0.4	13
Nuclear power reactor operators	4	4	0.0	0.0	0	-0.5	1
Power distributors and dispatchers	8	8	0.0	0.0	0	0.0	2
Power plant operators	34	34	0.0	0.0	0	-0.4	9
Stationary engineers and boiler operators	50	52	0.0	0.0	2	3.4	11
Water and liquid waste treatment plant and system operators	94	110	0.1	0.1	15	16.2	48
Miscellaneous plant and system operators	129	117	0.1	0.1	-12	-9.6	42
Chemical plant and system operators	60	49	0.0	0.0	-11	-17.7	19
Gas plant operators	11	12	0.0	0.0	1	7.7	4
Petroleum pump system operators, refinery operators, and gaugers	43	39	0.0	0.0	-4	-8.6	13
Plant and system operators, all other	15	16	0.0	0.0	1	7.1	6
Other production	2 909	2 920	2.0	1.8	10	0.4	775
Chemical processing machine setters, operators, and tenders	87	85	0.1	0.1	-2	-1.8	28
Chemical equipment operators and tenders	49	47	0.0	0.0	-2	-4.5	16
Separating, filtering, clarifying, precipitating, and still machine setters, operators, and tenders	38	38	0.0	0.0	1	1.6	13
Crushing, grinding, polishing, mixing, and blending	208	207	0.1	0.1	-1	-0.6	57
Crushing, grinding, and polishing machine setters, operators, and tenders	43	43	0.0	0.0	0	0.8	12
Grinding and polishing workers, hand	45	41	0.0	0.0	-4	-8.7	12
Mixing and blending machine setters, operators, and tenders	120	122	0.1	0.1	2	2.0	34
Cutting	104	103	0.1	0.1	-1	-1.3	22
Cutters and trimmers, hand	29	30	0.0	0.0	1	2.4	7
Cutting and slicing machine setters, operators, and tenders	75	73	0.1	0.0	-2	-2.7	16
Extruding, forming, pressing, and compacting machine setters, operators, and tenders	74	72	0.1	0.0	-2	-2.2	20
Furnace, kiln, oven, drier, and kettle operators and tenders	30	29	0.0	0.0	-1	-4.2	7
Inspectors, testers, sorters, samplers, and weighers	508	494	0.3	0.3	-13	-2.6	116
Jewelers and precious stone and metal	42	42	0.0	0.0	0	0.0	8
Medical, dental, and ophthalmic laboratory technicians	87	94	0.1	0.1	7	8.4	26
Dental laboratory technicians	50	54	0.0	0.0	4	7.6	15
Medical appliance technicians	11	13	0.0	0.0	2	13.2	4
Ophthalmic laboratory technicians	25	27	0.0	0.0	2	7.8	7
Packaging and filling machine operators and tenders	412	422	0.3	0.3	9	2.3	91
Painting workers	186	192	0.1	0.1	6	3.4	58
Coating, painting, and spraying machine setters, operators, and tenders	103	100	0.1	0.1	-3	-3.4	27
Painters, transportation equipment	53	61	0.0	0.0	7	14.1	21
Painting, coating, and decorating workers	29	31	0.0	0.0	2	7.9	10
Photographic process workers and processing machine operators	86	66	0.1	0.0	-20	-23.6	21
Photographic process workers	32	28	0.0	0.0	-4	-11.4	8
Photographic processing machine operators	54	38	0.0	0.0	-17	-30.7	13
Semiconductor processors	45	42	0.0	0.0	-3	-7.5	10
Miscellaneous production	1 040	1 072	0.7	0.7	31	3.0	310
Cementing and gluing machine operators and tenders	25	25	0.0	0.0	0	1.9	7
Cleaning, washing, and metal pickling equipment operators, and tenders	18	18	0.0	0.0	0	1.0	5
Cooling and freezing equipment operators and tenders	9	9	0.0	0.0	0	0.8	2
Etchers and engravers	12	12	0.0	0.0	0	2.1	3
Molders, shapers, and casters, except metal and plastic	47	43	0.0	0.0	-3	-7.0	11
Paper goods machine setters, operators, and tenders	111	113	0.1	0.1	3	2.4	26
Tire builders	18	15	0.0	0.0	-3	-16.6	4
Helpers—production	484	522	0.3	0.3	38	7.9	174
Production workers, all other	319	315	0.2	0.2	-4	-1.3	76
Transportation and Material Moving	10 098	11 214	6.9	6.8	1 116	11.1	3 449
Supervisors of transportation and material moving workers	408	458	0.3	0.3	50	12.3	146
Aircraft cargo handling supervisors	8	9	0.0	0.0	1	17.3	3
First-line supervisors/managers of helpers, laborers, and material movers, hand	173	187	0.1	0.1	14	8.1	55
First-line supervisors/managers of transportation and material moving machine and vehicle operators	228	262	0.2	0.2	35	15.3	88
Air transportation	135	157	0.1	0.1	22	16.5	58
Aircraft pilots and flight engineers	106	124	0.1	0.1	18	17.2	46
Airline pilots, copilots, and flight engineers	84	98	0.1	0.1	14	17.2	37
Commercial pilots	22	26	0.0	0.0	4	16.8	10
Air traffic controllers and airfield operations specialists	29	34	0.0	0.0	4	14.4	12
Air traffic controllers	24	28	0.0	0.0	3	14.3	10
Airfield operations specialists	5	6	0.0	0.0	1	15.0	2
Motor vehicle operators	4 182	4 810	2.9	2.9	629	15.0	1 256
Ambulance drivers and attendants, except emergency medical technicians	20	26	0.0	0.0	6	28.0	8
Bus drivers	653	757	0.4	0.5	104	15.9	246
Bus drivers, transit and intercity	190	231	0.1	0.1	41	21.7	83
Bus drivers, school	463	526	0.3	0.3	63	13.6	164
Driver/sales workers and truck drivers	3 232	3 681	2.2	2.2	449	13.9	902
Driver/sales workers	451	513	0.3	0.3	62	13.8	136
Truck drivers, heavy and tractor trailer	1 738	1 962	1.2	1.2	223	12.9	507
Truck drivers, light or delivery services	1 042	1 206	0.7	0.7	164	15.7	259
Taxi drivers and chauffeurs	188	235	0.1	0.1	47	24.8	64
Motor vehicle operators, all other	88	111	0.1	0.1	23	25.7	35

Note: Data may not sum to totals or 100 percent due to rounding.

[1]Total job openings represent the sum of employment increases and net replacements. If employment change is negative, job openings due to growth are zero and total job openings equal net replacements.

Table 4-7. Employment, by Occupation, 2004 and Projected 2014—*Continued*

(Numbers in thousands, percent.)

Occupation	Employment				Change, 2004–2014		Total job openings due to growth and net replacements, 2004–2014[1]
	Number		Percent distribution		Number	Percent	
	2004	2014	2004	2014			
Transportation and Material Moving—*Continued*							
Rail transportation	112	111	0.1	0.1	-1	-1.1	39
Locomotive engineers and operators	40	39	0.0	0.0	-1	-2.5	13
Railroad brake, signal, and switch operators	17	11	0.0	0.0	-7	-38.5	2
Railroad conductors and yardmasters	38	45	0.0	0.0	8	20.3	18
Subway and streetcar operators	9	10	0.0	0.0	1	13.7	4
Rail transportation workers, all other	8	6	0.0	0.0	-2	-30.8	2
Water transportation	72	77	0.0	0.0	4	6.2	29
Sailors and marine oilers	28	30	0.0	0.0	1	5.2	11
Ship and boat captains and operators	32	34	0.0	0.0	2	4.7	11
Captains, mates, and pilots of water vessels	29	30	0.0	0.0	1	4.8	10
Motorboat operators	3	4	0.0	0.0	1	4.4	1
Ship engineers	12	13	0.0	0.0	1	12.7	7
Other transportation	301	309	0.2	0.2	8	2.5	120
Bridge and lock tenders	4	4	0.0	0.0	0	7.2	1
Parking lot attendants	122	111	0.1	0.1	-11	-8.7	36
Service station attendants	91	98	0.1	0.1	7	7.5	48
Traffic technicians	6	7	0.0	0.0	1	14.1	3
Transportation inspectors	26	29	0.0	0.0	3	11.4	9
Transportation workers, all other	52	60	0.0	0.0	7	13.9	23
Material moving	4 887	5 292	3.4	3.2	405	8.3	1 801
Conveyor operators and tenders	53	58	0.0	0.0	4	7.7	19
Crane and tower operators	44	48	0.0	0.0	4	8.2	13
Dredge, excavating, and loading machine operators	92	99	0.1	0.1	7	7.1	32
Dredge operators	3	3	0.0	0.0	0	3.7	1
Excavating and loading machine and dragline operators	86	92	0.1	0.1	7	8.0	30
Loading machine operators, underground mining	4	4	0.0	0.0	0	-8.3	1
Hoist and winch operators	6	6	0.0	0.0	0	7.0	2
Industrial truck and tractor operators	635	685	0.4	0.4	50	7.9	170
Laborers and material movers, hand	3 803	4 142	2.6	2.5	339	8.9	1 485
Cleaners of vehicles and equipment	347	376	0.2	0.2	29	8.3	150
Laborers and freight, stock, and material movers hand	2 430	2 678	1.7	1.6	248	10.2	1 042
Machine feeders and offbearers	148	122	0.1	0.1	-27	-18.0	40
Packers and packagers, hand	877	966	0.6	0.6	89	10.1	253
Pumping station operators	27	21	0.0	0.0	-6	-22.6	6
Gas compressor and gas pumping station operators	5	4	0.0	0.0	-1	-21.3	1
Pump operators, except wellhead pumpers	11	8	0.0	0.0	-2	-22.2	2
Wellhead pumpers	11	8	0.0	0.0	-3	-23.6	3
Refuse and recyclable material collectors	149	163	0.1	0.1	13	8.9	52
Shuttle car operators	3	2	0.0	0.0	-1	-42.4	1
Tank car, truck, and ship loaders	17	15	0.0	0.0	-2	-11.0	5
Material moving workers, all other	58	55	0.0	0.0	-3	-5.3	16

Note: Data may not sum to totals or 100 percent due to rounding.

[1]Total job openings represent the sum of employment increases and net replacements. If employment change is negative, job openings due to growth are zero and total job openings equal net replacements.

CHAPTER FIVE

PRODUCTIVITY AND COSTS

PRODUCTIVITY AND COSTS

HIGHLIGHTS

This chapter covers two kinds of productivity measures produced by the Bureau of Labor Statistics (BLS): output per hour (or labor productivity) and multifactor productivity. Multifactor productivity is designed to ensure the joint influence of technological change, efficiency improvements, returns to scale, and other factors on economic growth. For some measures, there is a lag in the available data. Industry data are based on the North American Industry Classification System (NAICS).

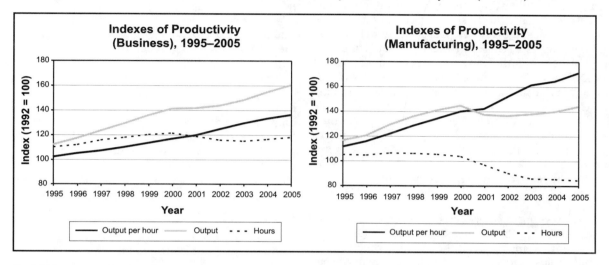

In 2005, output in the business sector rose 3.8 percent, a slower rate than in 2004. Hours also rose, leading to a slower increase in output per hour (2.3 percent, compared to 3.1 percent in 2004). In manufacturing, output rose more quickly than it did during the previous year and hours continued the downward trend that began in 1998. This resulted in a substantial rise of 4.1 percent in output per hour. (See Table 5-1.)

OTHER HIGHLIGHTS

- In 2005, unit labor costs in the business sector rose almost 3 times as fast as it did during the previous year (2.0 percent versus 0.7 percent). In manufacturing, unit labor costs increased 0.5 percent after increasing just 0.1 percent during the previous year. (See Table 5-1.)

- Wholesale trade had only a small increase in output per hour, as output increased slightly faster than hours from 2004 to 2005. (See Table 5-3.)

- Retail trade had a 3.4 percent increase in output per hour, as output increased at a much faster rate than hours from 2004 to 2005. (See Table 5-3.)

- The increase in multifactor productivity in private nonfarm business was higher in 2004 than in the previous year as a result of a larger increase in output per unit of capital as well as an increase in output per hour. (See Table 5-4.)

NOTES AND DEFINITIONS

Concepts and Definitions

Output per hour for the business, nonfarm business, and manufacturing sectors describes the relationship between real output and the labor time involved in production. The output measures for the business sectors and nonfinancial corporations are based on series prepared by the Bureau of Economic Analysis (BEA) of the U.S. Department of Commerce as part of the national income and product accounts (NIPAs). The Bureau of Labor Statistics (BLS) derives manufacturing output indexes by combining data from the Census Bureau, BEA, and the Federal Reserve Board. All of the output measures are chain-type annual-weighted indexes. This means that the relative prices (weights) used to combine output changes into an aggregate output measure are revised annually, thus minimizing the bias that arises from using fixed weights over long periods of time.

Business sector output is constructed by excluding the following outputs from gross domestic product (GDP): general government, nonprofit institutions, paid employees of private households, and the rental value of owner-occupied dwellings. Corresponding exclusions are also made in labor inputs. These activities are excluded because theoretical or practical difficulties make it impossible to use them as a basis for the computation of meaningful productivity measures. Business output accounted for about 78 percent of GDP and nonfarm business output accounted for about 77 percent of GDP in 2000. Manufacturing indexes are constructed by deflating current-dollar industry value of production data from the Census Bureau with deflators from BLS. These deflators are based on data from the BLS producer price program and other sources. To avoid duplication, intrasector transactions are removed when industry shipments are aggregated.

Productivity measures show the changes from period to period in the amount of goods and services produced per hour. Although these measures relate output to hours of persons engaged in a sector, they do not measure the specific contributions of labor, capital, or any other factor of production. Rather, they reflect the joint effects of many influences, including changes in technology, capital, economies of scale, utilization of capacity, the substitution of capital or intermediates for labor, the organization of production, managerial skill, and the characteristics and effort of the work force.

Labor input measures are based mainly on the monthly BLS survey of nonagricultural establishments. Measures of employment and average weekly hours paid for employees of these establishments are drawn from this survey. Weekly hours paid are adjusted to hours at work using information from the National Compensation Survey program for 2000 onward and the annual Hours at Work Survey for years prior to 2000. (The Hours at Work

Survey was terminated in 2000.) Supplementary information for farm workers, the self-employed, and unpaid family workers is obtained from the Current Population Survey, the monthly survey of households conducted by the Census Bureau for BLS.

The *indexes of hourly compensation* are based mainly on the BLS hours data, discussed above, and employee compensation data from the NIPAs. Compensation includes wages and salaries and supplemental payments such as employer contributions to Social Security and private health and pension funds. The all persons' compensation data include estimates of proprietors' salaries and contributions for supplementary benefits. Real compensation per hour is derived by adjusting the compensation data with the Consumer Price Index Research Series Using Current Methods (CPI-U-RS) in order to reflect changes in purchasing power. (See Chapter 7 for more information on the CPI-U-RS.)

The *indexes of unit labor costs* are computed by dividing compensation per hour by output per hour.

Nonlabor payments are calculated by subtracting total compensation from current dollar output and thus include profits, depreciation, interest, and indirect taxes.

The *implicit deflator* reflects changes in all of the costs of production and distribution (unit labor costs plus unit nonlabor payments). To construct the implicit price deflator, the current-dollar measure of output in a sector is divided by the real output series.

Output Per Hour and Related Series in Selected Industries

The BLS industry productivity program produces annual indexes of labor productivity, labor compensation, and unit labor costs for selected 4-, 5-, and 6-digit North American Industry Classification System (NAICS) industries. These data series cover 60 percent of employment in the private nonfarm business sector and 100 percent of employment in the manufacturing, retail trade, and wholesale trade sectors. The data sources used in the industry measures differ from those used in the productivity and cost measures for the major sectors.

Output per hour indexes are obtained by dividing an output index by an index of aggregate hours. Although the measures relate output to one input (labor time), they do not measure the specific contribution of labor or any other factor of production. Rather, they reflect the joint effect of a number of interrelated influences, such as changes in technology, capital investment per worker, and capacity utilization. Caution is necessary when analyzing year-to-year changes in output per hour; the annual changes can be irregular and are not necessarily indicative of long-term trends. Conversely, long-term trends are not necessarily applicable to any one year or period in the future.

An *output index* for a particular industry is calculated using the Tornqvist index formula that aggregates the growth rates of the industry products between two periods of time, with weights based on the products' shares in industry value of production. The weight for each product equals its average value share in the two periods. The formula yields the ratio of output in a given period to output in the previous period. The ratios for successive years must be chained together to form a time series. The quantities of products used in the output index are measured with either deflated values of production or actual quantities.

Indexes of labor input are employee hours indexes or all person hours indexes. In manufacturing industries, employee hours are used. In nonmanufacturing industries where self-employed workers play a significant role, all person hours are used. For most industries, the hours series are based on hours paid. Total hours are calculated by multiplying the number of workers by average weekly hours. Employee hours are treated as homogenous and additive, with no distinction made between the hours worked by different groups. Annual indexes are developed by dividing the aggregate hours for each year by the base period aggregate.

Indexes of unit labor costs are calculated as the ratio of total labor compensation to real output, or equivalently as the ratio of hourly compensation to labor productivity (output per hour). Unit labor costs measure the cost of labor input required to produce one unit of output.

Indexes of total compensation measure the change in the total costs to the employer of securing labor. Compensation is defined as payroll plus supplemental payments. Payroll includes salaries, wages, commissions, dismissal pay, bonuses, vacation and sick-leave pay, and compensation-in-kind. Supplemental payments are divided into legally required expenditures and payments for voluntary programs. The legally required expenditures include employers' contributions to Social Security, unemployment insurance taxes, and workers' compensation. Payments for voluntary programs include all programs not specifically required by legislation, such as the employer portion of private health insurance and pension plans.

Multifactor Productivity

BLS calculates the annual growth of multifactor productivity for the U.S. private business sector. This measure is generally released about 14 months after the end of the measured, or target, year. The lag occurs because the process of calculating multifactor productivity requires detailed data from many sources. BLS uses a simplified methodology to make preliminary estimates of private business sector multifactor productivity changes available within a few months after the end of target year.

Multifactor productivity measures refer to the ratio of an output index to an index of combined labor and capital services inputs. These measures are produced for the private business and private nonfarm business sectors for which multifactor productivity indexes are prepared exclude government enterprises.

Multifactor productivity growth reflects the amount of output growth that cannot be accounted for by the growth of weighted labor and capital inputs. The weights are associated cost shares. Labor's share is the ratio of compensation to current-dollar output. Capital's share is equal to the ratio of capital cost to current-dollar output. As with the output measures, the multifactor productivity growth weights are updated annually.

Capital services measure the services derived from the stock of physical assets and software. Physical assets included are fixed business equipment, structures, inventories, and land. Structures include nonresidential structures and residential capital that is rented out by profit-making firms or persons. Software includes prepackaged, custom, and own-account software. Financial assets are excluded, as are owner-occupied residential structures. Data on investments in physical assets and gross product originating by industry, which are used in measuring the rental prices, are obtained from BEA.

Labor input in private business and private nonfarm business is obtained by weighting the hours worked by all persons, classified by education, work experience, gender, and their shares of labor compensation. Additional information concerning data sources and methods of measuring labor composition can be found in BLS Bulletin 2426 (December 1993), "Labor Composition and U.S. Productivity Growth, 1948-90."

The *manufacturing multifactor productivity index* is derived by dividing an output index by a weighted index of combined hours, capital services, energy, materials, and purchased business services. Weights (shares of total costs) are updated annually. The labor hours for the manufacturing measure are directly added and thus do not include the effect of changing labor composition, unlike those used for business multifactor productivity. The manufacturing sector coverage is the same in both the multifactor and the labor productivity series.

Sources of Additional Information

Productivity concepts and methodology are described in Chapters 10 and 11 of the *BLS Handbook of Methods*. More information on productivity can be found in BLS news release USDL 06-1555, "Productivity and Costs." Additional information on multifactor productivity can be found in the June 2005 edition of the *Monthly Labor Review*. All of these resources can be found on the BLS Web site at <http://www.bls.gov>.

Table 5-1. Indexes of Productivity and Related Data, 1947–2005

(1992 = 100.)

Year	Business											
	Output per hour	Output	Hours	Hourly compensation	Real hourly compensation	Unit labor costs	Unit nonlabor payments	Implicit price deflator	Employment	Output per person	Compensation in current dollars	Nonlabor payments in current dollars
1947	32.2	20.4	63.4	7.0	40.7	21.8	18.6	20.6	55.7	36.7	4.4	3.8
1948	33.7	21.5	63.8	7.6	40.9	22.6	20.6	21.8	56.3	38.2	4.9	4.4
1949	34.5	21.3	61.8	7.7	42.0	22.4	20.4	21.6	55.1	38.7	4.8	4.4
1950	37.3	23.4	62.6	8.3	44.4	22.1	21.5	21.9	55.6	42.0	5.2	5.0
1951	38.5	24.9	64.6	9.0	45.1	23.5	23.7	23.6	57.1	43.6	5.8	5.9
1952	39.6	25.7	64.8	9.6	46.9	24.2	23.2	23.8	57.3	44.8	6.2	5.9
1953	41.0	26.9	65.6	10.2	49.5	24.9	22.6	24.0	58.1	46.3	6.7	6.1
1954	41.9	26.6	63.4	10.5	50.7	25.2	22.5	24.2	56.7	46.8	6.7	6.0
1955	43.6	28.7	65.8	10.8	52.2	24.8	24.0	24.5	58.3	49.2	7.1	6.9
1956	43.6	29.1	66.8	11.5	54.8	26.4	23.5	25.3	59.5	49.0	7.7	6.8
1957	45.0	29.6	65.8	12.3	56.5	27.2	24.2	26.1	59.4	49.9	8.1	7.2
1958	46.3	29.1	62.9	12.8	57.4	27.7	24.7	26.6	57.1	50.9	8.1	7.2
1959	48.0	31.4	65.5	13.3	59.4	27.8	25.2	26.8	58.9	53.4	8.7	7.9
1960	48.9	32.0	65.6	13.9	60.8	28.4	24.9	27.1	59.2	54.1	9.1	8.0
1961	50.6	32.7	64.6	14.4	62.5	28.5	25.3	27.3	58.6	55.8	9.3	8.3
1962	52.9	34.8	65.8	15.1	64.6	28.5	26.1	27.6	59.3	58.6	9.9	9.1
1963	55.0	36.4	66.2	15.6	66.1	28.4	26.6	27.7	59.6	61.0	10.3	9.7
1964	56.8	38.7	68.1	16.2	67.7	28.5	27.3	28.1	60.8	63.7	11.0	10.6
1965	58.8	41.4	70.4	16.8	69.1	28.6	28.4	28.5	62.5	66.3	11.8	11.8
1966	61.2	44.2	72.3	17.9	71.7	29.3	29.0	29.2	64.3	68.8	13.0	12.8
1967	62.5	45.1	72.1	19.0	73.5	30.3	29.5	30.0	65.2	69.1	13.7	13.3
1968	64.7	47.3	73.2	20.5	76.2	31.7	30.4	31.2	66.5	71.2	15.0	14.4
1969	65.0	48.8	75.0	21.9	77.3	33.7	30.8	32.6	68.6	71.1	16.4	15.0
1970	66.3	48.7	73.5	23.6	78.8	35.6	31.5	34.1	68.4	71.3	17.4	15.3
1971	69.0	50.6	73.3	25.1	80.2	36.3	34.1	35.5	68.5	73.9	18.4	17.3
1972	71.2	53.9	75.6	26.7	82.6	37.4	35.7	36.8	70.5	76.4	20.2	19.2
1973	73.4	57.6	78.5	28.9	84.3	39.4	37.5	38.7	73.5	78.4	22.7	21.6
1974	72.3	56.8	78.7	31.7	83.3	43.9	40.0	42.4	74.7	76.1	24.9	22.7
1975	74.8	56.3	75.3	34.9	84.1	46.7	46.3	46.6	72.4	77.7	26.3	26.1
1976	77.1	60.0	77.8	38.0	86.4	49.2	48.7	49.0	74.7	80.3	29.5	29.2
1977	78.5	63.3	80.7	41.0	87.6	52.2	51.5	52.0	77.9	81.3	33.1	32.6
1978	79.3	67.3	84.9	44.5	89.1	56.2	54.8	55.6	82.2	81.9	37.8	36.9
1979	79.3	69.6	87.7	48.9	89.3	61.6	58.2	60.4	85.4	81.5	42.9	40.5
1980	79.2	68.8	87.0	54.1	89.1	68.4	61.3	65.8	85.6	80.4	47.1	42.2
1981	80.8	70.7	87.6	59.3	89.3	73.5	69.1	71.8	86.4	81.8	52.0	48.9
1982	80.1	68.6	85.6	63.6	90.4	79.4	70.1	75.9	85.0	80.7	54.4	48.1
1983	83.0	72.3	87.1	66.3	90.3	79.8	76.3	78.5	85.8	84.3	57.7	55.2
1984	85.2	78.6	92.2	69.1	90.7	81.1	80.2	80.8	90.1	87.2	63.7	63.0
1985	87.1	82.2	94.3	72.5	92.0	83.2	82.0	82.7	92.3	89.0	68.4	67.4
1986	89.7	85.3	95.1	76.1	94.9	84.9	82.6	84.1	93.9	90.8	72.4	70.4
1987	90.1	88.3	97.9	79.0	95.2	87.6	83.1	85.9	96.4	91.5	77.3	73.3
1988	91.5	92.1	100.6	83.0	96.5	90.7	85.1	88.6	99.3	92.7	83.5	78.4
1989	92.4	95.4	103.3	85.2	95.0	92.2	91.3	91.9	101.5	94.0	88.0	87.1
1990	94.4	96.9	102.7	90.6	96.2	96.0	93.7	95.1	102.2	94.8	93.0	90.8
1991	95.9	96.1	100.2	95.1	97.4	99.1	96.7	98.2	100.6	95.6	95.3	92.9
1992	100.0	100.0	100.0	100.0	100.0	100.0	100.0	100.0	100.0	100.0	100.0	100.0
1993	100.4	103.1	102.7	102.2	99.7	101.8	102.6	102.1	102.1	101.0	105.0	105.8
1994	101.3	108.2	106.8	103.6	99.0	102.3	106.7	103.9	105.6	102.5	110.7	115.5
1995	101.5	111.4	109.7	105.8	98.7	104.2	108.3	105.7	108.5	102.6	116.1	120.6
1996	104.5	116.5	111.5	109.5	99.4	104.8	111.9	107.4	110.9	105.0	122.0	130.4
1997	106.5	122.7	115.2	113.0	100.5	106.1	113.8	109.0	113.9	107.7	130.2	139.7
1998	109.5	128.6	117.5	119.9	105.2	109.5	110.0	109.7	116.2	110.7	140.8	141.4
1999	112.8	135.2	119.8	125.8	108.0	111.5	109.4	110.7	118.1	114.5	150.7	147.9
2000	116.1	140.5	121.0	134.7	112.0	116.0	107.2	112.7	120.1	117.0	163.0	150.7
2001	119.1	141.0	118.4	140.4	113.5	117.9	110.0	114.9	119.0	118.4	166.1	155.0
2002	124.0	143.1	115.4	145.4	115.7	117.3	114.1	116.1	116.3	123.0	167.8	163.3
2003	128.7	147.5	114.6	151.2	117.7	117.5	118.3	117.8	116.0	127.1	173.4	174.5
2004	132.7	154.0	116.1	157.0	119.0	118.3	125.1	120.8	117.6	131.0	182.2	192.7
2005	135.7	159.8	117.7	163.8	120.2	120.7	130.3	124.3	119.5	133.7	192.9	208.2

Table 5-1. Indexes of Productivity and Related Data, 1947–2005—*Continued*

(1992 = 100.)

Year	Nonfarm business											
	Output per hour	Output	Hours	Hourly compensation	Real hourly compensation	Unit labor costs	Unit nonlabor payments	Implicit price deflator	Employment	Output per person	Compensation in current dollars	Nonlabor payments in current dollars
1947	37.0	20.1	54.2	7.5	43.3	20.2	17.8	19.3	47.1	42.5	4.0	3.6
1948	38.0	20.9	55.1	8.1	43.6	21.3	19.4	20.6	48.2	43.5	4.5	4.1
1949	39.3	20.8	53.0	8.3	45.4	21.2	20.0	20.8	46.8	44.5	4.4	4.2
1950	41.9	22.9	54.7	8.8	47.5	21.1	20.8	21.0	47.9	47.8	4.8	4.8
1951	43.0	24.6	57.2	9.6	47.8	22.3	22.5	22.4	50.1	49.2	5.5	5.5
1952	43.8	25.3	57.9	10.1	49.5	23.1	22.3	22.8	50.7	50.0	5.9	5.6
1953	44.8	26.6	59.3	10.7	51.9	23.9	22.2	23.3	52.2	50.9	6.3	5.9
1954	45.6	26.1	57.3	11.0	53.1	24.2	22.3	23.5	50.8	51.5	6.3	5.8
1955	47.5	28.3	59.6	11.4	55.3	24.1	23.7	23.9	52.3	54.1	6.8	6.7
1956	47.2	28.8	61.1	12.1	57.8	25.8	23.1	24.8	53.8	53.5	7.4	6.6
1957	48.4	29.4	60.7	12.8	59.2	26.6	23.8	25.6	54.1	54.3	7.8	7.0
1958	49.4	28.7	58.2	13.4	59.8	27.0	24.1	26.0	52.2	55.1	7.8	6.9
1959	51.3	31.2	60.9	13.9	61.8	27.1	25.0	26.3	54.1	57.7	8.5	7.8
1960	51.9	31.8	61.2	14.5	63.3	27.9	24.3	26.6	54.7	58.1	8.9	7.7
1961	53.5	32.4	60.6	15.0	64.8	28.0	24.8	26.8	54.3	59.7	9.1	8.0
1962	55.9	34.6	61.9	15.6	66.7	27.8	25.8	27.1	55.3	62.6	9.6	8.9
1963	57.8	36.2	62.6	16.1	68.1	27.8	26.3	27.3	55.9	64.8	10.1	9.5
1964	59.6	38.7	64.9	16.6	69.3	27.9	27.2	27.6	57.3	67.5	10.8	10.5
1965	61.4	41.4	67.4	17.1	70.5	27.9	28.1	28.0	59.3	69.9	11.6	11.6
1966	63.6	44.4	69.8	18.2	72.6	28.6	28.7	28.6	61.6	72.0	12.7	12.7
1967	64.7	45.1	69.7	19.2	74.5	29.7	29.2	29.5	62.6	72.1	13.4	13.2
1968	66.9	47.5	71.0	20.7	77.1	31.0	30.2	30.7	64.1	74.1	14.7	14.4
1969	67.0	48.9	73.0	22.1	78.1	33.0	30.5	32.1	66.4	73.7	16.2	14.9
1970	68.0	48.9	71.9	23.7	79.2	34.9	31.2	33.5	66.4	73.6	17.0	15.2
1971	70.7	50.7	71.7	25.2	80.7	35.7	33.8	35.0	66.6	76.1	18.1	17.1
1972	73.1	54.1	74.0	26.9	83.2	36.8	34.9	36.1	68.6	78.8	19.9	18.9
1973	75.3	58.0	77.0	29.1	84.7	38.6	35.3	37.4	71.7	81.0	22.4	20.5
1974	74.2	57.3	77.2	31.9	83.8	43.0	38.1	41.2	72.8	78.6	24.6	21.8
1975	76.2	56.3	73.9	35.1	84.5	46.0	44.9	45.6	70.7	79.6	25.9	25.3
1976	78.7	60.2	76.5	38.1	86.6	48.3	47.8	48.1	73.2	82.3	29.1	28.8
1977	80.0	63.6	79.5	41.2	88.0	51.5	50.7	51.2	76.5	83.1	32.7	32.3
1978	81.0	67.8	83.7	44.8	89.6	55.3	53.4	54.6	80.7	84.0	37.5	36.2
1979	80.7	70.0	86.6	49.1	89.7	60.8	56.5	59.2	84.2	83.1	42.5	39.5
1980	80.6	69.2	85.9	54.4	89.5	67.5	60.4	64.9	84.4	82.0	46.7	41.8
1981	81.7	70.7	86.6	59.7	89.8	73.1	67.7	71.1	85.4	82.8	51.7	47.9
1982	80.8	68.4	84.7	63.9	90.8	79.1	69.3	75.5	84.0	81.4	54.1	47.4
1983	84.5	72.9	86.3	66.6	90.9	78.9	76.1	77.9	84.9	85.9	57.5	55.4
1984	86.1	78.9	91.6	69.5	91.1	80.7	79.2	80.1	89.4	88.2	63.6	62.4
1985	87.5	82.2	94.0	72.6	92.2	83.0	81.5	82.5	92.0	89.4	68.2	67.0
1986	90.2	85.4	94.7	76.4	95.2	84.7	82.4	83.9	93.6	91.2	72.3	70.3
1987	90.6	88.4	97.6	79.2	95.5	87.4	82.8	85.7	96.2	91.9	77.3	73.2
1988	92.1	92.4	100.4	83.1	96.7	90.2	85.0	88.3	99.3	93.1	83.4	78.6
1989	92.8	95.7	103.1	85.3	95.1	91.9	90.9	91.5	101.5	94.3	87.9	87.0
1990	94.5	97.1	102.7	90.4	96.1	95.7	93.5	94.9	102.2	95.0	92.9	90.8
1991	96.1	96.3	100.2	95.0	97.4	98.9	96.8	98.1	100.6	95.8	95.2	93.2
1992	100.0	100.0	100.0	100.0	100.0	100.0	100.0	100.0	100.0	100.0	100.0	100.0
1993	100.4	103.4	102.9	102.0	99.5	101.6	103.1	102.1	102.4	101.0	105.0	106.5
1994	101.5	108.3	106.6	103.7	99.1	102.1	107.3	104.0	105.7	102.5	110.6	116.1
1995	102.0	111.8	109.6	105.9	98.8	103.8	109.3	105.8	108.7	102.9	116.0	122.2
1996	104.7	116.8	111.5	109.4	99.4	104.5	112.1	107.3	111.2	105.0	122.0	130.9
1997	106.4	122.8	115.4	112.8	100.3	106.0	114.5	109.1	114.3	107.4	130.2	140.7
1998	109.4	128.9	117.9	119.6	104.9	109.3	111.0	109.9	116.9	110.3	140.9	143.1
1999	112.5	135.6	120.5	125.2	107.5	111.3	110.9	111.1	119.0	113.9	150.8	150.4
2000	115.7	140.8	121.7	134.2	111.5	116.0	108.7	113.3	121.1	116.3	163.3	153.1
2001	118.6	141.3	119.2	139.5	112.8	117.7	111.6	115.4	120.2	117.6	166.3	157.7
2002	123.5	143.4	116.1	144.6	115.1	117.1	116.0	116.7	117.4	122.2	167.9	166.4
2003	128.0	147.8	115.4	150.4	117.1	117.5	119.6	118.3	117.2	126.1	173.7	176.8
2004	131.8	154.2	117.0	155.9	118.2	118.3	126.0	121.1	118.8	129.8	182.4	194.3
2005	134.9	160.0	118.7	162.7	119.3	120.7	132.2	124.9	120.7	132.6	193.1	211.5

Table 5-1. Indexes of Productivity and Related Data, 1947–2005—Continued

(1992 = 100.)

Year	Nonfinancial corporations												
	Output per hour	Output	Hours	Hourly compensation	Real hourly compensation	Unit labor costs	Unit nonlabor costs	Unit profits	Implicit price deflator	Employment	Output per person	Compensation in current dollars	Nonlabor payments in current dollars
1947	...	...	...	...	...	...	...	...	...	...	...	...	...
1948	...	...	...	...	...	...	...	...	...	...	...	...	...
1949	...	...	...	...	...	...	...	...	...	...	...	...	...
1950	...	...	...	...	...	...	...	...	...	...	...	...	...
1951	...	...	...	...	...	...	...	...	...	...	...	...	...
1952	...	...	...	...	...	...	...	...	...	...	...	...	...
1953	...	...	...	...	...	...	...	...	...	...	...	...	...
1954	...	...	...	...	...	...	...	...	...	...	...	...	...
1955	...	...	...	...	...	...	...	...	...	...	...	...	...
1956	...	...	...	...	...	...	...	...	...	...	...	...	...
1957	...	...	...	...	...	...	...	...	...	...	...	...	...
1958	52.8	25.4	48.0	15.0	67.2	28.4	23.5	47.2	28.9	43.6	58.2	7.2	7.6
1959	55.3	28.2	50.9	15.6	69.3	28.1	22.3	55.8	29.2	45.6	61.8	7.9	8.8
1960	56.2	29.1	51.7	16.2	70.8	28.8	23.3	50.2	29.4	46.6	62.4	8.4	8.9
1961	57.9	29.7	51.3	16.7	72.4	28.8	23.8	50.3	29.5	46.3	64.2	8.6	9.2
1962	60.4	32.2	53.3	17.4	74.4	28.7	23.4	54.5	29.7	47.8	67.3	9.3	10.2
1963	62.6	34.1	54.5	17.9	75.7	28.6	23.4	57.3	29.9	48.8	69.9	9.8	11.1
1964	63.6	36.5	57.4	18.2	76.2	28.7	23.3	59.7	30.1	50.6	72.1	10.5	12.1
1965	65.1	39.5	60.7	18.8	77.1	28.8	23.1	64.1	30.6	53.3	74.1	11.4	13.5
1966	66.2	42.3	63.9	19.8	79.2	29.9	23.3	63.6	31.3	56.3	75.2	12.7	14.4
1967	67.1	43.4	64.6	20.9	81.1	31.2	24.7	59.9	32.2	57.9	74.9	13.5	14.8
1968	69.5	46.1	66.4	22.5	83.8	32.4	26.2	60.0	33.4	59.9	76.9	14.9	16.3
1969	69.5	47.9	69.0	24.0	84.8	34.6	28.6	54.0	34.8	62.7	76.5	16.6	16.9
1970	69.8	47.4	67.9	25.7	85.9	36.9	32.2	44.4	36.4	62.8	75.5	17.5	16.8
1971	72.7	49.3	67.8	27.3	87.4	37.6	33.6	50.5	37.8	63.0	78.4	18.5	18.8
1972	74.2	53.1	71.6	28.8	89.2	38.8	33.9	54.1	39.0	66.1	80.3	20.6	20.9
1973	74.8	56.3	75.2	31.0	90.4	41.4	35.7	54.9	41.2	69.7	80.7	23.3	23.0
1974	73.3	55.3	75.5	33.9	89.2	46.3	41.1	48.4	45.2	71.1	77.8	25.6	23.8
1975	76.2	54.6	71.7	37.3	89.7	49.0	46.6	63.1	49.6	68.4	79.8	26.7	27.8
1976	78.6	58.9	75.0	40.3	91.8	51.3	46.4	71.4	51.9	71.5	82.4	30.2	31.3
1977	80.6	63.2	78.4	43.5	93.0	54.0	48.4	77.3	54.7	75.1	84.2	34.1	35.5
1978	81.7	67.4	82.5	47.6	95.1	58.2	51.2	79.1	58.4	79.3	84.9	39.2	39.5
1979	81.0	69.5	85.8	51.9	94.9	64.1	55.8	74.0	62.9	83.3	83.4	44.6	42.2
1980	80.8	68.8	85.2	57.2	94.1	70.8	64.9	66.9	69.0	83.6	82.3	48.7	45.0
1981	82.9	71.6	86.4	62.4	93.9	75.3	73.5	81.0	75.4	85.1	84.2	53.9	54.0
1982	83.1	69.9	84.1	66.5	94.4	80.0	81.3	75.2	79.9	83.1	84.0	55.9	55.7
1983	85.7	73.1	85.3	68.9	94.0	80.4	81.6	91.2	81.7	83.5	87.6	58.8	61.6
1984	87.8	79.7	90.8	71.9	94.3	81.9	81.3	107.6	84.1	88.4	90.1	65.3	70.4
1985	89.6	83.2	92.9	75.2	95.4	83.9	83.6	102.3	85.5	90.9	91.5	69.8	73.7
1986	91.4	85.2	93.2	78.9	98.3	86.3	86.3	90.2	86.6	92.2	92.3	73.5	74.4
1987	93.3	89.7	96.1	81.6	98.3	87.4	85.8	100.1	88.1	94.8	94.6	78.4	80.4
1988	95.7	94.9	99.1	84.9	98.7	88.7	86.8	111.6	90.3	97.9	96.9	84.2	88.6
1989	94.6	96.6	102.2	87.0	97.0	92.0	93.3	101.2	93.2	100.4	96.2	88.9	92.2
1990	95.4	97.8	102.5	91.1	96.8	95.5	97.3	96.9	96.1	102.2	95.8	93.4	95.1
1991	97.4	97.0	99.6	95.5	97.9	98.0	102.7	93.2	98.7	100.0	97.1	95.1	97.2
1992	100.0	100.0	100.0	100.0	100.0	100.0	100.0	100.0	100.0	100.0	100.0	100.0	100.0
1993	100.3	102.8	102.4	101.8	99.3	101.4	99.9	114.1	102.2	102.0	100.8	104.2	106.6
1994	102.2	109.2	106.8	103.5	98.9	101.3	100.8	131.7	103.9	105.7	103.2	110.6	119.1
1995	103.3	114.3	110.6	105.3	98.2	101.9	101.2	136.9	104.9	109.5	104.4	116.5	126.6
1996	107.1	120.6	112.6	108.5	98.5	101.3	100.0	150.0	105.3	112.3	107.4	122.1	136.7
1997	109.9	128.4	116.9	111.7	99.4	101.7	99.7	154.3	105.9	115.8	110.9	130.6	146.9
1998	113.7	135.8	119.5	118.3	103.8	104.1	99.5	137.0	105.9	118.7	114.5	141.4	148.8
1999	117.9	144.0	122.2	124.1	106.6	105.3	100.4	129.1	106.2	121.2	118.8	151.7	155.6
2000	122.4	151.5	123.7	133.0	110.5	108.6	104.2	108.7	107.5	123.6	122.6	164.5	159.7
2001	124.7	150.2	120.4	138.6	112.1	111.2	112.6	82.2	108.9	122.1	123.0	166.9	156.9
2002	129.7	151.5	116.7	143.6	114.3	110.7	110.8	98.0	109.6	118.6	127.7	167.7	162.7
2003	134.5	154.7	115.0	149.4	116.3	111.1	111.2	110.0	111.0	117.4	131.8	171.9	171.5
2004	139.4	162.5	116.6	154.3	116.9	110.7	109.2	138.8	112.8	118.8	136.7	179.8	190.4
2005	144.9	171.3	118.2	161.0	118.1	111.1	110.9	154.3	114.9	120.9	141.7	190.3	209.8

. . . = Not available.

Table 5-1. Indexes of Productivity and Related Data, 1947–2005—*Continued*

(1992 = 100.)

Year	Manufacturing											
	Output per hour	Output	Hours	Hourly compensation	Real hourly compensation	Unit labor costs	Unit nonlabor payments	Implicit price deflator	Employment	Output per person	Compensation in current dollars	Nonlabor payments in current dollars
1947	...	...	...	...	...	...	...	...	...	...	...	...
1948	...	...	...	...	...	...	...	...	...	...	...	...
1949	...	...	...	...	...	...	...	...	...	...	...	...
1950	...	...	...	...	...	...	...	...	...	...	...	...
1951	...	...	...	...	...	...	...	...	...	...	...	...
1952	...	...	...	...	...	...	...	...	...	...	...	...
1953	...	...	...	...	...	...	...	...	...	...	...	...
1954	...	...	...	...	...	...	...	...	...	...	...	...
1955	...	...	...	...	...	...	...	...	...	...	...	...
1956	...	...	...	...	...	...	...	...	...	...	...	...
1957	...	...	...	...	...	...	...	...	...	...	...	...
1958	...	...	...	...	...	...	...	...	...	...	...	...
1959	...	...	...	...	...	...	...	...	...	...	...	...
1960	...	...	...	...	...	...	...	...	...	...	...	...
1961	...	...	...	...	...	...	...	...	...	...	...	...
1962	...	...	...	...	...	...	...	...	...	...	...	...
1963	...	...	...	...	...	...	...	...	...	...	...	...
1964	...	...	...	...	...	...	...	...	...	...	...	...
1965	...	...	...	...	...	...	...	...	...	...	...	...
1966	...	...	...	...	...	...	...	...	...	...	...	...
1967	...	...	...	...	...	...	...	...	...	...	...	...
1968	...	...	...	...	...	...	...	...	...	...	...	...
1969	...	...	...	...	...	...	...	...	...	...	...	...
1970	...	...	...	...	...	...	...	...	...	...	...	...
1971	...	...	...	...	...	...	...	...	...	...	...	...
1972	...	...	...	...	...	...	...	...	...	...	...	...
1973	...	...	...	...	...	...	...	...	...	...	...	...
1974	...	...	...	...	...	...	...	...	...	...	...	...
1975	...	...	...	...	...	...	...	...	...	...	...	...
1976	...	...	...	...	...	...	...	...	...	...	...	...
1977	...	...	...	...	...	...	...	...	...	...	...	...
1978	...	...	...	...	...	...	...	...	...	...	...	...
1979	...	...	...	...	...	...	...	...	...	...	...	...
1980	...	...	...	...	...	...	...	...	...	...	...	...
1981	...	...	...	...	...	...	...	...	...	...	...	...
1982	...	...	...	...	...	...	...	...	...	...	...	...
1983	...	...	...	...	...	...	...	...	...	...	...	...
1984	...	...	...	...	...	...	...	...	...	...	...	...
1985	...	...	...	...	...	...	...	...	...	...	...	...
1986	...	...	...	...	...	...	...	...	...	...	...	...
1987	89.0	92.5	103.8	81.3	98.0	91.2	86.7	88.2	104.6	88.5	84.4	80.2
1988	91.0	97.4	107.0	84.1	97.8	92.4	90.2	90.9	106.4	91.5	90.0	87.8
1989	92.0	99.0	107.6	86.6	96.6	94.2	95.5	95.1	107.0	92.5	93.2	94.5
1990	93.9	98.6	105.0	90.5	96.1	96.3	99.5	98.4	105.4	93.6	95.0	98.1
1991	96.3	96.8	100.5	95.6	98.0	99.2	99.3	99.3	101.7	95.2	96.1	96.2
1992	100.0	100.0	100.0	100.0	100.0	100.0	100.0	100.0	100.0	100.0	100.0	100.0
1993	102.5	103.9	101.4	102.0	99.5	99.6	101.3	100.7	100.1	103.8	103.5	105.2
1994	106.1	110.0	103.8	105.3	100.6	99.3	102.8	101.6	101.5	108.5	109.2	113.1
1995	110.7	115.8	104.6	107.3	100.1	96.9	106.5	103.3	102.8	112.7	112.2	123.3
1996	115.0	119.8	104.2	109.3	99.3	95.1	108.3	103.9	102.6	116.7	113.9	129.7
1997	121.2	128.6	106.0	112.2	99.8	92.6	107.0	102.2	103.7	124.0	119.0	137.6
1998	127.9	135.3	105.7	118.8	104.2	92.8	102.0	99.0	104.6	129.3	125.6	137.9
1999	133.6	140.3	105.1	123.4	106.0	92.4	102.5	99.2	103.0	136.3	129.7	143.9
2000	139.4	144.1	103.4	134.7	112.0	96.7	104.7	102.0	102.5	140.6	139.3	150.8
2001	141.5	136.8	96.6	137.9	111.5	97.4	103.1	101.3	97.8	139.9	133.2	141.1
2002	151.4	135.9	89.8	147.8	117.7	97.6	100.8	99.7	90.6	150.0	132.7	137.0
2003	160.8	137.3	85.4	158.2	123.2	98.4	103.3	101.7	86.3	159.1	135.1	141.9
2004	163.8	139.1	84.9	161.4	122.3	98.5	109.5	105.9	85.2	163.4	137.1	152.3
2005	170.5	143.3	84.0	168.8	123.8	99.0	...	...	84.8	169.1	141.9	...

. . . = Not available.

Table 5-2. Average Annual Percent Change in Output Per Hour and Related Series, 1987–2004 and 2003–2004

(Number, percent.)

Industry	NAICS code	2004 employment (thousands)	Average annual percent change, 1987–2004			Annual percent change, 2003–2004		
			Output per hour	Output	Hours	Output per hour	Output	Hours
Mining								
Mining	21	523	1.3	-0.2	-1.5	-7.7	-1.2	7.1
Oil and gas extraction	211	123	2.0	-0.9	-2.9	-13.7	-2.6	12.9
Mining, except oil and gas	212	205	3.0	1.0	-2.0	1.2	3.4	2.2
Coal mining	2121	71	3.9	0.0	-3.7	-0.3	3.8	4.1
Metal ore mining	2122	28	4.0	2.2	-1.7	-4.7	0.9	5.9
Nonmetallic mineral mining and quarrying	2123	107	1.4	1.1	-0.3	4.1	4.1	-0.1
Utilities								
Power generation and supply	2211	409	2.9	1.1	-1.8	2.2	-0.5	-2.7
Natural gas distribution	2212	109	3.3	1.5	-1.8	3.9	0.2	-3.6
Manufacturing								
Food	311	1 495	1.3	1.6	0.3	1.5	-0.1	-1.5
Animal food	3111	50	3.5	2.1	-1.3	9.0	3.9	-4.6
Grain and oilseed milling	3112	60	2.8	1.5	-1.2	4.8	-1.2	-5.8
Sugar and confectionery product	3113	84	1.7	1.1	-0.5	3.4	0.7	-2.6
Fruit and vegetable preserving and specialty	3114	181	1.8	1.7	-0.2	2.7	-0.7	-3.4
Dairy product	3115	131	1.5	0.7	-0.8	-3.4	-3.3	0.1
Animal slaughtering and processing	3116	505	0.7	2.2	1.6	2.0	-1.2	-3.2
Seafood product preparation and packaging	3117	42	1.5	0.7	-0.8	-8.4	0.6	9.9
Bakery and tortilla manufacturing	3118	285	0.7	0.7	0.0	2.9	4.1	1.2
Other food product	3119	156	1.2	2.2	1.0	-0.2	1.0	1.1
Beverage and tobacco product	312	195	1.1	-0.1	-1.1	2.8	1.5	-1.3
Beverages	3121	166	2.2	1.5	-0.7	3.4	2.8	-0.6
Tobacco and tobacco product	3122	29	0.8	-2.4	-3.2	4.7	-0.7	-5.2
Textile mills	313	237	3.7	-1.2	-4.7	0.0	-7.7	-7.7
Fiber, yarn, and thread mills	3131	54	4.9	0.2	-4.5	1.4	0.1	-1.3
Fabric mills	3132	115	4.3	-1.4	-5.5	1.7	-9.7	-11.2
Textile and fabric finishing mills	3133	68	1.7	-1.8	-3.4	-3.4	-9.3	-6.2
Textile product mills	314	176	1.6	0.7	-0.9	7.6	3.6	-3.7
Textile furnishings mills	3141	101	1.7	0.7	-0.9	5.5	1.6	-3.7
Other textile product mills	3149	74	1.4	0.6	-0.9	12.7	8.5	-3.7
Apparel	315	286	2.2	-4.9	-7.0	-6.7	-14.4	-8.3
Apparel knitting mills	3151	42	1.2	-4.9	-6.0	-12.9	-17.5	-5.3
Cut and sew apparel	3152	221	2.8	-4.9	-7.5	-5.4	-14.3	-9.3
Accessories and other apparel	3159	23	-1.7	-4.6	-3.0	-7.0	-10.6	-3.8
Leather and allied product	316	42	2.5	-4.6	-6.9	8.9	-0.6	-8.7
Leather and hide tanning and finishing	3161	7	0.3	-3.6	-3.9	3.5	-4.3	-7.5
Footwear	3162	19	1.6	-7.3	-8.8	-2.0	-8.6	-6.8
Other leather product	3169	16	1.5	-3.4	-4.8	27.3	12.7	-11.5
Wood product	321	550	1.1	0.9	-0.2	0.0	1.7	1.7
Sawmills and wood preservation	3211	119	2.5	1.0	-1.5	-3.3	-1.6	1.7
Plywood and engineered wood product	3212	118	0.1	1.1	1.0	-5.1	-1.4	3.9
Other wood product	3219	313	0.9	0.8	-0.1	4.4	5.2	0.8
Paper and paper product	322	496	2.1	0.5	-1.6	2.7	-0.3	-2.9
Pulp, paper, and paperboard mills	3221	146	3.4	0.2	-3.1	2.9	-0.2	-3.0
Converted paper product	3222	350	1.4	0.7	-0.7	2.7	-0.4	-2.9
Printing and related support activities	323	663	0.9	0.1	-0.8	2.5	0.0	-2.4
Petroleum and coal product	324	112	3.2	1.3	-1.9	3.3	2.4	-0.9
Chemicals	325	887	2.2	1.7	-0.4	4.7	3.4	-1.2
Basic chemicals	3251	156	2.7	0.3	-2.3	9.2	6.0	-2.9
Resin, rubber, and artificial fibers	3252	110	2.8	1.2	-1.5	0.9	4.4	3.5
Agricultural chemicals	3253	42	2.2	1.0	-1.1	6.8	7.5	0.6
Pharmaceuticals and medicines	3254	290	1.0	4.2	3.1	3.6	1.0	-2.5
Paints, coatings, and adhesives	3255	68	1.7	0.6	-1.1	3.5	5.3	1.7
Soaps, cleaning compounds, and toiletries	3256	115	2.5	2.1	-0.4	8.3	5.6	-2.4
Other chemical product and preparations	3259	107	2.7	0.6	-2.1	-3.5	-4.5	-1.1
Plastics and rubber product	326	806	2.7	2.8	0.1	0.9	0.1	-0.8
Plastics product	3261	634	2.7	3.2	0.5	0.9	0.1	-0.8
Rubber product	3262	173	2.3	1.3	-1.1	1.0	0.1	-0.9
Nonmetallic mineral product	327	506	1.2	1.2	-0.1	-2.9	1.5	4.5
Clay product and refractories	3271	65	1.4	-0.3	-1.7	5.6	1.1	-4.3

Table 5-2. Average Annual Percent Change in Output Per Hour and Related Series, 1987–2004 and 2003–2004—*Continued*

(Number, percent.)

Industry	NAICS code	2004 employment (thousands)	Average annual percent change, 1987–2004			Annual percent change, 2003–2004		
			Output per hour	Output	Hours	Output per hour	Output	Hours
Manufacturing—*Continued*								
Glass and glass product	3272	113	1.9	0.8	-1.1	-1.0	0.9	2.0
Cement and concrete product	3273	235	0.5	1.8	1.2	-5.8	0.6	6.8
Lime and gypsum product	3274	20	0.9	0.3	-0.6	-3.1	3.3	6.5
Other nonmetallic mineral product	3279	75	1.5	1.1	-0.4	-4.3	4.1	8.8
Primary metal	331	467	2.8	0.7	-2.1	10.1	9.6	-0.4
Iron and steel mills and ferroalloy production	3311	95	5.4	1.8	-3.4	21.1	18.3	-2.3
Steel product from purchased steel	3312	61	1.0	0.2	-0.8	0.1	1.8	1.7
Alumina and aluminum production	3313	74	2.5	0.1	-2.3	8.0	6.7	-1.3
Other nonferrous metal production	3314	72	1.3	-1.0	-2.3	0.5	-0.2	-0.7
Foundries	3315	165	2.5	1.1	-1.3	6.4	6.8	0.4
Fabricated metal product	332	1 497	1.5	1.3	-0.3	-1.8	0.0	1.9
Forging and stamping	3321	110	2.9	1.7	-1.2	5.2	5.8	0.6
Cutlery and hand tools	3322	59	1.5	0.0	-1.5	-1.4	-2.6	-1.3
Architectural and structural metal	3323	389	0.9	1.4	0.5	-4.9	-3.9	1.1
Boilers, tanks, and shipping containers	3324	92	0.9	-0.2	-1.0	-8.0	-4.2	4.1
Hardware	3325	38	2.0	-1.0	-2.9	-1.4	-4.4	-3.1
Spring and wire product	3326	62	2.9	1.6	-1.3	-3.6	-6.2	-2.7
Machine shops and threaded product	3327	327	2.3	3.1	0.8	-2.5	4.2	6.9
Coating, engraving, and heat treating metal	3328	144	3.0	3.3	0.3	5.9	7.6	1.6
Other fabricated metal product	3329	278	1.2	0.2	-1.0	-0.1	-0.3	-0.2
Machinery	333	1 143	2.5	1.5	-1.0	0.5	3.3	2.8
Agriculture, construction, and mining machinery	3331	195	3.2	2.7	-0.4	9.1	15.2	5.6
Industrial machinery	3332	121	3.0	2.1	-0.9	6.9	8.6	1.6
Commercial and service industry machinery	3333	115	1.2	-0.4	-1.6	1.5	1.5	0.0
HVAC and commercial refrigeration equipment	3334	153	2.6	2.1	-0.5	0.3	1.4	1.1
Metalworking machinery	3335	201	1.9	0.4	-1.5	1.4	2.4	1.0
Turbine and power transmission equipment	3336	93	2.6	1.6	-1.0	-13.3	-11.4	2.1
Other general purpose machinery	3339	265	2.4	1.3	-1.0	-3.3	1.6	5.1
Computer and electronic product	334	1 312	13.5	10.6	-2.6	11.5	7.9	-3.3
Computer and peripheral equipment	3341	210	24.1	19.2	-3.9	15.0	7.0	-7.0
Communications equipment	3342	148	7.8	4.9	-2.7	0.2	-0.5	-0.7
Audio and video equipment	3343	33	8.4	4.5	-3.6	42.3	33.9	-5.9
Semiconductors and electronic components	3344	454	19.7	17.9	-1.5	11.7	9.0	-2.5
Electronic instruments	3345	431	4.2	1.3	-2.8	12.7	9.7	-2.7
Magnetic media manufacturing and reproduction	3346	36	2.9	3.0	0.1	11.2	6.4	-4.4
Electrical equipment and appliances	335	445	2.9	0.5	-2.4	4.5	0.9	-3.4
Electric lighting equipment	3351	65	1.7	0.2	-1.5	7.8	2.4	-5.0
Household appliances	3352	89	4.6	2.1	-2.4	6.9	3.0	-3.6
Electrical equipment	3353	154	2.8	-0.1	-2.9	6.7	2.1	-4.3
Other electrical equipment and components	3359	138	2.3	0.2	-2.1	-0.3	-1.8	-1.5
Transportation equipment	336	1 767	2.9	1.8	-1.1	-2.3	-1.5	0.8
Motor vehicles	3361	256	3.8	2.7	-1.0	0.9	-1.9	-2.8
Motor vehicle bodies and trailers	3362	165	1.4	2.6	1.2	-1.5	9.3	10.9
Motor vehicle parts	3363	692	3.4	3.9	0.5	1.1	0.3	-0.8
Aerospace product and parts	3364	442	1.8	-1.9	-3.6	-6.0	-4.8	1.3
Railroad rolling stock	3365	25	4.9	4.6	-0.3	-9.8	2.8	14.0
Ship and boat building	3366	148	2.1	0.9	-1.2	2.2	3.6	1.4
Other transportation equipment	3369	39	5.0	5.3	0.3	3.1	4.3	1.1
Furniture and related product	337	573	2.1	1.8	-0.3	2.8	4.4	1.5
Household and institutional furniture	3371	385	1.9	1.7	-0.2	2.8	6.9	4.0
Office furniture and fixtures	3372	135	2.4	1.5	-0.9	2.3	-0.8	-3.0
Other furniture-related product	3379	53	2.0	2.7	0.6	10.1	5.5	-4.2
Miscellaneous manufacturing	339	658	3.1	3.1	0.1	1.3	0.3	-1.0
Medical equipment and supplies	3391	304	3.8	4.8	1.0	1.6	0.6	-1.0
Other miscellaneous manufacturing	3399	354	2.3	1.7	-0.6	1.0	0.0	-1.0

Table 5-2. Average Annual Percent Change in Output Per Hour and Related Series, 1987–2004 and 2003–2004—*Continued*

(Number, percent.)

Industry	NAICS code	2004 employment (thousands)	Average annual percent change, 1987–2004			Annual percent change, 2003–2004		
			Output per hour	Output	Hours	Output per hour	Output	Hours
Transportation and Warehousing								
Air transportation	481	483	2.6	3.4	0.8	11.4	11.5	0.0
Line-haul railroads	482111	178	5.5	2.6	-2.7	3.1	5.6	2.5
General freight trucking, long distance	48412	864	1.5	3.2	1.7	-0.8	6.1	6.9
Used household and office goods, moving	48421	104	-1.1	0.3	1.4	2.9	5.7	2.7
Postal service	491	782	1.1	1.2	0.1	2.1	0.1	-1.9
Couriers and messengers	492	598	-0.9	2.6	3.5	-5.7	-2.3	3.6
Information								
Publishing	511	953	4.3	5.1	0.8	3.9	4.3	0.4
Newspaper, book, and directory publishers	5111	718	0.1	-0.4	-0.4	-2.4	0.6	3.0
Software publishers	5112	236	17.7	26.4	7.4	17.0	9.5	-6.5
Motion picture and video exhibition	51213	140	0.8	2.5	1.7	3.3	-3.1	-6.2
Broadcasting, except Internet	515	338	0.5	2.0	1.5	1.5	2.0	0.5
Radio and television broadcasting	5151	249	-0.4	-0.1	0.3	-3.1	-0.8	2.4
Cable and other subscription programming	5152	88	2.4	8.2	5.6	8.5	6.9	-1.5
Wired telecommunications carriers	5171	558	5.0	3.8	-1.2	0.8	-4.5	-5.3
Wireless telecommunications carriers	5172	195	8.2	24.0	14.6	19.1	16.5	-2.2
Cable and other program distribution	5175	132	0.5	5.8	5.3	12.4	8.7	-3.3
Finance and Insurance								
Commercial banking	52211	1 281	2.4	2.0	-0.4	5.3	4.8	-0.5
Real Estate Rental and Leasing								
Passenger car rental	532111	125	1.6	3.8	2.1	-1.8	9.3	11.3
Truck, trailer, and RV rental and leasing	53212	62	4.8	4.6	-0.2	18.3	13.0	-4.5
Videotape and disc rental	53223	158	4.2	7.4	3.1	4.2	6.6	2.3
Professional and Technical Services								
Tax preparation services	541213	131	1.2	4.3	3.1	-7.9	6.4	15.4
Architectural services	54131	207	1.6	3.7	2.1	5.2	5.3	0.1
Engineering services	54133	831	1.1	3.0	1.9	7.4	10.5	2.9
Advertising agencies	54181	180	1.9	1.8	-0.2	10.3	9.4	-0.8
Photography studios, portrait	541921	78	-0.4	2.5	2.9	-11.6	2.6	16.1
Administrative and Support Services								
Travel agencies	56151	128	3.8	2.9	-0.8	13.9	7.7	-5.4
Janitorial services	56172	1 129	3.1	4.6	1.4	-1.4	3.0	4.5
Health Care and Social Assistance[1]								
Medical and diagnostic laboratories	6215	198	4.5	7.5	2.9	0.1	4.7	4.6
Medical laboratories	621511	136	3.6	6.2	2.5	1.6	4.4	2.7
Diagnostic imaging centers	621512	62	5.6	9.8	4.0	-3.7	5.3	9.4
Accommodation and Food Services								
Traveler accommodations	7211	1 750	2.3	3.1	0.8	5.7	6.0	0.4
Other Services								
Automotive repair and maintenance	8111	1 155	1.6	2.6	1.0	7.8	1.2	-6.1
Hair, nail, and skin care services	81211	899	2.5	3.5	1.0	5.7	8.9	3.0
Funeral homes and funeral services	81221	111	-0.6	0.3	1.0	-2.4	-5.9	-3.5
Dry-cleaning and laundry services	8123	382	0.8	0.5	-0.3	7.4	0.6	-6.3
Photofinishing	81292	43	0.4	-3.6	-4.0	2.5	-11.8	-13.9

[1]For NAICS industries 6215, 621511, and 621512, average annual percent changes are for 1994–2004.

Table 5-3. Average Annual Percent Change in Output Per Hour and Related Series, Retail Trade, Wholesale Trade, and Food Services and Drinking Places, 1987–2005 and 2004–2005

(Number, percent.)

Industry	NAICS code	2005 employment (thousands)	Average annual percent change, 1987–2005			Annual percent change, 2004–2005		
			Output per hour	Output	Hours	Output per hour	Output	Hours
Wholesale Trade	42	5 987	3.5	4.1	0.6	0.6	3.1	2.5
Durable goods	423	3 109	5.5	6.0	0.4	3.1	5.0	1.8
Motor vehicles and parts	4231	361	4.1	4.0	-0.1	6.3	4.8	-1.3
Furniture and furnishings	4232	120	2.6	2.7	0.1	-2.0	0.7	2.8
Lumber and construction supplies	4233	261	1.0	2.9	1.8	-5.3	0.8	6.4
Commercial equipment	4234	650	15.2	15.7	0.4	8.1	7.7	-0.4
Metals and minerals	4235	125	0.2	0.4	0.2	-3.6	1.9	5.7
Electric goods	4236	352	9.0	8.9	-0.1	3.6	4.4	0.7
Hardware and plumbing	4237	251	1.4	2.6	1.2	-1.6	3.5	5.3
Machinery and supplies	4238	681	2.6	2.6	0.0	5.6	6.9	1.3
Miscellaneous durable goods	4239	308	2.3	3.1	0.7	0.7	5.2	4.5
Nondurable goods	424	2 132	1.3	1.6	0.3	0.6	0.9	0.3
Paper and paper product	4241	159	3.0	2.3	-0.6	10.5	3.8	-6.1
Druggists' goods	4242	223	2.6	5.1	2.5	5.3	5.9	0.5
Apparel and piece goods	4243	161	2.9	2.6	-0.3	10.2	6.3	-3.5
Grocery and related product	4244	734	0.8	1.7	0.9	-1.7	0.5	2.2
Farm product (raw materials)	4245	80	1.2	-1.4	-2.6	-7.8	-2.3	6.0
Chemicals	4246	136	-0.1	0.9	1.1	-2.2	2.3	4.6
Petroleum	4247	103	3.4	0.3	-3.0	-8.5	-8.7	-0.2
Alcoholic beverages	4248	149	0.5	2.0	1.5	5.7	6.6	0.9
Miscellaneous nondurable goods	4249	387	0.7	0.7	0.0	5.8	3.3	-2.4
Electronic markets and agents and brokers	425	745	2.4	5.1	2.7	-8.6	2.7	12.4
Retail Trade	44-45	16 461	3.3	4.2	0.9	3.4	4.3	0.9
Motor vehicle and parts dealers	441	2 024	2.8	4.0	1.2	0.5	1.3	0.7
Automobile dealers	4411	1 319	2.5	3.8	1.3	-1.0	-0.6	0.5
Other motor vehicle dealers	4412	186	4.3	7.2	2.8	5.4	18.4	12.3
Auto parts, accessory, and tire stores	4413	519	2.8	3.4	0.6	7.5	5.1	-2.2
Furniture and home furnishings stores	442	640	3.9	5.2	1.2	1.7	5.9	4.2
Furniture stores	4421	324	3.3	4.5	1.1	-0.7	5.4	6.2
Home furnishings stores	4422	316	4.7	6.1	1.3	4.2	6.5	2.1
Electronics and appliance stores	443	570	13.4	15.4	1.7	9.1	15.5	5.9
Building material and garden supply stores	444	1 346	3.3	5.3	2.0	0.4	6.6	6.2
Building material and supplies dealers	4441	1 174	3.1	5.5	2.3	0.5	6.5	5.9
Lawn and garden equipment and supplies stores	4442	172	4.2	4.2	0.0	-0.6	7.8	8.4
Food and beverage stores	445	2 922	0.4	0.3	-0.1	5.3	2.6	-2.5
Grocery stores	4451	2 503	0.3	0.3	0.0	4.5	2.1	-2.3
Specialty food stores	4452	268	0.0	0.3	0.3	13.5	10.7	-2.5
Beer, wine, and liquor stores	4453	152	2.5	0.6	-1.8	13.6	5.7	-7.0
Health and personal care stores	446	999	2.6	3.9	1.3	-0.9	2.5	3.5
Gasoline stations	447	892	2.4	1.9	-0.5	5.9	3.6	-2.2
Clothing and clothing accessories stores	448	1 527	4.5	4.9	0.4	5.9	6.9	0.9
Clothing stores	4481	1 129	4.7	5.4	0.7	9.0	8.5	-0.4
Shoe stores	4482	183	3.9	2.6	-1.2	3.7	1.4	-2.1
Jewelry, luggage, and leather goods stores	4483	216	4.3	4.8	0.5	-5.1	3.7	9.2
Sporting goods, hobby, book, and music stores	451	720	4.5	4.9	0.4	8.7	3.4	-4.8
Sporting goods and musical instrument stores	4511	501	5.1	5.4	0.3	7.9	4.3	-3.3
Book, periodical, and music stores	4512	218	3.2	4.0	0.7	10.8	1.6	-8.3
General merchandise stores	452	2 951	3.9	5.6	1.7	3.8	5.9	1.9
Department stores	4521	1 620	1.3	2.7	1.4	0.6	0.2	-0.4
Other general merchandise stores	4529	1 331	7.6	9.6	1.9	5.5	10.2	4.4
Miscellaneous store retailers	453	1 117	4.4	5.1	0.7	8.3	5.8	-2.3
Florists	4531	127	2.8	0.8	-1.9	23.8	8.8	-12.1
Office supply, stationery, and gift stores	4532	443	6.2	6.8	0.5	5.5	4.5	-1.0
Used merchandise stores	4533	185	5.5	6.6	1.1	8.0	8.9	0.9
Other miscellaneous store retailers	4539	362	2.4	4.3	1.8	7.3	5.7	-1.5
Nonstore retailers	454	752	8.6	9.4	0.8	2.8	8.8	5.8
Electronic shopping and mail-order houses	4541	311	11.6	16.1	4.0	4.2	12.3	7.8
Vending machine operators	4542	69	0.9	-0.9	-1.8	2.1	4.1	2.0
Direct selling establishments	4543	373	3.4	2.7	-0.7	-2.3	2.3	4.8
Food Services and Drinking Places	722	9 336	0.7	2.4	1.7	1.6	3.5	1.9
Full-service restaurants	7221	4 359	0.9	2.7	1.8	2.6	3.9	1.3
Limited-service eating places	7222	3 947	0.6	2.5	2.0	-0.1	3.3	3.5
Special food services	7223	651	1.8	2.6	0.8	3.4	4.7	1.3
Drinking places, alcoholic beverages	7224	380	-0.7	-0.4	0.3	6.4	0.1	-5.9

Table 5-4. Indexes of Multifactor Productivity and Related Measures, 1987–2004

(2000 = 100, unless otherwise indicated.)

Sector	1987	1988	1989	1990	1991	1992	1993	1994	1995	1996	1997	1998	1999	2000	2001	2002	2003	2004
PRIVATE BUSINESS																		
Productivity																		
Output per hour of all persons	77.5	78.7	79.5	81.1	82.5	86.0	86.4	87.3	87.5	90.1	91.8	94.4	97.2	100.0	102.8	107.0	111.2	115.0
Output per unit of capital	104.9	105.6	105.6	104.0	100.7	102.6	102.9	104.4	103.3	103.5	103.7	103.0	102.0	100.0	96.3	95.2	96.4	98.6
Multifactor productivity	89.5	90.2	90.5	91.0	90.3	92.7	93.0	93.7	93.5	95.1	96.0	97.5	98.7	100.0	100.2	101.8	104.7	107.7
Output	62.4	65.2	67.6	68.6	68.1	70.9	73.2	76.8	79.2	82.8	87.2	91.5	96.2	100.0	100.5	102.0	105.5	110.6
Inputs																		
Labor input	75.2	77.9	80.3	80.4	79.4	80.2	82.5	86.2	88.7	90.5	94.1	96.3	98.9	100.0	98.6	97.3	97.2	98.7
Capital services	59.5	61.7	64.0	66.0	67.6	69.1	71.2	73.6	76.6	80.0	84.1	88.8	94.3	100.0	104.4	107.1	109.4	112.1
Combined units of labor and capital inputs	69.8	72.3	74.7	75.4	75.4	76.5	78.7	82.0	84.7	87.1	90.8	93.9	97.5	100.0	100.3	100.2	100.8	102.7
Capital services per hour for all persons	73.8	74.5	75.3	78.0	81.9	83.9	84.0	83.6	84.7	87.1	88.5	91.6	95.3	100.0	106.8	112.3	115.3	116.6
PRIVATE NONFARM BUSINESS																		
Productivity																		
Output per hour of all persons	78.0	79.4	80.0	81.5	82.9	86.4	86.8	87.8	88.3	90.7	92.1	94.7	97.3	100.0	102.7	106.9	111.1	114.9
Output per unit of capital	106.4	107.6	107.3	105.5	101.9	103.5	103.9	105.2	104.3	104.2	104.1	103.4	102.3	100.0	96.3	95.1	96.3	98.6
Multifactor productivity	90.2	91.1	91.2	91.6	91.0	93.2	93.5	94.3	94.3	95.6	96.3	97.7	98.8	100.0	100.1	101.8	104.6	107.7
Output	62.4	65.3	67.6	68.6	68.1	70.8	73.2	76.7	79.3	82.8	87.2	91.5	96.3	100.0	100.5	102.1	105.5	110.6
Inputs																		
Labor input	74.7	77.4	79.9	80.0	78.9	79.7	82.2	85.6	88.1	90.1	93.7	96.0	98.9	100.0	98.7	97.3	97.3	98.9
Capital services	58.7	60.7	63.0	65.0	66.8	68.4	70.5	72.9	76.0	79.5	83.7	88.5	94.2	100.0	104.5	107.3	109.6	112.3
Combined units of labor and capital inputs	69.2	71.7	74.1	74.9	74.8	76.0	78.3	81.4	84.1	86.6	90.5	93.7	97.5	100.0	100.4	100.2	100.9	102.8
Capital services per hour for all persons	73.3	73.8	74.5	77.3	81.4	83.5	83.6	83.5	84.7	87.0	88.5	91.5	95.2	100.0	106.7	112.4	115.4	116.6
MANUFACTURING[1]																		
Productivity																		
Output per hour of all persons	78.3	79.9	80.0	82.2	84.1	88.6	90.2	93.0	96.5	100.0	103.8	108.9	114.0	118.3	119.7	...	...	...
Output per unit of capital	97.6	100.7	99.2	97.5	93.6	95.9	96.9	99.7	100.6	100.0	101.4	101.7	101.7	101.0	95.1	...	...	...
Multifactor productivity	93.6	95.3	93.5	93.3	92.4	94.0	95.1	97.3	99.2	100.0	103.1	105.7	108.7	111.3	110.3	...	...	...
Output	78.3	82.2	82.6	83.2	81.5	85.5	88.3	92.9	96.9	100.0	105.6	110.5	114.7	117.4	112.1	...	...	...
Inputs																		
Hours at work of all persons	100.0	102.8	103.3	101.1	96.9	96.5	97.8	99.9	100.4	100.0	101.7	101.5	100.7	99.2	93.6	...	...	...
Capital services	80.2	81.6	83.2	85.3	87.1	89.1	91.1	93.2	96.4	100.0	104.1	108.7	112.8	116.2	117.9	...	...	...
Energy	86.5	89.9	90.2	93.1	93.2	93.1	96.6	99.9	102.3	100.0	97.5	100.6	102.9	104.3	98.9	...	...	...
Non-energy materials	70.9	71.9	75.0	77.5	78.5	83.5	86.5	90.3	93.1	100.0	101.9	107.5	105.5	...	...	...	...	...
Purchased business services	70.8	77.4	82.6	84.7	84.6	92.0	92.9	96.0	100.4	100.0	103.9	103.1	105.4	106.5	97.7	...	...	...
Combined units of all inputs	83.7	86.2	88.3	89.1	88.3	90.9	92.8	95.5	97.7	100.0	102.4	104.6	105.5	105.5	101.6	...	...	...

[1]1996 = 100.

. . . = Not available.

Table 5-5. Indexes of Multifactor Productivity and Related Measures, Manufacturing Industries, 1985–2001

(1996 = 100.)

Industry	1985	1986	1987	1988	1989	1990	1991	1992	1993	1994	1995	1996	1997	1998	1999	2000	2001
NONDURABLE GOODS																	
Total Nondurable Goods																	
Output per hour of all persons	79.6	81.9	83.6	84.9	84.5	86.5	88.2	91.9	92.4	94.3	97.1	100.0	103.1	105.8	107.4	110.8	112.1
Output per unit of capital	101.0	101.9	104.3	105.7	104.0	102.9	99.9	101.9	101.3	102.2	101.7	100.0	100.5	98.7	96.5	95.0	90.8
Multifactor productivity	98.8	99.4	101.2	102.4	100.0	99.1	98.1	98.6	99.1	99.6	100.5	100.0	101.0	101.0	101.5	100.4	98.1
Sector output	78.0	80.5	84.0	86.5	87.0	88.6	88.5	92.9	94.5	97.3	99.2	100.0	103.2	104.4	104.9	105.5	101.7
Hours of all persons at work	98.0	98.3	100.4	102.0	103.0	102.5	100.3	101.0	102.3	103.2	102.2	100.0	100.0	98.6	97.7	95.2	90.7
Capital services	77.3	79.0	80.5	81.8	83.6	86.1	88.6	91.1	93.4	95.2	97.6	100.0	102.7	105.8	108.7	111.1	112.1
Energy	76.5	77.6	80.9	83.4	85.3	89.6	90.6	92.6	96.5	98.9	102.4	100.0	95.7	97.1	98.0	97.8	94.8
Non-energy materials	73.9	76.9	77.9	77.3	79.6	82.5	83.5	89.3	91.0	95.2	95.5	100.0	103.8	107.0	106.1	110.2	111.4
Purchased business services	57.4	59.8	65.5	73.2	80.7	87.1	90.3	97.9	96.2	96.6	101.5	100.0	102.7	101.5	102.2	106.8	103.2
Combined units of all inputs	79.0	81.0	83.0	84.5	87.0	89.5	90.2	94.1	95.4	97.7	98.7	100.0	102.1	103.3	103.4	105.1	103.7
Food and Kindred Product																	
Output per hour of all persons	89.0	89.0	89.5	91.9	89.4	90.1	93.2	98.1	98.3	98.8	100.8	100.0	102.2	106.1	104.3	104.7	105.0
Output per unit of capital	102.2	101.2	100.4	102.5	100.7	101.1	100.8	103.6	103.4	103.1	104.2	100.0	101.9	100.2	98.1	95.1	93.6
Multifactor productivity	103.9	102.3	102.9	106.4	102.2	100.9	101.8	101.4	102.7	100.5	104.5	100.0	101.2	100.1	102.9	100.2	97.1
Sector output	81.9	83.1	84.5	87.2	86.9	89.3	90.9	95.8	97.5	98.4	101.8	100.0	103.4	106.6	107.1	106.8	106.6
Hours of all persons at work	92.0	93.4	94.5	94.9	97.2	99.1	97.5	97.6	99.1	99.7	101.0	100.0	101.1	100.4	102.7	102.0	101.4
Capital services	80.1	82.2	84.2	85.1	86.3	88.3	90.2	92.5	94.2	95.5	97.7	100.0	101.5	106.4	109.1	112.3	113.9
Energy	78.9	81.7	84.5	87.1	88.0	88.4	91.3	93.4	96.1	100.1	104.8	100.0	101.3	105.2	105.2	105.6	106.0
Non-energy materials	77.1	79.1	80.6	79.0	81.9	85.6	86.1	92.9	92.5	97.4	95.5	100.0	102.7	109.1	104.2	107.6	112.8
Purchased business services	62.0	69.4	63.9	71.0	79.8	87.3	93.5	102.5	103.9	101.9	101.4	100.0	101.8	103.1	97.2	100.0	102.0
Combined units of all inputs	78.8	81.2	82.2	81.9	85.0	88.4	89.3	94.5	94.9	97.9	97.4	100.0	102.2	106.5	104.1	106.6	109.7
Textile Mill Product																	
Output per hour of all persons	70.1	71.2	72.6	73.6	76.5	78.9	79.7	85.7	88.9	91.2	95.1	100.0	101.0	104.1	109.4	111.2	114.5
Output per unit of capital	84.8	88.4	95.0	94.7	96.5	93.6	93.1	100.3	104.0	105.1	101.8	100.0	98.9	94.3	90.6	89.6	82.4
Multifactor productivity	84.1	85.9	87.1	89.8	90.3	91.0	91.2	95.1	96.5	97.2	98.5	100.0	101.4	100.7	104.7	107.8	110.0
Sector output	77.0	80.4	86.5	86.4	88.3	86.2	85.8	92.9	97.6	101.5	100.5	100.0	100.7	99.6	96.9	95.2	85.3
Hours of all persons at work	109.9	112.8	119.1	117.4	115.5	109.3	107.6	108.5	109.8	111.4	105.7	100.0	99.7	95.7	88.5	85.6	74.5
Capital services	90.8	90.9	91.1	91.2	91.5	92.0	92.1	92.6	93.9	96.5	98.8	100.0	101.8	105.6	106.9	106.2	103.5
Energy	79.5	83.0	91.3	91.3	92.0	88.5	90.5	94.5	98.8	104.7	106.2	100.0	95.9	94.1	91.7	90.3	81.1
Non-energy materials	87.0	88.5	95.1	88.0	90.7	88.2	86.6	91.9	97.4	101.9	99.7	100.0	99.0	101.5	93.7	87.9	76.3
Purchased business services	53.2	55.6	61.2	68.5	77.9	79.2	84.2	95.2	98.3	102.3	102.7	100.0	97.2	92.2	85.2	80.3	68.3
Combined units of all inputs	91.5	93.5	99.4	96.2	97.8	94.7	94.0	97.7	101.1	104.5	102.0	100.0	99.3	98.9	92.5	88.3	77.5
Apparel and Related Product																	
Output per hour of all persons	72.7	75.0	76.0	76.2	72.4	75.1	75.6	81.4	85.2	89.9	95.5	100.0	113.7	117.1	129.1	141.4	144.4
Output per unit of capital	102.9	103.3	105.9	102.6	99.4	97.8	98.1	102.5	101.4	102.9	99.5	100.0	108.0	97.1	95.8	91.8	83.8
Multifactor productivity	94.4	95.4	96.5	96.3	94.9	94.4	92.6	92.1	93.1	95.8	98.2	100.0	102.9	103.6	105.0	108.7	111.5
Sector output	88.6	91.0	93.5	92.3	87.7	87.0	86.2	93.4	96.2	100.8	101.6	100.0	107.0	103.0	104.2	102.1	92.6
Hours of all persons at work	121.9	121.3	123.0	121.1	121.2	115.8	114.1	114.8	112.9	112.1	106.3	100.0	94.1	88.0	80.7	72.2	64.1
Capital services	86.1	88.1	88.3	89.9	88.3	88.9	87.9	91.1	94.9	98.0	102.1	100.0	99.1	106.1	108.8	111.2	110.5
Energy	62.0	66.1	68.7	69.2	60.5	59.8	61.1	95.6	105.9	103.4	110.4	100.0	84.0	81.0	81.7	80.1	73.5
Non-energy materials	98.2	100.9	103.4	98.6	89.3	88.0	87.9	97.4	100.7	103.7	102.0	100.0	110.6	105.8	109.6	106.2	92.5
Purchased business services	31.3	32.5	31.6	39.7	47.5	58.7	70.5	91.8	95.6	99.2	102.1	100.0	108.1	100.9	101.6	93.6	80.6
Combined units of all inputs	93.8	95.4	96.9	95.8	92.5	92.1	93.1	101.3	103.3	105.2	103.4	100.0	104.0	99.4	99.2	93.9	83.1
Paper and Allied Product																	
Output per hour of all persons	81.3	86.6	86.5	88.3	88.1	88.3	90.6	93.0	94.8	98.4	99.1	100.0	101.3	104.8	105.8	108.4	108.2
Output per unit of capital	103.5	105.0	105.6	107.4	104.9	101.0	98.3	100.2	101.3	104.8	103.3	100.0	100.3	99.0	99.0	96.5	91.2
Multifactor productivity	97.9	100.2	99.8	100.8	98.4	97.4	98.2	99.5	103.0	104.1	98.1	100.0	102.7	101.6	101.7	100.0	98.2
Sector output	78.7	82.4	84.5	87.8	89.1	89.5	90.2	94.0	96.3	100.6	100.4	100.0	102.2	103.7	105.1	102.8	97.2
Hours of all persons at work	96.9	95.2	97.8	99.4	101.2	101.4	99.6	101.2	101.6	102.2	101.3	100.0	100.9	98.9	99.3	94.9	89.9
Capital services	76.1	78.5	80.1	81.7	84.9	88.6	91.8	93.9	95.0	96.0	97.2	100.0	102.0	104.7	106.2	106.5	106.6
Energy	77.8	81.2	84.9	86.4	88.8	94.2	94.9	96.8	99.2	101.3	104.5	100.0	98.2	99.5	101.3	99.0	93.8
Non-energy materials	76.8	79.9	81.7	83.3	87.0	87.5	86.9	90.2	87.7	93.5	103.1	100.0	98.3	104.5	106.8	109.0	105.6
Purchased business services	57.1	62.7	69.0	79.2	89.1	89.6	90.1	94.9	90.2	93.9	113.4	100.0	97.0	97.8	97.4	98.1	90.9
Combined units of all inputs	80.4	82.2	84.8	87.1	90.6	91.9	91.8	94.5	93.5	96.6	102.3	100.0	99.6	102.1	103.3	102.8	99.0

Table 5-5. Indexes of Multifactor Productivity and Related Measures, Manufacturing Industries, 1985–2001
—Continued

(1996 = 100.)

Industry	1985	1986	1987	1988	1989	1990	1991	1992	1993	1994	1995	1996	1997	1998	1999	2000	2001
Printing and Publishing																	
Output per hour of all persons	103.3	104.2	106.6	101.5	99.5	98.0	96.9	100.5	98.4	97.1	97.2	100.0	96.4	97.0	99.0	100.8	97.1
Output per unit of capital	142.9	139.5	138.8	131.6	123.1	117.6	108.4	107.5	105.3	104.3	102.1	100.0	92.4	91.1	86.5	82.3	73.7
Multifactor productivity	114.2	112.8	112.7	110.8	109.5	107.0	104.6	106.0	102.0	102.6	100.9	100.0	95.7	95.7	97.7	98.0	93.1
Sector output	93.4	96.6	101.1	101.4	100.0	99.7	95.3	97.7	98.0	98.5	99.2	100.0	98.4	98.1	99.9	100.4	92.9
Hours of all persons at work	90.3	92.6	94.9	99.9	100.5	101.7	98.3	97.2	99.6	101.4	102.1	100.0	102.2	101.1	100.9	99.6	95.6
Capital services	65.3	69.2	72.8	77.0	81.3	84.8	88.0	90.9	93.0	94.4	97.2	100.0	106.5	107.7	115.5	121.9	126.0
Energy	65.1	70.2	81.9	87.6	87.8	91.6	90.7	91.5	94.4	98.2	102.9	100.0	70.6	70.7	71.2	72.0	66.9
Non-energy materials	82.4	87.0	91.3	88.6	85.3	87.6	85.8	87.5	94.2	90.6	92.4	100.0	104.1	104.7	101.4	99.4	99.6
Purchased business services	74.8	80.9	89.2	88.8	88.3	89.2	84.3	88.1	93.0	92.4	100.4	100.0	101.4	99.8	97.5	100.0	91.6
Combined units of all inputs	81.7	85.6	89.7	91.5	91.3	93.2	91.1	92.2	96.1	96.0	98.4	100.0	102.9	102.5	102.3	102.4	99.7
Chemicals and Allied Product																	
Output per hour of all persons	72.9	78.3	85.1	86.4	86.1	87.5	87.5	89.0	89.2	94.9	97.9	100.0	107.1	106.4	107.4	110.6	108.9
Output per unit of capital	97.0	99.5	107.6	111.3	110.3	109.0	103.5	103.7	101.1	102.4	101.7	100.0	103.0	99.3	97.4	95.9	91.7
Multifactor productivity	92.8	96.7	102.8	101.9	99.7	100.1	97.2	96.9	95.4	98.2	99.1	100.0	102.9	101.8	100.9	97.5	96.4
Sector output	71.2	74.6	82.1	86.2	87.8	90.2	89.5	92.6	93.0	96.6	98.5	100.0	106.5	106.8	107.9	108.8	105.3
Hours of all persons at work	97.7	95.3	96.5	99.7	102.0	103.1	102.3	104.0	104.2	101.8	100.6	100.0	99.4	100.4	100.5	98.4	96.7
Capital services	73.4	75.0	76.3	77.5	79.6	82.8	86.5	89.3	92.0	94.3	96.9	100.0	103.4	107.6	110.7	113.4	114.8
Energy	75.6	73.9	79.6	83.1	85.7	90.7	90.4	91.2	95.7	97.7	99.5	100.0	92.1	93.0	93.1	93.7	91.8
Non-energy materials	72.3	73.6	76.6	82.4	85.7	86.0	88.2	93.0	95.9	99.2	98.3	100.0	108.3	108.4	114.8	131.6	126.0
Purchased business services	55.3	57.6	63.5	75.7	84.7	89.5	93.0	99.4	100.0	99.5	104.5	100.0	105.3	104.2	100.8	103.1	99.0
Combined units of all inputs	76.8	77.1	79.9	84.6	88.1	90.1	92.1	95.6	97.5	98.4	99.4	100.0	103.5	104.9	106.9	111.6	109.3
Petroleum Refining																	
Output per hour of all persons	68.2	76.1	78.8	82.7	83.3	83.0	82.3	84.5	90.1	91.6	96.8	100.0	106.2	108.4	112.8	120.2	118.6
Output per unit of capital	92.0	98.6	102.3	105.0	105.6	105.3	102.3	101.3	101.3	99.3	99.0	100.0	103.2	107.2	107.1	110.2	110.6
Multifactor productivity	96.2	98.7	98.7	99.4	99.2	98.5	98.5	99.2	100.1	99.7	99.9	100.0	101.1	104.1	103.3	102.5	102.8
Sector output	83.1	88.3	90.2	92.1	92.1	92.5	91.5	93.3	96.3	96.0	97.4	100.0	103.3	105.7	104.1	105.7	104.7
Hours of all persons at work	121.9	116.1	114.5	111.3	110.5	111.4	111.1	110.4	106.9	104.8	100.6	100.0	97.3	97.5	92.3	87.9	88.2
Capital services	90.4	89.6	88.2	87.7	87.3	87.8	89.4	92.1	94.8	96.7	98.4	100.0	100.0	98.6	97.2	95.9	94.6
Energy	100.9	102.5	90.2	93.9	93.9	106.3	104.5	100.3	103.3	99.6	103.8	100.0	100.5	101.2	104.1	102.1	101.5
Non-energy materials	83.8	89.3	91.9	93.7	93.5	93.4	92.0	93.6	96.8	96.4	97.6	100.0	103.1	105.6	103.6	105.2	104.3
Purchased business services	70.7	53.4	68.4	70.2	79.8	97.4	90.9	84.8	80.5	83.0	88.6	100.0	104.1	75.6	90.1	123.5	114.2
Combined units of all inputs	86.4	89.5	91.4	92.7	92.9	94.0	92.9	94.0	96.3	96.3	97.5	100.0	102.2	101.5	100.7	103.1	101.8
Rubber and Plastics Product																	
Output per hour of all persons	73.3	74.1	78.3	78.8	79.6	81.9	83.1	90.3	91.7	94.5	95.7	100.0	104.1	106.9	109.6	113.4	113.7
Output per unit of capital	94.8	93.9	99.4	100.6	99.6	97.5	92.1	100.6	103.1	106.7	102.5	100.0	99.4	95.8	93.2	90.5	81.8
Multifactor productivity	88.6	88.6	90.1	90.6	92.4	92.5	93.7	95.7	96.4	97.9	98.1	100.0	102.3	103.4	104.0	105.6	104.5
Sector output	60.4	62.2	67.6	70.1	72.0	73.4	72.0	81.2	86.7	94.3	96.4	100.0	106.1	109.8	114.0	116.7	109.1
Hours of all persons at work	82.3	83.9	86.3	89.0	90.4	89.7	86.6	89.9	94.6	99.8	100.7	100.0	101.9	102.7	104.1	103.0	95.9
Capital services	63.7	66.2	68.0	69.7	72.3	75.3	78.1	80.7	84.1	88.4	94.0	100.0	106.7	114.6	122.4	128.9	133.4
Energy	66.9	70.0	75.4	78.5	81.0	81.4	79.9	83.5	90.3	96.6	101.9	100.0	101.0	104.2	108.6	111.0	104.5
Non-energy materials	64.6	66.8	72.9	74.6	73.7	75.7	72.1	83.0	88.7	95.8	97.1	100.0	104.0	107.0	111.1	112.3	105.7
Purchased business services	46.2	48.0	54.9	61.3	64.7	68.7	69.4	83.1	87.7	95.7	100.6	100.0	106.0	104.3	106.1	106.8	96.8
Combined units of all inputs	68.1	70.2	74.9	77.4	77.9	79.4	76.8	84.8	90.0	96.3	98.3	100.0	103.8	106.2	109.6	110.6	104.4

Table 5-5. Indexes of Multifactor Productivity and Related Measures, Manufacturing Industries, 1985–2001
—Continued

(1996 = 100.)

Industry	1985	1986	1987	1988	1989	1990	1991	1992	1993	1994	1995	1996	1997	1998	1999	2000	2001
DURABLE GOODS																	
Total Durable Goods																	
Output per hour of all persons	68.1	71.7	74.4	76.1	76.2	78.2	79.4	84.6	87.4	91.4	95.7	100.0	105.2	112.6	120.8	126.0	126.9
Output per unit of capital	92.2	91.7	92.4	96.4	95.0	92.6	87.7	90.9	93.5	98.1	99.9	100.0	102.3	104.2	105.7	105.4	97.5
Multifactor productivity	82.0	84.1	87.5	89.4	88.3	88.9	88.1	90.6	92.2	95.5	98.1	100.0	104.6	109.4	114.4	120.3	121.0
Sector output	70.0	71.8	74.2	78.7	78.9	78.3	75.1	79.0	82.8	89.3	94.9	100.0	108.2	116.6	124.1	128.5	121.4
Hours of all persons at work	102.7	100.1	99.7	103.4	103.5	100.2	94.5	93.3	94.7	97.7	99.1	100.0	102.9	103.5	102.7	102.0	95.7
Capital services	75.9	78.3	80.2	81.7	83.1	84.6	85.6	86.9	88.5	91.0	95.0	100.0	105.8	111.9	117.4	121.9	124.5
Energy	88.1	88.1	95.4	100.2	97.8	98.6	97.3	94.4	97.2	101.7	102.6	100.0	99.4	105.4	110.2	113.6	106.3
Non-energy materials	72.5	73.2	68.4	71.3	73.5	74.0	73.0	77.7	82.5	86.7	92.4	100.0	102.3	109.3	112.2	105.3	98.1
Purchased business services	67.0	71.4	76.5	81.9	84.7	82.3	78.9	86.0	89.5	95.4	99.3	100.0	105.1	104.7	108.6	106.1	91.9
Combined units of all inputs	85.4	85.4	84.7	88.1	89.3	88.1	85.2	87.1	89.8	93.4	96.7	100.0	103.5	106.6	108.5	106.8	100.3
Lumber and Wood Product																	
Output per hour of all persons	101.4	106.4	107.9	105.4	102.5	103.8	105.9	106.2	100.0	99.3	99.5	100.0	98.6	99.5	100.9	100.6	101.5
Output per unit of capital	85.5	93.1	101.9	102.7	101.4	100.1	93.6	98.4	98.6	102.3	102.2	100.0	97.2	99.8	101.4	98.4	93.5
Multifactor productivity	102.0	105.9	110.7	111.7	110.9	111.6	111.3	110.7	101.8	101.1	102.3	100.0	98.5	97.5	96.4	95.6	94.5
Sector output	87.7	94.9	102.1	101.0	97.9	96.2	88.8	92.3	92.1	97.2	99.5	100.0	99.7	103.9	107.6	106.1	100.9
Hours of all persons at work	86.5	89.2	94.6	95.9	95.5	92.8	83.9	86.9	92.2	97.8	100.0	100.0	101.2	104.5	106.7	105.4	99.4
Capital services	102.6	101.9	100.3	98.4	96.5	96.1	94.9	93.7	93.5	95.0	97.4	100.0	102.6	104.2	106.2	107.8	107.9
Energy	69.8	75.8	85.7	90.4	88.5	89.6	89.5	83.1	92.3	97.9	103.3	100.0	88.5	92.5	96.6	94.8	90.6
Non-energy materials	87.7	92.7	94.2	89.1	83.7	80.8	73.6	78.8	85.9	93.8	94.6	100.0	100.8	110.4	119.6	119.8	119.0
Purchased business services	47.4	55.7	59.6	58.0	62.8	63.0	60.4	69.5	100.3	102.6	98.0	100.0	104.5	106.9	112.8	106.8	93.2
Combined units of all inputs	86.0	89.6	92.3	90.4	88.3	86.2	79.8	83.4	90.5	96.1	97.3	100.0	101.3	106.6	111.6	110.9	106.8
Furniture and Fixtures																	
Output per hour of all persons	81.6	84.1	86.8	85.5	85.4	87.6	88.0	91.7	93.5	93.8	98.2	100.0	107.2	111.3	113.0	114.0	116.6
Output per unit of capital	100.4	102.9	104.7	101.0	100.0	96.7	90.5	97.0	99.7	100.5	101.2	100.0	107.0	109.3	108.1	105.5	96.4
Multifactor productivity	95.0	94.5	95.9	95.5	95.4	95.4	95.7	98.7	100.5	99.3	99.9	100.0	103.4	103.2	103.7	103.4	103.0
Sector output	78.6	82.5	87.2	87.1	87.8	86.4	80.9	87.4	92.0	95.0	98.7	100.0	111.0	119.0	123.9	126.1	116.3
Hours of all persons at work	96.3	98.1	100.5	101.9	102.7	98.6	91.9	95.3	98.4	101.3	100.5	100.0	103.5	106.9	109.6	110.6	99.8
Capital services	78.3	80.2	83.3	86.3	87.8	89.4	89.3	90.2	92.3	94.6	97.5	100.0	103.7	108.9	114.5	119.4	120.7
Energy	71.4	76.3	89.6	92.7	97.2	91.3	90.4	91.2	96.3	98.5	103.9	100.0	110.5	118.0	122.7	125.0	117.1
Non-energy materials	74.4	79.8	83.2	82.9	83.9	84.2	78.6	83.5	86.8	92.2	97.5	100.0	109.4	121.2	126.3	129.9	121.6
Purchased business services	90.5	103.0	111.8	108.4	106.1	101.6	90.4	93.4	95.3	97.8	101.3	100.0	112.2	118.1	120.7	120.9	107.4
Combined units of all inputs	82.7	87.3	90.9	91.3	92.0	90.6	84.5	88.6	91.6	95.7	98.8	100.0	107.3	115.3	119.4	122.0	113.0
Stone, Clay, and Glass																	
Output per hour of all persons	85.5	88.9	91.1	90.2	89.9	92.1	90.9	95.7	95.8	96.1	97.3	100.0	103.9	108.4	108.5	107.0	102.3
Output per unit of capital	81.0	84.2	86.4	88.3	87.4	87.0	80.9	86.5	90.1	95.2	96.8	100.0	98.4	97.9	93.7	88.5	80.4
Multifactor productivity	89.6	92.9	94.5	94.7	95.7	96.6	94.4	98.8	97.4	99.2	99.9	100.0	103.9	103.2	102.2	100.1	94.9
Sector output	82.7	86.2	88.4	90.2	89.6	88.7	81.7	85.7	87.6	91.9	94.5	100.0	103.5	108.9	110.4	109.9	104.6
Hours of all persons at work	96.7	97.0	97.0	100.0	99.7	96.4	89.9	89.5	91.4	95.6	97.1	100.0	99.6	100.5	101.8	102.7	102.3
Capital services	102.1	102.4	102.2	102.2	102.5	102.0	101.0	99.1	97.2	96.5	97.6	100.0	105.2	111.3	117.8	124.1	130.1
Energy	95.2	100.4	102.6	104.5	101.7	101.6	97.0	99.6	100.6	98.7	104.3	100.0	101.7	107.1	108.4	108.1	104.5
Non-energy materials	87.2	86.4	86.7	87.6	84.3	83.4	78.3	78.5	84.7	87.8	89.7	100.0	97.3	108.7	111.2	113.1	114.5
Purchased business services	72.6	78.1	85.3	88.0	87.8	86.8	81.6	85.5	87.9	90.3	94.0	100.0	97.4	102.3	102.4	100.2	96.1
Combined units of all inputs	92.3	92.8	93.5	95.3	93.6	91.9	86.6	86.7	89.9	92.7	94.6	100.0	99.6	105.5	108.0	109.8	110.3
Primary Metal Industries																	
Output per hour of all persons	76.0	81.4	85.2	87.8	85.3	85.3	86.0	91.4	95.2	96.1	97.7	100.0	100.9	106.5	105.8	104.0	102.8
Output per unit of capital	74.0	75.3	82.1	90.2	88.6	86.5	82.2	86.1	91.4	97.2	98.5	100.0	101.6	103.9	102.0	100.3	92.1
Multifactor productivity	92.0	98.1	97.0	96.4	94.6	96.2	96.6	99.8	103.4	102.2	99.9	100.0	100.3	102.7	103.4	99.8	101.2
Sector output	81.5	81.0	86.5	93.7	91.1	88.5	83.7	86.6	91.0	96.2	97.7	100.0	102.6	106.3	105.7	104.2	94.4
Hours of all persons at work	107.3	99.6	101.5	106.8	106.8	103.7	97.3	94.8	95.5	100.2	100.0	100.0	101.7	99.8	99.9	100.2	91.9
Capital services	110.1	107.5	105.3	103.9	102.8	102.3	101.8	100.6	99.5	99.0	99.2	100.0	101.0	102.3	103.7	103.9	102.5
Energy	103.5	95.5	98.9	111.5	103.2	105.2	107.0	99.7	99.0	110.2	99.9	100.0	94.6	97.6	97.7	95.9	87.0
Non-energy materials	75.0	69.4	78.6	88.2	86.8	80.9	75.8	78.2	80.2	87.4	94.9	100.0	103.8	107.9	106.4	112.5	98.3
Purchased business services	73.2	70.9	84.0	100.6	101.2	92.9	81.4	83.9	85.0	93.6	101.6	100.0	103.6	100.9	94.1	91.4	76.0
Combined units of all inputs	88.6	82.6	89.1	97.6	96.3	91.9	86.6	86.8	88.0	94.1	97.7	100.0	102.3	103.5	102.3	104.4	93.3
Fabricated Metal Product																	
Output per hour of all persons	84.6	87.6	91.4	90.3	87.1	87.8	87.5	92.7	94.5	96.6	98.2	100.0	103.2	106.6	106.3	107.6	106.0
Output per unit of capital	98.0	95.4	95.5	98.4	95.6	92.5	87.3	91.9	94.7	100.0	100.2	100.0	103.5	103.9	101.3	101.4	93.6
Multifactor productivity	94.9	95.7	98.7	99.4	96.6	95.3	93.4	95.1	96.2	99.6	100.3	100.0	101.3	100.7	99.8	101.1	98.0
Sector output	83.3	83.3	85.1	87.7	85.3	83.4	79.1	83.7	86.9	93.5	96.8	100.0	106.4	110.8	111.5	114.0	105.9
Hours of all persons at work	98.4	95.1	93.1	97.2	97.9	95.0	90.3	90.2	92.0	96.8	98.6	100.0	103.1	103.9	104.9	106.0	99.9
Capital services	85.0	87.3	89.1	89.1	89.2	90.1	90.6	91.1	91.9	93.5	96.6	100.0	102.8	106.7	110.1	112.5	113.1
Energy	79.8	80.7	89.6	93.3	93.0	92.3	91.2	88.4	92.8	96.1	102.7	100.0	102.5	106.4	107.3	109.7	102.8
Non-energy materials	82.7	82.6	80.7	81.5	80.9	81.4	79.4	85.2	88.7	91.7	94.3	100.0	106.9	116.1	118.7	119.5	115.1
Purchased business services	79.8	80.3	85.2	89.9	90.7	88.0	83.1	89.5	91.0	94.8	99.2	100.0	106.9	109.5	106.0	105.6	96.0
Combined units of all inputs	87.8	87.0	86.2	88.3	88.2	87.5	84.7	87.9	90.4	93.9	96.5	100.0	105.0	110.0	111.7	112.8	108.1

Table 5-5. Indexes of Multifactor Productivity and Related Measures, Manufacturing Industries, 1985–2001
—Continued

(1996 = 100.)

Industry	1985	1986	1987	1988	1989	1990	1991	1992	1993	1994	1995	1996	1997	1998	1999	2000	2001
Industrial Machinery and Computer Equipment																	
Output per hour of all persons	49.7	53.1	55.7	60.1	60.9	62.4	62.3	69.1	74.1	81.2	89.6	100.0	108.5	120.6	132.0	146.4	145.5
Output per unit of capital	75.6	73.5	75.0	81.9	80.9	79.0	73.3	77.2	81.6	88.2	95.1	100.0	104.3	105.8	101.6	103.0	90.5
Multifactor productivity	69.1	71.4	76.2	80.2	80.9	81.7	79.8	84.1	86.3	90.8	95.1	100.0	106.8	118.0	125.2	137.6	139.5
Sector output	50.1	50.4	52.2	59.0	60.5	60.6	57.6	62.3	68.4	77.6	89.0	100.0	113.0	126.2	132.3	143.4	131.8
Hours of all persons at work	100.9	94.9	93.7	98.2	99.3	97.1	92.4	90.2	92.3	95.5	99.4	100.0	104.2	104.6	100.2	98.0	90.6
Capital services	66.2	68.5	69.7	72.0	74.7	76.7	78.5	80.7	83.8	88.0	93.5	100.0	108.3	119.3	130.3	139.3	145.6
Energy	86.1	86.9	92.0	94.9	99.2	99.1	97.7	89.9	92.7	99.5	102.8	100.0	99.9	111.2	117.2	125.6	117.0
Non-energy materials	54.4	53.5	50.1	55.9	56.7	57.0	56.3	60.9	68.4	76.5	88.6	100.0	107.8	108.3	107.9	105.8	92.3
Purchased business services	72.2	74.0	75.2	80.4	80.6	76.1	70.7	73.9	79.8	88.9	95.7	100.0	100.4	96.7	93.2	90.0	77.4
Combined units of all inputs	72.5	70.5	68.6	73.6	74.8	74.2	72.2	74.1	79.2	85.4	93.6	100.0	105.8	106.9	105.7	104.2	94.5
Electrical and Electronic Equipment																	
Output per hour of all persons	38.3	40.7	44.4	46.4	47.9	51.0	54.8	61.9	67.0	75.6	88.8	100.0	113.9	126.3	152.1	184.6	185.0
Output per unit of capital	67.9	65.9	66.0	68.3	67.8	66.8	66.6	71.8	76.2	84.6	94.3	100.0	105.6	110.0	122.1	142.0	123.2
Multifactor productivity	59.8	61.6	65.6	67.6	69.2	70.9	72.7	76.2	79.3	86.6	94.4	100.0	108.7	112.5	126.4	140.0	146.2
Sector output	41.5	42.6	45.2	48.3	49.2	50.0	50.7	55.9	61.5	71.7	86.4	100.0	115.4	128.9	151.2	187.4	172.8
Hours of all persons at work	108.3	104.6	102.0	104.1	102.8	98.2	92.5	90.4	91.7	94.9	97.4	100.0	101.3	102.1	99.4	101.5	93.4
Capital services	61.1	64.6	68.6	70.7	72.7	74.9	76.1	78.0	80.7	84.7	91.7	100.0	109.2	117.3	123.8	131.9	140.3
Energy	75.1	77.7	87.5	88.5	90.8	92.1	90.8	89.8	95.2	97.8	102.6	100.0	107.7	120.8	144.2	178.2	163.7
Non-energy materials	46.2	45.8	44.6	47.1	46.4	47.2	48.7	55.9	62.6	68.7	83.8	100.0	106.9	130.0	139.9	179.6	146.0
Purchased business services	55.7	58.7	62.1	64.5	63.5	60.9	57.9	66.9	70.7	82.1	95.0	100.0	111.8	112.4	132.1	150.1	114.1
Combined units of all inputs	69.3	69.1	68.9	71.4	71.1	70.6	69.7	73.5	77.5	82.8	91.6	100.0	106.1	114.6	119.6	133.8	118.2
Transportation Equipment																	
Output per hour of all persons	72.8	75.9	77.9	78.7	78.6	80.4	80.3	87.8	92.9	97.8	98.0	100.0	106.6	114.7	123.7	119.8	121.4
Output per unit of capital	95.4	94.6	93.2	95.7	94.1	90.9	84.5	90.3	94.2	100.6	100.8	100.0	107.1	110.1	115.1	106.7	101.2
Multifactor productivity	102.3	102.3	103.7	102.8	100.1	99.1	98.0	98.1	100.4	101.8	101.4	100.0	102.5	105.8	108.1	108.4	109.5
Sector output	78.4	81.6	83.2	88.0	88.1	86.4	81.1	86.6	90.5	97.2	98.3	100.0	111.1	120.2	131.2	123.4	116.5
Hours of all persons at work	107.7	107.5	106.7	111.9	112.1	107.5	101.0	98.6	97.4	99.4	100.3	100.0	104.3	104.7	106.1	103.0	96.0
Capital services	82.2	86.2	89.3	92.0	93.6	95.0	95.9	95.9	96.1	96.6	97.5	100.0	103.8	109.1	114.0	115.7	115.2
Energy	75.8	78.1	100.8	97.3	95.2	95.7	92.6	95.9	101.2	101.7	104.9	100.0	103.9	112.6	122.3	114.1	108.5
Non-energy materials	63.7	66.9	66.6	71.8	74.1	74.7	70.0	79.1	83.2	91.2	94.0	100.0	111.6	120.1	131.8	120.9	112.1
Purchased business services	57.1	66.7	71.3	81.3	90.7	91.1	91.3	102.0	100.8	105.5	102.5	100.0	107.6	108.5	118.5	103.9	93.9
Combined units of all inputs	76.7	79.7	80.3	85.6	88.0	87.2	82.7	88.2	90.1	95.4	96.9	100.0	108.4	113.6	121.5	113.9	106.4
Instruments																	
Output per hour of all persons	64.6	68.7	73.5	74.0	74.3	77.4	80.6	87.2	88.3	91.5	95.3	100.0	99.2	103.0	108.3	116.1	113.3
Output per unit of capital	117.1	116.6	125.5	126.1	117.0	112.0	106.3	104.6	100.9	99.1	98.9	100.0	96.7	94.5	91.2	90.8	84.3
Multifactor productivity	90.8	92.1	95.4	99.1	96.6	98.9	98.9	100.0	98.7	99.5	98.9	100.0	98.8	102.6	105.6	112.4	111.4
Sector output	77.4	79.9	84.9	88.3	87.8	89.1	89.3	92.8	92.6	92.5	94.7	100.0	102.1	105.2	108.6	114.1	110.0
Hours of all persons at work	119.9	116.4	115.5	119.3	118.2	115.2	110.7	106.4	104.9	101.1	99.4	100.0	103.0	102.1	100.2	98.3	97.1
Capital services	66.1	68.5	67.7	70.0	75.0	79.6	84.0	88.7	91.8	93.4	95.7	100.0	105.6	111.4	119.0	125.6	130.5
Energy	98.6	102.0	96.3	100.1	99.7	104.2	100.6	99.4	100.5	99.2	104.5	100.0	98.6	100.9	104.3	109.5	107.3
Non-energy materials	60.8	65.0	68.4	65.8	68.7	69.3	72.2	78.7	80.6	82.4	89.7	100.0	104.9	104.3	106.1	104.7	101.3
Purchased business services	80.1	82.3	89.6	89.4	94.8	92.6	92.8	99.8	104.5	103.7	104.3	100.0	99.1	95.3	95.4	94.8	86.5
Combined units of all inputs	85.3	86.7	89.0	89.0	90.9	90.2	90.3	92.8	93.8	93.0	95.7	100.0	103.4	102.6	102.8	101.5	98.8
Miscellaneous Manufacturing																	
Output per hour of all persons	84.2	85.5	89.4	90.4	87.7	90.9	90.0	90.6	92.0	91.1	97.5	100.0	96.9	99.9	104.8	112.5	108.9
Output per unit of capital	87.0	89.9	91.9	96.9	93.6	93.8	91.2	92.3	95.6	96.2	98.5	100.0	100.2	99.9	100.1	102.4	95.7
Multifactor productivity	98.8	97.9	100.0	103.3	101.8	100.9	97.2	95.0	95.4	96.7	99.7	100.0	100.2	99.6	102.7	109.2	105.9
Sector output	77.0	79.7	83.5	88.9	87.0	87.6	84.6	87.6	92.4	94.4	97.1	100.0	102.1	103.9	106.9	111.4	104.7
Hours of all persons at work	91.4	93.2	93.4	98.4	99.2	96.4	94.0	96.7	100.5	103.6	99.6	100.0	105.3	104.0	102.0	99.0	96.1
Capital services	88.5	88.6	90.9	91.7	93.0	93.4	92.7	94.9	96.7	98.1	98.6	100.0	101.9	104.0	106.8	108.8	109.4
Energy	67.8	73.4	90.1	91.9	94.4	95.6	93.3	84.7	95.6	96.2	107.9	100.0	83.8	84.7	87.3	90.4	85.8
Non-energy materials	65.7	69.6	71.0	72.3	71.1	75.9	79.1	87.5	94.0	93.4	94.7	100.0	100.0	107.2	108.2	105.2	101.0
Purchased business services	72.8	83.2	92.1	95.3	91.1	90.3	86.0	92.5	97.6	95.4	97.9	100.0	100.4	98.3	93.7	90.6	84.0
Combined units of all inputs	77.9	81.4	83.6	86.0	85.5	86.9	87.0	92.2	96.9	97.6	97.4	100.0	101.9	104.3	104.1	102.0	98.8

CHAPTER SIX

COMPENSATION OF EMPLOYEES

COMPENSATION OF EMPLOYEES

HIGHLIGHTS

This chapter discusses the Employment Cost Index (ECI), which covers changes in wages and salaries, and benefits; the Employer Costs for Employee Compensation (ECEC); employee participation in various benefit plans; and occupational wage data from the National Compensation Survey (NCS).

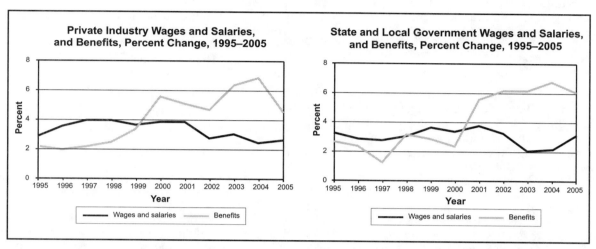

In 2005, in a trend that has been occurring since 2000, the ECI reported increases in benefits exceeded increases in wages and salaries. In private industry, wages and salaries rose 2.6 percent in 2005, which was somewhat faster than the rate during the previous year. Benefits increased 4.2 percent, far slower than the rate during the previous year. Wage costs for state and local governments increased 3.1 percent, while benefit costs increased at a rapid rate of 6.0 percent. (See Tables 6-1, 6-3, and 6-4.)

OTHER HIGHLIGHTS

• Wage increases in most industries hovered between 2 and 3 percent in 2005. Sales occupations experienced the greatest increase at 3.8 percent. Wage increases in hospitals, nursing homes, educational services, and colleges and universities, all exceeded 3 percent. (See Table 6-1.)

• In 2005, the rise in benefit costs in the aircraft manufacturing industry (39.9 percent) continued to vastly exceed the increases in any other industry. This rise in benefit costs was also an increase from 2004, when benefits in aircraft manufacturing rose by close to 25 percent. (See Table 6-4.)

• Health insurance costs for state and local governments are considerably higher than the costs in private industry—$3.91 cents per hour, compared to $1.72 per hour. (See Tables 6-5 and 6-7.)

• Service-providing industries spent $1.54 per hour on health insurance (compared to $2.47 per hour in goods-producing industries) in March 2006, indicating less or no coverage for many workers in the services sector. (See Table 6-5.)

NOTES AND DEFINITIONS

EMPLOYMENT COST INDEX

The National Compensation Survey (NCS) provides data for the Employment Cost Index (ECI), the Employer Costs for Employee Compensation (ECEC), employee benefits, and occupational wages. In 2005, the NCS classified workers into one of 480 occupations based on job duties.

Collection and Coverage

The ECI is a quarterly measure of the rate of change in compensation per hour worked and includes wages and salaries and the employer costs of employee benefits. It uses a fixed market basket of labor—similar in concept to the Consumer Price Index's fixed market basket of goods and services—to measure the change over time in the employer costs of employing labor.

Statistical series on total compensation costs, wages and salaries, and benefit costs are available for private nonfarm workers, excluding business proprietors, the self-employed, and household workers. The total compensation costs and wages and salaries series are also available for state and local government workers and for the civilian nonfarm economy, which consists of private industry and state and local government workers. Federal workers are excluded.

The variables included in the ECI probability sample changed from 1990 to 2005. The ECI probability sample for December 2005 consisted of about 11,300 private industry establishments (which provided about 50,400 occupational observations) and from approximately 3,500 occupations within about 800 sample establishments in state and local governments. On average, each reporting unit provided wage and compensation information on five well-specified occupations. These occupations were defined narrowly enough to ensure that all workers in the job carried out the same task at roughly the same level of skill. Data were collected each quarter for the pay periods that contained the 12th days of March, June, September, and December.

From June 1986 to March 1995, fixed employment weights from the 1980 decennial census were used each quarter to calculate the civilian and private indexes and the index for state and local governments. In March 1995, employment weights from the 1990 decennial census were introduced. Prior to June 1986, the employment weights came from the 1970 decennial census. These fixed weights, also used to derive all of the industry and occupation series indexes,

ensure that changes in these indexes reflect only changes in compensation—not employment shifts among industries or occupations with different levels of wages and compensation. However, for the bargaining status, region, and metropolitan/nonmetropolitan area series, employment data by industry and occupation are not available from the census. Instead, the 1980 employment weights are reallocated quarterly within these series, based on the current sample. Therefore, these indexes are not strictly comparable to indexes for the aggregate, industry, and occupation series.

The ECI was converted to the North American Industry Classification System (NAICS) in 2006.

Concepts and Definitions

Total compensation costs include wages and salaries, and the employer costs of employee benefits.

Wages and salaries consist of earnings before payroll deductions, including production bonuses, incentive earnings, commissions, and cost-of-living adjustments.

Benefits include the cost to employers for paid leave, supplemental pay (including nonproduction bonuses), insurance, retirement and savings plans, and legally required benefits such as Social Security, workers' compensation, and unemployment insurance.

Excluded from wages and salaries and employee benefit costs are items such as payment-in-kind, free room and board, and tips.

Bonuses. In June 2000, the Bureau of Labor Statistics (BLS) expanded the definition of nonproduction bonuses in the ECI to better represent the compensation packages offered to employees. In addition to the traditional types of nonproduction bonuses (such as attendance bonuses and lump-sum payments), the ECI will include hiring bonuses and referral bonuses. Hiring bonuses are payments made by the employer to induce an individual to accept employment; referral bonuses are made by the employer to an employee for recommending an applicant who is hired by the establishment.

Sources of Additional Information

Additional information on ECI methodology and data is available in BLS news releases. BLS's e-publication, *Compensation and Working Conditions*, contains articles on all aspects of the NCS. All of these resources are available on the BLS Web site at <http://www.bls.gov>.

Table 6-1. Employment Cost Index, Private Industry Workers,[1] Total Compensation and Wages and Salaries, by Occupation and Industry, 1990–2005

(December 2005 = 100.)

Characteristic and year	Total compensation					Wages and salaries				
	Indexes				Percent change for 12 months (ended December)	Indexes				Percent change for 12 months (ended December)
	March	June	September	December		March	June	September	December	
WORKERS BY INDUSTRY										
Private Industry Workers										
1990	57.6	58.3	58.9	59.3	4.6	60.6	61.3	61.9	62.3	4.0
1991	60.1	60.9	61.5	61.9	4.4	63.0	63.6	64.1	64.6	3.7
1992	62.7	63.1	63.6	64.1	3.6	65.1	65.5	65.8	66.3	2.6
1993	64.9	65.4	66.0	66.4	3.6	66.8	67.3	67.9	68.3	3.0
1994	67.1	67.6	68.2	68.5	3.2	68.8	69.3	69.9	70.2	2.8
1995	69.0	69.5	70.0	70.2	2.5	70.8	71.3	71.8	72.2	2.8
1996	70.9	71.5	72.0	72.4	3.1	73.0	73.7	74.2	74.7	3.5
1997	73.0	73.6	74.2	74.9	3.5	75.5	76.1	76.9	77.6	3.9
1998	75.6	76.2	77.1	77.5	3.5	78.5	79.2	80.2	80.6	3.9
1999	77.8	78.7	79.4	80.2	3.5	81.0	82.0	82.7	83.5	3.6
2000	81.4	82.3	83.1	83.6	4.2	84.4	85.3	86.2	86.7	3.8
2001	84.8	85.6	86.4	87.1	4.2	87.7	88.6	89.3	90.0	3.8
2002	88.1	89.1	89.6	90.0	3.3	90.8	91.7	92.1	92.4	2.7
2003	91.5	92.2	93.2	93.6	4.0	93.5	94.1	94.9	95.2	3.0
2004	95.0	95.9	96.7	97.1	3.7	95.9	96.5	97.4	97.5	2.4
2005	98.2	98.9	99.6	100.0	3.0	98.2	98.8	99.5	100.0	2.6
Private Industry Workers, Excluding Sales Occupations										
1990	57.5	58.2	58.9	59.3	5.0	60.6	61.3	61.9	62.4	4.3
1991	60.1	60.8	61.5	62.0	4.6	63.1	63.7	64.2	64.7	3.7
1992	62.7	63.2	63.7	64.2	3.5	65.2	65.6	66.1	66.5	2.8
1993	65.1	65.6	66.2	66.6	3.7	67.1	67.5	68.1	68.5	3.0
1994	67.2	67.7	68.3	68.6	3.0	69.0	69.5	70.1	70.5	2.9
1995	69.2	69.6	70.0	70.4	2.6	71.1	71.5	72.0	72.5	2.8
1996	71.0	71.5	72.1	72.4	2.8	73.2	73.8	74.5	74.9	3.3
1997	73.0	73.6	74.3	74.9	3.5	75.5	76.3	77.0	77.7	3.7
1998	75.5	76.1	76.9	77.2	3.1	78.5	79.2	80.0	80.4	3.5
1999	77.8	78.6	79.3	80.0	3.6	81.2	82.0	82.7	83.4	3.7
2000	81.1	82.1	82.9	83.6	4.5	84.3	85.2	86.0	86.7	4.0
2001	84.7	85.5	86.4	87.0	4.1	87.8	88.5	89.4	90.0	3.8
2002	88.0	88.9	89.5	89.9	3.3	91.0	91.7	92.2	92.5	2.8
2003	91.4	92.2	93.1	93.6	4.1	93.6	94.2	95.0	95.4	3.1
2004	95.0	95.9	96.7	97.2	3.8	96.0	96.6	97.4	97.8	2.5
2005	98.4	99.1	99.6	100.0	2.9	98.4	99.1	99.6	100.0	2.2
WORKERS BY OCCUPATIONAL GROUP										
White-Collar Occupations										
1990	56.6	57.4	58.1	58.4	4.8	59.4	60.2	60.8	61.2	4.3
1991	59.3	60.0	60.6	61.0	4.5	61.9	62.6	63.2	63.5	3.8
1992	61.7	62.1	62.6	63.1	3.4	64.1	64.4	64.8	65.2	2.7
1993	63.9	64.4	65.0	65.4	3.6	65.8	66.3	67.0	67.4	3.4
1994	66.1	66.6	67.2	67.5	3.2	67.9	68.4	69.0	69.3	2.8
1995	68.2	68.7	69.1	69.4	2.8	69.8	70.4	70.9	71.3	2.9
1996	70.2	70.7	71.3	71.7	3.3	72.2	72.9	73.4	73.8	3.5
1997	72.4	73.0	73.6	74.4	3.8	74.7	75.3	76.1	77.0	4.3
1998	75.1	75.8	76.8	77.3	3.9	77.9	78.6	79.7	80.3	4.3
1999	77.5	78.4	79.2	79.9	3.4	80.5	81.5	82.3	83.1	3.5
2000	81.2	82.2	83.0	83.6	4.6	84.1	85.1	85.9	86.4	4.0
2001	84.7	85.6	86.3	87.1	4.2	87.4	88.2	88.8	89.6	3.7
2002	88.1	89.1	89.6	89.9	3.2	90.5	91.5	91.8	92.0	2.7
2003	91.5	92.2	93.1	93.6	4.1	93.3	94.0	94.8	95.2	3.5
2004	94.8	95.6	96.5	96.9	3.5	95.9	96.5	97.4	97.5	2.4
2005	98.2	98.8	99.6	100.0	3.2	98.3	98.9	99.5	100.0	2.6
White-Collar Occupations, Excluding Sales Occupations										
1990	56.4	57.0	57.8	58.2	5.2	59.2	59.8	60.6	61.0	4.8
1991	59.1	59.7	60.5	61.0	4.8	61.7	62.3	63.0	63.5	4.1
1992	61.5	62.0	62.6	63.1	3.4	63.9	64.3	64.9	65.3	2.8
1993	64.0	64.5	65.0	65.4	3.6	66.0	66.4	67.0	67.4	3.2
1994	66.2	66.7	67.3	67.7	3.5	67.9	68.4	69.0	69.4	3.0
1995	68.3	68.7	69.1	69.6	2.8	70.1	70.4	70.9	71.4	2.9
1996	70.3	70.7	71.4	71.7	3.0	72.3	72.8	73.6	73.8	3.4
1997	72.3	72.9	73.5	74.3	3.6	74.6	75.3	76.1	76.9	4.2
1998	75.1	75.7	76.4	76.7	3.2	77.8	78.4	79.3	79.7	3.6
1999	77.3	78.2	79.0	79.7	3.9	80.4	81.3	82.1	82.8	3.9
2000	80.8	81.8	82.7	83.3	4.5	83.7	84.7	85.5	86.2	4.1
2001	84.6	85.5	86.3	87.0	4.4	87.3	88.1	88.8	89.5	3.8
2002	88.0	88.9	89.4	89.7	3.1	90.5	91.3	91.7	92.0	2.8
2003	91.5	92.2	93.1	93.6	4.3	93.3	94.0	94.8	95.3	3.6
2004	94.8	95.6	96.4	97.1	3.7	95.9	96.5	97.3	97.8	2.6
2005	98.4	99.1	99.6	100.0	3.0	98.5	99.1	99.5	100.0	2.2

[1] Excludes farm and household workers.

Table 6-1. Employment Cost Index, Private Industry Workers,[1] Total Compensation and Wages and Salaries, by Occupation and Industry, 1990–2005—*Continued*

(December 2005 = 100.)

Characteristic and year	Total compensation					Wages and salaries				
	Indexes				Percent change for 12 months (ended December)	Indexes				Percent change for 12 months (ended December)
	March	June	September	December		March	June	September	December	
Professional Specialty and Technical Occupations										
1990	57.2	57.7	58.6	59.2	5.5	60.6	61.0	62.0	62.6	4.9
1991	60.0	60.5	61.5	62.1	4.9	63.2	63.8	64.7	65.2	4.2
1992	62.8	63.4	64.3	64.9	4.5	65.8	66.4	67.2	67.6	3.7
1993	65.6	66.1	66.6	67.0	3.2	68.2	68.7	69.2	69.6	3.0
1994	67.9	68.3	68.8	69.1	3.1	70.1	70.6	71.2	71.6	2.9
1995	69.6	70.0	70.5	70.8	2.5	72.0	72.5	73.0	73.4	2.5
1996	71.7	72.3	72.6	72.9	3.0	74.4	75.0	75.5	75.7	3.1
1997	73.4	74.1	74.5	75.1	3.0	76.3	77.1	77.9	78.5	3.7
1998	75.6	76.3	77.2	77.7	3.5	79.1	79.8	80.8	81.4	3.7
1999	77.9	78.5	79.1	79.9	2.8	81.9	82.6	83.1	83.9	3.1
2000	80.9	82.1	82.9	83.8	4.9	84.5	85.8	86.5	87.5	4.3
2001	85.2	85.8	86.8	87.4	4.3	88.6	89.2	90.2	90.8	3.8
2002	88.0	88.6	89.2	89.6	2.5	91.3	91.7	92.1	92.3	1.7
2003	90.7	91.4	92.3	92.9	3.7	92.9	93.5	94.4	94.9	2.8
2004	94.5	95.2	96.3	97.1	4.5	95.9	96.4	97.6	97.8	3.1
2005	98.5	99.0	99.7	100.0	3.0	98.7	99.0	99.7	100.0	2.2
Executive, Administrative, and Managerial Occupations										
1990	55.9	56.8	57.5	57.8	5.7	57.5	58.4	59.1	59.5	5.3
1991	58.7	59.5	60.1	60.5	4.7	60.2	60.9	61.6	62.0	4.2
1992	60.8	61.0	61.4	61.7	2.0	62.1	62.4	62.6	63.0	1.6
1993	62.8	63.2	63.7	64.1	3.9	63.9	64.2	64.7	65.1	3.3
1994	64.9	65.4	66.1	66.5	3.7	65.6	66.1	66.8	67.1	3.1
1995	67.3	67.6	68.0	68.4	2.9	67.9	68.2	68.7	69.3	3.3
1996	69.0	69.4	70.6	70.8	3.5	70.1	70.6	71.8	72.0	3.9
1997	71.7	72.2	72.9	74.1	4.7	72.9	73.6	74.4	75.6	5.0
1998	75.1	75.5	76.5	76.4	3.1	76.7	77.2	78.5	78.2	3.4
1999	77.5	78.6	79.6	80.4	5.2	79.0	80.3	81.5	82.2	5.1
2000	81.5	82.3	83.2	83.7	4.1	83.1	83.9	84.8	85.2	3.6
2001	84.8	85.9	86.4	87.2	4.2	86.1	87.1	87.5	88.3	3.6
2002	88.6	89.8	90.0	90.1	3.3	89.8	91.1	91.5	91.6	3.7
2003	92.8	93.3	94.3	94.8	5.2	94.2	94.8	95.7	96.0	4.8
2004	95.3	96.0	96.6	97.1	2.4	96.2	96.8	97.4	97.8	1.9
2005	98.7	99.3	99.6	100.0	3.0	98.7	99.3	99.5	100.0	2.2
Sales Occupations										
1990	58.0	59.1	59.3	59.4	2.8	60.7	61.8	61.9	61.8	1.5
1991	60.5	61.5	61.5	61.4	3.4	62.7	63.7	63.5	63.4	2.6
1992	62.5	62.8	62.6	63.0	2.6	64.4	64.7	64.4	65.0	2.5
1993	63.2	63.7	64.7	65.2	3.5	64.9	65.5	66.8	67.4	3.7
1994	65.6	66.5	66.7	67.0	2.8	67.4	68.2	68.4	68.5	1.6
1995	67.3	68.5	69.0	69.0	3.0	68.6	70.1	70.8	70.7	3.2
1996	69.9	71.1	70.9	71.7	3.9	71.6	73.0	72.8	73.9	4.5
1997	72.8	73.2	74.0	74.7	4.2	75.0	75.3	76.2	77.2	4.5
1998	75.8	76.9	78.6	79.8	6.8	78.2	79.4	81.5	83.0	7.5
1999	78.2	79.8	80.7	81.4	2.0	80.6	82.5	83.4	84.1	1.3
2000	83.4	84.2	84.7	84.8	4.2	86.1	86.8	87.5	87.3	3.8
2001	85.3	86.5	86.8	87.7	3.4	87.6	89.0	88.8	89.6	2.6
2002	88.3	90.5	90.5	90.6	3.3	90.2	92.2	92.1	92.1	2.8
2003	91.5	92.4	93.6	93.6	3.3	92.8	93.5	94.9	94.6	2.7
2004	94.7	95.9	96.9	96.0	2.6	95.5	96.2	97.4	96.3	1.8
2005	96.9	97.6	99.1	100.0	4.2	96.8	97.5	99.2	100.0	3.8
Administrative Support Occupations, Including Clerical Occupations										
1990	55.9	56.5	57.1	57.6	4.9	59.2	59.8	60.4	60.8	4.1
1991	58.3	59.0	59.6	60.1	4.3	61.5	62.1	62.6	63.1	3.8
1992	61.0	61.4	62.0	62.5	4.0	63.8	64.2	64.7	65.1	3.2
1993	63.4	64.0	64.6	65.1	4.2	65.8	66.3	66.9	67.4	3.5
1994	65.8	66.3	66.8	67.1	3.1	68.0	68.5	69.1	69.5	3.1
1995	67.9	68.3	68.8	69.2	3.1	70.2	70.6	71.0	71.6	3.0
1996	69.8	70.2	70.9	71.1	2.7	72.3	72.7	73.4	73.8	3.1
1997	71.8	72.3	72.9	73.5	3.4	74.6	75.3	75.9	76.5	3.7
1998	74.2	74.9	75.5	75.9	3.3	77.3	78.1	78.8	79.4	3.8
1999	76.5	77.1	77.8	78.5	3.4	80.2	80.8	81.5	82.2	3.5
2000	80.0	80.8	81.7	82.3	4.8	83.4	84.3	85.2	85.8	4.4
2001	83.8	84.6	85.6	86.3	4.9	87.0	87.8	88.7	89.4	4.2
2002	87.4	88.1	88.9	89.5	3.7	90.4	91.0	91.6	92.2	3.1
2003	90.7	91.7	92.5	92.9	3.8	92.9	93.7	94.3	94.7	2.7
2004	94.5	95.6	96.3	97.0	4.4	95.5	96.3	97.0	97.6	3.1
2005	98.1	98.9	99.5	100.0	3.1	98.3	99.0	99.5	100.0	2.5

[1] Excludes farm and household workers.

Table 6-1. Employment Cost Index, Private Industry Workers,[1] Total Compensation and Wages and Salaries, by Occupation and Industry, 1990–2005—Continued

(December 2005 = 100.)

Characteristic and year	Total compensation					Wages and salaries				
	Indexes				Percent change for 12 months (ended December)	Indexes				Percent change for 12 months (ended December)
	March	June	September	December		March	June	September	December	
Blue-Collar Occupations										
1990	59.1	59.8	60.3	60.7	4.3	62.7	63.3	63.8	64.2	3.5
1991	61.6	62.2	62.9	63.4	4.4	64.9	65.5	65.9	66.4	3.4
1992	64.2	64.7	65.2	65.6	3.5	66.9	67.4	67.8	68.1	2.6
1993	66.6	67.2	67.8	68.1	3.8	68.6	69.1	69.6	70.0	2.8
1994	68.7	69.2	69.8	70.0	2.8	70.5	71.1	71.7	72.0	2.9
1995	70.5	71.0	71.4	71.7	2.4	72.6	73.3	73.7	74.1	2.9
1996	72.3	72.8	73.1	73.6	2.6	74.7	75.5	75.8	76.3	3.0
1997	74.0	74.7	75.2	75.5	2.6	76.9	77.7	78.3	78.8	3.3
1998	76.0	76.7	77.2	77.6	2.8	79.4	80.1	80.8	81.3	3.2
1999	78.1	78.9	79.6	80.2	3.4	81.9	82.7	83.5	84.0	3.3
2000	81.4	82.2	83.0	83.6	4.2	84.9	85.7	86.6	87.1	3.7
2001	84.6	85.2	86.2	86.7	3.7	88.2	89.0	90.0	90.5	3.9
2002	87.7	88.5	89.2	89.8	3.6	91.3	92.1	92.6	93.0	2.8
2003	91.2	92.1	92.9	93.4	4.0	93.7	94.3	94.9	95.2	2.4
2004	95.3	96.3	97.1	97.5	4.4	95.9	96.6	97.3	97.6	2.5
2005	98.3	99.1	99.7	100.0	2.6	98.1	98.9	99.5	100.0	2.5
Precision Production, Craft, and Repair Occupations										
1990	58.7	59.5	60.0	60.3	4.1	62.6	63.3	63.8	64.1	3.2
1991	61.3	62.0	62.7	63.0	4.5	64.9	65.4	65.9	66.2	3.3
1992	63.7	64.2	64.9	65.3	3.7	66.8	67.3	67.8	68.1	2.9
1993	66.2	66.8	67.4	67.5	3.4	68.7	69.2	69.8	70.1	2.9
1994	68.3	68.8	69.6	69.6	3.1	70.6	71.2	72.0	72.0	2.7
1995	70.1	70.6	71.2	71.4	2.6	72.6	73.2	73.9	74.2	3.1
1996	71.8	72.5	72.8	73.3	2.7	74.8	75.6	75.9	76.4	3.0
1997	73.6	74.3	74.8	74.9	2.2	76.8	77.8	78.3	78.6	2.9
1998	75.5	76.3	76.9	77.3	3.2	79.3	80.1	80.8	81.2	3.3
1999	77.9	78.6	79.3	79.8	3.2	82.0	82.8	83.5	84.0	3.4
2000	80.8	81.8	82.8	83.3	4.4	84.9	85.9	86.7	87.2	3.8
2001	84.4	85.0	86.2	86.6	4.0	88.3	89.0	90.2	90.7	4.0
2002	87.3	88.4	89.1	89.6	3.5	91.1	92.2	92.7	93.0	2.5
2003	90.9	92.0	92.6	93.2	4.0	93.7	94.5	95.0	95.4	2.6
2004	94.9	96.0	96.6	97.2	4.3	96.0	96.7	97.3	97.6	2.3
2005	98.3	99.3	99.7	100.0	2.9	98.0	99.0	99.5	100.0	2.5
Machine Operator, Assembler, and Inspector Occupations										
1990	59.1	59.8	60.3	60.9	5.0	62.3	63.0	63.4	64.0	4.2
1991	61.7	62.3	63.0	63.6	4.4	64.8	65.3	65.7	66.4	3.8
1992	64.9	65.3	65.5	66.0	3.8	67.0	67.5	67.5	68.0	2.4
1993	67.1	67.8	68.4	68.8	4.2	68.4	68.8	69.3	69.9	2.8
1994	69.1	69.6	70.0	70.3	2.2	70.3	70.9	71.3	71.8	2.7
1995	70.8	71.1	71.3	71.9	2.3	72.3	73.1	73.4	73.9	2.9
1996	72.4	73.0	73.3	73.8	2.6	74.6	75.3	75.8	76.4	3.4
1997	74.1	74.8	75.3	75.8	2.7	76.9	77.7	78.3	79.0	3.4
1998	76.1	76.8	77.3	77.9	2.8	79.6	80.2	80.9	81.6	3.3
1999	78.2	78.9	79.7	80.6	3.5	82.0	82.6	83.6	84.3	3.3
2000	82.1	82.6	83.2	83.6	3.7	85.1	85.6	86.4	86.9	3.1
2001	84.5	85.0	85.7	86.3	3.2	88.0	88.8	89.5	90.1	3.7
2002	87.5	88.1	88.5	89.3	3.5	91.0	91.7	91.9	92.6	2.8
2003	91.1	91.8	92.6	93.0	4.1	93.5	93.9	94.8	94.9	2.5
2004	96.1	97.2	98.1	98.3	5.7	95.9	96.6	97.7	97.7	3.0
2005	98.7	99.0	99.7	100.0	1.7	98.3	99.0	99.5	100.0	2.4
Transportation and Material Moving Occupations										
1990	61.7	62.4	62.7	63.1	4.1	64.6	65.3	65.7	66.0	3.0
1991	63.6	64.4	64.8	65.2	3.3	66.2	66.9	67.2	67.6	2.4
1992	66.0	66.6	67.3	67.6	3.7	68.1	68.6	69.3	69.5	2.8
1993	68.1	68.9	69.3	70.0	3.6	69.7	70.5	70.8	71.4	2.7
1994	70.9	71.2	71.9	72.1	3.0	71.9	72.2	73.0	73.3	2.7
1995	72.8	73.2	73.5	73.6	2.1	74.1	74.7	75.1	75.2	2.6
1996	74.1	74.6	74.7	74.9	1.8	76.0	76.4	76.7	76.7	2.0
1997	75.4	75.8	76.6	77.1	2.9	77.5	77.9	78.6	79.3	3.4
1998	77.3	77.7	78.2	78.2	1.4	79.8	80.1	80.9	81.0	2.1
1999	78.7	79.9	80.4	80.9	3.5	81.8	83.0	83.6	84.1	3.8
2000	82.2	82.9	83.7	84.4	4.3	85.0	85.7	86.5	87.2	3.7
2001	85.3	86.1	87.1	87.5	3.7	88.4	89.2	90.1	90.5	3.8
2002	88.9	89.5	90.3	90.8	3.8	91.8	92.0	92.7	93.1	2.9
2003	91.6	92.8	93.7	93.8	3.3	93.7	94.4	94.9	94.9	1.9
2004	94.8	96.1	96.8	97.1	3.5	95.3	96.2	96.9	97.1	2.3
2005	97.9	99.1	99.9	100.0	3.0	97.8	98.9	99.7	100.0	3.0

[1]Excludes farm and household workers.

Table 6-1. Employment Cost Index, Private Industry Workers,[1] Total Compensation and Wages and Salaries, by Occupation and Industry, 1990–2005—*Continued*

(December 2005 = 100.)

Characteristic and year	Total compensation					Wages and salaries				
	Indexes				Percent change for 12 months (ended December)	Indexes				Percent change for 12 months (ended December)
	March	June	September	December		March	June	September	December	
Handler, Equipment Cleaner, Helper, and Laborer Occupations										
1990	57.5	58.1	58.7	59.2	4.4	61.2	62.1	62.6	63.1	4.1
1991	60.0	60.7	61.3	61.8	4.4	63.8	64.5	64.9	65.3	3.5
1992	62.5	62.9	63.6	64.0	3.6	65.8	66.2	66.6	66.9	2.5
1993	64.8	65.3	65.7	66.1	3.3	67.5	68.0	68.3	68.8	2.8
1994	66.7	67.4	68.1	68.2	3.2	69.3	69.7	70.1	70.7	2.8
1995	68.9	69.5	69.9	70.4	3.2	71.4	72.1	72.2	72.9	3.1
1996	71.3	71.8	72.1	72.9	3.6	73.8	74.4	74.8	75.6	3.7
1997	73.7	74.0	74.5	75.4	3.4	76.3	76.9	77.4	78.4	3.7
1998	76.0	76.4	76.9	77.2	2.4	79.2	79.5	80.3	80.7	2.9
1999	78.2	79.0	79.5	80.1	3.8	81.6	82.2	82.9	83.5	3.5
2000	81.2	82.2	82.9	83.5	4.2	84.3	85.4	86.2	86.9	4.1
2001	84.5	85.1	86.0	86.8	4.0	88.0	89.1	89.8	90.6	4.3
2002	88.1	88.7	89.6	90.4	4.1	91.7	92.2	92.7	93.5	3.2
2003	91.5	92.6	93.6	94.1	4.1	94.2	94.5	95.1	95.5	2.1
2004	95.3	96.1	96.7	97.3	3.4	96.2	96.7	97.3	97.8	2.4
2005	98.2	98.7	99.4	100.0	2.8	98.5	98.6	99.3	100.0	2.2
Service Occupations										
1990	59.8	60.4	60.9	61.8	4.7	62.8	63.5	63.9	64.8	4.0
1991	62.3	63.3	64.2	64.7	4.7	65.1	66.0	66.9	67.4	4.0
1992	65.3	65.7	66.4	66.7	3.1	67.8	68.0	68.6	68.8	2.1
1993	67.5	67.9	68.5	68.8	3.1	69.2	69.5	70.0	70.3	2.2
1994	69.4	69.7	70.1	70.8	2.9	70.9	71.2	71.7	72.4	3.0
1995	71.0	71.4	71.8	72.1	1.8	72.8	73.1	73.6	74.0	2.2
1996	72.4	72.8	73.3	74.2	2.9	74.5	75.0	75.6	76.6	3.5
1997	74.7	75.4	76.6	77.2	4.0	77.1	77.8	79.2	79.9	4.3
1998	77.9	78.3	79.0	79.4	2.8	80.5	81.0	81.9	82.4	3.1
1999	80.3	80.9	81.2	82.1	3.4	83.3	84.0	84.1	85.1	3.3
2000	82.8	83.7	84.4	85.3	3.9	85.9	86.8	87.4	88.3	3.8
2001	86.4	87.1	87.9	89.1	4.5	89.2	89.9	90.6	91.8	4.0
2002	90.0	90.6	91.5	92.0	3.3	92.6	93.1	93.8	94.1	2.5
2003	93.1	93.6	94.3	94.9	3.2	94.8	95.1	95.7	96.2	2.2
2004	96.1	96.8	97.2	97.7	3.0	96.5	97.1	97.4	97.9	1.8
2005	98.4	99.0	99.5	100.0	2.4	98.4	98.9	99.5	100.0	2.1
Production and Nonsupervisory Occupations										
1990	58.3	59.1	59.6	60.1	4.3	61.6	62.2	62.8	63.2	3.6
1991	60.9	61.6	62.3	62.7	4.3	63.8	64.5	65.0	65.4	3.5
1992	63.5	64.0	64.5	64.9	3.5	66.0	66.4	66.8	67.2	2.8
1993	65.7	66.3	66.9	67.3	3.7	67.7	68.1	68.8	69.2	3.0
1994	67.8	68.4	68.9	69.2	2.8	69.6	70.1	70.7	71.1	2.7
1995	69.8	70.3	70.7	71.0	2.6	71.5	72.2	72.7	73.0	2.7
1996	71.7	72.3	72.6	73.1	3.0	73.8	74.5	74.9	75.5	3.4
1997	73.7	74.3	74.9	75.4	3.1	76.2	76.8	77.6	78.3	3.7
1998	76.1	76.8	77.6	78.1	3.6	78.9	79.7	80.7	81.4	4.0
1999	78.3	79.1	79.8	80.4	2.9	81.6	82.5	83.1	83.8	2.9
2000	81.7	82.6	83.4	84.0	4.5	84.8	85.7	86.5	87.1	3.9
2001	85.1	85.8	86.7	87.4	4.0	88.1	88.9	89.7	90.4	3.8
2002	88.3	89.2	89.8	90.2	3.2	91.1	91.9	92.3	92.6	2.4
2003	91.4	92.2	93.1	93.6	3.8	93.3	93.9	94.7	95.1	2.7
2004	95.2	96.1	96.9	97.2	3.8	95.9	96.5	97.3	97.5	2.5
2005	98.1	98.8	99.6	100.0	2.9	98.2	98.7	99.5	100.0	2.6
WORKERS BY INDUSTRY										
Goods-Producing Industries[2]										
1990	57.7	58.4	59.0	59.4	4.8	61.8	62.5	63.0	63.4	3.6
1991	60.2	61.0	61.6	62.1	4.5	64.1	64.7	65.2	65.8	3.8
1992	63.0	63.5	64.0	64.5	3.9	66.4	66.8	67.2	67.6	2.7
1993	65.5	66.1	66.6	67.0	3.9	68.2	68.6	69.1	69.6	3.0
1994	67.6	68.3	68.8	69.0	3.0	70.1	70.7	71.3	71.7	3.0
1995	69.6	69.9	70.2	70.7	2.5	72.2	72.8	73.2	73.7	2.8
1996	71.2	71.8	72.2	72.7	2.8	74.3	75.0	75.6	76.0	3.1
1997	73.0	73.7	74.2	74.5	2.5	76.4	77.3	77.9	78.3	3.0
1998	75.0	75.6	76.1	76.5	2.7	79.1	79.9	80.5	81.1	3.6
1999	77.1	77.7	78.3	79.1	3.4	81.7	82.3	83.0	83.8	3.3
2000	80.4	81.4	82.1	82.6	4.4	84.7	85.7	86.5	87.1	3.9
2001	83.7	84.5	85.0	85.7	3.8	88.1	89.1	89.6	90.2	3.6
2002	86.7	87.5	88.1	88.9	3.7	90.9	91.8	92.3	92.9	3.0
2003	90.5	91.3	92.0	92.4	3.9	93.7	94.4	94.9	95.1	2.4
2004	94.6	95.4	96.2	96.8	4.8	95.9	96.5	97.3	97.4	2.4
2005	98.2	99.1	99.8	100.0	3.3	98.1	98.8	99.5	100.0	2.7

[1]Excludes farm and household workers.
[2]Includes mining, construction, and manufacturing.

Table 6-1. Employment Cost Index, Private Industry Workers,[1] Total Compensation and Wages and Salaries, by Occupation and Industry, 1990–2005—*Continued*

(December 2005 = 100.)

Characteristic and year	Total compensation					Wages and salaries				
	Indexes				Percent change for 12 months (ended December)	Indexes				Percent change for 12 months (ended December)
	March	June	September	December		March	June	September	December	
Goods-Producing Industries, Excluding Sales Occupations										
1990	57.9	58.6	59.1	59.6	4.6	62.1	62.8	63.3	63.7	3.6
1991	60.4	61.2	61.8	62.3	4.5	64.4	65.0	65.5	66.1	3.8
1992	63.2	63.6	64.2	64.6	3.7	66.6	67.0	67.5	67.9	2.7
1993	65.7	66.2	66.7	66.9	3.6	68.4	68.8	69.3	69.7	2.7
1994	67.7	68.3	68.8	69.1	3.3	70.2	70.8	71.4	71.8	3.0
1995	69.6	70.0	70.3	70.8	2.5	72.3	72.9	73.3	73.8	2.8
1996	71.3	71.9	72.4	72.7	2.7	74.4	75.1	75.8	76.1	3.1
1997	73.1	73.7	74.2	74.5	2.5	76.6	77.3	77.9	78.4	3.0
1998	75.0	75.6	76.1	76.5	2.7	79.1	79.9	80.5	81.0	3.3
1999	77.1	77.6	78.3	79.0	3.3	81.7	82.3	83.1	83.7	3.3
2000	80.4	81.3	82.1	82.6	4.6	84.7	85.7	86.4	87.2	4.2
2001	83.7	84.4	85.0	85.7	3.8	88.2	89.1	89.6	90.2	3.4
2002	86.7	87.5	88.0	88.7	3.5	91.0	91.7	92.2	92.8	2.9
2003	90.5	91.3	92.0	92.5	4.3	93.7	94.3	94.9	95.2	2.6
2004	94.6	95.4	96.2	96.8	4.6	96.0	96.6	97.2	97.4	2.3
2005	98.3	99.2	99.8	100.0	3.3	98.1	98.9	99.6	100.0	2.7
Goods-Producing Industries, White-Collar Occupations										
1990	55.9	56.5	57.3	57.6	5.3	60.6	61.3	61.9	62.3	4.4
1991	58.4	59.1	59.7	60.3	4.7	62.9	63.6	64.1	64.7	3.9
1992	61.0	61.5	62.0	62.6	3.8	65.4	65.9	66.3	66.9	3.4
1993	63.7	64.2	64.7	65.0	3.8	67.6	68.2	68.7	69.2	3.4
1994	66.0	66.7	67.1	67.6	4.0	69.8	70.5	70.9	71.5	3.3
1995	68.3	68.5	68.8	69.2	2.4	72.1	72.5	72.9	73.4	2.7
1996	69.8	70.3	71.0	71.3	3.0	73.9	74.6	75.3	75.6	3.0
1997	71.7	72.4	72.8	73.1	2.5	76.2	77.0	77.5	77.9	3.0
1998	73.9	74.5	75.0	75.3	3.0	79.1	79.8	80.5	81.0	4.0
1999	76.1	76.6	77.2	78.1	3.7	81.7	82.3	83.0	83.8	3.5
2000	79.5	80.6	81.2	81.5	4.4	84.9	86.0	86.6	87.1	3.9
2001	82.9	84.0	84.2	84.9	4.2	88.2	89.2	89.4	90.0	3.3
2002	85.9	86.9	87.4	88.2	3.9	90.8	91.7	92.3	92.9	3.2
2003	90.1	90.8	91.3	91.5	3.7	93.7	94.6	94.8	95.0	2.3
2004	93.1	93.8	94.7	95.4	4.3	95.6	96.4	97.2	97.2	2.3
2005	97.8	98.9	99.8	100.0	4.8	98.0	98.7	99.6	100.0	2.9
Goods-Producing Industries, White-Collar Occupations, Excluding Sales Occupations										
1990	56.3	57.0	57.6	58.0	4.9	61.3	62.0	62.7	63.0	4.1
1991	58.8	59.6	60.2	60.8	4.8	63.6	64.4	65.0	65.6	4.1
1992	61.3	61.7	62.4	62.9	3.5	66.1	66.5	67.0	67.5	2.9
1993	64.0	64.5	64.8	65.0	3.3	68.2	68.6	69.1	69.3	2.7
1994	66.0	66.7	67.2	67.7	4.2	69.9	70.5	71.1	71.7	3.5
1995	68.4	68.6	68.9	69.4	2.5	72.3	72.7	73.1	73.7	2.8
1996	70.1	70.5	71.2	71.6	3.2	74.4	75.0	75.8	76.0	3.1
1997	71.8	72.5	72.9	73.1	2.1	76.5	77.2	77.7	78.1	2.8
1998	73.8	74.4	74.9	75.2	2.9	79.1	79.9	80.5	80.9	3.6
1999	76.1	76.5	77.2	78.0	3.7	81.8	82.4	83.1	83.9	3.7
2000	79.4	80.4	81.0	81.5	4.5	85.0	86.0	86.6	87.4	4.2
2001	82.9	84.0	84.1	84.8	4.0	88.4	89.3	89.5	90.0	3.0
2002	85.8	86.8	87.3	87.9	3.7	90.7	91.7	92.2	92.8	3.1
2003	90.1	90.7	91.3	91.7	4.3	93.8	94.5	94.9	95.2	2.6
2004	93.3	93.9	94.5	95.6	4.3	95.8	96.6	97.1	97.4	2.3
2005	98.0	99.1	100.1	100.0	4.6	98.1	98.9	99.7	100.0	2.7
Goods-Producing Industries, Blue-Collar Occupations										
1990	59.0	59.7	60.2	60.7	4.5	62.6	63.4	63.7	64.2	3.5
1991	61.6	62.3	62.9	63.4	4.4	65.0	65.5	65.9	66.5	3.6
1992	64.4	64.8	65.4	65.8	3.8	67.0	67.4	67.8	68.1	2.4
1993	66.8	67.4	67.9	68.3	3.8	68.7	69.0	69.4	69.9	2.6
1994	68.8	69.4	69.9	70.1	2.6	70.4	71.0	71.5	71.9	2.9
1995	70.5	70.9	71.3	71.7	2.3	72.3	73.0	73.5	73.9	2.8
1996	72.2	72.9	73.2	73.6	2.6	74.5	75.3	75.8	76.3	3.2
1997	73.9	74.6	75.2	75.4	2.4	76.7	77.5	78.1	78.6	3.0
1998	75.8	76.4	76.9	77.4	2.7	79.2	79.9	80.5	81.1	3.2
1999	77.9	78.5	79.2	79.9	3.2	81.7	82.4	83.1	83.7	3.2
2000	81.1	82.0	82.8	83.4	4.4	84.6	85.5	86.4	87.1	4.1
2001	84.2	84.8	85.6	86.3	3.5	88.1	88.9	89.7	90.3	3.7
2002	87.2	87.9	88.5	89.3	3.5	91.1	91.7	92.2	92.9	2.9
2003	90.8	91.7	92.5	93.1	4.3	93.6	94.2	94.9	95.2	2.5
2004	95.5	96.4	97.3	97.7	4.9	96.0	96.5	97.3	97.4	2.3
2005	98.5	99.2	99.7	100.0	2.4	98.1	98.8	99.5	100.0	2.7

[1]Excludes farm and household workers.

Table 6-1. Employment Cost Index, Private Industry Workers,[1] Total Compensation and Wages and Salaries, by Occupation and Industry, 1990–2005—*Continued*

(December 2005 = 100.)

Characteristic and year	Total compensation					Wages and salaries				
	Indexes				Percent change for 12 months (ended December)	Indexes				Percent change for 12 months (ended December)
	March	June	September	December		March	June	September	December	
Construction										
1990	59.4	60.1	60.6	60.9	3.2	63.0	63.6	63.9	64.1	2.1
1991	61.9	62.5	63.0	63.3	3.9	64.9	65.4	65.7	66.0	3.0
1992	63.7	64.4	65.2	65.6	3.6	66.2	66.6	67.1	67.3	2.0
1993	66.2	66.9	67.3	67.1	2.3	67.6	68.2	68.7	68.6	1.9
1994	68.4	69.3	70.0	69.6	3.7	69.3	70.2	70.8	70.8	3.2
1995	69.8	70.3	71.0	71.1	2.2	70.9	71.5	72.1	72.5	2.4
1996	71.6	72.2	72.6	72.9	2.5	73.1	73.9	74.4	74.6	2.9
1997	73.3	74.2	74.8	74.8	2.6	75.4	76.3	77.0	77.1	3.4
1998	75.3	76.5	76.9	77.4	3.5	77.8	79.1	79.4	79.9	3.6
1999	78.2	78.9	79.5	79.9	3.2	80.7	81.5	82.1	82.5	3.3
2000	81.2	82.5	83.6	84.6	5.9	84.0	85.2	86.1	86.9	5.3
2001	85.4	86.6	87.4	88.2	4.3	87.8	88.9	89.6	90.4	4.0
2002	88.8	89.5	90.1	91.0	3.2	90.8	91.5	92.0	92.8	2.7
2003	91.7	92.9	93.5	94.1	3.4	93.0	94.1	94.9	95.1	2.5
2004	94.9	95.6	96.3	96.4	2.4	95.8	96.3	97.0	97.0	2.0
2005	97.5	98.6	99.7	100.0	3.7	97.4	98.3	99.4	100.0	3.1
Manufacturing										
1990	57.4	58.1	58.7	59.1	5.0	61.4	62.1	62.7	63.1	4.1
1991	59.9	60.7	61.3	61.9	4.7	63.9	64.4	65.0	65.6	4.0
1992	62.9	63.3	63.8	64.3	3.9	66.3	66.7	67.1	67.6	3.0
1993	65.4	66.0	66.5	66.9	4.0	68.2	68.7	69.1	69.7	3.1
1994	67.6	68.1	68.6	69.0	3.1	70.2	70.7	71.3	71.8	3.0
1995	69.6	70.0	70.2	70.8	2.6	72.5	73.1	73.4	73.9	2.9
1996	71.3	71.9	72.4	72.9	3.0	74.6	75.2	75.9	76.3	3.2
1997	73.1	73.8	74.2	74.6	2.3	76.8	77.5	78.1	78.6	3.0
1998	75.2	75.7	76.2	76.6	2.7	79.5	80.0	80.9	81.3	3.4
1999	77.2	77.7	78.4	79.2	3.4	82.0	82.6	83.4	84.1	3.4
2000	80.5	81.4	82.0	82.3	3.9	85.0	85.9	86.6	87.1	3.6
2001	83.5	84.2	84.6	85.3	3.6	88.3	89.2	89.6	90.2	3.6
2002	86.4	87.2	87.8	88.5	3.8	91.0	91.9	92.4	93.0	3.1
2003	90.5	91.2	91.8	92.2	4.2	93.9	94.5	94.9	95.2	2.4
2004	94.7	95.5	96.5	96.7	4.9	95.9	96.6	97.4	97.5	2.4
2005	98.3	99.1	99.7	100.0	3.4	98.3	98.9	99.5	100.0	2.6
Manufacturing, White-Collar Occupations										
1990	56.1	56.8	57.6	57.9	5.3	60.9	61.4	62.1	62.4	4.5
1991	58.7	59.4	60.0	60.6	4.7	63.1	63.8	64.4	65.0	4.2
1992	61.3	61.8	62.3	62.9	3.8	65.7	66.3	66.7	67.3	3.5
1993	64.0	64.6	65.0	65.4	4.0	68.1	68.6	69.1	69.7	3.6
1994	66.2	66.8	67.4	68.0	4.0	70.1	70.8	71.4	72.0	3.3
1995	68.7	69.0	69.4	69.8	2.6	72.7	73.2	73.5	74.0	2.8
1996	70.4	71.0	71.6	72.1	3.3	74.6	75.2	76.1	76.3	3.1
1997	72.2	72.9	73.2	73.7	2.2	76.6	77.4	77.9	78.4	2.8
1998	74.5	75.0	75.6	75.8	2.8	79.6	80.3	81.2	81.6	4.1
1999	76.5	77.1	77.8	78.6	3.7	82.2	83.0	83.7	84.5	3.6
2000	79.9	81.0	81.7	81.7	3.9	85.6	86.7	87.3	87.6	3.7
2001	83.2	84.1	84.1	84.6	3.5	88.7	89.6	89.7	90.0	2.7
2002	85.8	86.9	87.5	88.1	4.1	90.9	91.9	92.5	93.1	3.4
2003	90.1	91.0	91.4	91.5	3.9	94.0	94.8	95.1	95.1	2.1
2004	93.4	94.2	95.1	95.3	4.2	95.8	96.7	97.5	97.5	2.5
2005	97.8	98.9	99.7	100.0	4.9	98.4	99.0	99.7	100.0	2.6
Manufacturing, White-Collar Occupations, Excluding Sales Occupations										
1990	56.7	57.3	58.0	58.4	5.0	61.6	62.2	62.9	63.3	4.3
1991	59.1	60.0	60.6	61.2	4.8	63.8	64.7	65.3	65.9	4.1
1992	61.6	62.1	62.7	63.2	3.3	66.3	66.8	67.3	67.9	3.0
1993	64.4	64.8	65.2	65.4	3.5	68.7	69.0	69.5	69.8	2.8
1994	66.2	66.8	67.4	68.1	4.1	70.3	70.9	71.6	72.3	3.6
1995	68.8	69.1	69.5	70.0	2.8	72.9	73.4	73.8	74.3	2.8
1996	70.6	71.2	71.9	72.3	3.3	75.0	75.6	76.5	76.8	3.4
1997	72.4	73.0	73.4	73.8	2.1	77.0	77.7	78.2	78.7	2.5
1998	74.5	74.9	75.5	75.7	2.6	79.7	80.4	81.2	81.7	3.8
1999	76.4	77.1	77.7	78.5	3.7	82.4	83.1	83.9	84.6	3.5
2000	79.8	80.9	81.5	81.7	4.1	85.6	86.7	87.3	87.8	3.8
2001	83.0	84.0	83.9	84.4	3.3	88.8	89.6	89.6	89.9	2.4
2002	85.5	86.5	87.1	87.7	3.9	90.7	91.7	92.3	92.9	3.3
2003	90.1	90.8	91.3	91.5	4.3	93.9	94.6	95.0	95.3	2.6
2004	93.5	94.2	95.0	95.3	4.2	96.0	96.8	97.4	97.6	2.4
2005	97.9	99.0	99.8	100.0	4.9	98.3	99.2	99.9	100.0	2.5

[1]Excludes farm and household workers.

Table 6-1. Employment Cost Index, Private Industry Workers,[1] Total Compensation and Wages and Salaries, by Occupation and Industry, 1990–2005—Continued

(December 2005 = 100.)

Characteristic and year	Total compensation					Wages and salaries				
	Indexes				Percent change for 12 months (ended December)	Indexes				Percent change for 12 months (ended December)
	March	June	September	December		March	June	September	December	
Manufacturing, Blue-Collar Occupations										
1990	58.4	59.1	59.6	60.2	5.1	62.0	62.7	63.2	63.8	4.1
1991	60.9	61.7	62.4	62.9	4.5	64.5	65.0	65.5	66.1	3.6
1992	64.1	64.5	65.0	65.4	4.0	66.8	67.1	67.5	68.0	2.9
1993	66.5	67.2	67.7	68.1	4.1	68.4	68.8	69.2	69.8	2.6
1994	68.7	69.2	69.6	69.9	2.6	70.3	70.8	71.3	71.8	2.9
1995	70.4	70.7	70.9	71.6	2.4	72.4	73.1	73.4	74.0	3.1
1996	72.1	72.7	73.1	73.6	2.8	74.6	75.4	75.9	76.5	3.4
1997	73.9	74.6	75.1	75.4	2.4	76.9	77.6	78.2	78.8	3.0
1998	75.8	76.3	76.8	77.3	2.5	79.5	80.0	80.7	81.3	3.2
1999	77.8	78.3	78.9	79.8	3.2	81.9	82.5	83.2	84.0	3.3
2000	81.1	81.8	82.4	83.0	4.0	84.6	85.3	86.2	86.9	3.5
2001	83.7	84.2	85.0	85.7	3.3	88.0	88.8	89.6	90.3	3.9
2002	86.8	87.5	88.0	88.9	3.7	91.2	91.8	92.2	93.0	3.0
2003	90.7	91.4	92.1	92.7	4.3	93.9	94.3	94.9	95.3	2.5
2004	95.7	96.6	97.5	97.9	5.6	96.0	96.5	97.4	97.6	2.4
2005	98.7	99.2	99.7	100.0	2.1	98.3	99.0	99.5	100.0	2.5
Manufacturing, Durable Goods										
1990	56.9	57.5	58.1	58.6	4.8	61.1	61.7	62.3	62.8	4.1
1991	59.3	60.1	60.8	61.3	4.6	63.5	64.1	64.6	65.2	3.8
1992	62.4	62.8	63.3	63.8	4.1	65.8	66.2	66.7	67.1	2.9
1993	65.1	65.6	66.2	66.6	4.4	67.7	68.1	68.6	69.3	3.3
1994	67.2	67.7	68.4	68.8	3.3	69.7	70.2	70.9	71.5	3.2
1995	69.4	69.8	70.1	70.5	2.5	72.1	72.7	73.1	73.6	2.9
1996	70.9	71.7	72.1	72.5	2.8	74.0	74.9	75.6	76.0	3.3
1997	72.7	73.3	73.8	74.2	2.3	76.3	77.0	77.6	78.0	2.6
1998	74.6	75.1	75.7	76.1	2.6	78.9	79.6	80.4	81.0	3.8
1999	76.5	77.1	77.8	78.7	3.4	81.6	82.3	83.1	83.9	3.6
2000	80.1	81.1	81.7	82.1	4.3	84.6	85.6	86.4	87.2	3.9
2001	83.0	83.7	84.2	84.9	3.4	88.2	89.1	89.6	90.3	3.6
2002	85.8	86.6	86.9	87.8	3.4	91.1	91.9	92.3	93.1	3.1
2003	89.9	90.5	91.1	91.5	4.2	94.0	94.5	95.0	95.2	2.3
2004	94.3	95.1	96.1	96.4	5.4	95.8	96.4	97.3	97.5	2.4
2005	98.1	99.1	99.7	100.0	3.7	98.2	98.9	99.5	100.0	2.6
Aircraft Manufacturing										
1990	44.2	44.8	45.5	45.5	4.8	58.1	59.0	59.5	60.2	4.7
1991	46.2	46.8	47.4	48.1	5.7	61.0	61.8	62.4	63.4	5.3
1992	49.0	49.9	50.3	51.5	7.1	63.9	64.8	65.3	66.0	4.1
1993	52.0	52.2	53.1	52.5	1.9	66.3	66.9	67.8	68.4	3.6
1994	52.9	53.2	53.9	54.1	3.0	68.9	69.4	69.8	70.2	2.6
1995	54.7	54.9	55.1	56.1	3.7	70.7	71.2	71.7	72.1	2.7
1996	57.4	57.9	57.9	57.6	2.7	72.6	73.3	73.5	73.7	2.2
1997	57.5	58.0	57.7	57.4	-0.3	74.3	75.1	75.0	75.4	2.3
1998	57.5	58.2	58.4	58.9	2.6	76.0	77.0	77.2	77.8	3.2
1999	58.9	59.7	60.2	61.5	4.4	78.4	79.6	80.3	80.8	3.9
2000	63.3	64.6	65.4	65.1	5.9	82.3	83.6	84.4	85.3	5.6
2001	66.9	67.2	67.2	68.5	5.2	86.8	87.3	88.1	89.1	4.5
2002	70.2	70.8	70.7	72.2	5.4	90.8	91.4	91.4	91.8	3.0
2003	76.7	77.0	77.3	76.3	5.7	93.4	93.9	94.2	94.4	2.8
2004	83.3	84.2	84.5	84.6	10.9	96.0	96.7	97.0	97.1	2.9
2005	98.1	98.2	98.5	100.0	18.2	98.8	99.1	99.4	100.0	3.0
Aircraft Manufacturing, White-Collar Occupations										
1990	45.4	45.9	46.5	46.3	3.8	59.6	60.5	60.7	61.2	3.6
1991	46.9	47.6	47.9	48.6	5.0	61.8	62.6	62.9	63.5	3.8
1992	49.5	50.5	50.8	51.6	6.2	64.1	65.0	65.4	65.9	3.8
1993	52.3	52.6	53.4	52.8	2.3	66.4	67.1	68.0	68.4	3.8
1994	53.2	53.7	54.4	54.4	3.0	68.8	69.4	69.8	70.0	2.3
1995	55.0	55.2	55.4	56.0	2.9	70.5	70.9	71.5	71.8	2.6
1996	57.4	58.1	58.0	58.0	3.6	72.3	73.4	73.5	73.7	2.6
1997	57.9	58.5	58.4	58.3	0.5	74.5	75.5	75.3	75.6	2.6
1998	58.4	59.5	59.6	59.6	2.2	76.5	77.9	78.0	78.4	3.7
1999	59.6	60.5	60.7	61.5	3.2	79.0	80.4	80.6	81.1	3.4
2000	63.6	65.4	65.9	65.6	6.7	82.8	84.6	85.1	85.2	5.1
2001	68.2	68.2	67.8	69.0	5.2	87.3	87.5	87.9	88.7	4.1
2002	70.8	71.2	71.0	71.7	3.9	90.9	91.1	90.9	91.0	2.6
2003	77.2	76.9	77.0	76.8	7.1	93.5	93.4	93.4	93.6	2.9
2004	84.1	84.6	84.7	84.7	10.3	96.0	96.4	96.6	96.7	3.3
2005	98.8	99.1	99.2	100.0	18.1	99.1	99.3	99.4	100.0	3.4

[1] Excludes farm and household workers.

Table 6-1. Employment Cost Index, Private Industry Workers,[1] Total Compensation and Wages and Salaries, by Occupation and Industry, 1990–2005—*Continued*

(December 2005 = 100.)

Characteristic and year	Total compensation					Wages and salaries				
	Indexes				Percent change for 12 months (ended December)	Indexes				Percent change for 12 months (ended December)
	March	June	September	December		March	June	September	December	
Aircraft Manufacturing, Blue-Collar Occupations										
1990	42.5	43.3	43.9	44.2	5.7	55.9	57.1	57.6	58.8	6.5
1991	45.2	45.8	46.5	47.4	7.2	59.9	60.7	61.7	63.1	7.3
1992	48.2	49.0	49.5	51.1	7.8	63.6	64.4	65.0	65.9	4.4
1993	51.5	51.5	52.5	51.8	1.4	66.3	66.4	67.4	68.4	3.8
1994	52.2	52.5	53.1	53.5	3.3	68.8	69.2	69.6	70.4	2.9
1995	54.1	54.3	54.4	56.0	4.7	71.0	71.4	71.7	72.2	2.6
1996	57.2	57.5	57.6	56.8	1.4	72.8	72.9	73.3	73.3	1.5
1997	56.8	57.0	56.6	55.7	-1.9	73.6	74.2	74.0	74.7	1.9
1998	55.7	55.9	56.2	57.6	3.4	74.9	75.1	75.4	76.6	2.5
1999	57.6	58.1	59.4	61.6	6.9	77.3	77.8	79.6	80.2	4.7
2000	62.9	63.2	64.4	64.0	3.9	81.2	81.3	82.9	85.2	6.2
2001	64.6	65.3	65.9	67.5	5.5	85.7	86.7	88.2	89.5	5.0
2002	68.8	69.7	70.0	72.7	7.7	90.4	91.7	92.1	92.6	3.5
2003	75.7	76.7	77.3	75.1	3.3	92.8	94.4	95.1	95.3	2.9
2004	81.6	83.1	84.1	84.5	12.5	95.4	96.6	97.9	98.0	2.8
2005	96.7	96.8	97.2	100.0	18.3	98.3	98.8	99.5	100.0	2.0
Manufacturing, Nondurable Goods										
1990	58.4	59.2	59.8	60.2	5.2	62.1	62.8	63.4	63.7	4.4
1991	61.0	61.7	62.4	63.0	4.7	64.5	65.1	65.6	66.3	4.1
1992	63.8	64.3	64.7	65.2	3.5	67.0	67.6	67.9	68.5	3.3
1993	66.1	66.7	67.1	67.5	3.5	69.2	69.7	70.1	70.4	2.8
1994	68.3	68.9	69.1	69.4	2.8	70.9	71.6	72.1	72.4	2.8
1995	69.9	70.3	70.5	71.2	2.6	73.1	73.7	73.9	74.6	3.0
1996	72.0	72.3	72.9	73.5	3.2	75.4	75.8	76.5	77.0	3.2
1997	73.9	74.6	75.0	75.4	2.6	77.5	78.3	78.8	79.5	3.2
1998	76.2	76.7	77.2	77.5	2.8	80.5	80.9	81.5	82.0	3.1
1999	78.3	78.7	79.4	80.1	3.4	82.7	83.2	83.8	84.5	3.0
2000	81.3	81.9	82.7	82.8	3.4	85.6	86.3	86.9	87.2	3.2
2001	84.4	85.0	85.2	85.9	3.7	88.4	89.3	89.5	90.0	3.2
2002	87.5	88.3	89.3	89.9	4.7	91.1	91.8	92.6	93.0	3.3
2003	91.5	92.5	93.1	93.4	3.9	93.9	94.6	94.9	95.1	2.3
2004	95.6	96.3	97.1	97.4	4.3	96.2	96.9	97.6	97.7	2.7
2005	98.6	99.2	99.7	100.0	2.7	98.6	99.1	99.7	100.0	2.4
Service-Producing Industries[3]										
1990	57.6	58.4	58.9	59.4	4.6	60.1	60.8	61.5	61.8	3.9
1991	60.2	60.9	61.6	61.9	4.2	62.5	63.2	63.8	64.1	3.7
1992	62.6	63.0	63.5	63.9	3.2	64.6	65.0	65.3	65.7	2.5
1993	64.6	65.1	65.8	66.2	3.6	66.3	66.7	67.4	67.8	3.2
1994	66.8	67.3	67.9	68.1	2.9	68.2	68.8	69.3	69.6	2.7
1995	68.8	69.3	69.8	70.0	2.8	70.2	70.7	71.3	71.7	3.0
1996	70.8	71.4	71.9	72.3	3.3	72.5	73.2	73.7	74.2	3.5
1997	73.0	73.5	74.3	75.1	3.9	75.0	75.7	76.5	77.4	4.3
1998	75.9	76.5	77.5	78.0	3.9	78.2	78.9	80.0	80.5	4.0
1999	78.2	79.2	80.0	80.6	3.3	80.8	81.9	82.7	83.4	3.6
2000	81.8	82.7	83.6	84.2	4.5	84.4	85.2	86.0	86.6	3.8
2001	85.3	86.2	87.1	87.8	4.3	87.6	88.4	89.1	89.9	3.8
2002	88.7	89.8	90.3	90.5	3.1	90.8	91.7	92.1	92.3	2.7
2003	91.9	92.7	93.7	94.2	4.1	93.4	94.1	95.0	95.3	3.3
2004	95.2	96.2	96.9	97.3	3.3	96.0	96.6	97.4	97.7	2.5
2005	98.3	98.8	99.5	100.0	2.8	98.3	98.9	99.5	100.0	2.4
Service-Producing Industries, Excluding Sales Occupations										
1990	57.3	58.0	58.7	59.2	5.2	59.8	60.4	61.2	61.7	4.8
1991	60.0	60.7	61.4	61.9	4.6	62.3	62.9	63.6	64.0	3.7
1992	62.5	62.9	63.5	64.0	3.4	64.5	64.9	65.4	65.8	2.8
1993	64.7	65.3	65.8	66.3	3.6	66.4	66.9	67.4	67.9	3.2
1994	67.0	67.4	68.0	68.3	3.0	68.4	68.8	69.5	69.8	2.8
1995	69.0	69.4	69.9	70.2	2.8	70.4	70.9	71.4	71.8	2.9
1996	70.9	71.3	71.9	72.2	2.8	72.6	73.2	73.8	74.2	3.3
1997	73.0	73.6	74.2	75.1	4.0	75.0	75.7	76.5	77.4	4.3
1998	75.8	76.4	77.3	77.6	3.3	78.2	78.8	79.8	80.1	3.5
1999	78.2	79.1	79.8	80.5	3.7	80.9	81.8	82.5	83.2	3.9
2000	81.5	82.5	83.4	84.0	4.3	84.0	85.0	85.8	86.4	3.8
2001	85.3	86.1	87.1	87.7	4.4	87.5	88.3	89.2	89.9	4.1
2002	88.8	89.6	90.2	90.5	3.2	90.9	91.7	92.1	92.3	2.7
2003	91.9	92.7	93.7	94.2	4.1	93.5	94.2	95.0	95.4	3.4
2004	95.2	96.1	96.9	97.4	3.4	96.0	96.6	97.5	97.9	2.6
2005	98.5	99.0	99.5	100.0	2.7	98.6	99.1	99.5	100.0	2.1

[1]Excludes farm and household workers.
[3]Includes transportation, communication, and public utilities; wholesale and retail trade; finance, insurance, and real estate; and service industries.

Table 6-1. Employment Cost Index, Private Industry Workers,[1] Total Compensation and Wages and Salaries, by Occupation and Industry, 1990–2005—*Continued*

(December 2005 = 100.)

Characteristic and year	Total compensation					Wages and salaries				
	Indexes				Percent change for 12 months (ended December)	Indexes				Percent change for 12 months (ended December)
	March	June	September	December		March	June	September	December	
Service-Producing Industries, White-Collar Occupations										
1990	57.0	57.7	58.4	58.8	4.8	59.2	60.0	60.6	61.0	4.1
1991	59.7	60.4	61.0	61.3	4.3	61.8	62.5	63.0	63.3	3.8
1992	62.0	62.4	62.9	63.3	3.3	63.8	64.1	64.5	64.9	2.5
1993	63.9	64.4	65.1	65.5	3.5	65.4	65.8	66.6	67.0	3.2
1994	66.2	66.7	67.2	67.5	3.1	67.4	67.9	68.5	68.8	2.7
1995	68.2	68.7	69.2	69.5	3.0	69.3	69.9	70.4	70.9	3.1
1996	70.3	70.9	71.4	71.7	3.2	71.8	72.5	73.0	73.4	3.5
1997	72.6	73.1	73.8	74.7	4.2	74.3	75.0	75.8	76.7	4.5
1998	75.5	76.2	77.2	77.8	4.1	77.5	78.3	79.5	80.1	4.4
1999	77.8	78.9	79.8	80.4	3.3	80.2	81.3	82.2	82.9	3.5
2000	81.7	82.6	83.5	84.1	4.6	83.9	84.9	85.7	86.2	4.0
2001	85.2	86.1	87.0	87.7	4.3	87.1	88.0	88.7	89.4	3.7
2002	88.7	89.7	90.1	90.3	3.0	90.4	91.4	91.7	91.8	2.7
2003	91.8	92.6	93.7	94.1	4.2	93.1	93.8	94.9	95.2	3.7
2004	95.2	96.1	97.0	97.3	3.4	95.9	96.5	97.4	97.6	2.5
2005	98.3	98.9	99.5	100.0	2.8	98.3	98.9	99.5	100.0	2.5
Service-Producing Industries, White-Collar Occupations, Excluding Sales Occupations										
1990	56.4	57.1	57.9	58.4	5.6	58.5	59.2	60.0	60.5	5.0
1991	59.2	59.8	60.6	61.1	4.6	61.2	61.8	62.5	62.9	4.0
1992	61.7	62.1	62.8	63.1	3.3	63.4	63.8	64.3	64.7	2.9
1993	64.0	64.5	65.1	65.6	4.0	65.4	65.9	66.4	66.9	3.4
1994	66.3	66.7	67.4	67.6	3.0	67.5	67.9	68.5	68.9	3.0
1995	68.3	68.7	69.2	69.6	3.0	69.5	69.8	70.3	70.8	2.8
1996	70.3	70.8	71.5	71.7	3.0	71.7	72.3	73.0	73.3	3.5
1997	72.4	73.0	73.7	74.6	4.0	74.2	74.8	75.7	76.6	4.5
1998	75.4	76.0	76.9	77.2	3.5	77.4	78.1	79.1	79.4	3.7
1999	77.7	78.6	79.5	80.2	3.9	80.1	81.0	81.8	82.6	4.0
2000	81.2	82.2	83.2	83.8	4.5	83.4	84.4	85.3	85.9	4.0
2001	85.1	86.0	87.0	87.7	4.7	87.0	87.8	88.7	89.5	4.2
2002	88.7	89.5	90.0	90.3	3.0	90.5	91.1	91.7	91.8	2.6
2003	91.8	92.6	93.6	94.2	4.3	93.2	93.9	94.9	95.3	3.8
2004	95.2	96.1	97.0	97.5	3.5	96.0	96.6	97.5	97.9	2.7
2005	98.6	99.0	99.5	100.0	2.6	98.7	99.2	99.5	100.0	2.1
Service-Producing Industries, Blue-Collar Occupations										
1990	59.3	60.0	60.5	60.9	4.3	62.6	63.3	63.8	64.2	3.9
1991	61.6	62.2	62.8	63.2	3.8	64.7	65.3	65.7	66.1	3.0
1992	63.8	64.5	64.9	65.4	3.5	66.6	67.2	67.6	68.0	2.9
1993	66.0	66.7	67.4	67.7	3.5	68.6	69.2	69.9	70.2	3.2
1994	68.4	68.8	69.7	69.7	3.0	70.8	71.2	72.0	72.1	2.7
1995	70.5	71.1	71.6	71.6	2.7	73.0	73.7	74.2	74.4	3.2
1996	72.3	72.8	73.0	73.5	2.7	75.2	75.7	75.9	76.5	2.8
1997	74.1	74.6	75.1	75.6	2.9	77.2	77.9	78.4	79.0	3.3
1998	76.3	76.9	77.6	77.9	3.0	79.8	80.3	81.1	81.4	3.0
1999	78.7	79.6	80.4	80.8	3.7	82.4	83.3	83.9	84.4	3.7
2000	81.9	82.7	83.5	83.9	3.8	85.2	86.0	86.8	87.1	3.2
2001	85.3	85.9	87.2	87.5	4.3	88.4	89.0	90.4	90.7	4.1
2002	88.5	89.7	90.5	90.6	3.5	91.5	92.6	93.0	93.1	2.6
2003	91.7	92.9	93.7	93.9	3.6	93.9	94.5	95.0	95.2	2.3
2004	94.8	96.1	96.7	97.1	3.4	95.7	96.7	97.4	97.7	2.6
2005	98.2	99.1	99.6	100.0	3.0	98.1	99.0	99.5	100.0	2.4
Service-Producing Industries, Service Occupations										
1990	60.1	60.7	61.2	62.1	4.7	63.1	63.8	64.2	65.1	4.0
1991	62.7	63.6	64.5	65.1	4.8	65.4	66.3	67.3	67.7	4.0
1992	65.6	66.0	66.6	66.9	2.8	68.1	68.3	68.9	69.1	2.1
1993	67.6	68.1	68.6	68.9	3.0	69.4	69.8	70.3	70.5	2.0
1994	69.5	69.8	70.2	70.9	2.9	71.1	71.4	71.7	72.6	3.0
1995	71.1	71.5	71.8	72.2	1.8	73.0	73.3	73.8	74.2	2.2
1996	72.5	72.9	73.5	74.4	3.0	74.6	75.1	75.8	76.8	3.5
1997	74.9	75.5	76.7	77.4	4.0	77.4	78.0	79.4	80.1	4.3
1998	78.1	78.5	79.2	79.7	3.0	80.8	81.3	82.1	82.7	3.2
1999	80.6	81.3	81.4	82.4	3.4	83.6	84.3	84.4	85.4	3.3
2000	83.1	83.9	84.6	85.5	3.8	86.3	87.2	87.8	88.6	3.7
2001	86.5	87.2	88.0	89.2	4.3	89.4	90.0	90.8	91.9	3.7
2002	90.2	90.8	91.7	92.1	3.3	92.7	93.2	93.9	94.3	2.6
2003	93.2	93.7	94.4	95.0	3.1	94.9	95.2	95.8	96.3	2.1
2004	96.1	96.8	97.2	97.7	2.8	96.6	97.1	97.5	98.0	1.8
2005	98.4	99.0	99.5	100.0	2.4	98.4	99.0	99.6	100.0	2.0

[1]Excludes farm and household workers.

Table 6-1. Employment Cost Index, Private Industry Workers,[1] Total Compensation and Wages and Salaries, by Occupation and Industry, 1990–2005—*Continued*

(December 2005 = 100.)

Characteristic and year	Total compensation					Wages and salaries				
	Indexes				Percent change for 12 months (ended December)	Indexes				Percent change for 12 months (ended December)
	March	June	September	December		March	June	September	December	
Transportation and Public Utilities										
1990	58.0	58.1	58.6	59.1	3.9	63.1	63.4	64.0	64.3	3.4
1991	59.7	60.6	61.3	61.7	4.4	64.8	65.5	66.2	66.6	3.6
1992	62.5	63.0	63.5	63.9	3.6	67.4	68.0	68.3	68.7	3.2
1993	64.6	65.3	65.7	66.1	3.4	69.4	70.1	70.5	70.9	3.2
1994	67.1	67.4	68.3	68.7	3.9	71.5	72.0	73.1	73.5	3.7
1995	69.8	70.2	70.9	71.2	3.6	74.5	75.0	75.5	76.0	3.4
1996	72.0	72.3	72.8	73.4	3.1	76.6	76.8	77.4	78.1	2.8
1997	73.9	74.1	74.8	75.5	2.9	78.8	79.2	80.0	80.7	3.3
1998	76.4	77.2	77.9	78.4	3.8	81.2	81.6	82.5	83.0	2.9
1999	78.6	79.3	79.8	80.1	2.2	83.2	84.1	84.5	84.8	2.2
2000	81.0	82.0	82.9	83.5	4.2	85.1	86.0	86.8	87.5	3.2
2001	84.7	85.8	86.4	87.5	4.8	88.3	89.6	90.2	91.7	4.8
2002	88.5	89.4	90.5	91.0	4.0	92.5	93.5	94.3	94.7	3.3
2003	91.8	93.1	93.7	94.0	3.3	95.1	95.6	95.9	96.2	1.6
2004	95.6	97.1	97.7	97.6	3.8	96.9	97.8	98.6	98.6	2.5
2005	98.2	98.9	99.8	100.0	2.5	98.2	99.0	99.8	100.0	1.4
Transportation										
1990	61.3	61.4	61.9	62.3	3.7	65.5	65.5	66.2	66.3	2.8
1991	62.7	63.6	64.2	64.7	3.9	66.8	67.6	68.3	68.5	3.3
1992	65.5	65.9	66.6	66.6	2.9	69.4	70.0	70.3	70.4	2.8
1993	67.2	68.0	68.4	69.0	3.6	71.0	71.7	72.1	72.6	3.1
1994	69.8	70.1	71.3	71.7	3.9	73.2	73.5	74.8	75.3	3.7
1995	72.9	73.3	74.3	74.6	4.0	76.2	76.7	77.5	77.9	3.5
1996	75.6	76.1	76.4	77.0	3.2	78.7	78.9	79.3	79.9	2.6
1997	77.8	78.0	78.7	79.5	3.2	81.0	81.3	82.3	83.0	3.9
1998	79.9	80.4	81.5	81.8	2.9	83.3	83.5	84.8	85.1	2.5
1999	81.5	82.3	82.7	83.1	1.6	84.8	85.7	86.1	86.4	1.5
2000	83.7	84.5	85.1	85.8	3.2	86.4	87.3	88.0	88.8	2.8
2001	86.7	87.5	88.3	90.0	4.9	89.6	90.7	91.4	93.3	5.1
2002	90.9	91.7	92.6	93.0	3.3	94.4	95.2	95.8	96.2	3.1
2003	94.0	94.7	95.0	95.1	2.3	96.4	96.5	96.3	96.6	0.4
2004	96.5	98.2	99.0	99.0	4.1	97.2	98.3	99.3	99.4	2.9
2005	98.6	99.0	100.0	100.0	1.0	98.3	99.0	101.1	100.0	0.6
Public Utilities										
1990	53.9	54.3	54.8	55.3	3.9	60.1	60.7	61.2	61.8	4.0
1991	55.9	56.9	57.7	58.1	5.1	62.3	63.0	63.6	64.1	3.7
1992	58.9	59.4	59.8	60.4	4.0	65.0	65.5	65.9	66.5	3.7
1993	61.4	61.8	62.3	62.7	3.8	67.3	67.9	68.3	68.7	3.3
1994	63.6	64.1	64.6	65.0	3.7	69.4	70.0	70.8	71.3	3.8
1995	65.9	66.3	66.6	67.2	3.4	72.2	72.6	73.0	73.5	3.1
1996	67.4	67.5	68.2	68.8	2.4	73.8	74.1	74.9	75.7	3.0
1997	69.0	69.3	69.9	70.6	2.6	75.9	76.3	77.0	77.8	2.8
1998	72.1	73.0	73.5	74.2	5.1	78.4	79.1	79.6	80.3	3.2
1999	75.0	75.6	76.2	76.4	3.0	81.2	82.0	82.5	82.7	3.0
2000	77.7	78.9	80.2	80.6	5.5	83.5	84.5	85.4	85.8	3.7
2001	82.2	83.5	84.0	84.4	4.7	86.7	88.0	88.6	89.6	4.4
2002	85.7	86.5	87.9	88.4	4.7	90.0	91.2	92.2	92.9	3.7
2003	89.1	91.1	92.2	92.5	4.6	93.5	94.5	95.3	95.7	3.0
2004	94.3	95.7	96.0	95.9	3.7	96.4	97.0	97.7	97.7	2.1
2005	97.7	98.9	99.5	100.0	4.3	98.1	99.1	99.4	100.0	2.4
Communications										
1990	54.0	54.0	54.6	55.1	3.6	59.9	60.5	61.0	61.6	4.2
1991	55.5	56.5	57.5	58.0	5.3	61.8	62.5	63.0	63.6	3.2
1992	58.5	59.0	59.4	60.1	3.6	64.3	64.9	65.2	65.9	3.6
1993	61.0	61.5	62.0	62.4	3.8	66.6	67.1	67.7	68.0	3.2
1994	63.4	63.9	64.3	64.9	4.0	68.8	69.4	70.3	70.9	4.3
1995	66.1	66.3	66.7	67.2	3.5	72.2	72.4	72.8	73.3	3.4
1996	67.0	66.8	67.6	68.6	2.1	73.2	73.5	74.4	75.7	3.3
1997	68.2	68.3	69.0	70.2	2.3	75.4	75.8	76.5	77.8	2.8
1998	71.5	72.9	73.6	74.2	5.7	78.0	78.9	79.4	80.1	3.0
1999	75.0	75.9	76.5	76.4	3.0	81.0	81.9	82.4	82.6	3.1
2000	77.7	79.0	80.6	81.0	6.0	83.3	84.2	85.2	85.6	3.6
2001	82.9	84.3	85.2	85.5	5.6	86.6	88.2	89.0	90.1	5.3
2002	86.9	87.0	88.5	89.1	4.2	90.2	91.2	92.7	93.3	3.6
2003	89.7	91.9	93.4	93.7	5.2	94.0	94.9	96.1	96.3	3.2
2004	95.4	96.1	96.2	96.1	2.6	97.0	97.3	98.0	97.7	1.5
2005	97.4	98.6	99.5	100.0	4.1	97.8	98.9	99.3	100.0	2.4

[1]Excludes farm and household workers.

Table 6-1. Employment Cost Index, Private Industry Workers,[1] Total Compensation and Wages and Salaries, by Occupation and Industry, 1990–2005—*Continued*

(December 2005 = 100.)

Characteristic and year	Total compensation					Wages and salaries				
	Indexes				Percent change for 12 months (ended December)	Indexes				Percent change for 12 months (ended December)
	March	June	September	December		March	June	September	December	
Electric, Gas, and Sanitary Services										
1990	53.9	54.6	55.1	55.4	4.3	60.3	61.0	61.5	61.9	3.9
1991	56.5	57.3	57.9	58.3	5.2	62.9	63.6	64.1	64.7	4.5
1992	59.3	60.0	60.5	60.9	4.5	65.7	66.4	66.9	67.3	4.0
1993	61.9	62.3	62.7	63.0	3.4	68.1	68.8	69.2	69.6	3.4
1994	64.0	64.3	64.9	65.1	3.3	70.2	70.8	71.4	71.7	3.0
1995	65.7	66.3	66.6	67.2	3.2	72.3	72.9	73.3	73.8	2.9
1996	67.9	68.4	68.9	69.1	2.8	74.4	74.8	75.3	75.6	2.4
1997	70.0	70.4	71.0	71.2	3.0	76.4	76.9	77.4	77.9	3.0
1998	72.9	73.2	73.6	74.2	4.2	78.9	79.4	79.8	80.5	3.3
1999	74.8	75.3	75.7	76.3	2.8	81.4	82.0	82.5	82.8	2.9
2000	77.7	78.8	79.8	80.1	5.0	83.8	84.8	85.5	85.9	3.7
2001	81.4	82.5	82.5	83.0	3.6	86.8	87.8	88.1	88.9	3.5
2002	84.2	86.0	87.3	87.7	5.7	89.6	91.1	91.7	92.2	3.7
2003	88.5	90.1	90.7	91.1	3.9	92.9	94.0	94.3	94.8	2.8
2004	93.0	95.2	95.7	95.7	5.0	95.7	96.7	97.2	97.6	3.0
2005	98.1	99.3	99.5	100.0	4.5	98.4	99.1	99.5	100.0	2.5
Wholesale and Retail Trade										
1990	59.3	60.2	60.5	60.9	3.6	61.8	62.6	62.9	63.2	2.8
1991	61.5	62.6	63.2	63.4	4.1	63.8	64.9	65.5	65.6	3.8
1992	63.8	64.5	64.8	65.2	2.8	65.8	66.5	66.7	67.2	2.4
1993	65.7	66.4	66.7	67.1	2.9	67.6	68.3	68.6	69.1	2.8
1994	67.4	68.4	69.1	69.1	3.0	69.1	70.3	70.8	70.9	2.6
1995	69.7	70.4	70.9	71.2	3.0	71.5	72.2	72.8	73.2	3.2
1996	71.9	72.4	73.1	73.7	3.5	74.1	74.7	75.3	76.0	3.8
1997	74.6	75.2	75.9	76.2	3.4	76.9	77.6	78.3	78.8	3.7
1998	77.2	77.8	78.9	79.2	3.9	79.8	80.6	81.7	82.0	4.1
1999	79.6	80.9	81.5	82.2	3.8	82.4	83.5	84.2	85.0	3.7
2000	83.4	84.4	85.0	85.6	4.1	86.1	87.1	87.6	88.2	3.8
2001	86.5	87.4	88.1	89.1	4.1	88.8	89.8	90.1	91.0	3.2
2002	89.7	91.4	91.5	91.5	2.7	91.6	93.2	93.1	93.1	2.3
2003	92.4	93.1	94.2	94.6	3.4	93.8	94.3	95.3	95.5	2.6
2004	95.3	96.3	96.9	96.9	2.4	95.9	96.7	97.2	97.0	1.6
2005	97.9	98.4	99.4	100.0	3.2	97.8	98.2	99.3	100.0	3.1
Wholesale and Retail Trade, Excluding Sales Occupations										
1990	58.8	59.7	60.2	60.6	3.9	60.9	61.8	62.3	62.6	3.5
1991	61.5	62.3	62.9	63.3	4.5	63.4	64.3	64.8	65.0	3.8
1992	63.7	64.4	64.8	65.2	3.0	65.3	66.1	66.5	66.8	2.8
1993	65.9	66.4	66.8	67.4	3.4	67.4	67.9	68.4	68.9	3.1
1994	67.7	68.4	69.0	69.0	2.4	69.1	69.9	70.4	70.5	2.3
1995	69.9	70.3	70.9	71.4	3.5	71.3	71.8	72.3	73.1	3.7
1996	71.9	72.2	73.1	73.7	3.2	73.8	74.1	75.1	75.8	3.7
1997	74.5	75.3	76.0	76.5	3.8	76.7	77.8	78.5	79.1	4.4
1998	77.4	77.8	78.9	79.3	3.7	79.9	80.5	81.7	82.0	3.7
1999	79.9	81.0	81.6	82.4	3.9	82.8	83.7	84.2	85.0	3.7
2000	83.6	84.6	85.4	86.0	4.4	86.2	87.1	88.0	88.4	4.0
2001	87.2	87.9	88.7	89.7	4.3	89.4	90.1	90.9	91.8	3.8
2002	89.9	91.4	91.5	91.6	2.1	91.9	93.2	93.2	93.2	1.5
2003	92.4	92.9	94.2	94.7	3.4	93.7	94.2	95.4	95.7	2.7
2004	95.6	96.3	96.9	97.3	2.7	96.3	96.7	97.0	97.4	1.8
2005	98.4	98.9	99.7	100.0	2.8	98.2	98.7	99.5	100.0	2.7
Wholesale Trade										
1990	57.3	57.6	57.8	58.2	1.9	60.3	60.7	60.8	61.2	0.8
1991	58.9	59.9	60.5	60.7	4.3	61.9	63.0	63.7	63.6	3.9
1992	61.5	62.0	61.9	62.5	3.0	64.2	64.9	64.5	65.5	3.0
1993	63.0	63.6	63.7	64.4	3.0	65.7	66.4	66.4	67.1	2.4
1994	64.4	65.4	65.9	66.4	3.1	67.0	68.2	68.6	69.1	3.0
1995	67.3	68.2	68.9	69.4	4.5	69.7	70.8	71.5	72.4	4.8
1996	69.7	70.7	71.0	71.5	3.0	72.7	73.8	74.1	74.7	3.2
1997	72.6	73.1	73.6	73.8	3.2	75.8	76.2	76.7	77.0	3.1
1998	75.2	75.7	76.9	78.0	5.7	78.5	79.1	80.3	81.5	5.8
1999	78.0	79.0	79.9	81.1	4.0	81.1	82.1	83.2	84.5	3.7
2000	82.0	83.0	83.1	84.4	4.1	85.0	86.2	86.3	87.4	3.4
2001	84.8	86.2	86.7	87.2	3.3	87.4	89.1	88.9	89.3	2.2
2002	88.5	90.9	90.7	91.1	4.5	90.7	93.0	92.5	92.8	3.9
2003	92.6	93.6	94.0	94.0	3.2	94.2	95.0	95.0	95.3	2.7
2004	95.0	96.1	97.2	96.5	2.7	95.8	96.8	97.9	96.6	1.4
2005	97.9	98.0	99.3	100.0	3.6	97.8	97.7	99.0	100.0	3.5

[1] Excludes farm and household workers.

Table 6-1. Employment Cost Index, Private Industry Workers,[1] Total Compensation and Wages and Salaries, by Occupation and Industry, 1990–2005—*Continued*

(December 2005 = 100.)

Characteristic and year	Total compensation					Wages and salaries				
	Indexes				Percent change for 12 months (ended December)	Indexes				Percent change for 12 months (ended December)
	March	June	September	December		March	June	September	December	
Wholesale Trade, Excluding Sales Occupations										
1990	57.4	58.1	58.3	58.7	3.5	59.7	60.6	60.9	61.3	3.4
1991	59.8	60.6	61.0	61.5	4.8	62.4	63.2	63.5	63.9	4.2
1992	62.2	62.8	63.1	63.6	3.4	64.5	65.2	65.6	66.0	3.3
1993	64.2	64.6	65.0	65.7	3.3	66.4	66.8	67.3	68.0	3.0
1994	66.0	66.5	67.1	67.5	2.7	68.2	68.8	69.2	69.6	2.4
1995	68.8	69.2	69.8	70.3	4.1	70.7	71.1	71.6	72.7	4.5
1996	70.5	71.2	71.9	72.4	3.0	73.1	73.8	74.6	75.1	3.3
1997	73.3	73.9	74.4	74.9	3.5	76.3	76.9	77.5	78.1	4.0
1998	75.8	76.4	77.4	78.1	4.3	79.0	79.7	80.8	81.5	4.4
1999	78.8	79.6	80.6	81.5	4.4	82.1	82.8	83.8	84.7	3.9
2000	82.7	83.6	84.5	85.7	5.2	85.6	86.6	87.6	88.7	4.7
2001	86.8	87.7	88.5	88.8	3.6	89.6	90.6	91.1	91.4	3.0
2002	89.8	90.9	91.9	92.5	4.2	92.2	93.3	94.1	94.7	3.6
2003	93.1	94.0	94.7	94.7	2.4	94.8	95.6	95.9	96.2	1.6
2004	96.1	96.2	97.0	97.5	3.0	97.1	97.0	97.6	97.7	1.6
2005	99.1	99.3	99.8	100.0	2.6	99.2	99.2	99.7	100.0	2.4
Retail Trade										
1990	60.7	61.8	62.2	62.5	4.3	62.7	63.7	64.1	64.2	3.5
1991	63.3	64.3	64.9	65.2	4.3	64.8	65.9	66.5	66.6	3.7
1992	65.3	66.1	66.6	66.9	2.6	66.7	67.5	67.9	68.2	2.4
1993	67.5	68.2	68.5	68.9	3.0	68.7	69.4	69.9	70.2	2.9
1994	69.3	70.3	71.0	70.8	2.8	70.3	71.4	72.0	71.9	2.4
1995	71.3	71.8	72.3	72.3	2.1	72.4	73.0	73.5	73.6	2.4
1996	73.4	73.6	74.4	75.1	3.9	74.9	75.1	75.9	76.8	4.3
1997	75.8	76.5	77.3	77.7	3.5	77.5	78.4	79.3	79.7	3.8
1998	78.5	79.2	80.1	80.0	3.0	80.5	81.3	82.5	82.2	3.1
1999	80.7	82.0	82.5	83.0	3.8	83.1	84.4	84.7	85.2	3.6
2000	84.4	85.4	86.2	86.4	4.1	86.7	87.6	88.3	88.6	4.0
2001	87.7	88.3	89.0	90.3	4.5	89.6	90.2	90.8	91.9	3.7
2002	90.5	91.7	92.0	91.9	1.8	92.1	93.2	93.3	93.2	1.4
2003	92.3	92.8	94.3	94.9	3.3	93.4	93.8	95.4	95.5	2.5
2004	95.6	96.5	96.8	97.1	2.3	96.0	96.6	96.8	97.2	1.8
2005	98.0	98.6	99.4	100.0	3.0	97.8	98.5	99.4	100.0	2.9
General Merchandise Stores										
1990	58.9	60.7	60.8	61.4	5.3	63.5	65.2	65.5	66.0	4.9
1991	62.2	63.2	63.8	63.8	3.9	66.8	68.2	68.8	68.6	3.9
1992	64.1	64.8	65.0	65.0	1.9	68.9	69.2	69.2	69.3	1.0
1993	65.5	65.8	66.3	66.8	2.8	69.7	70.3	71.0	71.3	2.9
1994	66.2	67.7	68.1	68.5	2.5	70.7	72.2	72.2	72.8	2.1
1995	68.9	69.3	69.5	69.9	2.0	73.1	73.5	73.8	74.5	2.3
1996	70.3	71.0	71.5	72.5	3.7	75.0	75.4	76.0	77.3	3.8
1997	72.6	73.3	73.8	74.6	2.9	77.5	78.2	78.5	79.6	3.0
1998	75.3	76.3	76.5	76.9	3.1	80.2	81.5	82.0	82.5	3.6
1999	77.5	77.8	78.8	79.4	3.3	82.9	83.3	84.1	84.7	2.7
2000	80.2	80.9	81.6	82.9	4.4	85.4	85.9	86.6	88.2	4.1
2001	84.6	85.8	85.9	86.6	4.5	89.2	90.2	90.3	90.8	2.9
2002	87.5	88.5	89.6	89.0	2.8	91.7	92.3	93.1	92.5	1.9
2003	89.8	91.4	92.5	95.1	6.9	92.9	94.2	94.9	95.2	2.9
2004	95.2	95.4	96.9	97.3	2.3	95.5	96.0	97.6	98.0	2.9
2005	98.9	98.8	98.7	100.0	2.8	98.8	98.6	98.6	100.0	2.0
Food Stores										
1990	61.5	62.3	63.0	63.4	4.6	64.9	65.8	66.3	66.8	4.0
1991	64.0	65.1	65.7	66.5	4.9	67.4	68.6	69.0	69.7	4.3
1992	67.1	67.7	68.0	68.6	3.2	70.0	70.9	71.2	71.7	2.9
1993	69.0	69.8	69.7	70.5	2.8	72.3	72.8	72.5	73.1	2.0
1994	71.2	71.8	71.6	71.5	1.4	73.8	74.3	74.1	74.0	1.2
1995	71.9	71.9	72.5	72.9	2.0	74.3	74.2	74.8	75.1	1.5
1996	73.6	74.1	75.6	76.5	4.9	76.0	76.5	77.7	78.7	4.8
1997	76.4	76.4	77.3	77.1	0.8	78.7	78.7	79.9	80.1	1.8
1998	78.2	79.2	79.6	79.0	2.5	81.4	82.3	83.1	82.3	2.7
1999	80.0	80.8	81.6	82.3	4.2	83.2	83.8	84.5	85.1	3.4
2000	83.4	84.9	85.4	86.1	4.6	86.2	88.0	88.5	89.3	4.9
2001	87.0	88.3	89.2	90.4	5.0	90.4	91.2	91.9	92.6	3.7
2002	91.1	92.0	93.1	93.1	3.0	93.4	93.9	94.7	94.8	2.4
2003	93.8	94.5	94.9	95.5	2.6	95.3	95.6	96.0	96.4	1.7
2004	96.5	97.4	97.4	97.7	2.3	97.0	97.4	97.5	97.8	1.5
2005	98.3	98.8	99.2	100.0	2.4	98.3	98.9	99.4	100.0	2.2

[1] Excludes farm and household workers.

Table 6-1. Employment Cost Index, Private Industry Workers,[1] Total Compensation and Wages and Salaries, by Occupation and Industry, 1990–2005—*Continued*

(December 2005 = 100.)

Characteristic and year	Total compensation					Wages and salaries				
	Indexes				Percent change for 12 months (ended December)	Indexes				Percent change for 12 months (ended December)
	March	June	September	December		March	June	September	December	
Finance, Insurance, and Real Estate										
1990	53.4	54.3	54.8	54.9	4.2	56.0	56.9	57.7	57.6	3.4
1991	56.3	56.9	57.0	57.2	4.2	58.8	59.4	59.4	59.6	3.5
1992	58.1	57.6	57.8	57.9	1.2	60.2	59.5	59.5	59.5	-0.2
1993	58.6	58.8	60.2	60.5	4.5	60.1	60.1	61.7	62.1	4.4
1994	61.2	61.2	61.6	61.8	2.1	62.5	62.2	62.6	62.8	1.1
1995	62.5	63.3	63.8	64.0	3.6	63.2	64.3	64.9	65.1	3.7
1996	64.7	65.7	65.9	65.5	2.3	65.9	67.0	67.2	67.2	3.2
1997	66.9	67.3	67.9	69.9	6.7	68.4	68.9	69.5	71.8	6.8
1998	71.1	72.0	73.3	74.1	6.0	72.9	74.1	75.9	76.9	7.1
1999	73.6	75.8	76.8	77.1	4.0	75.4	78.3	79.4	79.8	3.8
2000	79.0	79.6	80.7	81.0	5.1	81.7	82.2	83.4	83.4	4.5
2001	82.1	82.9	83.7	83.9	3.6	84.6	85.0	85.7	85.8	2.9
2002	85.9	87.0	87.4	87.6	4.4	88.1	89.1	89.3	89.4	4.2
2003	91.9	92.7	93.7	94.1	7.4	94.1	94.8	95.7	95.9	7.3
2004	94.9	95.5	96.1	96.7	2.8	96.3	96.4	97.0	97.7	1.9
2005	98.2	99.3	99.3	100.0	3.4	98.5	99.6	99.5	100.0	2.4
Finance, Insurance, and Real Estate, Excluding Sales Occupations										
1990	52.7	53.3	54.2	54.4	5.6	55.5	56.0	57.0	57.2	5.1
1991	55.3	55.8	56.3	56.7	4.2	58.0	58.4	59.0	59.5	4.0
1992	57.3	57.2	57.3	57.6	1.6	59.6	59.2	59.2	59.4	-0.2
1993	58.5	59.3	59.9	60.2	4.5	60.3	60.9	61.4	61.7	3.9
1994	61.0	61.3	61.9	62.0	3.0	62.2	62.5	63.1	63.3	2.6
1995	63.0	63.5	63.9	64.0	3.2	64.3	64.8	65.2	65.4	3.3
1996	65.0	65.5	66.1	65.8	2.8	66.5	67.1	67.9	67.5	3.2
1997	67.0	67.4	68.0	70.1	6.5	68.5	69.0	69.7	72.0	6.7
1998	71.4	72.0	72.9	73.0	4.1	73.2	74.1	75.3	75.2	4.4
1999	74.2	75.8	76.9	77.2	5.8	76.0	78.0	79.5	79.7	6.0
2000	78.6	79.2	80.2	80.7	4.5	80.9	81.6	82.6	83.0	4.1
2001	82.1	83.1	83.9	84.1	4.2	84.4	84.9	85.7	85.7	3.3
2002	86.5	87.3	87.7	88.2	4.9	88.6	89.3	89.5	90.1	5.1
2003	92.7	93.7	94.4	94.8	7.5	95.2	96.2	96.6	96.9	7.5
2004	95.1	96.1	96.8	97.4	2.7	96.6	97.3	98.0	98.5	1.7
2005	99.0	99.9	99.4	100.0	2.7	99.5	100.5	99.5	100.0	1.5
Banking, Savings and Loan, and Other Credit Agencies										
1990	47.5	48.4	48.6	49.2	4.9	48.1	49.0	49.2	49.9	4.4
1991	50.0	49.8	50.0	50.0	1.6	50.4	50.1	50.4	50.3	0.8
1992	51.3	51.2	51.7	51.8	3.6	51.2	51.0	51.4	51.6	2.6
1993	53.3	54.0	54.4	54.8	5.8	53.1	53.4	53.8	54.2	5.0
1994	55.2	55.6	56.2	56.1	2.4	54.3	54.4	55.1	55.0	1.5
1995	57.5	57.7	58.1	57.9	3.2	56.4	56.6	57.0	56.8	3.3
1996	59.1	59.7	60.6	59.6	2.9	58.1	58.8	60.0	58.6	3.2
1997	60.8	61.2	61.9	65.4	9.7	59.6	60.0	61.0	65.5	11.8
1998	66.7	67.6	69.1	68.3	4.4	66.7	67.8	69.6	68.3	4.3
1999	69.2	72.3	74.1	74.4	8.9	69.1	73.1	75.3	75.5	10.5
2000	75.7	76.4	77.2	77.5	4.2	76.7	77.3	78.1	78.4	3.8
2001	79.5	80.4	81.6	81.1	4.6	80.2	80.8	82.0	81.3	3.7
2002	84.7	85.7	85.9	86.2	6.3	85.8	86.5	86.5	87.0	7.0
2003	95.1	96.0	96.6	97.3	12.9	97.7	98.8	99.0	99.5	14.4
2004	96.4	97.2	98.0	98.8	1.5	97.8	98.2	99.1	100.0	0.5
2005	99.4	101.1	99.4	100.0	1.2	99.7	101.9	99.5	100.0	0.0
Insurance										
1990	54.3	55.4	56.1	55.8	4.9	58.7	59.7	60.7	60.3	4.3
1991	56.5	57.6	57.6	58.3	4.5	60.6	61.8	61.6	62.3	3.3
1992	59.6	60.4	60.5	60.6	3.9	63.8	64.6	64.6	64.6	3.7
1993	60.2	61.1	61.8	63.0	4.0	63.8	64.7	65.3	66.9	3.6
1994	63.1	63.4	63.9	64.4	2.2	66.5	67.0	67.5	68.0	1.6
1995	65.0	65.6	65.7	66.3	3.0	68.7	69.3	69.4	70.1	3.1
1996	67.2	67.5	68.1	68.2	2.9	70.9	71.2	71.9	72.2	3.0
1997	69.4	69.5	70.1	70.9	4.0	73.3	73.4	73.8	74.7	3.5
1998	72.3	73.1	74.7	74.6	5.2	76.3	77.3	79.5	79.4	6.3
1999	74.6	75.8	76.1	76.7	2.8	78.8	80.2	80.4	81.1	2.1
2000	78.9	79.6	81.5	81.7	6.5	83.4	84.1	86.4	86.5	6.7
2001	82.9	83.8	84.2	84.9	3.9	87.4	87.9	88.1	88.9	2.8
2002	86.3	87.4	87.9	88.4	4.1	90.1	90.9	91.5	91.2	2.6
2003	90.6	91.5	92.2	92.7	4.9	92.7	93.5	94.0	94.3	3.4
2004	93.6	95.0	95.8	96.6	4.2	94.7	95.9	96.8	97.7	3.6
2005	98.1	99.4	99.5	100.0	3.5	98.5	99.6	99.7	100.0	2.4

[1] Excludes farm and household workers.

Table 6-1. Employment Cost Index, Private Industry Workers,[1] Total Compensation and Wages and Salaries, by Occupation and Industry, 1990–2005—*Continued*

(December 2005 = 100.)

Characteristic and year	Total compensation					Wages and salaries				
	Indexes				Percent change for 12 months (ended December)	Indexes				Percent change for 12 months (ended December)
	March	June	September	December		March	June	September	December	
Insurance, Excluding Sales Occupations										
1990	56.1	57.0	57.3	57.8	5.9	61.3	62.2	62.6	62.9	4.8
1991	58.3	59.2	59.8	60.4	4.5	63.3	64.2	64.7	65.3	3.8
1992	61.1	62.1	62.3	62.9	4.1	66.0	67.0	67.3	67.9	4.0
1993	63.7	64.7	65.4	65.9	4.8	68.4	69.5	69.9	70.4	3.7
1994	66.8	67.1	67.6	67.9	3.0	71.3	71.7	72.3	72.5	3.0
1995	68.5	69.2	69.6	69.9	2.9	73.2	74.0	74.3	74.6	2.9
1996	70.9	71.2	71.6	71.7	2.6	75.7	76.0	76.4	76.7	2.8
1997	73.0	73.3	73.8	74.4	3.8	77.8	78.1	78.5	79.0	3.0
1998	75.1	75.6	76.0	76.5	2.8	79.6	80.2	80.7	81.5	3.2
1999	77.6	78.0	78.5	78.9	3.1	82.2	82.7	83.3	83.7	2.7
2000	80.2	80.8	81.7	82.2	4.2	84.6	85.2	86.1	86.6	3.5
2001	83.5	84.6	84.8	85.6	4.1	87.6	88.4	88.5	89.4	3.2
2002	87.5	88.2	88.6	88.9	3.9	91.2	91.7	92.1	92.1	3.0
2003	91.0	92.2	92.8	93.2	4.8	93.3	94.3	94.8	95.0	3.1
2004	94.1	95.6	96.1	96.8	3.9	95.6	96.7	97.3	97.8	2.9
2005	98.2	99.3	99.6	100.0	3.3	98.8	99.6	99.8	100.0	2.2
Service Industries										
1990	57.6	58.4	59.3	59.9	6.2	59.3	60.1	60.9	61.6	5.7
1991	60.7	61.1	62.0	62.5	4.3	62.3	62.6	63.4	63.8	3.6
1992	63.2	63.8	64.6	65.2	4.3	64.4	64.8	65.5	66.0	3.4
1993	65.8	66.3	67.1	67.5	3.5	66.6	66.9	67.6	68.0	3.0
1994	68.2	68.5	69.0	69.4	2.8	68.7	69.0	69.5	70.0	2.9
1995	69.9	70.3	70.7	70.9	2.2	70.5	70.8	71.3	71.7	2.4
1996	71.7	72.2	72.8	73.1	3.1	72.6	73.2	73.8	74.2	3.5
1997	73.8	74.4	75.1	75.9	3.8	75.0	75.7	76.6	77.5	4.4
1998	76.4	76.9	77.7	78.2	3.0	78.0	78.7	79.6	80.1	3.4
1999	78.7	79.3	80.1	80.9	3.5	80.9	81.5	82.2	83.0	3.6
2000	81.9	82.9	83.8	84.5	4.4	83.8	84.8	85.7	86.3	4.0
2001	85.8	86.5	87.7	88.3	4.5	87.5	88.2	89.4	90.0	4.3
2002	89.1	89.7	90.4	90.7	2.7	90.7	91.2	91.9	92.0	2.2
2003	91.6	92.3	93.4	94.0	3.6	92.6	93.3	94.4	94.8	3.0
2004	95.1	96.0	97.0	97.5	3.7	95.6	96.3	97.3	97.8	3.2
2005	98.5	99.0	99.6	100.0	2.6	98.6	99.1	99.6	100.0	2.2
Business Services										
1990	57.1	58.1	58.6	59.2	5.9	58.3	59.5	59.9	60.8	6.1
1991	60.8	60.9	60.7	61.3	3.5	62.1	62.0	61.7	62.3	2.5
1992	62.1	62.7	63.5	63.9	4.2	62.9	63.3	64.2	64.5	3.5
1993	64.3	64.8	65.1	65.4	2.3	64.7	64.9	65.3	65.5	1.6
1994	66.9	67.3	67.5	67.8	3.7	67.3	67.6	67.9	68.2	4.1
1995	68.7	69.1	69.3	69.7	2.8	69.1	69.6	70.0	70.4	3.2
1996	71.1	71.3	71.8	72.7	4.3	71.9	72.3	72.8	73.7	4.7
1997	73.5	74.0	75.2	76.4	5.1	74.4	75.0	76.4	77.7	5.4
1998	76.9	77.6	79.2	80.5	5.4	77.9	78.8	80.3	81.6	5.0
1999	81.4	82.0	83.1	83.8	4.1	82.3	82.8	84.1	84.8	3.9
2000	85.1	86.2	86.9	87.4	4.3	86.1	87.3	87.9	88.3	4.1
2001	88.5	89.9	91.1	91.7	4.9	89.6	91.1	92.2	92.7	5.0
2002	91.7	91.9	92.2	92.4	0.8	92.9	92.9	93.2	93.3	0.6
2003	92.9	93.3	94.8	95.2	3.0	93.8	94.2	95.8	96.1	3.0
2004	96.4	97.6	98.5	98.8	3.8	96.8	97.8	98.7	99.1	3.1
2005	99.3	99.8	99.9	100.0	1.2	99.4	99.9	99.9	100.0	0.9
Health Services										
1990	57.4	58.1	59.1	60.1	6.7	59.4	60.0	61.0	61.9	6.0
1991	61.1	61.6	62.6	63.2	5.2	62.7	63.1	64.0	64.6	4.4
1992	64.0	64.5	65.4	66.1	4.6	65.2	65.6	66.5	67.1	3.9
1993	66.7	67.3	67.8	68.4	3.5	67.6	68.1	68.6	69.1	3.0
1994	68.7	69.0	69.4	69.8	2.0	69.4	69.7	70.1	70.7	2.3
1995	70.4	70.7	71.2	71.7	2.7	71.2	71.5	71.9	72.4	2.4
1996	71.9	72.4	72.8	73.0	1.8	72.9	73.4	73.8	74.1	2.3
1997	73.5	73.7	74.3	74.9	2.6	74.7	75.1	75.7	76.4	3.1
1998	75.0	75.3	75.4	75.4	0.7	76.8	77.0	77.6	77.5	1.4
1999	76.2	76.7	77.4	78.2	3.7	78.2	78.7	79.3	80.2	3.5
2000	79.1	80.0	80.8	81.7	4.5	80.9	82.0	82.7	83.5	4.1
2001	82.9	83.9	85.1	85.9	5.1	84.5	85.6	86.6	87.6	4.9
2002	87.1	87.9	88.6	89.2	3.8	88.7	89.3	90.0	90.6	3.4
2003	90.3	91.1	91.9	92.7	3.9	91.3	92.0	92.8	93.5	3.2
2004	94.0	94.8	96.0	96.6	4.2	94.6	95.2	96.4	97.0	3.7
2005	97.8	98.5	99.2	100.0	3.5	97.8	98.5	99.2	100.0	3.1

[1]Excludes farm and household workers.

Table 6-1. Employment Cost Index, Private Industry Workers,[1] Total Compensation and Wages and Salaries, by Occupation and Industry, 1990–2005—*Continued*

(December 2005 = 100.)

Characteristic and year	Total compensation					Wages and salaries				
	Indexes				Percent change for 12 months (ended December)	Indexes				Percent change for 12 months (ended December)
	March	June	September	December		March	June	September	December	
Hospitals										
1990	55.3	55.9	57.1	58.0	6.8	58.3	58.9	60.1	61.0	6.3
1991	58.8	59.4	60.3	60.9	5.0	61.5	62.0	62.9	63.5	4.1
1992	61.7	62.1	63.0	63.8	4.8	64.1	64.4	65.1	65.7	3.5
1993	64.3	64.7	65.3	65.9	3.3	66.2	66.6	67.2	67.7	3.0
1994	66.4	66.6	67.0	67.4	2.3	68.2	68.5	68.8	69.3	2.4
1995	67.6	68.0	68.3	68.9	2.2	69.6	69.9	70.3	70.9	2.3
1996	69.3	69.6	70.0	70.1	1.7	71.3	71.7	72.0	72.3	2.0
1997	70.3	70.5	71.0	71.6	2.1	72.6	72.8	73.4	74.0	2.4
1998	71.7	72.5	72.9	73.4	2.5	74.2	74.8	75.4	75.8	2.4
1999	74.0	74.5	75.0	75.8	3.3	76.4	76.8	77.3	78.2	3.2
2000	76.5	77.3	78.2	79.2	4.5	78.7	79.6	80.5	81.5	4.2
2001	80.5	81.8	83.1	84.1	6.2	82.5	83.8	85.1	86.3	5.9
2002	85.4	86.3	87.2	88.1	4.8	87.2	88.1	89.0	90.0	4.3
2003	89.6	90.1	91.2	92.2	4.7	90.8	91.4	92.4	93.2	3.6
2004	93.4	94.2	95.3	96.1	4.2	94.1	94.7	95.7	96.5	3.5
2005	97.4	98.2	99.2	100.0	4.1	97.4	98.1	99.1	100.0	3.6
Nursing Homes										
1990	. . .	. . .	. . .	. . .	. . .	. . .	. . .	. . .	. . .	. . .
1991	. . .	. . .	. . .	. . .	. . .	. . .	. . .	. . .	. . .	. . .
1992	. . .	61.0	61.6	62.2	. . .	. . .	61.2	61.7	62.3	. . .
1993	63.0	63.5	64.0	64.6	3.9	63.0	63.5	64.0	64.5	3.5
1994	65.4	65.9	66.3	66.6	3.1	65.5	66.0	66.5	66.9	3.7
1995	67.4	67.8	68.2	68.9	3.5	67.6	68.2	68.5	69.1	3.3
1996	69.2	69.9	70.0	70.7	2.6	69.7	70.1	70.4	71.1	2.9
1997	71.2	71.5	72.0	72.5	2.5	71.9	72.2	72.7	73.3	3.1
1998	73.1	73.7	74.4	74.9	3.3	74.3	74.9	75.6	76.0	3.7
1999	75.8	76.5	77.2	78.1	4.3	77.1	77.8	78.5	79.3	4.3
2000	79.1	80.3	81.6	82.9	6.1	80.3	81.6	82.9	83.9	5.8
2001	84.4	85.0	86.3	87.1	5.1	85.4	86.0	87.2	88.2	5.1
2002	88.3	89.3	89.9	90.6	4.0	89.4	90.2	91.0	91.8	4.1
2003	91.7	92.4	93.2	93.7	3.4	92.5	93.2	93.8	94.4	2.8
2004	94.9	95.5	96.0	96.6	3.1	95.1	95.7	96.2	96.7	2.4
2005	97.2	98.0	98.9	100.0	3.5	97.4	98.3	99.0	100.0	3.4
Educational Services										
1990	53.9	54.1	56.3	56.9	7.0	57.3	57.5	59.8	60.4	6.2
1991	57.2	57.0	58.7	59.1	3.9	60.4	60.1	61.9	62.3	3.1
1992	59.2	59.4	61.0	61.3	3.7	62.1	62.2	63.8	64.1	2.9
1993	61.6	61.6	63.3	63.4	3.4	64.3	64.3	66.1	66.2	3.3
1994	63.6	64.1	65.5	65.6	3.5	66.4	66.9	68.4	68.5	3.5
1995	65.8	66.6	68.1	68.3	4.1	68.8	68.9	70.4	70.9	3.5
1996	68.7	68.9	70.3	70.5	3.2	71.2	71.4	73.0	73.3	3.4
1997	70.8	70.9	72.4	72.9	3.4	73.7	73.8	75.5	75.8	3.4
1998	73.3	73.5	75.1	75.5	3.6	76.2	76.5	78.2	78.6	3.7
1999	75.8	76.0	77.8	78.2	3.6	78.8	79.0	80.8	81.2	3.3
2000	78.7	79.2	81.1	81.7	4.5	81.5	81.9	84.0	84.5	4.1
2001	82.9	83.1	85.0	85.6	4.8	85.1	85.5	87.4	88.0	4.1
2002	86.1	86.4	88.7	89.5	4.6	88.3	88.3	90.5	91.2	3.6
2003	90.1	90.5	92.1	92.6	3.5	91.5	91.8	93.3	93.6	2.6
2004	93.6	94.1	95.6	96.3	4.0	94.1	94.5	96.1	96.8	3.4
2005	97.1	97.5	99.6	100.0	3.8	97.4	97.8	99.7	100.0	3.3
Colleges and Universities										
1990	54.5	54.7	56.8	57.2	6.5	58.3	58.5	60.7	61.0	5.4
1991	57.6	58.0	59.8	60.2	5.2	61.2	61.5	63.4	63.7	4.4
1992	60.5	60.8	62.3	62.5	3.8	63.7	63.9	65.5	65.6	3.0
1993	62.9	62.9	64.7	64.9	3.8	65.8	65.7	67.7	67.9	3.5
1994	65.1	65.2	66.5	66.7	2.8	68.1	68.2	69.5	69.7	2.7
1995	66.9	68.0	69.7	70.0	4.9	70.0	70.3	72.0	72.6	4.2
1996	70.3	70.5	71.7	72.0	2.9	72.9	73.0	74.4	74.7	2.9
1997	72.2	72.4	73.8	74.4	3.3	75.1	75.3	76.9	77.4	3.6
1998	74.7	74.9	76.5	76.9	3.4	77.6	78.0	79.7	80.1	3.5
1999	77.2	77.4	79.0	79.3	3.1	80.4	80.6	82.1	82.5	3.0
2000	80.0	80.5	82.1	82.4	3.9	83.1	83.4	85.1	85.3	3.4
2001	84.0	84.2	86.0	86.7	5.2	86.0	86.5	88.4	89.1	4.5
2002	87.0	87.2	89.0	89.9	3.7	89.2	89.2	91.0	91.7	2.9
2003	90.3	90.8	92.3	92.9	3.3	91.7	92.1	93.5	94.0	2.5
2004	93.8	94.5	95.9	96.4	3.8	94.6	94.9	96.5	96.9	3.1
2005	97.1	97.6	99.5	100.0	3.7	97.4	97.9	99.6	100.0	3.2

[1]Excludes farm and household workers.
. . . = Not available.

Table 6-1. Employment Cost Index, Private Industry Workers,[1] Total Compensation and Wages and Salaries, by Occupation and Industry, 1990–2005—*Continued*

(December 2005 = 100.)

Characteristic and year	Total compensation					Wages and salaries				
	Indexes				Percent change for 12 months (ended December)	Indexes				Percent change for 12 months (ended December)
	March	June	September	December		March	June	September	December	
Nonmanufacturing Industries										
1990	57.8	58.5	59.1	59.5	4.6	60.5	61.2	61.7	62.2	3.8
1991	60.4	61.0	61.7	62.0	4.2	62.9	63.5	64.0	64.3	3.4
1992	62.7	63.2	63.7	64.1	3.4	64.9	65.2	65.6	66.0	2.6
1993	64.7	65.2	65.9	66.2	3.3	66.4	66.9	67.6	68.0	3.0
1994	66.9	67.4	68.1	68.2	3.0	68.4	69.0	69.5	69.8	2.6
1995	68.8	69.3	69.8	70.1	2.8	70.3	70.8	71.4	71.8	2.9
1996	70.8	71.3	71.8	72.2	3.0	72.6	73.3	73.8	74.3	3.5
1997	73.0	73.5	74.2	75.0	3.9	75.1	75.7	76.6	77.4	4.2
1998	75.7	76.3	77.3	77.7	3.6	78.1	78.9	80.0	80.5	4.0
1999	78.1	79.0	79.8	80.4	3.5	80.8	81.8	82.6	83.2	3.4
2000	81.6	82.6	83.5	84.1	4.6	84.3	85.2	86.1	86.6	4.1
2001	85.2	86.1	87.0	87.7	4.3	87.6	88.4	89.2	89.9	3.8
2002	88.6	89.6	90.2	90.4	3.1	90.8	91.7	92.1	92.3	2.7
2003	91.8	92.6	93.5	94.0	4.0	93.4	94.0	95.0	95.3	3.3
2004	95.1	96.0	96.8	97.2	3.4	95.9	96.5	97.4	97.6	2.4
2005	98.2	98.8	99.6	100.0	2.9	98.2	98.8	99.5	100.0	2.5
Nonmanufacturing, White-Collar Occupations										
1990	56.8	57.6	58.2	58.6	4.6	59.3	60.1	60.7	61.0	4.1
1991	59.6	60.3	60.9	61.2	4.4	61.8	62.5	63.0	63.3	3.8
1992	61.9	62.3	62.7	63.2	3.3	63.8	64.1	64.5	64.9	2.5
1993	63.9	64.4	65.0	65.4	3.5	65.4	65.9	66.6	67.0	3.2
1994	66.1	66.6	67.2	67.4	3.1	67.4	68.0	68.5	68.8	2.7
1995	68.1	68.6	69.1	69.3	2.8	69.3	69.9	70.4	70.8	2.9
1996	70.1	70.7	71.2	71.6	3.3	71.7	72.4	73.0	73.4	3.7
1997	72.4	72.9	73.6	74.5	4.1	74.3	74.9	75.7	76.7	4.5
1998	75.3	76.0	77.0	77.5	4.0	77.5	78.3	79.5	80.0	4.3
1999	77.7	78.7	79.5	80.2	3.5	80.1	81.2	82.1	82.8	3.5
2000	81.4	82.4	83.3	83.9	4.6	83.8	84.8	85.6	86.2	4.1
2001	85.0	86.0	86.8	87.6	4.4	87.1	88.0	88.7	89.5	3.8
2002	88.5	89.6	90.0	90.2	3.0	90.4	91.3	91.6	91.8	2.6
2003	91.7	92.4	93.4	93.9	4.1	93.1	93.8	94.8	95.1	3.6
2004	95.0	95.9	96.7	97.2	3.5	95.8	96.5	97.3	97.5	2.5
2005	98.3	98.8	99.5	100.0	2.9	98.2	98.8	99.4	100.0	2.6
Nonmanufacturing, White-Collar Occupations, Excluding Sales Occupations										
1990	56.3	57.0	57.7	58.3	5.6	58.7	59.4	60.1	60.6	5.0
1991	59.1	59.7	60.5	60.9	4.5	61.3	61.8	62.6	63.0	4.0
1992	61.6	62.0	62.6	63.1	3.6	63.5	63.9	64.4	64.8	2.9
1993	64.0	64.4	65.0	65.5	3.8	65.5	65.9	66.5	67.0	3.4
1994	66.3	66.7	67.3	67.5	3.1	67.5	67.9	68.6	68.9	2.8
1995	68.2	68.6	69.1	69.4	2.8	69.5	69.8	70.3	70.9	2.9
1996	70.2	70.6	71.3	71.5	3.0	71.7	72.2	73.0	73.3	3.4
1997	72.3	72.9	73.5	74.4	4.1	74.2	74.8	75.6	76.6	4.5
1998	75.2	75.8	76.6	77.0	3.5	77.4	78.1	79.0	79.3	3.5
1999	77.5	78.4	79.2	79.9	3.8	80.0	80.9	81.7	82.5	4.0
2000	81.1	82.0	83.0	83.7	4.8	83.3	84.3	85.2	85.9	4.1
2001	85.0	85.9	86.8	87.6	4.7	87.0	87.8	88.7	89.5	4.2
2002	88.6	89.4	89.9	90.2	3.0	90.5	91.2	91.6	91.9	2.7
2003	91.7	92.5	93.5	94.0	4.2	93.2	93.9	94.8	95.3	3.7
2004	95.1	95.9	96.8	97.5	3.7	95.9	96.5	97.4	97.9	2.7
2005	98.6	99.1	99.6	100.0	2.6	98.6	99.2	99.5	100.0	2.1

[1]Excludes farm and household workers.

Table 6-1. Employment Cost Index, Private Industry Workers,[1] Total Compensation and Wages and Salaries, by Occupation and Industry, 1990–2005—*Continued*

(December 2005 = 100.)

Characteristic and year	Total compensation					Wages and salaries				
	Indexes				Percent change for 12 months (ended December)	Indexes				Percent change for 12 months (ended December)
	March	June	September	December		March	June	September	December	
Nonmanufacturing, Blue-Collar Occupations										
1990	59.8	60.5	61.0	61.3	3.7	63.3	63.9	64.4	64.6	3.0
1991	62.3	62.8	63.4	63.8	4.1	65.3	65.8	66.3	66.6	3.1
1992	64.3	64.9	65.5	65.9	3.3	67.0	67.6	67.9	68.2	2.4
1993	66.6	67.1	67.7	68.0	3.2	68.8	69.3	70.0	70.2	2.9
1994	68.6	69.2	70.0	70.0	2.9	70.7	71.3	72.1	72.1	2.7
1995	70.6	71.1	71.7	71.8	2.6	72.8	73.4	73.9	74.2	2.9
1996	72.4	72.9	73.1	73.6	2.5	74.9	75.5	75.8	76.2	2.7
1997	74.0	74.7	75.1	75.6	2.7	76.8	77.7	78.3	78.7	3.3
1998	76.1	76.9	77.5	77.8	2.9	79.4	80.2	80.8	81.2	3.2
1999	78.5	79.4	80.1	80.5	3.5	82.0	83.0	83.7	84.1	3.6
2000	81.6	82.6	83.6	84.1	4.5	85.1	86.0	86.9	87.2	3.7
2001	85.3	86.0	87.2	87.5	4.0	88.4	89.1	90.3	90.7	4.0
2002	88.4	89.4	90.2	90.5	3.4	91.3	92.3	92.8	93.0	2.5
2003	91.5	92.7	93.6	93.9	3.8	93.6	94.4	95.0	95.2	2.4
2004	94.9	96.1	96.6	97.2	3.5	95.8	96.7	97.3	97.5	2.4
2005	98.0	99.1	99.7	100.0	2.9	98.0	98.9	99.5	100.0	2.6
Nonmanufacturing, Service Occupations										
1990	60.1	60.7	61.2	62.1	4.9	63.2	63.8	64.3	65.2	4.2
1991	62.7	63.6	64.6	65.1	4.8	65.5	66.3	67.3	67.7	3.8
1992	65.6	66.0	66.6	66.9	2.8	68.1	68.4	68.9	69.1	2.1
1993	67.6	68.1	68.6	68.9	3.0	69.4	69.8	70.3	70.4	1.9
1994	69.5	69.8	70.2	70.8	2.8	71.2	71.4	71.8	72.6	3.1
1995	71.1	71.4	71.8	72.1	1.8	72.9	73.3	73.8	74.2	2.2
1996	72.5	72.9	73.5	74.4	3.2	74.7	75.1	75.8	76.8	3.5
1997	74.8	75.5	76.7	77.4	4.0	77.4	78.0	79.4	80.1	4.3
1998	78.0	78.5	79.2	79.6	2.8	80.8	81.3	82.1	82.7	3.2
1999	80.5	81.2	81.4	82.3	3.4	83.5	84.3	84.4	85.4	3.3
2000	83.0	83.9	84.6	85.5	3.9	86.2	87.1	87.8	88.6	3.7
2001	86.5	87.2	88.0	89.1	4.2	89.4	90.0	90.7	91.9	3.7
2002	90.2	90.7	91.6	92.1	3.4	92.7	93.2	93.9	94.2	2.5
2003	93.2	93.7	94.4	95.0	3.1	94.9	95.2	95.8	96.3	2.2
2004	96.0	96.8	97.2	97.7	2.8	96.6	97.1	97.4	98.0	1.8
2005	98.4	98.9	99.5	100.0	2.4	98.4	99.0	99.6	100.0	2.0

[1]Excludes farm and household workers.

Table 6-2. Employment Cost Index, Private Industry Workers,[1] Total Compensation and Wages and Salaries, by Bargaining Status, Industry, Region,[2] and Area Size, 1990–2005

(December 2005 = 100.)

Characteristic and year	Total compensation					Wages and salaries				
	Indexes				Percent change for 12 months (ended December)	Indexes				Percent change for 12 months (ended December)
	March	June	September	December		March	June	September	December	
WORKERS BY BARGAINING STATUS										
Union Workers										
1990	57.0	57.5	58.0	58.6	4.3	62.4	62.9	63.4	64.0	3.6
1991	59.4	60.1	60.8	61.3	4.6	64.6	65.2	65.7	66.3	3.6
1992	62.5	62.9	63.6	64.0	4.4	66.8	67.4	68.0	68.4	3.2
1993	65.0	65.8	66.3	66.8	4.4	68.8	69.3	69.9	70.4	2.9
1994	67.3	67.9	68.4	68.6	2.7	70.9	71.6	72.2	72.5	3.0
1995	69.1	69.5	70.0	70.5	2.8	72.9	73.4	74.0	74.4	2.6
1996	71.0	71.6	71.8	72.2	2.4	74.7	75.6	76.0	76.3	2.6
1997	72.3	72.8	73.6	73.7	2.1	76.7	77.2	78.1	78.5	2.9
1998	74.0	74.7	75.5	75.9	3.0	78.9	79.5	80.6	81.0	3.2
1999	76.2	76.8	77.4	78.0	2.8	81.3	82.0	82.6	83.1	2.6
2000	79.0	79.7	80.7	81.1	4.0	83.5	84.3	85.2	85.9	3.4
2001	81.7	82.6	83.4	84.5	4.2	86.5	87.5	88.3	89.7	4.4
2002	85.5	86.3	87.3	88.1	4.3	90.3	91.2	92.1	92.8	3.5
2003	89.5	90.6	91.5	92.1	4.5	93.3	93.9	94.5	95.1	2.5
2004	94.6	96.0	96.8	97.3	5.6	95.7	96.6	97.4	97.7	2.7
2005	98.0	98.8	99.6	100.0	2.8	97.9	98.7	99.5	100.0	2.4
Union Workers, Blue-Collar Occupations										
1990	57.7	58.3	58.7	59.3	4.0	63.2	63.9	64.2	64.9	3.3
1991	60.2	60.8	61.5	62.0	4.6	65.5	66.0	66.4	67.0	3.2
1992	63.2	63.8	64.3	64.7	4.4	67.5	68.0	68.6	68.9	2.8
1993	65.8	66.5	67.1	67.6	4.5	69.3	69.8	70.4	70.9	2.9
1994	67.9	68.6	69.0	69.1	2.2	71.2	71.9	72.6	72.8	2.7
1995	69.5	69.9	70.4	70.8	2.5	73.1	73.7	74.3	74.4	2.2
1996	71.0	71.7	71.9	72.2	2.0	74.8	75.5	76.0	76.4	2.7
1997	72.2	72.8	73.5	73.7	2.1	76.5	77.2	78.0	78.4	2.6
1998	73.8	74.7	75.4	75.8	2.8	78.7	79.5	80.4	80.8	3.1
1999	76.0	76.6	77.2	77.8	2.6	81.2	82.0	82.7	83.2	3.0
2000	79.0	79.8	80.8	81.2	4.4	83.7	84.5	85.5	86.1	3.5
2001	81.7	82.5	83.3	84.0	3.4	86.8	87.7	88.7	89.5	3.9
2002	85.0	86.0	86.9	87.7	4.4	90.1	91.1	91.8	92.6	3.5
2003	89.2	90.4	91.4	92.0	4.9	93.1	93.8	94.6	95.0	2.6
2004	94.7	95.9	96.7	97.2	5.7	95.5	96.2	97.0	97.3	2.4
2005	98.0	98.9	99.6	100.0	2.9	97.6	98.6	99.3	100.0	2.8
Union Workers, Goods-Producing Industries[3]										
1990	56.8	57.4	57.8	58.4	4.3	62.5	63.3	63.6	64.2	3.4
1991	59.3	60.0	60.6	61.2	4.8	64.9	65.5	65.8	66.4	3.4
1992	62.7	63.0	63.6	64.0	4.6	67.0	67.4	67.9	68.3	2.9
1993	65.3	66.0	66.5	67.0	4.7	68.6	69.1	69.6	70.2	2.8
1994	67.3	68.1	68.4	68.6	2.4	70.5	71.3	71.8	72.1	2.7
1995	68.8	69.2	69.7	70.1	2.2	72.4	72.9	73.5	73.7	2.2
1996	70.3	70.9	71.0	71.4	1.9	74.1	74.9	75.3	75.6	2.6
1997	71.5	72.1	72.7	72.8	2.0	75.9	76.7	77.4	77.7	2.8
1998	73.0	73.8	74.5	75.0	3.0	78.2	79.1	80.1	80.5	3.6
1999	75.2	76.0	76.5	77.4	3.2	80.9	81.8	82.5	83.2	3.4
2000	78.8	79.6	80.7	81.0	4.7	83.9	84.6	85.7	86.4	3.8
2001	81.3	82.1	82.8	83.5	3.1	87.0	88.1	88.8	89.4	3.5
2002	84.3	85.0	85.9	86.8	4.0	90.0	90.8	91.7	92.4	3.4
2003	88.7	89.8	90.5	91.2	5.1	93.2	94.1	94.6	95.0	2.8
2004	94.7	96.0	96.8	97.1	6.5	95.5	96.3	97.0	97.1	2.2
2005	98.0	98.8	99.5	100.0	3.0	97.6	98.5	99.1	100.0	3.0
Union Workers, Service-Producing Industries[4]										
1990	57.3	57.6	58.3	58.9	4.2	62.2	62.3	63.1	63.6	3.4
1991	59.5	60.2	61.0	61.6	4.6	64.1	64.7	65.5	66.0	3.8
1992	62.2	62.9	63.7	64.0	3.9	66.6	67.4	68.0	68.4	3.6
1993	64.8	65.4	65.9	66.4	3.8	69.0	69.6	70.1	70.6	3.2
1994	67.2	67.7	68.3	68.7	3.5	71.3	71.8	72.6	72.9	3.3
1995	69.3	69.8	70.4	71.1	3.5	73.5	73.9	74.5	75.1	3.0
1996	71.7	72.4	72.8	73.2	3.0	75.5	76.3	76.7	77.1	2.7
1997	73.3	73.6	74.4	74.7	2.0	77.5	77.9	78.8	79.3	2.9
1998	75.2	75.7	76.7	76.9	2.9	79.7	79.9	81.1	81.5	2.8
1999	77.3	77.6	78.3	78.6	2.2	81.9	82.1	82.7	83.0	1.8
2000	79.2	79.9	80.7	81.3	3.4	83.2	84.0	84.7	85.6	3.1
2001	82.0	83.1	84.0	85.7	5.4	86.0	86.9	87.9	90.0	5.1
2002	86.7	87.6	88.8	89.5	4.4	90.7	91.5	92.4	93.2	3.6
2003	90.3	91.4	92.5	93.1	4.0	93.5	93.8	94.5	95.1	2.0
2004	94.6	96.1	96.9	97.4	4.6	95.8	96.9	97.8	98.3	3.4
2005	98.1	98.8	99.7	100.0	2.7	98.1	98.9	99.7	100.0	1.7

[1]Excludes farm and household workers.
[2]The regional coverage is as follows: Northeast—Connecticut, Maine, Massachusetts, New Hampshire, New Jersey, New York, Pennsylvania, Rhode Island, and Vermont; South—Alabama, Arkansas, Delaware, District of Columbia, Florida, Georgia, Kentucky, Louisiana, Maryland, Mississippi, North Carolina, Oklahoma, South Carolina, Tennessee, Texas, Virginia, and West Virginia; Midwest—Illinois, Indiana, Iowa, Kansas, Michigan, Minnesota, Missouri, Nebraska, North Dakota, Ohio, South Dakota, and Wisconsin; and West—Alaska, Arizona, California, Colorado, Hawaii, Idaho, Montana, Nevada, New Mexico, Oregon, Utah, Washington, and Wyoming.
[3]Includes mining, construction, and manufacturing workers.
[4]Includes transportation, communication, and public utilities workers; wholesale and retail trade workers; finance, insurance, and real estate workers; and service industry workers.

Table 6-2. Employment Cost Index, Private Industry Workers,[1] Total Compensation and Wages and Salaries, by Bargaining Status, Industry, Region,[2] and Area Size, 1990–2005—*Continued*

(December 2005 = 100.)

Characteristic and year	Total compensation					Wages and salaries				
	Indexes				Percent change for 12 months (ended December)	Indexes				Percent change for 12 months (ended December)
	March	June	September	December		March	June	September	December	
Union Workers, Manufacturing Industries										
1990	56.5	57.1	57.4	58.1	4.5	62.0	62.8	63.1	63.8	3.7
1991	58.9	59.7	60.3	60.9	4.8	64.5	65.0	65.5	66.1	3.6
1992	62.6	62.8	63.3	63.7	4.6	66.7	67.0	67.5	68.0	2.9
1993	65.3	66.0	66.5	67.1	5.3	68.4	68.9	69.3	70.1	3.1
1994	67.4	68.0	68.3	68.6	2.2	70.5	71.2	71.6	72.1	2.9
1995	68.9	69.0	69.3	69.8	1.7	72.4	72.9	73.3	73.8	2.4
1996	70.2	70.8	70.8	71.2	2.0	74.3	74.9	75.3	75.7	2.6
1997	71.3	71.8	72.5	72.7	2.1	75.9	76.5	77.3	77.8	2.8
1998	72.8	73.4	74.2	74.6	2.6	78.4	78.8	79.9	80.4	3.3
1999	74.7	75.3	75.8	76.9	3.1	80.8	81.4	82.1	83.1	3.4
2000	78.8	79.3	80.2	80.4	4.6	83.9	84.5	85.5	86.2	3.7
2001	80.6	81.1	81.7	82.6	2.7	87.0	88.0	88.7	89.5	3.8
2002	83.6	84.3	85.0	86.1	4.2	90.1	90.8	91.7	92.6	3.5
2003	88.5	89.3	90.0	90.7	5.3	93.5	94.3	94.7	95.0	2.6
2004	95.4	96.5	97.3	97.5	7.5	95.6	96.3	97.0	97.2	2.3
2005	98.5	99.1	99.6	100.0	2.6	97.6	98.4	99.0	100.0	2.9
Union Workers, Manufacturing, Blue-Collar Occupations										
1990	57.1	57.7	58.0	58.8	4.6	62.6	63.3	63.6	64.3	3.5
1991	59.7	60.4	61.0	61.6	4.8	65.0	65.6	66.0	66.7	3.7
1992	63.3	63.5	64.0	64.5	4.7	67.3	67.6	68.1	68.6	2.8
1993	66.0	66.8	67.2	67.8	5.1	69.0	69.4	69.8	70.6	2.9
1994	68.2	68.8	69.0	69.3	2.2	71.0	71.8	72.2	72.5	2.7
1995	69.6	69.8	70.0	70.5	1.7	72.9	73.3	73.8	74.2	2.3
1996	70.8	71.4	71.5	71.8	1.8	74.7	75.4	75.8	76.3	2.8
1997	72.0	72.5	73.2	73.4	2.2	76.5	77.0	77.9	78.3	2.6
1998	73.5	74.1	74.8	75.3	2.6	78.7	79.3	80.2	80.8	3.2
1999	75.3	75.9	76.4	77.5	2.9	81.1	81.8	82.4	83.5	3.3
2000	79.4	79.9	80.8	81.1	4.6	84.1	84.6	85.7	86.5	3.6
2001	81.3	81.7	82.5	83.3	2.7	87.2	88.0	89.0	89.7	3.7
2002	84.2	84.8	85.5	86.6	4.0	90.2	90.9	91.7	92.6	3.2
2003	88.9	89.7	90.3	91.1	5.2	93.5	94.2	94.7	95.1	2.7
2004	95.9	97.1	97.8	98.1	7.7	95.6	96.3	97.1	97.1	2.1
2005	98.6	99.1	99.6	100.0	1.9	97.6	98.4	99.0	100.0	3.0
Union Workers, Nonmanufacturing Industries										
1990	57.5	57.9	58.5	59.1	4.2	62.6	62.9	63.6	64.0	3.2
1991	59.8	60.4	61.2	61.7	4.4	64.6	65.2	65.9	66.3	3.6
1992	62.4	63.1	63.9	64.2	4.1	66.8	67.6	68.2	68.5	3.3
1993	64.9	65.5	66.1	66.6	3.7	69.0	69.6	70.2	70.6	3.1
1994	67.2	67.8	68.4	68.6	3.0	71.1	71.7	72.4	72.7	3.0
1995	69.2	69.8	70.4	70.9	3.4	73.2	73.7	74.3	74.7	2.8
1996	71.4	72.1	72.5	72.8	2.7	75.0	75.9	76.3	76.7	2.7
1997	72.9	73.4	74.2	74.3	2.1	77.0	77.6	78.6	78.9	2.9
1998	74.7	75.5	76.4	76.7	3.2	79.2	79.9	80.9	81.3	3.0
1999	77.1	77.7	78.3	78.6	2.5	81.7	82.2	82.8	83.0	2.1
2000	79.1	80.0	80.9	81.6	3.8	83.3	84.2	85.0	85.8	3.4
2001	82.2	83.4	84.3	85.7	5.0	86.2	87.2	88.1	89.9	4.8
2002	86.5	87.4	88.6	89.2	4.1	90.5	91.4	92.3	92.9	3.3
2003	90.1	91.4	92.4	92.9	4.1	93.2	93.8	94.4	95.1	2.4
2004	94.2	95.8	96.5	97.2	4.6	95.7	96.8	97.5	98.0	3.0
2005	97.8	98.7	99.7	100.0	2.9	97.9	98.8	99.6	100.0	2.0
Nonunion Workers, Total										
1990	57.8	58.5	59.2	59.5	4.8	60.3	61.1	61.7	62.0	4.2
1991	60.4	61.1	61.7	62.1	4.4	62.7	63.4	64.0	64.3	3.7
1992	62.8	63.2	63.7	64.1	3.2	64.8	65.2	65.5	65.9	2.5
1993	64.8	65.3	65.9	66.3	3.4	66.5	66.9	67.6	68.0	3.2
1994	67.0	67.5	68.1	68.4	3.2	68.5	69.0	69.5	69.9	2.8
1995	69.0	69.5	69.9	70.2	2.6	70.4	71.0	71.5	71.9	2.9
1996	70.9	71.4	72.0	72.4	3.1	72.8	73.4	74.0	74.5	3.6
1997	73.1	73.7	74.3	75.1	3.7	75.3	76.0	76.7	77.6	4.2
1998	75.9	76.5	77.3	77.7	3.5	78.4	79.1	80.1	80.6	3.9
1999	78.1	79.1	79.8	80.6	3.7	81.0	82.0	82.8	83.6	3.7
2000	81.8	82.7	83.6	84.1	4.3	84.6	85.5	86.4	86.9	3.9
2001	85.3	86.2	87.0	87.6	4.2	87.9	88.7	89.4	90.0	3.6
2002	88.6	89.6	90.0	90.3	3.1	90.9	91.8	92.2	92.4	2.7
2003	91.8	92.6	93.5	93.8	3.9	93.5	94.2	95.0	95.3	3.1
2004	95.1	95.8	96.7	97.1	3.5	96.0	96.6	97.4	97.6	2.4
2005	98.3	98.9	99.6	100.0	3.0	98.3	98.9	99.5	100.0	2.5

[1]Excludes farm and household workers.
[2]The regional coverage is as follows: Northeast—Connecticut, Maine, Massachusetts, New Hampshire, New Jersey, New York, Pennsylvania, Rhode Island, and Vermont; South—Alabama, Arkansas, Delaware, District of Columbia, Florida, Georgia, Kentucky, Louisiana, Maryland, Mississippi, North Carolina, Oklahoma, South Carolina, Tennessee, Texas, Virginia, and West Virginia; Midwest—Illinois, Indiana, Iowa, Kansas, Michigan, Minnesota, Missouri, Nebraska, North Dakota, Ohio, South Dakota, and Wisconsin; and West—Alaska, Arizona, California, Colorado, Hawaii, Idaho, Montana, Nevada, New Mexico, Oregon, Utah, Washington, and Wyoming.

Table 6-2. Employment Cost Index, Private Industry Workers,[1] Total Compensation and Wages and Salaries, by Bargaining Status, Industry, Region,[2] and Area Size, 1990–2005—*Continued*

(December 2005 = 100.)

Characteristic and year	Total compensation					Wages and salaries				
	Indexes				Percent change for 12 months (ended December)	Indexes				Percent change for 12 months (ended December)
	March	June	September	December		March	June	September	December	
Nonunion Workers, Blue-Collar Occupations										
1990	59.9	60.7	61.3	61.6	4.6	62.2	63.0	63.5	63.7	3.6
1991	62.5	63.1	63.8	64.1	4.1	64.5	65.1	65.6	66.0	3.6
1992	64.7	65.2	65.7	66.1	3.1	66.5	66.9	67.3	67.6	2.4
1993	66.8	67.4	67.9	68.2	3.2	68.2	68.6	69.1	69.5	2.8
1994	69.0	69.4	70.2	70.3	3.1	70.0	70.5	71.1	71.5	2.9
1995	70.9	71.5	71.8	72.1	2.6	72.2	72.9	73.4	73.8	3.2
1996	72.8	73.4	73.7	74.3	3.1	74.7	75.3	75.6	76.3	3.4
1997	74.9	75.7	76.0	76.5	3.0	77.0	77.9	78.4	78.9	3.4
1998	77.2	77.7	78.1	78.6	2.7	79.8	80.3	81.0	81.5	3.3
1999	79.4	80.2	80.9	81.5	3.7	82.3	83.1	83.8	84.4	3.6
2000	82.7	83.6	84.3	84.9	4.2	85.4	86.3	87.1	87.6	3.8
2001	86.2	86.7	87.8	88.2	3.9	88.9	89.5	90.6	90.9	3.8
2002	89.2	90.0	90.5	90.9	3.1	91.8	92.5	92.9	93.2	2.5
2003	92.2	93.0	93.8	94.1	3.5	94.0	94.6	95.2	95.3	2.3
2004	95.6	96.5	97.2	97.6	3.7	96.1	96.8	97.5	97.7	2.5
2005	98.5	99.3	99.7	100.0	2.5	98.3	99.1	99.5	100.0	2.4
Nonunion Workers, Goods-Producing Industries[3]										
1990	58.0	58.7	59.4	59.8	4.9	61.5	62.1	62.7	63.0	3.8
1991	60.6	61.3	62.0	62.5	4.5	63.8	64.3	64.9	65.4	3.8
1992	63.1	63.5	64.1	64.6	3.4	66.1	66.5	66.9	67.3	2.9
1993	65.5	66.0	66.5	66.8	3.4	68.0	68.4	68.9	69.3	3.0
1994	67.7	68.3	68.8	69.1	3.4	69.9	70.5	71.0	71.5	3.2
1995	69.7	70.1	70.4	70.8	2.5	72.1	72.6	73.0	73.6	2.9
1996	71.4	72.0	72.6	73.1	3.2	74.2	74.9	75.6	76.1	3.4
1997	73.5	74.2	74.6	75.0	2.6	76.6	77.4	78.0	78.4	3.0
1998	75.7	76.2	76.7	77.0	2.7	79.4	80.0	80.6	81.1	3.4
1999	77.8	78.2	79.0	79.7	3.5	81.9	82.5	83.2	83.8	3.3
2000	81.0	82.0	82.6	83.1	4.3	84.9	86.0	86.6	87.2	4.1
2001	84.4	85.2	85.7	86.5	4.1	88.4	89.3	89.8	90.4	3.7
2002	87.5	88.3	88.8	89.5	3.5	91.2	92.0	92.4	93.0	2.9
2003	91.1	91.8	92.5	92.8	3.7	93.8	94.4	94.9	95.1	2.3
2004	94.5	95.2	96.0	96.6	4.1	95.9	96.5	97.3	97.4	2.4
2005	98.3	99.1	99.8	100.0	3.5	98.2	98.9	99.5	100.0	2.7
Nonunion Workers, Service-Producing Industries[4]										
1990	57.7	58.6	59.1	59.5	4.6	59.9	60.8	61.4	61.7	4.2
1991	60.4	61.1	61.7	62.1	4.4	62.5	63.1	63.7	64.0	3.7
1992	62.7	63.1	63.5	64.0	3.1	64.4	64.7	65.1	65.5	2.3
1993	64.6	65.1	65.7	66.2	3.4	65.9	66.4	67.1	67.6	3.2
1994	66.8	67.2	67.9	68.1	2.9	67.9	68.4	68.9	69.2	2.4
1995	68.7	69.3	69.7	70.0	2.8	69.8	70.4	70.9	71.3	3.0
1996	70.7	71.2	71.7	72.1	3.0	72.2	72.8	73.3	73.9	3.6
1997	73.0	73.6	74.2	75.1	4.2	74.8	75.4	76.2	77.2	4.5
1998	75.9	76.6	77.6	78.1	4.0	78.0	78.7	79.9	80.4	4.1
1999	78.3	79.4	80.2	80.9	3.6	80.7	81.9	82.6	83.4	3.7
2000	82.2	83.1	84.0	84.6	4.6	84.5	85.3	86.2	86.7	4.0
2001	85.7	86.6	87.5	88.1	4.1	87.7	88.5	89.3	89.9	3.7
2002	89.0	90.1	90.4	90.7	3.0	90.8	91.7	92.1	92.1	2.4
2003	92.1	92.8	93.8	94.3	4.0	93.4	94.0	95.0	95.3	3.5
2004	95.3	96.2	96.9	97.2	3.1	95.9	96.5	97.3	97.6	2.4
2005	98.3	98.8	99.4	100.0	2.9	98.3	98.9	99.5	100.0	2.5
Nonunion Workers, Manufacturing Industries										
1990	57.7	58.4	59.2	59.6	5.5	61.2	61.9	62.6	62.9	4.5
1991	60.2	61.0	61.7	62.2	4.4	63.6	64.3	64.8	65.4	4.0
1992	62.9	63.4	64.0	64.5	3.7	66.1	66.6	67.0	67.5	3.2
1993	65.4	65.9	66.4	66.8	3.6	68.2	68.6	69.1	69.6	3.1
1994	67.6	68.1	68.7	69.1	3.4	70.1	70.6	71.2	71.8	3.2
1995	69.8	70.3	70.5	71.0	2.7	72.5	73.1	73.4	74.0	3.1
1996	71.6	72.3	72.9	73.4	3.4	74.6	75.3	76.1	76.6	3.5
1997	73.7	74.4	74.8	75.2	2.5	77.0	77.8	78.3	78.9	3.0
1998	76.0	76.4	76.9	77.2	2.7	79.8	80.4	81.1	81.6	3.4
1999	77.9	78.5	79.2	80.0	3.6	82.3	83.0	83.7	84.4	3.4
2000	81.1	82.1	82.6	83.0	3.8	85.3	86.3	86.9	87.4	3.6
2001	84.4	85.1	85.5	86.1	3.7	88.7	89.5	89.9	90.4	3.4
2002	87.3	88.1	88.6	89.3	3.7	91.4	92.2	92.6	93.2	3.1
2003	91.1	91.8	92.4	92.6	3.7	94.1	94.6	95.0	95.3	2.3
2004	94.5	95.2	96.2	96.5	4.2	96.0	96.7	97.6	97.6	2.4
2005	98.3	99.1	99.7	100.0	3.6	98.5	99.1	99.7	100.0	2.5

[1]Excludes farm and household workers.
[2]The regional coverage is as follows: Northeast—Connecticut, Maine, Massachusetts, New Hampshire, New Jersey, New York, Pennsylvania, Rhode Island, and Vermont; South—Alabama, Arkansas, Delaware, District of Columbia, Florida, Georgia, Kentucky, Louisiana, Maryland, Mississippi, North Carolina, Oklahoma, South Carolina, Tennessee, Texas, Virginia, and West Virginia; Midwest—Illinois, Indiana, Iowa, Kansas, Michigan, Minnesota, Missouri, Nebraska, North Dakota, Ohio, South Dakota, and Wisconsin; and West—Alaska, Arizona, California, Colorado, Hawaii, Idaho, Montana, Nevada, New Mexico, Oregon, Utah, Washington, and Wyoming.
[3]Includes mining, construction, and manufacturing workers.
[4]Includes transportation, communication, and public utilities workers; wholesale and retail trade workers; finance, insurance, and real estate workers; and service industry workers.

Table 6-2. Employment Cost Index, Private Industry Workers,¹ Total Compensation and Wages and Salaries, by Bargaining Status, Industry, Region,² and Area Size, 1990–2005—*Continued*

(December 2005 = 100.)

Characteristic and year	Total compensation					Wages and salaries				
	Indexes				Percent change for 12 months (ended December)	Indexes				Percent change for 12 months (ended December)
	March	June	September	December		March	June	September	December	
Nonunion Workers, Manufacturing, Blue-Collar Occupations										
1990	59.4	60.2	60.9	61.3	5.3	61.6	62.4	63.0	63.4	4.3
1991	62.0	62.7	63.5	64.0	4.4	64.1	64.7	65.2	65.8	3.8
1992	64.7	65.2	65.7	66.1	3.3	66.5	66.9	67.2	67.6	2.7
1993	66.8	67.3	67.9	68.2	3.2	68.1	68.5	69.0	69.4	2.7
1994	68.9	69.3	69.9	70.2	2.9	69.9	70.2	70.8	71.3	2.7
1995	70.8	71.3	71.5	72.2	2.8	72.1	72.9	73.2	73.8	3.5
1996	72.8	73.5	74.1	74.7	3.5	74.6	75.3	76.0	76.6	3.8
1997	75.2	75.9	76.3	76.6	2.5	77.2	78.0	78.5	79.1	3.3
1998	77.3	77.7	78.1	78.6	2.6	79.9	80.3	81.0	81.6	3.2
1999	79.3	79.7	80.5	81.2	3.3	82.3	82.8	83.5	84.2	3.2
2000	82.1	82.9	83.4	84.1	3.6	84.9	85.7	86.4	87.2	3.6
2001	85.2	85.7	86.5	87.3	3.8	88.4	89.2	90.0	90.7	4.0
2002	88.5	89.1	89.5	90.3	3.4	91.7	92.3	92.6	93.2	2.8
2003	91.8	92.4	93.3	93.7	3.8	94.1	94.4	95.0	95.4	2.4
2004	95.6	96.2	97.3	97.7	4.3	96.3	96.7	97.6	97.8	2.5
2005	98.8	99.3	99.7	100.0	2.4	98.7	99.2	99.6	100.0	2.2
Nonunion Workers, Nonmanufacturing Industries										
1990	57.9	58.7	59.3	59.7	4.7	60.2	61.0	61.6	61.9	3.9
1991	60.5	61.3	61.9	62.2	4.2	62.7	63.3	63.8	64.1	3.6
1992	62.8	63.2	63.6	64.1	3.1	64.6	64.9	65.2	65.6	2.3
1993	64.7	65.2	65.8	66.2	3.3	66.1	66.6	67.3	67.6	3.0
1994	66.9	67.4	68.0	68.2	3.0	68.1	68.6	69.1	69.4	2.7
1995	68.8	69.3	69.7	69.9	2.5	69.9	70.5	71.0	71.4	2.9
1996	70.7	71.2	71.7	72.1	3.1	72.3	72.9	73.4	74.0	3.6
1997	73.0	73.6	74.2	75.1	4.2	74.8	75.5	76.4	77.2	4.3
1998	75.8	76.5	77.4	77.9	3.7	78.0	78.8	79.8	80.4	4.1
1999	78.2	79.2	80.0	80.7	3.6	80.7	81.8	82.6	83.3	3.6
2000	82.0	83.0	83.9	84.5	4.7	84.4	85.4	86.2	86.7	4.1
2001	85.6	86.5	87.4	88.0	4.1	87.8	88.5	89.3	89.9	3.7
2002	89.0	90.0	90.4	90.7	3.1	90.8	91.7	92.1	92.2	2.6
2003	92.0	92.8	93.8	94.2	3.9	93.4	94.1	95.0	95.3	3.4
2004	95.2	96.0	96.8	97.2	3.2	95.9	96.5	97.3	97.6	2.4
2005	98.3	98.9	99.6	100.0	2.9	98.3	98.8	99.5	100.0	2.5
WORKERS BY REGION²										
Northeast										
1990	57.9	58.4	59.1	59.7	4.6	61.3	61.8	62.4	63.0	4.0
1991	60.7	61.4	62.0	62.4	4.5	63.8	64.5	65.0	65.4	3.8
1992	63.2	63.5	64.1	64.6	3.5	65.8	66.1	66.6	67.0	2.4
1993	65.4	66.1	66.7	67.0	3.7	67.5	68.2	68.8	69.1	3.1
1994	67.5	68.1	68.8	69.0	3.0	69.4	70.0	70.7	70.8	2.5
1995	69.7	70.3	70.7	70.9	2.8	71.5	72.0	72.5	72.8	2.8
1996	71.5	72.0	72.5	72.8	2.7	73.6	74.2	74.8	75.3	3.4
1997	73.4	73.9	74.4	74.9	2.9	75.9	76.5	77.0	77.5	2.9
1998	75.5	76.0	77.0	77.4	3.3	78.1	78.8	79.8	80.4	3.7
1999	78.0	78.5	79.5	80.1	3.5	80.8	81.4	82.4	83.0	3.2
2000	81.2	81.9	82.9	83.4	4.1	83.9	84.7	85.6	86.0	3.6
2001	84.1	85.3	86.1	86.7	4.0	86.8	87.9	88.7	89.4	4.0
2002	87.8	88.7	89.1	89.5	3.2	90.5	91.3	91.4	91.8	2.7
2003	90.9	91.7	92.6	93.2	4.1	92.7	93.3	94.3	94.8	3.3
2004	94.5	95.6	96.4	96.7	3.8	95.5	96.4	97.2	97.2	2.5
2005	97.7	98.6	99.3	100.0	3.4	97.8	98.6	99.3	100.0	2.9
South										
1990	59.6	60.6	60.9	61.3	4.6	62.5	63.6	63.9	64.1	3.9
1991	62.1	62.9	63.4	63.7	3.9	64.9	65.6	66.0	66.2	3.3
1992	64.5	64.9	65.4	65.8	3.3	66.9	67.4	67.7	68.1	2.9
1993	66.6	67.0	67.7	68.1	3.5	68.6	69.1	69.7	70.1	2.9
1994	68.8	69.2	69.8	70.2	3.1	70.5	70.9	71.6	72.0	2.7
1995	70.9	71.2	71.7	72.0	2.6	72.5	73.0	73.6	74.0	2.8
1996	72.8	73.2	73.8	74.3	3.2	75.0	75.6	76.1	76.7	3.6
1997	75.0	75.4	75.9	77.1	3.8	77.6	78.2	78.9	80.4	4.8
1998	77.7	78.2	78.9	79.1	2.6	81.0	81.5	82.5	82.6	2.7
1999	79.7	80.6	81.3	81.9	3.5	83.3	84.2	84.7	85.5	3.5
2000	83.1	84.1	84.6	85.2	4.0	86.4	87.4	87.8	88.4	3.4
2001	86.6	87.3	88.0	88.6	4.0	89.6	90.2	90.8	91.4	3.4
2002	89.5	90.3	91.1	91.1	2.8	92.1	92.8	93.5	93.4	2.2
2003	92.0	92.6	93.5	93.9	3.1	93.8	94.3	95.1	95.4	2.1
2004	95.4	96.2	97.1	97.8	4.2	96.1	96.7	97.6	98.1	2.8
2005	98.9	99.4	99.7	100.0	2.2	98.9	99.3	99.7	100.0	1.9

¹Excludes farm and household workers.
²The regional coverage is as follows: Northeast—Connecticut, Maine, Massachusetts, New Hampshire, New Jersey, New York, Pennsylvania, Rhode Island, and Vermont; South—Alabama, Arkansas, Delaware, District of Columbia, Florida, Georgia, Kentucky, Louisiana, Maryland, Mississippi, North Carolina, Oklahoma, South Carolina, Tennessee, Texas, Virginia, and West Virginia; Midwest—Illinois, Indiana, Iowa, Kansas, Michigan, Minnesota, Missouri, Nebraska, North Dakota, Ohio, South Dakota, and Wisconsin; and West—Alaska, Arizona, California, Colorado, Hawaii, Idaho, Montana, Nevada, New Mexico, Oregon, Utah, Washington, and Wyoming.

Table 6-2. Employment Cost Index, Private Industry Workers,[1] Total Compensation and Wages and Salaries, by Bargaining Status, Industry, Region,[2] and Area Size, 1990–2005—*Continued*

(December 2005 = 100.)

Characteristic and year	Total compensation					Wages and salaries				
	Indexes				Percent change for 12 months (ended December)	Indexes				Percent change for 12 months (ended December)
	March	June	September	December		March	June	September	December	
Midwest										
1990	56.3	57.0	57.8	58.2	5.1	58.7	59.3	60.1	60.5	4.1
1991	59.0	59.7	60.5	61.0	4.8	61.2	61.6	62.3	62.9	4.0
1992	61.9	62.3	62.7	63.1	3.4	63.3	63.7	64.0	64.4	2.4
1993	64.1	64.9	65.3	65.9	4.4	64.9	65.6	65.9	66.6	3.4
1994	66.8	67.2	67.8	68.0	3.2	67.2	67.7	68.4	68.7	3.2
1995	68.4	69.0	69.4	69.8	2.6	69.2	69.9	70.4	70.7	2.9
1996	70.4	71.1	71.4	71.8	2.9	71.6	72.2	72.6	73.1	3.4
1997	72.5	73.2	74.1	74.4	3.6	73.8	74.6	75.6	76.1	4.1
1998	75.2	75.9	76.6	76.9	3.4	77.1	77.8	78.7	78.9	3.7
1999	77.1	78.1	78.8	79.6	3.5	79.5	80.7	81.5	82.2	4.2
2000	81.0	81.9	82.8	83.4	4.8	83.1	84.2	85.0	85.6	4.1
2001	84.2	84.8	85.6	86.2	3.4	86.3	87.1	87.9	88.5	3.4
2002	87.6	88.4	88.9	89.5	3.8	89.9	90.7	91.1	91.6	3.5
2003	91.9	92.7	93.4	93.8	4.8	93.9	94.4	95.0	95.3	4.0
2004	95.0	95.8	96.6	96.7	3.1	95.5	95.9	96.8	96.8	1.6
2005	97.9	98.4	99.5	100.0	3.4	97.6	98.0	99.3	100.0	3.3
West										
1990	56.0	56.7	57.3	57.6	4.3	59.3	60.2	60.6	61.0	4.1
1991	58.3	59.1	59.7	60.1	4.3	61.5	62.2	62.8	63.3	3.8
1992	60.7	61.2	61.9	62.3	3.7	63.7	64.3	64.9	65.2	3.0
1993	63.0	63.1	63.9	64.0	2.7	65.7	65.8	66.7	66.9	2.6
1994	64.8	65.3	65.8	66.0	3.1	67.4	68.2	68.3	68.8	2.8
1995	66.5	66.9	67.2	67.8	2.7	69.3	69.9	70.2	71.0	3.2
1996	68.3	69.0	69.6	69.9	3.1	71.3	72.2	72.8	73.2	3.1
1997	70.7	71.3	71.9	72.3	3.4	73.9	74.6	75.3	75.9	3.7
1998	73.3	74.1	75.1	75.9	5.0	76.9	77.8	79.1	80.0	5.4
1999	76.1	77.1	77.7	78.5	3.4	79.9	81.1	81.7	82.5	3.1
2000	79.7	80.7	81.8	82.3	4.8	83.7	84.6	85.7	86.3	4.6
2001	83.7	84.6	85.5	86.4	5.0	87.5	88.4	89.2	90.2	4.5
2002	87.0	88.3	88.8	89.5	3.6	90.5	91.8	92.1	92.6	2.7
2003	90.7	91.9	93.0	93.4	4.4	93.3	94.3	95.3	95.5	3.1
2004	95.1	95.9	96.6	97.1	4.0	96.5	97.1	97.8	98.0	2.6
2005	98.4	99.4	99.8	100.0	3.0	98.5	99.4	99.6	100.0	2.0
WORKERS BY AREA SIZE										
Metropolitan Areas[5]										
1990	57.5	58.2	58.9	59.3	4.8	60.5	61.2	61.7	62.2	4.0
1991	60.1	60.8	61.5	61.9	4.4	62.9	63.5	64.0	64.5	3.7
1992	62.6	63.1	63.6	64.0	3.4	65.0	65.4	65.8	66.1	2.5
1993	64.8	65.4	65.9	66.3	3.6	66.7	67.2	67.8	68.2	3.2
1994	66.9	67.5	68.1	68.3	3.0	68.7	69.2	69.8	70.1	2.8
1995	68.9	69.4	69.9	70.2	2.8	70.7	71.2	71.7	72.2	3.0
1996	70.9	71.5	72.0	72.3	3.0	73.0	73.7	74.2	74.6	3.3
1997	72.9	73.5	74.1	74.8	3.5	75.4	76.1	76.8	77.5	3.9
1998	75.5	76.1	77.0	77.4	3.5	78.4	79.1	80.2	80.7	4.1
1999	77.7	78.6	79.3	80.1	3.5	81.0	82.0	82.7	83.5	3.5
2000	81.3	82.3	83.1	83.6	4.4	84.4	85.4	86.2	86.7	3.8
2001	84.8	85.6	86.4	87.2	4.3	87.8	88.6	89.3	90.0	3.8
2002	88.1	89.1	89.6	90.0	3.2	90.9	91.8	92.2	92.5	2.8
2003	91.5	92.2	93.2	93.6	4.0	93.5	94.1	95.0	95.3	3.0
2004	95.0	95.8	96.7	97.1	3.7	96.0	96.6	97.4	97.6	2.4
2005	98.2	98.9	99.6	100.0	3.0	98.2	98.9	99.5	100.0	2.5
Other Areas										
1990	58.0	58.9	59.4	59.8	4.7	61.3	62.3	62.7	63.1	4.0
1991	60.7	61.6	62.0	62.3	4.2	63.8	64.5	64.9	65.1	3.2
1992	63.4	63.7	64.3	64.8	4.0	65.9	66.2	66.7	67.1	3.1
1993	65.5	66.0	66.5	67.1	3.5	67.6	68.1	68.5	68.9	2.7
1994	68.0	68.6	69.0	69.2	3.1	69.6	70.3	70.6	70.8	2.8
1995	69.9	70.2	70.6	70.9	2.5	71.7	72.2	72.7	72.9	3.0
1996	71.3	71.7	72.1	72.9	2.8	73.5	73.9	74.4	75.3	3.3
1997	73.6	74.2	75.0	75.8	4.0	76.0	76.7	77.6	78.6	4.4
1998	76.1	76.8	77.4	78.1	3.0	78.9	79.4	80.2	81.0	3.1
1999	78.7	79.4	80.2	80.4	2.9	81.6	82.4	83.2	83.5	3.1
2000	81.8	82.7	83.4	84.2	4.7	84.6	85.5	86.1	86.9	4.1
2001	85.2	86.1	86.7	87.2	3.6	87.7	88.6	89.1	89.6	3.1
2002	88.2	88.8	89.6	90.1	3.3	90.3	90.8	91.5	92.1	2.8
2003	91.6	92.4	93.1	93.5	3.8	93.3	94.0	94.6	94.9	3.0
2004	95.4	96.4	97.1	97.6	4.4	95.7	96.5	97.2	97.5	2.7
2005	98.8	99.3	99.8	100.0	2.5	98.3	99.0	99.5	100.0	2.6

[1]Excludes farm and household workers.
[2]The regional coverage is as follows: Northeast—Connecticut, Maine, Massachusetts, New Hampshire, New Jersey, New York, Pennsylvania, Rhode Island, and Vermont; South—Alabama, Arkansas, Delaware, District of Columbia, Florida, Georgia, Kentucky, Louisiana, Maryland, Mississippi, North Carolina, Oklahoma, South Carolina, Tennessee, Texas, Virginia, and West Virginia; Midwest—Illinois, Indiana, Iowa, Kansas, Michigan, Minnesota, Missouri, Nebraska, North Dakota, Ohio, South Dakota, and Wisconsin; and West—Alaska, Arizona, California, Colorado, Hawaii, Idaho, Montana, Nevada, New Mexico, Oregon, Utah, Washington, and Wyoming.
[5]A metropolitan area can be a Metropolitan Statistical Area (MSA) or a Consolidated Metropolitan Statistical Area (CMSA), as defined by the Office of Management and Budget in 1994.

Table 6-3. Employment Cost Index, State and Local Government Workers, Total Compensation and Wages and Salaries, by Occupation and Industry, 1990–2005

(December 2005 = 100.)

Characteristic and year	Total compensation					Wages and salaries				
	Indexes				Percent change for 12 months (ended December)	Indexes				Percent change for 12 months (ended December)
	March	June	September	December		March	June	September	December	
WORKERS BY INDUSTRY										
State and Local Government Workers										
1990	58.9	59.3	60.9	61.5	5.9	61.7	62.0	63.7	64.2	5.2
1991	62.2	62.4	63.4	63.7	3.6	64.9	65.1	66.2	66.4	3.4
1992	64.1	64.4	65.6	66.0	3.6	66.8	67.0	68.0	68.4	3.0
1993	66.4	66.6	67.6	67.9	2.9	68.8	68.9	70.0	70.2	2.6
1994	68.3	68.5	69.6	69.9	2.9	70.7	70.8	72.1	72.4	3.1
1995	70.4	70.7	71.7	72.0	3.0	72.9	73.1	74.3	74.7	3.2
1996	72.3	72.5	73.4	73.9	2.6	75.0	75.2	76.3	76.8	2.8
1997	74.2	74.2	75.2	75.6	2.3	77.1	77.2	78.4	78.9	2.7
1998	76.0	76.2	77.4	77.8	2.9	79.3	79.5	80.8	81.3	3.0
1999	78.2	78.5	79.7	80.5	3.5	81.6	81.9	83.5	84.2	3.6
2000	81.0	81.2	82.3	82.9	3.0	84.7	84.9	86.4	87.0	3.3
2001	83.7	84.2	85.9	86.4	4.2	87.6	88.1	89.8	90.2	3.7
2002	86.9	87.2	89.1	89.9	4.1	90.6	90.9	92.5	93.1	3.2
2003	90.5	90.9	92.4	92.9	3.3	93.4	93.7	94.7	95.0	2.0
2004	93.5	93.9	95.5	96.1	3.4	95.4	95.5	96.5	97.0	2.1
2005	96.9	97.3	99.1	100.0	4.1	97.6	97.8	99.1	100.0	3.1
WORKERS BY OCCUPATIONAL GROUP										
White-Collar Occupations										
1990	59.7	60.0	61.8	62.4	6.1	62.1	62.4	64.2	64.6	5.4
1991	63.1	63.2	64.2	64.5	3.4	65.3	65.4	66.5	66.8	3.4
1992	64.9	65.1	66.4	66.9	3.7	67.1	67.2	68.4	68.8	3.0
1993	67.2	67.3	68.3	68.6	2.5	69.1	69.2	70.4	70.5	2.5
1994	69.0	69.1	70.2	70.6	2.9	70.9	71.1	72.3	72.7	3.1
1995	71.0	71.2	72.3	72.6	2.8	73.2	73.3	74.6	74.9	3.0
1996	72.9	73.1	74.1	74.5	2.6	75.2	75.4	76.6	77.1	2.9
1997	74.7	74.8	75.8	76.2	2.3	77.3	77.4	78.6	79.1	2.6
1998	76.5	76.6	77.8	78.3	2.8	79.4	79.5	80.9	81.5	3.0
1999	78.6	78.9	80.2	81.0	3.4	81.7	81.9	83.6	84.4	3.6
2000	81.5	81.7	82.8	83.4	3.0	84.8	85.0	86.5	87.1	3.2
2001	84.1	84.6	86.4	86.8	4.1	87.6	88.1	89.8	90.2	3.6
2002	87.3	87.6	89.6	90.4	4.1	90.5	90.8	92.6	93.2	3.3
2003	90.9	91.2	92.7	93.2	3.1	93.5	93.6	94.7	95.0	1.9
2004	93.8	94.2	95.6	96.3	3.3	95.4	95.5	96.5	97.0	2.1
2005	97.1	97.4	99.0	100.0	3.8	97.6	97.8	99.0	100.0	3.1
Professional Specialty and Technical Occupations										
1990	60.4	60.7	62.6	63.1	6.2	62.1	62.4	64.4	64.9	5.9
1991	63.7	63.8	64.9	65.2	3.3	65.4	65.6	66.8	67.0	3.2
1992	65.5	65.8	67.2	67.6	3.7	67.2	67.4	68.7	69.0	3.0
1993	67.8	67.9	69.0	69.2	2.4	69.3	69.4	70.7	70.8	2.6
1994	69.5	69.6	70.9	71.2	2.9	71.1	71.2	72.5	72.9	3.0
1995	71.5	71.6	72.8	73.1	2.7	73.2	73.4	74.8	75.1	3.0
1996	73.2	73.5	74.6	75.0	2.6	75.3	75.5	76.9	77.3	2.9
1997	75.2	75.2	76.3	76.6	2.1	77.4	77.5	78.9	79.3	2.6
1998	76.9	76.9	78.1	78.6	2.6	79.5	79.6	80.9	81.4	2.6
1999	78.7	79.0	80.5	81.2	3.3	81.5	81.8	83.6	84.3	3.6
2000	81.7	82.0	83.2	83.6	3.0	84.7	84.9	86.5	87.0	3.2
2001	84.2	84.6	86.7	86.9	3.9	87.5	87.9	89.8	90.0	3.4
2002	87.1	87.4	89.7	90.4	4.0	90.1	90.4	92.4	93.0	3.3
2003	90.9	91.2	92.7	93.1	3.0	93.2	93.4	94.5	94.7	1.8
2004	93.6	93.9	95.5	96.1	3.2	95.1	95.2	96.5	96.8	2.2
2005	96.7	97.1	98.8	100.0	4.1	97.2	97.5	98.8	100.0	3.3
Executive, Administrative, and Managerial Occupations										
1990	58.7	59.1	60.7	61.2	5.9	61.6	62.0	63.6	63.9	4.9
1991	62.3	62.2	62.9	63.2	3.3	64.9	65.0	65.7	65.9	3.1
1992	63.9	64.0	64.9	65.4	3.5	66.5	66.6	67.3	67.8	2.9
1993	66.1	66.2	67.2	67.6	3.4	68.4	68.4	69.4	69.7	2.8
1994	68.2	68.6	69.3	69.6	3.0	70.3	70.6	71.4	71.8	3.0
1995	70.5	70.8	71.7	72.2	3.7	72.8	72.9	73.9	74.5	3.8
1996	72.6	72.8	73.3	73.8	2.2	74.9	75.1	75.9	76.4	2.6
1997	74.5	74.7	75.3	75.8	2.7	77.1	77.3	78.1	78.7	3.0
1998	76.4	76.6	78.0	78.7	3.8	79.3	79.6	81.0	81.7	3.8
1999	79.2	79.3	80.3	81.2	3.2	82.2	82.5	83.7	84.7	3.7
2000	81.7	81.8	82.9	83.7	3.1	85.0	85.2	86.4	87.3	3.1
2001	84.7	85.4	86.9	87.6	4.7	88.1	88.9	90.3	91.0	4.2
2002	88.6	88.8	90.2	91.0	3.9	91.9	92.0	93.3	94.0	3.3
2003	91.8	92.1	93.3	93.9	3.2	94.4	94.5	95.4	95.8	1.9
2004	94.5	95.0	95.6	96.8	3.1	96.0	96.1	96.4	97.5	1.8
2005	98.2	98.1	99.3	100.0	3.3	98.7	98.6	99.6	100.0	2.6

Table 6-3. Employment Cost Index, State and Local Government Workers, Total Compensation and Wages and Salaries, by Occupation and Industry, 1990–2005—*Continued*

(December 2005 = 100.)

Characteristic and year	Total compensation					Wages and salaries				
	Indexes				Percent change for 12 months (ended December)	Indexes				Percent change for 12 months (ended December)
	March	June	September	December		March	June	September	December	
Administrative Support Occupations, Including Clerical Occupations										
1990	58.0	58.4	59.9	60.7	6.1	62.5	62.7	64.2	64.6	4.9
1991	61.6	61.5	62.5	62.8	3.5	65.5	65.6	66.7	66.9	3.6
1992	63.5	63.7	64.7	65.3	4.0	67.4	67.6	68.3	68.8	2.8
1993	65.6	65.9	66.6	67.0	2.6	69.1	69.4	70.1	70.5	2.5
1994	67.6	67.9	68.8	69.2	3.3	71.2	71.5	72.4	72.8	3.3
1995	69.5	69.9	70.7	71.1	2.7	73.3	73.5	74.4	74.9	2.9
1996	71.6	71.8	72.6	73.2	3.0	75.3	75.5	76.4	77.2	3.1
1997	73.4	73.5	74.5	74.9	2.3	77.3	77.5	78.6	79.2	2.6
1998	75.4	75.6	76.8	77.3	3.2	79.6	79.8	81.0	81.7	3.2
1999	77.9	77.8	78.7	79.8	3.2	82.2	82.3	83.5	84.8	3.8
2000	80.3	80.7	81.7	82.3	3.1	85.2	85.6	86.8	87.5	3.2
2001	83.0	83.5	84.9	85.7	4.1	88.0	88.3	89.6	90.3	3.2
2002	86.4	87.0	88.7	89.4	4.3	90.9	91.4	92.8	93.4	3.4
2003	90.2	90.5	92.5	92.8	3.8	93.9	94.1	95.2	95.5	2.2
2004	93.8	94.6	96.0	96.6	4.1	96.0	96.2	97.3	97.5	2.1
2005	97.6	97.9	99.3	100.0	3.5	98.1	98.1	99.4	100.0	2.6
Blue-Collar Occupations										
1990	59.2	59.6	60.7	61.0	4.8	62.8	63.4	64.5	64.8	4.2
1991	61.9	62.2	63.0	63.3	3.8	65.7	66.2	66.9	67.2	3.7
1992	64.0	64.7	65.6	66.1	4.4	67.7	68.5	69.2	69.6	3.6
1993	66.3	66.6	67.6	68.1	3.0	70.0	70.1	71.3	71.6	2.9
1994	68.6	68.8	69.7	69.9	2.6	72.1	72.3	73.3	73.8	3.1
1995	70.3	70.8	71.3	71.8	2.7	74.1	74.5	75.1	75.7	2.6
1996	72.3	72.6	73.1	73.6	2.5	76.2	76.5	77.0	77.5	2.4
1997	74.1	74.2	74.8	75.3	2.3	78.0	78.1	79.0	79.7	2.8
1998	75.7	75.8	76.7	77.3	2.7	80.1	80.4	81.3	81.9	2.8
1999	77.8	78.2	79.0	79.9	3.4	82.4	82.8	83.9	84.7	3.4
2000	80.6	80.9	81.8	82.6	3.4	85.2	85.6	86.6	87.4	3.2
2001	83.3	83.6	85.0	85.9	4.0	87.9	88.2	89.8	90.8	3.9
2002	86.4	86.8	88.8	89.6	4.3	91.3	91.6	93.0	93.4	2.9
2003	90.5	90.7	91.8	92.7	3.5	94.0	94.2	94.9	95.3	2.0
2004	93.5	93.9	95.3	95.9	3.5	95.7	95.8	96.7	97.2	2.0
2005	96.8	97.5	99.5	100.0	4.3	97.8	98.3	99.5	100.0	2.9
Service Occupations										
1990	55.4	55.7	57.1	57.7	5.3	59.4	59.5	61.0	61.5	4.6
1991	58.7	58.8	59.9	60.3	4.5	62.5	62.9	64.0	64.4	4.7
1992	60.8	61.1	62.1	62.4	3.5	64.7	65.0	65.7	66.0	2.5
1993	62.9	63.3	64.2	64.5	3.4	66.5	66.9	67.6	67.9	2.9
1994	65.1	65.5	66.6	66.9	3.7	68.4	68.8	70.1	70.5	3.8
1995	67.4	68.1	68.8	69.2	3.4	71.2	71.5	72.3	72.7	3.1
1996	69.7	69.9	70.6	71.1	2.7	73.2	73.5	74.3	74.9	3.0
1997	71.7	71.7	72.4	72.8	2.4	75.7	75.7	76.7	77.3	3.2
1998	73.7	74.5	75.6	75.8	4.1	78.0	78.4	79.5	80.0	3.5
1999	76.3	76.8	77.5	78.5	3.6	80.6	81.2	82.3	83.3	4.1
2000	79.0	79.1	80.1	80.8	2.9	83.7	83.8	85.5	86.4	3.7
2001	82.1	82.7	84.0	84.8	5.0	87.3	87.8	89.2	89.9	4.1
2002	85.4	85.8	87.3	87.9	3.7	90.5	91.0	91.8	92.1	2.4
2003	88.8	89.3	90.9	91.4	4.0	93.0	93.6	94.2	94.7	2.8
2004	92.2	92.7	94.8	95.4	4.4	95.3	95.4	96.3	96.8	2.2
2005	96.2	96.7	99.2	100.0	4.8	97.4	97.8	99.4	100.0	3.3
WORKERS BY INDUSTRY										
Service Industries										
1990	59.8	60.2	62.1	62.7	6.3	61.9	62.2	64.2	64.7	5.7
1991	63.3	63.4	64.7	65.0	3.7	65.3	65.4	66.7	66.9	3.4
1992	65.2	65.5	66.9	67.4	3.7	67.1	67.3	68.6	68.9	3.0
1993	67.6	67.7	68.8	69.1	2.5	69.3	69.3	70.6	70.7	2.6
1994	69.4	69.5	70.8	71.0	2.7	71.0	71.1	72.5	72.8	3.0
1995	71.4	71.6	72.8	73.0	2.8	73.3	73.4	74.8	75.2	3.3
1996	73.2	73.4	74.6	75.0	2.7	75.4	75.6	77.0	77.4	2.9
1997	75.0	75.1	76.3	76.6	2.1	77.5	77.5	79.0	79.4	2.6
1998	76.9	77.0	78.3	78.7	2.7	79.6	79.7	81.2	81.6	2.8
1999	78.9	79.2	80.7	81.4	3.4	81.8	82.1	83.8	84.5	3.6
2000	81.8	82.0	83.4	83.9	3.1	84.8	85.0	86.7	87.2	3.2
2001	84.5	84.8	87.0	87.3	4.1	87.7	88.1	90.1	90.4	3.7
2002	87.6	87.8	90.0	90.6	3.8	90.7	90.9	92.9	93.4	3.3
2003	91.2	91.4	92.9	93.4	3.1	93.5	93.7	94.8	95.1	1.8
2004	93.8	94.0	95.6	96.2	3.0	95.4	95.4	96.7	97.1	2.1
2005	96.8	97.1	99.0	100.0	4.0	97.5	97.7	99.1	100.0	3.0

Table 6-3. Employment Cost Index, State and Local Government Workers, Total Compensation and Wages and Salaries, by Occupation and Industry, 1990–2005—*Continued*

(December 2005 = 100.)

Characteristic and year	Total compensation					Wages and salaries				
	Indexes				Percent change for 12 months (ended December)	Indexes				Percent change for 12 months (ended December)
	March	June	September	December		March	June	September	December	
Service Industries, Excluding Schools										
1990	58.6	59.1	60.4	61.2	6.8	61.0	61.5	62.9	63.4	6.4
1991	62.3	62.1	63.2	63.6	3.9	64.4	64.4	65.6	66.0	4.1
1992	63.9	64.2	65.3	65.9	3.6	66.4	66.6	67.3	67.9	2.9
1993	66.4	66.7	67.4	67.7	2.7	68.5	68.7	69.5	69.6	2.5
1994	68.2	68.5	69.4	69.8	3.1	70.2	70.5	71.3	71.7	3.0
1995	70.2	70.9	71.6	71.9	3.0	72.3	72.6	73.4	73.7	2.8
1996	72.4	72.7	73.3	73.3	1.9	74.1	74.4	75.2	75.5	2.4
1997	73.6	73.8	74.7	75.2	2.6	75.9	76.1	77.1	77.7	2.9
1998	75.6	75.7	77.1	77.1	2.5	78.3	78.4	79.7	79.9	2.8
1999	77.6	77.9	79.2	79.9	3.6	80.4	80.7	82.2	82.8	3.6
2000	80.7	81.0	82.0	82.7	3.5	83.5	83.7	84.8	85.5	3.3
2001	83.4	84.4	85.8	86.7	4.8	86.2	87.2	88.6	89.6	4.8
2002	87.7	88.2	89.4	90.4	4.3	90.6	91.0	92.0	92.7	3.5
2003	91.1	91.2	92.7	93.4	3.3	93.3	93.6	94.4	95.1	2.6
2004	94.1	94.5	96.1	96.6	3.4	95.5	95.8	96.9	97.3	2.3
2005	97.6	98.0	99.6	100.0	3.5	98.0	98.4	99.5	100.0	2.8
Health Services										
1990	58.0	58.4	60.0	60.7	6.7	60.3	60.6	62.2	62.6	5.7
1991	61.5	61.3	62.2	62.8	3.5	63.4	63.8	64.5	65.1	4.0
1992	63.3	63.8	64.8	65.2	3.8	65.6	66.1	66.6	67.0	2.9
1993	65.6	65.9	66.7	67.2	3.1	67.4	67.8	68.8	69.1	3.1
1994	67.8	68.4	69.5	69.7	3.7	69.6	70.2	71.2	71.6	3.6
1995	70.1	70.9	71.5	71.9	3.2	72.0	72.3	73.0	73.4	2.5
1996	72.4	72.7	73.2	73.2	1.8	73.8	74.2	74.9	75.0	2.2
1997	73.5	73.7	74.3	74.9	2.3	75.4	75.7	76.5	77.3	3.1
1998	75.3	75.4	76.6	76.8	2.5	77.8	78.0	79.2	79.5	2.8
1999	77.1	77.6	78.8	79.6	3.6	79.8	80.2	81.6	82.4	3.6
2000	80.4	80.8	81.9	82.8	4.0	83.0	83.2	84.4	85.3	3.5
2001	83.1	84.3	85.8	86.6	4.6	85.6	86.8	88.1	89.0	4.3
2002	87.6	88.1	89.3	90.4	4.4	90.1	90.7	91.7	92.6	4.0
2003	90.9	91.0	92.6	93.4	3.3	93.0	93.4	94.3	95.2	2.8
2004	94.0	94.4	96.0	96.6	3.4	95.6	95.8	96.9	97.5	2.4
2005	97.7	98.1	99.6	100.0	3.5	98.2	98.6	99.4	100.0	2.6
Hospitals										
1990	57.8	58.3	59.8	60.7	6.7	60.0	60.5	62.1	62.7	5.7
1991	61.1	61.1	62.2	62.8	3.5	63.3	63.6	64.5	65.2	4.0
1992	63.2	63.6	64.6	65.1	3.7	65.4	65.8	66.6	66.9	2.6
1993	65.4	65.6	66.5	67.2	3.2	67.2	67.5	68.5	69.0	3.1
1994	67.4	67.8	69.2	69.6	3.6	69.3	69.7	71.0	71.5	3.6
1995	70.0	70.8	71.4	71.8	3.2	71.9	72.2	72.9	73.4	2.7
1996	72.3	72.6	73.1	73.2	1.9	73.8	74.1	74.8	75.0	2.2
1997	73.5	73.7	74.3	75.0	2.5	75.4	75.7	76.4	77.3	3.1
1998	75.4	75.4	76.7	76.9	2.5	77.9	78.0	79.2	79.5	2.8
1999	77.2	77.8	78.9	79.7	3.6	79.8	80.3	81.6	82.3	3.5
2000	80.6	80.9	82.1	82.8	3.9	83.0	83.2	84.4	85.3	3.6
2001	82.9	84.3	85.8	86.7	4.7	85.4	86.7	88.1	89.0	4.3
2002	87.6	88.2	89.4	90.6	4.5	90.1	90.7	91.8	92.9	4.4
2003	91.0	91.2	92.8	93.4	3.1	93.2	93.6	94.6	95.3	2.6
2004	94.0	94.4	96.1	96.7	3.5	95.7	95.9	97.1	97.7	2.5
2005	97.6	98.0	99.5	100.0	3.4	98.3	98.6	99.4	100.0	2.4
Educational Services										
1990	60.1	60.4	62.4	63.0	6.1	62.1	62.4	64.5	65.0	5.7
1991	63.6	63.7	65.0	65.3	3.7	65.5	65.6	66.9	67.1	3.2
1992	65.5	65.7	67.3	67.7	3.7	67.2	67.4	68.8	69.2	3.1
1993	67.9	68.0	69.2	69.4	2.5	69.4	69.5	70.8	70.9	2.5
1994	69.6	69.7	71.0	71.3	2.7	71.1	71.2	72.7	73.1	3.1
1995	71.6	71.8	73.0	73.2	2.7	73.4	73.5	75.1	75.5	3.3
1996	73.4	73.6	74.9	75.3	2.9	75.6	75.8	77.2	77.6	2.8
1997	75.3	75.4	76.6	76.9	2.1	77.7	77.8	79.3	79.6	2.6
1998	77.1	77.2	78.6	79.0	2.7	79.8	79.9	81.4	81.9	2.9
1999	79.2	79.4	81.0	81.7	3.4	82.1	82.2	84.1	84.7	3.4
2000	82.1	82.2	83.7	84.2	3.1	85.0	85.2	87.1	87.5	3.3
2001	84.7	84.9	87.2	87.4	3.8	87.9	88.2	90.4	90.6	3.5
2002	87.6	87.8	90.1	90.7	3.8	90.7	90.9	93.0	93.5	3.2
2003	91.2	91.5	93.0	93.4	3.0	93.6	93.7	94.8	95.1	1.7
2004	93.8	93.9	95.5	96.2	3.0	95.3	95.4	96.6	97.0	2.0
2005	96.7	97.0	99.0	100.0	4.0	97.4	97.5	99.0	100.0	3.1

Table 6-3. Employment Cost Index, State and Local Government Workers, Total Compensation and Wages and Salaries, by Occupation and Industry, 1990–2005—*Continued*

(December 2005 = 100.)

Characteristic and year	Total compensation					Wages and salaries				
	Indexes				Percent change for 12 months (ended December)	Indexes				Percent change for 12 months (ended December)
	March	June	September	December		March	June	September	December	
Schools										
1990	60.1	60.4	62.5	63.0	5.9	62.0	62.2	64.5	64.9	5.5
1991	63.5	63.7	65.0	65.3	3.7	65.3	65.5	66.8	67.0	3.2
1992	65.5	65.7	67.3	67.7	3.7	67.2	67.3	68.7	69.0	3.0
1993	67.9	67.9	69.2	69.4	2.5	69.3	69.3	70.7	70.9	2.8
1994	69.6	69.7	71.1	71.3	2.7	71.1	71.2	72.7	73.0	3.0
1995	71.6	71.8	73.1	73.3	2.8	73.4	73.5	75.1	75.4	3.3
1996	73.4	73.6	74.9	75.3	2.7	75.6	75.7	77.2	77.7	3.1
1997	75.3	75.4	76.6	76.9	2.1	77.7	77.7	79.3	79.6	2.4
1998	77.1	77.2	78.5	79.0	2.7	79.8	79.9	81.4	82.0	3.0
1999	79.2	79.4	81.0	81.7	3.4	82.0	82.3	84.1	84.7	3.3
2000	82.0	82.2	83.7	84.1	2.9	85.0	85.1	87.0	87.5	3.3
2001	84.6	85.0	87.2	87.4	3.9	88.0	88.2	90.4	90.5	3.4
2002	87.6	87.7	90.1	90.7	3.8	90.7	90.8	93.0	93.4	3.2
2003	91.1	91.5	93.0	93.3	2.9	93.5	93.7	94.8	95.1	1.8
2004	93.7	93.9	95.5	96.2	3.1	95.2	95.4	96.5	96.9	1.9
2005	96.7	97.0	98.9	100.0	4.0	97.3	97.5	98.9	100.0	3.2
Elementary and Secondary Schools										
1990	60.5	60.9	63.1	63.7	6.3	62.2	62.4	64.9	65.4	5.8
1991	64.1	64.2	65.7	66.0	3.6	65.8	65.8	67.4	67.6	3.4
1992	66.3	66.5	68.1	68.6	3.9	67.7	67.9	69.5	69.8	3.3
1993	68.6	68.6	69.9	70.2	2.3	69.9	70.0	71.4	71.7	2.7
1994	70.3	70.3	71.8	71.9	2.4	71.7	71.8	73.4	73.6	2.6
1995	72.2	72.4	73.8	73.9	2.8	74.0	74.1	75.8	76.1	3.4
1996	74.0	74.1	75.3	75.6	2.3	76.2	76.3	77.8	78.0	2.5
1997	75.6	75.7	77.0	77.2	2.1	78.0	78.1	79.7	80.0	2.6
1998	77.3	77.4	78.9	79.1	2.5	80.1	80.2	81.7	82.1	2.6
1999	79.3	79.5	81.2	81.9	3.5	82.2	82.4	84.3	84.9	3.4
2000	82.1	82.2	83.7	84.1	2.7	85.2	85.2	87.2	87.5	3.1
2001	84.4	84.7	86.8	87.0	3.4	87.8	88.1	90.0	90.2	3.1
2002	87.2	87.3	89.6	90.2	3.7	90.4	90.5	92.8	93.2	3.3
2003	90.6	90.9	92.6	93.0	3.1	93.2	93.4	94.6	94.8	1.7
2004	93.4	93.5	95.5	96.1	3.3	95.1	95.2	96.5	96.9	2.2
2005	96.5	96.8	98.9	100.0	4.1	97.1	97.3	98.9	100.0	3.2
Colleges and Universities										
1990	59.0	59.1	60.7	61.3	5.3	61.7	61.9	63.3	63.8	4.9
1991	61.9	62.6	63.1	63.1	2.9	64.4	64.8	65.4	65.4	2.5
1992	63.4	63.5	65.0	65.2	3.3	65.6	65.6	66.6	66.8	2.1
1993	65.9	65.9	67.2	67.1	2.9	67.5	67.5	68.8	68.8	3.0
1994	67.6	67.9	69.2	69.8	4.0	69.3	69.6	71.0	71.6	4.1
1995	70.1	70.1	71.2	71.6	2.6	72.0	71.8	73.0	73.5	2.7
1996	72.0	72.2	73.7	74.5	4.1	74.1	74.2	75.8	76.6	4.2
1997	74.7	74.6	75.8	76.3	2.4	76.8	76.8	78.0	78.6	2.6
1998	76.7	76.8	77.9	78.7	3.1	79.0	79.1	80.4	81.5	3.7
1999	78.8	79.0	80.5	81.5	3.6	81.5	81.7	83.3	84.3	3.4
2000	82.0	82.1	83.7	84.4	3.6	84.6	85.0	86.6	87.3	3.6
2001	85.5	85.8	88.4	88.8	5.2	88.4	88.7	91.4	91.5	4.8
2002	89.0	89.2	91.6	92.2	3.8	91.6	91.9	93.9	94.4	3.2
2003	92.9	93.2	94.1	94.5	2.5	94.7	94.7	95.5	95.8	1.5
2004	94.9	95.1	95.9	96.3	1.9	96.0	96.0	96.6	97.1	1.4
2005	97.4	97.7	99.2	100.0	3.8	98.1	98.2	99.3	100.0	3.0
Public Administration[1]										
1990	57.4	57.6	58.9	59.4	5.3	61.8	62.0	63.1	63.6	4.4
1991	60.5	60.6	61.3	61.5	3.5	64.6	64.9	65.5	65.7	3.3
1992	62.3	62.6	63.2	63.5	3.3	66.3	66.6	67.0	67.3	2.4
1993	64.2	64.4	65.2	65.5	3.1	67.8	68.1	68.7	69.1	2.7
1994	66.4	66.7	67.6	67.8	3.5	69.8	70.2	71.0	71.4	3.3
1995	68.5	68.9	69.6	70.1	3.4	72.2	72.5	73.0	73.5	2.9
1996	70.6	70.8	71.4	72.0	2.7	74.0	74.2	75.0	75.7	3.0
1997	72.6	72.6	73.2	73.8	2.5	76.4	76.4	77.2	77.8	2.8
1998	74.5	75.0	75.9	76.4	3.5	78.6	78.9	79.9	80.5	3.5
1999	76.9	77.3	77.8	78.9	3.3	81.1	81.6	82.6	83.8	4.1
2000	79.6	79.8	80.2	81.0	2.7	84.4	84.7	85.7	86.6	3.3
2001	82.3	83.0	84.0	84.8	4.7	87.4	88.1	89.0	89.8	3.7
2002	85.5	86.0	87.5	88.3	4.1	90.3	90.9	91.7	92.3	2.8
2003	89.2	89.7	91.4	91.8	4.0	93.1	93.6	94.4	94.8	2.7
2004	92.9	93.6	95.1	95.8	4.4	95.4	95.6	96.3	96.9	2.2
2005	97.0	97.4	98.9	100.0	4.4	97.7	98.1	99.2	100.0	3.2

[1]Includes executive, legislative, judicial, administrative, and regulatory activities of state and local governments (SIC 91 and 96).

Table 6-4. Employment Cost Index, Benefits, by Occupation, Industry, and Bargaining Status, 1990–2005

(December 2005 = 100.)

Characteristic and year	Indexes				Percent change for 12 months (ended December)
	March	June	September	December	
Civilian Workers[1]					
1990	51.4	52.1	52.9	53.5	6.8
1991	54.5	55.2	56.0	56.5	5.6
1992	57.6	58.1	59.0	59.5	5.3
1993	60.7	61.3	61.9	62.2	4.5
1994	63.2	63.6	64.3	64.4	3.5
1995	65.0	65.3	65.7	65.8	2.2
1996	66.1	66.5	66.9	67.1	2.0
1997	67.5	67.8	68.1	68.5	2.1
1998	69.0	69.5	69.9	70.3	2.6
1999	70.6	71.2	71.8	72.6	3.3
2000	74.1	74.9	75.7	76.2	5.0
2001	77.6	78.3	79.5	80.2	5.2
2002	81.4	82.3	83.4	84.2	5.0
2003	86.4	87.4	88.8	89.5	6.3
2004	92.3	93.7	94.8	95.7	6.9
2005	97.8	98.5	99.6	100.0	4.5
State and Local Government Workers					
1990	53.2	53.6	55.1	55.8	6.9
1991	56.8	56.7	57.7	58.0	3.9
1992	58.7	59.1	60.6	61.1	5.3
1993	61.5	61.7	62.5	62.9	2.9
1994	63.3	63.6	64.5	64.6	2.7
1995	64.9	65.5	66.2	66.3	2.6
1996	66.7	66.9	67.4	67.8	2.3
1997	68.1	68.1	68.4	68.6	1.2
1998	69.2	69.5	70.4	70.7	3.1
1999	71.1	71.3	71.8	72.7	2.8
2000	73.4	73.6	73.8	74.4	2.3
2001	75.4	76.0	77.9	78.5	5.5
2002	79.2	79.5	82.1	83.3	6.1
2003	84.4	85.0	87.6	88.4	6.1
2004	89.7	90.6	93.3	94.3	6.7
2005	95.6	96.1	99.0	100.0	6.0
Private Industry Workers[2]					
1990	51.0	51.7	52.3	52.9	6.7
1991	53.9	54.9	55.7	56.2	6.2
1992	57.3	57.9	58.6	59.1	5.2
1993	60.5	61.2	61.7	62.0	4.9
1994	63.2	63.7	64.2	64.3	3.7
1995	65.0	65.3	65.5	65.7	2.2
1996	66.0	66.4	66.7	67.0	2.0
1997	67.4	67.7	68.1	68.5	2.2
1998	68.9	69.5	69.8	70.2	2.5
1999	70.5	71.2	71.8	72.6	3.4
2000	74.3	75.3	76.1	76.7	5.6
2001	78.1	78.9	79.8	80.6	5.1
2002	81.8	82.9	83.7	84.4	4.7
2003	86.8	88.0	89.1	89.8	6.4
2004	92.9	94.4	95.2	96.0	6.9
2005	98.3	99.0	99.8	100.0	4.2
White-Collar Occupations					
1990	50.0	50.8	51.5	52.0	7.0
1991	53.1	53.9	54.6	55.2	6.2
1992	56.1	56.6	57.3	57.8	4.7
1993	59.1	59.7	60.1	60.5	4.7
1994	61.8	62.4	62.9	63.2	4.5
1995	64.1	64.5	64.7	64.8	2.5
1996	65.3	65.6	66.1	66.2	2.2
1997	66.7	67.1	67.3	68.0	2.7
1998	68.6	69.0	69.5	69.9	2.8
1999	70.1	70.8	71.6	72.3	3.4
2000	74.1	75.1	76.0	76.5	5.8
2001	78.3	79.3	80.3	81.1	6.0
2002	82.2	83.5	84.0	84.6	4.3
2003	87.0	87.9	89.0	89.7	6.0
2004	92.1	93.6	94.4	95.3	6.2
2005	98.0	98.8	99.7	100.0	4.9

[1]Includes private industry and state and local government workers and excludes farm, household, and federal government workers.
[2]Excludes farm and household workers.

Table 6-4. Employment Cost Index, Benefits, by Occupation, Industry, and Bargaining Status, 1990–2005
   —Continued

(December 2005 = 100.)

Characteristic and year	Indexes				Percent change for 12 months (ended December)
	March	June	September	December	
Blue-Collar Occupations					
1990	52.5	53.2	53.9	54.4	6.3
1991	55.4	56.3	57.4	57.8	6.3
1992	59.3	59.8	60.5	61.0	5.5
1993	62.7	63.6	64.1	64.4	5.6
1994	65.2	65.7	66.3	66.2	2.8
1995	66.6	66.7	66.9	67.2	1.5
1996	67.5	67.9	68.0	68.4	1.8
1997	68.5	68.9	69.3	69.4	1.5
1998	69.4	70.1	70.4	70.7	1.9
1999	71.0	71.7	72.3	73.0	3.3
2000	74.9	75.7	76.4	76.9	5.3
2001	77.7	78.0	79.0	79.5	3.4
2002	81.0	81.9	83.0	83.8	5.4
2003	86.2	87.9	89.1	89.8	7.2
2004	94.0	95.8	96.5	97.3	8.4
2005	98.8	99.6	100.0	100.0	2.8
Service Occupations					
1990	51.9	52.4	53.0	53.8	6.5
1991	55.0	56.1	57.1	57.7	7.2
1992	58.8	59.6	60.6	61.0	5.7
1993	62.6	63.4	63.9	64.4	5.6
1994	65.1	65.2	65.8	66.0	2.5
1995	66.1	66.4	66.5	66.6	0.9
1996	66.5	66.8	66.7	67.3	1.1
1997	67.8	68.4	69.3	69.6	3.4
1998	70.2	70.4	70.9	70.9	1.9
1999	71.7	72.3	72.7	73.4	3.5
2000	73.9	74.8	75.6	76.6	4.4
2001	78.1	78.9	80.0	81.3	6.1
2002	82.8	83.5	85.0	85.7	5.4
2003	88.3	89.2	90.2	91.3	6.5
2004	94.8	96.1	96.8	97.1	6.4
2005	98.4	99.0	99.5	100.0	3.0
Goods-Producing Industries[3]					
1990	50.3	51.0	51.7	52.3	7.2
1991	53.2	54.2	55.1	55.5	6.1
1992	56.9	57.3	58.2	58.7	5.8
1993	60.5	61.3	61.8	62.0	5.6
1994	63.1	63.7	64.1	64.1	3.4
1995	64.6	64.6	64.8	65.2	1.7
1996	65.5	65.9	66.0	66.4	1.8
1997	66.5	67.0	67.3	67.3	1.4
1998	67.3	67.8	68.0	68.1	1.2
1999	68.6	69.0	69.6	70.5	3.5
2000	72.4	73.3	74.0	74.3	5.4
2001	75.4	75.9	76.5	77.3	4.0
2002	78.8	79.6	80.3	81.3	5.2
2003	84.6	85.7	86.7	87.4	7.5
2004	92.1	93.3	94.2	95.7	9.5
2005	98.4	99.6	100.3	100.0	4.5
Manufacturing					
1990	50.2	50.9	51.6	52.1	7.0
1991	52.9	53.9	54.9	55.2	6.0
1992	56.8	57.1	57.8	58.3	5.6
1993	60.3	61.2	61.7	61.8	6.0
1994	62.8	63.3	63.7	63.9	3.4
1995	64.4	64.3	64.5	65.0	1.7
1996	65.4	65.9	66.0	66.5	2.3
1997	66.6	67.1	67.3	67.4	1.4
1998	67.4	67.7	67.8	67.9	0.7
1999	68.3	68.7	69.3	70.3	3.5
2000	72.5	73.2	73.7	73.6	4.7
2001	74.7	75.1	75.4	76.3	3.7
2002	77.9	78.7	79.4	80.4	5.4
2003	84.2	85.2	86.2	86.7	7.8
2004	92.5	93.7	94.8	95.3	9.9
2005	98.3	99.3	100.0	100.0	4.9

[3]Includes mining, construction, and manufacturing workers.

Table 6-4. Employment Cost Index, Benefits, by Occupation, Industry, and Bargaining Status, 1990–2005
—Continued

(December 2005 = 100.)

Characteristic and year	Indexes				Percent change for 12 months (ended December)
	March	June	September	December	
Aircraft Manufacturing					
1990	29.6	29.9	30.8	30.1	5.2
1991	30.7	31.2	31.6	32.2	7.0
1992	33.4	34.2	34.7	36.3	12.7
1993	37.0	36.8	37.7	35.8	-1.4
1994	36.1	36.4	37.3	37.2	3.9
1995	37.9	37.8	37.8	39.3	5.6
1996	41.5	41.8	41.6	40.8	3.8
1997	39.9	40.0	39.7	38.4	-5.9
1998	38.1	38.5	38.7	39.1	1.8
1999	38.3	38.8	39.1	41.4	5.9
2000	43.5	44.8	45.3	43.8	5.8
2001	46.1	46.2	45.2	46.9	7.1
2002	48.6	49.1	49.1	51.7	10.2
2003	59.2	59.2	59.5	57.4	11.0
2004	70.1	71.0	71.3	71.5	24.6
2005	97.3	97.3	97.5	100.0	39.9
Aircraft Manufacturing, White-Collar Occupations					
1990	29.5	29.8	30.7	29.9	5.3
1991	30.4	30.9	31.2	32.0	7.0
1992	33.3	34.2	34.5	35.7	11.6
1993	36.6	36.3	37.2	35.6	-0.3
1994	35.8	36.2	37.0	36.9	3.7
1995	37.6	37.6	37.6	38.3	3.8
1996	40.8	41.0	40.8	40.5	5.7
1997	39.4	39.5	39.4	38.9	-4.0
1998	38.4	38.9	39.1	38.6	-0.8
1999	37.9	38.3	38.4	39.6	2.6
2000	42.1	43.9	44.4	43.7	10.4
2001	47.0	46.8	45.3	47.0	7.6
2002	48.5	49.0	48.9	50.2	6.8
2003	59.0	58.6	58.7	58.1	15.7
2004	70.9	71.2	71.4	71.4	22.9
2005	98.5	98.9	99.1	100.0	40.1
Aircraft Manufacturing, Blue-Collar Occupations					
1990	29.9	30.3	31.0	30.5	4.8
1991	31.2	31.7	32.3	32.6	6.9
1992	33.6	34.4	35.0	37.2	14.1
1993	37.7	37.6	38.4	36.1	-3.0
1994	36.5	36.7	37.6	37.7	4.4
1995	38.3	38.1	38.0	40.8	8.2
1996	42.4	42.8	42.8	41.2	1.0
1997	40.8	40.7	40.1	37.8	-8.3
1998	37.6	37.7	38.1	39.7	5.0
1999	39.0	39.6	40.4	44.1	11.1
2000	45.8	46.1	46.9	44.0	-0.2
2001	44.6	45.1	44.9	46.6	5.9
2002	48.6	49.1	49.2	53.9	15.7
2003	59.5	60.0	60.6	56.1	4.1
2004	68.5	70.3	71.1	71.7	27.8
2005	95.2	94.8	95.0	100.0	39.5
Service-Producing Industries[4]					
1990	51.6	52.2	52.8	53.4	6.4
1991	54.6	55.3	56.1	56.7	6.2
1992	57.6	58.2	59.0	59.4	4.8
1993	60.4	61.0	61.6	62.0	4.4
1994	63.1	63.5	64.3	64.4	3.9
1995	65.2	65.7	66.0	66.0	2.5
1996	66.4	66.7	67.2	67.3	2.0
1997	67.8	68.2	68.5	69.2	2.8
1998	69.9	70.4	71.0	71.4	3.2
1999	71.5	72.4	73.2	73.8	3.4
2000	75.4	76.4	77.3	78.1	5.8
2001	79.6	80.6	81.8	82.5	5.6
2002	83.6	84.9	85.7	86.1	4.4
2003	88.1	89.3	90.5	91.2	5.9
2004	93.3	95.1	95.7	96.2	5.5
2005	98.2	98.7	99.5	100.0	4.0

[4]Includes transportation, communication, and public utilities workers; wholesale and retail trade workers; finance, insurance, and real estate workers; and service industry workers.

Table 6-4. Employment Cost Index, Benefits, by Occupation, Industry, and Bargaining Status, 1990–2005
  —*Continued*

(December 2005 = 100.)

Characteristic and year	Indexes				Percent change for 12 months (ended December)
	March	June	September	December	
Nonmanufacturing Industries					
1990	51.4	52.1	52.7	53.3	6.4
1991	54.5	55.3	56.1	56.6	6.2
1992	57.6	58.2	59.0	59.5	5.1
1993	60.5	61.2	61.6	62.1	4.4
1994	63.3	63.7	64.4	64.5	3.9
1995	65.3	65.6	66.0	65.9	2.2
1996	66.3	66.6	67.0	67.2	2.0
1997	67.7	68.0	68.3	69.0	2.7
1998	69.5	70.1	70.7	71.1	3.0
1999	71.3	72.1	72.8	73.4	3.2
2000	75.0	76.1	77.0	77.8	6.0
2001	79.4	80.4	81.6	82.3	5.8
2002	83.4	84.6	85.4	85.9	4.4
2003	87.9	89.1	90.2	91.0	5.9
2004	93.0	94.7	95.4	96.3	5.8
2005	98.2	98.9	99.7	100.0	3.8
Union Workers					
1990	48.9	49.4	49.9	50.6	5.9
1991	51.5	52.5	53.3	53.9	6.5
1992	55.8	56.2	56.9	57.3	6.3
1993	59.2	60.1	60.7	61.1	6.6
1994	61.7	62.2	62.4	62.6	2.5
1995	63.1	63.4	63.9	64.6	3.2
1996	65.1	65.5	65.5	65.8	1.9
1997	65.6	65.9	66.5	66.4	0.9
1998	66.5	67.3	67.9	68.1	2.6
1999	68.2	68.7	69.4	70.1	2.9
2000	71.9	72.8	73.7	73.7	5.1
2001	74.2	74.9	75.8	76.5	3.8
2002	77.9	78.7	79.9	80.8	5.6
2003	83.6	85.5	86.8	87.6	8.4
2004	93.0	95.1	95.9	96.6	10.3
2005	98.3	99.1	99.9	100.0	3.5
Nonunion Workers					
1990	51.7	52.4	53.2	53.7	7.0
1991	54.8	55.7	56.5	56.9	6.0
1992	57.8	58.3	59.1	59.6	4.7
1993	60.8	61.5	62.0	62.2	4.4
1994	63.5	64.0	64.7	64.8	4.2
1995	65.5	65.8	66.0	66.0	1.9
1996	66.3	66.7	67.1	67.3	2.0
1997	67.8	68.2	68.5	69.1	2.7
1998	69.6	70.0	70.4	70.8	2.5
1999	71.1	71.8	72.5	73.2	3.4
2000	75.0	75.9	76.8	77.4	5.7
2001	79.1	79.9	81.0	81.6	5.4
2002	82.9	84.0	84.7	85.3	4.5
2003	87.6	88.6	89.7	90.4	6.0
2004	92.9	94.2	95.0	95.9	6.1
2005	98.3	99.1	99.8	100.0	4.3

NOTES AND DEFINITIONS

EMPLOYER COSTS FOR EMPLOYEE COMPENSATION

The Employer Costs for Employee Compensation (ECEC) measures the average cost per employee hour worked that employers pay for wages and salaries and benefits.

Definitions

Wages and salaries are defined as the hourly straight-time wage rate or (for workers not paid on an hourly basis) straight-time earnings divided by the corresponding hours. Straight-time wage and salary rates are total earnings before payroll deductions and include production bonuses, incentive earnings, commission payments, and cost-of-living adjustments. Not included in straight-time earnings are nonproduction bonuses, such as lump-sum payments provided in lieu of wage increases, shift differentials, and premium pay for overtime and for work on weekends and holidays; these payments are included in the benefits component.

Benefits include paid leave—vacations, holidays, sick leave, and other leave; supplemental pay—premium pay for work in addition to the regular work schedule (such as overtime, weekends, and holidays), shift differentials, and nonproduction bonuses (such as referral bonuses and attendance bonuses); insurance benefits—life, health, short-term disability, and long-term disability insurance; retirement and savings benefits—defined benefit and defined contribution plans; and legally required benefits—Social Security, Medicare, federal and state unemployment insurance, and workers' compensation. The collection of other benefits, such as severance pay and supplemental unemployment plans, were discontinued with the release of the March 2006 estimates.

Survey Scope

The ECEC consists of data for the civilian economy obtained from both private industry and state and local government. Excluded from private industry are the self-employed and farm and private household workers. Federal government workers are excluded from the public sector. The private industry series and the state and local government series provide separate data for the two sectors.

The cost levels for March 2006 were collected from a probability sample of about 50,000 occupational observations within approximately 11,300 sample establishments in private industry, and from approximately 3,500 occupations within about 800 sample establishments in state and local governments. Data were collected for the pay periods containing the 12th days of the survey months of March, June, September, and December.

Current employment weights are used to calculate cost levels. The March 2006 cost levels were calculated using the March 2006 employment counts from the Bureau of Labor Statistics (BLS) Current Employment Statistics (CES) program, benchmarked to the March 2005 universe of all private nonfarm establishments.

The ECEC was converted to the North American Industry Classification System (NAICS) in 2004.

Sources of Additional Information

Additional information may be obtained from BLS news release 06-1049 "Employer Costs for Employee Compensation—March 2006," and in various articles in the BLS e-publication, *Compensation and Working Conditions*. These resources are available on the BLS Web site at <http://www.bls.gov>.

Table 6-5. Employer Compensation Costs Per Hour Worked for Employee Compensation and Costs as a Percent of Total Compensation: Private Industry Workers, by Major Industry Group, March 2006

(Dollars, percent of total cost.)

Compensation component	All workers		Goods-producing[1]						Service-providing[2]			
			All goods-producing[1]		Construction		Manufacturing		All service-providing[2]		Trade, transportation, and utilities	
	Cost	Percent	Cost	Percent	Cost	Percent	Cost	Percent	Cost	Percent	Cost	Percent
TOTAL COMPENSATION	25.09	100.0	29.36	100.0	28.65	100.0	29.40	100.0	24.05	100.0	20.89	100.0
WAGES AND SALARIES	17.73	70.7	19.44	66.2	19.67	68.6	19.18	65.2	17.31	72.0	14.88	71.2
TOTAL BENEFITS	7.36	29.3	9.92	33.8	8.98	31.4	10.22	34.8	6.73	28.0	6.01	28.8
Paid Leave	1.71	6.8	1.85	6.3	1.02	3.6	2.26	7.7	1.67	7.0	1.25	6.0
Vacation	0.85	3.4	0.97	3.3	0.57	2.0	1.16	3.9	0.83	3.4	0.63	3.0
Holiday	0.57	2.3	0.66	2.2	0.35	1.2	0.81	2.8	0.54	2.3	0.41	1.9
Sick	0.21	0.8	0.16	0.5	0.07	0.2	0.20	0.7	0.23	0.9	0.17	0.8
Other	0.08	0.3	0.07	0.2	0.02	0.1	0.09	0.3	0.08	0.3	0.05	0.2
Supplemental Pay	0.73	2.9	1.16	4.0	1.15	4.0	1.15	3.9	0.63	2.6	0.49	2.4
Overtime and premium pay[3]	0.26	1.0	0.56	1.9	0.57	2.0	0.54	1.8	0.19	0.8	0.24	1.1
Shift differentials	0.06	0.2	0.09	0.3	(4)	(5)	0.13	0.5	0.05	0.2	0.03	0.1
Nonproduction bonuses	0.41	1.6	0.51	1.7	0.57	2.0	0.47	1.6	0.39	1.6	0.23	1.1
Insurance	1.85	7.4	2.64	9.0	2.11	7.3	2.87	9.8	1.66	6.9	1.59	7.6
Life insurance	0.04	0.2	0.06	0.2	0.05	0.2	0.06	0.2	0.04	0.2	0.04	0.2
Health insurance	1.72	6.9	2.47	8.4	2.00	7.0	2.67	9.1	1.54	6.4	1.49	7.1
Short-term disability	0.05	0.2	0.08	0.3	0.04	0.1	0.09	0.3	0.04	0.2	0.04	0.2
Long-term disability	0.04	0.1	0.04	0.1	(4)	(5)	0.05	0.2	0.04	0.2	0.02	0.1
Retirement and Savings	0.91	3.6	1.48	5.0	1.42	5.0	1.44	4.9	0.77	3.2	0.75	3.6
Defined benefit plans	0.44	1.8	0.96	3.3	0.93	3.3	0.90	3.1	0.32	1.3	0.41	2.0
Defined contribution plans	0.47	1.9	0.52	1.8	0.49	1.7	0.53	1.8	0.45	1.9	0.33	1.6
Legally Required Benefits	2.15	8.6	2.78	9.5	3.29	11.5	2.51	8.5	2.00	8.3	1.93	9.2
Social Security and Medicare	1.49	5.9	1.66	5.7	1.63	5.7	1.67	5.7	1.44	6.0	1.24	5.9
Social Security[6]	1.19	4.8	1.34	4.6	1.32	4.6	1.34	4.6	1.16	4.8	1.00	4.8
Medicare	0.29	1.2	0.32	1.1	0.32	1.1	0.32	1.1	0.29	1.2	0.24	1.2
Federal unemployment insurance	0.03	0.1	0.03	0.1	0.03	0.1	0.03	0.1	0.03	0.1	0.04	0.2
State unemployment insurance	0.16	0.6	0.22	0.7	0.26	0.9	0.20	0.7	0.15	0.6	0.14	0.7
Workers' compensation	0.47	1.9	0.87	3.0	1.36	4.8	0.61	2.1	0.38	1.6	0.51	2.4

Note: Individual items may not sum to totals due to rounding.

[1]Includes mining, construction, and manufacturing. The agriculture, forestry, farming, and hunting sector is excluded.
[2]Includes utilities; wholesale trade; retail trade; transportation and warehousing; information; finance and insurance; real estate and rental and leasing; professional and technical services; management of companies and enterprises; administrative and waste services; educational services; health care and social assistance; arts, entertainment, and recreation; accommodation and food services; and other services, except public administration.
[3]Includes premium pay for work in addition to the regular work schedule (such as overtime, weekends, and holidays).
[4]Cost per hour worked is $0.01 or less.
[5]Less than 0.05 percent.
[6]Comprises the Old Age, Survivors, and Disability Insurance (OASDI) program.

Table 6-5. Employer Compensation Costs Per Hour Worked for Employee Compensation and Costs as a Percent of Total Compensation: Private Industry Workers, by Major Industry Group, March 2006—*Continued*

(Dollars, percent of total cost.)

| Compensation component | Service-providing[2] | | | | | | | | | | | |
| | Information | | Financial activities | | Professional and business services | | Education and health services | | Leisure and hospitality | | Other services | |
	Cost	Percent	Cost	Percent	Cost	Percent	Cost	Percent	Cost	Percent	Cost	Percent
TOTAL COMPENSATION	37.01	100.0	34.18	100.0	29.61	100.0	26.62	100.0	10.69	100.0	21.59	100.0
WAGES AND SALARIES	25.64	69.3	23.15	67.7	21.70	73.3	19.25	72.3	8.47	79.3	15.79	73.1
TOTAL BENEFITS	11.36	30.7	11.04	32.3	7.90	26.7	7.37	27.7	2.21	20.7	5.81	26.9
Paid Leave	3.50	9.5	2.75	8.0	2.16	7.3	2.01	7.5	0.34	3.2	1.49	6.9
Vacation	1.72	4.7	1.37	4.0	1.06	3.6	0.96	3.6	0.20	1.8	0.70	3.2
Holiday	1.07	2.9	0.88	2.6	0.73	2.5	0.65	2.4	0.10	0.9	0.53	2.5
Sick	0.45	1.2	0.36	1.1	0.29	1.0	0.30	1.1	0.04	0.4	0.19	0.9
Other	0.25	0.7	0.14	0.4	0.08	0.3	0.10	0.4	0.02	0.1	0.06	0.3
Supplemental Pay	0.92	2.5	1.85	5.4	0.81	2.7	0.48	1.8	0.13	1.2	0.33	1.5
Overtime and premium pay[3]	0.35	1.0	0.13	0.4	0.20	0.7	0.19	0.7	0.08	0.7	0.11	0.5
Shift differentials	0.04	0.1	0.02	(5)	0.03	0.1	0.17	0.6	(4)	(5)	0.02	0.1
Nonproduction bonuses	0.52	1.4	1.70	5.0	0.57	1.9	0.12	0.5	0.05	0.4	0.20	0.9
Insurance	2.89	7.8	2.58	7.6	1.72	5.8	1.97	7.4	0.45	4.2	1.49	6.9
Life insurance	0.06	0.2	0.07	0.2	0.05	0.2	0.03	0.1	(4)	(5)	0.06	0.3
Health insurance	2.60	7.0	2.38	7.0	1.56	5.3	1.85	6.9	0.43	4.0	1.38	6.4
Short-term disability	0.16	0.4	0.07	0.2	0.06	0.2	0.04	0.2	(4)	(5)	0.02	0.1
Long-term disability	0.08	0.2	0.06	0.2	0.05	0.2	0.05	0.2	(4)	(5)	0.03	0.1
Retirement and Savings	1.35	3.7	1.59	4.7	0.87	3.0	0.77	2.9	0.10	0.9	0.57	2.6
Defined benefit plans	0.66	1.8	0.67	2.0	0.33	1.1	0.22	0.8	0.02	0.2	0.17	0.8
Defined contribution plans	0.69	1.9	0.92	2.7	0.55	1.8	0.55	2.1	0.08	0.8	0.40	1.8
Legally Required Benefits	2.70	7.3	2.27	6.6	2.34	7.9	2.14	8.0	1.19	11.1	1.94	9.0
Social Security and Medicare	2.17	5.9	1.88	5.5	1.77	6.0	1.61	6.1	0.76	7.1	1.31	6.1
Social Security[6]	1.73	4.7	1.48	4.3	1.41	4.8	1.30	4.9	0.62	5.8	1.06	4.9
Medicare	0.43	1.2	0.40	1.2	0.36	1.2	0.31	1.2	0.15	1.4	0.26	1.2
Federal unemployment insurance	0.03	0.1	0.03	0.1	0.03	0.1	0.03	0.1	0.04	0.4	0.03	0.1
State unemployment insurance	0.19	0.5	0.15	0.4	0.18	0.6	0.14	0.5	0.12	1.1	0.15	0.7
Workers' compensation	0.31	0.8	0.20	0.6	0.36	1.2	0.36	1.3	0.27	2.5	0.44	2.0

Note: Individual items may not sum to totals due to rounding.

[2]Includes utilities; wholesale trade; retail trade; transportation and warehousing; information; finance and insurance; real estate and rental and leasing; professional and technical services; management of companies and enterprises; administrative and waste services; educational services; health care and social assistance; arts, entertainment, and recreation; accommodation and food services; and other services, except public administration.
[3]Includes premium pay for work in addition to the regular work schedule (such as overtime, weekends, and holidays).
[4]Cost per hour worked is $0.01 or less.
[5]Less than 0.05 percent.
[6]Comprises the Old Age, Survivors, and Disability Insurance (OASDI) program.

Table 6-6. Employer Compensation Costs Per Hour Worked for Employee Compensation and Costs as a Percent of Total Compensation: Private Industry Workers, by Census Region and Area, March 2006

(Dollars, percent of total costs.)

Compensation component	Census region and division[1]					
	Northeast		Northeast divisions			
			New England		Middle Atlantic	
	Cost	Percent	Cost	Percent	Cost	Percent
TOTAL COMPENSATION	28.75	100.0	27.96	100.0	29.08	100.0
WAGES AND SALARIES	20.12	70.0	19.86	71.0	20.23	69.6
TOTAL BENEFITS	8.63	30.0	8.11	29.0	8.85	30.4
Paid Leave	2.18	7.6	2.04	7.3	2.24	7.7
Vacation	1.05	3.7	0.99	3.5	1.08	3.7
Holiday	0.71	2.5	0.70	2.5	0.72	2.5
Sick	0.30	1.0	0.25	0.9	0.32	1.1
Other	0.11	0.4	0.09	0.3	0.12	0.4
Supplemental Pay	0.93	3.2	0.81	2.9	0.98	3.4
Overtime and premium pay[2]	0.26	0.9	0.26	0.9	0.27	0.9
Shift differentials	0.06	0.2	0.06	0.2	0.07	0.2
Nonproduction bonuses	0.60	2.1	0.50	1.8	0.64	2.2
Insurance	2.07	7.2	1.91	6.8	2.14	7.3
Life insurance	0.05	0.2	0.05	0.2	0.05	0.2
Health insurance	1.92	6.7	1.78	6.4	1.97	6.8
Short-term disability	0.07	0.2	0.04	0.2	0.08	0.3
Long-term disability	0.04	0.1	0.03	0.1	0.04	0.1
Retirement and Savings	1.06	3.7	1.00	3.6	1.09	3.8
Defined benefit	0.48	1.7	0.41	1.5	0.51	1.7
Defined contribution	0.59	2.0	0.59	2.1	0.59	2.0
Legally Required Benefits	2.39	8.3	2.35	8.4	2.41	8.3
Social Security and Medicare	1.68	5.8	1.66	5.9	1.68	5.8
Social Security[3]	1.34	4.7	1.33	4.8	1.34	4.6
Medicare	0.34	1.2	0.33	1.2	0.34	1.2
Federal unemployment insurance	0.03	0.1	0.03	0.1	0.03	0.1
State unemployment insurance	0.22	0.8	0.22	0.8	0.22	0.8
Workers' compensation	0.46	1.6	0.43	1.5	0.47	1.6

Note: Individual items may not sum to totals due to rounding.

[1]The states that comprise the Census divisions are: New England—Connecticut, Maine, Massachusetts, New Hampshire, Rhode Island, and Vermont; Middle Atlantic—New Jersey, New York, and Pennsylvania; South Atlantic—Delaware, District of Columbia, Florida, Georgia, Maryland, North Carolina, South Carolina, Virginia, and West Virginia; East South Central—Alabama, Kentucky, Mississippi, and Tennessee; West South Central—Arkansas, Louisiana, Oklahoma, and Texas; East North Central—Illinois, Indiana, Michigan, Ohio, and Wisconsin; West North Central—Iowa, Kansas, Minnesota, Missouri, Nebraska, North Dakota, and South Dakota; Mountain—Arizona, Colorado, Idaho, Montana, Nevada, New Mexico, Utah, and Wyoming; and Pacific—Alaska, California, Hawaii, Oregon, and Washington.
[2]Includes premium pay for work in addition to the regular work schedule (such as overtime, weekends, and holidays).
[3]Comprises the Old-Age, Survivors, and Disability Insurance (OASDI) program.

Table 6-6. Employer Compensation Costs Per Hour Worked for Employee Compensation and Costs as a Percent of Total Compensation: Private Industry Workers, by Census Region and Area, March 2006—*Continued*

(Dollars, percent of total costs.)

Compensation component	Census region and division[1]							
	South		South divisions					
			South Atlantic		East South Central		West South Central	
	Cost	Percent	Cost	Percent	Cost	Percent	Cost	Percent
TOTAL COMPENSATION	22.35	100.0	23.43	100.0	19.82	100.0	21.83	100.0
WAGES AND SALARIES	16.11	72.1	16.93	72.3	14.07	71.0	15.76	72.2
TOTAL BENEFITS	6.24	27.9	6.49	27.7	5.74	29.0	6.07	27.8
Paid Leave	1.42	6.4	1.54	6.6	1.14	5.8	1.37	6.3
Vacation	0.72	3.2	0.78	3.3	0.61	3.1	0.67	3.1
Holiday	0.48	2.1	0.51	2.2	0.37	1.9	0.48	2.2
Sick	0.17	0.8	0.19	0.8	0.11	0.6	0.18	0.8
Other	0.06	0.2	0.06	0.3	0.05	0.3	0.05	0.2
Supplemental Pay	0.57	2.6	0.57	2.4	0.58	2.9	0.59	2.7
Overtime and premium pay[2]	0.23	1.0	0.23	1.0	0.23	1.1	0.24	1.1
Shift differentials	0.05	0.2	0.05	0.2	0.07	0.4	0.04	0.2
Nonproduction bonuses	0.29	1.3	0.28	1.2	0.28	1.4	0.31	1.4
Insurance	1.61	7.2	1.66	7.1	1.65	8.3	1.52	7.0
Life insurance	0.04	0.2	0.04	0.2	0.05	0.2	0.05	0.2
Health insurance	1.49	6.7	1.53	6.5	1.52	7.7	1.41	6.4
Short-term disability	0.04	0.2	0.05	0.2	0.05	0.3	0.04	0.2
Long-term disability	0.04	0.2	0.04	0.2	0.03	0.2	0.03	0.2
Retirement and Savings	0.75	3.3	0.76	3.3	0.62	3.1	0.78	3.6
Defined benefit	0.34	1.5	0.31	1.3	0.24	1.2	0.43	2.0
Defined contribution	0.41	1.8	0.45	1.9	0.38	1.9	0.35	1.6
Legally Required Benefits	1.88	8.4	1.97	8.4	1.75	8.9	1.81	8.3
Social Security and Medicare	1.35	6.0	1.42	6.1	1.21	6.1	1.30	6.0
Social Security[3]	1.08	4.8	1.14	4.9	0.97	4.9	1.04	4.8
Medicare	0.26	1.2	0.28	1.2	0.23	1.2	0.26	1.2
Federal unemployment insurance	0.03	0.1	0.03	0.1	0.03	0.2	0.03	0.1
State unemployment insurance	0.11	0.5	0.11	0.4	0.10	0.5	0.12	0.5
Workers' compensation	0.40	1.8	0.41	1.8	0.41	2.1	0.36	1.7

Note: Individual items may not sum to totals due to rounding.

[1]The states that comprise the Census divisions are: New England—Connecticut, Maine, Massachusetts, New Hampshire, Rhode Island, and Vermont; Middle Atlantic—New Jersey, New York, and Pennsylvania; South Atlantic—Delaware, District of Columbia, Florida, Georgia, Maryland, North Carolina, South Carolina, Virginia, and West Virginia; East South Central—Alabama, Kentucky, Mississippi, and Tennessee; West South Central—Arkansas, Louisiana, Oklahoma, and Texas; East North Central—Illinois, Indiana, Michigan, Ohio, and Wisconsin; West North Central—Iowa, Kansas, Minnesota, Missouri, Nebraska, North Dakota, and South Dakota; Mountain—Arizona, Colorado, Idaho, Montana, Nevada, New Mexico, Utah, and Wyoming; and Pacific—Alaska, California, Hawaii, Oregon, and Washington.
[2]Includes premium pay for work in addition to the regular work schedule (such as overtime, weekends, and holidays).
[3]Comprises the Old-Age, Survivors, and Disability Insurance (OASDI) program.

Table 6-6. Employer Compensation Costs Per Hour Worked for Employee Compensation and Costs as a Percent of Total Compensation: Private Industry Workers, by Census Region and Area, March 2006—*Continued*

(Dollars, percent of total costs.)

Compensation component	Census region and division[1]					
	Midwest		Midwest divisions			
			East North Central		West North Central	
	Cost	Percent	Cost	Percent	Cost	Percent
TOTAL COMPENSATION	24.65	100.0	26.03	100.0	21.50	100.0
WAGES AND SALARIES	17.10	69.4	17.96	69.0	15.13	70.4
TOTAL BENEFITS	7.56	30.6	8.07	31.0	6.37	29.6
Paid Leave	1.67	6.8	1.80	6.9	1.39	6.5
Vacation	0.85	3.4	0.90	3.5	0.73	3.4
Holiday	0.55	2.2	0.60	2.3	0.45	2.1
Sick	0.19	0.8	0.20	0.8	0.15	0.7
Other	0.09	0.4	0.10	0.4	0.06	0.3
Supplemental Pay	0.76	3.1	0.84	3.2	0.57	2.7
Overtime and premium pay[2]	0.30	1.2	0.31	1.2	0.26	1.2
Shift differentials	0.08	0.3	0.09	0.3	0.06	0.3
Nonproduction bonuses	0.38	1.5	0.43	1.7	0.26	1.2
Insurance	2.02	8.2	2.16	8.3	1.71	8.0
Life insurance	0.05	0.2	0.05	0.2	0.04	0.2
Health insurance	1.88	7.6	2.00	7.7	1.60	7.4
Short-term disability	0.06	0.2	0.06	0.2	0.04	0.2
Long-term disability	0.04	0.1	0.04	0.1	0.03	0.1
Retirement and Savings	1.01	4.1	1.11	4.3	0.79	3.7
Defined benefit	0.57	2.3	0.66	2.5	0.38	1.8
Defined contribution	0.44	1.8	0.45	1.7	0.41	1.9
Legally Required Benefits	2.09	8.5	2.17	8.3	1.90	8.8
Social Security and Medicare	1.45	5.9	1.52	5.8	1.29	6.0
Social Security[3]	1.17	4.7	1.22	4.7	1.04	4.8
Medicare	0.28	1.1	0.30	1.1	0.25	1.2
Federal unemployment insurance	0.03	0.1	0.03	0.1	0.03	0.1
State unemployment insurance	0.16	0.7	0.17	0.7	0.14	0.7
Workers' compensation	0.44	1.8	0.44	1.7	0.43	2.0

Note: Individual items may not sum to totals due to rounding.

[1] The states that comprise the Census divisions are: New England—Connecticut, Maine, Massachusetts, New Hampshire, Rhode Island, and Vermont; Middle Atlantic—New Jersey, New York, and Pennsylvania; South Atlantic—Delaware, District of Columbia, Florida, Georgia, Maryland, North Carolina, South Carolina, Virginia, and West Virginia; East South Central—Alabama, Kentucky, Mississippi, and Tennessee; West South Central—Arkansas, Louisiana, Oklahoma, and Texas; East North Central—Illinois, Indiana, Michigan, Ohio, and Wisconsin; West North Central—Iowa, Kansas, Minnesota, Missouri, Nebraska, North Dakota, and South Dakota; Mountain—Arizona, Colorado, Idaho, Montana, Nevada, New Mexico, Utah, and Wyoming; and Pacific—Alaska, California, Hawaii, Oregon, and Washington.
[2] Includes premium pay for work in addition to the regular work schedule (such as overtime, weekends, and holidays).
[3] Comprises the Old-Age, Survivors, and Disability Insurance (OASDI) program.

Table 6-6. Employer Compensation Costs Per Hour Worked for Employee Compensation and Costs as a Percent of Total Compensation: Private Industry Workers, by Census Region and Area, March 2006—*Continued*

(Dollars, percent of total costs.)

Compensation component	Census region and division[1]						Area[4]			
	West		West divisions				Metropolitan area		Nonmetropolitan area	
			Mountain		Pacific					
	Cost	Percent	Cost	Percent	Cost	Percent	Cost	Percent	Cost	Percent
TOTAL COMPENSATION	26.56	100.0	23.12	100.0	28.02	100.0	26.00	100.0	18.85	100.0
WAGES AND SALARIES	18.85	71.0	16.68	72.1	19.77	70.6	18.37	70.7	13.33	70.7
TOTAL BENEFITS	7.71	29.0	6.44	27.9	8.25	29.4	7.63	29.3	5.52	29.3
Paid Leave	1.76	6.6	1.40	6.0	1.92	6.8	1.80	6.9	1.10	5.8
Vacation	0.89	3.4	0.72	3.1	0.96	3.4	0.90	3.4	0.57	3.0
Holiday	0.59	2.2	0.46	2.0	0.64	2.3	0.60	2.3	0.37	2.0
Sick	0.23	0.9	0.17	0.8	0.25	0.9	0.23	0.9	0.11	0.6
Other	0.05	0.2	0.04	0.2	0.06	0.2	0.08	0.3	0.05	0.2
Supplemental Pay	0.77	2.9	0.67	2.9	0.82	2.9	0.76	2.9	0.54	2.9
Overtime and premium pay[2]	0.25	0.9	0.21	0.9	0.27	1.0	0.26	1.0	0.28	1.5
Shift differentials	0.05	0.2	0.05	0.2	0.05	0.2	0.06	0.2	0.06	0.3
Nonproduction bonuses	0.47	1.8	0.41	1.8	0.50	1.8	0.44	1.7	0.20	1.1
Insurance	1.82	6.9	1.62	7.0	1.91	6.8	1.89	7.3	1.55	8.2
Life insurance	0.04	0.2	0.03	0.1	0.04	0.2	0.05	0.2	0.03	0.2
Health insurance	1.71	6.4	1.53	6.6	1.79	6.4	1.76	6.8	1.46	7.8
Short-term disability	0.03	0.1	0.03	0.1	0.04	0.1	0.05	0.2	0.04	0.2
Long-term disability	0.03	0.1	0.03	0.1	0.04	0.1	0.04	0.1	0.02	0.1
Retirement and Savings	0.90	3.4	0.72	3.1	0.98	3.5	0.96	3.7	0.57	3.0
Defined benefit	0.43	1.6	0.26	1.1	0.51	1.8	0.47	1.8	0.26	1.4
Defined contribution	0.47	1.8	0.45	2.0	0.47	1.7	0.49	1.9	0.31	1.6
Legally Required Benefits	2.45	9.2	2.04	8.8	2.62	9.4	2.21	8.5	1.76	9.3
Social Security and Medicare	1.57	5.9	1.39	6.0	1.65	5.9	1.54	5.9	1.15	6.1
Social Security[3]	1.26	4.7	1.12	4.8	1.32	4.7	1.23	4.7	0.93	4.9
Medicare	0.31	1.2	0.27	1.2	0.33	1.2	0.30	1.2	0.22	1.2
Federal unemployment insurance	0.03	0.1	0.03	0.1	0.03	0.1	0.03	0.1	0.03	0.2
State unemployment insurance	0.19	0.7	0.13	0.6	0.21	0.8	0.17	0.6	0.14	0.7
Workers' compensation	0.66	2.5	0.48	2.1	0.73	2.6	0.48	1.8	0.44	2.3

Note: Individual items may not sum to totals due to rounding.

[1]The states that comprise the Census divisions are: New England—Connecticut, Maine, Massachusetts, New Hampshire, Rhode Island, and Vermont; Middle Atlantic—New Jersey, New York, and Pennsylvania; South Atlantic—Delaware, District of Columbia, Florida, Georgia, Maryland, North Carolina, South Carolina, Virginia, and West Virginia; East South Central—Alabama, Kentucky, Mississippi, and Tennessee; West South Central—Arkansas, Louisiana, Oklahoma, and Texas; East North Central—Illinois, Indiana, Michigan, Ohio, and Wisconsin; West North Central—Iowa, Kansas, Minnesota, Missouri, Nebraska, North Dakota, and South Dakota; Mountain—Arizona, Colorado, Idaho, Montana, Nevada, New Mexico, Utah, and Wyoming; and Pacific—Alaska, California, Hawaii, Oregon, and Washington.
[2]Includes premium pay for work in addition to the regular work schedule (such as overtime, weekends, and holidays).
[3]Comprises the Old-Age, Survivors, and Disability Insurance (OASDI) program.
[4]A metropolitan area can be a Metropolitan Statistical Area (MSA) or a Consolidated Metropolitan Statistical Area (CMSA), as defined by the Office of Management and Budget in 1994. Nonmetropolitan areas are counties that do not fit the definitions above.

Table 6-7. Employer Compensation Costs Per Hour Worked for Employee Compensation and Costs as a Percent of Total Compensation: State and Local Government, by Major Occupational and Industry Group, March 2006

(Dollars, percent of total cost.)

Compensation component	All workers		Occupational group[1]						Industry group	
	Cost	Percent	Management, professional, and related		Sales and office		Service		Service-providing[2]	
			Cost	Percent	Cost	Percent	Cost	Percent	Cost	Percent
TOTAL COMPENSATION	36.96	100.0	45.07	100.0	25.23	100.0	28.21	100.0	37.14	100.0
WAGES AND SALARIES	25.01	67.6	31.95	70.9	15.73	62.4	17.19	60.9	25.15	67.7
TOTAL BENEFITS	11.96	32.4	13.11	29.1	9.50	37.6	11.02	39.1	11.99	32.3
Paid Leave	2.88	7.8	3.16	7.0	2.41	9.6	2.58	9.2	2.89	7.8
Vacation	1.00	2.7	0.92	2.0	0.98	3.9	1.11	3.9	1.00	2.7
Holiday	0.92	2.5	1.02	2.3	0.77	3.1	0.81	2.9	0.92	2.5
Sick	0.73	2.0	0.92	2.1	0.50	2.0	0.48	1.7	0.73	2.0
Other	0.24	0.6	0.29	0.7	0.16	0.6	0.19	0.7	0.24	0.6
Supplemental Pay	0.32	0.9	0.19	0.4	0.17	0.7	0.62	2.2	0.32	0.9
Overtime and premium pay[3]	0.16	0.4	0.05	0.1	0.08	0.3	0.33	1.2	0.15	0.4
Shift differentials	0.07	0.2	0.05	0.1	0.02	0.1	0.15	0.5	0.07	0.2
Nonproduction bonuses	0.10	0.3	0.10	0.2	0.07	0.3	0.14	0.5	0.10	0.3
Insurance	4.03	10.9	4.39	9.7	3.80	15.1	3.35	11.9	4.03	10.9
Life insurance	0.06	0.2	0.07	0.1	0.05	0.2	0.04	0.1	0.06	0.2
Health insurance	3.91	10.6	4.26	9.4	3.70	14.7	3.23	11.5	3.91	10.5
Short-term disability	0.02	0.1	0.02	(4)	0.02	0.1	0.04	0.1	0.02	0.1
Long-term disability	0.04	0.1	0.05	0.1	0.03	0.1	0.03	0.1	0.04	0.1
Retirement and Savings	2.54	6.9	2.86	6.3	1.53	6.1	2.71	9.6	2.56	6.9
Defined benefit plans	2.27	6.1	2.52	5.6	1.36	5.4	2.57	9.1	2.28	6.1
Defined contribution plans	0.28	0.8	0.34	0.8	0.16	0.6	0.14	0.5	0.28	0.8
Legally Required Benefits	2.18	5.9	2.51	5.6	1.59	6.3	1.76	6.2	2.18	5.9
Social Security and Medicare	1.66	4.5	2.07	4.6	1.21	4.8	1.08	3.8	1.67	4.5
Social Security[5]	1.28	3.5	1.59	3.5	0.95	3.8	0.81	2.9	1.28	3.5
Medicare	0.38	1.0	0.48	1.1	0.26	1.0	0.26	0.9	0.38	1.0
Federal unemployment insurance	(6)	(4)	(6)	(4)	(6)	(4)	(6)	(4)	(6)	(4)
State unemployment insurance	0.06	0.2	0.06	0.1	0.05	0.2	0.07	0.2	0.06	0.2
Workers' compensation	0.46	1.2	0.38	0.8	0.32	1.3	0.62	2.2	0.46	1.2

Note: Individual items may not sum to totals due to rounding.

[1]This table presents data for the three major occupational groups in state and local government: management, professional, and related occupations, including teachers; sales and office occupations, including clerical workers; and service occupations, including police and firefighters.
[2]Service-providing industries, which include health and educational services, employ a large proportion of the state and local government workforce.
[3]Includes premium pay for work in addition to the regular work schedule (such as overtime, weekends, and holidays).
[4]Less than 0.05 percent.
[5]Comprises the Old Age, Survivors, and Disability Insurance (OASDI) program.
[6]Cost per hour worked is $0.01 or less.

Table 6-8. Employer Compensation Costs Per Hour Worked for Employee Compensation and Costs as a Percent of Total Compensation: State and Local Government Workers, by Occupational and Industry Workers, March 2006

(Dollars, percent of total compensation.)

Characteristic	Total compensation	Wages and salaries	Cost per hour worked					
			Total	Paid leave	Supplemental pay	Insurance	Retirement and savings	Legally required benefits
COSTS PER HOUR WORKED								
State and Local Government Workers	36.96	25.01	11.96	2.88	0.32	4.03	2.54	2.18
Occupational Group								
Management, professional, and related	45.07	31.95	13.11	3.16	0.19	4.39	2.86	2.51
Professional and related	44.87	32.13	12.74	2.87	0.20	4.38	2.82	2.47
Teachers[1]	50.12	36.86	13.26	2.67	0.12	4.57	3.26	2.65
Primary, secondary, and special education school teachers	48.24	35.19	13.05	2.47	0.11	4.86	3.12	2.49
Sales and office	25.23	15.73	9.50	2.41	0.17	3.80	1.53	1.59
Office and administrative support	25.24	15.74	9.50	2.41	0.17	3.80	1.53	1.58
Service	28.21	17.19	11.02	2.58	0.62	3.35	2.71	1.76
Industry Group								
Education and health services	38.96	27.43	11.53	2.71	0.21	4.07	2.37	2.17
Educational services	39.58	28.14	11.45	2.54	0.14	4.16	2.45	2.16
Elementary and secondary schools	38.62	27.47	11.15	2.21	0.12	4.37	2.38	2.08
Junior colleges, colleges, and universities	42.85	30.36	12.49	3.58	0.20	3.59	2.70	2.42
Health care and social assistance	34.98	22.96	12.02	3.78	0.68	3.49	1.85	2.22
Hospitals	31.39	20.46	10.93	3.24	0.75	3.19	1.66	2.09
Public administration	33.88	21.19	12.69	3.19	0.49	3.96	2.95	2.10
PERCENT OF TOTAL COMPENSATION								
State and Local Government Workers	100.0	67.6	32.4	7.8	0.9	10.9	6.9	5.9
Occupational Group								
Management, professional, and related	100.0	70.9	29.1	7.0	0.4	9.7	6.3	5.6
Professional and related	100.0	71.6	28.4	6.4	0.5	9.8	6.3	5.5
Teachers[1]	100.0	73.5	26.5	5.3	0.2	9.1	6.5	5.3
Primary, secondary, and special education school teachers	100.0	72.9	27.1	5.1	0.2	10.1	6.5	5.2
Sales and office	100.0	62.4	37.6	9.6	0.7	15.1	6.1	6.3
Office and administrative support	100.0	62.4	37.6	9.6	0.7	15.0	6.1	6.3
Service	100.0	60.9	39.1	9.2	2.2	11.9	9.6	6.2
Industry Group								
Education and health services	100.0	70.4	29.6	7.0	0.5	10.4	6.1	5.6
Educational services	100.0	71.1	28.9	6.4	0.4	10.5	6.2	5.5
Elementary and secondary schools	100.0	71.1	28.9	5.7	0.3	11.3	6.2	5.4
Junior colleges, colleges, and universities	100.0	70.9	29.1	8.4	0.5	8.4	6.3	5.6
Health care and social assistance	100.0	65.6	34.4	10.8	1.9	10.0	5.3	6.4
Hospitals	100.0	65.2	34.8	10.3	2.4	10.2	5.3	6.7
Public administration	100.0	62.5	37.5	9.4	1.4	11.7	8.7	6.2

Note: Individual items may not sum to totals due to rounding.

[1] Includes postsecondary teachers; primary, secondary, and special education teachers; and other teachers and instructors.

NOTES AND DEFINITIONS

EMPLOYEE BENEFITS SURVEY

The Employee Benefits Survey is now part of the National Compensation Survey (NCS), which also includes the Employment Cost Index.

Collection and Coverage

The statistics in this chapter represent the integration of data on employee benefits into the NCS. Prior to 1999, surveys of different sectors of the economy were conducted in alternating years; medium and large private establishments were studied during odd-numbered years, and small private establishments were studied during even-numbered years. Since these surveys have been replaced by the new survey, the tables previously presented in this *Handbook* have been discontinued. Data for all private workers are now collected annually.

Definitions

Incidence refers to different methods of computing the number or percentage of employees who receive a benefit plan or specific benefit feature.

Access to a benefit is determined on an occupational basis within an establishment. An employee is considered to have access to a benefit if it is available for his or her use.

Participation refers to the proportion of employees covered by a benefit. There will be cases where employees with access to a plan will not participate. For example, some employees may decline to participate in a health insurance plan if there is an employee cost involved.

Survey Scope

The 2000 NCS benefits incidence survey obtained data from 1,436 private industry establishments, representing over 107 million workers. Of this total, nearly 86 million were full-time workers; the remainder—nearly 22 million—was made up of part-time workers.

The NCS uses the establishment's definition of full- and part-time status. For purposes of this survey, an establishment is an economic unit that produces goods or services, a central administrative office, or an auxiliary unit providing support services to a company. For private industries, the establishment is usually at a single physical location.

Sources of Additional Information

For more information, see BLS news release USDL-06-1482, "Employee Benefits in Private Industry, 2006." For a listing of selected benefit definitions, see the *Glossary of Compensation Terms*. Additional data and further information on methodology and sampling are available in BLS Bulletin 2555, "National Compensation Survey: Employee Benefits in Private Industry in the United States, 2000." These resources are available on the BLS Web site at <http://www.bls.gov>. The NCS was described in an article in the fifth edition of this *Handbook*.

Table 6-9. Percent of Workers with Access to or Participating in Selected Benefits, March 2006

(Percent.)

Characteristic	Retirement benefits			Health care benefits				Life insurance	Disability benefits	
	All plans[1]	Defined benefit	Defined contribution	Medical care	Dental care	Vision care	Outpatient prescription drug coverage		Short-term disability	Long-term disability
ACCESS TO SELECTED BENEFITS										
All workers	60	21	54	71	46	29	67	52	39	30
Worker Characteristics										
White-collar occupations	69	23	65	77	53	32	72	60	43	42
Blue-collar occupations	62	25	53	77	46	31	73	54	43	23
Service occupations	34	8	30	45	27	19	43	30	22	12
Full-time	69	24	63	85	55	34	81	64	46	38
Part-time	29	9	25	22	15	11	21	13	13	6
Union	84	70	50	89	69	54	86	63	63	30
Nonunion	57	15	55	68	43	26	64	51	36	30
Average wage less than $15 per hour	47	11	43	57	34	20	54	40	27	17
Average wage $15 per hour or higher	77	34	69	88	62	40	84	67	54	48
Establishment Characteristics										
Goods-producing	73	32	63	86	56	35	82	62	53	31
Service-producing	56	18	52	66	43	27	62	49	35	30
1 to 99 workers	44	9	41	59	31	20	56	38	27	19
100 workers or more	78	35	70	84	64	40	80	69	53	43
Geographic Areas[2]										
Metropolitan areas[3]	61	22	55	71	47	30	68	53	40	32
Nonmetropolitan areas[3]	55	14	51	66	40	25	63	50	32	21
New England	58	20	53	71	54	31	69	49	38	34
Middle Atlantic	61	27	52	71	45	32	65	47	73	27
South Atlantic	60	17	57	72	45	28	68	57	34	33
East South Central	63	15	60	72	47	32	69	56	35	28
West South Central	54	15	50	66	36	19	60	52	25	28
East North Central	63	25	56	71	46	27	69	57	42	34
West North Central	64	20	57	66	43	22	64	52	33	29
Mountain	63	20	59	70	47	30	67	50	26	29
Pacific	56	21	49	73	55	39	70	46	28	28
PARTICIPATING IN SELECTING BENEFITS										
All workers	51	20	43	52	36	22	49	50	37	29
Worker Characteristics										
White-collar occupations	60	22	53	57	41	24	54	58	41	40
Blue-collar occupations	52	25	40	60	38	25	57	51	42	22
Service occupations	24	7	20	27	18	13	27	26	21	11
Full-time	60	23	51	64	44	26	60	61	45	36
Part-time	21	8	16	13	10	7	12	10	12	5
Union	80	68	44	80	63	48	77	62	62	29
Nonunion	47	14	43	49	33	19	46	48	35	29
Average wage less than $15 per hour	36	10	31	38	23	14	35	37	26	16
Average wage $15 per hour or higher	70	33	58	71	52	32	67	66	52	46
Establishment Characteristics										
Goods-producing	64	31	51	70	49	29	66	60	52	31
Service-producing	47	17	40	47	32	20	44	47	33	28
1 to 99 workers	37	9	33	43	24	14	40	36	25	18
100 workers or more	67	33	54	63	50	31	60	66	52	42
Geographic Areas[2]										
Metropolitan areas[3]	52	21	44	53	37	22	50	50	39	31
Nonmetropolitan areas[3]	44	13	39	48	31	19	46	47	31	20
New England	50	19	43	51	41	21	48	48	37	31
Middle Atlantic	55	26	43	52	35	24	48	45	72	27
South Atlantic	49	16	43	53	33	20	49	54	31	31
East South Central	47	14	42	55	37	26	53	53	33	26
West South Central	43	15	37	49	27	15	44	48	24	26
East North Central	56	24	46	53	36	21	52	54	41	32
West North Central	56	20	47	50	34	17	48	50	32	28
Mountain	52	18	46	51	36	24	49	44	25	27
Pacific	47	20	38	55	44	30	52	44	27	27

Note: Individual items may not sum to totals due to rounding.

[1] Includes defined benefit pension plans and defined contribution retirement plans. The total is less than the sum of the individual items because many employees have access to both types of plans.

[2] The states that comprise the Census divisions are: New England—Connecticut, Maine, Massachusetts, New Hampshire, Rhode Island, and Vermont; Middle Atlantic—New Jersey, New York, and Pennsylvania; South Atlantic—Delaware, District of Columbia, Florida, Georgia, Maryland, North Carolina, South Carolina, Virginia, and West Virginia; East South Central—Alabama, Kentucky, Mississippi, and Tennessee; West South Central—Arkansas, Louisiana, Oklahoma, and Texas; East North Central—Illinois, Indiana, Michigan, Ohio, and Wisconsin; West North Central—Iowa, Kansas, Minnesota, Missouri, Nebraska, North Dakota, and South Dakota; Mountain—Arizona, Colorado, Idaho, Montana, Nevada, New Mexico, Utah, and Wyoming; and Pacific—Alaska, California, Hawaii, Oregon, and Washington.

[3] A metropolitan area can be a Metropolitan Statistical Area (MSA) or a Consolidated Metropolitan Statistical Area (CMSA), as defined by the Office of Management and Budget in 1994. Nonmetropolitan areas are counties that do not fit the definitions above.

Table 6-10. Percent of Medical Plan Participants and Employer Premiums Per Participant, by Requirements for Employee Contributions for Single and Family Coverage, Private Industry, March 2006

(Dollars, percent.)

Characteristic	Total		Employee contribution not required		Employee contribution required		
	Percent of participating employees	Average flat monthly employer premium	Percent of participating employees	Average flat monthly employer premium	Percent of participating employees	Average flat monthly employer premium	Average flat monthly employee contribution
SINGLE COVERAGE							
All workers	100	266.50	25	327.45	75	246.72	76.05
Worker Characteristics							
White-collar occupations	100	265.93	20	322.78	80	251.35	76.69
Blue-collar occupations	100	265.85	33	323.33	67	237.70	73.20
Service occupations	100	271.75	20	376.10	80	246.43	80.41
Full-time	100	265.69	25	324.80	75	246.25	75.39
Part-time	100	280.35	21	381.10	79	254.15	86.75
Union	100	333.13	49	390.42	51	278.15	57.28
Nonunion	100	253.75	20	297.67	80	242.89	78.34
Average wage less than $15 per hour	100	249.97	20	296.93	80	237.95	77.50
Average wage $15 per hour or higher	100	277.75	27	342.92	73	253.25	74.97
Establishment Characteristics							
Goods-producing	100	266.96	30	320.77	70	243.75	70.00
Service-producing	100	266.31	22	331.28	78	247.84	78.35
1 to 99 workers	100	257.39	32	320.29	68	227.31	83.66
100 workers or more	100	273.76	18	337.55	82	259.51	71.04
Geographic Areas[1]							
Metropolitan areas[2]	100	267.36	24	333.73	76	245.87	75.91
Nonmetropolitan areas[2]	100	261.60	25	291.88	75	251.60	76.86
New England	100	258.74	16	337.19	84	243.56	83.92
Middle Atlantic	100	285.37	28	359.34	72	256.96	73.87
South Atlantic	100	251.79	21	301.04	79	238.68	79.67
East South Central	100	243.70	22	277.63	78	234.40	79.13
West South Central	100	263.02	20	311.06	80	251.38	75.42
East North Central	100	274.38	23	359.28	77	248.45	76.08
West North Central	100	272.02	27	310.39	73	257.96	71.26
Mountain	100	269.78	23	333.84	77	251.00	77.54
Pacific	100	267.02	34	318.44	66	240.25	70.49
FAMILY COVERAGE							
All workers	100	617.18	13	788.53	87	592.38	296.88
Worker Characteristics							
White-collar occupations	100	624.40	9	754.51	91	611.90	303.36
Blue-collar occupations	100	620.62	20	827.94	80	567.43	279.03
Service occupations	100	567.18	9	676.90	91	556.76	311.79
Full-time	100	618.51	13	793.97	87	593.04	294.46
Part-time	100	593.33	12	686.13	88	580.60	339.90
Union	100	750.88	40	870.66	60	670.05	196.60
Nonunion	100	592.39	8	706.91	92	583.08	308.88
Average wage less than $15 per hour	100	558.64	8	648.37	92	551.06	311.29
Average wage $15 per hour or higher	100	656.66	16	834.72	84	622.94	286.23
Establishment Characteristics							
Goods-producing	100	654.66	19	851.25	81	607.63	260.76
Service-producing	100	601.51	10	737.17	90	586.67	310.40
1 to 99 workers	100	553.37	15	787.46	85	512.52	344.12
100 workers or more	100	667.32	11	789.68	89	652.34	261.41
Geographic Areas[1]							
Metropolitan areas[2]	100	621.93	13	799.86	87	595.74	296.89
Nonmetropolitan areas[2]	100	590.22	12	717.36	88	573.54	296.81
New England	100	652.63	10	805.78	90	635.70	279.34
Middle Atlantic	100	661.40	17	803.01	83	632.36	282.84
South Atlantic	100	590.83	7	814.61	93	574.72	309.91
East South Central	100	564.05	9	753.25	91	544.75	304.20
West South Central	100	577.70	6	716.26	94	568.74	317.10
East North Central	100	668.73	16	902.78	84	624.93	283.02
West North Central	100	609.19	16	658.08	84	599.91	281.28
Mountain	100	592.99	10	821.06	90	566.41	320.07
Pacific	100	592.56	18	713.31	82	565.93	295.88

Note: Individual items may not sum to totals due to rounding.

[1]The states that comprise the Census divisions are: New England—Connecticut, Maine, Massachusetts, New Hampshire, Rhode Island, and Vermont; Middle Atlantic—New Jersey, New York, and Pennsylvania; South Atlantic—Delaware, District of Columbia, Florida, Georgia, Maryland, North Carolina, South Carolina, Virginia, and West Virginia; East South Central—Alabama, Kentucky, Mississippi, and Tennessee; West South Central—Arkansas, Louisiana, Oklahoma, and Texas; East North Central—Illinois, Indiana, Michigan, Ohio, and Wisconsin; West North Central—Iowa, Kansas, Minnesota, Missouri, Nebraska, North Dakota, and South Dakota; Mountain—Arizona, Colorado, Idaho, Montana, Nevada, New Mexico, Utah, and Wyoming; and Pacific—Alaska, California, Hawaii, Oregon, and Washington.
[2]A metropolitan area can be a Metropolitan Statistical Area (MSA) or a Consolidated Metropolitan Statistical Area (CMSA), as defined by the Office of Management and Budget in 1994. Nonmetropolitan areas are counties that do not fit the definitions above.

NOTES AND DEFINITIONS

NATIONAL COMPENSATION SURVEY: OCCUPATIONAL WAGES

Collection and Coverage

The occupational wages in this section are from the National Compensation Survey (NCS). In 2005, the NCS included 25,723 establishments and represented over 84 million workers. Private sector establishments with one or more workers were included in the survey. State and local governments with 50 or more workers within a survey area were also included.

The survey covered goods-producing industries (mining, construction, and manufacturing), service-producing industries (transportation, communications, electric, gas, and sanitary services; wholesale trade; retail trade; finance, insurance, and real estate; and service industries), and state and local governments. Agriculture, private households, and the federal government were excluded from the scope of the NCS.

For the purposes of this survey, an establishment is an economic unit that produces goods or services, a central administrative office, or an auxiliary unit providing support services to a company. For private industries in this survey, the establishment is usually at a single physical location. For state and local governments, an establishment is defined as all locations of a government entity. The geographic scope of the NCS includes all 50 states and the District of Columbia.

Identification of the occupations for which wage data were collected for the 2005 NCS was a multistep process:

1. Probability-proportional-to-size selection of establishment jobs
2. Classification of jobs into occupations based on the Census of Population system
3. Characterization of jobs as full time versus part time, union versus nonunion, and time versus incentive
4. Determination of the level of work of each job

For each occupation, wage data were collected for workers who met the unique set of characteristics identified in the last three steps. Special procedures were developed for jobs for which a level could not be determined.

In step one, the jobs to be sampled were selected at each establishment by a Bureau of Labor Statistics (BLS) field economist during a personal visit. A complete list of employees was used for sampling, with each selected worker representing a job within the establishment.

The second step of the process entailed classifying the selected jobs into occupations based on their duties. A selected job may have been categorized into any one of about 480 occupational classifications.

In step three, certain job characteristics (such as full-time versus part-time employment, time versus incentive pay, and union versus non-union status) were determined.

In the last step before wage data were collected, the work level of each selected job was determined using a "point factor leveling" process. Point factor leveling matches certain aspects of a job to specific levels of work with assigned point values. Points for each factor are then totaled to determine the overall work level for the job.

Definitions

A *full-time worker* is any employee whom the employer considers to be working full time.

A *part-time worker* is any employee whom the employer considers to be working part time.

An *incentive worker* is any employee whose earnings are tied, at least in part, to commissions, piece rates, production bonuses, or other incentives based on production or sales.

A *level* is a ranking of an occupation based on the requirements of the position.

A *nonunion worker* is any employee in an occupation who does not meet the conditions for union coverage. (See below.)

A *time-based worker* is any employee whose earnings are tied to an hourly rate or salary and not to a specific level of production.

A *union worker* is any employee who works in an unionized occupation and meets all of the following conditions:

- A labor organization is recognized as the bargaining agent for all workers in the occupation.
- Wage and salary rates are determined through collective bargaining or negotiations.
- Settlement terms, which must include earnings provisions and may include benefit provisions, are embodied in a signed, mutually binding collective bargaining agreement.

Earnings are defined as regular payments from the employer to the employee as compensation for straight-time hourly work, or for any salaried work performed. The following components were included as part of earnings:

- Incentive pay, including commissions, production bonuses, and piece rates
- Cost-of-living allowances
- Hazard pay
- Payments of income deferred due to participation in a salary reduction plan
- Deadhead pay, defined as pay given to transportation workers returning in a vehicle without freight or passengers.

Weighting and Estimation

Sample weights were calculated for each establishment and occupation in the survey. These weights reflected the relative size of the occupation within the establishment and of the establishment within the sample universe. Weights were used to aggregate data for the individual establishments or occupations into the various data series.

The wage series in the tables are computed by combining the wages for each sampled occupation. Before being combined, individual wage rates are weighted by the number of workers; the sample weight, adjusted for non-responding establishments and other factors; and the occupations scheduled hours of work.

Sources of Additional Information

An extensive description of the steps and additional detailed tables are available in BLS Bulletin 2581, "National Compensation Survey: Occupational Wages in the United States, June 2005," available on the BLS Web site at <http://www.bls.gov>.

Table 6-11. Mean Hourly Earnings[1] and Weekly Hours, by Selected Characteristics, Private Industry and State and Local Government, National Compensation Survey,[2] June 2005

(Dollars, number of hours.)

Characteristic	Total		Private		State and local government	
	Mean hourly earnings	Mean weekly hours	Mean hourly earnings	Mean weekly hours	Mean hourly earnings	Mean weekly hours
TOTAL	18.62	35.7	17.82	35.5	23.31	36.8
Worker Characteristics[3]						
White-collar occupations[4]	22.96	36.0	22.21	35.9	26.32	36.5
Professional specialty and technical	30.24	36.2	29.80	36.2	31.25	36.1
Executive, administrative, and managerial	33.69	39.8	34.21	40.0	31.04	38.6
Sales	15.32	32.4	15.33	32.4	13.75	33.3
Administrative support	14.53	36.5	14.44	36.5	14.98	36.6
Blue-collar occupations[4]	15.87	38.1	15.75	38.1	17.96	37.7
Precision production, craft, and repair	19.95	39.6	19.93	39.6	20.24	39.7
Machine operators, assemblers, and inspectors	14.19	39.0	14.17	39.0	17.59	38.0
Transportation and material moving	15.28	37.7	15.10	38.1	17.01	34.5
Handlers, equipment cleaners, helpers, and laborers	11.63	35.3	11.43	35.1	14.90	38.6
Service occupations	10.89	31.7	9.38	30.6	17.55	37.0
Full-time	19.70	39.6	18.95	39.7	23.73	38.8
Part-time	10.52	20.5	10.15	20.6	15.80	19.1
Union	22.65	36.7	20.67	36.6	25.49	36.8
Nonunion	17.77	35.5	17.43	35.4	21.22	36.8
Time	18.33	35.5	17.43	35.3	23.31	36.8
Incentive	24.12	38.7	24.11	38.7	. . .	. . .
Establishment Characteristics						
Goods-producing	(5)	(5)	19.60	39.5	(5)	(5)
Service-producing	(5)	(5)	17.19	34.3	(5)	(5)
1 to 99 workers[6]	15.73	34.4	15.69	34.4	18.86	36.6
100 to 499 workers	18.13	36.4	17.72	36.4	21.79	35.9
500 to 999 workers	20.79	36.9	19.94	37.2	23.83	35.8
1,000 to 2,499 workers	21.65	36.9	21.07	37.0	23.37	36.4
2,500 workers or more	25.44	37.3	27.05	37.1	24.06	37.5
Geographic Areas[7]						
Metropolitan[8]	19.37	35.7	18.58	35.5	24.20	36.7
Nonmetropolitan[8]	14.63	35.7	13.57	35.5	19.53	36.9
New England	20.81	34.3	19.97	34.1	26.72	35.5
Middle Atlantic	21.19	35.1	20.27	35.0	26.67	35.7
South Atlantic	17.72	36.2	17.19	35.9	20.40	38.1
East South Central	14.66	37.0	14.06	37.0	19.16	37.3
West South Central	16.36	36.6	15.73	36.3	19.64	38.3
East North Central	18.91	35.3	18.11	35.2	24.27	36.1
West North Central	17.09	35.4	16.18	35.0	22.13	37.2
Mountain	17.30	35.8	16.31	35.5	23.27	37.1
Pacific	20.83	35.4	19.74	35.4	27.10	35.6

[1]Earnings are the straight-time hourly wages or salaries paid to employees. They include incentive pay, cost-of-living adjustments, and hazard pay. Excluded are premium pay for overtime, vacations, and holidays; nonproduction bonuses; and tips. The mean is computed by totaling the pay of all workers and dividing by the number of workers, weighted by hours.

[2]This survey covers all 50 states. Data collection was conducted between December 2004 and January 2006. The average reference period was June 2005.

[3]Employees are classified as working either a full-time or part-time schedule based on the definition used by each establishment. Union workers are those whose wages are determined through collective bargaining. Wages of time workers are based solely on hourly rate or salary; incentive workers are those whose wages are at least partly based on productivity payments such as piece rates, commissions, and production bonuses.

[4]A classification system including about 480 individual occupations is used to cover all workers in the civilian economy.

[5]Classification of establishments into goods-producing and service-producing industries applies to private industry only.

[6]Estimates include private establishments employing 1 to 99 workers and state and local government establishments employing 50 to 99 workers.

[7]The states that comprise the Census divisions are: New England—Connecticut, Maine, Massachusetts, New Hampshire, Rhode Island, and Vermont; Middle Atlantic—New Jersey, New York, and Pennsylvania; South Atlantic—Delaware, District of Columbia, Florida, Georgia, Maryland, North Carolina, South Carolina, Virginia, and West Virginia; East South Central—Alabama, Kentucky, Mississippi, and Tennessee; West South Central—Arkansas, Louisiana, Oklahoma, and Texas; East North Central—Illinois, Indiana, Michigan, Ohio, and Wisconsin; West North Central—Iowa, Kansas, Minnesota, Missouri, Nebraska, North Dakota, and South Dakota; Mountain—Arizona, Colorado, Idaho, Montana, Nevada, New Mexico, Utah, and Wyoming; and Pacific—Alaska, California, Hawaii, Oregon, and Washington.

[8]A metropolitan area can be a Metropolitan Statistical Area (MSA) or a Consolidated Metropolitan Statistical Area (CMSA), as defined by the Office of Management and Budget in 1994. Nonmetropolitan areas are counties that do not fit the definitions above.

. . . = Not available.

Table 6-12. Mean Hourly Earnings[1] and Weekly Hours for Selected Characteristics, Metropolitan and Nonmetropolitan Areas,[2] National Compensation Survey,[3] June 2005

(Dollars, number of hours.)

Characteristic	Total		Metropolitan areas		Nonmetropolitan areas	
	Mean hourly earnings	Mean weekly hours	Mean hourly earnings	Mean weekly hours	Mean hourly earnings	Mean weekly hours
TOTAL	18.62	35.7	19.37	35.7	14.63	35.7
Industry						
Private industry	17.82	35.5	18.58	35.5	13.57	35.5
State and local government	23.31	36.8	24.20	36.7	19.53	36.9
Worker Characteristics[4]						
White-collar occupations[5]	22.96	36.0	23.68	36.1	17.88	35.7
Professional specialty and technical	30.24	36.2	31.00	36.2	24.56	36.0
Executive, administrative, and managerial	33.69	39.8	34.32	39.8	27.75	40.1
Sales	15.32	32.4	16.01	32.3	11.49	32.9
Administrative support	14.53	36.5	14.86	36.5	12.32	36.1
Blue-collar occupations[5]	15.87	38.1	16.25	38.0	14.30	38.4
Precision production, craft, and repair	19.95	39.6	20.49	39.5	17.51	39.9
Machine operators, assemblers, and inspectors	14.19	39.0	14.42	39.0	13.30	39.1
Transportation and material moving	15.28	37.7	15.52	37.6	14.27	38.4
Handlers, equipment cleaners, helpers, and laborers	11.63	35.3	11.87	35.2	10.57	35.7
Service occupations[5]	10.89	31.7	11.26	31.5	9.37	32.2
Full-time	19.70	39.6	20.50	39.6	15.40	39.7
Part-time	10.52	20.5	10.82	20.5	8.92	20.6
Union	22.65	36.7	23.07	36.5	19.56	38.0
Nonunion	17.77	35.5	18.55	35.5	13.87	35.4
Time	18.33	35.5	19.05	35.5	14.51	35.5
Incentive	24.12	38.7	25.17	38.5	17.18	40.4
Establishment Characteristics						
Goods-producing[6]	19.60	39.5	...	...	...	...
Service-producing[6]	17.19	34.3	...	...	...	...
1 to 99 workers[7]	15.73	34.4	16.28	34.5	13.17	33.9
100 to 499 workers	18.13	36.4	18.62	36.2	15.68	37.0
500 to 999 workers	20.79	36.9	21.58	36.7	17.23	37.4
1,000 to 2,499 workers	21.65	36.9	23.31	36.5	15.05	38.4
2,500 workers or more	25.44	37.3	25.75	37.2	17.65	39.9
Geographic Areas[8]						
New England	20.81	34.3	21.41	34.4	16.88	33.9
Middle Atlantic	21.19	35.1	21.44	35.1	16.74	34.4
South Atlantic	17.72	36.2	18.41	36.1	14.13	36.7
East South Central	14.66	37.0	15.93	36.5	12.88	37.9
West South Central	16.36	36.6	16.89	36.8	13.61	35.6
East North Central	18.91	35.3	19.49	35.3	15.68	35.3
West North Central	17.09	35.4	18.28	35.6	14.11	34.7
Mountain	17.30	35.8	17.73	35.9	15.80	35.2
Pacific	20.83	35.4	21.15	35.5	16.30	34.1

[1]Earnings are the straight-time hourly wages or salaries paid to employees. They include incentive pay, cost-of-living adjustments, and hazard pay. Excluded are premium pay for overtime, vacations, and holidays; nonproduction bonuses; and tips. The mean is computed by totaling the pay of all workers and dividing by the number of workers, weighted by hours.

[2]A metropolitan area can be a Metropolitan Statistical Area (MSA) or a Consolidated Metropolitan Statistical Area (CMSA), as defined by the Office of Management and Budget in 1994. Nonmetropolitan areas are counties that do not fit the definitions above.

[3]This survey covers all 50 states. Data collection was conducted between December 2004 and January 2006. The average reference period was June 2005.

[4]Employees are classified as working either a full-time or a part-time schedule based on the definition used by each establishment. Union workers are those whose wages are determined through collective bargaining. Wages of time workers are based solely on hourly rate or salary; incentive workers are those whose wages are at least partly based on productivity payments such as piece rates, commissions, and production bonuses.

[5]A classification system including about 480 individual occupations is used to cover all workers in the civilian economy.

[6]Classification of establishments into goods-producing and service-producing industries applies to private industry only.

[7]Estimates include private establishments employing 1 to 99 workers and state and local government establishments employing 50 to 99 workers.

[8]The states that comprise the Census divisions are: New England—Connecticut, Maine, Massachusetts, New Hampshire, Rhode Island, and Vermont; Middle Atlantic—New Jersey, New York, and Pennsylvania; South Atlantic—Delaware, District of Columbia, Florida, Georgia, Maryland, North Carolina, South Carolina, Virginia, and West Virginia; East South Central—Alabama, Kentucky, Mississippi, and Tennessee; West South Central—Arkansas, Louisiana, Oklahoma, and Texas; East North Central—Illinois, Indiana, Michigan, Ohio, and Wisconsin; West North Central—Iowa, Kansas, Minnesota, Missouri, Nebraska, North Dakota, and South Dakota; Mountain—Arizona, Colorado, Idaho, Montana, Nevada, New Mexico, Utah, and Wyoming; and Pacific—Alaska, California, Hawaii, Oregon, and Washington.

. . . = Not available.

Table 6-13. Mean Hourly Earnings[1] and Weekly Hours for Selected Occupations, Full-Time and Part-Time Workers,[2] National Compensation Survey,[3] June 2005

(Dollars, number of hours.)

Occupation[4]	Total		Full-time		Part-time	
	Mean hourly earnings	Mean weekly hours	Mean hourly earnings	Mean weekly hours	Mean hourly earnings	Mean weekly hours
ALL OCCUPATIONS	18.62	35.7	19.70	39.6	10.52	20.5
White-Collar Occupations	22.96	36.0	24.03	39.5	13.46	20.3
Professional specialty and technical	30.24	36.2	30.66	39.0	24.80	18.6
Executive, administrative, and managerial	33.69	39.8	33.78	40.3	26.43	20.0
Sales	15.32	32.4	17.84	40.1	8.14	20.9
Administrative support, including clerical	14.53	36.5	14.82	39.3	11.62	21.1
Blue-Collar Occupations	15.87	38.1	16.27	40.1	9.60	21.3
Precision production, craft, and repair	19.95	39.6	20.04	40.0	12.60	21.2
Machine operators, assemblers, and inspectors	14.19	39.0	14.32	39.8	9.39	23.7
Transportation and material moving	15.28	37.7	15.69	40.9	10.80	20.5
Handlers, equipment cleaners, helpers, and laborers	11.63	35.3	12.14	39.9	8.69	21.3
Service	10.89	31.7	12.01	38.9	7.59	20.4

[1]Earnings are the straight-time hourly wages or salaries paid to employees. They include incentive pay, cost-of-living adjustments, and hazard pay. Excluded are premium pay for overtime, vacations, and holidays; nonproduction bonuses; and tips. The mean is computed by totaling the pay of all workers and dividing by the number of workers, weighted by hours.
[2]Total includes full-time and part-time workers. Employees are classified as working either a full-time or a part-time schedule based on the definition used by each establishment. Therefore, a worker with a 35-hour-per-week schedule might be considered a full-time employee in one establishment but a part-time employee in another establishment, where a 40-hour week is the minimum full-time schedule.
[3]This survey covers all 50 states. Data collection was conducted between December 2004 and January 2006. The average reference period was June 2005.
[4]A classification system including about 480 individual occupations is used to cover all workers in the civilian economy.

CHAPTER SEVEN

PRICES

PRICES

HIGHLIGHTS

This chapter examines the movement of prices, which is one of the most important indicators of the state of the economy. Several indexes are covered: the Producer Price Index (PPI), which gives information about prices received by producers; the Consumer Price Index (CPI), which gives information about prices paid by consumers; and the Import Price Index (MPI) and the Export Price Index (XPI), which give information about prices involved in various foreign trade, export, and import price indexes.

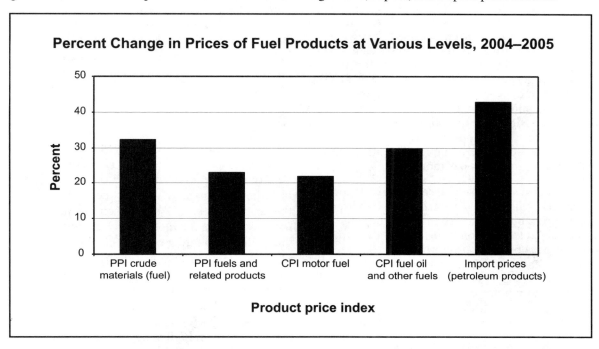

The price indexes show the sharp increase in the price of fuel and fuel products from 2004 to 2005. The content of these products in the various indexes may not be identical; however, they essentially refer to petroleum fuel products. (See Tables 7-1, 7-8, and 7-13.)

OTHER HIGHLIGHTS

- While a great deal of attention has been paid to energy prices, another important component, materials and components for construction, has increased significantly in the last two years. This value rose 8.3 percent in 2004 and 6.1 percent in 2005. (See Table 7-1.)

- In 2005, the PPI for capital equipment continued to grow at a much slower rate (2.3 percent) than the PPI for consumer goods (5.7 percent). (See Table 7-1.)

- The PPI for all commodities rose 7.3 percent in 2005. Since 1999, it has increased 25.4 percent. However, from 1994 to 1999, it only increased 4.2 percent. (See Table 7-2.)

- While prices of imported commodities rose 8 percent between December 2004 and December 2005, petroleum products rose 42.8 percent and natural and manufactured gas rose 50.2 percent. (See Table 7-13.)

NOTES AND DEFINITIONS

PRODUCER PRICE INDEX

Collection and Coverage

The *Producer Price Index (PPI)* measures average changes in prices received by domestic producers of goods and services. Most of the information used in calculating the indexes is obtained through the systematic sampling of nearly every industry in the manufacturing and mining sectors of the economy. The PPI program also includes data from other sectors, including agriculture, fishing, and forestry; services; and gas and electricity. As producer price indexes are designed to measure only the change in prices received for the output of domestic industries, imports are not included. The sample currently contains about 80,000 price quotations per month.

Producer price indexes are based on selling prices reported by establishments of all sizes as selected by probability sampling, with the probability of selection proportional to size. Individual items and transaction terms from these firms are also chosen by probability proportionate to size. The Bureau of Labor Statistics (BLS) strongly encourages cooperating companies to supply actual transaction prices at the time of shipment to minimize the use of list prices. Prices are normally reported monthly by mail questionnaire for the Tuesday of the week containing the 13th of the month

Price data are always provided on a voluntary and confidential basis; only BLS employees, prohibited from revealing, are allowed access to individual company price reports. BLS publishes price indexes instead of unit dollar prices. All producer price indexes are routinely subject to revision four months after the original publication to reflect the availability of late reports and corrections by respondents.

There are three primary systems of indexes within the PPI program: (1) stage-of-processing indexes; (2) indexes for the net output of industries and their products; and (3) commodity indexes. The commodity-based stage-of-processing structure organizes products by class of buyer and degree of fabrication. The entire output of various industries is sampled to derive price indexes for the net output of industries and their products. The commodity structure organizes products by similarity of end-use or material composition.

Within the commodity-based stage-of-processing system, finished goods are commodities that will not undergo further processing and they are ready for sale to the final demand user—either an individual consumer or a business firm. Consumer foods include unprocessed foods, such as eggs and fresh vegetables, as well as processed foods, such as bakery products and meats. Other finished consumer goods include durable goods, such as automobiles, household furniture, and appliances; and nondurable goods, such as apparel and home heating oil. Capital equipment includes producer durable goods, such as heavy motor trucks, tractors, and machine tools.

Producer price indexes for the net output of industries and their products are grouped according to the Standard Industrial Classification (SIC) system and the Census Bureau product code extensions of the SIC. Industry price indexes are compatible with other economic time series organized by SIC codes, such as data on employment, wages, and productivity.

Net output values of shipments are used as weights for industry indexes and refer to the value of shipments from establishments in one industry shipped to establishments classified in another industry. However, *weights for commodity price indexes* are based on gross shipment values, including shipment values between establishments within the same industry. As a result, commodity aggregate indexes, such as the *all commodities index*, are affected by the multiple counting of price change at successive stages of processing. This can lead to exaggerated or misleading signals about inflation. Stage-of-processing indexes partly correct this defect, but industry indexes consistently correct this weakness at all levels of aggregation. Therefore, industry and stage-of-processing indexes are more appropriate than commodity aggregate indexes for economic analysis of general price trends.

Weights for most traditional commodity groupings of the PPI, as well as all indexes calculated from traditional commodity groupings (such as stage-of-processing indexes), are currently and primarily calculated with 1997 net output weights and 1992 input-output relationships.

With the release of data for January 2004, the PPI program changed its basis for industry classification from the 1987 SIC system to the North American Industry Classification System (NAICS). The PPI treats the SIC-to-NAICS comparison as continuous if 80 percent or more of the weight of the SIC-based index comprises at least 80 percent of the weight of the NAICS-based index. All index series that have passed this test are published under the NAICS structure using the index base date and price index history established by the SIC-based index.

Sources of Additional Information

Additional information is published monthly by the BLS in the *Producer Price Index Detailed Report*. For information on the underlying concepts and methodology of the Producer Price Index, see Chapter 14 in the *BLS Handbook of Methods*, which is available on the BLS Web site at <http://www.bls.gov>.

Table 7-1. Producer Price Indexes, by Stage of Processing, 1947–2005

(1982 = 100.)

Year	Crude materials for further processing				Intermediate materials, supplies, and components						Finished goods		
	Total	Foodstuffs and feedstuffs	Nonfood materials, except fuel	Fuel	Total	Materials and components for construction	Components for manufacturing	Processed fuels and lubricants	Containers	Supplies	Total	Consumer goods	Capital equipment
1947	31.7	45.1	24.0	7.5	23.3	22.5	21.3	14.4	23.4	28.5	26.4	28.6	19.8
1948	34.7	48.8	26.7	8.9	25.2	24.9	23.0	16.4	24.4	29.8	28.5	30.8	21.6
1949	30.1	40.5	24.3	8.8	24.2	24.9	23.4	14.9	24.5	28.0	27.7	29.4	22.7
1950	32.7	43.4	27.8	8.8	25.3	26.2	24.3	15.2	25.2	29.0	28.2	29.9	23.2
1951	37.6	50.2	32.0	9.0	28.4	28.7	27.6	15.9	29.6	32.6	30.8	32.7	25.5
1952	34.5	47.3	27.8	9.0	27.5	28.5	27.6	15.7	28.0	32.6	30.6	32.3	25.9
1953	31.9	42.3	26.6	9.3	27.7	29.0	28.1	15.8	28.0	31.0	30.3	31.7	26.3
1954	31.6	42.3	26.1	8.9	27.9	29.1	28.3	15.8	28.5	31.7	30.4	31.7	26.7
1955	30.4	38.4	27.5	8.9	28.4	30.3	29.5	15.8	28.9	31.2	30.5	31.5	27.4
1956	30.6	37.6	28.6	9.5	29.6	31.8	32.2	16.3	31.0	32.0	31.3	32.0	29.5
1957	31.2	39.2	28.2	10.1	30.3	32.0	33.5	17.2	32.4	32.3	32.5	32.9	31.3
1958	31.9	41.6	27.1	10.2	30.4	32.0	33.8	16.2	33.2	33.1	33.2	33.6	32.1
1959	31.1	38.8	28.1	10.4	30.8	32.9	34.2	16.2	33.0	33.5	33.1	33.3	32.7
1960	30.4	38.4	26.9	10.5	30.8	32.7	34.0	16.6	33.4	33.3	33.4	33.6	32.8
1961	30.2	37.9	27.2	10.5	30.6	32.2	33.7	16.8	33.2	33.7	33.4	33.6	32.9
1962	30.5	38.6	27.1	10.4	30.6	32.1	33.4	16.7	33.6	34.5	33.5	33.7	33.0
1963	29.9	37.5	26.7	10.5	30.7	32.2	33.4	16.6	33.2	35.0	33.4	33.5	33.1
1964	29.6	36.6	27.2	10.5	30.8	32.5	33.7	16.2	32.9	34.7	33.5	33.6	33.4
1965	31.1	39.2	27.7	10.6	31.2	32.8	34.2	16.5	33.5	35.0	34.1	34.2	33.8
1966	33.1	42.7	28.3	10.9	32.0	33.6	35.4	16.8	34.5	36.5	35.2	35.4	34.6
1967	31.3	40.3	26.5	11.3	32.2	34.0	36.5	16.9	35.0	36.8	35.6	35.6	35.8
1968	31.8	40.9	27.1	11.5	33.0	35.7	37.3	16.5	35.9	37.1	36.6	36.5	37.0
1969	33.9	44.1	28.4	12.0	34.1	37.7	38.5	16.6	37.2	37.8	38.0	37.9	38.3
1970	35.2	45.2	29.1	13.8	35.4	38.3	40.6	17.7	39.0	39.7	39.3	39.1	40.1
1971	36.0	46.1	29.4	15.7	36.8	40.8	41.9	19.5	40.8	40.8	40.5	40.2	41.7
1972	39.9	51.5	32.3	16.8	38.2	43.0	42.9	20.1	42.7	42.5	41.8	41.5	42.8
1973	54.5	72.6	42.9	18.6	42.4	46.5	44.3	22.2	45.2	51.7	45.6	46.0	44.2
1974	61.4	76.4	54.5	24.8	52.5	55.0	51.1	33.6	53.3	56.8	52.6	53.1	50.5
1975	61.6	77.4	50.0	30.6	58.0	60.1	57.8	39.4	60.0	61.8	58.2	58.2	58.2
1976	63.4	76.8	54.9	34.5	60.9	64.1	60.8	42.3	63.1	65.8	60.8	60.4	62.1
1977	65.5	77.5	56.3	42.0	64.9	69.3	64.5	47.7	65.9	69.3	64.7	64.3	66.1
1978	73.4	87.3	61.9	48.2	69.5	76.5	69.2	49.9	71.0	72.9	69.8	69.4	71.3
1979	85.9	100.0	75.5	57.3	78.4	84.2	75.8	61.6	79.4	80.2	77.6	77.5	77.5
1980	95.3	104.6	91.8	69.4	90.3	91.3	84.6	85.0	89.1	89.9	88.0	88.6	85.8
1981	103.0	103.9	109.8	84.8	98.6	97.9	94.7	100.6	96.7	96.9	96.1	96.6	94.6
1982	100.0	100.0	100.0	100.0	100.0	100.0	100.0	100.0	100.0	100.0	100.0	100.0	100.0
1983	101.3	101.8	98.8	105.1	100.6	102.8	102.4	95.4	100.4	101.8	101.6	101.3	102.8
1984	103.5	104.7	101.0	105.1	103.1	105.6	105.0	95.7	105.9	104.1	103.7	103.3	105.2
1985	95.8	94.8	94.3	102.7	102.7	107.3	106.4	92.8	109.0	104.4	104.7	103.8	107.5
1986	87.7	93.2	76.0	92.2	99.1	108.1	107.5	72.7	110.3	105.6	103.2	101.4	109.7
1987	93.7	96.2	88.5	84.1	101.5	109.8	108.8	73.3	114.5	107.7	105.4	103.6	111.7
1988	96.0	106.1	85.9	82.1	107.1	116.1	112.3	71.2	120.1	113.7	108.0	106.2	114.3
1989	103.1	111.2	95.8	85.3	112.0	121.3	116.4	76.4	125.4	118.1	113.6	112.1	118.8
1990	108.9	113.1	107.3	84.8	114.5	122.9	119.0	85.9	127.7	119.4	119.2	118.2	122.9
1991	101.2	105.5	97.5	82.9	114.4	124.5	121.0	85.3	128.1	121.4	121.7	120.5	126.7
1992	100.4	105.1	94.2	84.0	114.7	126.5	122.0	84.5	127.7	122.7	123.2	121.7	129.1
1993	102.4	108.4	94.1	87.1	116.2	132.0	123.0	84.7	126.4	125.0	124.7	123.0	131.4
1994	101.8	106.5	97.0	82.4	118.5	136.6	124.3	83.1	129.7	127.0	125.5	123.3	134.1
1995	102.7	105.8	105.8	72.1	124.9	142.1	126.5	84.2	148.8	132.1	127.9	125.6	136.7
1996	113.8	121.5	105.7	92.6	125.7	143.6	126.9	90.0	141.1	135.9	131.3	129.5	138.3
1997	111.1	112.2	103.5	101.3	125.6	146.5	126.4	89.3	136.0	135.9	131.8	130.2	138.2
1998	96.8	103.9	84.5	86.7	123.0	146.8	125.9	81.1	140.8	134.8	130.7	128.9	137.6
1999	98.2	98.7	91.1	91.2	123.2	148.9	125.7	84.6	142.5	134.2	133.0	132.0	137.6
2000	120.6	100.2	118.0	136.9	129.2	150.7	126.2	102.0	151.6	136.9	138.0	138.2	138.8
2001	121.0	106.1	101.5	151.4	129.7	150.6	126.4	104.5	153.1	138.7	140.7	141.5	139.7
2002	108.1	99.5	101.0	117.3	127.8	151.3	126.1	96.3	152.1	138.9	138.9	139.4	139.1
2003	135.3	113.5	116.9	185.7	133.7	153.6	125.9	112.6	153.7	141.5	143.3	145.3	139.5
2004	159.0	127.0	149.2	211.4	142.6	166.4	127.4	124.3	159.3	146.7	148.5	151.7	141.4
2005	182.2	122.7	176.7	279.7	154.0	176.6	129.9	150.0	167.1	151.9	155.7	160.4	144.6

Table 7-2. Producer Price Indexes, by Commodity Group, 1913–2005

(1982 = 100.)

Year	All com-modities	Farm products	Processed foods and feeds	Industrial commodities													
				Total	Textile products and apparel	Hides, leather, and related products	Fuels and related products and power	Chemi-cals and related products	Rubber and plastics products	Lumber and wood products	Pulp, paper, and allied products	Metals and metal products	Machin-ery and equip-ment	Furniture and house-hold durables	Non-metallic mineral products	Trans-porta-tion equip-ment	Miscel-laneous products
1913	12.0	18.0	...	11.9	...	...	...	...	...	...	...	...	...	...	...	...	...
1914	11.8	17.9	...	11.3	...	...	...	...	...	...	...	...	...	...	...	...	...
1915	12.0	18.0	...	11.6	...	...	...	...	...	...	...	...	...	...	...	...	...
1916	14.7	21.3	...	15.0	...	...	...	...	...	...	...	...	...	...	...	...	...
1917	20.2	32.6	...	19.5	...	...	...	...	...	...	...	...	...	...	...	...	...
1918	22.6	37.4	...	21.1	...	...	...	...	...	...	...	...	...	...	...	...	...
1919	23.9	39.8	...	22.0	...	...	...	...	...	...	...	...	...	...	...	...	...
1920	26.6	38.0	...	27.4	...	...	...	...	...	...	...	...	...	...	...	...	...
1921	16.8	22.3	...	17.8	...	...	...	...	...	...	...	...	...	...	...	...	...
1922	16.7	23.7	...	17.4	...	...	...	...	...	...	...	...	...	...	...	...	...
1923	17.3	24.9	...	17.8	...	...	...	...	...	...	...	...	...	...	...	...	...
1924	16.9	25.2	...	17.0	...	...	...	...	...	...	...	...	...	...	...	...	...
1925	17.8	27.7	...	17.5	...	...	...	...	...	...	...	...	...	...	...	...	...
1926	17.2	25.3	...	17.0	...	17.1	10.3	...	47.1	9.3	...	13.7	...	28.6	16.4	...	...
1927	16.5	25.1	...	16.0	...	18.4	9.1	...	35.7	8.8	...	12.9	...	27.9	15.7	...	...
1928	16.7	26.7	...	15.8	...	20.7	8.7	...	28.3	8.5	...	12.9	...	27.2	16.2	...	...
1929	16.4	26.4	...	15.6	...	18.6	8.6	...	24.6	8.8	...	13.3	...	27.0	16.0	...	...
1930	14.9	22.4	...	14.5	...	17.1	8.1	...	21.5	8.0	...	12.0	...	26.5	15.9	...	...
1931	12.6	16.4	...	12.8	...	14.7	7.0	...	18.3	6.5	...	10.8	...	24.4	14.9	...	...
1932	11.2	12.2	...	11.9	...	12.5	7.3	...	15.9	5.6	...	9.9	...	21.5	13.9	...	...
1933	11.4	13.0	...	12.1	...	13.8	6.9	16.2	16.7	6.7	...	10.2	...	21.6	14.7	...	...
1934	12.9	16.5	...	13.3	...	14.8	7.6	17.0	19.5	7.8	...	11.2	...	23.4	15.7	...	...
1935	13.8	19.8	...	13.3	...	15.3	7.6	17.7	19.6	7.5	...	11.2	...	23.2	15.7	...	...
1936	13.9	20.4	...	13.5	...	16.3	7.9	17.8	21.1	7.9	...	11.4	...	23.6	15.8	...	...
1937	14.9	21.8	...	14.5	...	17.9	8.0	18.6	24.9	9.3	...	13.1	...	26.1	16.1	...	...
1938	13.5	17.3	...	13.9	...	15.8	7.9	17.7	24.4	8.5	...	12.6	...	25.5	15.6	...	...
1939	13.3	16.5	...	13.9	...	16.3	7.5	17.6	25.4	8.7	...	12.5	14.8	25.4	15.3	...	...
1940	13.5	17.1	...	14.1	...	17.2	7.4	17.9	23.7	9.6	...	12.5	14.9	26.0	15.3	...	...
1941	15.1	20.8	...	15.1	...	18.4	7.9	19.5	25.5	11.5	...	12.8	15.1	27.6	15.7	...	...
1942	17.0	26.7	...	16.2	...	20.1	8.1	21.7	29.7	12.5	...	13.0	15.4	29.9	16.3	...	...
1943	17.8	30.9	...	16.5	...	20.1	8.3	21.9	30.5	13.2	...	12.9	15.2	29.7	16.4	...	...
1944	17.9	31.2	...	16.7	...	19.9	8.6	22.2	30.1	14.3	...	12.9	15.1	30.5	16.7	...	...
1945	18.2	32.4	...	17.0	...	20.1	8.7	22.3	29.2	14.5	...	13.1	15.1	30.5	17.4	...	...
1946	20.8	37.5	...	18.6	...	23.3	9.3	24.1	29.3	16.6	...	14.7	16.6	32.4	18.5	...	...
1947	25.6	45.1	33.0	22.7	50.6	31.7	11.1	32.1	29.2	25.8	25.1	18.2	19.3	37.2	20.7	...	26.6
1948	27.7	48.5	35.3	24.6	52.8	32.1	13.1	32.8	30.2	29.5	26.2	20.7	20.9	39.4	22.4	...	27.7
1949	26.3	41.9	32.1	24.1	48.3	30.4	12.4	30.0	29.2	27.3	25.1	20.9	21.9	40.1	23.0	...	28.2
1950	27.3	44.0	33.2	25.0	50.2	32.9	12.6	30.4	35.6	31.4	25.7	22.0	22.6	40.9	23.5	...	28.6
1951	30.4	51.2	36.9	27.6	56.0	37.7	13.0	34.8	43.7	34.1	30.5	24.5	25.3	44.4	25.0	...	30.3
1952	29.6	48.4	36.4	26.9	50.5	30.5	13.0	33.0	39.6	33.2	29.7	24.5	25.3	43.5	25.0	...	30.2
1953	29.2	43.8	34.8	27.2	49.3	31.0	13.4	33.4	36.9	33.1	29.6	25.3	25.9	44.4	26.0	...	31.0
1954	29.3	43.2	35.4	27.2	48.2	29.5	13.2	33.8	37.5	32.5	29.6	25.5	26.3	44.9	26.6	...	31.3
1955	29.3	40.5	33.8	27.8	48.2	29.4	13.2	33.7	42.4	34.1	30.4	27.2	27.2	45.1	27.3	...	31.3
1956	30.3	40.0	33.8	29.1	48.2	31.2	13.6	33.9	43.0	34.6	32.4	29.6	29.3	46.3	28.5	...	31.7
1957	31.2	41.1	34.8	29.9	48.3	31.2	14.3	34.6	42.8	32.8	33.0	30.2	31.4	47.5	29.6	...	32.6
1958	31.6	42.9	36.5	30.0	47.4	31.6	13.7	34.9	42.8	32.5	33.4	30.0	32.1	47.9	29.9	...	33.3
1959	31.7	40.2	35.6	30.5	48.1	35.9	13.7	34.8	42.6	34.7	33.7	30.6	32.8	48.0	30.3	...	33.4
1960	31.7	40.1	35.6	30.5	48.6	34.6	13.9	34.8	42.7	33.5	34.0	30.6	33.0	47.8	30.4	...	33.6
1961	31.6	39.7	36.2	30.4	47.8	34.9	14.0	34.5	41.1	32.0	33.0	30.5	33.0	47.5	30.5	...	33.7
1962	31.7	40.4	36.5	30.4	48.2	35.3	14.0	33.9	39.9	32.2	33.4	30.2	33.0	47.2	30.5	...	33.9
1963	31.6	39.6	36.8	30.3	48.2	34.3	13.9	33.5	40.1	32.8	33.1	30.3	33.1	46.9	30.3	...	34.2
1964	31.6	39.0	36.7	30.5	48.5	34.4	13.5	33.6	39.6	33.5	33.0	31.1	33.3	47.1	30.4	...	34.4

. . . = Not available.

Table 7-2. Producer Price Indexes, by Commodity Group, 1913–2005—*Continued*

(1982 = 100.)

Year	All commodities	Farm products	Processed foods and feeds	Industrial commodities													
				Total	Textile products and apparel	Hides, leather, and related products	Fuels and related products and power	Chemicals and related products	Rubber and plastics products	Lumber and wood products	Pulp, paper, and allied products	Metals and metal products	Machinery and equipment	Furniture and household durables	Nonmetallic mineral products	Transportation equipment	Miscellaneous products
1965	32.3	40.7	38.0	30.9	48.8	35.9	13.8	33.9	39.7	33.7	33.3	32.0	33.7	46.8	30.4	. . .	34.7
1966	33.3	43.7	40.2	31.5	48.9	39.4	14.1	34.0	40.5	35.2	34.2	32.8	34.7	47.4	30.7	. . .	35.3
1967	33.4	41.3	39.8	32.0	48.9	38.1	14.4	34.2	41.4	35.1	34.6	33.2	35.9	48.3	31.2	. . .	36.2
1968	34.2	42.3	40.6	32.8	50.7	39.3	14.3	34.1	42.8	39.8	35.0	34.0	37.0	49.7	32.4	. . .	37.0
1969	35.6	45.0	42.7	33.9	51.8	41.5	14.6	34.2	43.6	44.0	36.0	36.0	38.2	50.7	33.6	40.4	38.1
1970	36.9	45.8	44.6	35.2	52.4	42.0	15.3	35.0	44.9	39.9	37.5	38.7	40.0	51.9	35.3	41.9	39.8
1971	38.1	46.6	45.5	36.5	53.3	43.4	16.6	35.6	45.2	44.7	38.1	39.4	41.4	53.1	38.2	44.2	40.8
1972	39.8	51.6	48.0	37.8	55.5	50.0	17.1	35.6	45.3	50.7	39.3	40.9	42.3	53.8	39.4	45.5	41.5
1973	45.0	72.7	58.9	40.3	60.5	54.5	19.4	37.6	46.6	62.2	42.3	44.0	43.7	55.7	40.7	46.1	43.3
1974	53.5	77.4	68.0	49.2	68.0	55.2	30.1	50.2	56.4	64.5	52.5	57.0	50.0	61.8	47.8	50.3	48.1
1975	58.4	77.0	72.6	54.9	67.4	56.5	35.4	62.0	62.2	62.1	59.0	61.5	57.9	67.5	54.4	56.7	53.4
1976	61.1	78.8	70.8	58.4	72.4	63.9	38.3	64.0	66.0	72.2	62.1	65.0	61.3	70.3	58.2	60.5	55.6
1977	64.9	79.4	74.0	62.5	75.3	68.3	43.6	65.9	69.4	83.0	64.6	69.3	65.2	73.2	62.6	64.6	59.4
1978	69.9	87.7	80.6	67.0	78.1	76.1	46.5	68.0	72.4	96.9	67.7	75.3	70.3	77.5	69.6	69.5	66.7
1979	78.7	99.6	88.5	75.7	82.5	96.1	58.9	76.0	80.5	105.5	75.9	86.0	76.7	82.8	77.6	75.3	75.5
1980	89.8	102.9	95.9	88.0	89.7	94.7	82.8	89.0	90.1	101.5	86.3	95.0	86.0	90.7	88.4	82.9	93.6
1981	98.0	105.2	98.9	97.4	97.6	99.3	100.2	98.4	96.4	102.8	94.8	99.6	94.4	95.9	96.7	94.3	96.1
1982	100.0	100.0	100.0	100.0	100.0	100.0	100.0	100.0	100.0	100.0	100.0	100.0	100.0	100.0	100.0	100.0	100.0
1983	101.3	102.4	101.8	101.1	100.3	103.2	95.9	100.3	100.8	107.9	103.3	101.8	102.7	103.4	101.6	102.8	104.8
1984	103.7	105.5	105.4	103.3	102.7	109.0	94.8	102.9	102.3	108.0	110.3	104.8	105.1	105.7	105.4	105.2	107.0
1985	103.2	95.1	103.5	103.7	102.9	108.9	91.4	103.7	101.9	106.6	113.3	104.4	107.2	107.1	108.6	107.9	109.4
1986	100.2	92.9	105.4	100.0	103.2	113.0	69.8	102.6	101.9	107.2	116.1	103.2	108.8	108.2	110.0	110.5	111.6
1987	102.8	95.5	107.9	102.6	105.1	120.4	70.2	106.4	103.0	112.8	121.8	107.1	110.4	109.9	110.0	112.5	114.9
1988	106.9	104.9	112.7	106.3	109.2	131.4	66.7	116.3	109.3	118.9	130.4	118.7	113.2	113.1	111.2	114.3	120.2
1989	112.2	110.9	117.8	111.6	112.3	136.3	72.9	123.0	112.6	126.7	137.8	124.1	117.4	116.9	112.6	117.7	126.5
1990	116.3	112.2	121.9	115.8	115.0	141.7	82.3	123.6	113.6	129.7	141.2	122.9	120.7	119.2	114.7	121.5	134.2
1991	116.5	105.7	121.9	116.5	116.3	138.9	81.2	125.6	115.1	132.1	142.9	120.2	123.0	121.2	117.2	126.4	140.8
1992	117.2	103.6	122.1	117.4	117.8	140.4	80.4	125.9	115.1	146.6	145.2	119.2	123.4	122.2	117.3	130.4	145.3
1993	118.9	107.1	124.0	119.0	118.0	143.7	80.0	128.2	116.0	174.0	147.3	119.2	124.0	123.7	120.0	133.7	145.4
1994	120.4	106.3	125.5	120.7	118.3	148.5	77.8	132.1	117.6	180.0	152.5	124.8	125.1	126.1	124.2	137.2	141.9
1995	124.7	107.4	127.0	125.5	120.8	153.7	78.0	142.5	124.3	178.1	172.2	134.5	126.6	128.2	129.0	139.7	145.4
1996	127.7	122.4	133.3	127.3	122.4	150.5	85.8	142.1	123.8	176.1	168.7	131.0	126.5	130.4	131.0	141.7	147.7
1997	127.6	112.9	134.0	127.7	122.6	154.2	86.1	143.6	123.2	183.8	167.9	131.8	125.9	130.8	133.2	141.6	150.9
1998	124.4	104.6	131.6	124.8	122.9	148.0	75.3	143.9	122.6	179.1	171.7	127.8	124.9	131.3	135.4	141.2	156.0
1999	125.5	98.4	131.1	126.5	121.1	146.0	80.5	144.2	122.5	183.6	174.1	124.6	124.3	131.7	138.9	141.8	166.6
2000	132.7	99.5	133.1	134.8	121.4	151.5	103.5	151.0	125.5	178.2	183.7	128.1	124.0	132.6	142.5	143.8	170.8
2001	134.2	103.8	137.3	135.7	121.3	158.4	105.3	151.8	127.2	174.4	184.8	125.4	123.7	133.2	144.3	145.2	181.3
2002	131.1	99.0	136.2	132.4	119.9	157.6	93.2	151.9	126.8	173.3	185.9	125.9	122.9	133.5	146.2	144.6	182.4
2003	138.1	111.5	143.4	139.1	119.8	162.3	112.9	161.8	130.1	177.4	190.0	122.1	121.9	133.9	148.2	145.7	179.6
2004	146.7	123.3	151.2	147.6	121.0	164.5	126.9	174.4	133.8	195.6	195.7	149.6	122.1	135.1	153.2	148.6	183.2
2005	157.4	118.5	153.1	160.2	122.8	165.4	156.4	192.0	143.8	196.5	202.6	160.8	123.7	139.4	164.2	151.0	195.1

. . . = Not available.

Table 7-3. Producer Price Indexes for the Net Output of Selected Industries, 1995–2005

(December 2003 = 100, unless otherwise indicated.)

Industry	1995	1996	1997	1998	1999	2000	2001	2002	2003	2004	2005
Agriculture, Forestry, Fishing, and Hunting											
Logging[1]	194.3	185.7	191.2	188.1	182.7	177.5	167.5	165.0	168.7	175.2	179.0
Mining											
Oil and gas extraction[2]	66.6	84.8	87.5	68.3	78.5	126.8	127.5	107.0	160.1	192.7	262.0
Mining (except oil and gas)	...	...	...	...	...	...	...	...	...	109.5	126.6
Coal mining[2]	91.6	91.4	92.2	89.5	87.3	84.8	91.3	93.9	94.4	104.1	118.2
Metal ore mining[3]	101.4	92.1	85.8	73.2	70.3	73.8	70.8	73.6	81.6	111.8	146.0
Iron ore mining[3]	91.0	95.7	95.3	94.5	94.0	93.9	95.2	94.2	95.0	97.2	115.7
Gold ore and silver ore mining[3]	77.1	78.6	67.9	61.1	58.2	57.0	55.2	62.6	72.6	82.6	89.5
Copper, nickel, lead, and zinc mining[4]	157.1	117.0	110.4	76.8	71.3	88.7	81.7	80.1	90.1	147.7	195.2
Other metal ore mining[2]	33.6	31.9	29.9	27.6	25.9	26.4	24.7	28.9	34.9	80.0	159.1
Nonmetallic mineral mining and quarrying[3]	123.8	127.1	128.8	132.2	134.0	137.0	141.0	143.5	146.4	151.2	161.3
Stone mining and quarrying[3]	130.7	133.2	135.4	138.8	142.1	147.3	152.2	156.1	160.2	166.1	176.7
Sand, gravel, clay, and refractory minerals mining	...	...	...	...	...	...	...	...	...	102.4	108.8
Other nonmetallic mineral mining and quarrying[3]	104.2	108.6	107.6	110.1	108.0	106.8	107.1	107.7	108.4	111.4	120.8
Mining support activities	...	...	...	...	...	...	...	...	...	104.8	133.9
Utilities											
Electric power generation, transmission, and distribution	...	...	...	...	...	...	...	...	...	104.9	117.6
Electric power generation	...	...	...	...	...	...	...	...	...	103.3	111.3
Electric power transmission, control, and distribution	...	...	...	...	...	...	...	...	...	105.2	121.6
Natural gas distribution	...	...	...	...	...	...	...	...	...	102.5	107.1
										107.3	126.6
Manufacturing											
Food[3]	121.7	127.1	127.9	126.3	126.3	128.5	132.8	132.0	137.4	144.3	146.1
Animal food	...	...	...	...	...	...	...	...	...	103.3	98.2
Grain and oilseed milling	...	...	...	...	...	...	...	...	...	103.1	99.8
Flour milling and malt	...	...	...	...	...	...	...	...	...	102.6	100.5
Starch and vegetable fats and oils	...	...	...	...	...	...	...	...	...	103.6	97.9
Breakfast cereal manufacturing	...	...	...	...	...	...	...	...	...	101.7	105.0
Sugar and confectionery product[3]	123.3	127.7	129.3	128.8	129.4	127.5	129.3	133.7	139.5	141.4	147.3
Sugar	...	...	...	...	...	...	...	...	...	99.7	105.6
Chocolate and confectionery from cacao beans	...	...	...	...	...	...	...	...	...	100.1	101.7
Confectionery from purchased chocolate	...	...	...	...	...	...	...	...	...	100.1	102.2
Nonchocolate confectionery	...	...	...	...	...	...	...	...	...	104.0	111.0
Fruit and vegetable preserving and specialty food[3]	125.5	129.7	129.9	130.1	131.7	132.1	133.3	135.2	136.6	139.2	141.7
Fruit and vegetable canning, pickling, and drying	...	...	...	...	...	...	...	...	...	100.5	104.0
Dairy product[3]	115.8	125.0	123.9	133.1	133.8	129.9	141.2	133.3	135.8	151.0	151.3
Ice cream and frozen dessert	...	...	...	...	...	...	...	...	...	103.3	104.7
Animal slaughtering and processing[3]	109.3	114.6	116.1	109.2	108.9	115.0	120.3	114.0	125.8	134.2	135.8
Seafood product preparation and packaging	...	...	...	...	...	...	...	...	...	102.4	106.2
Bakery and tortilla	...	...	...	...	...	...	...	...	...	100.8	102.6
Bread and bakery product	...	...	...	...	...	...	...	...	...	101.1	103.4
Cookie, cracker, and pasta	...	...	...	...	...	...	...	...	...	100.5	101.3
Tortilla	...	...	...	...	...	...	...	...	...	100.4	102.5
Other food	...	...	...	...	...	...	...	...	...	101.1	105.4
Snack food	...	...	...	...	...	...	...	...	...	101.4	108.4
Coffee and tea	...	...	...	...	...	...	...	...	...	101.7	115.1
Flavoring syrup and concentrate	...	...	...	...	...	...	...	...	...	101.0	103.1
Seasoning and dressing	...	...	...	...	...	...	...	...	...	101.1	101.3
All other food	...	...	...	...	...	...	...	...	...	100.4	100.8
Beverage and tobacco product	...	...	...	...	...	...	...	...	...	101.0	104.8
Beverage[3]	123.1	125.5	126.3	127.2	129.8	134.4	138.6	140.8	142.7	146.4	150.4
Soft drink and ice	...	...	...	...	...	...	...	...	...	102.1	104.1
Breweries	...	...	...	...	...	...	...	...	...	101.3	105.6
Wineries	...	...	...	...	...	...	...	...	...	100.7	104.2
Distilleries	...	...	...	...	...	...	...	...	...	100.1	100.6
Tobacco[3]	193.2	199.1	210.8	243.1	325.7	345.8	386.1	401.9	377.9	379.7	401.0
Tobacco stemming and redrying[5]	112.2	109.7	106.5	104.2	104.7	109.0	112.3	114.7	117.5	119.4	119.9
Tobacco product[6]	204.3	210.5	223.3	260.4	356.7	379.3	425.8	442.8	411.7	412.5	436.3
Textile mills	...	...	...	...	...	...	...	...	...	101.1	103.6
Fiber, yarn, and thread mills[3]	112.1	113.6	114.1	112.1	106.9	105.5	103.0	99.8	100.9	105.6	108.8
Fabric mills	...	...	...	...	...	...	...	...	...	101.0	103.0
Broadwoven fabric mills	...	...	...	...	...	...	...	...	...	101.1	103.2
Narrow fabric mills and schiffli mach embroidery[5]	119.7	121.2	122.7	123.8	124.3	125.3	126.2	126.0	125.1	126.2	129.3
Nonwoven fabric mills	...	...	...	...	...	...	...	...	...	101.5	105.6
Knit fabric mills	...	...	...	...	...	...	...	...	...	100.4	100.5
Textile fabric finishing/fabric coating mills	...	...	...	...	...	...	...	...	...	99.9	102.8
Textile and fabric finishing mills	...	...	...	...	...	...	...	...	...	99.8	102.4
Fabric coating mills	...	...	...	...	...	...	...	...	...	100.2	104.9
Textile product mills	...	...	...	...	...	...	...	...	...	101.4	105.3
Textile furnishings mills	...	...	...	...	...	...	...	...	...	101.1	105.1
Carpet and rug mills[3]	111.6	114.1	115.7	116.3	115.4	117.8	118.9	119.0	121.8	124.6	132.9
Curtain and linen mills	...	...	...	...	...	...	...	...	...	100.2	100.3
Other textile product mills	...	...	...	...	...	...	...	...	...	102.0	105.4
Textile bag and canvas mills	...	...	...	...	...	...	...	...	...	102.7	104.9
All other textile product mills	...	...	...	...	...	...	...	...	...	101.7	105.6

[1]December 1981 = 100.
[2]December 1985 = 100.
[3]December 1984 = 100.
[4]June 1988 = 100.
[5]June 1984 = 100.
[6]December 1982 = 100.
. . . = Not available.

Table 7-3. Producer Price Indexes for the Net Output of Selected Industries, 1995–2005—*Continued*

(December 2003 = 100, unless otherwise indicated.)

Industry	1995	1996	1997	1998	1999	2000	2001	2002	2003	2004	2005
Manufacturing—*Continued*											
Apparel	...	...	...	...	...	...	...	...	...	100.0	100.0
Apparel knitting mills[3]	115.7	116.6	117.0	116.6	114.0	113.9	113.7	112.7	111.6	110.3	109.6
Hosiery and sock mills[3]	115.7	116.6	117.0	116.6	114.0	113.9	113.7	112.7	111.6	111.4	110.9
Cut and sew apparel	...	...	...	...	...	...	...	...	...	100.2	100.2
Cut and sew apparel contractors	...	...	...	...	...	...	...	...	...	100.2	103.0
Men's/boys' cut and sew apparel	...	...	...	...	...	...	...	...	...	100.4	104.8
Women's/girls' cut and sew apparel	...	...	...	...	...	...	...	...	...	100.1	102.4
Other cut and sew apparel	...	...	...	...	...	...	...	...	...	100.2	102.3
Apparel accessories and other apparel	...	...	...	...	...	...	...	...	...	100.5	101.6
Leather and allied product[3]	134.1	134.7	137.1	137.1	136.5	137.9	141.3	141.1	142.8	143.6	144.5
Leather and hide tanning and finishing[7]	183.9	172.4	176.9	171.6	168.8	174.6	191.7	191.4	200.5	205.7	204.8
Footwear	...	...	...	...	...	...	...	...	...	100.1	101.1
Other leather and allied product	...	...	...	...	...	...	...	...	...	99.8	100.7
Wood product	...	...	...	...	...	...	...	...	...	106.7	108.6
Sawmills and wood preservation	...	...	...	...	...	...	...	...	...	110.5	110.7
Veneer, plywood, and engineered wood product	...	...	...	...	...	...	...	...	...	107.0	105.2
Other wood product	...	...	...	...	...	...	...	...	...	104.7	108.3
Millwork	...	...	...	...	...	...	...	...	...	104.8	105.4
Wood container and pallet	...	...	...	...	...	...	...	...	...	102.8	107.1
All other wood product	...	...	...	...	...	...	...	...	...	105.0	111.3
Paper	...	...	...	...	...	...	...	...	...	102.6	106.9
Pulp, paper, and paperboard mills	...	...	...	...	...	...	...	...	...	103.8	109.4
Pulp mills[6]	182.4	135.5	131.0	125.1	122.7	143.4	122.9	116.5	120.9	131.3	137.4
Paper mills[7]	164.8	152.2	143.2	144.5	139.7	148.8	150.5	144.1	145.7	151.1	161.0
Paperboard mills[6]	203.1	169.7	158.2	165.1	166.9	192.2	187.3	179.5	180.2	189.9	196.0
Converted paper product	...	...	...	...	...	...	...	...	...	101.9	105.5
Paper container[3]	148.5	140.4	132.9	141.1	144.1	157.1	158.9	157.0	157.3	161.5	167.1
Paper bag and coated and treated paper	...	...	...	...	...	...	...	...	...	101.7	105.8
Stationery product	...	...	...	...	...	...	...	...	...	101.7	106.8
Other converted paper product	...	...	...	...	...	...	...	...	...	97.0	98.7
Printing and related support activities	...	...	...	...	...	...	...	...	...	101.1	103.1
Printing	...	...	...	...	...	...	...	...	...	101.2	103.3
Printing support activities	...	...	...	...	...	...	...	...	...	100.4	100.0
Petroleum and coal product[3]	77.2	87.4	85.6	66.3	76.8	112.8	105.3	98.8	122.0	149.9	200.4
Petroleum refineries[8]	74.5	85.3	83.1	62.3	73.6	111.6	103.1	96.3	121.2	151.5	205.3
Asphalt paving, roofing, and saturated materials[3]	98.1	99.4	102.2	102.0	102.8	113.5	116.9	119.7	125.1	127.1	138.6
Other petroleum and coal product[3]	136.3	140.9	142.0	142.5	142.1	150.3	159.3	160.5	165.3	172.0	197.8
Chemical[3]	143.4	145.8	147.1	148.7	149.7	156.7	158.4	157.3	164.6	172.8	187.3
Basic chemical[3]	158.1	164.0	163.9	160.1	161.4	177.3	173.5	170.6	183.0	197.7	225.9
Petrochemical	...	...	...	...	...	...	...	...	...	120.7	151.0
Industrial gas	...	...	...	...	...	...	...	...	...	108.3	118.3
Synthetic dye and pigment	...	...	...	...	...	...	...	...	...	104.2	108.7
Other basic inorganic chemical	...	...	...	...	...	...	...	...	...	103.1	120.4
Resin, synthetic rubber, and artificial and synthetic fiber and filament[3]	127.8	123.1	124.4	115.9	115.4	128.0	126.2	119.7	131.0	145.5	169.4
Resin and synthetic rubber	...	...	...	...	...	...	...	...	...	115.1	136.5
Artificial and synthetic fiber and filament	...	...	...	...	...	...	...	...	...	101.2	107.8
Pesticide, fertilizer, and other agricultural chemical[3]	129.7	133.4	131.9	128.5	123.2	124.9	132.0	127.0	135.3	142.7	151.3
Fertilizer	...	...	...	...	...	...	...	...	...	107.3	118.1
Pesticide and other agricultural chemical	...	...	...	...	...	...	...	...	...	100.6	102.2
Pharmaceutical and medicine[3]	178.7	181.2	184.8	203.1	210.1	215.7	220.5	226.3	235.4	244.2	255.2
Paint, coating, and adhesive	...	...	...	...	...	...	...	...	...	101.9	108.8
Adhesive	...	...	...	...	...	...	...	...	...	100.5	106.4
Soap, cleaners, and toilet preparation[3]	125.0	126.6	127.3	128.7	130.3	132.5	134.2	134.2	134.9	136.9	140.5
Soap and cleaning compound	...	...	...	...	...	...	...	...	...	102.0	105.8
Toilet preparation	...	...	...	...	...	...	...	...	...	100.0	101.2
Other chemical product and preparation	...	...	...	...	...	...	...	...	...	101.6	108.6
Printing ink	...	...	...	...	...	...	...	...	...	100.0	103.0
All other chemical product and preparation	...	...	...	...	...	...	...	...	...	101.8	109.4
Plastics and rubber product[3]	123.3	123.1	122.8	122.1	122.2	124.6	125.9	125.5	128.4	131.7	141.2
Plastics product[9]	108.3	108.0	107.6	106.8	107.1	109.8	111.0	110.2	113.0	116.2	125.8
Unsupported plastics film, sheet, and bag	...	...	...	...	...	...	...	...	...	104.2	116.9
Plastics pipe, fitting, and unsupported shape	...	...	...	...	...	...	...	...	...	108.5	122.6
Laminated plastics plate, sheet, and shape	...	...	...	...	...	...	...	...	...	101.7	105.0
Polystyrene foam product	...	...	...	...	...	...	...	...	...	104.6	117.0
Foam product (except polystyrene)	...	...	...	...	...	...	...	...	...	100.2	110.0
Plastics bottle	...	...	...	...	...	...	...	...	...	103.1	114.8
Other plastics product	...	...	...	...	...	...	...	...	...	101.3	107.1
Rubber product	...	...	...	...	...	...	...	...	...	102.1	106.7
Tire[7]	108.5	105.2	103.4	102.0	100.4	100.4	101.5	102.7	105.6	110.5	116.9
Rubber and plastics hose and belting	...	...	...	...	...	...	...	...	...	102.3	107.4
Nonmetallic mineral product[3]	124.3	125.8	127.4	129.3	132.6	134.7	136.0	137.1	138.0	142.7	152.0
Clay product and refractory	...	...	...	...	...	...	...	...	...	101.5	105.1
Pottery, ceramics, and plumbing fixture[3]	129.3	130.0	131.8	133.5	138.1	139.7	150.2	150.1	150.6	152.1	154.3
Clay building material and refractories	...	...	...	...	...	...	...	...	...	102.2	107.8
Glass and glass product	...	...	...	...	...	...	...	...	...	100.1	101.6
Cement and concrete product	...	...	...	...	...	...	...	...	...	104.2	114.8
Cement[10]	127.2	132.9	138.1	144.2	149.1	148.6	148.7	151.1	150.5	155.4	175.2

[3]December 1984 = 100.
[6]December 1982 = 100.
[7]June 1981 = 100.
[8]June 1985 = 100.
[9]June 1993 = 100.
[10]June 1982 = 100.
. . . = Not available.

Table 7-3. Producer Price Indexes for the Net Output of Selected Industries, 1995–2005—*Continued*

(December 2003 = 100, unless otherwise indicated.)

Industry	1995	1996	1997	1998	1999	2000	2001	2002	2003	2004	2005
Manufacturing—*Continued*											
Ready-mix concrete	...	...	...	...	...	...	...	...	...	104.5	117.3
Concrete pipe, brick, and block	...	...	...	...	...	...	...	...	...	102.5	109.2
Other concrete products	...	...	...	...	...	...	...	...	...	104.7	111.3
Lime and gypsum product	...	...	...	...	...	...	...	...	...	110.0	124.5
Lime	...	...	...	...	...	...	...	...	...	103.5	112.4
Gypsum product	...	...	...	...	...	...	...	...	...	111.9	127.9
Other nonmetallic mineral product[3]	123.6	125.6	126.2	127.4	131.3	130.9	132.0	132.6	133.4	137.2	142.5
Abrasive product	...	...	...	...	...	...	...	...	...	100.2	103.1
All other nonmetallic mineral product	...	...	...	...	...	...	...	...	...	103.5	108.0
Primary metal[3]	128.2	123.7	124.7	120.9	115.8	119.8	116.1	116.2	118.4	142.8	156.3
Iron and steel mills and ferroalloy	...	...	...	...	...	...	...	...	...	127.7	136.7
Steel product from purchased steel	...	...	...	...	...	...	...	...	...	133.1	146.2
Iron/steel pipe and tube from purchased steel	...	...	...	...	...	...	...	...	...	147.9	160.1
Rolling and drawing of purchased steel	...	...	...	...	...	...	...	...	...	123.7	137.5
Nonferrous (except aluminum) production and processing	...	...	...	...	...	...	...	...	...	113.6	137.6
Copper rolling, drawing, extruding, and alloying	...	...	...	...	...	...	...	...	...	118.2	138.9
Other nonferrous rolling, drawing, extruding, and alloying	...	...	...	...	...	...	...	...	...	110.3	136.2
Ferrous metal foundries[3]	124.0	127.6	129.2	129.7	130.4	132.1	132.7	133.0	133.5	140.4	152.5
Nonferrous metal foundries[3]	132.8	131.4	133.8	132.7	131.6	133.5	134.1	134.4	135.6	140.0	145.0
Fabricated metal product[3]	124.8	126.2	127.6	128.7	129.1	130.3	131.0	131.7	132.9	141.3	149.5
Forging and stamping	...	...	...	...	...	...	...	...	...	107.0	113.3
Architectural and structural metals	...	...	...	...	...	...	...	...	...	111.2	118.0
Plate work and fabricated structural product	...	...	...	...	...	...	...	...	...	115.2	124.2
Ornamental and architectural metal product	...	...	...	...	...	...	...	...	...	108.3	113.5
Boiler, tank, and shipping container	...	...	...	...	...	...	...	...	...	106.8	115.7
Light gauge metal container[3]	109.4	103.9	102.7	102.3	100.7	101.0	100.8	102.7	105.4	110.4	117.5
Hardware	...	...	...	...	...	...	...	...	...	103.4	107.2
Spring and wire product	...	...	...	...	...	...	...	...	...	108.9	114.4
Machine shops; turned product; and screw, nut, and bolt	...	...	...	...	...	...	...	...	...	102.8	108.4
Machine shops	...	...	...	...	...	...	...	...	...	102.4	107.4
Turned product and screw, nut, and bolt[3]	120.0	121.6	122.6	122.7	121.8	122.9	122.8	123.4	123.6	128.4	136.6
Coating, engraving, heat treating, and other activity	...	...	...	...	...	...	...	...	...	102.0	104.2
Other fabricated metal product	...	...	...	...	...	...	...	...	...	103.8	109.8
Metal valve	...	...	...	...	...	...	...	...	...	103.0	109.8
All other fabricated metal product	...	...	...	...	...	...	...	...	...	104.5	109.9
Machinery	...	...	...	...	...	...	...	...	...	101.9	105.6
Agricultural, construction, and mining machinery	...	...	...	...	...	...	...	...	...	102.4	107.4
Agricultural implement	...	...	...	...	...	...	...	...	...	101.8	105.8
Construction machinery	...	...	...	...	...	...	...	...	...	102.9	107.7
Mining and oil and gas field machinery	...	...	...	...	...	...	...	...	...	102.7	110.6
Industrial machinery[3]	137.3	140.5	143.0	145.4	147.2	148.7	149.9	149.6	150.1	153.0	155.9
Sawmill and woodworking machinery	...	...	...	...	...	...	...	...	...	101.5	105.0
Plastics and rubber industry machinery	...	...	...	...	...	...	...	...	...	102.8	106.3
Other industrial machinery[3]	137.3	140.5	143.0	145.4	147.2	148.7	149.9	149.6	150.1	152.7	155.3
Commercial and service industry machinery	...	...	...	...	...	...	...	...	...	101.3	102.9
HVAC and commercial refrigeration equipment	...	...	...	...	...	...	...	...	...	101.9	108.0
Metalworking machinery	...	...	...	...	...	...	...	...	...	100.8	103.3
Engine, turbine, and power transmission equipment[3]	130.8	132.3	133.6	133.9	135.7	136.6	137.7	138.9	139.1	140.8	143.2
Other general purpose machinery	...	...	...	...	...	...	...	...	...	103.0	107.6
Pump and compressor	...	...	...	...	...	...	...	...	...	102.2	108.4
Material handling equipment	...	...	...	...	...	...	...	...	...	104.6	110.6
All other general purpose machinery	...	...	...	...	...	...	...	...	...	102.5	105.7
Computer and electronic product	...	...	...	...	...	...	...	...	...	99.0	97.5
Computer and peripheral equipment[3]	70.5	63.4	55.9	48.8	44.0	41.3	39.0	35.5	31.6	29.4	27.4
Communications equipment[2]	113.9	115.0	115.7	115.0	113.0	110.4	108.6	105.0	101.7	98.4	97.0
Telephone apparatus	...	...	...	...	...	...	...	...	...	95.3	93.2
Radio/TV broadcast and wireless communication equipment	...	...	...	...	...	...	...	...	...	99.4	98.7
Other communications equipment	...	...	...	...	...	...	...	...	...	99.8	99.7
Audio and video equipment	...	...	...	...	...	...	...	...	...	98.1	95.6
Semiconductor and other electronic component[3]	102.5	99.3	95.1	91.9	90.1	88.8	86.4	84.9	81.1	78.3	76.5
Navigation, measuring, medical, and control instruments	...	...	...	...	...	...	...	...	...	100.6	101.9
Manufacturing and reproducing magnetic and optical media	...	...	...	...	...	...	...	...	...	98.0	97.0
Electrical equipment, appliance and component	...	...	...	...	...	...	...	...	...	103.2	108.0
Electric lighting equipment	...	...	...	...	...	...	...	...	...	100.8	103.5
Electric lamp bulb and part	...	...	...	...	...	...	...	...	...	98.1	100.2
Lighting fixture	...	...	...	...	...	...	...	...	...	101.7	104.6
Household appliance[3]	108.8	109.7	108.3	107.5	107.2	106.2	104.6	104.2	103.1	103.1	106.3
Small electrical appliance	...	...	...	...	...	...	...	...	...	99.9	101.8
Major appliance	...	...	...	...	...	...	...	...	...	100.6	104.2
Electrical equipment	...	...	...	...	...	...	...	...	...	101.9	107.2
Other electrical equipment and component	...	...	...	...	...	...	...	...	...	106.6	112.5
Battery	...	...	...	...	...	...	...	...	...	102.2	105.7
Communications and energy wire and cable	...	...	...	...	...	...	...	...	...	106.8	115.8
Wiring device	...	...	...	...	...	...	...	...	...	113.6	118.9
All other electrical equipment and component	...	...	...	...	...	...	...	...	...	101.7	105.4
Transportation equipment	...	...	...	...	...	...	...	...	...	100.9	102.5
Motor vehicle	...	...	...	...	...	...	...	...	...	99.4	98.7
Automobile and light duty motor vehicle	...	...	...	...	...	...	...	...	...	99.2	98.2
Heavy duty truck	...	...	...	...	...	...	...	...	...	102.2	106.4
Motor vehicle body and trailer	...	...	...	...	...	...	...	...	...	104.0	109.7
Motor vehicle parts	...	...	...	...	...	...	...	...	...	101.4	102.7
Motor vehicle steering and suspension parts	...	...	...	...	...	...	...	...	...	101.8	105.1
Aerospace product and parts[8]	137.3	140.8	142.7	143.4	144.8	149.9	154.7	157.3	162.2	168.0	176.0

[2]December 1985 = 100.
[3]December 1984 = 100.
[8]June 1985 = 100.
. . . = Not available.

Table 7-3. Producer Price Indexes for the Net Output of Selected Industries, 1995–2005—*Continued*

(December 2003 = 100, unless otherwise indicated.)

Industry	1995	1996	1997	1998	1999	2000	2001	2002	2003	2004	2005
Manufacturing—*Continued*											
Railroad rolling stock[5]	127.6	129.7	127.4	127.6	128.2	128.6	128.3	127.7	129.0	135.8	150.5
Ship and boat building[3]	135.0	138.2	142.0	144.1	145.6	149.0	152.6	156.8	163.0	169.6	175.0
Other transportation equipment	. . .	. . .	. . .	. . .	. . .	. . .	. . .	. . .	. . .	101.1	103.6
Furniture and related product[3]	133.3	136.2	138.2	139.7	141.3	143.3	145.1	146.3	147.4	151.5	157.8
Household and institutional furniture and kitchen cabinet[3]	132.2	134.7	136.4	138.4	140.3	142.5	144.4	146.2	147.0	148.6	152.6
Wood kitchen cabinet and countertop	. . .	. . .	. . .	. . .	. . .	. . .	. . .	. . .	. . .	101.1	103.2
Household and institutional furniture	. . .	. . .	. . .	. . .	. . .	. . .	. . .	. . .	. . .	101.1	104.0
Office furniture (including fixtures)	. . .	. . .	. . .	. . .	. . .	. . .	. . .	. . .	. . .	105.1	111.5
Other furniture-related product	. . .	. . .	. . .	. . .	. . .	. . .	. . .	. . .	. . .	104.0	110.6
Mattress	. . .	. . .	. . .	. . .	. . .	. . .	. . .	. . .	. . .	105.6	115.0
Blind and shade	. . .	. . .	. . .	. . .	. . .	. . .	. . .	. . .	. . .	101.3	103.9
Miscellaneous	. . .	. . .	. . .	. . .	. . .	. . .	. . .	. . .	. . .	101.2	102.9
Medical equipment and supplies	. . .	. . .	. . .	. . .	. . .	. . .	. . .	. . .	. . .	101.3	102.5
Other miscellaneous[2]	125.9	127.8	129.0	129.7	130.3	130.9	132.4	133.3	133.9	135.2	138.4
Jewelry and silverware[2]	126.3	128.0	128.0	127.1	126.4	127.1	128.0	129.1	131.0	134.6	138.7
Sporting and athletic goods	. . .	. . .	. . .	. . .	. . .	. . .	. . .	. . .	. . .	101.3	102.0
Doll, toy, and game	. . .	. . .	. . .	. . .	. . .	. . .	. . .	. . .	. . .	100.3	101.7
Office supplies (except paper)[2]	127.4	130.2	129.8	130.9	132.0	132.0	131.4	132.8	132.9	133.1	135.8
Sign	. . .	. . .	. . .	. . .	. . .	. . .	. . .	. . .	. . .	100.9	104.6
All other miscellaneous	. . .	. . .	. . .	. . .	. . .	. . .	. . .	. . .	. . .	101.0	103.7
Wholesale Trade											
Merchant wholesalers, durable goods	. . .	. . .	. . .	. . .	. . .	. . .	. . .	. . .	. . .	. . .	102.0
Merchant wholesalers, nondurable goods	. . .	. . .	. . .	. . .	. . .	. . .	. . .	. . .	. . .	. . .	. . .
Retail Trade											
Motor vehicle and parts dealers	. . .	. . .	. . .	. . .	. . .	. . .	. . .	. . .	. . .	103.5	106.9
Automobile dealers	. . .	. . .	. . .	. . .	. . .	. . .	. . .	. . .	. . .	102.9	105.4
New car dealers[11]	. . .	. . .	. . .	. . .	. . .	99.7	103.1	108.7	111.5	113.5	116.3
Recreational vehicle dealers[12]	. . .	. . .	. . .	. . .	. . .	. . .	. . .	112.2	109.7	121.4	133.6
Automotive parts, accessories, and tire stores[13]	. . .	. . .	. . .	. . .	. . .	. . .	. . .	100.9	104.2	109.4	115.1
Automotive parts and accessories stores	. . .	. . .	. . .	. . .	. . .	. . .	. . .	. . .	. . .	106.8	110.9
Tire dealers	. . .	. . .	. . .	. . .	. . .	. . .	. . .	. . .	. . .	102.0	110.7
Furniture and home furnishings stores	. . .	. . .	. . .	. . .	. . .	. . .	. . .	. . .	. . .	102.4	110.7
Furniture stores	. . .	. . .	. . .	. . .	. . .	. . .	. . .	. . .	. . .	100.8	108.0
Floor covering stores	. . .	. . .	. . .	. . .	. . .	. . .	. . .	. . .	. . .	104.6	114.4
Electronics and appliance stores	. . .	. . .	. . .	. . .	. . .	. . .	. . .	. . .	. . .	99.0	98.9
Appliance, TV, and other electronics stores	. . .	. . .	. . .	. . .	. . .	. . .	. . .	. . .	. . .	101.8	103.5
Computer and software stores	. . .	. . .	. . .	. . .	. . .	. . .	. . .	. . .	. . .	95.2	92.4
Camera and photographic supplies stores	. . .	. . .	. . .	. . .	. . .	. . .	. . .	. . .	. . .	88.6	82.0
Building material and garden equipment and supplies dealers	. . .	. . .	. . .	. . .	. . .	. . .	. . .	. . .	. . .	108.3	109.9
Building material and supplies dealers	. . .	. . .	. . .	. . .	. . .	. . .	. . .	. . .	. . .	108.7	109.9
Home centers	. . .	. . .	. . .	. . .	. . .	. . .	. . .	. . .	. . .	107.0	109.6
Paint and wallpaper stores	. . .	. . .	. . .	. . .	. . .	. . .	. . .	. . .	. . .	99.5	104.4
Hardware stores	. . .	. . .	. . .	. . .	. . .	. . .	. . .	. . .	. . .	103.1	108.2
Other building material dealers	. . .	. . .	. . .	. . .	. . .	. . .	. . .	. . .	. . .	111.4	110.8
Lawn and garden equipment and supplies stores	. . .	. . .	. . .	. . .	. . .	. . .	. . .	. . .	. . .	105.8	110.3
Nursery, garden, and farm supply stores	. . .	. . .	. . .	. . .	. . .	. . .	. . .	. . .	. . .	105.8	110.3
Food and beverage stores[11]	. . .	. . .	. . .	. . .	. . .	103.8	109.6	113.4	117.6	123.2	131.0
Grocery stores	. . .	. . .	. . .	. . .	. . .	. . .	. . .	. . .	. . .	103.5	110.7
Grocery (except convenience) stores	. . .	. . .	. . .	. . .	. . .	. . .	. . .	. . .	. . .	103.5	110.7
Specialty food stores	. . .	. . .	. . .	. . .	. . .	. . .	. . .	. . .	. . .	107.1	110.2
Beer, wine, and liquor stores[14]	. . .	. . .	. . .	. . .	. . .	. . .	102.9	103.5	106.9	110.7	111.0
Health and personal care stores	. . .	. . .	. . .	. . .	. . .	. . .	. . .	. . .	. . .	101.7	107.6
Pharmacies and drug stores[14]	. . .	. . .	. . .	. . .	. . .	. . .	102.4	112.4	116.6	119.8	127.9
Optical goods stores	. . .	. . .	. . .	. . .	. . .	. . .	. . .	. . .	. . .	99.8	100.1
Gasoline stations[12]	. . .	. . .	. . .	. . .	. . .	. . .	. . .	66.8	54.1	51.3	51.0
Gasoline stations with convenience stores	. . .	. . .	. . .	. . .	. . .	. . .	. . .	. . .	. . .	102.5	104.3
Other gasoline stations	. . .	. . .	. . .	. . .	. . .	. . .	. . .	. . .	. . .	132.8	118.1
Clothing and clothing accessories stores	. . .	. . .	. . .	. . .	. . .	. . .	. . .	. . .	. . .	100.5	103.3
Clothing stores	. . .	. . .	. . .	. . .	. . .	. . .	. . .	. . .	. . .	99.3	102.4
Men's clothing stores	. . .	. . .	. . .	. . .	. . .	. . .	. . .	. . .	. . .	100.2	102.1
Women's clothing stores	. . .	. . .	. . .	. . .	. . .	. . .	. . .	. . .	. . .	102.9	103.3
Family clothing stores	. . .	. . .	. . .	. . .	. . .	. . .	. . .	. . .	. . .	97.8	102.2
Shoe stores	. . .	. . .	. . .	. . .	. . .	. . .	. . .	. . .	. . .	103.9	105.0
Jewelry, luggage, and leather goods stores	. . .	. . .	. . .	. . .	. . .	. . .	. . .	. . .	. . .	101.8	104.9
Jewelry stores	. . .	. . .	. . .	. . .	. . .	. . .	. . .	. . .	. . .	101.8	104.8
Luggage and leather goods stores	. . .	. . .	. . .	. . .	. . .	. . .	. . .	. . .	. . .	101.4	106.5
Sporting goods, hobby, book, and music stores	. . .	. . .	. . .	. . .	. . .	. . .	. . .	. . .	. . .	96.6	96.6
Sporting goods, hobby, and musical instrument stores	. . .	. . .	. . .	. . .	. . .	. . .	. . .	. . .	. . .	97.8	99.0
Sporting goods stores	. . .	. . .	. . .	. . .	. . .	. . .	. . .	. . .	. . .	95.0	96.1
Hobby, toy, and game stores	. . .	. . .	. . .	. . .	. . .	. . .	. . .	. . .	. . .	100.5	101.7
Sewing, needlework, and piece goods stores	. . .	. . .	. . .	. . .	. . .	. . .	. . .	. . .	. . .	103.2	104.7
Book, periodical, and music stores	. . .	. . .	. . .	. . .	. . .	. . .	. . .	. . .	. . .	94.7	92.5
Bookstores and news dealers	. . .	. . .	. . .	. . .	. . .	. . .	. . .	. . .	. . .	95.0	92.0
Prerecorded tape, CD, and record stores	. . .	. . .	. . .	. . .	. . .	. . .	. . .	. . .	. . .	93.9	93.8
General merchandise stores	. . .	. . .	. . .	. . .	. . .	. . .	. . .	. . .	. . .	103.1	103.4
Department stores	. . .	. . .	. . .	. . .	. . .	. . .	. . .	. . .	. . .	105.4	105.1
Other general merchandise stores	. . .	. . .	. . .	. . .	. . .	. . .	. . .	. . .	. . .	97.7	99.5
Florists	. . .	. . .	. . .	. . .	. . .	. . .	. . .	. . .	. . .	100.2	100.2

[2]December 1985 = 100.
[3]December 1984 = 100.
[5]June 1984 = 100.
[11]December 1999 = 100.
[12]June 2001 = 100.
[13]December 2001 = 100.
[14]June 2000 = 100.
. . . = Not available.

Table 7-3. Producer Price Indexes for the Net Output of Selected Industries, 1995–2005—*Continued*

(December 2003 = 100, unless otherwise indicated.)

Industry	1995	1996	1997	1998	1999	2000	2001	2002	2003	2004	2005
Retail Trade—*Continued*											
Office supplies, stationery, and gift stores	...	...	...	...	...	...	...	...	...	99.7	101.7
Office supplies and stationery stores	...	...	...	...	...	...	...	...	...	100.4	102.9
Gift, novelty, and souvenir stores	...	...	...	...	...	...	...	...	...	98.7	100.0
Manufactured (mobile) home dealers	...	...	...	...	...	...	...	...	...	107.7	116.7
Nonstore retailers	...	...	...	...	...	...	...	...	...	107.5	119.8
Vending machine operators	...	...	...	...	...	...	...	...	...	101.5	104.4
Fuel dealers[14]	...	...	...	...	...	...	120.5	113.8	122.7	129.4	147.3
Transportation and Warehousing											
Air transportation[15]	113.7	121.1	125.3	124.5	130.8	147.7	157.2	157.8	162.1	162.3	171.0
Scheduled air transportation[16]	135.9	145.5	150.8	149.3	157.3	180.1	193.0	193.3	198.5	198.6	209.3
Nonscheduled air transportation[17]	...	...	97.8	99.2	102.2	107.3	112.7	114.7	117.8	119.9	126.7
Rail transportation[17]	...	...	100.5	101.7	101.3	102.6	104.5	106.6	108.8	113.4	125.2
Water transportation	...	...	...	...	...	...	...	...	...	101.3	106.4
Inland water transportation	...	...	...	...	...	...	...	...	...	103.2	119.3
Truck transportation	...	...	...	...	...	...	...	...	...	103.1	109.0
General freight trucking	...	...	...	...	...	...	...	...	...	103.5	110.0
General freight trucking, local	...	...	...	...	...	...	...	...	...	105.2	111.5
General freight trucking, long distance	...	...	...	...	...	...	...	...	...	103.2	109.7
Specialized freight trucking	...	...	...	...	...	...	...	...	...	102.3	107.0
Used household and office goods moving	...	...	...	...	...	...	...	...	...	102.6	106.0
Specialized freight (except used) trucking, local	...	...	...	...	...	...	...	...	...	102.7	107.1
Specialized freight (except used) trucking, long distance	...	...	...	...	...	...	...	...	...	101.7	107.5
Pipeline transportation of crude oil	...	...	...	...	...	...	...	...	...	103.9	113.3
Other pipeline transportation	...	...	...	...	...	...	...	...	...	101.4	105.2
Pipeline transportation of refined petroleum products	...	...	...	...	...	...	...	...	...	101.4	105.2
Transportation support activities	...	...	...	...	...	...	...	...	...	101.1	104.1
Air transportation support activities[17]	...	...	102.5	105.2	108.6	114.2	117.5	121.4	125.1	128.1	134.2
Airport operations	...	...	...	...	...	...	...	...	...	101.1	104.8
Other air transportation support activities	...	...	...	...	...	...	...	...	...	102.0	107.5
Water transportation support activities	...	...	...	...	...	...	...	...	...	101.0	103.5
Port and harbor operations	...	...	...	...	...	...	...	...	...	102.4	105.9
Marine cargo handling	...	...	...	...	...	...	...	...	...	100.5	102.2
Navigational services to shipping	...	...	...	...	...	...	...	...	...	101.5	105.7
Freight transportation arrangement[17]	...	...	99.4	97.7	97.3	98.3	98.2	97.5	97.9	98.9	99.1
Postal service[18]	132.2	132.3	132.3	132.3	135.3	135.2	143.4	150.2	155.0	155.0	155.0
Couriers and messengers	...	...	...	...	...	...	...	...	...	106.1	113.8
Couriers	...	...	...	...	...	...	...	...	...	106.6	115.0
Local messengers and local delivery	...	...	...	...	...	...	...	...	...	101.1	102.7
Warehousing and storage	...	...	...	...	...	...	...	...	...	100.3	101.5
Refrigerated warehousing and storage	...	...	...	...	...	...	...	...	...	100.5	101.0
Farm product warehousing and storage	...	...	...	...	...	...	...	...	...	100.2	101.5
Information											
Publishing industries, except Internet	...	...	...	...	...	...	...	...	...	101.5	104.1
Newspaper, periodical, book, and directory publishers	...	...	...	...	...	...	...	...	...	102.1	105.5
Newspaper publishers[19]	286.7	306.9	317.7	328.7	339.3	351.3	367.9	381.9	395.7	409.7	426.2
Periodical publishers[19]	246.3	253.1	263.2	276.9	284.9	292.6	305.9	320.4	332.4	339.1	347.6
Book publishers[3]	162.3	169.4	174.0	178.9	184.7	190.2	195.6	201.5	208.2	215.7	224.3
Directory and mailing list publishers	...	...	...	...	...	...	...	...	...	101.3	103.3
Other publishers	...	...	...	...	...	...	...	...	...	100.7	103.9
Software publishers	...	...	...	...	...	...	...	...	...	99.8	99.8
Broadcasting, except Internet	...	...	...	...	...	...	...	...	...	101.2	102.1
Radio and television broadcasting[12]	...	...	...	...	...	...	98.2	97.1	99.8	102.8	101.9
Radio broadcasting	...	...	...	...	...	...	...	...	...	102.7	106.3
Television broadcasting	...	...	...	...	...	...	...	...	...	100.5	97.3
Cable networks	...	...	...	...	...	...	...	...	...	101.4	104.3
Telecommunications	...	...	...	...	...	...	...	...	...	99.8	98.1
Wired telecommunications carriers[20]	...	...	...	...	...	96.4	93.6	89.9	88.1	86.3	85.8
Wireless telecommunications carriers	...	...	...	...	...	...	...	...	...	98.4	86.4
Cable and other program distribution	...	...	...	...	...	...	...	...	...	102.2	106.5
Data processing and related services	...	...	...	...	...	...	...	...	...	98.8	98.8
Financial Activities											
Security, commodity contracts, and like activity	...	...	...	...	...	...	...	...	...	103.4	109.4
Security and commodity contracts, intermediation and brokerage[14]	...	...	...	...	...	...	88.1	81.8	82.5	84.2	88.1
Investment banking and securities dealing	...	...	...	...	...	...	...	...	...	102.6	109.1
Securities brokerage	...	...	...	...	...	...	...	...	...	100.0	102.2
Portfolio management	...	...	...	...	...	...	...	...	...	108.1	117.8
Investment advice	...	...	...	...	...	...	...	...	...	102.0	104.8
Other direct insurance carriers[21]	...	...	...	...	100.7	101.9	104.3	108.7	115.0	118.7	121.0
Insurance agencies and brokerages	...	...	...	...	...	...	...	...	...	100.8	101.8
Lessors of nonresidential building (except miniwarehouse)	...	...	...	...	...	...	...	...	...	102.3	105.1
Lessors of miniwarehouse and self-storage units	...	...	...	...	...	...	...	...	...	102.0	105.6
Offices of real estate agents and brokers	...	...	...	...	...	...	...	...	...	101.8	108.1

[3]December 1984 = 100.
[12]June 2001 = 100.
[14]June 2000 = 100.
[15]December 1992 = 100.
[16]December 1989 = 100.
[17]December 1996 = 100.
[18]June 1989 = 100.
[19]December 1979 = 100.
[20]June 1999 = 100.
[21]December 1998 = 100.
... = Not available.

Table 7-3. Producer Price Indexes for the Net Output of Selected Industries, 1995–2005—*Continued*

(December 2003 = 100, unless otherwise indicated.)

Industry	1995	1996	1997	1998	1999	2000	2001	2002	2003	2004	2005
Financial Activities—*Continued*											
Real estate property managers	. . .	. . .	. . .	. . .	. . .	. . .	. . .	. . .	. . .	100.9	102.2
Offices of real estate appraisers	. . .	. . .	. . .	. . .	. . .	. . .	. . .	. . .	. . .	102.7	104.2
Automotive equipment rental and leasing[12]	. . .	. . .	. . .	. . .	. . .	. . .	. . .	103.9	106.6	107.8	109.0
Passenger car rental and leasing	. . .	. . .	. . .	. . .	. . .	. . .	. . .	. . .	. . .	98.2	99.9
Truck, utility trailer, and RV rental and leasing	. . .	. . .	. . .	. . .	. . .	. . .	. . .	. . .	. . .	99.9	99.9
Legal services[17]	. . .	. . .	102.5	106.1	108.7	112.5	117.9	121.7	125.6	131.8	138.5
Offices of lawyers[17]	. . .	. . .	102.5	106.1	108.7	112.5	117.9	121.7	125.6	131.8	138.5
Architectural, engineering, and related services[17]	. . .	. . .	102.2	105.1	108.5	111.8	115.9	121.1	124.3	126.8	129.2
Architectural services	. . .	. . .	. . .	. . .	. . .	. . .	. . .	. . .	. . .	99.7	102.0
Engineering services	. . .	. . .	. . .	. . .	. . .	. . .	. . .	. . .	. . .	101.5	103.4
Advertising agencies	. . .	. . .	. . .	. . .	. . .	. . .	. . .	. . .	. . .	100.1	101.4
Employment services[17]	. . .	. . .	101.0	103.2	105.2	107.3	108.2	108.9	111.4	113.9	116.3
Employment placement agencies	. . .	. . .	. . .	. . .	. . .	. . .	. . .	. . .	. . .	102.2	104.4
Temporary help services	. . .	. . .	. . .	. . .	. . .	. . .	. . .	. . .	. . .	101.7	104.0
Employee leasing services	. . .	. . .	. . .	. . .	. . .	. . .	. . .	. . .	. . .	101.3	102.9
Travel agencies	. . .	. . .	. . .	. . .	. . .	. . .	. . .	. . .	. . .	96.9	95.9
Janitorial services	. . .	. . .	. . .	. . .	. . .	. . .	. . .	. . .	. . .	100.9	101.9
Waste collection	. . .	. . .	. . .	. . .	. . .	. . .	. . .	. . .	. . .	101.3	102.5
Health Care and Social Assistance											
Offices of physicians[17]	. . .	. . .	101.0	103.2	105.5	107.3	110.4	110.3	112.1	114.3	116.4
Medical and diagnostic laboratories	. . .	. . .	. . .	. . .	. . .	. . .	. . .	. . .	. . .	100.0	104.1
Home health care services[17]	. . .	. . .	103.3	106.2	107.1	111.1	114.0	116.6	117.0	119.8	121.1
Hospitals[15]	110.0	112.6	113.6	114.4	116.4	119.4	123.0	127.5	134.9	141.5	146.9
General medical and surgical hospitals	. . .	. . .	. . .	. . .	. . .	. . .	. . .	. . .	. . .	102.9	106.7
Psychiatric and substance abuse hospitals	. . .	. . .	. . .	. . .	. . .	. . .	. . .	. . .	. . .	101.1	103.7
Other specialty hospitals	. . .	. . .	. . .	. . .	. . .	. . .	. . .	. . .	. . .	103.8	109.6
Nursing care facilities	. . .	. . .	. . .	. . .	. . .	. . .	. . .	. . .	. . .	102.6	106.4
Residential mental retardation facilities	. . .	. . .	. . .	. . .	. . .	. . .	. . .	. . .	. . .	101.2	104.5
Accommodations[17]	. . .	. . .	104.2	108.1	112.7	116.2	121.3	121.3	122.0	125.2	131.9
Hotels (except casino hotels) and motels	. . .	. . .	. . .	. . .	. . .	. . .	. . .	. . .	. . .	103.5	110.0
Casino hotels	. . .	. . .	. . .	. . .	. . .	. . .	. . .	. . .	. . .	105.0	107.5

[12]June 2001 = 100.
[15]December 1992 = 100.
[17]December 1996 = 100.
. . . = Not available.

CONSUMER PRICE INDEX

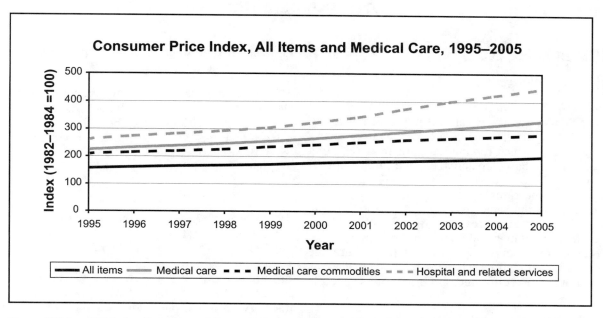

Consumer Price Index, All Items and Medical Care, 1995–2005

From 2004 to 2005, the Consumer Price Index (CPI) for hospital and related services continued to rise at a faster rate (5.3 percent) than other components of medical care prices. The CPI for medical services rose 4.8 percent, the CPI for professional services increased by 3.8 percent, and the CPI for medical care commodities grew by 2.5 percent. (See Table 7-8.)

OTHER HIGHLIGHTS

- In 2005, the CPI for all items rose 3.4 percent, but the CPI for all items excluding energy prices only increased 2.2 percent. From 1999 to 2005, prices for nondurables less food and apparel and medical care services grew rapidly (36.4 percent and 31.9 percent, respectively). The CPI for apparel declined 9 percent from 1999 to 2005. (See Tables 7-4 and 7-5.)

- Food and beverages, housing, and transportation made up 76.1 percent of the CPI in 2005, rising from 75.8 percent in 2004. (See Table 7-9.)

- The CPI Research Series Using Current Methods (CPI-U-RS) rose more slowing than the CPI for All Urban Consumers (CPI-U). From 1995 to 2005, the CPI-U-RS grew 27.2 percent, compared to 28.1 percent for the CPI-U. (See Tables 7-4 and 7-11.)

NOTES AND DEFINITIONS

CONSUMER PRICE INDEX

Collection and Coverage

The Consumer Price Index (CPI) measures the average change in prices of goods and services purchased by urban consumers for day-to-day living. The weights used in calculating the index, which remain fixed for relatively long periods of time, are based on actual expenditures reported in the Consumer Expenditure Survey (CE). The quantities and qualities of the sample items in the market basket remain essentially the same between consecutive pricing periods. The index measures only the effect of price change on the cost of living and does not measure changes in the total amount families spend for living. Geographic area indexes measure price changes in individual areas over time, not relative differences in prices or living costs between areas.

Periodic Updating

The index for the years 1913–1935 used a study of 1917–1919 spending by households of wage earners and clerical workers as the basis for its weights. Since then, there have been six revisions to bring the market basket of goods and services up to date and to revise the weights and improve the sampling methods used in the survey. Over the past 20 years, several major changes have been introduced into the CPI.

The 1978 revision of the CPI updated the Consumer Price Index for Urban Wage Earners and Clerical Workers (CPI-W) and introduced a new index for the Consumer Price Index for All Urban Consumers (CPI-U), which includes salaried workers, the self-employed, the retired, the unemployed, and wage earners and clerical workers. The CPI-W now represents the spending patterns of 32 percent of the population; the CPI-U represents the spending patterns of 87 percent of the population. Before 1978, changes in the CPI-U were based on changes in the CPI-W. The 1978 revision also instituted sampling for all levels of the index, right down to the selection of individual items within each retail outlet.

Beginning with the index for January 1983, the Bureau of Labor Statistics (BLS) changed the way the CPI-U measures homeowners' costs; the CPI-W implemented the same change in January 1985. The change converted the homeownership component from an asset approach, which includes both the investment and consumption aspects of homeownership, to a flow-of-services approach, which only measures the cost of shelter services consumed by homeowners. The new approach uses a rental equivalence method to calculate homeowner shelter costs by estimating the implicit rent owners would have to pay to rent the homes in which they live. The old method calculated homeowners' costs as home purchase, mortgage interest costs, property taxes, property insurance, and maintenance and repair.

The 1987 major revision of both the CPI-U and the CPI-W introduced weights based upon data from the 1982, 1983, and 1984 CE Surveys. The 1998 CPI revision, which went into effect with the index for January 1998, uses expenditure data from the 1993–1995 CE Surveys and population data from the 1990 decennial census.

Current Methodology

The CPI uses 87 pricing areas in 38 different index areas from around the United States. BLS revises the outlets and items in its sample on a five-year rotating basis. Before rotating the sample, the Census Bureau conducts a Point-of-Purchase Survey for BLS. This survey determines the locations of retail outlets at which consumers buy goods and services in various categories; it also determines how much they spend on each category in each reported outlet. BLS then draws outlet samples from the Point-of-Purchase Survey information. Field agents visit the selected retail outlets and sample the applicable item categories with checklists, which exhaustively define these categories of goods and services. A data collector, who uses the checklists in systematic stages, generally selects the items to be priced in a specific retail store. Information provided by the respondent is taken into account at each stage. Outlets may be located outside of the pricing area to represent out-of-town purchases.

After the initial selection, the same item (or a close substitute) is priced from period to period in order to ensure the greatest extent possible that differences in reported prices are measures of price change only. All taxes directly associated with the purchase, or with the continued use of the items priced, are included in the indexes. Foods, fuels, rents, and other items are priced monthly in all areas. Prices of most other commodities and services are obtained monthly in the three largest geographical areas and every other month in the remaining areas, with half obtained in odd-numbered months and half obtained in even-numbered months. Between scheduled survey dates, prices are held at the level of their last pricing. BLS agents also collect data for a sample of rental units drawn from the Decennial Census of Population and Housing. This sample is heavily augmented with renter-occupied housing units in areas where there are many owner-occupied units. This survey is the basis for the rent and owner-equivalent rent components of the CPI.

BLS calculates basic indexes (elementary aggregates) for the 211 item strata in each of the 38 index areas. Basic indexes are combined with weights based on the 1993–1995 Consumer Expenditure Surveys and the 1990 decennial census.

BLS publishes CPI indexes for a variety of commodities and services by region, by size of city, by cross-classifications of regions and population size classes, and for 26 metropolitan areas.

The purchasing power of the consumer dollar for any given date is calculated as the reciprocal of the index for that date, expressed in dollars, with the dollar's value in 1982–1984 equal to $1.00. It shows changes in the value of the dollar resulting from changes in prices of consumer goods and services. Dividing the index for the desired base date by the index for the current date and expressing the result in dollars can calculate the purchasing power of the dollar; this allows for clear comparisons to other base dates.

The relative importance figures are percentage distributions of the cost or value weights used in the index calculation. The cost weights represent average expenditures by consumers for specific classes of goods and services. However, in the subsequent pricing periods, the value weights and the corresponding relative importance figures change as prices change differentially. (In other words, the relative importance increases for an item or group having a greater than average price increase and decreases for an item having a less than average price increase.) Historically, the weights in the CPI have been updated about once every 10 years. Since 2002, the CPI expenditure weights have been updated every other year to keep the weights more current with consumer spending habits.

Since the CPI traditionally measured price changes for a fixed market basket of goods and services, it was criticized as overstating inflation, because it did not account for the fact that consumers can substitute (buy more or less) as relative prices change. In 1999, the CPI began using a geometric mean formula to average the prices within most item categories. This formula assumes a modest degree of substitution within CPI item categories as relative prices change.

In 2002, BLS created an additional price index using a "superlative" formula to be address consumer substitution across CPI item categories. BLS began publishing this index, called the Chained Consumer Price Index for All Urban Consumers effective with release of July data in August 2002. Designated the C-CPI-U, the index will supplement—not replace—the CPI-U and the CPI-W.

The Consumer Price Index Research Series Using Current Methods (CPI-U-RS) presents an estimate of the CPI for All Urban Consumers (CPI-U) from 1978 to the present that incorporates most of the improvements made over that time span into the entire series.

Sources of Additional Information

An extensive description of the methodology is available in the updated version of Chapter 17 in the *BLS Handbook of Methods*. Additional detailed data is in the *Consumer Price Index Detailed Report* (published monthly) and other special reports. All of these resources can be found on the BLS Web site at <http://www.bls.gov>.

Table 7-4. Consumer Price Indexes, All Urban Consumers (CPI-U): U.S. City Average, Major Groups, 1967–2005

(1982–1984 = 100, unless otherwise indicated.)

Year	All items	Food and beverages	Housing	Apparel	Transportation	Medical care	Recreation[1]	Education and communi- cation[1]	Other goods and services
1967	33.4	35.0	30.8	51.0	33.3	28.2	. . .	. . .	35.1
1968	34.8	36.2	32.0	53.7	34.3	29.9	. . .	. . .	36.9
1969	36.7	38.1	34.0	56.8	35.7	31.9	. . .	. . .	38.7
1970	38.8	40.1	36.4	59.2	37.5	34.0	. . .	. . .	40.9
1971	40.5	41.4	38.0	61.1	39.5	36.1	. . .	. . .	42.9
1972	41.8	43.1	39.4	62.3	39.9	37.3	. . .	. . .	44.7
1973	44.4	48.8	41.2	64.6	41.2	38.8	. . .	. . .	46.4
1974	49.3	55.5	45.8	69.4	45.8	42.4	. . .	. . .	49.8
1975	53.8	60.2	50.7	72.5	50.1	47.5	. . .	. . .	53.9
1976	56.9	62.1	53.8	75.2	55.1	52.0	. . .	. . .	57.0
1977	60.6	65.8	57.4	78.6	59.0	57.0	. . .	. . .	60.4
1978	65.2	72.2	62.4	81.4	61.7	61.8	. . .	. . .	64.3
1979	72.6	79.9	70.1	84.9	70.5	67.5	. . .	. . .	68.9
1980	82.4	86.7	81.1	90.9	83.1	74.9	. . .	. . .	75.2
1981	90.9	93.5	90.4	95.3	93.2	82.9	. . .	. . .	82.6
1982	96.5	97.3	96.9	97.8	97.0	92.5	. . .	. . .	91.1
1983	99.6	99.5	99.5	100.2	99.3	100.6	. . .	. . .	101.1
1984	103.9	103.2	103.6	102.1	103.7	106.8	. . .	. . .	107.9
1985	107.6	105.6	107.7	105.0	106.4	113.5	. . .	. . .	114.5
1986	109.6	109.1	110.9	105.9	102.3	122.0	. . .	. . .	121.4
1987	113.6	113.5	114.2	110.6	105.4	130.1	. . .	. . .	128.5
1988	118.3	118.2	118.5	115.4	108.7	138.6	. . .	. . .	137.0
1989	124.0	124.9	123.0	118.6	114.1	149.3	. . .	. . .	147.7
1990	130.7	132.1	128.5	124.1	120.5	162.8	. . .	. . .	159.0
1991	136.2	136.8	133.6	128.7	123.8	177.0	. . .	. . .	171.6
1992	140.3	138.7	137.5	131.9	126.5	190.1	. . .	. . .	183.3
1993	144.5	141.6	141.2	133.7	130.4	201.4	90.7	85.5	192.9
1994	148.2	144.9	144.8	133.4	134.3	211.0	92.7	88.8	198.5
1995	152.4	148.9	148.5	132.0	139.1	220.5	94.5	92.2	206.9
1996	156.9	153.7	152.8	131.7	143.0	228.2	97.4	95.3	215.4
1997	160.5	157.7	156.8	132.9	144.3	234.6	99.6	98.4	224.8
1998	163.0	161.1	160.4	133.0	141.6	242.1	101.1	100.3	237.7
1999	166.6	164.6	163.9	131.3	144.4	250.6	102.0	101.2	258.3
2000	172.2	168.4	169.6	129.6	153.3	260.8	103.3	102.5	271.1
2001	177.1	173.6	176.4	127.3	154.3	272.8	104.9	105.2	282.6
2002	179.9	176.8	180.3	124.0	152.9	285.6	106.2	107.9	293.2
2003	184.0	180.5	184.8	120.9	157.6	297.1	107.5	109.8	298.7
2004	188.9	186.6	189.5	120.4	163.1	310.1	108.6	111.6	304.7
2005	195.3	191.2	195.7	119.5	173.9	323.2	109.4	113.7	313.4

[1]December 1997 = 100.
. . . = Not available.

Table 7-5. Consumer Price Indexes, All Urban Consumers (CPI-U): U.S. City Average, Commodity, Service, and Special Groups, 1967–2005

(1982–1984 = 100, unless otherwise indicated.)

Year	All items less food	All items less shelter	All items less medical care	All items less energy	All items less food and energy	Commodities	Commodities less food and beverages	Commodities less food and energy	Energy commodities	Nondurables	Nondurables less food	Nondurables less food and apparel
1967	33.4	35.2	33.7	34.4	34.7	36.8	38.3	41.3	23.9	35.7	37.6	32.6
1968	34.9	36.7	35.1	35.9	36.3	38.1	39.7	42.9	24.4	37.1	39.1	33.7
1969	36.8	38.4	37.0	38.0	38.4	39.9	41.4	44.7	25.2	38.9	40.9	34.9
1970	39.0	40.3	39.2	40.3	40.8	41.7	43.1	46.7	25.6	40.8	42.5	36.3
1971	40.8	42.0	40.8	42.0	42.7	43.2	44.7	48.5	26.1	42.1	44.0	37.6
1972	42.0	43.3	42.1	43.4	44.0	44.5	45.8	49.7	26.4	43.5	45.0	38.6
1973	43.7	46.2	44.8	46.1	45.6	47.8	47.3	51.1	29.1	47.5	46.9	40.3
1974	48.0	51.4	49.8	50.6	49.4	53.5	52.4	55.0	40.4	54.0	52.9	46.9
1975	52.5	56.0	54.3	55.1	53.9	58.2	57.3	60.1	43.4	58.3	57.0	51.5
1976	56.0	59.3	57.2	58.2	57.4	60.7	60.2	63.2	45.4	60.5	59.5	54.1
1977	59.6	63.1	60.8	61.9	61.0	64.2	63.6	66.5	48.7	64.0	62.5	57.2
1978	63.9	67.4	65.4	66.7	65.5	68.8	67.3	70.5	51.0	68.6	65.5	60.4
1979	71.2	74.2	72.9	73.4	71.9	76.6	75.2	76.4	68.7	77.2	74.6	71.2
1980	81.5	82.9	82.8	81.9	80.8	86.0	85.7	83.5	95.2	87.6	88.4	87.1
1981	90.4	91.0	91.4	90.1	89.2	93.2	93.1	90.0	107.6	95.2	96.7	96.8
1982	96.3	96.2	96.8	96.1	95.8	97.0	96.9	95.3	102.9	97.8	98.3	98.2
1983	99.7	99.8	99.6	99.6	99.6	99.8	100.0	100.2	99.0	99.7	100.0	100.0
1984	104.0	103.9	103.7	104.3	104.6	103.2	103.1	104.4	98.1	102.5	101.7	101.8
1985	108.0	107.0	107.2	108.4	109.1	105.4	105.2	107.1	98.2	104.8	104.1	104.1
1986	109.8	108.0	108.8	112.6	113.5	104.4	101.4	108.6	77.2	103.5	98.5	96.9
1987	113.6	111.6	112.6	117.2	118.2	107.7	104.0	111.8	80.2	107.5	101.8	100.3
1988	118.3	115.9	117.0	122.3	123.4	111.5	107.3	115.8	80.8	111.8	105.8	104.0
1989	123.7	121.6	122.4	128.1	129.0	116.7	111.6	119.6	87.9	118.2	111.7	111.3
1990	130.3	128.2	128.8	134.7	135.5	122.8	117.0	123.6	101.2	126.0	119.9	120.9
1991	136.1	133.5	133.8	140.9	142.1	126.6	120.4	128.8	99.1	130.3	124.5	125.7
1992	140.8	137.3	137.5	145.4	147.3	129.1	123.2	132.5	98.3	132.8	127.6	128.9
1993	145.1	141.4	141.2	150.0	152.2	131.5	125.3	135.2	97.3	135.1	129.3	130.7
1994	149.0	144.8	144.7	154.1	156.5	133.8	126.9	137.1	97.6	136.8	129.7	131.6
1995	153.1	148.6	148.6	158.7	161.2	136.4	128.9	139.3	98.8	139.3	130.9	134.1
1996	157.5	152.8	152.8	163.1	165.6	139.9	131.5	141.3	105.7	143.5	134.5	139.5
1997	161.1	155.9	156.3	167.1	169.5	141.8	132.2	142.3	105.7	146.4	136.3	141.8
1998	163.4	157.2	158.6	170.9	173.4	141.9	130.5	143.2	92.1	146.9	134.6	139.2
1999	167.0	160.2	162.0	174.4	177.0	144.4	132.5	144.1	100.0	151.2	139.4	147.5
2000	173.0	165.7	167.3	178.6	181.3	149.2	137.7	144.9	129.5	158.2	149.1	162.9
2001	177.8	169.7	171.9	183.5	186.1	150.7	137.2	145.3	125.2	160.6	149.1	164.1
2002	180.5	170.8	174.3	187.7	190.5	149.7	134.2	143.7	117.1	161.1	147.4	163.3
2003	184.7	174.6	178.1	190.6	193.2	151.2	134.5	140.9	136.7	165.3	151.9	172.1
2004	189.4	179.3	182.7	194.4	196.6	154.7	136.7	139.6	161.2	172.2	159.3	183.8
2005	196.0	186.1	188.7	198.7	200.9	160.2	142.5	140.3	197.4	180.2	170.1	201.2

Table 7-5. Consumer Price Indexes, All Urban Consumers (CPI-U): U.S. City Average, Commodity, Service, and Special Groups, 1967–2005—*Continued*

(1982–1984 = 100, unless otherwise indicated.)

Year	Total services[1]	Rent of shelter[2]	Gas (piped) and electricity	Transportation services	Medical care services	Other services	Services less medical care	Energy	Services less energy
1967	28.8	. . .	23.7	32.6	26.0	36.0	29.3	23.8	29.3
1968	30.3	. . .	23.9	33.9	27.9	38.1	30.8	24.2	30.9
1969	32.4	. . .	24.3	36.3	30.2	40.0	32.9	24.8	33.2
1970	35.0	. . .	25.4	40.2	32.3	42.2	35.6	25.5	36.0
1971	37.0	. . .	27.1	43.4	34.7	44.4	37.5	26.5	38.0
1972	38.4	. . .	28.5	44.4	35.9	45.6	38.9	27.2	39.4
1973	40.1	. . .	29.9	44.7	37.5	47.7	40.6	29.4	41.1
1974	43.8	. . .	34.5	46.3	41.4	51.3	44.3	38.1	44.8
1975	48.0	. . .	40.1	49.8	46.6	55.1	48.3	42.1	48.8
1976	52.0	. . .	44.7	56.9	51.3	58.4	52.2	45.1	52.7
1977	56.0	. . .	50.5	61.5	56.4	62.1	55.9	49.4	56.5
1978	60.8	. . .	55.0	64.4	61.2	66.4	60.7	52.5	61.3
1979	67.5	. . .	61.0	69.5	67.2	71.9	67.5	65.7	68.2
1980	77.9	. . .	71.4	79.2	74.8	78.7	78.2	86.0	78.5
1981	88.1	. . .	81.9	88.6	82.8	86.1	88.7	97.7	88.7
1982	96.0	. . .	93.2	96.1	92.6	93.5	96.4	99.2	96.3
1983	99.4	102.7	101.5	99.1	100.7	100.0	99.2	99.9	99.2
1984	104.6	107.7	105.4	104.8	106.7	106.5	104.4	100.9	104.5
1985	109.9	113.9	107.1	110.0	113.2	113.0	109.6	101.6	110.2
1986	115.4	120.2	105.7	116.3	121.9	119.4	114.6	88.2	116.5
1987	120.2	125.9	103.8	121.9	130.0	125.7	119.1	88.6	122.0
1988	125.7	132.0	104.6	128.0	138.3	132.6	124.3	89.3	127.9
1989	131.9	138.0	107.5	135.6	148.9	140.9	130.1	94.3	134.4
1990	139.2	145.5	109.3	144.2	162.7	150.2	136.8	102.1	142.3
1991	146.3	152.1	112.6	151.2	177.1	159.8	143.3	102.5	149.8
1992	152.0	157.3	114.8	155.7	190.5	168.5	148.4	103.0	155.9
1993	157.9	162.0	118.5	162.9	202.9	177.0	153.6	104.2	161.9
1994	163.1	167.0	119.2	168.6	213.4	185.4	158.4	104.6	167.6
1995	168.7	172.4	119.2	175.9	224.2	193.3	163.5	105.2	173.7
1996	174.1	178.0	122.1	180.5	232.4	201.4	168.7	110.1	179.4
1997	179.4	183.4	125.1	185.0	239.1	209.6	173.9	111.5	185.0
1998	184.2	189.6	121.2	187.9	246.8	216.9	178.4	102.9	190.6
1999	188.8	195.0	120.9	190.7	255.1	223.1	182.7	106.6	195.7
2000	195.3	201.3	128.0	196.1	266.0	229.9	188.9	124.6	202.1
2001	203.4	208.9	142.4	201.9	278.8	238.0	196.6	129.3	209.6
2002	209.8	216.7	134.4	209.1	292.9	246.4	202.5	121.7	217.5
2003	216.5	221.9	145.0	216.3	306.0	254.4	208.7	136.5	223.8
2004	222.8	227.9	150.6	220.6	321.3	261.3	214.5	151.4	230.2
2005	230.1	233.7	166.5	225.7	336.7	268.4	221.2	177.1	236.6

[1]Includes tenants, household insurance, water, sewer, trash, and household operations services, not shown separately.
[2]December 1982 = 100.
. . . = Not available.

Table 7-6. Consumer Price Indexes, All Urban Consumers (CPI-U): U.S. City Average, Selected Groups and Purchasing Power of the Consumer Dollar, 1913–2005

(1982–1984 = 100, unless otherwise indicated.)

Year	All items	Food	Rent of primary residence	Owners' equivalent of primary residence[1]	Apparel	Purchasing power of the consumer dollar[2]
1913	9.9	10.0	21.0	. . .	14.9	10.08
1914	10.0	10.2	21.0	. . .	15.0	9.94
1915	10.1	10.0	21.1	. . .	15.3	9.84
1916	10.9	11.3	21.3	. . .	16.8	9.15
1917	12.8	14.5	21.2	. . .	20.2	7.79
1918	15.1	16.7	21.5	. . .	27.3	6.64
1919	17.3	18.6	23.3	. . .	36.2	5.78
1920	20.0	21.0	27.4	. . .	43.1	4.99
1921	17.9	15.9	31.5	. . .	33.2	5.59
1922	16.8	14.9	32.4	. . .	27.0	5.96
1923	17.1	15.4	33.2	. . .	27.1	5.86
1924	17.1	15.2	34.4	. . .	26.8	5.85
1925	17.5	16.5	34.6	. . .	26.3	5.70
1926	17.7	17.0	34.2	. . .	25.9	5.65
1927	17.4	16.4	33.7	. . .	25.3	5.76
1928	17.1	16.3	32.9	. . .	25.0	5.83
1929	17.1	16.5	32.1	. . .	24.7	5.83
1930	16.7	15.6	31.2	. . .	24.2	5.99
1931	15.2	12.9	29.6	. . .	22.0	6.56
1932	13.7	10.7	26.5	. . .	19.5	7.32
1933	13.0	10.4	22.9	. . .	18.8	7.71
1934	13.4	11.6	21.4	. . .	20.6	7.46
1935	13.7	12.4	21.4	. . .	20.8	7.28
1936	13.9	12.6	21.9	. . .	21.0	7.21
1937	14.4	13.1	22.9	. . .	22.0	6.96
1938	14.1	12.1	23.7	. . .	21.9	7.09
1939	13.9	11.8	23.7	. . .	21.6	7.20
1940	14.0	12.0	23.7	. . .	21.8	7.13
1941	14.7	13.1	24.2	. . .	22.8	6.79
1942	16.3	15.4	24.7	. . .	26.7	6.13
1943	17.3	17.1	24.7	. . .	27.8	5.78
1944	17.6	16.9	24.8	. . .	29.8	5.68
1945	18.0	17.3	24.8	. . .	31.4	5.55
1946	19.5	19.8	25.0	. . .	34.4	5.12
1947	22.3	24.1	25.8	. . .	39.9	4.47
1948	24.1	26.1	27.5	. . .	42.5	4.15
1949	23.8	25.0	28.7	. . .	40.8	4.19
1950	24.1	25.4	29.7	. . .	40.3	4.15
1951	26.0	28.2	30.9	. . .	43.9	3.85
1952	26.5	28.7	32.2	. . .	43.5	3.77
1953	26.7	28.3	33.9	. . .	43.1	3.74
1954	26.9	28.2	35.1	. . .	43.1	3.72
1955	26.8	27.8	35.6	. . .	42.9	3.73
1956	27.2	28.0	36.3	. . .	43.7	3.68
1957	28.1	28.9	37.0	. . .	44.5	3.55
1958	28.9	30.2	37.6	. . .	44.6	3.46
1959	29.1	29.7	38.2	. . .	45.0	3.43

[1]December 1982 = 100.
[2]Purchasing power in 1982–1984 = $1.00.
. . . = Not available.

Table 7-6. Consumer Price Indexes, All Urban Consumers (CPI-U): U.S. City Average, Selected Groups and Purchasing Power of the Consumer Dollar, 1913–2005—*Continued*

(1982–1984 = 100, unless otherwise indicated.)

Year	All items	Food	Rent of primary residence	Owners' equivalent of primary residence[1]	Apparel	Purchasing power of the consumer dollar[2]
1960	29.6	30.0	38.7	. . .	45.7	3.37
1961	29.9	30.4	39.2	. . .	46.1	3.34
1962	30.2	30.6	39.7	. . .	46.3	3.30
1963	30.6	31.1	40.1	. . .	46.9	3.27
1964	31.0	31.5	40.5	. . .	47.3	3.22
1965	31.5	32.2	40.9	. . .	47.8	3.17
1966	32.4	33.8	41.5	. . .	49.0	3.08
1967	33.4	34.1	42.2	. . .	51.0	2.99
1968	34.8	35.3	43.3	. . .	53.7	2.87
1969	36.7	37.1	44.7	. . .	56.8	2.73
1970	38.8	39.2	46.5	. . .	59.2	2.57
1971	40.5	40.4	48.7	. . .	61.1	2.47
1972	41.8	42.1	50.4	. . .	62.3	2.39
1973	44.4	48.2	52.5	. . .	64.6	2.25
1974	49.3	55.1	55.2	. . .	69.4	2.03
1975	53.8	59.8	58.0	. . .	72.5	1.86
1976	56.9	61.6	61.1	. . .	75.2	1.76
1977	60.6	65.5	64.8	. . .	78.6	1.65
1978	65.2	72.0	69.3	. . .	81.4	1.53
1979	72.6	79.9	74.3	. . .	84.9	1.38
1980	82.4	86.8	80.9	. . .	90.9	1.22
1981	90.9	93.6	87.9	. . .	95.3	1.10
1982	96.5	97.4	94.6	. . .	97.8	1.04
1983	99.6	99.4	100.1	102.5	100.2	1.00
1984	103.9	103.2	105.3	107.3	102.1	0.96
1985	107.6	105.6	111.8	113.2	105.0	0.93
1986	109.6	109.0	118.3	119.4	105.9	0.91
1987	113.6	113.5	123.1	124.8	110.6	0.88
1988	118.3	118.2	127.8	131.1	115.4	0.85
1989	124.0	125.1	132.8	137.4	118.6	0.81
1990	130.7	132.4	138.4	144.8	124.1	0.77
1991	136.2	136.3	143.3	150.4	128.7	0.73
1992	140.3	137.9	146.9	155.5	131.9	0.71
1993	144.5	140.9	150.3	160.5	133.7	0.69
1994	148.2	144.3	154.0	165.8	133.4	0.68
1995	152.4	148.4	157.8	171.3	132.0	0.66
1996	156.9	153.3	162.0	176.8	131.7	0.64
1997	160.5	157.3	166.7	181.9	132.9	0.62
1998	163.0	160.7	172.1	187.8	133.0	0.61
1999	166.6	164.1	177.5	192.9	131.3	0.60
2000	172.2	167.8	183.9	198.7	129.6	0.58
2001	177.1	173.1	192.1	206.3	127.3	0.57
2002	179.9	176.2	199.7	214.7	124.0	0.56
2003	184.0	180.0	205.5	219.9	120.9	0.54
2004	188.9	186.2	211.0	224.9	120.4	0.53
2005	195.3	190.7	217.3	230.2	119.5	0.51

[1]December 1982 = 100.
[2]Purchasing power in 1982–1984 = $1.00.
. . . = Not available.

Table 7-7. Consumer Price Indexes, Urban Wage Earners and Clerical Workers (CPI-W): U.S. City Average, Major Groups, 1913–2005

(1982–1984 = 100, unless otherwise indicated.)

Year	All items	Food and beverages	Housing	Apparel	Transportation	Medical care	Recreation[1]	Education and communication[1]	Other goods and services
1913	10.0	. . .	. . .	15.0	. . .	. . .	. . .	. . .	. . .
1914	10.1	. . .	. . .	15.1	. . .	. . .	. . .	. . .	. . .
1915	10.2	. . .	. . .	15.4	. . .	. . .	. . .	. . .	. . .
1916	11.0	. . .	. . .	16.9	. . .	. . .	. . .	. . .	. . .
1917	12.9	. . .	. . .	20.3	. . .	. . .	. . .	. . .	. . .
1918	15.1	. . .	. . .	27.5	. . .	. . .	. . .	. . .	. . .
1919	17.4	. . .	. . .	36.4	. . .	. . .	. . .	. . .	. . .
1920	20.1	. . .	. . .	43.3	. . .	. . .	. . .	. . .	. . .
1921	18.0	. . .	. . .	33.4	. . .	. . .	. . .	. . .	. . .
1922	16.9	. . .	. . .	27.2	. . .	. . .	. . .	. . .	. . .
1923	17.2	. . .	. . .	27.2	. . .	. . .	. . .	. . .	. . .
1924	17.2	. . .	. . .	26.9	. . .	. . .	. . .	. . .	. . .
1925	17.6	. . .	. . .	26.4	. . .	. . .	. . .	. . .	. . .
1926	17.8	. . .	. . .	26.0	. . .	. . .	. . .	. . .	. . .
1927	17.5	. . .	. . .	25.5	. . .	. . .	. . .	. . .	. . .
1928	17.2	. . .	. . .	25.1	. . .	. . .	. . .	. . .	. . .
1929	17.2	. . .	. . .	24.8	. . .	. . .	. . .	. . .	. . .
1930	16.8	. . .	. . .	24.3	. . .	. . .	. . .	. . .	. . .
1931	15.3	. . .	. . .	22.1	. . .	. . .	. . .	. . .	. . .
1932	13.7	. . .	. . .	19.6	. . .	. . .	. . .	. . .	. . .
1933	13.0	. . .	. . .	18.9	. . .	. . .	. . .	. . .	. . .
1934	13.5	. . .	. . .	20.7	. . .	. . .	. . .	. . .	. . .
1935	13.8	. . .	. . .	20.9	14.1	10.2	. . .	. . .	. . .
1936	13.9	. . .	. . .	21.1	14.2	10.3	. . .	. . .	. . .
1937	14.4	. . .	. . .	22.1	14.5	10.4	. . .	. . .	. . .
1938	14.2	. . .	. . .	22.0	14.6	10.4	. . .	. . .	. . .
1939	14.0	. . .	. . .	21.7	14.2	10.4	. . .	. . .	. . .
1940	14.1	. . .	. . .	21.9	14.1	10.4	. . .	. . .	. . .
1941	14.8	. . .	. . .	23.0	14.6	10.5	. . .	. . .	. . .
1942	16.4	. . .	. . .	26.8	15.9	10.8	. . .	. . .	. . .
1943	17.4	. . .	. . .	28.0	15.8	11.3	. . .	. . .	. . .
1944	17.7	. . .	. . .	30.0	15.8	11.6	. . .	. . .	. . .
1945	18.1	. . .	. . .	31.5	15.8	11.9	. . .	. . .	. . .
1946	19.6	. . .	. . .	34.6	16.6	12.6	. . .	. . .	. . .
1947	22.5	. . .	. . .	40.1	18.4	13.6	. . .	. . .	. . .
1948	24.2	. . .	. . .	42.7	20.4	14.5	. . .	. . .	. . .
1949	24.0	. . .	. . .	41.0	22.0	14.9	. . .	. . .	. . .
1950	24.2	. . .	. . .	40.5	22.6	15.2	. . .	. . .	. . .
1951	26.1	. . .	. . .	44.1	24.0	15.9	. . .	. . .	. . .
1952	26.7	. . .	. . .	43.7	25.6	16.8	. . .	. . .	. . .
1953	26.9	. . .	. . .	43.3	26.3	17.4	. . .	. . .	. . .
1954	27.0	. . .	. . .	43.3	25.9	17.9	. . .	. . .	. . .
1955	26.9	. . .	. . .	43.1	25.6	18.3	. . .	. . .	. . .
1956	27.3	. . .	. . .	44.0	26.1	19.0	. . .	. . .	. . .
1957	28.3	. . .	. . .	44.7	27.6	19.8	. . .	. . .	. . .
1958	29.1	. . .	. . .	44.8	28.4	20.7	. . .	. . .	. . .
1959	29.3	. . .	. . .	45.2	29.6	21.6	. . .	. . .	. . .

[1]December 1997 = 100.
. . . = Not available.

Table 7-7. Consumer Price Indexes, Urban Wage Earners and Clerical Workers (CPI-W): U.S. City Average, Major Groups, 1913–2005—*Continued*

(1982–1984 = 100, unless otherwise indicated.)

Year	All items	Food and beverages	Housing	Apparel	Transportation	Medical care	Recreation[1]	Education and communication[1]	Other goods and services
1960	29.8	...	...	45.9	29.6	22.4	...	...	...
1961	30.1	...	...	46.3	30.0	23.0	...	...	...
1962	30.4	...	...	46.6	30.6	23.6	...	...	...
1963	30.8	...	...	47.1	30.8	24.2	...	...	...
1964	31.2	...	...	47.5	31.2	24.7	...	...	...
1965	31.7	...	...	48.0	31.7	25.3	...	...	...
1966	32.6	...	...	49.2	32.2	26.4	...	...	...
1967	33.6	35.0	31.1	51.2	33.1	28.3	...	...	35.4
1968	35.0	36.2	32.3	54.0	34.1	30.0	...	...	37.2
1969	36.9	38.0	34.3	57.1	35.5	32.1	...	...	39.1
1970	39.0	40.1	36.7	59.5	37.3	34.1	...	...	41.3
1971	40.7	41.3	38.3	61.4	39.2	36.3	...	...	43.3
1972	42.1	43.1	39.8	62.7	39.7	37.5	...	...	45.1
1973	44.7	48.8	41.5	65.0	41.0	39.0	...	...	46.9
1974	49.6	55.5	46.2	69.8	45.5	42.6	...	...	50.2
1975	54.1	60.2	51.1	72.9	49.8	47.7	...	...	54.4
1976	57.2	62.0	54.2	75.6	54.7	52.3	...	...	57.6
1977	60.9	65.7	57.9	79.0	58.6	57.3	...	...	60.9
1978	65.6	72.1	62.9	81.7	61.5	62.1	...	...	64.8
1979	73.1	79.9	70.7	85.2	70.4	68.0	...	...	69.4
1980	82.9	86.9	81.7	90.9	82.9	75.6	...	...	75.6
1981	91.4	93.6	91.1	95.6	93.0	83.5	...	...	82.5
1982	96.9	97.3	97.7	97.8	97.0	92.5	...	...	90.9
1983	99.8	99.5	100.0	100.2	99.2	100.5	...	...	101.3
1984	103.3	103.2	102.2	102.0	103.8	106.9	...	...	107.9
1985	106.9	105.5	106.6	105.0	106.4	113.6	...	...	114.2
1986	108.6	108.9	109.7	105.8	101.7	122.0	...	...	120.9
1987	112.5	113.3	112.8	110.4	105.1	130.2	...	...	127.8
1988	117.0	117.9	116.8	114.9	108.3	139.0	...	...	136.5
1989	122.6	124.6	121.2	117.9	113.9	149.6	...	...	147.4
1990	129.0	131.8	126.4	123.1	120.1	162.7	...	...	158.9
1991	134.3	136.5	131.2	127.4	123.1	176.5	...	...	171.7
1992	138.2	138.3	135.0	130.7	125.8	189.6	...	...	183.3
1993	142.1	141.2	138.5	132.4	129.4	200.9	91.2	86.0	192.2
1994	145.6	144.4	142.0	132.2	133.4	210.4	93.0	89.1	196.4
1995	149.8	148.3	145.4	130.9	138.8	219.8	94.7	92.3	204.2
1996	154.1	153.2	149.6	130.9	142.8	227.6	97.5	95.4	212.2
1997	157.6	157.2	153.4	132.1	143.6	234.0	99.7	98.5	221.6
1998	159.7	160.4	156.7	131.6	140.5	241.4	100.9	100.4	236.1
1999	163.2	163.8	160.0	130.1	143.4	249.7	101.3	101.5	261.9
2000	168.9	167.7	165.4	128.3	152.8	259.9	102.4	102.7	276.5
2001	173.5	173.0	172.1	126.1	153.6	271.8	103.6	105.3	289.5
2002	175.9	176.1	175.7	123.1	151.8	284.6	104.6	107.6	302.0
2003	179.8	179.9	180.4	120.0	156.3	296.3	105.5	109.0	307.0
2004	184.5	186.2	185.0	120.0	161.5	309.5	106.3	110.0	312.6
2005	191.0	190.5	191.2	119.1	173.0	322.8	106.8	111.4	322.2

[1]December 1997 = 100.
. . . = Not available.

Table 7-8. Consumer Price Indexes, All Urban Consumers (CPI-U): U.S. City Average, by Expenditure Category, 1990–2005

(1982–1984 = 100, unless otherwise indicated.)

Expenditure category	1990	1991	1992	1993	1994	1995	1996	1997	1998	1999	2000	2001	2002	2003	2004	2005
ALL ITEMS	130.7	136.2	140.3	144.5	148.2	152.4	156.9	160.5	163.0	166.6	172.2	177.1	179.9	184.0	188.9	195.3
Food and Beverages	132.1	136.8	138.7	141.6	144.9	148.9	153.7	157.7	161.1	164.6	168.4	173.6	176.8	180.5	186.6	191.2
Food	132.4	136.3	137.9	140.9	144.3	148.4	153.3	157.3	160.7	164.1	167.8	173.1	176.2	180.0	186.2	190.7
Food at home	132.3	135.8	136.8	140.1	144.1	148.8	154.3	158.1	161.1	164.2	167.9	173.4	175.6	179.4	186.2	189.8
Cereals and bakery products	140.0	145.8	151.5	156.6	163.0	167.5	174.0	177.6	181.1	185.0	188.3	193.8	198.0	202.8	206.0	209.0
Meats, poultry, fish, and eggs	130.0	132.6	130.9	135.5	137.2	138.8	144.8	148.5	147.3	147.9	154.5	161.3	162.1	169.3	181.7	184.7
Dairy and related products	126.5	125.1	128.5	129.4	131.7	132.8	142.1	145.5	150.8	159.6	160.7	167.1	168.1	167.9	180.2	182.4
Fruits and vegetables	149.0	155.8	155.4	159.0	165.0	177.7	183.9	187.5	198.2	203.1	204.6	212.2	220.9	225.9	232.7	241.4
Nonalcoholic beverages and beverage materials	113.5	114.1	114.3	114.6	123.2	131.7	128.6	133.4	133.0	134.3	137.8	139.2	139.2	139.8	140.4	144.4
Other food at home	123.4	127.3	128.8	130.5	135.6	140.8	142.9	147.3	150.8	153.5	155.6	159.6	160.8	162.6	164.9	167.0
Sugar and sweets	124.7	129.3	133.1	133.4	135.2	137.5	143.7	147.8	150.2	152.3	154.0	155.7	159.0	162.0	163.2	165.2
Fats and oils	126.3	131.7	129.8	130.0	133.5	137.3	140.5	141.7	146.9	148.3	147.4	155.7	155.4	157.4	167.8	167.7
Other foods	131.2	137.1	140.1	143.7	147.5	151.1	156.2	161.2	165.5	168.9	172.2	176.0	177.1	178.8	179.7	182.5
Other miscellaneous foods[1]	...	...	...	...	...	...	...	...	102.6	104.9	107.5	108.9	109.2	110.3	110.4	111.3
Food away from home	133.4	137.9	140.7	143.2	145.7	149.0	152.7	157.0	161.1	165.1	169.0	173.9	178.3	182.1	187.5	193.4
Other food away from home[1]	...	...	...	...	...	...	...	...	101.6	105.2	109.0	113.4	117.7	121.3	125.3	131.3
Alcoholic beverages	129.3	142.8	147.3	149.6	151.5	153.9	158.5	162.8	165.7	169.7	174.7	179.3	183.6	187.2	192.1	195.9
Housing	128.5	133.6	137.5	141.2	144.8	148.5	152.8	156.8	160.4	163.9	169.6	176.4	180.3	184.8	189.5	195.7
Shelter	140.0	146.3	151.2	155.7	160.5	165.7	171.0	176.3	182.1	187.3	193.4	200.6	208.1	213.1	218.8	224.4
Rent of primary residence	138.4	143.3	146.9	150.3	154.0	157.8	162.0	166.7	172.1	177.5	183.9	192.1	199.7	205.5	211.0	217.3
Lodging away from home[1]	...	...	...	...	...	...	...	...	109.0	112.3	117.5	118.6	118.3	119.3	125.9	130.3
Owners' equivalent rent of primary residence[2]	144.8	150.4	155.5	160.5	165.8	171.3	176.8	181.9	187.8	192.9	198.7	206.3	214.7	219.9	224.9	230.2
Tenants' and household insurance[1]	...	...	...	...	...	...	...	...	99.8	101.3	103.7	106.2	108.7	114.8	116.2	117.6
Fuels and utilities	111.6	115.3	117.8	121.3	122.8	123.7	127.5	130.8	128.5	128.8	137.9	150.2	143.6	154.5	161.9	179.0
Fuels	104.5	106.7	108.1	111.2	111.7	111.5	115.2	117.9	113.7	113.5	122.8	135.4	127.2	138.2	144.4	161.6
Fuel oil and other fuels	99.3	94.6	90.7	90.3	88.8	88.1	99.2	99.8	90.0	91.4	129.7	129.3	115.5	139.5	160.5	208.6
Gas (piped) and electricity	109.3	112.6	114.8	118.5	119.2	119.2	122.1	125.1	121.2	120.9	128.0	142.4	134.4	145.0	150.6	166.5
Water, sewer, and trash collection services[1]	...	...	...	...	...	...	...	...	101.6	104.0	106.5	109.6	113.0	117.2	124.0	130.3
Household furnishings and operations	113.3	116.0	118.0	119.3	121.0	123.0	124.7	125.4	126.6	126.7	128.2	129.1	128.3	126.1	125.5	126.1
Household operations[1]	...	...	...	...	...	...	...	...	101.5	104.5	110.5	115.6	119.0	121.8	125.0	130.3
Apparel	124.1	128.7	131.9	133.7	133.4	132.0	131.7	132.9	133.0	131.3	129.6	127.3	124.0	120.9	120.4	119.5
Men's and boys' apparel	120.4	124.2	126.5	127.5	126.4	126.2	127.7	130.1	131.8	131.1	129.7	125.7	121.7	118.0	117.5	116.1
Women's and girls' apparel	122.6	127.6	130.4	132.6	130.9	126.9	124.7	126.1	126.0	123.3	121.5	119.3	115.8	113.1	113.0	110.8
Infants' and toddlers' apparel	125.8	128.9	129.3	127.1	128.1	127.2	129.7	129.0	126.1	129.0	130.6	129.2	126.4	122.1	118.5	116.7
Footwear	117.4	120.9	125.0	125.9	126.0	125.4	126.6	127.6	128.0	125.7	123.8	123.0	121.4	119.6	119.3	122.6
Transportation	120.5	123.8	126.5	130.4	134.3	139.1	143.0	144.3	141.6	144.4	153.3	154.3	152.9	157.6	163.1	173.9
Private transportation	118.8	121.9	124.6	127.5	131.4	136.3	140.0	141.0	137.9	140.5	149.1	150.0	148.8	153.6	159.4	170.2
New and used motor vehicles[1]	...	...	...	91.8	95.5	99.4	101.0	100.5	100.1	100.1	100.8	101.3	99.2	96.5	94.2	95.6
New vehicles	121.4	126.0	129.2	132.7	137.6	141.0	143.7	144.3	143.4	142.9	142.8	142.1	140.0	137.9	137.1	137.9
Used cars and trucks	117.6	118.1	123.2	133.9	141.7	156.5	157.0	151.1	150.6	152.0	155.8	158.7	152.0	142.9	133.3	139.4
Motor fuel	101.2	99.4	99.0	98.0	98.5	100.0	106.3	106.2	92.2	100.7	129.3	124.7	116.6	135.8	160.4	195.7
Gasoline (all types)	101.0	99.2	99.0	97.7	98.2	99.8	105.9	105.8	91.6	100.1	128.6	124.0	116.0	135.1	159.7	194.7
Motor vehicle parts and equipment	100.9	102.2	103.1	101.6	101.4	102.1	102.2	101.9	101.1	100.5	101.5	104.8	106.9	107.8	108.7	111.9
Motor vehicle maintenance and repair	130.1	136.0	141.3	145.9	150.2	154.0	158.4	162.7	167.1	171.9	177.3	183.5	190.2	195.6	200.2	206.9
Public transportation	142.6	148.9	151.4	167.0	172.0	175.9	181.9	186.7	190.3	197.7	209.6	210.6	207.4	209.3	209.1	217.3
Medical Care	162.8	177.0	190.1	201.4	211.0	220.5	228.2	234.6	242.1	250.6	260.8	272.8	285.6	297.1	310.1	323.2
Medical care commodities	163.4	176.8	188.1	195.0	200.7	204.5	210.4	215.3	221.8	230.7	238.1	247.6	256.4	262.8	269.3	276.0
Medical care services	162.7	177.1	190.5	202.9	213.4	224.2	232.4	239.1	246.8	255.1	266.0	278.8	292.9	306.0	321.3	336.7
Professional services	156.1	165.7	175.8	184.7	192.5	201.0	208.3	215.4	222.2	229.2	237.7	246.5	253.9	261.2	271.5	281.7
Hospital and related services	178.0	196.1	214.0	231.9	245.6	257.8	269.5	278.4	287.5	299.5	317.3	338.3	367.8	394.8	417.9	439.9
Recreation[1]	...	...	...	90.7	92.7	94.5	97.4	99.6	101.1	102.0	103.3	104.9	106.2	107.5	108.6	109.4
Video and audio[1]	...	...	...	96.5	95.4	95.1	96.6	99.4	101.1	100.7	101.0	101.5	102.8	103.6	104.2	104.2
Education and Communication[1]	...	...	...	85.5	88.8	92.2	95.3	98.4	100.3	101.2	102.5	105.2	107.9	109.8	111.6	113.7
Education[1]	...	...	...	78.4	83.3	88.0	92.7	97.3	102.1	107.0	112.5	118.5	126.0	134.4	143.7	152.7
Educational books and supplies	171.3	180.3	190.3	197.6	205.5	214.4	226.9	238.4	250.8	261.7	279.9	295.9	317.6	335.4	351.0	365.6
Tuition, other school fees, and childcare	175.7	191.4	208.5	225.3	239.8	253.8	267.1	280.4	294.2	308.4	324.0	341.1	362.1	386.7	414.3	440.9
Communication[1]	...	...	...	96.7	97.6	98.8	99.6	100.3	98.7	96.0	93.6	93.3	92.3	89.7	86.7	84.7
Information and information processing[1]	...	...	...	97.7	98.6	98.7	99.5	100.4	98.5	95.5	92.8	92.3	90.8	87.8	84.6	82.6
Telephone services[1]	...	...	...	...	...	...	...	...	100.7	100.1	98.5	99.3	99.7	98.3	95.8	94.9
Information technology, hardware, and services[3]	93.5	88.6	83.7	78.8	72.0	63.8	57.2	50.1	39.9	30.5	25.9	21.3	18.3	16.1	14.8	13.6
Personal computers and peripheral equipment[1]	...	...	...	...	...	...	...	...	78.2	53.5	41.1	29.5	22.2	17.6	15.3	12.8
Other Goods and Services	159.0	171.6	183.3	192.9	198.5	206.9	215.4	224.8	237.7	258.3	271.1	282.6	293.2	298.7	304.7	313.4
Tobacco and smoking products	181.5	202.7	219.8	228.4	220.0	225.7	232.8	243.7	274.8	355.8	394.9	425.2	461.5	469.0	478.0	502.8
Personal care	130.4	134.9	138.3	141.5	144.6	147.1	150.1	152.7	156.7	161.1	165.6	170.5	174.7	178.0	181.7	185.6
Personal care products	128.2	132.8	136.5	139.0	141.5	143.1	144.3	144.2	148.3	151.8	153.7	155.1	154.7	153.5	153.9	154.4
Personal care services	132.8	137.0	140.0	144.0	147.9	151.5	156.6	162.4	166.0	171.4	178.1	184.3	188.4	193.2	197.6	203.9
Miscellaneous personal services	158.4	168.8	177.5	186.1	195.9	205.9	215.6	226.1	234.7	243.0	252.3	263.1	274.4	283.5	293.9	303.0

[1]December 1997 = 100.
[2]December 1982 = 100.
[3]December 1988 = 100.
... = Not available.

Table 7-9. Relative Importance of Components in the Consumer Price Index: U.S. City Average, Selected Groups, December 1997–December 2005

(Percent distribution.)

Index and year	All items	Food and beverages	Housing	Apparel	Transportation	Medical care	Recreation	Education and communication	Other goods and services
ALL URBAN CONSUMERS (CPI-U)									
December 1997	100.0	16.3	39.6	4.9	17.6	5.6	6.1	5.5	4.3
December 1998	100.0	16.4	39.8	4.8	17.0	5.7	6.1	5.5	4.6
December 1999	100.0	16.3	39.6	4.7	17.5	5.8	6.0	5.4	4.7
December 2000	100.0	16.2	40.0	4.4	17.6	5.8	5.9	5.3	4.8
December 2001[1]	100.0	16.4	40.5	4.2	16.6	6.0	5.9	5.4	4.9
December 2001[2]	100.0	15.7	40.9	4.4	17.1	5.8	6.0	5.8	4.3
December 2002	100.0	15.6	40.9	4.2	17.3	6.0	5.9	5.8	4.4
December 2003	100.0	15.4	42.1	4.0	16.9	6.1	5.9	5.9	3.8
December 2004	100.0	15.3	42.0	3.8	17.4	6.1	5.7	5.8	3.8
December 2005	100.0	15.1	42.2	3.7	17.7	6.2	5.6	5.8	3.7
URBAN WAGE EARNERS AND WORKERS (CPI-W)									
December 1997	100.0	17.9	36.5	5.3	19.8	4.6	6.0	5.4	4.5
December 1998	100.0	18.0	36.7	5.2	19.2	4.7	5.9	5.4	5.0
December 1999	100.0	17.9	36.5	5.0	19.7	4.7	5.8	5.3	5.1
December 2000	100.0	17.8	36.8	4.8	19.9	4.7	5.7	5.2	5.2
December 2001[1]	100.0	18.0	37.3	4.6	18.8	4.9	5.7	5.3	5.4
December 2001[2]	100.0	17.2	38.1	4.8	19.4	4.6	5.6	5.6	4.5
December 2002	100.0	17.1	38.1	4.6	19.7	4.7	5.6	5.6	4.6
December 2003	100.0	17.2	39.1	4.4	19.1	5.0	5.7	5.6	3.9
December 2004	100.0	17.0	39.0	4.2	19.8	5.0	5.5	5.5	3.9
December 2005	100.0	16.8	39.2	4.0	20.1	5.1	5.4	5.4	3.9

[1]1993–1995 weights.
[2]1999–2000 weights.

Table 7-10. Consumer Price Indexes, All Urban Consumers (CPI-U), All Items: Selected Metropolitan Statistical Areas, Selected Years, 1960–2005

(1982–1984 = 100, unless otherwise indicated.)

Area	1960	1965	1970	1975	1980	1981	1982	1983	1984	1985	1986	1987	1988	1989	1990
NORTHEAST															
Boston-Brockton-Nashua, MA-NH-ME-CT	29.8	32.5	40.2	55.8	82.6	91.8	95.5	99.8	104.7	109.4	112.2	117.1	124.2	131.3	138.9
New York-Northern New Jersey-Long Island, NY-NJ-CT-PA	30.2	32.6	41.2	57.6	82.1	90.1	95.3	99.8	104.8	108.7	112.3	118.0	123.7	130.6	138.5
Philadelphia-Wilmington-Atlantic City, PA-NJ-DE-MD	30.6	32.8	40.8	56.8	83.6	92.1	96.6	99.4	104.1	108.8	111.5	116.8	122.4	128.3	135.8
Pittsburgh, PA	29.7	31.4	38.1	52.4	81.0	89.3	94.4	101.1	104.5	106.9	108.2	111.4	114.9	120.1	126.2
NORTH CENTRAL															
Chicago-Gary-Kenosha, IL-IN-WI	30.4	31.7	38.9	52.8	82.2	90.0	96.2	100.0	103.8	107.7	110.0	114.5	119.0	125.0	131.7
Cincinnati-Hamilton, OH-KY-IN	29.1	30.5	37.4	51.8	82.1	87.9	94.9	100.8	104.3	106.6	107.6	111.9	116.1	120.9	126.5
Cleveland-Akron, OH	28.3	29.6	37.2	50.2	78.9	87.2	94.0	101.2	104.8	107.8	109.4	112.7	116.7	122.7	129.0
Detroit-Ann Arbor-Flint, MI	29.7	31.2	39.5	53.9	85.3	93.2	97.0	99.8	103.2	106.8	108.3	111.7	116.1	122.3	128.6
Kansas City, MO-KS	29.3	32.2	39.0	53.2	83.6	90.5	95.0	100.5	104.5	107.7	108.7	113.1	117.4	121.6	126.0
Milwaukee-Racine, WI	29.2	31.0	37.5	50.8	81.4	90.7	95.9	100.2	103.8	107.0	107.4	111.5	115.5	120.8	126.2
Minneapolis-St. Paul, MN-WI	28.3	30.1	37.4	51.2	78.9	88.6	97.4	99.5	103.1	107.0	108.4	111.6	117.2	122.0	127.0
St. Louis, MO-IL	29.5	31.7	38.8	52.6	82.5	90.1	96.6	100.1	103.3	107.1	108.6	112.2	115.7	121.8	128.1
SOUTH															
Atlanta, GA	29.6	31.2	38.6	53.6	80.3	90.2	96.0	99.9	104.1	108.9	112.2	116.5	120.4	126.1	131.7
Dallas-Fort Worth, TX	. . .	29.9	37.6	50.4	81.5	90.8	96.0	99.7	104.3	108.2	109.9	112.9	116.1	119.5	125.1
Houston-Galveston-Brazoria, TX	27.8	29.6	36.4	51.4	82.7	91.0	97.3	100.0	102.7	104.9	103.9	106.5	109.5	114.1	120.6
Miami-Fort Lauderdale, FL	. . .	. . .	. . .	. . .	81.1	90.5	96.7	99.9	103.5	106.5	107.9	111.8	116.8	121.5	128.0
Tampa-St. Petersburg-Clearwater, FL[1]	. . .	. . .	. . .	. . .	. . .	. . .	. . .	. . .	. . .	. . .	. . .	. . .	100.0	103.7	107.2	111.7
Washington-Baltimore, DC-MD-VA-WV[2]	. . .	. . .	. . .	. . .	. . .	. . .	. . .	. . .	. . .	. . .	. . .	. . .	. . .	. . .	. . .
WEST															
Anchorage, AK	. . .	35.3	41.1	57.1	85.5	92.4	97.4	99.2	103.3	105.8	107.8	108.2	108.6	111.7	118.6
Denver-Boulder-Greeley, CO	. . .	28.8	34.5	48.4	78.4	87.2	95.1	100.5	104.3	107.1	107.9	110.8	113.7	115.8	120.9
Honolulu, HI	. . .	34.4	41.5	56.3	83.0	91.7	97.2	99.3	103.5	106.8	109.4	114.9	121.7	128.7	138.1
Los Angeles-Riverside-Orange County, CA	30.0	32.4	38.7	53.3	83.7	91.9	97.3	99.1	103.6	108.4	111.9	116.7	122.1	128.3	135.9
Phoenix-Mesa, AZ	. . .	. . .	. . .	. . .	. . .	. . .	. . .	. . .	. . .	. . .	. . .	. . .	. . .	. . .	. . .
Portland-Salem, OR-WA	29.8	32.3	38.7	53.5	87.2	95.0	98.0	99.1	102.8	106.7	108.2	110.9	114.7	120.4	127.4
San Diego, CA	. . .	28.2	34.1	47.6	79.4	90.1	96.2	99.0	104.8	110.4	113.5	117.5	123.4	130.6	138.4
San Francisco-Oakland-San Jose, CA	28.6	30.8	37.7	51.8	80.4	90.8	97.6	98.4	104.0	108.4	111.6	115.4	120.5	126.4	132.1
Seattle-Tacoma-Bremerton, WA	28.8	31.0	37.4	51.1	82.7	91.8	97.7	99.3	103.0	105.6	106.7	109.2	112.8	118.1	126.8

Area	1991	1992	1993	1994	1995	1996	1997	1998	1999	2000	2001	2002	2003	2004	2005
NORTHEAST															
Boston-Brockton-Nashua, MA-NH-ME-CT	145.0	148.6	152.9	154.9	158.6	163.3	167.9	171.7	176.0	183.6	191.5	196.5	203.9	209.5	216.4
New York-Northern New Jersey-Long Island, NY-NJ-CT-PA	144.8	150.0	154.5	158.2	162.2	166.9	170.8	173.6	177.0	182.5	187.1	191.9	197.8	204.8	212.7
Philadelphia-Wilmington-Atlantic City, PA-NJ-DE-MD	142.2	146.6	150.2	154.6	158.7	162.8	166.5	168.2	171.9	176.5	181.3	184.9	188.8	196.5	204.2
Pittsburgh, PA	131.3	136.0	139.9	144.6	149.2	153.2	157.0	159.2	162.5	168.0	172.5	174.0	177.5	183.0	189.8
NORTH CENTRAL															
Chicago-Gary-Kenosha, IL-IN-WI	137.0	141.1	145.4	148.6	153.3	157.4	161.7	165.0	168.4	173.8	178.3	181.2	184.5	188.6	194.3
Cincinnati-Hamilton, OH-KY-IN	131.4	134.1	137.8	142.4	146.2	149.6	152.1	155.1	159.2	164.8	167.9	170.0	173.4	176.5	181.6
Cleveland-Akron, OH	134.2	136.8	140.3	144.4	147.9	152.0	156.1	159.8	162.5	168.0	172.9	173.3	176.2	181.6	187.9
Detroit-Ann Arbor-Flint, MI	133.1	135.9	139.6	144.0	148.6	152.5	156.3	158.9	163.9	169.8	174.4	178.9	182.5	185.4	190.8
Kansas City, MO-KS	131.2	134.3	138.1	141.3	145.3	151.6	155.8	157.8	160.1	166.6	172.2	174.0	177.0	180.7	185.3
Milwaukee-Racine, WI	132.2	137.1	142.1	147.0	151.0	154.7	157.7	160.3	163.7	168.6	171.7	174.0	177.7	180.2	185.2
Minneapolis-St. Paul, MN-WI	130.4	135.0	139.2	143.6	147.0	151.9	155.4	158.3	163.3	170.1	176.5	179.6	182.7	187.9	193.1
St. Louis, MO-IL	132.1	134.7	137.5	141.3	145.2	149.6	152.9	154.5	157.6	163.1	167.3	169.1	173.4	180.3	186.2
SOUTH															
Atlanta, GA	135.9	138.5	143.4	146.7	150.9	156.0	158.9	161.2	164.8	170.6	176.2	178.2	180.8	183.2	188.9
Dallas-Fort Worth, TX	130.8	133.9	137.3	141.2	144.9	148.8	151.4	153.6	158.0	164.7	170.4	172.7	176.2	178.7	184.7
Houston-Galveston-Brazoria, TX	125.1	129.1	133.4	137.9	139.8	142.7	145.4	146.8	148.7	154.2	158.8	159.2	163.7	169.5	175.6
Miami-Fort Lauderdale, FL	132.3	134.5	139.1	143.6	148.9	153.7	158.4	160.5	162.4	167.8	173.0	175.5	180.6	185.6	194.3
Tampa-St. Petersburg-Clearwater, FL[1]	116.4	119.2	124.0	126.5	129.7	131.6	134.0	137.5	140.6	145.7	148.8	153.9	158.1	162.0	168.5
Washington-Baltimore, DC-MD-VA-WV[2]	. . .	. . .	. . .	. . .	. . .	. . .	100.8	102.1	104.2	107.6	110.4	113.0	116.2	119.5	124.3
WEST															
Anchorage, AK	124.0	128.2	132.2	135.0	138.9	142.7	144.8	146.9	148.4	150.9	155.2	158.2	162.5	166.7	171.8
Denver-Boulder-Greeley, CO	125.6	130.3	135.8	141.8	147.9	153.1	158.1	161.9	166.6	173.2	181.3	184.8	186.8	187.0	190.9
Honolulu, HI	148.0	155.1	160.1	164.5	168.1	170.7	171.9	171.5	173.3	176.3	178.4	180.3	184.5	190.6	197.8
Los Angeles-Riverside-Orange County, CA	141.4	146.5	150.3	152.3	154.6	157.5	160.0	162.3	166.1	171.6	177.3	182.2	187.0	193.2	201.8
Phoenix-Mesa, AZ	. . .	. . .	. . .	. . .	. . .	. . .	. . .	. . .	. . .	. . .	101.2	103.3	105.2	108.3
Portland-Salem, OR-WA	133.9	139.8	144.7	148.9	153.2	158.6	164.0	167.1	172.6	178.0	182.4	183.8	186.3	191.1	196.0
San Diego, CA	143.4	147.4	150.6	154.5	156.8	160.9	163.7	166.9	172.8	182.8	191.2	197.9	205.3	212.8	220.6
San Francisco-Oakland-San Jose, CA	137.9	142.5	146.3	148.7	151.6	155.1	160.4	165.5	172.5	180.2	189.9	193.0	194.4	198.8	202.7
Seattle-Tacoma-Bremerton, WA	134.1	139.0	142.9	147.8	152.3	157.5	163.0	167.7	172.8	179.2	185.7	189.3	192.3	194.7	200.2

[1]1987 = 100.
[2]November 1996 = 100.
. . . = Not available.

Table 7-11. Consumer Price Index Research Series, Using Current Methods (CPI-U-RS), by Month and Annual Average, 1977–2005

(December 1977 = 100.)

Year	January	February	March	April	May	June	July	August	September	October	November	December	Annual average
1977	. . .	. . .	. . .	. . .	. . .	. . .	. . .	. . .	. . .	. . .	. . .	100.0	. . .
1978	100.5	101.1	101.8	102.6	103.6	104.5	105.0	105.4	106.0	106.6	107.2	107.7	104.3
1979	108.6	109.6	110.5	111.6	112.8	114.0	114.9	115.8	116.8	117.6	118.2	119.2	114.1
1980	120.6	122.1	123.5	124.4	125.4	126.4	127.2	128.2	129.6	130.3	131.1	131.9	126.7
1981	133.1	134.8	135.9	136.6	137.4	138.1	139.2	140.1	141.2	141.8	142.3	142.8	138.6
1982	143.5	144.0	144.2	144.3	145.4	146.8	147.7	148.0	148.7	149.4	149.6	149.8	146.8
1983	150.2	150.3	150.3	151.5	152.3	152.8	153.4	153.8	154.6	154.9	155.1	155.3	152.9
1984	156.1	156.9	157.2	157.9	158.4	158.8	159.3	159.9	160.6	161.0	160.9	161.1	159.0
1985	161.3	161.9	162.6	163.3	163.9	164.4	164.7	165.0	165.6	166.0	166.5	166.9	164.3
1986	167.4	166.9	166.1	165.7	166.3	167.1	167.1	167.3	168.2	168.3	168.4	168.5	167.3
1987	169.5	170.1	170.9	171.7	172.2	172.9	173.2	174.1	174.9	175.3	175.4	175.3	173.0
1988	175.8	176.1	176.8	177.7	178.3	178.9	179.6	180.4	181.5	181.9	182.1	182.2	179.3
1989	183.0	183.7	184.7	185.9	186.8	187.3	187.8	187.9	188.6	189.3	189.6	189.9	187.0
1990	191.7	192.6	193.6	193.9	194.2	195.2	196.0	197.6	199.3	200.4	200.6	200.7	196.3
1991	201.5	201.8	201.9	202.2	202.7	203.1	203.3	203.9	204.7	204.9	205.3	205.4	203.4
1992	205.8	206.4	207.2	207.6	207.9	208.3	208.7	209.2	209.8	210.4	210.7	210.5	208.5
1993	211.1	211.9	212.5	213.1	213.5	213.7	213.8	214.3	214.6	215.3	215.5	215.3	213.7
1994	215.6	216.2	216.9	217.2	217.4	218.0	218.5	219.3	219.6	219.8	220.0	219.9	218.2
1995	220.7	221.4	222.1	222.8	223.2	223.7	223.8	224.2	224.6	225.2	225.0	224.9	223.5
1996	226.0	226.8	227.9	228.7	229.2	229.4	229.8	230.0	230.8	231.4	231.8	231.8	229.5
1997	232.5	233.2	233.6	233.9	233.9	234.2	234.3	234.7	235.5	235.9	235.8	235.4	234.4
1998	235.9	236.2	236.6	237.1	237.4	237.6	237.8	238.2	238.5	239.0	238.9	238.7	237.7
1999	239.4	239.7	240.4	242.1	242.0	242.2	242.8	243.5	244.6	245.1	245.2	245.2	242.7
2000	245.9	247.3	249.3	249.5	249.7	251.1	251.6	251.6	253.0	253.4	253.6	253.4	250.8
2001	255.0	256.0	256.6	257.6	258.7	259.3	258.4	258.5	259.6	258.7	258.3	257.3	257.8
2002	257.9	258.9	260.3	261.8	261.7	262.0	262.3	263.1	263.5	264.0	264.0	263.4	261.9
2003	264.5	266.6	268.2	267.6	267.2	267.5	267.8	268.8	269.6	269.4	268.7	268.4	267.9
2004	269.7	271.2	272.9	273.8	275.3	276.2	275.9	275.9	276.5	278.0	278.2	277.1	275.1
2005	277.6	279.3	281.4	283.3	283.1	283.2	284.5	285.9	289.4	290.1	287.8	286.5	284.3

. . . = Not available.

NOTES AND DEFINITIONS

EXPORT AND IMPORT PRICE INDEXES

Collection and Coverage

United States Export Price Indexes (XPI) and Import Price Indexes (MPI) cover nonmilitary goods transactions between the United States and the rest of the world. The XPI provides a measure of price change for U.S. products sold to other countries, and the MPI provides a measure of price change for goods purchased by U.S. residents from other countries

Bureau of Labor Statistics (BLS) field representatives use personal visits to initially collect the prices used in constructing the indexes. Thereafter, the prices are generally collected each month by mail questionnaire or telephone. To the greatest extent possible, products are priced at the U.S. border for exports and at both the foreign border and the U.S. border for imports. Only one price basis series is used in constructing the index for each given product. For most products, prices refer to transactions completed during the first week of the month. Indexes published in this volume are based on the Standard Industrial Trade Classification System (SITC), a United Nations product classification system. The SITC is especially useful for international comparisons. The Bureau of Economic Analysis's End-Use Category and Harmonized System both publish these indexes.

Prices are collected according to a specification method. The specifications for each product include detailed descriptions of the product's physical and functional characteristics. The terms of transaction include information on the number of units bought or sold, discounts, credit terms, packaging, and class of buyer or seller. When there are changes in either the specifications or terms of transaction for a product, the dollar value of each change is deleted from the total price change in order to obtain the "pure price change." Once this value is determined, a linking procedure is employed, which allows for the continued repricing of the item.

At the elementary level, the price changes for individual items within a given company/classification group cell are generally averaged together using equal weights in order to produce an index at the cell level. These cells are then averaged together using the relative importance of a given company's trade in the product area to produce an index at the classification group level. These classification group indexes are then averaged together using weights derived from these company weights in order to produce the lowest-level publication strata. Successively higher levels of publication strata are then averaged together using their relative importance based on 2004 U.S. trade values.

A limited number of import price indexes based on locality of origin indexes are also produced. BLS also publishes indexes for selected categories of internationally traded services; these indexes are calculated on an international basis.

Sources of Additional Information

Concepts and methodology are described in Chapter 15 of the *BLS Handbook of Methods* and in monthly BLS press releases. These resources are available on the BLS Web site at <http://www.bls.gov>.

Table 7-12. U.S. Export Price Indexes for Selected Categories of Goods, by Standard International Trade Classification, 1990–2005

(2000 = 100.)

Commodity	Relative impor- tance	1990				1991				1992			
		March	June	Septem- ber	Decem- ber	March	June	Septem- ber	Decem- ber	March	June	Septem- ber	Decem- ber
ALL COMMODITIES	100.0	94.8	95.1	95.8	96.3	96.4	96.1	95.6	95.7	96.2	96.5	96.6	96.3
Food and Live Animals	5.7	101.1	102.4	96.2	93.3	96.4	99.0	98.0	100.3	104.3	101.0	98.8	98.2
Meat and meat preparations	0.7	82.8	81.4	81.8	84.7	85.0	84.2	85.3	82.8	86.6	87.7	86.4	88.2
Fish, crustaceans, aquatic invertebrates, and preparations thereof	0.5	89.9	86.8	88.8	87.2	86.7	83.5	77.6	83.2	90.0	86.5	84.5	80.0
Cereals and cereal preparations	1.8	122.1	126.5	112.4	104.7	107.9	112.7	112.7	119.6	127.4	122.0	115.3	114.2
Vegetables and fruit and nuts, fresh or dried	1.2	92.6	93.2	90.2	89.5	104.0	111.0	103.4	95.6	97.0	91.4	92.0	94.1
Feeding stuff for animals (not including unmilled cereals)	0.5	102.3	99.5	101.0	104.9	105.6	101.9	107.2	108.0	103.9	104.1	107.0	105.8
Miscellaneous edible products and preparations	0.5	93.4	94.0	93.8	95.0	93.9	94.5	93.8	94.0	93.4	94.2	94.9	95.1
Beverages and Tobacco	0.6	83.4	84.9	85.6	88.0	89.9	90.4	90.9	92.6	93.1	93.8	94.7	95.5
Tobacco and tobacco manufactures	0.3	83.4	85.0	85.7	87.9	89.9	90.3	90.7	92.4	92.9	93.7	94.5	95.4
Crude Materials, Inedible, Except Fuels	5.0	96.4	96.7	97.1	94.7	94.6	91.8	88.2	86.2	87.6	89.9	90.4	90.0
Oil seeds and oleaginous fruits	0.7	115.2	116.1	123.5	123.3	124.1	118.7	116.8	111.8	113.8	117.6	110.1	110.2
Cork and wood	0.5	77.1	76.5	74.2	71.9	73.2	73.4	74.3	74.2	78.9	82.5	89.8	93.7
Textile fibers and their waste	0.7	111.2	118.2	116.0	115.3	120.3	123.2	112.5	102.6	97.9	99.1	94.7	94.1
Metalliferous ores and metal scrap	1.4	102.8	105.9	111.9	103.5	102.2	94.5	92.3	87.2	91.0	90.2	91.0	87.0
Mineral Fuels, Lubricants, and Related Materials	3.6	68.9	67.2	78.3	80.7	69.1	66.3	66.3	67.0	61.3	63.8	64.7	63.6
Petroleum, petroleum products, and related materials	2.7	60.1	57.5	77.2	79.2	59.3	54.9	54.9	56.1	47.4	52.9	54.6	52.2
Chemicals and Related Products n.e.s.	15.5	90.4	90.4	93.3	97.1	96.1	92.5	91.0	90.3	90.2	90.4	90.1	89.0
Organic chemicals	3.7	97.4	93.9	99.5	105.1	100.7	93.6	88.6	88.6	88.5	90.5	91.9	89.7
Inorganic chemicals	1.0	. . .	. . .	. . .	. . .	. . .	. . .	. . .	. . .	. . .	. . .	. . .	87.9
Medicinal and pharmaceutical products	3.0	91.4	91.7	92.0	92.5	92.2	92.4	94.0	94.0	95.1	95.7	95.6	95.8
Essential oils, polishing, and cleansing preparations	1.0	86.2	87.4	87.6	87.9	88.1	88.2	88.8	88.5	90.0	90.5	89.6	89.5
Fertilizers	0.4	. . .	. . .	. . .	. . .	. . .	. . .	. . .	. . .	. . .	. . .	. . .	. . .
Plastics in primary forms	2.8	. . .	. . .	. . .	. . .	. . .	. . .	. . .	. . .	. . .	. . .	. . .	78.8
Plastics in nonprimary forms	1.0	. . .	. . .	. . .	. . .	. . .	. . .	. . .	. . .	. . .	. . .	. . .	92.9
Chemical materials and products n.e.s.	1.9	85.8	86.4	88.0	90.0	91.7	90.5	89.6	89.5	90.1	90.1	90.5	90.6
Manufactured Goods, Classified Chiefly by Material	10.8	86.7	86.8	87.2	87.1	87.3	87.0	86.7	86.7	87.2	87.5	87.8	87.7
Rubber manufactures n.e.s.	0.7	81.3	81.4	82.2	84.2	85.7	86.4	86.6	87.0	86.8	86.9	87.5	87.7
Uncoated paper, paperboard, and linerboard	1.4	91.1	90.8	91.3	91.5	91.1	90.7	90.0	90.2	89.9	89.7	89.2	88.8
Textile yarn, fabrics, and made-up articles n.e.s.	1.6	91.7	91.2	91.2	92.1	94.1	95.3	94.8	95.1	96.5	96.7	97.0	97.3
Nonmetallic mineral manufactures n.e.s.	1.8	86.3	85.8	85.8	86.6	87.2	87.2	87.2	88.0	88.2	89.2	89.3	89.4
Iron and steel	1.2	. . .	. . .	. . .	. . .	. . .	. . .	. . .	. . .	. . .	. . .	. . .	. . .
Nonferrous metals	1.5	86.1	87.1	89.2	85.0	81.0	76.5	76.0	73.9	75.4	76.3	76.4	73.9
Manufactures of metals n.e.s.	2.2	80.9	81.2	81.3	82.0	83.1	83.5	83.7	84.0	84.2	84.2	84.8	85.6
Machinery and Transport Equipment	46.7	97.4	97.9	98.3	98.8	100.3	101.0	101.4	101.7	102.1	102.4	102.6	102.6
Power-generating machinery and equipment	4.7	76.3	77.0	77.2	77.8	79.8	80.7	81.4	81.8	82.9	84.5	84.4	84.6
Machinery specialized for particular industries	4.1	82.6	82.7	83.4	84.5	85.3	86.1	86.2	86.6	87.3	88.0	88.4	89.0
Metalworking machinery	0.8	81.1	82.1	82.2	84.2	85.9	87.7	87.9	88.3	89.4	89.9	89.9	89.8
General industrial machinery, equipment, and parts n.e.s.	4.8	81.8	82.5	83.0	83.4	85.3	85.8	86.4	86.4	87.6	87.8	88.1	88.6
Computer equipment and office machines	4.8	193.4	193.2	192.9	190.5	190.9	189.4	187.2	185.0	183.8	182.2	180.9	176.9
Telecommunications and sound recording and reproducing apparatus and equipment	3.3	95.5	97.3	97.8	98.3	100.7	103.4	104.9	105.8	104.5	105.3	105.7	105.8
Electrical machinery and equipment	10.8	113.1	112.7	112.4	112.7	112.8	113.4	115.5	116.3	117.6	116.8	117.4	117.2
Road vehicles	8.6	88.2	88.7	89.1	90.1	90.9	91.2	91.4	92.1	92.2	92.6	92.8	93.2
Miscellaneous Manufactured Articles	11.2	89.7	90.5	91.8	93.2	94.4	95.1	95.4	95.9	96.6	97.0	97.2	97.3
Furniture and parts thereof	0.6	92.3	93.6	93.4	95.2	96.9	97.6	97.7	97.5	98.4	98.2	97.8	98.1
Articles of apparel and clothing accessories	0.6	. . .	. . .	. . .	. . .	. . .	. . .	. . .	. . .	. . .	. . .	. . .	. . .
Professional, scientific, and controlling instruments and apparatus n.e.s.	4.5	80.5	81.9	83.8	85.6	86.6	87.8	88.0	88.8	89.7	90.1	90.0	90.1
Photographic apparatus, equipment, and supplies, and optical goods n.e.s.	0.9	95.0	94.6	96.0	98.4	98.8	98.6	98.4	99.4	99.3	98.2	99.1	99.7
Miscellaneous manufactured articles n.e.s.	4.1	97.6	98.1	98.7	99.4	101.1	101.2	101.9	101.7	102.1	103.0	103.6	103.3

n.e.s. = Not elsewhere specified.

. . . = Not available.

Table 7-12. U.S. Export Price Indexes for Selected Categories of Goods, by Standard International Trade Classification, 1990–2005—*Continued*

(2000 = 100.)

Commodity	1993				1994				1995			
	March	June	September	December	March	June	September	December	March	June	September	December
ALL COMMODITIES	96.6	96.9	96.9	97.3	98.2	98.5	99.1	101.1	103.0	104.5	104.4	104.4
Food and Live Animals	97.7	96.1	100.4	105.9	106.7	102.0	100.6	104.9	106.3	112.1	121.6	126.5
Meat and meat preparations	89.8	92.2	88.4	88.5	91.3	88.7	89.0	90.1	92.9	95.7	99.4	101.4
Fish, crustaceans, aquatic invertebrates, and preparations thereof	81.5	85.1	79.8	77.8	83.1	86.5	93.4	97.8	106.8	107.1	105.6	96.3
Cereals and cereal preparations	112.7	105.8	111.8	129.4	130.4	118.5	111.9	121.0	120.1	133.2	149.6	167.9
Vegetables and fruit and nuts, fresh or dried	94.7	94.1	107.8	104.5	102.5	100.1	100.1	103.5	106.8	107.2	122.7	111.2
Feeding stuff for animals (not including unmilled cereals)	101.9	102.7	109.6	112.0	108.8	108.2	105.9	101.0	99.1	104.9	107.1	122.4
Miscellaneous edible products and preparations	93.9	94.4	94.0	90.6	91.9	92.0	93.1	93.1	92.9	94.8	94.0	95.3
Beverages and Tobacco	96.4	96.7	97.5	96.5	96.9	97.0	96.8	96.9	97.9	98.2	98.7	98.5
Tobacco and tobacco manufactures	96.3	96.4	97.2	96.1	96.6	96.7	96.4	96.5	97.5	98.1	98.6	98.3
Crude Materials, Inedible, Except Fuels	93.4	95.8	94.3	95.0	100.7	104.0	104.8	112.4	122.6	125.4	119.0	116.0
Oil seeds and oleaginous fruits	114.4	117.0	130.0	133.9	134.2	134.9	115.0	109.8	112.0	115.6	123.1	136.0
Cork and wood	110.0	121.0	111.4	110.0	114.7	112.0	111.8	113.6	117.9	117.5	111.4	112.0
Textile fibers and their waste	97.8	96.1	93.3	95.6	113.3	120.9	117.3	127.3	152.6	154.3	141.2	142.2
Metalliferous ores and metal scrap	87.8	89.0	89.0	90.3	96.0	96.7	106.2	123.5	132.4	132.2	125.0	116.4
Mineral Fuels, Lubricants, and Related Materials	64.5	64.9	63.2	60.4	61.8	64.5	64.6	65.9	65.6	68.5	67.5	68.5
Petroleum, petroleum products, and related materials	53.5	55.3	52.6	48.2	50.1	55.0	55.6	56.7	56.1	59.6	57.4	59.2
Chemicals and Related Products n.e.s.	89.1	89.2	88.5	88.6	89.5	91.9	96.4	101.3	107.1	108.4	104.3	102.1
Organic chemicals	89.2	89.5	87.8	86.7	87.7	91.8	97.9	107.4	117.0	122.8	112.6	105.8
Inorganic chemicals	86.0	85.1	82.5	82.5	79.7	82.8	88.2	90.4	102.4	100.9	101.7	102.2
Medicinal and pharmaceutical products	97.2	98.3	98.7	99.5	100.0	99.6	99.2	98.7	99.5	100.4	100.5	99.9
Essential oils, polishing, and cleansing preparations	90.6	90.5	91.0	91.6	92.9	95.3	95.8	95.5	96.4	96.4	96.8	97.7
Fertilizers	...	...	...	...	...	...	...	...	...	...	...	...
Plastics in primary forms	78.7	80.5	79.9	79.2	80.1	83.9	95.8	105.6	111.8	110.6	99.7	94.4
Plastics in nonprimary forms	92.6	90.0	90.7	90.6	91.3	92.5	94.2	97.4	99.0	101.8	102.0	101.3
Chemical materials and products n.e.s.	91.9	92.5	92.6	92.6	94.7	95.2	95.4	97.1	99.2	100.7	101.4	101.3
Manufactured Goods, Classified Chiefly by Material	88.4	87.6	88.1	87.6	89.5	90.8	92.6	96.4	99.0	100.6	100.6	99.4
Rubber manufactures n.e.s.	88.7	89.3	89.6	89.5	89.7	89.9	90.7	90.9	95.3	95.7	97.1	98.3
Uncoated paper, paperboard, and linerboard	87.5	85.6	84.7	84.9	85.5	87.7	92.9	101.2	108.0	115.6	114.0	109.0
Textile yarn, fabrics, and made-up articles n.e.s.	97.3	97.8	97.8	97.0	97.7	97.7	97.0	97.2	99.0	102.8	102.6	103.7
Nonmetallic mineral manufactures n.e.s.	89.6	90.8	91.9	91.2	92.1	92.4	92.7	93.5	94.1	94.3	94.4	95.2
Iron and steel	...	...	...	93.4	95.3	96.4	97.2	99.0	101.7	104.0	104.0	104.7
Nonferrous metals	74.3	70.6	72.3	68.6	76.3	80.3	85.7	96.7	100.1	98.2	98.9	93.7
Manufactures of metals n.e.s.	86.1	85.5	86.2	86.8	87.5	87.3	87.7	89.4	91.6	92.3	92.7	93.2
Machinery and Transport Equipment	102.3	102.5	102.2	102.4	102.4	102.1	101.7	101.7	102.2	102.8	103.0	103.2
Power-generating machinery and equipment	85.2	85.3	85.7	86.2	86.8	86.9	87.6	88.4	88.3	88.5	88.7	90.3
Machinery specialized for particular industries	89.6	90.0	90.5	91.0	91.1	91.5	91.6	91.6	93.0	94.0	94.8	95.2
Metalworking machinery	91.3	91.4	91.2	91.3	91.1	91.2	90.5	91.1	92.0	92.3	92.8	92.8
General industrial machinery, equipment, and parts n.e.s.	89.2	89.6	90.1	90.6	90.9	91.0	91.3	91.3	90.9	91.0	91.3	91.3
Computer equipment and office machines	171.0	168.9	165.3	162.9	158.9	156.0	151.8	150.4	148.1	147.5	144.7	142.9
Telecommunications and sound recording and reproducing apparatus and equipment	105.0	106.4	105.7	105.6	104.6	104.4	103.8	103.4	103.4	103.8	103.2	102.4
Electrical machinery and equipment	116.1	116.7	115.9	116.6	116.8	116.3	114.8	114.4	115.2	117.2	117.5	116.8
Road vehicles	93.6	93.7	93.7	94.0	94.5	94.7	94.9	95.5	96.0	96.1	96.2	97.1
Miscellaneous Manufactured Articles	97.5	97.6	97.6	97.6	97.5	97.8	98.1	98.1	98.3	98.6	98.6	98.8
Furniture and parts thereof	95.9	94.3	94.2	94.4	94.6	94.9	95.4	94.1	94.0	94.7	94.8	95.1
Articles of apparel and clothing accessories	...	...	...	102.4	102.5	103.3	103.2	103.6	103.4	102.5	104.4	102.6
Professional, scientific, and controlling instruments and apparatus n.e.s.	90.8	91.3	92.0	91.9	92.4	92.6	93.3	93.4	93.9	94.3	94.4	94.5
Photographic apparatus, equipment and supplies, and optical goods n.e.s.	98.8	101.0	101.2	101.4	101.8	102.0	103.4	102.8	103.3	103.5	102.3	102.1
Miscellaneous manufactured articles n.e.s.	102.8	102.5	101.7	101.5	100.6	100.9	100.6	100.7	100.9	101.0	100.9	101.9

n.e.s. = Not elsewhere specified.

. . . = Not available.

Table 7-12. U.S. Export Price Indexes for Selected Categories of Goods, by Standard International Trade Classification, 1990–2005—*Continued*

(2000 = 100.)

Commodity	1996				1997				1998			
	March	June	September	December	March	June	September	December	March	June	September	December
ALL COMMODITIES	104.6	105.4	103.9	103.2	103.6	103.2	102.9	102.0	100.7	99.9	98.5	98.5
Food and Live Animals	131.8	140.4	123.4	117.3	119.0	113.3	114.4	111.3	106.4	104.6	99.8	103.0
Meat and meat preparations	94.0	97.4	94.4	93.7	92.4	91.3	91.3	90.7	88.3	93.7	92.3	86.2
Fish, crustaceans, aquatic invertebrates, and preparations thereof	91.2	92.8	96.9	100.5	92.5	88.5	102.9	96.6	86.0	83.8	99.5	99.3
Cereals and cereal preparations	183.0	203.3	152.6	140.4	146.4	128.9	132.7	131.9	126.3	115.4	98.0	110.2
Vegetables and fruit and nuts, fresh or dried	114.9	117.8	119.0	112.6	112.8	113.3	108.8	102.6	102.3	109.8	110.6	111.1
Feeding stuff for animals (not including unmilled cereals)	129.5	130.7	135.5	128.0	133.7	135.7	128.9	121.1	107.8	101.3	94.4	98.4
Miscellaneous edible products and preparations	96.0	96.6	96.2	97.1	96.7	96.9	98.3	98.2	98.1	98.3	99.5	100.0
Beverages and Tobacco	98.7	98.8	98.8	98.7	98.4	99.1	99.3	98.8	98.4	98.2	98.0	99.0
Tobacco and tobacco manufactures	98.5	98.6	98.6	98.5	98.1	98.9	99.1	98.4	98.2	97.8	97.5	98.4
Crude Materials, Inedible, Except Fuels	109.6	108.7	109.3	106.8	112.2	112.4	110.3	105.6	101.4	98.7	93.8	91.8
Oil seeds and oleaginous fruits	143.0	152.0	157.6	137.5	159.3	161.1	143.8	139.4	129.7	122.8	109.8	114.4
Cork and wood	113.0	109.0	110.9	112.3	110.5	107.3	104.7	98.6	96.8	94.5	94.7	93.7
Textile fibers and their waste	133.4	131.6	125.1	120.5	122.9	120.3	121.2	115.5	112.5	114.4	110.2	101.9
Metalliferous ores and metal scrap	114.8	113.4	108.6	108.7	113.8	116.4	119.8	106.5	101.2	97.2	88.4	86.1
Mineral Fuels, Lubricants, and Related Materials	71.8	73.3	75.6	78.4	74.8	74.5	75.1	75.8	71.3	69.3	62.8	63.0
Petroleum, petroleum products, and related materials	64.1	65.4	69.6	73.9	68.7	68.7	70.1	68.5	63.6	61.4	52.3	53.0
Chemicals and Related Products n.e.s.	102.5	102.6	101.8	101.5	102.3	102.0	100.9	100.3	99.0	97.9	97.0	96.2
Organic chemicals	103.9	100.9	97.6	97.6	99.0	97.6	96.2	96.0	91.2	88.7	86.4	85.3
Inorganic chemicals	105.6	106.1	103.3	103.5	100.9	101.1	100.3	100.9	103.7	105.2	104.9	105.1
Medicinal and pharmaceutical products	101.9	101.6	101.7	101.7	100.8	101.4	101.0	100.7	102.2	101.4	101.5	100.4
Essential oils, polishing, and cleansing preparations	96.8	97.6	98.5	98.3	99.0	99.7	100.4	98.7	98.4	98.2	99.4	98.5
Fertilizers	. . .	. . .	. . .	133.3	128.2	128.1	126.6	125.6	122.7	128.0	130.5	127.8
Plastics in primary forms	96.4	100.7	101.3	99.0	103.1	102.4	98.8	98.2	96.7	93.7	92.4	90.2
Plastics in nonprimary forms	101.5	100.8	98.9	98.3	99.6	100.0	99.8	99.6	100.6	98.7	98.1	96.3
Chemical materials and products n.e.s.	101.5	102.6	103.5	103.8	104.2	104.6	104.2	102.6	101.2	101.2	100.6	101.8
Manufactured Goods, Classified Chiefly by Material	98.5	97.7	97.0	96.8	97.4	98.1	98.5	98.4	98.2	97.7	96.7	96.3
Rubber manufactures n.e.s.	98.0	98.6	98.5	98.7	98.5	99.0	97.7	97.9	97.9	97.7	98.2	101.6
Uncoated paper, paperboard, and linerboard	103.6	97.7	97.9	95.0	93.0	93.4	95.1	95.2	94.7	93.7	91.0	91.0
Textile yarn, fabrics, and made-up articles n.e.s.	104.8	105.5	104.8	104.1	103.4	105.0	105.0	104.8	105.3	104.9	103.0	102.7
Nonmetallic mineral manufactures n.e.s.	96.1	95.4	96.3	97.9	98.0	98.3	100.0	100.9	100.8	100.6	100.7	101.1
Iron and steel	104.7	106.0	104.8	104.9	106.7	106.0	106.2	106.3	103.9	103.7	102.9	100.0
Nonferrous metals	91.6	91.9	87.3	86.9	90.3	92.0	91.8	89.6	89.8	86.7	84.1	82.6
Manufactures of metals n.e.s.	94.4	93.6	93.6	93.7	95.1	96.3	96.2	96.3	96.8	98.6	98.4	98.1
Machinery and Transport Equipment	103.3	103.6	103.3	103.2	103.3	103.3	102.9	102.5	102.0	101.4	100.9	100.9
Power-generating machinery and equipment	91.9	92.9	92.8	93.1	94.0	94.4	94.5	94.6	95.1	95.3	95.2	96.6
Machinery specialized for particular industries	95.9	96.5	97.0	96.8	97.6	98.0	98.3	98.7	98.8	99.0	99.2	98.9
Metalworking machinery	93.7	94.4	94.6	94.5	96.7	96.3	96.4	97.5	99.5	100.0	100.1	100.5
General industrial machinery, equipment, and parts n.e.s.	94.0	94.8	95.0	95.4	96.3	97.3	97.3	97.5	97.9	98.1	98.4	98.5
Computer equipment and office machines	139.7	137.2	132.3	128.7	126.9	123.9	122.5	119.5	116.9	112.0	109.4	108.9
Telecommunications and sound recording and reproducing apparatus and equipment	104.6	104.6	103.7	104.2	103.4	103.0	102.6	102.1	102.0	102.1	101.6	100.9
Electrical machinery and equipment	116.2	115.3	113.9	113.5	112.5	112.3	110.7	109.9	108.3	107.2	106.1	105.4
Road vehicles	97.1	97.2	97.2	97.6	98.0	98.0	97.9	98.2	98.0	98.1	98.2	98.3
Miscellaneous Manufactured Articles	99.4	99.4	99.5	99.9	100.2	100.3	100.4	100.4	100.0	99.4	99.2	99.2
Furniture and parts thereof	96.7	96.0	96.4	96.4	97.0	97.9	97.9	98.1	98.7	98.4	98.5	98.5
Articles of apparel and clothing accessories	103.0	103.8	104.2	104.4	105.0	104.9	107.1	107.2	107.4	107.4	106.2	104.4
Professional, scientific, and controlling instruments and apparatus n.e.s.	95.4	95.8	96.1	96.7	97.8	97.5	97.4	97.6	97.7	97.8	97.8	98.1
Photographic apparatus, equipment and supplies, and optical goods n.e.s.	102.2	101.4	101.7	102.2	101.4	102.0	101.6	101.0	98.4	96.5	95.2	97.3
Miscellaneous manufactured articles n.e.s.	102.0	101.9	101.7	101.9	101.4	101.8	101.6	101.5	100.6	99.3	99.5	99.3

n.e.s. = Not elsewhere specified.

. . . = Not available.

Table 7-12. U.S. Export Price Indexes for Selected Categories of Goods, by Standard International Trade Classification, 1990–2005—*Continued*

(2000 = 100.)

Commodity	1999				2000				2001			
	March	June	September	December	March	June	September	December	March	June	September	December
ALL COMMODITIES	97.9	98.2	98.5	99.0	100.0	100.1	100.4	100.1	100.0	99.4	99.0	97.6
Food and Live Animals	101.1	102.6	99.6	98.5	99.9	100.6	98.8	102.1	102.5	101.1	103.3	101.2
Meat and meat preparations	86.2	87.6	93.4	96.7	95.3	104.8	100.8	101.5	102.6	106.1	107.8	97.8
Fish, crustaceans, aquatic invertebrates, and preparations thereof	109.8	123.0	100.8	102.6	98.9	100.6	100.1	98.4	99.0	90.8	90.4	88.6
Cereals and cereal preparations	105.9	106.0	101.5	95.7	103.9	100.0	94.7	105.8	107.9	102.6	106.4	107.2
Vegetables and fruit and nuts, fresh or dried	105.8	109.9	105.1	101.7	98.8	97.9	102.5	99.1	97.9	98.6	100.8	100.6
Feeding stuff for animals (not including unmilled cereals)	96.8	92.5	93.6	97.4	98.2	100.4	99.2	104.6	100.7	101.1	103.6	102.4
Miscellaneous edible products and preparations	100.0	100.1	100.6	100.7	99.8	100.0	100.0	100.2	100.1	100.1	100.1	100.1
Beverages and Tobacco	99.5	99.4	99.8	100.1	100.2	100.0	99.9	99.8	98.9	98.4	98.4	98.3
Tobacco and tobacco manufactures	99.3	99.2	99.7	100.1	100.1	99.9	99.9	99.9	98.9	98.2	98.2	98.1
Crude Materials, Inedible, Except Fuels	89.1	90.2	93.5	94.9	100.2	101.6	100.7	99.4	96.0	92.6	89.5	87.1
Oil seeds and oleaginous fruits	93.7	94.8	101.7	95.2	102.9	103.3	100.3	101.8	94.5	95.6	99.0	90.9
Cork and wood	93.8	94.4	95.4	97.9	100.4	99.8	100.1	98.9	96.1	92.8	90.2	88.0
Textile fibers and their waste	100.7	99.1	92.9	90.2	99.1	100.5	104.3	105.7	97.6	90.9	87.7	84.0
Metalliferous ores and metal scrap	88.6	89.7	93.3	99.5	102.6	99.2	99.9	94.8	92.0	91.0	85.1	81.9
Mineral Fuels, Lubricants, and Related Materials	62.5	68.5	77.5	85.0	102.2	97.4	111.7	105.8	102.4	103.2	103.3	82.4
Petroleum, petroleum products, and related materials	52.3	61.9	74.0	80.6	103.1	96.8	117.0	105.6	99.2	101.8	103.6	74.6
Chemicals and Related Products n.e.s.	95.7	96.4	97.6	98.9	99.7	100.9	99.8	98.3	98.7	96.2	93.8	92.8
Organic chemicals	84.7	86.4	90.6	96.3	98.8	102.1	99.9	96.0	95.9	90.6	84.9	83.9
Inorganic chemicals	104.7	102.7	100.4	99.7	99.6	101.2	99.8	101.4	104.1	103.3	103.2	102.8
Medicinal and pharmaceutical products	100.3	100.4	99.6	100.1	100.0	99.5	100.0	100.0	99.2	99.5	101.1	100.9
Essential oils, polishing, and cleansing preparations	98.3	98.7	98.9	100.1	99.8	99.6	100.1	100.0	100.2	99.7	99.1	98.8
Fertilizers	125.2	119.4	113.2	97.8	96.5	96.1	105.3	102.0	105.3	94.9	91.8	94.0
Plastics in primary forms	89.0	93.2	97.2	100.2	100.8	103.4	97.8	94.9	97.8	93.9	88.6	86.5
Plastics in nonprimary forms	97.3	98.1	98.4	98.9	101.0	100.2	100.2	99.2	97.6	97.4	97.2	95.8
Chemical materials and products n.e.s.	101.1	100.3	99.9	99.7	100.3	99.7	99.8	100.5	99.1	99.1	99.0	97.6
Manufactured Goods, Classified Chiefly by Material	96.3	96.7	97.3	98.1	99.6	100.2	100.9	100.3	100.2	99.5	98.2	96.7
Rubber manufactures n.e.s.	102.4	101.2	102.5	104.0	99.4	100.1	100.4	99.5	100.4	99.8	101.0	100.9
Uncoated paper, paperboard, and linerboard	90.5	93.3	96.6	97.6	98.9	100.5	100.7	99.7	98.4	97.4	95.6	95.1
Textile yarn, fabrics, and made-up articles n.e.s.	101.3	100.8	100.3	100.3	100.0	100.2	100.1	98.4	98.8	98.5	98.8	97.5
Nonmetallic mineral manufactures n.e.s.	100.3	100.2	99.9	99.7	100.1	100.4	100.0	99.5	99.8	100.8	101.1	102.1
Iron and steel	98.7	97.5	97.6	97.7	99.9	101.2	100.0	99.5	96.8	97.8	98.3	95.7
Nonferrous metals	82.7	83.7	86.6	90.9	100.3	98.5	103.4	103.3	104.9	98.0	90.2	83.1
Manufactures of metals n.e.s.	99.8	100.2	99.0	98.8	98.6	100.9	101.5	101.1	100.9	101.5	101.8	101.7
Machinery and Transport Equipment	100.6	100.3	99.9	99.9	99.9	100.0	100.1	100.1	100.6	100.3	100.0	99.6
Power-generating machinery and equipment	97.4	97.6	98.0	98.8	99.5	99.7	100.0	101.2	102.0	102.3	103.0	103.9
Machinery specialized for particular industries	99.4	99.8	99.5	98.4	99.8	100.2	100.0	100.3	100.5	100.3	99.5	100.5
Metalworking machinery	100.6	100.4	100.4	100.1	100.1	99.3	100.1	99.8	101.1	101.0	101.2	100.7
General industrial machinery, equipment, and parts n.e.s.	99.1	99.2	99.5	99.8	99.9	100.1	100.0	100.3	101.0	101.3	101.9	101.7
Computer equipment and office machines	106.9	104.8	102.8	102.7	100.5	99.9	99.3	99.0	97.8	95.9	94.8	92.9
Telecommunications and sound recording and reproducing apparatus and equipment	100.9	100.2	100.2	100.0	99.9	100.3	100.1	99.6	99.8	99.8	98.5	97.7
Electrical machinery and equipment	104.0	103.1	102.0	100.9	100.5	99.8	99.9	99.3	99.2	98.3	97.6	95.9
Road vehicles	98.4	98.6	98.6	99.3	100.1	100.0	100.2	100.1	100.2	100.2	100.2	100.3
Miscellaneous Manufactured Articles	99.6	99.6	99.8	99.9	99.6	99.7	100.2	100.2	100.0	100.1	100.4	100.4
Furniture and parts thereof	98.5	99.0	99.7	99.5	99.4	100.1	99.8	101.1	101.0	101.0	101.8	101.6
Articles of apparel and clothing accessories	104.7	103.8	103.9	103.7	100.1	99.8	99.0	99.5	96.9	96.6	98.1	98.2
Professional, scientific, and controlling instruments and apparatus n.e.s.	99.0	99.2	99.4	99.3	99.6	99.7	100.4	100.4	100.8	100.9	100.9	100.9
Photographic apparatus, equipment and supplies, and optical goods n.e.s.	97.9	97.2	98.6	100.3	97.9	98.0	101.6	101.3	99.1	98.2	98.7	97.6
Miscellaneous manufactured articles n.e.s.	99.2	99.5	99.4	99.5	99.7	99.9	100.0	99.9	100.3	100.5	100.6	101.0

n.e.s. = Not elsewhere specified.

Table 7-12. U.S. Export Price Indexes for Selected Categories of Goods, by Standard International Trade Classification, 1990–2005—*Continued*

(2000 = 100.)

Commodity	2002				2003			
	March	June	September	December	March	June	September	December
ALL COMMODITIES	97.6	98.0	98.8	98.6	99.7	99.5	99.8	100.8
Food and Live Animals	100.3	99.8	107.7	105.8	105.9	107.5	112.1	116.5
Meat and meat preparations	93.2	90.0	89.8	90.3	96.4	102.9	117.2	123.0
Fish, crustaceans, aquatic invertebrates, and preparations thereof	94.3	97.9	98.6	101.7	108.2	108.2	103.3	103.1
Cereals and cereal preparations	105.4	106.5	133.4	126.3	122.2	118.5	124.2	130.8
Vegetables and fruit and nuts, fresh or dried	102.5	99.0	98.9	98.3	95.1	99.6	101.4	103.2
Feeding stuff for animals (not including unmilled cereals)	99.6	101.2	106.8	103.5	105.5	108.8	112.7	123.2
Miscellaneous edible products and preparations	100.7	100.7	100.7	100.5	101.0	101.5	101.0	100.3
Beverages and Tobacco	97.4	98.2	98.8	98.7	97.4	98.2	97.8	100.6
Tobacco and tobacco manufactures	96.8	97.6	98.0	97.8	95.9	96.6	96.2	99.7
Crude Materials, Inedible, Except Fuels	87.7	95.3	97.3	98.5	102.3	103.9	106.2	116.9
Oil seeds and oleaginous fruits	92.0	102.9	114.1	116.2	116.6	122.7	121.1	152.5
Cork and wood	87.2	87.1	90.0	90.3	91.2	90.4	91.6	93.7
Textile fibers and their waste	86.2	88.6	93.1	98.3	105.0	103.2	109.6	121.2
Metalliferous ores and metal scrap	87.3	99.8	93.9	96.3	105.8	109.0	119.9	136.6
Mineral Fuels, Lubricants, and Related Materials	89.8	93.9	102.8	99.5	130.1	107.6	108.7	110.7
Petroleum, petroleum products, and related materials	83.6	87.9	98.0	92.2	130.2	102.7	104.2	106.2
Chemicals and Related Products n.e.s.	93.2	95.3	96.8	96.6	100.6	100.8	100.3	101.4
Organic chemicals	84.9	90.8	95.3	94.9	103.4	103.1	100.4	103.3
Inorganic chemicals	101.6	102.1	101.0	96.9	98.1	98.6	99.1	99.1
Medicinal and pharmaceutical products	100.5	100.4	101.4	101.2	104.1	104.8	105.4	105.8
Essential oils, polishing, and cleansing preparations	97.6	97.3	97.4	97.3	96.2	97.3	98.2	100.1
Fertilizers	98.1	95.5	100.9	104.3	108.2	117.2	122.8	123.1
Plastics in primary forms	87.6	92.5	92.9	92.9	99.5	96.6	95.4	96.5
Plastics in nonprimary forms	95.8	96.0	96.9	95.9	97.2	98.8	98.2	97.2
Chemical materials and products n.e.s.	98.0	97.5	98.3	98.8	100.7	101.6	101.9	102.6
Manufactured Goods, Classified Chiefly by Material	96.7	98.1	99.1	99.0	99.4	100.0	100.2	100.8
Rubber manufactures n.e.s.	100.8	102.7	105.6	105.6	108.4	110.1	109.2	109.9
Uncoated paper, paperboard, and linerboard	92.5	94.8	96.3	96.8	96.7	98.3	98.3	97.6
Textile yarn, fabrics, and made-up articles n.e.s.	97.8	100.0	100.6	101.1	102.0	102.7	102.1	102.5
Nonmetallic mineral manufactures n.e.s.	102.1	102.2	102.2	101.3	100.2	100.4	99.5	99.8
Iron and steel	96.6	101.0	103.6	104.3	104.5	106.8	106.1	109.6
Nonferrous metals	85.1	85.3	84.4	83.5	84.3	80.3	81.6	84.5
Manufactures of metals n.e.s.	101.9	102.5	103.4	103.3	103.5	104.8	104.4	104.4
Machinery and Transport Equipment	99.5	98.9	98.7	98.5	98.5	97.8	97.9	97.8
Power-generating machinery and equipment	104.6	104.5	104.4	105.1	106.9	107.2	107.5	108.7
Machinery specialized for particular industries	101.1	101.8	101.8	101.7	102.2	102.6	103.1	103.4
Metalworking machinery	100.0	99.9	100.2	100.5	101.7	101.0	100.8	100.7
General industrial machinery, equipment, and parts n.e.s. ...	102.2	102.3	102.3	101.6	102.1	102.4	102.6	102.8
Computer equipment and office machines	93.1	90.4	89.4	88.6	88.6	88.1	87.8	88.6
Telecommunications and sound recording and reproducing apparatus and equipment	97.5	97.7	96.4	95.8	95.0	93.8	93.3	92.0
Electrical machinery and equipment	94.7	93.9	93.5	92.9	92.2	89.7	89.4	88.1
Road vehicles	100.3	100.3	100.6	101.0	100.9	101.1	101.4	101.5
Miscellaneous Manufactured Articles	100.5	100.4	100.4	100.6	100.5	101.2	100.7	101.1
Furniture and parts thereof	101.7	101.6	101.5	101.4	101.1	101.4	102.6	102.5
Articles of apparel and clothing accessories	98.3	98.8	97.8	97.2	97.5	97.0	96.8	97.1
Professional, scientific, and controlling instruments and apparatus n.e.s.	101.2	101.3	101.4	101.7	101.5	102.2	102.2	102.3
Photographic apparatus, equipment and supplies, and optical goods n.e.s.	96.6	97.5	97.3	97.4	97.1	98.9	94.4	95.6
Miscellaneous manufactured articles n.e.s.	100.9	100.4	100.5	101.1	100.9	101.6	101.2	101.6

n.e.s. = Not elsewhere specified.

Table 7-12. U.S. Export Price Indexes for Selected Categories of Goods, by Standard International Trade Classification, 1990–2005—*Continued*

(2000 = 100.)

Commodity	2004				2005			
	March	June	September	December	March	June	September	December
ALL COMMODITIES	103.0	103.4	103.8	104.8	106.4	106.7	107.5	107.7
Food and Live Animals	122.7	123.9	117.6	118.1	120.1	124.3	123.8	122.8
Meat and meat preparations	127.1	127.3	124.8	124.6	128.5	140.2	142.7	136.9
Fish, crustaceans, aquatic invertebrates, and preparations thereof	107.2	108.6	108.8	110.3	111.2	110.1	114.8	116.6
Cereals and cereal preparations	110.1	111.1	119.8	129.9	121.4	118.7	117.0	121.1
Vegetables and fruit and nuts, fresh or dried	139.6	141.2	122.0	116.4	125.1	133.6	129.2	123.9
Feeding stuff for animals (not including unmilled cereals)	133.6	131.9	109.8	107.5	113.7	118.1	120.1	123.2
Miscellaneous edible products and preparations	102.0	101.6	102.1	102.6	107.1	108.1	107.5	107.4
Beverages and Tobacco	102.1	101.6	101.7	101.5	102.2	103.3	103.6	101.2
Tobacco and tobacco manufactures	100.5	100.0	100.3	100.6	101.4	101.6	101.7	101.0
Crude Materials, Inedible, Except Fuels	129.0	125.7	119.4	119.4	127.5	130.3	126.4	131.3
Oil seeds and oleaginous fruits	181.6	168.5	125.1	111.1	128.9	136.5	121.7	119.7
Cork and wood	96.5	98.3	99.1	98.8	98.9	97.6	96.9	97.3
Textile fibers and their waste	121.9	108.7	102.1	96.4	104.1	103.1	104.8	109.2
Metalliferous ores and metal scrap	171.4	167.5	178.5	195.0	206.4	212.9	206.2	227.8
Mineral Fuels, Lubricants, and Related Materials	123.0	131.8	141.2	146.5	169.3	181.0	231.9	205.5
Petroleum, petroleum products, and related materials	120.1	129.7	138.0	144.6	174.9	188.7	239.3	206.3
Chemicals and Related Products n.e.s.	104.9	105.8	109.7	114.0	117.0	115.7	118.8	119.6
Organic chemicals	110.8	114.6	120.5	128.4	130.6	128.6	137.0	132.8
Inorganic chemicals	99.5	98.7	107.6	113.7	120.0	120.9	121.5	120.1
Medicinal and pharmaceutical products	105.5	105.8	108.0	107.2	107.9	107.6	107.3	107.1
Essential oils, polishing, and cleansing preparations	104.3	104.3	105.6	109.1	111.3	112.4	112.6	111.8
Fertilizers	138.1	137.4	143.9	148.3	143.5	149.1	162.1	165.3
Plastics in primary forms	102.1	103.2	109.9	118.9	128.3	122.1	126.9	135.3
Plastics in nonprimary forms	97.4	96.5	97.4	99.9	103.2	103.3	104.9	108.0
Chemical materials and products n.e.s.	104.8	104.9	105.5	105.8	106.0	106.1	106.3	107.7
Manufactured Goods, Classified Chiefly by Material	104.1	107.0	110.5	112.2	113.7	113.9	113.9	116.0
Rubber manufactures n.e.s.	110.4	111.2	111.4	112.9	114.4	115.5	116.9	117.8
Uncoated paper, paperboard, and linerboard	97.9	99.2	102.7	104.2	103.8	103.9	103.7	102.8
Textile yarn, fabrics, and made-up articles n.e.s.	104.1	105.4	105.7	107.2	109.1	111.7	110.8	111.1
Nonmetallic mineral manufactures n.e.s.	99.7	99.9	100.4	101.6	102.2	103.5	104.2	105.5
Iron and steel	124.9	145.4	166.8	170.6	164.1	158.5	155.2	160.8
Nonferrous metals	94.1	95.4	99.0	101.5	107.2	106.1	108.5	118.2
Manufactures of metals n.e.s.	105.5	108.4	111.6	113.5	117.7	118.3	118.8	119.6
Machinery and Transport Equipment	98.2	98.2	98.2	98.5	98.7	98.7	98.0	98.1
Power-generating machinery and equipment	109.4	108.7	109.0	110.4	111.5	111.3	111.2	112.4
Machinery specialized for particular industries	104.2	105.4	106.1	108.0	109.4	110.7	112.1	114.1
Metalworking machinery	100.9	100.0	101.0	101.9	102.6	103.7	103.6	103.6
General industrial machinery, equipment, and parts n.e.s. ...	102.1	102.4	102.6	102.8	108.3	109.3	109.4	109.9
Computer equipment and office machines	88.4	87.2	86.0	83.8	82.3	80.9	79.1	77.1
Telecommunications and sound recording and reproducing apparatus and equipment	92.4	91.8	90.7	90.4	90.5	89.7	89.4	89.5
Electrical machinery and equipment	88.6	88.2	88.1	87.9	87.7	87.4	84.9	84.6
Road vehicles	101.9	102.4	102.4	103.0	103.0	103.0	103.5	103.8
Miscellaneous Manufactured Articles	100.9	100.9	101.2	102.3	102.7	102.1	102.5	102.7
Furniture and parts thereof	102.4	102.3	102.8	104.4	104.2	104.2	104.5	103.5
Articles of apparel and clothing accessories	96.8	96.9	96.9	97.1	97.1	96.9	96.6	96.6
Professional, scientific, and controlling instruments and apparatus n.e.s.	102.3	102.0	101.8	102.6	103.4	103.1	103.8	103.7
Photographic apparatus, equipment and supplies, and optical goods n.e.s.	95.0	94.5	95.7	97.0	96.3	96.4	95.8	95.2
Miscellaneous manufactured articles n.e.s.	101.4	101.6	102.3	104.0	104.3	102.9	103.5	104.4

n.e.s. = Not elsewhere specified.

Table 7-13. U.S. Import Price Indexes for Selected Categories of Goods, by Standard International Trade Classification, 1990–2005

(2000 = 100.)

Commodity	Relative impor-tance	1990				1991				1992			
		March	June	Septem-ber	Decem-ber	March	June	Septem-ber	Decem-ber	March	June	Septem-ber	Decem-ber
ALL COMMODITIES	100.0	92.4	90.8	96.5	98.4	95.0	93.4	93.3	94.3	93.9	94.8	95.9	94.4
Food and Live Animals	3.3	91.9	92.1	93.9	95.7	95.7	95.6	94.6	95.6	97.4	91.4	92.1	93.2
Meat and meat preparations	0.4	113.1	118.4	121.7	120.5	120.9	125.0	119.5	115.9	114.8	112.3	111.5	109.5
Fish, crustaceans, aquatic invertebrates, and preparations thereof	0.8	70.7	70.9	74.5	77.1	79.7	78.9	78.2	78.3	79.1	79.1	80.3	78.3
Vegetables and fruit and nuts, fresh or dried	0.8	90.7	87.0	83.1	90.6	88.3	91.4	91.9	95.6	107.7	89.9	89.6	91.7
Coffee, tea, cocoa, spices, and manufactures thereof	0.4	103.7	105.4	110.6	104.5	104.7	98.8	98.2	98.5	90.0	82.0	81.6	96.1
Beverages and Tobacco	0.9	74.7	76.5	77.6	79.6	84.2	85.4	85.3	86.3	87.1	87.5	88.3	87.2
Beverages	0.8	77.3	78.9	80.0	81.5	86.6	87.6	87.2	88.2	89.0	89.4	90.5	89.1
Crude Materials, Inedible, Except Fuels	1.8	91.3	90.4	88.0	85.0	84.4	85.0	81.8	81.5	84.6	85.0	86.3	85.9
Cork and wood	0.7	66.0	66.7	66.2	61.6	62.9	70.1	66.6	68.0	75.3	76.1	77.1	79.1
Wood pulp and recovered paper	0.2	118.9	116.6	112.5	105.6	97.1	89.8	80.7	78.6	81.2	84.4	88.2	83.9
Metalliferous ores and metal scrap	0.4	97.5	93.2	90.2	89.1	89.1	86.6	86.8	86.2	86.0	84.3	85.4	83.7
Crude animal and vegetable materials n.e.s.	0.2	. . .	. . .	. . .	. . .	. . .	. . .	. . .	. . .	. . .	. . .	. . .	. . .
Mineral Fuels, Lubricants, and Related Materials	20.0	64.3	54.7	87.3	93.0	65.8	62.3	63.6	63.3	56.8	64.9	65.3	60.0
Petroleum, petroleum products, and related materials	17.6	64.6	54.8	89.8	95.1	66.3	63.0	64.5	63.9	57.4	66.0	66.2	60.2
Gas, natural and manufactured	2.3	63.7	54.9	57.7	69.2	61.5	54.1	53.4	57.8	49.7	51.4	55.4	58.1
Chemicals and Related Products n.e.s.	8.0	94.3	93.7	94.9	97.6	97.4	95.8	95.4	95.6	96.2	96.8	97.5	97.1
Organic chemicals	2.6	98.7	98.1	100.0	104.7	101.8	98.6	96.1	97.1	97.0	96.8	96.5	94.4
Inorganic chemicals	0.7	95.4	95.8	97.0	100.7	101.5	100.2	98.1	94.9	95.5	94.1	93.7	99.0
Medicinal and pharmaceutical products	2.3	80.5	80.6	81.5	83.6	83.2	81.7	83.2	86.4	87.3	87.6	90.1	89.8
Essential oils, polishing, and cleansing preps	0.5	90.5	91.6	92.1	94.6	93.4	93.2	96.0	95.2	97.5	98.6	98.8	98.8
Plastics in primary forms	0.7	. . .	. . .	. . .	. . .	. . .	. . .	. . .	. . .	. . .	. . .	. . .	96.8
Plastics in nonprimary forms	0.4	. . .	. . .	. . .	. . .	. . .	. . .	. . .	. . .	. . .	. . .	. . .	109.9
Chemical materials and products n.e.s.	0.6	97.2	92.9	91.6	90.2	89.6	88.1	88.3	90.1	94.0	97.1	101.0	100.1
Manufactured Goods Classified Chiefly by Material	12.2	90.5	91.3	93.2	92.3	92.7	91.1	90.3	90.6	91.0	91.3	92.0	90.4
Rubber manufactures n.e.s.	0.7	102.9	103.3	103.3	104.6	104.3	104.1	103.7	104.8	105.7	105.6	107.0	106.8
Cork and wood manufactures, other than furniture	0.8	84.7	86.4	87.8	85.3	84.1	84.8	85.9	86.3	90.0	93.0	95.1	92.4
Paper and paperboard, cut to size	1.2	86.5	89.3	89.8	90.2	92.2	89.9	88.2	87.8	85.1	83.7	84.3	84.3
Textile yarn, fabrics, made-up articles, and related products n.e.s.	1.3	90.6	91.4	93.4	94.8	96.3	95.4	96.8	98.4	98.9	98.1	100.9	99.3
Nonmetallic mineral manufactures n.e.s.	2.0	87.7	88.9	89.4	90.3	91.9	92.1	92.2	93.0	93.3	94.0	94.9	94.6
Iron and steel	1.8	100.4	98.2	97.1	98.4	98.1	97.8	96.9	97.2	96.6	96.1	94.8	94.8
Nonferrous metals	2.2	80.9	84.2	92.6	83.6	82.1	75.9	72.9	70.8	73.7	75.6	75.6	70.0
Manufactures of metals n.e.s.	2.1	94.6	93.9	95.2	96.0	96.8	96.1	95.5	96.9	97.6	97.8	99.6	97.9
Machinery and Transport Equipment	37.8	101.6	100.8	101.8	104.2	105.4	103.7	103.8	105.4	105.6	105.6	106.9	106.1
Power-generating machinery and equipment	2.4	. . .	. . .	. . .	. . .	. . .	. . .	. . .	. . .	. . .	. . .	. . .	. . .
Machinery specialized for particular industries	1.8	86.3	87.1	90.4	94.1	95.6	91.0	90.7	93.4	94.2	94.3	99.0	95.4
Metalworking machinery	0.4	86.9	87.8	89.2	92.1	92.8	89.6	89.6	92.1	92.3	92.5	94.8	93.7
General industrial machinery, equipment, and machine parts n.e.s.	3.1	86.5	87.6	90.9	93.6	94.5	91.0	91.1	93.7	94.0	94.0	96.8	95.0
Computer equipment and office machines	5.3	200.8	198.5	196.8	199.2	197.3	193.4	191.2	191.7	192.2	190.2	190.9	189.0
Telecommunications and sound recording and reproducing apparatus and equipment	5.3	122.5	120.9	119.3	120.1	118.7	118.0	117.3	117.8	117.4	117.3	117.3	117.6
Electrical machinery and equipment	6.0	113.1	111.3	112.7	114.0	115.5	113.4	112.8	114.5	114.3	115.1	116.3	114.6
Road vehicles	12.3	83.2	82.0	82.9	85.4	87.1	86.3	86.8	88.1	88.2	88.0	88.6	88.8
Miscellaneous Manufactured Articles	15.4	94.5	94.7	96.2	97.5	97.7	96.3	96.5	98.0	99.1	99.3	101.0	99.9
Prefabricated buildings; plumbing and heat and lighting fixtures n.e.s.	0.5	102.7	102.0	104.2	105.6	101.9	101.6	101.4	102.8	103.8	105.2	106.8	105.5
Furniture and parts thereof	1.8	95.1	96.0	97.2	99.1	99.6	98.0	98.4	99.0	99.8	100.1	102.6	100.7
Travel goods, handbags, and similar containers	0.4	89.7	89.8	88.8	90.6	90.7	91.1	91.0	91.8	92.9	96.2	96.6	94.5
Articles of apparel and clothing accessories	4.7	95.7	96.5	96.4	95.5	95.5	94.8	95.4	95.9	96.9	97.7	97.5	97.9
Footwear	1.1	95.2	96.5	98.2	100.0	100.2	98.4	98.1	98.8	99.4	100.0	101.5	98.7
Professional, scientific, and controlling instruments and apparatus n.e.s.	1.8	87.7	89.1	92.0	96.9	98.0	93.4	93.0	95.6	95.7	95.4	101.2	98.4
Photographic apparatus, equipment and supplies, and optical goods n.e.s.	0.8	93.7	94.0	97.0	98.8	99.1	96.0	96.3	98.6	99.3	98.6	102.1	100.5
Miscellaneous manufactured articles n.e.s.	4.3	95.6	94.3	96.6	98.6	98.5	98.0	98.3	100.8	102.6	102.0	104.1	103.1

n.e.s. = Not elsewhere specified.

. . . = Not available.

Table 7-13. U.S. Import Price Indexes for Selected Categories of Goods, by Standard International Trade Classification, 1990–2005—*Continued*

(2000 = 100.)

Commodity	1993				1994				1995			
	March	June	September	December	March	June	September	December	March	June	September	December
ALL COMMODITIES	94.7	95.0	94.5	93.5	94.0	96.3	97.2	98.4	99.9	101.4	100.8	101.0
Food and Live Animals	91.2	94.4	95.6	95.3	96.3	101.8	110.9	110.8	112.6	108.6	106.7	104.7
Meat and meat preparations	113.4	117.6	115.9	111.3	114.3	107.8	108.8	108.5	104.9	100.8	97.3	99.6
Fish, crustaceans, aquatic invertebrates, and preparations thereof	78.9	79.1	79.9	83.6	85.5	88.9	90.6	93.8	93.6	92.5	89.2	86.5
Vegetables and fruit and nuts, fresh or dried	85.4	96.6	93.6	89.3	88.0	90.1	88.0	99.0	100.5	97.6	101.0	106.4
Coffee, tea, cocoa, spices, and manufactures thereof	89.8	86.1	104.2	107.8	109.3	145.4	214.4	182.7	194.8	176.3	165.7	141.9
Beverages and Tobacco	86.8	86.8	86.2	86.9	86.6	87.3	87.5	87.5	88.2	88.6	89.4	90.6
Beverages	89.1	89.6	89.0	89.3	89.2	89.6	90.1	90.2	91.0	91.2	91.7	92.0
Crude Materials, Inedible, Except Fuels	92.2	84.5	85.9	90.7	93.4	94.7	96.2	101.6	107.6	109.5	113.6	111.0
Cork and wood	105.9	84.9	92.4	110.9	108.7	104.1	101.3	97.4	93.4	85.3	94.7	88.5
Woodpulp and recovered paper	74.3	72.2	68.5	66.2	69.8	79.5	90.8	102.9	118.8	131.6	134.8	138.4
Metalliferous ores and metal scrap	82.8	81.7	80.6	77.0	83.5	82.9	85.4	90.0	98.6	98.4	101.5	100.2
Crude animal and vegetable materials n.e.s.	...	...	...	...	...	...	...	...	...	...	...	...
Mineral Fuels, Lubricants, and Related Materials	61.5	59.8	55.0	47.7	48.2	57.1	55.0	56.4	59.2	61.9	57.6	59.2
Petroleum, petroleum products, and related materials	62.1	60.3	55.0	47.0	47.7	57.6	55.2	56.7	60.1	63.0	58.5	60.2
Gas, natural and manufactured	54.9	55.4	56.3	57.7	55.6	51.4	53.6	54.2	48.8	49.3	47.1	49.1
Chemicals and Related Products n.e.s.	97.1	97.8	97.1	96.4	96.3	97.6	100.5	103.5	105.4	106.8	106.6	106.4
Organic chemicals	94.0	94.6	94.3	92.8	92.6	95.2	100.0	104.5	102.5	100.6	101.0	100.3
Inorganic chemicals	99.1	97.9	97.7	97.5	96.9	97.9	99.9	104.6	110.0	111.1	110.9	110.2
Medicinal and pharmaceutical products	91.0	95.9	94.4	95.1	95.8	95.9	97.6	98.3	99.2	104.4	104.1	105.6
Essential oils, polishing, and cleansing preps	100.9	102.2	100.2	101.4	99.6	99.9	101.9	104.6	107.7	113.8	114.7	115.5
Plastics in primary forms	97.7	95.8	96.5	96.5	97.6	97.9	98.4	99.6	103.4	106.1	105.1	107.9
Plastics in nonprimary forms	109.0	109.3	108.5	107.1	104.7	108.0	112.9	117.7	126.9	129.6	124.5	117.4
Chemical materials and products n.e.s.	98.7	98.0	96.1	94.5	95.4	94.5	97.8	96.4	96.5	98.7	101.6	104.2
Manufactured Goods Classified Chiefly by Material	90.8	91.2	90.7	89.8	91.2	92.8	94.6	97.7	100.2	102.7	105.0	104.3
Rubber manufactures n.e.s.	107.6	107.5	106.8	106.9	105.2	106.0	105.0	105.9	106.4	108.7	110.0	110.4
Cork and wood manufactures, other than furniture	100.5	103.8	104.8	103.9	106.1	108.8	101.7	99.4	101.4	102.7	100.1	100.9
Paper and paperboard, cut to size	85.6	86.0	84.9	83.8	83.6	85.1	88.4	93.6	101.8	111.3	120.5	121.6
Textile yarn, fabrics, made-up articles, and related products n.e.s.	99.4	100.0	98.9	98.2	98.8	100.8	101.8	102.0	103.2	106.3	106.4	106.1
Nonmetallic mineral manufactures n.e.s.	95.1	96.2	96.0	96.2	96.1	96.7	97.8	98.4	98.7	99.2	99.6	99.9
Iron and steel	95.1	96.7	96.6	96.4	97.3	97.6	99.7	101.6	104.0	106.9	110.7	108.1
Nonferrous metals	68.3	65.4	64.8	61.7	68.5	72.7	77.6	88.0	90.3	88.5	90.5	87.2
Manufactures of metals n.e.s.	98.1	99.2	99.0	98.7	98.6	99.3	100.7	101.0	102.9	105.1	105.2	105.9
Machinery and Transport Equipment	106.1	107.2	107.7	108.4	108.6	109.1	109.7	110.3	110.8	112.4	112.1	112.0
Power-generating machinery and equipment	...	...	...	...	...	...	...	...	...	...	...	...
Machinery specialized for particular industries	...	96.2	95.8	96.0	96.9	98.1	99.8	100.6	102.0	104.7	103.8	105.6
Metalworking machinery	93.5	95.9	96.4	96.9	97.1	98.0	100.3	101.4	103.1	108.9	108.3	108.9
General industrial machinery, equipment, and machine parts n.e.s.	94.4	95.9	95.9	96.7	97.2	97.7	98.9	100.0	101.3	104.5	104.7	105.5
Computer equipment and office machines	186.2	182.8	180.1	178.0	175.5	173.2	171.1	168.5	167.0	167.2	165.9	163.4
Telecommunications and sound recording and reproducing apparatus and equipment	117.3	118.3	119.5	118.5	117.5	117.6	117.7	118.0	117.8	119.1	119.0	118.0
Electrical machinery and equipment	115.2	117.2	119.4	118.9	119.1	119.6	120.2	120.1	120.5	122.9	120.7	119.7
Road vehicles	89.1	90.4	90.9	92.9	93.3	94.0	94.7	96.0	96.6	97.3	97.9	98.2
Miscellaneous Manufactured Articles	99.7	100.7	100.7	100.5	100.6	100.9	101.3	101.5	102.2	103.2	103.1	103.7
Prefabricated buildings; plumbing and heat and lighting fixtures n.e.s.	104.4	105.7	105.9	105.6	104.9	103.2	104.4	103.3	107.2	107.4	108.3	109.7
Furniture and parts thereof	100.2	100.8	100.2	99.7	100.2	100.6	100.9	101.2	101.7	103.1	102.9	103.5
Travel goods, handbags, and similar containers	94.8	95.5	95.8	94.9	94.8	94.5	95.7	96.0	96.4	98.5	100.5	99.3
Articles of apparel and clothing accessories	97.5	98.1	98.2	97.8	97.7	97.8	97.9	98.2	98.8	99.0	99.0	99.5
Footwear	98.0	98.7	97.8	97.6	97.1	97.7	98.4	98.5	98.5	99.3	99.6	100.1
Professional, scientific, and controlling instruments and apparatus n.e.s.	98.9	101.0	100.2	100.9	102.0	103.3	104.2	105.1	105.1	107.2	107.5	107.1
Photographic apparatus, equipment and supplies, and optical goods n.e.s.	100.5	102.5	103.5	104.2	104.0	104.6	106.2	106.0	106.4	110.6	109.9	109.9
Miscellaneous manufactured articles n.e.s.	103.1	104.2	104.4	104.3	104.4	104.4	104.7	104.8	106.1	106.5	106.1	107.2

n.e.s. = Not elsewhere specified.

. . . = Not available.

Table 7-13. U.S. Import Price Indexes for Selected Categories of Goods, by Standard International Trade Classification, 1990–2005—*Continued*

(2000 = 100.)

Commodity	1996				1997				1998			
	March	June	September	December	March	June	September	December	March	June	September	December
ALL COMMODITIES	101.6	100.7	101.8	102.5	100.0	98.8	98.4	97.2	94.1	93.1	92.2	91.0
Food and Live Animals	103.2	102.7	104.8	102.6	110.4	112.5	109.8	108.0	106.1	106.3	103.5	103.2
Meat and meat preparations	93.7	92.0	102.6	100.7	105.3	103.6	105.7	106.0	103.0	100.0	98.9	93.4
Fish, crustaceans, aquatic invertebrates, and preparations thereof	86.8	88.8	88.3	89.4	90.7	94.3	95.2	96.1	97.4	99.6	94.4	91.2
Vegetables and fruit and nuts, fresh or dried	102.4	98.8	107.1	102.4	111.8	102.2	104.0	103.1	96.2	104.0	107.3	111.2
Coffee, tea, cocoa, spices, and manufactures thereof	144.3	143.7	135.8	129.0	169.7	203.7	172.1	158.5	161.8	141.3	133.1	129.2
Beverages and Tobacco	91.2	92.1	93.2	93.4	95.0	95.5	95.8	96.5	97.0	97.4	97.5	97.6
Beverages	92.1	92.5	93.5	93.9	94.3	94.9	95.2	96.1	96.6	97.0	97.1	97.3
Crude Materials, Inedible, Except Fuels	105.8	103.4	106.4	105.6	108.5	106.8	106.0	102.6	99.9	96.2	94.0	92.2
Cork and wood	91.3	104.5	115.9	110.9	116.2	112.7	111.5	104.1	101.8	93.1	98.7	98.4
Woodpulp and recovered paper	100.2	79.2	84.9	84.4	82.7	83.9	86.9	87.6	81.8	84.2	77.5	73.7
Metalliferous ores and metal scrap	100.3	100.1	95.9	96.0	101.4	104.1	102.9	100.7	98.8	97.0	91.5	91.3
Crude animal and vegetable materials n.e.s.	. . .	. . .	. . .	94.2	99.1	91.7	97.1	100.8	103.7	106.6	99.2	93.6
Mineral Fuels, Lubricants, and Related Materials	66.3	65.1	72.6	79.8	67.1	61.6	63.0	60.8	47.3	45.7	45.6	38.0
Petroleum, petroleum products, and related materials	67.4	66.3	74.3	80.0	67.6	62.2	63.0	59.8	45.5	43.9	44.2	35.1
Gas, natural and manufactured	54.7	52.7	56.3	76.7	61.3	55.1	60.2	65.0	55.9	54.5	51.8	53.9
Chemicals and Related Products n.e.s.	106.5	104.9	105.1	105.1	103.7	102.3	102.1	101.1	99.2	99.3	97.4	96.7
Organic chemicals	100.7	99.9	100.4	100.9	101.3	97.3	98.5	96.7	93.5	93.6	92.7	91.1
Inorganic chemicals	111.5	109.2	109.9	113.3	111.0	108.4	109.0	106.4	103.7	107.0	102.8	99.5
Medicinal and pharmaceutical products	103.9	102.7	104.4	102.0	98.9	99.3	98.7	99.8	98.8	98.3	97.5	98.7
Essential oils, polishing, and cleansing preps	116.8	112.8	112.8	112.6	110.5	109.2	109.1	109.7	106.2	106.7	105.6	107.1
Plastics in primary forms	108.2	102.6	98.8	100.3	96.7	96.7	97.8	97.1	99.6	99.2	96.8	96.4
Plastics in nonprimary forms	110.8	108.6	108.1	108.2	107.4	110.6	108.5	103.3	101.7	98.7	92.4	92.0
Chemical materials and products n.e.s.	107.4	107.1	107.5	105.3	104.1	103.0	102.7	102.6	101.2	100.9	100.1	99.0
Manufactured Goods Classified Chiefly by Material	103.3	102.0	99.8	98.2	98.7	99.5	99.6	98.7	97.3	96.7	95.4	94.3
Rubber manufactures n.e.s.	108.7	108.8	108.2	107.0	105.7	106.0	103.2	103.7	102.8	103.1	102.4	102.5
Cork and wood manufactures, other than furniture	101.4	104.4	103.7	101.7	102.2	102.0	102.4	102.1	95.7	95.6	98.6	98.0
Paper and paperboard, cut to size	118.9	112.7	104.0	96.3	95.0	97.7	99.2	98.9	98.2	97.8	97.2	96.2
Textile yarn, fabrics, made-up articles, and related products n.e.s.	105.9	105.4	105.5	105.8	105.8	105.8	105.2	104.5	103.1	102.3	101.8	101.4
Nonmetallic mineral manufactures n.e.s.	100.9	100.8	101.6	102.3	102.5	101.9	101.4	101.0	100.0	99.9	99.4	100.0
Iron and steel	105.7	104.8	104.8	104.1	103.2	103.3	103.3	103.3	101.9	99.7	96.7	93.5
Nonferrous metals	85.4	84.2	77.8	76.0	81.8	85.4	87.1	82.7	81.9	81.6	77.5	74.5
Manufactures of metals n.e.s.	106.0	105.0	105.8	105.7	104.0	103.6	102.6	103.1	101.8	101.0	101.0	101.1
Machinery and Transport Equipment	111.2	110.1	110.2	109.6	107.8	106.9	105.9	105.0	103.8	102.6	101.6	102.0
Power-generating machinery and equipment	. . .	. . .	. . .	100.2	99.7	99.4	99.0	99.2	100.1	98.1	97.4	98.1
Machinery specialized for particular industries	106.3	104.7	104.9	105.1	103.2	102.8	102.0	102.6	101.6	101.1	100.2	102.0
Metalworking machinery	108.3	108.1	108.4	108.0	104.4	104.9	103.8	105.3	104.1	103.4	103.0	104.2
General industrial machinery, equipment, and machine parts n.e.s.	104.9	104.4	105.2	104.6	102.2	102.1	101.0	101.0	100.3	100.3	100.3	102.1
Computer equipment and office machines	158.5	152.8	149.7	146.9	140.6	135.3	130.2	128.0	121.5	117.2	114.5	111.1
Telecommunications and sound recording and reproducing apparatus and equipment	116.5	115.3	114.3	113.5	111.9	110.6	109.8	108.7	107.5	105.9	105.3	104.6
Electrical machinery and equipment	118.0	115.6	114.8	112.1	109.9	109.1	107.9	104.7	103.4	102.2	100.6	101.8
Road vehicles	97.9	97.8	98.3	98.1	98.1	98.1	98.6	98.8	98.8	98.4	98.1	98.8
Miscellaneous Manufactured Articles	103.7	103.5	103.5	103.2	102.9	103.0	102.7	102.5	102.0	101.4	101.0	101.0
Prefabricated buildings; plumbing and heat and lighting fixtures n.e.s.	108.6	106.5	108.7	106.2	102.7	103.0	101.9	103.1	103.5	102.7	102.2	100.9
Furniture and parts thereof	103.2	103.3	103.3	104.3	104.9	105.4	104.9	105.6	105.4	102.6	102.6	102.8
Travel goods, handbags, and similar containers	99.6	99.6	99.6	99.2	99.9	99.7	99.5	98.9	98.0	99.6	98.7	99.5
Articles of apparel and clothing accessories	99.9	100.4	100.1	99.9	100.6	101.5	101.7	101.7	101.5	101.5	101.7	100.9
Footwear	100.7	100.6	100.3	100.2	100.3	100.3	100.0	100.5	100.0	100.0	100.2	100.1
Professional, scientific, and controlling instruments and apparatus n.e.s.	107.4	105.9	107.0	106.5	103.9	103.6	103.4	102.8	101.4	101.3	100.8	101.4
Photographic apparatus, equipment and supplies, and optical goods n.e.s.	108.4	106.3	106.7	105.7	104.0	103.0	102.1	101.6	100.1	99.3	98.3	99.4
Miscellaneous manufactured articles n.e.s.	107.1	107.2	107.2	106.5	105.9	105.6	104.7	104.2	103.5	102.2	101.1	101.4

n.e.s. = Not elsewhere specified.

. . . = Not available.

Table 7-13. U.S. Import Price Indexes for Selected Categories of Goods, by Standard International Trade Classification, 1990–2005—*Continued*

(2000 = 100.)

Commodity	1999				2000				2001			
	March	June	September	December	March	June	September	December	March	June	September	December
ALL COMMODITIES	91.5	92.9	95.8	97.4	99.9	100.2	101.6	100.5	98.3	97.6	95.9	91.4
Food and Live Animals	101.1	101.2	99.3	102.7	101.0	99.0	99.0	100.2	100.9	96.0	95.1	94.8
Meat and meat preparations	95.7	96.1	101.2	100.1	100.9	100.8	100.7	99.1	102.2	106.2	113.5	109.8
Fish, crustaceans, aquatic invertebrates, and preparations thereof	94.0	94.9	93.9	97.2	98.3	99.3	102.5	99.3	93.0	90.0	86.3	82.9
Vegetables and fruit and nuts, fresh or dried	102.3	103.7	102.2	104.2	101.8	96.2	98.4	105.1	110.1	97.6	98.5	99.3
Coffee, tea, cocoa, spices, and manufactures thereof	122.1	119.4	105.7	121.4	105.0	102.3	93.9	87.4	88.7	85.8	80.1	78.5
Beverages and Tobacco	98.1	98.1	99.7	99.5	99.2	100.4	100.9	100.5	100.4	101.7	102.0	103.0
Beverages	97.6	97.9	99.6	99.3	99.1	100.5	101.0	100.9	100.8	102.4	102.4	103.1
Crude Materials, Inedible, Except Fuels	94.7	99.1	100.5	101.1	103.5	99.4	97.5	97.0	94.5	102.8	96.6	89.9
Cork and wood	104.2	112.5	112.0	109.3	109.2	101.3	91.8	93.6	89.8	122.1	112.2	91.7
Woodpulp and recovered paper	73.5	77.3	84.1	86.9	92.3	102.0	104.5	106.3	102.5	87.1	77.3	77.7
Metalliferous ores and metal scrap	88.5	90.4	92.8	97.4	102.3	99.1	100.0	97.3	96.6	93.9	92.8	91.2
Crude animal and vegetable materials n.e.s.	103.1	95.8	104.7	105.5	105.5	87.4	97.0	91.5	92.0	92.9	83.8	96.0
Mineral Fuels, Lubricants, and Related Materials	43.1	54.6	74.5	83.2	97.4	101.3	111.3	106.1	90.8	90.4	85.8	61.2
Petroleum, petroleum products, and related materials	41.9	54.6	75.1	84.5	99.5	102.2	112.1	97.9	86.5	89.3	86.8	59.8
Gas, natural and manufactured	47.5	51.8	69.2	73.1	83.1	95.2	106.2	161.6	119.1	97.4	77.8	68.6
Chemicals and Related Products n.e.s.	96.4	96.2	96.9	97.6	98.5	99.8	101.2	100.7	102.4	100.5	98.3	97.4
Organic chemicals	91.7	91.6	93.2	94.3	95.9	100.4	102.5	102.1	101.5	102.1	99.3	96.1
Inorganic chemicals	97.0	94.9	94.8	96.3	97.2	100.1	101.2	103.0	107.2	100.1	98.1	97.6
Medicinal and pharmaceutical products	99.7	99.1	100.0	100.3	100.3	99.8	99.7	98.6	97.5	96.7	97.0	97.0
Essential oils, polishing, and cleansing preps	105.3	104.1	103.9	101.6	101.0	100.8	100.0	96.2	99.7	98.4	99.7	100.1
Plastics in primary forms	97.1	98.8	99.1	99.2	99.2	99.6	100.6	101.2	101.1	102.1	99.7	99.8
Plastics in nonprimary forms	91.3	94.4	97.2	99.5	100.3	100.8	100.8	98.0	105.3	102.4	99.3	100.9
Chemical materials and products n.e.s.	97.4	97.0	97.6	99.1	100.2	99.2	100.7	100.1	101.4	99.9	99.0	98.0
Manufactured Goods Classified Chiefly by Material	94.5	94.6	95.2	96.6	100.8	100.4	100.6	100.0	100.0	98.0	94.8	92.0
Rubber manufactures n.e.s.	102.6	102.4	103.1	102.5	100.2	99.7	99.6	99.7	99.7	99.0	98.7	97.9
Cork and wood manufactures, other than furniture	103.5	107.7	106.8	102.8	106.3	99.2	95.8	94.1	92.0	96.2	90.4	88.3
Paper and paperboard, cut to size	95.8	93.6	93.5	96.3	97.3	99.6	102.1	103.0	103.6	102.7	99.3	96.2
Textile yarn, fabrics, made-up articles, and related products n.e.s.	100.6	99.7	99.9	99.8	100.7	99.7	99.8	99.5	99.1	98.8	98.1	97.1
Nonmetallic mineral manufactures n.e.s.	100.6	100.2	100.4	100.5	100.1	99.8	100.1	99.5	99.9	99.4	99.3	97.4
Iron and steel	91.2	92.0	92.5	95.5	100.4	103.9	100.7	97.9	95.5	93.5	94.0	92.5
Nonferrous metals	77.1	78.8	81.8	85.9	103.4	99.4	102.7	102.7	104.6	95.3	82.2	73.8
Manufactures of metals n.e.s.	100.3	100.6	100.2	100.3	100.6	100.1	99.8	99.4	99.3	100.1	99.3	99.0
Machinery and Transport Equipment	101.6	100.9	100.5	100.3	100.2	100.1	99.8	99.4	99.2	98.5	98.0	97.7
Power-generating machinery and equipment	98.8	98.5	98.6	99.3	99.5	100.4	99.9	100.1	99.2	98.8	98.6	98.5
Machinery specialized for particular industries	101.8	101.1	101.1	101.3	100.7	99.5	99.3	98.7	99.7	99.1	99.1	98.7
Metalworking machinery	102.6	100.9	100.6	101.5	100.2	98.8	100.3	99.8	100.6	99.4	100.1	99.7
General industrial machinery, equipment, and machine parts n.e.s.	102.1	101.3	101.1	100.7	100.7	99.9	99.7	99.0	99.3	98.2	98.0	97.8
Computer equipment and office machines	107.3	105.1	102.7	102.7	101.6	99.9	99.5	97.8	95.7	93.6	90.0	88.8
Telecommunications and sound recording and reproducing apparatus and equipment	104.8	103.8	103.2	101.4	100.6	100.2	99.6	99.0	98.1	97.2	96.8	96.3
Electrical machinery and equipment	101.3	100.1	99.8	99.3	99.4	100.7	99.9	99.4	99.9	98.8	98.6	97.8
Road vehicles	99.2	99.6	99.5	99.6	99.9	100.1	99.9	100.1	100.1	99.8	100.0	100.3
Miscellaneous Manufactured Articles	101.1	100.5	100.7	100.7	100.3	99.7	99.7	99.7	100.2	99.8	99.6	99.1
Prefabricated buildings; plumbing and heat and lighting fixtures n.e.s.	99.9	99.5	97.6	99.4	100.9	99.2	99.5	99.2	98.8	99.2	98.3	98.4
Furniture and parts thereof	102.6	101.1	100.8	100.1	100.5	99.6	100.3	99.7	99.8	98.5	98.9	98.9
Travel goods, handbags, and similar containers	99.2	100.3	100.9	100.1	100.5	99.8	99.9	99.8	100.1	99.0	99.3	98.7
Articles of apparel and clothing accessories	101.1	100.6	101.1	100.8	100.4	99.6	99.7	99.9	101.1	100.6	100.1	100.2
Footwear	100.4	100.0	100.1	100.1	100.0	99.6	100.2	99.8	100.8	100.1	100.4	100.3
Professional, scientific, and controlling instruments and apparatus n.e.s.	101.0	100.4	100.8	101.3	100.1	99.8	99.8	99.2	99.1	98.7	98.5	98.5
Photographic apparatus, equipment and supplies, and optical goods n.e.s.	100.1	99.6	99.7	100.9	100.1	99.9	99.7	98.9	99.7	98.5	98.2	98.4
Miscellaneous manufactured articles n.e.s.	101.5	100.9	100.9	100.8	100.3	99.8	99.5	99.7	99.7	99.7	99.6	97.8

n.e.s. = Not elsewhere specified.

Table 7-13. U.S. Import Price Indexes for Selected Categories of Goods, by Standard International Trade Classification, 1990–2005—*Continued*

(2000 = 100.)

Commodity	2002				2003			
	March	June	September	December	March	June	September	December
ALL COMMODITIES	92.8	94.1	95.5	95.2	99.1	96.2	96.2	97.5
Food and Live Animals	96.4	94.5	98.8	98.8	101.2	99.4	100.0	101.0
Meat and meat preparations	109.8	104.0	103.4	106.8	108.5	102.9	112.8	120.4
Fish, crustaceans, aquatic invertebrates, and preparations thereof	80.4	79.8	84.9	82.5	81.4	81.3	82.2	79.2
Vegetables and fruit and nuts, fresh or dried	104.0	102.2	106.7	105.6	110.7	108.9	105.0	109.4
Coffee, tea, cocoa, spices, and manufactures thereof	83.3	84.6	93.5	99.9	100.2	94.8	98.6	96.0
Beverages and Tobacco	102.1	103.0	102.6	102.7	104.0	103.9	104.0	104.4
Beverages	102.5	102.8	102.2	102.4	103.0	103.7	103.9	104.3
Crude Materials, Inedible, Except Fuels	95.8	96.4	96.4	94.5	98.5	99.5	106.1	107.9
Cork and wood	106.6	103.1	98.3	94.0	95.0	94.4	113.0	108.0
Woodpulp and recovered paper	74.9	77.1	82.3	78.9	86.5	95.3	90.4	92.8
Metalliferous ores and metal scrap	93.7	95.9	93.3	94.7	99.9	99.7	103.7	115.3
Crude animal and vegetable materials n.e.s.	92.3	92.8	104.0	101.4	102.6	104.9	95.7	99.6
Mineral Fuels, Lubricants, and Related Materials	76.4	86.1	96.3	94.9	126.0	101.7	101.5	108.2
Petroleum, petroleum products, and related materials	77.4	85.9	97.8	94.2	118.1	97.6	99.4	106.9
Gas, natural and manufactured	64.8	83.6	81.1	97.0	185.9	130.1	114.4	113.9
Chemicals and Related Products n.e.s.	96.3	97.0	98.7	98.2	101.1	100.1	99.2	101.1
Organic chemicals	96.6	97.2	99.7	98.5	99.4	97.0	97.0	97.5
Inorganic chemicals	97.8	98.6	100.1	102.5	110.8	106.4	105.4	114.0
Medicinal and pharmaceutical products	96.0	98.0	99.6	99.2	101.3	102.5	101.9	103.4
Essential oils, polishing, and cleansing preps	99.8	99.9	98.4	99.2	98.4	99.4	91.6	91.6
Plastics in primary forms	91.5	91.8	97.9	94.8	99.3	106.1	102.7	105.5
Plastics in nonprimary forms	100.6	100.3	99.4	99.6	100.4	100.8	101.4	101.8
Chemical materials and products n.e.s.	93.6	93.6	92.4	91.6	97.6	92.3	91.8	93.3
Manufactured Goods Classified Chiefly by Material	92.2	92.8	93.5	93.7	94.1	94.4	95.7	97.8
Rubber manufactures n.e.s.	97.6	98.2	99.3	99.3	99.0	99.2	98.5	98.8
Cork and wood manufactures, other than furniture	96.2	93.2	93.9	89.8	94.4	95.8	113.7	112.0
Paper and paperboard, cut to size	93.4	91.7	93.7	93.0	93.0	93.5	94.5	93.7
Textile yarn, fabrics, made-up articles, and related products n.e.s.	97.3	96.9	97.0	97.8	100.3	100.8	100.6	101.8
Nonmetallic mineral manufactures n.e.s.	96.9	96.9	97.5	97.7	97.6	97.9	97.8	98.1
Iron and steel	90.9	94.6	99.9	101.9	99.0	101.2	99.9	105.1
Nonferrous metals	76.9	79.7	76.4	77.3	80.0	78.1	80.7	87.7
Manufactures of metals n.e.s.	98.5	98.3	98.6	98.3	97.9	98.3	98.5	99.5
Machinery and Transport Equipment	97.1	97.1	96.7	96.1	95.8	95.8	95.5	95.3
Power-generating machinery and equipment	98.0	98.2	99.4	98.7	99.1	99.9	99.7	100.4
Machinery specialized for particular industries	98.5	99.0	98.3	99.2	100.7	101.4	102.2	103.6
Metalworking machinery	98.4	100.8	102.4	101.4	104.0	105.2	103.6	105.0
General industrial machinery, equipment, and machine parts n.e.s.	97.5	97.8	98.4	98.6	99.8	100.8	100.2	101.2
Computer equipment and office machines	88.1	87.8	86.4	84.2	82.7	81.8	80.5	78.2
Telecommunications and sound recording and reproducing apparatus and equipment	94.8	94.4	92.8	92.0	90.0	89.3	88.6	86.7
Electrical machinery and equipment	96.8	97.1	96.5	95.6	95.3	95.4	96.0	95.3
Road vehicles	100.1	100.2	100.3	100.5	100.6	100.7	100.6	101.6
Miscellaneous Manufactured Articles	98.8	98.6	98.7	99.0	99.5	99.7	99.6	99.9
Prefabricated buildings; plumbing and heat and lighting fixtures n.e.s.	98.9	98.5	96.5	95.6	95.8	94.8	95.1	93.2
Furniture and parts thereof	99.1	98.8	98.8	99.4	99.5	100.2	100.4	100.1
Travel goods, handbags, and similar containers	99.3	99.0	100.5	99.6	101.5	101.6	102.9	103.8
Articles of apparel and clothing accessories	100.1	99.7	99.5	100.5	100.8	100.6	100.5	100.7
Footwear	99.5	99.2	99.4	99.6	99.8	100.0	99.9	100.1
Professional, scientific, and controlling instruments and apparatus n.e.s.	97.9	97.8	98.2	98.2	98.5	99.5	99.3	100.0
Photographic apparatus, equipment and supplies, and optical goods n.e.s.	97.2	97.8	98.4	98.5	99.4	100.0	99.2	99.9
Miscellaneous manufactured articles n.e.s.	97.3	97.1	97.6	97.5	98.1	98.3	98.3	98.8

n.e.s. = Not elsewhere specified.

Table 7-13. U.S. Import Price Indexes for Selected Categories of Goods, by Standard International Trade Classification, 1990–2005—*Continued*

(2000 = 100.)

Commodity	2004				2005			
	March	June	September	December	March	June	September	December
ALL COMMODITIES	100.2	101.7	104.1	104.0	107.8	109.2	114.4	112.3
Food and Live Animals	105.4	106.9	109.2	111.9	117.5	113.9	113.5	117.4
Meat and meat preparations	120.4	128.9	134.9	133.0	135.9	138.5	140.8	140.4
Fish, crustaceans, aquatic invertebrates, and preparations thereof	83.3	84.1	86.0	85.0	88.5	87.8	91.4	91.7
Vegetables and fruit and nuts, fresh or dried	111.3	105.9	109.2	112.2	121.6	109.0	106.2	120.6
Coffee, tea, cocoa, spices, and manufactures thereof	101.7	107.0	105.6	114.4	130.2	127.8	119.1	120.3
Beverages and Tobacco	105.3	105.3	106.2	107.1	107.8	108.5	108.9	108.5
Beverages	105.5	105.6	106.7	107.6	108.2	109.1	109.5	109.3
Crude Materials, Inedible, Except Fuels	120.0	125.8	135.1	125.5	135.0	130.5	132.0	133.7
Cork and wood	123.3	136.1	151.1	124.7	136.9	127.0	124.5	123.6
Woodpulp and recovered paper	95.4	106.5	105.5	100.3	108.7	103.6	102.2	106.0
Metalliferous ores and metal scrap	148.0	140.4	162.6	167.3	176.9	176.0	193.3	195.2
Crude animal and vegetable materials n.e.s.	99.7	98.0	98.7	98.3	109.9	111.7	106.0	111.3
Mineral Fuels, Lubricants, and Related Materials	120.8	131.5	146.8	140.6	166.5	179.0	223.5	202.3
Petroleum, petroleum products, and related materials	120.0	130.0	149.5	137.0	169.0	182.4	225.1	195.7
Gas, natural and manufactured	122.9	140.0	121.9	163.5	145.8	148.5	209.1	245.5
Chemicals and Related Products n.e.s.	103.8	103.8	106.7	109.6	112.2	112.4	114.6	115.0
Organic chemicals	98.7	99.8	106.1	109.3	111.9	110.2	113.5	110.0
Inorganic chemicals	120.5	119.8	124.1	126.7	130.2	138.2	151.7	162.0
Medicinal and pharmaceutical products	108.1	107.1	106.6	108.9	110.2	110.3	111.0	110.2
Essential oils, polishing, and cleansing preps	93.7	93.5	93.4	94.4	95.5	94.5	95.2	94.7
Plastics in primary forms	106.9	104.6	109.6	116.1	125.9	125.1	125.5	138.0
Plastics in nonprimary forms	102.9	102.3	103.8	105.7	106.4	107.2	106.6	106.9
Chemical materials and products n.e.s.	95.8	95.2	94.4	96.1	99.2	102.4	101.8	103.1
Manufactured Goods Classified Chiefly by Material	103.6	106.1	108.9	110.4	112.8	112.8	112.8	114.4
Rubber manufactures n.e.s.	99.7	100.5	100.8	101.9	103.5	104.5	104.4	104.6
Cork and wood manufactures, other than furniture	127.8	118.7	116.6	113.0	123.5	116.1	116.9	113.5
Paper and paperboard, cut to size	95.0	95.5	97.9	99.0	100.3	102.1	103.7	104.4
Textile yarn, fabrics, made-up articles, and related products n.e.s.	103.7	103.8	104.0	104.1	104.5	104.0	103.9	105.3
Nonmetallic mineral manufactures n.e.s.	99.0	99.4	100.4	100.7	100.9	101.4	101.9	101.8
Iron and steel	119.2	144.6	157.4	160.1	161.9	161.9	152.2	150.3
Nonferrous metals	102.6	101.6	106.3	111.0	116.1	117.7	121.1	133.3
Manufactures of metals n.e.s.	101.1	102.4	103.9	106.7	108.7	108.6	109.0	108.4
Machinery and Transport Equipment	95.5	95.1	95.0	95.2	95.1	95.0	94.4	94.1
Power-generating machinery and equipment	101.3	101.5	101.4	102.5	103.8	103.8	104.2	104.1
Machinery specialized for particular industries	106.7	106.6	107.4	109.5	110.8	110.9	111.0	111.1
Metalworking machinery	107.4	106.2	108.0	112.5	113.9	120.2	118.2	116.9
General industrial machinery, equipment, and machine parts n.e.s.	103.3	103.5	104.3	105.3	106.8	107.2	107.3	107.3
Computer equipment and office machines	77.7	75.5	73.9	72.8	71.2	70.5	68.3	67.3
Telecommunications and sound recording and reproducing apparatus and equipment	85.1	84.7	83.8	83.1	82.7	82.1	80.5	79.8
Electrical machinery and equipment	95.6	94.7	94.6	94.6	94.5	94.4	94.0	94.0
Road vehicles	102.0	102.4	103.1	103.7	103.7	103.8	104.1	104.1
Miscellaneous Manufactured Articles	100.1	99.9	100.1	100.5	101.0	101.0	101.2	101.3
Prefabricated buildings; plumbing and heat and lighting fixtures n.e.s.	93.2	93.5	93.5	94.8	96.2	96.4	96.3	96.2
Furniture and parts thereof	100.8	102.3	103.1	104.7	106.5	106.4	106.4	106.3
Travel goods, handbags, and similar containers	103.6	103.4	103.6	105.2	106.9	106.4	106.3	105.8
Articles of apparel and clothing accessories	100.6	100.7	100.8	100.7	100.7	100.6	100.9	100.7
Footwear	100.6	100.4	100.5	100.5	100.3	100.5	100.9	100.9
Professional, scientific, and controlling instruments and apparatus n.e.s.	99.6	99.6	99.9	100.2	101.0	101.4	101.5	101.3
Photographic apparatus, equipment and supplies, and optical goods n.e.s.	100.0	99.0	98.2	98.6	99.1	99.0	98.1	98.0
Miscellaneous manufactured articles n.e.s.	99.0	97.2	97.2	97.4	99.3	99.5	99.8	100.7

n.e.s. = Not elsewhere specified.

Table 7-14. U.S. Import Price Indexes for Selected Categories of Goods, by Locality of Origin, 1995–2005

(2000 = 100.)

Category and year	Percent of U.S. imports[1]	Month			
		March	June	September	December
INDUSTRIALIZED COUNTRIES	46.4				
Total Goods					
1995		97.4	99.8	100.0	100.0
1996		99.7	98.8	99.3	99.4
1997		97.4	96.5	96.4	96.1
1998		94.6	94.0	93.3	93.8
1999		94.1	94.8	96.4	97.5
2000		99.5	100.1	100.9	101.4
2001		100.2	99.0	96.5	93.7
2002		94.3	95.7	96.9	96.7
2003		100.0	98.4	98.6	100.0
2004		103.4	104.7	106.3	107.5
2005		109.7	110.0	113.5	114.1
Nonmanufactured Goods	4.0				
1995		66.3	67.6	65.2	66.0
1996		71.6	72.3	76.0	84.3
1997		73.3	68.9	69.4	68.5
1998		59.3	56.8	57.2	55.7
1999		56.9	65.1	78.7	83.2
2000		92.7	102.2	107.5	118.2
2001		103.9	97.2	85.2	69.9
2002		82.9	93.8	102.4	102.7
2003		134.3	113.7	108.9	112.4
2004		122.9	133.1	138.7	147.1
2005		156.7	158.0	203.0	199.2
Manufactured Goods	41.9				
1995		100.0	102.6	102.9	102.9
1996		102.1	101.1	101.4	100.7
1997		99.5	98.9	98.8	98.6
1998		97.8	97.5	96.7	97.3
1999		97.6	97.7	98.1	98.9
2000		100.2	99.9	100.2	99.8
2001		99.9	99.2	97.6	96.0
2002		95.6	96.3	96.9	96.7
2003		97.8	97.7	98.2	99.4
2004		102.1	102.8	104.0	104.6
2005		106.3	106.6	106.7	107.7
OTHER COUNTRIES	53.7				
Total Goods					
1995		97.5	98.7	97.4	97.6
1996		99.8	99.0	101.3	102.7
1997		100.6	99.4	98.7	96.6
1998		92.4	90.7	89.5	86.8
1999		87.7	90.3	94.5	96.9
2000		99.8	100.4	102.5	99.5
2001		97.0	96.6	95.0	88.6
2002		90.9	92.2	94.3	93.4
2003		96.7	93.1	93.3	94.1
2004		96.3	97.9	101.5	99.7
2005		105.0	107.0	112.1	109.5
Nonmanufactured Goods	9.3				
1995		69.5	70.3	66.1	67.3
1996		73.7	72.1	80.9	84.5
1997		75.8	72.6	72.2	68.8
1998		57.1	54.9	54.5	46.8
1999		53.0	63.6	80.3	89.2
2000		99.9	102.4	109.2	97.4
2001		88.9	89.7	86.1	65.3
2002		81.3	88.2	99.6	96.4
2003		113.3	98.0	98.8	106.5
2004		118.1	123.2	141.5	130.3
2005		158.0	169.5	199.8	181.3
Manufactured Goods	44.2				
1995		107.3	108.8	108.6	108.4
1996		108.9	108.4	107.9	108.6
1997		108.4	107.8	107.0	105.3
1998		103.5	102.2	100.6	99.6
1999		98.8	98.9	99.0	99.3
2000		99.8	99.7	100.3	100.2
2001		99.6	98.8	97.9	96.0
2002		95.6	95.9	96.2	95.8
2003		96.5	95.1	95.1	94.5
2004		95.2	96.2	97.2	97.1
2005		98.4	98.7	99.3	99.6

[1]Percentages are based on 2004 trade values.

Table 7-14. U.S. Import Price Indexes for Selected Categories of Goods, by Locality of Origin, 1995–2005
—*Continued*

(2000 = 100.)

Category and year	Percent of U.S. imports[1]	Month			
		March	June	September	December
CANADA	17.1				
Total Goods					
1995		92.1	93.8	94.8	94.7
1996		94.3	93.5	93.8	95.1
1997		93.2	92.6	93.2	92.0
1998		90.1	89.7	89.3	88.7
1999		88.8	90.6	93.5	94.7
2000		97.2	99.8	102.4	105.6
2001		102.6	101.8	97.0	93.2
2002		96.1	97.8	99.6	99.2
2003		106.6	103.1	103.9	104.4
2004		110.0	112.3	114.4	116.6
2005		120.1	119.6	128.2	129.6
Nonmanufactured Goods	3.2				
1995		61.7	64.4	63.9	64.8
1996		70.3	70.7	74.4	84.3
1997		69.9	66.6	68.1	66.4
1998		58.4	56.6	56.5	56.3
1999		56.5	64.2	76.8	79.9
2000		89.3	103.6	107.6	124.4
2001		108.1	97.9	83.1	69.8
2002		83.8	96.8	104.1	104.9
2003		143.1	119.0	111.5	114.0
2004		126.1	138.0	138.9	150.5
2005		157.9	159.8	210.8	207.4
Manufactured Goods	13.6				
1995		98.0	99.4	100.7	100.5
1996		99.0	98.0	97.7	97.4
1997		98.0	98.0	98.3	97.3
1998		96.7	96.6	96.3	95.5
1999		95.5	96.1	96.9	97.7
2000		98.8	98.9	101.3	101.8
2001		101.6	102.8	99.9	98.1
2002		99.1	98.7	99.5	98.9
2003		100.9	101.1	103.2	103.3
2004		107.4	108.2	110.3	110.7
2005		113.7	112.9	113.1	115.6
EUROPEAN UNION	18.7				
Total Goods					
1995		97.7	99.5	99.7	100.4
1996		101.3	101.0	101.7	101.9
1997		100.5	100.0	99.1	100.1
1998		98.9	98.8	98.7	99.4
1999		98.8	99.1	99.9	100.3
2000		100.8	100.1	100.0	98.9
2001		99.0	98.8	98.2	97.4
2002		97.4	99.2	101.0	100.9
2003		103.2	102.8	102.8	104.3
2004		107.4	108.5	110.0	111.6
2005		113.8	114.1	115.7	114.5
Nonmanufactured Goods	0.4				
1995		72.8	74.5	71.2	73.0
1996		78.8	80.6	85.7	91.7
1997		89.3	82.2	76.5	78.4
1998		65.6	58.7	58.8	53.4
1999		53.6	66.6	81.3	88.7
2000		100.4	102.9	107.9	106.2
2001		96.0	99.5	89.1	75.7
2002		86.6	88.7	99.6	104.1
2003		118.8	106.7	111.5	118.8
2004		128.4	135.1	157.9	163.1
2005		177.1	177.5	209.7	191.1
Manufactured Goods	18.2				
1995		98.6	100.4	100.9	101.5
1996		102.3	101.8	102.4	102.3
1997		101.0	100.8	100.1	101.0
1998		100.4	100.6	100.5	101.5
1999		100.9	100.6	100.8	100.8
2000		100.8	99.9	99.6	98.6
2001		99.2	98.8	98.7	98.4
2002		98.1	99.9	101.5	101.4
2003		103.3	103.2	103.2	104.5
2004		107.4	108.4	109.3	110.9
2005		112.8	113.0	113.8	112.9

[1]Percentages are based on 2004 trade values.

Table 7-14. U.S. Import Price Indexes for Selected Categories of Goods, by Locality of Origin, 1995–2005
—Continued

(2000 = 100.)

Category and year	Percent of U.S. imports[1]	Month			
		March	June	September	December
LATIN AMERICA	17.4				
Total Goods					
1995		. . .	. . .	. . .	. . .
1996		. . .	. . .	. . .	. . .
1997		. . .	. . .	. . .	89.0
1998		84.3	83.9	83.0	80.4
1999		81.7	85.3	90.7	94.2
2000		98.9	100.9	103.5	99.5
2001		99.5	98.9	97.2	90.6
2002		94.0	96.2	100.0	98.9
2003		104.8	99.6	99.8	102.6
2004		106.3	108.6	114.7	113.1
2005		122.1	126.3	133.8	131.0
Nonmanufactured Goods	4.2				
1995		. . .	. . .	. . .	. . .
1996		. . .	. . .	. . .	. . .
1997		. . .	. . .	. . .	70.8
1998		60.8	59.7	59.4	51.9
1999		59.3	67.2	82.1	90.2
2000		100.2	103.5	107.8	93.6
2001		89.3	89.0	86.0	67.3
2002		83.5	90.7	103.0	99.3
2003		111.7	103.5	100.9	109.8
2004		121.1	125.9	144.6	130.1
2005		161.0	175.1	205.1	184.6
Manufactured Goods	13.2				
1995		. . .	. . .	. . .	. . .
1996		. . .	. . .	. . .	. . .
1997		. . .	. . .	. . .	97.2
1998		94.8	95.0	93.8	93.5
1999		92.0	93.6	94.6	96.0
2000		98.3	99.6	101.6	102.3
2001		104.2	103.5	102.5	101.4
2002		101.5	102.4	104.2	103.8
2003		108.2	103.6	104.4	105.8
2004		107.5	109.1	112.0	113.9
2005		117.1	118.6	120.1	122.2
JAPAN	8.9				
Total Goods					
1995		108.6	112.5	112.0	111.0
1996		110.1	108.4	107.8	106.5
1997		104.6	103.2	102.7	101.0
1998		99.8	98.2	96.8	98.0
1999		98.2	98.2	98.6	99.6
2000		99.6	100.0	99.9	99.9
2001		99.4	98.6	97.8	97.0
2002		95.6	95.4	95.0	94.6
2003		94.4	94.2	93.8	94.7
2004		95.2	95.1	95.3	95.9
2005		95.9	95.8	95.8	95.2
ASIAN NEWLY INDUSTRALIZED COUNTRIES[2]	7.2				
Total Goods					
1995		120.9	121.3	121.5	120.8
1996		120.6	119.6	118.1	117.3
1997		116.6	115.3	113.8	111.3
1998		108.7	105.2	103.0	102.0
1999		101.3	100.8	100.7	100.8
2000		100.6	99.9	100.0	99.3
2001		97.3	96.4	95.2	93.8
2002		93.3	92.6	92.5	91.3
2003		91.2	91.5	91.7	90.9
2004					
2005		90.9	90.0	89.7	88.5

[1]Percentages are based on 2004 trade values.
[2]The Asian Newly Industrialized Countries are Hong Kong, Korea, Singapore, and Taiwan.
. . . = Not available.

Table 7-15. U.S. International Price Indexes for Selected Transportation Services, 1995–2005

(2000 = 100.)

Category and year	March	June	September	December
AIR FREIGHT				
Import Air Freight				
1995	115.8	118.7	112.9	115.1
1996	113.7	112.2	112.0	110.6
1997	104.1	104.5	102.5	100.1
1998	93.0	94.2	92.8	100.2
1999	101.5	98.7	100.6	102.8
2000	100.7	100.1	100.2	99.0
2001	98.9	96.0	95.9	95.6
2002	96.7	99.7	101.2	106.9
2003	110.2	111.5	116.8	114.9
2004	117.1	117.5	120.0	126.8
2005	128.6	128.4	129.7	128.9
Export Air Freight				
1995	. . .	. . .	. . .	. . .
1996	. . .	. . .	. . .	112.9
1997	111.1	110.4	109.0	105.4
1998	107.1	106.6	108.0	109.2
1999	102.1	102.5	100.8	99.1
2000	99.1	100.8	100.8	99.4
2001	99.7	98.4	98.6	97.9
2002	95.5	97.9	98.3	95.2
2003	96.3	95.2	95.1	95.4
2004	97.1	99.1	100.3	106.1
2005	106.4	110.1	110.9	112.0
Inbound Air Freight				
1995	113.6	116.5	111.0	111.7
1996	108.6	107.7	108.2	107.6
1997	101.3	101.8	100.3	97.9
1998	93.9	94.4	92.7	99.0
1999	99.6	97.6	99.5	102.8
2000	100.7	100.1	100.2	99.0
2001	97.9	95.1	94.9	95.1
2002	93.9	98.3	100.3	105.9
2003	108.8	109.4	112.5	112.9
2004	116.2	116.6	118.7	125.1
2005	126.3	125.6	127.5	124.6
Outbound Air Freight				
1995	108.2	108.1	108.6	107.8
1996	107.3	107.6	107.0	107.3
1997	108.0	107.3	107.7	105.7
1998	105.2	103.8	103.7	103.0
1999	100.3	100.4	100.3	99.2
2000	99.2	100.3	100.2	100.2
2001	100.1	98.0	97.6	97.8
2002	95.9	98.4	97.3	95.4
2003	97.2	95.4	95.5	94.9
2004	96.1	99.0	100.7	104.7
2005	103.8	107.2	112.4	112.0
AIR PASSENGER FARES				
Import Air Passenger Fares				
1995	80.2	88.1	86.4	82.6
1996	82.0	88.1	86.8	84.3
1997	84.7	95.5	94.0	88.0
1998	87.1	94.9	95.1	88.6
1999	87.5	98.9	99.5	89.7
2000	92.5	103.5	105.1	98.9
2001	101.1	112.8	116.4	105.7
2002	103.1	119.1	125.2	107.2
2003	108.6	122.3	125.9	107.0
2004	103.6	123.1	121.0	111.7
2005	110.0	128.1	124.0	116.3

. . . = Not available.

Table 7-15. U.S. International Price Indexes for Selected Transportation Services, 1995–2005—*Continued*

(2000 = 100.)

Category and year	March	June	September	December
Export Air Passenger Fares				
1995	92.4	99.4	96.4	91.6
1996	93.0	94.4	97.7	94.7
1997	85.3	97.7	95.0	87.4
1998	89.5	90.2	90.6	93.1
1999	95.5	96.8	100.6	98.6
2000	98.1	101.5	102.6	97.7
2001	99.6	100.4	102.5	98.4
2002	97.5	103.2	108.1	103.2
2003	108.4	117.0	118.0	118.4
2004	123.2	123.8	130.1	134.0
2005	136.3	136.2	139.5	128.3
CRUDE OIL TANKER FREIGHT				
Inbound Crude Oil Tanker Freight				
1995	71.2	73.7	70.8	81.4
1996	78.8	77.3	68.8	74.4
1997	79.7	80.3	72.7	76.7
1998	76.9	64.9	61.5	61.4
1999	55.4	53.0	53.0	57.7
2000	73.2	86.3	107.5	133.0
2001	119.3	96.7	74.3	72.4
2002	60.2	59.9	58.5	77.2
2003	133.2	101.9	73.7	90.2
2004	133.4	104.3	119.1	186.9
2005	130.7	116.8	99.8	154.8
OCEAN LINER FREIGHT				
Inbound Ocean Liner Freight				
1995	68.7	71.1	71.9	71.6
1996	71.9	70.5	69.4	69.7
1997	69.1	68.5	67.2	65.8
1998	65.9	73.1	74.4	73.8
1999	72.7	94.7	104.8	98.7
2000	96.6	101.3	101.1	101.0
2001	102.8	100.8	98.1	92.8
2002	91.7	90.3	93.5	93.3
2003	94.0	116.1	116.2	117.8
2004	119.1	121.1	120.3	122.7
2005	121.3	128.5	127.9	126.8

CHAPTER EIGHT

CONSUMER EXPENDITURES

CONSUMER EXPENDITURES

HIGHLIGHTS

The principal objective of the Consumer Expenditure Survey is to collect information about the buying habits of American households. This survey breaks down expenditures for different demographic categories, such as income, age, family size, and geographic location. These data are used in a variety of government, business, and academic research projects and provide important weights for the periodic revisions of the Consumer Price Index.

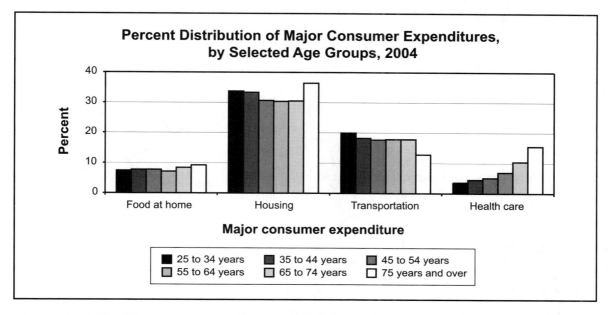

The most notable differences in expenditure spending among different age groups can be found when comparing the 75 years old and over age group to younger age groups. As expected, the 75 years old and over age group expended a much higher percentage on health care in 2004, spending twice the share of the 55- to 64-year-old age group and more than three times the share of the 45-to 54-year-old age group. (See Table 8-10.)

OTHER HIGHLIGHTS

- Much of the difference in expenditure shares can be associated with income and with changing needs. For instance, the spending shares of the 65 years old and over age group in 2004 reflected the fact that the income of that group was about one-third less than the income of the 55- to 64-year-old age group. (See Table 8-10.)

- While the proportion of all households without a mortgage was 25 percent in 2004, this number rose to 62 percent for the 65 years old and over age group. (See Tables 8-2 and 8-10.)

- From 2003 to 2004, the proportion of all households with incomes over $100,000 increased from 11.8 percent to 12.8 percent, and the share of aggregate expenditures of these households rose from 25.9 percent to 27.9 percent. In 2004, 4.4 percent of all households had incomes of $150,000 or more and accounted for 11.9 percent of total spending. (See Table 8-4.)

- Single women spent 8.1 percent of their income on health care and single men spent 5.1 percent of their income on health care in 2004. Typically, single women were older and had lower incomes than single men. However, single men spent more on transportation and entertainment than single women. Even in the same income bracket ($30,000–$39,999), single men spent a greater percentage of their total income on transportation (20.2 percent) than single women (16.4 percent). (See Tables 8-21 and 8-22.)

NOTES AND DEFINITIONS

Purpose, Collection, and Coverage

The buying habits of American consumers change over time because of changes in relative prices, real income, family size and composition, and other determinants of tastes and preferences. The introduction of new products into the marketplace and the emergence of new concepts in retailing also have influence on consumer buying habits. Data from the Consumer Expenditure Survey (CE), the only national survey that relates family expenditures to demographic characteristics, are of great importance to researchers. The survey data are also used to revise the Consumer Price Index market baskets and item samples.

Until the 1970s, the Bureau of Labor Statistics (BLS) conducted surveys of consumer expenditures roughly once every 10 years. The last such survey was conducted in 1972–1973. In late 1979, in a significant departure from previous methodology, BLS initiated a survey to be conducted on a continuous basis with rotating panels of respondents.

The current CE is similar to its 1972–1973 predecessor in that it consists of two separate components. Each component has its own questionnaire and sample: (1) the Interview Survey, in which an interviewer visits each consumer unit every three months for a 12-month period; and (2) the Diary Survey, a record-keeping survey completed by other consumer units for two consecutive one-week periods. The Census Bureau, under contract to BLS, collects the data for both components of the survey. Beginning in 1999, the sample was increased from 5,000 to 7,500 households.

In 2003, the survey modified the questions on race and Hispanic origin to comply with the new standards for maintaining, collecting, and presenting federal data on race and ethnicity for federal statistical agencies. Beginning with the 2003 data, the CE tables have used data collected from the new race and ethnicity questions. A number of new classifications were made with publication of the 2003 data.

Beginning with the publication of the 2004 tables, the CE has been implementing multiple imputations of income data. Prior to 2004, the CE only published income data collected from complete income reporters. The introduction of multiply imputed income data affects the CE published tables in several ways, because income data are now published for all consumer units (instead of complete reporters only). The most obvious result of this change is seen on the tables showing expenditures categorized by income before taxes, including income by quintile. Starting in 2004, columns describing income, expenditures, and characteristics for "Total complete reporting" and "Incomplete reporting of income" no longer appear in these tables, and the column entitled, "All consumer units" appears on the income tables. Due to the implementation of income imputation, data for 2004 are not strictly comparable to those of prior years, especially for the income tables. Averages for demographic characteristics and annual expenditures will change, due to differences between the incomplete and complete income reporters in these categories. Furthermore, certain expenditures (such as personal insurance and pensions) are computed using income data. As a result of imputation, average annual values for these expenditures may be substantially different in the 2004 CE tables than in tables for previous years. The regular flow of data resulting from this design substantially enhances the usefulness of the survey by providing more timely information on consumption patterns within different kinds of consumer units.

The *Interview Survey* is designed to collect data on the types of expenditures that respondents can be expected to recall after a period of three months or longer. These include relatively large expenditures (such as those for property, travel, automobiles, and major appliances) and expenditures that occur on a regular basis (such as those for rent, utilities, insurance premiums, and clothing). The interview also obtains "global estimates" of food expenditures for both food at home and food away from home. For food-at-home expenditures, respondents are asked to estimate their typical weekly spending at the grocery store and to determine how much was spent on nonfood items. Nonfood items are then subtracted from the total. Convenience and specialty stores are also included in the food-at-home estimates. The survey also collects data for approximately 95 percent of total expenditures. Excluded from the Interview Survey are nonprescription drugs, household supplies, and personal care products.

The *Diary Survey* is designed to collect data on expenditures for frequently purchased items that are more difficult to recall over longer periods of time. Respondents keep detailed records of expenses for food and beverages at home and meals in eating places away from home. Expenditures for tobacco, drugs (including nonprescription drugs), and personal care supplies and services are also collected in the Diary Survey.

Participants in both surveys record dollar amounts for goods and services purchased during the reporting period, regardless of whether payment was made at the time of purchase. Excluded from both surveys are business-related expenditures and expenditures for which the family is reimbursed. Information is collected on demographic and family characteristics at the initial interview for each survey.

The tables in this chapter present integrated data from the Diary and Interview Surveys and provide a complete accounting of consumer expenditures and income, which neither survey component is designed to do alone. Data for some expenditure items are only collected in either the

Diary Survey or Interview Survey. For example, the Diary Survey does not collect data for expenditures on overnight travel or information on reimbursements, while the Interview Survey records these purchases. Examples of expenditures for which reimbursements are netted out include those for medical care, auto repair, and construction, repairs, alterations, and maintenance of property.

For items unique to one survey or the other, the choice of which survey to use as the source of data is obvious. However, there is considerable overlap in coverage between the two surveys. Integrating the data thus presents the problem of determining the appropriate survey component. When data are available from both survey sources, the more reliable of the two (as determined by statistical methods) is selected. As a result, some items are selected from the Interview Survey and others are selected from the Diary Survey.

Research is underway to evaluate survey methodology; this research is described in *Consumer Expenditure Survey Anthology, 2005*, which can be found on the BLS Web site at <http://www.bls.gov>.

Data Included in This Book

Data for single characteristics are for calendar year 2004, and data for two cross-classified characteristics are for an average of calendar years 2003–2004. Income values from the survey are derived from "complete income reporters" only. Complete income reporters are defined as consumer units that provide values for at least one of the major sources of their income: wages and salaries, self-employment income, retirement income, dividends and interest, and welfare benefits. Some consumer units are defined as complete income reporters, even though they may not have provided a full accounting of all income from all sources.

Consumer units are classified by quintiles of income before taxes, age of reference person, size of consumer unit, region, composition of consumer unit, number of earners in consumer unit, housing tenure, race, type of area (urban or rural), and occupation.

Concepts and Definitions

A *consumer unit* comprises either (1) all members of a particular household related by blood, marriage, adoption, or other legal arrangements; (2) a person living alone, sharing a household with others, living as a roomer in a private home or lodging house or in permanent living quarters in a hotel or motel, but who is financially independent; or (3) two or more persons living together who pool their income to make joint expenditure decisions. Financial independence is determined by the three major expense categories: housing, food, and other living expenses. To be considered financially independent, at least two of the three major expense categories have to be provided by the respondent. The terms "family," "household," and "consumer unit" are used interchangeably in descriptions of the CE.

The *householder* or *reference person* is the first member of the consumer unit mentioned by the respondent as owner or renter of the premises at the time of the initial interview.

Total expenditures include the transaction costs, including excise and sales taxes of goods and services acquired during the interview period. Estimates include expenditures for gifts and contributions and payments for pensions and personal insurance.

An *earner* is a consumer unit member, 14 years of age or older, who reported having worked at least 1 week during the 12 months prior to the interview date.

Sources of Additional Information

More extensive descriptions and tables are contained in BLS Report 992, "Consumer Expenditures in 2004"; in an updated version of Chapter 16 in the *BLS Handbook of Methods*; and in an anthology of articles relating to consumer expenditures. All of these resources can be found on the BLS Web site at <http://www.bls.gov>.

Table 8-1. Consumer Expenditures, Annual Average of All Consumer Units, 1994–2004

(Number, dollar, percent.)

Item	1994	1995	1996	1997	1998	1999	2000	2001	2002	2003	2004
NUMBER OF CONSUMER UNITS (THOUSANDS)	102 210	103 123	104 212	105 576	107 182	108 465	109 367	110 339	112 108	115 356	116 282
CONSUMER UNIT CHARACTERISTICS											
Income Before Taxes	36 181	36 918	38 014	39 926	41 622	43 951	44 649	47 507	49 430	51 128	54 453
Age of Reference Person	47.6	48.0	47.7	47.7	47.6	47.9	48.2	48.1	48.1	48.0	48.5
Average Number in Consumer Unit											
Persons	2.5	2.5	2.5	2.5	2.5	2.5	2.5	2.5	2.5	2.5	2.5
Children under 18 years	0.7	0.7	0.7	0.7	0.7	0.7	0.7	0.7	0.7	0.6	0.6
Persons 65 years and over	0.3	0.3	0.3	0.3	0.3	0.3	0.3	0.3	0.3	0.3	0.3
Earners	1.3	1.3	1.3	1.3	1.3	1.3	1.4	1.4	1.4	1.3	1.3
Vehicles	1.9	1.9	1.9	2.0	2.0	1.9	1.9	1.9	2.0	1.9	1.9
Percent Homeowner	63	64	64	64	64	65	66	66	66	67	68
With mortgage	37	38	38	38	39	38	39	40	41	41	42
Without mortgage	26	26	26	26	26	27	27	26	26	26	25
AVERAGE ANNUAL EXPENDITURES	31 731	32 264	33 797	34 819	35 535	36 995	38 045	39 518	40 677	40 817	43 395
Food	4 411	4 505	4 698	4 801	4 810	5 031	5 158	5 321	5 375	5 340	5 781
Food at home	2 712	2 803	2 876	2 880	2 780	2 915	3 021	3 086	3 099	3 129	3 347
Cereals and bakery products	429	441	447	453	425	448	453	452	450	442	461
Meats, poultry, fish, and eggs	429	441	447	453	425	448	453	452	798	825	880
Dairy products	289	297	312	314	301	322	325	332	328	328	371
Fruits and vegetables	437	457	490	476	472	500	521	522	552	535	561
Other food at home	825	856	889	895	858	896	927	952	970	999	1 075
Food away from home	1 698	1 702	1 823	1 921	2 030	2 116	2 137	2 235	2 276	2 211	2 434
Alcoholic Beverages	278	277	309	309	309	318	372	349	376	391	459
Housing	10 106	10 458	10 747	11 272	11 713	12 057	12 319	13 011	13 283	13 432	13 918
Shelter	5 686	5 928	6 064	6 344	6 680	7 016	7 114	7 602	7 829	7 887	7 998
Owned dwellings	3 492	3 749	3 783	3 935	4 245	4 525	4 602	4 979	5 165	5 263	5 324
Rented dwellings	1 799	1 788	1 864	1 983	1 978	2 027	2 034	2 134	2 160	2 179	2 201
Other lodging	395	391	417	426	458	465	478	489	505	445	473
Utilities, fuels, and public services	2 189	2 191	2 347	2 412	2 405	2 377	2 489	2 767	2 684	2 811	2 927
Household operations	490	509	522	548	546	666	684	676	706	707	753
Housekeeping supplies	393	430	464	455	482	498	482	509	545	529	594
Household furnishings and equipment	1 348	1 401	1 350	1 512	1 601	1 499	1 549	1 458	1 518	1 497	1 646
Apparel and Services	1 644	1 704	1 752	1 729	1 674	1 743	1 856	1 743	1 749	1 640	1 816
Transportation	6 044	6 014	6 382	6 457	6 616	7 011	7 417	7 633	7 759	7 781	7 801
Vehicle purchases (net outlay)	2 725	2 638	2 815	2 736	2 964	3 305	3 418	3 579	3 665	3 732	3 397
Gasoline and motor oil	986	1 006	1 082	1 098	1 017	1 055	1 291	1 279	1 235	1 333	1 598
Other vehicle expenses	1 953	2 015	2 058	2 230	2 206	2 254	2 281	2 375	2 471	2 331	2 365
Public transportation	381	355	427	393	429	397	427	400	389	385	441
Health Care	1 755	1 732	1 770	1 841	1 903	1 959	2 066	2 182	2 350	2 416	2 574
Health insurance	815	860	827	881	913	923	983	1 061	1 168	1 252	1 332
Medical services	571	512	543	531	542	558	568	573	590	591	648
Drugs	286	280	303	320	346	370	416	449	487	467	480
Medical supplies	83	80	97	108	102	109	99	100	105	107	114
Entertainment	1 567	1 612	1 834	1 813	1 746	1 891	1 863	1 953	2 079	2 060	2 218
Personal Care Products and Services	397	403	513	528	401	408	564	465	526	527	581
Reading	165	162	159	164	161	159	146	141	139	127	130
Education	460	471	524	571	580	635	632	648	752	783	905
Tobacco Products and Smoking Supplies	259	269	255	264	273	300	319	308	320	290	288
Miscellaneous	749	766	855	847	860	867	776	750	792	606	690
Cash Contributions	960	925	940	1 001	1 109	1 181	1 192	1 258	1 277	1 370	1 408
Personal Insurance and Pensions	2 938	2 964	3 060	3 223	3 381	3 436	3 365	3 737	3 899	4 055	4 823
Life and other personal insurance	398	373	353	379	398	394	399	410	406	397	390
Pensions and Social Security	2 540	2 591	2 707	2 844	2 982	3 042	2 966	3 326	3 493	3 658	4 433

Table 8-2. Shares of Annual Average Consumer Expenditures and Characteristics of All Consumer Units, 1994–2004

(Number, dollar, percent.)

Item	1994	1995	1996	1997	1998	1999	2000	2001	2002	2003	2004
NUMBER OF CONSUMER UNITS (THOUSANDS)	102 210	103 123	104 212	105 576	107 182	108 465	109 367	110 339	112 108	115 356	116 282
CONSUMER UNIT CHARACTERISTICS											
Income Before Taxes	36 181	36 918	38 014	39 926	41 622	43 951	44 649	47 507	49 430	51 128	54 453
Age of Reference Person	47.6	48.0	47.7	47.7	47.6	47.9	48.2	48.1	48.1	48.4	48.5
Average Number in Consumer Unit											
Persons	2.5	2.5	2.5	2.5	2.5	2.5	2.5	2.5	2.5	2.5	2.5
Children under 18 years	0.7	0.7	0.7	0.7	0.7	0.7	0.7	0.7	0.7	0.6	0.6
Persons 65 years and over	0.3	0.3	0.3	0.3	0.3	0.3	0.3	0.3	0.3	0.3	0.3
Earners	1.3	1.3	1.3	1.3	1.3	1.3	1.4	1.4	1.4	1.3	1.3
Vehicles	1.9	1.9	1.9	2.0	2.0	1.9	1.9	1.9	2.0	1.9	1.9
Percent Homeowner	63	64	64	64	64	65	66	66	66	67	68
With mortgage	37	38	38	38	39	38	39	40	41	41	42
Without mortgage	26	26	26	26	26	27	27	26	26	26	25
AVERAGE ANNUAL EXPENDITURES	31 731	32 264	33 797	34 819	35 535	36 995	38 045	39 518	40 677	40 817	43 395
Food	13.9	14.0	13.9	13.8	13.5	13.6	13.6	13.5	13.2	13.1	13.3
Food at home	8.5	8.7	8.5	8.3	7.8	7.9	7.9	7.8	7.6	7.7	7.7
Cereals and bakery products	1.4	1.4	1.3	1.3	1.2	1.2	1.2	1.1	1.1	1.1	1.1
Meats, poultry, fish, and eggs	2.3	2.3	2.2	2.1	2.0	2.0	2.1	2.1	2.0	2.0	2.0
Dairy products	0.9	0.9	0.9	0.9	0.8	0.9	0.9	0.8	0.8	0.8	0.9
Fruits and vegetables	1.4	1.4	1.4	1.4	1.3	1.4	1.4	1.3	1.4	1.3	1.3
Other food at home	2.6	2.7	2.6	2.6	2.4	2.4	2.4	2.4	2.4	2.4	2.5
Food away from home	5.4	5.3	5.4	5.5	5.7	5.7	5.6	5.7	5.6	5.4	5.6
Alcoholic Beverages	0.9	0.9	0.9	0.9	0.9	0.9	1.0	0.9	0.9	1.0	1.1
Housing	31.8	32.4	31.8	32.4	33.0	32.6	32.4	32.9	32.7	32.9	32.1
Shelter	17.9	18.4	17.9	18.2	18.8	19.0	18.7	19.2	19.2	19.3	18.4
Owned dwellings	11.0	11.6	11.2	11.3	11.9	12.2	12.1	12.6	12.7	12.9	12.3
Rented dwellings	5.7	5.5	5.5	5.7	5.6	5.5	5.3	5.4	5.3	5.3	5.1
Other lodging	1.2	1.2	1.2	1.2	1.3	1.3	1.3	1.2	1.2	1.1	1.1
Utilities, fuels, and public services	6.9	6.8	6.9	6.9	6.8	6.4	6.5	7.0	6.6	6.9	6.7
Household operations	1.5	1.6	1.5	1.6	1.5	1.8	1.8	1.7	1.7	1.7	1.7
Housekeeping supplies	1.2	1.3	1.4	1.3	1.4	1.3	1.3	1.3	1.3	1.3	1.4
Household furnishings and equipment	4.2	4.3	4.0	4.3	4.5	4.1	4.1	3.7	3.7	3.7	3.8
Apparel and Services	5.2	5.3	5.2	5.0	4.7	4.7	4.9	4.4	4.3	4.0	4.2
Transportation	19.0	18.6	18.9	18.5	18.6	19.0	19.5	19.3	19.1	19.1	18.0
Vehicle purchases (net outlay)	8.6	8.2	8.3	7.9	8.3	8.9	9.0	9.1	9.0	9.1	7.8
Gasoline and motor oil	3.1	3.1	3.2	3.2	2.9	2.9	3.4	3.2	3.0	3.3	3.7
Other vehicle expenses	6.2	6.2	6.1	6.4	6.2	6.1	6.0	6.0	6.1	5.7	5.5
Public transportation	1.2	1.1	1.3	1.1	1.2	1.1	1.1	1.0	1.0	0.9	1.0
Health Care	5.5	5.4	5.2	5.3	5.4	5.3	5.4	5.5	5.8	5.9	5.9
Health insurance	2.6	2.7	2.4	2.5	2.6	2.5	2.6	2.7	2.9	3.1	3.1
Medical services	1.8	1.6	1.6	1.5	1.5	1.5	1.5	1.4	1.5	1.4	1.5
Drugs	0.9	0.9	0.9	0.9	1.0	1.0	1.1	1.1	1.2	1.1	1.1
Medical supplies	0.3	0.2	0.3	0.3	0.3	0.3	0.3	0.3	0.3	0.3	0.3
Entertainment	4.9	5.0	5.4	5.2	4.9	5.1	4.9	4.9	5.1	5.0	5.1
Personal Care Products and Services	1.3	1.2	1.5	1.5	1.1	1.1	1.5	1.2	1.3	1.3	1.3
Reading	0.5	0.5	0.5	0.5	0.5	0.4	0.4	0.4	0.3	0.3	0.3
Education	1.4	1.5	1.6	1.6	1.6	1.7	1.7	1.6	1.8	1.9	2.1
Tobacco Products and Smoking Supplies	0.8	0.8	0.8	0.8	0.8	0.8	0.8	0.8	0.8	0.7	0.7
Miscellaneous	2.4	2.4	2.5	2.4	2.4	2.3	2.0	1.9	1.9	1.5	1.6
Cash Contributions	3.0	2.9	2.8	2.9	3.1	3.2	3.1	3.2	3.1	3.4	3.2
Personal Insurance and Pensions	9.3	9.2	9.1	9.3	9.5	9.3	8.8	9.5	9.6	9.9	11.1
Life and other personal insurance	1.3	1.2	1.0	1.1	1.1	1.1	1.0	1.0	1.0	1.0	0.9
Pensions and Social Security	8.0	8.0	8.0	8.2	8.4	8.2	7.8	8.4	8.6	9.0	10.2

Table 8-3. Consumer Expenditures, Averages by Income Before Taxes, 2004

(Number, dollar, percent.)

Item	All consumer units	Less than $5,000	$5,000 to $9,999	$10,000 to $14,999	$15,000 to $19,999	$20,000 to $29,999	$30,000 to $39,999	$40,000 to $49,999	$50,000 to $69,999	$70,000 and over
NUMBER OF CONSUMER UNITS (THOUSANDS)	116 282	4 553	7 218	8 950	8 177	14 172	13 125	11 374	18 069	30 644
CONSUMER UNIT CHARACTERISTICS										
Income Before Taxes	54 453	1 097	7 812	12 499	17 417	24 767	34 739	44 645	59 259	118 482
Income After Taxes	52 287	1 177	7 800	12 619	17 480	24 298	34 199	43 689	57 122	112 266
Age of Reference Person	48.5	38.9	51.6	56.2	53.9	50.5	47.5	47.3	45.8	47.0
Average Number in Consumer Unit										
Persons	2.5	1.6	1.6	1.8	2.0	2.2	2.4	2.6	2.8	3.1
Children under 18 years	0.6	0.3	0.3	0.4	0.5	0.5	0.6	0.7	0.7	0.8
Persons 65 years and over	0.3	0.2	0.4	0.5	0.5	0.4	0.3	0.3	0.2	0.2
Earners	1.3	0.6	0.4	0.5	0.7	1.0	1.3	1.4	1.7	2.0
Vehicles	1.9	0.8	0.8	1.1	1.3	1.5	1.8	2.1	2.4	2.8
Percent Distribution										
Male	48	39	34	32	43	44	49	50	54	56
Female	52	61	66	68	57	56	51	50	46	44
Percent Homeowner	68	26	36	51	54	57	63	70	78	90
With mortgage	42	10	9	14	16	23	36	45	57	72
Without mortgage	25	15	27	37	38	35	27	25	20	18
AVERAGE ANNUAL EXPENDITURES	43 395	17 029	14 596	19 444	23 023	27 741	33 273	38 204	47 750	76 954
Food	5 781	3 173	2 409	2 981	3 567	4 076	4 986	5 452	6 312	9 042
Food at home	3 347	2 030	1 695	2 105	2 435	2 591	3 056	3 263	3 640	4 734
Cereals and bakery products	461	300	259	294	351	359	430	456	506	628
Meats, poultry, fish, and eggs	880	558	476	562	640	698	827	900	936	1 209
Dairy products	371	229	177	230	268	289	349	361	403	521
Fruits and vegetables	561	346	272	385	419	425	519	549	592	794
Other food at home	1 075	597	512	633	757	819	930	997	1 202	1 582
Food away from home	2 434	1 143	714	876	1 132	1 485	1 930	2 189	2 672	4 308
Alcoholic Beverages	459	219	156	207	193	262	323	449	484	824
Housing	13 918	6 300	5 645	7 513	8 370	9 639	11 143	12 383	14 699	23 547
Shelter	7 998	3 952	3 379	4 245	4 783	5 538	6 371	7 074	8 421	13 571
Owned dwellings	5 324	1 354	971	1 577	2 052	2 479	3 406	4 363	5 917	11 053
Rented dwellings	2 201	2 409	2 272	2 550	2 599	2 893	2 753	2 457	2 085	1 362
Other lodging	473	189	136	118	132	166	212	255	419	1 156
Utilities, fuels, and public services	2 927	1 340	1 506	1 988	2 148	2 425	2 645	2 935	3 270	4 125
Household operations	753	180	151	420	318	452	453	487	690	1 597
Housekeeping supplies	594	325	223	316	398	381	513	542	645	948
Household furnishings and equipment	1 646	505	386	544	724	843	1 161	1 345	1 672	3 306
Apparel and Services	1 816	915	722	809	915	1 047	1 384	1 490	1 774	3 349
Transportation	7 801	2 270	2 052	3 000	3 758	5 114	6 288	7 031	9 700	13 513
Vehicle purchases (net outlay)	3 397	712	700	1 209	1 328	2 186	2 671	2 867	4 539	6 017
Gasoline and motor oil	1 598	690	620	782	964	1 190	1 432	1 621	1 953	2 411
Other vehicle expenses	2 365	690	648	872	1 301	1 525	1 942	2 259	2 795	4 092
Public transportation	441	178	86	137	165	212	243	283	413	992
Health Care	2 574	886	1 171	1 806	2 010	2 157	2 383	2 552	2 874	3 630
Health insurance	1 332	383	651	953	1 081	1 147	1 223	1 440	1 521	1 791
Medical services	648	254	181	328	379	466	558	519	728	1 107
Drugs	480	211	288	466	471	476	495	484	488	557
Medical supplies	114	39	52	59	79	68	107	110	138	175
Entertainment	2 218	853	582	852	901	1 512	1 525	1 756	2 587	4 119
Personal Care Products and Services	581	279	207	282	333	410	451	550	600	985
Reading	130	48	52	59	76	83	95	118	137	234
Education	905	1 023	637	494	383	316	316	417	706	2 031
Tobacco Products and Smoking Supplies	288	178	189	239	274	291	320	329	339	285
Miscellaneous	690	347	278	255	463	502	522	735	748	1 128
Cash Contributions	1 408	276	213	414	828	738	844	1 284	1 360	2 929
Personal Insurance and Pensions	4 823	261	282	533	951	1 594	2 692	3 656	5 430	11 338
Life and other personal insurance	390	89	78	141	156	183	270	316	417	804
Pensions and Social Security	4 433	172	205	392	795	1 411	2 422	3 340	5 013	10 535

Table 8-4. Consumer Expenditures, Averages by Higher Income Before Taxes, 2004

(Number, dollar, percent.)

Item	All consumer units	Less than $70,000	$70,000 to $79,000	$80,000 to $99,999	$100,000 and over	$100,000 to $119,000	$120,000 to $149,999	$150,000 and over
NUMBER OF CONSUMER UNITS (THOUSANDS)	116 282	85 638	6 461	9 246	14 937	5 625	4 245	5 067
CONSUMER UNIT CHARACTERISTICS								
Income Before Taxes	54 453	31 541	74 437	88 811	155 901	108 751	132 292	228 021
Income After Taxes	52 287	30 825	72 236	84 884	146 530	103 801	124 273	212 610
Age of Reference Person	48.5	49.0	45.8	46.6	47.7	47.2	47.6	48.4
Average Number in Consumer Unit								
Persons	2.5	2.3	3.0	3.1	3.2	3.1	3.3	3.2
Children under 18 years	0.6	0.6	0.8	0.9	0.8	0.8	0.9	0.8
Persons 65 years and over	0.3	0.3	0.2	0.2	0.2	0.2	0.1	0.2
Earners	1.3	1.1	1.8	2.0	2.1	2.1	2.2	2.1
Vehicles	1.9	1.6	2.6	2.7	2.9	2.8	2.9	2.9
Percent Distribution								
Male	48	45	55	56	57	57	60	54
Female	52	55	45	44	43	43	40	46
Percent Homeowner	68	60	85	90	93	90	93	95
With mortgage	42	32	66	73	74	72	76	74
Without mortgage	25	28	19	16	19	18	17	21
AVERAGE ANNUAL EXPENDITURES	43 395	31 280	55 012	65 446	93 526	75 213	87 299	119 449
Food	5 781	4 562	7 337	7 467	10 733	9 444	10 419	12 555
Food at home	3 347	2 825	4 079	4 043	5 435	5 014	5 542	5 840
Cereals and bakery products	461	398	522	545	724	672	741	772
Meats, poultry, fish, and eggs	880	756	1 097	1 033	1 363	1 271	1 396	1 442
Dairy products	371	314	426	451	604	560	620	641
Fruits and vegetables	561	473	645	659	941	860	932	1 049
Other food at home	1 075	884	1 389	1 355	1 803	1 651	1 853	1 935
Food away from home	2 434	1 737	3 259	3 424	5 299	4 429	4 877	6 715
Alcoholic Beverages	459	323	617	702	987	724	887	1 405
Housing	13 918	10 456	17 422	20 397	28 140	22 273	26 339	36 246
Shelter	7 998	6 004	10 213	11 761	16 143	12 871	14 869	20 843
Owned dwellings	5 324	3 275	8 051	9 604	13 249	10 421	12 527	16 992
Rented dwellings	2 201	2 501	1 638	1 325	1 266	1 496	1 019	1 219
Other lodging	473	229	524	833	1 628	954	1 323	2 633
Utilities, fuels, and public services	2 927	2 498	3 552	3 903	4 511	3 977	4 446	5 159
Household operations	753	451	895	1 332	2 064	1 407	1 799	3 016
Housekeeping supplies	594	461	677	862	1 118	893	1 051	1 461
Household furnishings and equipment	1 646	1 042	2 085	2 539	4 304	3 125	4 174	5 767
Apparel and Services	1 816	1 248	2 219	2 666	4 253	3 644	3 675	5 502
Transportation	7 801	5 756	9 965	12 446	15 707	13 520	15 515	18 308
Vehicle purchases (net outlay)	3 397	2 459	4 218	5 516	7 106	6 013	7 028	8 384
Gasoline and motor oil	1 598	1 307	2 131	2 366	2 559	2 452	2 686	2 573
Other vehicle expenses	2 365	1 747	3 184	3 812	4 659	4 162	4 582	5 278
Public transportation	441	244	432	752	1 383	894	1 219	2 073
Health Care	2 574	2 195	3 029	3 384	4 042	3 732	3 812	4 581
Health insurance	1 332	1 167	1 532	1 766	1 918	1 778	1 799	2 173
Medical services	648	484	867	945	1 311	1 163	1 221	1 551
Drugs	480	452	511	528	596	569	594	629
Medical supplies	114	92	119	145	217	222	197	228
Entertainment	2 218	1 534	2 870	3 677	4 932	3 613	4 716	6 570
Personal Care Products and Services	581	433	658	852	1 207	1 030	1 191	1 427
Reading	130	93	159	197	290	227	298	353
Education	905	502	940	1 540	2 806	1 865	2 166	4 382
Tobacco Products and Smoking Supplies	288	289	337	303	252	279	290	189
Miscellaneous	690	532	809	894	1 411	1 132	1 140	1 968
Cash Contributions	1 408	864	1 551	2 052	4 067	2 445	2 672	7 037
Personal Insurance and Pensions	4 823	2 492	7 099	8 871	14 699	11 284	14 178	18 927
Life and other personal insurance	390	242	430	645	1 063	785	904	1 505
Pensions and Social Security	4 433	2 249	6 670	8 225	13 636	10 498	13 274	17 422

Table 8-5. Consumer Expenditures, Averages by Quintiles of Income Before Taxes, 2004

(Number, dollar, percent.)

Item	All consumer units	Lowest 20 percent	Second 20 percent	Third 20 percent	Fourth 20 percent	Highest 20 percent
NUMBER OF CONSUMER UNITS (THOUSANDS)	116 282	23 223	23 266	23 252	23 263	23 277
CONSUMER UNIT CHARACTERISTICS						
Income Before Taxes	54 453	9 168	24 102	41 614	65 100	132 158
Income After Taxes	52 287	9 220	23 751	40 802	62 847	124 698
Age of Reference Person	48.5	51.1	50.9	47.2	45.7	47.4
Average Number in Consumer Unit						
Persons	2.5	1.7	2.2	2.6	2.9	3.2
Children under 18 years	0.6	0.4	0.5	0.7	0.8	0.8
Persons 65 years and over	0.3	0.4	0.4	0.3	0.2	0.2
Earners	1.3	0.5	0.9	1.4	1.7	2.1
Vehicles	1.9	0.9	1.5	2.0	2.4	2.8
Percent Distribution						
Male	48	35	45	50	55	56
Female	52	65	55	50	45	44
Percent Homeowner	68	41	57	68	80	91
With mortgage	42	12	23	42	61	73
Without mortgage	25	30	35	25	20	18
AVERAGE ANNUAL EXPENDITURES	43 395	17 837	27 410	36 980	50 974	83 710
Food	5 781	2 967	4 139	5 378	6 762	9 653
Food at home	3 347	2 044	2 659	3 209	3 836	4 984
Cereals and bakery products	461	296	371	451	522	664
Meats, poultry, fish, and eggs	880	548	731	863	1 004	1 252
Dairy products	371	222	299	361	416	555
Fruits and vegetables	561	354	438	546	614	853
Other food at home	1 075	624	820	989	1 280	1 660
Food away from home	2 434	923	1 480	2 169	2 926	4 669
Alcoholic Beverages	459	194	264	408	554	876
Housing	13 918	6 760	9 505	12 144	15 741	25 424
Shelter	7 998	3 941	5 478	6 902	9 031	14 629
Owned dwellings	5 324	1 358	2 517	4 091	6 659	11 986
Rented dwellings	2 201	2 448	2 802	2 555	1 906	1 295
Other lodging	473	135	159	255	466	1 348
Utilities, fuels, and public services	2 927	1 720	2 371	2 868	3 370	4 301
Household operations	753	278	406	493	771	1 814
Housekeeping supplies	594	314	407	530	712	1 009
Household furnishings and equipment	1 646	507	843	1 351	1 856	3 670
Apparel and Services	1 816	837	1 058	1 477	2 052	3 654
Transportation	7 801	2 629	5 005	6 827	9 954	14 580
Vehicle purchases (net outlay)	3 397	951	2 130	2 797	4 546	6 555
Gasoline and motor oil	1 598	730	1 157	1 579	2 020	2 500
Other vehicle expenses	2 365	821	1 499	2 180	2 951	4 372
Public transportation	441	126	218	271	437	1 153
Health Care	2 574	1 421	2 139	2 529	2 969	3 810
Health insurance	1 332	745	1 146	1 346	1 556	1 864
Medical services	648	265	439	578	778	1 181
Drugs	480	357	477	493	499	575
Medical supplies	114	53	77	113	136	190
Entertainment	2 218	764	1 377	1 728	2 735	4 484
Personal Care Products and Services	581	271	400	507	641	1 086
Reading	130	55	82	112	145	256
Education	905	641	314	396	811	2 363
Tobacco Products and Smoking Supplies	288	214	287	340	327	272
Miscellaneous	690	312	482	646	766	1 243
Cash Contributions	1 408	343	790	1 106	1 422	3 376
Personal Insurance and Pensions	4 823	429	1 568	3 379	6 095	12 632
Life and other personal insurance	390	110	182	310	426	922
Pensions and Social Security	4 433	318	1 386	3 069	5 669	11 710

Table 8-6. Consumer Expenditures, Averages by Occupation of Reference Person, 2004

(Number, dollar, percent.)

Item	Self-employed workers	Wage and salary earners						Retired	All others, including those not reporting
		Total wage and salary earners	Managers and professional workers	Technical sales and clerical workers	Service workers	Construction workers and mechanics	Operators, fabricators, and laborers		
NUMBER OF CONSUMER UNITS (THOUSANDS)	5 262	76 790	28 960	21 461	11 309	4 443	10 616	20 060	14 170
CONSUMER UNIT CHARACTERISTICS									
Income Before Taxes	71 241	62 679	86 705	53 033	40 433	51 542	44 997	30 399	37 693
Income After Taxes	68 573	59 963	81 935	51 075	39 719	49 599	43 895	29 706	36 610
Age of Reference Person	50.3	42.3	43.8	41.6	41.2	39.9	41.7	73.8	45.5
Average Number in Consumer Unit									
Persons	2.6	2.6	2.6	2.5	2.7	2.7	2.8	1.7	2.8
Children under 18 years	0.7	0.7	0.7	0.7	0.8	0.8	0.9	0.1	0.9
Persons 65 years and over	0.3	0.1	0.1	0.1	0.1	(1)	0.1	1.2	0.2
Earners	1.7	1.7	1.7	1.7	1.7	1.8	1.8	0.2	0.7
Vehicles	2.3	2.1	2.2	2.0	1.7	2.4	2.1	1.6	1.6
Percent Distribution									
Male	59	52	51	40	44	95	72	45	26
Female	41	48	49	60	56	5	28	55	74
Percent Homeowner	82	66	76	62	50	66	59	80	56
With mortgage	51	50	61	47	33	50	41	19	32
Without mortgage	31	16	15	15	17	17	18	61	24
AVERAGE ANNUAL EXPENDITURES	55 464	47 576	61 111	43 271	34 695	42 722	35 253	30 450	34 684
Food	6 922	6 173	7 255	5 701	5 215	5 813	5 404	4 200	5 530
Food at home	3 853	3 437	3 733	3 218	3 143	3 506	3 378	2 711	3 598
Cereals and bakery products	508	469	495	459	451	456	444	386	510
Meats, poultry, fish, and eggs	1 032	901	943	797	902	957	974	688	990
Dairy products	450	377	418	357	325	391	357	310	395
Fruits and vegetables	670	564	638	517	504	532	539	502	588
Other food at home	1 194	1 127	1 240	1 088	959	1 171	1 063	825	1 114
Food away from home	3 069	2 736	3 522	2 483	2 072	2 307	2 027	1 489	1 931
Alcoholic Beverages	602	530	678	510	357	556	347	299	257
Housing	16 060	15 098	19 338	13 984	11 375	12 477	10 871	10 363	11 770
Shelter	9 229	8 840	11 393	8 237	6 643	7 136	6 143	5 329	6 762
Owned dwellings	6 879	5 933	8 489	5 258	3 389	4 543	3 619	3 526	3 996
Rented dwellings	1 483	2 413	2 085	2 596	3 000	2 317	2 354	1 398	2 455
Other lodging	867	493	820	383	254	277	171	406	311
Utilities, fuels, and public services	3 362	3 030	3 452	2 860	2 623	2 862	2 729	2 559	2 723
Household operations	863	822	1 250	681	457	580	427	668	460
Housekeeping supplies	736	612	789	566	433	461	484	536	529
Household furnishings and equipment	1 869	1 795	2 454	1 640	1 219	1 438	1 087	1 270	1 296
Apparel and Services	2 106	2 043	2 618	1 848	1 612	1 797	1 460	970	1 706
Transportation	9 530	8 799	10 556	8 343	6 481	9 704	7 021	4 976	5 751
Vehicle purchases (net outlay)	4 167	3 852	4 477	3 791	2 721	5 025	2 984	2 050	2 554
Gasoline and motor oil	1 825	1 791	1 952	1 688	1 523	2 023	1 751	998	1 312
Other vehicle expenses	2 950	2 671	3 299	2 524	1 963	2 432	2 109	1 571	1 616
Public transportation	587	485	828	340	274	224	177	357	269
Health Care	3 679	2 265	2 855	2 115	1 658	1 917	1 753	3 868	2 003
Health insurance	1 928	1 156	1 435	1 079	849	1 052	917	2 096	982
Medical services	966	631	832	586	431	528	432	738	498
Drugs	629	373	446	354	312	257	325	879	438
Medical supplies	155	105	142	96	66	80	79	155	85
Entertainment	2 850	2 410	3 366	2 000	1 686	1 763	1 679	1 722	1 651
Personal Care Products and Services	681	627	796	599	498	450	436	483	439
Reading	170	132	197	115	73	81	74	143	90
Education	1 099	1 101	1 692	945	703	646	422	167	821
Tobacco Products and Smoking Supplies	336	304	211	297	325	557	445	168	353
Miscellaneous	930	718	917	653	518	788	496	583	601
Cash Contributions	2 140	1 419	2 116	1 202	746	949	874	1 476	978
Personal Insurance and Pensions	8 359	5 957	8 516	4 961	3 448	5 223	3 971	1 031	2 734
Life and other personal insurance	688	411	593	354	211	377	255	339	241
Pensions and Social Security	7 671	5 546	7 923	4 607	3 237	4 846	3 716	692	2 492

[1]Value less than 0.05.

Table 8-7. Consumer Expenditures, Averages by Number of Earners, 2004

(Number, dollar, percent.)

Item	Single consumer		Consumer units of two or more persons			
	No earner	One earner	No earner	One earner	Two earners	Three or more earners
NUMBER OF CONSUMER UNITS (THOUSANDS)	12 607	21 079	10 012	23 873	39 198	9 513
CONSUMER UNIT CHARACTERISTICS						
Income Before Taxes	15 219	35 873	26 878	50 684	76 821	93 931
Income After Taxes	15 077	33 748	25 812	49 228	73 516	90 744
Age of Reference Person	68.9	41.7	65.9	46.7	42.7	46.4
Average Number in Consumer Unit						
Persons	1.0	1.0	2.3	3.0	3.0	4.3
Children under 18 years	X	X	0.3	1.1	0.9	1.1
Persons 65 years and over	0.7	0.1	1.2	0.3	0.1	0.1
Earners	X	1.0	X	1.0	2.0	3.3
Vehicles	0.8	1.2	1.8	2.0	2.5	3.2
Percent Distribution						
Male	32	52	53	42	52	55
Female	68	48	47	58	48	45
Percent Homeowner	59	47	77	68	76	81
With mortgage	10	30	19	43	59	67
Without mortgage	49	17	58	25	17	15
AVERAGE ANNUAL EXPENDITURES	18 398	29 640	32 404	43 955	55 718	66 606
Food	2 539	3 433	5 180	6 096	7 182	9 454
Food at home	1 708	1 664	3 537	3 742	3 977	5 475
Cereals and bakery products	250	215	494	541	531	756
Meats, poultry, fish, and eggs	421	405	987	979	1 035	1 542
Dairy products	192	178	394	418	444	591
Fruits and vegetables	321	284	625	629	648	897
Other food at home	524	582	1 036	1 175	1 320	1 690
Food away from home	831	1 769	1 643	2 354	3 205	3 979
Alcoholic Beverages	167	475	349	368	600	601
Housing	7 569	10 247	10 584	14 837	17 152	18 365
Shelter	4 350	6 732	5 277	8 440	9 739	10 221
Owned dwellings	2 041	3 440	3 359	5 591	7 152	7 721
Rented dwellings	2 141	2 969	1 486	2 334	2 008	1 794
Other lodging	168	323	432	515	580	706
Utilities, fuels, and public services	1 774	1 863	2 780	3 181	3 437	4 224
Household operations	619	337	454	761	1 101	711
Housekeeping supplies	316	314	626	648	744	803
Household furnishings and equipment	510	1 000	1 447	1 808	2 130	2 407
Apparel and Services	562	1 184	1 135	1 945	2 437	2 760
Transportation	2 133	5 022	5 431	7 676	10 337	13 838
Vehicle purchases (net outlay)	727	2 122	2 344	3 314	4 543	6 355
Gasoline and motor oil	477	1 003	1 115	1 607	2 103	2 800
Other vehicle expenses	768	1 587	1 623	2 282	3 139	4 009
Public transportation	161	310	348	472	552	673
Health Care	2 390	1 282	3 973	2 682	2 771	3 127
Health insurance	1 218	630	2 194	1 380	1 431	1 602
Medical services	485	334	674	684	785	880
Drugs	594	256	936	505	427	503
Medical supplies	92	62	169	113	129	142
Entertainment	746	1 411	2 196	2 222	2 920	3 096
Personal Care Products and Services	285	398	491	592	709	929
Reading	91	102	133	124	157	151
Education	376	781	146	820	1 083	2 166
Tobacco Products and Smoking Supplies	135	186	221	327	354	419
Miscellaneous	435	566	658	725	777	891
Cash Contributions	822	1 150	1 436	1 322	1 718	1 664
Personal Insurance and Pensions	148	3 403	471	4 219	7 522	9 143
Life and other personal insurance	132	154	379	412	520	681
Pensions and Social Security	[1]16	3 249	92	3 808	7 002	8 462

[1]Data are likely to have large sampling errors.
X = Not applicable.

Table 8-8. Consumer Expenditures, Averages by Size of Consumer Unit, 2004

(Number, dollar, percent.)

Item	One person	Two or more persons	Two persons	Three persons	Four persons	Five or more persons
NUMBER OF CONSUMER UNITS (THOUSANDS)	33 686	82 596	37 542	17 806	16 388	10 859
CONSUMER UNIT CHARACTERISTICS						
Income Before Taxes	28 143	65 183	58 307	66 762	74 970	71 600
Income After Taxes	26 761	62 698	55 393	64 220	72 627	70 473
Age of Reference Person	51.9	47.1	52.9	44.0	41.1	41.1
Average Number in Consumer Unit						
Persons	1.0	3.1	2.0	3.0	4.0	5.6
Children under 18 years	X	0.9	0.1	0.8	1.6	2.8
Persons 65 years and over	0.3	0.3	0.5	0.2	0.1	0.1
Earners	0.6	1.6	1.3	1.8	1.9	2.2
Vehicles	1.0	2.3	2.2	2.4	2.5	2.5
Percent Distribution						
Male	45	50	53	47	49	44
Female	55	50	47	53	51	56
Percent Homeowner	51	74	75	71	77	74
With mortgage	23	50	40	54	65	58
Without mortgage	29	24	35	17	12	16
AVERAGE ANNUAL EXPENDITURES	25 423	50 706	45 855	51 503	57 866	55 468
Food	3 095	6 866	5 808	6 930	8 171	8 516
Food at home	1 681	4 019	3 288	4 007	4 809	5 416
Cereals and bakery products	229	555	435	556	673	791
Meats, poultry, fish, and eggs	411	1 069	864	1 097	1 252	1 464
Dairy products	183	446	358	442	548	608
Fruits and vegetables	298	667	576	643	745	908
Other food at home	560	1 282	1 055	1 269	1 590	1 644
Food away from home	1 414	2 847	2 520	2 924	3 362	3 100
Alcoholic Beverages	359	500	569	468	478	345
Housing	9 244	15 822	14 036	16 177	18 360	17 593
Shelter	5 841	8 878	7 866	9 036	10 382	9 849
Owned dwellings	2 916	6 307	5 311	6 263	7 977	7 299
Rented dwellings	2 659	2 014	1 930	2 213	1 921	2 121
Other lodging	265	558	625	561	484	429
Utilities, fuels, and public services	1 830	3 374	3 004	3 470	3 757	3 917
Household operations	443	879	595	980	1 346	993
Housekeeping supplies	315	707	661	713	802	720
Household furnishings and equipment	816	1 983	1 909	1 977	2 073	2 114
Apparel and Services	949	2 167	1 758	2 266	2 601	2 784
Transportation	3 941	9 376	8 151	9 790	11 148	10 258
Vehicle purchases (net outlay)	1 600	4 130	3 412	4 297	5 298	4 575
Gasoline and motor oil	806	1 920	1 634	1 994	2 250	2 293
Other vehicle expenses	1 281	2 808	2 543	2 976	3 136	2 951
Public transportation	254	518	561	523	464	439
Health Care	1 697	2 932	3 212	2 865	2 635	2 520
Health insurance	850	1 528	1 648	1 476	1 443	1 328
Medical services	391	753	768	804	686	723
Drugs	383	520	651	472	384	352
Medical supplies	73	130	146	114	123	116
Entertainment	1 162	2 649	2 618	2 417	2 910	2 743
Personal Care Products and Services	355	673	631	650	740	753
Reading	97	144	161	129	138	118
Education	629	1 018	793	1 019	1 417	1 190
Tobacco Products and Smoking Supplies	167	338	309	374	346	365
Miscellaneous	517	761	780	763	745	714
Cash Contributions	1 027	1 563	1 888	1 393	1 162	1 327
Personal Insurance and Pensions	2 184	5 899	5 141	6 263	7 014	6 242
Life and other personal insurance	146	490	486	479	496	513
Pensions and Social Security	2 039	5 409	4 655	5 783	6 518	5 729

X = Not applicable.

Table 8-9. Consumer Expenditures, Averages by Composition of Consumer Unit, 2004

(Number, dollar, percent.)

Item	Husband and wife consumer units						Other husband and wife consumer units	One parent, at least one child under 18 years	Single person and other consumer units
	Total	Husband and wife only	Husband and wife with children						
			Total	Oldest child under 6 years	Oldest child 6 to 17 years	Oldest child 18 years or over			
NUMBER OF CONSUMER UNITS (THOUSANDS)	59 797	25 585	29 279	5 604	15 376	8 300	4 933	6 892	49 592
CONSUMER UNIT CHARACTERISTICS									
Income Before Taxes	73 001	64 434	79 764	75 293	78 508	85 109	77 287	31 055	35 341
Income After Taxes	70 047	61 108	76 883	72 403	75 771	81 967	75 837	30 951	33 838
Age of Reference Person	48.8	56.7	42.0	32.6	40.3	51.5	47.8	37.9	49.6
Average Number in Consumer Unit									
Persons	3.2	2.0	3.9	3.5	4.1	3.9	4.9	2.9	1.6
Children under 18 years	0.9	X	1.6	1.5	2.1	0.7	1.5	1.8	0.2
Persons 65 years and over	0.3	0.6	0.1	(1)	(1)	0.2	0.5	(1)	0.3
Earners	1.7	1.2	2.0	1.7	1.8	2.5	2.3	1.0	1.0
Vehicles	2.6	2.4	2.7	2.2	2.6	3.3	2.6	1.2	1.3
Percent Distribution									
Male	57	61	54	52	52	59	53	15	42
Female	43	39	46	48	48	41	47	85	58
Percent Homeowner	83	85	82	73	81	88	79	43	53
With mortgage	57	44	68	67	70	67	57	32	26
Without mortgage	26	41	13	6	12	21	22	11	27
AVERAGE ANNUAL EXPENDITURES	55 607	49 690	60 661	55 981	60 578	64 162	56 290	32 824	30 085
Food	7 379	6 268	8 089	6 300	8 484	8 682	8 950	4 873	3 946
Food at home	4 303	3 574	4 711	3 765	4 887	5 104	5 692	3 015	2 218
Cereals and bakery products	593	472	668	492	718	705	778	443	301
Meats, poultry, fish, and eggs	1 121	923	1 210	875	1 216	1 465	1 641	835	589
Dairy products	480	390	542	437	580	549	579	317	243
Fruits and vegetables	726	644	756	634	771	823	980	456	373
Other food at home	1 383	1 145	1 535	1 327	1 602	1 561	1 714	964	712
Food away from home	3 076	2 694	3 378	2 535	3 597	3 578	3 258	1 858	1 729
Alcoholic Beverages	493	567	443	330	455	506	410	219	452
Housing	17 005	14 706	18 912	21 045	18 900	17 503	17 595	12 030	10 451
Shelter	9 427	8 031	10 658	11 944	10 838	9 455	9 365	7 043	6 408
Owned dwellings	7 291	5 947	8 473	9 254	8 644	7 628	7 253	3 314	3 232
Rented dwellings	1 463	1 308	1 558	2 334	1 545	1 058	1 708	3 510	2 909
Other lodging	673	776	628	357	650	769	404	219	267
Utilities, fuels, and public services	3 572	3 176	3 839	3 325	3 809	4 240	4 041	2 755	2 173
Household operations	996	638	1 299	2 699	1 167	599	1 058	759	458
Housekeeping supplies	771	729	815	820	824	794	724	453	397
Household furnishings and equipment	2 238	2 133	2 301	2 257	2 262	2 415	2 407	1 020	1 015
Apparel and Services	2 263	1 745	2 680	2 583	2 757	2 617	2 463	1 859	1 263
Transportation	10 486	8 975	11 884	10 599	11 377	13 694	10 021	5 446	4 892
Vehicle purchases (net outlay)	4 724	3 806	5 579	5 142	5 370	6 263	4 402	2 304	1 949
Gasoline and motor oil	2 087	1 752	2 362	1 991	2 277	2 770	2 192	1 216	1 061
Other vehicle expenses	3 080	2 753	3 381	3 015	3 188	3 986	2 985	1 716	1 594
Public transportation	595	664	561	451	542	674	442	209	288
Health Care	3 345	3 761	3 009	2 369	2 948	3 554	3 191	1 384	1 809
Health insurance	1 750	1 945	1 589	1 275	1 579	1 820	1 693	705	914
Medical services	863	880	859	690	872	947	802	415	422
Drugs	581	762	427	305	372	611	565	213	395
Medical supplies	151	175	134	99	125	176	132	51	77
Entertainment	2 945	2 919	3 051	2 442	3 320	2 975	2 449	1 573	1 430
Personal Care Products and Services	711	656	748	604	732	891	773	517	432
Reading	166	186	153	139	158	154	135	68	97
Education	1 154	828	1 485	414	1 439	2 294	880	700	633
Tobacco Products and Smoking Supplies	301	249	324	211	318	413	429	277	274
Miscellaneous	800	790	757	687	650	1 011	1 101	643	564
Cash Contributions	1 836	2 316	1 481	1 189	1 517	1 610	1 459	587	1 006
Personal Insurance and Pensions	6 722	5 723	7 645	7 069	7 524	8 257	6 434	2 648	2 836
Life and other personal insurance	594	604	570	389	543	742	688	204	170
Pensions and Social Security	6 128	5 119	7 075	6 680	6 981	7 516	5 745	2 444	2 665

[1]Value less than 0.05.
X = Not applicable.

Table 8-10. Consumer Expenditures, Averages by Age of Reference Person, 2004

(Number, dollar, percent.)

Item	Under 25 years	25 to 34 years	35 to 44 years	45 to 54 years	55 to 64 years	65 years and over	65 to 74 years	75 years and over
NUMBER OF CONSUMER UNITS (THOUSANDS)	8 817	19 439	24 070	23 712	17 479	22 765	11 230	11 536
CONSUMER UNIT CHARACTERISTICS								
Income Before Taxes	22 840	52 484	65 515	70 434	61 031	34 988	42 137	28 028
Income After Taxes	22 507	50 819	63 202	66 761	58 043	34 040	41 126	27 142
Age of Reference Person	21.4	29.7	39.7	49.3	59.1	75.3	69.3	81.2
Average Number in Consumer Unit								
Persons	1.9	2.9	3.2	2.7	2.1	1.7	1.9	1.5
Children under 18 years	0.4	1.1	1.3	0.6	0.2	0.1	0.1	(1)
Persons 65 years and over	(1)	(1)	(1)	(1)	0.1	1.4	1.4	1.3
Earners	1.3	1.5	1.7	1.7	1.3	0.5	0.7	0.2
Vehicles	1.2	1.8	2.1	2.4	2.2	1.5	1.9	1.2
Percent Distribution								
Male	46	49	48	50	50	46	50	42
Female	54	51	52	50	50	54	50	58
Percent Homeowner	15	49	69	77	83	80	83	78
With mortgage	9	42	59	58	46	18	27	10
Without mortgage	5	7	11	19	37	62	56	68
AVERAGE ANNUAL EXPENDITURES	24 535	42 701	50 402	52 764	47 299	31 104	36 512	25 763
Food	3 715	5 705	6 752	7 038	5 898	4 206	4 871	3 518
Food at home	1 853	3 155	3 897	4 083	3 374	2 722	3 049	2 380
Cereals and bakery products	265	432	552	547	437	394	422	364
Meats, poultry, fish, and eggs	480	812	1 019	1 111	894	694	799	584
Dairy products	205	346	440	436	371	313	353	271
Fruits and vegetables	285	521	615	673	588	510	548	470
Other food at home	618	1 043	1 271	1 316	1 083	812	927	692
Food away from home	1 862	2 550	2 855	2 955	2 524	1 484	1 822	1 138
Alcoholic Beverages	503	522	535	502	457	261	329	190
Housing	7 649	14 379	16 794	16 164	14 339	10 259	11 152	9 381
Shelter	4 901	8 729	9 856	9 313	7 883	5 329	5 784	4 886
Owned dwellings	1 009	4 700	7 025	6 968	5 970	3 523	4 134	2 928
Rented dwellings	3 647	3 802	2 450	1 636	1 169	1 393	1 123	1 655
Other lodging	244	227	381	710	743	414	527	303
Utilities, fuels, and public services	1 413	2 687	3 309	3 413	3 222	2 580	2 881	2 287
Household operations	270	915	992	693	645	694	522	861
Housekeeping supplies	253	499	677	756	657	509	569	445
Household furnishings and equipment	812	1 548	1 960	1 989	1 932	1 147	1 395	901
Apparel and Services	1 371	2 134	2 142	2 217	1 863	907	1 200	604
Transportation	4 704	8 485	9 183	9 343	8 421	4 875	6 506	3 286
Vehicle purchases (net outlay)	2 035	4 033	4 190	3 790	3 616	1 966	2 822	1 132
Gasoline and motor oil	1 130	1 679	1 877	1 980	1 666	963	1 259	675
Other vehicle expenses	1 326	2 407	2 681	3 061	2 532	1 546	1 902	1 200
Public transportation	214	366	435	512	606	400	524	280
Health Care	654	1 519	2 263	2 695	3 262	3 899	3 799	3 995
Health insurance	321	842	1 199	1 291	1 567	2 142	2 171	2 115
Medical services	184	403	654	809	892	678	631	723
Drugs	118	212	318	461	642	920	854	985
Medical supplies	31	62	92	133	161	158	144	172
Entertainment	1 166	2 122	2 504	2 711	2 823	1 429	1 879	990
Personal Care Products and Services	334	552	660	690	628	468	514	421
Reading	51	94	123	149	177	146	158	135
Education	1 821	726	786	1 567	730	274	352	198
Tobacco Products and Smoking Supplies	236	283	350	375	301	147	197	98
Miscellaneous	297	600	773	774	825	641	735	547
Cash Contributions	310	815	1 265	1 625	1 752	2 000	2 471	1 542
Personal Insurance and Pensions	1 726	4 765	6 273	6 915	5 825	1 592	2 348	856
Life and other personal insurance	31	235	391	505	612	372	472	275
Pensions and Social Security	1 695	4 529	5 881	6 410	5 214	1 220	1 875	582

[1]Value less than 0.05.

Table 8-11. Consumer Expenditures, Averages by Race of Reference Person, 2004

(Number, dollar, percent.)

Item	White, Asian, and other races			Black
	Total	White and other races	Asian	
NUMBER OF CONSUMER UNITS (THOUSANDS)	102 509	98 552	3 957	13 773
CONSUMER UNIT CHARACTERISTICS				
Income Before Taxes	56 596	56 150	67 705	38 503
Income After Taxes	54 207	53 751	65 574	37 996
Age of Reference Person	48.7	49.0	41.7	46.6
Average Number in Consumer Unit				
Persons	2.5	2.4	2.8	2.6
Children under 18 years	0.6	0.6	0.7	0.8
Persons 65 years and over	0.3	0.3	0.2	0.2
Earners	1.3	1.3	1.5	1.2
Vehicles	2.0	2.0	1.7	1.3
Percent Distribution				
Male	50	50	58	36
Female	50	50	42	64
Percent Homeowner	70	71	58	49
With mortgage	44	44	47	32
Without mortgage	26	27	12	18
AVERAGE ANNUAL EXPENDITURES	45 135	44 962	49 459	30 481
Food	5 987	5 958	6 742	4 265
Food at home	3 428	3 418	3 689	2 749
Cereals and bakery products	471	469	527	388
Meats, poultry, fish, and eggs	877	872	1 021	898
Dairy products	387	391	286	249
Fruits and vegetables	577	566	870	442
Other food at home	1 116	1 121	985	772
Food away from home	2 559	2 539	3 053	1 516
Alcoholic Beverages	499	505	325	171
Housing	14 306	14 181	17 418	11 043
Shelter	8 212	8 071	11 728	6 411
Owned dwellings	5 615	5 530	7 734	3 165
Rented dwellings	2 081	2 022	3 537	3 097
Other lodging	516	519	458	149
Utilities, fuels, and public services	2 932	2 938	2 781	2 884
Household operations	791	788	885	466
Housekeeping supplies	625	630	472	374
Household furnishings and equipment	1 746	1 754	1 552	907
Apparel and Services	1 823	1 821	1 885	1 765
Transportation	8 181	8 166	8 556	4 976
Vehicle purchases (net outlay)	3 617	3 615	3 676	1 759
Gasoline and motor oil	1 647	1 647	1 637	1 231
Other vehicle expenses	2 455	2 460	2 330	1 696
Public transportation	462	443	913	290
Health Care	2 736	2 762	2 101	1 368
Health insurance	1 397	1 406	1 177	846
Medical services	706	714	502	220
Drugs	510	518	294	263
Medical supplies	124	124	127	39
Entertainment	2 377	2 401	1 789	1 040
Personal Care Products and Services	592	595	506	503
Reading	141	142	112	53
Education	950	904	2 087	573
Tobacco Products and Smoking Supplies	300	308	103	200
Miscellaneous	721	728	569	457
Cash Contributions	1 485	1 501	1 089	835
Personal Insurance and Pensions	5 037	4 991	6 176	3 230
Life and other personal insurance	404	408	306	292
Pensions and Social Security	4 634	4 584	5 871	2 938

Table 8-12. Consumer Expenditures, Averages by Hispanic Origin[1] of Reference Person, 2004

(Number, dollar, percent.)

Item	Hispanic[1]	Not Hispanic or Latino		
		Total	White, Asian, and other races	Black
NUMBER OF CONSUMER UNITS (THOUSANDS)	12 298	103 984	90 424	13 559
CONSUMER UNIT CHARACTERISTICS				
Income Before Taxes	43 693	55 726	58 314	38 464
Income After Taxes	42 798	53 410	55 728	37 950
Age of Reference Person	42.2	49.2	49.6	46.6
Average Number in Consumer Unit				
Persons	3.3	2.4	2.3	2.6
Children under 18 years	1.2	0.6	0.5	0.8
Persons 65 years and over	0.2	0.3	0.3	0.2
Earners	1.6	1.3	1.3	1.2
Vehicles	1.7	2.0	2.1	1.3
Percent Distribution				
Male	52	48	50	36
Female	48	52	50	64
Percent Homeowner	50	70	73	50
With mortgage	36	43	45	32
Without mortgage	14	27	28	18
AVERAGE ANNUAL EXPENDITURES	37 578	44 084	46 163	30 286
Food	5 911	5 764	5 999	4 230
Food at home	3 883	3 281	3 367	2 725
Cereals and bakery products	517	454	464	387
Meats, poultry, fish, and eggs	1 175	844	836	893
Dairy products	425	364	382	245
Fruits and vegetables	712	542	559	435
Other food at home	1 054	1 077	1 125	766
Food away from home	2 027	2 483	2 633	1 505
Alcoholic Beverages	320	476	523	172
Housing	12 884	14 042	14 503	10 977
Shelter	7 833	8 018	8 266	6 362
Owned dwellings	4 107	5 469	5 817	3 145
Rented dwellings	3 501	2 047	1 894	3 068
Other lodging	226	502	555	150
Utilities, fuels, and public services	2 671	2 957	2 966	2 894
Household operations	574	774	820	467
Housekeeping supplies	503	606	641	372
Household furnishings and equipment	1 303	1 687	1 809	881
Apparel and Services	1 817	1 816	1 830	1 724
Transportation	7 497	7 837	8 273	4 936
Vehicle purchases (net outlay)	3 445	3 391	3 639	1 741
Gasoline and motor oil	1 650	1 591	1 646	1 229
Other vehicle expenses	2 048	2 403	2 511	1 684
Public transportation	355	452	477	282
Health Care	1 588	2 691	2 891	1 362
Health insurance	850	1 389	1 471	838
Medical services	402	678	746	221
Drugs	252	507	544	263
Medical supplies	85	117	129	40
Entertainment	1 443	2 311	2 503	1 035
Personal Care Products and Services	519	588	602	501
Reading	53	140	152	54
Education	438	961	1 019	573
Tobacco Products and Smoking Supplies	155	304	319	201
Miscellaneous	477	715	754	459
Cash Contributions	710	1 491	1 589	836
Personal Insurance and Pensions	3 765	4 948	5 207	3 226
Life and other personal insurance	155	418	437	293
Pensions and Social Security	3 610	4 530	4 770	2 933

[1]May be of any race.

Table 8-13. Consumer Expenditures, Averages by Education of Reference Person, 2004

(Number, dollar, percent.)

Item		Less than a college graduate				College graduate or more		
	Total	Less than a high school graduate	High school graduate	High school graduate with some college	Associate degree	Total	Bachelor's degree	Master's, professional, or doctorate degree
NUMBER OF CONSUMER UNITS (THOUSANDS)	83 830	16 829	31 005	25 317	10 678	32 452	20 684	11 768
CONSUMER UNIT CHARACTERISTICS								
Income Before Taxes	43 083	29 094	42 334	46 756	58 593	83 825	75 647	98 201
Income After Taxes	41 818	28 951	41 131	45 118	56 268	79 332	71 857	92 470
Age of Reference Person	49.1	54.8	50.6	44.9	45.6	46.9	45.2	49.8
Average Number in Consumer Unit								
Persons	2.5	2.7	2.5	2.3	2.6	2.5	2.4	2.5
Children under 18 years	0.6	0.8	0.6	0.6	0.7	0.6	0.6	0.6
Persons 65 years and over	0.3	0.5	0.4	0.3	0.2	0.2	0.2	0.3
Earners	1.3	1.0	1.3	1.3	1.5	1.5	1.5	1.5
Vehicles	1.9	1.4	1.9	1.9	2.2	2.1	2.1	2.1
Percent Distribution								
Male	46	44	48	47	44	54	51	58
Female	54	56	52	53	56	46	49	42
Percent Homeowner	64	57	68	60	74	76	73	82
With mortgage	37	24	36	39	53	56	55	58
Without mortgage	28	33	32	21	21	20	18	23
AVERAGE ANNUAL EXPENDITURES	36 654	25 421	35 439	40 878	48 177	60 712	56 728	67 801
Food	5 213	4 260	5 182	5 505	6 218	7 206	6 848	7 877
Food at home	3 174	2 991	3 229	3 098	3 482	3 779	3 626	4 071
Cereals and bakery products	443	413	466	425	465	504	494	524
Meats, poultry, fish, and eggs	867	889	890	808	898	911	872	985
Dairy products	344	325	346	335	394	436	415	474
Fruits and vegetables	512	507	510	502	551	682	640	761
Other food at home	1 006	856	1 017	1 028	1 173	1 246	1 204	1 326
Food away from home	2 039	1 269	1 952	2 407	2 736	3 428	3 222	3 806
Alcoholic Beverages	359	202	345	452	448	711	693	746
Housing	11 682	8 724	11 208	12 915	14 855	19 676	18 305	22 110
Shelter	6 563	4 913	6 177	7 364	8 389	11 706	10 956	13 024
Owned dwellings	4 083	2 412	3 869	4 623	6 062	8 530	7 689	10 009
Rented dwellings	2 184	2 425	2 066	2 303	1 863	2 246	2 462	1 866
Other lodging	296	76	242	438	464	930	804	1 150
Utilities, fuels, and public services	2 759	2 414	2 837	2 717	3 172	3 361	3 232	3 586
Household operations	546	318	475	657	847	1 288	1 125	1 573
Housekeeping supplies	518	394	507	557	670	786	715	921
Household furnishings and equipment	1 297	685	1 212	1 621	1 777	2 536	2 277	3 004
Apparel and Services	1 535	1 150	1 405	1 806	1 948	2 526	2 436	2 690
Transportation	7 040	4 472	6 819	7 829	9 872	9 766	9 720	9 848
Vehicle purchases (net outlay)	3 205	1 922	3 046	3 590	4 776	3 893	4 072	3 580
Gasoline and motor oil	1 509	1 142	1 537	1 574	1 852	1 826	1 817	1 841
Other vehicle expenses	2 065	1 259	2 027	2 324	2 851	3 140	3 052	3 293
Public transportation	260	149	209	341	393	908	780	1 134
Health Care	2 328	1 874	2 450	2 325	2 703	3 208	3 031	3 522
Health insurance	1 219	994	1 308	1 183	1 405	1 622	1 585	1 686
Medical services	549	383	542	600	708	906	821	1 054
Drugs	466	433	507	440	467	515	485	571
Medical supplies	94	64	93	102	124	165	140	210
Entertainment	1 814	953	1 685	2 276	2 465	3 259	3 045	3 639
Personal Care Products and Services	503	361	481	554	684	779	754	825
Reading	92	45	85	116	130	229	193	292
Education	560	133	364	981	808	1 797	1 497	2 326
Tobacco Products and Smoking Supplies	343	347	380	308	312	147	166	113
Miscellaneous	602	382	607	674	760	918	827	1 084
Cash Contributions	968	544	949	1 094	1 390	2 546	2 046	3 425
Personal Insurance and Pensions	3 615	1 974	3 480	4 042	5 584	7 943	7 169	9 305
Life and other personal insurance	299	210	302	311	406	625	551	756
Pensions and Social Security	3 316	1 764	3 178	3 731	5 177	7 318	6 618	8 549

Table 8-14. Consumer Expenditures, Averages by Housing Tenure and Type of Area, 2004

(Number, dollar, percent.)

| Item | Housing tenure | | | | Type of area | | | |
| | Homeowner | | | Renter | Urban | | | Rural |
	Total	Homeowner with mortgage	Homeowner without mortgage		Total	Central city	Other urban	
NUMBER OF CONSUMER UNITS (THOUSANDS)	78 698	49 098	29 600	37 584	101 336	34 336	67 001	14 945
CONSUMER UNIT CHARACTERISTICS								
Income Before Taxes	65 436	76 571	46 967	31 455	55 769	46 596	60 470	45 530
Income After Taxes	62 574	73 104	45 107	30 748	53 542	44 668	58 090	43 779
Age of Reference Person	52.3	46.3	62.3	40.4	48.0	46.7	48.7	51.6
Average Number in Consumer Unit								
Persons	2.6	2.9	2.1	2.2	2.5	2.4	2.5	2.5
Children under 18 years	0.7	0.9	0.3	0.6	0.6	0.6	0.7	0.6
Persons 65 years and over	0.4	0.2	0.7	0.1	0.3	0.3	0.3	0.4
Earners	1.4	1.7	0.9	1.2	1.3	1.2	1.4	1.3
Vehicles	2.3	2.5	2.0	1.2	1.9	1.5	2.0	2.5
Percent Distribution								
Male	50	52	46	45	48	46	49	47
Female	50	48	54	55	52	54	51	53
Percent Homeowner	100	100	100	X	65	53	72	83
With mortgage	62	100	X	X	43	34	47	39
Without mortgage	38	X	100	X	23	19	25	43
AVERAGE ANNUAL EXPENDITURES	50 195	57 978	36 936	29 170	44 172	38 428	47 107	38 088
Food	6 451	7 095	5 197	4 383	5 854	5 325	6 122	5 263
Food at home	3 711	3 975	3 188	2 587	3 370	3 053	3 529	3 181
Cereals and bakery products	511	542	449	358	463	410	490	444
Meats, poultry, fish, and eggs	963	1 033	822	707	882	845	901	861
Dairy products	413	437	366	281	373	324	397	356
Fruits and vegetables	619	651	554	440	575	523	601	464
Other food at home	1 206	1 311	997	802	1 077	951	1 141	1 057
Food away from home	2 740	3 121	2 009	1 796	2 484	2 271	2 592	2 081
Alcoholic Beverages	492	547	386	391	484	473	489	287
Housing	15 653	19 169	9 786	10 290	14 487	12 866	15 316	10 059
Shelter	8 503	11 272	3 912	6 941	8 488	7 683	8 901	4 678
Owned dwellings	7 837	10 550	3 336	64	5 587	4 077	6 360	3 547
Rented dwellings	57	55	60	6 690	2 411	3 225	1 994	777
Other lodging	609	666	515	187	490	382	546	353
Utilities, fuels, and public services	3 442	3 722	2 979	1 847	2 940	2 632	3 098	2 834
Household operations	930	1 081	679	382	793	679	851	482
Housekeeping supplies	712	747	641	351	597	511	640	578
Household furnishings and equipment	2 066	2 347	1 575	770	1 669	1 361	1 826	1 488
Apparel and Services	2 007	2 346	1 373	1 416	1 867	1 770	1 915	1 464
Transportation	9 151	10 703	6 575	4 975	7 702	6 363	8 388	8 474
Vehicle purchases (net outlay)	4 057	4 849	2 744	2 014	3 290	2 535	3 677	4 125
Gasoline and motor oil	1 826	2 075	1 413	1 120	1 549	1 270	1 692	1 926
Other vehicle expenses	2 758	3 216	1 997	1 544	2 389	2 055	2 560	2 206
Public transportation	510	563	422	297	474	504	459	217
Health Care	3 196	2 966	3 582	1 272	2 498	2 102	2 701	3 090
Health insurance	1 653	1 524	1 866	660	1 303	1 089	1 413	1 526
Medical services	818	825	806	294	618	508	675	852
Drugs	582	486	744	268	463	406	492	599
Medical supplies	144	131	166	51	114	99	121	113
Entertainment	2 700	3 029	2 136	1 210	2 236	1 786	2 466	2 102
Personal Care Products and Services	659	730	528	418	598	555	620	461
Reading	156	162	147	76	134	124	139	108
Education	965	1 167	623	781	972	877	1 021	450
Tobacco Products and Smoking Supplies	274	293	242	319	279	275	281	348
Miscellaneous	783	791	770	495	692	578	750	677
Cash Contributions	1 788	1 629	2 052	612	1 438	1 183	1 568	1 206
Personal Insurance and Pensions	5 918	7 352	3 540	2 531	4 930	4 149	5 330	4 099
Life and other personal insurance	514	579	406	131	383	282	435	437
Pensions and Social Security	5 404	6 772	3 134	2 400	4 547	3 867	4 895	3 662

X = Not applicable.

Table 8-15. Consumer Expenditures, Averages by Population Size of Area of Residence, 2004

(Number, dollar, percent.)

Item	Outside urbanized area	All urbanized area consumer units	Urbanized area consumer units					
			Less than 100,000	100,000 to 249,000	250,000 to 999,999	1,000,000 to 2,499,000	2,500,000 to 4,999,999	5,000,000 and over
NUMBER OF CONSUMER UNITS (THOUSANDS)	44 925	71 357	8 850	12 565	10 739	16 815	10 047	12 340
CONSUMER UNIT CHARACTERISTICS								
Income Before Taxes	50 233	57 110	45 225	48 826	52 581	56 991	70 799	67 029
Income After Taxes	48 250	54 829	43 912	46 441	50 111	54 595	67 251	65 510
Age of Reference Person	49.6	47.8	48.5	44.9	48.3	48.5	46.8	49.8
Average Number in Consumer Unit								
Persons	2.5	2.5	2.3	2.4	2.4	2.5	2.6	2.7
Children under 18 years	0.6	0.6	0.6	0.6	0.6	0.6	0.7	0.7
Persons 65 years and over	0.3	0.3	0.3	0.2	0.3	0.3	0.2	0.3
Earners	1.3	1.3	1.2	1.3	1.3	1.3	1.4	1.4
Vehicles	2.3	1.7	1.8	1.8	1.8	1.8	1.7	1.5
Percent Distribution								
Male	48	48	46	51	49	48	49	46
Female	52	52	54	49	51	52	51	54
Percent Homeowner	76	62	63	60	64	65	64	57
With mortgage	43	42	38	41	42	45	45	39
Without mortgage	34	20	24	18	22	20	19	19
AVERAGE ANNUAL EXPENDITURES	40 895	44 951	37 010	41 010	41 389	44 865	51 629	52 351
Food	5 477	5 962	5 220	5 422	5 626	5 971	6 338	6 962
Food at home	3 247	3 406	3 002	3 158	3 250	3 538	3 414	3 875
Cereals and bakery products	452	466	398	445	430	473	474	549
Meats, poultry, fish, and eggs	837	905	821	764	862	907	912	1 129
Dairy products	367	373	325	351	356	401	356	418
Fruits and vegetables	507	593	463	512	544	624	630	730
Other food at home	1 084	1 069	996	1 086	1 058	1 133	1 043	1 050
Food away from home	2 230	2 556	2 218	2 264	2 376	2 433	2 924	3 087
Alcoholic Beverages	384	504	465	420	392	550	586	584
Housing	12 036	15 105	11 438	12 820	13 520	15 155	17 735	19 232
Shelter	6 270	9 086	6 012	7 465	7 613	9 055	11 069	12 653
Owned dwellings	4 699	5 718	3 789	4 693	4 800	5 756	7 201	7 688
Rented dwellings	1 149	2 863	1 879	2 367	2 448	2 794	3 184	4 270
Other lodging	422	505	344	406	366	505	684	695
Utilities, fuels, and public services	2 910	2 937	2 668	2 642	3 048	2 942	3 243	3 080
Household operations	617	838	561	718	729	829	1 024	1 116
Housekeeping supplies	608	587	655	517	614	611	568	567
Household furnishings and equipment	1 631	1 657	1 542	1 478	1 515	1 717	1 832	1 817
Apparel and Services	1 570	1 965	1 705	1 783	1 552	1 824	2 412	2 505
Transportation	8 140	7 587	6 830	7 249	7 413	7 410	8 346	8 240
Vehicle purchases (net outlay)	3 766	3 165	3 268	3 204	3 183	3 022	3 316	3 107
Gasoline and motor oil	1 797	1 472	1 389	1 436	1 498	1 481	1 514	1 498
Other vehicle expenses	2 277	2 421	1 948	2 202	2 353	2 415	2 816	2 723
Public transportation	300	529	225	407	379	493	700	911
Health Care	2 800	2 432	2 189	2 504	2 471	2 448	2 614	2 330
Health insurance	1 445	1 260	1 217	1 227	1 238	1 294	1 341	1 232
Medical services	691	621	413	705	592	591	737	659
Drugs	542	441	474	441	533	449	429	337
Medical supplies	121	110	85	131	108	113	109	102
Entertainment	2 431	2 087	1 933	2 034	1 898	2 170	2 255	2 169
Personal Care Products and Services	507	627	615	545	595	598	723	705
Reading	117	139	117	134	136	140	157	146
Education	776	987	605	911	745	1 006	1 358	1 216
Tobacco Products and Smoking Supplies	332	261	347	256	297	246	212	231
Miscellaneous	661	708	469	681	632	771	738	863
Cash Contributions	1 240	1 514	1 265	1 544	1 337	1 518	1 591	1 747
Personal Insurance and Pensions	4 425	5 074	3 811	4 708	4 774	5 060	6 563	5 421
Life and other personal insurance	424	369	337	332	359	382	490	324
Pensions and Social Security	4 001	4 705	3 475	4 376	4 415	4 678	6 073	5 096

Table 8-16. Consumer Expenditures, Averages by Region of Residence,[1] 2004

(Number, dollar, percent.)

Item	Northeast	Midwest	South	West
NUMBER OF CONSUMER UNITS (THOUSANDS)	22 051	26 539	41 801	25 891
CONSUMER UNIT CHARACTERISTICS				
Income Before Taxes	61 050	53 567	50 775	55 682
Income After Taxes	58 673	51 122	49 079	53 222
Age of Reference Person	50.3	49.1	48.2	46.7
Average Number in Consumer Unit				
Persons	2.4	2.4	2.5	2.6
Children under 18 years	0.6	0.6	0.6	0.7
Persons 65 years and over	0.3	0.3	0.3	0.3
Earners	1.3	1.4	1.3	1.4
Vehicles	1.7	2.2	1.9	2.0
Percent Distribution				
Males	48	50	45	50
Females	52	50	55	50
Percent Homeowner	65	73	69	62
With mortgage	39	46	41	43
Without mortgage	26	27	28	19
AVERAGE ANNUAL EXPENDITURES	46 115	43 371	39 174	47 922
Food	6 368	5 592	5 318	6 224
Food at home	3 634	3 189	3 119	3 634
Cereals and bakery products	521	446	427	480
Meats, poultry, fish, and eggs	1 008	781	849	922
Dairy products	417	358	329	411
Fruits and vegetables	638	510	501	645
Other food at home	1 050	1 094	1 013	1 177
Food away from home	2 733	2 403	2 199	2 590
Alcoholic Beverages	625	427	348	532
Housing	15 734	13 438	12 250	15 557
Shelter	9 626	7 339	6 621	9 513
Owned dwellings	6 387	5 260	4 456	5 887
Rented dwellings	2 674	1 556	1 826	3 066
Other lodging	565	523	339	560
Utilities, fuels, and public services	3 098	2 957	2 975	2 672
Household operations	793	707	673	894
Housekeeping supplies	586	661	549	606
Household furnishings and equipment	1 630	1 775	1 432	1 871
Apparel and Services	2 176	1 672	1 643	1 936
Transportation	7 622	7 710	7 233	8 966
Vehicle purchases (net outlay)	3 196	3 315	3 195	3 979
Gasoline and motor oil	1 386	1 620	1 598	1 755
Other vehicle expenses	2 396	2 413	2 160	2 622
Public transportation	644	363	280	609
Health Care	2 371	2 861	2 508	2 560
Health insurance	1 307	1 492	1 287	1 261
Medical services	597	714	583	731
Drugs	375	526	533	438
Medical supplies	92	128	106	131
Entertainment	2 017	2 208	2 134	2 538
Personal Care Products and Services	631	563	542	620
Reading	145	150	98	150
Education	1 152	928	631	1 115
Tobacco Products and Smoking Supplies	296	340	291	223
Miscellaneous	760	797	512	809
Cash Contributions	1 108	1 790	1 252	1 525
Personal Insurance and Pensions	5 110	4 895	4 414	5 167
Life and other personal insurance	364	439	394	357
Pensions and Social Security	4 746	4 456	4 020	4 809

[1]The states that comprise the Census regions are: Northeast—Connecticut, Maine, Massachusetts, New Hampshire, New Jersey, New York, Pennsylvania, Rhode Island, and Vermont; Midwest—Illinois, Indiana, Iowa, Kansas, Michigan, Minnesota, Missouri, Nebraska, North Dakota, Ohio, South Dakota, and Wisconsin; South—Alabama, Arkansas, Delaware, District of Columbia, Florida, Georgia, Kentucky, Louisiana, Maryland, Mississippi, North Carolina, Oklahoma, South Carolina, Tennessee, Texas, Virginia, and West Virginia; West—Alaska, Arizona, California, Colorado, Hawaii, Idaho, Montana, Nevada, New Mexico, Oregon, Utah, Washington, and Wyoming.

Table 8-17. Consumer Expenditures, Averages by Selected Metropolitan Statistical Areas: Northeast Region, 2003–2004

(Number, dollar, percent.)

Item	All consumer units in the Northeast	New York	Philadelphia	Boston	Pittsburgh
NUMBER OF CONSUMER UNITS (THOUSANDS)	22 116	7 503	2 441	2 636	1 117
CONSUMER UNIT CHARACTERISTICS					
Income Before Taxes[1]	59 187	71 247	62 647	61 778	52 703
Age of Reference Person	50.1	50.2	50.3	49.7	52.5
Average Number in Consumer Unit					
Persons	2.4	2.6	2.5	2.4	2.3
Children under 18 years	0.6	0.7	0.6	0.6	0.5
Persons 65 years and over	0.3	0.3	0.3	0.3	0.4
Earners	1.3	1.4	1.3	1.3	1.3
Vehicles	1.7	1.4	1.6	1.6	1.9
Percent Homeowner	65	57	71	62	72
AVERAGE ANNUAL EXPENDITURES	44 202	51 979	44 484	46 444	40 604
Food	6 049	7 054	5 622	6 578	5 527
Food at home	3 470	3 879	3 051	3 791	3 146
Cereals and bakery products	503	573	451	555	455
Meats, poultry, fish, and eggs	948	1 102	875	1 054	847
Dairy products	385	433	327	378	359
Fruits and vegetables	612	735	511	641	527
Other food at home	1 022	1 036	887	1 163	958
Food away from home	2 579	3 174	2 572	2 787	2 381
Alcoholic Beverages	526	563	608	802	440
Housing	15 271	19 708	15 200	16 337	12 021
Shelter	9 379	13 047	9 015	10 556	6 322
Owned dwellings	6 159	8 146	6 240	6 882	4 314
Rented dwellings	2 669	4 190	2 248	3 198	1 573
Other lodging	551	710	526	477	435
Utilities, fuels, and public services	2 993	3 248	3 312	2 822	2 964
Household operations	803	1 067	674	903	559
Housekeeping supplies	555	547	535	653	528
Household furnishings and equipment	1 541	1 799	1 664	1 403	1 649
Apparel and Services	2 018	2 682	2 310	2 103	1 850
Transportation	7 332	7 599	7 678	7 400	6 488
Vehicle purchases (net outlay)	3 118	2 672	3 623	3 443	2 483
Gasoline and motor oil	1 271	1 198	1 243	1 299	1 266
Other vehicle expenses	2 351	2 722	2 347	2 128	2 360
Public transportation	591	1 007	465	529	379
Health Care	2 248	2 224	2 126	2 274	2 527
Entertainment	2 067	2 283	1 822	1 922	2 159
Personal Care Products and Services	582	668	674	576	526
Reading	149	151	124	172	166
Education	1 096	1 347	1 166	1 410	881
Tobacco Products and Smoking Supplies	301	256	234	280	478
Miscellaneous	654	808	671	519	560
Cash Contributions	1 135	990	987	1 184	3 064
Personal Insurance and Pensions	4 776	5 647	5 263	4 887	3 916
Life and other personal insurance	409	496	377	301	444
Pensions and Social Security	4 367	5 151	4 886	4 586	3 472

[1]Components of income and taxes are derived from "complete income" reporters only through 2003. Beginning in 2004, income imputation was implemented. As a result, all consumer units are considered to be complete income reporters.

Table 8-18. Consumer Expenditures, Averages by Selected Metropolitan Statistical Areas: South Region, 2003–2004

(Number, dollar, percent.)

Item	All consumer units in the South	Washington, D.C.	Baltimore	Atlanta	Miami	Tampa	Dallas-Fort Worth	Houston
NUMBER OF CONSUMER UNITS (THOUSANDS)	41 563	2 283	1 238	1 847	1 855	900	2 166	1 760
CONSUMER UNIT CHARACTERISTICS								
Income Before Taxes[1]	49 110	81 531	58 545	56 094	51 521	50 958	63 098	63 981
Age of Reference Person	48.2	46.4	51.9	45.8	48.7	52.8	45.6	44.7
Average Number in Consumer Unit								
Persons	2.5	2.6	2.3	2.5	2.6	2.4	2.7	3.0
Children under 18 years	0.6	0.7	0.6	0.7	0.7	0.5	0.7	1.0
Persons 65 years and over	0.3	0.2	0.4	0.2	0.3	0.4	0.2	0.2
Earners	1.3	1.6	1.2	1.4	1.4	1.2	1.5	1.5
Vehicles	1.9	1.8	1.6	1.7	1.5	1.8	1.9	1.9
Percent Homeowner	69	70	69	73	65	75	68	64
AVERAGE ANNUAL EXPENDITURES	38 454	53 251	37 681	37 130	39 875	35 911	50 304	48 063
Food	5 142	6 049	4 688	5 241	5 758	4 750	6 111	5 737
Food at home	3 058	3 137	2 757	2 809	4 056	3 020	3 554	3 107
Cereals and bakery products	420	415	396	386	550	411	470	429
Meats, poultry, fish, and eggs	842	840	734	825	1 142	774	897	813
Dairy products	314	299	287	290	484	343	378	343
Fruits and vegetables	495	609	485	523	798	487	582	535
Other food at home	987	974	855	785	1 082	1 006	1 227	987
Food away from home	2 083	2 912	1 931	2 432	1 702	1 730	2 557	2 630
Alcoholic Beverages	346	630	370	353	389	519	507	297
Housing	12 130	19 461	13 640	13 711	15 907	13 123	15 891	15 512
Shelter	6 640	12 685	8 584	8 233	10 086	7 512	9 050	8 706
Owned dwellings	4 492	8 830	5 996	5 865	6 709	5 462	6 264	5 838
Rented dwellings	1 814	3 293	2 247	2 106	3 017	1 820	2 307	2 466
Other lodging	334	562	341	262	360	230	479	402
Utilities, fuels, and public services	2 933	3 361	2 846	3 372	3 109	3 008	3 604	3 594
Household operations	670	1 099	586	605	954	710	828	923
Housekeeping supplies	523	581	459	453	550	533	624	640
Household furnishings and equipment	1 364	1 735	1 165	1 049	1 208	1 360	1 785	1 650
Apparel and Services	1 548	2 158	1 564	1 520	1 096	1 143	2 051	2 100
Transportation	7 426	8 086	5 970	5 794	6 791	6 855	9 574	9 126
Vehicle purchases (net outlay)	3 542	3 280	2 290	2 320	2 386	3 078	4 624	4 250
Gasoline and motor oil	1 460	1 496	1 257	1 295	1 397	1 191	1 640	1 686
Other vehicle expenses	2 157	2 570	2 055	1 975	2 562	2 369	2 906	2 838
Public transportation	267	739	369	204	446	217	403	352
Health Care	2 453	2 419	2 077	1 760	1 924	2 241	3 063	2 642
Entertainment	1 974	2 469	1 542	1 794	1 479	1 592	2 064	2 212
Personal Care Products and Services	519	628	570	432	523	459	727	697
Reading	96	157	89	54	41	107	128	117
Education	606	1 509	654	693	558	292	902	937
Tobacco Products and Smoking Supplies	283	175	227	127	194	257	235	258
Miscellaneous	534	787	464	240	884	436	724	638
Cash Contributions	1 298	1 553	1 203	844	672	585	2 312	2 003
Personal Insurance and Pensions	4 101	7 169	4 623	4 566	3 659	3 555	6 016	5 787
Life and other personal insurance	388	611	308	418	196	324	455	431
Pensions and Social Security	3 713	6 558	4 315	4 148	3 463	3 231	5 561	5 356

[1]Components of income and taxes are derived from "complete income" reporters only through 2003. Beginning in 2004, income imputation was implemented. As a result, all consumer units are considered to be complete income reporters.

Table 8-19. Consumer Expenditures, Averages by Selected Metropolitan Statistical Areas: Midwest Region, 2003–2004

(Number, dollar, percent.)

Item	All consumer units in the Midwest	Chicago	Detroit	Milwaukee	Minneapolis-St. Paul	Cleveland	Cincinnati	St. Louis	Kansas City
NUMBER OF CONSUMER UNITS (THOUSANDS)	26 489	3 165	2 013	763	1 259	1 281	1 007	1 026	813
CONSUMER UNIT CHARACTERISTICS									
Income Before Taxes[1]	53 149	65 545	62 728	51 958	69 717	51 796	54 627	61 082	55 719
Age of Reference Person	48.9	49.2	49.0	49.3	47.1	49.1	49.4	49.5	48.1
Average Number in Consumer Unit									
Persons	2.4	2.7	2.7	2.5	2.4	2.5	2.3	2.5	2.6
Children under 18 years	0.6	0.7	0.8	0.7	0.6	0.6	0.5	0.6	0.7
Persons 65 years and over	0.3	0.3	0.3	0.3	0.2	0.3	0.3	0.3	0.3
Earners	1.4	1.5	1.4	1.3	1.5	1.4	1.3	1.4	1.4
Vehicles	2.1	1.8	2.1	2.1	2.6	1.8	2.0	2.1	2.1
Percent Homeowner	72	71	78	65	73	73	61	74	71
AVERAGE ANNUAL EXPENDITURES	41 881	50 627	46 731	42 111	55 951	37 070	40 594	47 793	46 308
Food	5 338	6 023	5 726	5 189	6 549	4 589	5 333	5 976	6 092
Food at home	3 045	3 427	3 287	3 062	3 566	2 824	3 025	3 397	3 615
Cereals and bakery products	428	472	470	460	509	388	413	463	513
Meats, poultry, fish, and eggs	758	855	863	837	779	854	773	920	923
Dairy products	341	366	339	309	431	310	315	365	395
Fruits and vegetables	491	606	542	506	610	449	462	548	570
Other food at home	1 028	1 128	1 073	950	1 236	822	1 062	1 101	1 214
Food away from home	2 293	2 597	2 439	2 126	2 983	1 765	2 308	2 579	2 477
Alcoholic Beverages	415	493	380	531	761	337	426	636	411
Housing	13 036	18 114	15 011	14 575	18 282	12 616	13 573	14 330	15 129
Shelter	7 212	10 737	8 930	8 993	10 697	7 237	8 046	7 904	7 626
Owned dwellings	5 084	7 840	6 588	6 228	7 552	5 271	4 654	5 621	5 236
Rented dwellings	1 638	2 225	1 622	2 287	2 188	1 581	2 877	1 652	2 001
Other lodging	490	672	720	477	957	385	515	631	388
Utilities, fuels, and public services	2 906	3 383	3 070	2 790	2 928	3 287	2 685	3 178	3 419
Household operations	661	1 066	823	497	950	384	563	937	713
Housekeeping supplies	618	731	552	664	748	460	513	485	853
Household furnishings and equipment	1 639	2 198	1 635	1 632	2 960	1 248	1 766	1 826	2 518
Apparel and Services	1 617	1 938	2 170	1 720	2 240	1 180	1 624	2 260	2 007
Transportation	7 763	8 179	8 974	7 145	9 202	6 753	7 268	8 978	8 518
Vehicle purchases (net outlay)	3 545	3 618	3 473	3 261	3 878	2 744	3 317	4 737	3 996
Gasoline and motor oil	1 489	1 449	1 639	1 444	1 610	1 244	1 400	1 450	1 689
Other vehicle expenses	2 363	2 445	3 403	2 028	2 972	2 515	2 242	2 391	2 599
Public transportation	367	667	460	412	742	250	309	400	234
Health Care	2 724	2 704	2 005	2 643	2 928	2 161	2 341	2 837	2 813
Entertainment	2 093	2 329	2 343	2 002	3 407	1 695	2 077	2 266	2 095
Personal Care Products and Services	531	611	603	582	706	428	572	580	638
Reading	146	152	143	146	192	128	173	157	169
Education	862	1 505	1 075	748	1 218	719	781	1 117	814
Tobacco Products and Smoking Supplies	352	323	411	314	322	346	278	354	292
Miscellaneous	722	727	775	935	1 184	713	556	578	653
Cash Contributions	1 630	2 860	1 317	1 103	1 563	980	1 536	2 484	1 811
Personal Insurance and Pensions	4 653	4 669	5 797	4 478	7 398	4 426	4 056	5 239	4 866
Life and other personal insurance	431	317	475	450	470	295	322	632	394
Pensions and Social Security	4 222	4 352	5 322	4 028	6 928	4 131	3 734	4 607	4 472

[1]Components of income and taxes are derived from "complete income" reporters only through 2003. Beginning in 2004, income imputation was implemented. As a result, all consumer units are considered to be complete income reporters.

Table 8-20. Consumer Expenditures, Averages by Selected Metropolitan Statistical Areas: West Region, 2003–2004

(Number, dollar, percent.)

Item	All consumer units in the West	Los Angeles	San Francisco	San Diego	Portland	Seattle	Honolulu	Anchorage	Phoenix	Denver
NUMBER OF CONSUMER UNITS (THOUSANDS)	25 651	5 086	2 632	910	1 030	1 650	273	98	1 341	1 253
CONSUMER UNIT CHARACTERISTICS										
Income Before Taxes[1]	54 416	59 557	75 390	62 122	54 137	61 564	64 082	66 399	53 531	62 990
Age of Reference Person	46.9	47.4	47.5	49.2	49.0	48.6	52.1	44.2	46.5	44.7
Average Number in Consumer Unit										
Persons	2.6	2.9	2.6	2.6	2.4	2.3	2.7	2.7	2.5	2.5
Children under 18 years	0.7	0.8	0.6	0.6	0.6	0.5	0.5	0.9	0.7	0.7
Persons 65 years and over	0.3	0.3	0.3	0.4	0.3	0.3	0.4	0.1	0.3	0.2
Earners	1.4	1.5	1.4	1.4	1.3	1.4	1.5	1.5	1.3	1.5
Vehicles	2.0	1.9	1.9	2.0	2.1	2.4	1.7	2.4	1.8	2.1
Percent Homeowner	62	57	61	62	63	65	57	68	66	66
AVERAGE ANNUAL EXPENDITURES	46 717	52 652	56 162	53 949	47 762	52 843	48 339	53 520	46 628	48 719
Food	6 051	7 194	7 108	6 545	6 276	6 854	6 666	6 585	5 698	6 263
Food at home	3 531	4 064	3 896	3 472	3 724	3 977	3 592	3 969	3 296	3 805
Cereals and bakery products	481	536	518	463	491	526	499	494	450	514
Meats, poultry, fish, and eggs	886	1 076	975	818	878	958	860	954	823	948
Dairy products	385	426	390	357	432	457	317	472	366	416
Fruits and vegetables	639	799	789	709	684	683	693	711	575	645
Other food at home	1 141	1 227	1 225	1 126	1 238	1 352	1 223	1 338	1 081	1 281
Food away from home	2 520	3 131	3 212	3 073	2 552	2 877	3 075	2 615	2 403	2 458
Alcoholic Beverages	477	563	643	445	526	615	367	543	469	748
Housing	15 465	18 714	21 075	19 365	15 655	16 703	15 874	17 438	14 524	15 762
Shelter	9 571	12 054	14 527	13 041	9 363	10 381	10 324	10 811	8 374	9 790
Owned dwellings	6 064	7 378	9 229	7 575	6 038	7 011	5 629	7 329	5 743	6 314
Rented dwellings	2 958	4 114	4 552	4 690	2 597	2 638	4 160	2 977	2 265	3 001
Other lodging	549	562	746	777	728	732	535	505	366	475
Utilities, fuels, and public services	2 621	2 713	2 670	2 633	2 794	2 631	2 606	2 824	2 851	2 878
Household operations	837	1 124	1 321	1 100	913	760	770	868	983	836
Housekeeping supplies	572	652	645	723	573	681	593	740	474	587
Household furnishings and equipment	1 865	2 172	1 912	1 868	2 012	2 249	1 582	2 196	1 843	1 670
Apparel and Services	1 885	2 514	2 321	2 114	1 929	2 098	1 467	1 645	1 797	1 656
Transportation	8 807	9 733	8 878	9 871	7 276	9 345	8 778	10 493	10 529	8 610
Vehicle purchases (net outlay)	4 004	4 096	3 441	4 532	2 845	4 204	4 356	5 129	5 612	3 583
Gasoline and motor oil	1 618	1 938	1 590	1 733	1 433	1 528	1 277	1 622	1 455	1 447
Other vehicle expenses	2 640	3 116	3 018	2 831	2 537	2 806	2 218	2 897	3 093	2 963
Public transportation	545	583	830	775	461	807	927	845	369	617
Health Care	2 543	2 309	2 775	2 605	2 972	2 992	2 668	2 858	2 609	2 647
Entertainment	2 516	2 373	2 496	2 412	2 443	2 992	2 941	3 182	2 226	3 048
Personal Care Products and Services	613	810	643	760	629	677	649	680	626	613
Reading	148	151	197	158	210	208	149	213	144	122
Education	996	896	1 072	1 271	1 048	1 110	1 020	775	542	1 015
Tobacco Products and Smoking Supplies	224	190	179	191	293	255	270	403	306	308
Miscellaneous	752	754	755	763	1 432	862	825	1 027	839	929
Cash Contributions	1 508	1 329	1 554	2 072	1 846	2 123	1 218	1 553	1 415	1 353
Personal Insurance and Pensions	4 733	5 121	6 467	5 377	5 228	6 008	5 447	6 125	4 902	5 645
Life and other personal insurance	352	313	471	323	542	413	554	531	444	333
Pensions and Social Security	4 381	4 808	5 996	5 054	4 685	5 595	4 893	5 594	4 458	5 312

[1]Components of income and taxes are derived from "complete income" reporters only through 2003. Beginning in 2004, income imputation was implemented. As a result, all consumer units are considered to be complete income reporters.

Table 8-21. Consumer Expenditures, Averages for Single Men by Income Before Taxes, 2003–2004

(Number, dollar, percent.)

Item	All single males	Complete reporting of income							
		Total	Less than $5,000	$5,000 to $9,999	$10,000 to $14,999	$15,000 to $19,999	$20,000 to $29,999	$30,000 to $39,999	$40,000 and over
NUMBER OF CONSUMER UNITS (THOUSANDS)	15 226	14 294	1 309	1 783	1 682	1 473	2 219	1 827	4 002
CONSUMER UNIT CHARACTERISTICS									
Income Before Taxes[1]	31 801	31 801	1 449	7 537	12 359	17 114	24 639	34 175	68 991
Income After Taxes[1]	29 961	29 961	1 411	7 506	12 271	16 840	23 647	32 571	63 867
Age of Reference Person	45.4	45.4	33.4	46.1	52.7	49.0	46.4	43.9	44.9
Average Number in Consumer Unit									
Persons	1.0	1.0	1.0	1.0	1.0	1.0	1.0	1.0	1.0
Children under 18 years	X	X	X	X	X	X	X	X	X
Persons 65 years and over	0.2	0.2	0.1	0.3	0.4	0.3	0.2	0.1	0.1
Earners	0.7	0.8	0.7	0.5	0.5	0.7	0.8	0.9	0.9
Vehicles	1.2	1.2	0.7	0.8	1.0	1.1	1.2	1.4	1.6
Percent Homeowner	45	45	17	29	41	40	43	50	64
With mortgage	23	23	5	5	8	12	16	28	49
Without mortgage	22	22	12	24	32	28	27	22	15
AVERAGE ANNUAL EXPENDITURES	26 325	26 948	13 673	13 407	16 760	18 925	23 627	28 433	45 077
Food	3 299	3 400	2 377	2 007	2 749	2 696	3 121	3 446	4 688
Food at home	1 513	1 542	1 099	1 062	1 604	1 351	1 514	1 615	1 824
Cereals and bakery products	202	208	151	154	265	191	189	222	227
Meats, poultry, fish, and eggs	390	391	253	279	422	348	408	422	439
Dairy products	158	164	126	104	177	134	172	171	190
Fruits and vegetables	258	263	193	167	261	232	260	271	319
Other food at home	505	516	376	357	479	446	485	530	648
Food away from home	1 786	1 858	1 279	944	1 145	1 345	1 607	1 831	2 865
Alcoholic Beverages	482	514	312	255	406	361	440	468	791
Housing	8 934	8 994	4 330	4 855	5 914	6 758	8 057	9 797	14 559
Shelter	6 017	6 038	3 008	3 309	3 713	4 484	5 350	6 524	9 954
Owned dwellings	2 791	2 809	639	861	1 192	1 448	1 819	2 808	6 114
Rented dwellings	2 927	2 922	2 093	2 246	2 344	2 959	3 379	3 572	3 173
Other lodging	300	308	276	201	177	78	151	144	667
Utilities, fuels, and public services	1 699	1 699	839	1 020	1 385	1 537	1 746	1 944	2 338
Household operations	274	279	112	100	234	156	240	337	472
Housekeeping supplies	230	245	139	140	263	222	166	284	326
Household furnishings and equipment	713	732	233	285	319	359	555	708	1 469
Apparel and Services	749	775	352	521	422	436	622	776	1 314
Transportation	4 622	4 728	2 056	2 325	2 763	3 388	4 626	5 743	7 579
Vehicle purchases (net outlay)	2 007	2 069	686	974	1 215	976	2 151	2 748	3 415
Gasoline and motor oil	906	911	563	574	640	821	937	1 099	1 221
Other vehicle expenses	1 451	1 487	676	660	767	1 469	1 365	1 673	2 407
Public transportation	258	262	132	117	142	122	173	223	537
Health Care	1 333	1 356	618	759	1 283	1 298	1 294	1 530	1 861
Health insurance	656	661	228	408	715	614	647	795	856
Medical services	387	397	229	153	214	359	331	451	662
Drugs	237	242	115	142	310	292	281	224	259
Medical supplies	53	56	45	56	43	32	35	59	84
Entertainment	1 317	1 339	769	524	816	806	1 468	1 346	2 208
Personal Care Products and Services	206	215	128	95	199	150	186	244	313
Reading	87	90	50	62	63	69	89	78	140
Education	728	750	1 773	1 028	877	595	322	369	698
Tobacco Products and Smoking Supplies	242	248	163	262	238	266	289	227	253
Miscellaneous	561	591	204	206	209	499	588	453	1 113
Cash Contributions	1 233	1 259	279	223	330	609	866	1 205	2 913
Personal Insurance and Pensions	2 533	2 690	261	285	492	995	1 660	2 751	6 647
Life and other personal insurance	135	137	34	37	73	112	93	124	282
Pensions and Social Security	2 399	2 553	227	248	419	883	1 567	2 627	6 364

[1]Components of income and taxes are derived from "complete income" reporters only through 2003. Beginning in 2004, income imputation was implemented. As a result, all consumer units are considered to be complete income reporters.
X = Not applicable.

Table 8-22. Consumer Expenditures, Averages for Single Women by Income Before Taxes, 2003–2004

(Number, dollar, percent.)

Item	All single females	Complete reporting of income							
		Total	Less than $5,000	$5,000 to $9,999	$10,000 to $14,999	$15,000 to $19,999	$20,000 to $29,999	$30,000 to $39,999	$40,000 and over
NUMBER OF CONSUMER UNITS (THOUSANDS)	18 581	17 338	1 689	3 136	3 289	1 965	2 619	1 639	3 000
CONSUMER UNIT CHARACTERISTICS									
Income Before Taxes[1]	24 256	24 256	2 352	7 895	12 357	17 311	24 475	34 222	65 650
Income After Taxes[1]	23 107	23 107	2 380	7 850	12 296	17 035	23 775	32 584	60 794
Age of Reference Person	56.8	56.8	41.4	59.6	66.8	62.5	56.4	51.5	51.1
Average Number in Consumer Unit									
Persons	1.0	1.0	1.0	1.0	1.0	1.0	1.0	1.0	1.0
Children under 18 years	X	X	X	X	X	X	X	X	X
Persons 65 years and over	0.4	0.4	0.2	0.5	0.7	0.6	0.4	0.2	0.2
Earners	0.5	0.5	0.5	0.3	0.3	0.5	0.7	0.8	0.9
Vehicles	0.9	0.9	0.5	0.5	0.8	0.9	1.0	1.1	1.2
Percent Homeowner	55	54	23	37	57	64	61	59	72
With mortgage	21	21	7	7	10	15	22	35	50
Without mortgage	34	34	17	30	48	49	39	25	22
AVERAGE ANNUAL EXPENDITURES	23 117	23 684	12 657	12 295	17 219	21 919	25 210	29 799	44 721
Food	2 709	2 794	1 991	1 940	2 158	2 680	2 867	3 320	4 297
Food at home	1 670	1 726	1 178	1 433	1 542	1 724	1 788	1 992	2 226
Cereals and bakery products	239	245	179	228	235	276	258	253	264
Meats, poultry, fish, and eggs	382	391	281	353	350	376	398	430	499
Dairy products	183	191	132	152	175	194	204	210	243
Fruits and vegetables	312	324	197	257	313	331	326	380	418
Other food at home	555	575	390	443	469	546	601	719	801
Food away from home	1 039	1 068	813	507	616	956	1 078	1 329	2 071
Alcoholic Beverages	198	211	122	99	124	163	126	248	527
Housing	9 051	9 163	5 101	5 106	7 142	8 696	9 776	11 668	16 183
Shelter	5 489	5 533	3 342	3 158	4 030	5 064	5 621	7 170	10 237
Owned dwellings	2 815	2 829	1 041	869	1 643	2 590	2 784	3 851	6 824
Rented dwellings	2 458	2 483	2 159	2 181	2 287	2 290	2 671	3 130	2 802
Other lodging	216	222	141	107	100	184	166	189	611
Utilities, fuels, and public services	1 872	1 876	988	1 298	1 756	1 996	2 142	2 237	2 602
Household operations	490	491	92	145	543	487	663	484	875
Housekeeping supplies	351	373	249	225	288	426	392	470	543
Household furnishings and equipment	849	890	429	280	525	723	958	1 307	1 925
Apparel and Services	997	1 045	669	548	550	892	915	1 272	2 265
Transportation	3 292	3 338	1 383	1 212	2 036	2 969	4 287	4 882	6 648
Vehicle purchases (net outlay)	1 350	1 362	393	342	795	1 142	2 036	2 037	2 784
Gasoline and motor oil	603	609	448	340	423	601	701	861	972
Other vehicle expenses	1 086	1 107	386	442	710	1 019	1 300	1 682	2 211
Public transportation	253	260	155	88	108	207	250	302	681
Health Care	1 866	1 905	801	1 361	2 356	2 275	2 198	1 856	2 118
Health insurance	944	950	376	720	1 235	1 254	1 074	856	942
Medical services	366	375	201	168	398	320	490	399	588
Drugs	477	496	196	420	655	600	553	451	467
Medical supplies	79	84	29	52	68	100	80	150	120
Entertainment	928	953	540	476	690	795	1 061	1 298	1 776
Personal Care Products and Services	437	455	257	235	316	426	506	519	858
Reading	102	104	42	44	83	104	124	124	196
Education	429	434	1 010	535	294	377	219	204	503
Tobacco Products and Smoking Supplies	129	132	110	127	113	131	154	144	146
Miscellaneous	400	416	207	179	266	392	527	505	813
Cash Contributions	863	898	263	227	702	1 143	929	907	1 980
Personal Insurance and Pensions	1 717	1 835	161	207	388	879	1 520	2 851	6 412
Life and other personal insurance	166	173	57	86	136	183	173	228	330
Pensions and Social Security	1 551	1 662	104	120	252	696	1 348	2 623	6 082

[1]Components of income and taxes are derived from "complete income" reporters only through 2003. Beginning in 2004, income imputation was implemented. As a result, all consumer units are considered to be complete income reporters.
X = Not applicable.

Table 8-23. Consumer Expenditures, Averages for Age Groups by Income Before Taxes: Reference Person Under 25 Years of Age, 2003–2004

(Number, dollar, percent.)

Item		Complete reporting of income						
	Total	Less than $5,000	$5,000 to $9,999	$10,000 to $14,999	$15,000 to $19,999	$20,000 to $29,999	$30,000 to $39,999	$40,000 and over
NUMBER OF CONSUMER UNITS (THOUSANDS)	8 175	1 736	1 425	978	791	1 153	739	1 353
CONSUMER UNIT CHARACTERISTICS								
Income Before Taxes[1]	21 855	2 613	7 169	12 082	17 262	24 510	34 700	62 488
Income After Taxes[1]	21 488	2 619	7 179	12 203	17 347	24 301	33 927	60 716
Age of Reference Person	21.4	20.3	20.8	21.5	21.8	21.8	22.2	22.4
Average Number in Consumer Unit								
Persons	1.9	1.2	1.3	1.6	1.9	2.3	2.4	2.7
Children under 18 years	0.4	0.1	0.2	0.4	0.5	0.7	0.6	0.5
Persons 65 years and over	(2)	(2)	(2)	(2)	(2)	(2)	(2)	(2)
Earners	1.3	0.9	0.9	1.1	1.2	1.4	1.6	2.0
Vehicles	1.1	0.5	0.7	1.1	1.2	1.4	1.6	2.0
Percent Distribution								
Male	48	45	49	44	49	47	47	51
Female	52	55	51	56	51	53	53	49
Percent Homeowner	15	3	6	7	17	17	24	39
With mortgage	9	1	2	1	9	9	17	30
Without mortgage	6	2	5	6	8	7	7	8
AVERAGE ANNUAL EXPENDITURES	24 051	11 642	14 838	20 368	22 709	26 294	31 822	45 598
Food	3 632	2 226	2 431	2 794	3 280	3 716	4 863	5 959
Food at home	1 826	1 094	1 152	1 481	1 582	2 080	2 371	2 909
Cereals and bakery products	262	165	169	190	210	311	356	409
Meats, poultry, fish, and eggs	456	257	243	366	396	482	634	792
Dairy products	201	118	118	170	163	236	257	325
Fruits and vegetables	282	179	177	209	227	344	369	439
Other food at home	626	374	444	546	584	707	755	944
Food away from home	1 806	1 132	1 280	1 314	1 699	1 635	2 492	3 050
Alcoholic Beverages	528	288	305	490	463	460	583	1 049
Housing	7 477	3 277	4 781	6 128	7 514	8 728	10 715	13 690
Shelter	4 778	2 231	3 298	3 982	4 958	5 611	6 748	8 292
Owned dwellings	905	103	199	153	788	666	1 381	3 232
Rented dwellings	3 643	1 870	2 724	3 554	4 004	4 840	5 261	4 834
Other lodging	231	257	375	274	166	105	106	226
Utilities, fuels, and public services	1 395	490	740	1 192	1 564	1 717	2 077	2 645
Household operations	253	41	83	190	247	353	461	552
Housekeeping supplies	242	140	136	219	169	249	328	433
Household furnishings and equipment	809	375	524	546	576	798	1 101	1 769
Apparel and Services	1 292	752	850	1 027	949	1 314	1 664	2 411
Transportation	4 832	1 535	2 108	4 584	5 248	5 958	6 612	9 935
Vehicle purchases (net outlay)	2 229	492	610	2 535	2 532	2 959	2 823	4 816
Gasoline and motor oil	1 059	534	745	911	1 080	1 240	1 451	1 789
Other vehicle expenses	1 338	368	643	978	1 437	1 610	2 062	2 885
Public transportation	207	141	110	159	199	148	276	445
Health Care	611	172	223	409	447	713	784	1 627
Health insurance	304	65	70	148	255	402	452	835
Medical services	159	31	65	151	90	145	182	466
Drugs	114	60	71	76	64	123	112	262
Medical supplies	34	16	16	34	[3]38	42	38	64
Entertainment	1 098	611	741	804	1 007	1 335	1 588	1 840
Personal Care Products and Services	333	204	217	369	294	305	341	603
Reading	53	37	45	48	46	64	54	81
Education	1 668	2 038	2 188	2 339	1 578	920	816	1 318
Tobacco Products and Smoking Supplies	238	111	141	228	306	319	342	342
Miscellaneous	276	155	252	195	215	279	275	557
Cash Contributions	342	86	154	222	177	362	431	987
Personal Insurance and Pensions	1 670	149	403	732	1 183	1 823	2 755	5 199
Life and other personal insurance	36	[3]3	[3]11	[3]26	29	41	57	102
Pensions and Social Security	1 634	146	391	706	1 154	1 782	2 698	5 098

[1]Components of income and taxes are derived from "complete income" reporters only through 2003. Beginning in 2004, income imputation was implemented. As a result, all consumer units are considered to be complete income reporters.
[2]Value less than 0.05.
[3]Data are likely to have large sampling errors.

Table 8-24. Consumer Expenditures, Averages for Age Groups by Income Before Taxes: Reference Person 25 to 34 Years of Age, 2003–2004

(Number, dollar, percent.)

Item	Total	Complete reporting of income								
		Less than $5,000	$5,000 to $9,999	$10,000 to $14,999	$15,000 to $19,999	$20,000 to $29,999	$30,000 to $39,999	$40,000 to $49,999	$50,000 to $69,999	$70,000 and over
NUMBER OF CONSUMER UNITS (THOUSANDS)	18 396	488	748	1 039	1 223	2 599	2 541	2 064	3 364	4 330
CONSUMER UNIT CHARACTERISTICS										
Income Before Taxes[1]	51 650	910	7 680	12 605	17 409	24 978	34 418	44 316	59 018	107 895
Income After Taxes[1]	49 863	1 327	7 947	13 107	17 919	25 057	33 443	43 052	56 826	102 775
Age of Reference Person	29.7	29.5	28.7	29.1	28.7	29.3	29.3	29.8	29.9	30.5
Average Number in Consumer Unit										
Persons	2.9	2.4	2.5	2.8	2.8	2.7	2.7	2.9	3.0	3.1
Children under 18 years	1.1	1.0	1.2	1.4	1.2	1.1	1.0	1.1	1.0	1.0
Persons 65 years and over	(2)	(2)	(2)	(2)	(2)	(2)	(2)	(2)	(2)	(2)
Earners	1.5	0.8	0.8	1.0	1.2	1.3	1.4	1.6	1.8	1.9
Vehicles	1.8	1.0	0.9	1.1	1.2	1.3	1.6	1.9	2.2	2.3
Percent Distribution										
Male	50	35	30	34	44	47	53	58	52	56
Female	50	65	70	66	56	53	47	42	48	44
Percent Homeowner	49	21	18	21	18	31	40	51	62	76
With mortgage	42	14	8	8	10	22	33	46	57	72
Without mortgage	7	7	11	13	7	8	7	5	5	5
AVERAGE ANNUAL EXPENDITURES	42 520	20 145	18 785	21 768	24 013	27 543	34 479	39 155	48 363	69 666
Food	5 627	3 846	3 635	4 018	4 262	4 009	5 160	5 330	5 945	7 867
Food at home	3 103	2 400	2 595	2 677	2 890	2 521	3 130	2 976	3 038	3 786
Cereals and bakery products	426	362	361	382	396	352	431	432	412	504
Meats, poultry, fish, and eggs	791	598	843	765	699	672	832	767	705	939
Dairy products	337	258	236	251	341	269	344	340	339	404
Fruits and vegetables	514	410	346	478	494	426	521	485	493	633
Other food at home	1 035	771	809	802	960	801	1 003	952	1 089	1 306
Food away from home	2 524	1 447	1 040	1 340	1 372	1 488	2 030	2 353	2 908	4 082
Alcoholic Beverages	517	189	163	212	285	292	439	494	584	859
Housing	14 511	7 900	6 697	7 928	8 867	10 216	11 838	13 369	15 563	23 578
Shelter	8 833	5 260	4 214	4 845	5 376	6 355	7 373	8 025	9 315	14 320
Owned dwellings	4 782	1 300	784	703	881	1 855	2 785	3 843	5 623	10 671
Rented dwellings	3 809	3 861	3 310	4 091	4 431	4 425	4 459	4 004	3 437	3 090
Other lodging	241	[3]99	[3]120	[3]51	64	74	129	177	255	560
Utilities, fuels, and public services	2 638	1 665	1 629	1 882	1 936	2 184	2 335	2 656	2 987	3 472
Household operations	919	197	202	347	345	478	596	738	993	1 905
Housekeeping supplies	498	345	262	271	479	286	417	441	587	724
Household furnishings and equipment	1 624	432	390	583	732	913	1 117	1 509	1 680	3 159
Apparel and Services	2 073	1 036	1 137	1 484	1 253	1 362	1 855	1 908	1 984	3 340
Transportation	8 400	3 320	3 537	3 922	3 619	5 364	7 182	7 536	11 140	13 054
Vehicle purchases (net outlay)	4 031	[3]933	1 571	1 794	1 006	2 403	3 555	3 270	5 815	6 427
Gasoline and motor oil	1 551	965	737	905	1 053	1 227	1 346	1 635	1 878	2 072
Other vehicle expenses	2 456	1 138	999	1 048	1 325	1 533	2 043	2 364	3 097	3 854
Public transportation	363	284	230	176	235	201	238	267	349	702
Health Care	1 514	483	431	517	612	919	1 297	1 654	1 974	2 366
Health insurance	829	245	185	192	336	480	698	908	1 093	1 341
Medical services	408	109	111	157	122	266	343	443	553	627
Drugs	215	102	98	140	126	138	209	257	250	289
Medical supplies	63	[3]28	[3]38	28	28	35	47	47	78	108
Entertainment	2 086	801	736	889	1 084	1 312	1 411	1 734	2 287	3 888
Personal Care Products and Services	542	364	241	350	338	376	449	522	559	856
Reading	98	57	41	52	40	56	79	88	106	176
Education	691	890	1 027	751	831	363	428	596	755	900
Tobacco Products and Smoking Supplies	290	169	233	331	401	333	287	394	284	205
Miscellaneous	592	284	242	300	459	439	445	706	728	818
Cash Contributions	804	545	228	206	614	476	657	827	878	1 346
Personal Insurance and Pensions	4 773	259	437	807	1 347	2 025	2 952	3 997	5 578	10 411
Life and other personal insurance	219	[3]78	[3]69	63	61	100	98	201	244	473
Pensions and Social Security	4 554	181	368	744	1 286	1 925	2 854	3 796	5 334	9 939

[1]Components of income and taxes are derived from "complete income" reporters only through 2003. Beginning in 2004, income imputation was implemented. As a result, all consumer units are considered to be complete income reporters.
[2]Value less than 0.05.
[3]Data are likely to have large sampling errors.

Table 8-25. Consumer Expenditures, Averages for Age Groups by Income Before Taxes: Reference Person 35 to 44 Years of Age, 2003–2004

(Number, dollar, percent.)

Item		Complete reporting of income								
	Total	Less than $5,000	$5,000 to $9,999	$10,000 to $14,999	$15,000 to $19,999	$20,000 to $29,999	$30,000 to $39,999	$40,000 to $49,999	$50,000 to $69,999	$70,000 and over
NUMBER OF CONSUMER UNITS (THOUSANDS)	22 669	631	760	923	884	2 347	2 628	2 448	4 320	7 729
CONSUMER UNIT CHARACTERISTICS										
Income Before Taxes[1]	63 597	-1 579	7 880	12 623	17 517	24 777	34 485	44 499	59 500	115 779
Income After Taxes[1]	61 086	-1 269	8 211	13 027	17 764	25 003	33 889	43 754	57 636	109 693
Age of Reference Person	39.7	40.0	39.6	40.0	39.8	39.7	39.5	39.7	39.5	39.8
Average Number in Consumer Unit										
Persons	3.2	2.6	2.5	2.6	3.0	2.8	3.0	3.2	3.3	3.6
Children under 18 years	1.3	1.1	1.1	1.1	1.3	1.2	1.2	1.3	1.3	1.5
Persons 65 years and over	(2)	(2)	(2)	(2)	(2)	(2)	(2)	(2)	(2)	(2)
Earners	1.6	0.9	0.7	1.0	1.1	1.3	1.5	1.7	1.8	2.0
Vehicles	2.1	1.0	0.9	1.1	1.2	1.5	1.8	2.2	2.4	2.7
Percent Distribution										
Male	50	37	36	39	45	42	46	53	56	54
Female	50	63	64	61	55	58	54	47	44	46
Percent Homeowner										
With mortgage	69	36	30	33	34	44	60	69	77	89
	58	21	15	18	22	30	49	57	66	81
Without mortgage	11	15	15	15	11	14	11	12	11	8
AVERAGE ANNUAL EXPENDITURES	49 826	23 357	17 320	21 899	22 415	28 181	33 901	40 466	49 589	76 493
Food	6 711	4 495	3 191	4 601	3 706	4 603	5 308	5 862	6 681	9 124
Food at home	3 844	3 165	2 035	3 413	2 549	3 053	3 166	3 604	3 707	4 852
Cereals and bakery products	552	481	305	468	411	430	458	516	530	692
Meats, poultry, fish, and eggs	991	883	601	1 058	730	878	820	997	952	1 165
Dairy products	429	377	201	367	292	318	359	394	419	547
Fruits and vegetables	616	504	306	498	384	487	553	593	559	787
Other food at home	1 256	921	621	1 022	733	940	975	1 103	1 247	1 660
Food away from home	2 867	1 330	1 156	1 188	1 156	1 549	2 142	2 258	2 975	4 272
Alcoholic Beverages	516	338	112	211	184	204	288	529	578	762
Housing	16 561	9 144	7 137	8 296	8 865	10 175	11 611	13 519	15 451	25 116
Shelter	9 781	5 755	4 355	4 948	5 553	6 324	7 113	8 015	8 955	14 682
Owned dwellings	6 978	2 434	1 166	1 290	1 549	2 469	3 972	5 256	6 458	12 447
Rented dwellings	2 405	3 219	3 156	3 576	3 918	3 787	3 015	2 532	2 159	1 421
Other lodging	399	[3]102	[3]33	[3]81	[3]86	67	126	227	337	814
Utilities, fuels, and public services	3 230	2 154	1 918	2 206	2 192	2 448	2 715	3 071	3 326	4 096
Household operations	977	190	194	228	271	286	370	487	759	1 982
Housekeeping supplies	678	257	291	405	303	394	496	510	669	1 014
Household furnishings and equipment	1 896	788	379	509	548	723	918	1 436	1 743	3 342
Apparel and Services	2 157	1 690	1 091	1 283	1 510	1 250	1 651	1 271	1 938	3 299
Transportation	9 097	3 815	2 499	3 415	3 417	5 208	6 431	7 848	10 358	13 281
Vehicle purchases (net outlay)	4 239	[3]1 717	[3]931	1 398	1 071	2 334	2 818	3 465	5 208	6 236
Gasoline and motor oil	1 739	866	718	930	1 032	1 182	1 455	1 708	1 902	2 274
Other vehicle expenses	2 691	1 074	695	926	1 187	1 500	1 936	2 426	2 900	3 984
Public transportation	428	158	156	161	126	193	223	249	347	787
Health Care	2 212	757	577	862	879	1 337	1 672	2 142	2 415	3 160
Health insurance	1 163	266	239	364	415	662	913	1 207	1 379	1 612
Medical services	631	259	154	235	245	404	447	484	605	994
Drugs	321	207	146	209	195	228	248	359	319	413
Medical supplies	97	[3]26	[3]38	[3]55	[3]25	43	64	93	112	141
Entertainment	2 547	720	633	771	869	1 258	1 484	2 005	2 469	4 244
Personal Care Products and Services	658	274	311	337	322	355	460	558	615	1 002
Reading	120	45	50	47	34	54	69	91	115	203
Education	750	242	242	316	139	232	262	350	566	1 512
Tobacco Products and Smoking Supplies	342	317	409	397	350	355	381	436	369	267
Miscellaneous	715	729	383	339	379	505	410	640	830	954
Cash Contributions	1 286	326	237	241	452	571	764	1 072	1 283	2 151
Personal Insurance and Pensions	6 155	465	450	784	1 308	2 075	3 110	4 144	5 921	11 419
Life and other personal insurance	386	153	70	62	136	127	196	279	360	694
Pensions and Social Security	5 770	312	380	722	1 171	1 948	2 914	3 865	5 562	10 725

[1]Components of income and taxes are derived from "complete income" reporters only through 2003. Beginning in 2004, income imputation was implemented. As a result, all consumer units are considered to be complete income reporters.
[2]Value less than 0.05.
[3]Data are likely to have large sampling errors.

Table 8-26. Consumer Expenditures, Averages for Age Groups by Income Before Taxes: Reference Person 45 to 54 Years of Age, 2003–2004

(Number, dollar, percent.)

Item	Total	Complete reporting of income								
		Less than $5,000	$5,000 to $9,999	$10,000 to $14,999	$15,000 to $19,999	$20,000 to $29,999	$30,000 to $39,999	$40,000 to $49,999	$50,000 to $69,999	$70,000 and over
NUMBER OF CONSUMER UNITS (THOUSANDS)	21 880	478	724	990	1 091	2 040	2 147	2 175	3 782	8 451
CONSUMER UNIT CHARACTERISTICS										
Income Before Taxes[1]	69 489	-1 636	7 817	12 622	17 251	24 772	34 860	44 555	59 259	122 796
Income After Taxes[1]	65 744	-1 892	7 834	12 945	17 282	24 266	33 953	42 894	56 106	115 263
Age of Reference Person	49.4	49.2	49.5	49.3	49.4	49.3	49.5	49.2	49.4	49.4
Average Number in Consumer Unit										
Persons	2.7	1.8	1.8	2.2	2.2	2.2	2.3	2.5	2.7	3.1
Children under 18 years	0.6	0.4	0.4	0.6	0.5	0.5	0.5	0.5	0.6	0.7
Persons 65 years and over	(2)	(2)	(2)	(2)	(2)	(2)	0.1	(2)	(2)	(2)
Earners	1.7	0.8	0.5	0.9	1.1	1.3	1.5	1.6	1.8	2.2
Vehicles	2.4	1.2	0.8	1.1	1.5	1.6	2.0	2.3	2.6	3.2
Percent Distribution										
Males	51	43	38	40	45	42	49	46	54	56
Females	49	57	62	60	55	58	51	54	46	44
Percent Homeowner	76	46	38	45	52	57	65	74	84	93
With mortgage	57	25	19	23	28	34	45	51	65	77
Without mortgage	19	21	19	22	24	23	20	23	19	17
AVERAGE ANNUAL EXPENDITURES	52 775	26 583	16 125	19 819	24 444	28 159	33 396	37 743	49 027	81 407
Food	6 907	4 720	2 877	3 432	4 761	4 410	4 927	5 567	6 811	9 590
Food at home	3 981	3 046	2 236	2 632	3 347	3 069	3 098	3 252	4 068	5 048
Cereals and bakery products	540	442	306	418	465	409	397	458	556	676
Meats, poultry, fish, and eggs	1 078	844	622	690	988	953	882	881	1 112	1 314
Dairy products	420	318	238	242	357	297	330	361	428	538
Fruits and vegetables	663	487	422	432	537	464	538	514	668	859
Other food at home	1 279	954	649	850	1 000	946	951	1 038	1 303	1 662
Food away from home	2 926	1 674	641	800	1 414	1 341	1 829	2 315	2 743	4 542
Alcoholic Beverages	509	194	134	169	177	211	278	378	421	848
Housing	16 070	9 869	6 591	7 663	8 756	9 499	11 403	12 065	14 725	23 592
Shelter	9 311	5 949	3 741	4 610	4 817	5 518	6 458	6 881	8 376	13 794
Owned dwellings	6 936	3 108	1 352	1 851	2 219	2 704	3 667	4 513	6 491	11 510
Rented dwellings	1 669	2 509	2 355	2 728	2 523	2 684	2 591	2 126	1 440	833
Other lodging	706	[3]333	[3]34	[3]32	76	131	199	243	444	1 450
Utilities, fuels, and public services	3 389	2 220	1 946	2 209	2 221	2 553	2 771	3 038	3 416	4 304
Household operations	669	299	138	147	198	234	309	362	478	1 219
Housekeeping supplies	721	559	249	286	439	379	587	533	648	1 061
Household furnishings and equipment	1 981	841	517	411	1 080	814	1 278	1 250	1 807	3 214
Apparel and Services	2 171	1 520	870	1 130	1 140	1 112	1 260	1 466	1 940	3 354
Transportation	9 676	4 630	2 377	3 284	3 914	5 795	6 130	6 971	9 638	14 631
Vehicle purchases (net outlay)	4 240	[3]2 393	[3]951	1 223	1 373	2 456	2 290	2 669	4 332	6 640
Gasoline and motor oil	1 839	802	645	900	1 104	1 250	1 451	1 574	1 945	2 467
Other vehicle expenses	3 091	1 132	643	1 057	1 281	1 889	2 170	2 515	2 988	4 603
Public transportation	505	302	139	104	156	200	219	212	374	921
Health Care	2 631	1 172	979	1 232	1 498	1 592	2 014	2 316	2 695	3 628
Health insurance	1 250	430	361	602	664	787	985	1 148	1 379	1 672
Medical services	770	262	276	360	405	342	515	603	723	1 168
Drugs	475	429	238	228	369	416	417	437	461	587
Medical supplies	136	50	103	42	59	47	97	128	133	200
Entertainment	2 651	1 865	555	768	962	1 259	1 494	1 680	2 470	4 273
Personal Care Products and Services	676	370	294	243	310	414	460	520	617	1 010
Reading	153	74	31	31	68	67	80	110	140	250
Education	1 479	265	123	163	173	279	359	416	835	3 125
Tobacco Products and Smoking Supplies	385	286	357	463	432	410	403	373	394	367
Miscellaneous	820	465	295	216	452	365	570	700	881	1 184
Cash Contributions	1 686	575	263	181	446	699	756	944	1 351	3 023
Personal Insurance and Pensions	6 960	578	381	843	1 355	2 046	3 262	4 237	6 111	12 533
Life and other personal insurance	563	221	86	114	229	204	316	338	454	975
Pensions and Social Security	6 397	357	294	729	1 126	1 842	2 946	3 899	5 657	11 558

[1]Components of income and taxes are derived from "complete income" reporters only through 2003. Beginning in 2004, income imputation was implemented. As a result, all consumer units are considered to be complete income reporters.
[2]Value less than 0.05.
[3]Data are likely to have large sampling errors.

Table 8-27. Consumer Expenditures, Averages for Age Groups by Income Before Taxes: Reference Person 55 to 64 Years of Age, 2003–2004

(Number, dollar, percent.)

Item		Complete reporting of income								
	Total	Less than $5,000	$5,000 to $9,999	$10,000 to $14,999	$15,000 to $19,999	$20,000 to $29,999	$30,000 to $39,999	$40,000 to $49,999	$50,000 to $69,999	$70,000 and over
NUMBER OF CONSUMER UNITS (THOUSANDS)	15 878	496	959	973	983	1 879	1 734	1 622	2 486	4 746
CONSUMER UNIT CHARACTERISTICS										
Income Before Taxes[1]	60 312	1 525	8 012	12 537	17 379	24 745	34 623	44 565	58 689	125 407
Income After Taxes[1]	57 438	1 496	7 940	12 543	17 316	24 390	33 576	43 149	56 333	118 063
Age of Reference Person	59.1	59.4	59.9	59.9	59.7	59.7	59.3	59.2	58.8	58.5
Average Number in Consumer Unit										
Persons	2.1	1.5	1.4	1.7	1.8	1.9	2.0	2.1	2.3	2.5
Children under 18 years	0.2	[2]0.1	[2]0.1	0.2	0.2	0.2	0.2	0.2	0.2	0.2
Persons 65 years and over	0.1	(3)	[2]0.1	0.1	0.1	0.1	0.1	0.1	0.1	0.1
Earners	1.3	0.5	0.3	0.5	0.8	1.0	1.2	1.4	1.5	1.9
Vehicles	2.2	1.3	1.0	1.5	1.5	1.8	2.2	2.2	2.5	2.9
Percent Distribution										
Males	51	40	40	35	42	39	47	51	57	63
Females	49	60	60	65	58	61	53	49	43	37
Percent Homeowner	82	56	47	64	65	78	83	85	90	95
With mortgage	45	22	15	22	25	33	40	48	55	62
Without mortgage	37	34	32	41	40	45	42	37	35	33
AVERAGE ANNUAL EXPENDITURES	46 869	20 703	16 172	22 832	23 083	30 266	34 211	38 298	47 573	79 616
Food	5 848	3 015	2 528	3 364	3 467	4 667	4 902	5 181	6 019	8 838
Food at home	3 404	2 047	1 730	2 291	2 262	2 969	3 140	3 140	3 797	4 528
Cereals and bakery products	441	321	265	307	288	395	429	414	493	555
Meats, poultry, fish, and eggs	914	428	457	609	580	844	847	886	1 125	1 143
Dairy products	361	207	192	247	239	342	341	313	382	481
Fruits and vegetables	601	387	284	407	436	494	540	568	636	825
Other food at home	1 088	704	532	721	719	894	982	959	1 160	1 525
Food away from home	2 444	968	797	1 074	1 205	1 698	1 762	2 041	2 222	4 310
Alcoholic Beverages	445	226	149	290	150	252	229	298	429	852
Housing	14 121	8 512	6 479	8 734	8 393	9 582	10 387	11 396	14 100	22 676
Shelter	7 752	4 870	3 688	4 818	4 713	5 114	5 467	6 240	7 878	12 437
Owned dwellings	5 869	2 864	1 598	2 645	2 547	3 386	3 967	4 615	6 358	10 246
Rented dwellings	1 192	1 885	1 977	2 018	1 912	1 483	1 225	1 270	965	608
Other lodging	691	121	113	155	254	245	275	355	554	1 583
Utilities, fuels, and public services	3 168	2 010	1 904	2 379	2 369	2 553	2 867	2 983	3 354	4 191
Household operations	639	444	124	226	193	289	310	458	503	1 332
Housekeeping supplies	667	325	284	404	489	578	539	571	612	1 025
Household furnishings and equipment	1 894	863	480	906	629	1 047	1 205	1 143	1 754	3 691
Apparel and Services	1 797	654	512	838	939	890	1 106	1 543	1 614	3 387
Transportation	8 665	2 946	2 876	4 167	4 406	5 644	7 112	7 773	8 724	14 280
Vehicle purchases (net outlay)	4 004	[2]856	[2]1 355	2 022	1 807	2 520	3 341	3 675	3 742	6 808
Gasoline and motor oil	1 563	735	588	892	961	1 163	1 476	1 498	1 771	2 213
Other vehicle expenses	2 536	1 200	818	1 113	1 441	1 696	2 032	2 245	2 700	4 077
Public transportation	561	155	115	139	198	265	263	355	512	1 182
Health Care	3 198	2 053	1 512	1 934	2 119	2 551	3 257	3 396	3 547	4 131
Health insurance	1 556	904	783	973	1 013	1 324	1 533	1 698	1 660	2 008
Medical services	835	757	234	348	498	515	851	855	1 007	1 158
Drugs	659	310	430	521	550	586	737	734	703	747
Medical supplies	149	[2]81	64	91	58	126	137	109	177	218
Entertainment	2 686	782	709	1 266	941	2 550	1 585	1 513	3 047	4 610
Personal Care Products and Services	607	277	198	335	281	431	398	586	609	1 008
Reading	174	66	64	63	77	94	121	164	171	308
Education	755	[2]318	[2]24	[2]79	95	202	178	258	428	1 996
Tobacco Products and Smoking Supplies	326	221	307	315	335	369	339	371	383	275
Miscellaneous	792	541	283	328	379	580	651	762	853	1 220
Cash Contributions	1 710	827	225	504	525	690	777	1 087	1 619	3 600
Personal Insurance and Pensions	5 746	265	307	614	976	1 764	3 169	3 971	6 030	12 435
Life and other personal insurance	601	176	141	272	208	312	378	440	641	1 118
Pensions and Social Security	5 145	89	166	342	768	1 452	2 791	3 531	5 389	11 317

[1]Components of income and taxes are derived from "complete income" reporters only through 2003. Beginning in 2004, income imputation was implemented. As a result, all consumer units are considered to be complete income reporters.
[2]Data are likely to have large sampling errors.
[3]Value less than 0.05.

Table 8-28. Consumer Expenditures, Averages for Age Groups by Income Before Taxes: Reference Person 65 Years of Age and Over, 2003–2004

(Number, dollar, percent.)

Item	Total	Less than $5,000	$5,000 to $9,999	$10,000 to $14,999	$15,000 to $19,999	$20,000 to $29,999	$30,000 to $39,999	$40,000 to $49,999	$50,000 to $69,999	$70,000 and over
					Complete reporting of income					
NUMBER OF CONSUMER UNITS (THOUSANDS)	21 375	689	2 618	3 701	2 866	3 819	2 351	1 573	1 751	2 007
CONSUMER UNIT CHARACTERISTICS										
Income Before Taxes[1]	33 076	1 955	8 087	12 460	17 520	24 536	34 777	44 601	58 930	119 223
Income After Taxes[1]	31 714	1 889	8 013	12 365	17 327	21 488	34 304	43 937	57 671	113 260
Age of Reference Person	75.2	76.0	77.0	77.3	76.1	75.5	74.1	73.4	72.6	71.8
Average Number in Consumer Unit										
Persons	1.7	1.4	1.2	1.3	1.6	1.7	1.9	2.0	2.2	2.5
Children under 18 years	0.1	(2)	(2)	(2)	(2)	(2)	0.1	0.1	0.1	0.2
Persons 65 years and over	1.4	1.2	1.1	1.1	1.3	1.5	1.5	1.5	1.5	1.5
Earners	0.5	0.1	0.1	0.1	0.2	0.4	0.6	0.7	0.9	1.4
Vehicles	1.5	0.8	0.7	0.9	1.3	1.6	2.0	2.1	2.3	2.5
Percent Distribution										
Males	46	32	26	28	42	50	57	58	64	68
Females	54	68	74	72	58	50	43	42	36	32
Percent Homeowner	80	61	57	70	82	85	89	91	93	95
With mortgage	18	12	7	9	13	17	20	26	35	38
Without mortgage	62	49	50	60	68	68	69	65	57	57
AVERAGE ANNUAL EXPENDITURES	30 893	18 369	13 096	17 466	22 998	28 496	33 876	39 366	47 378	74 885
Food	4 115	3 039	2 081	2 649	3 170	3 925	4 598	5 418	6 290	8 282
Food at home	2 683	2 056	1 615	1 998	2 291	2 560	2 980	3 411	3 825	4 502
Cereals and bakery products	394	295	266	304	353	370	422	495	576	601
Meats, poultry, fish, and eggs	682	557	424	485	568	655	748	880	997	1 158
Dairy products	301	229	164	226	245	298	342	409	417	496
Fruits and vegetables	507	398	311	414	452	481	567	585	631	890
Other food at home	799	577	450	569	674	757	901	1 043	1 204	1 358
Food away from home	1 432	983	465	651	879	1 365	1 618	2 008	2 465	3 781
Alcoholic Beverages	238	145	87	105	116	214	218	247	427	867
Housing	10 117	7 556	5 413	7 075	8 292	9 565	10 677	11 990	13 975	20 928
Shelter	5 308	4 597	3 098	3 714	4 415	4 852	5 340	5 907	7 345	11 226
Owned dwellings	3 542	2 344	1 390	1 857	2 921	3 250	3 843	4 489	5 538	8 473
Rented dwellings	1 369	2 114	1 656	1 743	1 343	1 334	1 137	910	963	1 139
Other lodging	396	139	51	114	152	268	360	507	844	1 614
Utilities, fuels, and public services	2 536	1 812	1 614	1 945	2 307	2 572	2 811	3 017	3 234	4 028
Household operations	667	313	181	577	521	682	600	578	921	1 695
Housekeeping supplies	518	348	259	352	435	461	588	787	741	970
Household furnishings and equipment	1 089	486	261	487	613	999	1 339	1 702	1 734	3 008
Apparel and Services	931	535	488	485	653	784	1 034	1 306	1 431	2 382
Transportation	4 954	2 085	1 409	1 941	3 454	4 731	5 724	6 871	10 032	11 857
Vehicle purchases (net outlay)	2 158	3704	3437	625	1 275	2 051	2 421	3 104	5 218	5 475
Gasoline and motor oil	890	438	361	465	737	872	1 107	1 269	1 507	1 680
Other vehicle expenses	1 545	772	535	739	1 294	1 474	1 906	2 087	2 664	3 282
Public transportation	361	170	76	112	148	333	290	412	643	1 420
Health Care	3 890	2 377	2 083	2 865	3 530	4 211	4 687	4 448	5 233	6 016
Health insurance	2 094	1 301	1 227	1 614	1 961	2 270	2 450	2 611	2 741	2 845
Medical services	702	461	226	422	504	754	929	707	989	1 583
Drugs	934	509	567	754	920	1 022	1 072	945	1 262	1 296
Medical supplies	160	107	62	75	146	165	236	184	240	292
Entertainment	1 494	571	435	632	811	1 443	2 156	2 309	2 207	3 783
Personal Care Products and Services	461	273	195	279	406	449	521	573	757	906
Reading	147	55	53	85	114	147	170	213	224	312
Education	212	3230	318	25	42	109	133	130	511	1 145
Tobacco Products and Smoking Supplies	158	117	112	110	138	166	191	187	208	231
Miscellaneous	611	260	241	254	528	639	747	827	791	1 477
Cash Contributions	2 042	747	329	700	1 167	1 434	1 769	2 932	2 249	9 045
Personal Insurance and Pensions	1 521	380	151	260	579	678	1 251	1 915	3 045	7 653
Life and other personal insurance	393	161	133	182	321	302	493	518	611	1 067
Pensions and Social Security	1 129	3220	18	78	258	376	758	1 397	2 434	6 586

[1]Components of income and taxes are derived from "complete income" reporters only through 2003. Beginning in 2004, income imputation was implemented. As a result, all consumer units are considered to be complete income reporters.
[2]Value less than 0.05.
[3]Data are likely to have large sampling errors.

CHAPTER NINE

OCCUPATIONAL SAFETY AND HEALTH

OCCUPATIONAL SAFETY AND HEALTH

HIGHLIGHTS

This chapter includes data on work-related injuries, illnesses, and fatalies from the annual Survey of Occupational Injuries and Illnesses and the Census of Fatal Occupations. Data are classified by industry and selected worker characteristics.

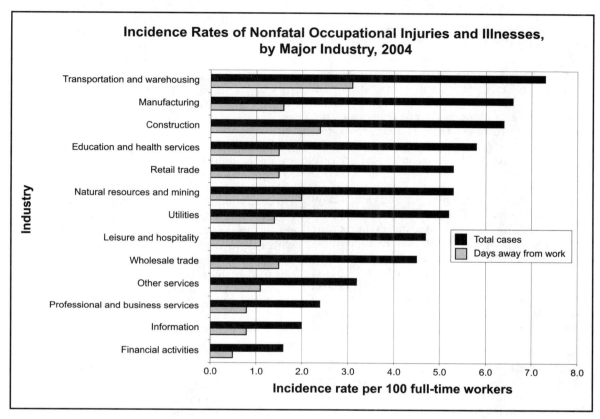

Transportation and warehousing continued to have the highest incidence rate of non-fatal occupational injuries and illnesses among all major industries, with 7.3 per 100 full-time workers in 2004. Financial activities had the lowest rate at 1.6 injuries and illnesses per 100 full-time workers. Most industries had injury and illness rates that were equal to or lower than their rates in 2003. Rates for injuries and illnesses requiring days away from work were much lower, ranging from 0.5 injuries and illnesses per 100 full-time workers for financial services to 3.1 injuries and illnesses per 100 full-time workers for transportation and warehousing. (See Table 9-1.)

OTHER HIGHLIGHTS

- In 2004, manufacturing had a higher injury incidence rate than construction, but construction had a higher rate of injuries and illnesses requiring days away from work. This indicates an occurance of more serious injuries and illnesses in that industry. (See Table 9-1.)

- Truck drivers had the highest number of days away from work as a result of occupational injuries and illnesses. They also had the highest percentage of being away from work for 31 days or more. (See Table 9-3.)

- Men suffered 93 percent of all fatal injuries and 66 percent of all non-fatal injuries in 2004. (See Tables 9-2 and 9-4.)

- In 2005, there was just 1 less fatal occupational injury than in 2004. The age distribution of workers suffering from fatal occupational injuries remained about the same in 2005, with those in the 45- to 54-year-old age group again suffering the highest number of fatalities. (See Table 9-4.)

NOTES AND DEFINITIONS

Collection and Coverage

Nonfatal Occupational Injuries and Illnesses

The Survey of Occupational Injuries and Illnesses is a federal/state program that collected employer reports from about 173,800 private industry establishments in 2004. The survey estimates are based on a probability sample and are then processed by state agencies in cooperation with the Bureau of Labor Statistics (BLS). The survey measures nonfatal injuries and illnesses only and excludes the self-employed, farms with fewer than 11 employees, private households, federal government agencies, and, for national estimates, employees in state and local government agencies

BLS has reported annually on the number and rate of days away from work injuries and illnesses in private industry since the early 1970s. The 2004 national survey marks the 13th year that BLS has collected additional detailed information concerning worker and case characteristics data, including data on lost work time. On January 19, 2001, the Occupational Safety and Health Administration (OSHA) promulgated revisions to its requirements for recording occupational injuries and illnesses. These revisions became effective January 1, 2002, and were reflected in the 2002 survey.

The term "lost workdays" was eliminated under these revisions, which instead require companies to record days away from work and days of restricted work or transfer to another job. In addition, the new rules for counting rely on calendar days instead of workdays. Employers are no longer required to count days away from work or days of job transfer or restriction beyond 180 days. These changes have affected the calculation of median days away from work from 2002 onward, making data from those years noncomparable to data from previous years.

The number and frequency (incidence rates) of days away from work cases are based on logs and other records kept by private industry employers throughout the year. These records reflect the year's overall injury and illness experience and the employers' understanding of which cases are work related under the current record-keeping guidelines of the U. S. Department of Labor. The number of injuries and illnesses reported in a given year can be influenced by changes in the level of economic activity, working conditions and work practices, worker experience and training, and the number of hours worked.

The Mine Safety and Health Administration and the Federal Railroad Administration furnish mining and railroad data to BLS. These data are therefore not comparable to data from other industries.

Industry data are classified according to the North American Industry Classification System (NAICS).

Concepts and Definitions

Recordable occupational injuries and illnesses include: (1) nonfatal occupational injuries that involve one or more of the following: loss of consciousness, restriction of work or motion, transfer to another job, or medical treatment (other than first aid). The annual survey measures only nonfatal injuries and illnesses. To better address fatalities, BLS implemented the Census of Fatal Occupational Injuries (described below); and (2) nonfatal occupational illnesses.

Occupational injury is any injury—such as a cut, fracture, sprain, or amputation—that results from a work accident or from exposure to an incident in the work environment.

Occupational illness is an abnormal condition or disorder (other than one resulting from an occupational injury) caused by exposure to environmental factors associated with employment. It includes acute and chronic illnesses and diseases that may have been caused by inhalation, absorption, ingestion, or direct contact. Long-term latent illnesses can be difficult to relate to the workplace and are believed to be understated in this survey.

Days away from work are cases that involve days away from work, days of restricted work activity, or both.

The data are presented in the form of incidence rates, defined as the number of injuries and illnesses or cases of days away from work per 100 full-time employees. The formula is $(N/EH) \times 200,000$, where N = number of injuries and illnesses or days away from work, EH = total hours worked by all employees during the calendar year, and 200,000 = the base for 100 full-time equivalent workers (working 40 hours per week, 50 weeks per year).

Comparable data for individual states are available from the BLS Office of Safety, Health, and Working Conditions.

Collection and Coverage

Fatal Occupational Injuries

Since 1992, BLS has been collected a comprehensive count of work-related deaths in the Census of Fatal Occupational Injuries (CFOI). The CFOI covers private workers in family businesses, and public sector workers.

The CFOI program is a cooperative venture between the state and federal governments. The program collects and cross checks fatality information from multiple sources, including death certificates, state and federal workers' compensation reports, Occupational Safety and Health Administration and Mine Safety and Health Administration records, medical examiner and autopsy reports, media accounts, state motor vehicle fatality records, and follow-up questionnaires to employers.

Fatality counts from the CFOI are combined with average annual employment from the Current Population Survey to produce a fatal work injury rate. Data for 2005 are preliminary. CFOI data include deaths that resulted from traumatic occupational injuries.

For a fatality to be included in the CFOI, the decedent must have been employed at the time of the event and present at the site of the incident as a job requirement. Due to the latency period of many occupational illnesses and the resulting difficulty associated with linking illnesses to work, it is difficult to compile a complete count of all fatal illnesses in a given year. Thus, information on illness-related deaths are excluded from the basic fatality count.

Industries are classified according to NAICS and occupations according to the Standard Occupational Classification (SOC) system.

Sources of Additional Information

For more extensive definitions and a description of collection methods see BLS news release USDL 05-2195, "Workplace Injuries and Illnesses in 2004," for injuries and illnesses; USDL 06-1364, "National Census of Fatal Occupational Injuries for Fatalities," for more information on the CFOI; and occasional articles in *Compensation and Working Conditions*. All of these resources are available on the BLS Web site at <http://www.bls.gov>.

Table 9-1. Incidence Rates Per 100 Full-Time Workers[1] of Nonfatal Occupational Injuries and Illnesses, by Selected Industries and Case Types, 2004

(Number, rate.)

Industry[2]	NAICS code[3]	2004 average annual employment (thousands)[4]	Total recordable cases	Cases with days away from work, job transfer, or restriction			Other recordable cases
				Total	Cases with days away from work[5]	Cases with job transfer or restriction	
PRIVATE INDUSTRY[6]		107 552	4.8	2.5	1.4	1.1	2.3
Goods-Producing[6]		22 656	6.5	3.5	1.9	1.7	2.9
Natural resources and mining[6,7]		1 482	5.3	3.1	2.0	1.1	2.2
Agriculture, forestry, fishing and hunting[6]	11	962	6.4	3.7	2.3	1.4	2.7
Crop production[6]	111	430	5.6	3.3	1.7	1.5	2.3
Animal production[6]	112	141	8.5	4.7	2.9	1.9	3.8
Support activities for agriculture and forestry	115	309	5.9	3.3	2.2	1.2	2.6
Mining[7]	21	520	3.8	2.3	1.6	0.6	1.5
Oil and gas extraction	211	121	2.6	1.2	0.9	0.3	1.4
Mining (except oil and gas)[8]	212	204	4.3	2.9	2.2	0.7	1.4
Support activities for mining	213	194	3.8	2.2	1.5	0.7	1.7
Construction	23	6 916	6.4	3.4	2.4	0.9	3.0
Construction of buildings	236	1 618	5.6	2.9	2.2	0.7	2.7
Heavy and civil engineering construction	237	895	5.9	3.2	2.1	1.0	2.8
Specialty trade contractors	238	4 403	6.8	3.6	2.6	1.0	3.2
Manufacturing	31	14 257	6.6	3.6	1.6	2.1	3.0
Food	311	1 490	8.2	5.3	1.9	3.4	3.0
Beverage and tobacco product	312	194	8.7	5.8	2.9	2.9	2.8
Textile mills	313	238	4.0	2.3	0.8	1.5	1.7
Textile product mills	314	176	5.4	2.9	1.0	1.9	2.5
Apparel	315	285	3.5	1.8	1.0	0.8	1.7
Leather and allied product	316	42	6.9	4.4	1.5	2.9	2.4
Wood product	321	548	10.0	5.4	2.7	2.7	4.6
Paper	322	493	4.9	2.9	1.4	1.5	2.1
Printing and related support activities	323	658	4.5	2.4	1.2	1.2	2.0
Petroleum and coal product	324	112	2.5	1.2	0.7	0.5	1.2
Chemical	325	882	3.5	2.0	0.9	1.0	1.5
Plastics and rubber product	326	804	7.7	4.7	2.0	2.7	3.0
Nonmetallic mineral product	327	498	8.0	4.8	2.3	2.5	3.1
Primary metal	331	466	10.0	5.2	2.2	3.0	4.8
Fabricated metal product	332	1 489	8.0	3.9	1.9	2.0	4.1
Machinery	333	1 137	6.7	3.1	1.5	1.6	3.6
Computer and electronic product	334	1 315	2.3	1.2	0.6	0.6	1.1
Electrical equipment, appliance, and component	335	444	5.5	2.9	1.2	1.7	2.6
Transportation equipment	336	1 763	8.5	4.6	1.6	3.0	3.9
Furniture and related product	337	568	8.3	4.7	2.3	2.5	3.6
Miscellaneous	339	654	4.5	2.5	1.2	1.3	2.0
Service-Providing		84 896	4.2	2.2	1.3	0.9	2.1
Trade, transportation, and utilities[9]		25 273	5.5	3.1	1.8	1.3	2.3
Wholesale trade	42	5 642	4.5	2.7	1.5	1.2	1.8
Merchant wholesalers, durable goods	423	2 942	4.1	2.2	1.3	0.9	1.9
Merchant wholesalers, nondurable goods	424	2 000	5.6	3.9	2.0	1.9	1.7
Wholesale electronic markets and agents and brokers	425	700	2.8	1.6	1.0	0.6	1.3
Retail trade	44	15 061	5.3	2.7	1.5	1.2	2.6
Motor vehicle and parts dealers	441	1 901	5.1	2.2	1.4	0.7	3.0
Furniture and home furnishings stores	442	564	5.7	3.2	1.9	1.3	2.5
Electronics and appliance stores	443	522	3.1	1.5	0.9	...	1.6
Building material and garden equipment and supplies dealers	444	1 234	8.1	4.3	2.3	2.0	3.8
Food and beverage stores	445	2 818	6.4	3.3	1.9	1.4	3.0
Health and personal care stores	446	941	2.3	1.1	0.7	0.4	1.2
Gasoline stations	447	873	3.4	1.5	1.0	0.5	1.9
Clothing and clothing accessories stores	448	1 368	2.6	0.9	0.6	0.3	1.6
Sporting goods, hobby, book, and music stores	451	646	3.9	1.3	0.8	0.5	2.6
General merchandise stores	452	2 851	7.0	4.3	1.9	2.4	2.7
Miscellaneous store retailers	453	918	3.2	1.6	0.9	0.6	1.6
Nonstore retailers	454	424	4.8	2.8	1.6	1.2	2.0
Transportation and warehousing[9]	48	4 006	7.3	4.9	3.1	1.8	2.4
Air transportation	481	513	10.1	7.7	5.3	2.5	2.4
Rail transportation[9]	482	...	2.7	2.0	1.8	0.2	0.7
Water transportation	483	55	4.4	2.6	1.8	0.8	1.8

Note: Due to rounding, components may not sum to totals.

[1] The incidence rates represent the number of injuries and illnesses per 100 full-time workers and were calculated as: (N/EH) x 200,000, where N = number of injuries and illnesses; EH = total hours worked by all employees during the calendar year; 200,000 = base for 100 equivalent full-time workers working 40 hours per week, 50 weeks per year.
[2] Totals include data for industries not shown separately.
[3] North American Industry Classification System—United States, 2002.
[4] Employment is expressed as an average annual value and is derived primarily from the Bureau of Labor Statistics's (BLS) Quarterly Census of Employment and Wages (QCEW) program.
[5] Days away from work cases include those that result in days away from work with or without job transfer or restriction.
[6] Excludes farms with fewer than 11 employees.
[7] Data for mining include establishments not governed by the Department of Labor's Mine Safety and Health Administration (MSHA) rules and reporting, such as those in oil and gas extraction and related support activities. Data for mining operators in coal, metal, and nonmetal mining are provided to BLS by MSHA. Independent mining contractors are excluded from the coal, metal, and nonmetal mining industries. These data do not reflect the changes the Occupational Safety and Health Administration (OSHA) made to its record keeping requirements effective January 1, 2002; thus, estimates for these industries are not comparable to estimates in other industries.
[8] Data for mining operators in this industry are provided to BLS by MSHA. Independent mining contractors are excluded. These data do not reflect the changes OSHA made to its record keeping requirements effective January 1, 2002; thus, estimates for these industries are not comparable to estimates in other industries.
[9] Data for employers in rail transportation are provided to BLS by the Department of Transportation's Federal Railroad Administration (FRA).
... = Not available.

Table 9-1. Incidence Rates Per 100 Full-Time Workers[1] of Nonfatal Occupational Injuries and Illnesses, by Selected Industries and Case Types, 2004—*Continued*

(Number, rate.)

Industry[2]	NAICS code[3]	2004 average annual employment (thousands)[4]	Total recordable cases	Cases with days away from work, job transfer, or restriction			Other recordable cases
				Total	Cases with days away from work[5]	Cases with job transfer or restriction	
Service-Providing—*Continued*							
Truck transportation	484	1 351	6.1	3.9	2.9	1.0	2.3
Transit and ground passenger transportation	485	378	6.1	3.6	2.8	0.8	2.5
Pipeline transportation	486	38	2.5	1.4	1.0	0.4	1.1
Scenic and sightseeing transportation	487	27	4.7	2.8	2.4	0.5	1.9
Support activities for transportation	488	531	5.3	3.5	2.2	1.3	1.9
Couriers and messengers	492	558	12.4	8.8	4.1	4.7	3.7
Warehousing and storage	493	556	9.3	5.8	2.8	3.0	3.4
Utilities	22	564	5.2	2.5	1.4	1.1	2.7
Information	51	3 100	2.0	1.1	0.8	0.4	0.9
Publishing industries (except Internet)	511	908	2.1	1.1	0.7	0.4	1.0
Motion picture and sound recording industries	512	380	. . .	. . .	0.7	0.2	. . .
Broadcasting (except Internet)	515	324	2.3	1.2	0.7	0.5	1.1
Internet publishing and broadcasting	516	29	2.4	0.7	0.5	. . .	1.7
Telecommunications	517	1 027	2.2	1.4	1.0	0.4	0.8
Internet service providers, Web search portals, and data processing	518	382	0.8	0.3	0.2	0.1	0.5
Other information services	519	49	1.6	1.0	1.0	. . .	0.6
Financial activities		7 891	1.6	0.7	0.5	0.2	0.9
Finance and insurance	52	5 813	0.9	0.3	0.2	0.1	0.6
Monetary authorities—central bank	521	22	1.9	1.2	0.6	0.6	0.7
Credit intermediation and related activities	522	2 813	1.0	0.4	0.3	0.1	0.6
Securities, commodity contracts, and other financial investments and related activities	523	765	0.3	0.1	0.1	. . .	0.2
Insurance carriers and related activities	524	2 128	1.1	0.4	0.3	0.1	0.7
Funds, trusts, and other financial vehicles	525	86	0.6	0.3	0.2	. . .	0.3
Real estate and rental and leasing	53	2 078	3.7	1.9	1.3	0.7	1.8
Real estate	531	1 410	3.3	1.7	1.2	0.5	1.6
Rental and leasing services	532	641	4.7	2.5	1.5	1.0	2.2
Professional and business services		16 295	2.4	1.3	0.8	0.5	1.1
Professional, scientific, and technical services	54	6 769	1.3	0.5	0.3	0.2	0.8
Management of companies and enterprises	55	1 696	2.7	1.5	0.7	. . .	1.2
Administrative and support and waste management and remediation services	56	7 829	3.7	2.2	1.4	0.8	1.5
Administrative and support services	561	7 504	3.4	2.0	1.3	0.7	1.4
Waste management and remediation services	562	326	7.6	5.3	2.9	2.4	2.4
Education and health services		16 085	5.8	2.7	1.5	1.2	3.1
Educational services	61	2 079	2.5	1.0	0.7	0.3	1.5
Health care and social assistance	62	14 006	6.2	2.9	1.6	1.3	3.3
Ambulatory health care services	621	4 938	3.3	1.2	0.8	0.4	2.0
Hospitals	622	4 247	8.3	3.4	1.9	1.5	4.9
Nursing and residential care facilities	623	2 810	9.7	5.8	2.9	2.8	3.9
Social assistance	624	2 011	3.9	2.1	1.2	0.8	1.8
Leisure and hospitality		12 468	4.7	1.9	1.1	0.8	2.8
Arts, entertainment, and recreation	71	1 853	5.9	3.1	1.5	1.5	2.9
Performing arts, spectator sports, and related industries	711	380	5.8	2.5	1.8	0.7	3.3
Museums, historical sites, and similar institutions	712	117	5.2	2.5	1.6	1.0	2.6
Amusement, gambling, and recreation industries	713	1 355	6.0	3.3	1.5	1.8	2.8
Accommodation and food services	72	10 615	4.5	1.7	1.1	0.6	2.8
Accommodation	721	1 785	5.8	3.1	1.6	1.5	2.7
Food services and drinking places	722	8 830	4.2	1.4	1.0	0.4	2.8
Other services		3 785	3.2	1.6	1.1	0.5	1.6
Other services, except public administration	81	3 785	3.2	1.6	1.1	0.5	1.6
Repair and maintenance	811	1 222	3.9	1.9	1.4	0.5	2.0
Personal and laundry services	812	1 266	2.8	1.6	1.0	0.7	1.2
Religious, grantmaking, civic, professional, and similar organizations	813	1 297	2.7	1.2	0.8	0.4	1.6

Note: Due to rounding, components may not sum to totals.

[1]The incidence rates represent the number of injuries and illnesses per 100 full-time workers and were calculated as: (N/EH) x 200,000, where N = number of injuries and illnesses; EH = total hours worked by all employees during the calendar year; 200,000 = base for 100 equivalent full-time workers working 40 hours per week, 50 weeks per year.
[2]Totals include data for industries not shown separately.
[3]North American Industry Classification System—United States, 2002.
[4]Employment is expressed as an average annual value and is derived primarily from the Bureau of Labor Statistics's (BLS) Quarterly Census of Employment and Wages (QCEW) program.
[5]Days away from work cases include those that result in days away from work with or without job transfer or restriction.
. . . = Not available.

Table 9-2. Number of Nonfatal Occupational Injuries and Illnesses Involving Days Away from Work,[1] by Selected Worker Characteristics and Private Industry Division, 2004

(Number.)

Characteristic	Total cases[2]	Goods-producing[2]			
		All goods-producing	Natural resources and mining[3]	Construction	Manufacturing
TOTAL CASES	1 259 320	408 400	29 100	153 200	226 090
Sex					
Men	829 300	348 220	25 410	149 430	173 380
Women	425 470	60 030	3 700	3 670	52 660
Age[4]					
14 to 15 years	200	. . .	. . .	. . .	. . .
16 to 19 years	38 230	9 540	830	3 720	5 000
20 to 24 years	141 730	46 950	3 890	21 530	21 530
25 to 34 years	303 880	101 750	7 330	45 700	48 710
35 to 44 years	331 610	114 690	7 000	44 030	63 660
45 to 54 years	272 250	88 330	6 460	26 010	55 870
55 to 64 years	128 810	37 600	2 750	9 250	25 600
65 years and over	23 950	3 810	420	840	2 550
Length of Service with Employer					
Fewer than 3 months	162 410	64 300	6 750	30 000	27 550
3 to 11 months	258 500	81 210	6 070	37 040	38 110
1 to 5 years	446 820	130 130	8 690	51 230	70 210
More than 5 years	383 050	131 200	7 350	34 390	89 450
Race and Hispanic Origin					
White only	591 570	224 270	9 810	90 020	124 430
Black only	103 820	25 190	580	7 160	17 450
Hispanic only[5]	164 390	71 070	9 560	27 990	33 520
Asian only	16 040	3 960	170	590	3 210
Native Hawaiian or Pacific Islander only	4 650	1 220	70	470	680
American Indian or Alaskan Native only	5 140	2 090	120	960	1 010
Hispanic[5] and other race	530	240	20	. . .	160
Multi-race	1 260	300	. . .	110	190
Not reported	371 920	80 060	8 760	25 850	45 450

Note: Due to rounding and nonclassifiable responses, components may not sum to totals.

[1] Days away from work cases include those that result in days away from work with or without restricted work activity.
[2] Excludes farms with fewer than 11 employees.
[3] Data for mining include establishments not governed by the Department of Labor's Mine Safety and Health Administration (MSHA) rules and reporting, such as those in oil and gas extraction and related support activities. Data for mining operators in coal, metal, and nonmetal mining are provided to the Bureau of Labor Statistics (BLS) by MSHA. Independent mining contractors are excluded from the coal, metal, and nonmetal mining industries. These data do not reflect the changes the Occupational Safety and Health Administration (OSHA) made to its record keeping requirements effective January 1, 2002; thus, estimates for these industries are not comparable to estimates in other industries.
[4] Data are not shown separately for injured workers under 14 years of age; these workers accounted for fewer than 50 cases.
[5] May be of any race.
. . . = Not available.

Table 9-2. Number of Nonfatal Occupational Injuries and Illnesses Involving Days Away from Work,[1] by Selected Worker Characteristics and Private Industry Division, 2004—*Continued*

(Number.)

Characteristic	Service-providing							
	All service-providing	Trade, transportation, and utilities[6]	Information	Financial activities	Professional and business services	Educational and health services	Leisure and hospitality	Other services
TOTAL CASES	850 930	387 650	21 150	34 930	90 500	189 980	95 380	31 350
Sex								
Men	481 090	278 290	14 890	19 580	60 100	39 410	47 040	21 790
Women	365 440	105 050	6 260	15 350	30 390	150 550	48 270	9 560
Age[4]								
14 to 15 years	180	80	. . .	. . .	. . .	. . .	80	. . .
16 to 19 years	28 690	12 450	500	550	1 930	3 190	8 790	1 280
20 to 24 years	94 780	43 480	1 230	2 930	9 820	16 360	17 490	3 470
25 to 34 years	202 130	91 250	5 020	7 830	26 690	43 450	20 820	7 070
35 to 44 years	216 920	102 810	5 390	9 160	24 520	48 150	19 150	7 740
45 to 54 years	183 920	82 350	6 150	8 090	17 060	47 740	15 190	7 340
55 to 64 years	91 210	40 970	2 320	4 390	6 970	23 640	9 560	3 360
65 years and over	20 140	8 960	410	1 470	1 830	4 460	2 110	890
Length of Service with Employer								
Fewer than 3 months	98 100	42 600	850	3 000	13 890	16 590	17 640	3 540
3 to 11 months	177 290	76 670	2 600	7 290	20 970	38 100	25 180	6 480
1 to 5 years	316 690	140 220	6 680	13 800	35 700	77 610	30 870	11 800
More than 5 years	251 850	122 670	10 950	10 810	19 800	57 020	21 300	9 290
Race and Hispanic Origin								
White only	367 300	165 230	8 010	15 110	38 360	85 560	37 260	17 770
Black only	78 630	24 950	920	3 190	9 090	30 940	7 170	2 370
Hispanic only[5]	93 320	34 770	1 000	4 450	18 830	15 590	14 650	4 020
Asian only	12 080	3 260	170	510	1 620	3 080	3 050	390
Native Hawaiian or Pacific Islander only	3 440	1 310	40	170	290	770	670	200
American Indian or Alaskan Native only	3 050	1 400	70	90	230	670	360	230
Hispanic[5] and other race	290	110	. . .	. . .	. . .	40	70	. . .
Multi-race	960	320	. . .	. . .	. . .	200	370	. . .
Not reported	291 860	156 290	10 920	11 410	22 000	53 140	31 780	6 320

Note: Due to rounding and nonclassifiable responses, components may not sum to totals.

[1]Days away from work cases include those that result in days away from work with or without restricted work activity.
[4]Data are not shown separately for injured workers under 14 years of age; these workers accounted for fewer than 50 cases.
[5]May be of any race.
[6]Data for employers in rail transportation are provided to BLS by the Department of Transportation's Federal Railroad Administration (FRA).
. . . = Not available.

Table 9-3. Number and Percent Distribution of Nonfatal Occupational Injuries and Illnesses Involving Days Away from Work,[1] by Selected Occupation and Number of Days Away from Work, Private Industry, 2004

(Number, percent.)

Occupation[2]	Total number of cases	Percent of days away from work cases involving:								Median days away from work
		Total	1 day	2 days	3 to 5 days	6 to 10 days	11 to 20 days	21 to 30 days	31 days and over	
TOTAL[3]	1 259 320	100.0	14.3	11.5	18.4	12.6	11.4	6.8	25.0	7
Labor and freight, stock, and material movers, hand	89 250	100.0	14.3	11.8	18.0	13.6	11.7	6.2	24.3	7
Truck drivers, heavy and tractor trailer	63 570	100.0	8.4	8.7	16.9	13.4	12.0	6.8	33.7	12
Nursing aides, orderlies, and attendants	51 940	100.0	15.0	14.3	21.7	13.8	11.4	5.4	18.5	5
Construction laborers	37 930	100.0	14.1	10.2	16.4	12.5	12.3	7.1	27.3	10
Truck drivers, light or delivery services	37 160	100.0	11.3	7.0	17.1	13.6	10.4	6.8	33.8	12
Janitors and cleaners, except maids and housekeeping cleaners	33 580	100.0	13.2	12.2	19.8	11.6	10.6	8.6	24.0	7
Retail salespersons	33 160	100.0	14.8	12.1	16.9	12.6	9.6	7.5	26.7	8
Carpenters	30 450	100.0	13.6	10.2	18.0	11.7	11.3	7.2	28.0	9
Stock clerks and order fillers	24 250	100.0	13.7	12.1	20.0	13.8	12.6	6.3	21.6	7
Maintenance and repair workers, general	21 050	100.0	14.1	11.7	20.8	13.7	11.0	5.9	22.9	7
Registered nurses	20 500	100.0	13.9	11.3	20.9	13.1	10.6	6.5	23.8	7
Maids and housekeeping cleaners	17 980	100.0	14.8	14.2	19.1	11.5	11.3	5.6	23.5	6
Cashiers	17 640	100.0	12.8	12.1	19.6	11.2	10.9	6.3	27.0	8
Automotive service technicians and mechanics	15 550	100.0	16.8	13.2	21.6	11.9	10.5	6.1	19.8	5
Combined food preparation and service workers, including fast food	14 180	100.0	12.8	14.0	22.4	11.3	11.0	5.1	23.3	6
First-line supervisors/managers of retail sales work	14 150	100.0	13.8	14.9	20.7	13.2	9.0	7.2	21.2	6
Landscaping and groundskeeping workers	14 000	100.0	15.4	14.6	22.6	12.0	9.7	4.2	21.5	5
Welders, cutters, solderers, and brazers	13 490	100.0	20.2	13.8	15.5	14.8	9.9	6.3	19.5	6
Electricians	11 310	100.0	10.8	13.4	15.7	11.1	12.5	6.6	29.9	10
Waiters and waitresses	11 060	100.0	16.9	16.9	20.0	10.4	6.4	5.2	24.2	5
Customer service representatives	10 830	100.0	19.0	11.4	15.4	15.1	9.7	4.3	24.9	7
Plumbers, pipefitters, and steamfitters	10 340	100.0	13.1	9.5	20.0	14.3	12.2	6.2	24.8	8
Driver/sales workers	10 270	100.0	10.6	10.5	23.1	11.3	10.8	6.5	27.2	7
Cooks, restaurant	10 000	100.0	19.1	17.6	20.5	9.5	9.3	8.1	16.0	4
Food preparation workers	9 950	100.0	19.0	10.9	22.3	14.0	7.1	6.4	20.5	5
Industrial truck and tractor operators	9 890	100.0	13.4	7.0	22.6	9.2	11.8	8.7	27.1	9
Industrial machinery mechanics	9 460	100.0	12.1	10.0	16.2	11.5	13.8	8.0	28.4	11

Note: Due to rounding and nonclassifiable responses, percentages may not sum to 100.

[1]Days away from work cases include those that result in days away from work with or without restricted work activity.
[2]Based on the 2000 Standard Occupational Classification (SOC) system.
[3]Total includes data from occupations not shown separately.

Table 9-4. Fatal Occupational Injuries, by Selected Worker Characteristics and Selected Event or Exposure, 2005

(Number, percent.)

Characteristic	Fatalities		Selected event or exposure[1] (percent of total for characteristic category)			
	Number	Percent	Highway[2]	Homicides	Falls	Struck by object
TOTAL	5 702	100	25	10	13	11
Employee Status						
Wage and salary workers[3]	4 568	80	28	9	14	10
Self-employed[4]	1 134	20	13	14	12	15
Sex						
Men	5 300	93	24	9	14	11
Women	402	7	33	24	9	4
Age[5]						
Under 16 years	24	(6)	. . .	. . .	. . .	12
16 to 17 years	30	1	13	13	10	20
18 to 19 years	112	2	21	10	16	11
20 to 24 years	403	7	26	10	10	9
25 to 34 years	1 005	18	24	12	11	10
35 to 44 years	1 239	22	26	12	12	11
45 to 54 years	1 383	24	26	9	14	10
55 to 64 years	924	16	28	8	16	10
65 years and over	575	10	20	6	17	15
Race and Hispanic Origin						
White	3 940	69	26	7	13	11
Black	577	10	29	20	8	8
Hispanic[7]	917	16	19	10	20	12
American Indian or Alaskan Native ...	49	1	31	. . .	8	10
Asian	153	3	12	46	9	6
Native Hawaiian or Pacific Islander ...	9	(6)	. . .	. . .	. . .	. . .
Other or not reported	55	1	15	25	11	7

Note: Totals for 2005 are preliminary. Totals for major categories may include subcategories not shown separately. Due to rounding, components may not sum to totals.

[1]The figure shown is the percentage of the total fatalities for that demographic group.
[2]"Highway" includes deaths to vehicle occupants resulting from traffic incidents that occur on the public roadway, shoulder, or surrounding area. It excludes incidents occurring entirely off the roadway, such as in parking lots and on farms; incidents involving trains; and deaths of pedestrians or other non-passengers.
[3]May include volunteers and other workers receiving compensation.
[4]Includes self-employed workers, owners of unincorporated businesses and farms, paid and unpaid family workers, and members of partnerships, and may include owners of incorporated businesses.
[5]There were seven fatalities for which there was insufficient information to determine the age of the decedent.
[6]Less than or equal to 0.5 percent.
[7]May be of any race.
. . . = Not available.

Table 9-5. Fatal Occupational Injuries, by Occupation and Selected Event or Exposure, 2005

(Number, percent.)

Occupation[1]	Fatalities		Selected event or exposure[2] (percent of total for characteristic category)			
	Number	Percent	Highway[3]	Homicide	Falls	Struck by object
Total	5 702	100	25	10	13	11
Management	567	10	15	7	9	13
Top executives	30	1	37	...	...	...
Advertising, marketing, promotions, public relations, and sales managers	7	(4)	57	...	...	...
Operations specialties managers	34	1	15	15	12	...
Other management	496	9	14	7	9	14
Business and financial operations	36	1	33	8	19	...
Business operations specialists	23	(4)	30	17	...	...
Financial specialists	13	(4)	38	...	23	...
Computer and mathematical	6	(4)	...	...	...	...
Computer specialists	6	(4)	...	...	...	...
Architecture and engineering	53	1	21	6	15	6
Architects, surveyors, and cartographers	9	(4)	...	...	...	...
Engineers	29	1	24	...	14	...
Drafters, engineering, and mapping techicians	15	(4)	20	...	27	...
Life, physical, and social science	17	(4)	41	18	...	...
Life scientists	4	(4)	...	...	...	...
Physical scientists	4	(4)	...	...	...	...
Social scientists and related workers	3	(4)	...	...	...	...
Life, physical, and social science technicians	6	(4)	50	...	...	...
Community and social services	25	(4)	36	16	12	...
Counselors, social workers, and other community and social service specialists	14	(4)	29	21	...	...
Religious workers	11	(4)	45	...	...	...
Legal	17	(4)	41	29	...	...
Lawyers, judges, and related workers	15	(4)	40	27	...	...
Education, training, and library	25	(4)	24	20	12	...
Postsecondary teachers	11	(4)	27	...	...	...
Primary, secondary, and special education teachers	6	(4)	...	...	...	...
Other teachers and instructors	3	(4)	...	...	...	...
Librarians, curators, and archivists	3	(4)	...	...	...	...
Arts, design, entertainment, sports, and media	52	1	17	10	21	10
Art and design workers	10	(4)	...	...	30	...
Entertainers and performers, sports and related workers	29	1	14	...	21	17
Media and communication workers	4	(4)	...	...	...	...
Media and communication equipment workers	9	(4)	...	...	...	...
Health care practitioners and technical operations	42	1	26	12	...	...
Health diagnosing and treating practitioners	23	(4)	22	13	...	...
Health technologists and technicians	19	(4)	32	...	...	...
Health care support	18	(4)	39	22	...	...
Nursing, psychiatric, and home health aides	17	(4)	41	18	...	...
Protective service	256	4	29	35	5	5
First-line supervisors and managers of protective service workers	15	(4)	47	...	...	...
Fire fighting and prevention workers	28	1	43	...	...	14
Law enforcement workers	141	2	32	40	4	4
Other protective service workers	72	1	15	43	7	6
Food preparation and serving related	58	1	5	62	12	...
Supervisors of food preparation and serving workers	26	(4)	...	65	...	...
Cooks and food preparation workers	15	(4)	...	53	20	...
Food and beverage serving workers	13	(4)	...	77	...	...
Other food preparation and serving related workers	4	(4)	...	...	...	...
Building and grounds cleaning and maintenance	264	5	12	4	23	12
Supervisors of building and grounds cleaning and maintenance workers	36	1	25	...	31	11
Building cleaning and pest control workers	58	1	9	10	36	...
Grounds maintenance workers	170	3	10	2	17	17
Personal care and service	61	1	13	33	7	7
Supervisors of personal care and service workers	6	(4)	...	67	...	...
Animal care and service workers	5	(4)	...	...	...	...
Entertainment attendants and related workers	7	(4)	...	...	...	...
Personal appearance workers	11	(4)	...	100	...	...
Transportation, tourism, and lodging attendants	12	(4)	25	...	...	...
Other personal care and service workers	19	(4)	21	26	...	...
Sales and related	320	6	22	54	6	3
Supervisors of sales workers	132	2	14	58	5	5
Retail sales workers	112	2	6	75	8	4
Sales representatives, services	17	(4)	59	...	...	...
Sales representatives, wholesale and manufacturing	26	(4)	85	...	...	...
Other sales and related workers	33	1	42	33	...	...
Office and administrative support	106	2	26	28	13	4
Supervisors of office and administrative support workers	8	(4)	...	62	...	...
Financial clerks	7	(4)	...	57	...	...
Information and record clerks	22	(4)	14	41	18	...
Material recording, scheduling, dispatching, and distributing workers	54	1	41	17	11	6
Secretaries and administrative asistants	9	(4)	...	...	...	...
Other office and administrative support workers	6	(4)	...	...	...	...

Note: Totals for 2005 are preliminary. Totals for major categories may include subcategories not shown separately. Due to rounding, components may not sum to totals.

[1]Based on the 2000 Standard Occupational Classification (SOC) system.
[2]The figure shown is the percentage of total fatalities for that occupation group.
[3]"Highway" includes deaths to vehicle occupants resulting from traffic incidents that occur on the public roadway, shoulder, or surrounding area. It excludes incidents occurring entirely off the roadway, such as in parking lots and on farms; incidents involving trains; and deaths of pedestrians or other non-passengers.
[4]Less than or equal to 0.5 percent.
. . . = Not available.

Table 9-5. Fatal Occupational Injuries, by Occupation and Selected Event or Exposure, 2005—*Continued*

(Number, percent.)

Occupation[1]	Fatalities		Selected event or exposure[2] (percent of total for characteristic category)			
	Number	Percent	Highway[3]	Homicide	Falls	Struck by object
Farming, fishing, and forestry	324	6	11	2	4	25
Supervisors of farming, fishing, and forestry workers	12	(4)	25	. . .	. . .	33
Agricultural workers	178	3	17	2	6	8
Fishing and hunting workers	48	1	. . .	. . .	. . .	. . .
Forest, conservation, and logging workers	86	2	5	. . .	. . .	74
Construction and extraction	1 180	21	11	2	33	12
Supervisors of construction and extraction workers	122	2	15	5	20	11
Construction trades workers	890	16	9	1	38	11
Helpers—construction trades	23	(4)	13	. . .	35	. . .
Other construction and related workers	64	1	20	5	11	. . .
Extraction workers	81	1	14	. . .	14	21
Installation, maintenance, and repair	396	7	17	3	13	16
Supervisors of installation, maintenance, and repair workers	19	(4)	16	. . .	16	. . .
Electrical and electronic equipment mechanics, installers, and repairers	17	(4)	24	. . .	29	. . .
Vehicle and mobile equipment, mechanics, installers, and repairers	138	2	17	2	5	29
Other installation, maintenance, and repair workers	222	4	17	3	17	9
Production	274	5	8	8	12	21
Supervisors of production workers	39	1	8	18	. . .	21
Assemblers and fabricators	26	(4)	. . .	. . .	15	31
Food processing workers	9	(4)	. . .	33	. . .	. . .
Metal workers and plastics workers	84	1	6	. . .	19	26
Printing workers	8	(4)	. . .	. . .	. . .	. . .
Textile, apparel, and furnishings workers	5	(4)	. . .	. . .	. . .	. . .
Woodworkers	7	(4)	. . .	. . .	. . .	71
Plant and system operators	15	(4)	33	. . .	. . .	. . .
Other production workers	81	1	5	9	11	15
Transportation and material moving	1 543	27	50	4	4	7
Supervisors of transportation and material moving workers	23	(4)	13	13	. . .	13
Air transportation workers	81	1	. . .	. . .	. . .	. . .
Motor vehicle operators	1 095	19	67	5	3	6
Rail transportation workers	23	(4)	. . .	. . .	. . .	. . .
Water transportation workers	35	1	. . .	. . .	. . .	. . .
Other transportation workers	15	(4)	. . .	27	. . .	. . .
Material moving workers	271	5	15	2	10	17
Military	47	1	17	. . .	. . .	. . .

Note: Totals for 2005 are preliminary. Totals for major categories may include subcategories not shown separately. Due to rounding, components may not sum to totals.

[1]Based on the 2000 Standard Occupational Classification (SOC) system.
[2]The figure shown is the percentage of total fatalities for that occupation group.
[3]"Highway" includes deaths to vehicle occupants resulting from traffic incidents that occur on the public roadway, shoulder, or surrounding area. It excludes incidents occurring entirely off the roadway, such as in parking lots and on farms; incidents involving trains; and deaths of pedestrians or other non-passengers.
[4]Less than or equal to 0.5 percent.
. . . = Not available.

CHAPTER TEN

LABOR MANAGEMENT RELATIONS

LABOR MANAGEMENT RELATIONS

HIGHLIGHTS

This chapter contains information on historical trends in union membership, earnings, and work stoppages.

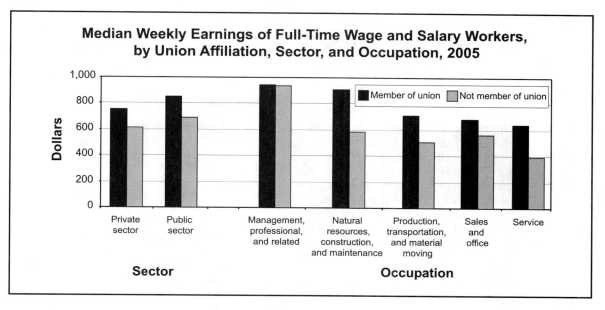

In both the public and private sectors, median weekly earnings of union members were about 23 percent higher than those of non-union workers in 2005. Union members in natural resources, construction, and manufacturing earned over 55 percent more than non-union members in the same occupational group. However, in management, professional, and related occupations, there was virtually no difference in median weekly earnings according to union status. (See Table 10-4.)

OTHER HIGHLIGHTS

- In 2005, the proportion of employed workers who were union members remained constant at 12.5 percent, making this the first year since 1999 that this percentage did not decline from the previous year. The decrease in the number of men belonging to unions was offset by an increase in the number of women belonging to unions. (See Tables 10-2 and 10-5.)

- The public sector, which typically has the highest percentage of union members, experienced increases in union membership at the state and local levels but suffered a decline at the federal level from 2004 to 2005. Local government employment, including teachers, librarians, and social service workers, made up more than half of all public sector employment. Nearly 42 percent of local government employees were union members in 2005. (See Table 10-3.)

- In five states, at least 20 percent of workers belonged to unions in 2005: New York (26.1 percent), Hawaii (25.8 percent), Alaska (22.8 percent), Michigan (20.5 percent), and New Jersey (20.5 percent). Of the five states, only Michigan experienced a decline in union membership from 2004 to 2005. (See Table 10-6.)

- Work stoppages were very rare in 2005, with days idle constituting only 0.01 percent of total working time. (See Table 10-1.)

NOTES AND DEFINITIONS

WORK STOPPAGES

Collection and Coverage

Data on work stoppages measure the number and duration of major strikes or lockouts (involving 1,000 workers or more) during the year, the number of workers involved in these stoppages, and the amount of time lost due to these stoppages.

Information on work stoppages is obtained from reports issued by the Federal Mediation and Conciliation Service, state labor market information offices, Bureau of Labor Statistics (BLS) Strike Reports from the Office of Employment and Unemployment Statistics, and media sources such as the *Daily Labor Report* and the *Wall Street Journal.* One or both parties involved in the work stoppage (employer and/or union) is contacted to verify the duration of the stoppage and number of workers idled by the stoppage.

The current series is not comparable with series terminated in 1981. The former series covered strikes involving six workers or more.

Concepts and Definitions

Major work stoppage includes both worker-initiated strikes and employer-initiated lockouts involving 1,000 workers or more. BLS does not distinguish between lockouts and strikes in its statistics.

Workers involved consists of workers directly involved in the stoppage. This category does not measure the indirect or secondary effect of stoppages on other establishments whose employees are idle from material shortages or lack of services.

Days of idleness is calculated by taking the number of workers involved in the strike or lockout and multiplying it by the number of days workers are off the job.

Sources of Additional Information

Additional information is available in BLS news release USDL 06-363, "Major Work Stoppages in 2005."

UNION MEMBERSHIP

Collection, Coverage, and Definitions

The estimates of union membership are obtained from the Current Population Survey (CPS). The union membership and earnings data are tabulated from one-quarter of the CPS monthly sample and are limited to wage and salary workers. Excluded are all self-employed workers.

Union members are members of a labor union or an employee association similar to a union.

Represented by unions refers to union members, as well as to workers who have no union affiliation but whose jobs are covered by a union contract.

Sources of Additional Information

Additional information is available in BLS news release USDL 06-99, "Union Members in 2005."

Table 10-1. Work Stoppages Involving 1,000 Workers or More, 1947–2005

(Number, percent.)

Year	Stoppages beginning during the year		Days idle during the year[1]	
	Number	Workers involved (thousands)[2]	Number (thousands)	Percent of estimated total working time[3]
1947	270	1 629	25 720	. . .
1948	245	1 435	26 127	0.22
1949	262	2 537	43 420	0.38
1950	424	1 698	30 390	0.26
1951	415	1 462	15 070	0.12
1952	470	2 746	48 820	0.38
1953	437	1 623	18 130	0.14
1954	265	1 075	16 630	0.13
1955	363	2 055	21 180	0.16
1956	287	1 370	26 840	0.20
1957	279	887	10 340	0.07
1958	332	1 587	17 900	0.13
1959	245	1 381	60 850	0.43
1960	222	896	13 260	0.09
1961	195	1 031	10 140	0.07
1962	211	793	11 760	0.08
1963	181	512	10 020	0.07
1964	246	1 183	16 220	0.11
1965	268	999	15 140	0.10
1966	321	1 300	16 000	0.10
1967	381	2 192	31 320	0.18
1968	392	1 855	35 367	0.20
1969	412	1 576	29 397	0.16
1970	381	2 468	52 761	0.29
1971	298	2 516	35 538	0.19
1972	250	975	16 764	0.09
1973	317	1 400	16 260	0.08
1974	424	1 796	31 809	0.16
1975	235	965	17 563	0.09
1976	231	1 519	23 962	0.12
1977	298	1 212	21 258	0.10
1978	219	1 006	23 774	0.11
1979	235	1 021	20 409	0.09
1980	187	795	20 844	0.09
1981	145	729	16 908	0.07
1982	96	656	9 061	0.04
1983	81	909	17 461	0.08
1984	62	376	8 499	0.04
1985	54	324	7 079	0.03
1986	69	533	11 861	0.05
1987	46	174	4 481	0.02
1988	40	118	4 381	0.02
1989	51	452	16 996	0.07
1990	44	185	5 926	0.02
1991	40	392	4 584	0.02
1992	35	364	3 989	0.01
1993	35	182	3 981	0.01
1994	45	322	5 021	0.02
1995	31	192	5 771	0.02
1996	37	273	4 889	0.02
1997	29	339	4 497	0.01
1998	34	387	5 116	0.02
1999	17	73	1 996	0.01
2000	39	394	20 419	0.06
2001	29	99	1 151	(4)
2002	19	46	660	(4)
2003	14	129	4 091	0.01
2004	17	171	3 344	0.01
2005	22	100	1 736	0.01

[1]Days idle include all stoppages in effect during the reference period. For work stoppages that are still ongoing at the end of the calendar year, only those days of idleness during the calendar year are counted.
[2]Workers are counted more than once if involved in more than one stoppage during the reference period.
[3]Agricultural and government workers are included in the calculation of estimated working time; private household, forestry, and fishery employees are excluded.
[4]Less than 0.005 percent.
. . . = Not available.

Table 10-2. Union Affiliation of Employed Wage and Salary Workers, by Selected Characteristics, 2000–2005

(Numbers in thousands, percent.)

Characteristic	2000					2001					2002				
	Total employed	Member of union[1]		Represented by union[2]		Total employed	Member of union[1]		Represented by union[2]		Total employed	Member of union[1]		Represented by union[2]	
		Total	Percent employed	Total	Percent employed		Total	Percent employed	Total	Percent employed		Total	Percent employed	Total	Percent employed
SEX AND AGE															
Both Sexes, 16 Years and Over	120 786	16 258	13.5	17 944	14.9	122 482	16 387	13.4	18 114	14.8	121 826	16 145	13.3	17 695	14.5
16 to 24 years	20 166	1 010	5.0	1 152	5.7	19 698	1 015	5.2	1 184	6.0	19 216	995	5.2	1 126	5.9
25 years and over	100 620	15 248	15.2	16 792	16.7	102 784	15 372	15.0	16 930	16.5	102 610	15 151	14.8	16 569	16.1
25 to 34 years	28 406	3 369	11.9	3 720	13.1	28 809	3 264	11.3	3 659	12.7	28 232	3 172	11.2	3 522	12.5
35 to 44 years	32 470	4 822	14.9	5 293	16.3	31 962	4 733	14.8	5 191	16.2	31 253	4 455	14.3	4 859	15.5
45 to 54 years	25 651	4 815	18.8	5 305	20.7	26 909	5 068	18.8	5 543	20.6	27 040	5 016	18.6	5 446	20.1
55 to 64 years	11 204	1 998	17.8	2 193	19.6	12 032	2 063	17.1	2 265	18.8	12 952	2 256	17.4	2 456	19.0
65 years and over	2 889	243	8.4	281	9.7	3 072	243	7.9	272	8.9	3 133	251	8.0	285	9.1
Men, 16 Years and Over	62 853	9 578	15.2	10 355	16.5	63 756	9 578	15.0	10 410	16.3	63 272	9 325	14.7	10 066	15.9
16 to 24 years	10 440	618	5.9	697	6.7	10 137	607	6.0	704	6.9	9 857	616	6.3	687	7.0
25 years and over	52 412	8 960	17.1	9 657	18.4	53 619	8 971	16.7	9 706	18.1	53 415	8 709	16.3	9 379	17.6
25 to 34 years	15 197	2 030	13.4	2 207	14.5	15 627	1 983	12.7	2 169	13.9	15 284	1 877	12.3	2 061	13.5
35 to 44 years	17 028	2 871	16.9	3 077	18.1	16 657	2 821	16.9	3 028	18.2	16 355	2 631	16.1	2 805	17.1
45 to 54 years	12 898	2 739	21.2	2 956	22.9	13 561	2 840	20.9	3 070	22.6	13 578	2 784	20.5	2 982	22.0
55 to 64 years	5 770	1 191	20.6	1 268	22.0	6 168	1 195	19.4	1 292	20.9	6 570	1 281	19.5	1 376	21.0
65 years and over	1 519	129	8.5	148	9.8	1 605	131	8.1	148	9.2	1 627	136	8.4	155	9.5
Women, 16 Years and Over	57 933	6 680	11.5	7 590	13.1	58 726	6 809	11.6	7 704	13.1	58 555	6 820	11.6	7 629	13.0
16 to 24 years	9 726	392	4.0	455	4.7	9 561	409	4.3	480	5.0	9 359	378	4.0	439	4.7
25 years and over	48 207	6 288	13.0	7 135	14.8	49 166	6 400	13.0	7 224	14.7	49 196	6 441	13.1	7 190	14.6
25 to 34 years	13 209	1 340	10.1	1 513	11.5	13 181	1 281	9.7	1 490	11.3	12 948	1 295	10.0	1 461	11.3
35 to 44 years	15 441	1 951	12.6	2 215	14.3	15 305	1 912	12.5	2 163	14.1	14 898	1 825	12.2	2 055	13.8
45 to 54 years	12 752	2 077	16.3	2 348	18.4	13 349	2 227	16.7	2 474	18.5	13 462	2 232	16.6	2 464	18.3
55 to 64 years	5 434	807	14.9	925	17.0	5 864	868	14.8	973	16.6	6 383	975	15.3	1 080	16.9
65 years and over	1 370	114	8.3	133	9.7	1 467	113	7.7	124	8.5	1 506	115	7.6	130	8.6
RACE, HISPANIC ORIGIN, AND SEX															
White, 16 Years and Over[3]	100 455	13 094	13.0	14 453	14.4	101 546	13 209	13.0	14 574	14.4	100 923	12 958	12.8	14 178	14.0
Men	53 105	7 911	14.9	8 541	16.1	53 731	7 909	14.7	8 585	16.0	53 198	7 689	14.5	8 284	15.6
Women	47 350	5 183	10.9	5 912	12.5	47 815	5 300	11.1	5 989	12.5	47 725	5 269	11.0	5 894	12.3
Black, 16 Years and Over[3]	14 544	2 489	17.1	2 744	18.9	14 261	2 409	16.9	2 668	18.7	14 108	2 386	16.9	2 624	18.6
Men	6 701	1 282	19.1	1 388	20.7	6 488	1 221	18.8	1 330	20.5	6 493	1 183	18.2	1 281	19.7
Women	7 843	1 208	15.4	1 356	17.3	7 773	1 188	15.3	1 338	17.2	7 615	1 204	15.8	1 343	17.6
Asian, 16 Years and Over[3]	. . .	. . .	. . .	. . .	. . .	. . .	. . .	. . .	. . .	. . .	. . .	. . .	. . .	. . .	. . .
Men	. . .	. . .	. . .	. . .	. . .	. . .	. . .	. . .	. . .	. . .	. . .	. . .	. . .	. . .	. . .
Women	. . .	. . .	. . .	. . .	. . .	. . .	. . .	. . .	. . .	. . .	. . .	. . .	. . .	. . .	. . .
Hispanic, 16 Years and Over[4]	13 609	1 554	11.4	1 740	12.8	15 174	1 679	11.1	1 876	12.4	15 486	1 639	10.6	1 810	11.7
Men	7 884	972	12.3	1 063	13.5	8 997	1 032	11.5	1 136	12.6	9 098	1 006	11.1	1 100	12.1
Women	5 725	582	10.2	677	11.8	6 177	647	10.5	740	12.0	6 387	633	9.9	710	11.1
FULL- OR PART-TIME STATUS[5]															
Full-time workers	99 917	14 822	14.8	16 306	16.3	101 187	14 921	14.7	16 445	16.3	100 081	14 622	14.6	16 005	16.0
Part-time workers	20 619	1 395	6.8	1 593	7.7	21 057	1 437	6.8	1 637	7.8	21 513	1 492	6.9	1 654	7.7

Note: Data refer to the sole or principal job of full- and part-time workers. Excluded are all self-employed workers, regardless of whether or not their businesses are incorporated.

[1]Data refer to members of a labor union or to an employee association similar to a union.
[2]Data refer to members of a labor union or to an employee association similar to a union, as well as to workers who report no union affiliation but whose jobs are covered by a union or an employee association contract.
[3]Beginning in 2003, persons who selected this race group only; persons who selected more than one race group are not included. Prior to 2003, persons who reported more than one race group were included in the group they identified as their main race. Additionally, estimates for the above race groups (White, Black, and Asian) do not sum to totals because data are not presented for all races.
[4]May be of any race.
[5]The distinction between full- and part-time workers is based on hours usually worked. Data will not sum to totals because full- or part-time status on the principal job is not identifiable for a small number of multiple jobholders.
. . . = Not available.

Table 10-2. Union Affiliation of Employed Wage and Salary Workers, by Selected Characteristics, 2000–2005—*Continued*

(Numbers in thousands, percent.)

Characteristic	2003					2004					2005				
	Total em-ployed	Member of union[1]		Represented by union[2]		Total em-ployed	Member of union[1]		Represented by union[2]		Total em-ployed	Member of union[1]		Represented by union[2]	
		Total	Percent em-ployed	Total	Percent em-ployed		Total	Percent em-ployed	Total	Percent em-ployed		Total	Percent em-ployed	Total	Percent em-ployed
SEX AND AGE															
Both Sexes, 16 Years and Over	122 358	15 776	12.9	17 448	14.3	123 554	15 472	12.5	17 087	13.8	125 889	15 685	12.5	17 223	13.7
16 to 24 years	18 904	966	5.1	1 124	5.9	19 109	890	4.7	1 019	5.3	19 283	878	4.6	1 019	5.3
25 years and over	103 454	14 810	14.3	16 324	15.8	104 444	14 581	14.0	16 069	15.4	106 606	14 808	13.9	16 204	15.2
25 to 34 years	28 179	3 097	11.0	3 455	12.3	28 202	2 982	10.6	3 316	11.8	28 450	3 044	10.7	3 368	11.8
35 to 44 years	30 714	4 308	14.0	4 717	15.4	30 470	4 173	13.7	4 590	15.1	30 654	4 211	13.7	4 579	14.9
45 to 54 years	27 567	4 848	17.6	5 307	19.3	28 039	4 771	17.0	5 233	18.7	28 714	4 731	16.5	5 158	18.0
55 to 64 years	13 633	2 300	16.9	2 547	18.7	14 239	2 390	16.8	2 617	18.4	15 158	2 496	16.5	2 732	18.0
65 years and over	3 361	258	7.7	297	8.8	3 495	264	7.5	314	9.0	3 631	325	8.9	366	10.1
Men, 16 Years and Over	63 236	9 044	14.3	9 848	15.6	64 145	8 878	13.8	9 638	15.0	65 466	8 870	13.5	9 597	14.7
16 to 24 years	9 683	595	6.1	685	7.1	9 835	557	5.7	627	6.4	9 860	523	5.3	603	6.1
25 years and over	53 553	8 450	15.8	9 163	17.1	54 310	8 321	15.3	9 010	16.6	55 606	8 347	15.0	8 994	16.2
25 to 34 years	15 263	1 826	12.0	2 005	13.1	15 391	1 722	11.2	1 873	12.2	15 559	1 754	11.3	1 915	12.3
35 to 44 years	16 080	2 535	15.8	2 735	17.0	16 035	2 449	15.3	2 658	16.6	16 196	2 422	15.0	2 582	15.9
45 to 54 years	13 723	2 684	19.6	2 891	21.1	14 026	2 699	19.2	2 903	20.7	14 421	2 658	18.4	2 849	19.8
55 to 64 years	6 776	1 271	18.8	1 377	20.3	7 117	1 309	18.4	1 414	19.9	7 606	1 346	17.7	1 458	19.2
65 years and over	1 710	133	7.8	155	9.0	1 741	142	8.2	163	9.4	1 824	167	9.1	190	10.4
Women, 16 Years and Over	59 122	6 732	11.4	7 601	12.9	59 408	6 593	11.1	7 450	12.5	60 423	6 815	11.3	7 626	12.6
16 to 24 years	9 221	371	4.0	439	4.8	9 274	333	3.6	391	4.2	9 423	354	3.8	417	4.4
25 years and over	49 901	6 360	12.7	7 161	14.4	50 134	6 260	12.5	7 058	14.1	51 000	6 461	12.7	7 210	14.1
25 to 34 years	12 916	1 270	9.8	1 451	11.2	12 811	1 261	9.8	1 443	11.3	12 891	1 290	10.0	1 454	11.3
35 to 44 years	14 634	1 773	12.1	1 982	13.5	14 435	1 725	11.9	1 931	13.4	14 457	1 790	12.4	1 997	13.8
45 to 54 years	13 844	2 163	15.6	2 416	17.5	14 014	2 072	14.8	2 330	16.6	14 293	2 073	14.5	2 309	16.2
55 to 64 years	6 857	1 029	15.0	1 170	17.1	7 122	1 081	15.2	1 203	16.9	7 552	1 150	15.2	1 274	16.9
65 years and over	1 651	125	7.6	142	8.6	1 753	121	6.9	151	8.6	1 806	158	8.8	176	9.8
RACE, HISPANIC ORIGIN, AND SEX															
White, 16 Years and Over[3]	100 589	12 535	12.5	13 849	13.8	101 340	12 381	12.2	13 657	13.5	102 967	12 520	12.2	13 755	13.4
Men	52 827	7 378	14.0	8 016	15.2	53 432	7 260	13.6	7 854	14.7	54 462	7 275	13.4	7 858	14.4
Women	47 762	5 157	10.8	5 834	12.2	47 908	5 121	10.7	5 803	12.1	48 505	5 245	10.8	5 897	12.2
Black, 16 Years and Over[3]	13 928	2 298	16.5	2 540	18.2	14 090	2 130	15.1	2 355	16.7	14 459	2 178	15.1	2 391	16.5
Men	6 302	1 153	18.3	1 249	19.8	6 409	1 085	16.9	1 185	18.5	6 603	1 062	16.1	1 166	17.7
Women	7 626	1 145	15.0	1 291	16.9	7 681	1 045	13.6	1 170	15.2	7 857	1 115	14.2	1 225	15.6
Asian, 16 Years and Over[3]	5 096	581	11.4	659	12.9	5 280	603	11.4	670	12.7	5 479	614	11.2	666	12.2
Men	2 699	296	11.0	346	12.8	2 815	328	11.7	371	13.2	2 881	314	10.9	337	11.7
Women	2 397	285	11.9	313	13.1	2 465	275	11.1	299	12.1	2 598	299	11.5	329	12.7
Hispanic, 16 Years and Over[4]	16 068	1 712	10.7	1 913	11.9	16 533	1 676	10.1	1 888	11.4	17 191	1 793	10.4	1 981	11.5
Men	9 567	1 050	11.0	1 160	12.1	9 857	1 016	10.3	1 130	11.5	10 324	1 093	10.6	1 185	11.5
Women	6 501	662	10.2	753	11.6	6 676	661	9.9	758	11.4	6 866	700	10.2	796	11.6
FULL- OR PART-TIME STATUS[5]															
Full-time workers	100 302	14 263	14.2	15 732	15.7	101 224	14 029	13.9	15 463	15.3	103 560	14 207	13.7	15 551	15.0
Part-time workers	21 809	1 479	6.8	1 679	7.7	22 047	1 406	6.4	1 587	7.2	22 052	1 441	6.5	1 630	7.4

Note: Data refer to the sole or principal job of full- and part-time workers. Excluded are all self-employed workers, regardless of whether or not their businesses are incorporated.

[1]Data refer to members of a labor union or to an employee association similar to a union.
[2]Data refer to members of a labor union or to an employee association similar to a union, as well as to workers who report no union affiliation but whose jobs are covered by a union or an employee association contract.
[3]Beginning in 2003, persons who selected this race group only; persons who selected more than one race group are not included. Prior to 2003, persons who reported more than one race group were included in the group they identified as their main race. Additionally, estimates for the above race groups (White, Black, and Asian) do not sum to totals because data are not presented for all races.
[4]May be of any race.
[5]The distinction between full- and part-time workers is based on hours usually worked. Data will not sum to totals because full- or part-time status on the principal job is not identifiable for a small number of multiple jobholders.

Table 10-3. Union Affiliation of Wage and Salary Workers, by Occupation and Industry, 2004–2005

(Thousands of people, percent.)

Occupation and industry	2004					2005				
	Total employed	Member of union[1]		Represented by union[2]		Total employed	Member of union[1]		Represented by union[2]	
		Total	Percent of employed	Total	Percent of employed		Total	Percent of employed	Total	Percent of employed
OCCUPATION										
Management, professional, and related	41 451	5 418	13.1	6 256	15.1	42 226	5 639	13.4	6 385	15.1
Management, business, and financial operations	15 758	732	4.6	895	5.7	15 955	793	5.0	939	5.9
Management	10 796	441	4.1	553	5.1	10 921	485	4.4	585	5.4
Business and financial operations	4 962	291	5.9	342	6.9	5 034	308	6.1	354	7.0
Professional and related	25 693	4 686	18.2	5 361	20.9	26 271	4 845	18.4	5 447	20.7
Computer and mathematical	2 962	128	4.3	171	5.8	3 067	142	4.6	172	5.6
Architecture and engineering	2 597	209	8.0	246	9.5	2 593	221	8.5	259	10.0
Life, physical, and social science	1 204	106	8.8	129	10.7	1 305	125	9.6	140	10.7
Community and social service	2 132	370	17.4	422	19.8	2 100	346	16.5	376	17.9
Legal	1 216	75	6.2	92	7.6	1 261	71	5.6	83	6.6
Education, training, and library	7 636	2 874	37.6	3 235	42.4	7 813	3 006	38.5	3 354	42.9
Arts, design, entertainment, sports, and media	1 894	162	8.6	184	9.7	1 957	152	7.8	171	8.8
Health care practitioner and technical	6 052	762	12.6	882	14.6	6 175	782	12.7	892	14.4
Services	20 724	2 371	11.4	2 552	12.3	21 074	2 446	11.6	2 659	12.6
Health care support	2 791	290	10.4	315	11.3	2 971	286	9.6	317	10.7
Protective service	2 840	1 059	37.3	1 118	39.4	2 843	1 051	37.0	1 109	39.0
Food preparation and serving related	7 164	294	4.1	337	4.7	7 361	316	4.3	362	4.9
Building and grounds cleaning and maintenance	4 597	490	10.7	529	11.5	4 525	504	11.1	553	12.2
Personal care and service	3 331	238	7.1	254	7.6	3 373	288	8.5	317	9.4
Sales and office	32 322	2 493	7.7	2 780	8.6	32 541	2 385	7.3	2 671	8.2
Sales and related	13 527	488	3.6	548	4.1	13 630	451	3.3	519	3.8
Office and administrative support	18 795	2 005	10.7	2 232	11.9	18 911	1 934	10.2	2 152	11.4
Natural resources, construction, and maintenance	12 081	2 222	18.4	2 343	19.4	12 907	2 129	16.5	2 238	17.3
Farming, fishing, and forestry	862	27	3.1	34	3.9	898	35	3.9	38	4.3
Construction and extraction	6 680	1 312	19.6	1 370	20.5	7 296	1 283	17.6	1 348	18.5
Installation, maintenance, and repair	4 540	883	19.4	939	20.7	4 713	811	17.2	851	18.1
Production, transportation, and material moving	16 976	2 968	17.5	3 156	18.6	17 142	3 086	18.0	3 271	19.1
Production	9 085	1 485	16.3	1 582	17.4	9 007	1 539	17.1	1 617	17.9
Transportation and material moving	7 891	1 483	18.8	1 574	20.0	8 135	1 547	19.0	1 655	20.3
INDUSTRY										
Private sector	103 584	8 205	7.9	8 956	8.6	105 508	8 255	7.8	8 962	8.5
Agriculture and related industries	1 023	23	2.2	30	2.9	1 021	28	2.7	30	3.0
Nonagricultural industries	102 560	8 182	8.0	8 926	8.7	104 487	8 227	7.9	8 931	8.5
Mining	496	57	11.4	58	11.7	600	48	8.0	57	9.5
Construction	7 550	1 110	14.7	1 162	15.4	8 053	1 057	13.1	1 111	13.8
Manufacturing	15 754	2 036	12.9	2 183	13.9	15 518	2 017	13.0	2 127	13.7
Durable goods	9 885	1 316	13.3	1 407	14.2	9 845	1 310	13.3	1 382	14.0
Nondurable goods	5 869	720	12.3	776	13.2	5 673	707	12.5	746	13.1
Wholesale and retail trade	18 754	1 028	5.5	1 107	5.9	18 989	1 021	5.4	1 122	5.9
Wholesale trade	4 083	189	4.6	214	5.2	4 017	236	5.9	259	6.4
Retail trade	14 671	839	5.7	893	6.1	14 973	785	5.2	864	5.8
Transportation and utilities	4 893	1 218	24.9	1 287	26.3	5 212	1 252	24.0	1 309	25.1
Transportation and warehousing	4 043	976	24.2	1 031	25.5	4 379	1 024	23.4	1 071	24.4
Utilities	850	241	28.4	256	30.1	833	228	27.4	239	28.6
Information[3]	3 058	433	14.2	470	15.4	2 934	398	13.6	422	14.4
Publishing, except Internet	778	52	6.7	59	7.6	765	68	8.8	74	9.7
Motion pictures and sound recording	329	52	15.7	54	16.4	277	42	15.0	43	15.5
Broadcasting, except Internet	502	47	9.3	53	10.5	534	46	8.6	48	9.0
Telecommunications	1 218	273	22.4	292	24.0	1 096	234	21.4	248	22.6
Financial activities	8 490	171	2.0	209	2.5	8 619	195	2.3	238	2.8
Finance and insurance	6 301	96	1.5	124	2.0	6 304	102	1.6	132	2.1
Finance	4 111	56	1.4	73	1.8	4 114	59	1.4	77	1.9
Insurance	2 191	40	1.8	51	2.3	2 190	44	2.0	54	2.5
Real estate and rental and leasing	2 188	76	3.5	85	3.9	2 315	92	4.0	107	4.6
Professional and business services	10 815	246	2.3	306	2.8	10 951	292	2.7	341	3.1
Professional and technical services	6 263	70	1.1	102	1.6	6 468	98	1.5	120	1.9
Management, administrative, and waste services	4 552	177	3.9	204	4.5	4 483	194	4.3	221	4.9
Education and health services	16 870	1 405	8.3	1 593	9.4	17 357	1 434	8.3	1 632	9.4
Educational services	3 243	421	13.0	475	14.6	3 312	435	13.1	511	15.4
Health care and social assistance	13 627	984	7.2	1 119	8.2	14 045	999	7.1	1 121	8.0
Leisure and hospitality	10 326	319	3.1	368	3.6	10 658	333	3.1	377	3.5
Arts, entertainment, and recreation	1 777	114	6.4	123	6.9	1 869	118	6.3	134	7.2
Accommodation and food services	8 548	205	2.4	245	2.9	8 790	215	2.4	243	2.8
Accommodation	1 431	117	8.2	132	9.2	1 459	122	8.3	130	8.9
Food services and drinking places	7 117	88	1.2	112	1.6	7 331	93	1.3	113	1.5
Other services[3]	5 556	158	2.8	183	3.3	5 596	181	3.2	194	3.5
Other services, except private households	4 782	148	3.1	172	3.6	4 799	175	3.7	188	3.9
Public sector	19 970	7 267	36.4	8 131	40.7	20 381	7 430	36.5	8 262	40.5
Federal government	3 298	985	29.9	1 153	35.0	3 427	954	27.8	1 134	33.1
State government	5 712	1 751	30.7	1 961	34.3	5 874	1 838	31.3	2 056	35.0
Local government	10 961	4 532	41.3	5 017	45.8	11 080	4 638	41.9	5 071	45.8

Note: Data refer to the sole or principal job of full- and part-time workers. Excluded are all self-employed workers, regardless of whether or not their businesses are incorporated.

[1]Data refer to members of a labor union or an employee association similar to a union.
[2]Data refer to members of a labor union or an employee association similar to a union, as well as to workers who report no union affiliation but whose jobs are covered by a union or an employee association contract.
[3]Includes other industries, not shown separately.

Table 10-4. Median Weekly Earnings of Full-Time Wage and Salary Workers, by Union Affiliation, Occupation, and Industry, 2004–2005

(Dollars.)

Occupation and industry	2004				2005			
	Total	Member of union[1]	Represented by union[2]	Non-union	Total	Member of union[1]	Represented by union[2]	Non-union
OCCUPATION								
Management, professional, and related	918	921	916	918	937	942	937	937
Management, business, and financial operations	965	963	972	965	997	1 015	1 029	995
Management	1 052	1 065	1 074	1 050	1 083	1 137	1 146	1 076
Business and financial operations	847	880	881	844	871	854	866	872
Professional and related	883	915	907	875	902	932	924	894
Computer and mathematical	1 114	1 000	983	1 124	1 132	1 009	1 029	1 141
Architecture and engineering	1 098	1 080	1 090	1 100	1 105	1 133	1 133	1 101
Life, physical, and social science	957	949	977	955	965	978	1 011	959
Community and social service	707	827	817	666	725	880	865	693
Legal	1 070	1 174	1 155	1 058	1 052	1 147	1 155	1 042
Education, training, and library	781	899	886	687	798	913	898	710
Arts, design, entertainment, sports, and media	768	953	972	754	819	983	925	808
Health care practitioner and technical	852	938	933	841	878	932	932	867
Services	411	655	647	389	413	643	629	392
Health care support	407	458	462	401	410	466	462	405
Protective service	700	907	897	567	678	896	886	568
Food preparation and serving related	360	445	435	355	356	439	442	350
Building and grounds cleaning and maintenance	385	515	513	368	394	528	518	378
Personal care and service	402	522	518	394	409	558	549	397
Sales and office	558	662	658	545	575	681	675	562
Sales and related	604	576	577	606	622	623	625	622
Office and administrative support	535	676	671	519	550	689	682	528
Natural resources, construction, and maintenance	621	867	858	581	623	910	903	585
Farming, fishing, and forestry	356	(3)	(3)	352	372	(3)	(3)	369
Construction and extraction	604	861	852	555	604	913	903	554
Installation, maintenance, and repair	704	886	880	662	705	915	913	666
Production, transportation, and material moving	523	687	681	498	540	709	704	510
Production	526	681	674	503	538	698	693	511
Transportation and material moving	520	695	689	491	543	721	717	508
INDUSTRY								
Private sector	615	739	734	604	625	757	752	615
Agriculture and related industries	403	(3)	(3)	402	402	(3)	(3)	402
Nonagricultural industries	617	740	735	606	629	758	753	617
Mining	874	905	911	865	885	(3)	989	870
Construction	618	893	884	588	619	933	926	590
Manufacturing	662	694	692	654	676	722	719	667
Durable goods	691	707	706	687	704	751	747	695
Nondurable goods	611	670	662	602	624	676	672	618
Wholesale and retail trade	550	596	590	547	566	615	610	562
Wholesale trade	677	722	709	674	692	678	676	694
Retail trade	509	567	560	507	515	590	585	513
Transportation and utilities	711	854	850	662	726	864	860	676
Transportation and warehousing	668	819	814	619	688	829	827	640
Utilities	957	979	978	948	941	960	954	931
Information[4]	828	893	887	808	832	931	925	810
Publishing, except Internet	720	844	829	710	755	860	867	740
Motion pictures and sound recording	805	(3)	(3)	762	751	(3)	(3)	691
Broadcasting, except Internet	763	(3)	(3)	749	749	(3)	(3)	738
Telecommunications	918	910	897	929	927	937	935	923
Financial activities	706	657	649	708	741	698	696	743
Finance and insurance	738	636	629	740	765	692	696	767
Finance	735	606	616	737	765	650	667	768
Insurance	743	(3)	(3)	744	764	(3)	(3)	766
Real estate and rental and leasing	615	677	670	613	653	711	696	649
Professional and business services	709	679	694	710	739	663	673	743
Professional and technical services	927	940	937	927	961	770	858	963
Management, administrative, and waste services	478	607	606	470	488	586	578	485
Education and health services	613	717	728	603	627	731	736	617
Educational services	716	828	831	679	737	818	809	718
Health care and social assistance	595	656	671	588	607	684	692	601
Leisure and hospitality	407	518	508	402	409	513	510	405
Arts, entertainment, and recreation	523	677	662	513	521	652	618	515
Accommodation and food services	391	477	473	387	388	487	486	384
Accommodation	432	481	490	422	455	515	510	438
Food services and drinking places	378	467	422	377	372	400	406	372
Other services[4]	528	749	750	521	535	694	698	524
Other services, except private households	560	764	764	551	579	698	701	572
Public sector	751	832	827	683	758	850	842	692
Federal government	856	840	848	869	882	873	879	887
State government	725	788	781	681	733	802	798	684
Local government	731	844	834	627	738	858	844	633

Note: Data refer to the sole or principal job of full- and part-time workers. Excluded are all self-employed workers, regardless of whether or not their businesses are incorporated.

[1]Data refer to members of a labor union or an employee association similar to a union.
[2]Data refer to members of a labor union or an employee association similar to a union, as well as to workers who report no union affiliation but whose jobs are covered by a union or an employee association contract.
[3]Data not shown where base is less than 50,000.
[4]Includes other industries, not shown separately.

Table 10-5. Union or Employee Association Members Among Wage and Salary Employees, 1977–2005

(Numbers in thousands, percent.)

Year	Total wage and salary employment	Union or employee association member	Union or association member as a percentage of wage and salary employment
1977	81 334	19 335	23.8
1978	84 968	19 548	23.0
1979	87 117	20 986	24.1
1980	87 480	20 095	23.0
1981	...	...	...
1982	...	...	...
1983[1]	88 290	17 717	20.1
1984	92 194	17 340	18.8
1985	94 521	16 996	18.0
1986	96 903	16 975	17.5
1987	99 303	16 913	17.0
1988	101 407	17 002	16.8
1989	103 480	16 980	16.4
1990	103 905	16 740	16.1
1991	102 786	16 568	16.1
1992	103 688	16 390	15.8
1993	105 087	16 598	15.8
1994[2]	107 989	16 748	15.5
1995	110 038	16 360	14.9
1996	111 960	16 269	14.5
1997	114 533	16 110	14.1
1998	116 730	16 211	13.9
1999	118 963	16 477	13.9
2000	120 786	16 258	13.5
2001	122 482	16 387	13.4
2002	121 826	16 145	13.3
2003	122 358	15 776	12.9
2004	123 554	15 472	12.5
2005	125 889	15 685	12.5

[1]Annual average data beginning in 1983 are not directly comparable with the May data for 1977–1980.
[2]Data beginning in 1994 are not strictly comparable with data for 1993 and earlier years because of the introduction of a major redesign of the Current Population Survey questionnaire and collection methodology and the introduction of 1990 census-based population controls.
. . . = Not available.

Table 10-6. Union Affiliation of Employed Wage and Salary Workers, by State, 2004–2005

(Numbers in thousands, percent.)

| State | 2004 | | | | | 2005 | | | | |
| | Total employed | Member of union[1] | | Represented by union[2] | | Total employed | Member of union[1] | | Represented by union[2] | |
		Total	Percent of employed	Total	Percent of employed		Total	Percent of employed	Total	Percent of employed
UNITED STATES	123 554	15 472	12.5	17 087	13.8	125 889	15 685	12.5	17 223	13.7
Alabama	1 861	181	9.7	213	11.5	1 909	195	10.2	223	11.7
Alaska	268	54	20.1	60	22.4	275	63	22.8	66	24.1
Arizona	2 323	145	6.3	183	7.9	2 366	145	6.1	181	7.7
Arkansas	1 058	51	4.8	65	6.2	1 138	54	4.8	68	6.0
California	14 414	2 385	16.5	2 588	18.0	14 687	2 424	16.5	2 610	17.8
Colorado	2 050	172	8.4	191	9.3	2 052	170	8.3	193	9.4
Connecticut	1 539	235	15.3	256	16.6	1 550	247	15.9	263	17.0
Delaware	373	46	12.4	49	13.2	386	46	11.8	50	12.9
District of Columbia	258	33	12.7	38	14.5	259	29	11.3	33	12.8
Florida	6 943	414	6.0	533	7.7	7 389	401	5.4	532	7.2
Georgia	3 773	242	6.4	282	7.5	3 765	190	5.0	226	6.0
Hawaii	533	126	23.7	132	24.8	545	141	25.8	145	26.7
Idaho	561	33	5.8	44	7.9	606	31	5.2	38	6.3
Illinois	5 410	908	16.8	971	17.9	5 473	927	16.9	965	17.6
Indiana	2 717	311	11.4	338	12.4	2 789	346	12.4	368	13.2
Iowa	1 345	141	10.5	171	12.7	1 369	157	11.5	185	13.5
Kansas	1 223	103	8.4	132	10.8	1 210	85	7.0	115	9.5
Kentucky	1 699	164	9.6	197	11.6	1 696	164	9.7	184	10.8
Louisiana	1 697	129	7.6	157	9.3	1 778	114	6.4	132	7.4
Maine	564	64	11.3	74	13.2	582	69	11.9	79	13.6
Maryland	2 502	272	10.9	313	12.5	2 530	337	13.3	379	15.0
Massachusetts	2 920	393	13.5	430	14.7	2 886	402	13.9	431	14.9
Michigan	4 305	930	21.6	966	22.4	4 288	880	20.5	916	21.4
Minnesota	2 429	424	17.5	443	18.3	2 494	392	15.7	410	16.4
Mississippi	1 108	53	4.8	70	6.3	1 089	77	7.1	105	9.7
Missouri	2 546	315	12.4	357	14.0	2 532	290	11.5	319	12.6
Montana	366	43	11.7	46	12.6	391	42	10.7	48	12.2
Nebraska	831	69	8.3	83	10.0	830	69	8.3	79	9.5
Nevada	1 006	126	12.5	144	14.3	1 051	145	13.8	158	15.1
New Hampshire	618	61	9.9	68	11.0	627	65	10.4	72	11.5
New Jersey	3 769	745	19.8	813	21.6	3 868	791	20.5	838	21.7
New Mexico	734	49	6.7	65	8.9	777	63	8.1	83	10.7
New York	7 901	1 996	25.3	2 085	26.4	8 008	2 090	26.1	2 201	27.5
North Carolina	3 549	97	2.7	127	3.6	3 631	107	2.9	143	3.9
North Dakota	292	22	7.7	26	9.0	289	21	7.3	26	9.2
Ohio	4 998	759	15.2	820	16.4	5 039	804	16.0	866	17.2
Oklahoma	1 402	86	6.1	100	7.1	1 432	77	5.4	91	6.4
Oregon	1 471	224	15.2	243	16.5	1 470	213	14.5	231	15.7
Pennsylvania	5 298	793	15.0	842	15.9	5 456	753	13.8	818	15.0
Rhode Island	487	79	16.3	83	17.0	494	79	15.9	83	16.8
South Carolina	1 765	54	3.0	74	4.2	1 739	40	2.3	58	3.3
South Dakota	347	21	6.0	27	7.7	350	21	5.9	29	8.2
Tennessee	2 465	164	6.7	191	7.7	2 368	128	5.4	156	6.6
Texas	9 072	457	5.0	573	6.3	9 485	506	5.3	590	6.2
Utah	1 001	58	5.8	67	6.7	1 035	51	4.9	63	6.1
Vermont	291	29	9.8	33	11.4	287	31	10.8	37	13.0
Virginia	3 308	176	5.3	218	6.6	3 406	165	4.8	211	6.2
Washington	2 645	510	19.3	536	20.3	2 746	523	19.1	559	20.4
West Virginia	700	99	14.2	110	15.7	688	99	14.4	107	15.5
Wisconsin	2 597	414	16.0	439	16.9	2 551	410	16.1	438	17.2
Wyoming	222	18	8.0	22	9.8	228	18	7.9	22	9.5

Note: Data refer to the sole or principal job of full and part-time workers. Excluded are all self-employed workers, regardless of whether or not their businesses are incorporated.

[1]Data refer to members of a labor union or an employee association similar to a union.
[2]Data refer to members of a labor union or an employee association similar to a union, as well as to workers who report no union affiliation but whose jobs are covered by a union or an employee association contract.

CHAPTER ELEVEN

FOREIGN LABOR AND PRICE STATISTICS

FOREIGN LABOR AND PRICE STATISTICS

HIGHLIGHTS

This chapter compares several summary statistics of labor force status, manufacturing productivity, and consumer prices for the United States with similar statistics for other countries. Different concepts and methodologies can make intercountry comparisons difficult, but the Bureau of Labor Statistics (BLS) makes adjustments to reconcile as much of the data as possible. There are lags in the receipt of data from other countries; thus, comparisons are based on the latest data available.

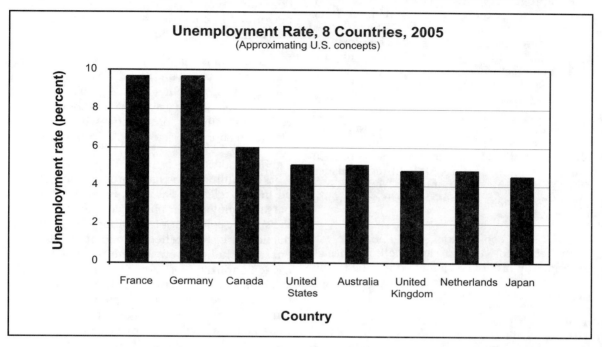

In 2005, unemployment rates declined or remained the same in 7 out of the 8 countries measured in Table 11-1. Unemployment data were not available for Italy or Sweden. Although unemployment rates dropped in several countries, Western Europe continued to struggle with relatively high unemployment. The unemployment rates in France and Germany in 2005 were both 9.7 percent in 2005, compared to 5.1 percent in the United States. (See Table 11-1.)

OTHER HIGHLIGHTS

- The decline in unemployment rates accompanied a rise in gross domestic product (GDP) per capita in all countries except Italy. However, even though GDP per capita increased in most countries, it generally grew at a much slower rate than in previous years. (See Table 11-9.)

- Stated in 2002 U.S. dollars, the United States had the highest real GDP per capita at $39,103 in 2005, followed closely by Norway at $38,338 (data adjusted to accommodate price differences and reflect purchasing power parity). The Republic of Korea had the lowest real GDP per capita at $20,422, but had the largest percentage increase from the previous year at 3.5 percent. (See Table 11-6.)

- Inflation appeared to be under control in the 16 countries from which data were collected; prices increased a small amount in most of these countries in 2005. (See Table 11-5.)

NOTES AND DEFINITIONS

Collection and Coverage

From its inception, the Bureau of Labor Statistics (BLS) has conducted a program of research and statistical analysis that compares labor conditions in the United States with those in selected foreign countries. The principal comparative measures cover the labor force, employment, and unemployment; trends in labor productivity and unit labor costs in manufacturing; and hourly compensation costs for manufacturing production workers. All of the measures are based upon statistical data and other source materials from (a) the statistical agencies of the foreign countries studied; (b) international and supranational bodies such as the United Nations, the International Labour Office (ILO), the Organisation for Economic Co-operation and Development (OECD), and the Statistical Office of the European Communities (EUROSTAT), which attempt to obtain comparable country data; and (c) other secondary sources.

International statistical comparisons should be made with caution, as the statistical concepts and methods in each country are primarily fashioned to meet domestic (rather than international) needs. Wherever possible, BLS adjusts the data to improve comparability.

The first table in this chapter provides BLS comparative measures of the civilian labor force participation rate, employment, and unemployment, approximating U.S. concepts. The second table provides trend indexes of manufacturing labor productivity (output per hour), hourly compensation, unit labor costs (labor compensation per unit of output), and related measures for the United States and 14 other countries. The third table is limited to production workers in manufacturing and shows hourly compensation costs in U.S. dollars for the United States and 31 other countries.

The fourth and fifth tables provide Consumer Price Indexes for selected countries. No adjustments for compa-

rability are made in the total indexes except to convert them to a uniform base year (1982–1984 = 100). The final tables present comparative levels and trends in real gross domestic product (GDP) per capita and per employed person for 15 countries. All GDP series are converted to U.S. dollars through the use of purchasing power parities.

U.S. data in this chapter have been revised from 1998 forward and are based on the 1997 North American Industry Classification System (NAICS). Output, a value-added measure, is based on a new methodology that balances and reconciles industry production with commodity usage. Canadian data are also on a NAICS basis for 1997 onward.

Labor productivity is defined as real output per hour worked. Although the labor productivity measure presented in this release relates output to the hours worked of persons employed in manufacturing, it does not measure the specific contributions of labor as a single factor of production. It instead reflects the joint effects of many influences, including new technology, capital investment, capacity utilization, energy use, managerial skills, and the skills and efforts of the workforce. Unit labor costs are defined as the cost of labor input required to produce one unit of output. They are computed as compensation in nominal terms divided by real output.

Sources of Additional Information

An extensive description of the methodology can be found in Chapter 12 in the *BLS Handbook of Methods*. For more information on manufacturing productivity, see BLS news release USDL 06-1655, "International Comparisons of Manufacturing Productivity and Unit Labor Costs Trends, 2005." Special reports on the BLS Web site at <http://www.bls.gov> describe the adjustments made to each country to conform the country's data to U.S. definitions.

Table 11-1. Employment Status of the Working-Age Population, Approximating U.S. Concepts, 10 Countries, 1970–2005

(Numbers in thousands, percent.)

Category and year	United States	Canada	Australia	Japan	France	Germany[1]	Italy	Nether-lands	Sweden	United Kingdom
Employed										
1970	78 678	7 919	5 388	50 140	20 270	26 100	19 080	. . .	3 850	24 330
1971	79 367	8 104	5 517	50 470	20 420	26 220	19 020	. . .	3 854	[2]24 315
1972	[2]82 153	8 344	5 601	50 590	20 540	26 280	18 710	. . .	3 856	24 385
1973	85 064	8 761	5 765	51 920	20 840	26 590	18 870	5 050	3 873	24 777
1974	86 794	9 125	5 891	51 710	21 030	26 240	19 280	5 100	3 956	24 849
1975	85 846	9 284	5 866	51 530	20 860	25 540	19 400	5 070	4 056	24 758
1976	88 752	[2]9 652	5 946	52 030	21 030	25 400	19 500	5 100	4 082	24 611
1977	92 017	9 825	6 000	52 720	21 220	25 430	19 670	5 210	4 093	24 638
1978	[2]96 048	10 124	6 038	53 370	21 320	25 650	19 720	5 260	4 109	24 774
1979	98 824	10 561	6 111	54 040	21 390	26 080	19 930	5 350	4 174	25 031
1980	99 303	10 872	6 284	54 600	21 440	26 490	20 200	5 520	4 226	24 917
1981	100 397	11 192	6 416	55 060	21 330	26 450	20 280	5 550	4 219	24 256
1982	99 526	10 847	6 415	55 620	[2]21 390	26 150	20 250	5 520	4 213	23 781
1983	100 834	10 936	6 300	56 550	21 380	[2]25 770	20 320	[2]5 420	4 218	23 607
1984	105 005	11 211	6 494	56 870	21 200	25 830	20 390	5 490	4 249	24 115
1985	107 150	11 526	6 697	57 260	21 150	26 010	20 490	5 650	4 293	24 422
1986	[2]109 597	11 873	[2]6 984	57 740	21 240	26 380	[2]20 610	5 740	4 326	24 578
1987	112 440	12 221	7 142	58 320	21 320	26 590	20 590	5 850	[2]4 340	25 072
1988	114 968	12 591	7 413	59 310	21 520	26 800	20 870	[2]5 884	4 410	25 905
1989	117 342	12 876	7 734	60 500	21 850	27 200	20 770	5 989	4 480	26 588
1990	[2]118 793	12 964	7 877	61 700	[2]22 075	27 950	21 080	6 267	4 513	26 713
1991	117 718	12 754	7 698	62 920	22 113	[2]36 871	[2]21 360	6 383	4 447	26 007
1992	118 492	12 643	7 660	63 620	22 000	36 390	21 230	6 549	4 265	25 384
1993	120 259	12 705	7 699	63 820	21 715	35 989	[2]20 543	6 572	4 028	25 158
1994	[2]123 060	12 975	7 942	63 860	21 746	35 756	20 171	6 664	3 992	25 685
1995	124 900	13 210	8 256	63 900	21 955	35 780	20 030	6 730	4 056	25 691
1996	126 708	13 338	8 364	64 200	22 036	35 637	20 120	6 858	4 019	25 941
1997	[2]129 558	13 637	8 444	64 900	22 176	35 508	20 165	7 163	3 973	26 413
1998	[2]131 463	13 973	8 618	64 450	22 597	36 059	20 366	7 321	4 034	26 686
1999	[2]133 488	14 331	8 762	63 920	23 056	[2]36 042	20 613	7 595	4 117	27 051
2000	[2]136 891	14 681	8 989	63 790	23 698	36 236	20 969	7 907	4 229	27 368
2001	136 933	14 866	9 091	63 460	24 142	36 350	21 356	7 947	4 303	27 599
2002	136 485	15 223	9 271	62 650	24 314	36 018	21 665	8 076	4 310	27 812
2003	[2]137 736	15 579	9 481	62 510	24 288	35 615	21 973	8 080	4 303	28 073
2004	[2]139 252	15 861	9 677	62 640	24 259	35 876	22 105	8 118	4 276	28 358
2005	141 730	16 080	9 987	62 910	. . .	. . .	. . .	8 036	. . .	28 637
Unemployed										
1970	4 093	476	91	590	530	140	640	. . .	59	770
1971	5 016	535	107	640	580	160	640	. . .	101	[2]1 059
1972	4 882	553	150	730	610	190	740	. . .	107	1 116
1973	4 365	515	136	680	590	190	720	160	98	946
1974	5 156	514	162	730	630	420	620	190	80	949
1975	7 929	690	302	1 000	910	890	690	270	67	1 174
1976	7 406	[2]716	298	1 080	1 020	890	790	290	66	1 414
1977	6 991	836	358	1 100	1 160	900	840	270	75	1 470
1978	6 202	898	405	1 240	1 220	870	850	280	94	1 453
1979	6 137	831	408	1 170	1 390	780	920	290	88	1 432
1980	7 637	854	409	1 140	1 490	770	920	350	86	1 833
1981	8 273	887	394	1 260	1 760	1 090	1 040	540	108	2 609
1982	10 678	1 298	495	1 360	[2]1 930	1 560	1 160	630	137	2 875
1983	10 717	1 437	697	1 560	2 020	[2]1 900	1 270	[2]700	151	3 081
1984	8 539	1 377	641	1 610	2 360	1 970	1 280	710	136	3 241
1985	8 312	1 309	603	1 560	2 470	2 010	1 310	600	125	3 151
1986	8 237	1 216	[2]601	1 670	2 520	1 860	[2]1 680	640	117	3 161
1987	7 425	1 123	612	1 730	2 570	1 800	1 760	650	[2]97	2 940
1988	6 701	999	558	1 550	2 460	1 810	1 790	[2]458	84	2 445
1989	6 528	982	490	1 420	2 320	1 640	1 760	427	72	2 082
1990	[2]7 047	1 083	563	1 340	[2]2 084	1 460	1 590	390	81	2 053
1991	8 628	1 386	788	1 360	2 210	[2]2 204	[2]1 580	373	144	2 530
1992	9 613	1 507	897	1 420	2 443	2 615	1 680	373	255	2 823
1993	8 940	1 533	914	1 660	2 776	3 113	[2]2 227	442	416	2 930
1994	[2]7 996	1 372	829	1 920	2 926	3 318	2 421	489	426	2 433
1995	7 404	1 246	739	2 100	2 787	3 200	2 544	478	404	2 439
1996	7 236	1 285	751	2 250	2 946	3 505	2 555	443	440	2 298
1997	[2]6 739	1 248	759	2 300	2 940	3 907	2 584	374	445	1 987
1998	[2]6 210	1 162	721	2 790	2 837	3 693	2 634	296	368	1 788
1999	[2]5 880	1 072	652	3 170	2 711	[2]3 333	2 559	253	313	1 726
2000	[2]5 692	956	602	3 200	2 385	3 065	2 388	230	260	1 584
2001	6 801	1 026	[2]661	3 400	2 226	3 110	2 164	183	227	1 486
2002	8 378	1 143	636	3 590	2 393	3 396	2 062	232	234	1 524
2003	[2]8 774	1 150	611	3 500	2 577	3 661	2 048	311	264	1 484
2004	[2]8 149	1 093	567	3 130	2 641	3 920	1 960	387	300	1 417
2005	7 591	1 028	537	2 940	. . .	. . .	. . .	405	. . .	1 458

[1]Unified Germany for 1991 and onward. Data for previous years relate to the former West Germany.
[2]Break in series.
. . . = Not available.

Table 11-1. Employment Status of the Working-Age Population, Approximating U.S. Concepts, 10 Countries, 1970–2005—*Continued*

(Numbers in thousands, percent.)

Category and year	United States	Canada	Australia	Japan	France	Germany[1]	Italy	Netherlands	Sweden	United Kingdom
Civilian Labor Force Participation Rate										
1970	60.4	57.8	62.1	64.5	57.5	56.9	49.0	...	64.0	61.1
1971	60.2	58.1	62.2	64.3	57.4	56.5	48.7	...	64.2	²62.8
1972	60.4	58.6	62.3	63.8	57.2	56.2	47.7	...	64.1	62.9
1973	60.8	59.7	62.6	64.0	57.3	56.3	47.6	53.4	64.1	63.1
1974	61.2	60.5	63.0	63.1	57.4	55.7	47.7	53.5	64.8	63.1
1975	61.2	61.1	63.2	62.4	57.2	55.0	47.7	54.5	65.9	63.1
1976	61.6	²62.5	62.7	62.4	57.5	54.6	48.0	54.1	66.0	63.0
1977	62.3	62.8	62.7	62.5	57.8	54.4	48.2	54.2	65.9	62.7
1978	63.2	63.7	61.9	62.8	57.7	54.4	47.8	54.0	66.1	62.6
1979	63.7	64.5	61.6	62.7	57.8	54.5	48.0	54.2	66.6	62.7
1980	63.8	65.0	62.1	62.6	57.5	54.7	48.2	55.4	66.9	62.8
1981	63.9	65.6	61.9	62.6	57.5	54.7	48.3	56.7	66.8	62.7
1982	64.0	64.9	61.7	62.7	²57.5	54.6	47.7	56.6	66.8	61.9
1983	64.0	65.2	61.4	63.1	57.2	²54.3	47.5	²55.7	66.7	61.6
1984	64.4	65.5	61.5	62.7	57.2	54.4	47.3	55.7	66.6	62.7
1985	64.8	65.9	61.7	62.3	56.8	54.7	47.2	55.5	66.9	62.9
1986	65.3	66.4	²62.8	62.1	56.7	54.9	²47.8	56.0	67.0	62.9
1987	65.6	66.7	62.9	61.9	56.5	55.0	47.6	56.3	²66.4	63.2
1988	65.9	67.1	63.3	61.9	56.2	55.1	47.4	²54.4	66.9	63.8
1989	66.5	67.4	64.1	62.2	56.1	55.2	47.3	54.6	67.3	64.3
1990	²66.5	67.3	64.7	62.6	²55.7	55.3	47.2	56.2	67.3	64.3
1991	66.2	66.7	64.2	63.2	55.7	²58.8	²47.7	56.6	67.0	63.7
1992	66.4	65.9	63.9	63.4	55.7	58.1	47.5	57.5	65.7	62.9
1993	66.3	65.5	63.5	63.3	55.4	57.8	²48.3	57.9	64.5	62.6
1994	²66.6	65.2	63.9	63.1	55.6	57.4	47.6	58.6	63.7	62.4
1995	66.6	64.8	64.5	62.9	55.4	57.1	47.3	58.8	64.1	62.4
1996	66.8	64.7	64.6	63.0	55.7	57.1	47.3	59.2	64.0	62.4
1997	67.1	65.0	64.3	63.2	55.6	57.3	47.3	60.8	63.3	62.5
1998	67.1	65.3	64.3	62.8	55.9	57.7	47.6	61.1	62.8	62.5
1999	67.1	65.8	64.0	62.4	56.3	²56.9	47.9	62.6	62.8	62.8
2000	67.1	65.8	64.4	62.0	56.5	56.7	48.1	64.4	63.8	62.9
2001	66.8	65.9	64.4	61.6	56.8	56.7	48.2	63.9	63.7	62.7
2002	66.6	66.7	64.4	60.8	57.1	56.4	48.5	64.9	64.0	62.9
2003	66.2	67.3	64.6	60.3	57.0	56.0	49.1	65.2	64.0	63.0
2004	66.0	67.3	64.7	60.0	56.9	56.5	49.1	65.7	63.7	63.0
2005	66.0	67.0	65.4	60.0	...	...	...	65.2	...	63.1
Unemployment Rate										
1970	4.9	5.7	1.6	1.2	2.5	0.5	3.2	...	1.5	3.1
1971	5.9	6.2	1.9	1.3	2.8	0.6	3.3	...	2.6	²4.2
1972	5.6	6.2	2.6	1.4	2.9	0.7	3.8	...	2.7	4.4
1973	4.9	5.5	2.3	1.3	2.8	0.7	3.7	3.1	2.5	3.7
1974	5.6	5.3	2.7	1.4	2.9	1.6	3.1	3.6	2.0	3.7
1975	8.5	6.9	4.9	1.9	4.2	3.4	3.4	5.1	1.6	4.5
1976	7.7	²6.9	4.8	2.0	4.6	3.4	3.9	5.4	1.6	5.4
1977	7.1	7.8	5.6	2.0	5.2	3.4	4.1	4.9	1.8	5.6
1978	6.1	8.1	6.3	2.3	5.4	3.3	4.1	5.1	2.2	5.5
1979	5.8	7.3	6.3	2.1	6.1	2.9	4.4	5.1	2.1	5.4
1980	7.1	7.3	6.1	2.0	6.5	2.8	4.4	6.0	2.0	6.9
1981	7.6	7.3	5.8	2.2	7.6	4.0	4.9	8.9	2.5	9.7
1982	9.7	10.7	7.2	2.4	²8.3	5.6	5.4	10.2	3.1	10.8
1983	9.6	11.6	10.0	2.7	8.6	²6.9	5.9	²11.4	3.5	11.5
1984	7.5	10.9	9.0	2.8	10.0	7.1	5.9	11.5	3.1	11.8
1985	7.2	10.2	8.3	2.7	10.5	7.2	6.0	9.6	2.8	11.4
1986	7.0	9.3	²7.9	2.8	10.6	6.6	²7.5	10.0	2.6	11.4
1987	6.2	8.4	7.9	2.9	10.8	6.3	7.9	10.0	²2.2	10.5
1988	5.5	7.4	7.0	2.5	10.3	6.3	7.9	²7.2	1.9	8.6
1989	5.3	7.1	6.0	2.3	9.6	5.7	7.8	6.7	1.6	7.3
1990	²5.6	7.7	6.7	2.1	²8.6	5.0	7.0	5.9	1.8	7.1
1991	6.8	9.8	9.3	2.1	9.1	²5.6	²6.9	5.5	3.1	8.9
1992	7.5	10.6	10.5	2.2	10.0	6.7	7.3	5.4	5.6	10.0
1993	6.9	10.8	10.6	2.5	11.3	8.0	²9.8	6.3	9.4	10.4
1994	²6.1	9.6	9.4	2.9	11.9	8.5	10.7	6.8	9.6	8.7
1995	5.6	8.6	8.2	3.2	11.3	8.2	11.3	6.6	9.1	8.7
1996	5.4	8.8	8.2	3.4	11.8	9.0	11.3	6.1	9.9	8.1
1997	4.9	8.4	8.3	3.4	11.7	9.9	11.4	5.0	10.1	7.0
1998	4.5	7.7	7.7	4.1	11.2	9.3	11.5	3.9	8.4	6.3
1999	4.2	7.0	6.9	4.7	10.5	²8.5	11.0	3.2	7.1	6.0
2000	4.0	6.1	6.3	4.8	9.1	7.8	10.2	2.8	5.8	5.5
2001	4.7	6.5	²6.8	5.1	8.4	7.9	9.2	2.2	5.0	5.1
2002	5.8	7.0	6.4	5.4	9.0	8.6	8.7	2.8	5.1	5.2
2003	6.0	6.9	6.1	5.3	9.6	9.3	8.5	3.7	5.8	5.0
2004	5.5	6.4	5.5	4.8	9.8	9.9	8.1	4.6	6.6	4.8
2005	5.1	6.0	5.1	4.5	9.7	9.7	...	...	4.8	4.8

[1]Unified Germany for 1991 and onward. Data for previous years relate to the former West Germany.
²Break in series.
. . . = Not available.

Table 11-2. Indexes of Manufacturing Productivity and Related Measures, 15 Countries, 1970 and 1990–2005

(1992 = 100.)

Category and year	United States	Canada	Japan	Korea, Republic of	Taiwan	Belgium	Denmark	France	Germany[1]	Italy	Netherlands	Norway	Sweden	United Kingdom	Australia
Output Per Hour															
1970	52.4	55.9	37.7	...	...	32.9	47.8	38.5	52.0	40.1	38.5	59.1	52.2	45.4	...
1990	93.5	93.4	94.4	82.7	89.8	96.8	98.5	92.7	99.0	97.7	98.7	98.1	94.6	90.1	91.6
1991	96.3	95.3	99.0	92.7	96.8	99.1	99.7	96.4	98.3	97.0	99.0	98.2	95.5	94.3	96.6
1992	100.0	100.0	100.0	100.0	100.0	100.0	100.0	100.0	100.0	100.0	100.0	100.0	100.0	100.0	100.0
1993	102.7	105.8	101.7	108.3	101.3	102.5	100.3	101.2	101.0	102.8	102.0	99.6	107.3	102.8	105.8
1994	108.1	110.8	103.3	118.1	105.2	108.4	112.7	109.4	108.5	107.6	113.1	99.6	118.2	105.4	104.9
1995	112.1	112.4	111.0	129.7	112.9	113.2	112.7	116.0	110.2	111.1	117.3	100.7	125.1	103.7	105.5
1996	116.8	109.7	116.1	142.6	121.5	116.0	109.0	116.7	113.3	112.5	120.5	102.5	130.2	102.8	112.8
1997	121.7	117.0	120.7	160.8	126.5	125.7	117.7	125.8	120.0	113.3	121.2	102.0	142.0	104.1	114.7
1998	130.2	120.7	120.4	179.3	132.7	126.9	117.1	132.6	120.4	112.5	124.5	99.9	150.7	105.6	117.6
1999	136.7	124.5	124.9	199.4	140.9	124.6	119.0	138.7	123.4	112.5	129.3	103.6	164.1	110.9	118.9
2000	147.7	129.8	131.7	216.4	148.4	129.3	123.2	148.2	132.0	116.0	138.5	106.6	176.8	117.9	127.1
2001	149.2	127.4	128.9	214.8	155.1	130.7	123.4	150.7	135.4	116.2	139.2	109.8	172.6	121.8	130.7
2002	165.0	129.8	133.1	235.8	166.7	136.9	124.2	157.4	137.0	114.2	143.4	112.8	190.7	125.1	135.2
2003	176.8	130.6	142.3	252.2	171.7	141.0	124.7	164.2	142.4	111.3	146.4	122.6	204.5	130.6	140.7
2004	186.3	135.9	150.4	281.2	179.9	145.5	125.8	170.0	149.0	112.4	153.7	128.8	224.6	137.9	139.7
2005	195.7	143.7	154.1	305.1	191.4	149.7	125.8	176.7	156.9	112.4	160.0	132.5	235.4	141.4	142.4
Output															
1970	54.5	59.9	39.4	6.4	12.9	57.6	74.0	56.9	70.9	41.7	59.8	91.0	80.7	90.3	...
1990	98.2	106.0	97.1	88.1	91.0	101.0	101.7	97.7	99.1	100.5	99.0	101.4	110.1	105.3	104.1
1991	96.8	99.0	102.0	96.0	96.4	100.7	100.3	99.2	102.4	100.2	99.8	99.0	104.1	100.1	100.9
1992	100.0	100.0	100.0	100.0	100.0	100.0	100.0	100.0	100.0	100.0	100.0	100.0	100.0	100.0	100.0
1993	104.2	105.9	96.3	105.1	100.9	97.0	97.0	95.9	92.0	97.6	97.7	101.7	101.9	101.4	103.5
1994	112.2	114.1	94.9	117.1	106.9	101.4	107.5	100.6	94.9	104.1	104.5	104.6	117.5	106.2	109.0
1995	117.3	119.6	98.9	130.8	112.7	104.2	112.7	106.2	94.0	109.1	108.2	107.3	132.5	107.9	108.4
1996	121.6	119.6	103.0	139.2	118.7	105.6	107.5	106.3	92.0	107.8	109.8	110.3	137.1	108.6	111.7
1997	129.0	127.7	106.1	146.0	125.5	112.5	116.3	113.3	96.1	109.6	111.3	114.2	147.6	110.6	114.7
1998	137.7	134.0	99.2	134.5	129.5	114.1	117.2	119.0	97.2	109.9	115.1	113.7	159.5	111.3	117.7
1999	143.7	145.5	99.9	163.7	139.0	113.3	118.2	123.1	98.2	109.6	119.4	113.6	173.9	112.3	117.3
2000	152.7	159.6	105.1	191.5	149.2	118.3	122.5	128.7	104.8	112.9	127.4	112.8	189.7	115.0	122.9
2001	144.2	153.2	99.3	195.7	138.1	118.3	122.5	130.0	106.6	111.8	127.2	112.3	185.6	113.5	122.2
2002	148.2	154.5	97.5	210.5	148.3	119.1	119.0	129.9	104.6	110.4	127.2	112.2	196.4	110.5	127.7
2003	151.0	154.4	102.7	222.2	155.9	118.1	114.6	132.3	105.7	107.8	125.8	115.6	203.6	110.7	130.2
2004	158.2	161.6	107.5	246.8	170.6	120.8	111.7	134.5	110.6	108.6	127.8	121.0	223.6	113.0	130.0
2005	164.5	165.1	108.7	264.1	180.5	120.3	111.7	136.5	113.9	106.3	128.1	124.1	229.3	111.7	129.9
Total Hours															
1970	104.0	107.1	104.3	...	...	174.7	154.9	147.5	136.3	104.0	155.5	153.9	154.7	198.7	...
1990	105.0	113.5	102.9	106.4	101.4	104.3	103.3	105.5	100.1	102.9	100.3	103.4	116.4	116.9	113.6
1991	100.5	103.9	103.1	103.6	99.6	101.5	100.6	102.9	104.1	103.3	100.8	100.8	109.0	106.2	104.4
1992	100.0	100.0	100.0	100.0	100.0	100.0	100.0	100.0	100.0	100.0	100.0	100.0	100.0	100.0	100.0
1993	101.4	100.1	94.7	97.1	99.6	94.7	96.8	94.8	91.1	95.0	95.8	102.1	94.9	98.7	97.8
1994	103.8	103.0	91.9	99.2	101.7	93.6	95.4	91.9	87.5	96.8	92.4	105.0	99.4	100.8	103.9
1995	104.6	106.4	89.1	100.9	99.8	92.0	100.0	91.6	85.3	98.2	92.3	106.6	105.9	104.0	102.8
1996	104.2	109.0	88.8	97.6	97.7	91.1	98.6	91.0	81.2	95.8	91.1	107.6	105.3	105.7	99.1
1997	106.0	109.1	87.9	90.8	99.2	89.6	98.8	90.1	80.1	96.7	91.8	112.0	103.9	106.3	100.0
1998	105.7	111.0	82.4	75.0	97.6	89.9	100.1	89.7	80.7	97.7	92.4	113.7	105.9	105.4	100.1
1999	105.1	116.9	79.9	82.1	98.7	90.9	99.4	88.7	79.6	97.4	92.3	109.6	106.0	101.2	98.7
2000	103.4	122.9	79.8	88.5	100.5	91.4	99.4	86.8	79.4	97.3	91.9	105.9	107.3	97.5	96.7
2001	96.6	120.2	77.1	91.1	89.0	90.5	99.3	86.3	78.7	96.2	91.4	102.3	107.5	93.2	93.5
2002	89.8	119.0	73.3	89.3	89.0	87.0	95.8	82.5	76.4	96.7	88.7	99.4	103.0	88.3	94.5
2003	85.4	118.2	72.2	88.1	90.8	83.8	91.9	80.6	74.3	96.8	85.9	94.3	99.6	84.8	92.5
2004	84.9	118.9	71.5	87.8	94.9	83.0	88.8	79.1	74.2	96.6	83.2	94.0	99.6	81.9	93.0
2005	84.0	114.8	70.5	86.5	94.3	80.4	88.8	77.2	72.6	94.5	80.0	93.7	97.4	79.0	91.2
Compensation Per Hour, National Currency Basis															
1970	24.0	17.2	16.4	...	...	13.7	10.8	9.3	20.7	5.3	19.4	11.8	10.7	6.8	...
1990	90.5	88.5	90.6	68.0	85.2	90.1	93.6	88.5	89.4	87.6	89.8	92.3	87.8	88.8	86.3
1991	95.6	95.0	96.5	85.5	93.5	97.3	97.8	93.9	91.4	94.2	94.8	97.5	95.5	99.8	94.0
1992	100.0	100.0	100.0	100.0	100.0	100.0	100.0	100.0	100.0	100.0	100.0	100.0	100.0	100.0	100.0
1993	102.0	102.0	102.7	115.9	105.9	104.8	102.4	104.3	106.2	105.7	104.5	101.5	97.4	103.2	105.9
1994	105.3	103.9	104.7	133.1	111.1	106.1	106.0	108.0	111.0	107.3	109.0	104.4	99.8	104.7	103.9
1995	107.3	106.5	108.3	161.6	120.2	109.2	112.7	110.7	117.0	112.0	112.1	109.2	106.8	106.5	112.7
1996	109.3	107.4	109.1	188.1	128.2	111.1	112.6	112.5	122.5	120.0	114.6	113.6	115.2	107.0	122.3
1997	112.2	111.7	112.7	204.5	132.1	115.5	116.5	116.3	124.9	124.1	117.6	118.7	121.0	110.9	124.0
1998	118.7	115.8	115.6	222.7	137.1	117.3	119.6	117.2	126.7	123.3	122.4	125.7	125.6	120.0	127.7
1999	123.4	116.6	115.5	223.9	139.6	118.8	122.6	121.0	129.6	125.6	126.5	133.0	130.3	127.3	132.2
2000	134.7	118.9	114.9	239.1	142.3	120.9	125.0	127.0	136.3	128.7	132.8	140.5	136.8	134.4	138.9
2001	137.9	122.7	116.4	246.7	151.4	127.3	130.9	130.6	140.6	133.5	138.9	148.9	143.8	140.0	147.7
2002	147.8	126.2	117.2	271.6	145.0	132.8	136.5	137.4	144.1	136.9	146.8	156.7	151.7	148.1	154.7
2003	158.2	130.5	114.6	285.0	147.3	136.7	142.5	141.4	147.2	140.6	152.8	163.3	159.2	154.9	164.5
2004	161.4	131.6	115.1	325.5	144.0	138.9	146.7	144.7	148.0	145.1	158.0	167.6	162.6	162.2	167.8
2005	168.8	138.2	117.0	345.6	149.5	144.8	150.1	148.7	150.6	149.5	163.2	173.4	169.2	169.1	177.6

[1]Unified Germany for 1991 and onward. Data for previous years relate to the former West Germany.
... = Not available.

Table 11-2. Indexes of Manufacturing Productivity and Related Measures, 15 Countries, 1970 and 1990–2005—*Continued*

(1992 = 100.)

Category and year	United States	Canada	Japan	Korea, Republic of	Taiwan	Belgium	Denmark	France	Germany[1]	Italy	Nether-lands	Norway	Sweden	United King-dom	Australia
Compensation Per Hour, U.S. Currency Basis															
1970	24.0	19.9	5.8	. . .	. . .	8.9	8.7	8.9	8.9	10.3	9.4	10.3	12.0	9.2	. . .
1990	90.5	91.6	79.2	75.0	79.6	86.6	91.2	86.0	86.4	90.1	86.7	91.7	86.4	89.6	91.7
1991	95.6	100.2	90.9	91.1	87.9	91.5	92.2	88.0	86.0	93.5	89.1	93.3	91.9	99.9	99.6
1992	100.0	100.0	100.0	100.0	100.0	100.0	100.0	100.0	100.0	100.0	100.0	100.0	100.0	100.0	100.0
1993	102.0	95.6	117.2	112.9	100.9	97.4	95.3	97.5	100.2	82.8	98.9	88.8	72.8	87.7	98.0
1994	105.3	91.9	129.9	129.5	105.6	102.1	100.7	103.1	106.9	82.1	105.4	91.9	75.3	90.8	103.4
1995	107.3	93.7	146.1	164.1	114.2	119.1	116.6	117.5	127.6	84.7	122.8	107.1	87.1	95.2	113.5
1996	109.3	95.2	127.2	183.4	117.4	115.3	117.2	116.4	127.2	95.8	119.6	109.3	100.1	94.5	130.2
1997	112.2	97.5	118.1	169.3	115.5	103.7	106.4	105.4	112.5	89.8	105.9	104.1	92.2	102.8	125.5
1998	118.7	94.3	111.9	124.8	102.8	103.8	107.7	105.1	112.5	87.5	108.5	103.4	92.0	112.6	109.2
1999	123.4	94.9	128.8	147.6	108.7	100.9	105.9	104.0	110.3	85.1	107.5	105.9	91.7	116.6	116.0
2000	134.7	96.8	135.1	165.9	114.6	88.9	93.2	94.6	100.5	75.6	97.9	99.1	86.9	115.4	109.9
2001	137.9	95.7	121.4	149.8	112.6	90.8	94.9	94.4	100.5	76.0	99.2	102.9	81.0	114.1	103.8
2002	147.8	97.1	118.6	170.4	105.6	100.1	104.5	104.8	108.8	82.3	110.8	121.9	90.9	126.0	114.4
2003	158.2	112.6	125.3	187.6	107.7	123.3	130.8	129.2	133.1	101.3	138.0	143.4	114.8	143.3	146.0
2004	161.4	122.2	135.0	223.0	108.6	137.7	147.9	145.3	147.0	114.9	156.9	154.6	128.9	168.3	168.1
2005	168.8	137.9	134.7	264.9	117.1	143.7	151.1	149.3	149.7	118.5	162.1	167.2	131.9	174.3	184.2
Unit Labor Costs, National Currency Basis															
1970	45.8	30.8	43.6	8.6	23.3	41.7	22.7	24.1	39.8	13.1	50.4	20.0	20.6	14.9	. . .
1990	96.8	94.8	95.9	82.1	94.9	93.0	95.0	95.5	90.3	89.7	91.1	94.1	92.9	98.5	94.2
1991	99.2	99.7	97.4	92.2	96.5	98.1	98.1	97.4	93.0	97.1	95.7	99.2	100.0	105.9	97.3
1992	100.0	100.0	100.0	100.0	100.0	100.0	100.0	100.0	100.0	100.0	100.0	100.0	100.0	100.0	100.0
1993	99.3	96.5	101.0	107.0	104.6	102.3	102.2	103.1	105.2	102.9	102.4	101.9	90.8	100.4	100.1
1994	97.4	93.8	101.4	112.7	105.6	97.9	94.1	98.7	102.4	99.8	96.4	104.8	84.4	99.4	99.1
1995	95.7	94.7	97.6	124.6	106.5	96.4	96.0	95.4	106.2	100.8	95.6	108.4	85.3	102.7	106.8
1996	93.6	97.9	94.0	131.9	105.5	95.8	103.3	96.4	108.2	106.6	95.1	110.8	88.5	104.1	108.4
1997	92.2	95.5	93.4	127.1	104.5	91.9	98.9	92.4	104.1	109.5	97.1	116.4	85.2	106.5	108.1
1998	91.2	95.9	96.1	124.2	103.4	92.4	102.1	88.3	105.2	109.6	98.3	125.7	83.3	113.6	108.5
1999	90.3	93.7	92.5	112.3	99.1	95.4	103.0	87.3	105.1	111.7	97.8	128.3	79.4	114.8	111.1
2000	91.2	91.6	87.3	110.5	95.9	93.5	101.4	85.7	103.3	110.9	95.9	131.9	77.4	114.0	109.3
2001	92.4	96.3	90.3	114.8	97.6	97.4	106.1	86.7	103.8	114.9	99.8	135.6	83.3	115.0	113.0
2002	89.6	97.2	88.0	115.2	87.0	97.0	109.9	87.3	105.1	119.8	102.4	138.8	79.5	118.4	114.4
2003	89.5	99.9	80.5	113.0	85.8	97.0	114.3	86.1	103.4	126.3	104.3	133.3	77.9	118.6	116.9
2004	86.7	96.8	76.5	115.8	80.1	95.4	116.6	85.1	99.3	129.2	102.8	130.2	72.4	117.6	120.1
2005	86.3	96.2	75.9	113.3	78.1	96.8	119.3	84.1	96.0	133.0	102.0	130.9	71.9	119.6	124.7
Unit Labor Costs, U.S. Currency Basis															
1970	45.8	35.7	15.4	21.7	14.6	27.0	18.3	23.1	17.1	25.8	24.5	17.4	23.1	20.2	. . .
1990	96.8	98.1	83.9	90.7	88.7	89.5	92.7	92.8	87.3	92.2	87.9	93.5	91.3	99.5	100.1
1991	99.2	105.2	91.8	98.2	90.8	92.3	92.5	91.3	87.5	96.4	90.0	95.0	96.3	106.0	103.1
1992	100.0	100.0	100.0	100.0	100.0	100.0	100.0	100.0	100.0	100.0	100.0	100.0	100.0	100.0	100.0
1993	99.3	90.4	115.3	104.2	99.6	95.1	95.1	96.3	99.3	80.6	96.9	89.1	67.8	85.3	92.6
1994	97.4	83.0	125.8	109.6	100.4	94.2	89.4	94.2	98.6	76.3	93.2	92.3	63.7	86.2	98.6
1995	95.7	83.4	131.7	126.5	101.1	105.2	103.5	101.3	115.8	76.2	104.8	106.4	69.6	91.8	107.6
1996	93.6	86.7	109.6	128.6	96.7	99.4	107.6	99.7	112.2	85.2	99.2	106.6	76.9	92.0	115.4
1997	92.2	83.3	97.8	105.3	91.3	82.5	90.4	83.8	93.8	79.2	87.4	102.1	64.9	98.8	109.3
1998	91.2	78.1	93.0	69.6	77.5	81.8	92.0	79.3	93.4	77.7	87.2	103.5	61.1	106.6	92.9
1999	90.3	76.2	103.1	74.0	77.2	81.0	89.0	75.0	89.4	75.7	83.2	102.2	55.9	105.1	97.5
2000	91.2	74.5	102.6	76.7	77.2	68.8	75.6	63.8	76.2	65.1	70.7	93.0	49.1	97.8	86.4
2001	92.4	75.1	94.2	69.7	72.6	69.5	76.9	64.2	74.2	65.5	71.3	93.7	46.9	93.7	79.5
2002	89.6	74.8	89.1	72.3	63.4	73.1	84.2	66.6	79.4	72.1	77.3	108.1	47.6	100.7	84.6
2003	89.5	86.2	88.1	74.4	62.7	87.5	104.9	78.7	93.5	91.0	94.3	117.0	56.2	109.7	103.7
2004	86.7	89.9	89.7	79.3	60.4	94.6	117.5	85.5	98.6	102.2	102.1	120.0	57.4	122.0	120.3
2005	86.3	95.9	87.4	86.8	61.2	96.0	120.1	84.5	95.4	105.4	101.3	126.3	56.0	123.3	129.3
Exchange Rates[2]															
1970	100.0	115.8	35.4	252.7	62.9	64.7	80.5	95.7	42.8	196.5	48.6	86.9	112.3	135.6	152.3
1990	100.0	103.6	87.4	110.4	93.5	96.2	97.5	97.2	96.6	102.8	96.6	99.4	98.4	101.0	106.3
1991	100.0	105.5	94.2	106.5	94.0	94.0	94.3	93.7	94.0	99.3	93.9	95.7	96.3	100.1	106.0
1992	100.0	100.0	100.0	100.0	100.0	100.0	100.0	100.0	100.0	100.0	100.0	100.0	100.0	100.0	100.0
1993	100.0	93.7	114.1	97.4	95.2	93.0	93.1	93.4	94.4	78.3	94.6	87.5	74.7	85.0	92.5
1994	100.0	88.4	124.1	97.2	95.1	96.2	95.0	95.4	96.3	76.5	96.7	88.1	75.5	86.7	99.5
1995	100.0	88.1	134.9	101.5	95.0	109.1	107.8	106.2	109.1	75.6	109.6	98.1	81.6	89.4	100.7
1996	100.0	88.6	116.5	97.5	91.6	103.8	104.1	103.5	103.8	79.9	104.3	96.2	86.8	88.4	106.5
1997	100.0	87.3	104.7	82.8	87.4	89.8	91.3	90.7	90.0	72.3	90.1	87.7	76.2	92.7	101.1
1998	100.0	81.5	96.8	56.0	75.0	88.5	90.1	89.7	88.8	70.9	88.7	82.3	73.3	93.8	85.6
1999	100.0	81.3	111.5	65.9	77.8	84.9	86.4	86.0	85.1	67.8	85.0	79.6	70.4	91.6	87.8
2000	100.0	81.4	117.6	69.4	80.5	73.6	74.6	74.5	73.7	58.7	73.7	70.5	63.5	85.8	79.1
2001	100.0	78.0	104.3	60.7	74.4	71.3	72.5	72.2	71.5	57.0	71.4	69.1	56.3	81.5	70.3
2002	100.0	77.0	101.2	62.8	72.9	75.3	76.6	76.3	75.5	60.2	75.4	77.8	59.9	85.1	73.9
2003	100.0	86.3	109.3	65.8	73.1	90.2	91.8	91.4	90.4	72.0	90.3	87.8	72.1	92.5	88.7
2004	100.0	92.8	117.2	68.5	75.4	99.1	100.8	100.4	99.3	79.2	99.3	92.2	79.3	103.8	100.2
2005	100.0	99.8	115.1	76.6	78.3	99.2	100.7	100.7	100.5	79.2	99.4	96.5	78.0	103.1	103.7

[1]Unified Germany for 1991 and onward. Data for previous years relate to the former West Germany.
[2]Index of value of foreign currency relative to the U.S. dollar.
. . . = Not available.

Table 11-3. Hourly Compensation Costs in U.S. Dollars for Production Workers in Manufacturing, 32 Countries and Selected Areas, Selected Years, 1975–2004

(Dollars.)

Region and country	1975	1980	1985	1990	1995	2000	2001	2002	2003	2004
Americas										
United States	6.16	9.63	12.71	14.84	17.21	19.70	20.58	21.40	22.27	23.17
Brazil	. . .	. . .	. . .	. . .	. . .	3.51	2.95	2.56	2.74	3.03
Canada	6.11	8.87	11.20	16.33	16.50	16.48	16.23	16.66	19.37	21.42
Mexico	1.45	2.19	1.58	1.56	1.47	2.20	2.54	2.60	2.49	2.50
Asia and Oceania										
Australia	5.60	8.44	8.18	13.09	15.36	14.39	13.30	15.41	19.78	23.09
Hong Kong SAR[1]	0.75	1.50	1.73	3.22	4.80	5.45	5.74	5.66	5.54	5.51
Israel	2.03	3.41	3.66	7.71	9.50	11.49	12.25	11.03	11.66	12.18
Japan	2.97	5.46	6.27	12.54	23.55	22.02	19.43	18.65	20.32	21.90
Korea, Republic of	0.32	0.95	1.23	3.70	7.28	8.24	7.72	8.77	10.03	11.52
New Zealand	3.10	5.14	4.30	8.01	9.78	7.91	7.53	8.60	11.04	12.89
Singapore	0.83	1.53	2.53	3.75	7.58	7.19	6.97	6.71	7.18	7.45
Sri Lanka	0.28	0.22	0.28	0.35	0.48	0.48	0.45	0.49	0.51	. . .
Taiwan	0.37	0.99	1.49	3.85	5.87	6.19	6.05	5.64	5.69	5.97
Europe										
Austria	4.50	8.87	7.57	17.91	25.26	19.17	19.08	20.69	25.32	28.29
Belgium	5.77	11.74	8.29	17.84	25.64	20.09	19.80	21.74	26.52	29.98
Czech Republic	. . .	. . .	. . .	. . .	2.53	2.83	3.13	3.83	4.72	5.43
Denmark	6.24	10.77	8.10	18.35	25.28	21.87	22.02	24.25	30.15	33.75
Finland	4.63	8.30	8.20	21.15	24.31	19.44	19.85	21.78	27.10	30.67
France	4.50	8.90	7.48	15.36	19.26	15.46	15.65	17.12	21.14	23.89
Germany[2]	6.26	12.16	9.46	21.71	30.09	22.67	22.48	24.20	29.63	32.53
Greece	1.69	3.73	3.67	6.82	9.07	. . .	. . .	. . .	. . .	. . .
Hungary	. . .	. . .	. . .	. . .	2.69	2.79	3.16	3.92	4.80	5.72
Ireland	3.06	6.02	6.00	11.77	13.75	12.72	13.60	15.26	19.09	21.94
Italy	4.64	8.09	7.56	17.28	15.69	13.84	13.61	14.75	18.11	20.48
Luxembourg	6.22	11.51	7.48	16.00	23.36	17.51	17.21	18.71	23.12	26.57
Netherlands	6.58	12.05	8.73	17.98	24.03	19.33	19.85	22.12	27.47	30.76
Norway	6.90	11.80	10.47	21.76	24.84	22.66	23.29	27.29	31.56	34.64
Portugal	1.52	1.98	1.46	3.59	5.09	4.49	4.59	5.07	6.24	7.02
Spain	2.52	5.86	4.64	11.30	12.70	10.65	10.76	11.92	14.97	17.10
Sweden	7.14	12.44	9.61	20.81	21.68	20.18	18.39	20.23	25.19	28.42
Switzerland	6.03	10.96	9.55	20.63	28.99	21.02	21.60	23.81	27.83	30.26
United Kingdom	3.35	7.52	6.22	12.61	13.79	16.73	16.75	18.25	21.20	24.71
Trade-Weighted Measures[3,4]										
All 31 foreign economies	3.85	6.54	6.65	11.90	15.05	13.78	13.43	14.00	16.28	18.02
All 31 foreign economies less Brazil, the Czech Republic, and Hungary	3.85	6.54	6.65	11.90	15.11	14.06	13.71	14.29	16.63	18.41
OECD[5,6]	4.16	7.05	7.12	12.69	15.93	14.73	14.34	15.03	17.58	19.51
Europe[6]	4.99	9.67	7.85	17.05	21.50	18.08	18.11	19.80	24.10	27.08
European Union-15[7]	4.92	9.59	7.74	16.84	21.40	18.13	18.12	19.78	24.14	27.17
Asian NIEs[8]	0.49	1.14	1.61	3.69	6.59	7.07	6.82	7.05	7.62	8.32

[1]Hong Kong Special Administrative Region of China.
[2]Unified Germany for 1995 onward. Data for previous years relate to the former West Germany.
[3]Since data for Germany are not available before 1993, data for the former West Germany are only included in the trade-weighted measures.
[4]The trade weights used to compute the average compensation cost measures for selected economic groups are new weights based on the relative dollar value of U.S. trade in manufactured commodities (exports plus imports) with each country or region in 2004. The trade data are compiled by the U.S. Census Bureau.
[5]Organisation for Economic Co-operation and Development.
[6]Data for the Czech Republic and Hungary are not included for 1975–1990.
[7]European Union-15 refers to European Union member countries prior to the European Union's expansion to 25 countries on May 1, 2004. It consisted of Austria, Belgium, Denmark, Finland, France, Germany, Greece, Ireland, Italy, Luxembourg, Netherlands, Portugal, Spain, Sweden, and the United Kingdom.
[8]The Asian Newly Industrialized Economies (NIEs) are Hong Kong, Korea, Singapore, and Taiwan.
. . . = Not available.

Table 11-4. Consumer Price Indexes, 16 Countries, 1950–2005

(1982–1984 = 100.)

Year	Consumer Price Index[1]															
	United States[2]	Canada[3]	Japan	Australia[4]	Austria	Belgium[5]	Denmark[6]	France[7]	Germany[8]	Italy	Netherlands[9]	Norway[10]	Spain[11]	Sweden	Switzerland[12]	United Kingdom
1950	24.1	21.6	14.8	12.6	...	24.0	12.3	11.1	...	...	...	13.6	5.5	13.4	33.2	9.8
1951	26.0	23.9	17.2	15.1	...	26.3	13.5	13.0	...	...	...	15.7	6.0	15.5	34.8	10.7
1952	26.5	24.5	18.0	17.7	...	26.5	14.0	14.6	...	...	...	17.1	5.9	16.7	35.7	11.7
1953	26.7	24.2	19.2	18.4	...	26.4	14.1	14.4	...	10.3	...	17.5	6.0	16.9	35.4	12.1
1954	26.9	24.4	20.5	18.5	...	26.9	14.2	14.3	...	10.6	...	18.2	6.1	17.1	35.7	12.3
1955	26.8	24.4	20.2	18.9	...	26.8	15.0	14.5	...	10.9	...	18.4	6.3	17.5	36.0	12.9
1956	27.2	24.8	20.3	20.1	...	27.4	15.8	14.8	...	11.2	...	19.1	6.7	18.4	36.5	13.5
1957	28.1	25.6	20.9	20.6	...	28.2	16.1	15.3	...	11.4	...	19.6	7.4	19.2	37.3	14.0
1958	28.9	26.3	20.8	20.9	31.6	28.6	16.3	17.6	...	11.7	...	20.6	8.4	20.0	37.9	14.4
1959	29.1	26.6	21.1	21.3	32.0	29.0	16.5	18.7	...	11.7	...	21.0	9.0	20.2	37.7	14.5
1960	29.6	26.9	21.8	22.1	32.6	29.1	16.7	19.4	...	11.9	...	21.1	9.1	21.0	38.2	14.6
1961	29.9	27.1	23.0	22.6	33.8	29.3	17.4	20.0	...	12.2	...	21.6	9.2	21.5	38.9	15.1
1962	30.2	27.4	24.6	22.6	35.3	29.8	18.8	21.0	43.1	12.7	...	22.8	9.7	22.5	40.6	15.8
1963	30.6	27.9	26.4	22.7	36.2	30.4	19.8	22.0	44.4	13.7	...	23.4	10.6	23.2	42.0	16.1
1964	31.0	28.4	27.4	23.2	37.6	31.7	20.5	22.7	45.4	14.5	...	24.7	11.3	23.9	43.3	16.6
1965	31.5	29.1	29.5	24.1	39.5	32.9	21.8	23.3	46.9	15.2	...	25.7	12.8	25.1	44.8	17.4
1966	32.4	30.2	31.0	24.9	40.3	34.3	23.3	23.9	48.6	15.5	...	26.6	13.6	26.8	46.9	18.1
1967	33.4	31.3	32.3	25.7	41.9	35.3	25.0	24.6	49.4	16.1	...	27.8	14.5	27.9	48.8	18.5
1968	34.8	32.5	34.0	26.3	43.1	36.3	27.0	25.7	50.2	16.3	...	28.7	15.2	28.4	50.0	19.4
1969	36.7	34.0	35.8	27.1	44.4	37.6	27.9	27.3	51.1	16.7	40.6	29.6	15.5	29.2	51.3	20.5
1970	38.8	35.1	38.5	28.2	46.4	39.1	29.8	28.8	52.8	17.5	42.1	32.8	16.4	31.3	53.1	21.8
1971	40.5	36.2	40.9	29.9	48.5	40.8	31.5	30.3	55.6	18.4	45.3	34.8	17.7	33.6	56.6	23.8
1972	41.8	37.9	42.9	31.6	51.6	43.0	33.6	32.2	58.7	19.4	48.9	37.3	19.2	35.6	60.4	25.5
1973	44.4	40.7	47.9	34.6	55.5	46.0	36.7	34.6	62.8	21.6	52.9	40.1	21.4	38.0	65.7	27.9
1974	49.3	45.2	59.1	39.9	60.8	51.9	42.3	39.3	67.2	25.7	58.1	43.8	24.8	41.7	72.1	32.3
1975	53.8	50.1	66.0	45.9	65.9	58.5	46.4	43.9	71.2	30.0	63.8	49.0	29.0	45.8	76.9	40.1
1976	56.9	53.8	72.2	52.1	70.8	63.8	50.5	48.2	74.2	35.1	69.6	53.5	34.1	50.5	78.2	46.8
1977	60.6	58.1	78.1	58.5	74.6	68.4	56.1	52.7	77.0	41.0	74.1	58.3	42.4	56.3	79.2	54.2
1978	65.2	63.3	81.4	63.1	77.3	71.4	61.8	57.5	79.0	46.0	77.2	63.1	50.8	61.9	80.1	58.7
1979	72.6	69.1	84.4	68.8	80.2	74.6	67.7	63.6	82.3	52.8	80.5	66.1	58.8	66.4	83.0	66.6
1980	82.4	76.1	90.9	75.8	85.3	79.6	76.1	72.3	86.7	64.0	86.1	73.3	67.9	75.5	86.3	78.5
1981	90.9	85.6	95.4	83.2	91.1	85.6	85.0	82.0	92.2	75.4	91.9	83.3	77.8	84.6	91.9	87.9
1982	96.5	94.9	98.0	92.4	96.0	93.1	93.6	91.6	97.1	87.8	97.2	92.7	89.0	91.9	97.1	95.4
1983	99.6	100.4	99.8	101.8	99.2	100.3	100.0	100.5	100.3	100.7	99.8	100.5	99.9	100.0	100.0	99.8
1984	103.9	104.7	102.1	105.8	104.8	106.6	106.4	107.9	102.7	111.5	103.0	106.8	111.1	108.1	102.9	104.8
1985	107.6	108.9	104.2	112.9	108.2	111.8	111.4	114.2	104.8	121.8	105.3	112.9	120.9	116.0	106.4	111.1
1986	109.6	113.4	104.8	123.2	110.0	113.3	115.4	117.2	104.7	129.0	105.6	121.0	131.5	121.0	107.2	114.9
1987	113.6	118.4	104.9	133.7	111.6	115.0	120.0	120.9	104.9	135.1	105.1	131.6	138.5	126.1	108.8	119.7
1988	118.3	123.2	105.7	142.9	113.8	116.4	125.5	124.2	106.3	141.9	106.1	140.4	145.1	133.4	110.8	125.6
1989	124.0	129.3	108.1	154.1	116.6	120.0	131.5	128.6	109.2	150.8	107.1	146.8	155.0	142.0	114.3	135.4
1990	130.7	135.5	111.4	165.3	120.5	124.1	135.0	133.0	112.1	160.5	109.9	152.8	165.4	156.7	120.5	148.2
1991	136.2	143.1	115.1	170.7	124.4	128.1	138.2	137.2	81.9	170.6	113.3	158.0	175.2	171.5	127.5	156.9
1992	140.3	145.3	117.0	172.4	129.5	131.2	141.1	140.6	86.1	179.4	116.9	161.7	185.6	175.6	132.7	162.7
1993	144.5	147.9	118.5	175.5	134.1	134.8	142.9	143.5	89.9	187.5	120.0	165.4	194.1	183.9	137.0	165.3
1994	148.2	148.2	119.3	178.8	138.2	138.0	145.8	145.9	92.3	195.0	123.3	167.7	203.3	187.8	138.3	169.3
1995	152.4	151.4	119.2	187.1	141.3	140.1	148.8	148.4	93.9	205.1	125.7	171.8	212.8	192.4	140.8	175.2
1996	156.9	153.8	119.3	192.0	143.9	142.9	151.9	151.3	95.3	213.4	128.2	174.0	220.3	193.5	141.9	179.4
1997	160.5	156.2	121.5	192.5	145.8	145.3	155.3	153.2	97.1	217.7	131.0	178.5	224.8	194.8	142.5	185.1
1998	163.0	157.7	122.2	194.1	147.1	146.7	158.2	154.3	98.0	222.0	133.6	182.5	228.8	194.2	142.7	191.4
1999	166.6	160.5	121.8	197.0	147.9	148.3	162.0	155.0	98.6	225.7	136.5	186.7	234.2	195.1	143.8	194.3
2000	172.2	164.8	121.0	205.8	151.4	152.1	166.8	157.7	100.0	231.4	140.0	192.5	242.1	196.9	146.0	200.1
2001	177.1	169.0	120.1	214.8	155.5	155.8	170.8	160.3	102.0	237.8	145.9	198.4	250.8	201.6	147.4	203.6
2002	179.9	172.8	119.1	221.2	158.2	158.4	174.8	163.4	103.4	243.7	150.7	200.9	259.6	206.0	148.4	207.0
2003	184.0	177.6	118.7	227.4	160.3	160.9	178.5	166.8	104.5	250.3	153.9	205.9	267.6	209.9	149.3	213.0
2004	188.9	180.9	118.7	232.7	163.7	164.3	180.7	170.3	106.2	255.8	155.7	206.8	275.7	210.7	150.5	219.4
2005	195.3	184.9	118.3	238.9	167.4	164.3	183.9	173.3	108.3	260.8	158.4	210.1	285.0	211.7	152.2	225.6

[1]The figures may differ from official indexes published by national statistical agencies due to rounding.
[2]Urban worker households prior to 1978.
[3]All households from January 1995, all urban households from September 1978 to December 1994, and middle-income urban households prior to September 1978.
[4]Urban worker households prior to September 1998.
[5]Excluding rent and several other services prior to 1976.
[6]Excluding rent prior to 1964.
[7]Urban worker households prior to 1991. Worker households in Paris only prior to 1962.
[8]Unified Germany for 1991 onward. Data for previous years relate to the former West Germany.
[9]Employee households from 2001, low-income employee households prior to 2001.
[10]Urban worker households prior to 1960.
[11]All family households from 1993, middle-income family households prior to 1963.
[12]Urban worker households prior to May 1993.
. . . = Not available.

Table 11-5. Consumer Price Indexes, Percent Change from Previous Year, 16 Countries, 1955–2005

(Percent.)

Year	\multicolumn{16}{c}{Percent change in Consumer Price Index[1]}															
	United States[2]	Canada[3]	Japan	Australia[4]	Austria	Bel- gium[5]	Den- mark[6]	France[7]	Ger- many[8]	Italy	Nether- lands[9]	Norway[10]	Spain[11]	Sweden	Switzer- land[12]	United Kingdom
1955	-0.4	0.0	-1.5	2.2	...	-0.4	5.6	1.4	...	2.8	...	1.1	3.3	2.3	0.8	4.9
1956	1.5	1.5	0.4	6.3	...	2.9	5.3	1.9	...	3.4	...	3.7	5.9	5.0	1.5	4.9
1957	3.3	3.2	3.1	2.7	...	3.1	2.2	3.5	...	1.3	...	2.7	10.8	4.3	1.9	3.7
1958	2.8	2.6	-0.5	1.1	...	1.3	0.7	15.1	...	2.8	...	4.8	13.4	4.4	1.8	3.0
1959	0.7	1.1	1.1	1.9	...	1.2	1.8	6.1	...	-0.4	...	2.2	7.3	0.8	-0.7	0.6
1960	1.7	1.2	3.7	4.0	...	0.3	1.2	3.6	...	2.3	...	0.3	1.2	4.1	1.4	1.0
1961	1.0	0.9	5.3	2.6	3.6	1.0	4.2	3.3	...	2.1	...	2.6	1.1	2.1	1.9	3.4
1962	1.0	1.2	6.8	-0.3	4.4	1.4	7.5	4.8	...	4.7	...	5.3	5.7	4.8	4.3	4.3
1963	1.3	1.8	7.6	0.5	2.7	2.1	5.3	4.8	2.9	7.5	...	2.5	8.8	2.9	3.4	2.0
1964	1.3	1.8	3.8	2.4	3.8	4.2	3.6	3.4	2.4	5.9	...	5.7	7.0	3.4	3.1	3.3
1965	1.6	2.4	7.6	4.0	5.0	4.1	6.5	2.5	3.1	4.6	...	4.3	13.2	5.0	3.4	4.8
1966	2.9	3.7	5.1	3.0	2.2	4.2	6.7	2.7	3.7	2.3	...	3.2	6.2	6.4	4.7	3.9
1967	3.1	3.5	4.0	3.2	4.0	2.9	7.5	2.7	1.7	3.7	...	4.4	6.4	4.2	4.0	2.5
1968	4.2	4.1	5.3	2.7	2.8	2.8	8.0	4.5	1.5	1.4	...	3.5	4.9	1.9	2.4	4.7
1969	5.5	4.5	5.2	2.9	3.1	3.7	3.5	6.4	1.9	2.7	...	3.1	2.2	2.7	2.5	5.4
1970	5.7	3.3	7.7	3.9	4.4	3.9	6.5	5.2	3.4	4.9	3.7	10.6	5.7	7.0	3.6	6.4
1971	4.4	2.9	6.3	6.1	4.7	4.3	5.8	5.5	5.3	4.8	7.6	6.2	8.2	7.4	6.6	9.4
1972	3.2	4.8	4.9	5.9	6.3	5.5	6.6	6.2	5.5	5.7	8.0	7.2	8.3	6.0	6.7	7.1
1973	6.2	7.5	11.7	9.5	7.6	7.0	9.3	7.3	6.9	10.8	8.1	7.5	11.5	6.8	8.7	9.2
1974	11.0	10.9	23.2	15.1	9.5	12.7	15.2	13.7	7.0	19.1	9.8	9.4	15.7	9.9	9.8	16.0
1975	9.1	10.8	11.7	15.1	8.4	12.8	9.6	11.8	6.0	17.0	9.9	11.7	17.0	9.8	6.7	24.2
1976	5.8	7.5	9.4	13.5	7.3	9.2	9.0	9.6	4.3	16.8	9.0	9.1	17.6	10.3	1.7	16.5
1977	6.5	8.0	8.1	12.3	5.5	7.1	11.1	9.4	3.7	17.0	6.4	9.1	24.5	11.4	1.3	15.8
1978	7.6	9.0	4.2	7.9	3.6	4.4	10.1	9.1	2.7	12.1	4.2	8.1	19.8	10.0	1.1	8.3
1979	11.3	9.1	3.7	9.1	3.7	4.5	9.6	10.8	4.1	14.8	4.3	4.8	15.7	7.2	3.6	13.4
1980	13.5	10.1	7.7	10.2	6.4	6.6	12.3	13.6	5.4	21.2	7.0	10.9	15.5	13.7	4.0	18.0
1981	10.3	12.5	4.9	9.7	6.8	7.6	11.7	13.4	6.3	17.8	6.7	13.6	14.6	12.1	6.5	11.9
1982	6.2	10.8	2.8	11.2	5.4	8.7	10.1	11.8	5.3	16.5	5.7	11.3	14.5	8.6	5.6	8.6
1983	3.2	5.8	1.9	10.1	3.3	7.7	6.9	9.6	3.3	14.7	2.7	8.4	12.2	8.9	2.9	4.6
1984	4.3	4.4	2.3	4.0	5.6	6.3	6.3	7.4	2.4	10.8	3.2	6.2	11.3	8.1	3.0	5.0
1985	3.6	4.0	2.0	6.7	3.2	4.9	4.7	5.8	2.1	9.2	2.3	5.7	8.8	7.3	3.4	6.1
1986	1.9	4.1	0.6	9.1	1.7	1.3	3.6	2.7	-0.1	5.9	0.2	7.2	8.8	4.3	0.7	3.4
1987	3.6	4.4	0.1	8.5	1.4	1.6	4.0	3.1	0.2	4.7	-0.4	8.7	5.3	4.2	1.5	4.2
1988	4.1	4.1	0.7	6.9	2.0	1.2	4.6	2.7	1.3	5.0	0.9	6.7	4.8	5.8	1.8	4.9
1989	4.8	5.0	2.3	7.9	2.5	3.1	4.8	3.6	2.8	6.3	1.0	4.6	6.8	6.5	3.2	7.8
1990	5.4	4.8	3.1	7.3	3.3	3.5	2.6	3.4	2.7	6.5	2.6	4.1	6.7	10.4	5.4	9.5
1991	4.2	5.6	3.3	3.2	3.3	3.2	2.4	3.2	3.7	6.3	3.1	3.4	6.0	9.4	5.8	5.9
1992	3.0	1.5	1.6	1.0	4.1	2.4	2.1	2.4	5.1	5.2	3.2	2.3	5.9	2.4	4.0	3.7
1993	3.0	1.8	1.3	1.8	3.6	2.8	1.2	2.1	4.4	4.5	2.6	2.3	4.6	4.7	3.3	1.6
1994	2.6	0.2	0.7	1.9	3.0	2.4	2.0	1.7	2.7	4.0	2.7	1.4	4.8	2.1	0.9	2.4
1995	2.8	2.1	-0.1	4.6	2.2	1.5	2.1	1.7	1.7	5.2	2.0	2.4	4.6	2.5	1.8	3.5
1996	3.0	1.6	0.1	2.6	1.9	2.1	2.1	2.0	1.5	4.0	2.0	1.3	3.6	0.5	0.8	2.4
1997	2.3	1.6	1.8	0.3	1.3	1.6	2.2	1.2	1.9	2.0	2.2	2.6	2.0	0.7	0.5	3.1
1998	1.6	0.9	0.6	0.9	0.9	1.0	1.9	0.7	0.9	2.0	2.0	2.3	1.8	-0.3	0.1	3.4
1999	2.2	1.7	-0.3	1.5	0.6	1.1	2.5	0.5	0.6	1.7	2.2	2.3	2.3	0.5	0.8	1.5
2000	3.4	2.7	-0.7	4.5	2.3	2.5	3.0	1.7	1.4	2.5	2.6	3.1	3.4	0.9	1.5	3.0
2001	2.8	2.6	-0.7	4.4	2.7	2.5	2.4	1.7	2.0	2.7	4.5	3.0	3.6	2.4	1.0	1.8
2002	1.6	2.2	-0.9	3.0	1.8	1.6	2.3	1.9	1.4	2.5	3.5	1.3	3.5	2.2	0.7	1.7
2003	2.3	2.8	-0.3	2.8	1.3	1.6	2.1	2.1	1.1	2.7	2.1	2.5	3.1	1.9	0.6	2.9
2004	2.7	1.9	0.0	2.3	2.1	2.1	1.2	2.1	1.6	2.2	1.2	0.4	3.0	0.4	0.8	3.0
2005	3.4	2.2	-0.3	2.7	2.3	0.0	1.8	1.8	2.0	2.0	1.7	1.6	3.4	0.5	1.2	2.8

[1]The figures may differ from official percent changes published by national statistical agencies due to rounding.
[2]Urban worker households prior to 1978.
[3]All households from January 1995, all urban households from September 1978 to December 1994, and middle-income urban households prior to September 1978.
[4]Urban worker households prior to September 1998.
[5]Excluding rent and several other services prior to 1976.
[6]Excluding rent prior to 1964.
[7]Urban worker households prior to 1991. Worker households in Paris only prior to 1962.
[8]Unified Germany for 1991 onward. Data for previous years relate to the former West Germany.
[9]Employee households from 2001, low-income employee households prior to 2001.
[10]Urban worker households prior to 1960.
[11]All family households from 1993, middle-income family households prior to 1963.
[12]Urban worker households prior to May 1993.
. . . = Not available.

Table 11-6. Real Gross Domestic Product (GDP) Per Capita, 15 Countries, 1960–2005

(2002 U.S. dollars.)

Year	United States	Canada	Australia	Japan	Korea, Republic of	Austria	Belgium	Denmark	France	Germany[1]	Italy	Netherlands	Norway	Sweden	United Kingdom
1960	14 420	11 448	11 747	5 366	1 684	9 285	9 451	11 464	9 483	11 346	7 240	11 757	10 237	11 484	11 700
1961	14 516	11 573	11 783	6 003	1 730	9 724	9 888	12 056	9 901	11 715	7 782	11 938	10 775	12 073	11 888
1962	15 161	12 136	11 687	6 458	1 718	9 897	10 361	12 626	10 374	12 119	8 209	12 278	10 976	12 518	11 918
1963	15 598	12 520	12 186	6 954	1 823	10 234	10 732	12 583	10 733	12 340	8 606	12 510	11 306	13 111	12 451
1964	16 278	13 090	12 813	7 650	1 948	10 780	11 371	13 603	11 316	13 029	8 774	13 406	11 783	13 901	13 055
1965	17 107	13 686	13 343	7 919	2 008	11 017	11 669	14 145	11 757	13 575	8 985	13 923	12 310	14 297	13 270
1966	18 014	14 314	13 405	8 746	2 196	11 557	11 957	14 358	12 268	13 829	9 449	14 127	12 674	14 458	13 458
1967	18 267	14 479	14 017	9 602	2 272	11 816	12 351	14 811	12 743	13 755	10 055	14 708	13 355	14 830	13 713
1968	18 958	15 020	14 489	10 626	2 472	12 280	12 820	15 335	13 188	14 453	10 645	15 534	13 542	15 284	14 226
1969	19 351	15 595	15 203	11 756	2 751	13 006	13 632	16 255	13 997	15 384	11 231	16 401	14 038	15 937	14 462
1970	19 162	15 782	15 968	12 701	2 928	13 884	14 492	16 489	14 667	16 003	11 765	17 133	14 214	16 811	14 744
1971	19 557	16 123	16 078	13 079	3 107	14 529	14 990	16 881	15 225	16 323	11 922	17 676	14 839	16 853	14 966
1972	20 374	16 789	16 204	13 983	3 186	15 341	15 723	17 541	15 761	16 909	12 289	18 038	15 476	17 188	15 459
1973	21 342	17 778	16 401	14 897	3 506	16 002	16 601	18 179	16 486	17 628	13 086	18 797	16 046	17 838	16 526
1974	21 040	18 258	16 844	14 519	3 694	16 605	17 228	18 011	16 888	17 640	13 774	19 407	16 616	18 355	16 300
1975	20 797	18 392	16 802	14 785	3 849	16 589	16 925	17 658	16 764	17 483	13 415	19 270	17 388	18 750	16 211
1976	21 694	19 148	17 075	15 216	4 188	17 379	17 840	18 689	17 407	18 503	14 300	20 022	18 322	18 880	16 650
1977	22 468	19 580	17 475	15 735	4 536	18 208	17 904	19 034	17 887	19 070	14 629	20 367	19 023	18 512	17 065
1978	23 470	20 177	17 451	16 417	4 882	18 197	18 379	19 341	18 406	19 665	15 058	20 749	19 611	18 782	17 632
1979	23 944	20 818	17 972	17 173	5 135	19 226	18 758	19 985	18 973	20 485	15 936	20 987	20 420	19 461	18 087
1980	23 615	20 836	18 330	17 521	4 980	19 569	19 547	19 959	19 216	20 616	16 493	21 168	21 362	19 746	17 685
1981	23 970	21 212	18 692	17 906	5 206	19 490	19 481	19 783	19 386	20 598	16 611	20 913	21 495	19 689	17 422
1982	23 282	20 362	18 971	18 273	5 501	19 855	19 591	20 432	19 825	20 419	16 681	20 551	21 461	19 908	17 776
1983	24 115	20 709	18 237	18 442	6 005	20 497	19 654	20 917	20 150	20 851	16 884	20 831	22 156	20 273	18 396
1984	25 623	21 707	18 847	18 895	6 412	20 494	20 139	21 808	20 372	21 524	17 439	21 399	23 398	21 126	18 839
1985	26 445	22 538	19 606	19 734	6 781	21 008	20 465	22 686	20 677	22 016	17 934	21 868	24 541	21 550	19 458
1986	27 114	22 856	20 190	20 216	7 427	21 458	20 830	23 731	21 074	22 516	18 425	22 429	25 334	22 090	20 181
1987	27 780	23 514	20 346	20 883	8 170	21 775	21 293	23 734	21 448	22 845	19 018	22 693	25 734	22 753	21 054
1988	28 667	24 365	21 124	22 204	8 952	22 497	22 184	23 638	22 316	23 552	19 810	23 218	25 585	23 234	22 058
1989	29 402	24 557	21 613	23 292	9 461	23 187	22 914	23 816	23 059	24 164	20 478	24 188	25 723	23 700	22 470
1990	29 620	24 235	22 110	24 423	10 226	24 070	23 563	24 245	23 554	25 062	20 866	25 001	26 169	23 775	22 570
1991	29 179	23 446	21 682	25 141	11 077	24 689	23 906	24 495	23 733	23 576	21 152	25 396	26 987	23 352	22 184
1992	29 752	23 371	21 438	25 291	11 606	24 995	24 174	24 897	24 038	23 919	21 290	25 581	27 717	22 811	22 189
1993	30 152	23 655	22 002	25 278	12 194	24 872	23 848	24 787	23 672	23 556	21 150	25 566	28 303	22 753	22 677
1994	30 987	24 520	22 682	25 491	13 102	25 436	24 541	26 074	24 066	24 110	21 625	26 143	29 622	22 967	23 616
1995	31 389	24 948	23 429	25 940	14 160	25 882	25 555	26 747	24 510	24 493	22 220	26 798	30 752	23 739	24 223
1996	32 174	25 088	24 089	26 769	15 008	26 524	25 801	27 337	24 689	24 666	22 355	27 495	32 205	24 019	24 823
1997	33 221	25 889	24 734	27 179	15 559	26 982	26 598	28 091	25 148	25 063	22 722	28 402	33 692	24 565	25 541
1998	34 208	26 726	25 563	26 827	14 388	27 912	27 050	28 599	25 928	25 579	23 019	29 456	34 373	25 451	26 296
1999	35 324	27 976	26 595	26 750	15 642	28 783	27 818	29 236	26 639	26 075	23 417	30 428	34 867	26 582	26 997
2000	36 215	29 166	27 332	27 332	16 828	29 677	28 824	30 166	27 538	26 879	24 240	31 259	35 624	27 690	27 989
2001	36 110	29 369	27 510	27 309	17 346	29 807	29 026	30 272	27 863	27 162	24 666	31 466	36 411	27 911	28 502
2002	36 321	29 937	28 191	27 196	18 453	29 943	29 331	30 310	27 961	27 132	24 718	31 288	36 615	28 375	28 969
2003	36 937	30 255	28 768	27 511	18 931	30 236	29 476	30 441	28 082	27 068	24 459	31 100	36 812	28 748	29 583
2004	38 125	30 845	29 576	28 129	19 731	30 758	30 108	30 932	28 552	27 516	24 536	31 536	37 721	29 708	30 419
2005	39 103	31 459	29 923	28 865	20 422	31 156	30 434	31 786	28 717	27 772	24 376	31 720	38 338	30 389	30 887

[1]Unified Germany for 1991 and onward. Data for previous years relate to the former West Germany.

Table 11-7. Real Gross Domestic Product (GDP) Per Employed Person, 15 Countries, 1960–2005

(2002 U.S. dollars.)

Year	United States	Canada	Australia	Japan	Korea, Republic of	Austria	Bel-gium	Den-mark	France	Ger-many[1]	Italy	Nether-lands	Norway	Sweden	United Kingdom
1960	38 168	32 583	. . .	10 745	. . .	17 573	24 574	24 416	22 278	24 133	17 410	29 293	24 221	23 646	25 381
1961	39 041	33 089	. . .	11 861	. . .	18 406	25 606	25 479	23 508	24 903	18 719	29 709	25 300	24 789	25 734
1962	40 687	34 409	. . .	12 734	. . .	18 936	26 530	26 478	25 082	25 974	19 939	30 378	25 835	25 705	25 912
1963	41 883	35 346	. . .	13 736	6 571	19 844	27 491	26 277	26 213	26 641	21 413	30 959	26 694	26 940	27 180
1964	43 365	36 388	. . .	15 049	7 080	21 077	28 990	28 048	27 617	28 392	22 088	33 041	27 942	28 370	28 314
1965	45 044	37 372	32 559	15 659	7 105	21 826	29 907	28 866	28 848	29 743	23 380	34 499	29 176	29 252	28 687
1966	46 587	38 240	32 108	16 900	7 766	23 251	30 743	29 050	30 127	30 667	25 191	35 191	30 147	29 822	29 186
1967	46 654	38 293	33 053	18 393	7 939	24 347	32 075	30 221	31 459	31 602	26 667	37 171	31 814	31 158	30 259
1968	47 898	39 628	33 926	20 200	8 413	25 774	33 459	31 257	32 896	33 297	28 427	39 296	32 491	31 953	31 687
1969	48 190	40 497	35 399	22 396	9 347	27 442	35 082	32 710	34 668	35 233	30 379	41 281	33 660	32 934	32 358
1970	48 003	41 132	36 736	24 420	9 815	29 338	37 284	33 015	36 163	36 545	31 844	43 144	33 788	34 392	33 183
1971	49 425	42 446	37 042	25 313	10 272	30 503	38 383	34 102	37 723	37 510	32 412	44 798	35 213	34 785	33 887
1972	50 553	43 465	37 773	27 301	10 283	32 159	40 496	34 988	39 163	38 949	33 687	46 592	36 581	35 465	35 006
1973	51 760	44 404	38 004	28 842	10 928	33 266	42 512	36 058	40 730	40 365	35 610	48 923	37 904	36 734	36 939
1974	50 554	44 421	38 867	28 609	11 222	34 134	43 599	36 195	41 634	40 940	37 151	50 417	38 966	37 172	36 360
1975	51 027	44 639	39 143	29 566	11 615	34 263	43 581	36 059	41 883	41 543	36 371	50 884	40 326	37 383	36 302
1976	52 049	46 167	40 074	30 492	12 097	35 712	46 257	37 644	43 320	43 988	38 574	53 021	41 302	37 649	37 496
1977	52 570	46 930	40 919	31 453	12 890	36 979	46 664	38 546	44 345	45 175	39 510	53 146	41 890	36 973	38 387
1978	53 227	47 408	40 965	32 792	13 458	36 745	47 902	39 011	45 606	46 153	40 678	53 938	42 592	37 480	39 453
1979	53 413	47 376	42 374	34 238	14 170	38 591	48 481	40 044	46 975	47 306	42 700	53 983	43 876	38 361	40 114
1980	53 033	46 671	42 711	34 963	13 877	38 924	50 639	40 345	47 699	47 045	43 652	53 223	44 931	38 573	39 446
1981	53 768	46 732	43 041	35 717	14 375	39 021	51 445	40 632	48 578	47 142	44 053	52 659	44 777	38 447	39 904
1982	53 160	46 826	43 838	36 406	15 046	40 331	52 436	41 841	49 907	47 261	44 180	52 252	44 866	38 970	41 486
1983	54 846	47 706	43 565	36 442	16 522	41 845	53 141	42 774	51 151	48 787	44 590	54 171	46 594	39 613	43 268
1984	56 490	49 253	45 198	37 451	17 955	41 875	54 558	43 923	52 081	50 080	46 070	55 172	48 986	40 975	43 452
1985	57 661	50 198	46 228	39 142	18 483	42 820	55 151	44 686	53 544	50 718	46 948	55 081	50 166	41 440	44 439
1986	58 350	49 921	46 339	40 095	19 740	43 635	55 785	45 737	54 643	51 199	47 905	55 918	50 334	42 316	45 915
1987	58 818	50 563	46 072	41 452	20 794	44 334	56 775	45 670	55 488	51 583	49 339	56 013	50 336	43 385	47 075
1988	59 945	51 532	47 209	43 749	22 304	45 475	58 605	45 820	57 541	53 089	50 873	57 287	50 534	43 904	47 853
1989	60 843	51 715	47 212	45 394	22 872	46 517	59 703	46 491	58 820	54 224	52 270	59 071	52 498	44 435	47 658
1990	61 263	51 465	47 304	46 972	24 241	47 742	60 689	47 770	59 929	55 662	52 471	58 802	54 034	44 511	47 793
1991	61 733	51 217	47 329	47 578	25 716	48 848	61 735	48 677	60 617	48 826	52 249	59 228	56 502	44 689	48 417
1992	63 456	52 124	48 221	47 504	26 711	49 717	62 966	50 233	62 057	50 650	52 883	58 596	58 493	45 954	49 742
1993	64 289	53 088	50 100	47 442	28 018	50 115	62 832	50 918	62 175	50 918	54 020	58 800	59 790	47 600	51 440
1994	65 426	54 496	51 210	47 913	29 469	51 433	65 105	53 998	63 347	52 326	56 170	59 792	62 081	49 908	52 664
1995	66 140	55 048	51 511	48 809	31 279	52 512	67 478	54 696	64 173	53 194	57 832	61 115	63 431	51 072	54 202
1996	67 655	55 430	52 239	50 276	32 763	53 694	68 046	55 513	64 621	53 871	57 870	61 850	65 433	52 198	55 168
1997	69 184	56 523	53 835	50 643	33 704	54 196	69 684	56 433	65 764	54 894	58 667	61 506	66 871	54 120	55 922
1998	71 053	57 435	55 492	50 445	33 403	55 427	69 676	56 758	67 029	55 347	58 870	62 873	66 932	55 248	57 151
1999	73 117	59 105	57 237	50 807	35 935	56 344	70 890	57 585	67 828	55 706	59 258	63 004	67 808	56 557	58 098
2000	73 944	60 733	58 307	52 081	37 391	57 678	72 208	59 277	68 715	56 436	60 201	62 653	69 445	57 610	59 749
2001	74 472	61 066	58 260	52 493	38 077	57 817	71 945	59 135	68 767	56 886	60 082	63 197	71 146	57 144	60 577
2002	75 895	61 476	59 737	53 074	39 634	58 443	73 132	59 400	69 043	57 240	59 379	62 271	71 859	58 195	61 319
2003	77 237	61 286	60 198	53 939	40 917	59 208	73 855	60 588	69 703	57 685	58 343	62 157	73 438	59 381	62 263
2004	79 625	61 962	61 475	55 067	42 058	60 667	75 331	61 676	71 286	58 406	58 905	62 927	75 445	61 933	63 581
2005	81 024	62 916	61 080	56 313	43 152	61 455	75 563	63 097	71 942	59 052	58 813	64 290	76 635	63 401	64 134

[1]Unified Germany for 1991 and onward. Data for previous years relate to the former West Germany.
. . . = Not available.

Table 11-8. Employment-Population Ratios, 15 Countries, 1960–2005

(Percent.)

Year	United States	Canada	Australia	Japan	Korea, Republic of	Austria	Bel- gium	Den- mark	France	Ger- many[1]	Italy	Nether- lands	Norway	Sweden	United Kingdom
1960	37.8	35.1	. . .	49.9	. . .	52.8	38.5	47.0	42.6	47.0	41.6	40.1	42.3	48.6	46.1
1961	37.2	35.0	. . .	50.6	. . .	52.8	38.6	47.3	42.1	47.0	41.6	40.2	42.6	48.7	46.2
1962	37.3	35.3	. . .	50.7	. . .	52.3	39.1	47.7	41.4	46.7	41.2	40.4	42.5	48.7	46.0
1963	37.2	35.4	. . .	50.6	27.7	51.6	39.0	47.9	40.9	46.3	40.2	40.4	42.4	48.7	45.8
1964	37.5	36.0	. . .	50.8	27.5	51.1	39.2	48.5	41.0	45.9	39.7	40.6	42.2	49.0	46.1
1965	38.0	36.6	41.0	50.6	28.3	50.5	39.0	49.0	40.8	45.6	38.4	40.4	42.2	48.9	46.3
1966	38.7	37.4	41.7	51.7	28.3	49.7	38.9	49.4	40.7	45.1	37.5	40.1	42.0	48.5	46.1
1967	39.2	37.8	42.4	52.2	28.6	48.5	38.5	49.0	40.5	43.5	37.7	39.6	42.0	47.6	45.3
1968	39.6	37.9	42.7	52.6	29.4	47.6	38.3	49.1	40.1	43.4	37.4	39.5	41.7	47.8	44.9
1969	40.2	38.5	42.9	52.5	29.4	47.4	38.9	49.7	40.4	43.7	37.0	39.7	41.7	48.4	44.7
1970	39.9	38.4	43.5	52.0	29.8	47.3	38.9	49.9	40.6	43.8	36.9	39.7	42.1	48.9	44.4
1971	39.6	38.0	43.4	51.7	30.2	47.6	39.1	49.5	40.4	43.5	36.8	39.5	42.1	48.4	44.2
1972	40.3	38.6	42.9	51.2	31.0	47.7	38.8	50.1	40.2	43.4	36.5	38.7	42.3	48.5	44.2
1973	41.2	40.0	43.2	51.6	32.1	48.1	39.0	50.4	40.5	43.7	36.7	38.4	42.3	48.6	44.7
1974	41.6	41.1	43.3	50.7	32.9	48.6	39.5	49.8	40.6	43.1	37.1	38.5	42.6	49.4	44.8
1975	40.8	41.2	42.9	50.0	33.1	48.4	38.8	49.0	40.0	42.1	36.9	37.9	43.1	50.2	44.7
1976	41.7	41.5	42.6	49.9	34.6	48.7	38.6	49.6	40.2	42.1	37.1	37.8	44.4	50.1	44.4
1977	42.7	41.7	42.7	50.0	35.2	49.2	38.4	49.4	40.3	42.2	37.0	38.3	45.4	50.1	44.5
1978	44.1	42.6	42.6	50.1	36.3	49.5	38.4	49.6	40.4	42.6	37.0	38.5	46.0	50.1	44.7
1979	44.8	43.9	42.4	50.2	36.2	49.8	38.7	49.9	40.4	43.3	37.3	38.9	46.5	50.7	45.1
1980	44.5	44.6	42.9	50.1	35.9	50.3	38.6	49.5	40.3	43.8	37.8	39.8	47.5	51.2	44.8
1981	44.6	45.4	43.4	50.1	36.2	49.9	37.9	48.7	39.9	43.7	37.7	39.7	48.0	51.2	43.7
1982	43.8	43.5	43.3	50.2	36.6	49.2	37.4	48.8	39.7	43.2	37.8	39.3	47.8	51.1	42.8
1983	44.0	43.4	41.9	50.6	36.3	49.0	37.0	48.9	39.4	42.7	37.9	38.5	47.6	51.2	42.5
1984	45.4	44.1	41.7	50.5	35.7	48.9	36.9	49.7	39.1	43.0	37.9	38.8	47.8	51.6	43.4
1985	45.9	44.9	42.4	50.4	36.7	49.1	37.1	50.8	38.6	43.4	38.2	39.7	48.9	52.0	43.8
1986	46.5	45.8	43.6	50.4	37.6	49.2	37.3	51.9	38.6	44.0	38.5	40.1	50.3	52.2	44.0
1987	47.2	46.5	44.2	50.4	39.3	49.1	37.5	52.0	38.7	44.3	38.5	40.5	51.1	52.4	44.7
1988	47.8	47.3	44.7	50.8	40.1	49.5	37.9	51.6	38.8	44.4	38.9	40.5	50.6	52.9	46.1
1989	48.3	47.5	45.8	51.3	41.4	49.8	38.4	51.2	39.2	44.6	39.2	40.9	49.0	53.3	47.1
1990	48.3	47.1	46.7	52.0	42.2	50.4	38.8	50.8	39.3	45.0	39.8	42.5	48.4	53.4	47.2
1991	47.3	45.8	45.8	52.8	43.1	50.5	38.7	50.3	39.2	48.3	40.5	42.9	47.8	52.3	45.8
1992	46.9	44.8	44.5	53.2	43.5	50.3	38.4	49.6	38.7	47.2	40.3	43.7	47.4	49.6	44.6
1993	46.9	44.6	43.9	53.3	43.5	49.6	38.0	48.6	38.1	46.3	39.2	43.5	47.3	46.8	44.1
1994	47.4	45.0	44.3	53.2	44.5	49.5	37.7	48.3	38.0	46.1	38.5	43.7	47.7	46.0	44.8
1995	47.5	45.3	45.5	53.1	45.3	49.3	37.9	48.9	38.2	46.0	38.4	43.8	48.5	46.5	44.7
1996	47.6	45.3	46.1	53.2	45.8	49.4	37.9	49.2	38.2	45.8	38.6	44.5	49.2	46.0	45.0
1997	48.0	45.8	45.9	53.7	46.2	49.8	38.2	49.8	38.2	45.7	38.7	46.2	50.4	45.4	45.7
1998	48.1	46.5	46.1	53.2	43.1	50.4	38.8	50.4	38.7	46.2	39.1	46.9	51.4	46.1	46.0
1999	48.3	47.3	46.5	52.6	43.5	51.1	39.2	50.8	39.3	46.8	39.5	48.3	51.4	47.0	46.5
2000	49.0	48.0	46.9	52.5	45.0	51.5	39.9	50.9	40.1	47.6	40.3	49.9	51.3	48.1	46.8
2001	48.5	48.1	47.2	52.0	45.6	51.6	40.3	51.2	40.5	47.7	41.1	49.8	51.2	48.8	47.1
2002	47.9	48.7	47.2	51.2	46.6	51.2	40.1	51.0	40.5	47.4	41.6	50.2	51.0	48.8	47.2
2003	47.8	49.4	47.8	51.0	46.3	51.1	39.9	50.2	40.3	46.9	41.9	50.0	50.1	48.4	47.5
2004	47.9	49.8	48.1	51.1	46.9	50.7	40.0	50.2	40.1	47.1	41.7	50.1	50.0	48.0	47.8
2005	48.3	50.0	49.0	51.3	47.3	50.7	40.3	50.4	39.9	47.0	41.4	49.3	50.0	47.9	48.2

[1]Unified Germany for 1991 and onward. Data for previous years relate to the former West Germany.

. . . = Not available.

Table 11-9. Real Gross Domestic Product (GDP) Per Capita and Per Employed Person, 15 Countries, Selected Years, 1980–2005

(Average annual percent change.)

Category and country	1980–2005	1980–1990	1990–1995	1995–2000	2000	2001	2002	2003	2004	2005
Real GDP Per Capita										
United States	2.0	2.3	1.2	2.9	2.5	-0.3	0.6	1.7	3.2	2.6
Canada	1.7	1.5	0.6	3.2	4.3	0.7	1.9	1.1	2.0	2.0
Australia	2.0	1.9	1.2	3.1	2.8	0.7	2.5	2.0	2.8	1.2
Japan	2.0	3.4	1.2	1.1	2.2	-0.1	-0.4	1.2	2.2	2.6
Korea, Republic of	5.8	7.5	6.7	3.5	7.6	3.1	6.4	2.6	4.2	3.5
Austria	1.9	2.1	1.5	2.8	3.1	0.4	0.5	1.0	1.7	1.3
Belgium	1.8	1.9	1.6	2.4	3.6	0.7	1.1	0.5	2.1	1.1
Denmark	1.9	2.0	2.0	2.4	3.2	0.4	0.1	0.4	1.6	2.8
France	1.6	2.1	0.8	2.4	3.4	1.2	0.4	0.4	1.7	0.6
Germany[1]	1.6	2.0	1.5	1.9	3.1	1.1	-0.1	-0.2	1.7	0.9
Italy	1.6	2.4	1.3	1.8	3.5	1.8	0.2	-1.0	0.3	-0.7
Netherlands	1.6	1.7	1.4	3.1	2.7	0.7	-0.6	-0.6	1.4	0.6
Norway	2.4	2.1	3.3	3.0	2.2	2.2	0.6	0.5	2.5	1.6
Sweden	1.7	1.9	0.0	3.1	4.2	0.8	1.7	1.3	3.3	2.3
United Kingdom	2.3	2.5	1.4	2.9	3.7	1.8	1.6	2.1	2.8	1.5
Real GDP Per Employed Person										
United States	1.7	1.5	1.5	2.3	1.1	0.7	1.9	1.8	3.1	1.8
Canada	1.2	1.0	1.4	2.0	2.8	0.5	0.7	-0.3	1.1	1.5
Australia	1.4	1.0	1.7	2.5	1.9	-0.1	2.5	0.8	2.1	-0.6
Japan	1.9	3.0	0.8	1.3	2.5	0.8	1.1	1.6	2.1	2.3
Korea, Republic of	4.6	5.7	5.2	3.6	4.1	1.8	4.1	3.2	2.8	2.6
Austria	1.8	2.1	1.9	1.9	2.4	0.2	1.1	1.3	2.5	1.3
Belgium	1.6	1.8	2.1	1.4	1.9	-0.4	1.6	1.0	2.0	0.3
Denmark	1.8	1.7	2.7	1.6	2.9	-0.2	0.4	2.0	1.8	2.3
France	1.7	2.3	1.4	1.4	1.3	0.1	0.4	1.0	2.3	0.9
Germany[1]	1.5	1.7	2.2	1.2	1.3	0.8	0.6	0.8	1.3	1.1
Italy	1.2	1.9	2.0	0.8	1.6	-0.2	-1.2	-1.7	1.0	-0.2
Netherlands	0.8	1.0	0.8	0.5	-0.6	0.9	-1.5	-0.2	1.2	2.2
Norway	2.2	1.9	3.3	1.8	2.4	2.5	1.0	2.2	2.7	1.6
Sweden	2.0	1.4	2.8	2.4	1.9	-0.8	1.8	2.0	4.3	2.4
United Kingdom	2.0	1.9	2.5	2.0	2.8	1.4	1.2	1.5	2.1	0.9

[1]Unified Germany for 1995–2000 and onward. Data for previous years relate to the former West Germany.

Table 11-10. Purchasing Power Parities (PPPs), Exchange Rates, and Relative Prices, 15 Countries, 2002

(United States = 1.0.)

Country	PPPs for gross domestic product (GDP)	Exchange rates	Relative prices[1]
United States	1.000	1.000	1.00
Canada	1.229	1.570	0.78
Australia	1.337	1.839	0.73
Japan	143.7	125.2	1.15
Korea, Republic of	778.8	1 250.3	0.62
Austria	0.912	1.058	0.86
Belgium	0.883	1.058	0.83
Denmark	8.425	7.886	1.07
France	0.900	1.058	0.85
Germany	0.959	1.058	0.91
Italy	0.825	1.058	0.78
Netherlands	0.921	1.058	0.87
Norway	9.142	7.984	1.15
Sweden	9.365	9.723	0.96
United Kingdom	0.610	0.666	0.92

[1]A number below 1.00 indicates that prices are lower in the specified country than in the United States, and a number greater than 1.00 indicates that prices are higher in the specified country than in the United States.

CHAPTER TWELVE

AMERICAN TIME USE SURVEY

AMERICAN TIME USE SURVEY

HIGHLIGHTS

This chapter presents data from the new American Time Use Survey (ATUS). The survey was introduced in the sixth edition of the *Handbook of Labor Statistics*. Its purpose is to collect data on the activities people do during the day and the amount of time they spend on each one.

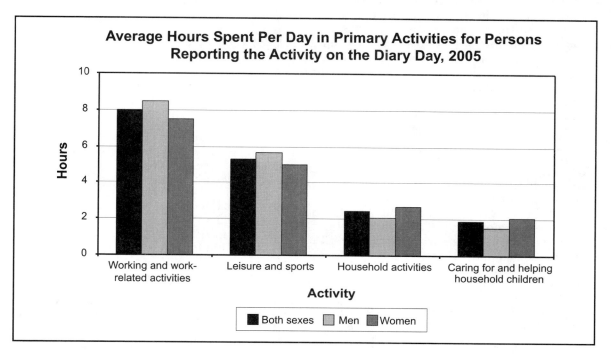

The results from the ATUS were similar in 2004 and 2005. Among those who reported having worked on the diary day, men worked 7.89 hours and women worked 7.07 hours per day in 2005. In 2004, men reported working 7.99 hours per day and women reported working 7.13 hours per day. Women were more likely to hold part-time jobs. Men spent more hours per day on leisure activities and sports, while women spent more time doing household activities and caring for children in both 2004 and 2005. (See Table 12-1.)

OTHER HIGHLIGHTS

• Persons with a bachelor's degree or higher spent less time on leisure activities and more time working in 2005 than those with lower levels of educational attainment. (See Table 12-2.)

• Management, business, and financial operations workers spent fewer hours at work on weekends and holidays than production or transportion and material moving workers. However, a greater percentage of management, business, and financial operations workers (31.5 percent) spent time working on weekends and holidays than transportation and material moving workers (25.6 percent) or production workers (20.8 percent). (See Table 12-4.)

• In 2005, men spent more time watching television than women. This disparity was the greater on the weekends, when men spent approximately 3.5 hours per day watching television and women spent approximately 2.7 hours per day watching television. (See Table 12-9.)

• In 2004 and 2005, women spent more time caring for children than men, regardless of their employment status. (See Table 12-8.)

NOTES AND DEFINITIONS

Survey Methodology

While the Bureau of Labor Statistics (BLS) has long produced statistics about the labor market, including information about employment, hours, and earnings, the American Time Use Survey (ATUS) marks the first time that a federal statistical agency has produced estimates on how Americans spend another critical resource—their time. Data collection for the ATUS began in January 2003. Sample cases for the survey are selected monthly, and interviews are conducted continuously throughout the year. In 2005, approximately 13,000 individuals were interviewed.

ATUS sample households are chosen from the households that have completed their eighth (final) interview for the Current Population Survey (CPS), the nation's monthly household labor force survey. (See Chapter 1 of this *Handbook* for a description of the CPS.) ATUS sample households are selected to ensure that estimates will be representative of the nation.

An individual age 15 years or over is randomly chosen from each sample household. This "designated person" takes part in a one-time telephone interview about his or her activities on the previous day (the "diary day").

Concepts and Definitions

Average hours per day. The average number of hours spent in a 24-hour day (between 4 a.m. on the diary day and 4 a.m. on the interview day) doing a specified activity.

Average hours per day, population. The average number of hours per day spent on a particular activity is computed using all responses from the sample population, including those from respondents who did not do the particular activity on their diary day. These estimates reflect the total number of respondents engaged in an activity and the total amount of time they spent on the activity.

Average hours per day, persons reporting the activity on the diary day. The average number of hours per day spent on a particular activity is computed using responses only from those engaged in the particular activity on the diary day.

Diary day. The diary day is the day about which the designated person reports. For example, the diary day of a designated person interviewed on Tuesday would be Monday.

Employment Status

Employed. All persons who, at any time during the seven days prior to the interview: 1) did any work at all as paid employees, worked in their own business profession, or on their own farm, or usually worked 15 hours or more as unpaid workers in a family-operated enterprise; and 2) all those who were not working but had jobs or businesses from which they were temporarily absent due to illness, bad weather, vacation, childcare problems, labor-management dispute, maternity or paternity leave, job training, or other family or personal reasons, whether or not they were paid for the time off or were seeking other jobs.

Employed full time. Full-time workers are those who usually work 35 hours or more per week at all jobs combined.

Employed part time. Part-time workers are those who usually work fewer than 35 hours per week at all jobs combined.

Not employed. Persons are not employed if they do not meet the conditions for employment. Not employed workers include those classified as unemployed as well as those classified as not in the labor force (using CPS definitions).

The numbers of employed and not employed persons in this report do not correspond to published totals from the CPS. While the information on employment from the ATUS is useful for assessing work in the context of other daily activities, the employment data are not intended for analysis of current employment trends. Compared to the CPS and other estimates of employment, the ATUS estimates are based on a much smaller sample and are only available with a substantial lag.

Household children. Household children are children under 18 years of age residing in the household of the ATUS respondent. The children may be related to the respondent (such as their own children, grandchildren, nieces, nephews, brothers, or sisters) or not related (such as foster children or children of roommates). For secondary childcare calculations, respondents are asked about care of household children under 13 years of age.

Primary activity. A primary activity is the main activity of a respondent at a specified time.

Major Activity Category Definitions

Personal care activities. Personal care activities include sleeping, bathing, dressing, health-related self-care, and personal or private activities. Receiving unpaid personal care from others (for example, "my sister put polish on my nails") is also classified in this category.

Eating and drinking. All time spent eating or drinking (except when identified by the respondent as part of a work or volunteer activity), whether alone, with others, at home, at a place of purchase, in transit, or somewhere else, in this category.

Household activities. Household activities are those done by respondents to maintain their households. These include housework, cooking, yard care, pet care, vehicle maintenance and repair, and home maintenance, repair, decoration, and renovation. Food preparation is always classified as a household activity. Household management and organizational activities—such as filling out paper-work, balancing a checkbook, and planning a party—are also included in this category.

Purchasing goods and services. This category includes the purchase of consumer goods as well as the purchase or use of professional and personal care services, household services, and government services. Most purchases and rentals of consumer goods, regardless of mode or place of purchase or rental (in person, via telephone, over the Internet, at home, or in a store), are classified in this category. Time spent obtaining, receiving, and purchasing professional and personal care services provided by someone else is also classified in this category. Time spent arranging for and purchasing household services provided by someone else is also classified in this category.

Caring for and helping household members. Time spent doing activities that involve caring for or helping to care for or that help any child or adult in the respondent's household, regardless of the relationship to the respondent or the physical or mental health status of the person being helped, are classified in this category. Household members are considered children if they are under 18 years of age. Caring for and helping household members also includes a range of activities done to benefit adult members of households, such as providing physical and medical care or obtaining medical services.

Caring for and helping non-household members. Time spent caring for and helping any child or adult who is not part of the respondent's household, regardless of the relationship to the respondent or the physical or mental health status of the person being helped, is classified in this category.

Working and work-related activities. This category includes time spent working, doing activities as part of one's job, engaging in income-generating activities (not as part of one's job), and job search activities. "Working" includes hours spent doing the specific tasks required of one's main or other job, regardless of location or time of day. Travel time related to working and work-related activities includes time spent commuting to and from one's job, as well as time spent traveling for work-related activities, generating income, and job searching.

Educational activities. Educational activities include taking classes (including Internet and other distance-learning courses), doing research and homework, and taking care of administrative tasks, such as registering for classes or obtaining a school ID. For high school students, before- and after-school extracurricular activities (except sports) also are classified as educational activities.

Organizational, civic, and religious activities. This category captures time spent volunteering for or through an organization, performing civic obligations, and participating in religious and spiritual activities.

Leisure and sports. The leisure and sports category includes sports, exercise, and recreation; socializing and communicating; and other leisure activities, such as watching television, reading or attending entertainment events.

Telephone calls, mail, and email. This category captures telephone communication and handling household or personal mail and email. Telephone and Internet purchases are classified in purchasing goods and services.

Other activities, not elsewhere classified. This residual category includes security procedures related to traveling, traveling not associated with a specific activity category, ambiguous activities that could not be coded, or missing activities that were considered too private to report.

Sources of Additional Information

Additional information, including expanded definitions and estimation methodology, is available from BLS news release USDL 06-1276, "American Time Use Survey, 2005"; the June 2005 edition of the *Monthly Labor Review*; and the *ATUS User's Guide*, July 2006 (all available on the BLS Web site at <http://www.bls.gov>).

Table 12-1. Average Hours Per Day Spent in Primary Activities[1] for the Total Population and for Persons Reporting the Activity on the Diary Day, by Activity Category and Sex, 2005 Annual Averages

(Number, percent.)

Activity	Hours per day, total population			Percent of population reporting the activity on the diary day			Hours per day, persons reporting the activity on the diary day		
	Both sexes	Men	Women	Both sexes	Men	Women	Both sexes	Men	Women
All Activities[2]	24.00	24.00	24.00	X	X	X	X	X	X
Personal care activities	9.43	9.22	9.62	100.0	100.0	100.0	9.43	9.22	9.62
Sleeping	8.63	8.54	8.70	99.9	99.9	100.0	8.63	8.55	8.71
Eating and drinking	1.24	1.30	1.19	97.1	97.4	96.8	1.28	1.33	1.23
Household activities	1.82	1.35	2.27	74.6	64.5	84.0	2.45	2.09	2.70
Housework	0.61	0.24	0.96	36.9	19.4	53.3	1.66	1.22	1.81
Food preparation and cleanup	0.51	0.26	0.75	52.0	37.1	66.0	0.98	0.70	1.13
Lawn and garden care	0.20	0.27	0.14	10.4	11.8	9.0	1.95	2.28	1.56
Household management	0.15	0.12	0.17	18.0	15.1	20.7	0.81	0.83	0.80
Purchasing goods and services	0.80	0.63	0.96	45.8	40.0	51.2	1.74	1.57	1.87
Consumer goods purchases	0.41	0.31	0.50	41.4	36.0	46.5	0.98	0.85	1.07
Professional and personal care services	0.08	0.06	0.11	8.9	6.7	10.9	0.93	0.83	0.99
Caring for and helping household members	0.54	0.34	0.72	26.2	20.5	31.5	2.04	1.63	2.29
Caring for and helping household children	0.42	0.25	0.57	22.2	16.4	27.7	1.88	1.51	2.08
Caring for and helping non-household members	0.23	0.21	0.25	13.7	12.1	15.2	1.70	1.78	1.65
Caring for and helping non-household adults	0.08	0.08	0.08	9.0	8.6	9.4	0.87	0.92	0.83
Working and work-related activities	3.69	4.44	3.00	46.1	52.6	40.1	8.01	8.45	7.47
Working	3.35	4.02	2.73	44.5	50.9	38.6	7.52	7.89	7.07
Educational activities	0.45	0.47	0.43	8.6	8.3	8.9	5.22	5.62	4.87
Attending class	0.27	0.28	0.25	6.0	6.1	5.9	4.45	4.61	4.29
Homework and research	0.14	0.15	0.14	5.3	5.1	5.5	2.70	2.86	2.56
Organizational, civic, and religious activities	0.31	0.27	0.35	13.3	11.7	14.9	2.31	2.30	2.33
Religious and spiritual activities	0.12	0.10	0.15	7.4	5.6	9.1	1.67	1.71	1.65
Volunteering (organizational and civic activities)	0.14	0.14	0.15	7.3	7.0	7.7	1.97	1.98	1.96
Leisure and sports	5.14	5.50	4.80	96.4	96.7	96.1	5.33	5.69	5.00
Socializing and communicating	0.75	0.71	0.78	40.4	37.6	43.0	1.86	1.89	1.82
Watching television	2.58	2.80	2.37	79.8	80.7	78.9	3.23	3.47	3.00
Participating in sports, exercise, and recreation	0.29	0.39	0.20	17.5	19.4	15.7	1.67	1.98	1.30
Telephone calls, mail, and email	0.18	0.12	0.23	24.3	18.0	30.2	0.73	0.69	0.76
Other activities n.e.c.	0.17	0.16	0.18	12.3	11.4	13.3	1.37	1.39	1.35

Note: Data refer to respondents age 15 years and over.

n.e.c. = Not elsewhere classified.

[1]A primary activity is designated by a respondent as his or her main activity. Other activities done simultaneously are not included.
[2]All major activity categories include related travel time.
X = Not applicable.

Table 12-2. Average Hours Per Day Spent in Primary Activities[1] for the Total Population, by Age, Sex, Race, Hispanic Origin, and Educational Attainment, 2005 Annual Averages

(Number.)

Characteristic	Hours per day spent in primary activities[2]											
	Personal care activities	Eating and drinking	Household activities	Purchasing goods and services	Caring for and helping household members	Caring for and helping non-household members	Working and work-related activities	Edu-cational activities	Organiza-tional, civic, and religious activities	Leisure activities	Telephone calls, mail, and email	Other activities n.e.c.
Both Sexes, 15 Years and Over	9.43	1.24	1.82	0.80	0.54	0.23	3.69	0.45	0.31	5.14	0.18	0.17
15 to 24 years	10.08	1.04	0.91	0.64	0.35	0.22	2.59	1.92	0.30	5.55	0.23	0.17
25 to 34 years	9.34	1.20	1.54	0.83	1.08	0.20	4.71	0.34	0.21	4.29	0.12	0.13
35 to 44 years	9.16	1.19	1.90	0.83	1.01	0.17	4.88	0.11	0.28	4.19	0.13	0.16
45 to 54 years	9.02	1.24	2.12	0.76	0.38	0.23	5.09	0.08	0.29	4.50	0.15	0.13
55 to 64 years	9.13	1.40	2.24	0.84	0.15	0.36	3.72	(3)	0.32	5.40	0.19	0.18
65 years and over	9.83	1.47	2.40	0.91	0.09	0.26	0.69	0.04	0.47	7.31	0.26	0.27
Men, 15 Years and Over	9.22	1.30	1.35	0.63	0.34	0.21	4.44	0.47	0.27	5.50	0.12	0.16
15 to 24 years	9.92	1.00	0.75	0.48	0.14	0.22	2.60	1.96	0.34	6.23	0.21	0.15
25 to 34 years	9.07	1.28	1.07	0.61	0.60	0.23	5.69	(3)	0.20	4.66	0.07	0.10
35 to 44 years	9.06	1.26	1.34	0.66	0.64	0.16	5.90	(3)	0.22	4.47	0.09	0.14
45 to 54 years	8.71	1.32	1.57	0.57	0.30	0.18	6.19	(3)	0.22	4.64	0.12	0.13
55 to 64 years	8.95	1.55	1.80	0.70	0.12	0.28	4.43	(3)	0.25	5.60	0.12	0.18
65 years and over	9.63	1.53	1.80	0.83	0.09	0.25	0.88	(3)	0.41	8.15	0.13	0.29
Women, 15 Years and Over	9.62	1.19	2.27	0.96	0.72	0.25	3.00	0.43	0.35	4.80	0.23	0.18
15 to 24 years	10.24	1.07	1.08	0.81	0.56	0.22	2.58	1.88	0.27	4.85	0.25	0.19
25 to 34 years	9.62	1.12	2.01	1.05	1.57	0.17	3.74	0.27	0.22	3.92	0.17	0.15
35 to 44 years	9.26	1.11	2.44	1.00	1.36	0.18	3.88	0.16	0.34	3.92	0.17	0.18
45 to 54 years	9.32	1.17	2.64	0.95	0.46	0.27	4.04	0.11	0.37	4.36	0.18	0.14
55 to 64 years	9.31	1.27	2.65	0.97	0.18	0.43	3.07	(3)	0.40	5.21	0.27	0.18
65 years and over	9.97	1.43	2.84	0.97	0.09	0.27	0.55	(3)	0.51	6.70	0.36	0.25
White, 15 Years and Over	9.32	1.29	1.91	0.81	0.54	0.24	3.74	0.43	0.29	5.08	0.17	0.17
Men	9.11	1.34	1.42	0.64	0.34	0.22	4.54	0.46	0.25	5.39	0.11	0.16
Women	9.52	1.23	2.37	0.97	0.72	0.26	2.99	0.40	0.33	4.79	0.23	0.18
Black, 15 Years and Over	10.09	0.88	1.29	0.73	0.45	0.23	3.30	0.50	0.47	5.69	0.21	0.15
Men	9.87	0.93	0.92	0.56	0.24	0.24	3.57	(3)	0.43	6.46	0.20	0.15
Women	10.27	0.84	1.60	0.87	0.63	0.22	3.09	0.55	0.50	5.06	0.22	0.15
Hispanic,[4] 15 Years and Over	9.78	1.18	1.75	0.79	0.65	0.17	3.89	0.44	0.28	4.80	0.10	0.18
Men	9.59	1.18	0.97	0.69	0.35	0.16	5.04	(3)	0.25	5.12	0.07	0.17
Women	9.99	1.18	2.57	0.90	0.95	0.18	2.67	0.47	0.31	4.46	0.13	0.19
Marital Status and Sex												
Married, spouse present	9.14	1.34	2.14	0.88	0.75	0.22	4.01	0.12	0.33	4.75	0.14	0.17
Men	8.93	1.40	1.54	0.70	0.51	0.19	5.06	0.10	0.29	5.04	0.08	0.16
Women	9.36	1.28	2.73	1.06	0.98	0.26	2.97	0.15	0.37	4.46	0.20	0.18
Other marital status	9.77	1.13	1.44	0.70	0.28	0.24	3.30	0.85	0.28	5.61	0.23	0.17
Men	9.60	1.16	1.09	0.53	0.10	0.25	3.62	0.96	0.24	6.11	0.18	0.16
Women	9.92	1.09	1.74	0.84	0.42	0.24	3.03	0.75	0.32	5.19	0.27	0.18
Educational Attainment, 25 Years and Over												
Less than a high school diploma	9.91	1.17	2.12	0.75	0.44	0.17	2.62	(3)	0.31	6.16	0.11	0.17
High school graduate, no college[5]	9.48	1.23	2.11	0.81	0.44	0.27	3.55	0.06	0.25	5.50	0.15	0.17
Less than a bachelor's degree	9.05	1.26	2.03	0.88	0.63	0.29	4.12	0.21	0.32	4.87	0.17	0.17
Bachelor's degree or higher[6]	9.00	1.43	1.87	0.85	0.74	0.18	4.78	0.18	0.37	4.22	0.21	0.16

Note: Unless otherwise specified, data refer to persons age 15 years and over.

n.e.c. = Not elsewhere classified.

[1]A primary activity is designated by a respondent as his or her main activity. Other activities done simultaneously are not included.
[2]All major activity categories include related travel time.
[3]Data not shown where base is less than 800,000.
[4]May be of any race.
[5]Includes persons with a high school diploma or equivalent.
[6]Includes persons with bachelor's, master's, professional, and doctoral degrees.

Table 12-3. Average Hours Worked Per Day by Employed Persons on Weekdays and Weekends, by Selected Characteristics, 2005 Annual Averages

(Number, percent.)

Characteristic	Total employed (thousands)	Worked on an average day			Worked on an average weekday			Worked on an average Saturday, Sunday, or holiday[1]		
		Number (thousands)	Percent	Hours per day[2]	Number[3] (thousands)	Percent	Hours per day[2]	Number[4] (thousands)	Percent	Hours per day[2]
Both Sexes[5]	150 748	102 146	67.8	7.53	124 653	82.7	7.86	47 788	31.7	5.48
Full-time worker	117 521	84 285	71.7	8.04	103 716	88.3	8.39	37 291	31.7	5.67
Part-time worker	33 227	17 861	53.8	5.13	20 926	63.0	5.20	10 497	31.6	4.81
Men[5]	79 988	56 302	70.4	7.90	68 486	85.6	8.26	27 144	33.9	5.74
Full-time worker	68 598	50 167	73.1	8.27	61 384	89.5	8.65	23 283	33.9	5.89
Part-time worker	11 390	6 135	53.9	4.85	7 093	62.3	4.85	3 861	33.9	4.86
Women[5]	70 760	45 844	64.8	7.08	56 181	79.4	7.37	20 620	29.1	5.13
Full-time worker	48 923	34 117	69.7	7.69	42 337	86.5	8.02	13 985	28.6	5.29
Part-time worker	21 837	11 727	53.7	5.28	13 832	63.3	5.38	6 633	30.4	4.78
Multiple Job Holding Status										
Single jobholder	135 474	90 399	66.7	7.53	111 479	82.3	7.83	38 647	28.5	5.40
Multiple jobholder	15 274	11 746	76.9	7.57	13 201	86.4	8.13	8 696	56.9	5.78
Educational Attainment, 25 Years and Over										
Less than a high school diploma	10 635	7 244	68.1	7.90	9 244	86.9	8.03	3 009	28.3	7.08
High school graduate, no college[6]	38 739	25 726	66.4	7.84	32 291	83.4	8.01	9 584	24.7	6.46
Less than a bachelor's degree	33 489	23 158	69.2	7.59	28 265	84.4	7.84	11 079	33.1	6.09
Bachelor's degree or higher[7]	44 026	32 495	73.8	7.37	39 121	88.9	7.97	16 014	36.4	3.74

Note: Unless otherwise specified, data refer to persons age 15 years and over.

[1]Holidays are New Year's Day, Easter, Memorial Day, the Fourth of July, Labor Day, Thanksgiving Day, and Christmas Day. In 2005, data were not collected for Thanksgiving Day.
[2]Includes work at main and other job(s) and excludes travel related to work.
[3]Number was derived by multiplying the "total employed" by the percent of employed persons who worked on an average weekday.
[4]Number was derived by multiplying the "total employed" by the percent of employed persons who worked on an average Saturday, Sunday, or holiday.
[5]Includes workers whose hours vary.
[6]Includes persons with a high school diploma or equivalent.
[7]Includes persons with bachelor's, master's, professional, and doctoral degrees.

Table 12-4. Average Hours Worked Per Day at Main Job Only by Employed Persons on Weekdays and Weekend Days, by Selected Characteristics, 2005 Annual Averages

(Number, percent.)

Characteristic	Total employed (thousands)	Worked on an average day			Worked on an average weekday			Worked on an average Saturday, Sunday, or holiday[1]		
		Number (thousands)	Percent	Hours per day[2]	Number[3] (thousands)	Percent	Hours per day[2]	Number[4] (thousands)	Percent	Hours per day[2]
Class of Worker										
Wage and salary workers	138 354	91 574	66.2	7.55	113 696	82.2	7.85	38 623	27.9	5.39
Self-employed workers	12 154	8 640	71.1	6.74	9 950	81.9	7.10	5 176	42.6	4.89
Occupation										
Management, business, and financial operations	22 156	16 437	74.2	7.66	20 223	91.3	8.14	6 968	31.5	4.20
Professional and related	31 532	21 365	67.8	7.23	26 375	83.6	7.78	9 801	31.1	3.79
Services	23 699	14 177	59.8	6.94	16 735	70.6	7.01	8 584	36.2	6.64
Sales and related	17 502	12 117	69.2	7.40	13 935	79.6	7.70	6 919	39.5	5.72
Office and administrative support	20 721	12 977	62.6	7.20	17 032	82.2	7.37	3 321	16.0	5.16
Farming, fishing, and forestry	1 578	(5)	(5)	(5)	(5)	(5)	(5)	(5)	(5)	(5)
Construction and extraction	9 073	6 120	67.5	8.13	7 877	86.8	8.36	(5)	(5)	(5)
Installation, maintenance, and repair	5 197	3 583	68.9	8.44	4 412	84.9	8.62	(5)	(5)	(5)
Production	10 878	7 208	66.3	7.89	9 324	85.7	7.97	2 265	20.8	7.17
Transportation and material moving	8 413	5 236	62.2	8.01	6 550	77.9	8.19	2 150	25.6	6.70
Earnings of Full-time Wage and Salary Earners[6]										
$0 to $450	27 781	18 149	65.3	7.81	22 860	82.3	7.99	7 598	27.3	6.57
$451 to $675	27 279	19 173	70.3	7.93	24 617	90.2	8.07	5 903	21.6	6.53
$676 to $1,050	23 863	16 201	67.9	7.99	20 366	85.3	8.35	5 863	24.6	4.91
$1,051 and higher	26 594	19 563	73.6	7.99	24 039	90.4	8.59	8 927	33.6	4.10

Note: Data refer to respondents age 15 years and over.

[1]Holidays are New Year's Day, Easter, Memorial Day, the Fourth of July, Labor Day, Thanksgiving Day, and Christmas Day. In 2005, data were not collected for Thanksgiving Day.
[2]Includes work at main job only and excludes travel related to work.
[3]Number was derived by multiplying the "total employed" by the percent of employed persons who worked on an average weekday.
[4]Number was derived by multiplying the "total employed" by the percent of employed persons who worked on an average Saturday, Sunday, or holiday.
[5]Data not shown where base is less than 800,000.
[6]These values represent usual weekly earnings. Each earnings range covers approximately 25 percent of full-time wage and salary workers.

Table 12-5. Average Hours Worked Per Day at All Jobs by Employed Persons at Workplace or at Home, by Selected Characteristics, 2005 Annual Averages

(Number, percent.)

Characteristic	Total employed (thousands)	Employed persons who reported working on the diary day[1]								
		Number (thousands)	Percent	Hours of work	Location of work[2]					
					Persons who reported working at the workplace on the diary day			Persons who reported working at home on the diary day[3]		
					Number (thousands)	Percent	Hours of work at workplace	Number (thousands)	Percent	Hours of work at home
Full and Part-time Status and Sex										
Both sexes[4]	150 748	102 146	67.8	7.53	89 154	87.3	7.81	20 048	19.6	2.58
Full-time worker	117 521	84 285	71.7	8.04	74 904	88.9	8.23	16 142	19.2	2.70
Part-time worker	33 227	17 861	53.8	5.13	14 251	79.8	5.61	3 906	21.9	2.10
Men[4]	79 988	56 302	70.4	7.90	49 417	87.8	8.13	11 781	20.9	2.57
Full-time worker	68 598	50 167	73.1	8.27	44 759	89.2	8.42	10 308	20.5	2.60
Part-time worker	11 390	6 135	53.9	4.85	4 658	75.9	5.31	1 472	24.0	2.38
Women[4]	70 760	45 844	64.8	7.08	39 737	86.7	7.41	8 267	18.0	2.59
Full-time worker	48 923	34 117	69.7	7.69	30 145	88.4	7.93	5 834	17.1	2.86
Part-time worker	21 837	11 727	53.7	5.28	9 593	81.8	5.76	2 434	20.8	1.94
Multiple Job Holding Status										
Single jobholder	135 474	90 399	66.7	7.53	79 492	87.9	7.80	16 376	18.1	2.57
Multiple jobholder	15 274	11 746	76.9	7.57	9 663	82.3	7.90	3 672	31.3	2.62
Educational Attainment, 25 Years and Over										
Less than a high school diploma	10 635	7 244	68.1	7.90	6 798	93.9	7.95	(5)	(5)	(5)
High school graduate, no college[6]	38 739	25 726	66.4	7.84	23 694	92.1	7.95	2 907	11.3	2.71
Some college or associate degree	33 489	23 158	69.2	7.59	19 877	85.8	7.90	4 676	20.2	3.02
Bachelor's degree or higher[7]	44 026	32 495	73.8	7.37	26 196	80.6	7.88	11 120	34.2	2.31

Note: Unless otherwise specified, data refer to persons age 15 years and over.

[1]Includes work at main and other job(s) and at locations other than home or the workplace. Excludes travel related to work.
[2]Respondents can report working at more than one location during the diary day.
[3]"Working at home" includes any time the respondent reported doing activities that were identified as "part of one's job"; this category is not restricted to persons whose usual workplace is their home.
[4]Includes workers whose hours vary.
[5]Data not shown where base is less than 800,000.
[6]Includes persons with a high school diploma or equivalent.
[7]Includes persons with bachelor's, master's, professional, and doctoral degrees.

Table 12-6. Average Hours Worked Per Day at Main Job Only by Employed Persons at Workplace or at Home, by Selected Characteristics, 2005 Annual Averages

(Number, percent.)

Characteristic	Total employed (thousands)	Employed persons who reported working on the diary day[1]								
		Number (thousands)	Percent	Hours of work	Location of work[2]					
					Persons who reported working at the workplace on the diary day			Persons who reported working at home on the diary day[3]		
					Number (thousands)	Percent	Hours of work at workplace	Number (thousands)	Percent	Hours of work at home
Class of Worker										
Wage and salary worker	138 354	91 574	66.2	7.55	82 519	90.1	7.81	14 118	15.4	2.19
Self-employed worker	12 154	8 640	71.1	6.74	5 229	60.5	7.24	4 245	49.1	3.92
Occupation										
Management, business, and financial operations	22 156	16 437	74.2	7.66	12 968	78.9	8.20	5 031	30.6	3.02
Professional and related	31 532	21 365	67.8	7.23	17 618	82.5	7.82	5 999	28.1	2.24
Services	23 699	14 177	59.8	6.94	12 628	89.1	7.14	1 634	11.5	3.16
Sales and related	17 502	12 117	69.2	7.40	10 654	87.9	7.57	2 400	19.8	2.57
Office and administrative support	20 721	12 977	62.6	7.20	12 168	93.8	7.44	1 224	9.4	1.57
Farming, fishing, and forestry	1 578	(4)	(4)	(4)	(4)	(4)	(4)	(4)	(4)	(4)
Construction and extraction	9 073	6 120	67.5	8.13	5 743	93.8	8.09	(4)	(4)	(4)
Installation, maintenance, and repair	5 197	3 583	68.9	8.44	3 411	95.2	8.49	(4)	(4)	(4)
Production	10 878	7 208	66.3	7.89	6 827	94.7	7.81	(4)	(4)	(4)
Transportation and material moving	8 413	5 236	62.2	8.01	4 915	93.9	8.20	(4)	(4)	(4)
Earnings of Full-time Wage and Salary Earners[5]										
$0 to $450	27 781	18 149	65.3	7.81	16 976	93.5	7.90	1 230	6.8	3.59
$451 to $675	27 279	19 173	70.3	7.93	17 990	93.8	8.14	1 823	9.5	2.23
$676 to $1,050	23 863	16 201	67.9	7.99	14 845	91.6	8.29	2 435	15.0	1.64
$1,051 and higher	26 594	19 563	73.6	7.99	16 729	85.5	8.45	5 236	26.8	1.83

Note: Unless otherwise specified, data refer to persons age 15 years and over.

[1]Includes work at main and other job(s) and at locations other than home or the workplace. Excludes travel related to work.
[2]Respondents can report working at more than one location during the diary day.
[3]"Working at home" includes any time the respondent reported doing activities that were identified as "part of one's job"; this category is not restricted to persons whose usual workplace is their home.
[4]Data not shown where base is less than 800,000.
[5]These values represent usual weekly earnings. Each earnings range covers approximately 25 percent of full-time wage and salary workers.

Table 12-7. Average Hours Per Day Spent by Persons Age 18 Years and Over Caring for Household Children Under 18 Years, by Sex of Respondent and Age of Youngest Household Child, 2005 Annual Averages

(Number.)

Activity	Hours per day caring for household children		
	Both sexes	Men	Women
Persons in Households with Children Under 18 Years			
Caring for household children as a primary activity	1.32	0.82	1.73
Physical care	0.44	0.23	0.61
Education-related activities	0.10	0.06	0.14
Reading to/with children	0.04	0.02	0.06
Talking to/with children	0.05	0.03	0.08
Playing/doing hobbies with children	0.24	0.21	0.27
Looking after children	0.08	0.07	0.10
Attending children's events	0.06	0.06	0.07
Travel related to care of household children	0.18	0.10	0.24
Other childcare activities	0.12	0.05	0.18
Persons in Households with Youngest Child 6 to 17 Years			
Caring for household children as a primary activity	0.80	0.46	1.09
Physical care	0.14	0.06	0.21
Education-related activities	0.13	0.07	0.17
Reading to/with children	0.02	(1)	0.03
Talking to/with children	0.07	0.03	0.10
Playing/doing hobbies with children	0.05	0.05	0.05
Looking after children	0.04	(1)	0.05
Attending children's events	0.08	0.07	0.09
Travel related to care of household children	0.17	0.10	0.24
Other childcare activities	0.09	0.04	0.15
Persons in Households with Youngest Child Under 6 Years			
Caring for household children as a primary activity	1.94	1.28	2.46
Physical care	0.79	0.45	1.06
Education-related activities	0.07	(1)	0.10
Reading to/with children	0.06	0.04	0.09
Talking to/with children	0.03	(1)	0.05
Playing/doing hobbies with children	0.47	0.41	0.51
Looking after children	0.14	0.12	0.15
Attending children's events	0.04	(1)	0.04
Travel related to care of household children	0.19	0.11	0.25
Other childcare activities	0.15	0.06	0.21

Note: Universe includes respondents age 18 years and over living in households with children under 18 years old, even if they did not report doing childcare on the diary day.

[1]Data not shown where base is less than 800,000.

Table 12-8. Average Hours Per Day Spent in Primary Activities[1] by the Total Population Age 18 Years and Over, by Activity Category, Employment Status, Presence and Age of Household Children, and Sex, 2005 Annual Averages

(Number.)

Activity	Hours spent per day in primary activities								
	Household with children under 6 years old			Household with children 6 to 17 years old			Household with no children under 18 years old		
	Both sexes	Men	Women	Both sexes	Men	Women	Both sexes	Men	Women
TOTAL									
All Activities[2]	24.00	24.00	24.00	24.00	24.00	24.00	24.00	24.00	24.00
Personal care activities	9.28	9.01	9.50	9.23	9.02	9.41	9.44	9.24	9.63
Sleeping	8.59	8.41	8.73	8.47	8.38	8.56	8.59	8.54	8.65
Eating and drinking	1.17	1.26	1.10	1.19	1.28	1.11	1.31	1.35	1.27
Household activities	1.89	1.17	2.46	1.92	1.32	2.45	1.90	1.49	2.30
Housework	0.76	0.26	1.15	0.70	0.27	1.07	0.58	0.23	0.93
Food preparation and cleanup	0.67	0.28	0.97	0.57	0.27	0.84	0.49	0.27	0.70
Lawn and garden care	0.12	0.18	0.08	0.18	0.26	0.12	0.25	0.32	0.18
Household management	0.11	0.09	0.12	0.16	0.13	0.19	0.16	0.14	0.18
Purchasing goods and services	0.85	0.70	0.96	0.83	0.62	1.03	0.80	0.64	0.95
Consumer goods purchases	0.47	0.38	0.54	0.42	0.29	0.55	0.39	0.31	0.47
Professional and personal care services	0.07	0.06	0.09	0.07	0.06	0.08	0.09	0.06	0.13
Caring for and helping household members	1.98	1.31	2.50	0.84	0.52	1.13	0.06	0.05	0.07
Caring for and helping household children	1.75	1.17	2.22	0.62	0.36	0.85	. . .	. . .	. . .
Caring for and helping non-household members	0.14	0.13	0.15	0.19	0.18	0.19	0.28	0.26	0.31
Caring for and helping non-household adults	0.06	0.06	0.06	0.07	0.08	0.06	0.09	0.09	0.09
Working and work-related activities	3.98	5.58	2.72	4.48	5.60	3.50	3.62	4.15	3.11
Working	3.60	5.01	2.48	4.04	5.01	3.18	3.30	3.78	2.83
Educational activities	0.23	(3)	0.27	0.33	0.32	0.33	0.23	0.26	0.20
Attending class	0.11	(3)	0.13	0.19	(3)	0.18	0.09	0.10	0.09
Homework and research	0.10	(3)	(3)	0.11	(3)	0.12	0.12	0.14	0.10
Organizational, civic, and religious activities	0.25	0.24	0.26	0.33	0.26	0.39	0.31	0.26	0.35
Religious and spiritual activities	0.11	0.07	0.13	0.12	0.08	0.15	0.13	0.10	0.16
Volunteering (organizational and civic activities)	0.11	0.13	0.09	0.17	0.15	0.19	0.13	0.12	0.15
Leisure and sports	3.99	4.27	3.77	4.39	4.70	4.13	5.66	5.98	5.35
Socializing and communicating	0.83	0.80	0.86	0.71	0.73	0.70	0.73	0.67	0.78
Watching television	2.04	2.19	1.92	2.16	2.30	2.04	2.90	3.15	2.65
Participating in sports, exercise, and recreation	0.20	0.26	0.16	0.26	0.33	0.19	0.29	0.37	0.20
Telephone calls, mail, and email	0.09	0.03	0.13	0.13	0.08	0.17	0.20	0.14	0.26
Other activities n.e.c.	0.15	0.13	0.18	0.14	0.11	0.17	0.19	0.18	0.19
EMPLOYED									
All Activities[2]	24.00	24.00	24.00	24.00	24.00	24.00	24.00	24.00	24.00
Personal care activities	9.11	8.90	9.37	8.97	8.76	9.19	9.14	8.99	9.31
Sleeping	8.40	8.29	8.53	8.24	8.16	8.33	8.32	8.28	8.35
Eating and drinking	1.19	1.28	1.09	1.20	1.32	1.07	1.29	1.35	1.22
Household activities	1.52	1.11	2.01	1.70	1.29	2.13	1.52	1.27	1.80
Housework	0.54	0.24	0.89	0.58	0.25	0.93	0.44	0.21	0.70
Food preparation and cleanup	0.51	0.27	0.79	0.48	0.26	0.72	0.35	0.23	0.50
Lawn and garden care	0.14	0.18	0.09	0.18	0.26	0.09	0.20	0.27	0.13
Household management	0.10	0.08	0.12	0.15	0.12	0.18	0.12	0.11	0.13
Purchasing goods and services	0.80	0.67	0.95	0.77	0.58	0.96	0.72	0.58	0.88
Consumer goods purchases	0.44	0.36	0.53	0.38	0.27	0.50	0.35	0.28	0.43
Professional and personal care services	0.07	0.06	0.09	0.07	0.05	0.08	0.08	0.05	0.11
Caring for and helping household members	1.70	1.31	2.17	0.74	0.50	0.99	0.04	0.05	0.04
Caring for and helping household children	1.49	1.16	1.88	0.54	0.36	0.74	. . .	. . .	. . .
Caring for and helping non-household members	0.11	0.11	0.11	0.18	0.18	0.19	0.25	0.22	0.28
Caring for and helping non-household adults	0.05	0.06	0.04	0.07	0.08	0.07	0.08	0.08	0.08
Working and work-related activities	5.33	6.12	4.41	5.67	6.46	4.84	5.79	6.17	5.37
Working	4.84	5.51	4.06	5.17	5.85	4.46	5.32	5.65	4.94
Educational activities	0.11	(3)	(3)	0.27	(3)	0.26	0.21	0.20	0.21
Attending class	(3)	(3)	(3)	0.15	(3)	(3)	0.07	(3)	0.08
Homework and research	(3)	(3)	(3)	0.10	(3)	(3)	0.12	(3)	0.11
Organizational, civic, and religious activities	0.24	0.24	0.24	0.33	0.27	0.39	0.23	0.21	0.25
Religious and spiritual activities	0.10	0.08	0.14	0.11	0.08	0.14	0.10	0.08	0.13
Volunteering (organizational and civic activities)	0.10	0.12	0.07	0.18	0.16	0.20	0.09	0.10	0.09
Leisure and sports	3.69	4.02	3.30	3.92	4.19	3.64	4.52	4.73	4.27
Socializing and communicating	0.73	0.73	0.72	0.63	0.64	0.63	0.66	0.60	0.73
Watching television	1.88	2.05	1.67	1.91	2.05	1.76	2.27	2.46	2.06
Participating in sports, exercise, and recreation	0.21	0.25	0.16	0.25	0.32	0.18	0.27	0.34	0.19
Telephone calls, mail, and email	0.07	0.04	0.10	0.12	0.08	0.17	0.17	0.13	0.21
Other activities n.e.c.	0.12	0.11	0.13	0.13	0.10	0.17	0.14	0.12	0.16

n.e.c. = Not elsewhere classified.

[1]A primary activity is designated by a respondent as his or her main activity. Other activities done simultaneously are not included.
[2]All major activity categories include related travel time.
[3]Data not shown where base is less than 800,000.
. . . = Not available.

Table 12-8. Average Hours Per Day Spent in Primary Activities[1] by the Total Population Age 18 Years and Over, by Activity Category, Employment Status, Presence and Age of Household Children, and Sex, 2005 Annual Averages—*Continued*

(Number.)

Activity	Hours spent per day in primary activities								
	Household with children under 6 years old			Household with children 6 to 17 years old			Household with no children under 18 years old		
	Both sexes	Men	Women	Both sexes	Men	Women	Both sexes	Men	Women
NOT EMPLOYED									
All Activities[2]	24.00	24.00	24.00	24.00	24.00	24.00	24.00	24.00	24.00
Personal care activities	9.76	10.05	9.71	10.12	10.47	9.96	9.93	9.75	10.06
Sleeping	9.13	9.62	9.04	9.29	9.60	9.15	9.04	9.05	9.04
Eating and drinking	1.10	1.03	1.11	1.15	1.06	1.20	1.35	1.36	1.35
Household activities	2.94	1.80	3.16	2.68	1.49	3.23	2.53	1.94	2.98
Housework	1.38	(3)	1.56	1.09	(3)	1.45	0.82	0.26	1.24
Food preparation and cleanup	1.13	(3)	1.26	0.88	0.29	1.15	0.70	0.36	0.96
Lawn and garden care	0.08	(3)	(3)	0.21	(3)	0.18	0.32	0.42	0.25
Household management	0.13	(3)	0.12	0.21	(3)	0.23	0.23	0.21	0.24
Purchasing goods and services	0.98	(3)	0.98	1.07	0.82	1.19	0.93	0.77	1.06
Consumer goods purchases	0.56	(3)	0.55	0.58	0.39	0.67	0.45	0.35	0.52
Professional and personal care services	0.08	(3)	(3)	(3)	(3)	(3)	0.12	0.08	0.16
Caring for and helping household members	2.75	1.38	3.00	1.19	0.61	1.46	0.09	0.06	0.10
Caring for and helping household children	2.51	1.27	2.74	0.90	0.39	1.14	. . .	. . .	. . .
Caring for and helping non-household members	0.22	(3)	0.20	0.20	(3)	0.20	0.34	0.33	0.35
Caring for and helping non-household adults	(3)	(3)	(3)	0.06	(3)	(3)	0.11	0.11	0.11
Working and work-related activities	(3)	(3)	(3)	(3)	(3)	(3)	0.09	(3)	(3)
Working	(3)	(3)	(3)	(3)	(3)	(3)	(3)	(3)	(3)
Educational activities	0.56	(3)	(3)	0.53	(3)	(3)	0.26	(3)	0.17
Attending class	(3)	(3)	(3)	(3)	(3)	(3)	0.12	(3)	0.09
Homework and research	(3)	(3)	(3)	(3)	(3)	(3)	(3)	(3)	(3)
Organizational, civic, and religious activities	0.29	(3)	0.29	0.33	(3)	0.39	0.43	0.37	0.48
Religious and spiritual activities	0.12	(3)	0.13	0.15	(3)	0.17	0.17	0.14	0.20
Volunteering (organizational and civic activities)	0.14	(3)	0.13	0.15	(3)	0.18	0.20	0.18	0.22
Leisure and sports	4.85	6.75	4.50	6.06	7.59	5.35	7.53	8.47	6.81
Socializing and communicating	1.12	(3)	1.07	1.00	1.24	0.89	0.84	0.81	0.85
Watching television	2.52	3.57	2.32	3.06	3.71	2.76	3.91	4.52	3.45
Participating in sports, exercise, and recreation	0.18	(3)	0.14	0.27	(3)	0.22	0.30	0.43	0.21
Telephone calls, mail, and email	0.16	(3)	0.19	0.16	(3)	0.19	0.26	0.17	0.34
Other activities n.e.c.	0.26	0.26	0.26	0.17	0.19	0.16	0.26	0.31	0.23

n.e.c. = Not elsewhere classified.

[1]A primary activity is designated by a respondent as his or her main activity. Other activities done simultaneously are not included.
[2]All major activity categories include related travel time.
[3]Data not shown where base is less than 800,000.
. . . = Not available.

Table 12-9. Average Hours Per Day Spent in Leisure and Sports Activities for the Total Population, by Selected Characteristics, 2005 Annual Averages

(Number.)

Characteristic	Total, all leisure and sports activities			Participating in sports, exercise, and recreation		Socializing and communicating		Watching TV	
	Total, all days	Weekdays	Weekends and holidays[1]	Weekdays	Weekends and holidays[1]	Weekdays	Weekends and holidays[1]	Weekdays	Weekends and holidays[1]
Sex									
Men	5.50	4.83	7.10	0.34	0.49	0.55	1.09	2.51	3.47
Women	4.80	4.39	5.80	0.21	0.18	0.60	1.22	2.24	2.68
Age									
Total, 15 years and over	5.14	4.60	6.43	0.27	0.33	0.58	1.16	2.37	3.07
15 to 24 years	5.55	5.03	6.82	0.51	0.57	0.77	1.51	2.18	2.66
25 to 34 years	4.29	3.55	5.91	0.24	0.29	0.53	1.21	1.94	2.89
35 to 44 years	4.19	3.59	5.59	0.22	0.29	0.50	1.15	1.91	2.72
45 to 54 years	4.50	3.84	6.15	0.20	0.35	0.47	1.03	2.12	3.17
55 to 64 years	5.40	4.87	6.66	0.22	0.27	0.56	1.09	2.59	3.27
65 years and over	7.31	7.11	7.81	0.25	0.19	0.65	0.91	3.73	3.89
Race and Hispanic Origin									
White	5.08	4.53	6.42	0.28	0.35	0.58	1.18	2.30	2.98
Black	5.69	5.29	6.63	0.21	0.25	0.67	1.04	2.92	3.82
Hispanic[2]	4.80	4.18	6.16	0.20	0.30	0.58	1.53	2.50	2.96
Employment Status									
Employed	4.23	3.55	5.87	0.23	0.36	0.47	1.15	1.84	2.72
Full-time workers	4.06	3.31	5.86	0.21	0.38	0.43	1.13	1.75	2.77
Part-time workers	4.84	4.41	5.89	0.31	0.27	0.62	1.23	2.14	2.56
Not employed	6.86	6.60	7.47	0.36	0.28	0.78	1.17	3.40	3.70
Earnings of Full-time Wage and Salary Earners[3]									
$0 to $450	4.34	3.68	5.82	0.17	0.30	0.51	1.26	1.95	2.85
$451 to $675	4.24	3.52	6.01	0.23	0.28	0.41	1.15	1.90	3.02
$676 to $1,050	4.10	3.38	5.88	0.21	0.43	0.50	1.17	1.76	2.64
$1,051 and higher	3.72	2.85	5.79	0.25	0.54	0.30	0.90	1.51	2.63
Presence and Age of Children									
No household children under 18 years ...	5.66	5.13	6.91	0.29	0.32	0.57	1.12	2.68	3.34
Household children under 18 years	4.37	3.80	5.72	0.26	0.34	0.59	1.22	1.92	2.66
Children 13 to 17 years, none younger ..	4.90	4.44	6.14	0.35	0.32	0.60	1.19	2.13	2.95
Children 6 to 12 years, none younger ...	4.37	3.74	5.81	0.27	0.42	0.53	1.10	1.83	2.64
Youngest child under 6 years	4.07	3.48	5.43	0.19	0.30	0.64	1.33	1.87	2.53
Marital Status and Sex									
Married, spouse present	4.75	4.18	6.13	0.23	0.29	0.54	1.17	2.20	2.91
Men	5.04	4.37	6.71	0.25	0.43	0.48	1.07	2.36	3.34
Women	4.46	3.99	5.57	0.20	0.16	0.60	1.26	2.04	2.49
Other marital status	5.61	5.11	6.79	0.33	0.38	0.63	1.15	2.58	3.25
Men	6.11	5.45	7.57	0.46	0.56	0.65	1.12	2.72	3.64
Women	5.19	4.83	6.06	0.22	0.21	0.61	1.18	2.47	2.90
Educational Attainment, 25 Years and Over									
Less than a high school diploma	6.16	5.82	6.90	0.21	0.16	0.56	1.17	3.36	3.92
High school graduates, no college[4] ...	5.50	4.95	6.83	0.17	0.26	0.58	1.09	2.79	3.67
Some college or associate degree	4.87	4.35	6.08	0.23	0.24	0.57	1.12	2.32	2.96
Bachelor's degree or higher[5]	4.22	3.58	5.78	0.29	0.40	0.45	1.00	1.68	2.36

Note: Unless otherwise specified, data refer to respondents age 15 years and over.

[1]Holidays are New Year's Day, Easter, Memorial Day, the Fourth of July, Labor Day, Thanksgiving Day, and Christmas Day. In 2005, data were not collected for Thanksgiving Day.
[2]May be of any race.
[3]These values represent usual weekly earnings. Each earnings range covers approximately 25 percent of full-time wage and salary workers.
[4]Includes persons with a high school diploma or equivalent.
[5]Includes persons with bachelor's, master's, professional, and doctoral degrees.

Table 12-9. Average Hours Per Day Spent in Leisure and Sports Activities for the Total Population, by Selected Characteristics, 2005 Annual Averages—*Continued*

(Number.)

Characteristic	Reading		Relaxing/thinking		Playing games and computer use for leisure		Other leisure and sports activities, including travel[6]	
	Weekdays	Weekends and holidays[1]	Weekdays	Weekends and holidays[1]	Weekdays	Weekends and holidays[1]	Weekdays	Weekends and holidays[1]
Sex								
Men	0.29	0.38	0.34	0.40	0.35	0.50	0.44	0.76
Women	0.39	0.52	0.30	0.29	0.27	0.28	0.37	0.62
Age								
Total, 15 years and over	0.34	0.45	0.32	0.35	0.31	0.39	0.41	0.69
15 to 24 years	0.14	0.16	0.19	0.21	0.57	0.71	0.68	1.00
25 to 34 years	0.13	0.20	0.17	0.25	0.24	0.41	0.30	0.65
35 to 44 years	0.21	0.30	0.20	0.21	0.22	0.29	0.32	0.63
45 to 54 years	0.30	0.37	0.25	0.31	0.15	0.29	0.36	0.63
55 to 64 years	0.43	0.68	0.41	0.39	0.32	0.31	0.33	0.64
65 years and over	0.92	1.18	0.77	0.80	0.36	0.31	0.43	0.53
Race and Hispanic Origin								
White	0.36	0.49	0.28	0.33	0.31	0.39	0.42	0.70
Black	0.24	0.15	0.59	0.52	0.30	0.29	0.37	0.56
Hispanic[2]	0.12	0.20	0.25	0.29	0.15	0.22	0.37	0.64
Employment Status								
Employed	0.22	0.34	0.23	0.27	0.23	0.36	0.34	0.67
Full-time workers	0.21	0.33	0.22	0.27	0.20	0.34	0.29	0.64
Part-time workers	0.27	0.38	0.24	0.25	0.32	0.43	0.51	0.78
Not employed	0.57	0.66	0.50	0.49	0.46	0.45	0.54	0.72
Earnings of Full-time Wage and Salary Earners[3]								
$0 to $450	0.18	0.19	0.30	0.23	0.28	0.39	0.28	0.60
$451 to $675	0.19	0.27	0.27	0.37	0.18	0.31	0.34	0.60
$676 to $1,050	0.20	0.38	0.16	0.24	0.24	0.40	0.32	0.63
$1,051 and higher	0.25	0.46	0.15	0.23	0.14	0.34	0.26	0.69
Presence and Age of Children								
No household children under 18 years ...	0.44	0.59	0.38	0.43	0.34	0.41	0.44	0.70
Household children under 18 years	0.19	0.25	0.22	0.22	0.26	0.36	0.36	0.66
Children 13 to 17 years, none younger ...	0.26	0.30	0.23	0.21	0.35	0.39	0.53	0.78
Children 6 to 12 years, none younger ...	0.20	0.29	0.25	0.26	0.29	0.40	0.38	0.70
Youngest child under 6 years	0.14	0.18	0.20	0.20	0.19	0.32	0.26	0.57
Marital Status and Sex								
Married, spouse present	0.33	0.52	0.30	0.35	0.26	0.31	0.33	0.60
Men	0.31	0.47	0.37	0.43	0.26	0.34	0.35	0.63
Women	0.35	0.56	0.23	0.27	0.26	0.27	0.31	0.56
Other marital status	0.35	0.37	0.34	0.34	0.37	0.49	0.50	0.79
Men	0.25	0.27	0.31	0.37	0.48	0.70	0.57	0.91
Women	0.44	0.47	0.37	0.32	0.27	0.30	0.45	0.69
Educational Attainment, 25 Years and Over								
Less than a high school diploma ...	0.33	0.23	0.84	0.68	0.18	(6)	0.34	0.60
High school graduates, no college[4]	0.35	0.43	0.42	0.48	0.31	0.28	0.33	0.61
Some college or associate degree ...	0.37	0.49	0.24	0.26	0.24	0.43	0.38	0.57
Bachelor's degree or higher[5]	0.45	0.76	0.15	0.21	0.22	0.37	0.34	0.69

Note: Unless otherwise specified, data refer to respondents age 15 years and over.

[1]Holidays are New Year's Day, Easter, Memorial Day, the Fourth of July, Labor Day, Thanksgiving Day, and Christmas Day. In 2005, data were not collected for Thanksgiving Day.
[2]May be of any race.
[3]These values represent usual weekly earnings. Each earnings range covers approximately 25 percent of full-time wage and salary workers.
[4]Includes persons with a high school diploma or equivalent.
[5]Includes persons with bachelor's, master's, professional, and doctoral degrees.
[6]Includes other leisure and sports activities, not elsewhere classified, and travel related to leisure and sports activities.

CHAPTER THIRTEEN

INCOME IN THE UNITED STATES
(CENSUS BUREAU)

INCOME IN THE UNITED STATES (CENSUS BUREAU)

HIGHLIGHTS

This chapter presents data on income collected by the Census Bureau. Total income consists of wages and income from pensions, investments, and other sources. Income is shown for various population groups and is measured as real income in 2005 dollars.

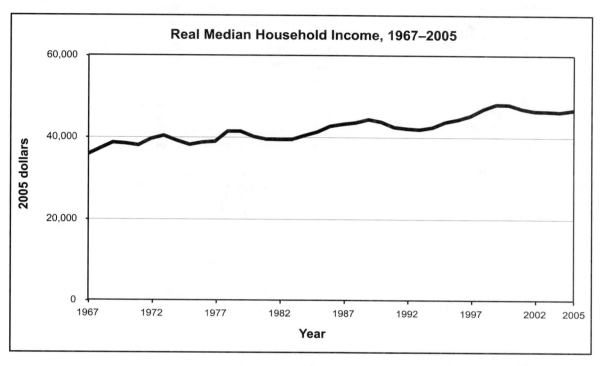

In 2005, real median income increased for the first time since 1999. It grew 1.1 percent, rising from $45,817 in 2004 to $46,326 in 2005. (See Table 13-1.)

OTHER HIGHLIGHTS

- Although real median income increased, earnings (as distinguished from income) of full-time workers decreased somewhat between 2004 and 2005. (See Table 13-1.)

- In 2005, Black households had the lowest real median income at $30,858 and Asian households had the highest real median income at $61,094. (See Table 13-1.)

- Also in 2005, households in the Northeast had the highest household income at $50,882, while households in the South had the lowest household income at $42,138. (See Table 13-1.)

- The Asian alone group had the highest percentage of households with incomes over $100,000 at 27.5 percent, compared with 19.7 percent of White alone, non-Hispanic households and 7.8 percent of Black alone households. (See Table 13-2.)

NOTES AND DEFINITIONS

Collection and Coverage

Data on income in the United States in this chapter are based on information collected in the 2006 and earlier Annual Social and Economic Supplements (ASEC) to the Census Bureau's Current Population Survey (CPS). The CPS is also the basis for the employment and unemployment data shown in Chapter 1 of this *Handbook*, which are collected by the Census Bureau for BLS. The basic CPS is described in the notes and definitions for Chapter 1. The sample universe for the CPS ASEC is slightly larger than the basic CPS, as it includes military personnel who live in a household with at least one other civilian adult, regardless of whether they live off post or on post.

For each person age 15 years and over in the sample, the ASEC asks questions about the amount of income received from all sources during the preceding calendar year from all sources. In addition to wage and salary earnings, which represent the largest component of income, other sources of income include Social Security, pensions, interest, dividends, and other money income. Excluded are certain money receipts, such as capital gains.

Although the income statistics refer to receipts during the previous calendar year, the demographic characteristics, such as age and household composition, are as of the survey date.

Data on income cover money income received before payments for personal income taxes, Social Security, Medicare, union dues, and the like. Therefore money income does not reflect the fact that some families receive noncash benefits, such as food stamps, health benefits, subsidized housing, and the like. In addition, money income does not reflect noncash benefits such payments by business for retirement programs, medical expenses, or other benefits.

The Census Bureau uses the research series of the BLS Consumer Price Index (CPI-U-RS) to adjust for changes in the cost of living. These indexes are shown in Table 7-11 of this *Handbook*.

Additional Information

Additional information is available in the Census publication "Income, Poverty, and Health Insurance Coverage in the United States: 2005," which can be found on the Census Bureau Web site at <http://www.census.gov/hhes>.

Table 13-1. Income and Earnings Summary Measures, by Selected Characteristics, 2004 and 2005

(Numbers in thousands, dollars, percent; income in 2005 dollars.)

| Characteristic | 2004[1] | | | 2005 | | | Percent change in real median income (2005 less 2004) | |
| | Number (thousands) | Median income (dollars) | | Number (thousands) | Median income (dollars) | | | |
		Estimate	90 percent confidence interval[2] (+/-)		Estimate	90 percent confidence interval[2] (+/-)	Estimate	90 percent confidence interval[2] (+/-)
Households								
All households	113 343	45 817	333	114 384	46 326	255	1.1	0.75
Type of Household								
Family households	76 858	57 179	338	77 402	57 278	332	0.2	0.67
Married-couple	57 975	65 946	490	58 179	66 067	401	0.2	0.78
Female householder, no husband present	13 981	30 823	530	14 093	30 650	431	-0.6	1.79
Male householder, no wife present	4 901	46 526	1 151	5 130	46 756	1 031	0.5	2.71
Nonfamily households	36 485	27 129	262	36 982	27 326	266	0.7	1.12
Female householder	19 942	22 594	321	20 230	22 688	413	0.4	1.90
Male householder	16 543	33 083	386	16 753	34 048	706	2.9	2.05
Race[3] and Hispanic Origin of Householder								
White	92 880	48 218	311	93 588	48 554	349	0.7	0.78
White, not Hispanic	81 628	50 546	381	82 003	50 784	283	0.5	0.76
Black	13 809	31 101	532	14 002	30 858	495	-0.8	1.84
Asian	4 123	59 427	2 077	4 273	61 094	1 171	2.8	3.42
Hispanic[4]	12 178	35 417	816	12 519	35 967	587	1.6	1.99
Age of Householder								
Under 65 years	90 192	52 562	253	90 926	52 287	242	-0.5	0.53
15 to 24 years	6 733	28 497	782	6 795	28 770	776	1.0	3.14
25 to 34 years	19 314	46 985	525	19 120	47 379	571	0.8	1.34
35 to 44 years	23 248	58 578	551	23 016	58 084	885	-0.8	1.47
45 to 54 years	23 393	63 068	559	23 731	62 424	724	-1.0	1.17
55 to 64 years	17 503	52 077	597	18 264	52 260	683	0.4	1.41
65 years and over	23 151	25 336	296	23 459	26 036	288	2.8	1.33
Nativity of Householder								
Native	98 842	46 786	304	99 579	46 897	271	0.2	0.70
Foreign-born	14 502	40 692	976	14 806	42 040	678	3.3	2.46
Naturalized citizen	6 741	47 642	1 448	6 990	50 030	1 341	5.0	3.43
Not a citizen	7 761	35 749	1 282	7 815	36 740	778	2.8	3.68
Region								
Northeast	21 187	49 462	819	21 054	50 882	610	2.9	1.72
Midwest	25 939	46 134	661	26 351	45 950	579	-0.4	1.54
South	41 224	42 108	374	41 805	42 138	349	0.1	0.98
West	24 993	49 245	668	25 174	50 002	609	1.5	1.50
Residence								
Inside metropolitan statistical areas	. . .	. . .	. . .	95 107	48 474	360	X	X
Inside principal cities	. . .	. . .	. . .	38 008	41 166	354	X	X
Outside principal cities	. . .	. . .	. . .	57 098	53 544	531	X	X
Outside metropolitan statistical areas[5]	. . .	. . .	. . .	19 278	37 564	683	X	X
Shares of Household Income, Quintiles, and Gini Index[6]								
Lowest quintile	22 669	3.4	0.04	22 877	3.4	0.04	-0.8	1.30
Second quintile	22 669	8.7	0.10	22 877	8.6	0.10	-0.7	1.25
Third quintile	22 669	14.7	0.16	22 877	14.6	0.16	-1.0	1.25
Fourth quintile	22 669	23.2	0.26	22 877	23.0	0.25	-1.6	1.25
Highest quintile	22 669	50.1	0.56	22 877	50.4	0.56	1.2	1.27
Gini index of income inequality	113 343	0.466	0.0047	114 384	0.469	0.0047	0.6	1.17
Earnings of Full-Time Year-Round Workers								
Men with earnings	60 088	42 160	153	61 500	41 386	148	-1.8	0.42
Women with earnings	42 380	32 285	134	43 351	31 858	133	-1.3	0.47
Per Capita Income[7]								
Total[3]	291 166	24 655	156	293 834	25 036	160	1.5	0.77
White	234 116	26 067	182	235 903	26 496	188	1.6	0.85
White, not Hispanic	195 347	28 357	209	195 893	28 946	219	2.1	0.91
Black	36 548	16 561	298	36 965	16 874	303	1.9	2.16
Asian	12 241	27 040	918	12 599	27 331	832	1.1	3.87
Hispanic[4]	41 840	14 577	304	43 168	14 483	253	-0.6	2.03

[1]The 2004 data have been revised to reflect a correction to the weights in the 2005 Annual Social and Economic Supplements (ASEC).
[2]A 90-percent confidence interval is a measure of an estimate's variability. The larger the confidence interval in relation to the size of the estimate, the less reliable the estimate.
[3]Federal surveys now give respondents the option of reporting more than one race. Therefore, two basic ways of defining a race group are possible. A group such as Asian may be defined as those who reported Asian and no other race (the race-alone or single-race concept) or as those who reported Asian regardless of whether they also reported another race (the race-alone-or-in-combination concept). This table shows data using the race-alone concept. The use of the single-race population does not imply that it is the preferred method of presenting or analyzing data. The Census Bureau uses a variety of approaches. Information on people who reported more than one race, such as White and American Indian and Alaska Native or Asian and Black or African American, is available from Census 2000 through American FactFinder. About 2.6 percent of people reported more than one race in Census 2000.
[4]May be of any race.
[5]The "outside metropolitan statistical areas" category includes both micropolitan statistical areas and territory outside of metropolitan and micropolitan statistical areas.
[6]The data shown in this section are shares of aggregate household income, the Gini index, and their respective confidence intervals. See the article by Paul Allison entitled "Measures of Inequality" from *American Sociological Review* 43 (December 1977), pp. 865–880, for an explanation of inequality measures.
[7]The data shown in this section are per capita incomes and their respective confidence intervals. Per capita income is the mean income computed for every man, woman, and child in a particular group. It is derived by dividing the total income of a particular group by the total population in that group (excluding patients or inmates in institutional quarters).
X = Not applicable.
. . . = Not available.

Table 13-2. Households, by Total Money Income, Race, and Hispanic Origin of Householder, 1967–2005

(Numbers in thousands, percent, dollars; income in 2005 CPI-U-RS adjusted dollars.)

Race and Hispanic origin of householder and year	Number (thousands)	Percent distribution										Median income (dollars)		Mean income (dollars)	
		Total	Under $5,000	$5,000 to $9,999	$10,000 to $14,999	$15,000 to $24,999	$25,000 to $34,999	$35,000 to $49,999	$50,000 to $74,999	$75,000 to $99,000	$100,000 and over	Value	Standard error	Value	Standard error
All Races															
1967[1]	60 813	100.0	4.9	8.2	7.4	14.0	15.7	21.8	18.3	5.7	4.1	35 379	129	39 569	129
1968	62 214	100.0	4.1	7.8	7.0	13.9	14.8	21.6	20.2	6.4	4.1	36 873	133	41 716	133
1969	63 401	100.0	3.9	7.7	6.8	13.1	14.1	20.8	21.3	7.4	4.9	38 282	141	43 553	137
1970	64 778	100.0	3.8	7.9	6.9	13.4	14.0	20.5	20.7	7.6	5.2	38 026	139	43 542	139
1971[2]	66 676	100.0	3.6	7.9	7.3	13.7	14.1	19.9	20.6	7.7	5.2	37 634	146	43 283	138
1972[3]	68 251	100.0	3.3	7.4	7.3	13.6	13.2	19.4	21.0	8.5	6.4	39 216	150	45 642	142
1973	69 859	100.0	3.0	7.0	7.4	13.6	12.8	19.1	21.1	9.4	6.7	40 008	152	46 268	141
1974[4,5]	71 163	100.0	2.5	7.3	7.7	14.0	13.8	18.8	21.1	8.5	6.2	38 774	149	45 343	142
1975[5]	72 867	100.0	2.7	7.7	8.1	14.6	13.6	19.0	20.5	8.5	5.5	37 736	154	44 065	138
1976[6]	74 142	100.0	2.6	7.7	7.5	14.8	13.3	18.4	21.0	8.9	6.0	38 368	142	45 131	139
1977	76 030	100.0	2.5	7.6	8.0	14.2	13.4	18.0	20.9	8.9	6.5	38 585	145	45 772	139
1978	77 330	100.0	2.3	7.0	7.5	13.7	12.7	17.5	21.4	10.1	7.8	41 061	166	48 328	185
1979[7]	80 776	100.0	2.6	7.0	7.2	13.4	12.9	17.2	21.5	9.9	8.3	41 015	194	48 722	184
1980	82 368	100.0	2.6	7.2	7.7	14.0	13.0	17.6	20.6	9.7	7.7	39 739	204	47 263	173
1981	83 527	100.0	2.9	7.2	7.8	14.6	13.1	17.0	20.4	9.4	7.7	39 125	205	46 741	170
1982	83 918	100.0	3.1	7.2	7.8	14.1	13.2	17.6	19.5	9.6	8.0	39 064	176	47 078	174
1983[8]	85 290	100.0	3.1	7.2	7.5	14.3	13.1	17.2	19.5	9.6	8.4	39 081	177	47 617	177
1984	86 789	100.0	2.9	6.8	7.7	13.6	13.1	16.9	19.6	10.2	9.2	40 079	182	49 107	181
1985[9]	88 458	100.0	2.9	6.8	7.5	13.3	13.0	16.4	19.9	10.5	9.7	40 868	221	50 295	199
1986	89 479	100.0	3.0	6.7	7.0	12.9	12.5	16.4	20.3	10.8	10.8	42 309	219	52 270	212
1987[10]	91 124	100.0	2.8	6.7	6.9	13.0	12.2	16.0	19.9	11.1	11.4	42 827	204	53 261	219
1988	92 830	100.0	2.7	6.7	6.6	13.0	12.1	16.1	19.8	11.2	11.8	43 168	211	53 938	241
1989	93 347	100.0	2.6	6.1	6.8	13.0	11.8	16.1	19.7	11.4	12.6	43 946	242	55 522	242
1990	94 312	100.0	2.7	6.4	6.8	12.8	12.2	16.4	19.7	10.9	12.0	43 366	222	54 171	229
1991	95 669	100.0	2.8	6.6	7.1	13.0	12.6	16.1	19.4	10.7	11.6	42 108	203	53 005	218
1992[11]	96 426	100.0	3.0	6.7	7.2	13.6	12.2	15.9	19.2	10.8	11.5	41 774	198	52 960	222
1993[12]	97 107	100.0	3.2	6.5	7.3	13.3	12.6	15.7	18.6	10.5	12.3	41 562	194	55 115	298
1994[13]	98 990	100.0	3.0	6.2	7.3	13.6	12.2	15.6	18.3	11.0	12.7	42 038	192	56 199	302
1995[14]	99 627	100.0	2.7	5.9	6.8	13.5	12.0	15.8	18.9	11.2	13.2	43 346	251	57 163	313
1996	101 018	100.0	2.7	5.9	6.9	13.3	12.0	15.2	19.0	11.4	13.6	43 967	222	58 375	327
1997	102 528	100.0	2.8	5.7	6.6	12.9	11.4	15.5	18.7	11.5	14.9	44 883	207	60 271	337
1998	103 874	100.0	2.8	5.4	6.3	12.3	11.4	15.2	19.0	11.7	15.9	46 508	275	62 021	335
1999[15]	106 434	100.0	2.5	4.9	6.2	12.4	11.2	15.1	18.7	11.9	17.0	47 671	223	64 119	333
2000[16]	108 209	100.0	2.6	4.8	6.3	12.0	11.6	14.9	18.7	11.9	17.2	47 599	150	64 767	255
2001	109 297	100.0	2.9	5.1	6.3	12.2	11.7	15.0	18.1	11.9	16.9	46 569	142	64 191	256
2002	111 278	100.0	3.0	5.2	6.4	12.4	11.8	14.7	17.9	11.9	16.6	46 036	151	62 800	236
2003	112 000	100.0	3.2	5.0	6.8	12.3	11.5	14.7	18.0	11.4	17.0	45 970	200	62 683	229
2004[17]	113 343	100.0	3.4	4.9	6.6	12.7	11.6	14.6	18.3	11.2	16.7	45 817	203	62 488	236
2005	114 384	100.0	3.3	5.0	6.4	12.4	11.4	14.9	18.4	11.1	17.2	46 326	155	63 344	239
White Alone[18]															
2002	91 645	100.0	2.4	4.6	6.1	12.0	11.6	14.6	18.5	12.6	17.6	48 942	199	65 312	266
2003	91 962	100.0	2.6	4.3	6.4	11.9	11.4	14.8	18.4	11.9	18.1	48 424	190	65 357	262
2004[17]	92 880	100.0	2.8	4.2	6.3	12.3	11.4	14.6	18.7	11.7	17.8	48 218	189	65 013	268
2005	93 588	100.0	2.6	4.1	6.1	12.0	11.4	14.9	18.9	11.6	18.3	48 554	212	65 962	273

[1]Implementation of a new Curent Population Survey (CPS) Annual Social and Economic Supplements (ASEC) processing system.
[2]Introduction of 1970 census sample design and population controls.
[3]Full implementation of 1970 census–based sample design.
[4]Implementation of a new CPS ASEC processing system. Questionnaire expanded to ask 11 income questions.
[5]Some of these estimates were derived using Pareto interpolation and may differ from published data that were derived using linear interpolation.
[6]First-year medians were derived using both Pareto and linear interpolation. Before this year, all medians were derived using linear interpolation.
[7]Implementation of 1980 census population controls. Questionnaire expanded to show 27 possible values from a list of 51 possible sources of income.
[8]Implementation of Hispanic population weighting controls and introduction of 1980 census–based sample design.
[9]Recording of amounts for earnings from longest job increased to $299,999. Full implementation of 1980 census–based sample design.
[10]Implementation of a new CPS ASEC processing system.
[11]Implementation of 1990 census population controls.
[12]Data collection method changed from paper and pencil to computer-assisted interviewing. In addition, the 1994 ASEC was revised to allow for the coding of different income amounts on selected questionnaire items. Limits either increased or decreased in the following categories: earnings limits increased to $999,999, Social Security limits increased to $49,999, Supplemental Security Income and public assistance limits increased to $24,999, veterans' benefits limits increased to $99,999, and child support and alimony limits decreased to $49,999.
[13]Introduction of 1990 census sample design.
[14]Full implementation of 1990 census–based sample design and metropolitan definitions, 7,000 household sample reduction, and revised editing of responses on race.
[15]Implementation of the 2000 census–based population controls.
[16]Implementation of a 28,000 household sample expansion.
[17]Data revised to reflect a correction to the weights in the 2005 ASEC.
[18]Beginning with the 2003 CPS, respondents were allowed to choose one or more races. White alone refers to people who reported White and did not report any other race category. The use of this single-race population does not imply that it is the preferred method of presenting or analyzing the data. The Census Bureau uses a variety of approaches. Information on people who reported more than one race, such as White and American Indian and Alaska Native or Asian and Black or African American, is available from Census 2000 through American FactFinder. About 2.6 percent of people reported more than one race in Census 2000.

Table 13-2. Households, by Total Money Income, Race, and Hispanic Origin of Householder, 1967–2005
—Continued

(Numbers in thousands, percent, dollars; income in 2005 CPI-U-RS adjusted dollars.)

Race and Hispanic origin of householder and year	Number (thousands)	Percent distribution										Median income (dollars)		Mean income (dollars)	
		Total	Under $5,000	$5,000 to $9,999	$10,000 to $14,999	$15,000 to $24,999	$25,000 to $34,999	$35,000 to $49,999	$50,000 to $74,999	$75,000 to $99,000	$100,000 and over	Value	Standard error	Value	Standard error
White[19]															
1967[1]	54 188	100.0	4.4	7.6	6.7	13.3	15.7	22.6	19.3	6.1	4.4	36 895	134	41 015	139
1968	55 394	100.0	3.7	7.2	6.4	13.1	14.8	22.3	21.3	6.8	4.5	38 392	143	43 216	143
1969	56 248	100.0	3.4	7.1	6.3	12.3	13.8	21.5	22.4	7.9	5.3	39 953	146	45 169	151
1970	57 575	100.0	3.3	7.3	6.4	12.8	13.8	21.1	21.7	8.0	5.6	39 606	152	45 066	148
1971[2]	59 463	100.0	3.3	7.2	6.8	13.1	13.9	20.5	21.6	8.2	5.6	39 364	150	44 850	146
1972[3]	60 618	100.0	2.9	6.7	6.6	12.9	13.0	19.9	21.9	9.1	6.9	41 141	158	47 417	154
1973	61 965	100.0	2.6	6.4	6.8	13.0	12.5	19.4	22.0	10.1	7.2	41 929	160	48 057	152
1974[4,5]	62 984	100.0	2.2	6.5	7.1	13.4	13.7	19.2	22.1	9.0	6.7	40 550	152	47 022	152
1975[5]	64 392	100.0	2.4	6.8	7.5	14.2	13.5	19.4	21.4	9.0	5.9	39 463	144	45 693	150
1976[6]	65 353	100.0	2.3	6.8	6.8	14.2	13.2	18.7	22.0	9.5	6.5	40 192	166	46 867	151
1977	66 934	100.0	2.2	6.6	7.5	13.6	13.2	18.4	21.9	9.5	7.1	40 575	171	47 561	154
1978	68 028	100.0	2.0	6.1	7.0	13.2	12.6	17.7	22.4	10.6	8.4	42 686	188	50 119	202
1979[7]	70 766	100.0	2.2	6.1	6.7	12.9	12.8	17.6	22.4	10.4	8.9	43 004	204	50 643	202
1980	71 872	100.0	2.2	6.2	7.1	13.5	13.0	17.8	21.6	10.2	8.3	41 925	215	49 170	188
1981	72 845	100.0	2.4	6.2	7.2	14.0	13.1	17.4	21.3	9.9	8.4	41 338	191	48 700	185
1982	73 182	100.0	2.6	6.3	7.2	13.5	13.3	17.9	20.3	10.2	8.6	40 896	186	49 019	192
1983[8]	74 170	100.0	2.6	6.1	7.0	13.8	13.1	17.8	20.4	10.2	9.1	40 972	184	49 607	192
1984	75 328	100.0	2.4	5.8	7.1	13.1	13.0	17.3	20.6	10.8	9.9	42 282	213	51 133	198
1985[9]	76 576	100.0	2.4	5.8	7.0	12.9	12.8	16.7	20.7	11.0	10.5	43 100	230	52 359	220
1986	77 284	100.0	2.4	5.8	6.5	12.5	12.4	16.3	21.0	11.5	11.6	44 480	216	54 447	233
1987[10]	78 519	100.0	2.3	5.6	6.4	12.5	12.1	16.4	20.8	11.8	12.1	45 123	228	55 537	240
1988	79 734	100.0	2.2	5.5	6.1	12.5	12.0	16.5	20.7	11.8	12.7	45 635	270	56 238	265
1989	80 163	100.0	2.0	5.0	6.3	12.6	11.8	16.4	20.5	11.9	13.5	46 227	225	57 835	268
1990	80 968	100.0	2.1	5.4	6.3	12.5	12.2	16.8	20.3	11.6	12.8	45 232	207	56 356	252
1991	81 675	100.0	2.1	5.5	6.6	12.7	12.6	16.4	20.2	11.3	12.5	44 125	214	55 243	240
1992[11]	81 795	100.0	2.3	5.6	6.8	13.2	12.2	16.2	19.9	11.5	12.4	43 919	213	55 352	247
1993[12]	82 387	100.0	2.5	5.5	6.7	13.0	12.5	16.0	19.4	11.1	13.2	43 849	255	57 585	333
1994[13]	83 737	100.0	2.4	5.2	6.9	13.2	12.1	16.0	18.9	11.6	13.7	44 336	249	58 676	341
1995[14]	84 511	100.0	2.1	5.1	6.4	13.2	11.9	16.0	19.5	11.7	14.2	45 496	238	59 441	345
1996	85 059	100.0	2.1	5.1	6.5	12.9	11.9	15.3	19.7	12.0	14.5	46 034	238	60 693	359
1997	86 106	100.0	2.3	4.9	6.3	12.6	11.3	15.6	19.1	12.0	15.9	47 269	300	62 951	383
1998	87 212	100.0	2.2	4.5	6.0	11.8	11.3	15.3	19.6	12.3	16.9	48 933	245	64 834	382
1999[15]	88 893	100.0	2.0	4.2	5.9	12.0	11.2	15.1	19.2	12.6	17.8	49 580	251	66 449	376
2000[16]	90 030	100.0	2.2	4.2	6.1	11.6	11.4	14.9	19.1	12.4	18.2	49 782	220	67 169	288
2001	90 682	100.0	2.3	4.4	6.1	11.8	11.5	15.0	18.5	12.4	18.0	49 093	230	66 732	287
White Alone, Not Hispanic[18]															
2002	81 166	100.0	2.2	4.4	6.0	11.4	11.1	14.4	18.7	13.1	18.8	50 911	200	67 428	287
2003	81 148	100.0	2.4	4.1	6.2	11.3	10.9	14.5	18.7	12.4	19.4	50 702	245	67 798	288
2004[17]	81 628	100.0	2.6	4.0	6.1	11.7	10.9	14.3	19.0	12.2	19.1	50 546	231	67 440	293
2005	82 003	100.0	2.5	3.9	5.9	11.3	10.9	14.6	19.1	12.1	19.7	50 784	172	68 603	303

[1]Implementation of a new Curent Population Survey (CPS) Annual Social and Economic Supplements (ASEC) processing system.
[2]Introduction of 1970 census sample design and population controls.
[3]Full implementation of 1970 census–based sample design.
[4]Implementation of a new CPS ASEC processing system. Questionnaire expanded to ask 11 income questions.
[5]Some of these estimates were derived using Pareto interpolation and may differ from published data that were derived using linear interpolation.
[6]First-year medians were derived using both Pareto and linear interpolation. Before this year, all medians were derived using linear interpolation.
[7]Implementation of 1980 census population controls. Questionnaire expanded to show 27 possible values from a list of 51 possible sources of income.
[8]Implementation of Hispanic population weighting controls and introduction of 1980 census–based sample design.
[9]Recording of amounts for earnings from longest job increased to $299,999. Full implementation of 1980 census–based sample design.
[10]Implementation of a new CPS ASEC processing system.
[11]Implementation of 1990 census population controls.
[12]Data collection method changed from paper and pencil to computer-assisted interviewing. In addition, the 1994 ASEC was revised to allow for the coding of different income amounts on selected questionnaire items. Limits either increased or decreased in the following categories: earnings limits increased to $999,999, Social Security limits increased to $49,999, Supplemental Security Income and public assistance limits increased to $24,999, veterans' benefits limits increased to $99,999, and child support and alimony limits decreased to $49,999.
[13]Introduction of 1990 census sample design.
[14]Full implementation of 1990 census–based sample design and metropolitan definitions, 7,000 household sample reduction, and revised editing of responses on race.
[15]Implementation of the 2000 census–based population controls.
[16]Implementation of a 28,000 household sample expansion.
[17]Data revised to reflect a correction to the weights in the 2005 ASEC.
[18]Beginning with the 2003 CPS, respondents were allowed to choose one or more races. White alone refers to people who reported White and did not report any other race category. The use of this single-race population does not imply that it is the preferred method of presenting or analyzing the data. The Census Bureau uses a variety of approaches. Information on people who reported more than one race, such as White and American Indian and Alaska Native or Asian and Black or African American, is available from Census 2000 through American FactFinder. About 2.6 percent of people reported more than one race in Census 2000.
[19]For 2001 and earlier years, the CPS allowed respondents to report only one race group.

Table 13-2. Households, by Total Money Income, Race, and Hispanic Origin of Householder, 1967–2005
—Continued

(Numbers in thousands, percent, dollars; income in 2005 CPI-U-RS adjusted dollars.)

Race and Hispanic origin of householder and year	Number (thousands)	Percent distribution										Median income (dollars)		Mean income (dollars)	
		Total	Under $5,000	$5,000 to $9,999	$10,000 to $14,999	$15,000 to $24,999	$25,000 to $34,999	$35,000 to $49,999	$50,000 to $74,999	$75,000 to $99,000	$100,000 and over	Value	Standard error	Value	Standard error
White, Not Hispanic[19]															
1972[3]	58 005	100.0	2.9	6.7	6.5	12.6	12.8	19.8	22.3	9.3	7.1	41 727	198	47 967	214
1973	59 236	100.0	2.5	6.4	6.7	12.7	12.3	19.4	22.3	10.3	7.4	42 299	198	48 594	206
1974[4,5]	60 164	100.0	2.2	6.4	7.0	13.1	13.5	19.2	22.4	9.2	6.9	40 896	201	47 545	208
1975[5]	61 533	100.0	2.3	6.7	7.3	13.9	13.3	19.4	21.7	9.3	6.1	39 760	211	46 243	224
1976[6]	62 365	100.0	2.2	6.7	6.7	14.0	13.1	18.7	22.2	9.7	6.7	41 012	239	47 484	212
1977	63 721	100.0	2.2	6.5	7.3	13.4	13.0	18.4	22.3	9.7	7.3	41 380	233	48 160	227
1978	64 836	100.0	2.0	6.0	6.9	13.0	12.4	17.7	22.6	10.9	8.6	43 490	229	50 700	218
1979[7]	67 203	100.0	2.1	6.0	6.6	12.7	12.6	17.5	22.7	10.6	9.2	43 609	242	51 229	224
1980	68 106	100.0	2.1	6.0	7.0	13.2	12.8	17.9	21.9	10.5	8.6	42 667	108	49 814	224
1981	68 996	100.0	2.3	6.1	7.0	13.8	13.0	17.4	21.6	10.1	8.7	41 935	213	49 311	205
1982	69 214	100.0	2.5	6.1	7.0	13.3	13.2	18.0	20.6	10.4	8.9	41 582	209	49 733	213
1983[8]	...	100.0	2.4	5.9	6.7	13.6	12.9	17.8	20.7	10.4	9.4	...	...	...	...
1984	70 586	100.0	2.2	5.5	6.9	12.8	13.0	17.3	20.8	11.1	10.3	43 160	240	52 014	232
1985[9]	71 540	100.0	2.3	5.6	6.8	12.5	12.7	16.7	21.1	11.3	11.0	44 069	225	53 382	242
1986	72 067	100.0	2.3	5.5	6.3	12.1	12.2	16.3	21.4	11.8	12.1	45 491	235	55 535	255
1987[10]	73 120	100.0	2.1	5.3	6.2	12.2	11.9	16.4	21.2	12.2	12.6	46 364	270	56 630	263
1988	74 067	100.0	2.0	5.3	5.9	12.2	11.8	16.5	20.9	12.2	13.2	46 893	263	57 383	270
1989	74 495	100.0	1.8	4.8	6.2	12.3	11.5	16.4	20.7	12.2	14.0	47 221	231	58 988	289
1990	75 035	100.0	1.9	5.2	6.0	12.2	12.0	16.8	20.6	11.9	13.3	46 266	216	57 599	261
1991	75 625	100.0	2.0	5.3	6.3	12.4	12.4	16.4	20.5	11.7	13.1	45 179	222	56 427	252
1992[11]	75 107	100.0	2.1	5.2	6.5	12.8	12.0	16.1	20.3	11.9	13.0	45 393	281	56 758	262
1993[12]	75 697	100.0	2.3	5.2	6.4	12.6	12.3	15.9	19.9	11.5	13.9	45 463	266	59 103	353
1994[13]	77 004	100.0	2.3	4.8	6.6	12.8	11.9	16.0	19.3	12.0	14.3	45 767	242	60 171	357
1995[14]	76 932	100.0	1.9	4.6	6.0	12.6	11.6	16.0	20.0	12.2	15.1	47 292	247	61 380	368
1996	77 240	100.0	1.9	4.7	6.2	12.4	11.6	15.2	20.1	12.5	15.4	48 049	330	62 529	...
1997	77 936	100.0	2.1	4.5	6.0	12.1	11.0	15.4	19.5	12.6	16.9	49 215	257	64 968	...
1998	78 577	100.0	2.0	4.1	5.7	11.3	10.9	15.1	20.0	12.8	18.0	50 759	292	66 910	409
1999[15]	79 819	100.0	1.9	3.9	5.7	11.5	10.8	14.9	19.5	13.0	19.0	51 726	327	68 628	406
2000[16]	80 527	100.0	2.1	4.0	6.0	11.0	11.1	14.6	19.2	12.8	19.3	51 717	207	69 213	311
2001	80 818	100.0	2.1	4.2	5.9	11.3	11.1	14.7	18.7	12.8	19.1	51 065	212	68 863	312
Black Alone or in Combination															
2002	13 778	100.0	6.4	10.0	8.9	15.6	13.8	15.5	14.0	7.7	8.1	31 672	417	43 784	510
2003	13 969	100.0	6.6	9.9	9.6	15.3	13.4	14.7	15.3	7.5	7.8	31 506	396	42 784	453
2004[17]	14 151	100.0	7.6	9.6	8.8	15.8	13.8	14.8	14.9	7.5	7.2	31 246	286	42 122	447
2005	14 399	100.0	6.8	10.3	8.9	16.1	12.5	15.0	15.2	7.4	7.9	30 954	295	42 727	465
Black Alone[20]															
2002	13 465	100.0	6.5	10.1	9.0	15.6	13.8	15.5	14.0	7.7	8.0	31 509	424	43 433	502
2003	13 629	100.0	6.7	10.0	9.5	15.3	13.4	14.7	15.2	7.5	7.7	31 460	410	42 588	456
2004[17]	13 809	100.0	7.6	9.7	8.9	15.9	13.8	14.7	14.8	7.4	7.2	31 101	323	41 992	455
2005	14 002	100.0	6.8	10.3	8.9	16.1	12.6	15.1	15.1	7.3	7.8	30 858	301	42 454	461

[3]Full implementation of 1970 census–based sample design.
[4]Implementation of a new CPS ASEC processing system. Questionnaire expanded to ask 11 income questions.
[5]Some of these estimates were derived using Pareto interpolation and may differ from published data that were derived using linear interpolation.
[6]First-year medians were derived using both Pareto and linear interpolation. Before this year, all medians were derived using linear interpolation.
[7]Implementation of 1980 census population controls. Questionnaire expanded to show 27 possible values from a list of 51 possible sources of income.
[8]Implementation of Hispanic population weighting controls and introduction of 1980 census–based sample design.
[9]Recording of amounts for earnings from longest job increased to $299,999. Full implementation of 1980 census–based sample design.
[10]Implementation of a new CPS ASEC processing system.
[11]Implementation of 1990 census population controls.
[12]Data collection method changed from paper and pencil to computer-assisted interviewing. In addition, the 1994 ASEC was revised to allow for the coding of different income amounts on selected questionnaire items. Limits either increased or decreased in the following categories: earnings limits increased to $999,999, Social Security limits increased to $49,999, Supplemental Security Income and public assistance limits increased to $24,999, veterans' benefits limits increased to $99,999, and child support and alimony limits decreased to $49,999.
[13]Introduction of 1990 census sample design.
[14]Full implementation of 1990 census–based sample design and metropolitan definitions, 7,000 household sample reduction, and revised editing of responses on race.
[15]Implementation of the 2000 census–based population controls.
[16]Implementation of a 28,000 household sample expansion.
[17]Data revised to reflect a correction to the weights in the 2005 ASEC.
[19]For 2001 and earlier years, the CPS allowed respondents to report only one race group.
[20]Black alone refers to persons who reported Black and did not report any other race category.
. . . = Not available.

Table 13-2. Households, by Total Money Income, Race, and Hispanic Origin of Householder, 1967–2005 —Continued

(Numbers in thousands, percent, dollars; income in 2005 CPI-U-RS adjusted dollars.)

Race and Hispanic origin of householder and year	Number (thousands)	Total	Under $5,000	$5,000 to $9,999	$10,000 to $14,999	$15,000 to $24,999	$25,000 to $34,999	$35,000 to $49,999	$50,000 to $74,999	$75,000 to $99,000	$100,000 and over	Median income Value	Median income Standard error	Mean income Value	Mean income Standard error
Black[19]															
1967[1]	5 728	100.0	9.4	14.3	13.5	20.6	16.3	13.7	8.7	2.0	1.4	21 422	357	25 741	287
1968	5 870	100.0	7.9	13.8	12.1	21.7	15.2	15.2	10.5	2.7	0.9	22 639	329	27 573	290
1969	6 053	100.0	7.8	13.6	11.3	20.3	16.6	15.0	11.4	3.1	0.9	24 150	356	28 749	306
1970	6 180	100.0	7.8	13.6	11.7	18.9	16.0	15.5	11.9	3.4	1.3	24 107	331	29 436	318
1971[2]	6 578	100.0	7.0	14.3	12.3	19.5	15.8	15.2	11.3	3.4	1.1	23 253	346	28 814	296
1972[3]	6 809	100.0	6.9	13.3	12.7	19.3	14.4	15.3	12.8	3.5	1.7	24 014	360	30 335	324
1973	7 040	100.0	6.1	12.8	12.3	19.1	15.1	16.0	12.8	3.8	2.0	24 681	384	30 649	304
1974[4,5]	7 263	100.0	5.3	14.6	12.5	19.7	15.2	15.5	12.2	3.7	1.4	24 115	291	29 992	267
1975[5]	7 489	100.0	5.5	15.4	13.4	18.0	14.7	15.6	12.4	3.5	1.4	23 691	349	29 572	262
1976[6]	7 776	100.0	4.9	15.1	12.7	19.8	13.4	15.6	13.0	4.0	1.6	23 899	296	30 535	272
1977	7 977	100.0	4.7	15.6	12.3	19.5	15.1	14.1	12.7	4.3	1.8	23 944	321	30 679	273
1978	8 066	100.0	4.6	15.1	12.5	17.3	13.5	15.9	13.0	5.7	2.4	25 652	542	32 783	428
1979[7]	8 586	100.0	5.5	14.7	11.9	18.1	14.1	14.2	14.0	5.1	2.4	25 248	461	32 397	399
1980	8 847	100.0	6.0	15.5	12.1	18.6	13.0	15.3	12.6	4.7	2.3	24 153	456	31 347	386
1981	8 961	100.0	6.7	12.6	12.7	18.7	12.9	13.8	12.7	4.9	2.0	23 197	390	30 473	369
1982	8 916	100.0	7.2	15.5	12.0	18.6	12.7	15.1	12.8	4.1	2.0	23 178	372	30 496	382
1983[8]	9 243	100.0	7.3	15.9	12.0	17.7	13.8	13.6	12.7	4.8	2.4	23 192	433	30 892	379
1984	9 480	100.0	6.4	15.2	12.2	18.1	13.7	14.1	11.7	5.4	3.2	24 087	463	32 124	395
1985[9]	9 797	100.0	6.3	15.0	11.0	17.1	14.3	13.8	13.3	6.0	3.1	25 642	498	33 457	434
1986	9 922	100.0	7.6	14.6	10.5	16.5	13.1	13.7	14.5	5.3	4.1	25 626	503	34 381	467
1987[10]	10 192	100.0	6.9	15.5	10.8	16.2	13.3	14.0	13.3	5.5	4.6	25 755	496	34 775	478
1988	10 561	100.0	6.1	15.8	10.5	16.3	13.1	13.4	13.6	6.5	4.6	26 015	542	35 640	520
1989	10 486	100.0	6.7	14.2	10.1	16.2	12.9	14.2	14.1	6.7	5.0	27 492	559	36 480	496
1990	10 671	100.0	6.9	14.4	10.9	15.3	12.9	14.0	14.9	5.6	5.1	27 048	617	35 938	485
1991	11 083	100.0	7.4	14.7	10.9	15.2	13.0	14.2	14.2	6.0	4.3	26 287	552	35 004	457
1992[11]	11 269	100.0	7.7	15.1	10.5	16.3	12.9	13.8	13.6	5.5	4.6	25 573	522	34 702	470
1993[12]	11 281	100.0	7.6	13.8	11.4	16.2	13.6	13.7	12.6	5.9	5.1	25 986	514	36 225	601
1994[13]	11 655	100.0	6.5	13.6	10.1	16.9	12.9	13.0	14.2	7.0	5.9	27 397	509	38 123	547
1995[14]	11 577	100.0	6.2	12.3	9.6	16.4	13.5	14.8	14.7	7.0	5.3	28 485	486	38 670	661
1996	12 109	100.0	6.3	11.6	10.1	17.0	13.0	14.6	15.1	6.4	6.0	29 089	572	40 211	785
1997	12 474	100.0	5.9	11.8	9.1	16.1	13.3	15.1	15.4	7.2	6.0	30 383	523	39 980	574
1998	12 579	100.0	6.3	11.8	8.9	16.2	12.7	14.7	14.9	7.1	7.3	30 321	475	40 832	545
1999[15]	12 838	100.0	5.4	10.3	8.7	15.3	12.8	15.1	15.6	7.5	9.3	32 694	609	45 055	647
2000[16]	13 174	100.0	5.5	9.4	8.2	15.8	13.3	15.5	16.2	7.8	8.2	33 630	445	44 411	450
2001	13 315	100.0	6.2	9.9	8.2	15.5	13.5	15.5	15.5	8.1	7.6	32 499	383	43 282	457
Asian Alone or in Combination															
2002	4 079	100.0	4.1	3.5	3.5	10.1	9.8	13.3	17.7	13.4	24.6	56 757	859	75 418	1 434
2003	4 235	100.0	4.8	4.9	4.7	9.3	6.9	12.9	17.9	13.1	25.3	58 645	1 307	73 661	1 267
2004[17]	4 346	100.0	3.7	3.7	3.9	8.9	8.5	12.9	19.6	12.6	26.0	59 370	1 197	78 677	1 485
2005	4 500	100.0	4.3	3.5	4.5	8.5	7.2	12.5	19.0	13.3	27.3	61 048	729	79 997	1 396
Asian Alone[21]															
2002	3 917	100.0	4.1	3.4	3.5	10.1	9.8	13.1	17.6	13.5	24.9	57 127	1 000	76 038	1 483
2003	4 040	100.0	4.9	5.0	4.7	9.3	6.7	12.9	17.9	13.1	25.6	59 109	1 161	74 257	1 315
2004[17]	4 123	100.0	3.7	3.7	4.0	8.9	8.5	12.7	19.5	12.6	26.4	59 427	1 263	79 076	1 529
2005	4 273	100.0	4.3	3.5	4.6	8.5	7.1	12.2	19.2	13.1	27.5	61 094	712	80 096	1 413

[1]Implementation of a new Curent Population Survey (CPS) Annual Social and Economic Supplements (ASEC) processing system.
[2]Introduction of 1970 census sample design and population controls.
[3]Full implementation of 1970 census–based sample design.
[4]Implementation of a new CPS ASEC processing system. Questionnaire expanded to ask 11 income questions.
[5]Some of these estimates were derived using Pareto interpolation and may differ from published data that were derived using linear interpolation.
[6]First-year medians were derived using both Pareto and linear interpolation. Before this year, all medians were derived using linear interpolation.
[7]Implementation of 1980 census population controls. Questionnaire expanded to show 27 possible values from a list of 51 possible sources of income.
[8]Implementation of Hispanic population weighting controls and introduction of 1980 census–based sample design.
[9]Recording of amounts for earnings from longest job increased to $299,999. Full implementation of 1980 census–based sample design.
[10]Implementation of a new CPS ASEC processing system.
[11]Implementation of 1990 census population controls.
[12]Data collection method changed from paper and pencil to computer-assisted interviewing. In addition, the 1994 ASEC was revised to allow for the coding of different income amounts on selected questionnaire items. Limits either increased or decreased in the following categories: earnings limits increased to $999,999, Social Security limits increased to $49,999, Supplemental Security Income and public assistance limits increased to $24,999, veterans' benefits limits increased to $99,999, and child support and alimony limits decreased to $49,999.
[13]Introduction of 1990 census sample design.
[14]Full implementation of 1990 census–based sample design and metropolitan definitions, 7,000 household sample reduction, and revised editing of responses on race.
[15]Implementation of the 2000 census–based population controls.
[16]Implementation of a 28,000 household sample expansion.
[17]Data revised to reflect a correction to the weights in the 2005 ASEC.
[19]For 2001 and earlier years, the CPS allowed respondents to report only one race group.
[21]Asian alone refers to persons who reported Asian and did not report any other race category.

Table 13-2. Households, by Total Money Income, Race, and Hispanic Origin of Householder, 1967–2005
—Continued

(Numbers in thousands, percent, dollars; income in 2005 CPI-U-RS adjusted dollars.)

Race and Hispanic origin of householder and year	Number (thousands)	Total	Under $5,000	$5,000 to $9,999	$10,000 to $14,999	$15,000 to $24,999	$25,000 to $34,999	$35,000 to $49,999	$50,000 to $74,999	$75,000 to $99,000	$100,000 and over	Median income Value	Median income Standard error	Mean income Value	Mean income Standard error
Asian and Pacific Islander[19]															
1987[10]	...	100.0	4.3	4.1	5.4	12.9	9.0	11.9	20.2	12.6	19.5	52 959	1 969	...	...
1988	1 913	100.0	3.0	4.2	4.6	12.3	9.3	15.6	19.8	12.2	19.0	51 163	2 103	63 965	1 911
1989	1 988	100.0	2.9	2.9	5.7	9.8	9.4	14.8	20.7	14.4	19.5	54 887	1 484	68 232	1 986
1990	1 958	100.0	3.8	3.2	5.0	9.8	8.3	13.6	23.1	13.1	20.0	55 687	1 650	67 218	1 903
1991	2 094	100.0	3.4	4.9	4.5	10.0	11.8	14.6	18.7	13.3	18.8	50 946	1 644	64 685	1 907
1992[11]	2 262	100.0	4.1	3.9	5.5	12.0	8.7	13.9	20.7	13.0	18.2	51 544	1 488	63 882	1 756
1993[12]	2 233	100.0	4.5	5.4	6.1	10.4	10.1	12.7	17.8	13.6	19.4	51 016	2 509	66 843	2 691
1994[13]	2 040	100.0	4.3	4.1	5.4	10.2	9.0	14.7	18.8	14.6	19.0	52 745	1 999	68 485	2 440
1995[14]	2 777	100.0	4.5	3.7	6.6	10.0	8.7	14.8	19.7	13.5	18.5	51 662	1 296	70 252	2 834
1996	2 998	100.0	3.7	4.9	4.6	9.8	9.2	15.2	17.4	14.2	20.9	53 609	1 921	70 049	2 512
1997	3 125	100.0	4.1	3.8	5.6	9.1	8.4	14.8	19.5	12.6	22.0	54 882	1 526	71 427	2 214
1998	3 308	100.0	4.2	3.7	4.3	9.5	9.0	14.4	18.0	14.2	22.9	55 780	1 552	72 012	2 080
1999[15]	3 742	100.0	3.9	3.6	4.2	8.6	8.2	15.1	16.9	13.5	26.0	59 695	2 104	78 937	2 001
2000[16]	3 963	100.0	3.5	2.9	4.1	8.0	9.1	13.2	18.0	14.6	26.6	63 205	1 078	82 521	1 713
2001	4 071	100.0	4.1	3.5	3.6	9.3	9.4	13.3	18.1	12.9	25.8	59 148	1 412	80 679	1 905
Hispanic[22]															
1972[3]	2 655	100.0	3.3	7.1	9.2	19.7	17.3	20.2	16.5	4.6	2.1	31 047	607	35 685	607
1973	2 722	100.0	2.7	8.0	10.1	19.8	17.2	19.5	15.6	4.7	2.3	30 995	704	36 011	586
1974[4,5]	2 897	100.0	2.7	8.0	10.1	19.8	17.2	19.5	15.6	4.7	2.3	30 840	675	35 726	582
1975[5]	2 948	100.0	3.8	10.0	10.2	20.5	16.7	19.0	14.2	3.7	1.9	28 350	627	33 655	598
1976[6]	3 081	100.0	3.2	10.3	10.5	19.6	16.3	17.9	15.9	4.0	2.3	28 941	617	34 201	557
1977	3 304	100.0	3.1	8.6	10.2	18.9	17.8	18.6	15.3	4.9	2.6	30 269	532	35 722	552
1978	3 291	100.0	3.0	8.1	9.5	17.5	16.7	18.3	18.1	5.7	3.2	32 173	780	38 003	769
1979[7]	3 684	100.0	3.1	8.3	8.8	17.5	15.9	18.9	16.8	6.4	4.1	32 496	937	39 319	790
1980	3 906	100.0	4.2	8.9	9.3	18.8	15.6	17.4	16.7	5.7	3.3	30 631	830	37 415	745
1981	3 980	100.0	3.7	8.1	10.6	17.9	14.9	18.6	16.2	6.4	3.5	31 384	859	37 687	720
1982	4 085	100.0	4.6	9.4	11.3	18.2	15.1	17.2	14.9	6.3	3.0	29 394	777	36 277	736
1983[8]	4 666	100.0	4.5	10.1	11.6	16.9	15.6	17.1	14.9	5.9	3.4	29 367	749	35 972	692
1984	4 883	100.0	4.7	9.8	10.4	16.6	13.9	17.9	16.5	6.2	4.1	30 383	762	37 780	737
1985[9]	5 213	100.0	4.1	9.7	10.8	17.9	14.5	16.7	15.6	6.5	4.4	30 221	706	37 762	614
1986	5 418	100.0	4.5	9.2	9.6	17.7	14.6	16.1	16.3	6.8	5.2	31 186	812	39 379	647
1987[10]	5 642	100.0	4.5	9.7	9.5	17.4	14.3	16.0	16.2	7.0	5.4	31 776	697	40 732	754
1988	5 910	100.0	4.6	9.4	8.5	17.4	13.8	17.0	17.0	6.5	5.8	32 281	796	41 215	874
1989	5 933	100.0	4.3	8.6	8.2	16.4	15.0	16.1	17.1	8.0	6.3	33 327	646	42 557	731
1990	6 220	100.0	3.8	8.8	9.9	16.9	14.6	17.3	16.4	6.7	5.6	32 340	663	40 512	668
1991	6 379	100.0	3.9	9.0	10.1	16.7	15.2	16.5	16.2	6.7	5.8	31 716	660	40 356	646
1992[11]	7 153	100.0	4.2	9.4	10.1	17.7	14.7	16.8	15.5	6.6	5.1	30 812	637	39 300	618
1993[12]	7 362	100.0	4.1	9.3	10.4	17.6	15.5	17.0	14.0	6.9	5.3	30 447	612	40 298	847
1994[13]	7 735	100.0	4.2	10.1	10.4	17.4	14.4	16.1	14.5	7.0	6.0	30 516	567	41 149	1 027
1995[14]	7 939	100.0	4.5	10.1	9.9	18.8	14.9	15.8	14.1	6.5	5.4	29 079	633	39 689	890
1996	8 225	100.0	4.0	9.5	9.4	18.5	14.5	15.9	15.2	7.0	6.1	30 853	598	42 125	975
1997	8 590	100.0	4.3	9.0	9.1	16.9	14.1	17.0	15.8	7.1	6.8	32 297	576	43 522	878
1998	9 060	100.0	4.2	8.0	8.7	16.3	14.6	16.5	16.5	7.6	7.6	33 884	653	45 785	974
1999[15]	9 579	100.0	3.5	6.2	7.9	16.5	14.6	17.4	17.0	8.8	8.2	36 016	524	47 313	840
2000[16]	10 034	100.0	3.2	5.9	7.4	16.2	14.1	17.6	18.1	9.2	8.3	37 598	542	49 852	718
2001	10 499	100.0	3.7	5.9	7.3	16.1	14.4	17.6	16.8	9.2	8.9	37 015	470	48 945	619
2002	11 339	100.0	4.0	6.1	6.9	16.6	15.5	16.4	17.1	8.7	8.7	35 934	523	48 726	651
2003	11 693	100.0	4.3	5.7	7.9	16.4	15.6	17.1	15.9	8.5	8.6	35 017	487	47 190	522
2004[17]	12 178	100.0	4.4	6.0	7.7	17.1	14.4	17.0	16.7	8.0	8.8	35 417	496	47 411	580
2005	12 519	100.0	3.9	6.1	7.4	16.2	15.0	17.1	17.2	8.2	8.8	35 967	357	47 138	474

3Full implementation of 1970 census–based sample design.
4Implementation of a new CPS ASEC processing system. Questionnaire expanded to ask 11 income questions.
5Some of these estimates were derived using Pareto interpolation and may differ from published data that were derived using linear interpolation.
6First-year medians were derived using both Pareto and linear interpolation. Before this year, all medians were derived using linear interpolation.
7Implementation of 1980 census population controls. Questionnaire expanded to show 27 possible values from a list of 51 possible sources of income.
8Implementation of Hispanic population weighting controls and introduction of 1980 census–based sample design.
9Recording of amounts for earnings from longest job increased to $299,999. Full implementation of 1980 census–based sample design.
10Implementation of a new CPS ASEC processing system.
11Implementation of 1990 census population controls.
12Data collection method changed from paper and pencil to computer-assisted interviewing. In addition, the 1994 ASEC was revised to allow for the coding of different income amounts on selected questionnaire items. Limits either increased or decreased in the following categories: earnings limits increased to $999,999, Social Security limits increased to $49,999, Supplemental Security Income and public assistance limits increased to $24,999, veterans' benefits limits increased to $99,999, and child support and alimony limits decreased to $49,999.
13Introduction of 1990 census sample design.
14Full implementation of 1990 census–based sample design and metropolitan definitions, 7,000 household sample reduction, and revised editing of responses on race.
15Implementation of the 2000 census–based population controls.
16Implementation of a 28,000 household sample expansion.
17Data revised to reflect a correction to the weights in the 2005 ASEC.
19For 2001 and earlier years, the CPS allowed respondents to report only one race group.
22Because Hispanics may be of any race, data in this report for Hispanics overlap with data for racial groups. Hispanic origin was reported by 12.1 percent of White householders who reported only one race, 2.9 percent of Black householders who reported only one race, 27.7 percent of Amerian Indian and Alaska Native householders who reported only one race, and 9.5 percent of Native Hawaiian and Other Pacific Islander householders who reported only one race. Data users should exercise caution when interpreting aggregate results for the Hispanic population and for race groups, because these populations consist of many distinct groups that differ in socioeconomic characteristics, culture, and recentness of immigration. Data were first collected for Hispanics in 1972.
. . . = Not available.

INDEX

INDEX